Biological Psychology

SIXTH EDITION

An Introduction to Behavioral, Cognitive, and Clinical Neuroscience

S. Marc Breedlove
Michigan State University

Neil V. Watson
Simon Fraser University

Mark R. Rosenzweig
Late, University of California, Berkeley

Sinauer Associates, Inc. Publishers • Sunderland, Massachusetts

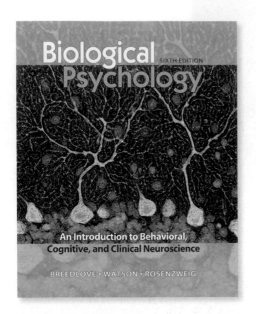

About the Cover:

Purkinje Cells of the Cerebellum   Alan Opsahl's photomicrograph of Purkinje cells in the cerebellum beautifully illustrates the astonishing complexity of these neurons. Named for their discoverer, Czech scientist Jan Evangelista Purkinje (1787–1869), the spectacularly branching dendrites of Purkinje cells greatly impressed neuroscientists of the nineteenth and early twentieth centuries, including the famed Spanish neuroanatomist Santiago Ramón y Cajal (1852–1934), whom we discuss in Chapter 2. We now know that these cells each receive up to a quarter million synaptic contacts from other neurons, and their output provides a major movement control signal. In addition to his contributions as a physiologist, Jan Purkinje pioneered new techniques for the microscopic study of extremely thin sections of brain tissue, so we think he would be delighted with the evolution of his work that our cover image represents. (Image by Alan Opsahl, © 2005 Pfizer, Inc.)

Library of Congress Cataloging-in-Publication Data

Breedlove, S. Marc.
  Biological psychology: an introduction to behavioral, cognitive, and clinical neuroscience/S. Marc Breedlove, Neil V. Watson, Mark R. Rosenzweig. -- 6th ed.
     p. cm.
  ISBN 978-0-87893-324-2 (hardcover)
  1. Psychobiology. I. Watson, Neil V. (Neil Verne), 1962- II. Rosenzweig, Mark R. III. Title.
  QP360.B727 2010
  612.8--dc22   2010007300

5   4   3   2   1

Biological Psychology

The brain is wider than the sky,
 For, put them side by side,
The one the other will include
 With ease, and you beside.

The brain is deeper than the sea,
 For, hold them, blue to blue,
The one the other will absorb,
 As sponges, buckets do.

The brain is just the weight of God,
 For, lift them, pound for pound,
And they will differ, if they do,
 As syllable from sound.

Emily Dickinson

We dedicate this book affectionately to our wives, children, and grandchildren. We appreciate their support and patience over the years of this project.

S.M.B.   **N.V.W.**

Cindy   *Maria*

Ben   Nick   Tessa   Kit   *Bix   Sophie   Lia*
Grace

Cristian
Johnathan

Mark R. Rosenzweig, September 12, 1922 – July 20, 2009

Our good friend and co-author Mark R. Rosenzweig passed away last July, just as we began revising this textbook, which he and Arnold L. Leiman first published in 1982. Born in 1922 in Rochester, NY, Mark earned his bachelor's and master's degrees in Psychology from the University of Rochester before serving in the Navy during World War II. After the war, he earned his Ph.D. from Harvard, where he demonstrated for the first time that electrodes placed outside the skull could detect auditory evoked potentials, a technique that is used to screen infants for deafness to this very day. In 1949 Mark joined the Psychology department at the University of California in Berkeley, where he would remain for his career.

Mark's most famous work, in collaboration with David Krech, Edward L. Bennett, and Marian Diamond, was in delineating the physical changes wrought in the brains of rats subjected to varying housing conditions. Rats raised in enriched conditions, with many peers and a rotation of stimulating toys, were found to have larger brains than rats kept in standard conditions. What's more, the brains of rats raised in enriched conditions displayed greater levels of cholinesterase activity, suggestive of more synaptic activity, than the brains of control rats. Initially greeted with loud skepticism from a field that had regarded the brain as fixed shortly after birth, these were among the first findings indicating the tremendous plasticity of the brain, ushering in our modern understanding of the crucial role of experience for brain development and function. Mark was elected to the National Academy of Sciences in 1979 and awarded the American Psychological Association's Distinguished Scientific Contribution Award in 1982.

Dedicated teachers, Mark and Arnie were prompted to write a new textbook, *Physiological Psychology*, out of dissatisfaction with existing texts. From the beginning they strove for outstanding, original illustrations, changing publishers twice before bringing the book to Sinauer Associates in 1996 with a new, richer illustration program as well as a new title, *Biological Psychology*, to emphasize a broader, more encompassing perspective.

A devoted family man, Mark married the French-born, Oxford-educated Janine Chappat in 1947. They had two daughters, Anne and Suzanne, and a son Philip, as well as several grandchildren and great-grandchildren. Mark and Janine were married over 60 years, until her death in 2008. An amazing scholar, devoted husband and father, a delightfully witty man and a faithful friend, Mark will be missed by many, including his surviving co-authors who will strive to maintain Mark's quality and enthusiasm in future editions of this book he began.

S. MARC BREEDLOVE AND NEIL V. WATSON, MARCH 2010

Brief Contents

Contents

PART II Evolution and Development of the Nervous System 149

PART IV Regulation and Behavior 349

PART VI Cognitive Neuroscience 509

Preface

The remarkable expansion of behavioral neuroscience research continues, with newspapers, magazines, YouTube and TV spilling over with stories about how the brain functions. Our website (**www.biopsychology.com/news**) boasts over 13,000 biopsychology news stories, all drawn from the mainstream media. There you can also find directions to receive email notifications or an RSS feed of new entries, posted 3–4 times per week.

As in the past, these new findings affect the stories we have to tell in every chapter. Since the previous edition, animal rights protesters have become more violent (Chapter 1). Intriguing and troubling findings with fMRI suggest that some people in comas may be more aware than we realized (Chapter 2). In some early chapters we focus less on new findings than on polishing presentations of what we already knew, as when we add figures illustrating different types of synapses and Otto Loewi's marvelous experiment in Chapter 3, and offer a new perspective on the dopaminergic "pleasure circuit" in Chapter 4. New reports confirm both the horrible ability of child abuse to stunt growth and the hope for at least partial recovery from psychosocial dwarfism when the child is rescued (Chapter 5). Chapter 6 offers more examples of how the size of brain regions mediating particular functions may vary with a species' ecological niche, and illustrates the important principle that the evolution of the vertebrate brain has consisted of prolongation of the later stages of development, that "late equals large." An exciting area of developmental research is epigenetics, which we now discuss in detail in Chapter 7, where we also describe new technology using dyes to non-invasively assess amyloid plaques in the aging brain. A class of free nerve endings has been discovered that seems to transmit itch information from the periphery to the spinal cord, and brain regions activated by placebo painkillers are rich in receptors for endogenous opioids (Chapter 8). The prospect for gene therapy to rescue or even regenerate hair cells to reverse deafness continues to improve (Chapter 9). We've reorganized Chapter 10 to offer a more streamlined discussion of vision, and added an intriguing hypothesis about why the smile portrayed in Da Vinci's *Mona Lisa* seems to come and go. A new, much less invasive surgical manipulation to reverse obesity has arisen, and the interplay of various hypothalamic peptides in regulating hunger has been better delineated (Chapter 13).

We've added a discussion of the mechanisms of anesthetic drugs to Chapter 14, relating those actions to sleep systems, and also report the recent discovery that the relationship between body size and sleep applies only to plant eaters, not meat eaters. Reports continue to cast doubt on the wisdom of using the newer, more expensive drugs for schizophrenia, and an exciting mouse model has arisen, expressing a gene implicated in human schizophrenia, which displays the enlarged lateral ventricles prominent in the disorder (Chapter 16). In Chapter 17 we now report that patient H.M.'s name was Henry Molaison and that he passed away in 2008. Thousands of people around the world watched via webcast as, following Henry's wishes, his brain was sectioned for study. Transcranial magnetic stimulation has revealed subregions of Broca's area that seem to mediate different aspects of language processing (Chapter 19).

But the biggest change in this edition is a reorganization, combining learning and memory materials into a single Chapter 17, and creating a new Chapter 18 devoted to attention and executive functioning. Almost entirely new material and figures explain how we can study so elusive a phenomenon as attention, and what we've learned about brain regions that are active as we shift attention from one domain to another. This chapter also includes all new material on consciousness, a topic once forbidden in psychological science that has blossomed with renewed findings and optimism about future discoveries. In our experience, students are as fascinated by the mysterious properties of consciousness as we are, and many students come to psychology hoping to learn more about consciousness. So we are very excited to talk about these wonderful new findings, even if they sometimes disturb our notions of free will.

We continue to offer vignettes to open each chapter, providing a human context to generate interest in the science. We have revised and replaced several of these with even more compelling tales of how the function of the brain affects us.

This explosion of knowledge in biological psychology shows no signing of slowing down. The field has made progress in answering so many formerly mysterious questions:

- Do prenatal events influence the probability that a child will develop a heterosexual or homosexual orientation?

- Does the brain make new neurons throughout life, in numbers large enough to make a functional difference?

- Can we improve memory performance with some drugs, and use other drugs to erase unwanted, traumatic memories?

- What happens in the brain as we develop trust in another person?

- Does strong liking for sweet foods involve the same brain mechanisms as addiction to drugs?

- How can we share so many genes with chimpanzees and other primates, and yet be so different from them?

- How can recent discoveries about the neural control of appetite help us to curb the obesity epidemic?

- Does a gene that predisposes for Alzheimer's disease in old age actually improve cognitive functioning earlier in life?

These are important questions, but the basic issues surrounding them cannot be reduced to "sound bites." A meaningful approach to questions like these requires an understanding of the bodily systems that underlie behavior and experience. Our aim in *Biological Psychology* is to provide a foundation that places these and other important problems in a unified scientific context.

This book explores the biological bases of our experience and behavior: the ways in which bodily states and processes produce and control behavior and cognition, and—just as important—the ways in which behavior, cognition, and the environment exert their influence on bodily systems. We treat biology in a broad sense. As in most textbooks of this sort, there is substantial coverage of the proximate, physiological underpinnings of behavior, but we have also related these systems to their ultimate, evolutionary origins whenever possible. The focus of the book is human behavior, but we include numerous discussions of other species' solutions to the problems of survival as well.

Many scientific disciplines contribute to these themes, so we draw on the research of psychologists, anatomists, biochemists, endocrinologists, engineers, geneticists, immunologists, neurologists, physiologists, evolutionary biologists, and zoologists. In order to gain a panoramic view of the questions that concern biological psychologists, we have tried to rise above the limits of any single specialty. Throughout the book we employ a five-fold approach to biological psychology—descriptive, comparative/evolutionary, developmental, mechanistic, and applied/clinical. We also emphasize the remarkable plasticity of the nervous system; it is increasingly evident that this mallcability is a general feature of neural tissue.

We've found that students enrolled in biological psychology courses have diverse academic backgrounds and personal interests, so we have taken pains to make the subject accessible to the widest spectrum of students by providing both the behavioral and biological foundations for each main topic. Some students will feel comfortable skipping or skimming some of this background material, but others will benefit from studying it carefully before moving on to the core of each chapter.

For instructors, specific suggestions for creating syllabi with different emphases can be found in the Instructor's Manual, along with detailed outlines for lectures and other helpful material. In addition, the Instructor's Resource Library contains many resources for use in the lecture, such as animations, videos, all the textbook figures, and Power-Point® presentations (For more information on the media and supplements, turn to page xviii.)

Many features of the text are designed to enhance students' mastery of the material:

- We have continued to develop what we believe is the finest full-color illustration program in any biological psychology text. This acclaimed art program has undergone hundreds of additions and refinements, always with a clear pedagogical goal in mind. Data from original sources have been recast in ways that are designed to aid the student's understanding. Many new photographs and drawings—clear, detailed, and consistent—are another feature of this edition.

- We have completely reorganized the summaries at the end of each chapter, recapitulating the organization of the chapter and directing students to the most important figures illustrating overarching principles.

- Key terms in the text are set in boldface type and the definition defined in the margin on the same page. Key terms are also included in an improved, more comprehensive glossary at the end of the book.

- "Boxes" describe interesting applications, important methods, sidelights, or refreshers on theoretical concepts relevant to biological psychology, or place the findings in the chapter in a historical perspective.

Learning Biological Psychology, our comprehensive electronic study guide, is now available online at www.biopsychology.com. Revised and updated by David Vago and Scott Baron, this website is a powerful companion to the textbook that enhances the learning experience with a variety of multimedia resources.

The creation of this new edition of our book has also been tinged with loss, as our dear friend Mark Rosenzweig passed away last year. The frontispiece in this edition relates just a few of Mark's many remarkable accomplishments as a scientist, teacher, world citizen and devoted family man. Mark and Arnie Leiman created the first two editions of this textbook. They were determined to infuse a wider scope than in any existing textbooks, emphasizing the pervasive imprints of evolution, the crucial role of experience, and creating figures that illuminate important principles in just a glance. Mindful of this legacy, we strive to push the book even further in the endeavors Mark and Arnie began.

Acknowledgments

In preparing this book we benefited from the help of many highly skilled people. These include members of the staff of Sinauer Associates: Graig Donini, Editor; Kathaleen Emerson, Production Editor; Christopher Small, Production Manager; Jefferson Johnson, Book Designer and Electronic Book Production; and Jason Dirks, Media and Supplements Editor. Copy Editor Stephanie Hiebert once again skillfully edited the text, and Photo Researcher David McIntyre sought out many of the photographs. Mike Demaray, Craig Durant and colleagues at Dragonfly Media Group, and Elizabeth Morales/Morales Studio transformed our rough sketches and wish list into the handsome and dynamic art program of this text.

We also want to thank our past undergraduate and graduate students for their helpful responses to our instruction, and the colleagues who provided information and critical comments about our manuscript: Brian Derrick, Karen De Valois, Russell De Valois, Jack Gallant, Ervin Hafter, Richard Ivry, Lucia Jacobs, Dacher Keltner, Raymond E. Kesner, Joe L. Martinez, Jr., John J. McDonald, James L. McGaugh, Frederick Seil, Arthur Shimamura, Richard D. Wright, and Irving Zucker.

We remain grateful to the reviewers whose comments helped shape the previous editions, including: Duane Albrecht, Anne E. Powell Anderson, Michael Antle, Benoit Bacon, Scott Baron, Mark S. Blumberg, Eliot A. Brenowitz, Chris Brill, Peter C. Brunjes, Rebecca D. Burwell, Catherine P. Cramer, Tiffany Donaldson, Loretta M. Flanagan-Cato, Francis W. Flynn, John D. E. Gabrieli, Kimberley P. Good, Diane C. Gooding, Janet M. Gray, James Gross, Mary E. Harrington, Wendy Heller, Mark Hollins, Janice Juraska, Keith R. Kluender, Leah A. Krubitzer, Joseph E. LeDoux, Michael A. Leon, Simon LeVay, Stephen G. Lomber, Donna Maney, Stephen A. Maren, Robert J. McDonald, Robert L. Meisel, Ralph Mistlberger, Jeffrey S. Mogil, Randy J. Nelson, Chris Newland, Miguel Nicolelis, Lee Osterhout, James Pfaus, Helene S. Porte, George V. Rebec, Scott R. Robinson, David A. Rosenbaum, Martin F. Sarter, Jeffrey D. Schall, Stan Schein, Dale R. Sengelaub, Matthew Shapiro, Rae Silver, Cheryl L. Sisk, Laura Smale, Robert L. Spencer, Steven K. Sutton, Harald K. Taukulis, Franco J. Vaccarino, David R. Vago, Cyma Van Petten, Charles J. Vierck, Robert Wickesberg, Christoph Wiedenmayer, Walter Wilczynski, S. Mark Williams, and Mark C. Zrull.

The following reviewers read and critiqued the Fifth Edition text to help direct our revision for the Sixth Edition, and we are grateful for their assistance:

Chalon E. Anderson, *University of Central Oklahoma*
Anthony Austin, *Ohio University*
A. Michael Babcock, *Montana State University*
John-Paul Baird, *Amherst College*
Terence J. Bazzett, *State University of New York, Geneseo*
Bruce Bridgeman, *University of California, Santa Cruz*
Judith Byrnes-Enoch, *Empire State College*
Deana Davalos, *Colorado State University*
Heather Dickinson-Anson, *University of California, Irvine*
Marcie Finkelstein, *University of South Florida*
Robert Flint, *The College of Saint Rose*
Philip Gasquoine, *University of Texas, Pan American*
Matthew Gendle, *Elon University*
Derek A. Hamilton, *University of New Mexico*
Michael J. Hawken, *New York University*
Christine Holler-Dinsmore, *Fort Peck Community College*
Katherine Hooper, *University of North Florida*
Anna Klintsova, *University of Delaware*
Kathleen B. Lustyk, *Seattle Pacific University*
Cyrille Magne, *Middle Tennessee State University*
Christopher May, *Carroll University*
Steven Meier, *University of Idaho*
Marilee Ogren, *Boston College*
M. Foster Olive, *College of Charleston*
Joseph H. Porter, *Virginia Commonwealth University*
Christian G. Reich, *Ramapo College*
Linda Rinaldini Head
Lawrence J. Ryan, *Oregon State University*
Fred Shaffer, *Truman State University*
David M. Smith, *Cornell University*
Sheralee Tershner, *Western New England College*
David G. Thomas, *Oklahoma State University*
Jeramy Townsley, *University of Indianapolis*
Charlene Wages, *Francis Marion University*
Jonathan D. Wallis, *University of California, Berkeley*
Leonard E. White, *Duke University*

Finally, we would like to thank all our colleagues who contribute research in the behavioral neurosciences.

S. MARC BREEDLOVE ■ NEIL V. WATSON

Media and Supplements

to accompany **Biological Psychology**, Sixth Edition

eBook *(ISBN 978-0-87893-555-0)*
www.sinauer.com/ebooks

New for the Sixth Edition, *Biological Psychology* is available as an online interactive ebook, at a substantial discount off the list price of the printed textbook. The interactive ebook features a variety of tools and resources that make it flexible for instructors and effective for students. For instructors, the eBook offers an unprecedented opportunity to easily customize the textbook with the addition of notes, Web links, images, documents, and more. Students can readily bookmark pages, highlight text, add their own notes, and customize display of the text. All of the Companion Website's resources are integrated into the eBook, so that students can easily access animations, study questions, quizzes, and more while reading the text.

Also available as a CourseSmart eBook (ISBN 978-0-87893-556-7). The CourseSmart eBook reproduces the look of the printed book exactly, and includes convenient tools for searching the text, highlighting, and notes. For more information, please visit www.coursesmart.com.

For the Student
Companion Website
www.biopsychology.com

Expanded for the Sixth Edition, the robust *Biological Psychology* Companion Website contains a wide range of study and review resources to help students master the material presented in the textbook. Access to the site is free and requires no passcode. Tightly integrated with the text, with content corresponding to every major heading in the book, this online resource greatly enhances the learning experience. (Instructor registration is required in order for students to access the online quizzes.)
The Companion Site includes:

- Detailed chapter outlines
- Extensive study questions
- Animated tutorials, activities, and videos
- Multiple-choice quizzes and essay quizzes
- Flashcards
- Complete glossary

Biological Psychology NewsLink
www.biopsychology.com/news

This invaluable online resource helps students make connections between the science of biological psychology and their daily lives, and keeps them apprised of the latest developments in the field. The site includes links to thousands of news stories, all organized both by keyword and by textbook chapter. The site is updated 3–4 times per week, so it includes up-to-the-minute information. NewsLink updates are also available via Twitter, at twitter.com/biologicalpsych.

For the Instructor
Instructor's Resource Library

The Sixth Edition Instructor's Resource Library includes a variety of resources to aid you in the planning of your course, the development of your lectures, and the assessment of your students. The Resource Library includes:

- Figures & Tables: All of the line-art illustrations, photos, and tables from the textbook are provided as both high-resolution and low-resolution JPEGs, all optimized for use in presentation software (such as PowerPoint®)
- PowerPoint Resources: Three different types of PowerPoint presentations are provided for each chapter of the textbook:
  - All figures, photos, and tables
  - A complete lecture outline, including selected figures
  - Animations and videos
- Videos: A collection of video segments for use in lecture
- Animations: These detailed animations help enliven lectures and illustrate dynamic processes
- Instructor's Manual and Test Bank in Word® format
- Computerized Test Bank: The entire Test Bank is provided in Diploma® format (software included), making it easy to quickly assemble exams using any combination of publisher-provided and custom questions. Includes the Companion Website quiz questions.

Instructor's Manual & Test Bank

(Included on the Instructor's Resource Library)

David Vago and Scott Baron

Included in the Instructor's Resource Library, the *Biological Psychology* Instructor's Manual & Test Bank includes useful resources for planning your course, lectures, and exams. For each chapter of the textbook, it includes the following:

- Chapter overview
- Complete chapter outline
- Key concepts
- Detailed lecture outlines
- Additional references for lecture/course development
- Comprehensive exam questions, including multiple choice, fill-in-the-blank, matching, essay, definition, and paragraph development questions

Online Quizzing

The Companion Website includes online quizzes that can be assigned by instructors or used as self-review exercises. Quizzes can be customized with any combination of the default questions and an instructor's own questions, and can be assigned as desired. Results of the quizzes are stored in the online gradebook. (Instructors must register in order for their students to be able to take the quizzes.)

Course Management System Support

e-Packs/Course Cartridges

New for the Sixth Edition, *Biological Psychology* now offers a complete e-pack/course cartridge for Blackboard® and WebCT®. This e-pack includes resources from the Companion Website and the Instructor's Resource Library, as well as the complete Test Bank, making it easy to quickly include a wide range of book-specific material into your Blackboard or WebCT course.

Assessment

Instructors using course management systems such as WebCT, Blackboard, and Angel® can easily create and export quizzes and exams (or the entire test bank) for integration into their online course. The entire test bank is provided in WebCT and Blackboard formats on the Instructor's Media Library, and other formats can be easily generated from the included Diploma software.

CHAPTER 1

Biological Psychology: Scope and Outlook

A Brain on the Ceiling of the Sistine Chapel?

Between 1508 and 1512, Michelangelo (1475–1564) painted the Sistine Chapel in the Vatican. One panel of the ceiling, his masterpiece *The Creation of Adam* (shown on the right), depicts God reaching out to bestow the gift of life upon humanity, through Adam. But the oddly shaped drapery behind God, and the arrangement of his attendants, has prompted speculation that Michelangelo was conveying a hidden message: God and attendants appear to be part of a human brain (Meshberger, 1990).

Only a little imagination is required to identify the broad outlines of a brain in Michelangelo's depiction of God (compare it with the midline section of a human brain in Figure 2.12*b*). During the Renaissance, when this fresco was created, the all-powerful church forbade depiction of the dissected human body, considering it to be a desecration. But there is no doubt that Michelangelo engaged in extensive dissections of cadavers, gaining the detailed knowledge of human anatomy that informs his sculpture and paintings. It is highly likely that he knew perfectly well what a dissected human brain looks like. So, was Michelangelo making a subtle commentary about the origins of behavior, God's most magnificent creation, or the secrets of nature? We probably will never know. But we can all agree that our uniquely human qualities—language, reason, emotion, and the rest—are products of the brain. The goal of this book is to give you some idea of how this mysterious organ enables humans to paint a masterpiece, sing an aria, or uncover some of the secrets of that very brain itself.

I n this book we explore the many ways in which the structures and actions of the brain produce mind and behavior. But that is only half of our task. We are also interested in the ways in which behavior in turn modifies the structures and actions of the brain. One of the most important lessons we hope to convey is that interactions between brain and behavior are reciprocal. The brain controls behavior and, in turn, behavior alters the brain.

We hope to give an interesting account of the main ideas and research in biological psychology, which is of great popular as well as scientific interest. Because there are so many pieces to tie together, we try to introduce a given piece of information when it makes a difference to the understanding of a subject—especially when it forms part of a story. Most important, we seek to communicate our own interest and excitement about the mysteries of mind and body.

What Is Biological Psychology?

No treaty or trade union agreement ever defined the boundaries of biological psychology. The first people to study the relationships between brain and behavior regarded themselves as philosophers, and their findings contributed to the births of biology and psychology. A merging of those disciplines, **biological psychology** is the field that relates behavior to bodily processes, especially the workings of the

biological psychology   Also called *behavioral neuroscience*. The study of the biological bases of psychological processes and behavior.

neuroscience   The study of the nervous system.

brain. Because study of the brain is known as **neuroscience** (the root *neuro-* comes from the Greek word *neuron*, meaning "nerve" or "cord"), biological psychology is also known as **behavioral neuroscience**. Whichever name is used, the main goal of this field is to understand the biology underlying behavior and experience.

Biological psychology is a field that includes many players who come from quite different backgrounds: psychologists, biologists, physiologists, engineers, neurolo-

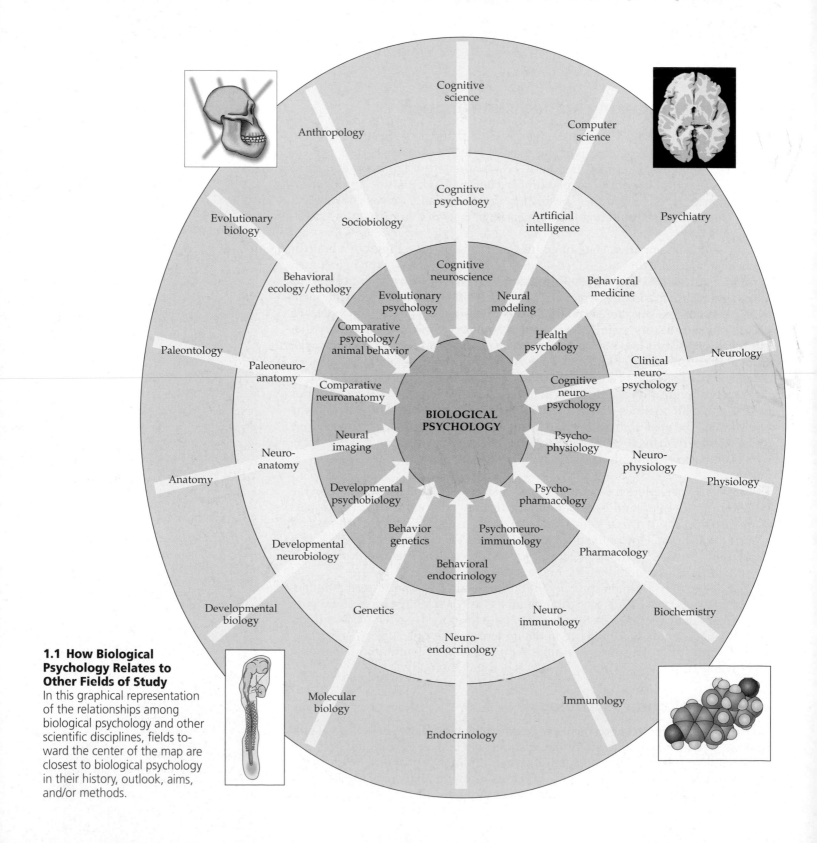

1.1 How Biological Psychology Relates to Other Fields of Study
In this graphical representation of the relationships among biological psychology and other scientific disciplines, fields toward the center of the map are closest to biological psychology in their history, outlook, aims, and/or methods.

gists, psychiatrists, and many others. Thus, there are many career opportunities, in both universities and private industry, for people with interests in this field (Hitt, 2007). **Figure 1.1** maps the relations of biological psychology to these many other disciplines. Clearly, the biological psychology umbrella is very wide.

Five Viewpoints Explore the Biology of Behavior

In our pursuit to understand the biological bases of behavior, we use several different perspectives. Because each one yields information that complements the others, the combination of perspectives is especially powerful. The five major perspectives are

1. *Describing* behavior
2. Studying the *evolution* of behavior
3. Observing the *development* of behavior and its biological characteristics over the life span
4. Studying the biological *mechanisms* of behavior
5. Studying *applications* of biological psychology—for example, its applications to dysfunctions of human behavior

These perspectives are discussed in the sections that follow, and **Table 1.1** shows how each perspective can be applied to three kinds of behavior.

Behavior can be described according to different criteria

Until we describe what we want to study, we cannot accomplish much. Depending on the goals of our investigation, we may describe behavior in terms of detailed acts or processes, or in terms of results or functions. An analytical description of arm movements might record the successive positions of the limb or the contraction of different muscles. A functional behavioral description, by contrast, would state whether the limb was being used in walking, running, hopping, swimming, or texting. To be useful for scientific study, a description must be precise and reveal the essential features of the behavior, using accurately defined terms and units.

TABLE 1.1 Five Research Perspectives Applied to Three Kinds of Behavior

Research perspective	Kind of behavior		
	Sexual behavior	**Learning and memory**	**Language and communication**
DESCRIPTION			
Structural	What are the main patterns of reproductive behavior and sex differences in behavior?	In what main ways does behavior change as a consequence of experience—for example, conditioning?	How are the sounds of speech patterned?
Functional	How do specialized patterns of behavior contribute to mating and to care of young?	How do certain behaviors lead to rewards or avoidance of punishment?	What behavior is involved in making statements or asking questions?
EVOLUTION	How does mating depend on hormones in different species?	How do different species compare in kinds and speed of learning?	How did the human speech apparatus evolve?
DEVELOPMENT	How do reproductive and secondary sex characteristics develop over the life span?	How do learning and memory change over the life span?	How do children learn to speak?
MECHANISMS	What neural circuits and hormones are involved in reproductive behavior?	What anatomical and chemical changes in the brain hold memories?	What brain regions are particularly involved in language?
APPLICATIONS	Low doses of testosterone restore libido in some postmenopausal women.	Gene therapy and behavioral therapy improve memory in some senile patients.	Speech therapy, in conjunction with amphetamine treatment, speeds language recovery following stroke.

We compare species to learn how the brain and behavior have evolved

Darwin's theory of evolution through natural selection is central to all modern biology and psychology. From this perspective emerge two rather different emphases: (1) the *continuity* of behavior and biological processes among species because of our common ancestry and (2) the species-specific *differences* in behavior and biology that have evolved as adaptations to different environments. At some points in this book we will concentrate on continuity—that is, features of behavior and its biological mechanisms that are common to many species. At other points, we will look at behaviors displayed by only a few species.

Nature is conservative. Once particular features of the body or behavior evolve, they may be maintained for millions of years and may be seen in animals that otherwise appear very different. For example, the electrical messages used by nerve cells (see Chapter 3) are essentially the same in a jellyfish, a cockroach, and a human being. Some of the chemical compounds that transmit messages through the bloodstream (hormones) are also the same in diverse animals (see Chapter 5). Species share these **conserved** characteristics because the features first arose in a shared ancestor (**Box 1.1**). But mere similarity of a feature between species does not guarantee that the feature came from a common ancestral species. Similar solutions to a problem may have evolved independently in different classes of animals.

The body and behavior develop over the life span

Ontogeny is the process by which an individual changes in the course of its lifetime—that is, grows up and grows old. Observing the way in which a particular behavior changes during ontogeny may give us clues to its functions and mechanisms. For example, we know that learning ability in monkeys increases over several years of development. Therefore, we can speculate that prolonged maturation of brain circuits is required for complex learning tasks. In rodents, the ability to form long-term memories lags somewhat behind the maturation of learning ability. So, young rodents learn well but forget more quickly than older ones, suggesting that learning and memory involve different processes. Studying the development of reproductive capacity and of differences in behavior between the sexes, along with changes in body structures and processes, enables us to throw light on body mechanisms underlying sex behaviors.

Biological mechanisms underlie all behavior

The history of a species tells us the evolutionary determinants of its behavior; the history of an individual tells us the developmental determinants. To learn about the mechanisms of an individual's behavior, we study how his or her *present* body works. To understand the underlying mechanisms of behavior, we must regard the organism (with all due respect) as a "machine," made up of billions of nerve cells, or **neurons** (the Greek word for "nerve" or "cord"). We must ask, How is this thing constructed to be able to do all that?

Our major aim in biological psychology is to examine body mechanisms that make particular behaviors possible. In the case of learning and memory, for example, we would like to know the sequence of electrical and biochemical processes that occur when we learn something and retrieve it from memory. What parts of the nervous system are involved in that process? In the case of reproductive behavior, we would like to know how the body grows to produce the capacity for sexual behavior. We also want to understand the neuronal and hormonal processes that underlie reproductive behavior.

Research can be applied to human problems

Like other sciences, biological psychology is also dedicated to improving the human condition. As Albert Einstein once said, concern for humanity and its fate must al-

conserved   In the context of evolution, referring to a trait that is passed on from a common ancestor to two or more descendant species.

ontogeny   The process by which an individual changes in the course of its lifetime—that is, grows up and grows old.

neuron   Also called *nerve cell*. The basic unit of the nervous system.

BOX 1.1 We Are All Alike, and We Are All Different

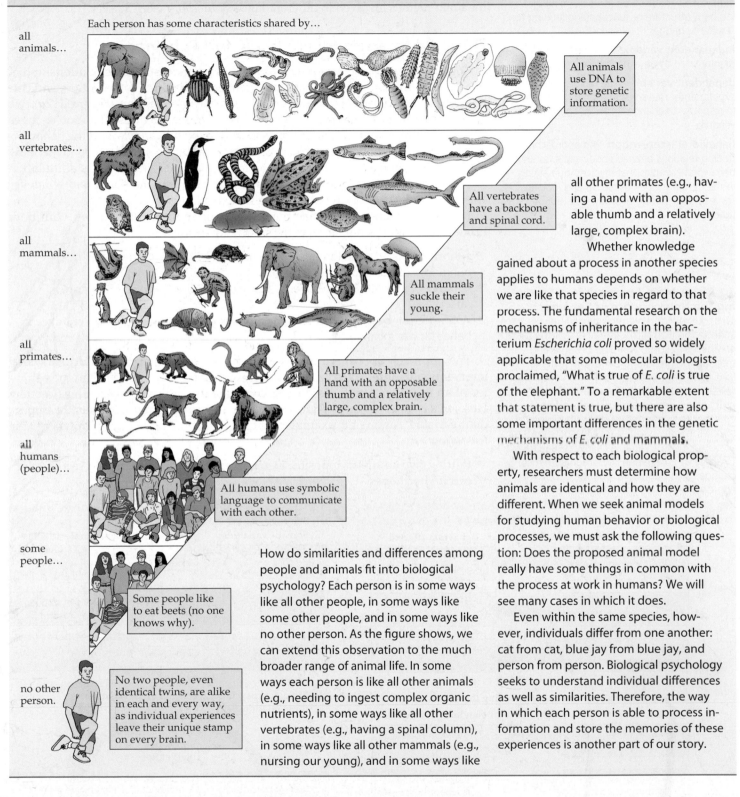

Each person has some characteristics shared by…

all animals…

All animals use DNA to store genetic information.

all vertebrates…

All vertebrates have a backbone and spinal cord.

all mammals…

All mammals suckle their young.

all primates…

All primates have a hand with an opposable thumb and a relatively large, complex brain.

all humans (people)…

All humans use symbolic language to communicate with each other.

some people…

Some people like to eat beets (no one knows why).

no other person.

No two people, even identical twins, are alike in each and every way, as individual experiences leave their unique stamp on every brain.

all other primates (e.g., having a hand with an opposable thumb and a relatively large, complex brain).

Whether knowledge gained about a process in another species applies to humans depends on whether we are like that species in regard to that process. The fundamental research on the mechanisms of inheritance in the bacterium *Escherichia coli* proved so widely applicable that some molecular biologists proclaimed, "What is true of *E. coli* is true of the elephant." To a remarkable extent that statement is true, but there are also some important differences in the genetic mechanisms of *E. coli* and mammals.

With respect to each biological property, researchers must determine how animals are identical and how they are different. When we seek animal models for studying human behavior or biological processes, we must ask the following question: Does the proposed animal model really have some things in common with the process at work in humans? We will see many cases in which it does.

Even within the same species, however, individuals differ from one another: cat from cat, blue jay from blue jay, and person from person. Biological psychology seeks to understand individual differences as well as similarities. Therefore, the way in which each person is able to process information and store the memories of these experiences is another part of our story.

How do similarities and differences among people and animals fit into biological psychology? Each person is in some ways like all other people, in some ways like some other people, and in some ways like no other person. As the figure shows, we can extend this observation to the much broader range of animal life. In some ways each person is like all other animals (e.g., needing to ingest complex organic nutrients), in some ways like all other vertebrates (e.g., having a spinal column), in some ways like all other mammals (e.g., nursing our young), and in some ways like

ways form the chief interest of all scientific endeavors "in order that the creations of our minds shall be a blessing and not a curse." Numerous human diseases involve malfunctioning of the brain. Many of these are already being alleviated as a result of research in the neurosciences, and the prospects for continuing advances are good.

somatic intervention   An approach to finding relations between body variables and behavioral variables that involves manipulating body structure or function and looking for resultant changes in behavior.

independent variable   The factor that is manipulated by an experimenter.

dependent variable   The factor that an experimenter measures to monitor a change in response to changes in an independent variable.

behavioral intervention   An approach to finding relations between body variables and behavioral variables that involves intervening in the behavior of an organism and looking for resultant changes in body structure or function.

1.2 Three Main Approaches to Studying the Neuroscience of Behavior
(a) In somatic intervention, investigators change the body structure or chemistry of an animal in some way and observe and measure any resulting behavioral effects. (b) Conversely, in behavioral intervention, researchers change an animal's behavior or its environment and try to ascertain whether the change results in physiological or anatomical changes. (c) Measurements of both kinds of variables allow researchers to arrive at correlations between somatic changes and behavioral changes. (d) Each approach enriches and informs the others.

Attempts to apply knowledge also benefit basic research. For example, the study of memory disorders in humans has pushed investigators to extend our knowledge of the brain regions involved in different kinds of memory (see Chapter 17).

Three Approaches Relate Brain and Behavior

Biological psychologists use three approaches to understand the relationship between brain and behavior: somatic intervention, behavioral intervention, and correlation. In the most common approach, **somatic intervention** (**Figure 1.2a**), we alter a structure or function of the brain or body to see how this alteration changes behavior. Here, somatic intervention is the **independent variable**, and the behavioral effect is the **dependent variable**; that is, the resulting behavior depends on how the brain has been altered. For example, in response to mild electrical stimulation of one part of her brain, not only did one patient laugh, but she found whatever she happened to be looking at amusing (Fried et al., 1998).

In later chapters we describe many kinds of somatic intervention with both humans and other animals, as in the following examples:

- A hormone is administered to some animals but not to others; various behaviors of the two groups are later compared.
- A part of the brain is stimulated electrically, and behavioral effects are observed.
- A connection between two parts of the nervous system is cut, and changes in behavior are measured.

The approach opposite to somatic intervention is psychological or **behavioral intervention** (**Figure 1.2b**). In this approach, the scientist intervenes in the behavior of an organism and looks for resulting changes in body structure or function. Here, behavior is the independent variable, and change in the body is the dependent variable. Among the examples that we will consider in later chapters are the following:

- Putting two adults of opposite sex together may lead to increased secretion of certain hormones.

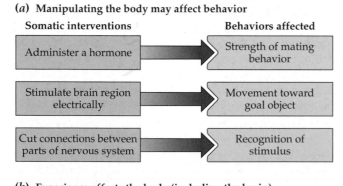

(a) Manipulating the body may affect behavior

Somatic interventions		Behaviors affected
Administer a hormone	→	Strength of mating behavior
Stimulate brain region electrically	→	Movement toward goal object
Cut connections between parts of nervous system	→	Recognition of stimulus

(b) Experience affects the body (including the brain)

Somatic effects		Behavioral interventions
Changes in hormone levels	←	Put male in presence of female
Changes in electrical activity of brain	←	Present a visual stimulus
Anatomical changes in nerve cells	←	Give training

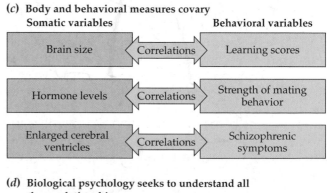

(c) Body and behavioral measures covary

Somatic variables		Behavioral variables
Brain size	⟷ Correlations	Learning scores
Hormone levels	⟷ Correlations	Strength of mating behavior
Enlarged cerebral ventricles	⟷ Correlations	Schizophrenic symptoms

(d) Biological psychology seeks to understand all these relationships

Somatic intervention

Somatic variables ⟷ Correlations ⟷ Behavioral variables

Behavioral intervention

- Exposing a person or animal to a visual stimulus provokes changes in electrical activity and blood flow in parts of the brain.
- Training of animals in a maze is accompanied by electrical, biochemical, and anatomical changes in parts of their brains.

The third approach to brain-behavior relations, **correlation** (**Figure 1.2c**), consists of finding the extent to which a given body measure varies with a given behavioral measure. Later we will examine the following questions, among others:

- Are people with large brains more intelligent than people with smaller brains?
- Are individual differences in sexual behavior correlated with levels of certain hormones in the individuals?
- Is the severity of schizophrenia correlated with the magnitude of changes in brain structure?

Such correlations should not be taken as proof of causal relationship. For one thing, even if a causal relation exists, the correlation does not reveal its direction—that is, which variable is independent and which is dependent. For another, two factors might be correlated only because a third, unknown factor affects the two factors measured. What a correlation does indicate is that the two variables are linked in some way—directly or indirectly. Such a correlation often stimulates investigators to formulate hypotheses and to test them by somatic or behavioral intervention.

Combining these three approaches yields the circle diagram of **Figure 1.2d**. This diagram incorporates the basic approaches to studying relationships between bodily processes and behavior. It also emphasizes the theme that the relations between brain and body are reciprocal: each affects the other in an ongoing cycle of bodily and behavioral interactions. We will see examples of this reciprocal relationship throughout the book.

Neuroplasticity: Behavior Can Change the Brain

The idea that there is a reciprocal relationship between brain and behavior has embedded within it a concept that is, for most people, startling. When we say that behavior and experience affect the brain, we mean that they, literally, physically alter the brain. The brain of a child growing up in a French-speaking household assembles itself into a configuration different from that of the brain of a child who hears only English. That's why the first child, as an adult, understands French effortlessly while the second does not. In this case we cannot tell you what the structural differences are exactly, but we do know one part of the brain that is being altered by these different experiences (see Chapter 19).

Numerous examples, almost all in animal subjects, show that experience can affect the number or size of neurons, or the number or size of connections between neurons. This ability of the brain, both in development and in adulthood, to be changed by the environment and by experience, is called **neuroplasticity** (or **neural plasticity**).

Today when we hear the word *plastic*, we think of the class of materials found in so many modern products. But originally, *plastic* meant "flexible, malleable" (from the Greek *plassein*, "to mold or form"), and the modern materials were named *plastics* because they can be molded into nearly any shape. In 1890, William James (1842–1910) described plasticity as the possession of a structure weak enough to yield to an influence but strong enough not to yield all at once:

> Nervous tissue seems endowed with a very extraordinary degree of plasticity of this sort; so that we may without hesitation lay down as our first proposition the following, that the phenomena of habit in living beings are due to the plasticity of the organic materials of which their bodies are composed. (p. 110)

correlation The covariation of two measures.

neuroplasticity or neural plasticity The ability of the nervous system to change in response to experience or the environment.

In the ensuing years, research has shown that the brain is even more plastic than James suspected. For example, parts of neurons known as dendritic spines (see Chapter 2) appear to be in constant motion, changing shape in the course of seconds (H. Fischer et al., 1998). We will see many examples in which experience alters the structure and/or function of the brain. In Chapter 5, hearing a baby cry will cause the mother's brain to secrete a hormone; in Chapter 7, visual experience in kittens will direct the formation of connections in the brain; in Chapter 12, a mother rat's grooming of her pups will affect the survival of spinal cord neurons; and in Chapter 17, a sea slug learning a task will strengthen the connections between two particular neurons.

Biological and social psychology are related

The plasticity of the human brain has a remarkable consequence: other individuals can affect the physical structure of your brain! Indeed, the whole point of coming to a lecture hall is to have the instructor use words and figures to alter your brain, so that you can retrieve that information in the future (in other words, she is teaching you something). Many of these alterations in your brain last only until you take an exam, but every once in a while the instructor may tell you something that you'll remember for the rest of your life. Most aspects of our social behavior are learned—from the language we speak to the clothes we wear and the kinds of food we eat—so our examination of the mechanisms of learning and memory (see Chapter 17) is important for understanding social behavior.

For an example from an animal model, consider the fact that rats spend a lot of time investigating the smells around them, including those coming from other rats. Cooke et al. (2000) took young rats, just weaned from their mother, and either raised each male in a cage alone, or raised them with other males to play with. Examination of these animals as adults found only one brain difference between the groups: a region of the brain known to process odors was smaller in the isolated males than in the males raised with playmates (**Figure 1.3**). Was it the lack of play (Gordon et al., 2003), the lack of odors to investigate, or the stress of isolation that made the region smaller? Whatever the mechanism, social experience affects this brain structure. In Chapter 17 we'll see that social experience also enhances the effects of environmental enrichment on brain growth.

Here's an example of how social influences can affect the human brain. When people were asked to put a hand into moderately hot water (47°C), part of the brain became active, presumably because of the discomfort involved (Rainville et al., 1997). But subjects who were led to believe the water would be *very* hot had a more activated brain than did subjects led to believe the discomfort would be minimal (**Figure 1.4**), even though the water was the same temperature for all subjects. The socially induced psychological expectation affected the magnitude of the brain

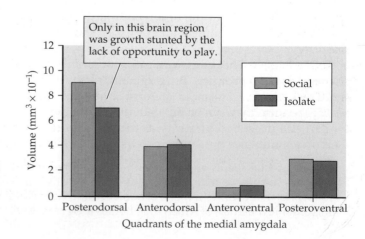

1.3 The Role of Play in Brain Development   A brain region involved in processing odors (the posterodorsal portion of the medial amygdala) was smaller in male rats housed individually compared to males housed together and allowed to play. Other nearby regions were identical in the two groups. (After Cooke et al., 2000.)

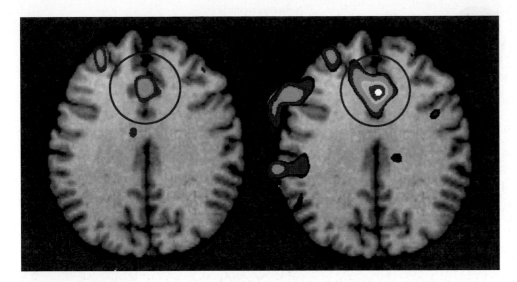

1.4 Pictures of Pain Subjects told to expect only mild discomfort from putting a hand into 47°C water (*left*) showed less activation in a particular brain region (the anterior cingulate cortex) than did subjects expecting more discomfort (*right*) from water of the very same temperature. Areas of high activation are indicated by orange, red, and white. (From Rainville et al., 1997; courtesy of Pierre Rainville.)

response, even though the physical stimulus was exactly the same. (By the way, the people with the more activated brains also reported that their hands hurt more.)

In most cases, biological and social factors continually interact and affect each other in an ongoing series of events as behavior unfolds. For example, the level of the hormone testosterone in a man's circulation affects his dominance behavior and aggression (see Chapter 15). The dominance may be exhibited in a great variety of social settings, ranging from playing chess to physical aggression. In humans and other primates, the level of testosterone correlates positively with the degree of dominance and with the amount of aggression exhibited. Winning a contest, whether a game of chess or a boxing match, raises the level of testosterone; losing a contest lowers the level. Thus, at any moment the level of testosterone is determined, in part, by recent dominant-submissive social experience; and the level of testosterone determines, in part, the degree of dominance and aggression in the future. Of course, social and cultural factors also help determine the frequency of aggression; cross-cultural differences in rates of aggression exist that cannot be correlated with hormone levels, and ways of expressing aggression and dominance are influenced by sociocultural factors.

Perhaps nothing distinguishes biological psychology from other neurosciences more clearly than this fascination with neuroplasticity and the role of experience. Biological psychologists have a pervasive interest in how experience physically alters the brain and therefore affects future behavior. We will touch on this theme in every chapter of this book and review some of these examples again in the Afterword.

Biological Psychologists Use Several Levels of Analysis

Scientific explanations usually involve analysis on a simpler or more basic level of organization than that of the structure or function to be explained. This approach is known as **reductionism**. In principle, it is possible to reduce each explanatory series down to the molecular or atomic level, though for practical reasons this extent of reductionism is rare. For example, most chemists deal with large, complex molecules and the laws that govern them; seldom do they seek explanations in terms of atoms.

Finding explanations for behavior often requires several levels of biological analysis. The units of each level of analysis are simpler in structure and organization than those of the level above. The **levels of analysis** range from social interactions to the brain, continuing to successively less complex units until we arrive at single nerve cells and their even simpler, molecular constituents.

reductionism The scientific strategy of breaking a system down into increasingly smaller parts in order to understand it.

levels of analysis The scope of experimental approaches. A scientist may try to understand behavior by monitoring molecules, nerve cells, brain regions, or social environments, or some combination of these levels of analysis.

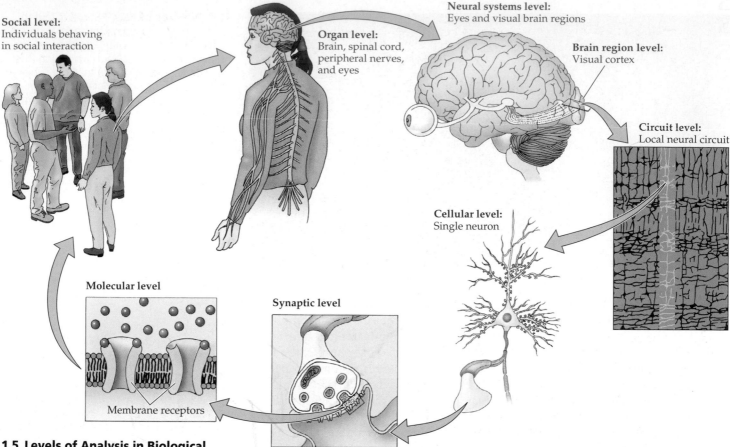

Social level:
Individuals behaving
in social interaction

Organ level:
Brain, spinal cord,
peripheral nerves,
and eyes

Neural systems level:
Eyes and visual brain regions

Brain region level:
Visual cortex

Circuit level:
Local neural circuit

Cellular level:
Single neuron

Molecular level

Synaptic level

Membrane receptors

1.5 Levels of Analysis in Biological Psychology   The scope of biological psychology ranges from the level of the individual interacting with others, to the level of the molecule. Depending on the question at hand, investigators use different techniques to focus on these many levels, but always with an eye toward how their findings apply to behavior.

Naturally, in all fields different problems are carried to different levels of analysis, and fruitful work is often being done simultaneously by different workers at several levels (**Figure 1.5**). Thus, in their research on visual perception, cognitive psychologists advance analytical descriptions of behavior. They try to determine how the eyes move while looking at a visual pattern, or how the contrast among parts of the pattern determines its visibility. Meanwhile, other biological psychologists study the differences in visual endowments among species and try to determine the adaptive significance of these differences. For example, how is the presence (or absence) of color vision related to the life of a species? At the same time, other investigators trace out brain structures and networks involved in different kinds of visual discrimination. Still other scientists try to ascertain the electrical and chemical events that occur in the brain during vision.

A Preview of the Book: Fables and Facts about the Brain

Here are some examples of research topics considered in this book:

- How does the brain grow, maintain, and repair itself over the life span, and how are these capacities related to the growth and development of the mind and behavior from the womb to the tomb?

- How does the nervous system capture, process, and represent information about the environment? For example, sometimes brain damage causes a person to lose the ability to identify other people's faces; what does that tell us about how the brain recognizes faces?

- How does sexual orientation develop? Some brain regions are different in heterosexual versus homosexual men; what do those differences tell us about the development of human sexual orientation?

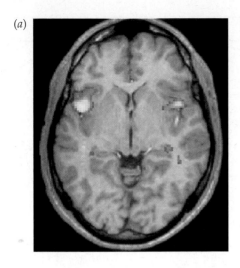

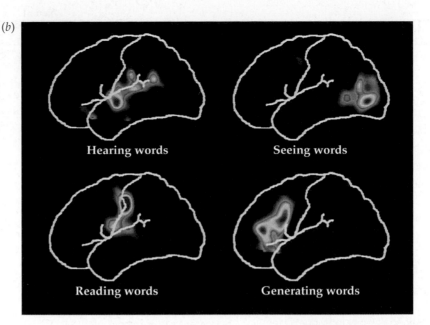

Hearing words

Seeing words

Reading words

Generating words

1.6 "Tell Me Where Is Fancy Bred?" (a) The parts of the brain highlighted here become especially active when a person thinks about his or her romantic partner. (b) Different brain regions are activated when people perform four different language tasks. The techniques used to generate such images are described in Chapter 2. (Part a from Bartels and Zeki, 2000; part b courtesy of Marcus Raichle.)

- What brain sites and activities underlie feelings and emotional expression? Are particular parts of the brain active in romantic love, for example (**Figure 1.6a**)?
- Some people suffer damage to the brain and afterward seem alarmingly unconcerned about dangerous situations and unable to judge the emotions of other people; what parts of the brain are damaged to cause such changes?
- How does the brain manage to change during learning, and how are memories retrieved?
- Why are different brain regions active during different language tasks (**Figure 1.6b**)?

The relationship between the brain and behavior is, on the one hand, very mysterious because it is difficult to understand how a physical device, the brain, could be responsible for our subjective experiences of fear, love, and awe. Yet despite this mystery, we all use our brains every day. Perhaps it is the "everyday miracle" aspect of the topic that has generated so much folk wisdom about the brain. Think of it as "neuromythology."

Sometimes these popular ideas about the brain are in line with our current knowledge, but in many cases we know they are false. For example, the notion that we normally use only a tenth (or a third, or a half, or some other fraction) of our brain is commonplace, but patent nonsense. Brain scans make it clear that the entire brain is activated by even fairly mundane tasks. Indeed, although the areas of activation shown in Figure 1.6 appear rather small and discrete, we will show in Box 2.3 that experimenters must work very hard to create images that separate activation related to a particular task from the background of widespread, ongoing brain activity.

In fact, it's fairly easy to reel off a host of commonly held beliefs about the relationships between the brain and behavior. **Table 1.2** presents a list of such beliefs that you may have heard, interspersed with some claims that are true but may sound improbable.

Neuroscience Contributes to Our Understanding of Psychiatric Disorders

One of the great promises of biological psychology is that it can help us understand brain disorders and devise treatment strategies. Like any other complex mechanism, the brain is subject to a variety of malfunctions and breakdowns. People

TABLE 1.2 Neuromythology: Facts or Fables?

Statement	True?	Chapter where discussed
Some human nerve cells are more than 3 feet long.	True	2
Nerve impulses travel at the speed of light.	False	3
More people die each year from the use of legal drugs than illegal drugs.	True	4
Only humans seek mind-altering substances.	False	4
Our bodies make chemicals that are similar in structure to heroin and marijuana	True	4
Testosterone is made only by males, and estrogen is made only by females.	False	5
Only humans have created cultures.	False	6
Once our brains are developed, we can never grow new nerve cells.	False	7
Some people are incapable of feeling pain.	True	8
Different parts of the tongue are specialized to recognize certain tastes.	False	9
Dogs are color-blind.	False	10
Each side of the brain controls the muscles on the opposite side of the body.	True	11
There are no anatomical differences between men's and women's brains.	False	12
In some animal species every individual is female.	True	12
Some people are "born gay."	Uncertain	12
Most of our energy is expended just maintaining our body temperature.	True	13
We can lose weight permanently by surgically removing fat from our bodies.	False	13
The peaks in cases of depression and suicide occur around Christmas holidays.	False	14
During sleep the brain is relatively inactive.	Not always	14
Sleepwalkers are acting out dreams.	False	14
Prolonged sleep deprivation will make you temporarily crazy.	False	14
Some animals can have half their brain asleep and the other half awake.	True	14
The left side of the face is more emotionally expressive than the right side.	True	15
Prolonged stress can cause heart disease.	True	15
All cultural groups recognize the same facial expressions for various emotions.	Uncertain	15
It is possible to determine scientifically whether someone is lying.	False (for now)	15
Scientists are not sure why antidepressant drugs work.	True	16
People in northern countries are more susceptible to seasonal depression.	Uncertain	16
Some people are incapable of producing any new memories.	True	17
We never really forget anything that we have experienced.	Uncertain	17
Each memory is stored in its own brain cells.	False (probably)	17
A stimulating environment can change the structure of an animal's brain.	True	17
We can take in a whole visual scene in just a single glance.	False	18
My brain decides what I will do next, before my conscious self is aware of the decision.	Uncertain	18
People are "right-brained" or "left-brained."	False	19
A child can have half of the brain removed and still develop normal intelligence.	True	19
Chimpanzees can use symbols to communicate.	True	19

afflicted by disorders of the brain are not an exotic few. At least one person in five around the world currently suffers from neurological and/or psychiatric disorders that vary in severity from complete disability to significant changes in quality of life. **Figure 1.7a** shows the estimated numbers of U.S. residents afflicted by some of the main neurological disorders. **Figure 1.7b** gives estimates of the numbers of U.S. adults who suffer from certain major psychiatric disorders. The percentage of U.S. adults suffering from mental illness may be increasing (Torrey, 2002).

The toll of these disorders is enormous, in terms of both individual suffering and social costs (Demyttenaere et al., 2004). The National Advisory Mental Health

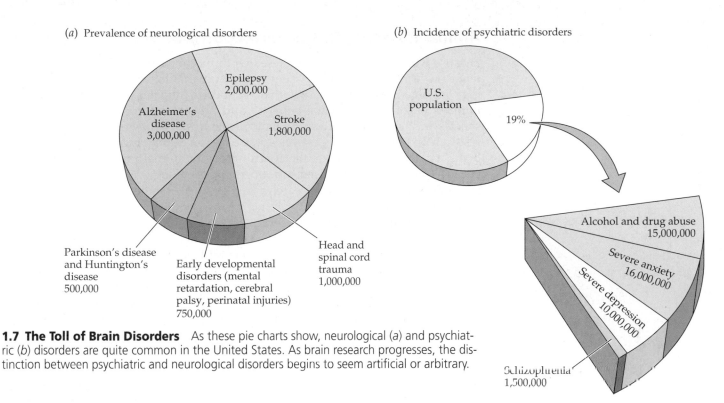

(a) Prevalence of neurological disorders

Epilepsy
2,000,000

Alzheimer's
disease
3,000,000

Stroke
1,800,000

Parkinson's disease
and Huntington's
disease
500,000

Early developmental
disorders (mental
retardation, cerebral
palsy, perinatal injuries)
750,000

Head and
spinal cord
trauma
1,000,000

(b) Incidence of psychiatric disorders

U.S.
population

19%

Alcohol and drug abuse
15,000,000

Severe anxiety
16,000,000

Severe depression
10,000,000

Schizophrenia
1,500,000

1.7 The Toll of Brain Disorders   As these pie charts show, neurological (a) and psychiatric (b) disorders are quite common in the United States. As brain research progresses, the distinction between psychiatric and neurological disorders begins to seem artificial or arbitrary.

Council estimated that direct and indirect costs of behavioral and brain disorders amount to $400 billion a year in the United States. For example, the cost for treatment of dementia (severely disordered thinking) exceeds the costs of treating cancer and heart disease combined. The World Health Organization (2004) estimates that over 15% of all disease burden, in terms of lost productivity, is due to mental disorders. The high cost in suffering and expense has compelled researchers to try to understand the mechanisms involved in these disorders and to try to alleviate or even prevent them.

In this quest, the distinction between clinical and laboratory approaches begins to fade away. For example, when clinicians encounter a pair of twins, one of whom has schizophrenia while the other seems healthy, the discovery of structural differences in their brains (**Figure 1.8**) immediately raises questions for laboratory scientists: Did the structural differences arise before the symptoms of schizophrenia, or the other way around? Were the brain differences present at birth or did they arise during puberty? Does medication that reduces symptoms affect brain structure? We'll consider these questions at length in Chapter 16.

(a) Person with
schizophrenia

(b) Normal

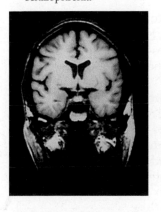
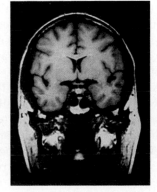

1.8 Identical Twins but Nonidentical Brains and Behavior   In these images of the brains of identical twins, the fluid-filled cerebral ventricles are prominent as dark "butterfly" shapes. The twin whose brain is imaged in (a) suffers from schizophrenia and has the enlarged cerebral ventricles that some researchers believe are characteristic of this disorder. The other twin does not suffer from schizophrenia; his brain (b) clearly has smaller ventricles. (Courtesy of E. Fuller Torrey.)

Animal Research Makes Vital Contributions

Because we will draw on animal research throughout this book, we should comment on some of the ethical issues of experimentation on animals. Human beings' involvement and concern with other species predates recorded history. Early humans had to study animal behavior and physiology in order to escape some species and hunt others. To study biological bases of behavior inevitably requires research on animals of other species as well as on human beings. Psychology students usually underestimate the contributions of animal research to psychology because the most widely used introductory psychology textbooks often present major findings from animal research as if they were obtained with human subjects (Domjan and Purdy, 1995).

Because of the importance of carefully regulated animal research for both human and animal health and well-being, the National Research Council (NRC Committee on Animals as Monitors of Environmental Hazards, 1991) undertook a study on the many uses of animals in research. The study notes that 93% of the mammals used in research are laboratory-reared rodents. It also reports that most Americans believe that animal research should continue. Of course, researchers have an obligation to minimize the discomfort of their animal subjects, and ironically enough, animal research has provided us with the drugs and techniques to make most research painless for the animal subjects (Sunstein and Nussbaum, 2004).

Nevertheless, a very active minority of people believe that research with animals, even if it does lead to lasting benefits, is unethical. For example, in his 1975 book *Animal Liberation*, Peter Singer asserts that research with animals can be justified only if it actually produces benefits. The trick, of course, is how to predict which experiment will lead to a breakthrough. Singer has repeatedly refused to say that animal experimentation is never justified (Neale, 2006). In the meantime, animal rights groups have vandalized labs, burned down buildings, and exploded bombs in laboratories (Conn and Parker, 2008). In 2008, animal rights extremists set off firebombs at the homes of two scientists in Santa Cruz, California. One scientist's family, including two young children, had to flee their home through a second-story window (Paddock and La Ganga, 2008).

The History of Research on the Brain and Behavior Begins in Antiquity

Only recently have scientists recognized the central role of the brain in controlling behavior. When Egyptian pharaoh Tutankhamen was mummified (about 1300 BCE), four important organs were preserved in alabaster jars in his tomb: liver, lungs, stomach, and intestines. The heart was preserved in its place within the body. All these organs were considered necessary to ensure the pharaoh's continued existence in the afterlife. The brain, however, was thrown away. Although the Egyptian version of the afterlife entailed considerable struggle, the brain was not considered an asset.

Neither the Hebrew Bible (written from the twelfth to the second century BCE) nor the New Testament ever mentions the brain. However, the Bible mentions the heart hundreds of times and makes several references each to the liver, the stomach, and the bowels as the seats of passion, courage, and pity, respectively. "Get thee a heart of wisdom," said the prophet.

The heart is also where Aristotle (about 350 BCE), the most prominent scientist of ancient Greece, located mental capacities. We still reflect this ancient notion when we call people *kindhearted, openhearted, fainthearted, hardhearted,* or *heartless,* and when we speak of learning *by heart.* Aristotle considered the brain to be only a cooling unit to lower the temperature of the hot blood from the heart. Around 400 BCE the great Greek physician Hippocrates was expressing the minority view when he wrote,

Not only our pleasure, our joy and our laughter but also our sorrow, pain, grief, and tears rise from the brain, and the brain alone. With it we think and understand, see and hear, and we discriminate between the ugly and the beautiful, between what is pleasant and what is unpleasant and between good and evil.

Around 350 BCE, the Greek physician Herophilus (called the "Father of Anatomy") advanced our knowledge of the nervous system by dissecting bodies of both people and animals. He traced nerves from muscles and skin into the spinal cord and noted that each region of the body is connected to separate nerves.

A second-century Greco-Roman physician, Galen (the "Father of Medicine"), treated the injuries of gladiators. His reports of behavioral changes caused by injuries to the heads of gladiators drew attention to the brain as the controller of behavior. Galen advanced the idea that animal spirits—a mysterious fluid—passed along nerves to all regions of the body. But Galen's ideas about the anatomy of the human brain were very inaccurate because he refused to dissect humans.

Renaissance scientists began to understand brain anatomy

The eminent Renaissance painter and scientist Leonardo da Vinci (1452–1519) studied the workings of the human body and laid the foundations of anatomical drawing. He especially pioneered in providing views from different angles and cross-sectional representations. His artistic renditions of the body included portraits of the nerves in the arm and the fluid-filled ventricles of the brain (**Figure 1.9**).

Renaissance anatomists emphasized the shape and appearance of the external surfaces of the brain because these were the parts that were easiest to see when the skull was removed. It was immediately apparent to anyone who looked that the brain has an extraordinarily complex shape. To Renaissance artists, this marvelous structure was God's greatest gift to humankind. So, in Michelangelo's painting on the ceiling of the Sistine Chapel, part of which is pictured at the beginning of this chapter, God seems to ride the form of the human brain when bestowing life to Adam.

In 1633, René Descartes (1596–1650) wrote an influential book (*De Homine* [*On Man*]) in which he tried to explain how the behavior of animals, and to some extent the behavior of humans, could be like the workings of a machine. In addition to tackling other topics, Descartes proposed the concept of spinal reflexes and a

1.9 Leonardo da Vinci's Changing View of the Brain (*a*) In an early representation, Leonardo simply copied old schematic drawings that represented the cerebral ventricles as a linear series of chambers. (*b*) Later he made a drawing based on direct observation: after making a cast of the ventricles of an ox brain by pouring melted wax into the brain and letting it set, he cut away the tissue to reveal the true shape of the ventricles.

(*a*) Early drawing

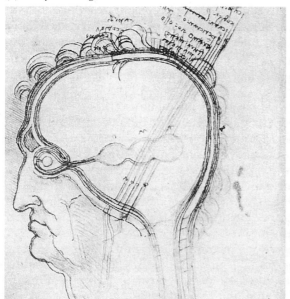

(*b*) Later drawing based on observation

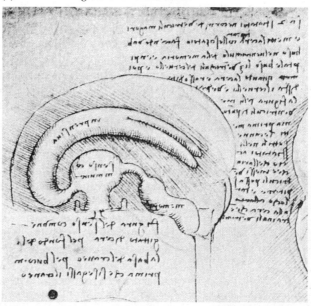

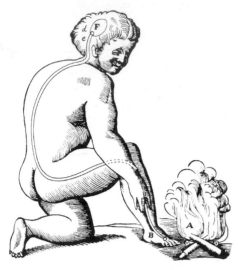

1.10 An Early Account of Reflexes
In this depiction of an explanation by Descartes, when a person's toe touches fire, the heat causes nervous activity to flow up the nerve to the brain. From there the nervous activity is "reflected" back down to the leg muscles, which contract, pulling the foot away from the fire; the idea of activity being reflected back is what gave rise to the word *reflex*. In Descartes's time, the difference between sensory and motor nerves had not yet been discovered, nor was it known that nerve fibers normally conduct in only one direction. Nevertheless, Descartes promoted thinking about bodily processes in scientific terms, and this focus led to steadily more accurate knowledge and concepts.

dualism   The notion, promoted by René Descartes, that the mind is subject only to spiritual interactions, while the body is subject only to material interactions.

phrenology   The belief that bumps on the skull reflect enlargements of brain regions responsible for certain behavioral faculties.

neural pathway for them (**Figure 1.10**). Attempting to relate the mind to the body, Descartes suggested that the two come into contact in the pineal gland, located within the brain. He suggested the pineal gland for this role because (1) whereas most brain structures are double, located symmetrically in the two hemispheres, the pineal gland is single, like consciousness; and (2) Descartes believed, erroneously, that the pineal gland exists only in humans and not in animals.

As Descartes was preparing to publish his book, he learned that the Pope had forced Galileo to renounce his teaching that Earth revolves around the sun, threatening to execute him if he did not recant. Fearful that his own speculations about mind and body could also incur the wrath of the church, Descartes withheld his book from publication. It did not appear in print until 1662, after his death. Descartes believed that, if people were nothing more than intricate machines, they could have about as much free will as a pocket watch, and no opportunity to make the moral choices that were so important to the church. He asserted that humans, at least, had a nonmaterial soul as well as a material body. This notion of **dualism** spread widely and left other philosophers with the task of determining how a nonmaterial soul could exert influence over a material body and brain. Biological psychologists reject dualism and insist that all the workings of the mind can also, in theory, be understood as purely physical processes in the material world, specifically in the brain.

The concept of localization of function arose in the nineteenth century

By the end of the 1600s, the English physician Thomas Willis (1621–1675), with his detailed descriptions of the structure of the human brain and his systematic study of brain disorders, convinced educated people in the Western world that the brain is the organ that coordinates and controls behavior (Zimmer, 2004). A popular notion of the nineteenth century, called **phrenology**, elaborated on this idea by asserting that the cerebral cortex consisted of separate functional areas, and that each area was responsible for a behavioral faculty such as love of family, perception of color, or curiosity. Investigators assigned functions to brain regions anecdotally, by observing the behavior of individuals and noting, from the shape of the skull, which underlying regions of the brain were more or less developed (**Figure 1.11***a*).

Opponents rejected the entire concept of localization of brain function, insisting that the brain, like the mind, functions as a whole. Today we know that the whole brain is indeed active when we are doing almost any task. When we are performing particular tasks, however (as we saw earlier in this chapter), certain brain regions become even more activated. Different tasks activate different brain regions. Modern brain maps of these places where *peaks* of activation occur (**Figure 1.11***b*) bear a passing resemblance to their phrenological predecessors, differing only in the specific locations of functions. But unlike the phrenologists, we confirm these modern maps by other methods, such as examining what happens after brain damage.

Even as far back as the 1860s, the French surgeon Paul Broca (1824–1880) argued that language ability was not a property of the entire brain but rather was localized in a restricted brain region. Broca presented a postmortem analysis of a patient who had been unable to talk for several years. The only portion of the patient's brain that appeared damaged was a small region within the frontal portions of the brain on the left side—a region now known as *Broca's area* (labeled "Speech production" in Figure 1.11*b*). The study of additional patients further convinced Broca that language expression is mediated by this specific brain region rather than reflecting activities of the entire brain.

These nineteenth-century observations form the background for a continuing theme of research in biological psychology—notably, the search for distinguishing differences among brain regions on the basis of their structure, and the effort to relate different kinds of behavior to different brain regions (M. Kemp, 2001). An

(a)

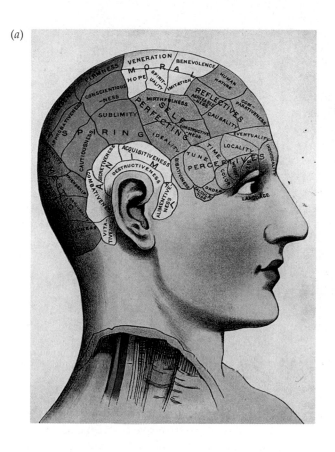

(b)

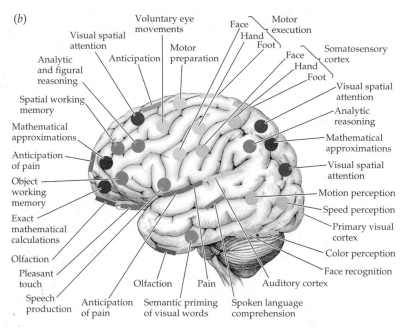

1.11 Old and New Phrenology (a) In the early nineteenth century, certain "faculties," such as skill at mathematics or a tendency toward aggression, were believed to be directly associated with particular brain regions. Phrenologists used diagrams like this one to measure bumps on the skull, which they took as an indication of how fully developed each brain region was in an individual, and hence how fully that person should display particular qualities. (b) Today, technology enables us to roughly gauge how active different parts of the brain are when a person is performing various tasks (see Chapter 2). But virtually the entire brain is active during any task, so the localization of function that such studies provide is really a measure of where *peak* activity occurs, rather than a suggestion of a single region involved in a particular task. (Part b after Nichols and Newsome, 1999.)

additional theme emerging from these studies is the relation of brain size to ability (**Box 1.2**).

In 1890, William James's book *Principles of Psychology* signaled the beginnings of a modern approach to biological psychology. The strength of the ideas described in this book is evident by the continuing frequent citation of the work, especially by contemporary cognitive neuroscientists. In James's work, psychological ideas such as consciousness and other aspects of human experience came to be seen as properties of the nervous system. A true biological psychology began to emerge from this approach.

Modern biological psychology arose in the twentieth century

The end of the nineteenth century brought many important developments for biological psychology. German psychologist Hermann Ebbinghaus showed in 1885 how to measure learning and memory in humans. In 1898, American psychologist Edward L. Thorndike demonstrated how to measure learning and memory in animals. Early in the twentieth century, Russian physiologist Ivan P. Pavlov announced research in his laboratory on conditioning in animals.

American psychologist Shepard I. Franz (1902) sought the site of learning and memory in the brain by removing different brain regions in animal subjects. This work started a search for the traces of experience in the brain—a quest that Karl S. Lashley (1890–1958) referred to as the "search for the engram." Lashley studied with Franz and took over the problem of investigating the locations and mechanisms of memory functions in the brain. In a long career, Lashley contributed many important findings and trained many students to study the biological mechanisms not only of learning and memory, but also of perception and motivation.

Biological psychology bears the strong imprint of Canadian psychologist Donald O. Hebb (1904–1985), a student of Lashley (P. M. Milner, 1993). In his book *The Organization of Behavior* (1949), Hebb showed, in principle, how complex cognitive behavior could be accomplished by networks of active neurons. He suggested

BOX 1.2 Is Bigger Better? The Case of the Brain and Intelligence

Does a bigger brain indicate greater intelligence? Brain size does seem to explain many species differences in complex behavior, as well as the remarkable expansion of the human brain over the past few million years (see Chapter 6). But do variations in brain size within our species correlate with intelligence? This question has been the subject of lively controversy for at least two centuries. Sir Francis Galton (1822–1911), who invented the correlation coefficient, stated that the greatest disappointment in his life was his failure to find a significant relationship between head size and intelligence. But Galton had to use head size, when he really wanted to measure brain size. In addition, he had to rely on teachers' estimates of their students' intelligence, and every student knows that teachers can be quite wrong. Other investigators in the nineteenth century measured the volumes of skulls (Figure A) of various groups and estimated intelligence on the basis of people's occupations or other doubtful criteria.

(A) A nineteenth-century apparatus for measuring the volume of the braincase

The development and standardization of intelligence quotient (IQ) tests in the twentieth century provided invaluable help for one side of the question, and these scores indeed correlate, with ranges from +0.08 to +0.22, with estimates of brain size from head size (Van Valen, 1974).

Newer, noninvasive techniques (discussed in detail in Chapter 2) to visualize the brains of living subjects now make it possible to directly measure brain size. One study found a significant correlation coefficient of about 0.26 between brain size and IQ (Posthuma et al., 2002). In another study, brain scans such as those shown in Figure B were used for measuring the sizes of different brain regions. After correction for body size, the correlation between brain size and IQ scores was 0.38 (Andreasen et al., 1993). IQ seems to correlate better with the volume of the front of the brain than the back (Colom et al., 2009). When the brains of children were measured at age 6 and again at 11, those with the highest IQ displayed the greatest thickening of the outer layer of the brain, especially in the front (P. Shaw et al., 2006).

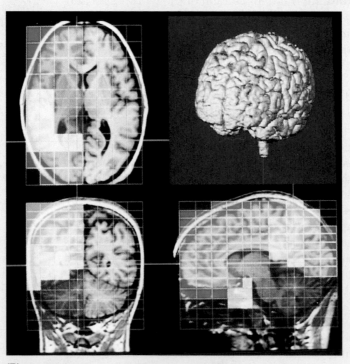

(B) Images from a modern brain measurement study

Another brain-imaging technique revealed correlations between IQ scores and the extent of *connectivity* between brain regions (Chiang et al., 2009).

Thus, on the basis of modern techniques, the long-standing controversy appears to have been settled in favor of a significant correlation between brain size and intelligence. Note, however, that the modest size of the correlations, while statistically significant, indicates that only about 10% of variability in IQ is accounted for by brain size. Thus, there is plenty of room for other factors to contribute to overall IQ. In addition, many people dispute whether IQ tests really measure a general property of intelligence (Stanovich, 2008).

Historically, scientists have misused information about brain size in racially or ethnically prejudicial ways (S. J. Gould, 1981). In fact, however, all racial groups show overlapping and widely varying intelligence and brain size. (Figure A from the Bettmann Archive; Figure B courtesy of Nancy Andreasen.)

how brain cell connections that are initially more or less random could become organized by sensory input and stimulation into strongly interconnected groups that he called *cell assemblies*. His hypothesis about how neurons strengthen their connections through use gave rise to the concept of the *Hebbian synapse*, a topic much studied by current neuroscientists (see Chapters 7 and 17).

Consciousness is a thorny problem

Almost anyone using this book has at some time wondered about **consciousness**: the personal, private awareness of our emotions, intentions, thoughts, and movements, and of the sensations that impinge upon us. How is it possible that you are aware of the words on this page, the room you are occupying, the goals you have in life?

In his review of theories of consciousness, Adam Zeman (2002) notes that almost all scientists agree on some aspects of consciousness:

1.12 How Blue the Sky? We would all agree that this sky is the color everyone calls "blue." But in Chapter 18 we will ask whether everyone who sees that sky has the same experience of color.

- Consciousness *matters*; it permits us to do certain important things, like planning and mentally "simulating" what might happen in the future.
- Consciousness is bound up somehow with the activity of the brain.
- We are not aware of all of our brain's activities. Some brain activity, and therefore some of our behavior, is unconscious.
- The deepest parts of our brain are important for arousal.
- The topmost parts of the brain are responsible for whatever we experience from moment to moment.

In the chapters to come, we will see many examples of experiments that demonstrate these properties of consciousness. However consciousness is brought about, any satisfying understanding would be able, for example, to explain why a certain pattern of activity in your brain causes you to experience the sensation of blue when looking at the sky (**Figure 1.12**), or the smell of cinnamon when entering a bakery. A good theory would let us predict that, by messing about with your brain, changing particular connections or activating particular neurons, you would now experience yellow when seeing the sky (and it's not fair to put colored goggles in front of your eyes; that's easy to understand).

Unfortunately, we are nowhere near understanding consciousness this clearly. We describe some intriguing (and disturbing) experiments explicitly directed at human consciousness in our new Chapter 18. In the rest of the book we rarely use the words *conscious* or *consciousness*. Normally we cannot say anything about the particulars of what human or animal subjects are *experiencing*, but only whether their behavior suggests that the brain detected a signal or event. Thus, we are in no position to know whether complicated machines like computers are, or might one day be, conscious.

Some people even doubt whether our "merely human" brains will ever be able to understand something as complicated as consciousness. Nevertheless, any gains we make in understanding how the brain works, which is the subject of this book, will bring us closer to that goal.

consciousness The state of awareness of one's own existence and experience.

Recommended Reading

Blackmore, S. (2004). *Consciousness: An introduction.* New York: Oxford University Press.

Carter, R. (2009). *The human brain book.* London: Dorling Kindersley.

Doidge, N. (2007). *The brain that changes itself.* New York: Penguin.

Finger, S. (1994). *Origins of neuroscience.* New York: Oxford University Press.

Gallagher, S. (2006). *How the body shapes the mind.* New York: Oxford University Press.

Zimmer, C. (2004). *The soul made flesh: The discovery of the brain—and how it changed the world.* New York: Basic Books.

Go to www.biopsychology.com for study questions, quizzes, key terms, and other resources.

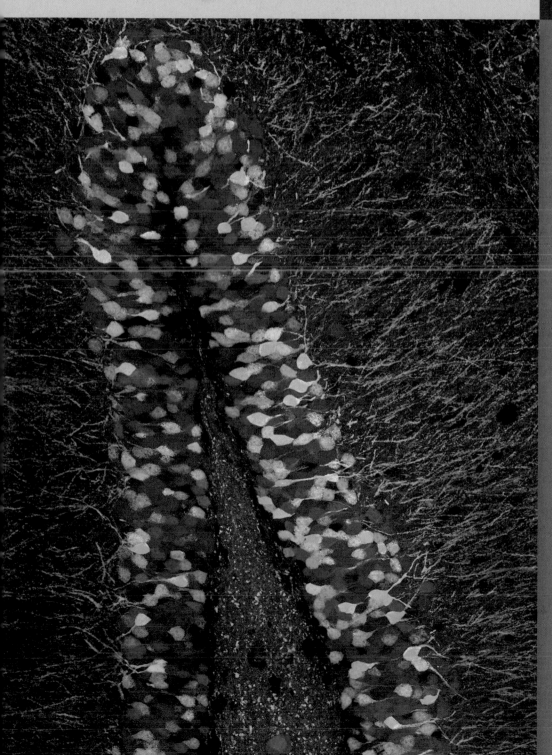

Biological Foundations of Behavior

Previous page   **A "brainbow" photomicrograph of the hippocampus.**   To create this image, four genes encoding differently-colored fluorescent labels were inserted into the DNA of mice, along with a genetic mechanism (called Cre-lox) that allowed a random combination of the four genes to be activated within each neuron. The 90 unique hues that resulted from the various combinations of the four transgenic labels vividly illustrate the complex cellular organization of the hippocampus. (Image by Tamily Weissman, Harvard University. Creation of the brainbow mouse is described in Livet et al., 2007.)

Functional Neuroanatomy: The Nervous System and Behavior

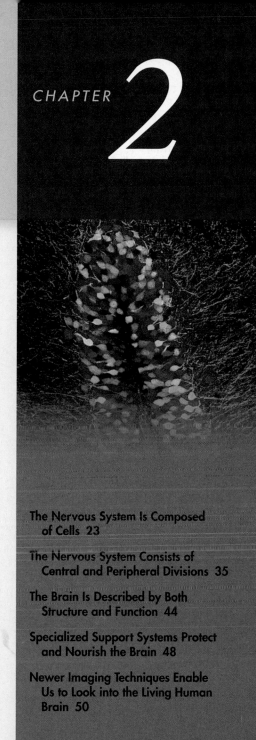

CHAPTER 2

Mapping the Human Brain

It's like a scene from a science fiction film: while you remain conscious and aware of your surroundings, the surface of your brain is exposed and electrically stimulated in precise locations, and your behavioral responses are carefully noted. With procedures perfected during the mid–twentieth century by neurosurgeon Wilder Penfield (1891–1976), thousands of people have undergone electrical-stimulation mapping of the brain to guide the removal of diseased brain tissue without harming neighboring regions critical for important functions like speech or movement. But Penfield and others realized that, beyond its utility as a surgical tool, stimulation mapping offered a way to ask more-profound questions about the organization of the brain.

Penfield found that stimulation of some brain regions reliably provoked specific movements, whereas stimulation of other regions produced specific sensations, like a tingling hand or flashes of blue light. Elsewhere, stimulations could evoke clear and nuanced vignettes of past experiences, such as the smell of a childhood haunt, or a fragment of a favorite song. Some regions were organized identically in different individuals; other regions defied attempts to create functional maps that could be generalized to other people.

Although we now know quite a bit about the organization of basic functions, the brain's control of complex cognition remains mostly a tantalizing mystery. However, the advent of sophisticated brain-imaging technology has infused new vigor into the search for answers to fundamental questions about brain organization: Does each brain region control a specific behavior? Conversely, can every behavior be linked to a particular brain region? Or do some regions act as general-purpose processors? How do the brains of men and women differ? Is everybody's brain organized in the same way?

Thoughts, feelings, perceptions, and acts—from the simplest movements to the most complex ideas—these are the products of the three-pound organ inside your head. In this chapter we begin our exploration of the biological basis of behavior by surveying the structure and basic functioning of this most complicated object. Neuroscientists adopt several different perspectives in describing the physical properties of the brain: accordingly, we open by introducing its microscopic, cellular anatomy. We then turn to the larger-scale neural structures, apparent to the naked eye, that are constructed from cellular building blocks.

In later chapters we will build on this information as we learn how cells within the brain communicate through electrical (Chapter 3), chemical (Chapter 4), and hormonal (Chapter 5) signals.

The Nervous System Is Composed of Cells

The nervous system extends throughout the body, contacting every organ and muscle. Like all other living tissue, the nervous system is made up of cells, the

neuron or nerve cell   The basic unit of the nervous system, each composed of a cell body, receptive extension(s) (dendrites), and a transmitting extension (axon).

neuron doctrine   The hypothesis that the brain is composed of separate cells that are distinct structurally, metabolically, and functionally.

synapse   The tiny gap between neurons where information is passed from one to the other.

most important of which are the **nerve cells**, or **neurons**. These cellular building blocks form circuits that underlie the simplest and the most complex of our abilities and talents. Each neuron receives inputs from many other nerve cells, integrates those inputs, and then distributes the processed information to other neurons. Your brain integrates vast amounts of information by assembling 100–150 billion of these tiny little information-processing units.

The neuron doctrine defines neurons and their connections

In the late nineteenth century, anatomists began looking at brain cells through microscopes, using special stains to make the normally transparent cells visible. They found that brains contain a large assembly of oddly shaped neurons. Unlike the cells of other organs, neurons are enormously varied in size and form.

The interconnection of nerve cells was a hotly debated question in the early days of modern neuroscience. Some nineteenth-century anatomists, notably Italian anatomist Camillo Golgi (1843–1926), thought that neurons were *continuous* with one another, forming a nearly endless network of connected tubes through which information flowed. But Spanish anatomist Santiago Ramón y Cajal (1852–1934), using Golgi's revolutionary staining techniques (see Box 2.1), developed a convincing alternative. On the basis of elegant studies of neurons, drawn so precisely that they remain accurate and useful to the present day (**Figure 2.1**), Ramón y Cajal argued that although neurons come very close to one another (i.e., they are *contiguous*), they are not quite continuous with one another. He insisted that at each point of contact between neurons a tiny gap keeps the cells separate.

From these studies emerged a new perspective—the **neuron doctrine**—which stated that (1) the brain is composed of separate neurons and other cells that are independent structurally, metabolically, and functionally; and (2) information is transmitted from cell to cell across tiny gaps. These gaps were later demonstrated by Charles Sherrington (1857–1957), who named them **synapses**.

It has been estimated that the brain has 10^{15} synapses. This is a remarkably large number: if you gathered that many grains of sand, each a millimeter in diameter, they would fill a cube with each side longer than an American football field. Such vast networks of connections are responsible for all of humanity's achievements.

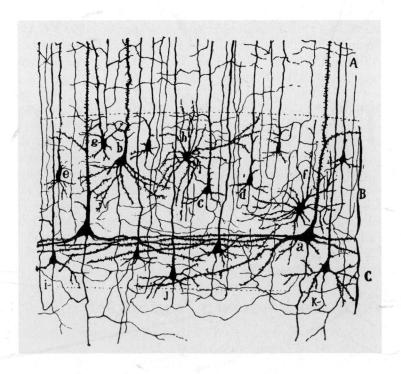

2.1 Nineteenth-Century Drawings of Neurons   The great Spanish neuroanatomist Santiago Ramón y Cajal created detailed renderings of the cells of the nervous system such as this drawing of mammalian brain neurons.

Glial cells (sometimes called *glia* or *neuroglia*) are another important type of cell within the nervous system. We'll see that glial cells are also important participants in information processing; but because neurons are larger and produce readily measured electrical signals, we know much more about them than about glia.

The neuron has four structural divisions specialized for information processing

Because they are cells, neurons contain the usual cellular components found in all cells of the body, including **mitochondria** (singular *mitochondrion*) that produce energy, the **cell nucleus** that contains genetic instructions, and the **ribosomes** and related machinery that translate genetic instructions into proteins. But neurons are specialized to collect signals from several sources, integrate this information, and distribute the processed information to other cells by means of its own electrochemical output signals. Therefore, all neurons share some distinctive structures that are directly related to this information processing. These structures, illustrated in **Figure 2.2**, represent four functional zones:

1. *Input zone*. Cellular extensions called **dendrites** (from the Greek *dendron*, "tree") serve as an **input zone**, receiving information from other neurons. Dendrites may be elaborately branched, to accommodate synapses from many other neurons.
2. *Integration zone*. A **cell body** region (or **soma**, plural *somata*), which contains the cell's nucleus, may receive additional synaptic contacts. In most types of neurons, inputs are combined and transformed in the cell body, which serves as an **integration zone**.

glial cells   Also called *glia* or *neuroglia*. Nonneuronal brain cells that provide structural, nutritional, and other types of support to the brain.

mitochondrion   A cellular organelle that provides metabolic energy for the cell's processes.

cell nucleus   The spherical central structure of a cell that contains the chromosomes.

ribosomes   Structures in the cell body where genetic information is translated to produce proteins.

dendrite   One of the extensions of the cell body that are the receptive surfaces of the neuron.

input zone   The part of a neuron that receives information, from other neurons or from specialized sensory structures. Usually corresponds to the cell's dendrites.

cell body or soma   The region of a neuron that is defined by the presence of the cell nucleus.

integration zone   The part of the neuron that initiates nerve electrical activity, described in detail in Chapter 3. Usually corresponds to the neuron's axon hillock.

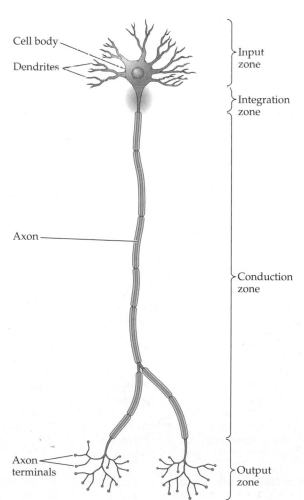

2.2 The Major Parts of the Neuron   The dendrites and cell bodies are covered with thousands of synapses providing information from other neurons. Likewise, each axon terminal branch forms a synapse to pass information to another cell.

axon   A single extension from the nerve cell that carries nerve impulses from the cell body to other neurons.

conduction zone   The part of the neuron over which the nerve's electrical signal may be actively propagated. Usually corresponds to the cell's axon.

axon terminal   Also called *synaptic bouton*. The end of an axon or axon collateral, which forms a synapse on a neuron or other target cell.

output zone   The part of a neuron, usually corresponding to the axon terminals, at which the cell sends information to another cell.

3. *Conduction zone.* A single extension, the **axon**, leads away from the cell body and serves as a **conduction zone**, transmitting the cell's electrical impulse away from the cell body. The details of the electrical signal traveling down the axon are described in Chapter 3.

4. *Output zone.* Specialized swellings at the ends of the axon, the **axon terminals** (sometimes called *synaptic boutons*), are a functional **output zone**. They communicate the cell's activity to other cells at synapses.

Neurons are remarkably diverse in shape; hundreds of geometrically distinguishable types of nerve cells are found in nature, as **Figure 2.3** illustrates.

In many neurons the axon is only a few micrometers (µm) long, but for the neurons that connect the spinal cord to the rest of the body, axons may reach more than a meter in length.* For example, the giraffe has axons that are, incredibly, several meters long. In order for you to wiggle your toes, individual axons must carry the instructions from the spinal cord to muscles in your foot. Long axons of sensory neurons then carry messages back to the spinal cord. The relative sizes of some of the neural structures that we will be discussing throughout the book are illustrated in **Figure 2.4**.

*The meter (m), the basic unit of length in the metric system, equals 39.37 inches. A centimeter (cm) is one-hundredth of a meter (10^{-2} m); a millimeter (mm) is one-thousandth of a meter (10^{-3} m); a micrometer, or micron (µm), is one-millionth of a meter (10^{-6} m); and a nanometer (nm) is one-billionth of a meter (10^{-9} m).

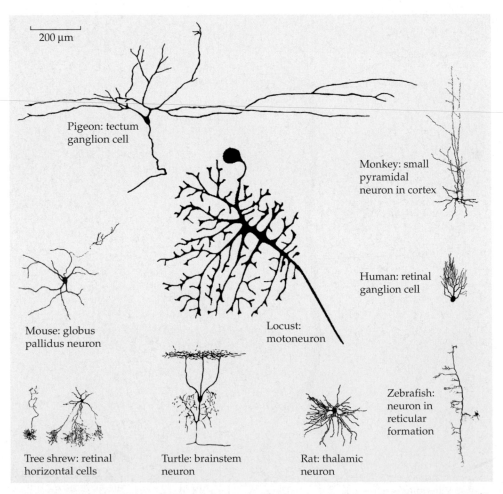

2.3 Variety in the Form of Nerve Cells   Note the considerable variety in the shape and size of these neurons (drawn to scale) from the brain or spinal cord of various animals.

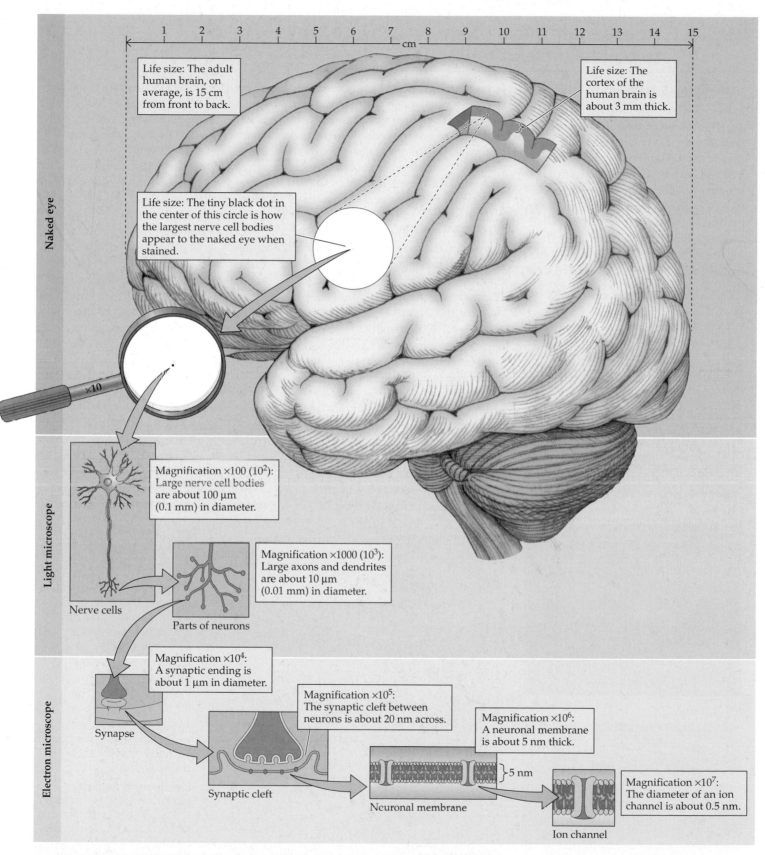

Life size: The adult human brain, on average, is 15 cm from front to back.

Life size: The cortex of the human brain is about 3 mm thick.

Life size: The tiny black dot in the center of this circle is how the largest nerve cell bodies appear to the naked eye when stained.

×10

Magnification ×100 (10^2): Large nerve cell bodies are about 100 μm (0.1 mm) in diameter.

Magnification ×1000 (10^3): Large axons and dendrites are about 10 μm (0.01 mm) in diameter.

Nerve cells

Parts of neurons

Magnification ×10^4: A synaptic ending is about 1 μm in diameter.

Magnification ×10^5: The synaptic cleft between neurons is about 20 nm across.

Magnification ×10^6: A neuronal membrane is about 5 nm thick.

Synapse

Synaptic cleft

5 nm

Neuronal membrane

Magnification ×10^7: The diameter of an ion channel is about 0.5 nm.

Ion channel

Naked eye

Light microscope

Electron microscope

2.4 Sizes of Some Neural Structures and the Units of Measure and Magnification Used in Studying Them

BOX 2.1 Neuroanatomical Methods Provide Ways to Make Sense of the Brain

Visualizing Structures in the Brain

In the mid-1800s, dyes used to color fabrics provided a breakthrough in anatomical analysis. Preserved nerve cells treated with these dyes suddenly become vivid, and hidden parts become evident. Different dyes have special affinities for different parts of the cell, such as membranes, the cell body, or the sheaths surrounding axons.

Golgi stains fill the whole cell, including details such as dendritic spines (Figure A). Golgi staining is often used to charac-

terize the variety of cell types in a region. For reasons that remain a mystery, this technique stains only a small number of cells, each of which stands out in dramatic contrast to adjacent unstained cells. Filling a cell with fluorescent molecules is a modern alternative (Figure B).

Nissl stains outline all cell bodies because the dyes are attracted to RNA, which encircles the nucleus. Nissl stains allow us to measure cell body size and the density of cells in particular regions (Figure C). Other stains are absorbed by myelin, the fatty sheaths that surround some axons (see, for example, the sections of spinal cord shown in Figure 2.10). Improved light microscopes and electron microscopy have also broadened our understanding of the fine structure of cells (e.g., see Figures 2.6 and 2.7).

In a procedure known as **autoradiography**, cells are manipulated into taking photographs of themselves. For example, in order to identify the parts of the brain that are affected by a newly discovered drug, experimenters might bathe thin sections of brain tissue in a solution with a radioactively labeled form of the drug. Time is

allowed for the radioactive drug to reach its target, and then the brain sections are placed on slides and covered with photographic emulsion. Radioactivity emitted by the labeled drug in the tissue "exposes" the emulsion—like light striking film—producing a collection of fine, dark grains wherever the drug has become selectively concentrated (see Box 5.1 and Figure 14.3).

Another way to label cells that have an attribute in common—termed **immunocytochemistry**—capitalizes on the affinity of antibodies for specific proteins. Brain slices are exposed to antibodies that are selective for a particular cellular protein of interest to the researchers (it is possible to make antibodies for almost any protein). After allowing time for the antibodies to attach to molecules of the target protein, unattached antibodies are rinsed off and chemical treatments make the antibodies visible. The process reveals only those cells that were making the specific protein (Figure D). This technique can even tell us where, within the cell, the protein is found. For example, if the protein is a neurotransmitter, the antibodies will detect it in axon terminals. A concep-

(A) Golgi stain

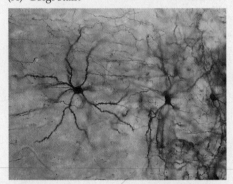

(B) Neuron injected with fluorescent dye

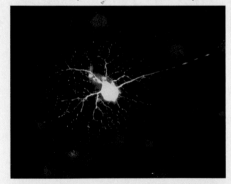

(C) Nissl stain

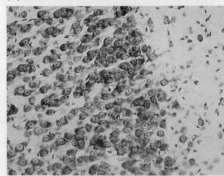

(D) Immunocytochemistry

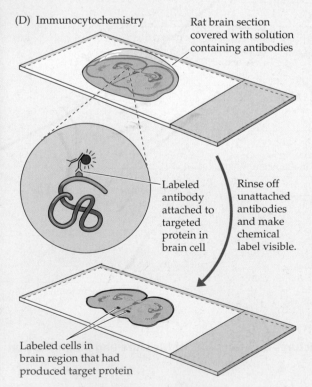

Rat brain section covered with solution containing antibodies

Labeled antibody attached to targeted protein in brain cell

Rinse off unattached antibodies and make chemical label visible.

Labeled cells in brain region that had produced target protein

Golgi stain   A histological stain that fills a small proportion of neurons with a dark, silver-based precipitate.

Nissl stain   A histological stain that outlines all cell bodies because the dyes are attracted to RNA, which encircles the nucleus.

autoradiography   A histological technique that shows the distribution of radioactive chemicals in tissues.

immunocytochemistry (ICC)   A method for detecting a particular protein in tissues in which an antibody recognizes and binds to the protein and then chemical methods are used to leave a visible reaction product around each antibody.

BOX 2.1 (*continued*)

tually related procedure called **in situ hybridization** (Figure E) goes a step further and, using radioactively labeled lengths of nucleic acid (RNA or DNA), identifies neurons that contain a specific mRNA message (see the Appendix). This technique is equivalent to identifying the cells in which a gene of interest has been turned on.

When neurons become more active, they tend to express **immediate early genes (IEGs)**, such as **c-fos**. Using immunocytochemistry to label the IEG product has become a very popular method for determining which neurons are active during particular behaviors. In this technique, animals are sacrificed shortly after performing a behavior of interest, and the distribution of IEG product in brain slices taken from these animals corresponds to the regions of the brain that were most likely involved in that behavior (Figure F).

Tracing Pathways in the Brain

The cells of the brain are interconnected through a complex web of axonal pathways. Gaining an understanding of neuronal circuitry required the development of techniques that clearly identify the origins or destinations of neural pathways. Tracing

pathways in the nervous system is difficult for several reasons: (1) axons have an even smaller diameter than cell bodies; (2) axons from different sources look alike; (3) the brain contains billions of axons; and (4) fibers with different destinations often travel together over parts of their routes, making it hard to disentangle one set from the rest.

Classic anatomical techniques for tracing pathways rely on visualization of the products of degenerating axons. Newer procedures accomplish the same goal by the injection of radioactively labeled amino acids into a collection of cell bodies. These radioactive molecules are taken up by the cell, incorporated into proteins, and transported to the tips of the axons (this process is termed *anterograde labeling*). Autoradiographic procedures, as described earlier in this box, are then used to visualize the locations of the transported substances, making the whole pathway known.

A powerful technique for determining the cells of origin of a particular set of axons employs a tracer such as **horseradish peroxidase (HRP)**, an enzyme found in the roots of horseradish. HRP acts as a tracer of pathways because it is taken up into the axon at the terminals and transported back

to the cell body. After HRP is injected into one part of the nervous system, any neurons that have axon terminals there transport the HRP back to the cell body (this process is termed *retrograde labeling*), and the HRP can be made visible by means of certain chemical reactions (Figure G). All along the way, visible reaction products are formed—akin to footprints along a pathway. (Figure A courtesy of Timothy DeVoogd; B courtesy of Carla Shatz; E courtesy of Brian Sauer and Suzanne Pham; F from Sunn et al., 2002; G courtesy of Dale Sengelaub.)

in situ hybridization   A method for detecting particular RNA transcripts in tissue sections by providing a nucleotide probe that is complementary to, and will therefore hybridize with, the transcript of interest.

immediate early genes (IEGs)   A class of genes that show rapid but transient increases in expression in cells that have become activated.

c-fos   An immediate early gene commonly used to identify activated neurons.

horseradish peroxidase (HRP)   An enzyme found in horseradish and other plants that is used to determine the cells of origin of a particular set of axons.

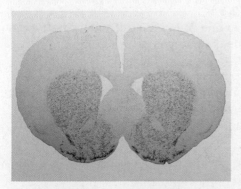

(E) In situ hybridization: enkephalin gene expression

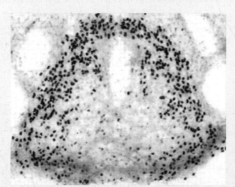

(F) Expression of *c-fos* in activated cells

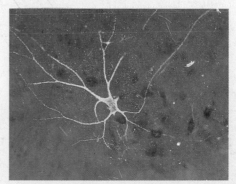

(G) HRP-filled motoneuron

A variety of techniques have been developed to help us visualize neuronal structure and activities. Some of these are described in **Box 2.1**.

Neurons can be classified by shape, size, or function

Anatomists use the *shapes* of cell bodies, dendrites, and axons to classify the many varieties of nerve cells into three principal types, each specialized for a particular kind of information processing.

2.5 A Classification of Neurons into Three Principal Types   (a) A multipolar neuron has many dendrites extending from the cell body, and a single axon. (b) A bipolar neuron has a single dendrite extending from the cell body, and a single axon. (c) A unipolar neuron has a single branch that emerges from the cell body and extends in two directions. Note the four functional zones (input, integration, conduction, and output), which are common to all neurons. In unipolar neurons the integration zone is not in the cell body, but at the trunk of the dendritic branches.

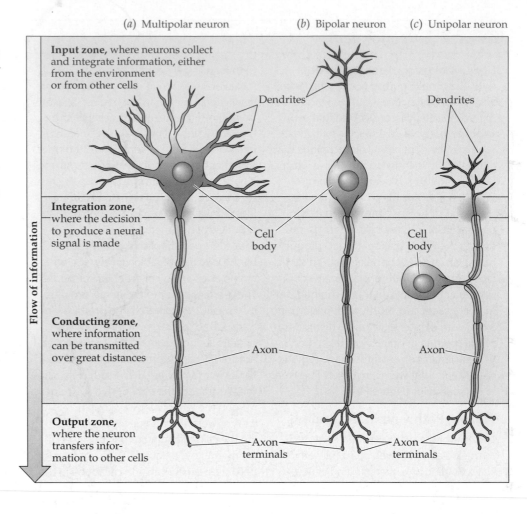

(a) Multipolar neuron   (b) Bipolar neuron   (c) Unipolar neuron

Input zone, where neurons collect and integrate information, either from the environment or from other cells

Dendrites

Dendrites

Flow of information

Integration zone, where the decision to produce a neural signal is made

Cell body

Cell body

Conducting zone, where information can be transmitted over great distances

Axon

Axon

Output zone, where the neuron transfers information to other cells

Axon terminals

Axon terminals

---

multipolar neuron   A nerve cell that has many dendrites and a single axon.

bipolar neuron   A nerve cell that has a single dendrite at one end and a single axon at the other end.

unipolar neuron   Also called *monopolar neuron*. A nerve cell with a single branch that leaves the cell body and then extends in two directions; one end is the receptive pole, the other end the output zone.

motoneuron   Also called *motor neuron*. A nerve cell that transmits motor messages, stimulating a muscle or gland.

sensory neuron   A neuron that is directly affected by changes in the environment, such as light, odor, or touch.

interneuron   A neuron that is neither a sensory neuron nor a motoneuron; it receives input from and sends output to other neurons.

1. **Multipolar neurons** have many dendrites and a single axon, and they are the most common type of neuron (**Figure 2.5a**).
2. **Bipolar neurons** have a single dendrite at one end of the cell and a single axon at the other end (**Figure 2.5b**). This type of neuron is especially common in sensory systems, such as vision.
3. **Unipolar neurons** (also called *monopolar*) have a single extension (or *process*), usually thought of as an axon, that branches in two directions after leaving the cell body (**Figure 2.5c**). One end is the input zone with branches like dendrites; the other, the output zone. Such cells transmit touch information from the body into the spinal cord.

In all three types of neurons, the dendrites are in the input zone; and in multipolar and bipolar cells, the cell body also is part of the input zone.

Another common way of classifying nerve cells is by *size*. Vertebrate nerve cell bodies range from as small as 10 μm to as large as 100 μm or more in diameter; the diversity in neuronal sizes is evident in Figure 2.3. Larger neurons tend to have more-complex inputs and outputs, cover greater distances, and/or convey information more rapidly than smaller neurons.

A third way to classify neurons is by *function*. For example, the axon terminals of **motoneurons** (or *motor neurons*) contact muscles or glands, providing a pathway for the brain and spinal cord to control body movements and organ function. Other neurons are directly affected by environmental stimuli; they respond to light, a particular odor, or touch. These cells are **sensory neurons**. The remaining neurons, which constitute the vast majority, receive input from and send their output to other neurons; thus they are called **interneurons**.

Some glial cells support neural activity

Glial cells were originally believed to hold the nervous system together (the Greek *glia* means "glue"). But glial cells can also communicate with each other and with neurons, and they directly affect neuronal functioning by providing neurons with raw materials and chemical signals that alter neuronal structure and excitability (**Figure 2.6**). In its exclusion of glial cells, the neuron doctrine was perhaps an oversimplification (Bullock et al., 2005).

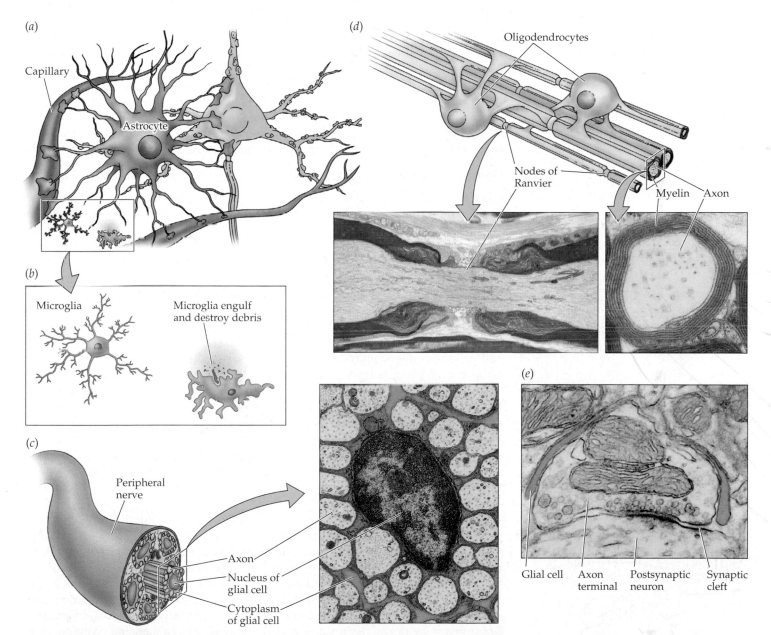

2.6 Representative Glial Cells (a) Star-shaped astrocytes detect neural activity and regulate adjacent capillaries to control blood flow, supplying neurons with more energy when they are active. (b) Tiny microglial cells surround and break down any debris that forms, especially after damage to the brain. (c) *Unmyelinated axons* are embedded in the troughs of glial cells. The light-colored circular shapes in the photograph are unmyelinated axons surrounded by the cytoplasm (blue) of a glial cell (the large dark area is the glial nucleus). (d) Extensions of oligodendrocytes form myelin wrapping (blue) on axons (yellow). The colorized electron micrograph of a myelinated axon (*lower right*) shows the many layers of the myelin sheath. The longitudinal micrograph of an axon (*lower left*) shows a node of Ranvier, the gap between adjacent myelinated segments. (e) Processes from astrocytes (blue) surround and insulate synapses, and directly modify synaptic activity. (Micrographs d [*left*] and e courtesy of Mark Ellisman and the National Center for Microscopy and Imaging Research; c and d [*right*] from Peters et al., 1991.)

astrocyte A star-shaped glial cell with numerous processes (extensions) that run in all directions.

microglial cells Also called *microglia*. Extremely small glial cells that remove cellular debris from injured or dead cells.

myelin The fatty insulation around an axon, formed by glial cells, that improves the speed of conduction of nerve impulses.

myelination The process of myelin formation.

node of Ranvier A gap between successive segments of the myelin sheath where the axon membrane is exposed.

multiple sclerosis Literally "many scars"; a disorder characterized by widespread degeneration of myelin.

oligodendrocyte A type of glial cell that forms myelin in the central nervous system.

Schwann cell The glial cell that forms myelin in the peripheral nervous system.

edema The swelling of tissue, especially in the brain, in response to injury.

arborization The elaborate branching of the dendrites of some neurons.

Compared to the hundreds of types of neurons, glial cells come in only four basic forms. One type, called an **astrocyte** (from the Greek *astron*, "star"), is a star-shaped cell with numerous processes extending in all directions (**Figure 2.6*a***), weaving among neurons. Some astrocytes form suckerlike end feet on blood vessels, regulating local blood flow to provide more supplies to neurons when they are active (Schummers et al., 2008). Astrocytes receive synapses directly from neurons and also monitor the activity of nearby neuronal synapses. They then communicate among themselves and with the neighboring neurons to modulate the neurons' responses (R. D. Fields and Stevens-Graham, 2002; Mauch et al., 2001; Zonta et al., 2003). Astrocytes are also involved in the formation of new synapses.

A second type of glial cell is the **microglial cell** (**Figure 2.6*b***). As the name suggests, microglial cells are very small. They are also remarkably active, continually extending and withdrawing very fine processes that, when they contact a site of damage, form a spherical containment zone around the injury (Davalos et al., 2005). The brain's cleanup crew, microglial cells migrate to sites of injury or disease in the nervous system to remove debris from injured or dead cells.

The third and fourth types of glial cells—*oligodendrocytes* and *Schwann cells*—perform a very different yet vital function for neurons, as the next section describes.

Some glial cells wrap around axons, forming myelin sheaths

All along the length of the axons of many neurons, adjacent glial cells wrap sections of the axon in sheaths of **myelin**, a fatty insulating substance, giving the axon the appearance of a string of slender beads. The process of ensheathing axons is termed **myelination**. Between each pair of myelinated segments is a small gap where the axonal membrane is exposed, called a **node of Ranvier** (**Figure 2.6*d***). As we will see in Chapter 3, the myelin sheathing and nodes of Ranvier greatly increase the speed at which axons can send information. So it's not surprising that anything that interferes with the myelin sheath, such as the demyelinating disease **multiple sclerosis**, can have catastrophic consequences for the individual.

Within the brain and spinal cord, the myelin sheath is formed by a type of glial cell called an **oligodendrocyte** (see Figure 2.6*d*). This cell is much smaller than an astrocyte and has fewer extensions (the Greek *oligos* means "few"). A single oligodendrocyte typically contributes sheathing to numerous adjacent axons, and oligodendrocytes are also commonly associated with nerve cell bodies. The regularity of the wrapping is nicely illustrated in cross sections of the axon (see Figure 2.6*b*). The process of myelination continues for a long time in humans—in some brain regions for 10–15 years after birth, and possibly throughout life. For axons outside the brain and spinal cord, myelin is provided by another type of glial cell: the **Schwann cell**. A single Schwann cell ensheathes a limited length of a single axon.

Many thin, short axons lack myelin but still are surrounded by oligodendrocytes or Schwann cells, which segregate the unmyelinated axons (**Figure 2.6*c***). Furthermore, the manner in which glial cells surround some synaptic contacts suggests that one of their roles is to insulate and isolate synapses to prevent one from affecting the other (**Figure 2.6*e***).

Glial cells are of clinical interest because they form many of the tumors that arise in the brain. Furthermore, some glial cells, especially astrocytes, respond to brain injury by changing in size—that is, by swelling. This **edema** damages neurons and is responsible for many symptoms of brain injuries.

The neuronal cell body and dendrites receive information across synapses

The arrangement of a neuron's dendrites—its tree branch–like **arborization**—reflects the cell's information-processing function. The surfaces of the dendrites are covered with contacts from other neurons, the synapses. Most neurons receive thousands of synaptic contacts, through which information is transmitted from

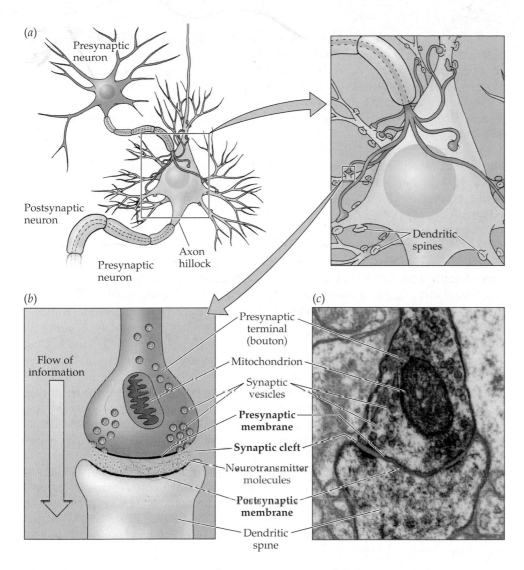

(a) Presynaptic neuron

Postsynaptic neuron

Presynaptic neuron

Axon hillock

Dendritic spines

(b) Flow of information

Presynaptic terminal (bouton)

Mitochondrion

Synaptic vesicles

Presynaptic membrane

Synaptic cleft

Neurotransmitter molecules

Postsynaptic membrane

Dendritic spine

(c)

2.7 Synapses (a) Axon terminals typically form synapses on the cell body or dendrites of a neuron. On dendrites, synapses may form on dendritic spines or on the shaft of a dendrite. (b) Information flows through a synapse from the presynaptic membrane across a gap called the *synaptic cleft* to the postsynaptic membrane. (c) This photomicrograph shows a synapse with some structures color coded.

presynaptic Referring to the region of the synapse that releases neurotransmitter.

postsynaptic Referring to the region of a synapse that receives and responds to neurotransmitter.

presynaptic membrane The specialized membrane of the axon terminal of the neuron that transmits information by releasing neurotransmitter.

postsynaptic membrane The specialized membrane on the surface of the cell that receives information by responding to neurotransmitter from a presynaptic neuron.

synaptic cleft The space between the presynaptic and postsynaptic elements.

synaptic vesicle A small, spherical structure that contains molecules of neurotransmitter.

neurotransmitter Also called *synaptic transmitter*, *chemical transmitter*, or simply *transmitter*. The chemical released from the presynaptic axon terminal that serves as the basis of communication between neurons.

receptor Also called *receptor molecule*. A protein that captures and reacts to molecules of a neurotransmitter or hormone.

presynaptic neurons to the **postsynaptic** neuron (**Figure 2.7a**). A synapse typically has three principal components (**Figure 2.7b**):

1. The **presynaptic membrane**, on the axon terminal of the presynaptic neuron

2. A specialized **postsynaptic membrane** on the surface of the dendrite or cell body of the postsynaptic neuron

3. A **synaptic cleft**, the gap of about 20–40 nanometers (nm) that separates the presynaptic and postsynaptic membranes

Presynaptic axon terminals contain many small spheres, called **synaptic vesicles**, each 30–140 nm in diameter. Each vesicle contains a specialized chemical substance, a **neurotransmitter**, which the neuron uses to communicate with postsynaptic neurons. In response to electrical activity in the axon, these vesicles fuse with the presynaptic membrane, releasing molecules of neurotransmitter into the cleft (see Figure 2.7b). After flowing across the cleft, the released neurotransmitter produces electrical changes in the postsynaptic cell, making it more or less likely to release neurotransmitter from its own axons. Many different substances are known to act as neurotransmitters, which we will discuss in depth in Chapter 4.

The postsynaptic membrane contains a high density of **receptors**, specialized protein molecules that capture and react to molecules of the neurotransmitter. Because each synapse occupies a very small patch of the postsynaptic neuron—less than 1 μm²—a large number of synapses can cover the surfaces of the dendrites and cell body. Some neurons receive as many as 100,000 synaptic contacts, although a more common number is about 5,000–10,000. As you might expect, neurons with elaborate dendrites tend to have more synaptic inputs.

Studding the dendrites of many neurons are outgrowths called dendritic spines (see Figure 2.7a), which, by effectively increasing the surface area of the dendrites, allow for extra synaptic contacts. Both the number and structure of dendritic spines may be rapidly altered by experience, such as training or exposure to sensory stimuli (see Chapter 17). This property of dendritic spines, a form of **neural plasticity**, has made them the focus of intensive research efforts. Some dendritic spines change from minute to minute, while others may be stable for a lifetime (Grutzendler et al., 2002; Trachtenberg et al., 2002).

The axon is a specialized output zone

A typical axon has several distinct regions (see Figure 2.5). The axon arises from the **axon hillock** ("little hill"), a cone-shaped projection of the cell body (see Figure 2.7a). The axon hillock is the neuron's integration zone, gathering information from all the synapses on the neuron's dendrites and soma, then triggering an electrical impulse that carries the neuron's message down the axon toward its targets (see Chapter 3). The axon beyond the hillock is tubular, with a diameter ranging from 0.5 to 20 μm in mammals and up to 500 μm in the "giant" axons of some invertebrates.

With very few exceptions, neurons have only one axon. But this solitary axon often divides into several branches, called **axon collaterals**, allowing the neuron to influence many other cells. The ends of axons or collaterals typically feature additional fine divisions, leading to the axon terminals that make synaptic contacts on other cells, or **innervate** them. **Table 2.1** compares the main structural features of axons and dendrites.

The cell body manufactures proteins under the guidance of the DNA (deoxyribonucleic acid) contained in the cell nucleus (see the Appendix). Therefore, proteins that are needed for the cell to function properly must be transported from the cell body to distant regions in the axon, and recycled materials must be returned to the cell body. The movement of materials within the axon is referred to as **axonal transport**. Some molecules are transported along axons at a "slow" rate (less than 8 mm per day); others are transported by a "fast" system (200–400 mm per day).

Neurons and glial cells form information-processing circuits

Supported and influenced by glial cells, and sharing information through synapses, neurons form ensembles that intricately process information. In Chapter 3 we will turn to the incredible processes by which the basic units of information—electrical signals—are formed, modified, and transmitted by neurons. For complicated high-level processes, these cell assemblies may involve vast numbers of cells and synaptic contacts, combined together in circuits and structures that are visible to

neural plasticity   Also called *neuroplasticity*. The ability of the nervous system to change in response to experience or the environment.

axon hillock   A cone-shaped area from which the axon originates out of the cell body. Functionally, the integration zone of the neuron.

axon collateral   A branch of an axon from a single neuron.

innervate   To provide neural input.

axonal transport   The transportation of materials from the neuronal cell body to distant regions in the dendrites and axons, and from the axon terminals back to the cell body.

TABLE 2.1	Distinctions between Axons and Dendrites	
Property	**Axons**	**Dendrites**
Number	Usually one per neuron, with many terminal branches	Usually many per neuron
Diameter	Uniform until start of terminal branching	Tapering progressively toward ending
Axon hillock	Present	No hillock-like region
Sheathing	Usually covered with myelin	No myelin sheath
Length	Ranging from practically non-existent to several meters long	Usually much shorter than axons

the naked eye as the major anatomical components of the central nervous system. These major divisions are our next topic.

The Nervous System Consists of Central and Peripheral Divisions

In this section we'll describe the **gross neuroanatomy** of the nervous system—the components that are visible to the unaided eye. **Figure 2.8a** presents a view of the entire human nervous system. This viewpoint reveals a natural subdivision into a **peripheral nervous system** (all nervous system parts that are outside the bony skull and spinal column) and a **central nervous system** (**CNS**), consisting of the brain and spinal cord (**Figure 2.8b**).

The peripheral nervous system has three components

The peripheral nervous system consists of **nerves**—collections of axons bundled together—that extend throughout the body. These nerves transmit information to muscles (in motor pathways) or arise from sensory surfaces (in sensory pathways). Three components make up the peripheral nervous system: (1) the **cranial nerves**, which are connected directly to the brain; (2) the **spinal nerves**, which are connected at regular intervals to the spinal cord; and (3) the **autonomic nervous system**, a regulatory system that primarily controls the viscera (internal organs). All three components communicate sensory information to the CNS and transmit commands from the CNS to the body.

gross neuroanatomy   Anatomical features of the nervous system that are apparent to the naked eye.

cauda equina   The caudal-most spinal nerves, which extend beyond the spinal cord proper to exit the spinal column.

peripheral nervous system   The portion of the nervous system that includes all the nerves and neurons outside the brain and spinal cord.

central nervous system (CNS)   The portion of the nervous system that includes the brain and the spinal cord.

nerve   A collection of axons bundled together outside the central nervous system.

cranial nerve   A nerve that is connected directly to the brain.

spinal nerve   Also called *somatic nerve*. A nerve that emerges from the spinal cord.

autonomic nervous system   The part of the peripheral nervous system that supplies neural connections to glands and to smooth muscles of internal organs.

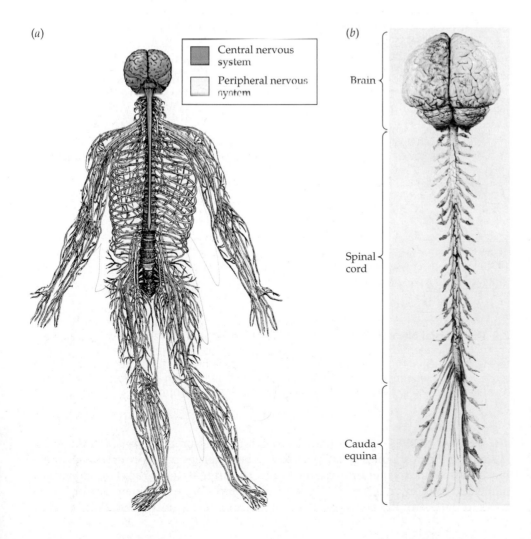

(a)

Central nervous system

Peripheral nervous system

(b)

Brain

Spinal cord

Cauda equina

2.8 The Central and Peripheral Nervous Systems   (a) This view of the nervous system is a composite of two drawings. A modern view of the central nervous system (the brain and spinal cord), shown in blue, is superimposed on a rendering of the peripheral nervous system by the great sixteenth-century anatomist Andreas Vesalius (1514–1564). The peripheral nervous system, shown in yellow, courses through the body and connects all body organs and systems to the central nervous system (CNS). (b) The brain and spinal cord together form the central nervous system. The spinal nerves have been spread out so that they're distinguishable, but they are normally inside the bony spinal column. Note that the solid part of the spinal cord ends in the middle of the lower back. Below this point a spray of fibers called the *cauda equina* (Latin for "horse's tail") continues downward inside the spinal column.

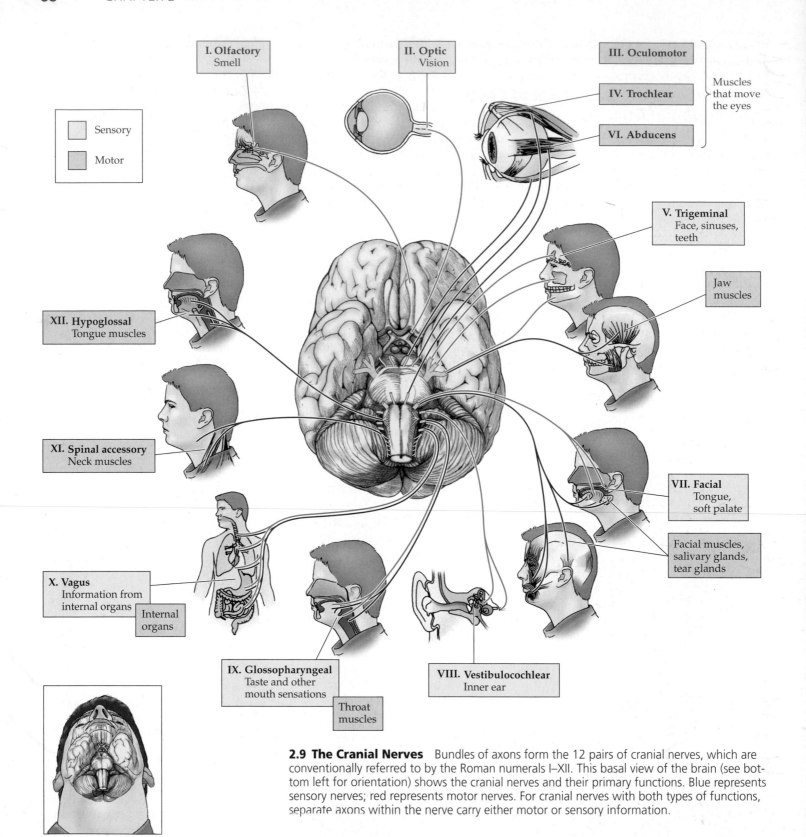

Sensory

Motor

I. Olfactory Smell

II. Optic Vision

III. Oculomotor

IV. Trochlear

VI. Abducens

Muscles that move the eyes

V. Trigeminal Face, sinuses, teeth

Jaw muscles

XII. Hypoglossal Tongue muscles

XI. Spinal accessory Neck muscles

X. Vagus Information from internal organs

Internal organs

IX. Glossopharyngeal Taste and other mouth sensations

Throat muscles

VIII. Vestibulocochlear Inner ear

VII. Facial Tongue, soft palate

Facial muscles, salivary glands, tear glands

2.9 The Cranial Nerves Bundles of axons form the 12 pairs of cranial nerves, which are conventionally referred to by the Roman numerals I–XII. This basal view of the brain (see bottom left for orientation) shows the cranial nerves and their primary functions. Blue represents sensory nerves; red represents motor nerves. For cranial nerves with both types of functions, separate axons within the nerve carry either motor or sensory information.

THE CRANIAL NERVES The 12 pairs of cranial nerves serve the sensory and motor systems of the head and neck (**Figure 2.9**). These nerves pass through small openings in the skull to enter or leave the brain. The cranial nerves are known both by name and by Roman numeral. Three cranial nerves are exclusively sensory pathways to the brain: the olfactory (I), optic (II), and vestibulocochlear (VIII) nerves.

Five are exclusively motor pathways from the brain: the oculomotor (III), trochlear (IV), and abducens (VI) nerves innervate muscles to move the eye; the spinal accessory (XI) nerves control neck muscles; and the hypoglossal (XII) nerves control the tongue.

The remaining cranial nerves have both sensory and motor functions. The trigeminal (V), for example, serves facial sensation through some axons, and it controls chewing movements through other axons. The facial (VII) nerves control facial muscles and receive taste sensation, and the glossopharyngeal (IX) nerves receive sensation from the throat and control the muscles there. The vagus (X) nerve extends far from the head, running to the heart, liver, and intestines. Its long, convoluted route is the reason for its name, which is Latin for "wandering."

THE SPINAL NERVES   Along the length of the spinal cord are 31 pairs of spinal nerves (also called *somatic nerves*), with one member of each pair for each side of the body (**Figure 2.10**). These nerves join the spinal cord at regularly spaced intervals through openings in the backbone. Each spinal nerve consists of the fusion of two distinct branches, called *roots*, which are functionally different. The **dorsal** (back) **root** of each spinal nerve consists of sensory projections from the body to the spinal cord. The **ventral** (front) **root** consists of motor projections from the spinal cord to the muscles.

dorsal root   The branch of a spinal nerve, entering the dorsal horn of the spinal cord, that carries sensory information from the peripheral nervous system to the spinal cord.

ventral root   The branch of a spinal nerve, arising from the ventral horn of the spinal cord, that carries motor messages from the spinal cord to the peripheral nervous system.

2.10 The Spinal Cord and Spinal Nerves   (*Middle*) The spinal column runs from the base of the brain to the coccyx (tailbone); a pair of nerves emerges from each level (see Figure 2.8b). (*Bottom right*) The spinal cord is surrounded by bony vertebrae and is enclosed in three membrane layers (the meninges). Each vertebra has an opening on each side through which the spinal nerves pass. (*Top right*) The spinal cord gray matter is located in the center of the cord and is surrounded by white matter. In the gray matter are interneurons and the motoneurons that send axons to the muscles. The white matter consists of myelinated axons that run up and down the spinal column. (*Left*) These stained cross sections show the spinal cord at the cervical, thoracic, lumbar, and sacral levels. (Photographs from Hanaway et al., 1998.)

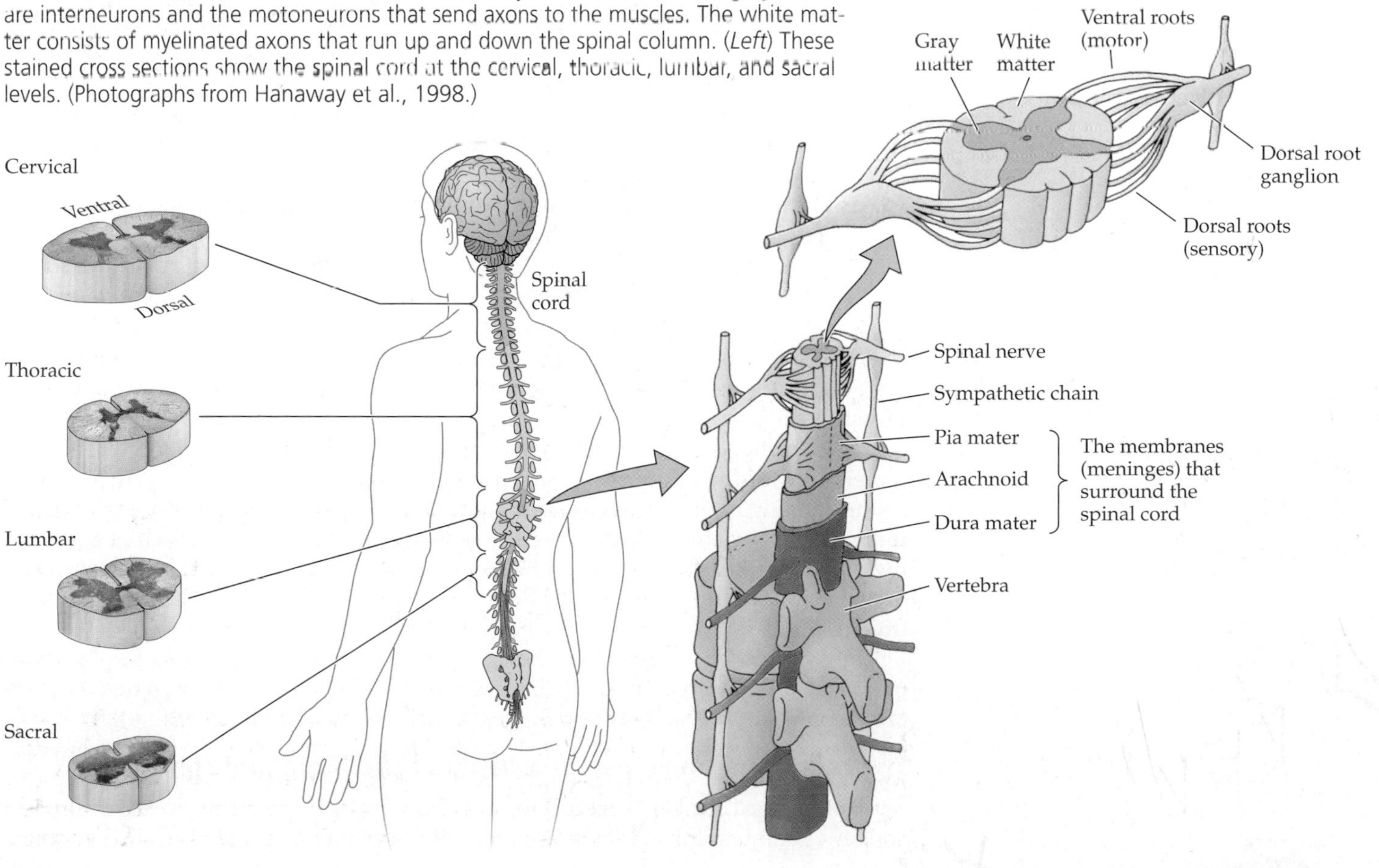

cervical Referring to the topmost 8 segments of the spinal cord, in the neck region.

thoracic Referring to the 12 spinal segments below the cervical (neck) portion of the spinal cord, corresponding to the chest.

lumbar Referring to the 5 spinal segments that make up the upper part of the lower back.

sacral Referring to the 5 spinal segments that make up the lower part of the lower back.

coccygeal Referring to the lowest spinal vertebra (also known as the tailbone).

autonomic ganglia Collections of nerve cell bodies, belonging to the autonomic division of the peripheral nervous system, that are found in various locations and innervate the major organs.

preganglionic Literally, "before the ganglion." Referring to neurons in the autonomic nervous system that run from the central nervous system to the autonomic ganglia.

postganglionic Literally, "after the ganglion." Referring to neurons in the autonomic nervous system that run from the autonomic ganglia to various targets in the body.

sympathetic nervous system A component of the autonomic nervous system that arises from the thoracic and lumbar spinal cord.

sympathetic chain A chain of ganglia that runs along each side of the spinal column; part of the sympathetic nervous system.

parasympathetic nervous system A component of the autonomic nervous system that arises from both the cranial nerves and the sacral spinal cord.

norepinephrine Also called *noradrenaline*. A neurotransmitter produced and released by sympathetic postganglionic neurons to accelerate organ activity. Also produced in the brainstem and found in projections throughout the brain.

acetylcholine A neurotransmitter produced and released by parasympathetic postganglionic neurons, by motoneurons, and by neurons throughout the brain.

enteric nervous system An extensive meshlike system of neurons that governs the functioning of the gut.

The name of a spinal nerve is the same as the segment of spinal cord to which it is connected: there are 8 **cervical** (neck), 12 **thoracic** (trunk), 5 **lumbar** (lower back), 5 **sacral** (pelvic), and 1 **coccygeal** (bottom) spinal segments. We refer to the spinal nerve that is connected to the twelfth segment of the thoracic portion of the spinal cord as *T12*, the nerve connected to the third segment of the sacral portion as *S3*, and so on. Fibers from different spinal nerves join to form peripheral nerves.

THE AUTONOMIC NERVOUS SYSTEM Aggregates of neurons called **autonomic** ("independent") **ganglia** (singular *ganglion*), are found in various locations in the body, outside of the CNS. Their name reflects the historical belief that these neural structures act independently of the brain, but today we know otherwise: the autonomic ganglia are controlled by the CNS. In fact, the autonomic nervous system spans both the central and the peripheral nervous systems.

Autonomic neurons within the brain and spinal cord send their axons to innervate neurons in the ganglia, which in turn send their axons to innervate all the major organs. The central neurons that innervate the ganglia are known as **preganglionic** autonomic neurons; the ganglionic neurons that innervate the body are known as **postganglionic** neurons.

The autonomic nervous system has three major divisions: the sympathetic nervous system, the parasympathetic nervous system, and the enteric nervous system. The preganglionic cells of the **sympathetic nervous system** are found exclusively in the spinal cord, specifically in the thoracic and lumbar regions. These cells send their axons a short distance to innervate the **sympathetic chain**, which consists of autonomic ganglia running along each side of the spinal column (**Figure 2.11 Left**). Cells of the sympathetic chain innervate smooth muscles in organs and in the walls of blood vessels. In general, sympathetic activation prepares the body for action: blood pressure increases, the pupils of the eyes widen, and the heart quickens. This set of reactions is sometimes called simply the "fight or flight" response.

The **parasympathetic nervous system** (from the Greek *para*, "around") gets its name because its preganglionic neurons are found above and below those of the sympathetic system—in the brain and the sacral spinal cord (**Figure 2.11 Right**). Parasympathetic ganglia are not collected in a chain as sympathetic ganglia are. Rather, parasympathetic ganglia are dispersed throughout the body, usually positioned near the organ affected.

For many body functions, the sympathetic and parasympathetic divisions act in opposite directions, because they use different neurotransmitters. The sympathetic system uses **norepinephrine** (also known as *noradrenaline*), which tends to accelerate activity, while the parasympathetic system uses **acetylcholine**, which tends to slow down activity. For example, the heartbeat is quickened by the activity of sympathetic nerves during exercise, but it is slowed by the parasympathetic system during rest. Sympathetic activation constricts blood vessels, raising blood pressure, while parasympathetic activation relaxes vessel walls; sympathetic activation inhibits digestion, while parasympathetic activation stimulates it. The simplified view of the parasympathetic division is that it prepares the body for rest.

Resembling a mesh embedded within the walls of the digestive organs, the **enteric nervous system** is a local network of sensory and motor neurons that regulates the functioning of the gut, under the control of the CNS. Because it regulates digestive activities of the gut, the enteric nervous system plays a key role in maintaining fluid and nutrient balances in the body (discussed in Chapter 13).

The sympathetic, parasympathetic, and enteric nervous systems are "autonomous" also in another sense: their functions are not subject to conscious, "voluntary" control in the same way that we can control our movements.

The central nervous system consists of the brain and spinal cord

The spinal cord funnels sensory information from the body up to the brain and conveys brain motor commands out to the body. The spinal cord also contains

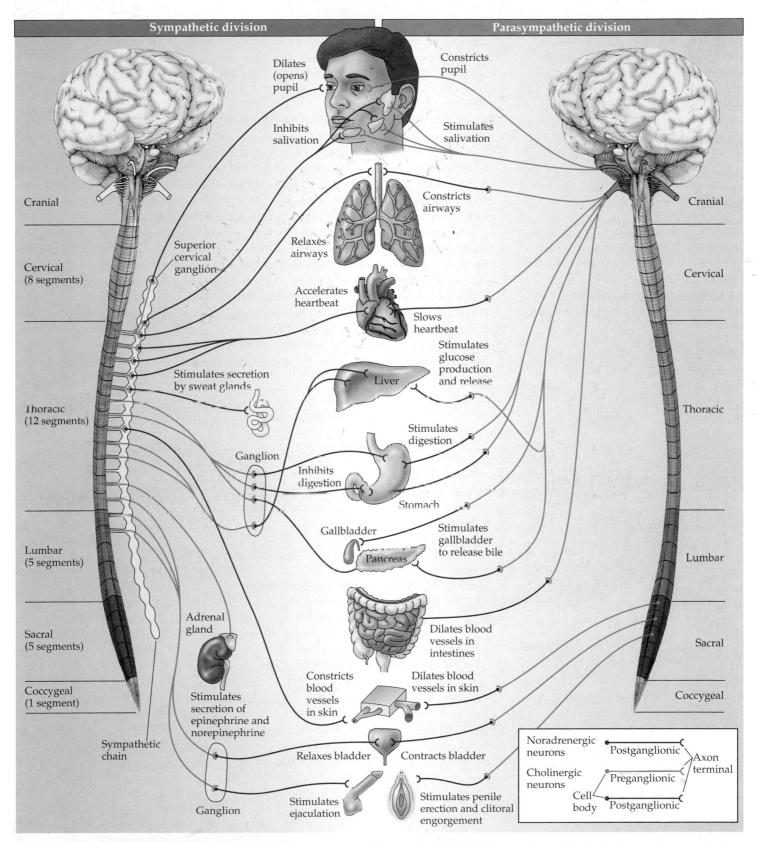

Dilates
(opens)
pupil

Constricts
pupil

Inhibits
salivation

Stimulates
salivation

Cranial

Cranial

Constricts
airways

Cervical
(8 segments)

Cervical

Superior
cervical
ganglion

Relaxes
airways

Accelerates
heartbeat

Slows
heartbeat

Stimulates
glucose
production
and release

Stimulates secretion
by sweat glands

Liver

Thoracic
(12 segments)

Thoracic

Stimulates
digestion

Ganglion

Inhibits
digestion

Stomach

Gallbladder

Stimulates
gallbladder
to release bile

Pancreas

Lumbar
(5 segments)

Lumbar

Adrenal
gland

Dilates blood
vessels in
intestines

Sacral
(5 segments)

Sacral

Stimulates
secretion of
epinephrine and
norepinephrine

Constricts
blood
vessels
in skin

Dilates blood
vessels in skin

Coccygeal
(1 segment)

Coccygeal

Sympathetic
chain

Relaxes bladder

Contracts bladder

Noradrenergic
neurons

Postganglionic

Axon
terminal

Cholinergic
neurons

Preganglionic

Cell
body

Postganglionic

Ganglion

Stimulates
ejaculation

Stimulates penile
erection and clitoral
engorgement

2.11 The Autonomic Nervous System (*Left*) The sympathetic division of the autonomic nervous system consists of the sympathetic chains and the nerve fibers that flow from them. (*Right*) The parasympathetic division arises from both the brain and the sacral parts of the spinal cord. All preganglionic axons, whether sympathetic or parasympathetic, produce and release acetylcholine (from which we get the adjective *cholinergic*) as a neurotransmitter, as do parasympathetic postganglionic cells. Sympathetic postganglionic cells produce and use norepinephrine (also known as noradrenaline; hence the adjective *noradrenergic*) as a neurotransmitter. The different postganglionic transmitters have opposing effects on target organs, allowing precise control. Neurotransmitters are discussed in detail in Chapter 4.

cerebral hemispheres   The right and left halves of the forebrain.

gyrus   A ridged or raised portion of a convoluted brain surface.

sulcus   A furrow of a convoluted brain surface.

frontal lobe   The most anterior portion of the cerebral cortex.

parietal lobes   Large regions of cortex lying between the frontal and occipital lobes of each cerebral hemisphere.

temporal lobes   Large lateral cortical regions of each cerebral hemisphere, continuous with the parietal lobes posteriorly, and separated from the frontal lobe by the Sylvian fissure.

occipital lobes   Large regions of cortex covering much of the posterior part of each cerebral hemisphere.

circuits that perform local processing and control simple units of behavior, such as reflexes. We will discuss the anatomy of the spinal cord later, when we're examining sensation (in Chapter 8) and movement (in Chapter 11). For now we will limit our focus to the executive portion of the CNS: the brain.

BRAIN FEATURES THAT ARE VISIBLE TO THE NAKED EYE   Given the importance of the adult human brain, it is surprising that, on average, it weighs a mere 1400 g, just 2% of the average body weight. However, even casual inspection reveals that what the brain lacks in weight it makes up for in intricacy. **Figure 2.12** offers three views of the human brain in standard orientations. These views will be helpful in our future discussions. Viewed from the side (see Figure 2.12a) or from the top, the human brain is dominated by the large **cerebral hemispheres**.

The convolutions of the paired cerebral hemispheres are the result of elaborate folding together of tissue. The resulting ridges of tissue, called **gyri** (singular *gyrus*), are separated from each other by furrows called **sulci** (singular *sulcus*). Such folding enormously increases the cerebral surface area; about two-thirds of the cerebral surface is hidden in the depths of these folds.

The major sectors of the cerebral hemispheres are four regions called the **frontal**, **parietal**, **temporal**, and **occipital lobes**. These lobes, named after the bones of the skull that overlie them, are distinguished by colors in Figure 2.12. In some cases, the boundaries between adjacent lobes are very clear; for example, the lat-

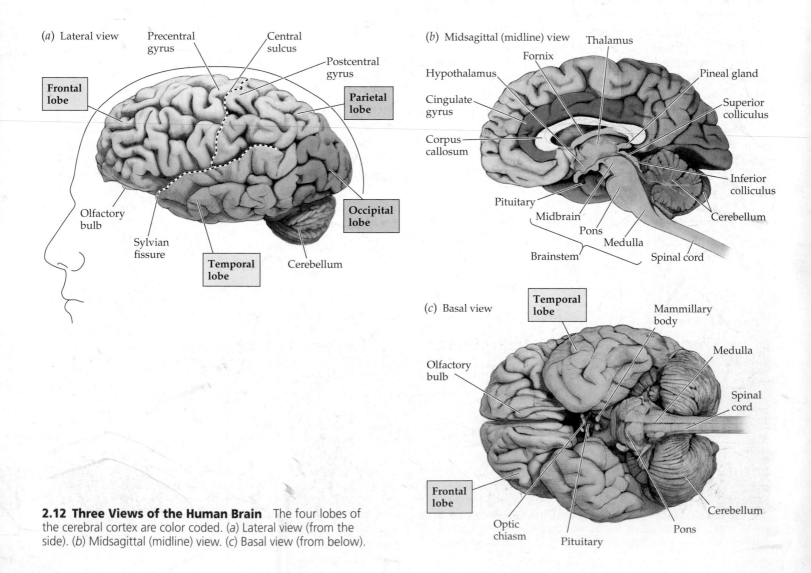

2.12 Three Views of the Human Brain   The four lobes of the cerebral cortex are color coded. (*a*) Lateral view (from the side). (*b*) Midsagittal (midline) view. (*c*) Basal view (from below).

eral sulcus, or **Sylvian fissure** (which demarcates the temporal lobe), and the **central sulcus** (which divides frontal from parietal lobes) are quite distinct. The boundaries dividing the occipital lobes from the parietal and temporal lobes are less well defined. The outer layer of the cerebrum is called the **cerebral cortex** (or sometimes just *cortex*), which consists largely of nerve cell bodies and their branches.

In general, the cortex may be regarded as the seat of complex cognition; damage to the cortex may impair "higher" functions such as speech, memory, or visual processing. In contrast, "lower" parts of the brain regulate respiration, heart rate, and other basic functions. Note that the four lobes of the brain normally collaborate with one another to serve myriad different processes. In a general sense, however, we can identify categories of processing that are particularly associated with specific lobes. For example, the occipital lobes receive and process information from the eyes, giving rise to the sense of vision. Auditory information is directed to the temporal lobes, and damage there can impair hearing (the temporal lobes are also particularly associated with the sense of smell, and with aspects of learning and memory).

The sense of touch is mediated by a strip of parietal cortex just behind the central sulcus called the **postcentral gyrus**. In front of the central sulcus, the **precentral gyrus** of the frontal lobe is crucial for motor control. In fact, Wilder Penfield's experiments with stimulation mapping of the brain, which we discussed at the beginning of the chapter, revealed that the precentral gyrus contains an orderly map of the muscles of the body (see Figure 11.12). Similarly, the postcentral gyrus contains a sensory map of the body (Penfield and Rasmussen, 1950). A large, C-shaped bundle of axons called the **corpus callosum** (see Figure 2.12*b*) crosses the midline and allows communication between the right and left cerebral hemispheres.

To get the most out of our discussion of these systems, you will need to understand the conventions that anatomists use for describing various viewpoints of the body and the brain. These conventions are described in **Box 2.2**.

When you slice into the brain, two distinct shades of color are evident (**Figure 2.13**). Beneath the outer surface is the lighter-colored **white matter**, which consists mostly of fiber tracts. It gains its appearance from the whitish fatty myelin that ensheathes and insulates the axons of many neurons. The darker-colored **gray matter** on the exterior is dominated more by nerve cell bodies and dendrites, which are devoid of myelin.

DEVELOPMENTAL SUBDIVISIONS OF THE BRAIN It can be difficult to understand some of the anatomical distinctions applied to the adult human brain. For exam-

Sylvian fissure Also called *lateral sulcus*. A deep fissure that demarcates the temporal lobe.

central sulcus A fissure that divides the frontal lobe from the parietal lobe.

cerebral cortex Sometimes called simply *cortex*. The outer covering of the cerebral hemispheres, which consists largely of nerve cell bodies and their branches.

postcentral gyrus The strip of parietal cortex, just behind the central sulcus, that receives somatosensory information from the entire body.

precentral gyrus The strip of frontal cortex, just in front of the central sulcus, that is crucial for motor control.

corpus callosum The main band of axons that connects the two cerebral hemispheres.

white matter A shiny layer underneath the cortex that consists largely of axons with white myelin sheaths.

gray matter Areas of the brain that are dominated by cell bodies and are devoid of myelin.

2.13 Inside the Brain (*a*) The colored lines here indicate the planes of section shown in (*b*) and (*c*). The lighter colored interior is white matter, packed with fatty myelin that surrounds axons sending information in and out of the cortex. Gray matter consists of cell bodies that form the outer layers of the cortex and nuclei within the brain. (Photographs courtesy of S. Mark Williams and Dale Purves, Duke University Medical Center.)

(*a*) Lateral view showing planes of section

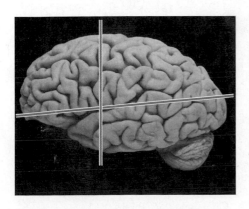

(*b*) Horizontal section

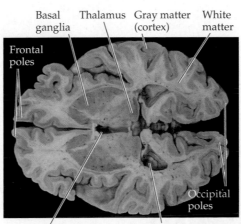

Basal ganglia Thalamus Gray matter (cortex) White matter

Frontal poles

Occipital poles

Third ventricle

Posterior horn of lateral ventricle

(*c*) Coronal (transverse) section

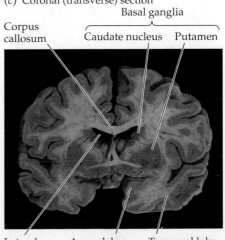

Basal ganglia

Corpus callosum

Caudate nucleus Putamen

Lateral ventricle

Amygdala

Temporal lobe

1/23 L3

BOX 2.2 Three Customary Orientations for Viewing the Brain and Body

Because the nervous system is a three-dimensional structure, two-dimensional illustrations and diagrams cannot represent it completely. The brain is usually cut in one of three main planes to obtain a two-dimensional section from this three-dimensional object. It is useful to know the terminology and conventions that apply to these sections, which are shown in the figure.

The plane that bisects the body into right and left halves is called the **sagittal plane** (from the Latin *sagitta*, "arrow"). The plane that divides the body into a front (anterior) and a back (posterior) part is called by several names: **coronal plane** (from the Latin *corona*, "crown"), *frontal plane*, or *transverse plane*. For clarity, we will view coronal sections from behind so that the right side of the figure represents the right side of the brain. (In medicine,

coronal sections are viewed as if you were facing the patient, with the patient's left on your right.) The third main plane, which divides the brain into upper and lower parts, is called the **horizontal plane**.

In addition, several directional terms are used. **Medial** means "toward the middle" and is contrasted with **lateral**, "toward the side." Relative to one location, a second location is **ipsilateral** if it is on the same side of the body and **contralateral** if on the opposite side of the body. The head end is referred to as **anterior** or **rostral** (from the Latin *rostrum*, "prow of a ship"). The tail end is called **posterior** or **caudal** (from the Latin *cauda*, "tail"). **Proximal** (from the Latin *proximus*, "nearest") means "near the trunk or center," and **distal** means "toward the periphery" or "toward the end of a limb" (distant from the origin or point of attachment).

Dorsal means "toward or at the back," and **ventral** means "toward or at the belly or front." In four-legged animals, such as the cat or the rat, *dorsal* refers to both the back of the body and the top of the head and brain. For consistency in comparing brains among species, this term is also used to refer to the top of the brain of a human or of a chimpanzee, even though in such two-legged animals the top of the brain is not at the back of the body. Similarly, *ventral* is understood to designate the bottom of the brain of a two-legged as well as of a four-legged animal.

An additional pair of words is important for describing the flow of information through the nervous system. We call an axon, tract, or nerve **afferent** if it carries information into a region that we are interested in, and **efferent** if it carries information away from the region of inter-

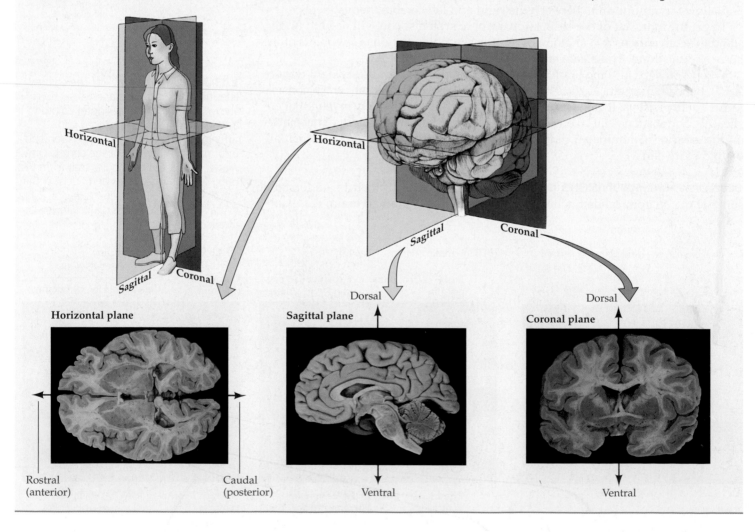

BOX 2.2 (continued)

est (a handy way to remember this is that *e*fferents *e*xit but *a*fferents *a*rrive, relative to the region of interest).

Although these terms may seem strange at first, they provide a means of describing anatomy without ambiguity. If you want to become adept with this terminology, you might find it helpful to get together with a friend and quiz each other about anatomical relations. "Where's the navel? In a medial position on the ventral surface, caudal to the rib cage, and rostral to the pelvis." (Photographs courtesy of S. Mark Williams and Dale Purves, Duke University Medical Center.)

---

ple, why is the part of the brain closest to the back of head identified as part of the *fore*brain? The key to understanding this confusing terminology is to consider how the brain develops early in life.

In a very young embryo of any vertebrate, the CNS looks like a tube. The walls of this **neural tube** are made of cells, and the interior is filled with fluid. A few weeks after conception, the human neural tube begins to show three separate swellings at the head end (**Figure 2.14a**): the **forebrain** (or *prosencephalon*), the **midbrain** (or *mesencephalon*), and the **hindbrain** (or *rhombencephalon*). (The term *encephalon*, meaning "brain," comes from the Greek *en*, "in," and *kephale*, "head.")

neural tube   An embryonic structure with subdivisions that correspond to the future forebrain, midbrain, and hindbrain.

forebrain   Also called *prosencephalon*. The frontal division of the neural tube, containing the cerebral hemispheres, the thalamus, and the hypothalamus.

midbrain   Also called *mesencephalon*. The middle division of the brain.

hindbrain   Also called *rhombencephalon*. The rear division of the brain, which, in the mature vertebrate, contains the cerebellum, pons, and medulla.

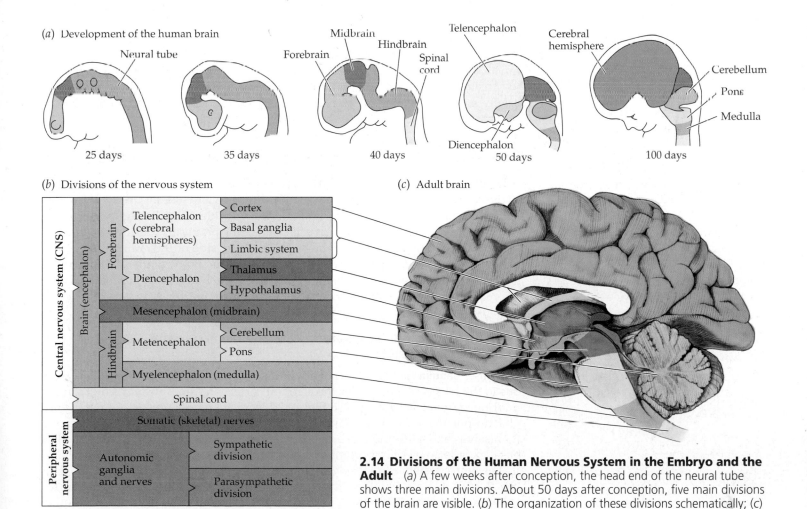

2.14 Divisions of the Human Nervous System in the Embryo and the Adult   (a) A few weeks after conception, the head end of the neural tube shows three main divisions. About 50 days after conception, five main divisions of the brain are visible. (b) The organization of these divisions schematically; (c) their positions in the adult brain.

telencephalon   The frontal subdivision of the forebrain that includes the cerebral hemispheres when fully developed.

diencephalon   The posterior part of the forebrain, including the thalamus and hypothalamus.

metencephalon   A subdivision of the hindbrain that includes the cerebellum and the pons.

cerebellum   A structure located at the back of the brain, dorsal to the pons, that is involved in the central regulation of movement.

pons   A portion of the metencephalon; part of the brainstem connecting midbrain to medulla.

myelencephalon or medulla   The posterior part of the hindbrain, continuous with the spinal cord.

brainstem   The region of the brain that consists of the midbrain, the pons, and the medulla.

nucleus   Here, a collection of neuronal cell bodies within the central nervous system (e.g., the caudate nucleus).

tract   A bundle of axons found within the central nervous system.

basal ganglia   A group of forebrain nuclei, including caudate nucleus, globus pallidus, and putamen, found deep within the cerebral hemispheres.

caudate nucleus   One of the basal ganglia; it has a long extension or tail.

putamen   One of the basal ganglia.

globus pallidus   One of the basal ganglia.

substantia nigra   A brainstem structure in humans that is related to the basal ganglia and is named for its dark pigmentation.

limbic system   A loosely defined, widespread group of brain nuclei that innervate each other to form a network.

amygdala   A group of nuclei in the medial anterior part of the temporal lobe.

About 50 days after conception, the forebrain and hindbrain have already developed clear subdivisions. At the very front of the developing brain is the **telencephalon**, which will become the cerebral hemispheres (consisting of cortex plus some deeper structures belonging to two functionally related groups: the basal ganglia and the limbic system). The other part of the forebrain is the **diencephalon** (or "between brain"), which will include regions called the *thalamus* and the *hypothalamus*.

The midbrain (mesencephalon) comes next. Behind it the hindbrain has two divisions: the **metencephalon**, which will develop into the **cerebellum** ("little brain") and the **pons** ("bridge"); and the **myelencephalon**, more commonly called the **medulla**. The term **brainstem** usually refers to the midbrain, pons, and medulla combined. **Figure 2.14c** shows the positions of these structures and their relative sizes in the adult human brain. Even when the brain achieves its adult form, it is still a fluid-filled tube, but a tube of very complicated shape.

Each of the five main sections (telencephalon, diencephalon, mesencephalon, metencephalon, and myelencephalon) can be subdivided in turn. We can work our way from the largest, most general divisions of the nervous system on the left of the schematic in **Figure 2.14b** to more-specific ones on the right.

Within each region are aggregations of neurons called **nuclei** (singular *nucleus*) and bundles of axons called **tracts**. Recall that in the periphery, aggregations of neurons are called *ganglia*, and bundles of axons are called *nerves*. Unfortunately, the same word *nucleus* can mean either "a collection of nerve cell bodies" or "the spherical center of a single cell," so you must rely on the context to understand which meaning is intended. Because brain tracts and nuclei are the same from individual to individual, and often from species to species, they have names too.

You are probably more interested in the functions of all these parts of the brain than in their names, but as we noted earlier, each region serves more than one function, and our knowledge of the functional organization of the brain is subject to constant revision as new findings are reported. With that caveat in mind, let's briefly survey functions of specific brain structures, leaving the detailed discussion for later chapters.

The Brain Is Described by Both Structure and Function

Although there are some single structures around the midline of the brain—such as the corpus callosum, pineal gland, and pituitary gland (see Figure 2.12b)—most structures are found in both the right and the left sides. One important principle of the brain in all vertebrates is that each side of the brain controls the opposite (or *contralateral*; see Box 2.2) side of the body: the right side of the brain controls and receives sensory information from the left side of the body, while the left side of the brain monitors and controls the right side of the body. We'll learn about how the two cerebral hemispheres interact in Chapter 19, but for now let's review the various components of the brain and their functions.

Within the cerebral hemispheres are the basal ganglia and the limbic system

The **basal ganglia** include the **caudate nucleus**, the **putamen**, and the **globus pallidus** in the telencephalon under the cerebral cortex, and the **substantia nigra** in the midbrain (**Figure 2.15a**; see also Figure 2.13b and c). These nuclei (not really ganglia, despite the unfortunate name *basal ganglia*) are reciprocally connected among themselves and with the cerebral cortex, forming a looping neural system. The basal ganglia are very important in motor control, as we will see in Chapter 11.

The **limbic system** is a loosely defined, widespread network of structures (**Figure 2.15b**) that are involved in emotion and learning. The **amygdala** (Latin for "almond," because it has that shape) consists of several subdivisions with quite diverse functions, including emotional regulation (Chapter 15) and the perception

(*a*) Basal ganglia

(*b*) Limbic system

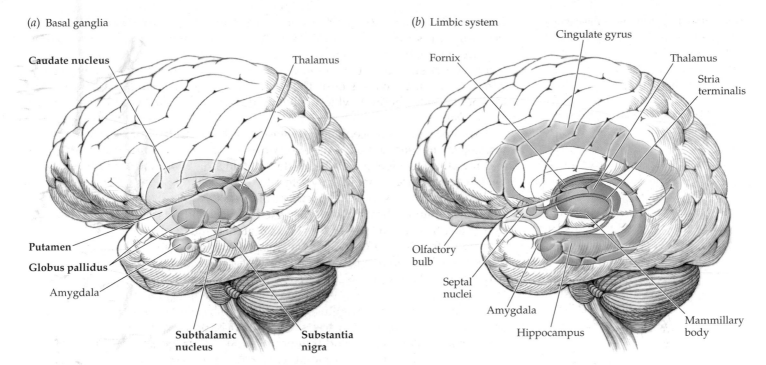

2.15 Two Important Brain Systems   (*a*) The basal ganglia—caudate nucleus, putamen, globus pallidus, subthalamic nucleus, and substantia nigra—are important in movement. (*b*) The limbic system—consisting of hippocampus, cingulate gyrus, fornix, septal nuclei, stria terminalis, olfactory bulb, amygdala, and mammillary bodies—is important for emotion, learning, and memory.

of odor (Chapter 9). The **hippocampus** (from the Greek *hippokampos*, "sea horse," which it resembles in shape) and the **fornix** are important for learning (Chapter 17). Other components of the limbic system include a strip of cortex in each hemisphere called the **cingulate gyrus**, which is implicated in diverse functions, including the direction of attention; and the **olfactory bulb**, which is involved in the sense of smell. The rest of the limbic system, including the hypothalamus and **mammillary bodies**, is found in the diencephalon.

The diencephalon is divided into thalamus and hypothalamus

The uppermost portion of the diencephalon is the **thalamus**, seen in the center of the adult brain in Figures 2.12*b*, 2.13*b*, and 2.15*b*. The thalamus is a complex cluster of nuclei that act as way stations to the cerebral cortex. Almost all sensory information enters the thalamus, where neurons send that information to the overlying cortex. The cortical cells in turn innervate the thalamus, controlling which sensory information is transmitted.

The second part of the diencephalon is known as the **hypothalamus** (see Figure 2.12*b*) because it is beneath the thalamus (the Greek *hypo* means "under"). The hypothalamus is relatively small, but it is packed with many distinct nuclei that have vital functions. It has been implicated in hunger, thirst, temperature regulation (Chapter 13), reproductive behaviors (Chapter 12), and much more. The hypothalamus also controls the pituitary gland, which in turn controls almost all hormone secretion, as we'll learn in Chapter 5.

The midbrain has sensory and motor systems

The most prominent features of the midbrain are two pairs of bumps on the dorsal surface—one pair in each hemisphere. The more rostral bumps are the **superior colliculi** (singular *colliculus*), and the caudal bumps are the **inferior colliculi** (see

hippocampus   A medial temporal lobe structure that is important for learning and memory.

fornix   A fiber tract that extends from the hippocampus to the mammillary body.

cingulate gyrus   A cortical portion of the limbic system, found in the frontal and parietal midline.

olfactory bulb   An anterior projection of the brain that terminates in the upper nasal passages and, through small openings in the skull, provides receptors for smell.

mammillary body   One of a pair of nuclei at the base of the brain.

thalamus   The brain regions that surround the third ventricle.

hypothalamus   Part of the diencephalon, lying ventral to the thalamus.

superior colliculi   Paired gray matter structures of the dorsal midbrain that receive visual information and are involved in direction of visual gaze and visual attention to intended stimuli.

inferior colliculi   Paired gray matter structures of the dorsal midbrain that receive auditory information.

tectum   The dorsal portion of the midbrain, including the inferior and superior colliculi.

red nucleus   A brainstem structure related to motor control.

reticular formation   An extensive region of the brainstem (extending from the medulla through the thalamus) that is involved in arousal (waking).

Purkinje cell   A type of large nerve cell in the cerebellar cortex.

granule cell   A type of small nerve cell.

parallel fiber   One of the axons of the granule cells that form the outermost layer of the cerebellar cortex.

Figure 2.12b); taken together the colliculi are referred to as the **tectum**. The superior colliculi process visual information; the inferior colliculi process information about sound.

Two important motor centers are embedded in the midbrain. One is the *substantia nigra*, which we mentioned as part of the basal ganglia (see Figure 2.15a), containing neurons that release the transmitter dopamine (loss of this system leads to Parkinson's disease, discussed in Chapter 11). The other motor center is the **red nucleus** (named for its reddish tint), which communicates with motoneurons in the spinal cord. The midbrain also contains several nuclei that send their axons out to form cranial nerves. Other such cranial nerve nuclei are found throughout the brainstem.

Also found in the midbrain is a distributed network of neurons collectively referred to as the **reticular formation** (from the Latin *reticulum*, "network"). The reticular formation stretches from the midbrain down to the medulla. Many varied functions have been attributed to different parts of this loose aggregation of neurons, including sleep and arousal (Chapter 14), temperature regulation (Chapter 13), and motor control.

The cerebellum is attached to the pons

The lateral, midsagittal, and basal views of the brain in Figure 2.12 show the cerebellum. Like the cerebral hemispheres, the surface of the cerebellum is elaborately folded. The arrangement of cells within this folded sheet is relatively simple, consisting of three layers (**Figure 2.16**). A middle layer is composed of a single row of enormous neurons called **Purkinje cells** after the anatomist who first described their elaborate, fan-shaped dendritic patterns. Axons from the small neurons of the **granule cell** layer, lying below the Purkinje cells, rise to the surface of the cerebellum to form the **parallel fibers** of the outermost layer (called the *molecular layer*). The cerebellum is particularly important for motor coordination and control, integration of some sensory and motor functions, and some aspects of cognition, including learning.

Immediately below (ventral to) the cerebellum lies the pons (see Figure 2.12b and c), a part of the brainstem. Within the pons are important motor control and sensory nuclei, including several cranial nerve nuclei. Information from the ear first enters the brain in the pons, via the nucleus of the vestibulocochlear (VIII) nerve.

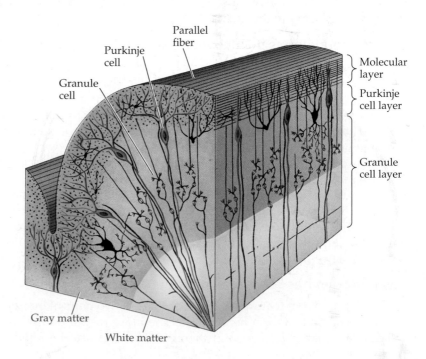

2.16 The Arrangement of Cells within the Cerebellum   Large Purkinje cells dominate the cerebellum, dividing it into three layers. Innervation between the various types of cells in the cerebellum forms a very consistent pattern. A variety of scattered cells, depicted here in black, inhibit the activity of other cells.

The medulla maintains vital body functions

The medulla is the most caudal portion of the brainstem and marks the transition from brainstem to spinal cord. Within the medulla are the nuclei of cranial nerves XI and XII—cell bodies of neurons that control the neck and tongue muscles, respectively. The reticular formation, which we first saw in the midbrain, stretches through the pons and ends in the medulla. Because the medulla contains nuclei that regulate breathing and heart rate, tissue damage there is often fatal. All axons passing between the brain and spinal cord necessarily course through the medulla, and several medullary nuclei add their own axons to the descending-fiber tracts.

The cerebral cortex performs complex cognitive processing

Neuroscientists agree that understanding human cognition depends on unraveling the structure and fundamental functions of the cerebral cortex. If the cerebral cortex were unfolded, it would occupy an area of about 2000 cm² (315 square inches), more than three times the area of this book's cover. How are these cells arranged? And how do the arrangements allow for particular feats of human information processing?

The neurons of the cerebral cortex are arranged in six distinct layers (**Figure 2.17a**). In mammals, these layers are collectively referred to sometimes as **neocortex** or **isocortex**, but in this book we will simply use the term **cortex** (Latin for "bark of a tree"). Each cortical layer is distinct because it consists of either a band of similar neurons, or a particular pattern of dendrites or axons. For example, the outermost layer, layer I, is distinct because it has few cell bodies, and layers V and VI stand out because of their many neurons with large cell bodies. Some other telencephalic structures are made up of **allocortex** (from the Greek *allos*, "other"), tissue with three layers or unlayered organization (previously known as *archi-* or *paleocortex*).

The most prominent kind of neuron in the cerebral cortex—the **pyramidal cell** (**Figure 2.17b**)—usually has its pyramid-shaped cell body in layer III or V. One dendrite of each pyramidal cell (called the **apical dendrite**) extends to the outer-

neocortex (isocortex) or cortex   Cerebral cortex that is made up of six distinct layers.

allocortex   Brain tissue with three layers or unlayered organization.

pyramidal cell   A type of large nerve cell that has a roughly pyramid-shaped cell body; found in the cerebral cortex.

apical dendrite   The dendrite that extends from a pyramidal cell to the outermost surface of the cortex.

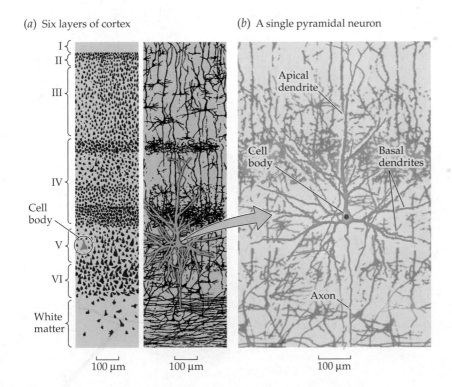

(*a*) Six layers of cortex

(*b*) A single pyramidal neuron

2.17 Layers of the Cerebral Cortex   (*a*) The six layers of cortex can be distinguished with stains that reveal all cell bodies (*left*), or with stains that reveal a few neurons in their entirety (*right*). (*b*) This pyramidal cell has been enlarged about 100 times.

basal dendrite   One of several dendrites on a pyramidal cell that extend horizontally from the cell body.

cortical column   One of the vertical columns that constitute the basic organization of the neocortex.

meninges   The three protective sheets of tissue—dura mater, pia mater, and arachnoid—that surround the brain and spinal cord.

dura mater   The outermost of the three meninges that surround the brain and spinal cord.

pia mater   The innermost of the three meninges that surround the brain and spinal cord.

arachnoid   The thin covering (one of the three meninges) of the brain that lies between the dura mater and pia mater.

cerebrospinal fluid (CSF)   The fluid that fills the cerebral ventricles.

meningitis   An acute inflammation of the meninges, usually caused by a viral or bacterial infection.

most surface of the cortex. The pyramidal cell also has several dendrites (called **basal dendrites**) that spread out horizontally from the cell body.

CORTICAL COLUMNS   In some regions of the cerebral cortex, neurons are organized into regular columns, perpendicular to the layers, that seem to serve as cohesive information-processing units (Horton and Adams, 2005). These **cortical columns** extend through the entire thickness of the cortex, from the white matter to the surface. Within each column, most of the synaptic interconnections of neurons are vertical, although there are some horizontal connections as well (Mountcastle, 1979).

Cortical regions communicate with one another via tracts of axons looping through the underlying white matter (**Figure 2.18**). Some of these connections are short pathways to nearby cortical regions; others travel longer distances through the cerebral hemispheres. Some pathways link corresponding areas in the two hemispheres, traversing the corpus callosum to go from one hemisphere to the other. Some longer links between cortical regions involve multisynaptic chains of neurons that loop through subcortical regions such as the thalamus and the basal ganglia, allowing processing and integration of information at several levels.

Specialized Support Systems Protect and Nourish the Brain

Within the bony skull and vertebrae, the brain and spinal cord are surrounded by three protective membranes called **meninges** (see Figure 2.10). The tough outermost sheet is the **dura mater** (in Latin, literally "hard mother"). The innermost layer, the delicate **pia mater** ("tender mother"), adheres tightly to the surface of the brain and follows all its contours. The weblike membrane between the dura mater and the pia mater is the **arachnoid** (literally, "spiderweb-like"). Space within the arachnoid is filled with a colorless liquid called **cerebrospinal fluid** (CSF). **Meningitis**, an inflammation of the meninges usually caused by viral infection, is a potentially lethal medical emergency characterized in early stages by headache, fever, and stiff neck.

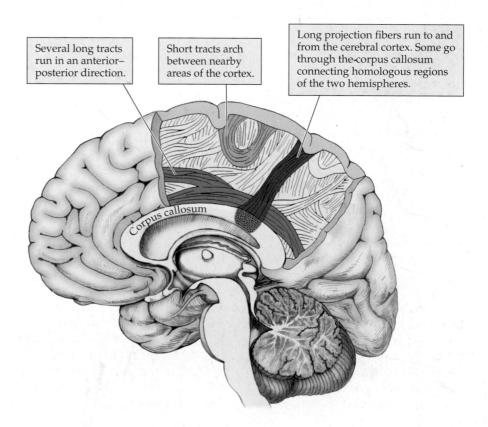

Several long tracts run in an anterior–posterior direction.

Short tracts arch between nearby areas of the cortex.

Long projection fibers run to and from the cerebral cortex. Some go through the corpus callosum connecting homologous regions of the two hemispheres.

Corpus callosum

2.18 Cortical Tracts Connect Cortical Regions

(*a*) Cerebral ventricles of the brain

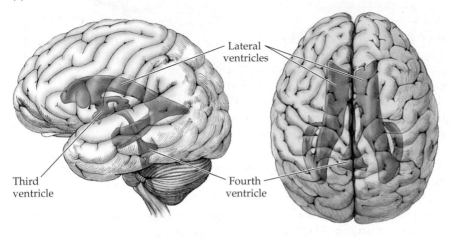

(*b*) A closer view

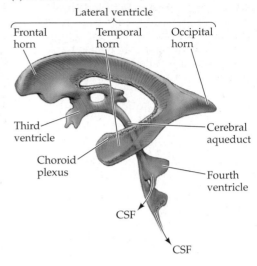

2.19 The Cerebral Ventricles   These views of an adult human brain show the position of the cerebral ventricles within it. Cerebrospinal fluid (CSF) is made by the choroid plexus in the lateral ventricles and exits from the fourth ventricle to surround the brain and spinal cord.

The cerebral ventricles are chambers filled with fluid

Inside the brain is a series of chambers—the **ventricular system**—filled with CSF (**Figure 2.19**). The CSF circulating through the ventricular system has at least two main functions. First, it acts mechanically as a shock absorber for the brain: floating in CSF, the brain is protected from sudden movements of the head that would smash it against the inside of the skull. Second, CSF provides a medium for the exchange of materials, including nutrients, between blood vessels and brain tissue.

Each hemisphere of the brain contains a **lateral ventricle**, extending into all four lobes of the hemisphere. The lateral ventricles are lined with a specialized membrane called the **choroid plexus**, which produces CSF by filtering blood. CSF flows from the lateral ventricles into the **third ventricle** (located in the midline) and continues down a narrow passage to the **fourth ventricle**, which lies anterior to the cerebellum. Just below the cerebellum are three small openings through which CSF leaves the ventricular system to circulate over the outer surface of the brain and spinal cord. CSF is absorbed back into the circulatory system through large veins beneath the top of the skull.

The brain has an elaborate vascular system

Although it accounts for only 2% of the weight of the average human body, the brain consumes more than 20% of the body's energy. However, the brain has very little reserve of the basic metabolic fuels oxygen and glucose, so it depends critically on its blood supply to provide them (**Figure 2.20**). The **carotid arteries** ascend the left and right sides of the neck and branch into external and internal carotid arteries. The internal carotid artery enters the skull and branches into **anterior** and **middle cerebral arteries**, which supply blood to about two-thirds of the cerebral hemispheres, indicated in purple and pink in Figure 2.20. The blood supply for the rest of the cortex (indicated in blue in the figure) is supplied by the **posterior cerebral arteries**. The blood supply for these arteries ascends through the **vertebral arteries**, which fuse to form the **basilar artery**, which, in addition to feeding the posterior cerebral arteries, has branches supplying blood to the hindbrain.

ventricular system   A system of fluid-filled cavities inside the brain.

lateral ventricle   A complexly shaped lateral portion of the ventricular system within each hemisphere of the brain.

choroid plexus   A highly vascular portion of the lining of the ventricles that secretes cerebrospinal fluid.

third ventricle   The midline ventricle that conducts cerebrospinal fluid from the lateral ventricles to the fourth ventricle.

fourth ventricle   The passageway within the pons that receives cerebrospinal fluid from the third ventricle and releases it to surround the brain and spinal cord.

carotid arteries   The major arteries that ascend the left and right sides of the neck to the brain, supplying blood to the anterior and middle cerebral arteries.

anterior cerebral arteries   Two large arteries, arising from the carotids, that provide blood to the anterior poles and medial surfaces of the cerebral hemispheres.

middle cerebral arteries   Two large arteries, arising from the carotids, that provide blood to most of the lateral surfaces of the cerebral hemispheres.

posterior cerebral arteries   Two large arteries, arising from the basilar artery, that provide blood to posterior aspects of the cerebral hemispheres, cerebellum, and brainstem.

vertebral arteries   Arteries that ascend the vertebrae, enter the base of the skull, and join together to form the basilar artery.

basilar artery   An artery, formed by the fusion of the vertebral arteries, that supplies blood to the brainstem and to the posterior cerebral arteries.

2.20 The Blood Supply of the Human Brain The anterior, middle, and posterior cerebral arteries—the three principal arteries that provide blood to the cerebral hemispheres—are depicted here in basal (*a*), midsagittal (*b*), and lateral (*c*) views of the brain. The basilar and internal carotid arteries form a circle at the base of the brain known as the circle of Willis.

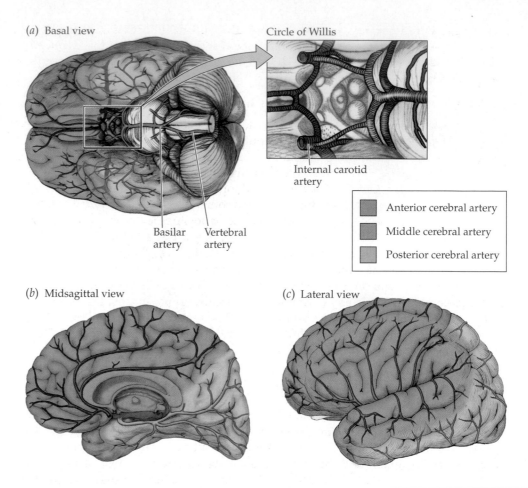

(*a*) Basal view

Circle of Willis

Internal carotid artery

Basilar artery   Vertebral artery

Anterior cerebral artery
Middle cerebral artery
Posterior cerebral artery

(*b*) Midsagittal view

(*c*) Lateral view

At the base of the brain, the major cerebral arteries join to form a structure called the **circle of Willis** (see Figure 2.20*a*). This joining of arterial paths may provide an alternate route for blood flow if any of the main arteries to the brain should be damaged or blocked by disease. In **stroke**—one of the most prevalent causes of disability and death—insufficient blood flow to a region of the brain is caused by the blockage or rupture of blood vessels. Although the exact effects of stroke depend on the region of the brain that is affected, the five most common warning signs are sudden numbness or weakness, altered vision, dizziness, severe headache, and confusion or difficulty speaking. Effective treatments are available to help restore blood flow and minimize the long-term effects of a stroke, but only if the victim is treated immediately.

Fine arteries branch off from the main arteries and in turn give rise to the very fine capillaries that deliver nutrients and other substances to brain cells and remove waste products. This exchange in the brain is quite different from exchanges between blood vessels and cells in other body organs. Because of very tight junctions between the cells that form their walls (endothelial cells), brain capillaries are much more resistant to the passage of large molecules across their walls than are capillaries found elsewhere in the body. This **blood-brain barrier** may have evolved to help protect the brain from infections and blood-borne toxins, but it also makes the delivery of drugs to the brain more difficult.

Newer Imaging Techniques Enable Us to Look into the Living Human Brain

Researchers have long sought ways to peer into the living human brain to see structures and how they work during different behaviors. X-rays of the head are of limited usefulness because they cannot resolve the brain's small variations in den-

circle of Willis A structure at the base of the brain that is formed by the joining of the carotid and basilar arteries.

stroke Damage to a region of brain tissue that results from blockage or rupture of vessels that supply blood to that region.

blood-brain barrier The mechanisms that make the movement of substances from blood vessels into brain cells more difficult than exchanges in other body organs, thus affording the brain greater protection from exposure to some substances found in blood.

sity. Attempts to improve contrast in X-rays through the injection of radiopaque (X-ray-blocking) dye led to a useful technique—**angiography** (from the Greek *angeion*, "blood vessel," and *graphein*, "to write")—that provides detailed views of the cerebral blood vessels and aids in the diagnosis of vascular disease.

CT uses X-rays to reveal brain structure

Although Wilder Penfield was able to make inferences about the functional organization of the brain by directly manipulating it during surgery, not until the advent of powerful computing techniques did the ability to visualize the form and functioning of the normal brain become a reality. In **computerized axial tomography** (**CAT** or **CT**; from the Greek *tomos*, "crosscut" or "section"), X-ray energy is used to generate images. In a CT scanner, an X-ray source is moved by steps in an arc around the head. At each point, detectors on the opposite side of the head measure the amount of X-ray radiation that is absorbed; this value is proportional to the density of the tissue through which the X-rays passed. When this process is repeated from many angles and the results are mathematically combined, an anatomical map of the brain based on tissue density can be generated by the computer (**Figure 2.21a**). CT scans are medium-resolution images, useful for visualizing problems such as strokes, tumors, or cortical atrophy. CT scanning has helped researchers identify brain regions that, when damaged, produce disorders of memory, language, attention, and other major cognitive functions.

MRI creates maps of the brain based on density

Magnetic resonance imaging (**MRI**) provides higher-resolution images that have replaced CTs for many applications. MRI images are derived from radio frequency

angiography   A brain-imaging technique in which a specialized X-ray image of the head is taken shortly after the cerebral blood vessels have been filled with a radiopaque dye by means of a catheter.

computerized axial tomography (CAT or CT)   A noninvasive technique for examining brain structure in humans through computer analysis of X-ray absorption at several positions around the head.

magnetic resonance imaging (MRI)   A noninvasive technique that uses magnetic energy to generate images that reveal some structural details in the living brain.

(*a*) Computerized tomography (CT)

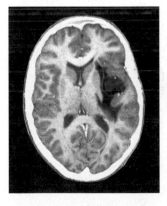

(*b*) Magnetic resonance imaging (MRI)

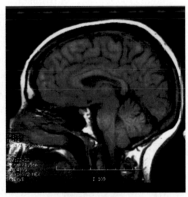

(*c*) Positron emission tomography (PET)

Normal (horizontal view)

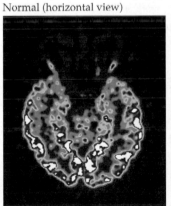

Patient with Alzheimer's disease

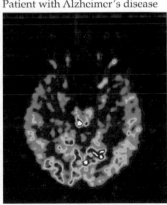

(*d*) Functional magnetic resonance imaging (fMRI)

Anterior 3-D view

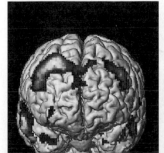

Lateral 3-D view of right hemisphere

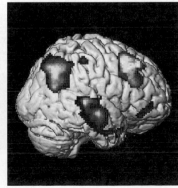

2.21 Visualizing the Living Human Brain   (*a*) CT scan from a patient with a brain tumor, visible as the dark area in the right hemisphere. (*b*) Midsagittal MRI image of a normal brain. (*c*) PET scans from a normal human and a patient with Alzheimer's, showing levels of metabolic activity in the brain. Note the greater level of activity in the normal brain. (*d*) Functional-MRI images showing changes in regional brain metabolism recorded during the presentation of visual or auditory stimuli. These images are three-dimensional renderings showing areas where brain activity changed in subjects viewing images of a romantic partner (see Figure 1.6). (Images in *d* courtesy of Semir Zeki.)

positron emission tomography (PET)   A technique for examining brain function by combining tomography with injections of radioactive substances used by the brain.

energy, so an additional benefit is that patients are not exposed to potentially damaging X-rays. An MRI scan involves three main steps. First the patient's head is placed in an extremely powerful magnet that causes all the protons in the brain's tissues to line up in parallel, instead of in their usual random orientations. Protons are found in the nuclei of atoms, and most protons in the brain are in the hydrogen atoms making up water. So the aim is to determine the density of protons in various regions because that reflects the density of water. First, the protons are knocked over by a powerful pulse of radio waves. Then, when this pulse is turned off, the protons relax back to their original configuration, emitting radio waves as they go. The emitted radio frequency energy, measured by detectors ringing the head, differs for tissues of varying densities. A powerful computer compiles this density-based information to generate a detailed cross-sectional view of the brain (**Figure 2.21*b***) (Elster and Burdette, 2001). With their higher resolution, MRI images can reveal subtle changes in the brain, such as the local demyelination that is characteristic of multiple sclerosis.

PET maps radioactive tracers to produce images of brain activity

In **positron emission tomography** (**PET**) the objective is to obtain images of the brain's *activity* rather than details of its structure, and it has proven to be very valuable for both experimental and diagnostic purposes. Short-lived radioactive chemicals are injected into the bloodstream, and a ring of detectors maps the destination of these chemicals in the brain by sensing their emissions of radiation. In one common

BOX 2.3 Isolating Specific Brain Activity

The advent of modern brain imaging has enabled dramatic images of the brain showing the particular brain regions that are activated during specific cognitive processes; there are many such images in this book. But in a normal person, as you might expect, almost all of the brain is active at any given moment (showing that the idea that "we use only 10% of our brain" is nonsense). So how do we get these highly specific images of brain activity?

The PET scan shown here beneath the box labeled "Visual stimulus" was made while a person looked at a fixation point surrounded by a flickering checkerboard ring. The scan next to it (beneath the box labeled "Control") was made while a person looked at a fixation point alone. In a comparison of the two it is hard to see differences, but subtracting the control values from the stimulation values yields an image such as that shown at the upper right ("Difference image"); in this scan it is easy to see that the main difference in activity is in the posterior part of the brain (the visual cortex).

The PET scans shown in the bottom row are difference images for five individuals

who performed the same two stimulation and control tasks. Averaging these five scans yields the mean difference image for all five subjects that is shown at far right.

Averaged images yield more-reliable results than individual images, but they lack some of the specificity of the individual images. (PET scans courtesy of Marcus Raichle.)

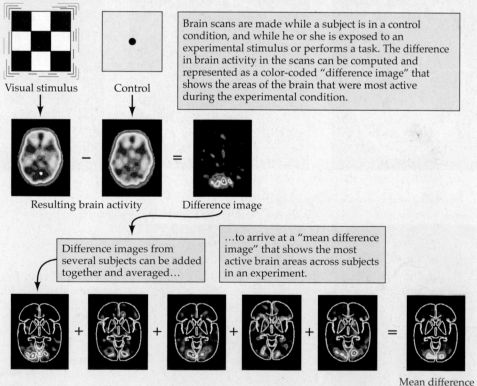

Visual stimulus   Control

Resulting brain activity   Difference image

Brain scans are made while a subject is in a control condition, and while he or she is exposed to an experimental stimulus or performs a task. The difference in brain activity in the scans can be computed and represented as a color-coded "difference image" that shows the areas of the brain that were most active during the experimental condition.

Difference images from several subjects can be added together and averaged…

…to arrive at a "mean difference image" that shows the most active brain areas across subjects in an experiment.

Mean difference image

technique, radioactive glucose is administered while a subject is performing a specific cognitive task. Because the radioactive glucose is particularly taken up and used by the brain regions that are most active from moment to moment, a computer-generated, color-coded portrait of brain activity can be created (**Figure 2.21c**) (P. E. Roland, 1993). Through precise experimental control and the use of special mathematical techniques (described in **Box 2.3**), we can generate metabolic maps of the brain that identify which brain regions contribute to specific functions.

Functional MRI uses local changes in metabolism to identify active brain regions

First introduced in the 1990s, **functional MRI** (**fMRI**) has revolutionized cognitive neuroscience research, producing images with reasonable speed (temporal resolution) and excellent sharpness (spatial resolution). Although the basic technology is the same as for MRI scanning (described earlier), it is applied differently. In fMRI scanning, high-powered, rapidly oscillating magnetic-field gradients are used to detect small changes in brain metabolism, particularly oxygen use by the most active regions of the brain. The amount of oxygen available is measured indirectly, on the basis of blood flow or the state of hemoglobin in blood. As with PET, scientists can use fMRI data to create images that reflect the *activity* of different parts of the brain while people engage in various experimental tasks (see Box 2.3). The detailed activity maps provided by fMRI reveal how networks of brain structures collaborate on complex cognitive processes (**Figure 2.21d**). The fMRI image generally reflects synaptic inputs and local processing, rather than the production of neural impulses (Logothetis, 2008), and is altered by aging and disease states (Rypma et al., 2005).

Light and magnetism can be used to study brain activity

Other investigators are using light to make images of brain activity within the head (Gratton and Fabiani, 2001; Villringer and Chance, 1997). In **optical imaging**, researchers capitalize on the observation that near-infrared light (having wavelengths of 700–1000 nm) passes easily through skin, scalp, and skull and penetrates a short distance into the cortex. When such light is transmitted into the brain and detectors pick up the reflections through the scalp, the responses reveal the activity of cortical regions. Some components of the optical responses represent the electrical signals of neurons, and other components represent blood flow.

The relatively low expense and small size of the optical imaging apparatus may allow many more laboratories to use brain imaging in their research. And because optical imaging is based on light, it is ideal for simultaneous use with other techniques: optical imaging has been coupled with **transcranial magnetic stimulation** (**TMS**) (**Figure 2.22**), in which focal magnetic currents are used to briefly stimulate the cortex of alert normal subjects directly, without a hole having to be made in the scalp or skull (Y. Noguchi et al., 2003). This approach enables experimenters to activate a discrete area of the brain through electromagnetic induction while simultaneously mapping the resulting pattern of activation. In *repetitive TMS* (*rTMS*), this focal magnetic stimulation of the brain is cycled several times per second, producing transient but measurable changes in behavior that may be of use in clinical settings, as well as in research.

Magnetism and brain function are linked in another way too. Like any electrical system, active circuits of the brain produce their own magnetic fields. Although they are minuscule, the magnetic fields created by activity in local circuits of neurons can be detected by ultra-

functional MRI (fMRI) Magnetic resonance imaging that detects changes in blood flow and therefore identifies regions of the brain that are particularly active during a given task.

optical imaging A method for visualizing brain activity in which near-infrared light is passed through the scalp and skull.

transcranial magnetic stimulation (TMS) Localized, noninvasive stimulation of cortical neurons through the application of strong magnetic fields.

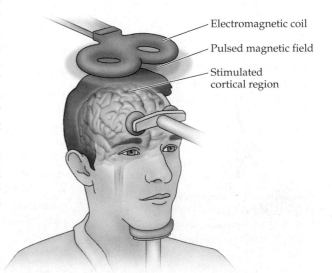

— Electromagnetic coil

— Pulsed magnetic field

— Stimulated cortical region

2.22 Transcranial Magnetic Stimulation Magnetic fields induced by electromagnetic coils stimulate neurons of the underlying cortical surface.

2.23 Animal Magnetism   Using measurements of the minuscule magnetic fields given off by ensembles of cortical cells during specific behavioral functions, magnetoencephalography (MEG) provides a real-time map of brain activity. In these images, MEG data have been superimposed on structural MRIs of a subject's brain, creating maps of brain activity associated with viewing faces (a) versus nonface objects (b). (Image courtesy of Drs. Mario Liotti and Anthony Herdman, Simon Fraser University, and Down Syndrome Research Foundation.)

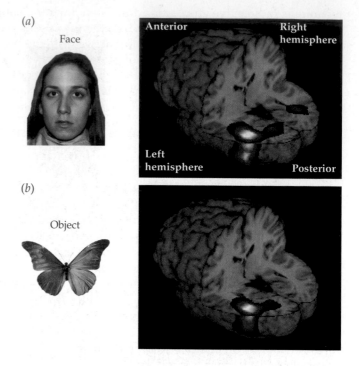

(a) Face

(b) Object

Anterior   Right hemisphere

Left hemisphere   Posterior

sensitive detectors called *SQUIDs* (*superconducting quantum interference devices*). In **magnetoencephalography** (**MEG**), a large array of SQUIDs is used to create real-time maps of brain activity from localized cortical magnetic fields during ongoing cognitive processing (**Figure 2.23**). Because the temporal resolution of MEG is so good—it responds very quickly to moment-by-moment changes in brain activity—it is excellent for studying rapidly shifting patterns of brain activity in cortical circuits, particularly when used in conjunction with MRI (F. H. Lin et al., 2004). Like optical imaging, MEG is noninvasive and thus suitable for studies of infants and children.

Sophisticated imaging techniques can overcome some of the limitations of other methods

To investigate many problems of biological psychology, imaging provides evidence to supplement studies of naturally occurring or experimental brain lesions. These kinds of investigation help overcome limitations on the other sources of evidence. One particularly difficult question has been the extent to which people in comas (or a vegetative state) are conscious of their condition and surroundings. When a 23-year-old woman in such a nonresponsive state was asked to imagine playing tennis, parts of her brain became active—the same regions that become active when control subjects imagine playing tennis (**Figure 2.24a**). When she was asked to imagine walking through her house, other brain regions became active (**Figure 2.24b**), matching the activation in control subjects doing this task (Owen et al., 2006). These results indicate that this young woman is indeed aware of what people are saying to her, and can imagine doing other things. She is also acting intentionally, so she seems to be consciously aware of herself and her surroundings. Functional MRI offers a way to communicate with this woman who is unable to speak or move.

It is important to keep in mind that although functional brain images seem unambiguous and easy to label, they are subject to a variety of procedural and experimental limitations (Racine et al., 2005). In particular, they are not actual images of the brain, but rather computer-generated composites based on measurements of blood flow, which reflects the metabolism and electrical activity of neurons. The origins of these neural signals are the topic of the next chapter.

magnetoencephalography (MEG)   A passive and noninvasive functional brain-imaging technique that measures the tiny magnetic fields produced by active neurons, in order to identify regions of the brain that are particularly active during a given task.

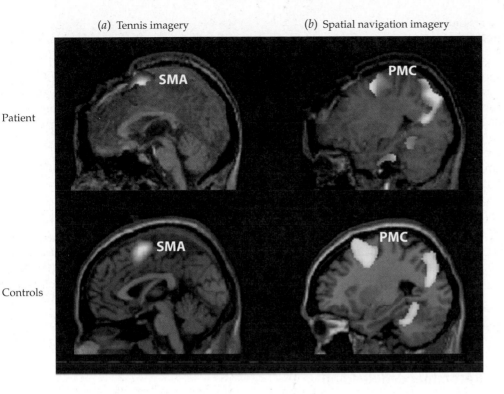

(a) Tennis imagery   (b) Spatial navigation imagery

Patient

Controls

2.24 Coma Consciousness A woman with brain injury appeared to be in a coma, but when researchers entered her room and asked her to imagine playing tennis (a) or walking through her home (b), her brain showed the same patterns of activity seen in control subjects imagining such activities. Note the damage to the patient's skull caused by the accident. SMA, supplementary motor area; PMC, premotor cortex. (Courtesy of Adrian Owen.)

SUMMARY

- The nervous system is extensive—monitoring, regulating, and modulating the activities of all parts and organs of the body.

The Nervous System Is Composed of Cells

- At the microscopic level, **neurons** are the basic units of the nervous system. The typical neuron of most vertebrate species has four main parts: (1) the **cell body**, which contains the **nucleus**; (2) **dendrites**, which receive information; (3) an **axon**, which carries impulses from the neuron; and (4) **axon terminals**, which transmit the neuron's impulses to other cells. Because of the variety of functions they serve, neurons are extremely varied in size, shape, and chemical activity. **Review Figures 2.2 and 2.5, Web Activity 2.1**

- The **axon** is generally tubular, branching at the end into many collaterals. Electrical signals, described in the next chapter, travel down the axon from the cell body to each **axon terminal.**

- Neurons make functional contacts with other neurons, or with muscles or glands, at specialized junctions called **synapses**. Synapses may be made onto dendritic spines, which exhibit **neural plasticity**, changing shape in response to experience. **Review Figure 2.7**

- At most synapses a chemical transmitter liberated by the presynaptic terminal diffuses across the **synaptic cleft** and binds to special **receptor molecules** in the **postsynaptic membrane.**

- **Glial cells** serve many functions, including the breakdown of transmitters, the production of **myelin** sheaths around axons, the exchange of nutrients and other materials with neurons, the direct regulation of the interconnections and activity of neurons, and the removal of cellular debris. **Review Figure 2.6**

The Nervous System Consists of Central and Peripheral Divisions

- At the gross anatomical level (i.e., to the naked eye), the nervous system of vertebrates is divided into peripheral and central nervous systems. **Review Figure 2.8**

- The **peripheral nervous system** includes the **cranial nerves**, **spinal nerves**, and **autonomic nervous system**. The **autonomic nervous system** consists of the **sympathetic nervous system**, which tends to ready the body for action; the **parasympathetic nervous system**, which tends to have an effect opposite to that of the sympathetic system; and the **enteric nervous system**, which innervates the gut. **Review Figures 2.9 and 2.11, Web Activities 2.2–2.4**

- The **central nervous system (CNS)** consists of the brain and spinal cord. The main divisions of the brain are the **forebrain** (telencephalon and diencephalon), the **midbrain** (mesencephalon), and the **hindbrain** (metencephalon and myelencephalon). **Review Web Activities 2.5–2.8**

The Brain Is Described by Both Structure and Function

■ The human brain is dominated by the **cerebral hemispheres**, which include the **cerebral cortex**, an extensive sheet of folded tissue. The six-layered cerebral cortex is responsible for higher-order functions such as vision, language, and memory. Other neural systems include the **basal ganglia**, which regulate movement; the **limbic system**, which controls emotional behaviors; and the **cerebellum**, which aids motor control. **Review Figure 2.15, Web Activities 2.9–2.11**

■ The brain and spinal cord, surrounded and protected by the three **meninges**, float in **cerebrospinal fluid (CSF)**, which surrounds and infiltrates the brain (via cerebral ventricles). **Review Figure 2.10, Web Activity 2.12**

Specialized Support Systems Protect and Nourish the Brain

■ The vascular system of the brain is an elaborate array of blood vessels that deliver nutrients and other substances to the brain. The walls of the blood vessels in the brain form the **blood-brain barrier**, restricting the flow of large, potentially harmful molecules into the brain. **Review Figure 2.20**

Newer Imaging Techniques Enable Us to Look into the Living Human Brain

■ Modern imaging techniques make it possible to visualize the anatomy of the living human brain and regional metabolic differences. These techniques include **computerized axial tomography (CT)**, **positron emission tomography (PET)**, **magnetic resonance imaging (MRI)**, **functional MRI (fMRI)**, infrared optical imaging, and **magnetoencephalography (MEG)**. **Review Figure 2.21, Web Activity 2.13**

Go to www.biopsychology.com for study questions, quizzes, key terms, and other resources.

Recommended Reading

Blumenfeld, H. (2010). *Neuroanatomy through clinical cases.* (2nd ed.) Sunderland, MA: Sinauer.

Brodal, P. (2003). *The central nervous system: Structure and function.* New York: Oxford University Press.

Cabeza, R., and Kingstone, A. (2006). *Handbook of functional neuroimaging of cognition* (2nd ed.). Cambridge MA: MIT Press.

Mai, J. K., Paxinos, G., and Voss, J. (2007). *Atlas of the human brain* (3rd ed.). San Diego, CA: Academic Press.

Mendoza, J., and Foundas, A. L. (2007). *Clinical neuroanatomy: A neurobehavioral approach.* Heidelberg: Springer.

Nolte, J. (2008). *The human brain: An introduction to its functional neuroanatomy* (6th ed.). St. Louis, MO: Mosby.

Posner, M. I., and Raichle, M. E. (1997). *Images of mind.* San Francisco: Freeman.

Woolsey, T. A., Hanaway, J., and Gado, M. H. (2007). *The brain atlas: A visual guide to the human central nervous system.* New York: Wiley-Liss.

CHAPTER 3

Neurophysiology: The Generation, Transmission, and Integration of Neural Signals

Finding an Answer in a Heartbeat

In the early twentieth century, debate raged over the basic nature of neural communication. The discovery that individual nerve cells contact each other at thousands of points was fresh knowledge. What happened at these synapses? Did an electrical current pass between the cells? Or did some mysterious substance waft across the synapse, carrying information from one cell to the other? A definitive answer to these questions seemed beyond the reach of the available technology.

A solution came to Otto Loewi (1873–1961) in a dream one night in 1921: a simple experiment that would definitively discriminate between the two candidate modes of transmission—chemical versus electrical. In excitement, Loewi sat up in bed and scribbled a few notes, but in the morning he was disappointed to find the notes indecipherable. When the dream came again the following night, Loewi got up and went straight to the lab, where he performed the experiment while it was still fresh in his mind.

Loewi had recently been studying cardiac function in frogs. So he electrically stimulated the vagus nerve of one frog, which he knew would decrease its heart rate, and collected a sample of the fluid surrounding that frog's heart. Then he bathed a second frog's heart with the fluid sample from the first frog. When the second frog's heart also slowed, Loewi knew he had a solution to the riddle of synaptic transmission. The stimulation of the first frog's nerve must have caused the release of a chemical—what Loewi initially called *Vagusstoff* ("substance from the vagus")—into the fluid. Thus scientists learned that the nervous system, long known to use electrical signals, also uses chemical signals. It was a breakthrough for which Loewi would receive a Nobel Prize in 1936.

I n this chapter we delve into **neurophysiology**, the life processes within neurons, which are specialized to use both electrical and chemical signals, as Loewi's experiment demonstrated. When a doctor uses a small rubber mallet to strike just below your knee and watches your leg kick upward, she is testing your neurophysiological function. Simple as it appears, a lot happens during this test. First, sensory neurons in the muscle detect the hammer tap and send a rapid electrical signal along their axons to your spinal cord. That rapid electrical signal along its axonal pathway from knee to spinal cord is a nerve impulse, or **action potential**. When the action potential reaches the axon terminals, it releases a chemical, called a **neurotransmitter**, to stimulate spinal motoneurons. In response to the neurotransmitter, the motoneurons send action potentials down their own axons to release yet another neurotransmitter onto muscles. In response to that neurotransmitter, the muscles contract, kicking your foot into the air a bit. Problems in the electrical or chemical signals might cause the kick to be either stronger or weaker than it should be.

So this "simple" behavior involves several rounds of signaling: first electrical (along sensory neuron axons), then chemical (sensory neurons to motoneurons), then electrical again (along motoneuron axons), and finally chemical again (motoneurons to muscle). Such alternating series of electrical and chemical signaling

neurophysiology   The study of the life processes of neurons.

action potential   The propagated electrical message of a neuron that travels along the axon to the presynaptic axon terminals.

neurotransmitter   Also called *synaptic transmitter*, *chemical transmitter*, *or* simply *transmitter*. The chemical released from the presynaptic axon terminal that serves as the basis of communication between neurons.

ion   An atom or molecule that has acquired an electrical charge by gaining or losing one or more electrons.

underlie all neuronal function. Information flows *within* a neuron via electrical signals, while information passes *between* neurons through chemical signals. This sequence reflects the organization of this chapter. First we explain how neurons produce action potentials and send them along their axons. Then we describe how the action potential causes axon terminals to release neurotransmitter into the synapse. Next we discuss how the neurotransmitter affects the neuron on the other side of the synapse. Finally, we talk about neuronal circuits in general, returning for a closing look at the knee jerk test of neurophysiological function.

Electrical Signals Are the Vocabulary of the Nervous System

All living cells possess an electrical charge—they are more negative on the inside than on the outside—that is a legacy of their evolutionary origins. Early single-celled organisms living in the primordial sea contained many proteins, which are negatively charged. Long ago, nerve cells began to exploit this electrical property to keep track of information. The bioelectrical communication system works in much the same way in neurons from human beings, insects, and jellyfish. These neural signals underlie the whole range of thought and action, from composing music or solving a mathematical problem to feeling an itch on the skin and swatting a mosquito. To understand this system, we'll first review the physical forces at work and then discuss some details of why nerve cells are electrically polarized, how neuronal polarity is influenced by other cells, and how a change of polarity in one part of a neuron can spread throughout the cell.

A balance of electrochemical forces produces the resting membrane potential of neurons

Let's start by considering a neuron at rest, neither perturbed by other neurons nor producing its own signals. Of the many **ions** (electrically charged molecules) that a neuron contains, a majority are **anions** (negatively charged ions), especially large

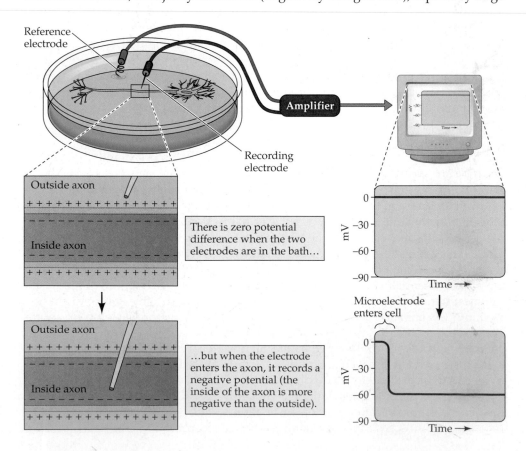

3.1 Measuring the Resting Potential

There is zero potential difference when the two electrodes are in the bath…

…but when the electrode enters the axon, it records a negative potential (the inside of the axon is more negative than the outside).

protein anions that cannot exit the cell; the rest are **cations** (positively charged ions), which we'll discuss shortly. All of these ions are dissolved in an **intracellular fluid**, which is separated from the **extracellular fluid** by the **cell membrane**.

If we insert a fine **microelectrode** into the interior of a neuron and compare it to the extracellular fluid (as illustrated in **Figure 3.1**), we find that the neuron is more negative on the inside than on the outside. Specifically, a neuron at rest exhibits a characteristic **resting membrane potential** (an electrical-potential difference across the membrane) of about –50 to –80 thousandths of a volt, or **millivolts (mV)** (the negative sign indicates the **negative polarity** of the cell's interior). To fully understand the basis of this membrane potential, we have to consider some special properties of the cell membrane, as well as two forces that drive ions across it.

Cell membranes are made up of a **lipid bilayer**—two layers of linked fatty molecules (see Figure 3.4)—within which many sorts of specialized proteins "float." One important type of membrane-spanning protein is the **ion channel**, a tubelike pore that allows ions of a specific type to pass through the membrane. As we'll see later, some types of ion channels are **gated**: they can open and close rapidly in response to various influences. But some ion channels stay open all the time, and the cell membrane of a neuron contains many such channels that selectively allow only **potassium ions (K⁺)** to cross the membrane. Because it is studded with these K⁺ channels, we say that the cell membrane of a neuron exhibits **selective permeability** to potassium; that is, K⁺ ions (but not other types of ions) can enter or exit the cell fairly freely, unimpeded by the cell membrane.

The resting potential of the neuron reflects a balancing act between two opposing forces that drive K⁺ ions in and out of the neuron. The first of these is **diffusion (Figure 3.2a)**, which is the force that causes molecules of a substance to diffuse from regions of high concentration to regions of low concentration. For example, if a drop of food coloring is placed in a glass of water, the mol-

(*a*) Diffusion

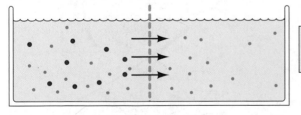

Particles move from areas of high concentration to areas of low concentration. That is, they move down their concentration gradient.

(*b*) Diffusion through semipermeable membranes

Cell membranes permit some substances to pass through, but not others.

(*c*) Electrostatic forces

Like charges repel each other.

Opposite charges are attracted to each other.

3.2 Ionic Forces Underlying Electrical Signaling in Neurons

---

anion   A negatively charged ion, such as a protein or chloride ion.

cation   A positively charged ion, such as a potassium or sodium ion.

intracellular fluid   Also called *cytoplasm*. The watery solution found within cells.

extracellular fluid   The fluid in the spaces between cells (interstitial fluid) and in the vascular system.

cell membrane   The lipid bilayer that ensheathes a cell.

microelectrode   An especially small electrode used to record electrical potentials from living cells.

resting membrane potential   A difference in electrical potential across the membrane of a nerve cell during an inactive period.

millivolt (mV)   A thousandth of a volt.

negative polarity   A negative electrical-potential difference relative to a reference electrode.

lipid bilayer   The structure of the neuronal cell membrane, which consists of two layers of lipid molecules, within which float various specialized proteins, such as receptors.

ion channel   A pore in the cell membrane that permits the passage of certain ions through the membrane when the channels are open.

gated   Referring to the property by which an ion channel may be opened or closed by factors such as chemicals, voltage changes, or mechanical actions.

potassium ion (K⁺)   A potassium atom that carries a positive charge because it has lost one electron.

selective permeability   The property of a membrane that allows some substances to pass through, but not others.

diffusion   The spontaneous spread of molecules of one substance among molecules of another substance until a uniform concentration is achieved.

concentration gradient Variation of the concentration of a substance within a region.

electrostatic pressure The propensity of charged molecules or ions to move, via diffusion, toward areas with the opposite charge.

sodium-potassium pump The energetically expensive mechanism that pushes sodium ions out of a cell, and potassium ions in.

sodium ion (Na⁺) A sodium atom that carries a positive charge because it has lost one electron.

ecules of dye tend to move from the drop, where they are highly concentrated, into the rest of the glass, where they are less concentrated. In other words, molecules tend to move down their **concentration gradient** until they are evenly distributed. If a selectively permeable membrane divides the fluid, particles that can pass through the membrane, such as K⁺, will diffuse across until they are equally concentrated on both sides (**Figure 3.2b**). Other ions, unable to cross the membrane, will remain concentrated on one side.

The second force at work is **electrostatic pressure** (**Figure 3.2c**), which arises from the distribution of electrical charges rather than the distribution of molecules. Charged particles exert electrical force on one another: like charges repel, and opposite charges attract. Positively charged cations are thus attracted to the negatively charged interior of the cell; and conversely, anions are repelled by the cell interior and so tend to exit to the extracellular fluid.

Now let's consider the situation across a neuron's cell membrane. Neurons use a mechanism, the **sodium-potassium pump**, that pumps three **sodium ions (Na⁺)** out of the cell for every two K⁺ ions pumped in (**Figure 3.3a**). This action consumes energy. In fact, a large fraction of the energy consumed by the brain—whether

(a) The sodium-potassium pump

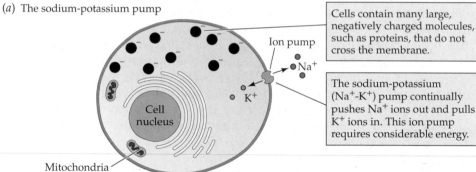

(b) Membrane permeability to ions

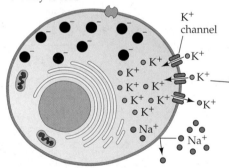

(c) Equilibrium potential

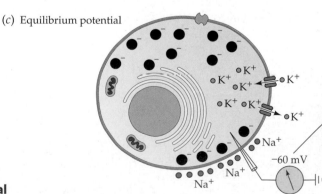

3.3 The Ionic Basis of the Resting Potential

waking or sleeping—is used to maintain these ionic differences across neuronal membranes.

The sodium-potassium pump causes a buildup of K⁺ ions inside the cell, but recall that, at rest, the membrane is selectively permeable to K⁺ ions (but not Na⁺ ions). That means K⁺ ions will tend to leave the interior, down their concentration gradient, causing a net buildup of negative charges inside the cell (**Figure 3.3b**). As negative charge builds up inside the cell, it begins to exert electrostatic pressure to pull positively charged K⁺ ions back inside. Eventually these opposing forces exerted by the K⁺ concentration gradient and by electrostatic pressure reach **equilibrium**, exactly balancing each other: any further movement of K⁺ ions into the cell (drawn by electrostatic pressure) is matched by the flow of K⁺ ions out of the cell (moving down the concentration gradient). This point corresponds to the cell's resting membrane potential of about –60 mV (values may range between –50 and –80 mV), as **Figure 3.3c** depicts.

The **Nernst equation** is a mathematical function predicting the voltage needed to just counterbalance the diffusion force pushing an ion across a semipermeable membrane (from the side with a high concentration to the side with a low concentration). In the case of K⁺ ions, the Nernst equation's prediction of the resting membrane potential that is required to balance the high concentration of K⁺ ions inside the cell is close to the potential actually recorded from neurons. If one also considers the diffusion force and permeability of other ions, the predicted voltage across neurons is quite close to what is observed in neurons.

The actions of the sodium potassium pump and the diffusion of K⁺ ions result in the distribution of ions inside and outside neurons that is illustrated in **Figure 3.4**. Notice the high intracellular concentration of K⁺ and the high extracellular concentration of Na⁺.

The resting potential of a neuron provides a baseline level of polarization found in all cells. But unlike most other cells, neurons routinely undergo a brief but radical *change* in polarization, sending an electrical signal from one end of the neuron to the other, as we'll discuss next.

A threshold amount of depolarization triggers an action potential

Action potentials are very brief but large changes in neuronal polarization that arise initially at the **axon hillock** (the specialized membrane located where the axon emerges from the cell body; see Figure 2.7a), which are propagated at high speed along the axon. The information that a neuron sends to its postsynaptic targets is encoded in patterns of these action potentials, so we need to understand their properties—where they come from, how they race down the axon, and how they communicate their information across synapses to other cells. Let's turn first to the creation of the action potential.

Two concepts are central to understanding how action potentials are triggered. **Hyperpolarization** is an increase in membrane potential (i.e., the neuron becomes even more negative on the inside, relative to the outside). So if the neuron already has a resting membrane potential of, say, –60 mV,

equilibrium Here, the point at which the movement of ions across the cell membrane is balanced, as the electrostatic pressure pulling ions in one direction is offset by the diffusion force pushing them in the opposite direction.

Nernst equation An equation predicting the voltage needed to just counterbalance the diffusion force pushing an ion across a semipermeable membrane from the side with a high concentration to the side with a low concentration.

axon hillock A cone-shaped area from which the axon originates out of the cell body. Functionally, the integration zone of the neuron.

hyperpolarization An increase in membrane potential (the interior of the neuron becomes even more negative).

3.4 The Distribution of Ions Inside and Outside of a Neuron Most potassium ions (K⁺) are found inside the neuron. Most sodium ions (Na⁺), chloride ions (Cl⁻), and calcium ions (Ca⁺) are in the extracellular space. These ions are exchanged through specialized channels in the cell membrane. The large, negatively charged protein molecules stay inside the neuron.

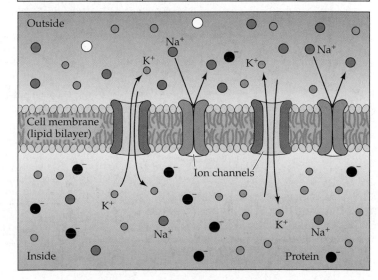

	Na⁺	K⁺	Cl⁻	Ca²⁺	Proteins
Outside cell	many	few	many	many	few
Inside cell	few	many	few	few	many

depolarization A reduction in membrane potential (the interior of the neuron becomes less negative).

hyperpolarization makes it even *farther from zero*, maybe –70 mV. **Depolarization** is the reverse, referring to a decrease in membrane potential. The depolarization of a neuron from a resting potential of –60 mV to, say, –50 mV makes the inside of the neuron more like the outside. In other words, depolarization of a neuron brings its membrane potential *closer to zero*.

Figure 3.5a illustrates an apparatus for experimentally applying hyperpolarizing and depolarizing stimuli to a neuron, via electrodes. (Later we'll talk about how synapses from other neurons produce similar hyperpolarizations and depolarizations.) Applying a *hyperpolarizing* stimulus to the membrane produces an immediate response that passively follows the stimulus pulse (**Figure 3.5b**; the distortions at the beginning and end of the neuron's response are caused by the membrane's ability to store electricity, known as *capacitance*). The greater the stimulus, the greater the response; so the neuron's change in potential is called a *graded response*.

If we measured the membrane response at locations successively farther and farther away from the stimulus location, we would see another way in which the membrane response seems passive. Like the ripples spreading from a pebble

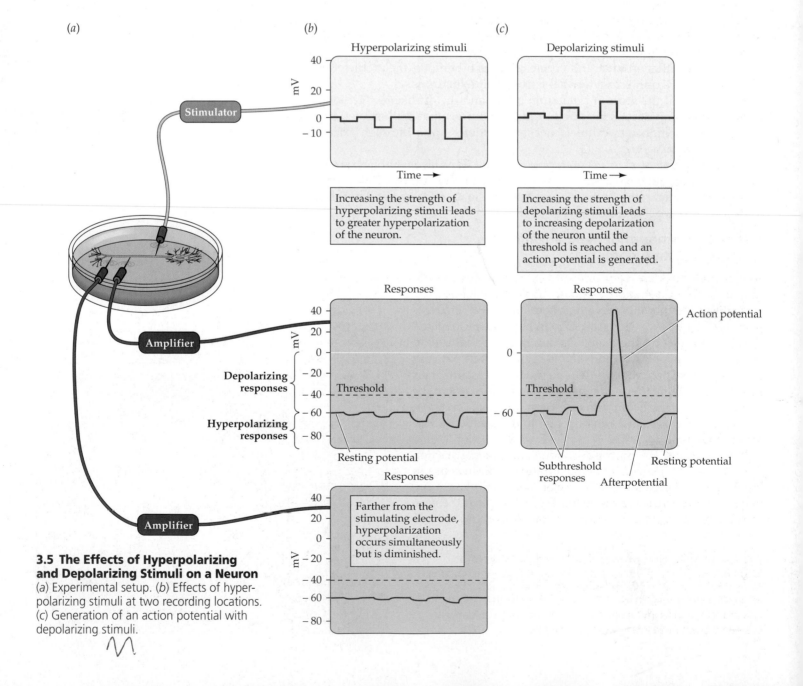

3.5 The Effects of Hyperpolarizing and Depolarizing Stimuli on a Neuron
(a) Experimental setup. (b) Effects of hyperpolarizing stimuli at two recording locations. (c) Generation of an action potential with depolarizing stimuli.

dropped in a pond, the potentials produced by stimulation of the membrane diminish as they spread away from the point of stimulation (see Figure 3.5*b*, bottom). A simple law of physics describes this phenomenon: as the potential spreads across the membrane, its size decays as a function of the square of the distance. Such **local potentials**, which are graded and diminish over time and distance, also arise at synapses in response to other neurons, as we will see later in this chapter.

Up to a point, the application of *depolarizing* pulses to the membrane follows the same pattern as for hyperpolarizing stimuli, producing local, graded responses. However, the situation changes suddenly if the stimulus depolarizes the cell to –40 mV or so (the exact value varies slightly among neurons). At this point, known as the **threshold**, a sudden and brief (0.5–2.0 ms) response—the action potential (**Figure 3.5***c*), sometimes referred to as a *spike* because of its shape—is provoked. An action potential is a rapid reversal of the membrane potential that momentarily makes the inside of the membrane *positive* with respect to the outside. Unlike the passive graded potentials that we have been discussing, the action potential is actively propagated (or regenerated) down the axon, through ionic mechanisms that we'll discuss shortly.

Applying strong stimuli to produce depolarizations that far exceed the neuron's threshold reveals another important property of action potentials: larger depolarizations do not produce larger action potentials. In other words, the size (or *amplitude*) of the action potential is independent of stimulus magnitude. This characteristic is referred to as the **all-or-none property** of the action potential: either it fires at its full amplitude, or it doesn't fire at all. It turns out that information is encoded by changes in the *frequency* of action potentials rather than in their amplitude. With stronger stimuli, more action potentials are produced, but the size of each action potential remains the same.

A closer look at the form of the action potential shows that the return to baseline membrane potential is not simple. Many axons exhibit electrical oscillations immediately following the spike; these changes are called **afterpotentials** (see Figure 3.5*c*), and they are also related to the movement of ions in and out of the cell.

Ionic mechanisms underlie the action potential

What events explain the action potential? To answer this question, English neurophysiologists Alan Hodgkin (1914–1998) and Andrew Huxley (1917–) took advantage of the giant axon of the squid, part of a neuron involved in the animal's emergency escape behavior. More than half a millimeter in diameter, the giant axon of the squid is readily apparent to the naked eye, and therefore much better suited to experimentation than mammalian axons, which range in size from 0.5 to 20 µm in diameter. Microelectrodes can be inserted into a giant axon without greatly altering the properties or activity of the axon; it is even possible to push the intracellular fluid out of the squid axon and replace it with other fluids to study various properties of the action potential.

Experimental evidence revealed that the action potential is created by the movement of sodium ions (Na^+) into the cell, through channels in the membrane (Hodgkin and Katz, 1949). At its peak, the action potential approaches the equilibrium potential for Na^+ as predicted by the Nernst equation: about +40 mV. At this point, the concentration gradient pushing Na^+ ions into the cell is exactly balanced by the positive charge pushing them out. The action potential thus involves a rapid shift in membrane properties, switching suddenly from the potassium-dependent resting state to a primarily sodium-dependent active state, and then swiftly returning to the resting state. This shift is accomplished through the actions of a very special ion channel: the voltage-gated Na^+ channel.

Like other ion channels, the **voltage-gated Na^+ channel** is a tubular, membrane-spanning protein, but its central Na^+-selective pore is ordinarily closed. When the cell membrane becomes depolarized to threshold levels, however, the channel's shape changes, opening the pore to allow Na^+ ions through. Consider what hap-

local potential   An electrical potential that is initiated by stimulation at a specific site, which is a graded response that spreads passively across the cell membrane, decreasing in strength with time and distance.

threshold   The stimulus intensity that is just adequate to trigger an action potential at the axon hillock.

all-or-none property   The fact that the amplitude of the action potential is independent of the magnitude of the stimulus.

afterpotential   The positive or negative change in membrane potential that may follow an action potential.

voltage-gated Na^+ channel   A Na^+-selective channel that opens or closes in response to changes in the voltage of the local membrane potential; it mediates the action potential.

refractory Transiently inactivated or exhausted.

absolute refractory phase A brief period of complete insensitivity to stimuli.

relative refractory phase A period of reduced sensitivity during which only strong stimulation produces an action potential.

pens when a patch of axonal membrane depolarizes (**Figure 3.6**). As long as the depolarization is below threshold, Na⁺ channels remain closed. But when the depolarization reaches threshold, a few Na⁺ channels open at first, allowing ions to start entering the neuron, depolarizing the membrane even further and opening still more Na⁺ channels. Thus, the process accelerates until the barriers are removed and Na⁺ ions rush in.

The voltage-gated Na⁺ channels stay open for a little less than a millisecond; then they close again. By this time the membrane potential has approached the sodium equilibrium potential of about +40 mV. Now, positive charges inside the nerve cell push K⁺ ions out, and voltage-gated K⁺ channels open, increasing the permeability to K⁺ even more, so the resting potential is quickly restored.

Applying very strong stimuli reveals another important property of axonal membranes. As we bombard the beleaguered axon with ever-greater stimuli, an upper limit to the frequency of action potentials becomes apparent at about 1200 spikes per second. (Many neurons have even slower maximum rates of response.) Similarly, applying pairs of stimuli that are spaced closer and closer together reveals a related phenomenon: beyond a certain point, only the first stimulus is able to elicit an action potential. The axonal membrane is said to be **refractory** (unresponsive) to the second stimulus.

Refractoriness has two phases: During the **absolute refractory phase**, a brief period immediately following the production of an action potential, no amount of stimulation can induce another action potential, because the voltage-gated Na⁺ channels are either still open or unresponsive (see Figure 3.6, step 3). The absolute phase is followed by a period of reduced sensitivity, the **relative refractory phase**, during which only a very strong stimulation can produce another action potential, because K⁺ ions are still flowing out, so the cell is temporarily hyperpolarized after firing an action potential (see Figure 3.6, step 4). The overall length of the refractory phase is what determines a neuron's maximal rate of firing. You might wonder if the repeated inrush of Na⁺ ions would allow them to build up, affecting the cell's resting potential. In fact, relatively few Na⁺ ions need to enter to

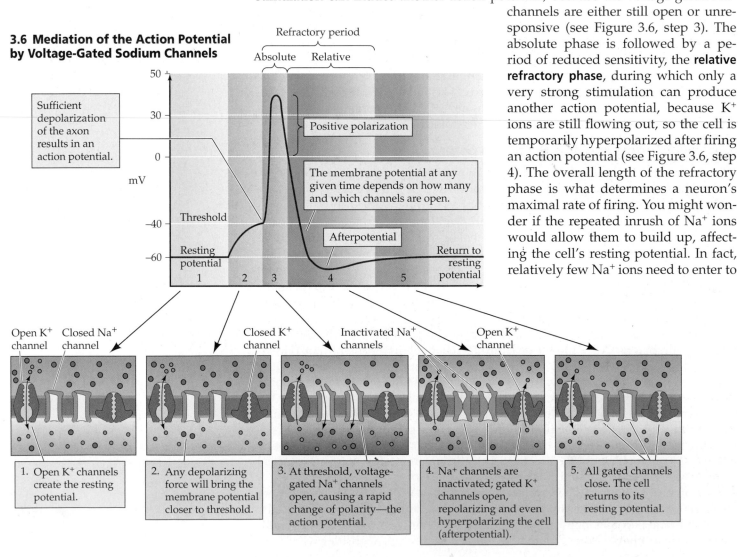

3.6 Mediation of the Action Potential by Voltage-Gated Sodium Channels

Sufficient depolarization of the axon results in an action potential.

Positive polarization

The membrane potential at any given time depends on how many and which channels are open.

Afterpotential

Refractory period

Absolute   Relative

mV

50
30
0
−40 Threshold
−60 Resting potential

1   2   3   4   5

Return to resting potential

Open K⁺ channel   Closed Na⁺ channel

Closed K⁺ channel

Inactivated Na⁺ channels

Open K⁺ channel

1. Open K⁺ channels create the resting potential.

2. Any depolarizing force will bring the membrane potential closer to threshold.

3. At threshold, voltage-gated Na⁺ channels open, causing a rapid change of polarity—the action potential.

4. Na⁺ channels are inactivated; gated K⁺ channels open, repolarizing and even hyperpolarizing the cell (afterpotential).

5. All gated channels close. The cell returns to its resting potential.

BOX 3.1 Changing the Channel

The cell membrane is made up of fatty molecules, so it tends to repel water. Because ions in body fluids are usually surrounded by clusters of water molecules, they cannot easily pass directly through neuronal membranes. Instead, they must pass through membrane-spanning ion channels, which are highly selective for particular types of ions. Research has begun to reveal some of the functional details of these channels, such as the K^+ channel shown in Figure A (Berneche and Roux, 2001; Morais-Cabral et al., 2001; Zhou et al., 2001). The inner surfaces of the K^+ channel are lined with oxygen atoms that mimic water molecules. With the oxygen atoms substituting for their usual escort of water molecules, K^+ ions fit exactly into this *selectivity filter*. Other ions, such as the smaller Na^+ ions, do not fit as comfortably and thus remain outside, in solution. The end result is a 10,000-fold selectivity for K^+ ions!

Given the extreme precision with which these ion channels must operate, it's no surprise that even the most minor alteration of channel functioning causes people serious health problems (Kass, 2005). **Channelopathy** is a medical condition in which the form and function of ion channels is altered as a result of mutation of the genes that encode those channels. Sodium channelopathy—a problem with sodium channels—is associated with a variety of seizure disorders, as well as heritable muscle diseases and certain types of cardiac ailments (S. C. Cannon, 1996; George, 2005; Kass, 2005). Chloride channel disorders can result in deafness, kidney problems, and neuromuscular disorders (T. J. Jentsch et al., 2005), as well as seizures. In fact, evidence is mounting that mutations in ion channel genes of all sorts may be a major cause of epilepsy (Steinlein, 2004), which we discuss later in this chapter.

The critical importance of channels is also exploited by a variety of potent animal toxins (Figure B). For example, **tetrodotoxin (TTX)** and **saxitoxin (STX)** selectively block voltage-gated sodium channels, thereby preventing the production of action potentials; paralysis and death rapidly follow. Tetrodotoxin is found in the ovaries of the puffer fish, which is esteemed as a delicacy in Japan. If the ovaries of the puffer fish are not removed properly and if the fish is not cleaned with great care, people who eat it may be poisoned by TTX. Saxitoxin is likewise a seafood threat: it derives from "red tide," a bloom of algae that sometimes affects shellfish. The extremely potent neurotoxin **batrachotoxin**, produced by South American poison arrow frogs, has the reverse effect and forces Na^+ channels to stay open, with equally lethal results. Scorpions are a rich source of channel-specific toxins; some species produce toxins that specifically block Na^+ channels, while others target K^+ channels.

Tiny quantities of any of these toxins can dramatically impede the ability of neurons to function. However, the same specificity that makes channel toxins so deadly also makes them useful tools in the laboratory. For example, the venom of the tarantula spider contains toxins that very specifically target the voltage sensor of certain voltage-gated ion channels; in the lab, these toxins have provided important clues about how those channels work (S.-Y. Lee and MacKinnon, 2004). The use of channel-selective toxins and other experimental techniques for studying ion channels is discussed on the website in **A Step Further: How Can We Study Ion Channels?**

channelopathy A genetic abnormality of ion channels, causing a variety of symptoms.

tetrodotoxin (TTX) A toxin from puffer fish ovaries that blocks the voltage-gated sodium channel, preventing action potential conduction.

saxitoxin (STX) An animal toxin that blocks sodium channels when applied to the outer surface of the cell membrane.

batrachotoxin A toxin, produced by poison arrow frogs, that selectively interferes with Na^+ channels.

(A) Potassium channel selectivity filter

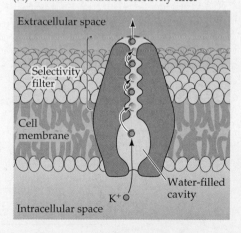

Extracellular space

Selectivity filter

Cell membrane

K^+

Water-filled cavity

Intracellular space

(B) Some sources of channel toxins

---

change the membrane potential, and the K^+ ions quickly restore the resting potential. In the long run, the sodium-potassium pump enforces the concentrations of ions that maintain the resting potential.

This tiny protein molecule, the voltage-gated Na^+ channel, is really quite a complicated machine. It monitors the axon's polarity, and at threshold the channel changes its shape to open the pore, shutting down again just a millisecond later. The channel then "remembers" that it was recently open and refuses to open again for a short time. These properties produce and enforce the properties of the action potential. As you might expect, anything that alters the functioning of neuronal ion channels can have dire consequences (**Box 3.1**).

In general, the transmission of action potentials is limited to axons. Cell bodies and dendrites usually have few voltage-gated Na⁺ channels, so they do not conduct action potentials. The ion channels on the cell body and dendrites are stimulated chemically at synapses, as we'll discuss later in this chapter. Because the axon has many such channels, once an action potential starts at the axon hillock, it regenerates itself down the length of the axon, as we discuss next.

Action potentials are actively propagated along the axon

Now that we have explored how voltage-gated channels underlie action potentials, we can turn to the question of how action potentials are transmitted down the axon—another function for which voltage-gated channels are crucial. Consider an experimental setup like the one pictured in **Figure 3.7**: recording electrodes are positioned along the length of the axon, allowing us to record an action potential at successive positions as it races toward the axon terminals. Recordings from this apparatus would show that an action potential initiated near the cell body spreads in a sort of chain reaction along the length of the axon, traveling at speeds that range from less than 1 meter per second (m/s) in some axons to more than 100 m/s in others.

How does the action potential travel? It is important to understand that the action potential is *regenerated* along the length of the axon. Remember, the action potential is a spike of depolarizing electrical activity (with a peak of about +40 mV), so it strongly depolarizes the next adjacent axon segment. Because this adjacent segment is similarly covered with voltage-gated Na⁺ channels, the depolarization immediately creates a new action potential, which in turn depolarizes the next patch of membrane, which generates yet another action potential, and so on all down the length of the axon. An analogy is the spread of fire along a row of closely

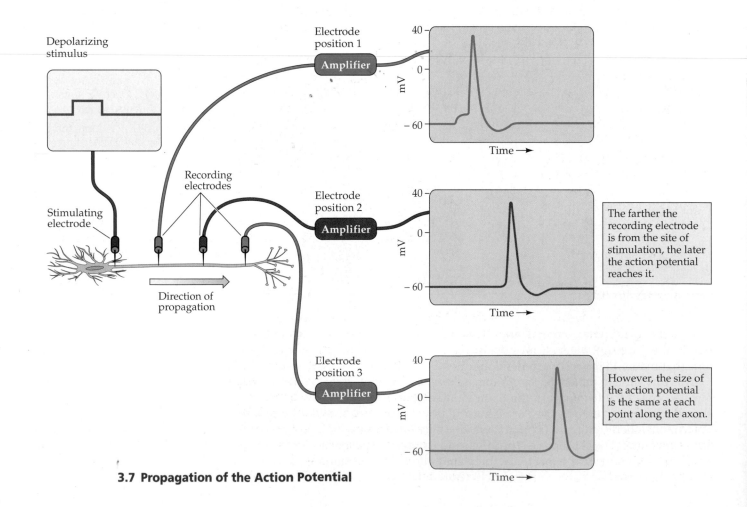

3.7 Propagation of the Action Potential

spaced match heads in a matchbook. When one match is lit, its heat is enough to ignite the next match and so on along the row. Voltage-gated Na^+ channels open when the axon is depolarized to threshold. In turn, the influx of Na^+ ions—the movement into the cell of positive charges—depolarizes the adjacent segment of axonal membrane and therefore opens new gates for the movement of Na^+ ions.

The axon normally conducts action potentials in only one direction—from the axon hillock toward the axon terminals—because as it progresses along the axon, the action potential leaves in its wake a stretch of refractory membrane (**Figure 3.8a**). Propagated activity does not spread from the axon hillock back over the cell body and dendrites, because the membrane there has very few voltage-gated Na^+ channels, so it cannot produce a regenerated action potential.

If we record the speed of action potentials along axons that differ in diameter, we see that **conduction velocity** varies with the diameter of the axon. Larger axons allow the depolarization to spread faster through the interior. In mammals, the conduction velocity in large fibers may be as fast as 150 m/s. (We discuss axon diameter and conduction velocity again in Chapter 8.) Although not as fast as the speed of light, as it was once believed to be, neural conduction is nevertheless very fast: up to about one-third the speed of sound in air. This relatively high rate of conduction ensures rapid sensory and motor processing.

The highest conduction velocities require more than just large axons. Myelin sheathing also greatly speeds conduction. As we described in Chapter 2, the myelin sheath that encases the axon is interrupted by **nodes of Ranvier**, small gaps spaced about every millimeter along the axon (see Figure 2.6h). Because the myelin insulation offers considerable resistance to the flow of ionic currents across the membrane, the action potential jumps from node to node. This process is called **saltatory conduction** (from the Latin *saltare*, "to leap or jump") (**Figure 3.8b**). The evolution of rapid saltatory conduction in vertebrates has given them a major behavioral advantage over invertebrates, in which axons are unmyelinated and mostly small in diameter, and thus slower in conduction.

To address this problem, many invertebrates have a few giant axons that mediate essential motor responses, such as escape behavior. Remember that the larger the axon, the faster the conduction velocity. The squid's giant axon, which we mentioned earlier, has an unusually high conduction rate for an invertebrate, but that rate is still only about 20 m/s, much slower than in myelinated axons (despite their smaller size).

To conduct action potentials as swiftly as a myelinated vertebrate axon does, an unmyelinated invertebrate axon would have to be 100 times larger in volume. It has been estimated that at least 10% of the volume of the human brain is occupied by myelinated axons. To maintain the conduction velocity of our cerebral neurons without the help of myelin, our brains would have to be 10 times as large as they are. This fact helps explain why myelination is an important index of maturation of the developing nervous system (see Chapter 7).

The function of synapses is to cause local changes in the postsynaptic membrane potential

At the beginning of the chapter, we related the tale of Otto Loewi's discovery of chemical signaling between neurons. Through painstaking experimentation, Loewi eventually proved that the chemical inhibiting the heart (which he called *Vagus-stoff*) was actually acetylcholine. Acetylcholine was thus the first demonstrated *neurotransmitter* (or *transmitter*), a chemical released by a neuron to affect a postsynaptic cell. We will discuss transmitters later in this chapter and in Chapter 4.

Neurotransmitters briefly alter the resting potential of the postsynaptic cell. We call these brief changes **postsynaptic potentials**. A given neuron, receiving synapses from hundreds of other cells, is subject to hundreds or thousands of postsynaptic potentials. When integrated, this massive array of local potentials determines whether the neuron will reach threshold and therefore generate an action potential

conduction velocity The speed at which an action potential is propagated along the length of an axon (or section of peripheral nerve).

node of Ranvier A gap between successive segments of the myelin sheath where the axon membrane is exposed.

saltatory conduction The form of conduction that is characteristic of myelinated axons, in which the action potential jumps from one node of Ranvier to the next.

postsynaptic potential A local potential that is initiated by stimulation at a synapse, can vary in amplitude, and spreads passively across the cell membrane, decreasing in strength with time and distance.

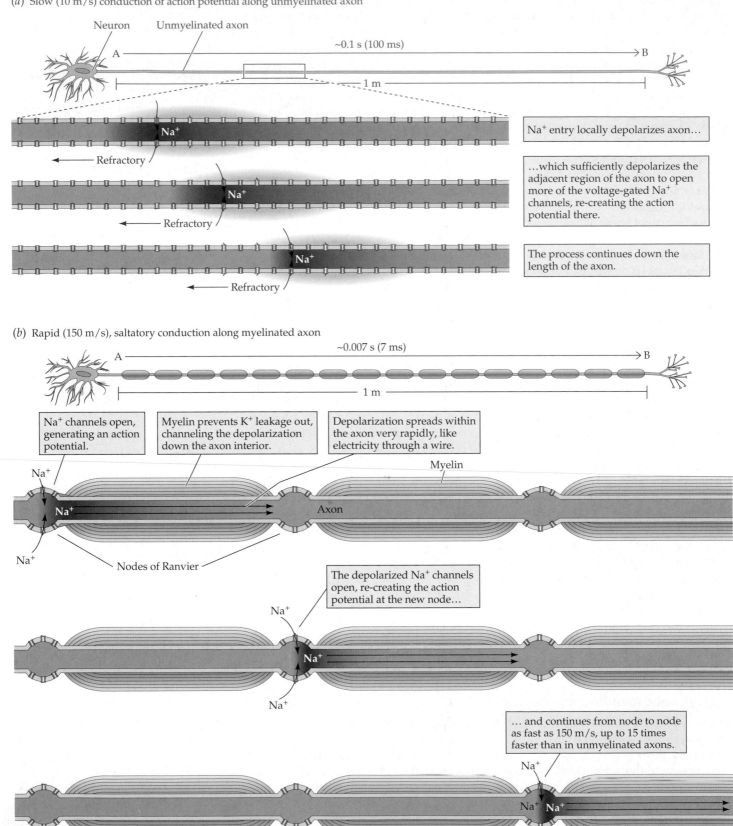

(*a*) Slow (10 m/s) conduction of action potential along unmyelinated axon

Neuron Unmyelinated axon

A ~0.1 s (100 ms) B

1 m

Na⁺ entry locally depolarizes axon…

Refractory

…which sufficiently depolarizes the adjacent region of the axon to open more of the voltage-gated Na⁺ channels, re-creating the action potential there.

Refractory

The process continues down the length of the axon.

Refractory

(*b*) Rapid (150 m/s), saltatory conduction along myelinated axon

A ~0.007 s (7 ms) B

1 m

Na⁺ channels open, generating an action potential.

Myelin prevents K⁺ leakage out, channeling the depolarization down the axon interior.

Depolarization spreads within the axon very rapidly, like electricity through a wire.

Myelin

Na⁺

Na⁺ Axon

Na⁺

Nodes of Ranvier

The depolarized Na⁺ channels open, re-creating the action potential at the new node…

Na⁺

Na⁺

Na⁺

… and continues from node to node as fast as 150 m/s, up to 15 times faster than in unmyelinated axons.

Na⁺

Na⁺ Na⁺

3.8 Conduction along Unmyelinated versus Myelinated Axons

BOX 3.2 Electrical Synapses Work with No Time Delay

Although we are focusing in this chapter on synapses that require a chemical substance to mediate synaptic transmission, electrical synapses are also widespread in the brain (M. V. Bennett, 2000). At **electrical synapses** (or **gap junctions**) the presynaptic membrane comes even closer to the postsynaptic membrane than it does at chemical synapses; the gap at an electrical synapse (Figure A) measures only 2–4 nm. In contrast, the synaptic cleft of a chemical synapse is 20–40 nm. At electrical synapses, the facing membranes of the two cells have relatively large channels arranged to allow ions to flow from one neuron directly into the other (Figure B). As a consequence, the electrical current that is associated with neural activity in one neuron can flow directly across the gap junction to affect the other neuron.

Transmission at these synapses closely resembles action potential conduction along the axon. Electrical synapses therefore work with practically no time delay, in contrast to chemical synapses, where the delay is on the order of a millisecond—slow in terms of neurons. Because of the speed of their transmission, electrical synapses are frequently found in neural circuits that mediate escape behaviors in invertebrates. They are also found where many fibers must be activated synchronously, as in the system for moving our eyes. Clinically, it is suspected that electrical synapses contribute to the spread of synchronized seizure discharges in epilepsy (Szente et al., 2002). (Figure A courtesy of Constantino Sotelo.)

(A) Electron micrograph of an electrical synapse

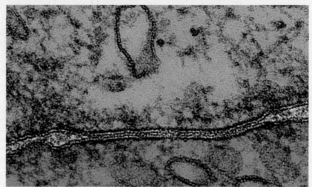

electrical synapse Also called *gap junction*. The region between neurons where the presynaptic and postsynaptic membranes are so close that the action potential can jump to the postsynaptic membrane without first being translated into a chemical message.

(B) Diagram of an electrical synapse

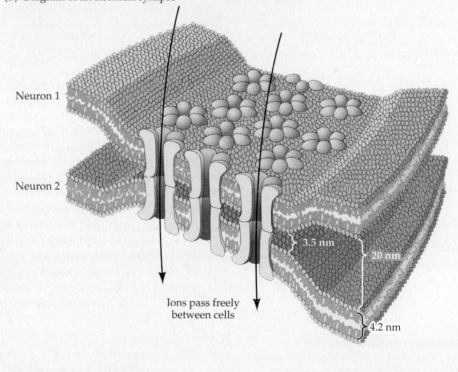

Neuron 1

Neuron 2

3.5 nm

20 nm

4.2 nm

Ions pass freely between cells

---

of its own. Eventually it was found that the nervous system also employs electrical synapses (**Box 3.2**), but the vast majority of synapses use neurotransmitters to produce postsynaptic potentials.

We can study postsynaptic potentials with a setup like that shown in **Figure 3.9**. This setup enables us to compare the effects of activity of excitatory versus inhibitory presynaptic terminals on the local membrane potential of a postsynaptic cell. The responses of the presynaptic and postsynaptic cells are shown on the same graphs in Figure 3.9 for easy comparison of their timing. It is important to remember that excitatory and inhibitory neurons get their names from their *actions on postsynaptic neurons*, not from their effects on behavior.

Stimulation of an excitatory presynaptic neuron (red) causes it to produce an all-or-none action potential that spreads to the end of the axon, releasing transmitter.

3.9 Recording Postsynaptic Potentials

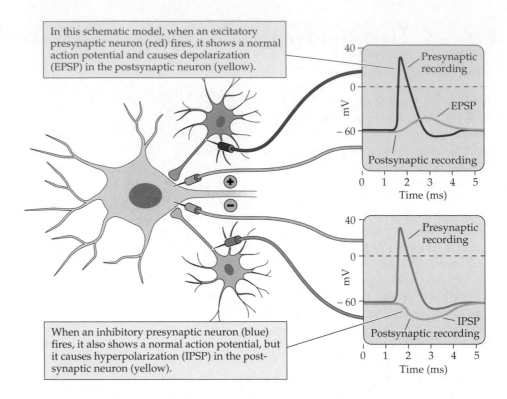

In this schematic model, when an excitatory presynaptic neuron (red) fires, it shows a normal action potential and causes depolarization (EPSP) in the postsynaptic neuron (yellow).

When an inhibitory presynaptic neuron (blue) fires, it also shows a normal action potential, but it causes hyperpolarization (IPSP) in the postsynaptic neuron (yellow).

After a brief delay, the postsynaptic cell (yellow) displays a small local depolarization, as Na^+ channels open to let the positive ions in. This postsynaptic membrane depolarization is known as an **excitatory postsynaptic potential** (**EPSP**) because it pushes the postsynaptic cell a little closer to the threshold for an action potential.

Generally, the combined effect of many excitatory synapses is required to elicit an action potential in a postsynaptic neuron. If EPSPs are elicited almost simultaneously by many neurons that converge on the postsynaptic cell, these potentials can sum and produce a depolarization large enough to reach threshold and trigger an action potential. Note that there is a delay: in the fastest cases, the postsynaptic depolarization begins about half a millisecond after the presynaptic action potentials arrive at the axon terminals. This **synaptic delay** reflects the time needed for the neurotransmitter to be released and diffuse across the synaptic cleft, as we'll discuss later.

The action potential of an inhibitory presynaptic neuron (blue) looks exactly like that of the excitatory presynaptic neuron; all neurons use the same kind of propagated signal (see Figure 3.9). But the effect on the *post*synaptic side is quite different. When the inhibitory neuron is stimulated, the postsynaptic effect is an *increase* of the resting membrane potential. This hyperpolarization moves the cell membrane potential away from threshold—it *decreases* the probability that the neuron will fire an action potential—so it is called an **inhibitory postsynaptic potential** (**IPSP**).

Usually IPSPs result from the opening of channels that permit **chloride ions** (Cl^-) to enter the cell. Because Cl^- ions are much more concentrated outside the cell than inside (see Figure 3.4), they rush into the cell, making it even more negative. Although in this discussion we have been paying more attention to excitation, inhibition also plays a vital role in the neural processing of information. Just as driving a car requires brakes as well as an accelerator, neural switches must be turned off as well as on. The nervous system treads a narrow path between overexcitation, which leads to seizures (see Box 3.3), and underexcitation, which leads to coma and death.

What determines whether a synapse excites or inhibits the postsynaptic cell? One factor is the particular neurotransmitter released by the presynaptic cell. Some

excitatory postsynaptic potential (EPSP) A depolarizing potential in the postsynaptic neuron that is caused by excitatory presynaptic potentials. EPSPs increase the probability that the postsynaptic neuron will fire an action potential.

synaptic delay The brief delay between the arrival of an action potential at the axon terminal and the creation of a postsynaptic potential.

inhibitory postsynaptic potential (IPSP) A hyperpolarizing potential in the postsynaptic neuron that is caused by inhibitory connections. IPSPs decrease the probability that the postsynaptic neuron will fire an action potential.

chloride ion (Cl^-) A chlorine atom that carries a negative charge because it has gained one electron.

transmitters generate an EPSP in the postsynaptic cells; others generate an IPSP. Whether a neuron fires an action potential at any given moment is decided by the balance between the number of excitatory and the number of inhibitory signals that it is receiving, and it receives many signals of both types at all times.

Spatial summation and temporal summation integrate synaptic inputs

Synaptic transmission is an impressive process, but complex behavior requires more than the simple conveyance of nerve signals across synapses. Neurons must also be able to integrate and transform the messages they receive. In other words, they perform *information processing*—by using a sort of neural algebra, in which each nerve cell adds and subtracts the myriad inputs it receives from other neurons. As we'll see next, these operations are possible because of the characteristics of synaptic inputs, the way in which the neuron integrates the postsynaptic potentials, and the trigger mechanism that determines whether a neuron will fire an action potential.

We have seen that postsynaptic potentials are caused by transmitter chemicals that can be either depolarizing (excitatory) or hyperpolarizing (inhibitory). From their points of origin on the dendrites and cell body, these EPSPs and IPSPs spread passively over the neuron, decreasing in strength over time and distance. Whether the postsynaptic neuron will fire an action potential is determined by whether a depolarization exceeding threshold reaches the axon hillock, the trigger zone in mammalian neurons.

The conceptual model in **Figure 3.10** illustrates the process of information processing by a neuron. For simplicity, no dendrites are shown, and all inputs synapse on the cell body. The presynaptic terminals are represented as simple contacts providing excitatory (depolarizing) or inhibitory (hyperpolarizing) stimulation to the postsynaptic cell membrane. The axon hillock contains a voltmeter; if the membrane potential rises (depolarizes) above a threshold level, an action potential is fired.

Suppose two excitatory endings are activated, as shown in **Figure 3.10a**, causing local depolarizations (in red) of the cell body. These depolarizations spread out over the neuron, dissipating as they spread, so that only a small proportion of the original depolarization reaches the axon hillock. Taken alone, neither would be sufficient to reach threshold depolarization, but when combined, the two depolarizations sum to push the hillock region to threshold.

Figure 3.10b shows what happens when inhibitory synapses also are active, creating postsynaptic hyperpolarizations. These hyperpolarizations also spread passively, dissipating as they travel. Because some potentials excite and others inhibit the hillock, these effects partially cancel each other. Thus, the net effect is the difference between the two: the neuron subtracts the IPSPs from the EPSPs. Simple arithmetic, right?

When summed, EPSPs and IPSPs do tend to cancel each other out. But because postsynaptic potentials spread passively and dissipate as they cross the cell membrane, the resulting sum is also influenced by *distance*. For example, simultaneous EPSPs from two synapses close to the hillock will produce a larger sum there than will two EPSPs from farther away. The summation of potentials originating from different physical locations across the cell body is called **spatial summation**. Only if the overall sum of *all* the potentials—both EPSPs and IPSPs—is sufficient to depolarize the cell to threshold at the axon hillock is an action potential triggered (**Figure 3.10c**). Usually the convergence of excitatory messages from many presynaptic neurons is required for a neuron to fire an action potential.

Postsynaptic effects that are not absolutely simultaneous can also be summed, because the postsynaptic potentials last a few milliseconds before fading away. The closer they are in time, the greater is the overlap and the more complete is the

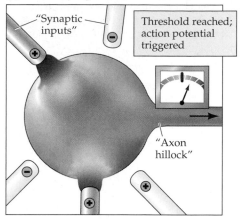

(a) Excitatory inputs cause the cell to fire

"Synaptic inputs"

Threshold reached; action potential triggered

"Axon hillock"

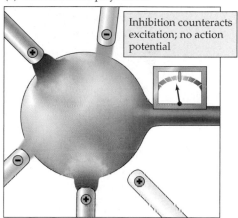

(b) Inhibition also plays a role

Inhibition counteracts excitation; no action potential

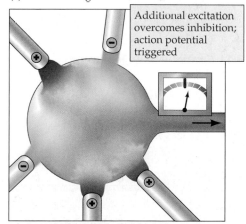

(c) The cell integrates excitation and inhibition

Additional excitation overcomes inhibition; action potential triggered

3.10 Integration of Excitatory and Inhibitory Inputs

spatial summation The summation at the axon hillock of postsynaptic potentials from across the cell body. If this summation reaches threshold, an action potential is triggered.

temporal summation The summation of postsynaptic potentials that reach the axon hillock at different times. The closer in time that the potentials occur, the more complete the summation.

summation, which in this case is called **temporal summation**. Temporal summation is easily understood if you imagine a neuron with only one input. If EPSPs arrive one right after the other, they sum and the postsynaptic cell eventually reaches threshold and produces an action potential (**Figure 3.11**). If too much time passes between EPSPs, the neuron will never fire.

It should now be clear that, although action potentials are all-or-none phenomena, the overall postsynaptic effect is graded in size and determined by the processing of numerous inputs occurring close together in time. The membrane potential at the axon hillock thus reflects the moment-to-moment integration of all the neuron's inputs, which the hillock encodes into an ongoing pattern of action potentials.

Dendrites add to the story of neuronal integration. A vast number of synaptic inputs, arrayed across the dendrites and cell body, can induce postsynaptic potentials. Dendrites therefore augment the receptive surface of the neuron and increase the amount of input information that the neuron can handle. We've already mentioned that proximity is an important factor in the summation of EPSPs and IPSPs. All other things being equal, then, the farther out on a dendrite a potential is produced, the less effect the potential should have at the axon hillock, because the potential decreases in amplitude (i.e., strength) as it passively spreads. When the potential arises at a dendritic spine, its effect is further reduced because it has to spread down the shaft of the spine. Thus, information arriving at various parts of the neuron is weighted in terms of the distance and path resistance to the axon hillock.

Interestingly, in some types of neurons, synapses that are distant from the axon hillock compensate by producing larger postsynaptic potentials. These large local potentials boost the effectiveness of the more distant synapses on the integration process occurring at the axon hillock, making the more distant synapses more comparable to nearer synapses. Furthermore, some neurons have *dendritic* integration zones, featuring voltage-gated ion channels, which sum and amplify local postsynaptic potentials, increasing their eventual impact at the axon hillock (S. R. Williams and Stuart, 2003). And finally, glial cells also play a role in synaptic transmission: they increase the strength of the postsynaptic potential (Pfrieger and Barres, 1997), overlying the presynaptic terminal and thereby preventing neurotransmitter from leaking out of the synaptic cleft.

Table 3.1 summarizes the many properties of action potentials, EPSPs, and IPSPs, noting the principal similarities and differences among the three kinds of neural potentials.

3.11 Spatial Versus Temporal Summation

(*a*) Spatial summation

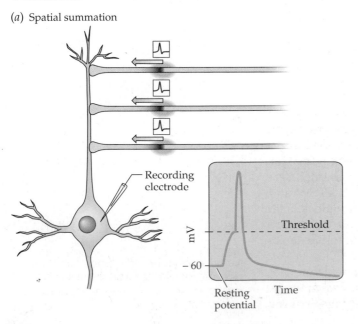

(*b*) Temporal summation

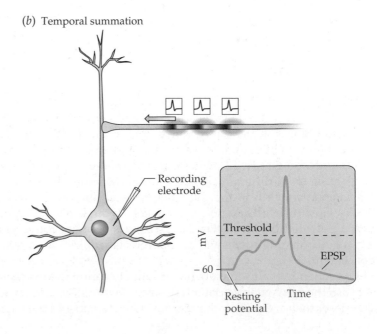

TABLE 3.1   Characteristics of Electrical Signals of Nerve Cells

Type of signal	Signaling role	Typical duration (ms)	Amplitude	Character	Mode of propagation	Ion channel opening	Channel sensitive to:
Action potential	Conduction along a neuron	1–2	Overshooting, 100 mV	All-or-none, digital	Actively propagated, regenerative	First Na^+, then $K+$, in different channels	Voltage (depolarization)
Excitatory postsynaptic potential (EPSP)	Transmission between neurons	10–100	Depolarizing, from less than 1 to more than 20 mV	Graded, analog	Local, passive spread	$Na^+–K^+$	Chemical (neurotransmitter)
Inhibitory postsynaptic potential (IPSP)	Transmission between neurons	10–100	Hyperpolarizing, from less than 1 to about 15 mV	Graded, analog	Local, passive spread	$Cl^-–K^+$	Chemical (neurotransmitter)

Synaptic Transmission Requires a Sequence of Events

The sequence of events during chemical synaptic transmission includes the following main steps:

1. The action potential is propagated into the presynaptic axon terminal.
2. Voltage-gated calcium channels in the membrane of the axon terminal open, and **calcium ions (Ca^{2+})** enter the axon terminal.
3. Ca^{2+} causes synaptic vesicles filled with neurotransmitter to fuse with the presynaptic membrane and rupture, releasing the transmitter molecules into the synaptic cleft.
4. Some transmitter molecules bind to special receptor molecules in the postsynaptic membrane, leading—directly or indirectly—to the opening of ion channels in the postsynaptic membrane. The resulting flow of ions creates a local EPSP or IPSP in the postsynaptic neuron.
5. The IPSPs and EPSPs in the postsynaptic cell spread toward the axon hillock, interacting with each other along the way. If the integration of all the EPSPs and IPSPs ultimately results in a depolarization sufficient to reach threshold, the neuron will fire an action potential.
6. Synaptic transmitter is either (a) inactivated (degraded) by enzymes; or (b) removed rapidly from the synaptic cleft by transporters, so the transmission is brief and accurately reflects the activity of the presynaptic cell.
7. Synaptic transmitter may also activate presynaptic autoreceptors, resulting in a decrease in transmitter release.

Action potentials cause the release of transmitter molecules into the synaptic cleft

When an action potential reaches a presynaptic terminal, it causes vesicles near the presynaptic membrane to fuse with the membrane and discharge their contents into the synaptic cleft. The key event in this process is an influx of calcium ions (Ca^{2+}), rather than K^+ or Na^+, into the axon terminal. These cations enter through voltage-gated Ca^{2+} channels that open in response to the arrival of an action potential. The higher the frequency of action potentials arriving at the terminal, the greater the influx of Ca^{2+}, and the greater the number of vesicles that dump their contents into the synapse. Most synaptic delay is caused by the time needed for Ca^{2+} to enter the terminal. Diffusion of the transmitter across the cleft, and the interaction of transmitter molecules with their receptors, also takes some time.

Synaptic vesicles are about 50 nanometers (nm) in diameter and are quite complex structures; one important component is a protein called *synaptotagmin* that binds

calcium ion (Ca^{2+}) A calcium atom that carries a double positive charge because it has lost two electrons.

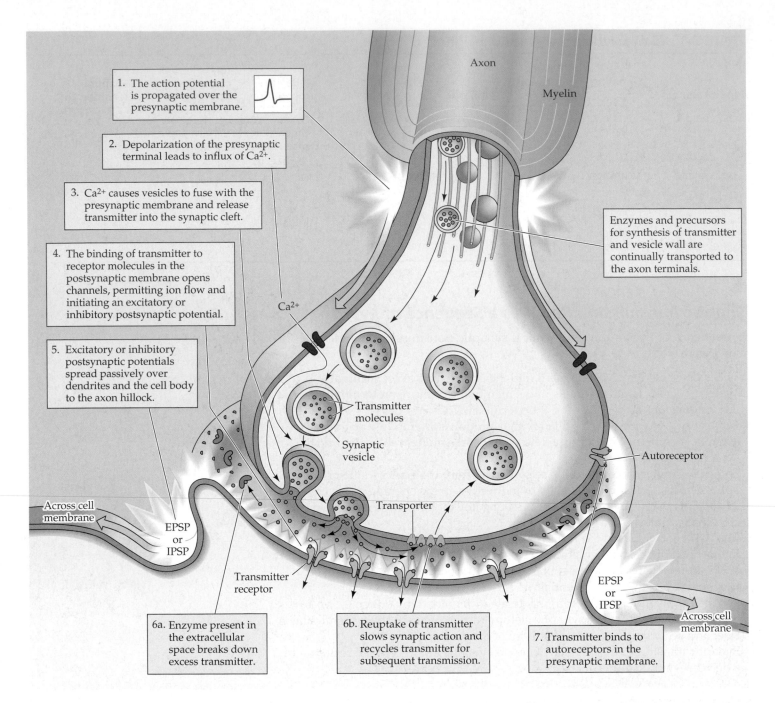

1. The action potential is propagated over the presynaptic membrane.

2. Depolarization of the presynaptic terminal leads to influx of Ca^{2+}.

3. Ca^{2+} causes vesicles to fuse with the presynaptic membrane and release transmitter into the synaptic cleft.

4. The binding of transmitter to receptor molecules in the postsynaptic membrane opens channels, permitting ion flow and initiating an excitatory or inhibitory postsynaptic potential.

5. Excitatory or inhibitory postsynaptic potentials spread passively over dendrites and the cell body to the axon hillock.

Axon

Myelin

Enzymes and precursors for synthesis of transmitter and vesicle wall are continually transported to the axon terminals.

Ca^{2+}

Transmitter molecules

Synaptic vesicle

Autoreceptor

Across cell membrane

EPSP or IPSP

Transporter

Transmitter receptor

6a. Enzyme present in the extracellular space breaks down excess transmitter.

6b. Reuptake of transmitter slows synaptic action and recycles transmitter for subsequent transmission.

7. Transmitter binds to autoreceptors in the presynaptic membrane.

EPSP or IPSP

Across cell membrane

3.12 Steps in Transmission at a Chemical Synapse

pinocytosis   The process by which synaptic neurotransmitter is repackaged into synaptic vesicles.

Ca^{2+}. Because all the synaptic vesicles in an axon terminal contain about the same number of molecules of transmitter, estimated to be tens of thousands, they all produce about the same change in postsynaptic potential when they rupture and release their contents. Typically, an action potential causes the release of several hundred vesicles at a time. **Figure 3.12** reviews the various steps in synaptic transmission.

The presynaptic terminal normally produces and stores enough transmitter to ensure that it is ready for activity. Intense activity of the neuron reduces the number of available vesicles, but soon more vesicles are produced to replace those that were discharged. This creation of new vesicles for transmitter molecules is called **pinocytosis**. Neurons differ in their ability to keep pace with a rapid rate of incoming action potentials. Furthermore, the rate of production of the transmitter chemical is governed by enzymes that are manufactured in the neuronal cell body and transported actively down the axons to the terminals. A neuron's maximal rate for producing and transporting these vital substances partly determines how long the neuron can sustain high levels of synaptic activity before becoming fatigued and less effective at stimulating its target.

Receptor molecules recognize transmitters

The action of a key in a lock is a good analogy for the action of a transmitter on a receptor protein. Just as a particular key can open a door, a molecule of the correct shape, called a **ligand** (see Chapter 4), can fit into a receptor protein and activate or block it. Neurotransmitters and hormones made inside the body are examples of **endogenous ligands**; drugs and toxins from outside the body are **exogenous ligands**. So, for example, at synapses where **acetylcholine (ACh)** is the transmitter, it fits into *ligand-binding sites* in **receptor molecules** located in the postsynaptic membrane (**Figure 3.13**).

The nature of the postsynaptic receptors at a given synapse determines the action of the transmitter (see Chapter 4). For example, ACh can function as either an inhibitory or an excitatory neurotransmitter, at different synapses. At excitatory synapses, binding of ACh opens channels for Na$^+$ and K$^+$ ions. At inhibitory synapses, ACh opens channels that allow chloride ions (Cl$^-$) to enter, thereby hyperpolarizing the membrane (i.e., making it more negative and so less likely to create an action potential).

The lock-and-key analogy is strengthened by the observation that various chemicals can fit onto receptor proteins and block the entrance of the key. Some of the preparations used in this research resemble the ingredients of a witches' brew. As an example, consider a couple of potent poisons that block ACh receptors: curare and bungarotoxin. **Curare** is an arrowhead poison used by native South Americans. Extracted from a plant, it greatly increases the efficiency of hunting: if the hunter hits any part of the prey, the arrow's poison soon blocks ACh receptors on muscles, paralyzing the animal. **Bungarotoxin**, another blocker of acetylcholine receptors, is

ligand A substance that binds to receptor molecules, such as those at the surface of the cell.

endogenous ligand Any substance, produced within the body, that selectively binds to the type of receptor that is under study.

exogenous ligand Any substance, originating from outside the body, that selectively binds to the type of receptor that is under study.

acetylcholine (ACh) A neurotransmitter produced and released by parasympathetic postganglionic neurons, by motoneurons, and by neurons throughout the brain.

receptor molecule Also called *receptor*. A protein that captures and reacts to molecules of a neurotransmitter or hormone.

curare An alkaloid neurotoxin that causes paralysis by blocking acetylcholine receptors in muscle.

bungarotoxin A neurotoxin, isolated from the venom of the banded krait, that selectively blocks acetylcholine receptors.

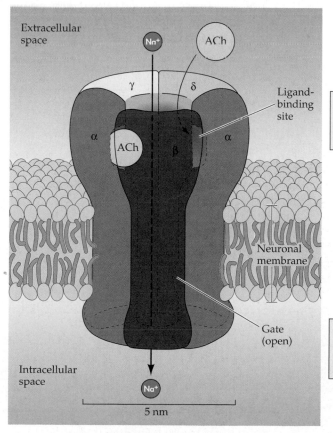

When ACh molecules occupy both binding sites, the sodium channel opens…

…allowing sodium ions to enter the cell. This results in a local depolarization.

3.13 A Nicotinic Acetylcholine Receptor
Each nicotinic ACh receptor consists of five subunits. The two ligand-binding sites normally bind ACh molecules, but they also bind nicotine and other nicotinic drugs. The ACh molecule and Na$^+$ ions are enlarged here for diagrammatic purposes.

agonist A molecule, usually a drug, that binds a receptor molecule and initiates a response like that of another molecule, usually a neurotransmitter.

antagonist A molecule, usually a drug, that interferes with or prevents the action of a transmitter.

cholinergic Referring to cells that use acetylcholine as their synaptic transmitter.

found in the venom of the banded krait (*Bungarus multicinctus*), a snake native to Taiwan. This toxin has proven very useful in research because a radioactive label can be attached to molecules of bungarotoxin without causing any change in their function. The labeled bungarotoxin can then be used to study the number, distribution, and functioning of acetylcholine receptor molecules.

Another poison, muscarine, mimics the action of ACh at some synapses. This poison is extracted from the mushroom *Amanita muscaria*. Molecules such as muscarine and nicotine that act like a transmitter at a receptor are called **agonists** (from the Greek *agon*, "contest" or "struggle") of that transmitter. Conversely, molecules that interfere with or prevent the action of a transmitter, in such a manner as curare or bungarotoxin block the action of ACh, are called **antagonists**.

Just as there are master keys that fit many different locks, there are submaster keys that fit a certain group of locks, and keys that fit only a single lock. Similarly, each chemical transmitter binds to several different receptor molecules. ACh acts on at least four kinds of **cholinergic** receptors; nicotinic and muscarinic are the two main kinds.

Nicotinic cholinergic receptors are found at synapses on muscles and in autonomic ganglia; it is the blockade of these receptors that is responsible for the paralysis caused by curare and bungarotoxin. Muscarinic cholinergic receptors are found on organs innervated by the parasympathetic division of the autonomic system (e.g., the intestines, the salivary gland, and heart muscle). These are the receptors that responded to ACh in the fluid transferred in Loewi's famous experiment (**Figure 3.14**). Most ACh receptors in the brain, too, are muscarinic. Most nicotinic sites are excitatory, but there are also inhibitory nicotinic synapses; and there are both excitatory and inhibitory muscarinic synapses, making at least four kinds of acetylcholine receptors. The existence of many types of receptors for each transmitter has evolved to provide specificity of transmitter action in the nervous system.

The nicotinic ACh receptor resembles a lopsided dumbbell with a tube running down its central axis (see Figure 3.13). The handle of the dumbbell spans the cell membrane (which is about 6 nm thick); the larger sphere extends about 5 nm above the surface of the membrane into the extracellular space, and the smaller sphere extends about 2 nm into the cell. The sides of the ion channel that runs through the

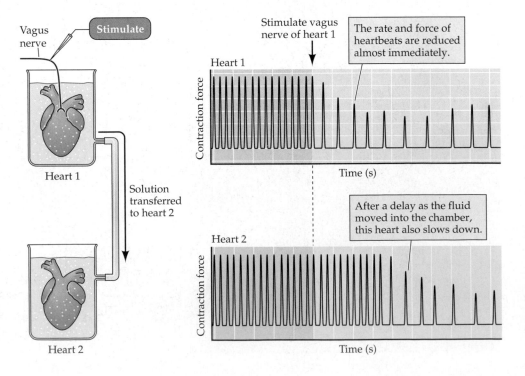

3.14 Loewi's Demonstration of a Chemical Messenger Loewi reasoned that some chemical released into the bath by stimulating the nerve to the first heart must have slowed down the second heart. We now know that chemical is the neurotransmitter acetylcholine (ACh) acting on inhibitory muscarinic receptors in heart muscle.

handle of the receptor consist of five protein subunits arranged like staves in a barrel. Two subunits are alike and, in conjunction with neighboring subunits, provide two recognition sites for ACh (Karlin, 2002); the other three subunits are all different. For the channel to open, both of the ACh-binding sites must be occupied.

After the structure of the nicotinic ACh receptor was determined, similar analyses were carried out for other receptors, including receptors for some of the synaptic transmitter molecules that we will be considering later, such as GABA (gamma-aminobutyric acid), glycine, and glutamate. Several of these receptors resemble each other, suggesting that they all belong to the same family and have a common evolutionary origin.

The coordination of different transmitter systems of the brain is incredibly complex. Each subtype of neurotransmitter receptor has a unique pattern of distribution within the brain. Different receptor systems become active at different times in fetal life. The number of any given type of receptor remains plastic in adulthood: not only are there seasonal variations, but many kinds of receptors show a regular daily variation of 50% or more in number, affecting the sensitivity of cells to that variety of transmitter. Similarly, the numbers of some receptors have been found to vary with the use of drugs (see Chapter 4). In general, an increase in receptor numbers is referred to as **up-regulation**, and a process that decreases receptor density is called **down-regulation** of that receptor type.

Transmitters bind to receptors, gating ion channels

The recognition of transmitter molecules by receptor molecules controls the opening of ion channels in two different ways. **Ionotropic receptors** (**Figure 3.15a**) directly control an ion channel. When bound by the transmitter, the ion channel opens and ions flow across the membrane. (Ionotropic receptors are also known as *chemically gated ion channels*, or **ligand-gated ion channels**.) **Metabotropic receptors** (**Figure 3.15b**) recognize the synaptic transmitter, but they do not directly control ion channels. Instead, they activate molecules known as **G proteins**.

up-regulation A compensatory increase in receptor availability at the synapses of a neuron.

down-regulation A compensatory reduction in receptor availability at the synapses of a neuron.

ionotropic receptor A receptor protein that includes an ion channel that is opened when the receptor is bound by an appropriate ligand.

ligand-gated ion channel Also known as *chemically gated ion channel*. An ion channel that opens or closes in response to the presence of a particular chemical.

metabotropic receptor A receptor protein that does not contain an ion channel but may, when activated, use a G protein system to alter the functioning of the postsynaptic cell.

G proteins A class of proteins that reside next to the intracellular portion of a receptor and that are activated when the receptor binds an appropriate ligand on the extracellular surface.

(a) Ionotropic receptor (ligand-gated ion channel; fast)

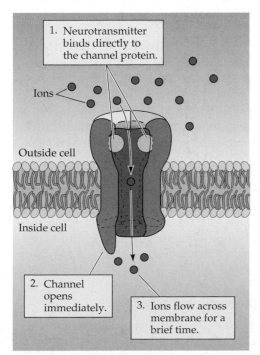

(b) Metabotropic receptor (G protein–coupled receptor; slow)

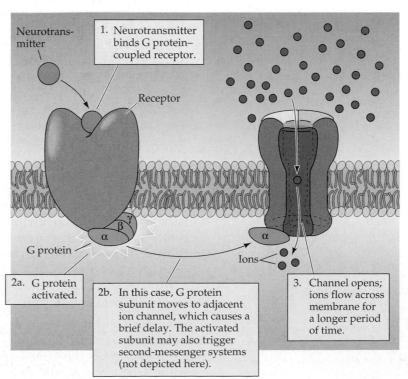

3.15 Two Types of Chemical Synapses

second messenger A slow-acting substance in the postsynaptic cell that amplifies the effects of synaptic activity and signals synaptic activity within the postsynaptic cell.

degradation The chemical breakdown of a neurotransmitter into inactive metabolites.

reuptake The process by which released synaptic transmitter molecules are taken up and reused by the presynaptic neuron, thus stopping synaptic activity.

transporters Specialized receptors in the presynaptic membrane that recognize transmitter molecules and return them to the presynaptic neuron for reuse.

axo-dendritic Referring to a synapse in which a presynaptic axon terminal synapses onto a dendrite of the postsynaptic neuron, either via a dendritic spine or directly onto the dendrite itself.

axo-somatic Referring to a synapse in which a presynaptic axon terminal synapses onto the cell body (soma) of the postsynaptic neuron.

axo-axonic Referring to a synapse in which a presynaptic axon terminal synapses onto another axon's terminal.

G protein is a convenient designation for proteins that bind the compounds guanosine diphosphate (GDP), guanosine triphosphate (GTP), and other guanine nucleotides. Sometimes the G protein itself acts to open ion channels, as in Figure 3.15*b*. But in other cases the G protein activates another, internal chemical signal to affect ion channels. If we think of the neurotransmitter as the first, external messenger arriving at the receptor on the cell's surface, then the next chemical signal, activated *inside* the cell, is a **second messenger**. Several different second messengers—such as cyclic adenosine monophosphate (cyclic AMP), diacylglycerol, or arachidonic acid—amplify the effect of the first messenger and can initiate processes that lead to changes in electrical potential at the membrane. An important feature of second-messenger systems is their ability to amplify and prolong the synaptic signals that a neuron receives.

About 80% of the known neurotransmitters and hormones activate cellular signal mechanisms through receptors coupled to G proteins, so this coupling device is very important (Birnbaumer et al., 1990). The G protein is located on the inner side of the neural membrane. When a transmitter molecule binds to a receptor that is coupled to a G protein, parts of the G protein complex separate from each other. One part, called the *alpha subunit*, migrates away within the cell and modulates the activity of its target molecules. Depending on the type of cell and receptor, the target may be a second-messenger system, an enzyme that works on an ion channel, or an ion pump. Many combinations of different receptors with different G proteins have already been identified, and more are being discovered at a rapid pace (Fredriksson et al., 2003; Wettschurek and Offermanns, 2005).

The action of synaptic transmitters is stopped rapidly

When a chemical transmitter such as ACh is released into the synaptic cleft, its postsynaptic action is not only prompt but usually very brief as well. This brevity ensures that the message is repeated faithfully. Accurate timing of synaptic transmission is necessary in many neural systems—for example, to drive the rapid cycles of muscle contraction and relaxation essential to many coordinated behaviors.

The prompt cessation of transmitter effects is achieved in one of two ways:

1. *Degradation*. Transmitter can be rapidly broken down and thus inactivated by a special enzyme—a process known as **degradation** (step 6a in Figure 3.12). For example, the enzyme that inactivates ACh is acetylcholinesterase (AChE). AChE breaks down ACh very rapidly into choline and acetic acid, and these products are recycled (at least in part) to make more ACh in the axon terminal. AChE is found especially at synapses, but also elsewhere in the nervous system. Thus, if any ACh escapes from a synapse where it is released, it is unlikely to reach other synapses intact, where it could start false messages.

2. *Reuptake*. Alternatively, transmitter molecules may be rapidly cleared from the synaptic cleft by being taken up into the presynaptic terminal—a process known as **reuptake** (step 6b in Figure 3.12). Norepinephrine, dopamine, and serotonin are examples of transmitters whose activity is terminated mainly by reuptake. In these cases, special receptors for the transmitter, called **transporters**, are located on the presynaptic axon terminal and bring the transmitter back inside. Once taken up into the presynaptic terminal, transmitter molecules may be repackaged into newly formed synaptic vesicles. Malfunction of reuptake mechanisms has been suspected to cause some kinds of mental illness, such as depression (see Chapter 16).

Nonclassic forms of synapses modulate neural activity

For simplicity, we have been focusing on the classic, directed **axo-dendritic** and **axo-somatic** synapses. But many nonclassic forms of chemical synapses exist in the nervous system. As the name implies, **axo-axonic** synapses form on axons, often near the axon terminal, allowing the presynaptic neuron to strongly facilitate or

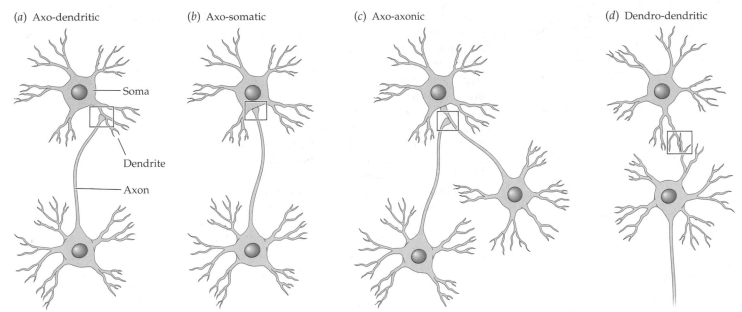

(a) Axo-dendritic   (b) Axo-somatic   (c) Axo-axonic   (d) Dendro-dendritic

Soma

Dendrite

Axon

inhibit the activity of the postsynaptic axon. Similarly, neurons may form **dendro-dendritic** contacts, allowing coordination of their activities (**Figure 3.16**).

At a **retrograde synapse**, transmission starts with classic axo-dendritic synaptic activity, but the postsynaptic cell subsequently releases a gas neurotransmitter, such as carbon monoxide or nitric oxide (see Chapter 4), which signals the presynaptic cell to release more transmitter.

Evidence is also mounting that **ectopic transmission** occurs between many neurons; in this mode of transmission, the location of transmitter release and the sites at which the transmitter acts are both well outside the conventional boundaries of nearby synapses (Coggan et al., 2005). And throughout the brain are found axons with regular swellings, called **varicosities**, along their length; like a drip-irrigation system, these **nondirected synapses** steadily release neurotransmitter to broadly affect surrounding areas.

Neurons and Synapses Combine to Make Circuits

Use of the term *circuit* for a group of neurons and their synaptic interconnections is an analogy to electronic circuits, in which an arrangement of components (e.g., resistors, capacitors, transistors, and their connecting wires) accomplishes a particular function. Electrical or electronic circuits can represent signals in either analog or digital ways—that is, in terms of continuously varying values or in terms of integers. Neurons similarly feature two kinds of processes: analog-like signals that vary in strength (such as graded potentials at synapses) and digital-like all-or-nothing signals (such as action potentials) that vary in frequency. The nervous system comprises many different types of neural circuits to accomplish basic functions in cognition, emotion, and action—all the categories of behavior and experience.

The simplest neural circuit that is routinely encountered in the nervous system is the **neural chain**, a straightforward linking of a series of neurons. (A look at some other simple neural circuits is presented on the website in **A Step Further: Circuits of Neurons Process Information**.) From the seventeenth century until well into the twentieth century, most attempts to understand behavior in neural terms were based on chains of neurons, which do indeed account for some behaviors. For example, the basic circuit for the stretch reflex, such as the **knee jerk reflex** we discussed at the start of the chapter, consists of a sensory neuron, a motor neuron, and a single synapse where the sensory neuron communicates with the motor neuron.

3.16 Different Types of Synaptic Connections   Most synapses are formed by an axon stimulating a dendrite, but axons also sometimes synapse upon cell bodies or even other axons. And in some instances, specialized dendrites synapse upon other dendrites.

dendro-dendritic   Referring to a type of synapse in which a synaptic connection forms between the dendrites of two neurons.

retrograde synapse   A synapse in which a signal (usually a gas neurotransmitter) flows from the postsynaptic neuron to the presynaptic neuron, thus counter to the usual direction of synaptic communication.

ectopic transmission   Cell-cell communication based on release of neurotransmitter in regions outside traditional synapses.

varicosity   The axonal swelling from which neurotransmitter diffuses in a nondirected synapse.

nondirected synapse   A type of synapse in which the presynaptic and postsynaptic cells are not in close apposition; instead, neurotransmitter is released by axonal varicosities and diffuses away to affect wide regions of tissue.

neural chain   A simple kind of neural circuit in which neurons are attached linearly, end-to-end.

knee jerk reflex   A variant of the stretch reflex in which stretching of the tendon beneath the knee leads to an upward kick of the leg.

3.17 The Knee Jerk Reflex

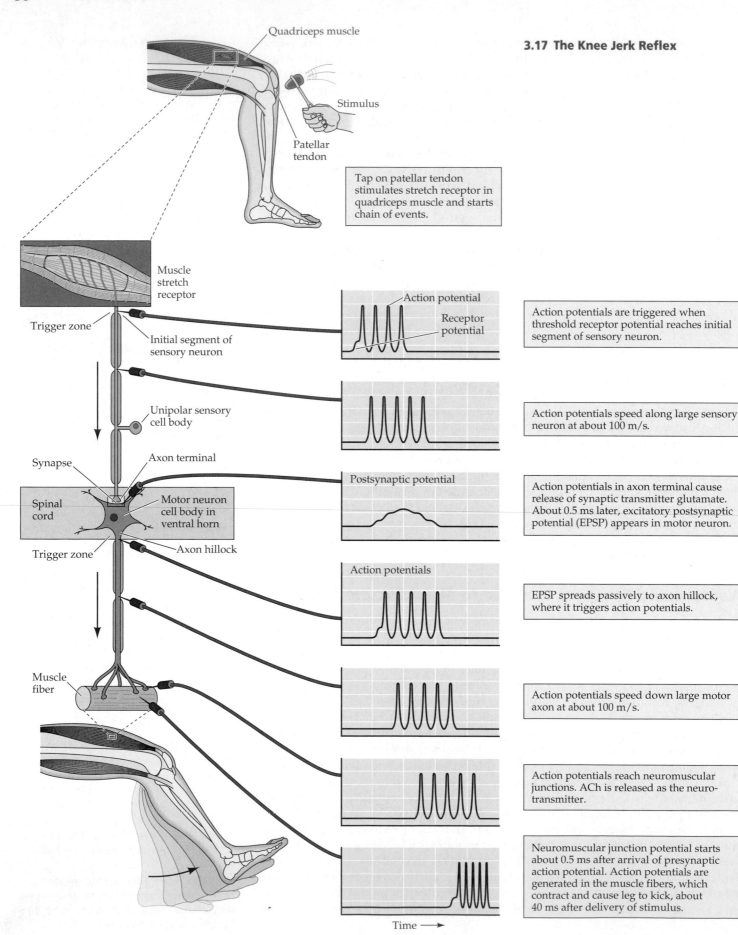

Quadriceps muscle

Stimulus

Patellar tendon

Tap on patellar tendon stimulates stretch receptor in quadriceps muscle and starts chain of events.

Muscle stretch receptor

Trigger zone

Initial segment of sensory neuron

Unipolar sensory cell body

Synapse

Axon terminal

Spinal cord

Motor neuron cell body in ventral horn

Trigger zone

Axon hillock

Muscle fiber

Action potential

Receptor potential

Action potentials are triggered when threshold receptor potential reaches initial segment of sensory neuron.

Action potentials speed along large sensory neuron at about 100 m/s.

Postsynaptic potential

Action potentials in axon terminal cause release of synaptic transmitter glutamate. About 0.5 ms later, excitatory postsynaptic potential (EPSP) appears in motor neuron.

Action potentials

EPSP spreads passively to axon hillock, where it triggers action potentials.

Action potentials speed down large motor axon at about 100 m/s.

Action potentials reach neuromuscular junctions. ACh is released as the neuro-transmitter.

Neuromuscular junction potential starts about 0.5 ms after arrival of presynaptic action potential. Action potentials are generated in the muscle fibers, which contract and cause leg to kick, about 40 ms after delivery of stimulus.

Time →

Figure 3.17 details the sequence and timing of events in the knee jerk reflex. Note that this reflex is extremely rapid: only about 40 ms elapse between the stimulus and the initiation of the response. Several factors account for this rapidity: (1) both the sensory and the motor axons involved are myelinated and of large diameter, so they conduct rapidly; (2) the sensory cells synapse directly on the motor neurons; and (3) both the central synapse and the neuromuscular junction are fast, ionotropic synapses.

For some purposes the afferent (input) parts of the visual system can be represented as a neural chain (**Figure 3.18a**) (in reality, however, the retina contains many kinds of neural circuits, which we will discuss in Chapter 10). A more accurate schematic diagram of the visual system (**Figure 3.18b**) highlights two other features that are common to many kinds of neural circuits: **convergence** and **divergence**.

In many parts of the nervous system, the axons from large numbers of neurons converge on certain cells. In the human eye, about 100 million receptor cells concentrate their information down on about 1 million ganglion cells; these ganglion cells convey the information from the eye to the brain (see Figure 3.18b). Higher in the visual system there is much divergence: the 1 million axons of the optic nerve communicate to billions of neurons in several different specialized regions of the cerebral cortex.

convergence The phenomenon of neural connections in which many cells send signals to a single cell.

divergence The phenomenon of neural connections in which one cell sends signals to many other cells.

Gross Electrical Activity of the Human Brain

The electrical activity of millions of cells working together combines to produce electrical potentials large enough that we can detect them at the surface of the skull. Recordings of electrical activity in the brain that are made with large electrodes either on the scalp or within the brain can provide useful glimpses of the simultaneous workings of large populations of neurons. Investigators divide these gross brain potentials into two principal classes: those that appear spontaneously without specific stimulation, and those that are evoked by particular stimuli.

(a) The visual system represented as a neural chain

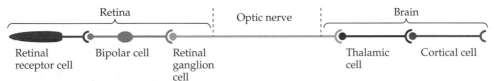

(b) A more realistic representation, showing convergence and divergence

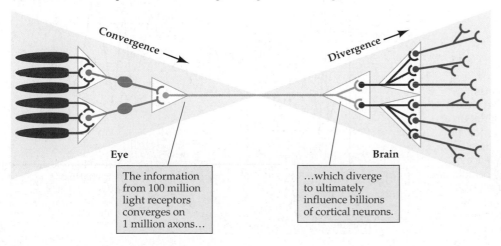

The information from 100 million light receptors converges on 1 million axons…

…which diverge to ultimately influence billions of cortical neurons.

3.18 Two Representations of Neural Circuitry (a) This simple representation shows the input part of the visual system. (b) This more complex representation illustrates convergence and divergence.

electroencephalogram (EEG) A recording of gross electrical activity of the brain recorded from large electrodes placed on the scalp.

event-related potential (ERP) Also called *evoked potential.* Averaged EEG recordings measuring brain responses to repeated presentations of a stimulus. Components of the ERP tend to be reliable because the background noise of the cortex has been averaged out.

A recording of spontaneous brain potentials, or *brain waves,* is called an **electroencephalogram (EEG)** (**Figure 3.19a**). As we will see in Chapter 14, EEG recordings of a sleeping person enable investigators to distinguish different kinds and stages of sleep. Brain potentials also provide significant diagnostic data—for example, in distinguishing forms of seizure disorders (**Box 3.3**). In addition, they may offer predictions about the functional effects of brain injury. In many jurisdictions, EEGs are used to determine death according to the legal definition.

Event-related potentials measure changes resulting from discrete stimuli

Gross potential changes evoked by discrete sensory stimuli, such as light flashes or clicks, are called **event-related potentials (ERPs)** (**Figure 3.19b**). Typically, in experiments that exploit this phenomenon, many ERPs are averaged to obtain a reliable estimate of stimulus-elicited brain activity. Sensory-evoked potentials have very distinctive characteristics of wave shape and *latency* (time delay) that reflect the type of stimulus, the state of the subject, and the site of recording. Subtler psychological processes, such as expectancy (anticipation that something is about to happen), also appear to influence some characteristics of evoked potentials.

(*a*) Multichannel EEG recording

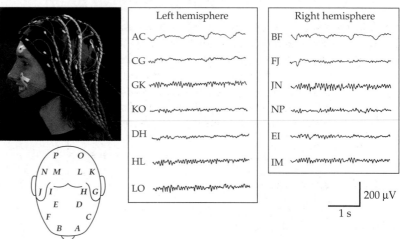

(*b*) Event-related potentials (average of many stimulus presentations)

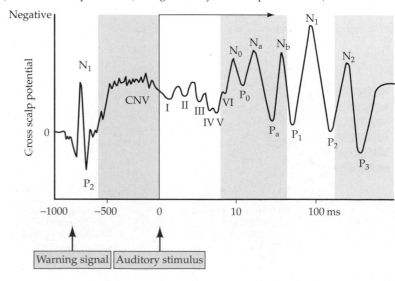

3.19 Gross Potentials of the Human Nervous System (*a*) (*Top left*) Electrode array for EEG recording. (*Bottom left*) Each electrode can be assigned a letter on a map of the scalp. (*Right*) Typical EEG recordings showing potential measured between various points on the scalp. (*b*) Following stimulus presentation, a fixed sequence of processing-related potentials is generated. Early components (labeled I–VI) are associated with brainstem activity, followed by large-amplitude negative- and positive-voltage events (labeled N_0–N_2 and P_0–P_3). The later-appearing components are associated with cognitive processing in the cortex.

BOX 3.3 Seizure Disorders

Epilepsy (from the Greek *epilepsia*, a form of the verb meaning "to seize") has provoked wonder and worry since the dawn of civilization. Through the ages the seizures that accompany this disease have spawned much speculation about the cause—from demons to gods. About 30 million people, worldwide, suffer from epilepsy.

Seizures are an unfortunate manifestation of the electrical character of the nervous system. Because of the extensive connections among its nerve cells, the brain can generate massive waves of intense nerve cell activity that seem to involve almost the entire brain. In the normal, active brain, electrical activity tends to be desynchronized; that is, different brain regions carry on their functions more or less independently. In contrast, a **seizure** features widespread synchronization of electrical activity: broad swaths of the brain start firing in simultaneous waves of excitation, which are evident in the EEGs as an abnormal "spike-and-wave" pattern of brain activity. Many abnormalities of the brain, such as trauma, injury, or metabolic problems, can predispose brain tissue to produce synchronized *epileptiform* activity, which can easily spread.

There are several major categories of seizure disorders. Generalized seizures are characterized by loss of consciousness and symmetrical involvement of body musculature. In **grand mal seizures**, abnormal EEG activity is evident all over the brain (Figure A). The person loses consciousness and makes characteristic movements: an enduring *tonic* contraction of the muscles for 1 or 2 minutes, followed by jerky, rhythmic *clonic* contractions and relaxations. Minutes or hours of confusion and sleep follow the seizure.

Petit mal seizures are a more subtle variant of generalized seizures, in which the characteristic spike-and-wave EEG activity is evident for 5–15 seconds at a time (Figure B), sometimes occurring many times per day. The person is unaware of the environment during these periods, and later cannot recall events that occurred during the petit mal episode. Behaviorally, the person does not show unusual muscle activity, except for a cessation of ongoing activity and sustained staring.

Complex partial seizures do not involve the entire brain and thus can produce a wide variety of symptoms, often preceded by an unusual sensation, or **aura**. In one example, a woman felt an unusual sensation in the abdomen, a sense of foreboding, and tingling in both hands before the seizure spread. At the height of it, she was unresponsive and rocked her body back and forth while speaking nonsensically, twisting her left arm, and looking toward the right. Figure C is a three-dimensional reconstruction showing where the seizures occurred in her brain. In some individuals, complex partial seizures may be provoked by environmental stimuli and may produce strikingly abnormal behavior.

Seizures affect nonhuman animals too, and such cases are studied as a model of human epilepsy. In **kindling** (McNamara, 1984), animals receive repeated electrical stimulation that is too weak to cause a seizure on its own. Although the individual stimuli are small, eventually their effects accumulate to cause spontaneous seizures. In other words, the kindling stimulations somehow change the tissue and make it more epilepsy-prone. Interestingly, after years of epilepsy some human patients develop multiple foci for the initiation of seizures, perhaps because of a kindling process (Morrell, 1991).

Many seizure disorders can be effectively controlled with the aid of antiepileptic drugs. Although these drugs have a wide variety of different targets, they have in common a tendency to selectively modulate the excitability of neurons, either by counteracting problems with ionic balance (see Box 3.1) or by promoting inhibitory processes (Rogawski and Löscher, 2004). (Figure C courtesy of Hal Blumenfeld, Rik Stokking, Susan Spencer, and George Zubal, Yale School of Medicine.)

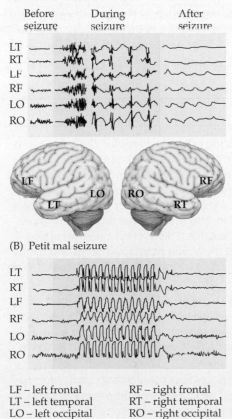

(A) Grand mal seizure

| Before seizure | During seizure | After seizure |

LT
RT
LF
RF
LO
RO

LF
LO
LT
RO
RF
RT

(B) Petit mal seizure

LT
RT
LF
RF
LO
RO

LF – left frontal   RF – right frontal
LT – left temporal   RT – right temporal
LO – left occipital   RO – right occipital

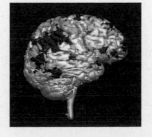

(C) Complete partial seizure

epilepsy   A brain disorder marked by major sudden changes in the electrophysiological state of the brain that are referred to as seizures.

seizure   An epileptic episode.

grand mal seizure   A type of generalized epileptic seizure in which nerve cells fire in high-frequency bursts.

petit mal seizure   Also called an *absence attack*. A seizure that is characterized by a spike-and-wave EEG and often involves a loss of awareness and inability to recall events surrounding the seizure.

complex partial seizure   In epilepsy, a type of seizure that doesn't involve the entire brain, and therefore can cause a wide variety of symptoms.

aura   In epilepsy, the unusual sensations or premonition that may precede the beginning of a seizure.

kindling   A method of experimentally inducing an epileptic seizure by repeatedly stimulating a brain region.

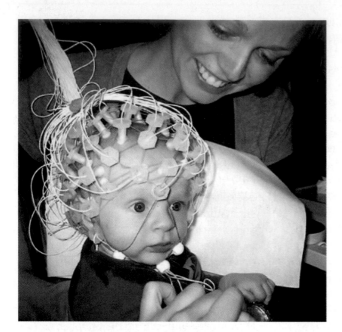

Figure 3.20 Did You Hear That? If this infant's hearing is normal, presentation of sounds should evoke an ERP from auditory centers in her (his) brain. (Courtesy of Brett Martin, Jen Gerometta, and Christine Rota-Donahue.)

Computer techniques enable researchers to record brain potentials using electrodes that are located a significant distance from the sites at which the potentials are generated. For example, *auditory-evoked brainstem potentials* (see Figure 3.19*b*) can be recorded through scalp electrodes located far from the neural generators of these waves in the cranial nerve and auditory parts of the brainstem. Decreases in the amplitude of certain waves or increases in their latency have been valuable for the detection of hearing impairments in very young children and noncommunicative persons (**Figure 3.20**). Infants with impaired hearing produce reduced auditory ERPs or no ERP at all in response to sounds. ERPs are also used in the assessment of brainstem injury or damage.

The long-latency components of scalp-recorded ERPs are thought to reflect the operation of information-processing mechanisms of the brain, such as attention, decision making, and other complex cognitive processes. In contrast, short-latency responses are determined more by exogenous factors, such as the physical characteristics of the stimulus. For example, dimensions like stimulus intensity have a bigger effect on early components of ERPs than on longer-latency components.

Although it is usually difficult to localize which brain region has produced a given component of the ERP, such changes are detected quickly, within a fraction of a second. In contrast, computer-coordinated imaging of brain activity, such as functional MRI (fMRI) (see Chapter 2), indicates clearly which brain region is active, but because such imaging techniques must average activity over seconds or minutes, they are slower than ERPs. Perhaps the greatest promise for future research is a melding of the two techniques—combining techniques that measure rapid changes in electrical activity, such as ERPs and magnetoencephalography (MEG) (Chapter 2), with slower but higher-resolution techniques such as fMRI or PET scans to identify probable sites of origin of the evoked activity (Liebenthal et al., 2003). These techniques have given us a better glimpse of brain functioning than Otto Loewi ever dreamed of.

SUMMARY

Electrical Signals Are the Vocabulary of the Nervous System

- Nerve cells are specialized for receiving, processing, and transmitting signals. Chemical signals transmit information *between* neurons; electrical signals transmit information *within* a neuron.

- Neurons exhibit a small electrical potential across the cell membrane; neural signals are changes in this potential.

- The different concentrations of **ions** inside and outside the neuron—especially **potassium ions (K+)**, to which the resting membrane is selectively permeable—account for the resting potential. At equilibrium, the electrostatic pressure pulling K+ ions into the neuron is balanced by the **concentration gradient** pushing them out; at this point, the membrane potential is about –60 mV, the resting potential. **Review Figure 3.3, Web Activity 3.1**

- The brain uses a great deal of energy maintaining ionic gradients through the operation of **sodium-potassium pumps**. **Review Web Activity 3.2**

- Reduction of the resting potential (**depolarization**) in axons opens voltage-gated channels. If the neuronal membrane is depolarized until it reaches a **threshold** value, **voltage-gated sodium (Na+)** channels of the axonal membrane open and the membrane becomes completely permeable to Na+. As a result, Na+ ions rush in, and the axon becomes briefly more positive inside than outside. This event is called an **action potential**. Following the action potential, the **resting membrane potential** is quickly restored. **Review Figure 3.6, Web Activity 3.3**

- The action potential strongly depolarizes the adjacent patch of axonal membrane, causing it to generate its own action potential. In this regenerative manner, the action potential spreads down the axon. **Review Figure 3.8, Web Activity 3.4**

- **Postsynaptic (local) potentials** spread very rapidly, but they are not regenerated. They diminish in amplitude as they spread passively along dendrites and the cell body.

- **Excitatory postsynaptic potentials (EPSPs)** are depolarizing (they decrease the resting potential) and increase the likelihood that the neuron will generate an action potential. **Inhibitory postsynaptic potentials (IPSPs)** are **hyperpolarizing** (they increase the resting potential) and decrease the likelihood that the neuron will fire. **Review Figure 3.5**

- Cell bodies process information by integrating (summing algebraically) the postsynaptic potentials moving across their surfaces. Postsynaptic potentials are integrated through both **spatial summation** (summing potentials that occur in different locations) and **temporal summation** (summing potentials across time). **Review Figure 3.11, Web Activity 3.5**

- An action potential is initiated at the **axon hillock** when the excess of EPSPs over IPSPs reaches threshold.

- During the action potential, the neuron cannot be excited by a second stimulus; it is absolutely **refractory**. For a few milliseconds afterward, the hyperpolarized neuron is relatively refractory, requiring a stronger stimulation than usual in order to fire.

- Some synapses use electrical transmission and do not require a chemical transmitter. At these electrical synapses, the cleft between presynaptic and postsynaptic cells is extremely small.

Synaptic Transmission Requires a Sequence of Events

- At most synapses, the transmission of information from one neuron to another requires a chemical transmitter that diffuses across the synaptic cleft and binds to **receptor molecules** in the postsynaptic membrane. A substance that binds to a receptor is called a **ligand**. **Review Box 3.2, Web Activity 3.6**

Neurons and Synapses Combine to Make Circuits

- At **ionotropic** synapses, the receptor molecule responds to recognition of a transmitter by opening an ion channel within its own structure. At **metabotropic** synapses, the binding of a transmitter molecule to a receptor molecule activates an intracellular second-messenger system that can have a variety of effects, including the opening of membrane channels. **Review Figure 3.15, Web Activity 3.7**

- Neurons and synapses are assembled into circuits that process information. Some circuits are very simple, involving only a few cells; others may be massive, involving millions of neurons. **Review Figures 3.17 and 3.18**

Gross Electrical Activity of the Human Brain

- The summation of electrical activity over millions of nerve cells can be detected by electrodes on the scalp. **Electroencephalograms (EEGs)** can reveal rapid changes in brain function, especially in response to a brief, controlled stimulus that evokes an **event-related potential (ERP)**. **Review Figure 3.19**

Go to www.biopsychology.com for study questions, quizzes, key terms, and other resources.

Recommended Reading

Cowan, W. M., Sudhof, T. C., and Stevens, C. F. (Eds.). (2003). *Synapses*. Baltimore: Johns Hopkins University Press.

Hille, B. (2001). *Ion channels of excitable membranes* (3rd ed.). Sunderland, MA: Sinauer.

Kandel, E. R., Schwartz, J. H., and Jessell, T. M. (2000). *Principles of neural science* (4th ed.). New York: McGraw-Hill.

LeDoux, J. (2002). *Synaptic self: How our brains become who we are.* New York: Penguin.

Nicholls, J. G., Martin, A. R., Wallace, B. G., and Fuchs, P. A. (2001). *From neuron to brain* (4th ed.). Sunderland, MA: Sinauer.

Purves, D., Augustine, G. J., Fitzpatrick, D., Hall, W. C., et al. (2008). *Neuroscience* (4th ed.). Sunderland, MA: Sinauer.

Shepherd, G. M. (Ed.). (2003). *The synaptic organization of the brain* (5th ed.). New York: Oxford University Press.

Valenstein, E. S. (2005). *The war of the soups and the sparks: The discovery of neurotransmitters and the dispute over how neurons communicate.* New York: Columbia University Press.

The Chemical Bases of Behavior: Neurotransmitters and Neuropharmacology

CHAPTER 4

The Birth of a Pharmaceutical Problem Child

Swiss pharmacologist Albert Hofmann was working for Sandoz Pharmaceuticals and studying compounds derived from ergot, a fungus that grows on grain, in the hope of synthesizing new and useful drugs from it. One day in April of 1943, Dr. Hofmann began to feel unwell at work and, believing he was coming down with a cold, he left for home. Soon, however, he began experiencing bizarre visual phenomena: "an uninterrupted stream of fantastic pictures, extraordinary shapes with intense, kaleidoscopic play of colors" (Hofmann, 1981). When he closed his eyes, the luridly colored, oddly shifting forms seemed to surge toward him. The state lasted about 2 hours. Suspecting that he had accidentally ingested a small amount of an experimental compound, Hofmann began to research its properties.

Although one could debate the wisdom of testing unknown drugs on oneself, Hofmann was breaking no laws in force at the time. Even a seemingly tiny dose of this stuff caused incapacitating changes in brain function and astonishing, sometimes frightening, visual apparitions. In addition to the visual phenomena, he reported sometimes feeling that his sense of self was "loosened." Careful analyses later revealed the new drug to be amazingly potent: a few millionths of a gram was enough to induce substantial effects. What was this substance? How could such tiny amounts exert so large an effect on the brain?

A s far back as we can trace human history, people have tasted, sipped, chewed, or swallowed all kinds of substances—animal, vegetable, and mineral. From these experiences, people have learned to consume some substances and shun others. Social customs and dietary codes evolved to protect people from consuming harmful substances. This long history of seeking, testing, and using different substances came not only from the need for nourishment but also from the desire to relieve pain, control anxiety, and pursue pleasure. We are not alone in this activity; "almost every species of animal has engaged in the natural pursuit of intoxicants" (R. K. Siegel, 1989, p. viii).

The brain is an electrochemical system, so it's no surprise that most drugs that affect the nervous system do so by altering brain chemistry and synaptic transmission. We begin our tour of **neurochemistry** and **neuropharmacology** by delving more deeply into the neurotransmitter systems that we introduced in Chapter 3. Then we review some of the major classes of drugs that affect the nervous system and behavior, and finally we turn to mechanisms of drug abuse and dependency.

Many Chemical Neurotransmitters Have Been Identified

We learned in Chapter 3 that neurons release a chemical known as a *neurotransmitter* (or simply *transmitter*) to communicate with target cells, usually other neurons. Identifying neurotransmitters and understanding how they act are continuing quests.

To be considered a classic neurotransmitter, a substance should meet the following criteria:

neurochemistry The branch of neuroscience concerned with the fundamental chemical composition and processes of the nervous system.

neuropharmacology Also called *psychopharmacology*. The scientific field concerned with the discovery and study of compounds that selectively affect the functioning of the nervous system.

amine neurotransmitter A neurotransmitter based on modifications of a single amino acid nucleus. Examples include acetylcholine, serotonin, or dopamine.

amino acid neurotransmitter A neurotransmitter that is itself an amino acid. Examples include GABA, glycine, or glutamate.

peptide neurotransmitter (neuropeptide) A neurotransmitter consisting of a short chain of amino acids.

gas neurotransmitter A soluble gas, such as nitric oxide or carbon monoxide, that is produced and released by a neuron to alter the functioning of another neuron.

receptor Also called *receptor molecule*. A protein that captures and reacts to molecules of a neurotransmitter or hormone.

ionotropic receptor A receptor protein that includes an ion channel that is opened when the receptor is bound by an agonist.

metabotropic receptor A receptor protein that does not contain an ion channel but may, when activated, use a G protein system to open a nearby ion channel.

- The substance exists in the presynaptic axon terminals.
- The presynaptic cell contains appropriate enzymes for synthesizing the substance.
- The substance is released in significant quantities when action potentials reach the terminals.
- Specific receptors that recognize the released substance exist on the postsynaptic membrane.
- Experimental application of the substance produces changes in postsynaptic potentials.
- Blocking release of the substance prevents presynaptic nerve impulses from affecting the activity of the postsynaptic cell.

Table 4.1 summarizes the major categories of some of the many neurotransmitters presently known. Substances that satisfy the criteria for transmitters include various **amine neurotransmitters**, such as acetylcholine, dopamine, and serotonin; **amino acid neurotransmitters**, like GABA and glutamate; and a wide variety of **peptide neurotransmitters** (or **neuropeptides**), made up of short chains of amino acids. As the search goes on, the number of probable synaptic transmitters continues to grow, and the effort occasionally yields surprises like the **gas neurotransmitters**, soluble gases that diffuse between neurons to alter ongoing processes.

Even if a substance is known to be a transmitter in one location, proving that it acts as a transmitter at another location may be difficult. For example, acetylcholine was long accepted as a transmitter agent in the peripheral nervous system (remember Otto Loewi's discoveries recounted in Chapter 3), but it was harder to prove that acetylcholine serves as a transmitter in the central nervous system as well. Now it is recognized that acetylcholine is widely distributed in the brain, and many scientists study its possible relationship to the cognitive deficits seen in Alzheimer's disease. Considering the rate at which these substances are being discovered and characterized, it would not be surprising if there turned out to be several hundred different neurotransmitters conveying information at synapses in different subsets of neurons.

As we discussed in Chapter 3, neurotransmitters affect their targets by interacting with **receptors**, protein molecules embedded in the postsynaptic membrane that recognize the transmitter. The transmitter molecule binds to the receptor, changing its shape to open an ion channel (fast, **ionotropic** receptors), or altering chemical reactions within the target cell (slow, **metabotropic** receptors) (see Figure 3.15). Receptors add to the complexity of neural signaling because any given trans-

TABLE 4.1 Some Synaptic Transmitters and Families of Transmitters

Family and subfamily	Transmitter(s)
AMINES	
Quaternary amines	Acetylcholine (ACh)
Monoamines	*Catecholamines*: norepinephrine (NE), epinephrine (adrenaline), dopamine (DA)
	Indoleamines: serotonin (5-hydroxytryptamine; 5-HT), melatonin
AMINO ACIDS	Gamma-aminobutyric acid (GABA), glutamate, glycine, histamine
NEUROPEPTIDES	
Opioid peptides	*Enkephalins*: met-enkephalin, leu-enkephalin
	Endorphins: β-endorphin
	Dynorphins: dynorphin A
Other neuropeptides	Oxytocin, substance P, cholecystokinin (CCK), vasopressin, neuropeptide Y (NPY), hypothalamic releasing hormones
GASES	Nitric oxide, carbon monoxide

4.1 The Versatility of Neuro-transmitters A single neurotransmitter may interact with many different receptors in different parts of the brain—binding to fast, ionotropic receptors on some target cells, and to slow, metabotropic receptors on other cells. Both types of receptors may either excite or inhibit the target cell.

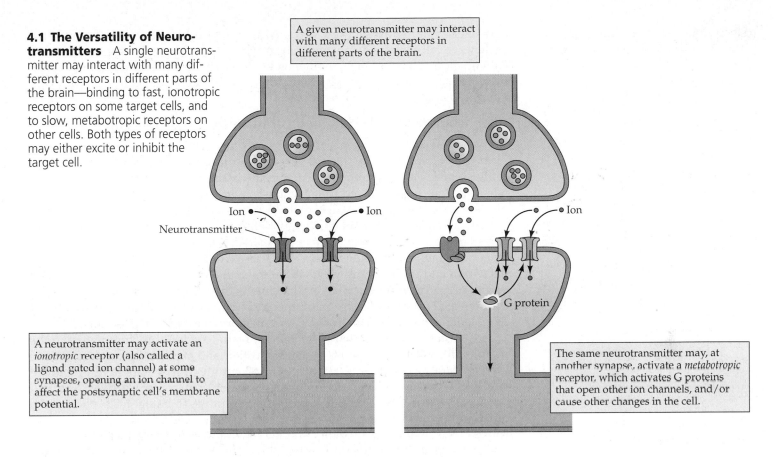

A given neurotransmitter may interact with many different receptors in different parts of the brain.

A neurotransmitter may activate an *ionotropic* receptor (also called a ligand-gated ion channel) at some synapses, opening an ion channel to affect the postsynaptic cell's membrane potential.

The same neurotransmitter may, at another synapse, activate a *metabotropic* receptor, which activates G proteins that open other ion channels, and/or cause other changes in the cell.

mitter may bind to a wide variety of receptor types. The different **receptor subtypes** may trigger very different responses in target cells (**Figure 4.1**), and they also often have different anatomical distributions within the nervous system. As we will see shortly, drug development capitalizes on the existence of receptor subtypes. Although a given neurotransmitter will interact with all the subtypes of its receptors, it is possible to design drugs that selectively affect only one of the subtypes, thereby producing the specific effects associated with that receptor subtype.

A substance that binds to a receptor is termed a **ligand** and typically has one of three effects:

1. A ligand that is classified as an **agonist** initiates the normal effects of the transmitter on that receptor.
2. A receptor **antagonist** is a ligand that binds to a receptor and does not activate it, thereby blocking it from being activated by other ligands (including the native neurotransmitter).
3. An **inverse agonist**—a less common type of ligand—binds to the receptor and initiates an effect that is the reverse of the normal function of the receptor.

First we will look at some of the substances that the brain itself produces, which we classify as *endogenous ligands* (the word **endogenous** means "occurring naturally within the body"). We will then turn to the major categories of drugs that affect the brain (drugs are **exogenous** substances; that is, they are introduced from outside the body).

Neurotransmitter Systems Form a Complex Array in the Brain

Powerful methods for probing the composition of neural tissue (see Box 2.1) are revealing that brain activity depends on a remarkably diverse assortment of neurotransmitters, distributed through intricate anatomical networks that overlap

receptor subtype Any type of receptor having functional characteristics that distinguish it from other types of receptors for the same neurotransmitter.

ligand A substance that binds to receptor molecules, such as those at the surface of the cell.

agonist A molecule, usually a drug, that binds a receptor molecule and initiates a response like that of another molecule, usually a neurotransmitter.

antagonist A molecule, usually a drug, that interferes with or prevents the action of a transmitter.

inverse agonist A substance that binds to a receptor and causes it to do the opposite of what the naturally occurring transmitter does.

endogenous Produced inside the body.

exogenous Arising from outside the body.

co-localization   Also called *co-release*. Here, the appearance of more than one neurotransmitter in a given presynaptic terminal.

acetylcholine (ACh)   A neurotransmitter produced and released by parasympathetic postganglionic neurons by motoneurons, and by neurons throughout the brain.

cholinergic   Referring to cells that use acetylcholine as their synaptic transmitter.

nicotinic   Referring to cholinergic receptors that respond to nicotine as well as to acetylcholine.

muscarinic   Referring to cholinergic receptors that respond to the chemical muscarine as well as to acetylcholine.

and interact in highly complex ways. Although at one time it was thought that each nerve cell contained only one transmitter, we now know that some nerve cells contain more than one—a phenomenon known as neurotransmitter **co-localization** or *co-release*. In this section we discuss the distribution of just a few of the major neurotransmitters, and their receptors.

Acetylcholine was the first neurotransmitter to be identified

Acetylcholine (ACh), the chemical at work in Otto Loewi's classic experiment (described in Chapter 3), was the first chemical substance to be identified as a neurotransmitter. The distribution of ACh in the brain was subsequently determined when the enzymes involved in its synthesis were mapped; **Figure 4.2** shows the distribution of **cholinergic** (ACh-containing) nerve cell bodies and their projections.

Several distinct clusters of cholinergic cells are apparent. The basal forebrain includes groups of cholinergic cells in the medial septal nucleus, the nucleus of the diagonal band, and the nucleus basalis. These cholinergic cells project to the hippocampus and amygdala, as well as throughout the cerebral cortex. Widespread loss of cholinergic neurons is evident in Alzheimer's disease, suggesting that cholinergic systems are crucial for learning and memory. Similarly, the cholinergic antagonist scopolamine interferes with learning and memory in experimental settings.

In Chapter 3 we noted that there are two broad classes of ACh receptors in the peripheral and central nervous systems: **nicotinic** and **muscarinic** receptors. Within each of these two groups are subtypes of receptors. Most nicotinic receptors are ionotropic, responding rapidly and usually having an excitatory effect (see Figure 4.1 *left*). Muscles also use nicotinic ACh receptors, so antagonists, such as the drug curare, cause widespread paralysis. Muscarinic ACh receptors are G protein–coupled (metabotropic) receptors, so they have slower responses when activated, and they can be either excitatory or inhibitory (see Figure 3.13b). Muscarinic receptors can be blocked by the drugs atropine or scopolamine, producing pronounced changes in cognition, including drowsiness, confusion, and blurred vision.

Five monoamines act as neurotransmitters

There are two principal classes of neurotransmitters that, because they are modified amino acids, are called monoamines: catecholamines and indoleamines. The

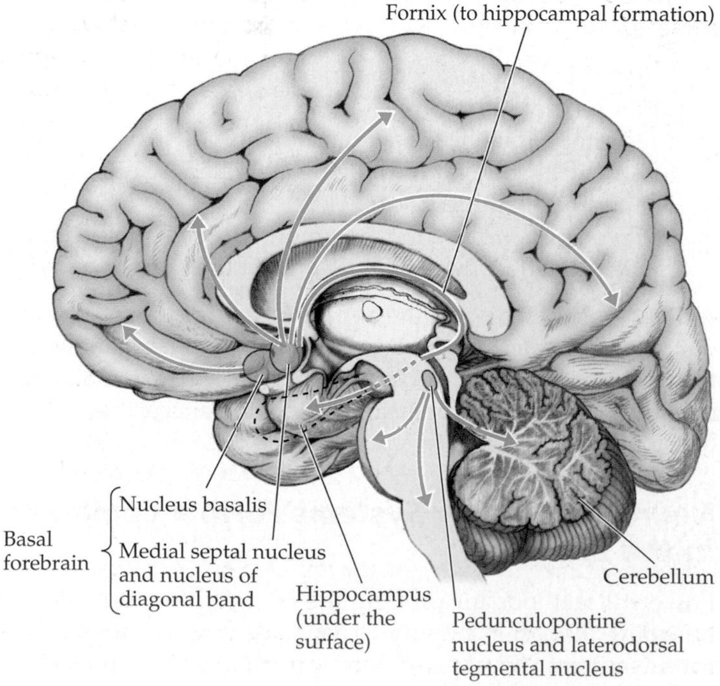

4.2 Cholinergic Pathways in the Brain   In this midsagittal view, the brain nuclei containing cell bodies of neurons that release ACh are shown in green; the projections of axons from these neurons are indicated by green arrows. Because they use ACh as a transmitter, these neurons are said to be *cholinergic*.

Fornix (to hippocampal formation)

Basal forebrain
Nucleus basalis
Medial septal nucleus and nucleus of diagonal band
Hippocampus (under the surface)
Pedunculopontine nucleus and laterodorsal tegmental nucleus
Cerebellum

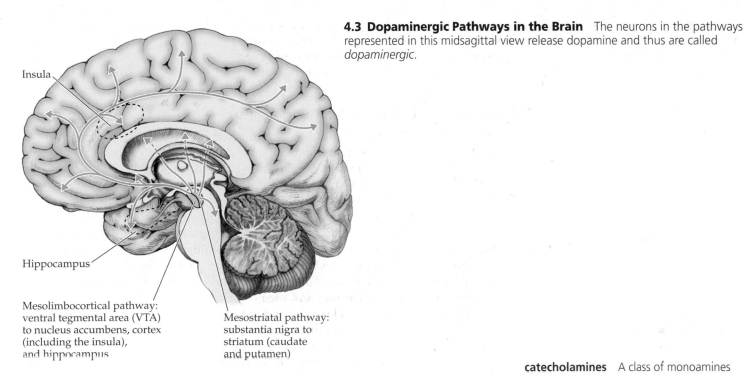

4.3 Dopaminergic Pathways in the Brain   The neurons in the pathways represented in this midsagittal view release dopamine and thus are called *dopaminergic*.

Insula

Hippocampus

Mesolimbocortical pathway: ventral tegmental area (VTA) to nucleus accumbens, cortex (including the insula), and hippocampus

Mesostriatal pathway: substantia nigra to striatum (caudate and putamen)

catecholamine neurotransmitters—derived from the amino acid tyrosine—are dopamine, epinephrine, and norepinephrine. The **indoleamines**—derived from the amino acid tryptophan—are melatonin and serotonin. Let's take a closer look at three important monoamines: dopamine, norepinephrine, and serotonin. (To learn more about the neuronal synthesis of the monoamines and ACh, see **A Step Further: Pathways for Neurotransmitter Synthesis** on the website.)

DOPAMINE   About a million nerve cells in the human brain contain **dopamine** (**DA**). **Figure 4.3** shows the locations of these cells and their projections in the brain. Several subtypes of DA receptors have been discovered and have been labeled D_1, D_2, D_3, D_4, and D_5, numbered in the order of their discovery. Dopaminergic neurons are found in several main groups; Figure 4.3 focuses on two of these groups: the **mesostriatal pathway** and the **mesolimbocortical pathway**.

The mesostriatal pathway, as the name indicates, originates from the mesencephalon (midbrain)—specifically the **substantia nigra** and nearby areas—and ascends as part of the medial forebrain bundle to innervate the **striatum**: the caudate nucleus and putamen (see Figure 4.3). All these structures are part of the *basal ganglia* described in Chapter 2 (see Figure 2.15*a*). Although the mesostriatal DA group contains relatively few nerve cells, a single axon can give rise to thousands of synapses. The mesostriatal DA pathway plays a crucial role in motor control, and significant loss of these neurons produces the movement problems of Parkinson's disease (described in Chapter 11).

The mesolimbocortical pathway also originates in the midbrain, in the **ventral tegmental area** (**VTA**) (see Figure 4.3), and projects to the limbic system (amygdala, nucleus accumbens, hippocampus) and the cortex. A rich research literature (e.g., Palmiter, 2008) implicates this system, especially via the dopamine D_2 receptor subtype, in reward and reinforcement; we revisit this topic at the end of the chapter. In humans, mesolimbocortical neurons release DA in the amygdala during verbal learning (Fried et al., 2001). Abnormalities in the mesolimbocortical pathway are associated with some of the symptoms of schizophrenia, as we discuss in Chapter 16.

NOREPINEPHRINE   The two main clusters of neurons in the brainstem releasing **norepinephrine** (**NE**) are the **locus coeruleus** in the pons, and the lateral tegmental

catecholamines   A class of monoamines that serve as neurotransmitters, including dopamine and norepinephrine.

indoleamines   A class of monoamines that serve as neurotransmitters, including serotonin and melatonin.

dopamine (DA)   A monoamine transmitter found in the midbrain—especially the substantia nigra—and basal forebrain.

mesostriatal pathway   A set of dopaminergic axons arising from the midbrain and innervating the basal ganglia, including those from the substantia nigra to the striatum.

mesolimbocortical pathway   A set of dopaminergic axons arising in the midbrain and innervating the limbic system and cortex.

substantia nigra   Literally, "black spot." A group of pigmented neurons in the midbrain that provides dopaminergic projections to areas of the forebrain, especially the basal ganglia.

striatum   The caudate nucleus and putamen together.

ventral tegmental area (VTA)   A portion of the midbrain that projects dopaminergic fibers to the nucleus accumbens.

norepinephrine (NE)   Also called *noradrenaline*. A neurotransmitter produced and released by sympathetic postganglionic neurons to accelerate organ activity. Also produced in the brainstem and found in projections throughout the brain.

locus coeruleus   Literally, "blue spot." A small nucleus in the brainstem whose neurons produce norepinephrine and modulate large areas of the forebrain.

4.4 Noradrenergic Pathways in the Brain The neurons in the pathways shown in this midsagittal view release norepinephrine (noradrenaline) as a transmitter and thus are said to be *noradrenergic*.

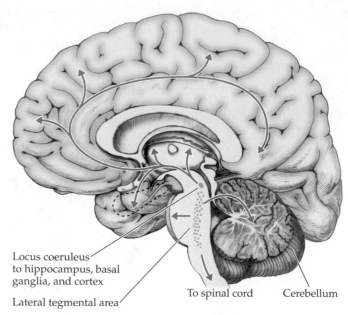

Locus coeruleus
to hippocampus, basal
ganglia, and cortex

Lateral tegmental area

To spinal cord   Cerebellum

system of the midbrain (**Figure 4.4**). Because norepinephrine is also known as *noradrenaline*, NE-producing cells are said to be **noradrenergic**. Recall from Chapter 2 that sympathetic fibers innervating the body are also noradrenergic (see Figure 2.11).

Fibers from the noradrenergic cells of the locus coeruleus project broadly throughout the cerebrum, including the cerebral cortex, limbic system, and thalamic nuclei. The cerebellum and spinal cord also receive noradrenergic innervation. The CNS contains four subtypes of NE receptors—α_1-, α_2-, β_1-, and β_2-adrenoceptors—all of which are metabotropic receptors. Because of their wide projections, noradrenergic systems are believed to modulate many behavioral and physiological processes, including mood, overall arousal, and sexual behavior.

SEROTONIN Because its chemical name is 5-hydroxytryptamine, **serotonin** is abbreviated **5-HT**. Large areas of the brain are innervated by **serotonergic** fibers, although 5-HT cell bodies are relatively few and are concentrated along the midline in the **raphe nuclei** (pronounced "ruh-FAY"; Latin for "seam") of the midbrain and brainstem. **Figure 4.5** shows the distribution of serotonergic cell bodies and their fiber projections. Only about 200,000 of the 100 billion neurons of the human brain are serotonergic, but they exert widespread influence through the rest of the brain.

Serotonin has been implicated in the control of sleep states (see Chapter 14), mood, sexual behavior, anxiety, and many other functions. Drugs that globally increase 5-HT activity are effective antidepressants; Prozac is an example (see Chapter 16). At least 19 types of 5-HT receptors ($5HT_1$, $5HT_2$, and so on) have been described, and all but one are metabotropic receptors. The effects of serotonergic drugs on behavior often depend on which subtypes of 5-HT receptors are affected (Gorzalka et al., 1990; Miczek et al., 2002).

Some amino acids act as neurotransmitters

The most common transmitters in the brain are amino acids. **Glutamate** and **aspartate** are important excitatory neurotransmitters. **Gamma-aminobutyric acid (GABA)** and **glycine** are major inhibitory transmitters. These transmitters are distributed throughout the central nervous system.

Glutamatergic transmission employs ionotropic *AMPA*, *kainate*, and *NMDA* receptors (their names refer to drugs that act as selective agonists). Because NMDA-type glutamate receptors are active in a fascinating model of learning and memory, they have been studied very closely. This topic is discussed more fully in Chapter

noradrenergic Referring to systems using norepinephrine (noradrenaline) as a transmitter.

serotonin (5-HT) A synaptic transmitter that is produced in the raphe nuclei and is active in structures throughout the cerebral hemispheres.

serotonergic Referring to neurons that use serotonin as their synaptic transmitter.

raphe nuclei A string of nuclei in the midline of the midbrain and brainstem that contain most of the serotonergic neurons of the brain.

glutamate An amino acid transmitter, the most common excitatory transmitter.

aspartate An amino acid transmitter that is excitatory at many synapses.

gamma-aminobutyric acid (GABA) A widely distributed amino acid transmitter, and the main inhibitory transmitter in the mammalian nervous system.

glycine An amino acid transmitter, often inhibitory.

glutamatergic Referring to cells that use glutamate as their synaptic transmitter.

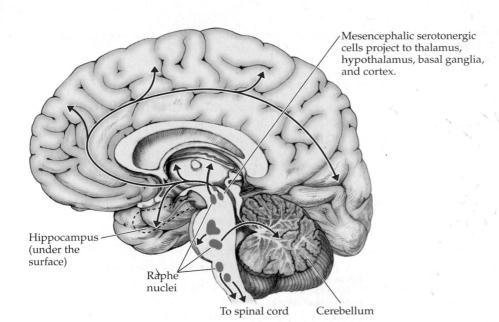

Mesencephalic serotonergic cells project to thalamus, hypothalamus, basal ganglia, and cortex.

Hippocampus (under the surface)

Raphe nuclei

To spinal cord   Cerebellum

4.5 Serotonergic Pathways in the Brain The neurons in the nuclei shown in this midsagittal view release serotonin (5-HT) and thus are said to be *serotonergic*.

17, and the details of the unique behavior of NMDA receptors are provided on the website in **A Step Further: A Receptor with a Long Memory**. There are also several metabotropic glutamate receptors (mGluR's), which act more slowly because they work through second messengers.

Glutamate is associated with **excitotoxicity**, a phenomenon in which neural injury, such as a stroke or trauma, provokes an excessive release of glutamate that produces prolonged depolarization of postsynaptic cells. This overexcitation ultimately kills the postsynaptic neurons, exacerbating the effects of the brain injury. Astrocytes overlying glutamatergic synapses clear the neurotransmitter from the cleft after synaptic transmission (Rothstein, 2000).

GABA receptors are divided into large classes designated $GABA_A$, $GABA_B$, and $GABA_C$ receptors. Although they all normally respond to GABA, the subtypes of receptors exhibit quite different properties.

$GABA_A$ receptors are ionotropic (they are ligand-gated chloride channels; see Figure 4.1 *left*), and when activated they produce fast inhibitory postsynaptic potentials. Each $GABA_A$ receptor is made up of five protein subunits surrounding a Cl^- ion channel that can be widened or narrowed depending on the state of the surrounding complex. By mixing and matching of the various protein subunits that make them up, the brain may in fact produce dozens of different kinds of $GABA_A$ receptors.

$GABA_B$ receptors are metabotropic receptors associated with a slow-occurring type of inhibitory postsynaptic potential (Tamás et al., 2003). $GABA_C$ receptors are ionotropic with a chloride channel, but they differ in certain details of their subunit structure from other GABA receptors. Given GABA's inhibitory actions, it is not surprising that some GABA agonists are potent tranquilizers (e.g., Valium), and that inverse agonists of GABA receptors can provoke seizures by blocking the important inhibitory influence of GABA.

Many peptides function as neurotransmitters

Among the many peptides that serve as neurotransmitters are several that we'll discuss in later chapters:

- **Opioid peptides** (peptides that can mimic opiate drugs such as morphine), including met-enkephalin, leu-enkephalin, β-endorphin, and dynorphin (Chapter 8)

- A group of peptides found in the gut and spinal cord or brain, including substance P, cholecystokinin (CCK), neurotensin, neuropeptide Y (NPY), and others (Chapter 13)

excitotoxicity The property by which neurons die when overstimulated, as with large amounts of glutamate.

opioid peptide A type of endogenous peptide that mimics the effects of morphine in binding to opioid receptors and producing marked analgesia and reward.

nitric oxide (NO)   A soluble gas that serves as a retrograde gas neurotransmitter in the nervous system.

retrograde transmitter   A neurotransmitter that diffuses from the postsynaptic neuron back to the presynaptic neuron.

- Pituitary hormones such as oxytocin and vasopressin, among others (Chapters 5 and 12)

Some neurotransmitters are gases

It may surprise you to learn that neurons use certain gas molecules that dissolve in water (and so are called *soluble gases*) to communicate information. The best studied of these is **nitric oxide**, or **NO** (distinct from *nitrous* oxide, or laughing gas, which is N_2O). The actions of gas neurotransmitters like NO are different from those of the classic transmitters in several important ways. First, nitric oxide is produced in cellular locations other than the axon terminals, especially the dendrites, and molecules of nitric oxide are not held in or released from vesicles; the substance simply diffuses out of the neuron as soon as it is produced. Second, the released NO doesn't interact with membrane-bound receptors on the surface of the target cell, but rather it diffuses into the target cell and stimulates the production of second messengers. And third, NO can serve as a **retrograde transmitter**: it diffuses from the postsynaptic neuron back to the presynaptic neuron, where it stimulates changes in synaptic efficacy that may be involved in learning and memory (this topic is covered in more detail in Chapter 17). Found widely throughout the body, NO has been implicated in processes as diverse as hair growth and penile erection (Burnett, 2006), in addition to its role in the brain.

Research on Drugs Ranges from Molecular Processes to Effects on Behavior

In everyday English, we use the term *drug* in different ways. One common meaning is "a medicine used in the treatment of a disease" (as in *prescription drug* or *over-the-counter drug*). Quite a different meaning of *drug*, but also a common one, is "a psychoactive agent," especially an addictive one—that is, a drug of abuse. The common element of these meanings is a substance that, taken in relatively small amounts, has clear effects on experience, mood, emotion, activity, and/or health.

Some drugs originally evolved in plants, often as a defense against being eaten. Other modern drugs are synthetic (human-made) and tuned to affect specific transmitter systems. To understand how drugs work, we must use many levels of analysis—from molecules to anatomical systems to behavioral effects and experiences.

Drugs fit like keys into molecular locks

Some drugs are effective because they interact with lipid molecules that make up the membrane, or because they directly alter the activity of particular enzymes, but most drugs of interest in biological psychology are ligands that interact with specific receptor molecules.

Recall that any given neurotransmitter interacts with a variety of different subtypes of receptors. This principle is crucial to neuropharmacology because, unlike the transmitter, which will act on *all* its receptor subtypes, a drug can be targeted to interact with just one or a few receptor subtypes. The various subtypes of receptors generally differ in their distribution within the brain, and they also serve very different cellular functions, so selectively activating or blocking specific subtypes of receptors can have widely varying effects. For example, treating someone with doses of serotonin would activate all of her serotonin receptors, regardless of subtype, and produce a variety of nonspecific effects. But drugs that are selective antagonists of 5-HT_3 receptors, showing little activity at other subtypes of serotonin receptors, produce a powerful and specific anti-nausea effect. We have also discussed how a single transmitter, GABA, may act on hundreds of different receptors. Apparently, evolution tinkers with the structure of receptors more than transmitters.

Drug molecules do not seek out particular receptor molecules; rather, drug molecules spread widely throughout the body, and when they come in contact with a

Receptor   Lower-affinity drug   Higher-affinity drug

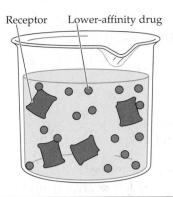 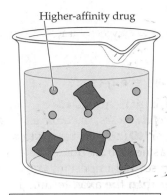 

If a particular drug has a low affinity for a receptor, then it will quickly uncouple from the receptor. To bind half the receptors at any given time, a higher concentration of the drug is needed.

If a drug has a high affinity for a receptor, the two will stay together for a longer time, and a lower concentration of drug will be sufficient to bind half the receptors.

If equal concentrations of the two drugs are present, the high- affinity drug will be bound to more receptors at any given time. If the drugs have an equivalent effect on the receptors, then the higher-affinity drug will be more potent.

receptor molecule possessing the specific shape that fits the drug molecule, the two molecules bind together briefly and begin a chain of events. The lock-and-key analogy is often used for this binding action, as mentioned in Chapter 3. In the case of receptor-selective drugs, though, we have to think of keys (drug molecules) trying to insert themselves in all the locks (receptor molecules) in the neighborhood; each such key fits into only a particular subset of the locks. Once the drug (the key) binds to the receptor (the lock), it alters the activity of the receptor, activating it or blocking it. But the binding is usually temporary, and when the drug or transmitter breaks away from the receptor, the receptor resumes its unbound shape and functioning.

Drug-receptor interactions vary in specificity and activity

The tuning of drug molecules to receptors is not absolutely specific. That is, a particular drug molecule will generally bind strongly to one kind of receptor, more weakly to some other types, and not at all to many others. A drug molecule that has more than one kind of action in the body exhibits this flexibility because it affects more than one kind of receptor molecule. For example, some drugs combat anxiety at low doses without producing sedation (relaxation, drowsiness), but at higher doses they cause sedation, probably because at those doses they activate additional types of receptors.

The degree of chemical attraction between a ligand and a receptor is termed **binding affinity** (or simply **affinity**). A drug with high affinity for a particular type of receptor will selectively bind to that type of receptor even at low doses, and will stay bound for a relatively long time. Lower-affinity drugs will bind fewer receptor molecules. **Figure 4.6** illustrates how binding affinity is measured.

After binding, the propensity of a ligand to *activate* the receptor to which it is bound is termed its **efficacy** (or **intrinsic activity**). As you might guess, agonists have high efficacy and antagonists have low efficacy (**Figure 4.7**). Partial agonists are drugs that produce a middling response regardless of dose. So, it is a combination of affinity and efficacy—where it binds and what it does—that determines the overall action of a drug. To some extent we can compare the effectiveness of different drugs by comparing their affinity for the receptor of interest (see Figure 16.10 for an example).

So far we have been talking about drugs that are **competitive ligands**: drugs that bind to the same receptor sites as the endogenous transmitter. To complicate things a bit further, some drugs bind to a part of the receptor complex that does not normally bind the transmitter (see Figure 4.7 *far right*). In such cases the drug does not directly compete with the transmitter for its binding site, so we say that the

binding affinity   Also called simply *affinity*. The propensity of molecules of a drug (or other ligand) to bind to receptors.

efficacy   Also called *intrinsic activity*. The extent to which a drug activates a response when it binds to a receptor.

partial agonist or partial antagonist   A drug that, when bound to a receptor, has less effect than the endogenous ligand would.

competitive ligand   A substance that directly competes with the endogenous ligand for the same binding site on a receptor molecule.

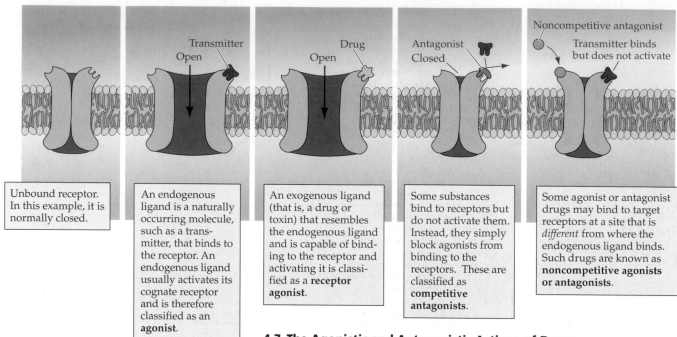

| Unbound receptor. In this example, it is normally closed. | An endogenous ligand is a naturally occurring molecule, such as a transmitter, that binds to the receptor. An endogenous ligand usually activates its cognate receptor and is therefore classified as an **agonist**. | An exogenous ligand (that is, a drug or toxin) that resembles the endogenous ligand and is capable of binding to the receptor and activating it is classified as a **receptor agonist**. | Some substances bind to receptors but do not activate them. Instead, they simply block agonists from binding to the receptors. These are classified as **competitive antagonists**. | Some agonist or antagonist drugs may bind to target receptors at a site that is *different* from where the endogenous ligand binds. Such drugs are known as **noncompetitive agonists or antagonists**. |

4.7 The Agonistic and Antagonistic Actions of Drugs

drug is a **noncompetitive ligand**, binding to a **modulatory site** on the receptor. Noncompetitive ligands may either activate the receptor, thereby acting as noncompetitive agonists, or prevent the receptor from being activated by the transmitter, thus acting as noncompetitive antagonists. We'll discuss the several modulatory sites on the GABA receptor later in this chapter.

Dose-response relationships reflect the potency and safety of drugs

As you would probably guess, administering larger doses of a drug ultimately increases the proportion of receptors that are bound and affected by the drug. Within certain limits, this increase in receptor binding also increases the response to the drug; in other words, greater doses tend to produce greater effects. When plotted as a graph, the relationship between drug doses and observed effects is called a **dose-response curve** (**DRC**). Careful analysis of DRCs reveals many aspects of a drug's activity and is one of the main tools for understanding **pharmacodynamics** (the functional relationships between drugs and their targets).

Figure 4.8 illustrates how DRCs are used to assess many important characteristics of drugs. For example, the DRC reveals the effective dose range of a drug (Figure 4.8*a*), allows comparison of the potencies of different drugs (Figure 4.8*b* and *c*). Sometimes the DRC gives us hints that the drug may be binding more than one type of receptor (Figure 4.8*d*). Comparing DRCs for two drugs can also indicate which drug would be safer to use (Figure 4.8*e*).

Repeated treatments can reduce the effectiveness of drugs

Our bodies are impressively adaptable. Many body systems change their functioning in order to accommodate environmental challenges, and in most ways drug treatments can be viewed as changes in the body's chemical environment. This adaptability is evident in the development of drug **tolerance**, in which successive treatments with a particular drug have decreasing effects.

Drug tolerance can develop in several different ways. Some drugs provoke **metabolic tolerance**, in which the body's metabolic organ systems (such as the liver) become increasingly effective at eliminating the drug before it has a chance to affect the brain or another target.

noncompetitive ligand   A drug that affects a transmitter receptor while binding at a site other than that bound by the endogenous ligand.

modulatory site   A portion of a receptor that, when bound by a compound, alters the receptor's response to its transmitter.

dose-response curve (DRC)   A formal plot of a drug's effects (on the *y*-axis) versus the dose given (on the *x*-axis).

pharmacodynamics   Collective name for the factors that affect the relationship between a drug and its target receptors, such as affinity and efficacy.

tolerance   A condition in which, with repeated exposure to a drug, an individual becomes less responsive to a constant dose.

metabolic tolerance   The form of drug tolerance that arises when repeated exposure to the drug causes the metabolic machinery of the body to become more efficient at clearing the drug.

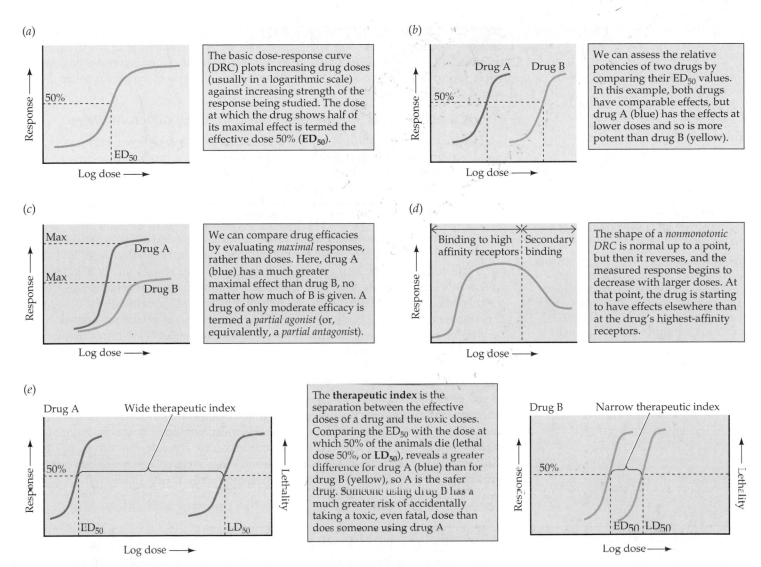

4.8 The Dose-Response Curve (DRC)

(a) The basic dose-response curve (DRC) plots increasing drug doses (usually in a logarithmic scale) against increasing strength of the response being studied. The dose at which the drug shows half of its maximal effect is termed the effective dose 50% (**ED$_{50}$**).

(b) We can assess the relative potencies of two drugs by comparing their ED$_{50}$ values. In this example, both drugs have comparable effects, but drug A (blue) has the effects at lower doses and so is more potent than drug B (yellow).

(c) We can compare drug efficacies by evaluating *maximal* responses, rather than doses. Here, drug A (blue) has a much greater maximal effect than drug B, no matter how much of B is given. A drug of only moderate efficacy is termed a *partial agonist* (or, equivalently, a *partial antagonist*).

(d) The shape of a *nonmonotonic* DRC is normal up to a point, but then it reverses, and the measured response begins to decrease with larger doses. At that point, the drug is starting to have effects elsewhere than at the drug's highest-affinity receptors.

(e) The **therapeutic index** is the separation between the effective doses of a drug and the toxic doses. Comparing the ED$_{50}$ with the dose at which 50% of the animals die (lethal dose 50%, or **LD$_{50}$**), reveals a greater difference for drug A (blue) than for drug B (yellow), so A is the safer drug. Someone using drug B has a much greater risk of accidentally taking a toxic, even fatal, dose than does someone using drug A.

Alternatively, the target tissue itself may show altered sensitivity to the drug, or **functional tolerance**. In neuropharmacology, an important source of functional tolerance is the regulation of receptor proteins—changing the number of receptors present in the cell membrane. This receptor regulation alters neuronal sensitivity in the direction opposite to the drug's effect. Thus, over the course of repeated exposures to an *agonist* drug, target neurons often **down-regulate** (decrease the number of available receptors to which the drug can bind), thereby countering the drug effect. If the drug is an *antagonist*, target neurons may instead **up-regulate** (increase the number of receptors).

Tolerance to a drug often generalizes to other drugs belonging to the same chemical class; this effect is termed **cross-tolerance**. For example, people who have developed tolerance to morphine tend to exhibit a degree of tolerance to all the other drugs in the opiate category, including codeine, heroin, and methadone. For drugs that have multiple effects in the body, tolerance to the various effects may develop at different rates.

Once established, drug tolerance is believed to be a major cause of **withdrawal symptoms**, the unpleasant sensations when one stops using a drug. As we will discuss later, many researchers believe that an important aspect of drug addiction is the avoidance of the physical discomfort of withdrawal symptoms. Furthermore,

functional tolerance Decreased responding to a drug after repeated exposures, generally as a consequence of up- or down-regulation of receptors.

down-regulation A compensatory decrease in receptor availability at the synapses of a neuron.

up-regulation A compensatory increase in receptor availability at the synapses of a neuron.

cross-tolerance A condition in which the development of tolerance for one drug causes an individual to develop tolerance for another drug.

withdrawal symptom An uncomfortable symptom that arises when a person stops taking a drug that he or she has used frequently, especially at high doses.

sensitization   A process in which the body shows an enhanced response to a given drug after repeated doses.

bioavailable   Referring to a substance, usually a drug, that is present in the body in a form that is able to interact with physiological mechanisms.

biotransformation   The process in which enzymes convert a drug into a metabolite that is itself active, possibly in ways that are substantially different from the actions of the original substance.

pharmacokinetics   Collective name for all the factors that affect the movement of a drug into, through, and out of the body.

blood-brain barrier   The mechanisms that make the movement of substances from blood vessels into brain cells more difficult than exchanges in other body organs, thus affording the brain greater protection from exposure to some substances found in blood.

some drug responses can become *stronger* with repeated treatments, rather than weaker. Termed **sensitization**, this effect is thought to contribute to the drug craving that addicts experience. This heightened sensitivity may last for a prolonged period, and it seems to reflect long-term brain changes in response to drugs of abuse (Peris et al., 1990).

Drugs are administered and eliminated in many different ways

The amount of drug that reaches the brain and the speed with which it starts acting are determined in part by the drug's route of administration. Some routes, such as smoking or intravenous injection, rapidly increase the concentration of drug in the body that is **bioavailable** (free to act on the target tissue, and therefore not bound to other proteins or in the process of being metabolized or excreted). With other routes, such as oral ingestion, the concentration of drug builds up more slowly over longer periods of time. Furthermore, the duration of a drug effect is largely determined by the manner in which the drug is metabolized and excreted from the body—via the kidneys, liver, lungs, and other routes. In some cases, the metabolites of drugs are themselves active; this **biotransformation** of drugs can be a source of unwanted side effects. Factors that affect the movement of a drug into, through, and out of the body are collectively referred to as **pharmacokinetics**.

Humans have devised an ingenious variety of techniques for introducing substances into the body; these are summarized in **Table 4.2**. In Chapter 2 we discussed the **blood-brain barrier**: the tight junctions between the endothelial cells of blood vessels within the CNS that inhibit the movement of larger molecules out of the bloodstream and into the brain. This barrier poses a major challenge for neuropharmacology because many drugs that might be clinically or experimentally useful are too large to pass the blood-brain barrier to enter the brain. To a limited extent this problem can be circumvented by the administration of drugs directly into the brain, but that is a drastic step. Alternatively, some drugs can take advantage of active transport systems that normally move nutrients out of the bloodstream and into the brain.

TABLE 4.2 The Relationship between Routes of Administration and Effects of Drugs

Route of administration	Examples and mechanisms	Typical speed of effects
INGESTION Tablets and capsules Syrups Infusions and teas Suppositories	Many sorts of drugs and remedies; depends on absorption by the gut, which is somewhat slower than most other routes.	Slow to moderate
INHALATION Smoking Nasal absorption Inhaled powders and sprays	Nicotine, cocaine, organic solvents such as airplane glue and gasoline, also used for a variety of prescription drugs and hormone treatments. Inhalation methods take advantage of the rich vascularization of the nose and lungs to convey drugs directly into the bloodstream.	Moderate to very fast
PERIPHERAL INJECTION Subcutaneous Intramuscular Intraperitoneal (abdominal) Intravenous	Many drugs; subcutaneous (under the skin) injections tend to have the slowest effects because they must diffuse into nearby tissue in order to reach the bloodstream; intravenous injections have very rapid effects because the drug is placed directly into circulation.	Moderate to very fast

CENTRAL INJECTION
Intracerebroventricular
  (into ventricular system)
Intrathecal (into spinal CSF)
Epidural (under the dura mater)
Intracerebral (directly into a
  brain region)
	Central methods involve injection directly into the CNS; used in order to circumvent the blood-brain barrier, to rule out peripheral effects, or to directly affect a discrete brain location.	Fast to very fast

Drugs Affect Each Stage of Neural Conduction and Synaptic Transmission

Local anesthetics, such as procaine (trade name Novocain) block sodium channels and therefore action potentials (see Chapter 3) in pain fibers from, say, that tooth your dentist is working on. But the great majority of drugs that act on the nervous system to produce changes in behavior do so by altering synaptic function. Some drugs act on the presynaptic terminal, affecting how much neurotransmitter is released into the synaptic cleft. Other drugs act on the postsynaptic membrane, altering how the target neuron responds to neurotransmitter. Let's consider these two sites of action in turn.

local anesthetic A drug, such as procaine or lidocaine, that blocks sodium channels to stop neural transmission in pain fibers.

Drugs affect presynaptic events

Figure 4.9 illustrates the presynaptic processes that are targeted by CNS drugs. Drugs that inhibit axonal transport (e.g., colchicine) prevent enzymes and other key compounds that originate in the cell body from being replaced in the axon terminals (step 3 in the figure). Because these supplies are needed to manufacture transmitter chemicals and vesicles, drugs that inhibit axonal transport prevent re-

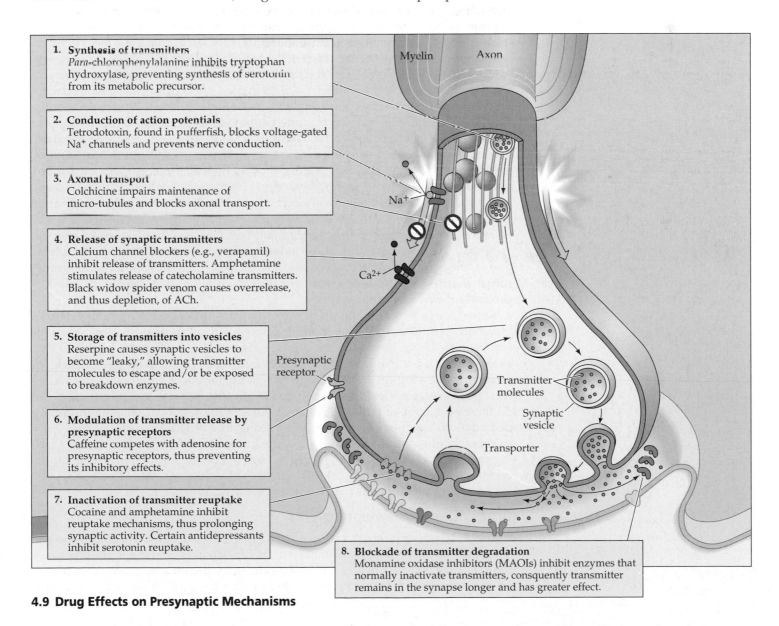

1. **Synthesis of transmitters**
   Para-chlorophenylalanine inhibits tryptophan hydroxylase, preventing synthesis of serotonin from its metabolic precursor.

2. **Conduction of action potentials**
   Tetrodotoxin, found in pufferfish, blocks voltage-gated Na^+ channels and prevents nerve conduction.

3. **Axonal transport**
   Colchicine impairs maintenance of micro-tubules and blocks axonal transport.

4. **Release of synaptic transmitters**
   Calcium channel blockers (e.g., verapamil) inhibit release of transmitters. Amphetamine stimulates release of catecholamine transmitters. Black widow spider venom causes overrelease, and thus depletion, of ACh.

5. **Storage of transmitters into vesicles**
   Reserpine causes synaptic vesicles to become "leaky," allowing transmitter molecules to escape and/or be exposed to breakdown enzymes.

6. **Modulation of transmitter release by presynaptic receptors**
   Caffeine competes with adenosine for presynaptic receptors, thus preventing its inhibitory effects.

7. **Inactivation of transmitter reuptake**
   Cocaine and amphetamine inhibit reuptake mechanisms, thus prolonging synaptic activity. Certain antidepressants inhibit serotonin reuptake.

8. **Blockade of transmitter degradation**
   Monoamine oxidase inhibitors (MAOIs) inhibit enzymes that normally inactivate transmitters, consequently transmitter remains in the synapse longer and has greater effect.

4.9 Drug Effects on Presynaptic Mechanisms

neuromodulator A substance that influences the activity of synaptic transmitters.

caffeine A stimulant compound found in coffee, cacao, and other plants.

adenosine In the context of neural transmission, a neuromodulator that alters synaptic activity.

autoreceptor A receptor for a synaptic transmitter that is located in the presynaptic membrane and tells the axon terminal how much transmitter has been released.

transporters Specialized receptors in the presynaptic membrane that recognize neurotransmitter molecules and return to the presynaptic neuron for reuse.

degradation The chemical breakdown of a neurotransmitter into inactive metabolites.

plenishment of the transmitter agent as it is used up, and synaptic transmission fails. Another drug, reserpine, interferes with the storage of catecholamine transmitters by making the vesicles leaky (step 5). Even if a presynaptic terminal has an adequate supply of transmitter stored in vesicles, various agents or conditions can prevent the *release* of transmitter when a nerve impulse reaches the terminal (step 6). For example, pharmacological blockade of calcium (Ca^{2+}) channels at the axon terminal inhibits transmitter release by preventing the Ca^{2+} influx that is required for transmitter release.

Some toxins prevent the release of specific kinds of transmitters (de Paiva et al., 1993). For instance, botulinum toxin, which is formed by bacteria that multiply in improperly canned food, poisons many people each year by blocking the release of ACh. Botulinum toxin binds to specialized receptors in nicotinic cholinergic membranes and is transported into the cell, where it blocks the Ca^{2+}-dependent release of transmitter (McMahon et al., 1992), resulting in muscle paralysis. In much-diluted form, botulinum toxin is marketed as Botox, which inhibits facial wrinkling by locally paralyzing facial muscles into which it has been injected. Tetanus (lockjaw) bacteria produce an often fatal toxin that blocks activity at inhibitory synapses and causes strong involuntary contractions of muscles.

Some agents stimulate or facilitate the release of certain transmitters. **Neuromodulators** are not transmitters themselves; rather they affect either the release of the transmitter or the receptor response to the transmitter. Perhaps the most beloved of all neuromodulators is the **caffeine** that we obtain from coffee and other beverages (worldwide, we drink about 400 *billion* cups of coffee each year). Caffeine acts as an exogenous neuromodulator, by blocking the effect of an endogenous neuromodulator, **adenosine**. By competing with adenosine for access to certain adenosine receptors on the surfaces of neurons, caffeine produces long-lasting changes in an internal signaling pathway (Lindskog et al., 2002). Because adenosine normally acts on presynaptic terminals to inhibit the release of catecholamine transmitters, caffeine *increases* catecholamine release, causing arousal. (Interestingly, by a different route, the stimulant drug amphetamine also facilitates catecholamine release.)

Where does adenosine normally come from? At least some catecholaminergic synapses co-release adenosine with the neurotransmitter. The adenosine binds to receptors on the same presynaptic terminal that released it (see Figure 4.9, step 6), so we say that the adenosine acts on **autoreceptors**. It may seem odd that a neuron that is releasing transmitter would also release a neuromodulator to inhibit transmitter release, but this type of complicated modulation of transmitter release is probably the rule, not the exception.

Other drugs work by affecting how long transmitters remain in the synapse. Some drugs interfere with **transporters**, the specialized proteins that remove neurotransmitter from the cleft for reuse (see Figure 4.9, step 7; see Chapter 3). For example, we'll see that the most common antidepressants inhibit the reuptake of serotonin, allowing the transmitter to have a bigger effect on postsynaptic receptors. Such drugs are said to work presynaptically, because the transporters are on the presynaptic terminal. Other drugs may have a similar affect by inhibiting **degradation**, the chemical process of breaking down neurotransmitter into inactive metabolites, which again can allow the transmitter to have a greater effect (see Figure 4.9, step 8). This type of drug action is usually considered postsynaptic, because it affects enzymes outside the presynaptic terminal, in the cleft itself. Let's explore other postsynaptic mechanisms of drug action.

Drugs affect postsynaptic events

Figure 4.10 illustrates how various CNS drugs can affect postsynaptic processes. For example, curare blocks nicotinic ACh receptors (step 3 in the figure). Because the synapses between nerves and skeletal muscles are nicotinic, curare paralyzes all skeletal muscles, including those used in breathing. We discussed several oth-

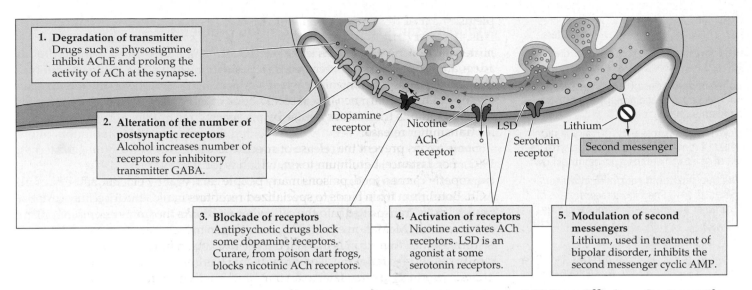

1. **Degradation of transmitter**
   Drugs such as physostigmine
   inhibit AChE and prolong the
   activity of ACh at the synapse.

2. **Alteration of the number of
   postsynaptic receptors**
   Alcohol increases number of
   receptors for inhibitory
   transmitter GABA.

Dopamine
receptor

Nicotine

ACh
receptor

LSD

Serotonin
receptor

Lithium

Second messenger

3. **Blockade of receptors**
   Antipsychotic drugs block
   some dopamine receptors.
   Curare, from poison dart frogs,
   blocks nicotinic ACh receptors.

4. **Activation of receptors**
   Nicotine activates ACh
   receptors. LSD is an
   agonist at some
   serotonin receptors.

5. **Modulation of second
   messengers**
   Lithium, used in treatment of
   bipolar disorder, inhibits the
   second messenger cyclic AMP.

**4.10 Drug Effects on Postsynaptic
Mechanisms**

er drugs that affect postsynaptic receptors when we described the different neurotransmitter systems at the start of this chapter. Behavior can be disrupted not only when transmitter-receptor action is blocked, but also when it is prolonged. For instance, agents that inhibit the enzyme acetylcholinesterase (AChE) allow ACh to remain active at the synapse and alter the timing of synaptic transmission. These *cholinesterase inhibitors*, including certain pesticides and chemical weapons, produce prolonged contraction of muscles and resultant paralysis, as well as overactivity of the parasympathetic nervous system.

Drugs That Affect the Brain Can Be Divided into Functional Classes

In addition to categorizing drugs on the basis of their cellular effects, we can classify them by their specific effects on behavior and therapeutic applications. In the sections that follow, we will briefly review some of the major categories of psychoactive substances.

Antipsychotic drugs relieve the symptoms of schizophrenia

Originally developed as an antihistamine in the 1950s, chlorpromazine was accidentally discovered to reduce some of the symptoms of schizophrenia. Subsequent research identified several other **antipsychotic** drugs (also known as **neuroleptics**). The neuroleptics revolutionized the treatment of schizophrenia because they greatly reduce many of the symptoms, such as delusions and hallucinations, that prevent patients with this condition from living on their own. These first-generation drugs, classified as **typical neuroleptics**, all share one key feature: they act as selective antagonists of dopamine D_2 receptors. One of the best-known typical neuroleptics, haloperidol (Haldol), exhibits a nearly 100-fold selectivity for D_2 over D_1 receptors.

   The 1990s saw the advent of second-generation antipsychotics, known as **atypical neuroleptics**, which feature nondopaminergic actions, especially the blockade of certain serotonin receptors. These atypical neuroleptics, such as clozapine, are claimed to reduce additional symptoms (termed *negative* symptoms, such as social withdrawal and blunted emotional responses) that typical neuroleptics generally do not relieve, although this claim has been disputed (Burton, 2006). Unfortunately, despite progress in its treatment, schizophrenia remains a major health problem. We return to the topic of schizophrenia and its treatment in Chapter 16.

antipsychotics A class of drugs that alleviate schizophrenia.

neuroleptics A class of antipsychotic drugs, traditionally dopamine receptor blockers.

typical neuroleptics A major class of antischizophrenic drugs that share antagonist activity at dopamine D_2 receptors.

atypical neuroleptics A class of antischizophrenic drugs that have actions other than the dopamine D_2 receptor antagonism that characterizes the typical neuroleptics.

antidepressants A class of drugs that relieve the symptoms of depression.

monoamine oxidase (MAO) An enzyme that breaks down and thereby inactivates monoamine transmitters.

tricyclic antidepressants A class of drugs that act by increasing the synaptic accumulation of serotonin and norepinephrine.

selective serotonin reuptake inhibitor (SSRI) A drug that blocks the reuptake of transmitter at serotonergic synapses.

anxiolytics A class of substances that are used to combat anxiety.

depressants A class of drugs that act to reduce neural activity.

benzodiazepine agonists A class of antianxiety drugs that bind to sites on GABA$_A$ receptors.

orphan receptor Any receptor for which no endogenous ligand has yet been discovered.

allopregnanolone A naturally occurring steroid that modulates GABA receptor activity in much the same way that benzodiazepine anxiolytics do.

Antidepressants relieve chronic mood problems

Disturbances of mood, or *affective disorders,* are among the most common of all psychiatric complaints (World Health Organization, 2001). The first generation of effective **antidepressant** medications, developed in the 1950s, were the **monoamine oxidase** (**MAO**) inhibitors, such as tranylcypromine (Parnate) and isocarboxazid (Marplan). MAOs break down monoamine neurotransmitters at synapses, thereby reducing transmitter activity. By blocking this process, MAO inhibitors allow monoamine neurotransmitters to accumulate at synapses (see Figure 4.9, step 8), with an associated improvement in mood.

Increasing synaptic monoamine availability appears to be a key activity of all antidepressants. The second generation of antidepressants—the **tricyclics**—combat depression by increasing the synaptic content of the monoamines norepinephrine and serotonin. Named for their three-ringed molecular structure, tricyclics such as imipramine (Tofranil) block the reuptake of neurotransmitters into presynaptic axon terminals (see Figure 4.9, step 7). More recently developed antidepressants, such as fluoxetine (Prozac), sertraline (Zoloft), and citalopram (Celexa), are **selective serotonin reuptake inhibitors** (**SSRIs**); as the name indicates, these drugs alleviate depression by selectively allowing serotonin to accumulate in synapses. These newer antidepressants lack some of the undesirable side effects of older drugs, but they can take as long as 6–8 weeks to have full effect. We will discuss the causes and treatment of affective disorders in more detail in Chapter 16.

Anxiolytics combat anxiety

Most of us occasionally suffer feelings of vague dissatisfaction or apprehension that we call anxiety, but some people are stricken by disabling emotional distress that resembles abject fear and terror. These clinical states of anxiety include panic attacks, phobias (such as the fear of taking an airplane or even of leaving the house), and generalized anxiety (see Chapter 16).

Humans have long sought relief from anxiety through the ingestion of **anxiolytics** (from the word *anxiety* and the Greek *lytikos,* "able to loosen"). Sometimes also called *tranquilizers,* anxiolytics belong to the general category of **depressants**: drugs that depress or reduce nervous system activity. Alcohol is perhaps the original anxiolytic, but its anxiety-fighting properties come at the cost of intoxication, addiction potential, and neuropsychological impairment with long-term abuse. Opiates and barbiturates have also been used to relieve anxiety, but they have strongly sedative effects, strong addiction potential, and significant risk of accidental overdose.

First discovered in the 1960s, **benzodiazepine agonists** have proven to be safe and effective anxiolytics, and they are among the most heavily prescribed drugs. One of the most familiar members of this class of drug, the benzodiazepine diazepam (trade name Valium), binds to specific sites on GABA$_A$ receptors and enhances the activity of GABA (Walters et al., 2000). Because GABA$_A$ receptors are inhibitory, benzodiazepines help GABA to produce larger inhibitory postsynaptic potentials than would be caused by GABA alone.

GABA$_A$ receptors have several different binding sites—some that facilitate and some that inhibit the effect of GABA (**Figure 4.11**); therefore, many different drugs can interact with this receptor complex. For example, benzodiazepines bind to a unique modulatory site on the receptor complex that is distant from where GABA itself binds. The benzodiazepine-binding site is thus an **orphan receptor**—a receptor for which an endogenous ligand has not been conclusively identified—and the hunt for its endogenous ligand has been intense. **Allopregnanolone**, a steroid derived from the hormone progesterone, acts on yet another site on the GABA$_A$ receptor. Allopregnanolone is elevated during stress and has a calming effect. Alcohol ingestion also increases brain concentrations of allopregnanolone (VanDoren et al., 2000), so this steroid may mediate some of the calming influence of alcohol.

4.11 The GABA_A Receptor Has Many Different Binding Sites The GABA_A complex is made up of five protein subunits that penetrate the cell membrane and surround a Cl⁻ ion channel at the core. These subunits contain many different recognition and receptor sites; some of the most important ones are labeled here. GABA_A receptors are widespread in the brain and are crucial for normal inhibitory processes. Many depressant drugs work by increasing the responsiveness of GABA_A receptors to GABA.

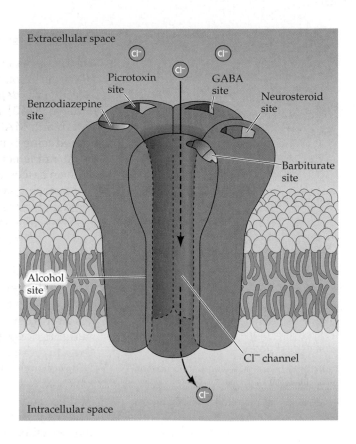

Several other progesterone-like **neurosteroids** (steroids produced in the brain) may act on GABA_A receptors to produce anxiolytic, analgesic, and anticonvulsant effects (Belelli and Lambert, 2005).

New generations of anxiolytics that are under development affect other transmitter systems, notably serotonin. The serotonergic agonist buspirone (Buspar) is an effective anxiolytic that lacks the sedative effects of benzodiazepines. Buspirone is known to be a $5HT_{1A}$ agonist and a partial agonist of dopamine D_2 receptors; but the exact mechanism of its anxiolytic action remains unknown.

Alcohol has several effects

Alcohol has traveled the full route of human history, no doubt because it is so easily produced by the fermentation of fruit or grains and thus is an ingredient of many types of pleasant beverages. Taken in moderation, alcohol is harmless or even beneficial to the health of adults; for example, consumption of one drink or so per day is associated with reduced risk of cardiovascular and Alzheimer's diseases, and with improved control of blood sugar levels (Davies et al., 2002; Leroi et al., 2002; Mukamal et al., 2003). *Excessive* alcohol consumption, however, is very damaging and linked to more than 60 disease processes.

The psychoactive effect of alcohol in the nervous system is biphasic: an initial stimulant phase is followed by a more prolonged depressant phase. In a manner similar to that of the benzodiazepines, but acting via a different recognition site, alcohol activates the GABA_A receptor–coupled chloride channel (see Figure 4.11), thereby increasing postsynaptic inhibition. This action contributes to social disinhibition, as well as the impairment of motor coordination that occurs after a few drinks (Hanchar et al., 2005). Alcohol also affects other transmitters. For example, low doses of alcohol stimulate dopamine pathways, and the resulting increase in dopamine may be related to the euphoria caused by alcohol.

Chronic abuse of alcohol damages nerve cells. Cells of the superior frontal cortex, Purkinje cells of the cerebellum, and hippocampal pyramidal cells show particularly prominent pathological changes. Some of these degenerative effects of chronic alcohol use may be due to a secondary consequence of alcoholism: poor diet. For example, chronic alcoholism is accompanied by severe thiamine deficiency, which can lead to neural degeneration and Korsakoff's syndrome (see Chapter 17). And alcohol abuse by expectant mothers can cause grievous permanent brain damage to the developing fetus (termed **fetal alcohol syndrome**), a topic to which we will return in Chapter 7 (see Figure 7.16). In fact, it is not clear whether it is safe for pregnant women to consume *any* alcohol, even small quantities; a few studies have suggested subtle changes in the cognitive function of babies exposed to only moderate levels of alcohol in utero (Day et al., 2002; Huizink and Mulder, 2006).

The frontal lobes—especially the superior frontal association cortex—are the brain areas that are most affected by chronic alcohol use (Kril et al., 1997). However, some of the anatomical changes associated with chronic alcoholism may be reversible with abstinence. In rats, chronic exposure to alcohol reduces the number of synapses on neurons in some regions, but this number returns to normal lev-

neurosteroids Steroids produced in the brain.

fetal alcohol syndrome (FAS) A disorder, including intellectual disability and characteristic facial anomalies, that affects children exposed to too much alcohol (through maternal ingestion) during fetal development.

4.12 The Effects of Alcohol on the Brain   MRI studies of humans who suffer from alcoholism show that abstaining from alcohol for 30 days increases the volume of cortical gray matter (*a*) and decreases the volume of the lateral ventricles (*b*). (After Pfefferbaum et al., 1995.)

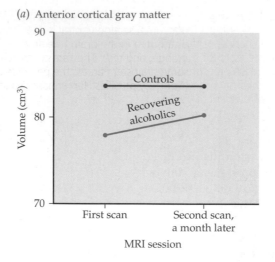

(*a*) Anterior cortical gray matter

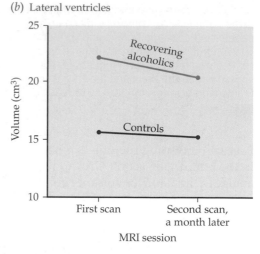

(*b*) Lateral ventricles

opium   A heterogeneous extract of the seedpod juice of the opium poppy, *Papaver somniferum*.

morphine   An opiate compound derived from the poppy flower.

analgesic   Referring to painkilling properties.

heroin   Diacetylmorphine; an artificially modified, very potent form of morphine.

opioid receptor   A receptor that responds to endogenous and/or exogenous opiates.

periaqueductal gray   The neuronal body–rich region of the midbrain surrounding the cerebral aqueduct that connects the third and fourth ventricles; involved in pain perception.

els after alcohol treatments stop (Dlugos and Pentney, 1997). Similarly, in humans suffering from alcoholism, MRI studies show an increase in the volume of cortical gray matter and an associated reduction in ventricular volume within weeks of giving up alcohol (**Figure 4.12**) (Pfefferbaum et al., 1995).

There is a strong hereditary component to alcoholism, as indicated by human studies and selective breeding experiments in rats (Schuckit and Smith, 1997). The combination of genetic vulnerability and a stressful environment probably explains many cases of alcoholism (McGue, 1999).

Even in the absence of clear-cut alcoholism, periodic overconsumption of alcohol—*bingeing*—may cause brain damage. After only 4 days of bingeing on alcohol, rats exhibit neural degeneration in several areas of the brain. Damage is especially evident in the olfactory bulbs and in limbic structures connected with the hippocampus, and it is associated with impairments of cognitive ability (Obernier et al., 2002). Alcohol bingeing also significantly reduces the rate of neurogenesis—the formation of new neurons—in the adult hippocampus (Nixon and Crews, 2002). Alcohol bingeing can depress breathing enough to kill. Many more college students die from alcohol-related accidents (Hingson et al., 2005).

Opiates help relieve pain

Opium, extracted from poppy flower seedpods (**Figure 4.13**), has been used by humans since at least the Stone Age. **Morphine**, the major active substance in opium, is a very effective **analgesic** (painkiller) that has brought relief from severe pain to many millions of people (see Chapter 8). Unfortunately, morphine also has a strong potential for addiction, as does its close relative **heroin** (diacetylmorphine).

Opiate drugs such as morphine bind to specific receptors—**opioid receptors**—that are concentrated in certain regions of the brain. Opioid receptors are found in the limbic and hypothalamic areas of the brain, and they are particularly rich in the locus coeruleus and in the gray matter that surrounds the aqueduct in the brainstem (known as the **periaqueductal gray**) (**Figure 4.14**). Injection of morphine directly into the periaqueductal gray produces strong analgesia, indicating that this is a region where morphine acts to reduce pain perception (see Chapter 8). The discovery of orphan receptors for opiates came as a surprise and, because the presence of these receptors implied that there must be an endogenous ligand

4.13 The Source of Opium and Morphine   The opium poppy has a distinctive flower and seedpod. The bitter flavor and CNS actions of opium may provide the poppy plant a defense against being eaten.

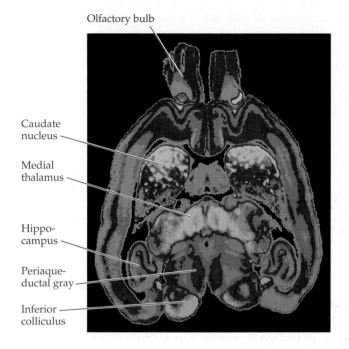

Olfactory bulb

Caudate nucleus

Medial thalamus

Hippo- campus

Periaque- ductal gray

Inferior colliculus

4.14 The Distribution of Opioid Receptors in the Rat Brain This horizontal section (rostral is at the top) shows opioid receptors widely distributed in the brain (the areas of highest binding are shown in yellow, orange, and red). They are concentrated in the medial thalamus and in some brainstem areas: the periaqueductal gray and the inferior colliculus. (Courtesy of Miles Herkenham, National Institute of Mental Health.)

endogenous opioids A family of peptide transmitters that have been called the body's own narcotics. The three kinds are enkepha- lins, endorphins, and dynorphins.

enkephalins One of three kinds of endog- enous opioids.

endorphins One of three kinds of endog- enous opioids.

dynorphins One of three kinds of endog- enous opioids.

marijuana A dried preparation of the *Can- nabis sativa* plant, usually smoked to obtain THC.

Δ9-tetrahydrocannabinol (THC) The major active ingredient in marijuana.

produced within the body, it prompted an intense scientific effort to identify **en- dogenous opioids**.

Two endogenous peptides that bind to opioid receptors were eventually identi- fied and named **enkephalins** (from the Greek *en*, "in," and *kephale*, "head") (Hughes et al., 1975). Research with animal subjects demonstrated that, like morphine, en- kephalins relieve pain and are addictive. Only a small part of the enkephalin mol- ecule is the same as the morphine molecule, but this common part is what binds to the opioid receptor. Further research uncovered additional families of endogenous opioids: the **endorphins** (a contraction of *endogenous morphine*) and the **dynorphins** (short for *dynamic endorphins*, in recognition of their potency and speed of action.)

There are three main kinds of opioid receptors—the delta (δ), kappa (κ), and mu (μ) opioid receptors—differing in their affinity for various *opiatergic* drugs (C. J. Evans et al., 1992; J. B. Wang et al., 1993; Yasuda et al., 1993). All three opioid re- ceptor subtypes are G protein–coupled metabotropic receptors. Several synthetic drugs act as *antagonists* at opioid receptors, including naltrexone. For some alco- holics, naltrexone treatment blocks the euphoria that normally results from alco- hol, suggesting that in these individuals alcohol causes the release of endogenous opioids that brings pleasure. Interestingly, only that minority of alcoholics who carry a gene for a particular variant of the mu opioid receptor benefit from naltrex- one treatment (Oroszi et al., 2009).

Cannabinoids have a wide array of effects

Marijuana and related preparations, such as hashish, obtained from the *Cannabis sativa* plant (**Figure 4.15**), have been used for thousands of years (Russo et al., 2008) and are today the most widely used of all illicit drugs. Typically ingested via smoking, marijuana contains dozens of active ingredients, chief among which is the compound **Δ9-tetrahydrocannabinol (THC)** (Gaoni and Mechoulam, 1964).

4.15 An Indoor Marijuana Farm Although growing the marijuana plant (*Cannabis sa- tiva*) is widely prohibited, it is believed to be the largest cash crop in several U.S. states, parts of Canada, and other locations around the globe. Growers have developed sophisticated hydroponic techniques for growing highly potent strains of cannabis in indoor "grow ops."

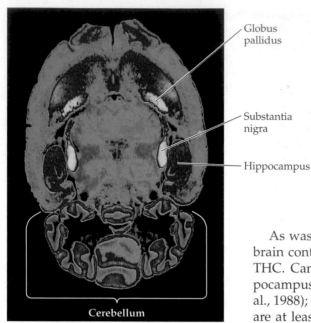

Globus
pallidus

Substantia
nigra

Hippocampus

Cerebellum

4.16 The Distribution of Cannabinoid Receptors in the Rat Brain   The areas of highest binding are indicated by yellow, orange, and red in this horizontal section. (Courtesy of Miles Herkenham, National Institute of Mental Health.)

The subjective experience of marijuana use is quite variable among individuals: relaxation and mood alteration are the most frequent effects; but stimulation, hallucination, and paranoia also occur in some cases. Sustained use of marijuana can cause addiction (Maldonado and Rodríguez de Fonseca, 2002); and frequent smoking of marijuana, like tobacco, can contribute to respiratory diseases. Adolescents who use marijuana are more likely to develop psychosis in adulthood (Murray et al., 2007), but it is not clear whether the drug causes psychosis or whether adolescents who are prepsychotic are more likely to turn to marijuana. In one longitudinal study, only those adolescents carrying a particular gene were more likely to become schizophrenic after using marijuana, suggesting that some people are genetically vulnerable to this devastating effect of the drug (Caspi et al., 2005).

As was the case with opiates and benzodiazepines, researchers found that the brain contains cannabinoid receptors that mediate the effects of compounds like THC. Cannabinoid receptors are concentrated in the substantia nigra, the hippocampus, the cerebellar cortex, and the cerebral cortex (**Figure 4.16**) (Devane et al., 1988); other regions, such as the brainstem, show few of these receptors. There are at least two subtypes of cannabinoid receptors—CB_1 and CB_2 (Gerard et al., 1991; Pertwee, 1997)—both of which are G protein–coupled metabotropic receptors. Genetic disruption of CB_1 receptors is sufficient to make mice unresponsive to the rewarding properties of cannabinoid drugs (Ledent et al., 1999). Only the CB_1 receptor is found in the nervous system; CB_2 receptors are especially prominent in the immune system.

The discovery of cannabinoid receptors touched off an intensive search for an endogenous ligand, and several such compounds—termed **endocannabinoids**—were identified. Interestingly, endocannabinoids can function as retrograde messengers, conveying messages from the postsynaptic cell to the presynaptic cell. This retrograde signal is thought to modulate the release of neurotransmitter by the presynaptic nerve terminal (Murray et al., 2007). The most studied endocannabinoid is **anandamide** (from the Sanskrit *ananda*, "bliss") (Devane et al., 1992), which has diverse functional effects, including alterations of memory formation, appetite stimulation, reduced sensitivity to pain, and protection from excitotoxic brain damage (Marsicano et al., 2003; P. B. Smith et al., 1994). Other endocannabinoids include 2-arachidonylglycerol (2-AG) (Stella et al., 1997) and oleamide (Leggett et al., 2004).

The study of endocannabinoids will aid the search for drugs that share the beneficial effects of marijuana: relieving pain, lowering blood pressure, combating nausea, lowering eye pressure in glaucoma, and so on. The documented use of cannabis for medicinal purposes spans over 6000 years, but treatment with "medical marijuana" remains illegal in most jurisdictions. It is ironic that synthetic cannabinoids patented by drug companies could eventually be legally prescribed to patients with these same medical conditions. In a sense, marijuana use is illegal therapy in these cases because no Wall Street company can profit from it. You can't file a patent for a plant that's already been in use for millennia.

Stimulants increase the activity of the nervous system

The degree of activity of the nervous system reflects a balance of excitatory and inhibitory influences. Stimulants are drugs that tip the balance toward the excitatory side; they therefore have an alerting, activating effect. Many naturally occurring and artificial stimulants are widely used, including amphetamine, nicotine, caffeine, and cocaine. Some stimulants act directly by increasing excitatory synaptic potentials. Others act by blocking normal inhibitory processes; we've already seen that caffeine blocks adenosine receptors. Other stimulants, such as **khat** (or *qat*, pronounced "cot"), an African shrub that is chewed, have several ac-

endocannabinoid   An endogenous ligand of cannabinoid receptors; thus, an analog of marijuana that is produced by the brain.

anandamide   An endogenous substance that binds the cannabinoid receptor molecule.

khat   Also spelled *qat*. An African shrub that, when chewed, acts as a stimulant.

tive ingredients that have not been well studied. Paradoxically, stimulants such as methylphenidate (Ritalin) have a calming effect in humans with attention deficit hyperactivity disorder (ADHD); this activity may be mediated by changes in serotonergic activity (Gainetdinov et al., 1999).

NICOTINE   Tobacco is native to the Americas, where European explorers first encountered smoking; these explorers brought tobacco back to Europe with them. Tobacco use became much more widespread following technological innovations that made it easier to smoke, in the form of cigarettes (W. Bennett, 1983). Exposed to the large surface of the lungs, the **nicotine** from cigarettes enters the blood and brain much more rapidly than does nicotine from other tobacco products. The nicotine increases the heart rate, blood pressure, secretion of hydrochloric acid in the stomach, and intestinal activity. In the short run, these effects make tobacco use pleasurable. But these neural effects on body function, quite apart from the effects of tobacco tar on the lungs, make prolonged tobacco use very unhealthful.

Nicotine activates one class of ACh receptors, which, as we learned earlier, are called nicotinic receptors. Most nicotinic receptors are found at neuromuscular junctions and in neurons of the autonomic ganglia, but many are also present in the central nervous system. This is one way in which nicotine enhances some aspects of cognitive performance. Astonishingly, the nicotine from one cigarette can occupy 88% of brain nicotinic receptors (Brody et al., 2006). Using a sophisticated genetic model in which certain nicotinic ACh receptors are expressed only in discrete brain regions, researchers found that nicotine acts on the ventral tegmental area (VTA; see Figure 4.3) to exert both its rewarding/addicting effects and improvements in cognitive performance (Maskos et al., 2005). (We will discuss the VTA in more detail when we discuss positive reward models later in the chapter.)

COCAINE   For hundreds of years, people in Bolivia, Colombia, and Peru have used the leaves of the coca shrub—either chewed or brewed as a tea—to increase endurance, alleviate hunger, and promote a sense of well-being. This use of coca leaves does not seem to cause problems. The artificially purified coca extract (**cocaine**), however, is a powerfully addictive alkaloid stimulant that has harmed millions of lives.

First isolated in 1859, cocaine was added to beverages (such as *Coca*-Cola) and tonics for its stimulant qualities, and subsequently it was used as a local anesthetic (it is in the same chemical family as procaine) and an antidepressant. In addition, it was widely used as a psychostimulant until 1932, when it gave way to amphetamine, which acts much like cocaine but was easier to obtain (amphetamine was sold in inhalers for nasal congestion, and some people cracked open inhalers to get the drug). When legal restrictions on amphetamine raised its price in the 1960s, cocaine use rose again. Many users snort cocaine powder, which rapidly enters the bloodstream via the nasal route (see Table 4.2).

Crack is a smokable form of cocaine that appeared in the mid-1980s. Because cocaine in this form enters the blood and the brain more rapidly, crack cocaine is even more addictive than cocaine powder. Like other psychostimulants, cocaine acts by blocking monoamine transporters, especially those for dopamine (**Figure 4.17**), slowing reuptake of the transmitters and therefore boosting their effects. Cocaine may have neurotoxic effects, and an overdose can provoke marked changes in cerebral blood flow, including strokes (Holman et al., 1993), as well as reduction in cortical gray matter density (Franklin et al., 2002). As a consequence of sensitization, which we discussed earlier, chronic cocaine use can provoke symptoms similar to psychosis. Cessation of cocaine use often produces very uncomfortable withdrawal symptoms: initial agitation and powerful drug cravings, followed by depression and an inability to enjoy anything

nicotine   A compound found in plants, including tobacco, that acts as an agonist on a large class of cholinergic receptors.

cocaine   A drug of abuse, derived from the coca plant, that acts by potentiating catecholamine stimulation.

4.17 Cocaine-Binding Sites in the Monkey Brain   This autoradiograph of a coronal section shows the distribution of cocaine-binding sites. The areas of the highest binding are shown by orange and yellow. (Courtesy of Bertha K. Madras.)

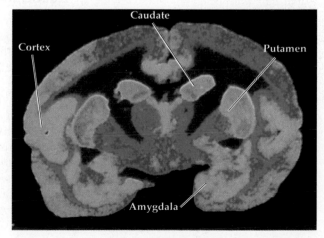

dual dependence Dependence for emergent drug effects that occur only when two drugs are taken simultaneously.

amphetamine A molecule that resembles the structure of the catecholamine transmitters and enhances their activity.

cocaine- and amphetamine-regulated transcript (CART) A peptide produced in the brain when an animal is injected with either cocaine or amphetamine. It is also associated with the appetite control circuitry of the hypothalamus.

hallucinogens A class of drugs that alter sensory perception and produce peculiar experiences.

LSD Also called *acid*. Lysergic acid diethylamide, a hallucinogenic drug.

else in life. Cerebral glucose metabolism is decreased for months after cocaine use is discontinued, and may contribute to that depression. People who use cocaine along with other substances run the additional risk of **dual dependence**, in which the interaction of two (or more) drugs produces an additional addictive state. For example, cocaine metabolized in the presence of ethanol (alcohol) yields an active metabolite called *cocaethylene*, to which the user may develop a further addiction (D. S. Harris et al., 2003).

AMPHETAMINE The molecular structure of the synthetic psychostimulant **amphetamine** closely resembles that of the catecholamine transmitters (norepinephrine, epinephrine, and dopamine). Amphetamine and the even more potent methamphetamine (*meth* or *speed*) cause the release of these transmitters from presynaptic terminals even in the absence of action potentials, and when action potentials *do* reach the axon terminals, amphetamine also potentiates the subsequent release of transmitter. Furthermore, once transmitter has been released, amphetamine enhances activity in two ways: (1) by blocking the reuptake of catecholamines into the presynaptic terminal, and (2) by providing an alternative target for the enzyme (monoamine oxidase) that normally inactivates them.

Because amphetamine stimulates and enhances the activity of the catecholamine transmitters, it has a variety of behavioral effects. On a short-term basis, it produces heightened alertness and even euphoria, and it promotes sustained effort without rest or sleep and with lowered fatigue. However, although a person may be able to accomplish more work and feel more confident by using amphetamine, most studies show that the quality of work is not improved by the drug—that is, that the drug increases motivation but not cognitive ability.

Tolerance to the effects of amphetamine develops rapidly, so chronic users have to take larger and larger doses, leading to sleeplessness, severe weight loss, and general deterioration of mental and physical condition. Prolonged use of amphetamine may lead to symptoms that closely resemble those of paranoid schizophrenia: compulsive, agitated behavior and irrational suspiciousness. In fact, some amphetamine users have been misdiagnosed as having schizophrenia (see Chapter 16). Amphetamine acts on the autonomic nervous system to produce high blood pressure, tremor, dizziness, sweating, rapid breathing, and nausea. Worst of all, people who chronically abuse speed display symptoms of brain damage long after they quit using the drug (Ernst et al., 2000).

Cocaine or amphetamine treatments induce the brain to produce a peptide called, naturally enough, **cocaine- and amphetamine-regulated transcript** (**CART**). Injection of CART into the ventral tegmental area is very rewarding for rats (Kimmel et al., 2000), suggesting that CART is involved in the pleasurable aspects of these drugs. The CART system also helps regulate appetite (see Chapter 13).

Hallucinogenic and dissociative drugs alter sensory perception

Drugs classified as **hallucinogens** alter sensory perceptions in dramatic ways and produce peculiar experiences. But the term *hallucinogen* is a misnomer because, whereas a hallucination is a novel perception that takes place in the absence of sensory stimulation (hearing voices, or seeing something that isn't there), the drugs in this category tend to alter or distort *existing* perceptions. The effects of lysergic acid diethylamide (**LSD**, or *acid*) and related substances like mescaline (*peyote*) and psilocybin (*magic mushrooms*), are predominantly visual. Users often see fantastic images with intense colors, and they are often aware that these strangely altered perceptions are not real events.

Hallucinogenic agents are diverse in their neural actions. For example, the Mexican herb salvia is unusual among hallucinogens because it acts on the opioid kappa receptor. Other hallucinogens, such as muscarine, found in some mushrooms, affect the ACh system. Mescaline, the drug extracted from the peyote plant, affects noradrenergic and serotonergic systems. Many hallucinogens, including LSD, mescaline, psilocybin, and others, act as serotonin receptor agonists or partial agonists, especially at $5HT_{2A}$ receptors.

You may have guessed that Albert Hofmann (**Figure 4.18**), whose story opened this chapter, was the discoverer of LSD. In fact, the study of LSD's activities became the focus of his professional career, summarized in his 1981 book, *LSD: My Problem Child*. Following its discovery, LSD was intensively studied as a possible psychiatric treatment. Starting in the 1950s, research to see if LSD could model psychosis did not bear fruit. But there has been a resurgence of interest in whether hallucinogens may relieve various psychiatric disorders, including depression and obsessive-compulsive disorder (Moreno et al., 2006).

The structure of LSD resembles that of serotonin, and LSD was soon found to act on serotonin receptors, probably evoking visual phenomena by activating $5HT_{2A}$ receptors in visual cortex. Former users of LSD sometimes report experiencing flashbacks—that is, having experiences as if they had taken a dose of drug, even though they are drug-free.

Phencyclidine (commonly known as **PCP** or *angel dust*) was developed in 1956 as a potent analgesic and anesthetic agent. Classified as a **dissociative drug** because it produces feelings of depersonalization and detachment from reality, it was soon dropped from use in anesthesia because it also causes agitation, excitement, delirium, hostility, and disorganization of perceptions. PCP continues to be used as a street drug, principally because of its hallucinogenic actions. Even at relatively low doses, PCP produces numerous undesirable effects, including combativeness and catatonia (stupor and immobility). Higher doses or repeated use can lead to long-lasting profound confusion, or convulsions and coma. The similarity between PCP's effects and psychosis has led some researchers to propose PCP as a chemical model of schizophrenia (see Chapter 16). In animal models, PCP causes degeneration in the hippocampus and the cingulate gyrus.

4.18 The Father of LSD Albert Hofmann discovered LSD in 1943 and devoted the remainder of his career to studying it. A prohibited drug in most jurisdictions, LSD is distributed on colorful blotter paper. This example, picturing Hofmann and the LSD molecule, is made up of 1036 individual doses (or "hits").

PCP antagonizes the NMDA receptor (see Figure 16.11), perhaps at a special binding site, and it stimulates release of the transmitter dopamine (Gorelick and Balster, 1995). PCP's molecular relative, **ketamine** (nicknamed *Special K*), is a less potent NMDA antagonist that is used as a dissociative anesthetic agent. PET studies indicate that ketamine increases metabolic activity in the prefrontal cortex (Breier, Malhotra, et al., 1997), so perhaps PCP also acts there. Like PCP, ketamine in high doses produces transient psychotic symptoms in volunteers. Ketamine is used as an anesthetic in humans and is also being explored as a possible antidepressant (Zarate et al., 2006).

Ecstasy is the street name for the hallucinogenic amphetamine derivative **MDMA** (3,4-methylenedioxymethamphetamine). Major actions of MDMA in the brain include an increase in the release of serotonin, stimulation of $5HT_{2A}$ receptors, and changes in the levels of dopamine and certain hormones, such as prolactin. Exactly how these activities account for the subjective effects of MDMA—positive emotions, empathy, euphoria, a sense of well-being, and colorful visual phenomena—remains to be established.

In lab animals, chronic use of Ecstasy produces persistent effects on serotonin-producing neurons, such as a prolonged reduction in serotonin metabolites. In addition, fine serotonergic axons and axon terminals are at least temporarily damaged, probably by metabolites of MDMA (T. J. Monks et al., 2004), although it's not clear whether the cell bodies of serotonergic cells also suffer longer-lasting

phencyclidine (PCP) Also called *angel dust*. An anesthetic agent that is also a psychedelic drug.

dissociative drug A type of drug that produces a dreamlike state in which consciousness is partly separated from sensory inputs.

ketamine A dissociative anesthetic drug, similar to PCP, that acts as an NMDA receptor antagonist.

MDMA Also called *Ecstasy*. A drug of abuse, 3,4-methylenedioxymethamphetamine.

(a) Control

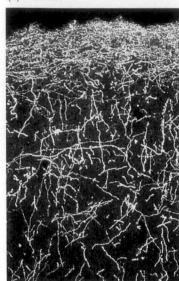

(b) Treated with Ecstasy

4.19 Long-Term Effects of a Single Dose of Ecstasy on the Monkey Brain Serotonin axons in the dorsal cortex of (a) a control squirrel monkey and (b) a squirrel monkey treated with a single dose of MDMA (Ecstasy) 18 months earlier. (C. Fischer et al., 1995; photo courtesy of George Ricaurte.)

damage. **Figure 4.19** shows a marked reduction in serotonin axons in the cortex and hippocampus of a squirrel monkey treated with MDMA 18 months earlier (C. Fischer et al., 1995). Humans who take MDMA also display reduced serotonin binding in the cortex (Semple et al., 1999). These changes may be related to the psychiatric and cognitive effects of MDMA use, including memory disturbances (Wareing et al., 2000) and depression (Sumnall and Cole, 2005).

Drug Abuse Is Pervasive

Substance abuse and addiction have become a social problem that afflicts many millions of people and disrupts the lives of their families, friends, and associates. Just one example reveals the extent of the problem: in the United States each year, more men and women die of smoking-related lung cancer than of colon, breast, and prostate cancers *combined*. In addition to the personal impact of so much illness and early death, there are dire social costs: huge expenses for medical and social services; millions of hours lost in the workplace; elevated rates of crime associated with illicit drugs; and scores of children who are damaged by their parents' substance abuse behavior, in the uterine environment as well as in the childhood home. In the discussion that follows, we will examine the mechanisms of drug abuse, the different approaches to understanding drug abuse, how individuals vary in their vulnerability to drug abuse, and how drug abuse can be prevented and treated.

The mechanisms of drug abuse have been studied extensively

The self-administration of intoxicating substances is a behavior that we share with a variety of wild animals (R. K. Siegel, 1989). Although the claim that wild elephants get drunk by eating fermented fruit is almost certainly a myth, it is nevertheless true that elephants like drinking alcohol if it's provided to them (S. Morris et al., 2006). Furthermore, when elephants on game preserves are stressed by a reduction in their ability to range, they self-medicate by increasing their intake of alcohol. Similarly, intoxicating mushrooms are eaten by cattle, reindeer, and rabbits. And as we will see, in the lab it is relatively easy to get experimental animals to dose themselves with intoxicating substances.

Researchers have proposed numerous models of substance abuse and addiction that vary in their emphasis on physiological, behavioral, and environmental factors (M. Glantz and Pickens, 1992). We will focus primarily on addiction to cocaine, the opiate drugs (such as morphine and heroin), nicotine, and alcohol because these substances have been studied the most thoroughly. According to the 2005 National Survey of Drug Use and Health, some 22.2 million people in the United States alone suffer from substance-related disorders (Substance Abuse and Mental Health Services Administration, 2006). Worldwide, the number is probably in the hundreds of millions. Some terminology specific to substance dependence (addiction) and substance abuse is clarified in **Box 4.1**.

Because addictive substances are no exception to the general rule that drugs produce multiple effects, it is difficult to determine which mechanisms are most important in producing dependence. For example, we have already noted that cocaine has the following major characteristics: (1) it is a local anesthetic; (2) it produces intensely pleasurable feelings, so it is a rewarding agent; and (3) it is a psychomotor stimulant. The opiate drugs, like morphine and heroin, also produce intensely rewarding sensations, but they are depressants, not stimulants. Like cocaine, the opiates produce a strong physical dependence and powerful withdrawal

BOX 4.1 The Terminology of Substance-Related Disorders

For definitions of mental disorders, psychiatrists, psychologists, and neuroscientists rely on the *Diagnostic and Statistical Manual of Mental Disorders* (fourth edition, text revised), known as the *DSM IV-TR* (American Psychiatric Association, 2000). The *DSM IV-TR* provides descriptions of a spectrum of substance-related disorders. Within this category, **dependence** (commonly called *addiction*) is a more severe disorder than **substance abuse**.

The essential feature of dependence on psychoactive substances (e.g., alcohol, tobacco, cocaine, marijuana) is "a cluster of cognitive, behavioral, and physiological symptoms indicating that the individual continues use of the substance despite significant substance-related problems." To be diagnosed as dependent, a person must meet at least three of seven criteria relating to patterns of consumption, craving, expenditure of time and energy in serving the addiction, and impact on the other aspects of the person's life. Furthermore, once dependence has been diagnosed, it is placed on a scale ranging from mild to moderate to severe, depending on how many of the seven criteria have been met.

When the minimum criteria for dependence have not been met but there is evidence of maladaptive patterns of substance use that have persisted at least a month or have occurred repeatedly, the diagnosis is substance abuse. The following situations are examples in which a diagnosis of substance abuse is appropriate:

- A student has substance-related absences, suspensions, or expulsion from school.
- A person is repeatedly intoxicated with alcohol in situations that are hazardous—for example, when driving a car, operating machinery, or engaging in risky recreational activities such as swimming or rock climbing.
- A person has recurrent substance-related legal problems—for example, arrests for disorderly conduct, assault and battery, or driving under the influence.

dependence Also called *addiction*. The strong desire to self-administer a drug of abuse.

substance abuse A maladaptive pattern of substance use that has lasted more than a month but does not fully meet the criteria for dependence.

---

symptoms on cessation of use. But opiates tend to produce only tolerance, whereas at least some of the actions of cocaine induce sensitization. So a comprehensive theory of drug abuse and addiction must be able to account for dependence across a wide variety of compounds with very different effects.

Several perspectives help us understand drug abuse

Any comprehensive model of drug abuse has to answer several difficult questions: What social and environmental factors in a person's life cause her to start abusing a substance? What factors cause her to continue? What physiological mechanisms make a substance rewarding? What is addiction, physiologically and behaviorally, and why is it so hard to quit? The major models that we sketch here each address some but not all of these issues; an integrative approach that addresses the entire problem of substance abuse is an urgent but elusive goal.

THE MORAL MODEL   The earliest approach to explaining drug abuse was to simply blame the substance abuser for a lack of moral character or a lack of self-control. Explanations of this sort often have a religious character and hold that only divine help will free a person from addiction. Applications based on the moral model can be effective. For example, the temperance movement in the United States, beginning around the 1830s, is estimated to have cut per capita consumption of alcohol to about one-third its level in the period from 1800 to 1820 (Rorabaugh, 1976). However, the "Just Say No" campaign championed by former U.S. First Lady Nancy Reagan in the 1980s did not appear to significantly reduce drug abuse.

THE DISEASE MODEL   In this view, the person who abuses drugs requires medical treatment rather than moral exhortation or punishment. This view also justifies spending money to research drug abuse in the same way that money is spent to research other diseases. However, usually the term *disease* is reserved for a state in which we can identify an abnormal physical or biochemical condition. No abnormal physical or biochemical condition has been found in the case of drug addiction, although mounting evidence suggests that some people are genetically

dysphoria   Unpleasant feelings; the opposite of euphoria.

more susceptible to addiction than others. Nevertheless, this model continues to appeal to many, and an intensive effort is under way to identify the physiological "switch" that establishes addiction after exposure to a drug.

THE PHYSICAL DEPENDENCE MODEL   The physical dependence model, sometimes called the *withdrawal avoidance model*, is based on the unpleasant withdrawal symptoms that occur when a person stops taking a drug that he or she has used frequently. The specific withdrawal symptoms depend on the drug, but they are often the opposite of the effects produced by the drug itself. For example, the withdrawal symptoms of morphine include irritability, tremor, and elevated heart rate and blood pressure. Waves of goose bumps occur, and the skin resembles that of a plucked turkey, which is why abrupt withdrawal without any treatment is called *cold turkey*.

Whereas most drugs of abuse produce pleasurable feelings, withdrawal usually induces the opposite: **dysphoria**. Withdrawal symptoms can be suppressed quickly (within 15–20 minutes in the case of morphine) by administration of the withdrawn drug, or a related compound (e.g., heroin withdrawal symptoms can be attenuated by its chemical cousin methadone, which reduces cravings without providing much of a "high"). This model provides one explanation of why addicts work compulsively to get drugs: to avoid or overcome withdrawal effects. Withdrawal symptoms can develop rapidly; some teenagers experience withdrawal symptoms only 2 days after their first cigarette (DiFranza et al., 2007).

Because withdrawal symptoms are so striking, some investigators have proposed that development of dependence is the basic characteristic of addiction. But it is clear that people can become dependent on drugs even in the absence of clear physical withdrawal symptoms (Wise, 1996). Are these people *psychologically* addicted rather than *physically* addicted? So far, such a distinction seems irrelevant because either form of addiction can have disastrous, even fatal, consequences. Indeed, the entire theme of this book is that *psychological* processes all have a physical basis in the brain, which is just as real as the muscular contractions that produce shivering or nausea. Clearly, a better explanation is needed.

4.20 Experimental Setup for Self-Administration of a Drug by an Animal   Here a computer is programmed to administer a small dose of the drug under study after a certain number of lever presses. The number of lever presses that the animal will perform to receive a drug is a measure of the rewarding properties and addictive potential of that drug; lab animals will press the lever many thousands of times to receive a single small dose of highly addictive compounds like cocaine and methamphetamine.

THE POSITIVE REWARD MODEL   The positive reward model of addictive behavior arose from animal research that was started in the 1950s (McKim, 1991). Before that time, researchers believed that animals could not become addicted to drugs, thinking (incorrectly) that animals were not capable of learning an association between the time a drug is injected and the onset of its effects. The subsequent development of a drug self-administration apparatus (**Figure 4.20**) made it possible to quantify the motivation of animals to consume drugs.

From the outset, it was clear that morphine-dependent rats or monkeys would quickly learn to repeatedly press a lever in order to receive a small morphine injection (T. Thompson and Schuster, 1964). The drug infusion therefore acted like any other experimental reward, such as food or water. Furthermore, even animals that are not already morphine-dependent learn to press a lever for morphine, and they will happily self-administer doses of morphine that are so low that no physical dependence ever develops (Schuster, 1970). Animals will also furiously press a lever to self-administer cocaine and other stimulants that do not produce withdrawal symptoms as marked as those that opiates produce (Koob, 1995; Pickens and Thompson, 1968; Tanda et al., 2000). In fact, cocaine supports some of the highest rates of lever pressing ever recorded.

These and other studies contradict the assumptions of both the disease model and the physical dependence model of drug addiction. Although physical dependence may be an important factor in the consumption of some drugs, it is not necessary for self-administration and cannot serve as the sole explanation for drug addiction. Furthermore, these studies indicate that drug self-administration can be interpreted as a behavior controlled by positive rewards (operant conditioning theory; see Box 17.1), without the need to implicate a disease process.

Many addictive drugs cause the release of dopamine in the **nucleus accumbens**, just like more-conventional rewards, such as food, sex, or winning money (D'Ardenne et al., 2008; Di Chiara et al., 1999); interestingly, dopamine release is also linked to pathological gambling (Dodd et al., 2005; Reuter et al., 2005). As we mentioned previously, dopamine released from axons originating from the ventral tegmental area (VTA), part of the mesolimbocortical dopaminergic pathway illustrated in Figure 4.3, has been widely implicated in the perception of reward (**Figure 4.21**). If the dopaminergic pathway from the VTA to the nucleus accumbens serves as a reward system for a wide variety of experiences, then the addictive power of drugs may come from their artificial stimulation of this pathway. When the drug "hijacks" this system, providing unnaturally powerful reinforcement, the user learns to associate the drug-taking behavior with that pleasure and begins seeking out drugs more and more until life's other pleasures fade into the background.

Exposure to cocaine produces long-lasting changes in dopaminergic circuitry (Dalley et al., 2007; Volkow et al., 2006), as well as other neurotransmitter systems

nucleus accumbens A region of the forebrain that receives dopaminergic innervation from the ventral tegmental area.

(a)

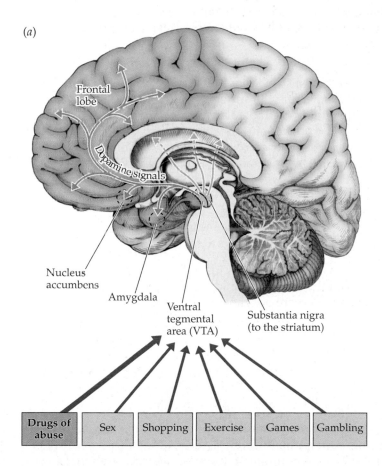

(b)

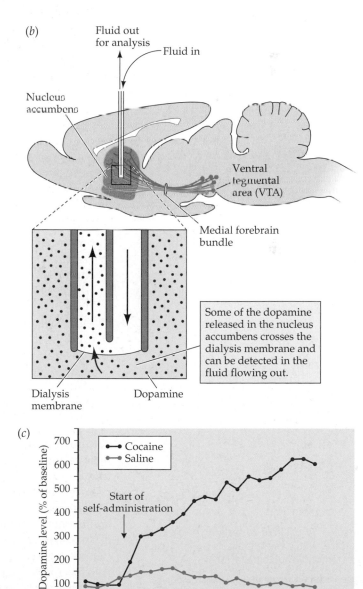

4.21 A Neural Pathway Implicated in Drug Abuse   (a) A variety of different behaviors, including sexual behavior, gambling and video game playing, normally activate the dopaminergic pathway that produces the experience of pleasure. Drugs of abuse exert a particularly strong influence on this system, and may eclipse other sources of pleasure. (b) The microdialysis technique makes use of a small, permanently implanted probe to monitor neurochemical changes in awake, behaving animals. The microdialysis probe inserted into the nucleus accumbens detects increased dopamine release in response to drug administration. (c) Dopamine levels in the nucleus accumbens rise sharply in rats during self-administration (begins at arrow) of cocaine. (Part c after Pettit and Justice, 1991.)

in the nucleus accumbens (K. L. Conrad et al., 2008; D. L. Graham et al., 2007), which seems to further augment the pleasure associated with drugs while decreasing the pleasure experienced from other behaviors. The drug's "pathological" reinforcement of associated behaviors leads to exclusive, compulsive drug seeking.

People suffering damage to a brain region tucked within the frontal cortex called the **insula** (Latin for "island") were able to effortlessly quit smoking (Naqvi et al., 2007), indicating that this brain region is also involved in addiction. The reciprocal connections between the VTA and the insula (Oades and Halliday, 1987) suggest that these two regions normally interact to mediate addiction.

People differ in their vulnerability to drug abuse

Not everyone who uses an addictive drug becomes addicted. For example, very, very few hospitalized patients treated with opiates for pain relief go on to abuse opiates after leaving the hospital (Brownlee and Schrof, 1997). Of Vietnam War veterans who had used heroin overseas, only a minority relapsed to dependence within 3 years after their return (Robins and Slobodyan, 2003). The individual and environmental factors that account for this differential susceptibility are the subject of active investigation (M. Glantz and Pickens, 1992; Karch, 2006); they fall into several general categories:

- *Biological factors.* Sex is a significant variable; males are more likely to abuse drugs than are females. There is also evidence for genetic predisposition. For example, having a biological parent who suffers from alcoholism makes drug abuse more likely, even for children adopted away soon after birth (Cadoret et al., 1986). A tendency to use opiates and cocaine also appears to be heritable (Kendler et al., 2000), and adolescents carrying a specific version of the gene for a specific serotonin transporter are more likely to abuse drugs (Caspi et al., 2003). Interestingly, living with two actively involved parents (regularly interacting with the child, involved in the child's school and after-school activities) reduces this risk for the gene carriers (Brody et al., 2009).
- *Family situation.* Family breakup, a poor relationship with parents, or the presence of an antisocial sibling are associated with drug abuse.
- *Personal characteristics.* Certain traits, such as aggressiveness and poor emotional control, are especially associated with drug abuse. Strong educational goals and maturity are associated with lower likelihood of drug abuse.
- *Environmental factors.* A high prevalence of drug use in the community, and especially in the peer group, predisposes an individual toward drug abuse. The effect of social factors is particularly marked with respect to the incidence of smoking: although seven of ten adult smokers in the United States say they want to quit, their success in doing so directly correlates with race, educational status, and whether their peers have also stopped smoking.

It is now clear that environmental stimuli—locations, social settings, sensory stimuli, and so on—can rapidly become strongly associated with the subjective effects of abused substances. These environmental stimuli can then become risk factors for deepening addiction or relapse: simply being in a setting where a person previously used drugs can trigger drug craving in that person (O'Brien et al., 1998). This phenomenon, termed **cue-induced drug use**, is not limited to longer-term users; in rats, exposure to environmental stimuli that were present *during their very first cocaine treatment* effectively and persistently cue drug-seeking behavior later (Ciccocioppo et al., 2004). Cue-induced drug use may be controlled by the central nucleus of the amygdala (Lu et al., 2005, 2006).

The greater the number of risk factors that apply, the more likely an individual will develop a substance abuse disorder (Brook et al., 1992). Furthermore, these risk factors do not necessarily operate independently; in some cases they interact to produce a more severe addiction that is resistant to interventions.

insula A region of cortex lying below the surface, within the lateral sulcus, of the frontal, temporal, and parietal lobes.

cue-induced drug use An increased likelihood to use a drug (especially an addictive drug) because of the presence of environmental stimuli that were present during previous use of the same drug.

Drug use, abuse, and dependence can be prevented or treated in multiple ways

Given the health and social costs of substance abuse, the development of effective treatment programs is a pressing concern. Many of those who become dependent are able to overcome their addiction without outside help: more than 90% of ex-smokers and about half of those who recover from alcoholism appear to have quit on their own (S. Cohen et al., 1989; Institute of Medicine, 1990). For those who require medical intervention, several categories of medication are available, including the following:

- *Drugs for detoxification.* For example, benzodiazepines and drugs that suppress central adrenergic activity (e.g., clonidine) help reduce withdrawal symptoms during the early drug-free period.
- *Agonist or partial agonist analogs of the addictive drug.* Analogs partially activate the same mechanisms that the addictive drug activates, to help wean the individual. For example, the opioid receptor agonist methadone reduces heroin appetite and lessens withdrawal symptoms; similarly, nicotine patches provide reduced doses of the addictive compound, without the other harmful components of cigarette smoke.
- *Antagonists to the addictive drug.* Specific antagonists block the effects of an abused drug (e.g., the opiate antagonist naloxone blocks heroin's actions), but they also may produce harsh withdrawal symptoms.
- Antabuse) accumulate acetaldehyde, a toxic metabolite of alcohol that can be quite unpleasant. Drinking then produces illness that counteracts the rewarding aspects of alcohol abuse.
- *Reward-blocking medications.* Researchers are looking at ways to block the positive reward associated with drugs of abuse, primarily by using dopamine receptor blockers to reduce the activity of the mesolimbocortical dopamine reward system that we discussed earlier. One problem with this approach is the tendency of treatments to produce a generalized loss of pleasurable feelings.
- *Anticraving medications.* These medications reduce the appetite for the abused substance; for example, naltrexone (trade name ReVia) blocks the rewarding aspects of consuming alcohol or other abused substances in some people, and acamprosate (trade name Campral) eases alcohol-associated withdrawal symptoms.
- *Immunization.* Vaccines against such drugs as cocaine, heroin, and nicotine have been developed and are being tested (Kosten and Owens, 2005; Maurer and Bachmann, 2007). Here the strategy is to prompt the individual's immune system to produce antibodies that remove the targeted drugs from circulation before they ever reach the brain.

No single approach appears to be uniformly effective, and rates of relapse remain high. Research breakthroughs are therefore badly needed.

SUMMARY

Many Chemical Neurotransmitters Have Been Identified

- The major categories of neurotransmitters are **amine, amino acid, peptide**, and soluble gas neurotransmitters. **Review Table 4.1, Web Activity 4.1**
- Because many drugs work by acting on **receptor molecules**, investigators search for the receptor molecules and for the **endogenous** substances that work on the receptors. A given

neurotransmitter may normally bind several different subtypes of receptors. **Review Figure 4.1**

- A **ligand** is any substance that binds to a receptor. **Agonists** activate transmitter pathways, **antagonists** block transmitter pathways, and **inverse agonists** have active effects that are opposite to a transmitter's normal effects. **Review Web Activity 4.2**

Neurotransmitter Systems Form a Complex Array in the Brain

■ The classic neurotransmitters are found in segregated regions that project widely throughout the brain. **Review Figures 4.2 – 4.5, Web Activity 4.3**

Research on Drugs Ranges from Molecular Processes to Effects on Behavior

■ Drugs vary in their **binding affinity** for different types of receptors, as well as in **efficacy**—their ability to produce effects—once they are bound. **Review Figure 4.6**

■ The relationship between concentrations of a drug and its physiological effects is formally studied by use of a **dose-response curve**. Dose-response relationships reveal a drug's activity, specificity, potency, and safety. **Review Figure 4.8**

■ Repeated treatments with a drug can produce tolerance to its effects, often through the **up-** or **down-regulation** of receptors. This compensatory mechanism is responsible for withdrawal symptoms. However, repeated use of some drugs produces **sensitization**, in which the drug's effects increase with use of the same dosage.

Drugs Affect Each Stage of Neural Conduction and Synaptic Transmission

■ Most CNS drugs alter neural transmission, such as by inhibiting axonal transport, affecting transmitter **reuptake**, or acting on postsynaptic receptors. **Neuromodulators** such as **caffeine** may affect the release of the transmitter or the receptor's response to the transmitter. **Review Figure 4.9**

Drugs That Affect the Brain Can Be Divided into Functional Classes

■ Effective drug treatments revolutionized the management of schizophrenia. Most **antipsychotic** medications block **dopamine** D_2 receptors, but some also block **serotonin** receptors. **Review Figure 4.10**

■ The main categories of antidepressants are **MAO** inhibitors, **tricyclics**, and **selective serotonin reuptake inhibitors**. All share the basic action of increasing the availability of monoamine transmitters in synapses.

■ Substances that are used to combat anxiety, such as the **benzodiazepines**, are called **anxiolytic** drugs. The benzodiazepines synergize the activity of the inhibitory transmitter **GABA** at some of its receptors. **Review Figure 4.11**

■ Alcohol acts on GABA receptors to produce some of its effects. Alcohol in moderation has beneficial effects; but in higher doses it is very harmful, damaging neurons in many areas of the brain. **Review Figure 4.12**

■ Opiates are potent painkillers; endogenous opioids include the **endorphins**, and exogenous opiates include **morphine** and **heroin**.

■ The active ingredient in **marijuana**, THC, acts on cannabinoid receptors to produce its effects. An endogenous cannabinoid, **anandamide**, serves as a **retrograde transmitter** in some synapses. **Review Figure 4.16**

■ Some stimulants, such as **nicotine**, imitate an excitatory synaptic transmitter. Others, such as **amphetamine**, cause the release of excitatory synaptic transmitters and block the reuptake of transmitters. Still others, such as **caffeine**, block the activity of an inhibitory **neuromodulator**.

■ Some drugs are called hallucinogens because they alter sensory perception and produce peculiar experiences. Different hallucinogens act on different kinds of synaptic receptors, and it is not yet clear what causes the hallucinogenic effects.

Drug Abuse Is Pervasive

■ Drug abuse and addiction are being studied intensively, and several models have been proposed: the moral model, the disease model, the physical dependence model, and the positive reward model. **Review Figure 4.21**

■ People differ in their vulnerability to drug abuse according to several factors: genetic predisposition, personality characteristics, and family and social context. Environmental stimuli can be associated with drug effects and potently cue subsequent drug use.

■ There are several medicinal approaches to treating drug addiction, including antiwithdrawal and anticraving medication and immunization.

Go to www.biopsychology.com for study questions, quizzes, key terms, and other resources.

Recommended Reading

Cooper, J. R., Bloom, F. E., and Roth, R. H. (2002). *The biochemical basis of neuropharmacology* (8th ed.). New York: Oxford University Press.

Grilly, D. M. (2005). *Drugs and human behavior* (5th ed.). Boston: Allyn & Bacon.

Julien, R. J. (2007). *A primer of drug action* (11th ed.). New York: Worth.

Karch, S. B. (2006). *Drug abuse handbook* (2nd ed.). Boca Raton, FL: CRC Press.

Meyer, J. S., and Quenzer, L. F. (2005). *Psychopharmacology: Drugs, the brain, and behavior.* Sunderland, MA: Sinauer.

Schatzberg, A. F., and Nemeroff, C. B. (Eds.). (2004). *Textbook of psychopharmacology.* Arlington, VA: American Psychiatric Publishing.

Thombs, D. L. (2006). *Introduction to addictive behaviors* (3rd ed.). New York: Guilford.

CHAPTER 5

Hormones and the Brain

Life-Threatening Lethargy

"Chuck's" mother finally became frightened and called 911. She told the emergency room staff that her son, a man in his 50s, had been lying on the sofa for weeks, watching TV and refusing to get up or do much else. He was sleepy most of the time, forgot appointments, and failed to finish chores that he started. This situation may sound familiar, but additional observations suggested that Chuck's problem was more than depression or mere laziness. His speech was slurred, his movements and heart rate were slow, and his cognitive abilities were so compromised that he couldn't name the month or the current president. In counting backward from 100 by sevens, he stalled at 93.

Chuck denied using drugs recreationally, and although he recalled taking an unknown medication previously, he was not currently taking any prescription drugs. Blood tests indicated no alcohol and no chronic infections that would affect the brain; MRI scans found no signs of stroke, tumor, or trauma. In the end, his diagnosis was suggested by one of the simplest and most familiar of tests: the knee jerk reflex in response to the tap of a rubber mallet. Chuck's knee jerk reflex was abnormally slow. A mysterious process appeared to be impeding the flow of information in his neurons, not only in the knee jerk circuitry but also, by extension, in the rest of his nervous system (Jauhar, 2003).

What was wrong with Chuck?

The cells in our body use chemicals to communicate, including an extensive array of hormones. Changes in hormone levels can produce striking changes in brain function. Cognitive abilities, emotions, our appetite for food or drink or sex, our aggressiveness or submissiveness, our care for children—the scope of hormonal influences on behavior is vast. Furthermore, hormones do more than influence adult behavior. Early in life, thyroid and sex hormones regulate brain development. Later in life, the changing outputs of endocrine glands and the body's changing sensitivity to hormones are prominent aspects of adolescence and aging.

In this chapter we consider the major hormones, their anatomical sources, their physiological actions, and their effects on behavior. This discussion sets the stage for topics in later chapters, such as hormonal effects in reproductive behavior (Chapter 12); feeding, drinking, and body maintenance (Chapter 13); and stress and emotion (Chapter 15).

Hormones Act in a Great Variety of Ways throughout the Body

Hormones (from the Greek *horman*, "to excite") are chemicals secreted by one group of cells and carried through the bloodstream to other parts of the body, where they act on specific target tissues to produce specific physiological effects. Many hormones are produced by **endocrine glands** (from the Greek *endon*, "within," and *krinein*, "to secrete"), so called because they release their hormones within the body.

hormone A chemical secreted by an endocrine gland that is conveyed by the bloodstream and regulates target organs or tissues.

endocrine gland A gland that secretes products into the bloodstream to act on distant targets.

exocrine gland A gland whose secretions exit the body via ducts.

castration Removal of the gonads, usually the testes.

Endocrine glands are sometimes contrasted with **exocrine glands** (tear glands, salivary glands, sweat glands), which use ducts to secrete fluid outside the body (the Greek *exo* means "out").

Our current understanding of hormones developed in stages

There's no doubt that the importance of hormones in various domains was anticipated in ancient civilization. In the fourth century BCE, Aristotle accurately described the effects of **castration** (removal of the testes) in birds, and he compared the behavioral and bodily effects with those seen in eunuchs (castrated men). Some cultures considered endocrine glands to have special medicinal properties: by 100 ACE, Chinese scholars recommended eating dog testes to combat impotence. Perhaps this practice built on prehistoric agricultural knowledge of the effects of castration on domestic livestock. Although no one knew what mechanism was involved, clearly the testes were important for the reproductive capacity and sexual characteristics of males.

The ancient Greeks emphasized body *humors*, or fluids, as an explanation of temperament and emotions. It was believed that these fluids—phlegm, blood, black bile, and yellow bile (also known as *choler*)—all interacted to produce health or disease. The notion of body fluids as the basis of human temperament lingers in our language in many now seldom-used terms, such as *phlegmatic* ("sluggish"), *sanguine* ("cheerful"; *sanguis* is Latin for "blood"), *bilious* ("irritable"), and *choleric* ("hot-tempered") to describe personalities. We routinely refer to other people as *good-humored* or *ill-humored*.

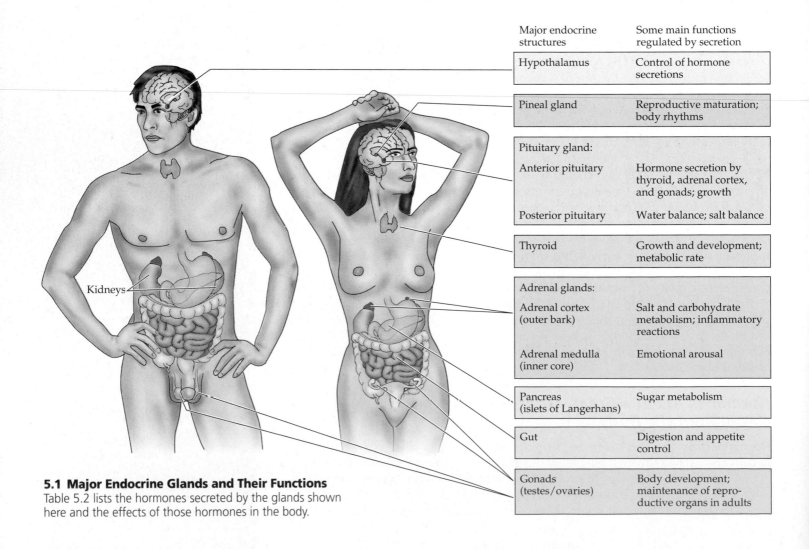

Major endocrine structures	Some main functions regulated by secretion
Hypothalamus	Control of hormone secretions
Pineal gland	Reproductive maturation; body rhythms
Pituitary gland:	
Anterior pituitary	Hormone secretion by thyroid, adrenal cortex, and gonads; growth
Posterior pituitary	Water balance; salt balance
Thyroid	Growth and development; metabolic rate
Adrenal glands:	
Adrenal cortex (outer bark)	Salt and carbohydrate metabolism; inflammatory reactions
Adrenal medulla (inner core)	Emotional arousal
Pancreas (islets of Langerhans)	Sugar metabolism
Gut	Digestion and appetite control
Gonads (testes/ovaries)	Body development; maintenance of reproductive organs in adults

Kidneys

5.1 Major Endocrine Glands and Their Functions
Table 5.2 lists the hormones secreted by the glands shown here and the effects of those hormones in the body.

Today we know there are many more than four hormones. Endocrine glands come in a variety of sizes, shapes, and locations in the body (**Figure 5.1**). Although the endocrine glands and their hormones are important, the definition of *hormone* is more inclusive than it used to be, reflecting the recognition that other tissues, such as the heart and kidneys, secrete hormones too. Even plants, which have no endocrine glands, use chemical signals that are considered to be hormones. We'll see that sometimes hormones can sometimes also act more locally, without traveling through the bloodstream, to affect other cells.

The first major endocrine experiment was carried out in 1849 by German physician Arnold Adolph Berthold (1803–1861), most likely replicating unpublished studies performed by John Hunter in England some 80 years previously (Sawin, 1996). When roosters are castrated as juveniles, they fail to develop normal reproductive behavior and secondary sexual characteristics, such as the rooster's comb, in adulthood (**Figure 5.2**). Berthold observed, however, that placing one testis into the body cavity of these young castrates could preserve normal development of adult anatomy and behavior. These animals began crowing and showed the usual male sexual behaviors. Because the nerve supply to the testis had not been reestablished, Berthold concluded that the testes release a chemical into the blood that affects both male behavior and male body structures. Today we know that the testes make and release the hormone testosterone, which exerts these effects.

Although Berthold didn't know it, experiments like this also illustrate another distinction in hormone action. If he had waited until the castrated chicks were adults before transplanting the testes, Berthold would have seen little effect. The testosterone must be present *early* in life to have such dramatic effects on the body

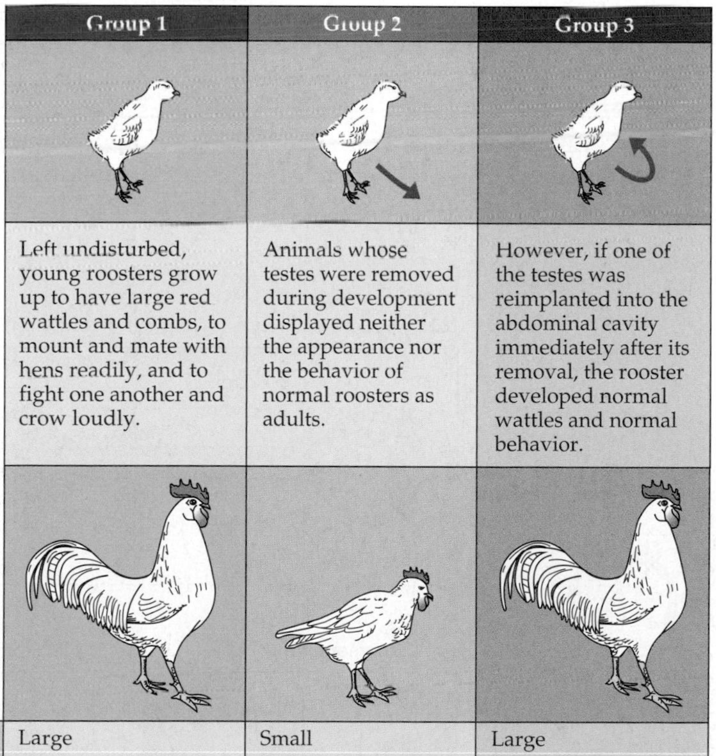

	Group 1	Group 2	Group 3
	Left undisturbed, young roosters grow up to have large red wattles and combs, to mount and mate with hens readily, and to fight one another and crow loudly.	Animals whose testes were removed during development displayed neither the appearance nor the behavior of normal roosters as adults.	However, if one of the testes was reimplanted into the abdominal cavity immediately after its removal, the rooster developed normal wattles and normal behavior.
Comb and wattles:	Large	Small	Large
Mount hens?	Yes	No	Yes
Aggressive?	Yes	No	Yes
Crowing?	Normal	Weak	Normal

Conclusion
Because the reimplanted testis in group 3 was in an abnormal body site, disconnected from normal innervation, and yet still affected development, Berthold reasoned that the testes release a chemical signal, which we would call a hormone, that has widespread effects.

5.2 The First Experiment in Behavioral Endocrinology   Berthold's nineteenth-century experiment demonstrated the importance of hormones for behavior.

endocrine Referring to glands that release chemicals to the interior of the body. These glands secrete the principal hormones.

neurocrine Referring to secretory functions of neurons, especially pertaining to synaptic transmission.

autocrine Referring to a signal that is secreted by a cell into its environment and that feeds back to the same cell.

paracrine Referring to cellular communication in which a chemical signal diffuses to nearby target cells through the intermediate extracellular space.

pheromone A chemical signal that is released outside the body of an animal and affects other members of the same species.

and behavior. We say that the brain and body are "organized" by exposure to hormones early in life, and sometimes these changes can be dramatic and long-lasting. If you wait until adulthood to provide hormones, they still affect the body and behavior, but the changes are less dramatic and tend to be short-lived. In that case, the hormones are said to "activate" behavior. We discuss organizational and activational effects of hormones in more detail in Chapter 12.

Organisms use several types of chemical communication

By reviewing the several categories of chemical signals used by the body, we can see how hormonal communication by endocrine glands compares to other methods of communication:

- *Endocrine communication.* In **endocrine** communication, our topic for this chapter, the chemical signal is a hormone released into the bloodstream to selectively affect distant target organs (**Figure 5.3a**).
- *Synaptic communication.* This form of communication was described in Chapters 3 and 4. In synaptic transmission (sometimes called **neurocrine** function), the released chemical signal diffuses across the synaptic cleft and causes a change in the postsynaptic membrane (**Figure 5.3b**). Typically, synaptic transmitter function is highly localized.
- *Autocrine communication.* In **autocrine** communication, a released chemical acts on the releasing cell itself and thereby affects its own activity (**Figure 5.3c**). For example, it is common for a neuron to contain autoreceptors that detect neurotransmitter molecules released by that neuron; the cell can thus monitor its own activity. In this case, the neurotransmitter serves both an autocrine and a synaptic communication function.
- *Paracrine communication.* In **paracrine** communication, the released chemical signal diffuses to nearby target cells (**Figure 5.3d**). The strongest impact is on the nearest cells.
- *Pheromone communication.* Chemicals can be used for communication not only within an individual, but also between individuals. **Pheromones** (from the Greek *pherein*, "to carry") are released into the outside environment to affect other individuals of the same species (**Figure 5.3e**). For example, ants produce

5.3 Chemical Communication Systems

(a) Endocrine function

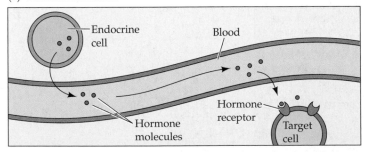

(b) Neurocrine function (synaptic transmission)

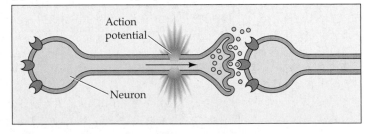

(c) Autocrine function

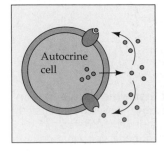

(d) Paracrine function

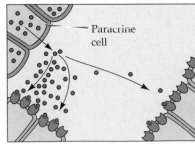

(e) Pheromone function

(f) Allomone function

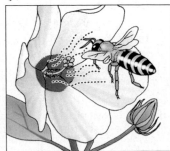

HORMONES AND THE BRAIN   **121**

5.4 Scents and Sensibility Skunks produce a very effective allomone.

pheromones that communicate the presence of intruders in the nest, or that identify the route to a rich food source (to the annoyance of picnickers). Dogs and wolves urinate on landmarks to designate their territory; other members of the species smell the pheromones in the urine and either respect or challenge the territory. In Chapters 9 and 12 we'll discuss pheromones in more detail.

- *Allomone communication.* Some chemical signals are released by members of one species to affect the behavior of individuals of another species. These substances are called **allomones** (from the Greek *allos*, "other") (**Figures 5.3f and 5.4**). Flowers exude scented allomones to attract insects and birds in order to distribute pollen. And the bolas spider—nature's femme fatale—releases a moth sex pheromone to attract male moths to their doom (Eberhard, 1977; Haynes et al., 2002).

Hormone actions can be organized according to nine general principles

Although there are some exceptions, the following nine rules are general principles of hormone action:

1. Hormones frequently act in a *gradual* fashion, activating behavioral and physiological responses hours or weeks after entering the bloodstream. The changes may persist for days, weeks, or years after hormone release is over.
2. When hormones alter behavior, they tend to act by changing the intensity or probability of evoked behaviors, rather than acting as a switch to turn behaviors on or off regardless of context.
3. Both the quantities and the types of hormones released are influenced by environmental factors. Therefore, *the relationship between behavior and hormones is clearly reciprocal;* that is, hormones change behaviors and behaviors change hormone levels. For example, high levels of testosterone are related to aggression, and in some species, males who lose in aggressive encounters show a reduction in testosterone levels, while the winners in these bouts show little change in testosterone levels. This example illustrates the reciprocal relation between behavioral and somatic (body) events that we discussed in Chapter 1 (see Figure 1.2).
4. A hormone may have multiple effects on different cells, organs, and behaviors; conversely, a single type of behavior or physiological change can be affected by many different hormones (**Figure 5.5**).
5. Hormones are produced in small amounts and often are secreted in bursts. This *pulsatile* secretion pattern is sometimes crucial for the small amount of hormone to be effective.
6. The levels of many hormones vary rhythmically throughout the day, and many hormonal systems are controlled by circadian "clocks" in the brain, as we'll see in Chapter 14.
7. Hormones interact; the effects of one hormone can be markedly changed by the actions of another hormone.
8. The chemical structure of a given hormone is similar in all vertebrates, but the *functions* served by that hormone can vary across species.
9. Hormones can affect only cells possessing receptor proteins that recognize the hormone and alter cell function.

allomone A chemical signal that is released outside the body by one species and affects the behavior of other species.

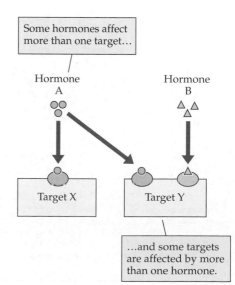

Some hormones affect more than one target…

Hormone A

Hormone B

Target X

Target Y

…and some targets are affected by more than one hormone.

5.5 The Multiplicity of Hormone Action A single hormone (hormone A in this illustration) may affect multiple target tissues in various locations throughout the body. Similarly, a single process or body organ (target Y here) may be sensitive to several hormones.

Neural and hormonal communications are similar in some ways and different in others

Neurotransmission—chemical communication between neurons—and hormonal communication are both secretory events, and they seem similar in several ways (**Figure 5.6**). For example, the neuron produces particular transmitter chemicals and stores them for later release, just as an endocrine gland stores its hormones for secretion. Another similarity between the two systems is that both neurotransmitters and hormones, upon binding to receptor molecules on the cell surface, often activate **second messengers** within the target cell to bring about changes in metabolism, membrane potentials, and other cellular functions. Moreover, the same chemicals act as second messengers in both the nervous and the endocrine systems.

Similarities between neuronal and hormonal communication are especially exemplified by the **neurosecretory** (or **neuroendocrine**) **cells** of the hypothalamus (see Figure 5.6c). These cells are neurons in almost every way except at their axon terminals, where instead of releasing transmitter into a synapse, they release hormones into the bloodstream. It is thus difficult to draw a firm line between neurons and endocrine cells. Indeed, some peptide hormones and **neuropeptides** (peptides used by neurons) are also found in single-celled organisms, suggesting that the nervous system and the endocrine system may share an evolutionary origin from chemical communication systems in our remote single-celled ancestors (LeRoith et al., 1992). Some investigators believe that the first endocrine glands may have been modified neurosecretory cells (Norman and Litwack, 1987).

Despite the many similarities between neural and hormonal communication, the two systems differ in five basic ways:

second messenger   A slow-acting substance in a target cell that amplifies the effects of synaptic or hormonal activity and regulates activity within the target cell.

neurosecretory cell or neuroendocrine cell   A neuron that releases hormones into local or systemic circulation.

neuropeptide   Also called *peptide neurotransmitter*.   A peptide that is used by neurons for signaling.

neuromodulator   A substance that influences the activity of synaptic transmitters.

1. *Neural communication* works somewhat like a telephone system: messages travel over fixed channels to precise destinations. The anatomical connections between neurons determine the source and destination of information. In contrast, *hormonal communication* works more like a radio broadcasting system: many different endocrine messages spread throughout the body and can then be picked up by scattered cells that have receptors for them.

2. Whereas neural messages are rapid and are measured in milliseconds, hormonal messages are slower and are measured in seconds and minutes. This distinction is blurred sometimes: **neuromodulators** alter the reactivity of cells to specific transmitters (see Chapter 4), acting more slowly and having a longer-lasting effect than neurotrans-

(*a*) Neurocrine communication (synaptic transmission)

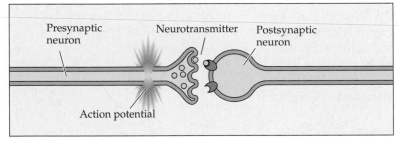

(*b*) Endocrine communication

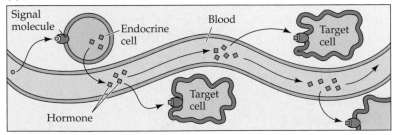

(*c*) Neuroendocrine communication

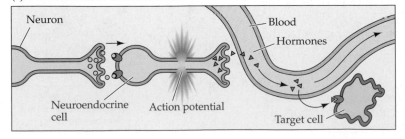

5.6 Neuroendocrine Cells Blend Neuronal and Endocrine Mechanisms   (*a*) Neurons can communicate only with the particular neurons, muscle cells, or glands on which they synapse. The target cell is determined by the synaptic anatomy. (*b*) Endocrine signals are transmitted through the bloodstream and are recognized by appropriate receptors wherever they occur in the body. (*c*) Neuroendocrine (neurosecretory) cells are the interface between neurons and endocrine glands. They receive synaptic signals from other neurons, yet secrete a hormone into the bloodstream. In this way electrical signals are converted into hormonal signals.

mitters have. So neuromodulators are something of a blend of neurotransmitter (because they're released into synapses) and hormone (because they act gradually).

3. The distance traveled by the chemical messengers differs enormously in the two cases; the synaptic cleft is only about 30 nm wide, but hormones may travel more than a meter to reach the target organ.
4. Most neural messages are *digital*, consisting of sequences of all-or-none action potentials. Hormonal messages are *analog*—that is, graded in strength.
5. Neural and hormonal communication also differs in terms of voluntary control. You cannot consciously change the secretion of hormones in the way that you can voluntarily lift your arm, blink your eyelids, or perform many other acts under neuromuscular control. This distinction between neural and hormonal systems, however, is not absolute. The autonomic nervous system regulates many activities—such as heart rate or intestinal action—but is not generally subject to conscious control.

Hormones can be classified by chemical structure

Most hormones fall into one of three categories: protein hormones, amine hormones, or steroid hormones. Like any other protein, a **protein hormone** is composed of a string of amino acids (**Figure 5.7a**). (Recall that a peptide is simply a small protein—i.e., a short string of amino acids.) Different protein hormones consist of different combinations of amino acids. **Amine hormones** are smaller and simpler, consisting of a modified version of a single amino acid (hence their alias, *monoamine* hormones) (**Figure 5.7b**). **Steroid hormones** are derivatives of cholesterol and thus share its structure of four rings of carbon atoms (**Figure 5.7c**). Different steroid hormones vary in the number and kinds of atoms attached to the rings. Steroids dissolve readily in lipids, so they can pass through membranes easily (recall from Chapter 2 that the cell membrane is a lipid bilayer).

The distinction between protein or amine hormones and steroid hormones is important because these hormone classes interact with different types of receptor mechanisms. **Table 5.1** gives examples of each class of hormones.

Hormones Act on a Wide Variety of Cellular Mechanisms

In later chapters we will be considering the effects of specific hormones on behavior. In preparation for that discussion, let's look briefly at three aspects of hormonal

protein hormones Also called *peptide hormones*. A class of hormones, molecules of which consist of a string of amino acids.

amine hormones Also called *monoamine hormones*. A class of hormones, each composed of a single amino acid that has been modified into a related molecule, such as melatonin or epinephrine.

steroid hormones A class of hormones, each of which is composed of four interconnected rings of carbon atoms.

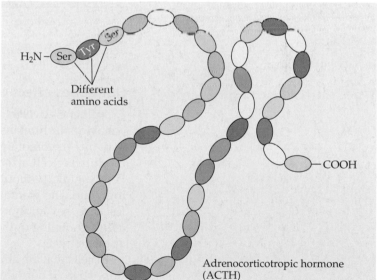

5.7 Chemical Structures of the Three Main Hormone Types (a) Protein hormones consist of strings of amino acids. If the string is short, as it is in adrenocorticotropic hormone (ACTH), it may be referred to as a *peptide hormone*. (b) Amine hormones, such as thyroxine, are modified single amino acids. (c) Steroid hormones, such as estradiol, are derived from cholesterol and consist of four interconnected rings of carbon atoms, to which are attached different numbers and types of atoms.

TABLE 5.1 Examples of Major Classes of Hormones

Class	Hormone
Protein hormones	Adrenocorticotropic hormone (ACTH)
	Follicle-stimulating hormone (FSH)
	Luteinizing hormone (LH)
	Thyroid-stimulating hormone (TSH)
	Growth hormone (GH)
	Prolactin
	Insulin
	Glucagon
	Oxytocin
	Vasopressin (arginine vasopressin, AVP; antidiuretic hormone, ADH)
	Releasing hormones, such as:
	Corticotropin-releasing hormone (CRH)
	Gonadotropin-releasing hormone (GnRH)
Amine hormones	Epinephrine (adrenaline)
	Norepinephrine (NE)
	Thyroid hormones
	Melatonin
Steroid hormones	Estrogens (e.g., estradiol)
	Progestins (e.g., progesterone)
	Androgens (e.g., testosterone, dihydrotestosterone)
	Glucocorticoids (e.g., cortisol)
	Mineralocorticoids (e.g., aldosterone)

activity: the effects of hormones on cells, the mechanisms by which hormones exercise these effects, and the regulation of hormone secretion.

Hormones affect cells by influencing their growth and activity

By influencing cells in various tissues and organs, hormones affect many everyday behaviors in humans and other animals. Hormones exert these far-reaching effects by (1) promoting the proliferation, growth, and differentiation of cells; and (2) modulating cell activity. Hormones shape many processes during development. For example, without thyroid hormones, fewer cells are produced in the developing brain, and mental development is stunted. Later in development, during adolescence, sex hormones cause secondary sexual characteristics to appear: breasts and broadening of the hips in women, facial hair and enlargement of the Adam's apple in men.

In cells that are already differentiated, hormones can modulate the rate of function. Thyroid hormones and insulin, for instance, regulate the metabolic activity of most of the cells in the human body. Other hormones modulate activity in certain types of cells. For example, luteinizing hormone (a hormone from the anterior pituitary gland) promotes the secretion of sex hormones by the testes and ovaries.

Hormones initiate actions by binding to receptor molecules

The three classes of hormones exert their influences on target organs in two different ways:

1. Protein and amine hormones bind to specific receptors (proteins that recognize only one hormone or class of hormones) that are usually found *on the surface* of target cell membranes and, when stimulated by the appropriate hormone,

cause the release of a second messenger inside the cell. (As we saw in Chapter 3, the release of a second messenger can also be caused by some synaptic transmitters.) Protein and amine hormones exert their effects by using this mechanism to alter proteins and processes within the target cell.

2. As we mentioned earlier, steroid hormones easily pass through cell membranes, so they generally bind to specific receptor proteins located *inside* the cell. The steroid-receptor complex binds to specific regions of the DNA in the nucleus of the cell, where it acts as a **transcription factor**, controlling the expression of specific genes, and thereby increasing or decreasing the rate of protein production (see the Appendix).

Let's look at these two main modes of action in a little more detail and examine the ways in which hormones affect cells.

PROTEIN AND AMINE HORMONES What determines whether a cell responds to a particular protein hormone? Only those cells that produce the appropriate receptor proteins for a hormone and insert them into the membrane can respond to that hormone. As we saw with neurotransmitter receptors in Chapters 3 and 4, the receptor protein spans the cellular membrane. When a hormone binds to the extracellular portion of the receptor, the receptor molecule changes its overall shape. The alteration in the intracellular portion of the receptor then changes the internal chemistry of the cell, most often by activating a second messenger (**Figure 5.8a**).

One second-messenger compound in particular—**cyclic adenosine monophosphate (cyclic AMP or cAMP)**—transmits the messages of many of the peptide and amine hormones. It may seem surprising that the same second messenger can mediate the effects of many different hormones, but a change in cAMP levels can cause many different outcomes, depending on which cells are affected, on which part of a cell is affected, and on the prior biochemical activity inside the cell. Other widespread second-messenger compounds include **cyclic guanosine monophosphate (cyclic GMP or cGMP)** and **phosphoinositides**.

The specificity of hormonal effects is determined in large part by the selectivity of receptors. Only a minority of cells produce the receptor that recognizes and reacts to a particular hormone, and thus only those cells can respond to it. For example, adrenocorticotropic hormone (ACTH) interacts with receptors on the membranes of cells in the adrenal gland, and in these cells an increase in cAMP leads to the synthesis and release of other hormones.

transcription factor A substance that binds to recognition sites on DNA and alters the rate of expression of particular genes.

cyclic adenosine monophosphate (cyclic AMP, or cAMP) A second messenger activated in target cells in response to synaptic or hormonal stimulation.

cyclic guanosine monophosphate (cyclic GMP, or cGMP) A second messenger activated in target cells in response to synaptic or hormonal stimulation.

phosphoinositides A class of common second-messenger compounds in post-synaptic cells.

(a) Protein hormone action

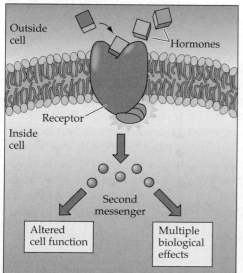

(b) Steroid hormone action

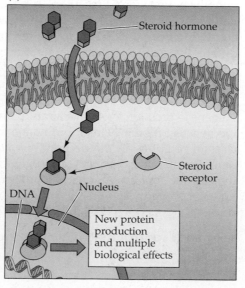

5.8 Two Main Mechanisms of Hormone Action (a) Protein hormone receptors are found in the cell membrane. When the hormone binds to the receptor, a second-messenger system is activated, which affects various cellular processes. (b) Steroid hormones diffuse passively into cells. Inside the target cells are large receptor molecules that bind to the steroid hormone. The steroid-receptor complex then binds to DNA, causing an increase in the production of some gene products and a decrease in the production of others. This is the mechanism by which steroids exert a genomic effect, which is distinct from the nongenomic effects mentioned in the text.

Protein hormones usually act relatively rapidly, within seconds to minutes. (Although rapid for a hormone, this action is much slower than neural activity.) There can also be prolonged effects. For example, ACTH promotes the proliferation and growth of some adrenal cells, thereby increasing their long-term capacity to produce hormones. A cell may increase or decrease the number of hormone receptors it makes, and these changes are sometimes referred to as *up-regulation* and *down-regulation*, respectively.

STEROID HORMONES Steroid hormones typically act more slowly than protein or amine hormones, requiring hours to take effect. The specificity of action of steroid hormones is determined by the receptors that reside *inside* target cells. These receptors are truly ancient, in an evolutionary sense; estrogen receptors may have arisen in primordial invertebrate species a billion years ago (Bridgham et al., 2006; J. W. Thornton et al., 2003).

Steroid hormones pass in and out of many cells in which they have no effect. If appropriate receptor proteins are inside, however, these receptors bind to the hormone, and the receptor-steroid complex then binds to DNA, so the complexes become concentrated in the nuclei of target cells (**Figure 5.8***b*). Thus, we can study where a steroid hormone is active by injecting radioactively tagged molecules of the steroid and observing where they accumulate. For example, tagged estradiol accumulates not only in the reproductive tract (as you might expect), but also in the nuclei of some neurons throughout the hypothalamus. Because neurons producing hormone receptors are found in only a limited number of brain regions, we can begin to learn how hormones affect behavior by finding those brain sites and asking what happens when the hormone arrives there. This strategy for learning about hormones and behavior is discussed in **Box 5.1**.

By altering protein production, steroids have slow but long-lasting effects on the development or adult function of cells. We will discuss such effects of steroids further in Chapter 12. There is a large "superfamily" of steroid receptor genes (Ribeiro et al., 1995), and some steroids act on more than one receptor. For example, a second estrogen **receptor isoform** (steroid receptor subtype) has been described and named estrogen receptor β (Kuiper et al., 1996) to distinguish it from the previously discovered estrogen receptor α. The brain contains both types of estrogen receptors, and they differ in their anatomical distribution within the brain. Scientists are trying to tease apart their separate effects on behavior.

Simple possession of appropriate steroid receptors is not enough to ensure that a given neuron will respond to the presence of that particular steroid hormone. Cells make a wide variety of **steroid receptor cofactors** that may be required, along with the bound steroid receptors, in order for the cell to respond. Furthermore, the nature of the target cell's response may be determined by the type of cofactor present: two different cells containing the same steroid receptors may respond quite differently to the steroid hormone if they are producing different steroid receptor cofactors (Molenda-Figueira et al., 2006; Tetel, 2000).

Steroids can also affect cells through mechanisms other than the classic nuclear steroid receptor. For example, estradiol, in addition to its slow, long-lasting action on gene expression, can have a rapid, brief effect on some neurons without affecting gene expression. This rapid **nongenomic effect** of steroids involves a separate class of receptors in the neuronal *membrane* (Toran-Allerand, 2005), modulating neural excitability. Similarly, androgenic steroids like testosterone can have effects that are too rapid to involve the transcription of genes and appear instead to involve androgen receptors localized in axons and other sites, distant from the cell nucleus and its DNA (DonCarlos et al., 2006).

Feedback control mechanisms regulate the secretion of hormones

One of the major features of almost all hormonal systems is that they don't just manufacture a hormone; they also detect and evaluate the effects of the hormone.

receptor isoform A version of a receptor protein (in this context, a hormone receptor) with slight differences in structure that give it different functional properties. Conceptually similar to a receptor subtype.

steroid receptor cofactors Proteins that affect the cell's response when a steroid hormone binds its receptor.

nongenomic effect An effect of a steroid hormone that is not mediated by direct changes in gene expression.

BOX 5.1 Techniques of Modern Behavioral Endocrinology

To establish that a particular hormone affects behavior, investigators usually begin with the type of experiment that Berthold performed in the nineteenth century: observing the behavior of the intact animal, and then removing the endocrine gland and looking for a change in behavior (see Figure 5.2). Berthold was limited to this type of experiment, but modern scientists have many additional options available. Let's imagine that we're investigating a particular effect of hormones on behavior to see how we might proceed.

Which Hormones Affect Which Behaviors?

First we must carefully observe the behavior of several individuals, seeking ways to classify and quantify the different types of behavior and to place them in the context of the behavior of other individuals. For example, most adult male rats will try to mount and copulate with a receptive female placed in their cage. If the testes are removed from the male rat, he will eventually stop copulating with females. We know that one of the hormones produced by the testes is testosterone. Is it the loss of testosterone that causes the loss of male copulatory behavior?

To explore this question, we inject some synthetic testosterone into castrated males and observe whether the copulatory behavior returns. (It does.) Another way to ask whether a steroid hormone is affecting a particular behavior is to examine the behavior of animals that lack the receptors for that steroid. We can delete the gene for a given hormone receptor, making a **knockout organism** (because the gene for the receptor has been "knocked out"), and ask which behaviors are different in the knockouts versus normal animals (see Box 7.3).

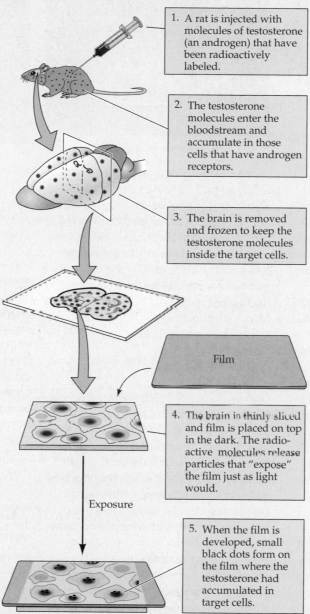

1. A rat is injected with molecules of testosterone (an androgen) that have been radioactively labeled.

2. The testosterone molecules enter the bloodstream and accumulate in those cells that have androgen receptors.

3. The brain is removed and frozen to keep the testosterone molecules inside the target cells.

Film

4. The brain is thinly sliced and film is placed on top in the dark. The radioactive molecules release particles that "expose" the film just as light would.

Exposure

5. When the film is developed, small black dots form on the film where the testosterone had accumulated in target cells.

(A) Steps in steroid autoradiography

Next we might examine individual male rats and ask whether the ones that copulate a lot have more testosterone circulating in their blood than those that copulate only a little. To investigate this question, we measure individual differences in the amount of copulatory behavior, take a sample of blood from each individual, and measure levels of testosterone with **radioimmunoassay** (**RIA**), a technique using an antibody that binds to a particular hormone. By adding many such antibodies to each blood sample and measuring how many of the antibodies find a hormone molecule to bind, we can estimate the total number of molecules of the hormone per unit volume of blood.

It turns out that individual differences in the sexual behavior of normal male rats (and normal male humans) do *not* correlate with differences in testosterone levels in the blood. In both rats and humans, a drastic loss of testosterone, as after castration, results in a gradual decline in sexual behavior. All normal males, however, appear to make more than enough testosterone to maintain sexual behavior, so something else must modulate this behavior. In other words, the hormone acts in a permissive manner: it permits the display of the behavior, but something else determines how much of the behavior each individual exhibits.

Where Are the Target Cells?

What does testosterone do to permit sexual behavior? One step toward answering this question is to ask another question: Which parts of the brain are normally affected by this hormone? We have several methods at our disposal for investigating this question.

First we might inject a castrated animal with radioactively labeled testosterone and wait for the hormone to accumulate in the brain regions that have receptors for the hormone. Then we can sacrifice the animal, remove

(*Continued on next page*)

knockout organism　An individual in which a particular gene has been disabled by an experimenter.

radioimmunoassay (RIA)　A technique that uses antibodies to measure the concentration of a substance, such as a hormone, in blood.

BOX 5.1 *(continued)*

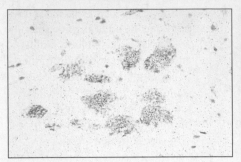

(B) An autoradiogram showing that spinal motoneurons (purple cell profiles) accumulate radioactive testosterone (small dots)

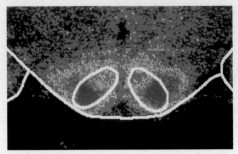

(C) An autoradiogram showing the concentration of oxytocin receptors in the ventromedial hypothalamus (oval outlines)

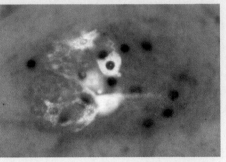

(D) Immunocytochemistry revealing cells with nuclei that contain androgen receptors (dark circles), to which testosterone can bind. The somata of these neurons have been labeled with the tracers fluorogold (white) and fluoro-ruby (red).

the brain, freeze it, cut thin sections from it, and place the thin sections on photographic film. Radioactive emissions from the tissue expose the film, revealing which brain regions had accumulated the most labeled testosterone. This method is known as **autoradiography** because the tissue "takes its own picture" with radioactivity (Figure A).

When the labeled hormone is a steroid like testosterone, the radioactivity accumulates in the nuclei of neurons and leaves small black specks on the film (Figure B). When the radiolabeled hormone is a protein hormone such as oxytocin, the radioactivity accumulates in the membranes of cells and appears in particular layers of the brain. Computers can generate color maps that highlight regions with high densities of receptors (Figure C).

Another method for detecting hormone receptors is **immunocytochemistry**. In this method (described in more detail in Box 2.1), we use antibodies that recognize the hormone receptor (Figure D). This method allows us to map the distribution of hormone receptors in the brain. We put the antibodies on slices of brain tissue, wait for them to bind to the receptors, wash off the unbound antibodies, and use chemical methods to visualize the antibodies by creating a tiny dark spot at each

one. When the antibodies recognize a steroid receptor, chemical reactions cause a dark coloration in the nuclei of target brain cells. We can also use **in situ hybridization** (see Box 2.1) to look for the neurons that make the mRNA for the steroid receptor. Because these cells make the transcript for the receptor, they are likely to possess the receptor protein itself.

What Happens at the Target Cells?

Once we have used autoradiography, immunocytochemistry, or in situ hybridization (or, better yet, all three) to identify brain regions that have receptors for the hormone, those regions become candidates for the places at which the hormone works to change behavior. Now we can take castrated males and implant tiny pellets of testosterone into one of those brain regions. We use RIA to ensure that the pellets are small enough that they have no effect on hormone levels in the blood. Then we ask whether the small implant in that brain region restores the behavior. If not, then in other animals we can implant pellets in a different region or try placing implants in a combination of brain sites.

It turns out that such implants can restore male sexual behavior in rats only if they are placed in the medial preoptic area

(mPOA) of the hypothalamus. Thus, we have found so far that testosterone does something to the mPOA to permit individual males to display sexual behavior. Now we can examine the mPOA in detail to learn what changes in the anatomy, physiology, or protein production of this region are caused by testosterone. We have more or less caught up to modern-day scientists who work on this very question. Some of the preliminary answers suggested by their research will be discussed in Chapter 12. (Figure C courtesy of Bruce McEwen; D courtesy of Cynthia Jordan.)

autoradiography A histological technique that shows the distribution of radioactive chemicals in tissues.

immunocytochemistry (ICC) A method for detecting a particular protein in tissues in which an antibody recognizes and binds to the protein and then chemical methods are then used to leave a visible reaction product around each antibody.

in situ hybridization A method for detecting particular RNA transcripts in tissue sections by providing a nucleotide probe that is complementary to, and will therefore hybridize with, the transcript of interest.

Thus, secretion is usually monitored and regulated so that the rate is appropriate to ongoing activities and needs of the body. The basic control used is a **negative feedback** system: output of the hormone *feeds back* to inhibit the drive for more of that same hormone. This negative feedback action of a hormonal system is like that of a thermostat, and just as the thermostat can be set to different temperatures

negative feedback The property by which some of the output of a system feeds back to reduce the effect of input signals.

at different times, the set points of a person's endocrine feedback systems can be changed to meet varying circumstances. We'll discuss negative feedback regulation of other processes in Chapter 13 (see Figure 13.1).

In the simplest kind of hormone regulation system, diagrammed in **Figure 5.9*a***, an endocrine cell releases a hormone that acts on target cells, but the same hormone also feeds back to inhibit the gland that released it. This is an autocrine response.

In other cases, the endocrine cell reacts not to its own hormone, but to the biological response that the hormone elicits from the target cells (**Figure 5.9*b***). If the initial effect is too small, additional hormone is released; if the effect is sufficient, no further hormone is released. For example, the hormone insulin is released to control the level of glucose circulating in our blood. After a meal, glucose from the food enters the bloodstream, causing insulin to be released from the pancreas. The insulin causes glucose to enter muscle and fat cells. As the level of glucose in the blood falls, the pancreas secretes less insulin, so a balance tends to be maintained (Chapter 13).

A more complex endocrine system includes the brain, usually the hypothalamus, as part of the circuit that controls an endocrine gland (**Figure 5.9*c***). When we are alarmed, for example, the hypothalamus directs the adrenal medulla to secrete the hormone epinephrine (also called adrenaline), which affects many target cells. The brain detects these effects and exerts negative feedback on the hypothalamus to reduce further hormone output.

An even greater degree of complexity is encountered when the anterior pituitary becomes involved (**Figure 5.9*d***). As we'll see in the next section, several anterior pituitary hormones regulate hormone secretion by other endocrine glands; all of these pituitary hormones are called **tropic hormones**. (*Tropic*, pronounced with a long *o* as in *toe*, means "directed toward.") The hypothalamus uses another set of hormones, called **releasing hormones**, to control the pituitary release of

tropic hormones A class of anterior pituitary hormones that affect the secretion of other endocrine glands.

releasing hormones A class of hormones, produced in the hypothalamus, that traverse the hypothalamic-pituitary portal system to control the pituitary's release of tropic hormones.

(*a*) Autocrine feedback

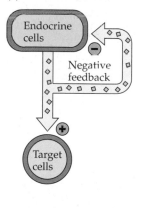

(*b*) Target cell feedback

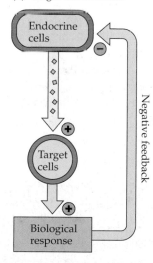

(*c*) Brain regulation

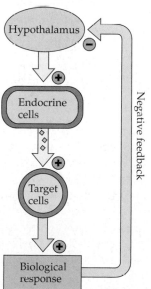

(*d*) Brain and pituitary regulation

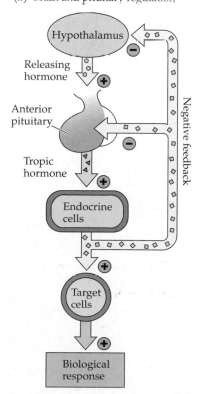

5.9 Endocrine Feedback Loops (*a*) In the simplest type of negative feedback control, an endocrine gland releases a hormone that not only acts on a target, but also feeds back in an autocrine fashion to inhibit further hormone secretion. (*b*) The hormone from the endocrine gland acts on target cells to produce a specific set of biological effects. The consequences of these effects may be detected by the endocrine gland, inhibiting further hormone release. (*c*) In many feedback systems the brain becomes involved. The hypothalamic region drives the endocrine gland via either neural or hormonal signals. The target organ signals the brain to inhibit this drive. (*d*) Highly complex feedback mechanisms involve the hypothalamus and the anterior pituitary, as well as the endocrine gland. Feedback is regulated by a variety of hormones via multiple routes.

TABLE 5.2 Examples of Major Classes of Hormones

Gland	Hormones	Principal effects
POSTERIOR PITUITARY (storage organ for certain hormones produced by hypothalamus)	Oxytocin	Stimulates contraction of uterine muscles; stimulates release of milk by mammary glands
	Vasopressin (AVP), or antidiuretic hormone (ADH)	Stimulates increased water reabsorption by kidneys; stimulates constriction of blood vessels
ANTERIOR PITUITARY	Growth hormone (GH)	Stimulates growth
	Thyroid-stimulating hormone (TSH)	Stimulates the thyroid
	Adrenocorticotropic hormone (ACTH)	Stimulates the adrenal cortex
	Follicle-stimulating hormone (FSH)	Stimulates growth of ovarian follicles and of seminiferous tubules of the testes
	Luteinizing hormone (LH)	Stimulates conversion of follicles into corpora lutea; stimulates secretion of sex hormones by gonads
	Prolactin	Stimulates milk secretion by mammary glands
HYPOTHALAMUS	Releasing hormones	Regulate hormone secretion by anterior pituitary
	Oxytocin; vasopressin	*See under* "Posterior pituitary" above
PINEAL	Melatonin	Regulates seasonal changes; regulates puberty
ADRENAL CORTEX	Glucocorticoids (corticosterone, cortisol, hydrocortisone, etc.)	Inhibit incorporation of amino acids into protein in muscle; stimulate formation and storage of glycogen; help maintain normal blood sugar level
	Mineralocorticoids (aldosterone, deoxycorticosterone, etc.)	Regulate metabolism of sodium and potassium
	Sex hormones (especially androstenedione)	Regulate facial and body hair
ADRENAL MEDULLA	Catecholamines (epinephrine, norepinephrine)	Prepare body for action
GONADS		
Testes	Androgens (testosterone, dihydrotestosterone, etc.)	Stimulate development and maintenance of male primary and secondary sexual characteristics and behavior
Ovaries	Estrogens (estradiol, estrone, etc.)	Stimulate development and maintenance of female secondary sexual characteristics and behavior
	Progestins (progesterone)	Stimulate female secondary sexual characteristics and behavior; maintain pregnancy
THYROID	Thyroxine (tetraiodothyronine); triiodothyronine	Stimulate oxidative metabolism
	Calcitonin	Prevents excessive rise in blood calcium
PANCREAS	Insulin	Stimulates glycogen formation and storage
	Glucagon	Stimulates conversion of glycogen into glucose
STOMACH	Secretin	Stimulates secretion of pancreatic juice
	Cholecystokinin (CCK)	Stimulates release of bile by gallbladder
	Gastrin	Stimulates secretion of gastric juice
	Ghrelin	Provides appetite signal to the hypothalamus appetite controller
HEART	Atrial natriuretic peptide	Promotes salt loss in urine

tropic hormones. Thus, the brain's releasing hormones affect the pituitary's tropic hormones, which affect the release of hormones from endocrine glands. Negative feedback in this case goes from the hormone of the endocrine gland to both the hypothalamus and the anterior pituitary (**Figure 5.10**).

5.10 An Example of Complex Endocrine Regulation The brain funnels information to the hypothalamus, which then controls the anterior pituitary, which in turn stimulates the thyroid gland. Note that three hormones and at least four cell groups are interacting in this instance.

Each Endocrine Gland Secretes Specific Hormones

We will restrict our account in this chapter to some of the main endocrine glands because a thorough treatment would fill an entire book (e.g., Hadley and Levine, 2006). **Table 5.2** gives a fuller but far from complete listing of hormones and their functions. We will discuss hormones from the pancreas and stomach in Chapter 13 when we consider hunger. Keep in mind that most hormones have more functions than are mentioned here and that several hormones may act together to produce effects in the same target cells.

The pituitary gland releases many important hormones

Resting in a socket in the base of the skull is the **pituitary gland** (or **hypophysis**; see Figure 5.1), occupying a volume of about 1 cm³ and weighing about 1 g. The hypothalamus sits just above it. The term *pituitary* comes from the Latin *pituita*, "mucus," reflecting the outmoded belief that waste products dripped down from the brain into the pituitary, which secreted them out through the nose. (The ancients may have thought you could literally sneeze your brains out!) The pituitary used to be referred to as the *master gland*, a reference to its regulatory role with regard to several other endocrine glands. But this gland is itself enslaved by the hypothalamus above it, as we'll see.

The pituitary gland consists of two main parts: the **anterior pituitary** (or **adenohypophysis**) and the **posterior pituitary** (or **neurohypophysis**). The anterior and posterior pituitary develop from different embryonic tissues and are completely separate in function. The pituitary is connected to the hypothalamus by a thin piece of tissue called the **pituitary stalk** or **infundibulum** (see Figure 5.11). The stalk contains many axons and is richly supplied with blood vessels. The axons extend only to the posterior pituitary, which we will consider next. The blood vessels, as we will see later, carry information exclusively to the anterior pituitary.

THE POSTERIOR PITUITARY The posterior pituitary gland secretes two principal hormones: **oxytocin** and **arginine vasopressin** (**AVP**), often called just **vasopressin**. Neurons in various hypothalamic nuclei, especially the supraoptic nuclei and the paraventricular nuclei, synthesize these two hormones and transport them along their axons to the axon terminals (**Figure 5.11**). Action potentials in these hypothalamic neurosecretory cells travel down the axons in the pituitary stalk and reach the axon terminals in the posterior pituitary, causing release of the hormone from the terminals into the rich vascular bed of the neurohypophysis. The axon terminals abut capillaries (small blood vessels), allowing the hormone to enter circulation immediately.

Some of the signals that activate the nerve cells of the supraoptic and paraventricular nuclei are related to thirst and water regulation, which we will discuss in Chapter 13. Secretion of vasopressin increases blood pressure by causing blood vessels to contract. Vasopressin also inhibits the formation of urine, so it is sometimes called *antidiuretic hormone*, or *ADH* (a *diuretic* is a food or drug that promotes urination). This action of vasopressin helps conserve water. In fact, the major physiological role of vasopressin is its potent antidiuretic activity; it exerts this effect with less than one-thousandth of the dose needed to alter blood pressure.

Oxytocin is involved in many aspects of reproductive and parental behavior. One of its functions is to stimulate contractions of the uterus in childbirth (the word *oxytocin* is derived from the Greek *oxys*, "rapid," and *tokos*, "childbirth"). In-

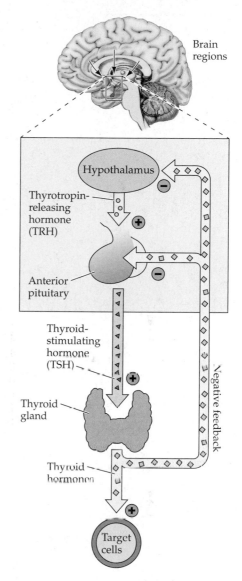

pituitary gland or hypophysis A small, complex endocrine gland located in a socket at the base of the skull.

anterior pituitary or adenohypophysis The front division of the pituitary gland; secretes tropic hormones.

posterior pituitary or neurohypophysis The rear division of the pituitary gland.

pituitary stalk or infundibulum A thin piece of tissue that connects the pituitary gland to the hypothalamus.

oxytocin A hormone, released from the posterior pituitary, that triggers milk letdown in the nursing female.

arginine vasopressin (AVP) or vasopressin Also called *antidiuretic hormone* (*ADH*). A peptide hormone from the posterior pituitary that promotes water conservation.

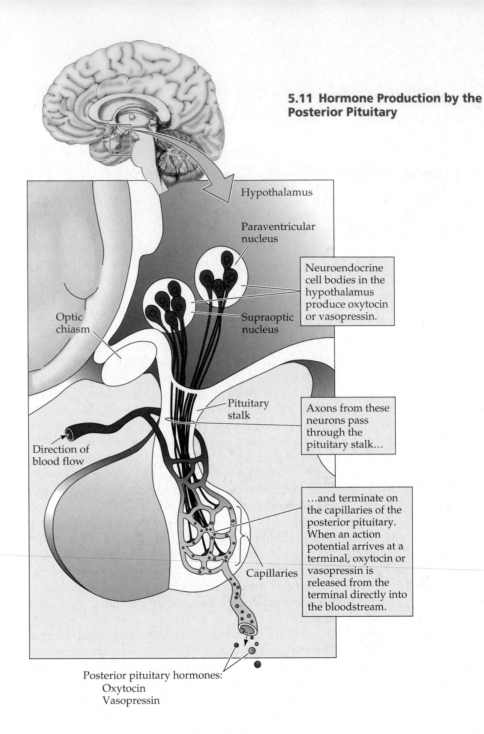

5.11 Hormone Production by the Posterior Pituitary

Hypothalamus

Paraventricular nucleus

Neuroendocrine cell bodies in the hypothalamus produce oxytocin or vasopressin.

Optic chiasm

Supraoptic nucleus

Pituitary stalk

Axons from these neurons pass through the pituitary stalk...

Direction of blood flow

...and terminate on the capillaries of the posterior pituitary. When an action potential arrives at a terminal, oxytocin or vasopressin is released from the terminal directly into the bloodstream.

Capillaries

Posterior pituitary hormones:
Oxytocin
Vasopressin

jections of oxytocin (or the synthetic version, Pitocin) are frequently used in medical settings to induce or accelerate labor and delivery.

Oxytocin also triggers the **milk letdown reflex**, the contraction of mammary gland cells that ejects milk into the breast ducts. This phenomenon exemplifies the reciprocal relationship between behavior and hormone release. When an infant or young animal first begins to suckle, the arrival of milk at the nipple is delayed by 30–60 seconds. This delay is caused by the sequence of steps that precedes letdown. Stimulation of the nipple activates receptors in the skin, which transmit this information through a chain of neurons and synapses to hypothalamic cells that contain oxytocin. Once these cells have been sufficiently stimulated, the hormone is released from the posterior pituitary and travels via the bloodstream to the mammary glands, where it produces a contraction of the tissues storing milk, making the milk available at the nipple (**Figure 5.12**).

For mothers, this reflex response to suckling frequently becomes conditioned to baby cries, so that milk appears promptly at the start of nursing. Because the

milk letdown reflex The reflexive release of milk in response to suckling, or to stimuli associated with suckling.

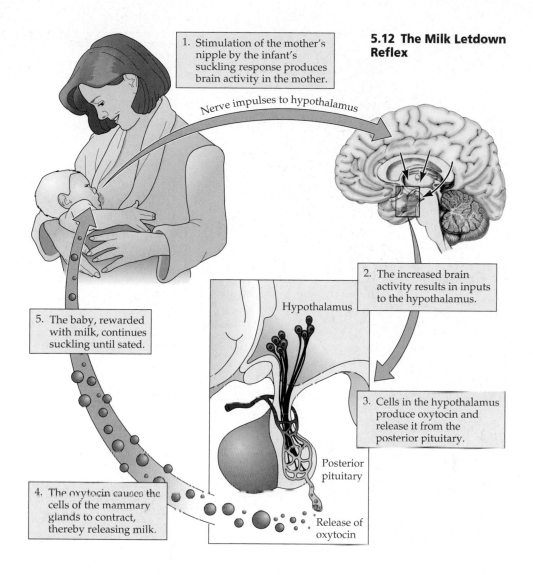

1. Stimulation of the mother's nipple by the infant's suckling response produces brain activity in the mother.

5.12 The Milk Letdown Reflex

Nerve impulses to hypothalamus

5. The baby, rewarded with milk, continues suckling until sated.

2. The increased brain activity results in inputs to the hypothalamus.

Hypothalamus

3. Cells in the hypothalamus produce oxytocin and release it from the posterior pituitary.

Posterior pituitary

4. The oxytocin causes the cells of the mammary glands to contract, thereby releasing milk.

Release of oxytocin

median eminence   Midline feature on the base of the brain marking the point at which the infundibulum exits the hypothalamus to connect to the pituitary. Contains elements of the hypophyseal portal system.

hypophyseal portal system   A duplex system of capillaries spanning between the neurosecretory cells of the hypothalamus and the secretory tissue of the anterior pituitary.

mother learns to release oxytocin *before* the suckling begins, sometimes the cries of someone else's baby in public trigger an inconvenient release of milk. Oxytocin and vasopressin also serve as neurotransmitters from hypothalamic cells (**Figure 5.13**), projecting widely through the nervous system. Oxytocin and vasopressin have been implicated in social behaviors, as we'll discuss near the end of this chapter.

THE ANTERIOR PITUITARY   Different cells of the anterior lobe of the pituitary synthesize and release different tropic hormones, which we'll discuss in the next section. Secretion of these tropic hormones, however, is under the control of releasing hormones, as mentioned earlier. We will briefly note some of the properties of these hypothalamic releasing hormones before further considering anterior pituitary actions.

Hypothalamic releasing hormones govern the anterior pituitary

The neurons that synthesize the different releasing hormones are neuroendocrine cells residing in various regions of the hypothalamus. The axons of these neuroendocrine cells converge on the **median eminence**, just above the pituitary stalk. This region contains an elaborate profusion of blood vessels that form the **hypophyseal portal system**. Here, in response to inputs from the rest of the brain, the axon terminals of the hypothalamic neuroendocrine cells secrete their releasing hormones into the local bloodstream (**Figure 5.14**).

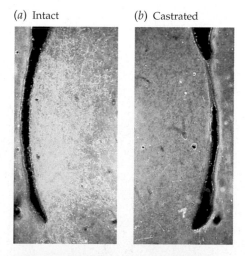

(a) Intact   (b) Castrated

5.13 Vasopressin Can Serve as a Neurotransmitter   Revealed here by immunocytochemistry are vasopressin-filled axonal fibers (yellow) in the septum of intact (a) and castrated (b) male rats. (Courtesy of Geert DeVries.)

5.14 Hormone Release by the Anterior Pituitary

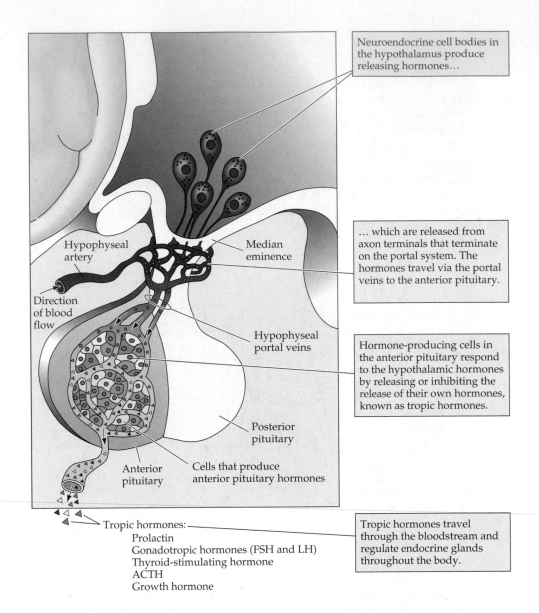

Neuroendocrine cell bodies in the hypothalamus produce releasing hormones…

… which are released from axon terminals that terminate on the portal system. The hormones travel via the portal veins to the anterior pituitary.

Hormone-producing cells in the anterior pituitary respond to the hypothalamic hormones by releasing or inhibiting the release of their own hormones, known as tropic hormones.

Tropic hormones travel through the bloodstream and regulate endocrine glands throughout the body.

Hypophyseal artery

Direction of blood flow

Median eminence

Hypophyseal portal veins

Posterior pituitary

Anterior pituitary

Cells that produce anterior pituitary hormones

Tropic hormones:
 Prolactin
 Gonadotropic hormones (FSH and LH)
 Thyroid-stimulating hormone
 ACTH
 Growth hormone

Blood carries the various releasing hormones only a very short distance, into the anterior pituitary. The rate at which releasing hormones arrive at their target cells in the anterior pituitary controls the rate at which the anterior pituitary cells, in turn, release their tropic hormones into the general circulation. These tropic hormones then regulate the activity of major endocrine organs throughout the body.

The hypothalamic neuroendocrine cells that synthesize the releasing hormones are themselves subject to two kinds of influences:

1. They are directly affected by *circulating messages*, such as other hormones (especially hormones that have themselves been secreted in response to tropic hormones), and by blood sugar and products of the immune system. The hypothalamus is not shielded by the blood-brain barrier (see Chapter 2) to the same extent that other brain regions are, which makes it possible for a wide variety of blood-borne material to access the hypothalamic neuroendocrine cells.

2. They receive *synaptic inputs* (either excitatory or inhibitory) from many other brain regions. A wide range of neural signals, reflecting both internal and external events, can thereby influence the endocrine system. As a result, hormonal actions can be coordinated with ongoing events, and conditioning (learning) can alter endocrine status. We saw an example of such influence in our discus-

sion of the milk letdown reflex, and we'll see other examples throughout the book.

The hypothalamic-releasing-hormone system therefore exerts high-level control over endocrine organs throughout the body and provides a route by which brain activity is translated into hormonal action. Cutting the pituitary stalk interrupts the portal blood vessels and the flow of releasing hormones, leading to profound atrophy of the pituitary, and major hormonal disruptions.

TROPIC HORMONES OF THE ANTERIOR PITUITARY Driven by various releasing hormones from the hypothalamus, the anterior pituitary gland secretes six main tropic hormones (**Figure 5.15**; see also Table 5.2). Two of these regulate the function of the adrenal cortex and the thyroid gland:

1. **Adrenocorticotropic hormone** (**ACTH**) controls the production and release of hormones of the adrenal cortex. The adrenal cortex, in turn, releases steroid hormones. The levels of ACTH and adrenal steroids show a marked daily rhythm (see Chapter 14).
2. **Thyroid-stimulating hormone** (**TSH**) increases the release of thyroid hormones from the thyroid gland and markedly affects thyroid gland size.

Two other tropic hormones of the anterior pituitary influence the gonads, and consequently are termed **gonadotropins**:

3. **Follicle-stimulating hormone** (**FSH**) gets its name from its actions in the ovary, where it stimulates the growth and maturation of egg-containing **follicles** and the secretion of estrogens from the follicles. In males, FSH governs sperm production.

adrenocorticotropic hormone (ACTH) A tropic hormone secreted by the anterior pituitary gland that controls the production and release of hormones of the adrenal cortex.

thyroid-stimulating hormone (TSH) A tropic hormone, released by the anterior pituitary gland, that signals the thyroid gland to secrete its hormones.

gonadotropin An anterior pituitary hormone that selectively stimulates the cells of the gonads to produce sex steroids and gametes.

follicle-stimulating hormone (FSH) A gonadotropin, named for its actions on ovarian follicles.

follicles Ovarian structures containing immature ova.

5.15 Secretions of the Anterior Pituitary Hormones produced in the anterior pituitary include tropic hormones, which control endocrine glands and directly affect other structures, such as bones.

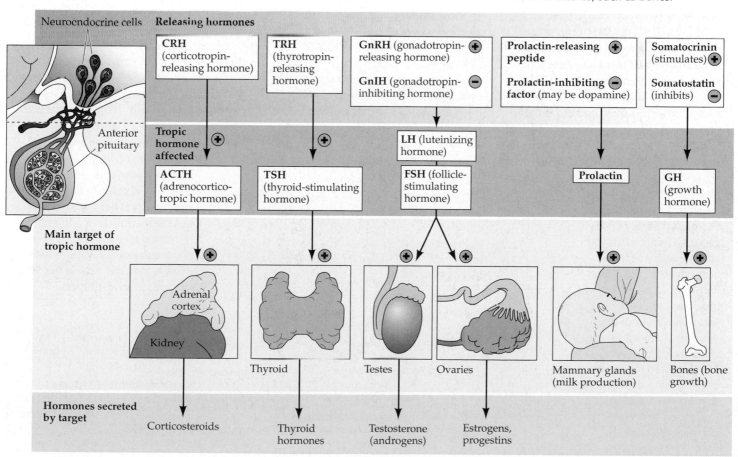

luteinizing hormone (LH) A gonadotropin, named for its stimulatory effects on the ovarian corpora lutea.

corpora lutea The structures formed from collapsed ovarian follicles subsequent to ovulation. The corpora lutea are a major source of progesterone.

prolactin A protein hormone, produced by the anterior pituitary, that promotes mammary development for lactation in female mammals.

4. **Luteinizing hormone** (**LH**) stimulates the follicles of the ovary to rupture, release their eggs, and form into structures called **corpora lutea** (singular **corpus luteum**) that secrete the sex steroid hormone progesterone. In males, LH stimulates the testes to produce testosterone. We will discuss the gonadal steroid hormones in more detail shortly.

The two remaining tropic hormones control milk production and body growth:

5. **Prolactin** is so named because it promotes lactation in female mammals. But prolactin has a number of roles in addition to its actions on breast tissue. For example, it is closely involved in the parental behavior of a wide variety of vertebrate species.

BOX 5.2 Stress and Growth: Psychosocial Dwarfism

Genie had a horrifically deprived childhood. For over 10 years, starting from the age of 20 months, she was isolated in a small, closed room, and much of the time she was tied to a potty chair. Her disturbed parents provided food, but nobody held Genie or spoke to her. When she was released from her confinement and observed by researchers at the age of 13, her size made her appear only 6 or 7 years old (Rymer, 1993).

Other less horrendous forms of family deprivation also result in failure of growth. This syndrome is referred to as **psychosocial dwarfism** to emphasize that the growth failure arises from psychological and social factors mediated through the CNS and its control over endocrine functions (W. H. Green et al., 1984). When children suffering from psychosocial dwarfism are removed from stressful circumstances, many begin to grow rapidly. The growth rates of five such children, before and after periods of emotional deprivation, are shown in the figure (asterisks indicate when each child was removed from the abusive situation). These children seem to have compensated for much of the growth deficit that occurred during prolonged stress periods (Sirotnak et al., 2004).

How do stress and emotional deprivation impair growth? Growth impairments appear to be mediated by changed outputs of several hormones, including growth hormone (GH), cortisol, and other hormones, known as **somatomedins** (which are normally released by the liver in response to GH). GH and the somatomedins normally stimulate cell growth; high levels of cortisol inhibit growth.

Some children with psychosocial dwarfism show almost a complete lack of GH release, which may be caused by an absence of the releasing hormone somatocrinin from the hypothalamus (Albanese et al., 1994). Disturbed sleep has also been suggested as a cause of this failure, because GH is typically released during certain stages of sleep, and children under stress show disturbed sleep patterns (L. I. Gardner, 1972). Other children who exhibit psychosocial dwarfism show normal levels of GH but low levels of somatomedins, and these hormones, along with GH, appear to be necessary for normal growth. Still other children with this condition show elevated levels of cortisol, probably as a result of stress, that inhibit growth. Some affected children show none of these hormonal disturbances, so there must also be other routes through which emotional experiences affect growth.

Growth is an example of a process that involves many factors—hormonal, metabolic, and dietary—and can therefore malfunction in a variety of ways. Cases of psychosocial dwarfism are more common than once was thought, and investigators who study this syndrome are calling for further awareness of and attention to it (W. H. Green et al., 1984). For Genie, relief came in time to restore much of her *body* growth, but her mental development remained severely limited; she never learned to say more than a few words and, now in her 50s, she lives in an institution.

psychosocial dwarfism Reduced stature caused by stress early in life that inhibits deep sleep.

somatomedins A group of proteins, released from the liver in response to growth hormone, that aid body growth and maintenance.

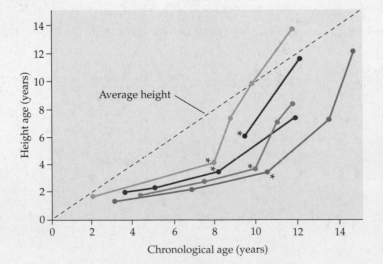

6. **Growth hormone** (**GH**; also known as *somatotropin* or *somatotropic hormone*) acts throughout the body to influence the growth of cells and tissues by affecting protein metabolism. GH is released almost exclusively during sleep. Other factors also affect GH secretion. The stomach secretes a hormone, called *ghrelin* (from the proto-Indo-European root for "grow"), which evokes GH release from the anterior pituitary (Kojima et al., 1999). Ghrelin is discussed in more detail in Chapter 13. Starvation, vigorous exercise, and intense stress can all profoundly inhibit GH release (**Box 5.2**).

Now let's consider three of the organ systems stimulated by tropic hormones of the anterior pituitary: the adrenal gland, the thyroid gland, and the gonads. Each of these glands secretes hormones of its own in response to the pituitary tropic hormones.

Two divisions of the adrenal gland produce hormones

Resting on top of each kidney is an **adrenal gland** (see Figure 5.1), which secretes a large variety of hormones (**Figure 5.16**). In mammals, the adrenal structure is divided into two major portions. The outer 80% of the gland, the **adrenal cortex**, is composed of distinct layers of cells, each producing different steroid hormones.

growth hormone (GH) Also called somatotropin or somatotropic hormone. A tropic hormone, secreted by the anterior pituitary, that influences the growth of cells and tissues.

adrenal gland An endocrine gland atop the kidney.

adrenal cortex The outer rind of the adrenal gland.

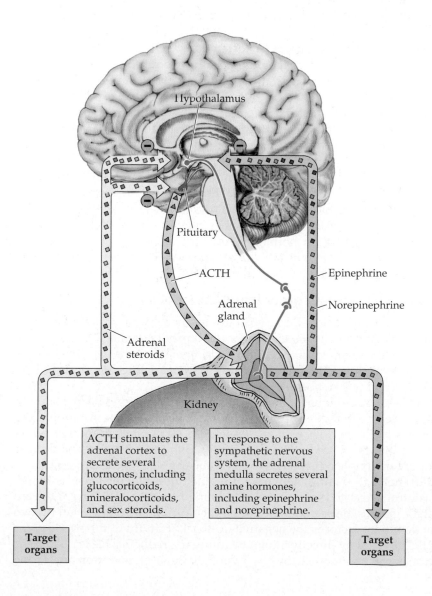

ACTH stimulates the adrenal cortex to secrete several hormones, including glucocorticoids, mineralocorticoids, and sex steroids.

In response to the sympathetic nervous system, the adrenal medulla secretes several amine hormones, including epinephrine and norepinephrine.

5.16 Regulation of Hormones Produced by the Adrenal Glands Situated above the kidneys, each adrenal gland consists of an outer cortex (in yellow) and an inner medulla (blue). The cortex secretes glucocorticoids, mineralocorticoids, and sex steroids under the control of ACTH, which is in turn regulated by corticotropin-releasing hormone from the hypothalamus. The cells of the adrenal medulla release epinephrine and norepinephrine under the control of the sympathetic nervous system.

adrenal medulla   The inner core of the adrenal gland.

epinephrine or adrenaline   A compound that acts both as a hormone (secreted by the adrenal medulla under the control of the sympathetic nervous system) and as a synaptic transmitter.

norepinephrine (NE) or noradrenaline   A neurotransmitter produced and released by sympathetic postganglionic neurons to accelerate organ activity.

adrenocorticoids   Also called *adrenal steroids*. A class of steroid hormones that are secreted by the adrenal cortex.

glucocorticoids   A class of steroid hormones, released by the adrenal cortex, that affect carbohydrate metabolism and inflammation.

cortisol   A glucocorticoid stress hormone of the adrenal cortex.

mineralocorticoids   A class of steroid hormones, released by the adrenal cortex, that affect ion concentrations in body tissues.

aldosterone   A mineralocorticoid hormone, secreted by the adrenal cortex, that induces the kidneys to conserve sodium ions.

sex steroids   Steroid hormones secreted by the gonads: androgens, estrogens, and progestins.

androstenedione   The chief sex hormone secreted by the human adrenal cortex.

thyroid gland   An endocrine gland, located in the throat, that regulates cellular metabolism throughout the body.

thyroid hormones   Two hormones, triiodothyronine and thyroxine (also called *tetraiodothyronine*), released from the thyroid gland that have widespread effects, including growth and maintenance of the brain.

thyrotropin-releasing hormone (TRH)   A hypothalamic hormone that regulates the release of thyroid-stimulating hormone from the anterior pituitary.

The core 20% of the gland is the **adrenal medulla**, which is richly supplied with autonomic nerves.

As part of the "fight or flight" reaction to threat, the adrenal medulla secretes hormones—the catecholamines **epinephrine** (adrenaline) and **norepinephrine** (noradrenaline)—that prepare the body for action, raising heart rate and respiration, among other things. Because emergencies demand quick action, secretion of these hormones is under direct control of the brain, via sympathetic nerve terminals that release acetylcholine in the adrenal medulla. In Chapter 4 we saw that epinephrine and norepinephrine are also synaptic transmitters at certain sites in the nervous system.

The adrenal cortex produces and secretes a variety of steroid hormones, collectively called the **adrenocorticoids** (or *adrenal steroids*). One subgroup consists of the **glucocorticoids**, so named because of their effects on the metabolism of carbohydrates, including glucose. Hormones of this type, such as **cortisol**, increase the level of blood glucose and accelerate the breakdown of proteins. In high concentrations, glucocorticoids have a marked anti-inflammatory effect; that is, they inhibit the swelling around injuries or infections. This action normally results in the temporary decrease of bodily responses to tissue injury, which is why synthetic glucocorticoids (such as prednisone) are important and useful drugs. However, sustained high levels of circulating glucocorticoids are harmful to the brain, as we'll see in Chapter 15 when we discuss stress.

A second subgroup of adrenal steroids consists of the **mineralocorticoids**, so named because of their effects on minerals such as sodium and potassium. The primary mineralocorticoid hormone is **aldosterone**, which acts on the kidneys to retain sodium and thus reduces the amount of urine produced, conserving water. This action helps maintain a homeostatic equilibrium of ions in blood and extracellular fluids (see Chapter 13).

The adrenal cortex also produces **sex steroids**, notably **androstenedione**. Androstenedione contributes to the adult pattern of body hair in men and women. In some females the adrenal cortex produces more than the normal amounts of sex hormones, causing a more masculine appearance (see Chapter 12).

Levels of circulating adrenal cortical hormones are regulated in several steps (see Figure 5.16). The pituitary hormone ACTH promotes steroid synthesis in the adrenal gland. Adrenal steroids in turn exert a negative feedback effect on ACTH release. As the level of adrenal cortical hormones increases, the secretion of ACTH is suppressed, so the output of hormones from the adrenal cortex diminishes. When the levels of adrenal steroids fall, the pituitary ACTH-secreting cells are released from suppression, and the concentration of ACTH in the blood rises again.

Thyroid hormones regulate growth and metabolism

Situated in the throat, just below the larynx (around the location of the Adam's apple) is the **thyroid gland** (see Figure 5.1). This gland produces and secretes several hormones. Two of these—*thyroxine* (or *tetraiodothyronine*) and *triiodothyronine*—are usually referred to as **thyroid hormones**; a third—*calcitonin*—promotes calcium deposition in bones and will not be discussed further.

The thyroid is unique among endocrine glands because it stores a large amount of hormone—at least a 100-day supply—which it slowly releases. Although thyroid hormones are amines, they behave like steroids. They bind to specialized receptors (part of the steroid receptor superfamily) found inside cells. The thyroid hormone–receptor complex then binds to DNA and regulates gene expression.

Figure 5.10 shows the control network for regulating thyroxine levels in blood. The major control is exerted by thyroid-stimulating hormone (TSH) from the anterior pituitary gland. The secretion of TSH by the pituitary is controlled by two factors. The dominant factor is the negative feedback from thyroid hormones circulating in the blood; they directly inhibit the pituitary, reducing TSH release. The second factor is the production (by the hypothalamus) of **thyrotropin-releasing** hormone (**TRH**), which stimulates the release of TSH from the pituitary. When the level of circulating thyroid hormone falls, both TRH and TSH are secreted; when TSH reaches the thyroid gland, it stimulates the production and release of thyroid hormones.

Thyroid hormones are the only substances produced by the body that contain iodine, and their manufacture is critically dependent on the supply of iodine. In parts of the world where foods contain little iodine, many people suffer from hypothyroidism. Driven by higher and higher TSH levels, the thyroid gland swells in its attempt to produce more thyroid hormones, causing a **goiter** to form. Because the soil in Switzerland has little iodine, through the nineteenth century even well-fed citizens there often had goiters (**Figure 5.17**). Today the addition of a small amount of iodine to table salt—producing *iodized salt*—ensures that we won't develop goiters even if we get insufficient iodine from our vegetables.

Remember Chuck at the start of this chapter? His problem was chronic hypothyroidism. He had been diagnosed years before and given thyroid hormone pills, but the prescription had run out and he had neglected to refill it. Six months later, when he showed up in the ER, he had not yet developed a goiter, but he was suffering. Thyroid hormones have a general effect on the nervous system, maintaining alertness and reflexes. Chuck's cognitive function became so impaired that he couldn't even remember that he had taken thyroid hormone before. But his slow knee jerk reflex suggested hypothyroidism, and blood tests confirmed that he had almost no thyroid hormone. Chuck was lucky that doctors caught his problem before he slipped into hypothyroid coma, which is fatal about 20% of the time, even when treated (Jauhar, 2003). People with less-severe hypothyroidism may appear depressed, so the hormonal imbalance is often overlooked in mild cases (C. G. Roberts and Ladenson, 2004).

Thyroid hormones also influence growth. When thyroid deficiency starts early in life, body growth is stunted and the face malformed. Thyroid deficiency also produces a marked reduction in brain size and in the branching of axons and dendrites. This state, called **cretinism** or *congenital hypothyroidism*, is accompanied by intellectual disability.

5.17 Isn't That a Stylish Collar? Because there is little iodine in the soil in Switzerland, vegetables grown there provide insufficient iodine even for prosperous people like the novelist Jeremias Gotthelf (1797–1854), who suffered from a large goiter that he routinely concealed behind elaborate collars. (Painting by Friedrich Dietler.)

The gonads produce steroid hormones, regulating reproduction

Almost all aspects of reproductive behavior, including mating and parental behaviors, depend on hormones. Since Chapter 12 is devoted to reproductive behavior and physiology, at this point we will only briefly note relevant hormones and some pertinent aspects of anatomy and physiology. Female and male **gonads** (ovaries and testes, respectively; see Figure 5.1) consist of two different subcompartments—one to produce hormones (the sex steroids we mentioned earlier) and another to produce gametes (eggs or sperm). The gonadal hormones are critical for triggering both reproductive behavior controlled by the brain and gamete production.

The hypothalamus controls gonadal hormone production by releasing **gonadotropin-releasing hormone (GnRH)**, which drives the anterior pituitary to release the gonadotropins FSH or LH, which we mentioned earlier. Although named for their effects on ovaries, FSH and LH drive development and steroid production in both testes and ovaries. The GnRH neurons in turn are stimulated by a recently identified hypothalamic peptide, **kisspeptin** (Kriegsfeld, 2006; J. T. Smith et al., 2006), which appears to play an important role in governing the onset of puberty (S. K. Han et al., 2005).

The hypothalamus uses GnRH to *stimulate* pituitary gonadotropin secretion, but it also uses a recently discovered hormone to *inhibit* gonadotropin secretion named, sensibly enough, **gonadotropin-inhibiting hormone (GnIH)** (Tsutsui et al., 2006). GnRH and GnIH thus work in opposition, translating inputs from the brain into controls on the pituitary, and therefore the gonads, like an accelerator and a brake, respectively.

goiter A swelling of the thyroid gland resulting from iodine deficiency.

cretinism Also called *congenital hypothyroidism*. Reduced stature and intellectual disability caused by thyroid deficiency during early development.

gonads The sexual organs (ovaries in females, testes in males), which produce gametes for reproduction.

gonadotropin-releasing hormone (GnRH) A hypothalamic hormone that controls the release of luteinizing hormone and follicle-stimulating hormone from the pituitary.

kisspeptin A hypothalamic peptide hormone that increases gonadotropin secretion by facilitating the release of gonadotropin-releasing hormone.

gonadotropin-inhibiting hormone (GnIH) A hypothalamic peptide hormone that reduces gonadotropin secretion by inhibiting the release of gonadotropin-releasing hormone.

5.18 The Influence of a Hormone
The antlers and combative behavior of male red deer, a subspecies of the North American elk, are both seasonally affected by testosterone.

THE TESTES   Within the **testes** are Sertoli cells, which produce sperm, and Leydig cells, which produce and secrete the sex steroid **testosterone**. Testosterone and other male hormones are called **androgens** (from the Greek *andro-*, "man," and *gennan*, "to produce").

Testosterone controls a wide range of bodily changes that become visible at puberty, including changes in voice, hair growth, and genital size. In species that breed only in certain seasons of the year, testosterone has especially marked effects on appearance and behavior—for example, the antlers and fighting between males that are displayed by many species of deer (**Figure 5.18**). **Figure 5.19***a* summarizes the regulation of testosterone secretion. As men age, testosterone levels tend to decline. Although elderly men who happen to maintain high levels of circulating testosterone perform better on tests of memory and attention than do those with low levels (Yaffe et al., 2002), there have been too few studies to tell whether taking supplemental testosterone actually helps aging men (Harder, 2003; Nair et al., 2006). Furthermore, taking supplemental testosterone can sometimes increase aggressive or manic behaviors (Pope et al., 2000), as well as possibly increasing prostate cancer risk.

THE OVARIES   The paired female gonads, the **ovaries**, also produce both the mature gametes—called *ova* (singular *ovum*) or eggs—and sex steroid hormones. However, hormone secretion is more complicated in ovaries than in testes. Ovarian hormones are produced in cycles, the duration of which varies with the species. Human ovarian cycles last about 4 weeks; rat cycles last only 4 days.

Normally, the ovary produces two major classes of steroid hormones: **progestins** (from the Latin *pro*, "favoring," and *gestare*, "to bear," because these hormones help to maintain pregnancy) and **estrogens** (from the Latin *oestrus*, "gadfly" or "frenzy"—*estrus* is the scientific term for the periodic sexual receptivity of females of many species—and the Greek *gennan*, "to produce"). The most important naturally occurring estrogen is **17β-estradiol** (or just **estradiol**). The primary progestin is **progesterone** (**Figure 5.19***b*). Interestingly, estrogens make the brain sensitive to progesterone by promoting the production of progestin receptors there.

Oral contraceptives contain small doses of synthetic estrogen and/or progestin, which exert a negative feedback effect on the hypothalamus, inhibiting the release of GnRH. The lack of GnRH prevents the release of FSH and LH from the pituitary, and therefore the ovary fails to release an egg for fertilization.

Estrogens may improve aspects of cognitive functioning (Maki and Resnick, 2000), although this topic is still debated (Dohanich, 2003). Estrogens may also protect the brain from some of the effects of stress and stroke (S. Suzuki et al.,

testes   The male gonads, which produce sperm and androgenic steroid hormones.

testosterone   A hormone, produced by male gonads, that controls a variety of bodily changes that become visible at puberty.

androgens   A class of hormones that includes testosterone and other male hormones.

ovaries   The female gonads, which produce eggs for reproduction.

progestins   A major class of steroid hormones that are produced by the ovary, including progesterone.

estrogens   A class of steroid hormones produced by female gonads.

17β-estradiol or estradiol   The primary type of estrogen that is secreted by the ovary.

progesterone   The primary type of progestin secreted by the ovary.

oral contraceptive   A birth control pill, typically consisting of steroid hormones to prevent ovulation.

(a) Male

(b) Female

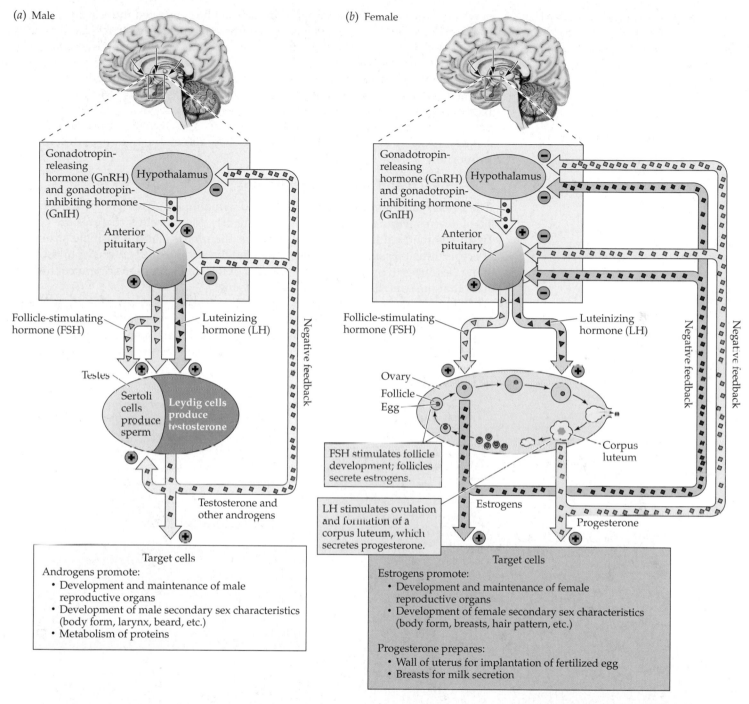

5.19 Regulation of Gonadal Steroid Hormones

2009). For these reasons and others, estrogen replacement therapy has been a popular postmenopausal treatment, but evidence that these treatments increase the risk of serious diseases like cancer and heart disease has raised questions about their safety (Christensen, 1999; Turgeon et al., 2004). Many synthetic estrogens are produced and tested in search of drugs that have only the beneficial effects of the hormone, without its harmful side effects.

RELATIONS AMONG GONADAL HORMONES   As we mentioned earlier, the steroid hormones—androgens, estrogens, progestins, and the adrenal steroids—are all based on the chemical structure of cholesterol, featuring a backbone of four interconnected carbon rings (see Figure 5.7c). Furthermore, progestins can be converted to androgens, and androgens in turn can be converted into estrogens. Each of these conversions is controlled by specific enzymes. The structural similarity among steroids reflects their evolutionary history: as enzymes evolved to modify old steroids, new steroids became available for signaling.

Different organs—and the two sexes—differ in the relative amounts of gonadal hormones that they produce. For example, whereas the testis converts only a relatively small proportion of testosterone into estradiol, the ovary converts most of the testosterone it makes into estradiol. But it is important to appreciate that *no steroid is found exclusively in either males or females*; rather, the two sexes differ in the proportion of these steroids.

The pineal gland secretes melatonin

The **pineal gland** sits atop the brainstem and in mammals is overlaid by the cerebral hemispheres (**Figure 5.20a**; see also Figure 5.1). Most brain structures are paired (with symmetrical left and right sides), but the pineal gland is a single structure. It is this unusual aspect of the pineal that led the seventeenth-century philosopher René Descartes to propose it to be "the seat of the soul"; religious dogma of his day held that the soul, like the pineal, is indivisible.

Today we know that the pineal plays a crucial role in biological rhythms. Governed by the superior cervical ganglion—part of the sympathetic nervous system—the pineal releases an amine hormone called **melatonin**. The melatonin receptor is a G protein–coupled receptor residing in cell membranes and is similar to

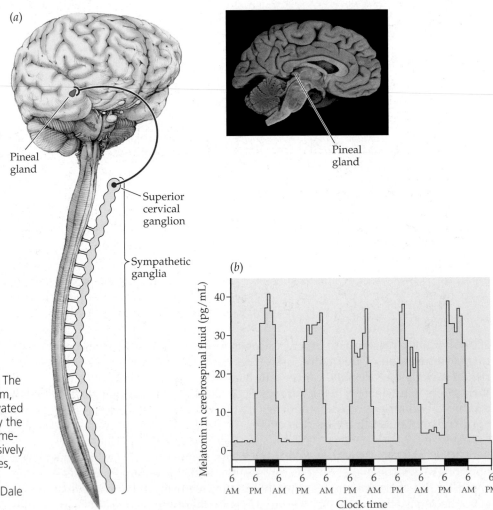

(a)

Pineal gland

Pineal gland

Superior cervical ganglion

Sympathetic ganglia

(b)

5.20 Regulation of the Pineal Gland (a) The pea-shaped pineal gland sits atop the brainstem, tucked under the cerebral hemispheres. Innervated by the sympathetic nervous system, specifically the superior cervical ganglion, the pineal releases melatonin. (b) Melatonin is released almost exclusively during the night in a wide variety of vertebrates, including humans. (After Reppert et al., 1979; photograph courtesy of S. Mark Williams and Dale Purves, Duke University Medical Center.)

receptors for peptide hormones. Because melatonin is released almost exclusively at night (**Figure 5.20***b*), it provides a signal that tracks day length and, by extension, the seasons.

Melatonin secretion controls breeding condition in many seasonally breeding mammals. In hamsters, for example, the lengthening nights of autumn affect activity in the superior cervical ganglion, which in turn causes the pineal to prolong its nocturnal release of melatonin. The hypothalamus responds to the prolonged exposure to melatonin by becoming extremely sensitive to the negative feedback effects of gonadal steroids (Revel et al., 2009). Consequently, less and less GnRH is released, resulting in less gonadotropin release, as well as atrophy of the gonads. In the spring, as days lengthen and the breeding season approaches, the process reverses: the hypothalamus becomes less sensitive to the negative feedback signal from sex steroids, the gonads swell, and the animal prepares to breed. Lesion of the pineal prevents seasonal gonadal regression, whereas chronic melatonin treatments induce regression.

In birds, light from the environment penetrates the thin skull and reaches the pineal gland directly. Photosensitive cells in the bird pineal gland monitor daily light durations (R. G. Foster and Soni, 1998). In several reptile species the pineal is close to the skull and even has an extension of photoreceptors providing a "third eye" in the back of the head. The pineal photoreceptors do not form images but simply monitor day length to regulate seasonal functions.

Humans are not, strictly speaking, seasonal breeders, but melatonin plays a role in our biological rhythms, especially the timing of sleep onset. Like other vertebrates, we release melatonin at night, and administering exogenous melatonin reportedly induces sleep sooner. This is why melatonin has been used to treat jet lag (Sack et al., 1992).

Hormones Affect Behavior in Many Different Ways

In later chapters we will discuss specific examples of the role of hormones in reproductive behavior (Chapter 12), eating and drinking (Chapter 13), biological rhythms (Chapter 14), and stress (Chapter 15). For now, to get an idea of how hormones affect behavior, let's briefly consider the role of hormones in social interaction, and the psychopathology that can result from too much or too little hormone.

Hormones can affect social behavior

We've already seen the role that the hormone oxytocin plays in the interaction of nursing babies and their mothers (see Figure 5.12). It turns out that this hormone is involved in several other social behaviors too. For one thing, a pulse of oxytocin is released during orgasm in both men and women (Carmichael et al., 1994), adding to the pleasurable feelings accompanying sexual encounters.

In nonhuman animals, oxytocin and vasopressin modulate many social processes (Lim and Young, 2006). Rodents given supplementary doses of oxytocin spend more time in physical contact with each other (Carter, 1992). Male mice with the oxytocin gene knocked out are unable to produce the hormone, and they display social amnesia: they seem unable to recognize the scent of female mice that they have met before (Ferguson et al., 2000). These oxytocin knockout males can be cured of their social amnesia with brain infusions of oxytocin, particularly in the medial amygdala (Winslow and Insel, 2002). In mice, the oxytocin released during delivery appears to protect fetal neurons from injury (Tyzio et al., 2006), and to improve the mother's ability to navigate a maze (Tomizawa et al., 2003).

In another rodent, the prairie vole (*Microtus ochrogaster*), in which couples form stable monogamous pair-bonds, oxytocin infusions in the brains of females help them bond to their mates. In male prairie voles, it is vasopressin rather than oxytocin that facilitates the formation of a preference for female partners. In fact, the

(a)

(b)

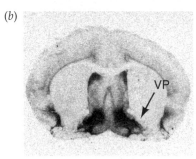

(c)

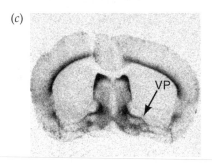

5.21 Vasopressin and the Monogamous Brain (a) Prairie voles form long-lasting pair-bonds. (b) Monogamy in male prairie voles seems to be due to the dense concentration of vasopressin receptors in the ventral pallidum (VP). (c) Males of the closely related meadow vole species have fewer vasopressin receptors in the VP, which may explain why they are not monogamous. (Photographs courtesy of Miranda Lim and Larry Young.)

distribution of vasopressin receptors in the brains of male prairie voles may be what makes them monogamous.

Supporting this idea is the finding that, in the closely related meadow voles (*M. pennsylvanicus*), which do not form pair-bonds and instead have multiple mating partners, the males have far fewer vasopressin receptors in certain brain regions than do prairie voles (**Figure 5.21**) (Lim et al., 2004). Furthermore, laboratory mice that have been genetically engineered to produce vasopressin receptors in their brains in the same pattern that is seen in prairie vole males are much more interested in associating with females, almost as if they were trying to form a pair-bond.

Thus, it appears that oxytocin and vasopressin regulate a range of social behaviors, and that natural selection sometimes alters the social behaviors of a species through changes in the brain distribution of receptors for these two peptides (Donaldson and Young, 2008).

Endocrine pathology can produce extreme effects on human behavior

Both deficient and excessive hormone secretion are associated with a variety of human physiological, anatomical, and behavioral disorders (Erhardt and Goldman, 1992). Many hormonal disorders resemble psychiatric disorders (**Table 5.3**). For example, parathyroid deficiency (the parathyroids are small glands, located behind the thyroid, that regulate calcium levels) results in calcium deposition in the basal ganglia and symptoms that resemble schizophrenia. Patients with excessive thyroid release frequently appear intensely anxious; we mentioned earlier that people like Chuck, with decreased thyroid release, may show cognitive impairments and depression. An inherited form of attention deficit hyperactivity disorder in children involves decreased sensitivity to thyroid hormone (Hauser et al., 1993).

A long-term excess of glucocorticoids results in **Cushing's syndrome**, a constellation of symptoms that includes fatigue, depression, *hirsutism* (unusual hair growth, such as beard growth in women), and various autonomic changes. The depression may precede other physiological effects of excessive cortisol secretion. Psychiatric symptoms including psychosis have been reported in people who take exogenous glucocorticoids for sustained periods of time. Excessive glucocorticoid exposure is also associated with *steroid dementia syndrome*, a long-lasting impairment of cognition, including memory and attention (Wolkowitz et al., 2004).

Cushing's syndrome   A condition in which levels of adrenal glucocorticoids are abnormally high.

TABLE 5.3   Hormonal Disorders and Associated Cognitive, Emotional, and Psychiatric Disorders

Hormonal disorder	Impaired cognition	Anxiety	Depression	Psychosis and delirium
Hyperthyroidism	+	++	+	+
Hypothyroidism	+	+	++	++
Hypercortisolism	+	++	++	++
Hypocortisolism	—	+	++	++
Panhypopituitarism[a]	—	+	++	++
Hyperparathyroidism	+	+	++	++
Hypoparathyroidism	?	++	++	++
Hyperinsulinism	+	++	—	++
Hypoinsulinism	+	—	—	+

Note: +, sometimes; ++, often.

[a]Undersecretion of all or nearly all anterior pituitary hormones.

Hormonal and Neural Systems Interact to Produce Integrated Responses

In many ways, the endocrine system and the nervous system can be viewed simply as divisions of a single master control mechanism. The two divisions work together, in an intimate and reciprocal manner, to seamlessly integrate the systems of the body and produce adaptive responses to environmental challenges.

Incoming environmental stimuli elicit activity in sensory pathways that project to a wide variety of brain regions, including the cerebral cortex, cerebellum, and hypothalamus. Our own behavioral responses to environmental circumstances bring further changes in stimulation. For example, if we approach an object or a sound source, we cause the visual image to become larger or the sound to become louder. Meanwhile the endocrine system is tuning our response characteristics to be consistent with the nature of the stimulus. If the stimulus calls for action—that faint buzzing sound turns out to be coming from a nest of angry wasps, for example—energy is mobilized through hormonal routes to prepare for appropriate behaviors (namely, sprinting and swatting and maybe yelling). The behaviors themselves, of course, are executed under the control of the nervous system. Sensory receptor organs are also subject to continual adjustment, thus modifying further processing of stimuli. Another example of neural and hormonal coordination is the milk letdown reflex (see Figure 5.12).

Four kinds of signals are possible between neurons and endocrine cells: neural-to-neural, neural-to-endocrine, endocrine-to-endocrine, and endocrine-to-neural. All four types are illustrated in the courtship behavior of the ringdove (**Figure 5.22**).

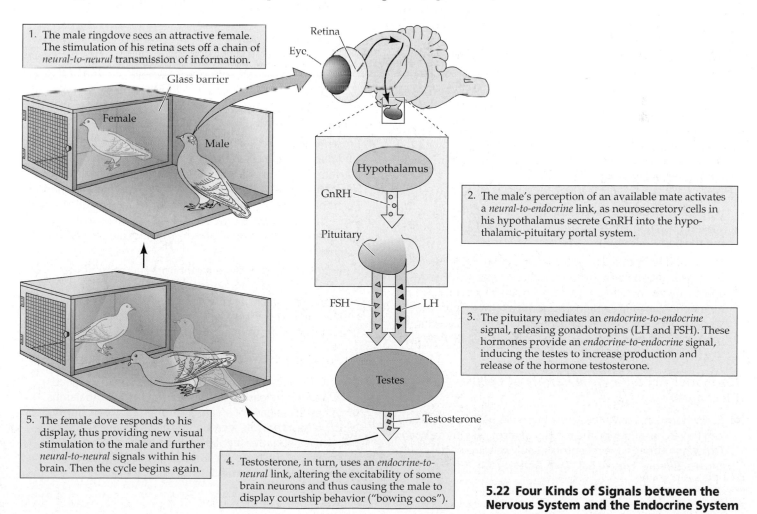

1. The male ringdove sees an attractive female. The stimulation of his retina sets off a chain of *neural-to-neural* transmission of information.

2. The male's perception of an available mate activates a *neural-to-endocrine* link, as neurosecretory cells in his hypothalamus secrete GnRH into the hypothalamic-pituitary portal system.

3. The pituitary mediates an *endocrine-to-endocrine* signal, releasing gonadotropins (LH and FSH). These hormones provide an *endocrine-to-endocrine* signal, inducing the testes to increase production and release of the hormone testosterone.

4. Testosterone, in turn, uses an *endocrine-to-neural* link, altering the excitability of some brain neurons and thus causing the male to display courtship behavior ("bowing coos").

5. The female dove responds to his display, thus providing new visual stimulation to the male and further *neural-to-neural* signals within his brain. Then the cycle begins again.

5.22 Four Kinds of Signals between the Nervous System and the Endocrine System

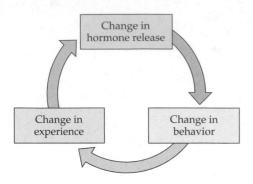

5.23 The Reciprocal Relations between Hormones and Behavior

The visual processing that occurs when a male dove sees an attractive female involves neural-to-neural transmission (step 1 in the figure). The details of the particular visual stimulus—namely, that it involves an opportunity for reproduction—activate a neural-to-endocrine link (step 2), which causes neurosecretory cells in the male's hypothalamus to secrete GnRH. The GnRH provides an endocrine-to-endocrine signal (step 3), stimulating the pituitary to release gonadotropins to induce the testes to release more testosterone. Testosterone, in turn, alters the excitability of neurons in the male's brain through an endocrine-to-neural link (step 4), causing the male to display courtship behavior. The female dove responds to this display (step 5), thus providing new visual stimulation to the male, triggering another cycle of signaling within him.

The interactions between endocrine activity and behavior are cyclical, as depicted by the circle schema in **Figure 5.23**. We saw earlier how Chuck's lack of thyroid hormone drastically affected his behavior and therefore what he experienced (i.e., not much except television). The level of circulating hormones can also be altered by experience, which in turn can affect future behavior and future experience. For example, starting to exercise or stepping out in the cold increases the release of thyroid hormones. Men rooting for a sports team will produce more testosterone if their team wins (Bernhardt et al., 1998). Physical stresses, pain, and unpleasant emotional situations decrease thyroid output and trigger the release of adrenal glucocorticoids (see Chapter 15).

Conversely, each of these hormonal events will affect the brain, shaping behavior, which will once more affect the person's future hormone production. Any thorough understanding of the relationship between hormones and behavior must come to grips with these reciprocal interactions.

SUMMARY

Hormones Act in a Great Variety of Ways throughout the Body

- **Hormones** are chemical compounds that act as signals in the body. Many are secreted by **endocrine glands** into the bloodstream and are taken up by receptor molecules in target cells. **Review Figure 5.1**, **Web Activity 5.1**

- Neural communication differs from hormonal communication in that neural signals travel rapidly over fixed pathways, whereas hormonal signals spread more slowly and throughout the body.

- Neural and hormonal communication systems have several characteristics in common: Both utilize chemical messages; some substances act as a hormone in some locations and as a synaptic transmitter in others. Both systems manufacture, store, and release chemical messengers. Both use specific receptors and may employ second messengers. **Review Figure 5.6**, **Web Activity 5.2**

Hormones Act on a Wide Variety of Cellular Mechanisms

- Some hormones have receptors in a wide variety of cells and can therefore influence the activity of most cells in the body. Other hormones have receptors in only certain special cells or organs. **Review Figure 5.8**, **Web Activity 5.3**

- Hormones act by promoting the proliferation and differentiation of cells and by modulating the activity of cells that have already differentiated.

- **Protein** and **amine hormones** typically bind to specific receptor molecules at the surface of the target cell membrane and activate second-messenger molecules inside the cell. **Steroid hormones** generally pass through the membrane and bind to receptor molecules inside the cell, ultimately regulating gene expression. However, some steroid actions involve other, more rapid signaling mechanisms that include cell surface receptors.

- A **negative feedback** system monitors and controls the rate of secretion of each hormone. In the simplest case the hormone acts on target cells, leading them to change the amount of a substance they release; this change in turn regulates output of the endocrine gland. **Review Figure 5.9**

Each Endocrine Gland Secretes Specific Hormones

- Several hormones are controlled by a more complex feedback system: a releasing hormone from the hypothalamus regulates the release of an anterior pituitary **tropic hormone**, which in turn controls secretion by an endocrine gland. In these cases, negative feedback of the endocrine hormone acts mainly at the hypothalamus and **anterior pituitary**. **Review Figures 5.10 and 5.15**, **Web Activity 5.4**

■ Endocrine influences on structures and functions often involve more than one hormone, as in growth, homeostasis, metabolism, and learning and memory. **Review Table 5.2**

Hormones Affect Behavior in Many Different Ways

■ Circulating hormones alter the probability of various behaviors, including regulating social behaviors. Abnormally high or low levels of hormones can result in symptoms of cognitive, emotional or psychiatric disorders. **Review Table 5.3**

Hormonal and Neural Systems Interact to Produce Integrated Responses

■ Many behaviors require the coordination of neural and hormonal components. Messages may be transmitted in the body via neural-to-neural, neural-to-endocrine, endocrine-to-endocrine, or endocrine-to-neural links. There are continuous, reciprocal influences between the endocrine system and the nervous system: experience affects hormone secretion, and hormones affect behavior and therefore future experiences. **Review Figures 5.22 and 5.23**

Go to www.biopsychology.com for study questions, quizzes, key terms, and other resources.

Recommended Reading

Becker, J. B., Breedlove, S. M., Crews, D., and McCarthy, M. M. (Eds.). (2002). *Behavioral endocrinology* (2nd ed.). Cambridge, MA: MIT Press.

Hadley, M. E., and Levine, J. (2006). *Endocrinology* (6th ed.). Englewood Cliffs, NJ: Prentice Hall.

Holt, R., and Hanley, N. (2006). *Essential endocrinology and diabetes*. Ames, IA: Blackwell.

Kronenberg, H. M., Melmed, S., Polonsky, K. S., and Larsen, P. R. (2007). *Williams textbook of endocrinology* (11th ed.). Philadelphia: Saunders.

Nelson, R. J. (2005). *An introduction to behavioral endocrinology* (3rd ed.). Sunderland, MA: Sinauer.

Pfaff, D. W., Phillips, I. M., and Rubin, R. T. (2004). *Principles of hormone/behavior relations*. San Diego, CA: Academic Press.

Evolution and Development of the Nervous System

PART II

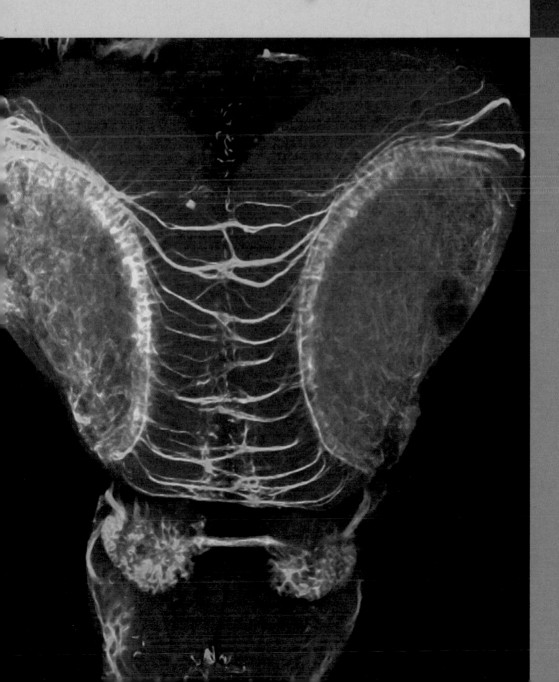

Previous page **Brain development in a three-day-old zebrafish embryo**   This whole-mount of an embryonic zebrafish brain was imaged using fluorescent dyes and confocal microscopy. The developing fiber tracts connecting homologous regions of the left and right hemispheres are clearly evident. (Image by Michael Hendricks, Center for Brain Science, Harvard University.)

Evolution of the Brain and Behavior

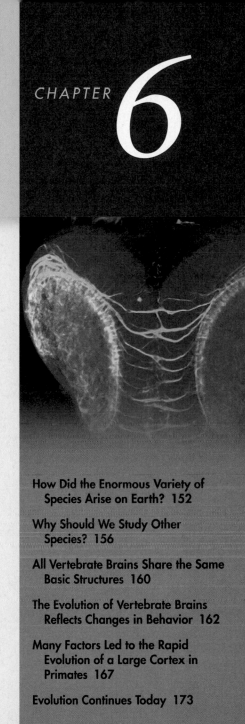

CHAPTER 6

We Are Not So Different, Are We?

If you have spent any length of time at the primate enclosure at the zoo, or watched a documentary about chimpanzees, you won't be surprised to learn that our closest animal relatives are the chimpanzees. After all, so many of their expressions and behaviors seem oddly, well, human. But despite the apparent similarities, humans and chimps are also strikingly dissimilar in many fundamental ways. Whereas humans have complex languages, chimps make only a small variety of vocal sounds. And whereas humans walk erect and have long legs, chimps travel mostly on all fours and have relatively long arms. The human brain is about twice the size of the chimp's. Humans have spread wide from their origins in Africa, populating (or overpopulating) the globe, but chimps have remained in Africa, their numbers now dwindling at an alarming rate.

Given the many differences between humans and chimps, you might be surprised to learn that the genetic material of the two species differs by only about 1.2%. One prominent scientist suggested that, since the genes of chimps and humans differ so little, the social context provided during the rearing of human children must be what causes them to come out so differently from chimpanzees. If that suggestion strikes you as unlikely, you are probably right. Several people have tried to rear chimpanzees like human children (see Chapter 19), and none of the chimps ever won a spelling bee or got a driver's license (not even a learner's permit).

Of course, social rearing is crucial for human development, but it cannot explain the vast differences between chimps and humans. So the problem remains: If human and chimp DNA is nearly 99% identical, how can we explain the striking differences in behavior, anatomy, and neurobiology? In other words, what makes humans human? Progress in neurobiological research is suggesting answers to this puzzle, as we will see.

O ur major objective in this chapter is to explore the intriguing story of how brains and behavior have evolved. We will see that brain size in primates, especially in humans, increased rapidly in our recent evolution. This enlarged brain doubtless increased our capacity for higher cognitive abilities, yet it is difficult to determine which expanded brain regions brought us which additional abilities. Thus, scientists study the nervous system in a wide variety of animals to understand how the evolution of a particular brain feature affects particular behaviors. But describing the relationships between the nervous system and behavior in even a small fraction of Earth's inhabitants would be an awesome (and dull) task unless we had a rationale beyond mere completeness. If we choose the right species to compare, however, we can learn about the principles of nervous system organization.

How Did the Enormous Variety of Species Arise on Earth?

Until about 200 years ago, it was generally believed that each species had been created separately. Then, some **naturalists**—students of animal life and structure— began to have doubts. For example, some naturalists observed that the limb bones of all mammals, no matter what the animal's way of life, are remarkably similar in many details (**Figure 6.1**). If these species had been specifically created for different ways of locomotion, the naturalists reasoned, they should have been built on different plans rather than all being modifications of a single plan.

As nineteenth-century geologists showed that Earth has been changing for millions of years, the newly discovered fossils of extinct species provided additional evidence for **evolution**—the gradual changing of one species into another. But a plausible *mechanism* for evolution was lacking.

Natural selection drives evolution

In 1858, Charles Darwin (1809–1892) and Alfred Russel Wallace (1823–1913) announced the hypothesis of **evolution by natural selection**. Darwin and Wallace had each hit upon the idea independently. The idea came to Wallace out of the blue, while he was suffering from a fever. In contrast, Darwin had been accumulating evidence to support the hypothesis for over 20 years, ever since he had voyaged on the HMS *Beagle* to South America and the Galápagos Islands, off the west coast of South America. The governor of the Galápagos had pointed out to Darwin that the giant tortoises differed in their shell patterns from island to island. Later, examining the specimens of finches that he had collected on different Galápagos islands, Darwin observed that the birds also differed from island to island. Although the birds resembled finches on the mainland, those on the Galápagos appeared to represent several different species, suited by their body sizes and beaks to obtaining different kinds of food, such as nuts or seeds or insects. Darwin speculated that the different birds had been a single species long ago and that, isolated on the islands, they had gradually diverged from their ancestors.

In 1859, Darwin published his revolutionary book *On the Origin of Species by Means of Natural Selection*. The hypothesis he stated was based on four main observations and one important inference. The observations were these:

1. Reproduction will tend to increase a population rapidly unless factors limit it.
2. Individuals of a given species are not identical.
3. Some of the variation among individuals is inherited.
4. Not all the offspring of a given generation survive to reproduce.

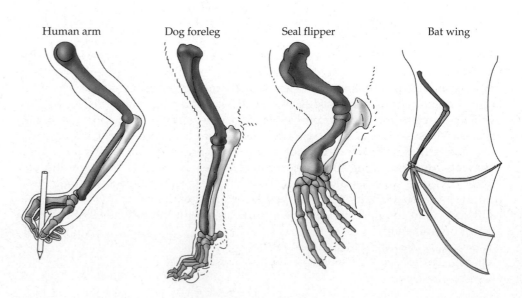

Human arm   Dog foreleg   Seal flipper   Bat wing

6.1 Homology of Forelimb Structures Bones of the same sort are shown here in the same color in all species. The sizes and shapes of the bones of the forelimb have evolved so that they are adapted to widely different functions: skilled manipulation in humans, locomotion in dogs, swimming in seals, flying in bats. The similarities among the sets of bones reflect descent from a common ancestor.

The inference was that the variations among individuals affect the probability of their surviving, reproducing, and passing on characteristics. The individuals better suited to the prevailing conditions will be those that reproduce and furnish the next generation. Therefore, individuals possessing **adaptations**, traits that increase the probability of having offspring, will predominate in the population. Over time, this selection at the level of individual organisms can yield substantial changes in the species.

The concept of evolution by natural selection has become one of the major organizing principles in all the life sciences, directing the study of behavior and its mechanisms, as well as the study of morphology (form and structure). Darwin (1859) felt confident that psychological functions are as much products of evolution as are the organs of the body.

Darwin later added another evolutionary principle: **sexual selection** (1871). This principle holds that members of each sex exert selective pressures on the other in terms of both anatomical and behavioral features that favor reproductive success. For example, female choices have led to the ornamental but costly tails of peacocks. We will discuss this principle later in this chapter.

Evolution may converge upon similar solutions

Adaptation to similar ecological features may bring about similarities in behavior or structure among animals that are only distantly related. These similarities are referred to as examples of **convergent evolution**. For example, the body forms of a tuna and a dolphin resemble each other because they each evolved for efficient swimming, even though the tuna is a fish and the dolphin is a mammal descended from terrestrial ancestors. Such a resemblance is an example of **homoplasy**, a resemblance between features that is due to convergent evolution. By contrast, a **homology** is a resemblance based on common *ancestry*, such as the similarities in forelimb structures of mammals that we described earlier (see Figure 6.1). **Analogy** refers to similar *function*, although the structures may look different (e.g., the hand of a human and the trunk of an elephant are analogous).

Modern evolutionary theory combines natural selection and genetics

A gap in Darwin's theory was his inability to specify either the source of variation by natural selection or the mechanism of biological inheritance. The pioneering work of an Austrian monk and botanist named Gregor Johann Mendel (1822–1884), however, accomplished a major step toward rounding out the theory of evolution. On the basis of his research with pea plants, Mendel published the laws of inheritance in an obscure journal in 1866 (Mendel, 1967). Not until 1900, however, was Mendel's work rediscovered and linked to evolution by the Dutch biologist Hugo de Vries (1848–1935), who was conducting experiments with primroses. De Vries went beyond Mendel in an important respect: he found that occasionally a new variety arose spontaneously and then passed its characteristics on to successive generations. In 1901, de Vries pointed out that, in such cases, evolution could occur by sudden jumps, or **mutations**, as he called these changes (**Figure 6.2**). (Nowadays, scientists deliberately induce mutations in plants and animals, as we discuss in Box 7.3.)

adaptation Here, a trait that increases the probability that an individual will leave offspring in subsequent generations.

sexual selection Darwin's theoretical mechanism for the evolution of anatomical and behavioral differences between males and females.

convergent evolution The evolutionary process by which responses to similar ecological features bring about similarities in behavior or structure among animals that are only distantly related (i.e., that differ in genetic heritage).

homoplasy A physical resemblance that is due to convergent evolution, such as the similar body form of tuna and dolphins.

homology A physical resemblance that is based on common ancestry, such as the similarity in forelimb structures of different mammals.

analogy Similarity of function, although the structures of interest may look different. The human hand and an elephant's trunk are analogous features.

mutation A change in the nucleotide sequence of a gene as a result of unfaithful replication.

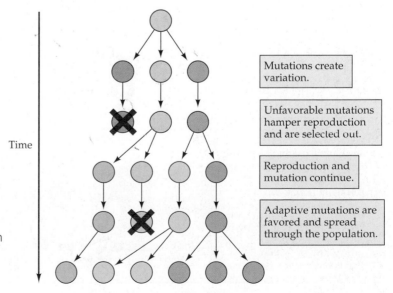

Time

Mutations create variation.

Unfavorable mutations hamper reproduction and are selected out.

Reproduction and mutation continue.

Adaptive mutations are favored and spread through the population.

6.2 Natural Selection at the Genetic Level A gene mutation that affects behavior may be selected for if the alteration in behavior is adaptive. Thus, not just physical traits, but also behaviors, evolve in a species over time.

genetics The study of inheritance, including the genes encoded in DNA.

chromosome A complex of condensed strands of DNA and associated protein molecules; found in the nucleus of cells.

Although **genetics**, the study of the mechanisms of inheritance, started with plants such as the pea and the primrose, investigators soon began to study organisms that reproduce more rapidly. An example is the fruit fly *Drosophila*, whose generation time is 10 days and whose salivary glands produce giant chromosomes that are visible under a light microscope. **Chromosomes** (from the Greek *chroma*, "color," and *soma*, "body") are rod-shaped assemblies of DNA in the nucleus of each cell that bear genetic information. Many of the findings about genetic mecha-

6.3 Linnaean Classification of the Domestic Dog

SPECIES. The basic (most specific) unit of taxonomic classification, consisting of a population or set of populations of closely related and similar organisms capable of interbreeding. The domestic dog is the species *Canis familiaris*. There are about 400 breeds of dogs, all considered to belong to one species.

Canis familiaris. 1 species

Domestic dogs

GENUS (plural *genera*). The main subdivision of a family; a group of similar, related species. Some genera in the family Canidae are *Canis* (dogs, coyotes, two species of wolves, four species of jackals) and *Vulpes* (ten species of foxes).

Canis. 8 species

Dogs, wolves, coyotes, jackals

FAMILY. The main subdivision of an order; a group of similar, related genera. Some families in the order Carnivora are **Canidae** (dogs, foxes, and related genera) and Felidae (domestic cats, lions, panthers, and related genera). Family names always end in *-idae*.

Canidae. Approximately 35 species

Canids

ORDER. The main subdivision of a class; a group of similar, related families. Some orders of the class Mammalia are **Carnivora** (meat eaters such as dogs, cats, bears, weasels, etc.) and Primates (humans, monkeys, and apes).

Carnivora. Approximately 235 species

Carnivores

CLASS. The main subdivision of a phylum; a group of similar, related orders. Some classes within the phylum Chordata are **Mammalia**, Aves (birds), and Reptilia. Mammals are characterized by production of milk by the female mammary glands and by hair for body covering.

Mammalia. Approximately 4300 species

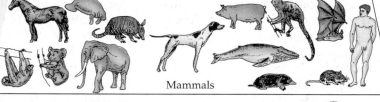
Mammals

PHYLUM (plural *phyla*). The main—and most inclusive—subdivision of a kingdom; a group of similar, related classes. Some phyla are **Chordata**, Mollusca, and Arthropoda. Chordates differ from members of the other phyla by having an internal skeleton.

Chordata. Approximately 40,000 species

Vertebrates

KINGDOM. All living beings can be divided into five kingdoms: **Animalia**, Plantae, Fungi, Monera (bacteria), and Protista.

Animalia. Approximately 1 million species of animals are known. The total number of existing species has been estimated to be as high as 30 million.

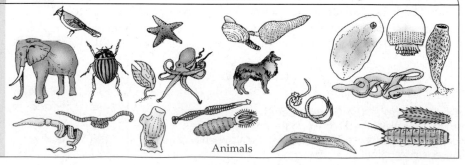
Animals

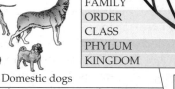
Dogs

SPECIES
GENUS
FAMILY
ORDER
CLASS
PHYLUM
KINGDOM

All animals alive today shared a common ancestor. Any chosen pair of species has been evolving since their last shared ancestor.

nisms made with *Drosophila* and even with bacteria hold true for larger organisms, such as humans, that reproduce much more slowly. Nowadays, we know that chromosomes are made up of supercoiled lengths of DNA, and that lengths of DNA contain the information to assemble the tens of thousands of proteins that make up the body (see the Appendix).

Both gradual changes within a species and the formation of new species can now be understood in the light of modern evolutionary theory, which combines Darwin's hypothesis of natural selection with modern genetics and molecular biology.

How closely related are two species?

People have probably always classified the animals around them and realized that some forms resemble each other more closely than others. The Swedish biologist Carolus Linnaeus (1707–1778) proposed the basic system that we use today. In Linnaeus's system, each species is assigned two names—the first name identifying the **genus** (plural *genera*), the second name indicating the **species**. Both names are always italicized, and the genus name is capitalized. According to this system, the modern human species is *Homo sapiens*.

The different levels of classification are illustrated and defined in **Figure 6.3**. The main trunk, the animal kingdom, includes all animal species. As branches divide and subdivide toward the outer reaches of the tree, each successive category includes fewer species, and the species are more closely related. The order of categories, from most broad to most narrow, is this: kingdom, phylum, class, order, family, genus, species. (Here's an aid to remembering the succession of classifications from broadest to most specific: *k*indly *p*ut *c*lothes *o*n, *f*or goodness' *s*ake.) Linnaeus classified animals mainly on the basis of gross anatomical similarities and differences; he did not mean to imply anything about evolution or common ancestry.

Today we understand that these levels of similarity that Linnaeus described reflect **phylogeny** (from the Greek *phylon*, "tribe" or "kind," and *genes*, "born"), the evolutionary history of a particular group of organisms. Phylogeny is often represented as a *family tree* that shows which species may have given rise to others. (Some scientists prefer to say *bush* rather than *tree* because the phylogeny branches so extensively.) Comparisons among extant animals, coupled with fragmentary but illuminating data from fossils, allow us to hypothesize about the history of the body and brain, and the forces that shaped them (Pennisi, 2003).

Newer methods aid in classifying animals and inferring evolution

In classifying animals, the field of **taxonomy** (from the Greek *taxis*, "arrangement," and *nomos*, "law")—or *classification*—these days makes use of our understanding of genetics to reconstruct phylogeny. DNA appears to change at a relatively steady average rate in all lineages of a given order of animals (Hillis et al., 1996). Thus, the proportion of differences between DNA samples from two species can be used as a "molecular clock" to estimate how long ago they diverged from a common ancestor. For example, **Figure 6.4** shows an attempt by Wildman et al. (2003) to reconstruct the family tree of apes and humans according to the genetic similarity of the species. Their diagram depicts humans and chimpanzees as more closely related to each other than either one is to the gorilla. The absolute times in Figure 6.4 should be considered with caution, however, because scientists are still discussing and testing ideas about calibration of the molecular clocks.

Estimates from fossil and DNA evidence do not always agree completely in dating branches of the evolutionary tree. Fossil dates tend to be too recent, because we can never find the first specimen of a given species. Molecular dates have tended to be too old, because of problems with calibrating rates of change of DNA over time. But Benton and Ayala (2003) show that these discrepancies are diminishing, and most paleontological and molecular dates now agree.

genus A group of species that resemble each other because of shared inheritance.

species A group of individuals that can readily interbreed to produce fertile offspring.

phylogeny The evolutionary history of a particular group of organisms.

taxonomy The classification of organisms.

6.4 Family Tree of Apes and Humans

This tree was derived from measurements of differences between pairs of species in samples of their genetic material, molecules of deoxyribonucleic acid (DNA). To see how different two species are in their genetic endowments, trace the lines from the two members of a pair to the point that connects them, and match the point with the scale on the left. For example, the line from humans and the line from chimpanzees converge at a point indicating that human DNA differs from chimpanzee DNA by just over 1%. The DNA of humans and of chimpanzees differs from that of the gorilla, in turn, by about 2.3%. The scale on the right gives the estimated amount of time, in millions of years, since any pair of species shared a common ancestor. For example, humans and chimpanzees diverged from a common ancestor about 4–6 million years ago. (After Wildman et al., 2003.)

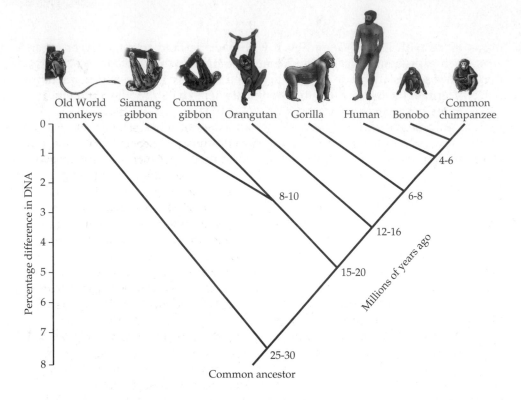

Why Should We Study Other Species?

One old-fashioned reason for comparing species was to investigate the question, Why do humans end up at the top of the animal order? This human-centered perspective was properly criticized because it implicitly pictured other animals as incomplete "little humans" (**Figure 6.5**). It also embraced the old idea that animals vary along a single scale from simple to complex, whereas scientists now see animal evolution as a multibranching set of radiations. Today we use comparisons of different species to gather clues about evolutionary history.

Comparisons of the behavior and neural mechanisms of different kinds of animals in different ecological niches appear in every chapter of this book. Comparing two or more carefully chosen species leads to a much deeper understanding because the evolutionary framework provides additional explanatory power. Each species is busily evolving adaptations to survive in its present environment. Species with varying biological histories show different solutions to the challenges of survival and reproduction. In many cases, these pressures to adapt have led to changes in brain structure. **Box 6.1** provides some reasons for studying a particular species.

One important adaptation is the ability to learn in order to successfully predict how to find food and to avoid danger. This capability must have arisen early in evolution, because even simple animals show lasting changes in behavior following important experiences. Understanding how the nervous systems of these simpler animals form and store memories provides insights into the mechanisms of memory in more-complex animals, including human beings, as we will see in Chapter 17. For now, let's look at a few examples of how comparing species can inform us about brain function.

In many songbirds, males sing to court females and persuade them to mate. In some species, each male may sing only a single song, while in other species males have repertoires of ten or more different tunes. The females prefer to mate with males with larger repertoires, so large

6.5 We Are Related, Aren't We?

BOX 6.1 Why Should We Study Particular Species?

With all the species that are available, why should we choose certain ones for study? In selecting species for their research, investigators usually use several criteria, including the following:

1. *Outstanding features.* Some species are champions at various behaviors and abilities, such as sensory discrimination (e.g., the acute auditory localization of the owl, or the extremely fine visual acuity of the eagle) or control of movement (e.g., the flight behavior of the housefly). These abilities are often linked to highly specialized neuronal structures that incorporate and optimize particular designs that may be less conspicuous in other organisms (Bullock, 1984, 1986). Study of such species may yield general principles that apply to other species. The female spotted hyena appears to have a penis and is dominant over the smaller male; this sex "reversal" is caused by unusual hormonal adaptations that help illuminate sexual development (see Box 12.1).

2. *Convenience.* Some species, such as the laboratory rat, are particularly convenient for study because they breed well in the laboratory, are relatively inexpensive to maintain, are not rare or endangered, have relatively short life spans, and have been studied extensively already, so there is a good base

of knowledge about them at the outset. In addition, they may serve as good models because their morphology and behavior show clear relationships to other species. Other species are convenient because they offer advantages for certain methods of study. For example, some mollusks have relatively simple nervous systems that aid in tracing neural circuits. The fruit fly *Drosophila* is excellent for genetic studies because it has a relatively simple genome and a short time period between generations; furthermore, investigators have been increasingly impressed by the large number of DNA sequences that *Drosophila* shares with mammals, including humans (R. Lewis, 1998).

3. *Comparison.* Close relationships between species that behave very differently enable the testing of hypotheses. For example, whereas in some closely related species of rodents the home ranges of males and females differ in size, in others they do not. Comparison of these species tests whether differences in maze-solving ability are associated with the size of the home range and with the size of the hippocampus (see Chapter 17).

4. *Preservation.* Studies of rare and/or endangered species can help set priorities and assess options for the conserva-

tion of biodiversity (Mace et al., 2003). Endangered species are seldom studied in the laboratory, but they may be investigated in field studies or in zoos.

5. *Economic importance.* Species that are economically important include agricultural animals (e.g., sheep and cows), animals that furnish valuable products (e.g., fishes), predators on agricultural animals (e.g., wolves), and destroyers of crops (e.g., elephants). Studying these animals can provide information that helps increase production and/or decrease losses.

6. *Treatment of disease.* Some species are subject to the same diseases as other species and therefore are valuable models for investigation. For diseases of the nervous system, examples include certain kinds of mice that provide a model for the behavior and anatomy of Down syndrome (see Chapter 7); baboons and certain breeds of dogs that are prone to seizures (see Chapter 3); several breeds of dogs that are afflicted by narcolepsy (see Chapter 14); some strains of rodents that provide models for depression (see Chapter 16); and *Drosophila* and mice, which now provide models for investigations of Parkinson's disease (see Chapter 11).

---

repertoires are definitely adaptive in those species. Across the closely related European warblers, there is a strong correlation between repertoire size and a brain region known as HVC (**Figure 6.6**). Without any other knowledge of HVC, this correlation provides evidence that it is important for song production in birds (as a variety of other experiments have indicated—HVC stands for "higher vocal center"). When females select males for large repertoires, they also select for larger HVCs to produce all those songs. This is also an example of sexual selection: large repertoires are adaptive only because the opposite sex prefers them. Next we'll see that the need for food affects brain evolution too.

Some ways of obtaining food require bigger brains than others

Most species of animals spend much of their time and energy in the pursuit of food, often using elaborate strategies.

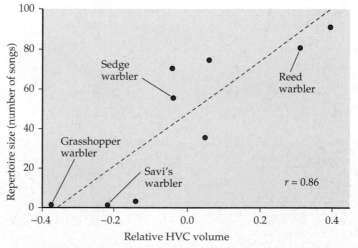

6.6 Brainy Warblers Sing More Songs (Data from Székely et al., 1996.)

Researchers have found that the strategies that different species use to obtain food are correlated to brain size and structure. For example, mammals that eat food distributed in clusters that are difficult to find (such as ripe fruit) tend to have brains larger than those of related species whose food is rather uniformly distributed and easy to find (such as grass or leaves). This relationship has been found within families of rodents, insectivores (such as shrews and moles), lagomorphs (such as rabbits and pikas) (Clutton-Brock and Harvey, 1980), and primates (Mace et al., 1981).

Finding novel ways of getting food is related to the size of the forebrain in different orders of birds (Lefebvre et al., 1997). Investigators collected accounts of novel behavior from ornithological journals, including magpies digging up potatoes, house sparrows searching car radiator grilles for insects, crows dropping palm nuts in the paths of cars that run over and open them. In data sets from both North America and the British Isles, more-innovative species have relatively larger forebrains. The results suggest selection for increased size of the forebrain to cope with environmental challenges and opportunities in new, flexible ways.

BOX 6.2 To Each Its Own Sensory World

Lifestyle differences among mammals are related to the organization of the cerebral cortex, as the examples here show. The rat (*Rattus norvegicus*) is nocturnal and uses its whiskers to find its way in the dark. About 28% of the representation of the rat's body surface in the cortex is devoted to the whiskers (vibrissae), compared to only about 9% in the squirrel (*Sciurus carolinensis*) (see Figure A) (Huffman et al., 1999). In addition, the nocturnal rat makes rather little use of vision, and its primary visual cortex (V1) is relatively small compared with that of the squirrel, which is diurnal.

The remarkable platypus (*Ornithorhynchus anatinus*) is an egg-laying mammal that lives in and around streams in eastern Australia and Tasmania. Because of its ducklike bill and webbed feet, some scientists thought it might be a hoax when the first skin preparations were brought to Europe at the beginning of the nineteenth century. The platypus is largely nocturnal and dives into murky waters, closing its eyes, ears, and nostrils as it hunts for insects, shrimp, and crayfish. How it senses its prey remained a mystery until the 1980s, when investigators found that the main sensory organ of the platypus is its bill, which is about 7 cm long in a 160-cm-long adult.

The bill has about 16 longitudinal stripes of receptors: stripes of touch (mechanosensory) receptors alternating with touch-electrical (electrosensory) receptors (see Figure B) (Manger et al., 1998). As the platypus moves its bill underwater, it can detect prey by both the mechanical ripples and the changes in electrical fields that they cause. In keeping with the importance of the bill in locating prey, almost all of the somatosensory cortex (S1 and S2) in the platypus is devoted to the bill (see Figure B), and the primary visual (V1) and auditory (A1) areas are small (Krubitzer et al., 1995).

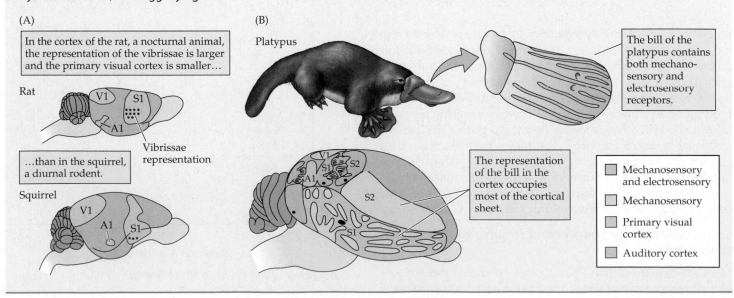

6.7 Food Storing in Birds as Related to Hippocampal Size Food-storing species of birds have twice as large a hippocampus in relation to their forebrain (telencephalon) as do species that do not store food. Note that both axes on this graph are logarithmic. (After Sherry et al., 1989.)

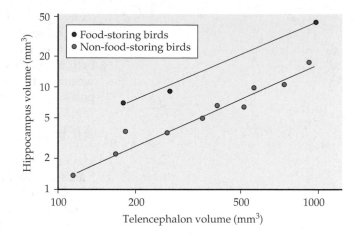

Later in the chapter we will see an extension of this kind of study to species of primates, showing that increased size of the forebrain seems to be related to innovation and sociality.

Other behavioral adaptations have also been related to differences in relative sizes of certain brain structures. For example, some species of bats find their way and locate prey by hearing; others rely almost entirely on vision. In the midbrain, the auditory center (inferior colliculus) is much larger in bats that depend on hearing; bats that depend on sight have a larger visual center (superior colliculus). Birds in families that store bits of food for later use (e.g., the acorn woodpecker, Clark's nutcracker, and the black-capped chickadee) have a larger hippocampus relative to the forebrain and to body weight than do birds in families that do not store food (Sherry, 1992). This difference has been found among both North American species (**Figure 6.7**) and European species. For more on hippocampal size and memory for food storage, see **A Step Further: Food Storing Depends on Hippocampal Size**, on the website.

Box 6.2 provides other examples of solutions that different species employ to solve the dilemmas of adaptation. As a general rule, the relative size of a brain region is a good guide to the importance of the function of that region for the adaptations of the species. Our understanding of how these differences in size and structure of the brain promote behavioral specializations should help us understand the neural basis of human behavior. For example, the sizes of some regions in the human temporal lobes seem related to language function (see Chapter 19).

Invertebrates offer simpler nervous systems

Most of the animals on Earth are invertebrates, animals without backbones. In fact, the order Coleoptera (beetles) contains far more species than any other order! The invertebrates far exceed vertebrates in many ways, including number, diversity of appearance, and variety of habitat. Whereas invertebrates make up 17 phyla, the vertebrates are only a part of one phylum: Chordata (chordates). The abundance of invertebrates is clearly demonstrated by the following estimate: for each person on Earth there are at least 1 billion insects, which are just one type of invertebrate.

Figure 6.8 shows the gross anatomy of the nervous systems of some representative animals. Faced with the enormous complexity of the vertebrate brain, with its billions of nerve cells, many researchers have turned instead to the nervous systems of some invertebrates that have only hundreds or thousands of neurons. Another advantage of studying invertebrates is that they possess elaborate sensory systems that permit some stimuli to be de-

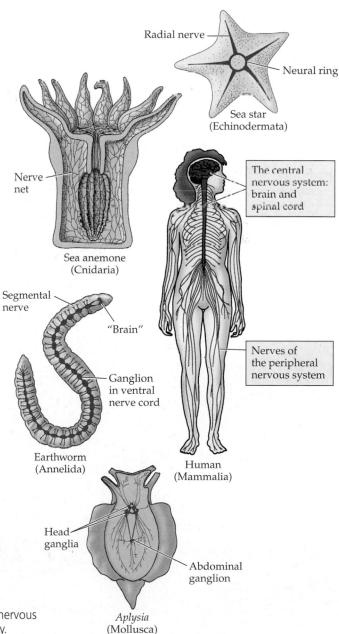

6.8 A Comparative View of Nervous Systems Gross anatomy of the nervous system in representative animals from several phyla shows some of the variety.

tected with exquisite sensitivity. You can learn more about insect nervous systems in **A Step Further: Insect Nervous Systems** on the website.

An exhaustive description of the "wiring diagram" of the nervous system and how it relates to behavior may someday be possible with invertebrates. But since we are primarily interested in understanding human behavior, let's start our comparison with brains more similar to our own.

All Vertebrate Brains Share the Same Basic Structures

Having compared aspects of the nervous systems of a few species, let's look more broadly at the variety of nervous systems of a few phyla of animals.

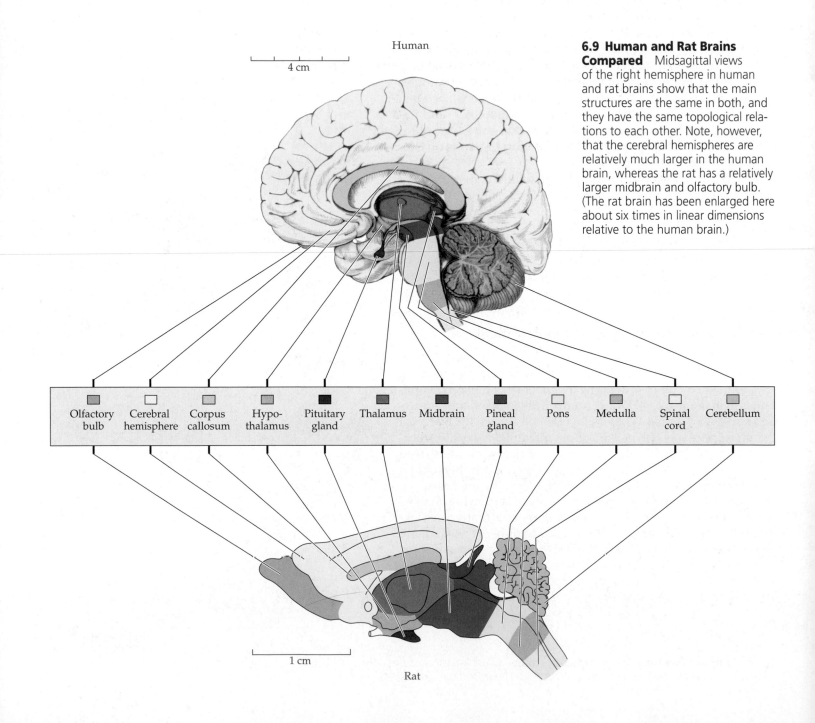

Human

4 cm

6.9 Human and Rat Brains Compared Midsagittal views of the right hemisphere in human and rat brains show that the main structures are the same in both, and they have the same topological relations to each other. Note, however, that the cerebral hemispheres are relatively much larger in the human brain, whereas the rat has a relatively larger midbrain and olfactory bulb. (The rat brain has been enlarged here about six times in linear dimensions relative to the human brain.)

| Olfactory bulb | Cerebral hemisphere | Corpus callosum | Hypo-thalamus | Pituitary gland | Thalamus | Midbrain | Pineal gland | Pons | Medulla | Spinal cord | Cerebellum |

1 cm

Rat

The main brain structures are the same in all mammals

A comparison of human and rat brains illustrates basic similarities and differences (**Figure 6.9**). Each of the main structures in the human brain has a counterpart in the rat brain. This comparison could be extended to much greater detail, down to nuclei, fiber tracts, and types of cells. Even small structures in the brains of one mammalian species are found to have exact correspondence in the brains of others. All mammals also have similar types of neurons and similar organization of the cerebellar cortex and the cerebral cortex. These similarities reflect the heritage of our evolution from a common ancestor. The diversity of mammalian brains can be seen on the Web at www.brainmuseum.org.

There are differences between the brains of humans and the brains of other mammals, of course, but they are mainly quantitative; that is, they concern both actual and relative sizes of the whole brain, brain regions, and brain cells. Whereas the brain of an adult human being weighs about 1400 g, that of an adult rat weighs a little less than 2 g. In each case, however, the brain represents about 2% of total body weight. The cerebral hemispheres occupy a much greater proportion of the brain in the human than in the rat, and the surface of the human brain shows prominent gyri and fissures, whereas the rat cerebral cortex is smooth and unfissured.

The olfactory bulb is relatively larger in rats than in humans. This difference is probably related to the rat's much greater use of the sense of smell. Neuron size also differs significantly between human and rat; in general, human neurons are much larger than rat neurons. In addition, there are great differences in the extent of dendritic trees. **Figure 6.10** shows some examples of size differences among neurons of different mammals.

All vertebrate nervous systems share certain main features but differ in others

Let's extend our view to the basic features of vertebrate nervous systems. The following are the main features of the vertebrate nervous system, including that of humans:

- *Development from a hollow dorsal neural tube* (see Chapters 2 and 7).
- *Bilateral symmetry*. The human cerebral hemispheres are almost mirror images. (We'll see some interesting exceptions in Chapter 19.)
- *Segmentation*. Pairs of spinal nerves extend from each level of the spinal cord.
- *Hierarchical control*. The cerebral hemispheres control or modulate the activity of the spinal cord.

6.10 The Same Kind of Neuron in Different Species These pyramidal neurons from the motor cortices of different mammals are all drawn to the same scale. (After Barasa, 1960.)

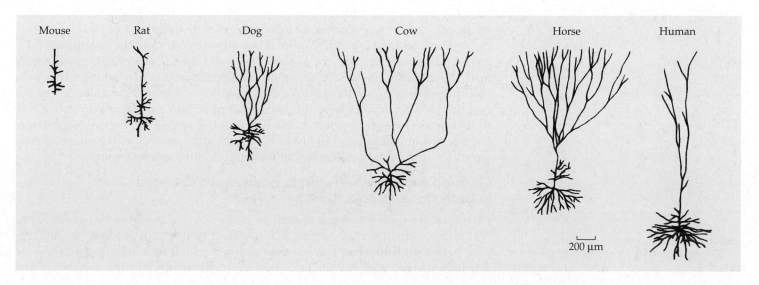

Mouse   Rat   Dog   Cow   Horse   Human

200 µm

- *Separate systems.* The central nervous system (brain and spinal cord) is clearly separate from the peripheral nervous system, as shown for humans in Figure 6.8.
- *Localization of function.* Certain functions are controlled by certain locations in the central nervous system.

Vertebrates have all of these features in common because they descended from a common ancestor that possessed them. In general, vertebrate species with larger bodies tend to possess larger brains, but we'll see that some classes of vertebrates have larger brains than others. No matter what the size, however, all vertebrate brains have the same major subdivisions. The main differences among vertebrates are the absolute and relative sizes of those regions.

The Evolution of Vertebrate Brains Reflects Changes in Behavior

During the course of evolution, the characteristics of the nervous system have changed progressively. One especially prominent change in the last 100 million years has been a general tendency for the brain size of vertebrates to increase, and the brains of our human ancestors have shown a particularly striking increase in size over the last 2 million years. How, then, has the evolution of the brain been related to changes in behavioral capacity?

Present-day animals and fossils reveal evolution of the brain

Theoretically, we could learn more about the evolution of the brain by studying the brains of fossil animals, but brains themselves do not fossilize—at least, not literally. Two methods of analysis have proven helpful. One is to use the cranial cavity of a fossil skull to make a cast of the brain that once occupied that space. These casts (called **endocasts**; the Greek *endon* means "within") give a reasonable indication of the size and shape of the brain, but no fine detail.

The other method is to study present-day animals, choosing species that show various degrees of similarity to (or difference from) ancestral forms. Although no modern animal is an ancestor of any other living form, some present-day species resemble ancestral forms more closely than others do. For example, present-day salamanders are much more similar to vertebrates of 300 million years ago than are any mammals. Among mammals, some species, such as the opossum, resemble fossil mammals of 50 million years ago more than do other species, such as the dog. Thus, a species such as the opossum is said to retain primitive or ancestral states of particular anatomical features. In studying the brains of living species, anatomists can obtain far more detailed information than they get from endocasts because they can investigate the internal structure of the brain: its nuclei, fiber tracts, and the circuitry formed by connections of its neurons.

We must be careful not to interpret the change in brain size over time as if it were a linear evolutionary sequence. The main classes of vertebrates in **Figure 6.11**, for example, represent different lines or radiations of evolution that have been proceeding separately and simultaneously for at least 200 million years. For example, today's sharks have much larger brains than primitive sharks had, but the evolution of large-brained sharks had nothing to do with the development of large brains in mammals. The line of descent that eventually led to mammals had separated from the shark line before the large-brained sharks evolved.

Through evolution, vertebrate brains have changed in both size and organization

Let's consider some examples of changes in the size and organization of vertebrate brains. Even the living vertebrate that has the most-primitive features—the lamprey (a jawless fish)—has a more complex brain than it used to be given credit for. The lamprey has not only the basic neural chassis of spinal cord, hindbrain, and

endocast A cast of the cranial cavity of a skull, especially useful for studying fossils of extinct species.

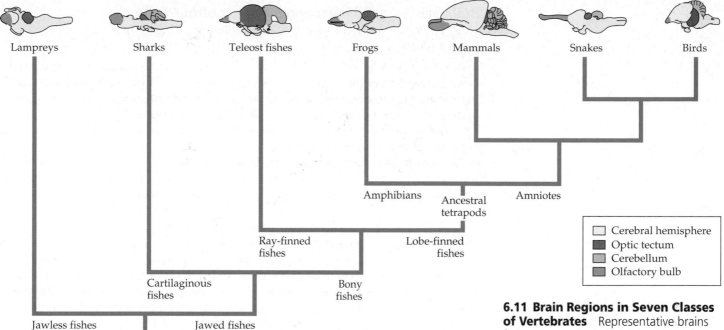

Lampreys   Sharks   Teleost fishes   Frogs   Mammals   Snakes   Birds

Amphibians   Ancestral tetrapods   Amniotes

Ray-finned fishes   Lobe-finned fishes

Cartilaginous fishes   Bony fishes

Jawless fishes   Jawed fishes

Ancestral vertebrates

☐ Cerebral hemisphere
■ Optic tectum
▨ Cerebellum
▨ Olfactory bulb

6.11 Brain Regions in Seven Classes of Vertebrates Representative brains from seven major vertebrate classes are shown here on a partial phylogenetic tree of the vertebrates; earlier evolutionary divergences appear lower in the tree. Note the relatively large sizes of the cerebral hemispheres (light blue) and the cerebellum (green) in the bird and mammal brains. (Brains are not drawn to the same scale.)

midbrain, but also a diencephalon and a telencephalon. Its telencephalon has cerebral hemispheres and other subdivisions that are also found in the mammalian brain. So all vertebrate brains appear to have these regions.

One difference in basic brain structure between the lamprey and other vertebrates is that the cerebellum in the lamprey is very small (too small to be depicted in Figure 6.11). The evolution of large cerebellar hemispheres in birds and mammals appears to be a case of independent evolution from the small cerebellum in their common reptilian ancestor; the increased size of the cerebellum may be responsible for increased complexity of sensory processing and increased motor agility.

The differences among the brains of vertebrate species, then, lie not in the existence of basic subdivisions, but in their relative size and elaboration. At what stages of vertebrate evolution do various brain regions first become important? Large, paired optic lobes in its midbrain probably represent the lamprey's highest level of visual integration. In bony fishes, amphibians, and reptiles, the relatively large optic tectum in the midbrain (see Figure 6.11) is the main brain center for vision. In birds and mammals, however, complex visual perception requires an enlarged telencephalon.

All mammals have a six-layered **neocortex** (from the Greek *neo*, "new," and the Latin *cortex*, "bark of a tree") also called **isocortex** (the Greek *iso* means "same"). In more-recent mammals the neocortex accounts for more than half the volume of the brain. In mammals the cortex is the structure mainly responsible for many complex functions, such as the perception of objects. Regions of the brain that were responsible for perceptual functions in less-encephalized animals—such as the midbrain optic lobes (in the lamprey) or the midbrain optic center (in the frog)—have in present-day mammals become visual reflex centers. (We will mention the neocortex or, more simply, the cortex, in almost every chapter in connection with perception and other complex cognitive functions.)

Reptiles were the first vertebrates to exhibit relatively large cerebral hemispheres. Reptiles were also the first vertebrates to have a cerebral cortex, but their cortex has only three layers, unlike the six cortical layers of mammals. Part of the cortex in reptiles may be homologous to the three-layered hippocampus in mammals.

neocortex or isocortex Cerebral cortex that is made up of six distinct layers.

Brain size evolved independently in multiple lineages

The brain is sometimes said to have increased in size with the appearance of each succeeding vertebrate class shown in Figure 6.11, but that statement is wrong in several respects. For one thing, there are exceptions among the present-day representatives of the various classes; for example, birds appeared later than mammals but do not have larger brains than mammals. For another, the generalization arose from the old way of viewing vertebrate evolution: as one linear series of increasing complexity rather than as numerous successive radiations occurring simultaneously.

If we compare animals of similar body size, we see considerable variation in brain size within each line of evolution. For example, within the ancient class of jawless fishes, the hagfishes, which are more-recent members of that class, have forebrains that are four times as large as those of lampreys of comparable body size. The increase of brain size in relation to behavioral capacity has been studied most thoroughly in mammals.

THE ENCEPHALIZATION FACTOR   The study of brain size is complicated by the wide range of body sizes, raising the question, How are body size and brain size related? A general relationship was found first for present-day species and then applied successfully to fossil species. This function turns out to be useful in understanding relationships between brain and behavior.

We humans long believed our own brains to be the largest, but this belief was upset in the seventeenth century when the elephant brain was found to weigh three times as much as our own. Later, whale brains were found to be even larger. These findings puzzled scholars of the time, who took it for granted that human beings are the most intelligent of animals and therefore must have the largest brains. To address this apparent discrepancy, they proposed that brain weight should be considered as a fraction of body weight. On this basis, humans outrank elephants, whales, and all other animals of large or moderate body size. But a mouse has about the same ratio of brain weight to body weight as a human, and the tiny shrew outranks a human on this measure. Without trying to prove that one species or another is "brainiest," we would like to know how much brain is needed to control and serve a body of a given size. From a comparative point of view, what is the general relation between brain size and body size?

When we plot brain weights and body weights for a large sample of mammals, we see some generalities (**Figure 6.12a**). All the plot points fall within a narrow polygon. Since both scales are logarithmic, the graph in Figure 6.12a encompass-

6.12 The Relation between Brain Weight and Body Weight (a) Brain weight is related here to body weight in several mammalian species. Note that both axes are logarithmic, so the graph includes a wide range of brain weights and body weights. A polygon has been drawn to connect the extreme cases and include the whole sample. The diagonal line shows the basic relationship, with brain weight related to the 0.69 power of body weight. (b) Brain weight is plotted here against body weight for various species in six classes of vertebrates. Each class is represented by a polygon that includes a large sample of species in that class. While the slope of each polygon is about the same, the other classes of animals fall below the mammals and birds, reflecting the fact that, relative to body weight, brain weight is smaller in those classes; they are less "brainy" than mammals and birds. (Part a after H. Stephan et al., 1981; b after Jerison, 1991.)

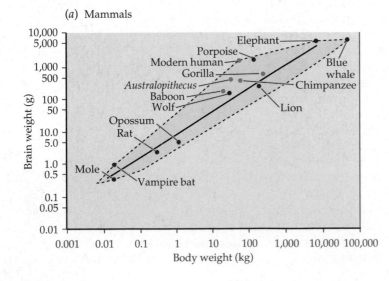

(a) Mammals

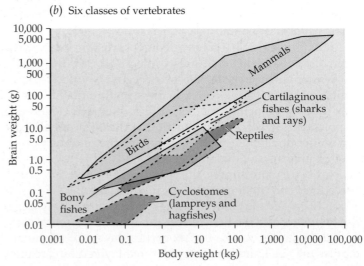

(b) Six classes of vertebrates

es a great variety of animal sizes, and departures from the general rule tend to be minimized. The line drawn through the center of the polygon has a slope of about 0.69 (Harvey and Krebs, 1990), representing the mathematical relationship between body weight and brain weight across all mammals.

Let's test the generality of this rule by examining the relation between brain weight and body weight for six vertebrate classes (**Figure 6.12b**). In each class the data yield a diagonal area with a slope that's about the same, so the relationship between brain weight and body weight is similar for all classes of vertebrates. But notice that the diagonal areas are displaced from each other vertically in Figure 6.12b: the mammals and birds are highest, the bony fishes and reptiles clearly lower, and cyclostomes (e.g., the lamprey) the lowest. This configuration reflects the fact that these classes have successively less brain weight for a body of the same size. Thus, a mammal or a bird that weighs about 100 g (e.g., a rat or blue jay) has a brain that weighs about 1 g, but a fish or a reptile of the same body weight has a brain that weighs only a little more than 0.1 g; a 100-g lamprey has an even smaller brain weight, 0.03 g.

To take into account the variation both between classes and within classes, we need a measure of vertical distance above or below the diagonal line on the graph. This distance is usually called k and is different for each class and for each species. Because k indicates the relative amount of brain, it is called the **encephalization factor**, which is illustrated in **Figure 6.13** as related to total brain weight and to brain weight as a percentage of body weight. The greater the encephalization factor is for a species, the higher its value is above the diagonal line for its class. In Figure 6.12a, the point for humans is farther from the black diagonal line than is the point for any other species. In terms of encephalization factor, human beings rate higher than any other species. In terms of the encephalization factor, humans are quite different from chimpanzees (see Figure 6.13c).

Brain size has been studied in many species of vertebrates, both living and fossil. These studies have yielded clues about some selection pressures that have led to larger brains. For example, you may have heard the statement that dinosaurs

encephalization factor A measure of brain size relative to body size.

6.13 Who Is the Brainiest? For this sample of small to large mammals, the answer depends on what measure is used: total brain weight (a), brain weight as a percentage of body weight (b), or the encephalization factor (c). For each measure, the animals are ranked here from lowest value to highest.

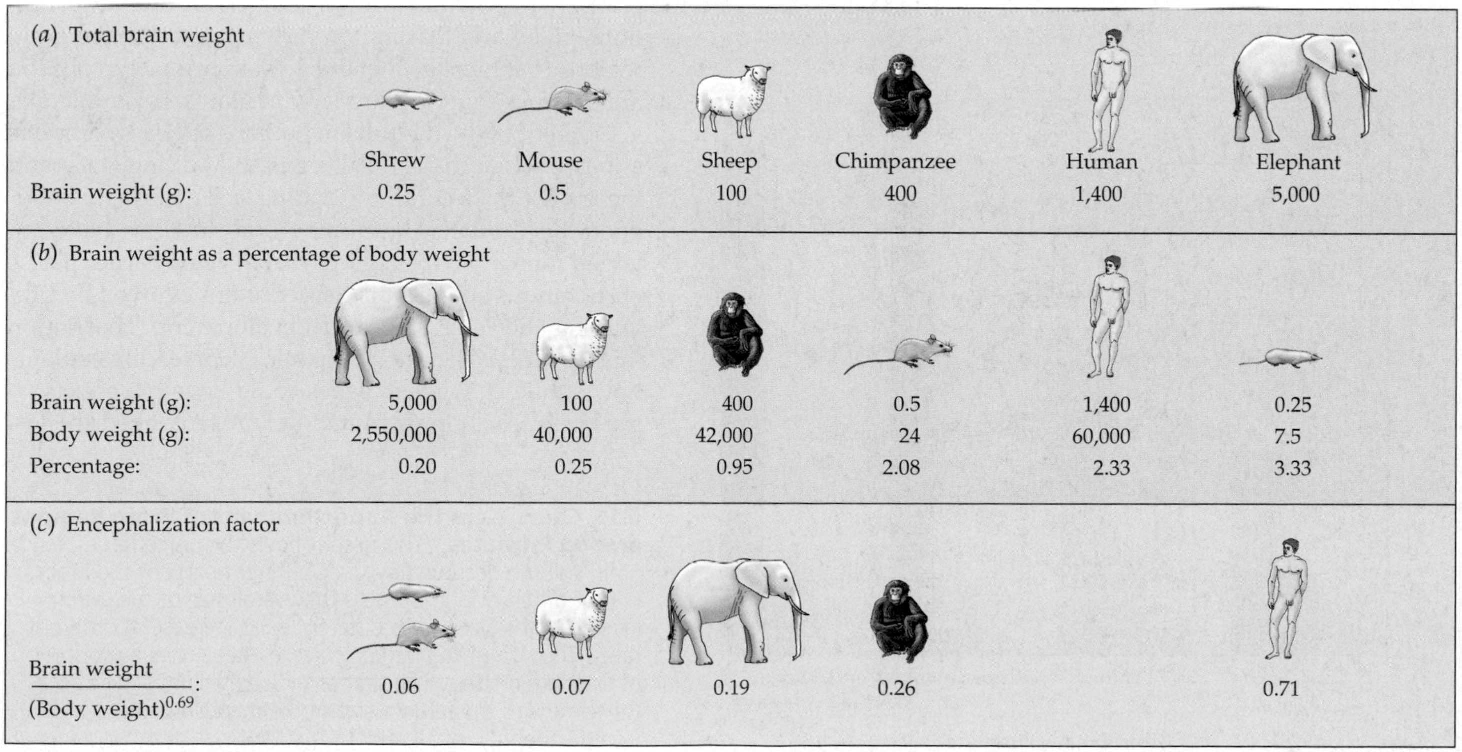

(a) Total brain weight

	Shrew	Mouse	Sheep	Chimpanzee	Human	Elephant
Brain weight (g):	0.25	0.5	100	400	1,400	5,000

(b) Brain weight as a percentage of body weight

	Elephant	Sheep	Chimpanzee	Mouse	Human	
Brain weight (g):	5,000	100	400	0.5	1,400	0.25
Body weight (g):	2,550,000	40,000	42,000	24	60,000	7.5
Percentage:	0.20	0.25	0.95	2.08	2.33	3.33

(c) Encephalization factor

$\dfrac{\text{Brain weight}}{(\text{Body weight})^{0.69}}$	0.06	0.07	0.19	0.26	0.71

THE FAR SIDE   By GARY LARSON

"The picture's pretty bleak, gentlemen... The world's climates are changing, the mammals are taking over, and we all have a brain about the size of a walnut."

6.14 Was the Dinosaur Being Too Modest?

became extinct because of the inadequacy of their small ("walnut-sized") brains (**Figure 6.14**). Is this hypothesis correct?

Examination of the endocasts of dinosaur brains shows that dinosaur brain weights fit the relationship for reptiles shown in Figure 6.12*b*. For example, the brain of *Tyrannosaurus rex* probably weighed about 700 g—only half the size of the human brain, but much heavier than a walnut and appropriate for a reptile of its size—so it seems unlikely that dinosaurs perished because of a lack of brains (Jerison, 1991).

THE EVOLUTION OF BRAIN SIZE   During its evolution, the brain has shown adaptive size changes both in specific regions and overall; this adaptation illustrates both the specificity and the continuity among species that we noted in Box 1.1. Certain capabilities, such as foraging for food or having a large repertoire of songs, have been linked to sizes of particular brain regions, as we saw earlier in this chapter. In contrast, some other capabilities are related to overall cortical volume rather than to the volume of any particular region of cortex; this relationship suggests that some capabilities could improve only as the result of an increase in total cortical volume, although this may seem like an inefficient way to add tissue related to a specific function. Using logarithmic scales, Finlay and Darlington (1995) found that the size of each brain structure shows a highly linear relation to brain weight, with correlations of 0.96 or higher. Thus, at the gross level a simple rule relates the size of the particular structure to total brain size for all parts of the brain. One exception is the olfactory bulb, which has a much larger relative size in some species, presumably because evolution has favored a very sensitive sense of smell in those species.

Although most parts of the brain increase roughly in proportion to total increases in brain size, the rates of increase do show subtle differences. In a comparison of primate brains from small to large, the medulla becomes *smaller* relative to brain weight, the cerebellum keeps pace with brain weight, and the cortex grows more than any other part (**Figure 6.15**). Thus, the proportion of brain devoted to each part differs in important ways from small to large brains, and the cortex has grown disproportionately in human evolution. Finlay and Darlington (1995) noted that the brain regions that have grown the most in primate evolution are the ones that develop later in life. For example, development of the medulla in humans appears complete at birth, while the cerebellum is still adding cells, and the cortex will continue adding cells through childhood. So the later-developing brain regions have enlarged more than the regions that develop earlier. These observations suggest that larger brains evolved by prolonging the later stages of development. The notion that "late equals large" (Striedter, 2005) readily explains how subtle changes in genes could have big effects on the brain. Any single mutation that prolonged the last

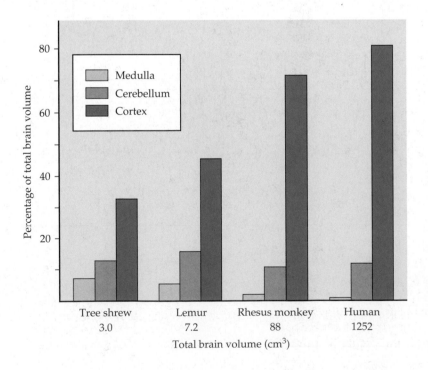

6.15 Changes in the Apportionment of Brain Regions among Primates   This graph shows the percentage of brain volume occupied by three different parts of the brain in four different primates. As the overall size of the brain increases, the sizes of its different parts increase at different rates. The size of the cortex increases steadily as a proportion of total brain size, while that of the cerebellum stays about the same and the relative size of the medulla *decreases*. (Data from H. Stephan et al., 1981.)

6.16 Evolution Allows Later-Developing Brain Regions to Grow Larger
The expansion of cortex that took place in mammals, especially among primates, is due primarily to greater growth of the outermost layers of cortex, which are the last to arise during development. Note the three-layered isocortex in reptiles and the basic six-layered neocortex in the insectivores. (From Hill and Walsh, 2005).

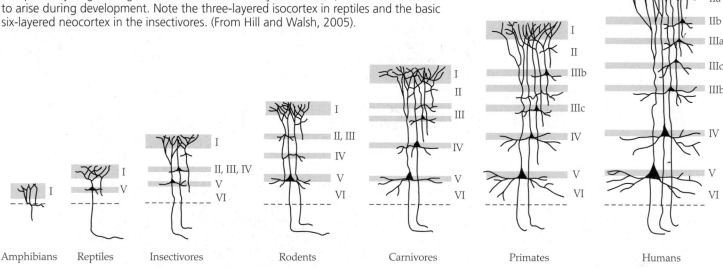

Amphibians   Reptiles   Insectivores   Rodents   Carnivores   Primates   Humans

stages of brain development, when neurons are being added almost exclusively in cortex, would result in a larger cortex relative to the rest of the brain.

Such a pattern of evolution may even explain changes in the fine structure of the cortex. During fetal development, the innermost layers of the cortex develop first and new neurons are added to form each subsequent outer layer. A comparison across mammals suggests that the later-added, outer layers of cortex have enlarged more in primates than the innermost layers (**Figure 6.16**). Let's consider primate evolution further to see if we can understand what selective pressures might favor the expansion of cortex in humans.

Many Factors Led to the Rapid Evolution of a Large Cortex in Primates

If you are convinced that humans really are quite brainy compared to other vertebrates, and that this additional brain power is responsible for our many cognitive abilities, then the question is, How did we come to evolve such a large cortex? The study of hominids—primates of the family Hominidae—of which we humans are the only living species, can help us understand how our body and brain adapted to the environment through natural selection.

Hominid brains enlarged rapidly in our recent evolution

The structural and behavioral features that we consider characteristic of humans did not develop simultaneously (Falk, 1993). Our large brain is a relatively late development. According to one estimate, the trunk and arms of hominids reached their present form about 10 million years ago. Although there remains some disagreement about precise dates, it appears that hominids began walking on two feet more than 4 million years ago, and the oldest manufactured stone tools date back more than 2.5 million years.

The early toolmakers and users were bipedal hominids called **australopithecines**. Endocasts of their skulls show a brain volume of about 350–400 cm^3, about the size of the modern chimpanzee brain. Chimpanzees do not make tools from stone, although some collect stones to use as tools, and one captive chimpanzee has been taught to make stone tools. But the australopithecines made and used crude stone tools in hunting and in breaking animal bones to eat. The ability to use tools reduced the selection pressure to maintain large jaws and teeth, and hominid jaws and teeth

australopithecine Of or related to *Australopithecus*, a primate genus, known only from the fossil record, thought to be an ancestor to humans.

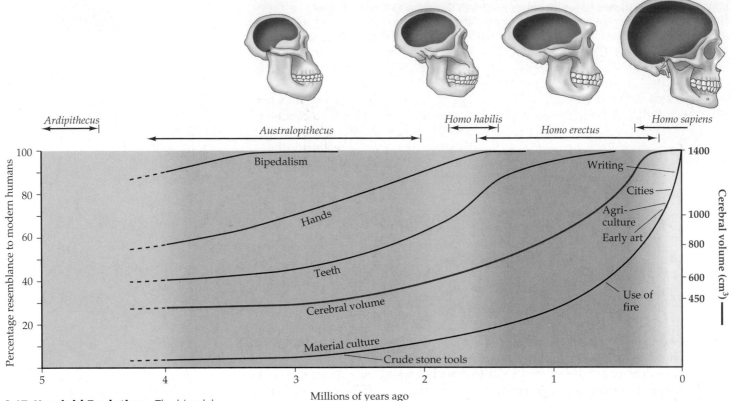

6.17 Hominid Evolution The bipedal (two-footed) gait was similar to that of modern humans even in *Australopithecus*, but cerebral volume reached its current size only in *Homo sapiens*. High culture (art, agriculture, cities, writing) emerged only relatively recently and was not associated with any further change in brain size. (After Tobias, 1980; updated with the assistance of Tim White.)

thus became steadily smaller than the ape's and more like those of modern human beings. Smaller teeth may also be related to increasing social tolerance, since the large canine teeth are often used in fighting among primate groups. Our australopithecine ancestors were successful animals, lasting—relatively unchanged—some 2 million years (**Figure 6.17**). Examination of ancient campsites suggests that these early hominids lived in nomadic groups of 20–50 individuals. They hunted and gathered plant foods—a new lifestyle that was continued by later hominids.

About 1.5–2 million years ago, as the australopithecines died out, the genus *Homo* appeared (see Figure 6.17). One early representative of the genus, *Homo erectus*, started with a cranial capacity of about 700 cm^3 and a smaller face than *Australopithecus* had. As *Homo erectus* evolved, the brain became steadily larger, reaching the present-day volume of about 1400 cm^3, and the face continued to become smaller. *Homo erectus* made elaborate stone tools, used fire, and killed large animals. Fossils and tools of *Homo erectus* are found throughout three continents, whereas australopithecine examples are found only in Africa. *Homo erectus* may have represented a level of capacity and of cultural adaptation that enabled the hominids to expand into new environmental niches and to overcome barriers that kept earlier hominids in a narrower range.

Evolution of the brain and increased behavioral capacity advanced rapidly during the time of *Homo erectus* (see Figure 6.17). By the time *Homo sapiens* appeared, about 150,000 years ago, brain volume had reached the modern level. Thus, after remaining little changed in size during about 2 million years of tool use by the australopithecines, the hominid brain almost tripled in volume during the next 1.5 million years.

The size of the human brain now appears to be at a plateau. The recent changes in human lifestyle shown in Figure 6.17—such as the appearance of language, the introduction of agriculture and animal husbandry (about 10,000 years ago), and urban living (the last few thousand years)—have all been accomplished and assimilated by a brain that does not seem to have altered in size since *Homo sapiens* first appeared. Subsequent changes in human behavior have been due to cultural evolution, as the ability of humans to pass hard-won knowledge along to the next generation has brought technology that has changed the face of Earth. In contrast, human brains seem the same as in prehistoric times. The lack of further increase in brain size may be related to the costs of a large brain, a topic we consider next.

THE COSTS OF A LARGE BRAIN Having a large brain entails costs as well as benefits. Growth of a large brain requires a long gestation period, which is a burden on the mother, and childbirth is difficult because of the large size of the baby's head. Much of the growth of the brain continues during the years after birth, which means prolonged dependence of the infant and prolonged parental care. Although the brain makes up only about 2% of our total adult body weight, when we are at rest it consumes a much bigger proportion of our metabolic budget.

Construction of the human brain is so complex that more than half of our genes contribute to the task. The complex genetic messages that are generated are vulnerable to accidents; mutations of any of them are likely to lead to behavioral disorders. The evolution of large brains is especially remarkable when viewed in the context of these costs.

SELECTION PRESSURES FOR INCREASED BRAIN SIZE Any change in an organ during evolution is assumed to confer advantages with respect to survival. A rapid change, as in the increase in size of the hominid brain, implies strong advantages for survival. However tiny the differences are between the genes of humans and chimpanzees, they have brought a big difference in brain size. What is the adaptive advantage of having such big brains?

One hypothesis is that selection pressure in the social domain may have led to increased brain size. Tool use is not very widespread in primates, but primates are extremely skilled in a variety of social interactions, such as cooperation, deception, and reciprocity. Anthropologist Robin Dunbar (1998) found a positive relationship between (1) group size in primates and (2) the size of the cortex relative to brain size. The *social brain hypothesis* suggests that a larger cortex is needed to handle the complex cognitive task of maintaining social relationships with other large-brained individuals (Dunbar, 2009). Indeed, across species primates show a correlation between the average size of a clique (a group of individuals that regularly socialize with one another) and the size of the cortex relative to overall brain size (**Figure 6.18**).

Using such relationships, for each primate species Dunbar estimated the *maximum* size of social group (as opposed to the smaller, more intimate cliques mentioned above) from the size of the cortex. For humans, this value was about 150. Dunbar inspected the anthropological literature and found that this number came

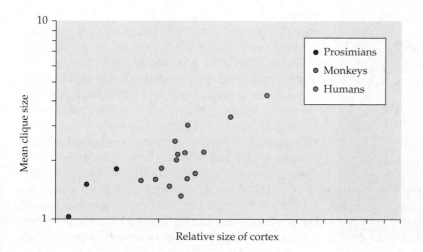

6.18 The Social Brain Hypothesis In primate species the average size of cliques (groups that individuals regularly associate with) is correlated with the relative size of the cortex. Did sociality drive human brain evolution? (After Dunbar, 1998.)

up frequently. For example, the average number of people in hunter-gatherer societies was close to 150. The same number holds true for many functional military units. So the ratio of cortex to brain may indicate the maximum number of individuals with whom we can have a meaningful social relationship. Perhaps our brains are too small to let us really keep tabs on more than about 150 "friends" on Facebook.

INNOVATION, TOOL USE, SOCIAL LEARNING, AND ENHANCED BRAIN SIZE IN PRIMATES
A major study correlated brain size in 116 species of primates with three different factors that have been proposed to account for the enhanced size of primate brains: (1) innovations in behavior, (2) use of tools, and (3) social learning—that is, learning by observing others (Reader and Laland, 2002). Rather than testing animals for these traits or observing them directly, Reader and Laland surveyed about 1000 articles in primate journals and other relevant literature and found 533 instances of innovation, 607 episodes of tool use, and 445 observations of social learning (**Figure 6.19**). In addition to using total brain weights, Reader and Laland used the ratio of what has been called the *executive brain* (the forebrain) to the brainstem.

Both total brain size and relative forebrain size correlated positively with the frequency of each of the behavioral indices, indicating that each of the behavioral factors is related to expansion of the primate brain. Thus, the results indicate that multiple sources of selection favored evolution of the large primate brain. Similar relationships between forebrain size and innovation may apply to birds as well, because members of the crow family have been observed to use tools (Bird and Emery, 2009), and they have larger relative forebrains than other birds have (Cnotka et al., 2008).

Brain size predicts success in adapting to a novel environment

We have seen that brain size correlates with the ability to find new ways to obtain food and with group size in primates, but is it possible to test the hypothesis that enlarged brains have evolved as an adaptation to cope with novel or altered environmental conditions? One way would be to introduce species with relatively large or small brains into novel environments and see whether they were able to establish themselves and thrive. Experimental introductions of species into novel environments are not considered ethical, however, because of problems that often occur when nonindigenous species are introduced. An alternative is to study the rich record of past human-mediated introductions. A comprehensive study that used a global database to examine more than 600 examples of introduction involving 195 bird species found that the species with larger brains, relative to body size, tended to be more successful in establishing themselves in novel environments (Sol et al., 2005).

SEXUAL SELECTION AND BRAIN SIZE Using a different approach, we can evaluate the rapid expansion of the human brain over the last 1.5 million years in terms of Darwin's second evolutionary principle: sexual selection. Geoffrey Miller (2000) suggests that natural selection to obtain food and shelter is not likely to account completely for the large brain and complex intelligence of *Homo sapiens*. In fact, he notes, brain size tripled in our ancestors between 2.5 million years ago and 200,000 years ago, yet during this period our ancestors continued to make the same kind of stone ax. Only

6.19 Transmitting Culture   Culture has been observed in nonhuman primates. For example, a population of Japanese macaques developed a set of behaviors that included washing food, playing in water, and eating marine food items; and they transmitted this culture of water-related behaviors from generation to generation. (Courtesy of Frans B. M. de Waal.)

after the human brain stopped expanding did technological progress develop, so brain growth did not correlate well with the supposed survival benefit of enlarged brains.

Rather, Miller proposes an additional factor to account for large human brains: in humans, he postulates, much creativity, along with related brain growth, is due to sexual selection for abilities to attract attention, stimulate, and surprise a potential mate. This hypothesis, Miller claims, has the further value of presenting an evolutionary theory for such characteristic human traits as humor, art, music, language, and creativity (**Box 6.3**).

BOX 6.3 Evolutionary Psychology

There's no doubt that humans looking for a mate find some traits more attractive than others, and such sexual selection has been used to explain, for example, why males tend to be larger than females in many species, or why in many bird species the males sing more elaborate songs and are more brightly colored than the females (see the figure). So speculation about selective pressure on reproductive behavior in various animals leads inevitably to questions about the extent to which our own behaviors have been affected by the difference between male and female reproductive strategies:

- *Are women inherently more selective than men about choosing mating partners?* Such a difference could be a result of the tremendous investment of time, energy, and resources that a female mammal must make in each offspring.

- *Are men more promiscuous than women?* It's easy to imagine that the low cost of producing sperm (and the potential for a man to expend no energy on child rearing) might favor such behavior.

- *Do romantic relationships tend to sour after about 7 years?* If so, the reason for this tendency may be that, in the ancestral environment in which hominids evolved, periodically selecting a new mate provided insurance that genetic defects from any one mate would not affect all of the offspring. Was 7 years how long it took for a couple to raise a child to self-sufficiency?

- *Is there an "ideal" waist-to-hip ratio that indicates maximal fertility in women?* Correlational studies suggest that a particular ratio is especially attractive to men, across different cultures and historical eras (Singh, 2002).

- *Are women attracted to power, and men to youth, because natural selection favored these preferences?*

Such speculations have given rise to a lively and controversial field called **evolutionary psychology** (Barkow et al., 1992; Buss, 2000). It's easy to spin plausible tales about how evolution might have shaped our behavior, but the challenge for theorists is to come up with ways to test and potentially disprove these hypotheses. Such an enterprise is especially daunting when ethical considerations mean that the investigator can never manipulate the variables ("Let's see; I'd like you to marry that person over there, and then I'll ask you some questions 7 years from now"). Researchers investigating questions of evolutionary psychology must often rely on correlations and surveys.

Geoffrey Miller (2000) proposes that sexual selection was crucial for evolution of the human brain. If early hominids had come to favor mates who sang, made jokes, or produced artistic works, such high-order functioning would have evolved rapidly in an "arms race," as the ever more discriminating brains of one sex demanded ever more impressive performances from the brains of the other sex. Did humor, song, and art originate from the drive to be sexually attractive? And does sexual selection account for the large size of the human brain?

evolutionary psychology   A field devoted to asking how natural selection has shaped behavior in humans.

This brightly colored peacock must impress the plain-colored peahen before she will accept his sperm.

6.20 A Bowerbird Nest To attract mates, male bowerbirds build elaborate bowers of twigs, such as this structure, and decorate them with colorful objects. The architectural complexity and ornate decoration of the bowers may be the reason for the relatively large brains of bowerbirds.

The hypothesis that sexual selection for artistry and creativity may lead to increased brain size is supported by findings from the bowerbird family (Ptilonorhynchidae). To attract and impress females, male bowerbirds construct elaborate structures of twigs, decorated with colorful objects such as shiny beetles, shells, and petals (**Figure 6.20**). Zoologist Joah Madden found that bowerbirds have large brains, compared with other birds (Madden, 2001). Even within the bowerbirds, species that build more-elaborate bowers have relatively larger brains.

Primate species differ in gene expression

At the start of this chapter we asked why humans and chimpanzees, which are identical in 99% of their genomic DNA sequences, differ in many morphological, behavioral, and cognitive aspects. One answer is that some genes affect brain development more than others. For example, the gene *ASPM* influences the size of the cerebral cortex. Humans inheriting one version of *ASPM* develop very small brains and are mentally disabled. The protein encoded by *ASPM* differs considerably between humans and chimps, suggesting that this gene evolved rapidly in the line leading to humans (P. D. Evans et al., 2004). So, even moderate changes in just a few crucial genes may make a big difference.

Another means by which similar genomes can produce different brains is the way the genes are *expressed*. Even small changes in DNA can result in big differences in when and where the gene is transcribed to produce its encoded protein. Researchers report that humans differ considerably from other primates in gene expression in the brain (Enard, Khaitovich, et al., 2002). To study this question, the investigators measured mRNA and protein expression patterns in brain, liver, and blood cells in humans and other primates. They could then quantify how similar or different two species are in the pattern of genes expressed in particular tissues.

In their blood cells and liver cells, humans and chimpanzees are more similar to each other than either species is to rhesus monkeys, as **Figure 6.21** shows. These relationships probably reflect the well-documented evolutionary relationships among the three species. A comparison of the pattern of gene expression in the *brain*, however, shows that we are more different from chimpanzees than they are from monkeys. These observations suggest that the pattern of gene expression in the brain has changed considerably, presumably under selective pressure, since

6.21 Differences in Gene Expression in Various Tissues Reveal the Extent of Similarity between Species (Enard, Khaitovich, et al., 2002.)

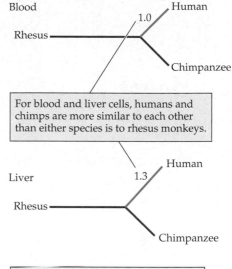

The distance between any two species indicates how different they are in the pattern of gene expression.

we shared a common ancestor with chimpanzees. The rate of evolutionary change in gene expression in the brain is accelerated in the human lineage relative to the chimpanzee and to other primates, whereas no such acceleration is evident in the liver or blood. The differences between humans and their closest relatives probably reflect differences not only in their DNA *sequences* but also in how those genes are *expressed* to construct a complex brain.

Even a small change in gene expression can cause a dramatic difference in brain development (Chenn and Walsh, 2002). For example, overexpression of just one gene in mice caused so much more growth in the cortex that the normally smooth surface developed gyri and sulci (**Figure 6.22**). To answer the question we raised at the start of this chapter, the pattern of gene expression has a tremendous effect on the developing brain and may be what makes humans unique.

For blood and liver cells, humans and chimps are more similar to each other than either species is to rhesus monkeys.

Evolution Continues Today

Although some examples of evolution have occurred slowly—over millions of years, as shown by the aspects of hominid evolution illustrated in Figure 6.17—other examples occur in a matter of years or decades. These rapid instances of evolution would have surprised Darwin, who thought that natural selection required vast periods of time to be effective. In some cases, selection is driven by natural causes. Other cases of rapid evolution are driven by human behavior, as reviewed by Bob Holmes (2005). For example, use of antibiotic medicines eliminates all but a very few resistant bacteria, but overuse of antibiotics speeds the evolution of resistant bacteria.

A striking example of evolution in action is the case of bighorn rams in the Rocky Mountains of Alberta, Canada. The massive, curling horns of these rams make them a prized hunting trophy. The rams become legal targets only after their horns reach an almost 360° curl. In some areas of Alberta, most rams are shot within a year or

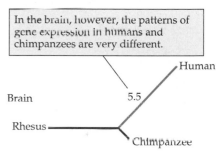

In the brain, however, the patterns of gene expression in humans and chimpanzees are very different.

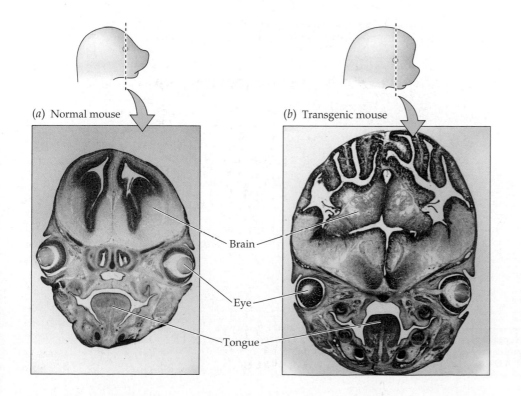

(a) Normal mouse

(b) Transgenic mouse

Brain

Eye

Tongue

6.22 Over Your Head Normally, mice at birth have a fairly simple cortex with no sulci or gyri (a), but increasing the expression of just one gene (that for β-catenin) in transgenic mice results in a monstrously complex, highly folded cortex (b). These animals die shortly after birth. (From Chenn and Walsh, 2002; photographs courtesy of Anjen Chenn.)

6.23 Bigger Is No Longer Better
Because human hunters prefer rams with large horns, the population of bighorn rams has changed. Males these days have smaller horns than males a few decades ago had. This is a disturbing example of evolution in action.

two after reaching this status. As a result, selection has worked in favor of rams whose horns never reach trophy status (**Figure 6.23**). In fact, the average horn size has dropped by about 25% over the past 30 years (Coltman et al., 2003).

Darwin's finches are continuing to evolve in the Galápagos Islands. In 1973, the medium ground finch (*Geospiza fortis*) predominated on one small island, eating both large and small seeds. Then, in 1982, a breeding population of the large ground finch (*G. magnirostris*) became established on the island. These larger birds eat large seeds more easily than the medium finches can, even those with relatively large beaks. For two decades there were not enough of the larger species to make much difference. But then in 2004, a drought sharply reduced the food supply. Competition for larger seeds became severe, and many of the medium finches with larger beaks died off. The smaller-beaked medium finches, however, survived and passed along the small-beaked trait to their offspring (Grant and Grant, 2006).

An economically important case of recent evolution concerns commercial fishing. In many regions, fishermen are allowed to keep only fish that are larger than a particular size. Atlantic cod off the coast of Newfoundland have been maturing at smaller sizes over several decades, probably because the largest fish are the ones being captured (E. M. Olsen et al., 2004). The remaining small fish produce fewer eggs than large fish, and this reduced egg production could help explain the collapse in the cod population.

New developments in radiocarbon dating have shown that the colonization of Europe and Asia by *Homo sapiens* was more rapid than previously believed (Mellars, 2006), occurring less than 50,000 years ago (**Figure 6.24**). Thus, the differences in skin color, stature, and facial traits that characterize Asian, African, and European populations evolved in less than 50,000 years in response to different climatic conditions. Human variation, then, is a reminder of both how quickly evolutionary processes can work and how very closely related we all are.

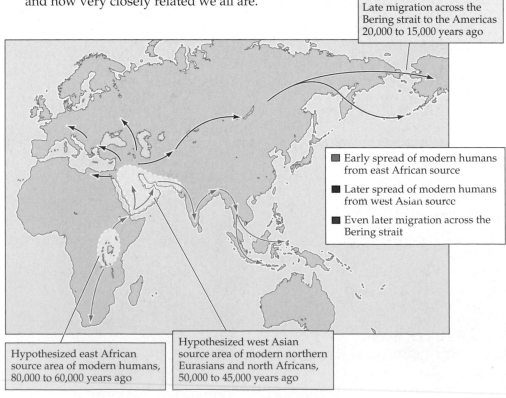

Late migration across the Bering strait to the Americas 20,000 to 15,000 years ago

■ Early spread of modern humans from east African source

■ Later spread of modern humans from west Asian source

■ Even later migration across the Bering strait

6.24 The Colonization of Europe and Asia by *Homo sapiens*
(After Goebel, 2007.)

Hypothesized east African source area of modern humans, 80,000 to 60,000 years ago

Hypothesized west Asian source area of modern northern Eurasians and north Africans, 50,000 to 45,000 years ago

SUMMARY

How Did the Enormous Variety of Species Arise on Earth?

■ Darwins' theory of **natural selection** posits that individuals with adaptive traits produce more offspring, so that species evolve over time. This process of natural selection favors newly arisen genes (mutations) that confer adaptive traits, including behavioral traits. By these gradual changes, all animal species arose from a common ancestor. **Review Figure 6.1**

■ Studies of the classification of animals help determine how closely related different **species** are. Knowing this relationship, in turn, helps us interpret similarities and differences in the behavior and structure of different species. **Review Figures 6.3 and 6.4**, **Web Activity 6.1**

Why Should We Study Other Species?

■ Size differences in specific brain regions are sometimes related to distinctive forms of behavioral **adaptation** in different species, such as song repertoires or food storing. **Review Figure 6.6 and 6.7**

■ Comparative studies help us understand the **evolution** of the nervous system, including the human brain. They also provide a perspective for understanding species-typical behavioral adaptations. **Review Box 6.2**

■ The nervous systems of invertebrate animals range in complexity from a simple nerve net to the complex structures of molluscs. The nervous systems of certain invertebrates may provide a simplified model for understanding some aspects of vertebrate nervous systems. **Review Figure 6.8**, **Web Activity 6.2**

All Vertebrate Brains Share the Same Basic Structures

■ The main divisions of the brain are the same in all vertebrates. Differences among these animals are largely quantitative, as reflected in the relative sizes of nerve cells and brain regions, and the amount of dendritic branching in neurons. **Review Figures 6.9 and 6.10**

The Evolution of Vertebrate Brains Reflects Changes in Behavior

■ Fossil **endocasts** of brains from extinct species indicate that the main result of mammalian evolution has been larger overall brain size.

■ The brain size of a species must be interpreted in terms of body size. As a rough rule of thumb, vertebrate brain weight is proportional to the 0.69 power of body weight. **Review Figure 6.12**

■ Some animals have larger brains and some have smaller brains than the general relation between brain and body weights predicts; that is, they differ in **encephalization factor**. Humans, in particular, have larger brains than their body size would predict. **Review Figure 6.13**

■ Primates have an especially large cortex relative to overall brain size. This relative enlargement of the cortex appears to have evolved because the later stages of brain development are prolonged, resulting in a disproportionately large cortex. **Review Figures 6.15 and 6.16**

Many Factors Led to the Rapid Evolution of a Large Cortex in Primates

■ Several factors, including tool use, innovation, and social relationships, are thought to have driven enlargement of the primate cortex. **Review Figures 6.17 and 6.18**

■ Not only natural selection, but also **sexual selection** has been proposed to account for the large size of the human brain, an issue central to **evolutionary psychology**. **Review Box 6.3**

■ Differences between humans and their nearest evolutionary relatives, the chimpanzees, reflect not only the small differences in their genomic DNA *sequences* but also differences in gene *expression* patterns. Humans differ from other primates especially in the large number of genes expressed in the brain. **Review Figures 6.21 and 6.22**

Evolution Continues Today

■ Evolution continues today in both human beings and nonhuman species.

Go to **www.biopsychology.com** for study questions, quizzes, key terms, and other resources.

Recommended Reading

Alcock, J. A. (2009). *Animal behavior: An evolutionary approach* (9th ed.). Sunderland, MA: Sinauer.

Bazzett, T. J. (2008). *An introduction to behavior genetics.* Sunderland, MA: Sinauer.

De Waal, F. (2001). *The ape and the sushi master: Cultural reflections by a primatologist.* New York: Basic Books.

Miller, G. F. (2000). *The mating mind: How sexual choice shaped the evolution of human nature.* New York: Doubleday.

Striedter, G. P. (2005). *Principles of brain evolution.* Sunderland, MA: Sinauer.

Understanding Evolution, http://evolution.berkeley.edu.

Life-Span Development of the Brain and Behavior

CHAPTER 7

Overcoming Blindness

As a 3-year-old, Michael May was injured by a chemical explosion that destroyed his left eye and damaged the surface of his right eye so badly that he was blind. He could tell whether it was day or night, but otherwise he couldn't see anything. An early attempt to restore his sight with corneal transplants failed, but Michael seemed undaunted. He learned to play Ping-Pong using his hearing alone (but only on the table at his parent's house, where he learned to interpret the sound cues). Michael also enjoyed riding a bicycle, until his parents made him stop after he crashed his brother's and his sister's bikes.

As an adult, Michael became a champion skier, marrying his instructor and raising two sons. He also started his own company, making equipment to help blind people navigate on their own. Then, when Michael was 46, technical advances made it possible to restore vision in his right eye. As soon as the bandages were removed, he could see his wife's blue eyes and blond hair. But even 3 years later, he could not recognize her face unless she spoke to him, or recognize three-dimensional objects like a cube or a sphere unless they were moving. Michael could still ski, but he found that he had to close his eyes to avoid falling over. On the slopes, seeing was more distracting than helpful.

The doctors could tell that images were focusing properly on Michael's retina, so why was his vision so poor?

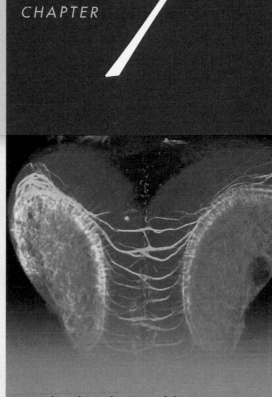

Age puts its stamp on the behavior of us all. Although the rate, progression, and orderliness of changes are especially prominent early in life, change is a feature of the entire life span. In this chapter we describe brains in terms of their progress through life from the womb to the tomb. The fertilization of an egg leads to a body with a brain that contains billions of neurons with an incredible number of connections. The pace of this process is extraordinary: during the height of prenatal growth of the human brain, more than 250,000 neurons are added per minute! We will describe the emergence of nerve cells, the formation of their connections, and the role of genes in shaping the nervous system. But we'll see that experience, gained through behavioral interactions with the environment, also sculpts the developing brain.

Growth and Development of the Brain Are Orderly Processes

Picture, if you can, the number of neurons in the mature human brain—about 100 billion. There are many types of neurons, each forming a vast array of hundreds or thousands of connections. The overall number of connections in the brain is over 100 trillion. Yet each of us began as a single microscopic cell, the fertilized egg. How can one cell divide and grow to form the most complicated machines on Earth, perhaps in the universe? Of course, some vital information was packed in the genes of that single cell, but we'll see that the developing nervous system also relies on its environment to guide the construction of this fabulous gadget between our ears.

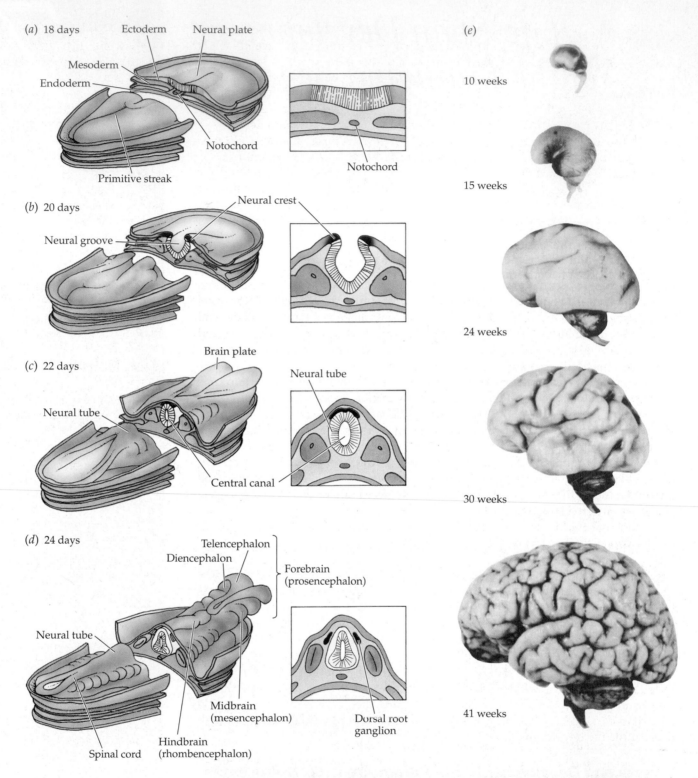

(a) 18 days
Ectoderm
Neural plate
Mesoderm
Endoderm
Notochord
Primitive streak
Notochord

(b) 20 days
Neural crest
Neural groove

(c) 22 days
Brain plate
Neural tube
Neural tube
Central canal

(d) 24 days
Telencephalon
Diencephalon
Forebrain (prosencephalon)
Neural tube
Midbrain (mesencephalon)
Dorsal root ganglion
Spinal cord
Hindbrain (rhombencephalon)

(e)
10 weeks
15 weeks
24 weeks
30 weeks
41 weeks

7.1 Development of the Nervous System in the Human Embryo and Fetus (a) At 18 days the embryo has begun to implant in the uterine wall and consists of three layers of cells: endoderm, mesoderm, and ectoderm. A thickening of the ectoderm leads to development of the neural plate (insets). (b) At 20 days the neural groove begins to develop. (c) At 22 days the neural groove has closed to form the neural tube with the rudimentary beginning of the brain at the anterior end. (d) A few days later, three major divisions of the brain—forebrain (prosencephalon, consisting of the telencephalon and diencephalon), midbrain (mesencephalon), and hindbrain (rhombencephalon)—are discernible. (e) In these lateral views of the human brain (shown at one-third size) at several stages of fetal development, note the gradual emergence of gyri and sulci. (Part e from Larroche, 1977.)

A new human being begins when a sperm penetrates the wall of an egg cell. The fertilized egg, or **zygote**, has 46 chromosomes—23 from each parent—which contain genetic recipes for the development of a new individual. (A summary of the life cycle of cells, including a discussion of the basic genetic materials and how they direct cell activities, is provided in the Appendix.) Within 12 hours after conception the single cell begins dividing, so after 3 days it has become a small mass of homogeneous cells, like a cluster of grapes, a mere 200 μm in diameter.

Within a week the emerging human embryo shows three distinct cell layers (**Figure 7.1a**). These layers are the beginnings of all the tissues of the embryo. The nervous system develops from the outer layer, called the **ectoderm** (from the Greek *ektos*, "out," and *derma*, "skin"). As the cell layers thicken, they grow into a flat oval plate. Uneven rates of cell division form a groove that will become the midline. At the head end of the groove, a thickened collection of cells forms. Ridges of ectoderm continue to bulge on both sides of the middle position, forming the **neural groove** between them (**Figure 7.1b**).

The pace of events then increases. The tops of the neural ridges come together to form the **neural tube** (**Figure 7.1c**). At the anterior part of the neural tube, three subdivisions become apparent. These subdivisions correspond to the future **forebrain** (prosencephalon, consisting of the telencephalon and diencephalon), **midbrain** (mesencephalon), and **hindbrain** (rhombencephalon, consisting of the metencephalon and myelencephalon) (**Figure 7.1d**), which were discussed in Chapter 2. The interior of the neural tube becomes the fluid-filled cerebral ventricles of the brain, the central canal of the spinal cord, and the passages that connect them.

By the end of the eighth week, the human embryo shows the rudimentary beginnings of most body organs. The rapid development of the brain is reflected in the fact that by this time the head is one-half the total size of the embryo. (Note that the developing human is called an **embryo** during the first 10 weeks after fertilization; thereafter it is called a **fetus**.) **Figure 7.1e** shows the prenatal development of the human brain from weeks 10–41. Even after this period, there are dramatic local changes as some brain regions grow more than others, well into the teenage years (P. M. Thompson et al., 2000).

zygote The fertilized egg.

ectoderm The outer cellular layer of the developing fetus, giving rise to the skin and the nervous system.

neural groove In the developing embryo, the groove between the neural folds.

neural tube An embryonic structure with subdivisions that correspond to the future forebrain, midbrain, and hindbrain.

forebrain Also called *prosencephalon*. The frontal division of the neural tube, containing the cerebral hemispheres, the thalamus, and the hypothalamus.

midbrain Also called *mesencephalon*. The middle division of the brain.

hindbrain Also called *rhombencephalon*. The rear division of the brain, which, in the mature vertebrate, contains the cerebellum, pons, and medulla.

embryo The earliest stage in a developing animal.

fetus A developing individual after the embryo stage.

neurogenesis The mitotic division of nonneuronal cells to produce neurons.

Development of the Nervous System Can Be Divided into Six Distinct Stages

From a cellular viewpoint it is useful to consider brain development as a sequence of distinct stages, most of which occur during prenatal life:

1. *Neurogenesis*, the mitotic division of nonneuronal cells to produce neurons
2. *Cell migration*, the massive movements of nerve cells or their precursors to establish distinct nerve cell populations (nuclei in the CNS, layers of the cerebral cortex, and so on)
3. *Differentiation* of cells into distinctive types of neurons or glial cells
4. *Synaptogenesis*, the establishment of synaptic connections as axons and dendrites grow
5. *Neuronal cell death*, the selective death of many nerve cells
6. *Synapse rearrangement*, the loss of some synapses and development of others, to refine synaptic connections

The six stages proceed at different rates and times in different parts of the nervous system. Some of the stages may overlap even within a region. In the discussion that follows, we will take up each stage in succession. This sequence is portrayed in **Figure 7.2**.

Cell proliferation produces cells that become neurons or glial cells

The production of nerve cells is called **neurogenesis**. Nerve cells themselves do not divide, but the cells that will give rise to neurons begin as a single layer of cells

7.2 The Six Stages of Neural Development

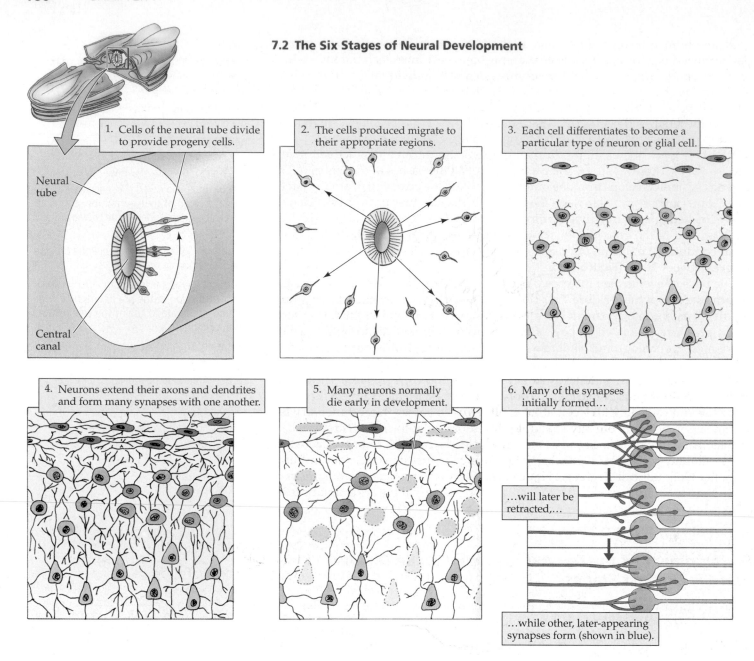

1. Cells of the neural tube divide to provide progeny cells.

Neural tube

Central canal

2. The cells produced migrate to their appropriate regions.

3. Each cell differentiates to become a particular type of neuron or glial cell.

4. Neurons extend their axons and dendrites and form many synapses with one another.

5. Many neurons normally die early in development.

6. Many of the synapses initially formed…

…will later be retracted,…

…while other, later-appearing synapses form (shown in blue).

along the inner surface of the neural tube. These cells divide (in a process called **mitosis**) and gradually form a closely packed layer of cells called the **ventricular zone** (**Figure 7.3**). All neurons and glial cells are derived from cells that originate from such ventricular mitosis. Eventually, some cells leave the ventricular zone and begin transforming into either a neuron or a glial cell.

Each part of an animal's brain has a species-characteristic "birth date." That is, there is an orderly chronological program for brain development, and it is possible to state the approximate days during development when particular cell groups stop dividing. Of course, given the complexity of vertebrate brains, it is difficult to trace individual cell development from the initial small population of ventricular cells. Descendants disappear in the crowd. But in some simpler invertebrate nervous systems that have very few neurons, mitotic lineages can be traced more easily and completely.

A favorite animal of researchers who study the lineage of nerve cells is the nematode *Caenorhabditis elegans*, a tiny worm with fewer than a thousand cells, 302 of which are neurons. Because the body of *C. elegans* is almost transparent (**Figure 7.4a**),

mitosis   The process of division of somatic cells that involves duplication of DNA.

ventricular zone   Also called *ependymal layer*. A region lining the cerebral ventricles that displays mitosis, providing neurons early in development and glial cells throughout life.

7.3 The Proliferation of Cellular Precursors of Neurons and Glial Cells   (*a*) In this small section of the wall of the neural tube at an early stage of embryonic development, only ventricular (V) and marginal (M) layers are visible. (*b*) Later an intermediate (I) layer develops as the wall thickens. (*c*) Nuclei (within their cells) migrate from the ventricular layer to the outer layers. Some cells then become neurons while others return to the ventricular zone to divide again.

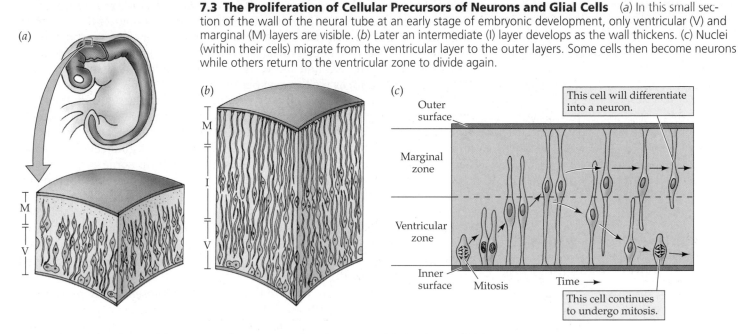

researchers have been able to trace the origins of each neuron (Wolinsky and Way, 1990). By observing successive cell divisions of a *C. elegans* zygote, investigators can exactly predict the fate of each cell in the adult—whether it will be a sensory neuron, muscle cell, skin cell, or other type of cell—on the basis of its mitotic "ancestors."

Whereas cell fate in *C. elegans* is a highly determined and stereotypical result of mitotic lineage (**Figure 7.4b**), in vertebrates the paths that cells take to form the completed nervous system are more complex. Anatomical and genetic studies

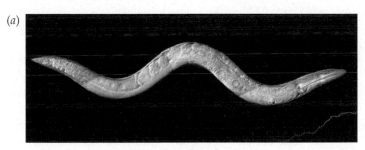

7.4 Cell Fate in a Simple Organism   (*a*) This montage of photomicrographs shows the transparent body of *Caenorhabditis elegans*. (*b*) In this mitotic lineage of cells that give rise to the body of the adult *C. elegans*, nervous system cells are highlighted in blue. The structure and function of every cell can be predicted from its mitotic lineage. Such mitotic determination of cell differentiation does not seem important to the development of vertebrates. (Part *a* courtesy of Paola Dal Santo and Erik M. Jorgensen, University of Utah; *b* after Pines, 1992.)

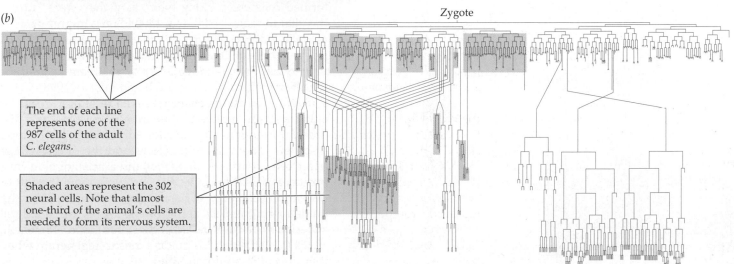

cell-cell interactions The general process during development in which one cell affects the differentiation of other, usually neighboring, cells.

adult neurogenesis The creation of new neurons in the brain of an adult.

cell migration The movement of cells from site of origin to final location.

radial glial cells Glial cells that form early in development, spanning the width of the emerging cerebral hemispheres, and guide migrating neurons.

cell adhesion molecule (CAM) A protein found on the surface of a cell that guides cell migration and/or axonal pathfinding.

7.5 Glial Spokes Guide Migrating Cells
Early in development, radial glial cells span the width of the emerging cerebral hemispheres. (*a*) This enlargement shows how radial glial cells act as guide wires for the migration of neurons. New cells shinny past established neurons to become neurons in successively higher (outer) layers of the cortex. (*b*) Further enlargement shows a single neuron migrating out along a radial glial fiber. (After Cowan, 1979, based on Rakic, 1971.)

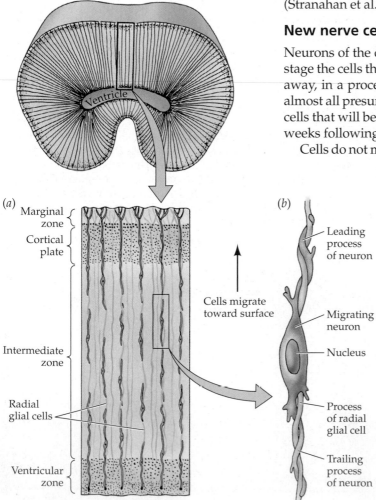

(*a*) Marginal zone / Cortical plate / Intermediate zone / Radial glial cells / Ventricular zone / Ventricle / Cells migrate toward surface

(*b*) Leading process of neuron / Migrating neuron / Nucleus / Process of radial glial cell / Trailing process of neuron

show that, in vertebrates, the paths of development include more-local regulatory mechanisms. The hallmark of vertebrate development is that cells sort themselves out via **cell-cell interactions**, taking on fates that are appropriate in the context of what neighboring cells are doing. Thus, vertebrate development is less hardwired and more susceptible to being shaped by environmental signals and, as we'll see, experience.

At birth, mammals have already produced most of the neurons they will ever have. The postnatal increase of human brain weight is primarily due to growth in the size of neurons, branching of dendrites, elaboration of synapses (see Figure 7.6), increase in myelin, and addition of glial cells. But early reports that new neurons are added just after birth in some brain regions (Altman, 1969) have been supplemented with findings of **adult neurogenesis**, the generation of new neurons in adulthood, in humans (Eriksson et al., 1998) and other animals (E. Gould, Reeves, et al., 1999; Magavi et al., 2000; Shingo et al., 2003). Likewise, nerve cells of the olfactory organ (which we use to detect odors) can be replaced throughout life (Sawamoto et al., 2006). Neurons are also added to the adult nervous system in songbirds (discussed in Chapters 12 and 19).

While the new neurons acquired in adulthood represent a tiny minority of neurons, there's reason to think they are important. Enriched experience, such as learning, increases the rate of neurogenesis in adult mammals (E. Gould, Beylin, et al., 1999). So by studying this chapter, you may be giving your brain a few more neurons to use on exam day! Physical exercise also boosts neurogenesis in rats—an effect that can be blocked by stresses such as social isolation (Stranahan et al., 2006)—so invest in exercise and a network of friends too.

New nerve cells migrate

Neurons of the developing nervous system are always on the move. At some stage the cells that form in the ventricular layer through mitotic division move away, in a process known as **cell migration**. In primates, by the time of birth almost all presumptive nerve cells have completed their migration; but in rats, cells that will become neurons continue to migrate in some regions for several weeks following birth.

Cells do not move in an aimless, haphazard manner. Cells in the developing brain move along the surface of a particular type of glial cell (Rakic, 1985). Like spokes (radii) of a wheel, these **radial glial cells** extend from the inner to the outer surfaces of the emerging nervous system (**Figure 7.5**). The radial glial cells act as a series of guide wires, and the newly formed cells creep along them, as if they were "riding the glial monorail" (Hatten, 1990). Some migrating cells move in a direction perpendicular to the radial glial cells (S. A. Anderson et al., 1997), like Tarzan swinging from vine to vine; others move in a rostral stream to produce the olfactory bulbs (C. M. Smith and Luskin, 1998).

Failures in the mechanism of cell migration result in either a vastly reduced population of neurons or a disorderly arrangement and, not surprisingly, behavioral disorders. The migration of cells and the outgrowth of nerve cell extensions (dendrites and axons) involve various chemicals. Molecules that promote the adhesion of developing elements of the nervous system, and thereby guide migrating cells and growing axons, are called **cell adhesion molecules** (**CAMs**) (Reichardt and Tomaselli, 1991). CAMs may also guide axons to regenerate when they are cut in adulthood (**Box 7.1**).

BOX 7.1 Degeneration and Regeneration of Nervous Tissue

When a mature nerve cell is injured, it can regrow in several ways. Complete replacement of injured nerve cells is rare in mammals, but Figures A and B illustrate two characteristic forms of degeneration and regeneration in the mammalian peripheral and central nervous systems. Injury close to the cell body of a neuron produces a series of changes resulting in the eventual destruction of the cell; this process is called **retrograde degeneration** (Figure A, 2 and 3). If the injured neuron dies, the target cells formerly innervated by that neuron may show signs of *transneuronal degeneration* (Figure A, 4).

Cutting through the axon also produces loss of the distal part of the axon (the part

that is separated from the cell body). This process is called *Wallerian degeneration*, or **anterograde degeneration** (Figure B, 2 and 3). The part of the axon that remains connected to the cell body may regrow. Severed axons in the peripheral nervous system regrow readily. Sprouts emerge from the part of the axon that is still connected to the nerve cell body and advance slowly toward the periphery (Figure B, 4). Cell adhesion molecules (CAMs) help guide the regenerating axons. Some fishes and amphibians have an enviable advantage over humans: after an injury to the brain they can regenerate many of the lost connections. In these cases, CAMs appear to guide the regeneration (as we'll see in Box 7.2).

One interesting thing about regeneration of the nervous system is that it involves processes that seem similar to those that take place during an organism's original development. Studying regeneration, then, may increase our understanding of the original processes of growth of the nervous system, and vice versa. From a therapeutic viewpoint, these studies may help scientists learn how to induce repair and regrowth of damaged neural tissue in humans.

retrograde degeneration Destruction of the nerve cell body following injury to its axon.

anterograde degeneration Also called *Wallerian degeneration*. The loss of the distal portion of an axon resulting from injury to the axon.

(A) Retrograde degeneration

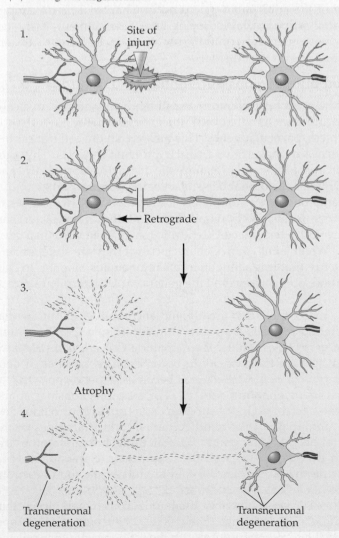

1. Site of injury
2. ← Retrograde
3. Atrophy
4. Transneuronal degeneration · Transneuronal degeneration

(B) Anterograde degeneration

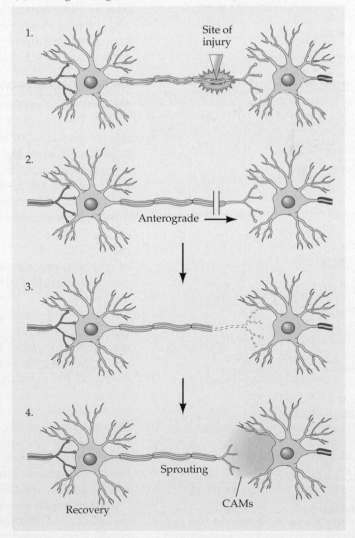

1. Site of injury
2. Anterograde →
3.
4. Sprouting · Recovery · CAMs

7.6 Cerebral Cortex Tissue in the Early Development of Humans These representations of cerebral cortex show the extent of neural connections and neuronal differentiation at birth (*a*), at 3 months of age (*b*), and at 2 years of age (*c*). Numerals refer to the six cortical layers. (From Conel, 1939, 1947, 1959.)

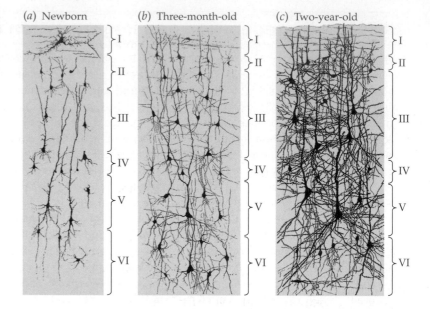

(*a*) Newborn   (*b*) Three-month-old   (*c*) Two-year-old

The single-file appearance of nerve cell precursors during cell migration (see Figure 7.5*a*) is followed by the aggregation, or grouping, of cells in a manner that foreshadows the nuclei of the adult brain discussed in Chapter 2. For example, cells of the cerebral cortex arrive in waves during fetal development, each successive wave forming a new outer layer, until the six layers of the adult cortex are formed, with the latest arrivals on the outside.

Cells in newly formed brain regions differentiate into neurons

Newly arrived cells in the brain bear no more resemblance to mature nerve cells than to the cells of other organs. Once they reach their destinations, however, the cells begin to use, or **express**, particular genes. This means that the cell transcribes a particular subset of genes to make the particular proteins it needs. This process of **cell differentiation** enables the cell to acquire the distinctive appearance and functions of neurons characteristic of that particular region (**Figure 7.6**).

What controls differentiation is not completely understood, but two classes of influence are known. First, intrinsic self-organization is an important factor; cerebellar Purkinje cells develop a very specific dendritic tree even **in vitro** (in a glass dish) (Seil et al., 1974). When a cell shows characteristics that are independent of neighboring cells, we say that it is acting in a **cell-autonomous** manner. In cell-autonomous differentiation, presumably only the genes within that cell are directing events.

However, the neural environment also greatly influences nerve cell differentiation. In other words, neighboring cells are a second major influence on the differentiation of neurons. In vertebrates (unlike the nematode *Caenorhabditis elegans*), young neural cells seem to have the capacity to become many varieties of neurons, and the particular type of neuron that a cell becomes depends on where it happens to be and what its neighboring cells are. For example, consider spinal motoneurons—cells in the spinal cord that send their axons out to control muscles. Motoneurons are large, multipolar cells found in the left and right sides of the spinal cord in the ventral horn of gray matter. Motoneurons are among the first recognizable neurons in the spinal cord, and they send their axons out early in fetal development. How do these cells "know" they should express motoneuron-specific genes and differentiate into motoneurons?

Examination of the late divisions giving rise to motoneurons makes it clear that the cells are not attending to mitotic lineage (Leber et al., 1990). Instead, some spinal cells are directed to become motoneurons under the influence of other cells ly-

expression The process by which a cell makes an mRNA transcript of a particular gene.

cell differentiation The developmental stage in which cells acquire distinctive characteristics, such as those of neurons, as the result of expressing particular genes.

in vitro Literally "in glass" (in Latin). Usually, in a laboratory dish; outside the body.

cell-autonomous Referring to cell processes that are directed by the cell itself rather than being under the influence of other cells.

7.7 The Induction of Spinal Motoneurons In this cross section of embryonic chick spinal cord, the notochord (green circle at bottom) lies just beneath the spinal cord and secretes a protein called Sonic hedgehog. A moderate concentration of this protein in the ventral spinal cord induces the cells there to develop as motoneurons (gold), forming columns of motoneurons on the left and right side. Another protein (blue) is expressed only in the dorsal spinal cord. (Courtesy of Thomas Jessell.)

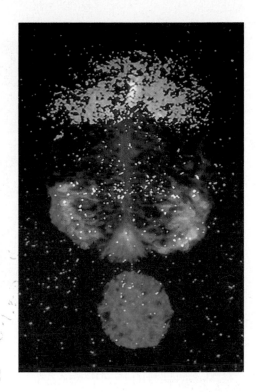

ing just ventral to the developing spinal cord—in the **notochord**, a rodlike structure that forms along the midline (see Figure 7.1*a*) (Roelink et al., 1994). The notochord releases a protein (playfully named Sonic hedgehog) that diffuses to the spinal cord and directs some (but not all) cells to become motoneurons (**Figure 7.7**).

The influence of one set of cells on the fate of neighboring cells is known as **induction**; the notochord induces some spinal cord cells to differentiate into motoneurons. Induction of this sort has been demonstrated many times in the developing vertebrate body and brain. Another way to describe the situation is that there is extensive cell-cell interaction, each cell taking cues from its neighbors. Because each cell influences the differentiation of others, vertebrate neural development is very complex, but also very flexible.

For example, cells differentiate into the type of neuron that is appropriate for wherever they happen to be in the brain; thus, cell-cell interaction coordinates development—directing differentiation to provide the right type of neuron for each part of the brain. Another consequence of the reliance of development on cell-cell interactions such as induction is that, if a few cells are injured or lost, other cells will "answer the call" of inducing factors and fill in for the missing cells.

This phenomenon can be observed in embryos from which some cells have been removed. For example, if cells are removed early enough from a developing limb bud in a chick embryo, other cells pitch in, and by the time the chick hatches the limb looks normal—with no parts missing. Embryologists refer to such adaptive responses to early injury as **regulation**: the developing animal compensates for missing or injured cells. Because cell fate is so tightly coupled with mitotic lineage in *C. elegans*, this organism shows little or no regulation. If a cell in *C. elegans* is killed (with a laser through the microscope), no other cells take its place; the worm must do without that cell.

The more complicated system of cells taking cues from their neighbors as to what genes they should express and what function they should fulfill has another consequence: if cells that have not yet differentiated extensively can be obtained and placed into a particular brain region, they will differentiate in an appropriate way and become properly integrated. Such undifferentiated cells, called **stem cells**, are present throughout embryonic tissues, so they can be gathered from umbilical-cord blood, miscarried embryos, or unused embryos produced during in vitro fertilization.

It may be possible to take cells from adult tissue and, by treating them with various factors in a dish, transform them into "adult" stem cells (Palmer et al., 2001). It is hoped that placing stem cells in areas of brain degeneration, such as loss of myelination in multiple sclerosis, or loss of dopaminergic neurons in Parkinson's disease, might reverse such degeneration as the implanted cells differentiate to fill in for the missing components (S. Liu et al., 2000).

The axons and dendrites of young neurons grow extensively and form synapses

The biggest change in brain cells early in life is the extensive growth of axons and dendrites (termed **process outgrowth**) and the proliferation of synapses (**synaptogenesis**). At the tips of both axons and dendrites are **growth cones**, swollen ends from which extensions emerge. The very fine outgrowths, called **filopodia** (singular *filopodium*, from the Latin *filum*, "thread," and the Greek *pous*, "foot"), are spikelike; the sheetlike extensions are called **lamellipodia** (singular *lamellipodium*, from a

notochord A midline structure arising early in the embryonic development of vertebrates.

induction The process by which one set of cells influences the fate of neighboring cells, usually by secreting a chemical factor that changes gene expression in the target cells.

regulation An adaptive response to early injury, as when developing individuals compensate for missing or injured cells.

stem cell A cell that is undifferentiated and therefore can take on the fate of any cell that a donor organism can produce.

process outgrowth The extensive growth of axons and dendrites.

synaptogenesis The establishment of synaptic connections as axons and dendrites grow.

growth cone The growing tip of an axon or a dendrite.

filopodia Very fine, tubular outgrowths from the growth cone.

lamellipodia Sheetlike extensions of a growth cone.

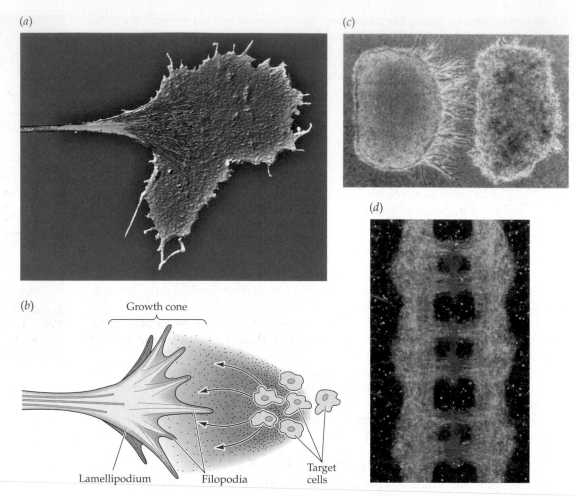

(a)

(c)

(d)

(b)

Growth cone

Lamellipodium   Filopodia   Target cells

7.8 The Growth Cones of Growing Axons and Dendrites (a) The fine, threadlike extensions pictured here are filopodia, which find adhesive surfaces and pull the growth cone, and therefore the growing axon, to the right. (b) Target cells release a chemical that creates a gradient (dots) around them. Growth cones orient to and follow the gradient to the cells. (c) The extensions visible here are growing out of a sensory ganglion (*left*) toward their normal target tissue. (d) The chemorepellent protein Slit (red), shown here in an embryo of the fruit fly, *Drosophila*, repels most axons (green), preventing them from crossing the midline. (Part *a* courtesy of Paul Bridgman; *b* after Tessier-Lavigne et al., 1988; *c* courtesy of Marc Tessier-Lavigne; *d* courtesy of Julie Simpson and Corey S. Goodman.)

form of the Latin *lamina*, "thin plate") (**Figure 7.8a and b**). Both the filopodia and the lamellipodia adhere to the extracellular environment, and then they contract to pull the growth cone in a particular direction (the growing axon or dendrite follows behind it). Dendritic growth cones are found in adults, mediating the continued elongation and change in dendrites that occurs throughout life in response to experience (see Chapter 17).

What guides axons along the paths they take? Axons are guided by chemicals released by the target nerve cells or other tissues, such as muscles (C. S. Goodman, 1996; Tessier-Lavigne and Placzek, 1991). The axon growth cone responds to the concentration gradients of these chemicals that provide directional guidance, as illustrated in **Figure 7.8b and c**. Chemical signals that attract certain growth cones are called **chemoattractants** (Hiramoto et al., 2000); chemicals that repel growth cones are **chemorepellents** (M. S. Chen et al., 2000; Keynes and Cook, 1992). For example, because it is important for some axons to remain on one side of the body and for others to cross over, a protein called Slit repels some axons to prevent them

chemoattractants Compounds that attract particular classes of growth cones.

chemorepellents Compounds that repel particular classes of growth cones.

(a) Rat visual cortex

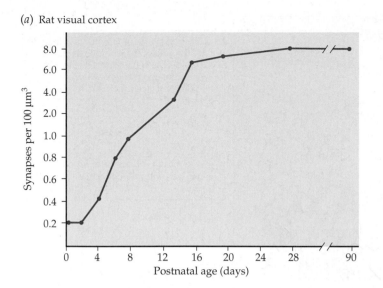

(b) Human visual cortex

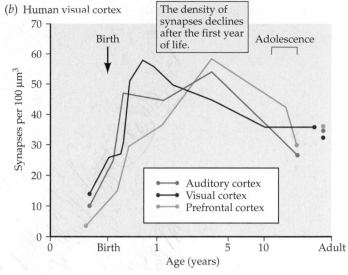

from crossing the midline (**Figure 7.8d**) (Brose et al., 1999). The same secreted protein may act as a chemoattractant to some growth cones and a chemorepellent to others (Polleux et al., 2000).

Synapses can form rapidly on dendrites and dendritic spines (**Figure 7.9**). The spines themselves proliferate rapidly after birth. These connections can be affected by postnatal experience, as we will see later in this chapter. To support the metabolic needs of the expanded dendritic tree, the nerve cell body greatly increases in volume.

The death of many neurons is a normal part of development

As strange as it may seem, cell death is a crucial phase of brain development, especially during embryonic stages. This developmental stage is not unique to the nervous system. Naturally occurring **cell death**, also called **apoptosis** (from the Greek *apo*, "away from," and *ptosis*, "act of falling"), is evident as a kind of sculpting process in the emergence of other tissues in both animals and plants (Oppenheim, 1991).

The number of neurons that die during early development is quite large. In some regions of the brain and spinal cord, *most* of the young nerve cells die during prenatal development. In 1958, Viktor Hamburger (1900–2001) first described naturally occurring neuronal cell death in chicks, in which nearly half the originally produced spinal motoneurons die before the chick hatches (**Figure 7.10**). Genetically interfering with neural apoptosis in fetal mice causes them to grow brains that are

7.9 The Postnatal Development of Synapses The rate of synapse development in the visual cortex of rats (a) and humans (b). In humans, note the decline in the density of synapses after the first year of life. (Part a after Blue and Parnavelas, 1983; b from Huttenlocher et al., 1982.)

cell death or apoptosis The developmental process during which "surplus" cells die.

7.10 Many Neurons Die during Normal Early Development The pattern of neuronal cell death in spinal motoneurons of chicks (a) and humans (b). Many neuronal populations show a similar pattern of apoptosis. (Part a from Hamburger, 1975; b from Forger and Breedlove, 1987.)

(a) Chick spinal motoneurons

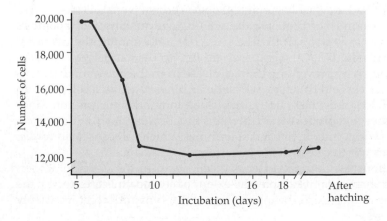

(b) Human spinal motoneurons

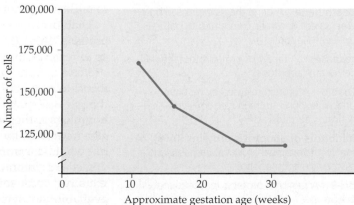

7.11 Death Genes Regulate Apoptosis

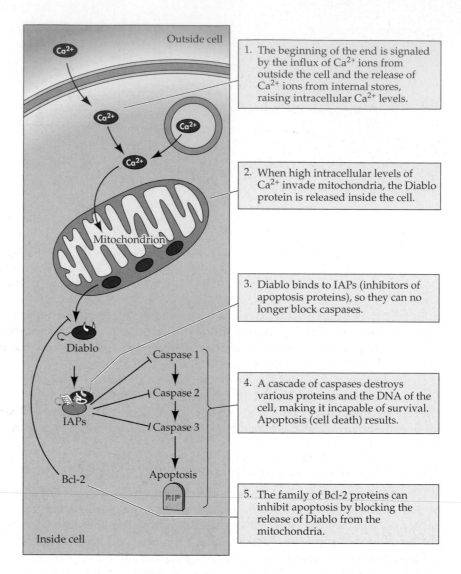

1. The beginning of the end is signaled by the influx of Ca^{2+} ions from outside the cell and the release of Ca^{2+} ions from internal stores, raising intracellular Ca^{2+} levels.

2. When high intracellular levels of Ca^{2+} invade mitochondria, the Diablo protein is released inside the cell.

3. Diablo binds to IAPs (inhibitors of apoptosis proteins), so they can no longer block caspases.

4. A cascade of caspases destroys various proteins and the DNA of the cell, making it incapable of survival. Apoptosis (cell death) results.

5. The family of Bcl-2 proteins can inhibit apoptosis by blocking the release of Diablo from the mitochondria.

too large to fit in the skull (Depaepe et al., 2005), so we can see how vital it is that some cells die.

These cells are not dying because of a defect. Rather, it appears that these cells have "decided" to die and are actively committing suicide. Your chromosomes carry **death genes**—genes that are expressed only when a cell undergoes apoptosis (Peter et al., 1997). For example, the **caspases** are a family of proteases (protein-dissolving enzymes) that cut up proteins and nuclear DNA. Apoptosis appears to begin with a sudden influx and release of Ca^{2+} ions that cause the mitochondria inside the cell to release a protein called, devilishly enough, **Diablo** (Verhagen et al., 2000).

Diablo binds to a family of proteins, the well-named **inhibitors of apoptosis proteins** (**IAPs**) (Earnshaw et al., 1999). The IAPs normally inhibit the caspases, so when Diablo binds the IAPs, the caspases are free to dismantle the cell. **Bcl-2** proteins block apoptosis by preventing Diablo release from the mitochondria. This intricate system of checks and balances, which determines whether a cell gives up the ghost (**Figure 7.11**), must have been established long ago in evolution, since homologs of the genes that produce these proteins function similarly in *Caenorhabditis elegans*. In the worm, mitotic lineage determines which cells are fated to die, but what determines which cells will die in vertebrates?

Cell-cell interactions regulate the extensive cell death in the developing nervous system of vertebrates. For example, the extent of cell death is affected by the availability of synaptic targets. Reducing the size of the synaptic target invariably

death gene A gene that is expressed only when a cell becomes committed to natural cell death (apoptosis).

caspases A family of proteins that regulate cell death (apoptosis).

Diablo A protein released by mitochondria, in response to high calcium levels, that activates apoptosis.

inhibitors of apoptosis proteins (IAPs) A family of proteins that inhibit caspases and thereby stave off apoptosis.

Bcl-2 A family of proteins that regulate apoptosis.

7.12 The Effects of Nerve Growth Factor If NGF is added to the solution bathing a spinal ganglion grown in vitro (in a glass dish), neuronal processes grow outward in an exuberant, radiating fashion. (From Levi-Montalcini, 1963.)

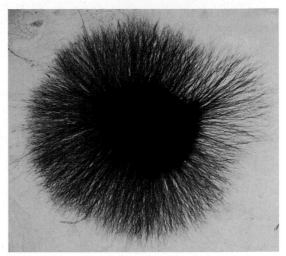

reduces the number of surviving nerve cells. If the leg of a tadpole is removed early in development, for instance, many more developing spinal motoneurons die than would die if the leg remained in position. Conversely, grafting on an extra leg—a technique that is possible with chicken embryos and tadpoles—reduces the usual loss of cells; in such cases the mature spinal cord has more than the usual number of motoneurons on that side.

Neurons compete for connections to target structures (other nerve cells or end organs, such as muscle). Cells that make adequate synapses remain; those without a place to form synaptic connections die. Apparently the cells compete not just for synaptic sites, but for a chemical that the target structure makes and releases. Neurons that receive enough of the chemical survive; those that do not, die. Such target-derived chemicals are called **neurotrophic factors** (or simply *trophic factors*) because they act as if they "feed" the neurons to help them survive (in Greek, *trophe* means "nourishment"). The neurotrophic factor that was the first to be identified prevents the death of developing sympathetic neurons, as we'll discuss next.

Neurotrophic factors allow neurons to survive and grow

In the 1950s, investigators discovered a substance—called **nerve growth factor** (**NGF**)—that markedly affects the growth of neurons in spinal ganglia and in the ganglia of the sympathetic nervous system (Levi-Montalcini, 1982). Administered to a chick embryo, NGF resulted in many more sympathetic neurons than usual. These cells were also larger and had more extensive processes (**Figure 7.12**).

Various target organs normally produce NGF during development. It is taken up by the axons of sympathetic neurons that innervate those organs and transported back to the cell body, where NGF prevents the sympathetic neurons from dying. The amount of NGF produced by targets during development is roughly correlated with the amount of sympathetic innervation that the targets maintain into adulthood. Thus, cell death, controlled by access to NGF, provides each target with an appropriate amount of sympathetic innervation.

There are additional neurotrophic factors, each one affecting the survival of a particular cell type during a specific developmental period. One such factor, purified from the brains of many animals, was named **brain-derived neurotrophic factor** (**BDNF**). The gene for BDNF turned out to be very similar to the gene for NGF. Investigators used molecular techniques to search for other NGF-related molecules and found several more. The family of NGF-like molecules was named the **neurotrophin** family, and its members are numbered: neurotrophin-1 (NGF), -2 (BDNF), -3, and -4/5 (the fifth neurotrophin discovered turned out to be identical with the fourth—oops). Neurotrophic factors that are unrelated to NGF also have been found, including ciliary neurotrophic factor (named after its ability to keep neurons from ciliary ganglia alive in vitro).

The exact role of these various factors (and other neurotrophic factors yet to be discovered) is under intense scientific scrutiny (Kafitz et al., 1999; Lewin and Barde, 1996). One role of neurotrophic factors seems to be guiding the rearrangement of synaptic connections, as we discuss next.

Synaptic connections are refined by synapse rearrangement

Just as not all the neurons produced by a developing individual are kept into adulthood, some of the synapses formed early in development are later retracted. Originally this process was described as synapse elimination, but later studies

neurotrophic factor Also called *trophic factor*. A target-derived chemical that acts as if it "feeds" certain neurons to help them survive.

nerve growth factor (NGF) A substance that markedly affects the growth of neurons in spinal ganglia and in the ganglia of the sympathetic nervous system.

brain-derived neurotrophic factor (BDNF) A protein purified from the brains of animals that can keep some classes of neurons alive.

neurotrophin A chemical that prevents neurons from dying.

7.13 A Model for the Action of Neurotrophic Factors

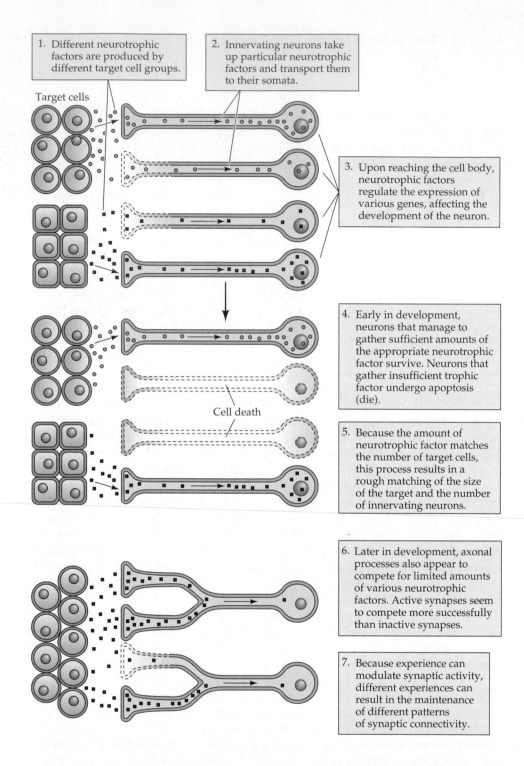

1. Different neurotrophic factors are produced by different target cell groups.

2. Innervating neurons take up particular neurotrophic factors and transport them to their somata.

Target cells

3. Upon reaching the cell body, neurotrophic factors regulate the expression of various genes, affecting the development of the neuron.

4. Early in development, neurons that manage to gather sufficient amounts of the appropriate neurotrophic factor survive. Neurons that gather insufficient trophic factor undergo apoptosis (die).

Cell death

5. Because the amount of neurotrophic factor matches the number of target cells, this process results in a rough matching of the size of the target and the number of innervating neurons.

6. Later in development, axonal processes also appear to compete for limited amounts of various neurotrophic factors. Active synapses seem to compete more successfully than inactive synapses.

7. Because experience can modulate synaptic activity, different experiences can result in the maintenance of different patterns of synaptic connectivity.

synapse rearrangement Also called *synaptic remodeling*. The loss of some synapses and the development of others; a refinement of synaptic connections that is often seen in development.

found that, although some original synapses are indeed lost, many new synapses are also formed as they compete for neurotropic factors (**Figure 7.13**). Thus, a more accurate term is **synapse rearrangement**, or *synaptic remodeling*. In most cases, synapse rearrangement takes place after the period of cell death.

For example, as we learned already, about half of the spinal motoneurons that form die later (see Figure 7.10). By the end of the cell death period, each surviving motoneuron innervates many muscle fibers, and every muscle fiber is innervated by several motoneurons. But later the surviving motoneurons retract many of their axon collaterals, until each muscle fiber comes to be innervated by only one motoneuron.

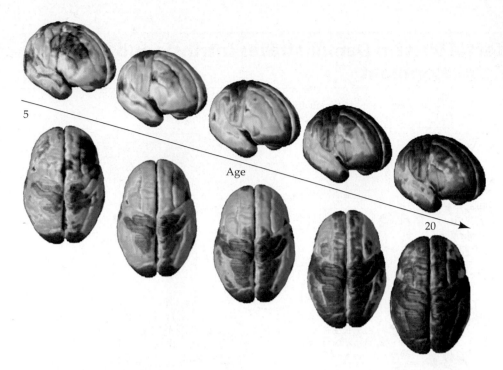

7.14 Synapse Rearrangement in the Developing Human Brain   Repeated measures from many subjects reveal that the layer of gray matter on the exterior of the cortex becomes thinner across development, as synapses are retracted. Purple and blue depict regions with little change in cortical thickness; yellow and red depict areas that are changing rapidly with age. Note that the prefrontal cortex, usually thought to be important in inhibiting behavior, does not finish maturation until adolescence. (From Gogtay et al., 2004, courtesy of Nitin Gogtay.)

Similar events have been documented in several neural regions, including the cerebellum (Mariani and Changeaux, 1981), the brainstem (Jackson and Parks, 1982), the visual cortex (Hubel et al., 1977), and the autonomic ganglia (Lichtman and Purves, 1980). In human cerebral cortex there seems to be a net loss of synapses from late childhood until midadolescence (see Figure 7.9b). This synaptic remodeling is evident in thinning of the gray matter in the cortex as pruning of dendrites and axon terminals progresses. The thinning process continues in a caudal–rostral direction during maturation (**Figure 7.14**), so prefrontal cortex is affected last (Gogtay et al., 2004). Since prefrontal cortex is important for inhibiting behavior (see Chapter 18), this delayed brain maturation may contribute to teenagers' impulsivity and lack of control. Furthermore, because the synaptic pruning going on at this stage is critical for future functioning of the brain, the tendency of psychiatric disorders, such as schizophrenia and mood disorders, to emerge in adolescence reflects the vulnerability of this developmental stage (Paus et al., 2008).

What determines which synapses are kept and which are lost? Although we don't know all the factors, one important influence is neural activity (**Box 7.2** describes an example). One theory is that active synapses take up some neurotrophic factor that maintains the synapse, while inactive synapses get too little trophic factor to remain stable (see Figure 7.13). Intellectual stimulation probably contributes, as suggested by the fact that teenagers with the highest IQ show an especially prolonged period of cortical thinning (P. Shaw et al., 2006).

Later in this chapter we'll see specific examples in which active synapses are maintained and inactive synapses are retracted in the mammalian visual system. And in Chapter 8 we'll review evidence that synapse rearrangement in the cerebral cortex continues throughout life.

Glial Cells Provide Myelin, Which Is Vital for Brain Function

As already noted, glial cells develop from the same populations of immature cells as neurons. Glial cells continue to be added to the nervous system throughout life. (Sometimes, however, the process becomes aberrant, resulting in glial tumors, or *gliomas*, of the brain.) In fact, the most intense phase of glial cell proliferation in many animals occurs *after* birth, when glial cells are added from immature cells located in the ventricular zone.

BOX 7.2 The Frog Retinotectal System Demonstrates Intrinsic and Extrinsic Factors in Neural Development

In the 1940s Roger Sperry (1913–1995) began a series of experiments that seemed to emphasize the importance of intrinsic factors, such as genes, for determining the pattern of connections in the brain. If the optic nerve that connects an eye to the brain is cut in an adult mammal, the animal is blinded in that eye and never recovers. In fishes and amphibians such as frogs, however, the animal is only temporarily blinded; in a few months the axons from the eye (specifically, from the ganglion cells of the retina) reinnervate the brain (specifically the dorsal portion of the midbrain, called the *tectum*) and the animal recovers its eyesight. When food is presented on the left or right, above or below, the animal flicks its tongue accurately to retrieve it. Thus, either (1) the retina reestablishes the same pattern of connections to the tectum that was there before surgery and the brain interprets visual information as before, or (2) the retina reinnervates the tectum at random but the rest of the brain learns to interpret the information presented in this new pattern.

Several lines of evidence established that the first hypothesis is correct. One such piece of evidence is that the first-arriving retinal axons sometimes pass over uninnervated tectum to reach their original targets. In the classic case illustrating this phenomenon, the optic nerve was cut and the eye was rotated 180°; when the animal recovered eyesight, it behaved as if the visual image had been rotated 180°, moving to the left when trying to get food presented on the right, and flicking its tongue up when food was presented below. The only explanation for this behavior is that the retinal axons had grown back to their *original* positions on the tectum, ignoring the rotation of the eye. Furthermore, once the original connections had been reestablished, the brain interpreted the information as if the eye were in its original position. Even years later, animals that underwent this treatment had not learned to make sense of information from the rotated eye.

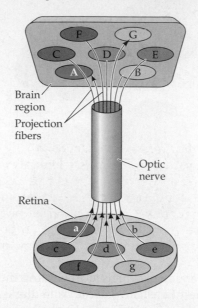

(A) Two possible mechanisms of chemoaffinity

Gradient 2

Gradient 1

Brain region

Projection fibers

Optic nerve

Retina

Sperry proposed the **chemoaffinity hypothesis** to explain how retinal axons know which part of the tectum to innervate. Suppose each retinal cell and each tectal cell had a specific chemical identity—an address of sorts. Then each retinal cell would need only to seek out the proper address in the tectum and the entire pattern would be reestablished; many chemical cues (represented by many colors in Figure A, *left*) or only a few (two colors in Figure A, *right*) may be involved. Cell adhesion molecules (CAMs) in tectal membranes direct the retinal axons to the roughly appropriate region of tectum (F. Bonhoeffer and Huf, 1985).

After arriving at the roughly appropriate region of tectum, however, retinal connections are fine-tuned by extrinsic factors, specifically by experience. Normally, each retina innervates only the tectum on the opposite side. When implantation of a third eye forces two retinas to innervate a single tectum (Figure B, *left*), they each do so in the same rough pattern, but they *segregate*; axons from one retina predominate in one area, and axons from the other retina predominate in neighboring tectum, so there are alternating stripes of innervation from the two eyes (Figure B, *right*).

This segregation depends on activity (Constantine-Paton et al., 1990). If neural activity in one eye is silenced (by injection of drugs), the eye loses its connections to the tectum and the other eye takes over, innervating the entire tectum. If both eyes are silenced (by keeping the animals in the dark), neither eye predominates, their axons fail to segregate in the tectum, and the detailed pattern of innervation fails

(B) This three-eyed frog has two eyes innervating the left tectum.

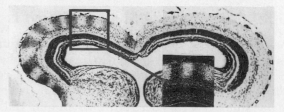

BOX 7.2 (*continued*)

to appear. Presumably the two eyes are competing for limited supplies of a neurotrophic factor from the tectum, and active synapses take up more of the factor(s).

Thus, the retinotectal system appears to reestablish the original pattern of innervation in two steps: (1) Chemical cues bring retinal axons to the approximately correct region of tectum. (2) The neural activity of the retinal cells, normally driven by visual experience, directs these axons to innervate or maintain innervation of the precise tectal region. As we'll see later in this chapter, a similar competition goes on in young mammals as information from the two eyes competes to form synapses in visual cortex. (Figure B courtesy of Martha Constantine-Paton.)

chemoaffinity hypothesis The notion that each cell has a chemical identity that directs it to synapse on the proper target cell during development.

The development of sheaths around axons—the process of **myelination** (**Figure 7.15**)—greatly changes the rate at which axons conduct messages (see Figure 3.8). Myelination has a strong impact on behavior because it allows large networks of cells to communicate rapidly. **Multiple sclerosis** is a disorder in which myelin is destroyed, probably by the person's own immune system, in random distinct patches (Manova and Kostadinova, 2000). The resultant desynchronization of activity in these locations can cause devastating disruptions of sensory and motor function.

In humans, the earliest myelination in the peripheral nervous system is evident in cranial and spinal nerves about 24 weeks after conception. But the most intense phase of myelination occurs shortly after birth. Furthermore, some investigators believe that myelin can be added to axons throughout life. The first nerve tracts in the human nervous system to become myelinated are in the spinal cord. Myelination then spreads successively into the hindbrain, midbrain, and forebrain. Within the cerebral cortex, sensory zones are myelinated before motor zones; correspondingly, sensory functions mature before motor functions.

myelination The process of myelin formation.

multiple sclerosis Literally, "many scars"; a disorder characterized by widespread degeneration of myelin.

Genes Interact with Experience to Guide Brain Development

Many factors influence the emergence of the form, arrangements, and connections of the developing brain. One influence is genes, which direct the production of every protein the cell can make. In the nematode *Caenorhabditis elegans*, genes are almost the only factors affecting development; the cells somehow keep track of their mitotic lineage and then simply express the genes that are appropriate for the cell fate their lineage directs.

7.15 Myelin Formation The repeated wrapping of a Schwann cell cytoplasm around an axon results in a many-layered sheath that insulates the axon electrically, speeding the conduction of electrical signals along its length.

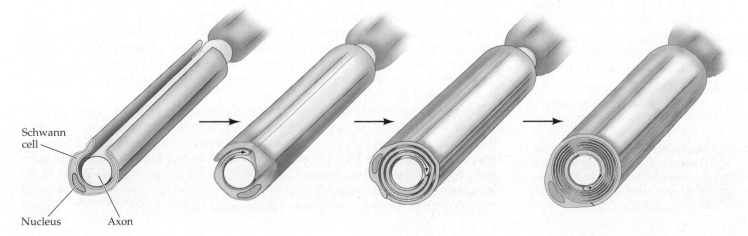

Schwann cell

Nucleus   Axon

Genes are also a major influence on the development of the vertebrate brain. An animal that has inherited an altered gene will make an altered protein, which will affect any cell structure that includes that protein. Thus, every neuronal structure, and therefore every behavior, can be altered by changes in the appropriate gene(s). It is useful to think of genes as *intrinsic* factors—that is, factors that originate within the developing cell itself. All other influences we can consider *extrinsic*—originating outside of the developing cell.

Two terms help illustrate how these intrinsic and extrinsic factors interact. The sum of all the intrinsic, genetic information that an individual has is its **genotype**. The sum of all the physical characteristics that make up an individual is its **phenotype**. Your genotype was determined at the moment of fertilization and remains the same throughout your life. But your phenotype changes constantly, as you grow up and grow old and even, in a tiny way, as you take each breath. In other words, phenotype is determined by the interaction of genotype and extrinsic factors, including experience. Thus, as we'll see, individuals who have identical genotypes do not have identical phenotypes, because they have not received identical extrinsic influences. And since their nervous system phenotypes are somewhat different, they do not behave exactly the same.

We'll start by considering some extrinsic factors that affect the developing brain, before sampling some of the powerful effects of those intrinsic factors called genes. Then we'll learn that extrinsic and intrinsic factors interact, because experience can control how genes are used in the developing brain. Thus, every behavior is affected not only by genes, but also by experience.

Environmental factors may limit brain development

One important extrinsic factor is whether the fetus is provided with the basic requirements to carry out the genetic instructions. For example, children who experience complicated delivery at birth, when a transient lack of oxygen (**hypoxia**) may affect the brain, are at greater risk for intellectual disability and schizophrenia than are children who have a problem-free birth. Similarly, if the mother does not get enough to eat, the fetal brain may have insufficient energy and nutrients to develop properly. For example, fetuses carried by malnourished Dutch women during the "hunger winter" of 1944 were underweight at birth, as would be expected, but as adults they were also more likely to suffer from schizophrenia. A similar outcome followed a famine in China (A. S. Brown and Susser, 2008). These results indicate that schizophrenia, which is known to be influenced by genetic factors, can also result from fetal malnutrition. We'll learn more about the interaction of genetic and environmental factors in schizophrenia in Chapter 16.

DRUGS CAN AFFECT BRAIN DEVELOPMENT   Even in the protected environment of the womb, the embryo and fetus are not immune to outside influence; what is taking place in the mother's body directly affects them. Maternal conditions such as viral infection and exposure to drugs are especially likely to result in developmental disorders in the unborn child. Concern with the maternal environment as a determinant of brain development spawned the field of **behavioral teratology** (*teratology*—from the Greek *teras*, "monster"—is the study of malformations). Investigators in this field are especially concerned with the pathological effects of drugs ingested during pregnancy.

There is a long history of concern about alcohol and pregnancy, dating back to classical times. About 40% of children born to alcoholic mothers show a distinctive profile of anatomical, physiological, and behavioral impairments known as **fetal alcohol syndrome** (**FAS**) (Abel, 1984; Colangelo and Jones, 1982). Prominent anatomical effects of fetal exposure to alcohol include distinctive changes in facial features (e.g., a sunken nasal bridge and altered shape of the nose and eyelids) and stunted growth. In some cases, the children may lack a corpus callosum (**Figure**

genotype   Also called *genome*. All the genetic information that one specific individual has inherited.

phenotype   The sum of an individual's physical characteristics at one particular time.

hypoxia   A transient lack of oxygen.

behavioral teratology   The study of impairments in behavior that are produced by embryonic or fetal exposure to toxic substances.

fetal alcohol syndrome (FAS)   A disorder, including intellectual disability and characteristic facial anomalies, that affects children exposed to too much alcohol (through maternal ingestion) during fetal development.

(*a*) Normal infant   Corpus callosum   (*b*) Infant with FAS

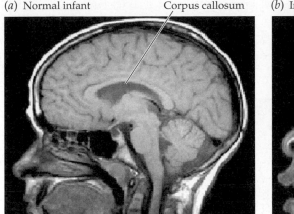 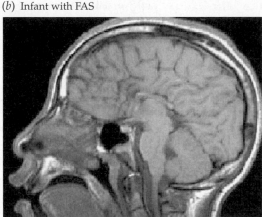

7.16 Abnormal Brain Development Associated with Fetal Alcohol Syndrome
(*a*) The brain of a normal infant. (*b*) The brain of an infant of the same age with FAS. The FAS brain shows microcephaly (abnormal smallness), fewer cerebral cortical gyri, and the absence of a corpus callosum connecting the two hemispheres. (Courtesy of E. Riley.)

7.16). Few FAS children catch up in the years following birth. The most common problem associated with FAS is intellectual disability, which varies in severity. No alcohol threshold has yet been established for this syndrome, but it can occur with relatively moderate intake during pregnancy. Even when FAS is not diagnosed, prenatal exposure to alcohol is correlated with neurophysiological impairments in language and fine motor skills (Mattson et al., 1998). Children with fetal alcohol syndrome may also show other neurological abnormalities, such as irritability, tremors, and hyperactivity.

Genes are the intrinsic factors that influence brain development

In addition to the powerful effects of the prenatal environment we just discussed, genes also have a profound influence on a variety of behaviors in many species (Rende and Plomin, 1995). We'll consider some of the best-studied influences of genes on brain development, including one genetic condition that can result in either severe intellectual disability or normal intelligence, depending on extrinsic factors in the diet.

EFFECTS OF MUTATIONS In rare instances, an animal inherits a sudden change in genetic structure, a **mutation**, that is related to marked anatomical or physiological change. Researchers can increase the frequency of mutations by exposing animals to radiation or chemicals that produce changes in genes. Animals with mutations are interesting to study because their changed behavioral phenotype may be quite specific and striking. For example, Greenspan et al. (1980) described mutants of the fruit fly, *Drosophila*, that seemed normal in every way except that they had memory problems. Affectionately labeled *dunce*, *amnesiac*, and *turnip*, these mutants either failed to learn or could learn but forgot rapidly. Biochemical deficits in these mutants (due to mutations that render specific genes, and therefore specific proteins, ineffective) cause the failure of memory (Dudai, 1988).

Many mutations in mice affect the nervous system. Individuals in one group of mouse mutants all have single-gene mutations that affect postnatal development of the cerebellum (Tissir and Goffinet, 2003). The names of these mutant mice—*reeler*, *staggerer*, and *weaver*—reflect the locomotor impairment that characterizes them (**Figure 7.17**). Today, scientists deliberately delete or introduce a particular gene in mice in order to study the effect of that gene on the nervous system (**Box 7.3**).

mutation A change in the nucleotide sequence of a gene as a result of unfaithful replication.

7.17 Cerebellar Mutants among Mice The cerebellum in a normal mouse (a) and two mutants (b, c) at two levels of magnification (top: ×25; bottom: ×250). In the mutant *weaver* (b), note the almost complete absence of the tiny granule cells (*bottom*), while the alignment of the large Purkinje cells (arrows) is normal. The mutant *reeler* (c) shows marked derangement of the customary layering of cells. Both mutants show overall shrinkage of the cerebellum (*top*). (From A. L. Leiman, unpublished observations.)

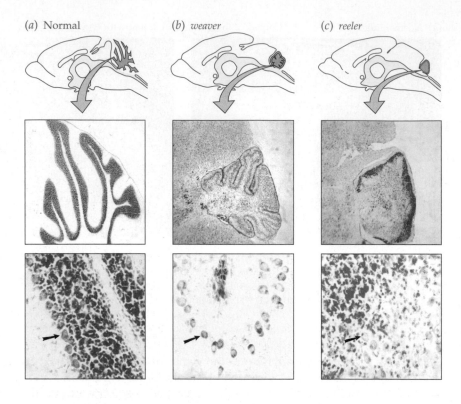

(a) Normal (b) *weaver* (c) *reeler*

Down syndrome Intellectual disability that is associated with an extra copy of chromosome 21.

fragile X syndrome A condition that is a frequent cause of inherited intellectual disability; produced by a fragile site on the X chromosome that seems prone to breaking because the DNA there is unstable.

CHROMOSOMAL EFFECTS A common form of cognitive disorder resulting from a chromosomal abnormality is **Down syndrome (Figure 7.18a)**. People with Down syndrome usually have an extra chromosome 21, for a total of three rather than the typical two copies. This disorder is strikingly related to the age of the mother at the time of conception: for women over 45 years old, the chance of having a baby with Down syndrome is nearly one in 40 (Karp, 1976). The behavioral dysfunctions are quite varied. Most individuals who have Down syndrome have a very low IQ, but some rare individuals attain an IQ as high as 80. Brain abnormalities in Down syndrome also vary. The cerebral cortex of patients with Down syndrome shows abnormal formation of dendritic spines. Mouse models of extra chromosomes result in structural changes that appear analogous to Down syndrome in humans (O'Doherty et al., 2005).

Probably the most frequent cause of inherited intellectual disability is the condition **fragile X syndrome (Figure 7.18b)**, which is more common in males than in

7.18 Atypical Chromosomes Have Widespread Effects (a) A young woman with Down syndrome. (b) A young man with fragile X syndrome.

(a)

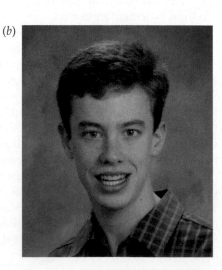

(b)

BOX 7.3 Transgenic and Knockout Mice

Animals with mutations in specific genes can offer clues about the role of genes in development and brain function. Until recently, the only types of mutants one could study were either the very rare cases of spontaneous mutations or the cases of mutations caused by animals being treated with radiation or chemicals to increase the rate of mutation. Unless very small, short-lived animals like *Drosophila* were the subject of the research, this process was tedious because very few of the induced mutations were in the gene of interest.

Among the many new tools brought by the revolution in molecular biology is **site-directed mutagenesis**, the ability to cause a mutation in a particular gene. Researchers using this technique must know the sequence of nucleotides in the gene of interest. Then they can use the tendency of complementary nucleotides to hybridize with that part of the gene to induce changes (see the Appendix for a refresher on hybridization).

The easiest change to understand is total disruption of the gene, making it nonfunctional. If this is done in special embryonic mouse cells, there are ways to introduce the manipulated cells into the testes or ovaries of a developing mouse. That mouse can then produce offspring that are missing one copy of the gene and, through inbreeding, grandchildren missing both copies of the gene. We call the resulting animal a **knockout organism** because the gene of interest has been *knocked out*.

By following the development of knockout mice, we can obtain clues about the roles of particular genes in normal animals. For example, the motoneurons of mice whose genes for brain-derived neurotrophic factor (BDNF) have been knocked out survive despite the absence of BDNF (Sendtner et al., 1996), so we know that trophic factor is not crucial for motoneuron survival. On the other hand, some parasympathetic ganglia fail to form in BDNF knockout mice (Erickson et al., 1996), suggesting that these neurons depend on BDNF for survival. As we'll see in Chapter 17, several genes suspected of playing a role in learning have been knocked out in mice, and the resulting animals indeed show deficits in learning.

There are some problems in interpreting such results, because the missing gene may have contributed only very indirectly to the learning process, or the animal's poor performance may have been due to a distraction caused by the knockout. For that matter, even normal behavior by animals missing the gene does not prove that the gene is unimportant for behavior. Perhaps the developing animal, in the absence of that gene, somehow has compensated for the loss and found a new way to solve the problem. This would be another example of the embryonic regulation that is so common in vertebrate development.

In other cases, a functional, manipulated copy of a gene can be introduced into the mouse. This animal is described as **transgenic** because a gene has been *trans*ferred into its genome. Sometimes the introduction of just a single new gene can have a dramatic effect on brain development; for example, compare the brains of newborn mice that are normal with those of transgenic mice carrying a modified gene for β-catenin (see Figure 6.22). Modifying this one gene caused the mouse to make far too many neurons, so extra gyri and sulci developed (Chenn and Walsh, 2002).

The transgenic approach is often used as a method for improving our understanding of genetic disorders. For example, in Chapter 11 we'll learn that when a human gene that causes severe motor impairments is transferred into mice, the mice develop symptoms similar to those that appear in humans. It may be possible to study the disease more closely in these mice and test possible therapies.

Knockout and transgenic animals have one limitation: they possess the genetic manipulation from the moment of conception and in every cell in the body. However, molecular neurobiologists have begun knocking out or replacing genes in adult animals—by injecting the animal with a triggering substance such as tetracycline, or by replacing or knocking out a gene in only one region of the brain. These manipulations allow the animal to develop with a normal genotype, thereby making it easier to interpret the result of the gene manipulation in adulthood. It may even be possible to knock out and then restore a gene in the same individual mouse, tracking its behavior as the gene is lost and regained.

site-directed mutagenesis   A technique in molecular biology that changes the sequence of nucleotides in an existing gene.

knockout organism   An individual in which a particular gene has been disabled by an experimenter.

transgenic   Referring to an animal in which a new or altered gene has been deliberately introduced into the genome.

females. At the end of the long arm of the X chromosome is a site that seems fragile—prone to breaking because the DNA there is unstable (Yu et al., 1991). People with this abnormality have a modified facial appearance, including elongation of the face, large prominent ears, and a prominent chin. A wide range of cognitive impairments—from mild to severe impairment—are associated with the syndrome (Baumgardner et al., 1994). Cortical neurons from the brains of people with fragile X syndrome, as well as mice genetically engineered to have this syndrome, possess an excess of small, immature dendritic spines (Bagni and Greenough, 2005). These findings suggest that the syndrome affects mental development by blocking the normal elimination of synapses after birth (see Figure 7.9).

The molecular basis of fragile X syndrome provided a surprise for geneticists because it demonstrated that we don't always pass on a faithful copy of our DNA to our offspring. The fragile site in the DNA consists of three nucleotides (CGG; see the Appendix for a review of nucleotides) repeated over and over. Most people have only 6–50 of these **trinucleotide repeats** at this site (Laxova, 1994). But during the production of sperm or eggs, the number of repeats sometimes changes, so a mother who has only 50 trinucleotide repeats may provide 100 repeats to her son. Any children who receive more than 200 repeats will display fragile X syndrome (Paulson and Fischbeck, 1996). Trinucleotide repeats in a different gene cause another behavioral disorder: Huntington's disease (see Chapter 11).

PHENYLKETONURIA   Several hundred different genetic disorders affect the metabolism of proteins, carbohydrates, or lipids, having a profound impact on the developing brain. Characteristically, the genetic defect is the absence of a particular enzyme that controls a critical biochemical step in the synthesis or breakdown of a vital body product.

An example is **phenylketonuria** (**PKU**), a recessive hereditary disorder of protein metabolism that at one time resulted in many people with intellectual disability. About one out of 100 persons is a carrier; one in 10,000 births produces an affected victim. The basic defect is the absence of an enzyme necessary to metabolize phenylalanine, an amino acid that is present in many foods. As a result, the brain is damaged by an enormous buildup of phenylalanine, which becomes toxic.

The discovery of PKU marked the first time that an inborn error of metabolism was associated with intellectual disability. Screening methods assess the level of phenylalanine in children a few days after birth. Early detection is important because brain impairment can be prevented simply by reducing phenylalanine in the diet. Such dietary control of PKU is critical during the early years of life, especially before age 2; after that, diet can be relaxed somewhat. Note this important example of the interaction of genes and the environment in PKU: the dysfunctional gene causes intellectual disability *only* in the presence of phenylalanine. Reducing phenylalanine consumption reduces or prevents this effect of the gene.

PKU illustrates one reason why, despite the importance of genes for nervous system development, understanding the genome alone could never enable an understanding of the developing brain. Knowing that a baby is born with PKU doesn't tell you anything about how that child's brain will develop *unless* you also know something about the child's diet. Another reason why genes alone cannot tell the whole story is that experience can affect the activity of genes, as we discuss next.

Experience regulates gene expression in the developing and mature brain

Genetically identical animals, called **clones**, used to be known mainly in science fiction and horror films. But life imitates fiction. In grasshopper clones, the basic shape of larger cells is similar in all clones, but many neurons show differences in neural connections despite the identical genotypes (C. Goodman, 1979). Likewise, genetically identical cloned pigs show as much variation in behavior and temperament as do normal siblings (G. S. Archer et al., 2003), and genetically identical mice raised in different laboratories behave very differently on a variety of tests (Crabbe et al., 1999; Finch and Kirkwood, 2000). If genes are so important to the developing nervous system, how can genetically identical individuals differ in their behavior?

EPIGENETICS   Recall that although nearly all of the cells in your body have a complete copy of your genome, each cell uses only a small subset of those genes at any one time. We told you earlier that when a cell transcribes a particular gene and makes the encoded protein, we say the cell has *expressed* that gene. **Epigenetics** is the study of factors that affect gene *expression* without making any changes in the nucleotide sequence of the genes themselves. One important epigenetic factor affecting

trinucleotide repeat   Repetition of the same three nucleotides within a gene, which can lead to dysfunction, as in the cases of Huntington's disease and fragile X syndrome.

phenylketonuria (PKU)   An inherited disorder of protein metabolism in which the absence of an enzyme leads to a toxic buildup of certain compounds, causing intellectual disability.

clones   Asexually produced organisms that are genetically identical.

epigenetics   The study of factors that affect gene expression without making any changes in the nucleotide sequence of the genes themselves.

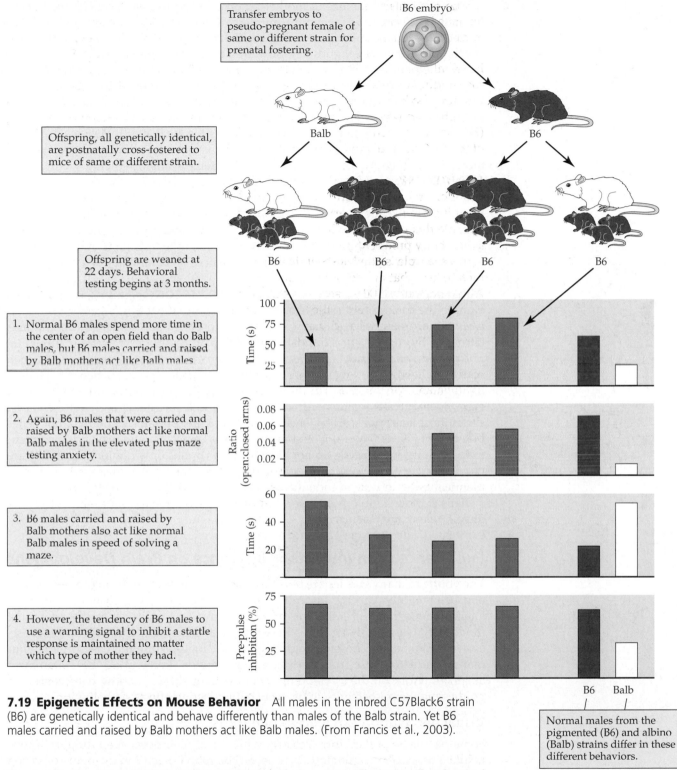

7.19 Epigenetic Effects on Mouse Behavior   All males in the inbred C57Black6 strain (B6) are genetically identical and behave differently than males of the Balb strain. Yet B6 males carried and raised by Balb mothers act like Balb males. (From Francis et al., 2003.)

Text boxes within the figure:

Transfer embryos to pseudo-pregnant female of same or different strain for prenatal fostering.

Offspring, all genetically identical, are postnatally cross-fostered to mice of same or different strain.

Offspring are weaned at 22 days. Behavioral testing begins at 3 months.

1. Normal B6 males spend more time in the center of an open field than do Balb males, but B6 males carried and raised by Balb mothers act like Balb males.

2. Again, B6 males that were carried and raised by Balb mothers act like normal Balb males in the elevated plus maze testing anxiety.

3. B6 males carried and raised by Balb mothers also act like normal Balb males in speed of solving a maze.

4. However, the tendency of B6 males to use a warning signal to inhibit a startle response is maintained no matter which type of mother they had.

Normal males from the pigmented (B6) and albino (Balb) strains differ in these different behaviors.

the developing brain in mice is the mothering they receive. If genetically identical embryos of one mouse strain are implanted into the womb of a foster mother of either their own strain or another strain, their behavior is affected (Francis et al., 2003). Strain B6 males carried and raised by mothers from the other strain (Balb) show significant differences in several behaviors, including maze running and measures of anxiety (**Figure 7.19**). Since the various males are genetically identical to one another, their different behaviors must be due to the effect of different prenatal environments and postnatal experiences on how those genes are expressed.

One particular influence of mothering on gene expression has been well documented. **Methylation** is a chemical modification of DNA that does not affect the nucleotide sequence of a gene but makes that gene less likely to be expressed. Michael Meaney and colleagues demonstrated that rodent pups provided with inattentive mothers, or subjected to interruptions in maternal care, secrete more glucocorticoids in response to stress as adults (Zhang and Meaney, 2010). Poor maternal care programs this heightened stress hormone response by inducing methylation of the glucocorticoid receptor gene in the brain. Reduced expression of that gene causes the pups to be hyperresponsive to stress for the rest of their lives.

A similar mechanism may apply to humans, because this same gene is also more likely to be methylated in the postmortem brains of suicide victims than of controls, *but only if the victim was subjected to childhood abuse*. Suicide victims that did not suffer childhood abuse were no more likely to have the gene methylated than were control subjects (McGowan et al., 2009). These results suggest that methylation of the gene in abused children may make them hyperresponsive to stress as adults—a condition that may have led them to take their own life. This is a powerful demonstration of epigenetic influences on behavior.

EXPERIENCE REGULATES GENE EXPRESSION IN ADULTS TOO Neurons in adults also alter gene expression in response to synaptic stimulation. Some genes, called *immediate early genes*, are expressed briefly by almost any neuron that has been stimulated (see Box 2.1). Neuroscientists exploit this process by exposing an animal to, say, a sound of a particular frequency, and then examining the brain to see which neurons altered gene expression in response to different frequencies. Likewise, lights, odors, or touches will all affect neuronal expression of immediate early genes in particular regions of the brain and spinal cord that receive information about those sensations. Experience also affects the expression of many other genes (Mayfield et al., 2002), not just immediate early genes. So one reason why genetically identical individuals do not have the same brains or behavior is that they are inevitably exposed to different experiences, and they grow up expressing their identical genes in very nonidentical ways (Ridley, 2003).

Let's explore a system where we can identify which experiences direct proper development: the visual system.

Experience Is an Important Influence on Brain Development

The young of many species are born in a highly immature state, both anatomically and behaviorally. Varying an individual's experience during early development alters many aspects of behavior, brain anatomy, and brain chemistry in animal models (G. Gottlieb, 1976; M. R. Rosenzweig and Bennett, 1977, 1978). Likewise, early-childhood enrichment programs produce long-lasting increases in IQ in humans, especially those from deprived backgrounds (Raine et al., 2002; Ramey et al., 2000). Work on the developing visual system shows us how experience can guide synaptic connectivity to have such long-lasting effects on behavior.

Visual deprivation can lead to blindness

Some people do not see forms clearly with one of their eyes, even though the eye is intact and a sharp image is focused on the retina. Such impairments of vision are known as **amblyopia** (from the Greek *amblys*, "dull" or "blunt," and *ops*, "eye"). Some people with this disorder have an eye that is turned inward (cross-eyed) or outward. Children born with such a misalignment see a double image rather than a single fused image. By the time an untreated person reaches the age of 7 or 8, pattern vision in the deviated eye is almost completely suppressed. If the eyes are realigned during childhood, the person learns to fuse the two images and has good depth perception. But if the realignment is not done until adulthood, it's too late to restore acute vision to the turned eye.

methylation A chemical modification of DNA that does not affect the nucleotide sequence of a gene but makes that gene less likely to be expressed.

amblyopia Reduced visual acuity that is not caused by optical or retinal impairments.

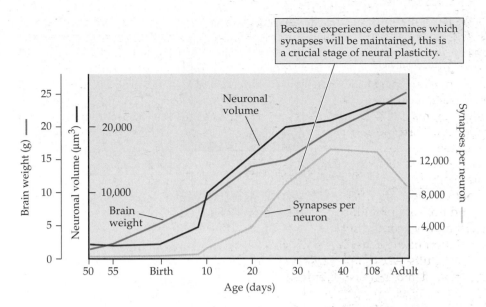

Because experience determines which synapses will be maintained, this is a crucial stage of neural plasticity.

7.20 Brain Development in the Visual Cortex of Cats Synaptic development in cats is most intense from 8 to 37 days after birth, a period during which visual experience can have profound influence. Note that increases in brain weight and cell volume are parallel and precede synaptic development. Note also the decline in synapse numbers after 108 days of age—evidence of synapse rearrangement. (After Cragg, 1975.)

Understanding the cause of amblyopia has been greatly advanced by visual-deprivation experiments with animals. These experiments revealed startling changes related to disuse of the visual system in early life. Depriving animals of light to both eyes (**binocular deprivation**) produces structural changes in visual cortical neurons: a loss of dendritic spines and a reduction in synapses. If such deprivation is maintained for several weeks during development, when the animal's eyes are opened it will be blind. Although light enters its eyes and the cells of the eyes send messages to the brain, the brain seems to ignore the messages and the animal is unable to detect visual stimuli. If the deprivation lasts long enough, the animal is *never* able to recover eyesight. Thus, early visual experience is crucial for the proper development of vision, and there is a **sensitive period** during which these manipulations of experience can exert long-lasting effects on the system. These effects are most extensive during the early period of synaptic development in the visual cortex (**Figure 7.20**). After the sensitive period, the manipulations have little or no effect.

Depriving only one eye of light (**monocular deprivation**) produces profound structural and functional changes in the thalamus and visual cortex. Monocular deprivation in an infant cat or monkey causes the deprived eye not to respond when the animal reaches adulthood. The effect of visual deprivation can be illustrated graphically by an **ocular dominance histogram**, which portrays the strength of response of a brain neuron to stimuli presented to either the left or the right eye. Normally, most cortical neurons (except those in layer IV) are excited equally by light presented to either eye (**Figure 7.21a**).

Monocular deprivation early in development, by keeping one eye closed or covered, results in a striking shift from the normal graph; most cortical neurons respond only to input from the nondeprived eye (**Figure 7.21b**). In cats the susceptible period for this effect is the first 4 months of life. In rhesus monkeys the sensitive period extends to age 6 months. After these ages, visual deprivation has little effect.

During early development, synapses are rearranged in the visual cortex, and axons representing input from each eye "compete" for synaptic places. Active, effective synapses predominate over inactive synapses. Thus, if one eye is "silenced," synapses carrying information from that eye are retracted while synapses driven by the other eye are maintained. Donald O. Hebb (1949) proposed that effective synapses (those that successfully drive the postsynaptic cell) might grow stronger at the expense of ineffective synapses. Thus, synapses that grow stronger or weaker depending on their effectiveness in driving their target cell are known as

binocular deprivation Depriving both eyes of form vision, as by sealing the eyelids.

sensitive period The period during development in which an organism can be permanently altered by a particular experience or treatment.

monocular deprivation Depriving one eye of light.

ocular dominance histogram A graph that portrays the strength of response of a brain neuron to stimuli presented to either the left eye or the right eye.

(a) Normal

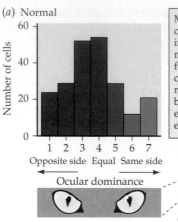

Most cells in visual cortex can be stimulated by light in either eye because, for most of the visual field, light from an object reaches corresponding spots on both retinas. So most cortical cells become binocular as the two eyes are stimulated by experience.

(b) Monocular deprivation

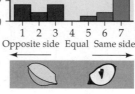

When one eye is closed in development, it quickly loses its connection to visual cortex. If deprived long enough, the animal will become blind in that eye. Similar deprivation in adulthood has virtually no effect on the connections from the eye or the ability of the cat to see.

(c) One eye deviated

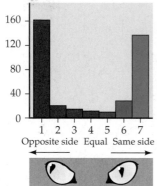

If the two eyes are not aligned properly, then light from the visual field may still reach both eyes, but it does not reach the *corresponding* parts of the two retinas. So each cortical cell comes to listen to only one eye or the other. This cat will have very poor depth perception.

(d) Binocular deprivation

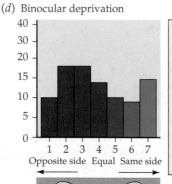

Ironically, briefly depriving *both* eyes during development may have less of an effect on the connections from the eye to the cortex than depriving one eye. The reason is that the two eyes are still evenly matched in their competition for connections to the cortex. However, *prolonged* binocular deprivation in development will lead to total blindness.

7.21 Ocular Dominance Histograms
These histograms show responses of cells in the visual cortex of cats: (a) normal adults; (b) after monocular deprivation through the early critical period; (c) after early deviation of one eye (squint); (d) after binocular deprivation. The numbers along the x-axis represent a gradation in response: Cells that respond *only* to stimulation of the opposite eye are class 1 cells. Cells that respond *mainly* to stimulation of the opposite eye are class 2. Cells that respond equally to either eye are class 4. Cells that respond only to stimulation of the eye on the same side are class 7, and so on. (After Hubel and Wiesel, 1965; Wiesel and Hubel, 1965.)

Hebbian synapse A synapse that is strengthened when it successfully drives the postsynaptic cell.

Hebbian synapses (**Figure 7.22**). In Chapter 17 we will see that the maintenance of active synapses and retraction of inactive synapses may also play a role in learning and memory.

Researchers offer a similar explanation for amblyopia produced by misalignment of the eyes. Hubel and Wiesel (1965) produced an animal replica of this human condition by surgically causing the eyes to diverge in kittens. The ocular dominance histogram of these animals reveals that the normal binocular sensitivity of visual cortical cells is greatly reduced (**Figure 7.21c**). A much larger proportion of visual cortical cells are excited by stimulation of either the right or the left eye in these animals than in control animals. The reason for this effect is that, after surgery, visual stimuli falling on the misaligned eyes no longer provide simultaneous, convergent input to the cells of the visual cortex.

The competitive interaction between the eyes results in a paradox: brief deprivation of *both* eyes can have less of an effect on neuronal connections than an equal period of deprivation to only one eye has (compare **Figure 7.21d** and b with the normal case depicted in part a). Presumably the binocular deprivation keeps both eyes on an equal footing for stimulating cells in the visual cortex, so the predominantly binocular input to the cortical cells is retained.

One popular notion is that neurotrophic factors may be playing a role in experience-driven synapse rearrangement. For example, if the postsynaptic cells are making a limited supply of a neurotrophic factor, and if active synapses take up more of the factor than inactive synapses do, then perhaps the inactive axons retract for lack of neurotrophic factor. BDNF has been implicated as the neurotrophic factor being competed for in the kitten visual cortex (McAllister et al., 1997) and in the frog retinotectal system (J. L. Du and Poo, 2004) (see Box 7.2). So perhaps ineffective synapses wither for lack of neurotrophic support.

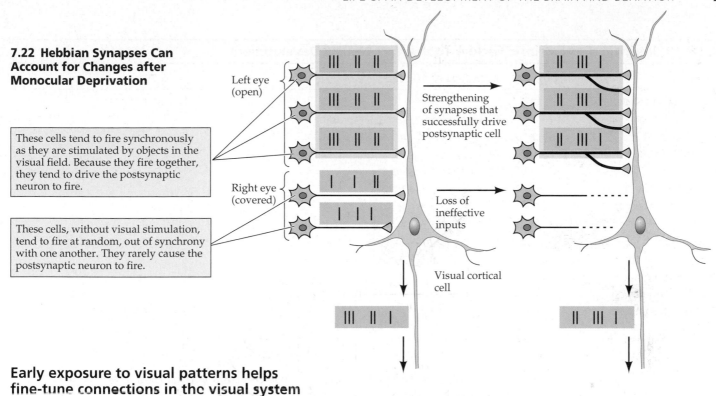

7.22 Hebbian Synapses Can Account for Changes after Monocular Deprivation

Left eye (open)

These cells tend to fire synchronously as they are stimulated by objects in the visual field. Because they fire together, they tend to drive the postsynaptic neuron to fire.

Right eye (covered)

These cells, without visual stimulation, tend to fire at random, out of synchrony with one another. They rarely cause the postsynaptic neuron to fire.

Strengthening of synapses that successfully drive postsynaptic cell

Loss of ineffective inputs

Visual cortical cell

Early exposure to visual patterns helps fine-tune connections in the visual system

Human disorders have also proven that early experience is crucial for vision. Babies born with cataracts (cloudy lenses) in industrialized countries usually have them removed a few months after birth and will have good vision. But if such a child grows up with the cataracts in place, removing them in adulthood is ineffective; the person never learns to make use of the information entering the eye (Bower, 2003). Early visual experience is known to be especially crucial for learning to perceive faces, because infants with cataracts that occlude vision for just the first 6 months of life are impaired at recognizing faces even 9 years later (Le Grand et al., 2001). These experience-dependent effects are probably mediated by synapse rearrangement within the visual cortex (Ruthazer et al., 2003).

Why does Michael May, whom we met at the start of the chapter, have such poor vision despite the clear images entering his eye? Had the accident happened to him as an adult, the surgery to let light back into his eye would have restored normal vision. But, like a kitten fitted with opaque contact lenses, Michael was deprived of form vision—in his case, for over 40 years. Because this deprivation began when he was a child, synaptic connections within his visual cortex were not strengthened by the patterns of light moving across the retina. In the absence of patterned stimulation, synapses between the eye and the brain languished and disappeared.

In one sense, Michael was lucky that his blindness came as late as it did. He had normal form vision for the first 3½ years of his life, and that stimulation may have been sufficient to maintain some synapses that would otherwise have been lost. These residual synapses are probably what allow him to make any sense whatsoever of his vision. Michael continues to learn to use sight more and more (Kurson, 2007). He loves having sight, but as he himself says, usually he has to "guess" what he's seeing.

One demonstration shows how visual experience in everyday life may affect our perception. In **Figure 7.23**, the numbers and letters along the bottom line appear more slanted than those above, but in fact the slant is the same. One theory of why we see a difference here that doesn't exist is that our experience reading digital clock readouts and italic fonts may tune synapses in our brain to perceive them as more upright than they really are—an effect lost if the figures are backward (Whitaker and McGraw, 2000).

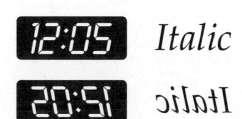

7.23 Which Line Is More Slanted? The numbers and letters on the lower line look more slanted than those on the upper line, but in fact the characters on the two lines are equally slanted. If you look at them in a mirror, the upper line will look more slanted. Is this optical illusion a result of the modification of synapses caused by a lifetime of looking at digital clocks and italic font?

TABLE 7.1 Intrinsic and Extrinsic Factors That Affect Neural Development

Factors	Examples of effects
INTRINSIC FACTORS (GENES)	
Chromosomal aberrations	Down syndrome, fragile X syndrome
Single-gene effects	Phenylketonuria, *Drosophila* mutations
EXTRINSIC FACTORS	
Basic biological factors	Malnutrition, hypoxia
Drugs, toxins	Fetal alcohol syndrome
Cell-cell interactions	
Induction directs differentiation	Motoneurons induced by notochord
Neurotrophic factors	NGF spares sympathetic neurons
Thyroid hormone	Deficiency causes intellectual disability (see Chapter 5)
Neural activity	
Non-sensory-driven	Eye segregation in layer IV cortex before birth
Sensory-driven (experience)	Ocular dominance outside layer IV after birth, maternal behavior affects gene methylation, increased IQ resulting from childhood enrichment

In **A Step Further: Experiences in Nonvisual Senses Also Affect Neural Development** on the website, you can learn how mouse whiskers compete for synapses in the cortex. As you review **Table 7.1**, which lists some of the intrinsic and extrinsic factors that we've discussed, consider how all of the extrinsic factors must regulate gene expression in order to have their effects on the developing brain. This review may give you a feel for how genes and environmental influences, including experience, are inextricably joined in their effects on development.

Developmental Disorders of the Brain Impair Behavior

Now that we understand how extrinsic factors like the environment, mothering, and experience can regulate gene expression and the developing brain, we are ready to consider two of the most common developmental disorders. Many genes have been implicated in both attention deficit disorder and autism, but it is equally clear that no single gene alone can cause either condition. Rather, many different genes each have a small, contributing effect, which means that extrinsic factors also play a role. What's more, both autism and attention deficit disorder are clearly part of a spectrum in which some children show very few symptoms and other children are affected severely. This range of behavior may cause you to wonder whether these are "disorders" at all.

Some children have a hard time paying attention in school

The core symptoms of **attention deficit hyperactivity disorder** (**ADHD**) are distractibility, hyperactivity, and impulsiveness. ADHD is seen in as many as 5% of children and is two to three times more common in boys than in girls. It is a controversial disorder for several reasons. For one thing, the symptoms are seen in all children at one time or another, so diagnosis depends on the extent to which these commonplace symptoms arise and interfere with normal functioning, rather than on the appearance of any rare or distinctive behavior.

When researchers compare children diagnosed with ADHD to other children, the differences they observe suggest that the syndrome is real. For example, children with ADHD have brain volumes that are 3%–4% smaller than those of controls (Castellanos et al., 2002). Differences are most prominent in prefrontal cortex (which is thought to play a role in inhibiting behavior; see Chapter 18) and the cerebellum (Arnsten, 2006). Children with ADHD also differ from controls in terms

attention deficit hyperactivity disorder (ADHD) Syndrome of distractibility, impulsiveness, and hyperactivity that, in children, interferes with school performance.

of brain activity (Ashtari et al., 2005), and they display a delay in the thinning of cortical thickness that is normal in development (see Figure 7.14) (P. Shaw et al., 2007). Children with ADHD also seem to have reduced signaling in the dopamine "reward" pathways we discussed in Chapter 4 (Volkow et al., 2009). But for all these differences, there is considerable overlap between the groups, so none of the differences can be used to diagnose the condition.

Because brain differences and symptoms of ADHD form part of a continuum, one can question whether it is a separate disorder or simply another way in which individuals differ from one another. Even the name may be a misnomer, since many people with ADHD have very good attention spans when they're doing something they find interesting, or something that is more "hands-on." But clearly children with ADHD have difficulty performing well in the traditional classroom.

There is also disagreement about whether ADHD should be treated with drugs, typically stimulants such as methylphenidate (Ritalin) or the amphetamine Adderall. Although the drugs improve attention in children with ADHD (as they do in adults, whether they have ADHD or not), some people question whether the improved performance in school is worth the risk of long-term exposure to psychoactive drugs. Reports of rare but serious side effects of stimulant treatment, such as hallucinations (Edelsohn, 2006) and heart attacks (Wilens et al., 2006), complicate the decision of whether to medicate children who have ADHD.

Autism is a disorder of social competence

Autism is a lifelong developmental disorder characterized by impaired social interactions and language, and a narrow range of interests and activities. The disorder is found in about one to two children per thousand, is much more common in males than females, and has a strong heritability (Weiss et al., 2009). Usually autism is discovered when apparently normal toddlers begin regressing, losing language skills, and withdrawing from family interaction. Children with autism may or may not appear mentally deficient, but they tend to **perseverate** (such as by continually nodding the head or making stereotyped finger movements), actively avoid making eye contact with other people, and have a difficult time judging other people's thoughts or feelings (Senju et al., 2009). When shown photos of the faces of family members, autistic individuals reveal a pattern of brain activation quite different from that exhibited by controls (Pierce et al., 2001), suggesting a very different brain organization for the fundamental social skill of recognizing others.

Several structural differences between the brains of people with autism and controls have been reported, including a reduction in the size of the corpus callosum and certain cerebellar regions (Egaas et al., 1995). Even though people with autism have fewer neurons in the amygdala than control subjects have (Schumann and Amaral, 2006), they show greater activation of the amygdala when they are gazing at faces (K. M. Dalton et al., 2005). The amygdala has been associated with fear (see Chapter 15), so this finding suggests that children with autism avoid making eye contact with people because they find it aversive.

The underlying problem with autism may be an inability to empathize with others, as reflected in the difficulty that individuals with autism display in making "copycat" movements of the fingers or body. When people with autism do this task, a particular part of the frontal cortex is less activated than in control subjects (Villalobos et al., 2005). The same region is also underactivated when people with autism try to mimic emotional facial expressions of others (**Figure 7.24**) (Dapretto et al., 2006). This hypoactivated region contains *mirror neurons* (discussed further in Chapters 10 and 11), which are active whenever the individual either makes a particular hand movement or sees someone else make that same hand movement. A child with a deficit in such a brain region underlying imitation and empathy might find other people's behaviors so bewildering that he or she would withdraw from social relations and language.

autism A disorder arising during childhood, characterized by social withdrawal and perseverative behavior.

perseverate To continue to show a behavior repeatedly.

7.24 Underactivation of Mirror Cells in Autism
(*a*) When control children are asked to imitate the emotional facial expressions displayed in photographs of other people, many brain regions show activation. (*b*) When children with autism do this task, the same brain regions are active except for a region in the inferior frontal cortex. (*c*) Mathematical subtraction pinpoints the site as the pars opercularis region that contains "mirror neurons" (see Chapters 10 and 11). This deficit in activating brain regions underlying imitation and empathy may be at the root of the social impairments of autism. (After Dapretto et al., 2006; courtesy of Mirella Dapretto.)

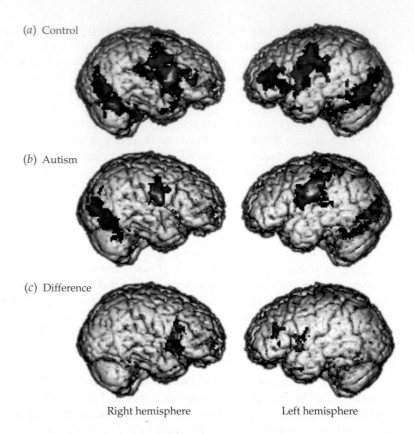

(*a*) Control

(*b*) Autism

(*c*) Difference

Right hemisphere   Left hemisphere

Autism seems to represent one end of a spectrum. **Asperger's syndrome** is also characterized by difficulties in understanding social interactions, yet children with Asperger's do not lose their language capabilities, and they may indeed be quite articulate. They have difficulty interpreting other people's emotional facial expressions, but they tend to be very good at classifying objects and noting details (Baron-Cohen, 2003). Not surprisingly, individuals with Asperger's tend to become scientists and engineers. The number of children diagnosed with autism and Asperger's is increasing steadily, but no one knows why. One hypothesis, that childhood vaccines may act as a neurotoxin to cause autism, is a favorite of celebrities and trial lawyers, but it has been thoroughly discredited (Aschner and Ceccatelli, 2009). There is no cure for autism, but some affected children are helped by highly structured training in language and behavior.

The Brain Continues to Change as We Grow Older

The passage of time brings us an accumulation of joys and sorrows—perhaps riches and fame—and a progressive decline in many of our abilities. Although slower responses seem inevitable with aging, many of our cognitive abilities show little change during the adult years, until we reach an advanced age. What happens to brain structure from adolescence to the day when we all become a little forgetful and walk more hesitantly?

Memory impairment correlates with hippocampal shrinkage during aging

In a study of healthy and cognitively normal people aged 55–87, investigators asked whether mild impairment in memory is specifically related to reduction in size of the hippocampal formation (HF) or is better explained by generalized shrinkage of brain tissue (Golomb et al., 1994). (In Chapter 17 we'll see that the hippocampus is implicated in memory.) Volunteers took a series of memory tests

Asperger's syndrome   Sometimes called *high-functioning autism*. A syndrome characterized by difficulties in social cognitive processing; usually accompanied by strong language skills.

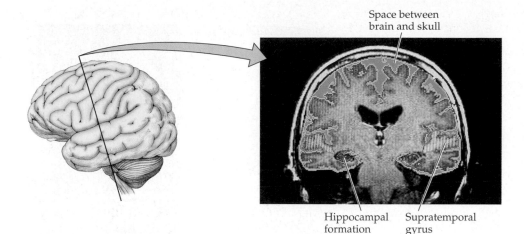

Space between
brain and skull

Hippocampal   Supratemporal
formation   gyrus

7.25 Hippocampal Shrinkage Correlates with Memory Decline in Aging
MRI images that illustrate the variables tested for correlation with memory decline in normal aged people are taken from the plane of section shown on the left. In the image on the right, the hippocampal formation is shaded red, the supratemporal gyrus orange, and the space between brain and skull yellow-green. Only shrinkage of the hippocampal formation correlated with memory decline. (From Golomb et al., 1994; MRI courtesy of James Golomb.)

and were scored for both immediate recall and delayed recall. A series of ten coronal MRI images for each subject was measured for three variables (**Figure 7.25**): (1) volume of the HF; (2) volume of the supratemporal gyrus, a region that is close to the HF and is known to shrink with age but has not been implicated in memory; and (3) volume of the subarachnoid cerebrospinal fluid (i.e., the fluid-filled space between the interior of the skull and the surface of the brain), which yields a measure of overall shrinkage of the brain. Immediate memory showed very little decline with age, but delayed memory did decline. When effects of sex, age, IQ, and overall brain atrophy were eliminated statistically, HF volume was the only brain measure that correlated significantly with the delayed memory score.

Two regions of the motor system show how different the effects of aging can be. In the motor cortex, a type of large neuron—the *Betz cell*—starts to decline in number by about age 50, and by the time a person reaches age 80, many of these cells have shriveled away (M. E. Scheibel et al., 1977). In contrast, other cells involved in motor circuitry—for example, those in an area of the brainstem called the *inferior olive*—remain about the same in number through at least eight decades of life.

PET scans of elderly people add a new perspective to aging-related changes. Studies of normal cases reveal that cerebral metabolism remains almost constant. This stability is in marked contrast to the decline of cerebral metabolism in Alzheimer's disease (see Figure 2.21c), which we will consider next.

Alzheimer's disease is associated with a decline in cerebral metabolism

The population of elderly people in the United States is increasing dramatically. Most people reaching an advanced age lead happy, productive lives, although at a slower pace than they did in their earlier years. In a growing number of elderly people, however, age has brought a particular agony: the disorder called **Alzheimer's disease**, named after Alois Alzheimer (1864–1915), the neurologist who first described a type of **dementia** (drastic failure of cognitive ability, including memory failure and loss of orientation) appearing before the age of 65. Alzheimer's disease is a type of **senile dementia**.

Over 4 million Americans suffer from Alzheimer's disease, and the progressive aging of our population means that these ranks will continue to swell. This disorder is found worldwide with almost no geographic differences. The frequency of Alzheimer's increases with aging up to age 85–90 (Rocca et al., 1991), but people who reach that age *without* symptoms become increasingly *less* likely ever to develop them (Breitner et al., 1999). This last finding indicates that Alzheimer's is in fact a disease, and not simply the result of wear and tear in the brain. The fact that remaining physically and mentally active reduces the risk of developing Alzheimer's disease (Smyth et al., 2004) also refutes the notion that brains simply "wear out" with age. Extensive use of the brain makes Alzheimer's *less* likely.

Alzheimer's disease   A form of dementia that may appear in middle age but is more frequent among the aged.

dementia   Drastic failure of cognitive ability, including memory failure and loss of orientation.

senile dementia   A neurological disorder of the aged that is characterized by progressive behavioral deterioration, including personality change and profound intellectual decline. It includes, but is not limited to, Alzheimer's disease.

7.26 Patients with Alzheimer's Show Structural Changes in the Brain (*a*) This representation of the brain shows the location of the basal forebrain nuclei and the distribution of their axons, which use acetylcholine as a neurotransmitter. These cells seem to disappear in Alzheimer's patients. (*b*) Neurofibrillary tangles (the flame-shaped objects) and senile plaques (the darkly stained clusters) are visible in this micrograph of the cerebral cortex of an aged patient with Alzheimer's. (From Roses, 1995; micrograph courtesy of Gary W. Van Hoesen.)

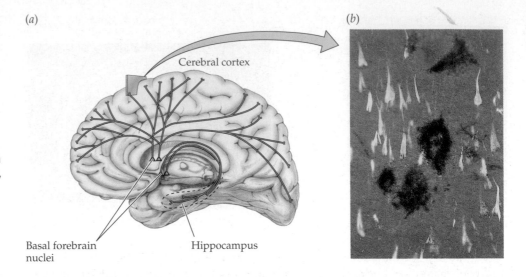

(*a*)

Cerebral cortex

Basal forebrain nuclei

Hippocampus

(*b*)

senile plaques Also called *amyloid plaques*. Senile plaques are small areas of the brain that have abnormal cellular and chemical patterns. Senile plaques correlate with senile dementia.

β-amyloid A protein that accumulates in senile plaques in Alzheimer's disease.

neurofibrillary tangle An abnormal whorl of neurofilaments within nerve cells.

tau A protein associated with neurofibrillary tangles in Alzheimer's disease.

amyloid precursor protein (APP) A protein that, when cleaved by several enzymes, produces β-amyloid.

β-secretase An enzyme that cleaves amyloid precursor protein, forming β-amyloid, which can lead to Alzheimer's disease.

presenilin An enzyme that cleaves amyloid precursor protein, forming β-amyloid, which can lead to Alzheimer's disease.

Alzheimer's disease begins as a loss of memory of recent events. Eventually this memory impairment becomes all-encompassing, so extensive that Alzheimer's patients cannot maintain any form of conversation because both the context and prior information are rapidly lost. They cannot answer simple questions such as, What year is it? Who is the president of the United States? or Where are you now? Cognitive decline is progressive and relentless. In time, patients become disoriented and easily lose themselves even in familiar surroundings.

Observations of whole brains of patients with Alzheimer's reveal striking cortical atrophy, especially in the frontal, temporal, and parietal areas. PET scans show marked reduction of metabolism in posterior parietal cortex and some portions of the temporal lobe (N. L. Foster et al., 1984). The brains of individuals suffering from Alzheimer's also reveal progressive changes at the cellular level (**Figure 7.26**):

- Strange patches termed **senile plaques** appear in frontal and temporoparietal cortex, the hippocampus, and associated limbic system sites. The plaques are formed by the buildup of a substance called **β-amyloid** (Selkoe, 1991), so they are sometimes called *amyloid plaques*.

- Some cells show abnormalities called **neurofibrillary tangles**, which are abnormal whorls of neurofilaments, including a protein called **tau**, that form a tangled array inside the cell. The number of neurofibrillary tangles is directly related to the magnitude of cognitive impairment, and they are probably a secondary response to amyloid plaques.

- These degenerative events cause the basal forebrain nuclei to disappear in Alzheimer's patients, either because the cells die or because they stop producing their transmitter, acetylcholine. The latter possibility is more likely, because providing these neurons with NGF restores their cholinergic characteristics in aged monkeys (D. E. Smith et al., 1999).

The only surefire diagnosis for Alzheimer's at present is postmortem examination of the brain for senile plaques and neurofibrillary tangles. But one innovative approach is to inject a dye, called Pittsburgh Blue (PiB) that has an affinity for β-amyloid. Then, a PET scan determines whether the dye accumulates in the brain (Wolk et al., 2009). The brain of virtually every patient diagnosed with Alzheimer's accumulates the dye, as do the brains of many elderly people showing mild cognitive impairment (**Figure 7.27**).

Amyloid plaques appear to be the primary cause of Alzheimer's disease, but what causes the buildup of β-amyloid? **Amyloid precursor protein** (**APP**) is cleaved by two enzymes—**β-secretase** and **presenilin**—to form extracellular β-amyloid that builds up. Some neurons take up the β-amyloid and then form neurofibrillary tan-

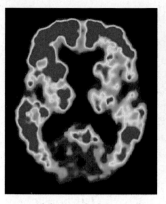 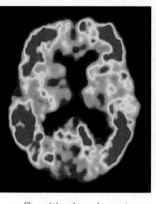 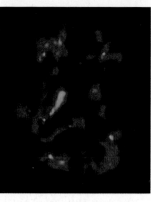 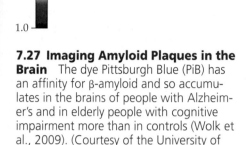

Alzheimer's disease

Cognitive impairment

Control subject

PiB accumulation

2.0

1.0

7.27 Imaging Amyloid Plaques in the Brain The dye Pittsburgh Blue (PiB) has an affinity for β-amyloid and so accumulates in the brains of people with Alzheimer's and in elderly people with cognitive impairment more than in controls (Wolk et al., 2009). (Courtesy of the University of Pittsburgh Amyloid Imaging Group.)

gles in response. Another enzyme, **apolipoprotein E (ApoE)**, works to break down β-amyloid (Bu, 2009). Mutations in each of the genes that produce these proteins have been associated with Alzheimer's disease, with presenilin mutations by far the most common (Bertram and Tanzi, 2008). Transgenic mice that produce extra β-amyloid show progressive memory deficits as they age (Lesné et al., 2006).

This scenario, depicted in **Figure 7.28**, suggests several treatment strategies, such as injection of antibodies that will bind β amyloid and slow the formation of plaques, but that does not seem to be effective (C. Holmes et al., 2008). Another strategy is to develop drugs that interfere with β-secretase and/or presenilin activity (O. Singer et al., 2005), reducing β-amyloid production. In the meantime, and in keeping with the repeated theme of this chapter that genes and experience interact, there is good evidence that physical activity (LaFerla et al., 2007), mental activity (Willis et al., 2006), and adequate sleep (J. E. Kang et al., 2009) can postpone the appearance of Alzheimer's disease.

apolipoprotein E (ApoE) A protein that may help break down amyloid.

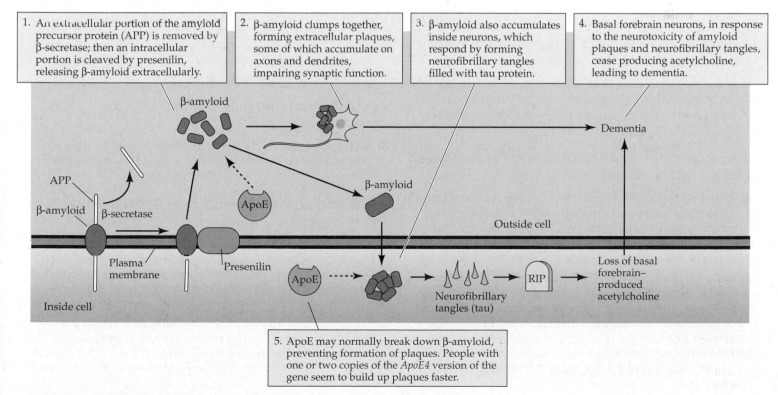

1. An extracellular portion of the amyloid precursor protein (APP) is removed by β-secretase; then an intracellular portion is cleaved by presenilin, releasing β-amyloid extracellularly.

2. β-amyloid clumps together, forming extracellular plaques, some of which accumulate on axons and dendrites, impairing synaptic function.

3. β-amyloid also accumulates inside neurons, which respond by forming neurofibrillary tangles filled with tau protein.

4. Basal forebrain neurons, in response to the neurotoxicity of amyloid plaques and neurofibrillary tangles, cease producing acetylcholine, leading to dementia.

5. ApoE may normally break down β-amyloid, preventing formation of plaques. People with one or two copies of the *ApoE4* version of the gene seem to build up plaques faster.

7.28 One Hypothesis of Alzheimer's Disease

Two Timescales Are Needed to Describe Brain Development

Chapters 6 and 7 present two very different timescales for the development of brain and behavior—the eons of evolution versus the days and years of individual development. These different timescales are analogous to the different but equally essential contributions of an architect and a contractor, respectively, in building a house.

In preparing his plans, the architect calls on a long history of human knowledge about structures that meet basic human needs. These plans incorporate hard-won information gathered over the centuries. Similarly, our genes carry a basic plan that has worked for thousands of generations (absolutely every one of your millions of ancestors managed to reproduce!).

The contractor's perspective is more like that of a developing individual. He must use the general plans of the architect to construct a particular house here and now. As he builds, the contractor's judgment and interpretation are necessary, so two houses built from the same blueprints will not be identical, just as two monozygotic twins will show differences. In fact, even the best architects rely on contractors to adjust and improvise to make their plans work. Similarly, the information in our genome relies on extrinsic factors such as experience to determine the fine wiring of the nervous system.

Long ago, well before the common ancestor of all the vertebrates emerged, developing animals began relying on cell-cell interactions to adjust the fate of individual cells on the basis of their position in the organism as a whole. Once this strategy was adopted, it was only a matter of time before the fate of some neurons would be affected by neural activity. So neural activity began determining which synapses and neurons would be retained and which would be eliminated. Eventually, it would be the neural activity derived from sensory neurons—experience itself—that would affect these decisions. That is how we humans came to have a nervous system so malleable, so plastic, that we can write, read, and think about our own origins.

SUMMARY

Growth and Development of the Brain Are Orderly Processes

■ In the human embryo, the brain develops from a **neural tube** with three subdivisions that will become the **forebrain**, **midbrain**, and **hindbrain**. **Review Figure 7.1**, **Web Activities 7.1–7.3**

Development of the Nervous System Can Be Divided into Six Distinct Stages

■ Early embryological events in the formation of the nervous system include a sequence of six cellular processes: (1) **neurogenesis**, (2) **cell migration**, (3) **cell differentiation**, (4) **synaptogenesis**, (5) neuronal **cell death**, and (6) **synapse rearrangement**. **Review Figure 7.2**, **Web Activities 7.4–7.6**

■ In simple animals such as the nematode *Caenorhabditis elegans*, neural pathways and synapses form according to an innate, genetic plan that specifies the precise relations between growing axons and particular target cells. In more-complicated animals—including all vertebrates—**cell-cell interactions** determine the fate of individual neurons and glia. **Review Figure 7.4 and Table 7.1**, **Web Activities 7.7 and 7.8**

■ Although in humans most neurons are present at birth, most synapses develop after birth and continue developing into adulthood. **Review Figure 7.9**

Glial Cells Provide Myelin, Which Is Vital for Brain Function

■ Fetal and postnatal changes in the brain include the **myelination** of axons by glial cells and the development of dendrites and synapses by neurons. **Review Figure 7.15**

Genes Interact with Experience to Guide Brain Development

■ Among the many determinants of brain development are (1) intrinsic genetic information and (2) a multitude of extrinsic factors, such as **neurotrophic factors**, nutrition, and experience. These factors interact extensively because extrinsic factors like experience can affect gene expression.

■ Impairments of fetal development that lead to intellectual disability can be caused by the use of drugs such as alcohol during pregnancy. **Review Figure 7.16**

- Maldevelopment of the brain can occur as a result of **mutations** or other genetically controlled disorders. Some, such as **Down syndrome** and **fragile X syndrome**, are related to disorders of chromosomes; others are metabolic disorders, such as **phenylketonuria (PKU)**. **Review Figure 7.18**

- Gene expression is affected by environmental factors and experience, so **epigenetic** influences can profoundly affect brain development without altering the sequence of nucleotides in any genes. Similarly, genetically identical individuals, either twins or **clones**, do not display identical behaviors. **Review Figure 7.19**

Experience Is an Important Influence on Brain Development

- Experience affects the growth and development of the nervous system. Experience can induce and modulate the formation of synapses, maintain synapses that are already formed, or determine which neurons and synapses will survive and which will be eliminated. **Review Figures 7.20–7.22**

Developmental Disorders of the Brain Impair Behavior

- **Attention deficit hyperactivity disorder (ADHD)**, which is characterized by distractibility, hyperactivity, and impulsiveness—exaggerations of traits common in childhood—is correlated with abnormalities in the prefrontal cortex and cerebellum, as well as in brain activity.

- **Autism** appears to be a disruption in the development of cognitive processing about social interactions, which impairs the development of language and other behaviors. **Review Figure 7.24**

The Brain Continues to Change as We Grow Older

- The brain continues to change throughout life. Old age is accompanied by the loss of neurons and synaptic connections in some regions of the brain. In some people the changes are more severe than in others; pathological changes characterize the condition of early-onset **senile dementia** known as **Alzheimer's disease**. **Review Figure 7.25**

- Alzheimer's seems to be caused by a buildup of **β-amyloid**, causing degenerative extracellular **senile plaques** and intracellular **neurofibrillary tangles** through much of the cortex. Several genes, including those that encode the enzymes **presenilin** and **apolipoprotein E (ApoE)**, influence the rate of amyloid accumulation and therefore the risk of Alzheimer's. Mental activity, physical activity, and adequate sleep seem to postpone the onset of Alzheimer's. **Review Figures 7.26–7.28**

Two Timescales Are Needed to Describe Brain Development

- The brain and behavior develop on two very different but equally essential timescales: eons of evolution versus days and years of individual development.

Go to **www.biopsychology.com** for study questions, quizzes, key terms, and other resources.

Recommended Reading

Anderson, V., Hendy, J., Northam, E., and Wrennall, J. (2001). *Developmental neuropsychology: A clinical approach.* Philadelphia: Psychology Press.

Gilbert, S. F. (2010). *Developmental biology* (9th ed.). Sunderland, MA: Sinauer.

Marcus, G. (2004). *The birth of the mind: How a tiny number of genes creates the complexities of human thought.* New York: Basic Books.

Nelson, C. A., and Luciana, M. (2001). *Handbook of developmental cognitive neuroscience.* Cambridge, MA: MIT Press.

Nigg, J. T. (2006) *What causes ADHD?* New York: Guilford.

Sanes, D. H., Reh, T. A., and Harris, W. A. (2005). *Development of the nervous system* (2nd ed.). San Diego, CA: Academic Press.

Turkington, C., Mitchell, D., and Glavin, J. (2010) *The encyclopedia of Alzheimer's disease.* New York: Facts on File.

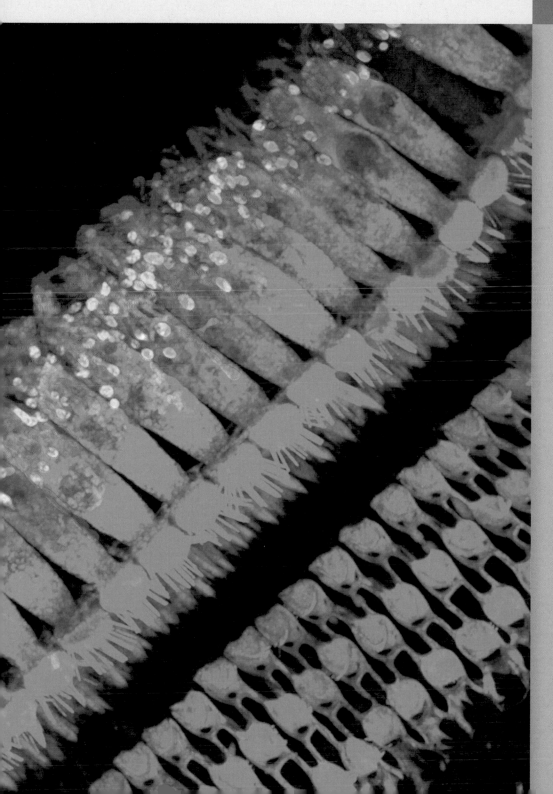

Perception and Action

Previous page   **Mammalian cochlear hair cells**   In this confocal image of the Organ of Corti—the part of the inner ear that encodes sounds—hair cells are labeled in green, with the brushy stereocilia protruding from the tops. Hair cell nuclei are labeled in blue, and fibers from auditory neurons are labeled in red. (Image by Sonja Pyott, Department of Biology and Marine Biology, University of North Carolina Wilmington.)

General Principles of Sensory Processing, Touch, and Pain

CHAPTER 8

What's Hot? What's Not?

It was a lovely warm summer evening, perfect for an after-dinner stroll. It was nice to see the neighbors out puttering in their yards, or sitting on the porch sipping cool drinks. When we came upon a woman in matching yellow shorts and blouse sprinkling something on her flowers, I noticed she was using what looked like a big salt shaker. I thought, "Gee, it's not very smart to put insecticide in a salt shaker. What if someone else in the house sprinkles it on food?"

Thinking I would sidle up to the topic to offer her my sage advice, I stopped to ask, "What are you putting on your flowers? Something to kill aphids?" She smiled and said, "No, it's red chili pepper flakes to keep the deer away." She assured me that her treatment worked: when she sprinkled the pepper flakes on the plants in the evening, the flowers would be intact in the morning. If she neglected to treat them in the evening, she would find blossoms missing and telltale bite marks on the bushes come dawn. "Why sprinkle every evening? Do the flakes blow away?" I asked. "Well," she said, "the main problem is that tomorrow the birds come and eat up all the pepper seeds, so I have to put some more on in the evening."

So it turned out she taught *me* something: deer hate chili pepper seeds, and birds love them. I was pretty sure I understood why the deer avoid the chili peppers: they contain a chemical called capsaicin that really burns my mouth when I eat spicy food. But why don't the birds avoid the peppers containing capsaicin? Doesn't it burn their mouths too?

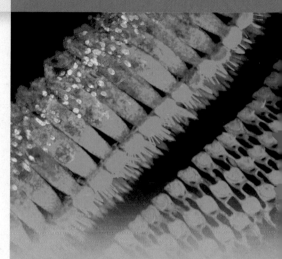

A ll around us, many different types of energy affect us in various ways. Some molecules traveling through the air cause us to note particular odors. We detect waves of compression and expansion of air as sounds. Our abilities to detect, recognize, and appreciate these varied energies depend on the characteristics of sensory systems. These systems include receptor cells specialized to detect specific energies, as well as brain systems that receive input from these receptors.

For each species, however, certain features of surrounding energies have become especially significant for adaptive success. For example, the bat darting through the evening sky is specially equipped to detect ultrasonic cries, which we humans are unable to hear. Some snakes have infrared-sensing organs in their faces that allow them to "see" heat sources in their surroundings, enabling them to locate warm-blooded prey in the dark. How do animals, including humans, detect changes in the world around them?

Sensory Processing

Each species has distinctive windows on the world based on which energies it detects and how its nervous system processes that information. We open this chapter by considering some of the basic principles of sensory processing. Then we look at how those principles apply first to touch and then to pain sensation.

Sensory Receptor Organs Detect Energy or Substances

sensory receptor organ   An organ (such as the eye or ear) specialized to receive particular stimuli.

stimulus   A physical event that triggers a sensory response.

receptor cell   A specialized cell that responds to a particular energy or substance in the internal or external environment, and converts this energy into a change in the electrical potential across its membrane.

All animals have specialized body parts that are particularly sensitive to some forms of energy. These **sensory receptor organs** act as filters of the environment: they detect and respond to some events but not others. We call the event that affected the sensory organ a **stimulus** (plural *stimuli*). Stimuli may be sound waves reaching the ear, light entering the eye, or food touching the tongue. **Receptor cells** within the organ detect particular kinds of stimuli and convert them into the language of the nervous system: electrical signals. Eventually, information from sensory receptor organs enters the brain as a series of action potentials traveling along millions of axons, and our brains must make sense of it all.

Across the animal kingdom, receptor organs offer enormous diversity. For some snakes, detectors of infrared radiation are essential; several species of fishes detect electrical energy; and some animals detect Earth's magnetic field (Holland et al., 2006; Gegear et al., 2008). The specialized sensors involved in these distinctive forms of detection have evolved to detect signals that are crucial for survival in particular environmental niches. Thus, receptor organs reflect strategies for success in particular worlds.

Even if we consider only a single receptor organ, such as the eye, a wide array of sizes, shapes, and forms reflects the varying survival needs of different animals (**Figure 8.1**). Different kinds of energy, such as light and sound, need different receptor organs to convert them into neural activity, just as taking a photograph requires a camera, not a sound recorder.

8.1 The Variety of Eyes   (*a*) Scanning electron micrograph of Simulian blackfly (*Simulium damnosum*) showing the compound eye x 13. (*b*) The panther chameleon can move its two eyes independently. (*c*) The eyes of the Philippine tarsier are specialized for nighttime foraging. (*d*) The eyes of the American bald eagle are particularly sharp.

TABLE 8.1 Classification of Sensory Systems

Type of sensory system	Modality	Adequate stimuli
Mechanical	Touch	Contact with or deformation of body surface
	Hearing	Sound vibrations in air or water
	Vestibular	Head movement and orientation
	Joint	Position and movement
	Muscle	Tension
Photic	Seeing	Visible radiant energy
Thermal	Cold	Decrease in skin temperature
	Warmth	Increase in skin temperature
Chemical	Smell	Odorous substances dissolved in air or water in the nasal cavity
	Taste	Substances in contact with the tongue or other taste receptor
	Common chemical	Changes in CO_2, pH, osmotic pressure
	Vomeronasal	Pheromones in air or water
Electrical	Electroreception	Differences in density of electrical currents

adequate stimulus The type of stimulus for which a given sensory organ is particularly adapted.

Table 8.1 classifies sensory systems, identifying the kinds of stimuli detected by sensory receptor organs in each system. An **adequate stimulus** is the type of stimulus for which a given sensory organ is particularly adapted. The adequate stimulus for the eye is photic (light) energy; an electrical shock or pressure on your eye can create an illusory sensation of light (called a *phosphene*), but neither electricity nor mechanical pressure is considered an adequate stimulus for the eye.

Sensory systems of particular animals have a restricted range of responsiveness

For any single form of physical energy, the sensory systems of a particular animal are quite selective. For example, humans do not hear sounds in the frequency range above 20,000 cycles per second (hertz, Hz)—a range we call *ultrasonic*. To a bat, however, air vibrations of 50,000 Hz would be sound waves, just as vibrations of 5000 Hz are sounds to humans. The range of hearing of larger mammals is even lower than that of humans. **Figure 8.2** compares the auditory ranges of some animals. In the visual realm, too, some animals can detect stimuli that humans cannot. For example, birds and bees see in the ultraviolet range of light.

What Type of Stimulus Was That?

We may appreciate the poet who writes, "The dawn came up like thunder," but usually we want to know whether a sudden dramatic sensory event was auditory or visual, a touch or a smell. How do we know whether a sudden event was a noise, a flash, or a smack on the head?

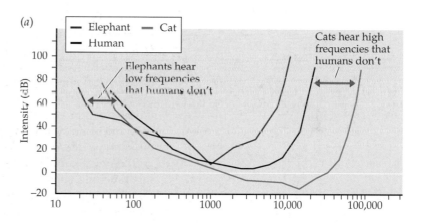

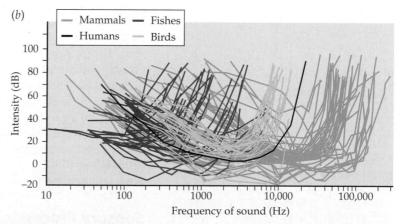

8.2 Do You Hear What I Hear?   For comparison, the auditory sensitivity ranges of three mammals (*a*) and of many species of fishes, birds, and mammals (*b*) are plotted here together. Note that the species within a class detect a similar range of frequencies. For a discussion of the measurement of sound, see Box 9.1. (After Fay, 1988.)

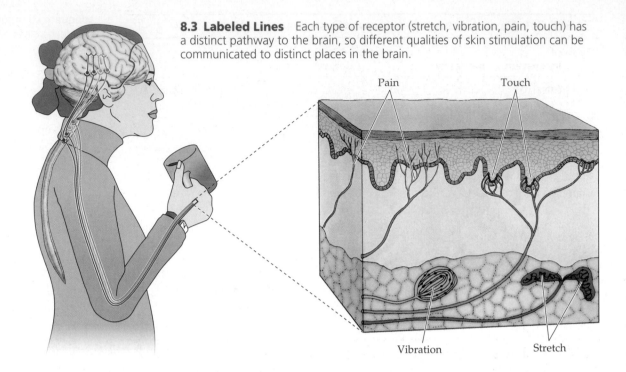

8.3 Labeled Lines Each type of receptor (stretch, vibration, pain, touch) has a distinct pathway to the brain, so different qualities of skin stimulation can be communicated to distinct places in the brain.

The physiologist Johannes Müller (1801–1858) proposed the doctrine of **specific nerve energies**, which states that the receptors and neural channels for the different senses are independent and that each uses a different nerve "energy." For example, no matter how the eye is stimulated—by light or mechanical pressure or by electrical shock—the resulting sensation is always visual. Müller formulated his hypothesis before anyone knew about action potentials. He imagined that different receptor organs might each use a different type of energy to communicate with the brain, and that the brain knew which type of stimulus had happened by which type of energy was received.

Today we know that the messages for the different senses—such as seeing, hearing, touching, sensing pain, and sensing temperature—all use the same type of "energy": action potentials. But the brain recognizes the modalities as separate and distinct because each modality sends its action potentials along separate nerve tracts. This is the concept of **labeled lines**: particular nerve cells are, at the outset, labeled for distinctive sensory experiences. Neural activity in one line signals a sound, activity in another line signals a smell, and activity in other lines signals touch. We can even distinguish different types of touch because some lines signal light touch, others signal vibration, and yet other lines signal stretching of the skin (**Figure 8.3**).

You can demonstrate this effect right now. If you take your finger and *gently* press on your eyelid, you'll see a dark blob appear on the edge of your field of view (it helps to look at a blank white wall). Of course, your skin also feels the touch of your finger, but why do you *see* a blob with your eye? The energy you applied, pressure, affected action potentials coming from your eye. Because your brain labels that line as always carrying visual information, what you *experienced* was a change in vision.

Sensory Processing Begins in Receptor Cells

Detection of energy starts with receptor cells. A given receptor cell is specialized to detect particular energies or chemicals. Upon exposure to a stimulus, a receptor cell converts that energy into a change in the electrical potential across its

specific nerve energies The doctrine that the receptors and neural channels for the different senses are independent and operate in their own special ways, and can produce only one particular sensation each.

labeled lines The concept that each nerve input to the brain reports only a particular type of information.

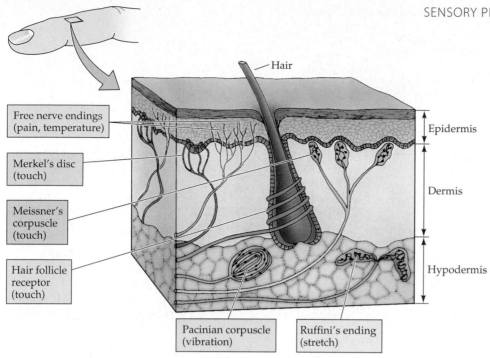

Hair

Free nerve endings
(pain, temperature)

Merkel's disc
(touch)

Meissner's
corpuscle
(touch)

Hair follicle
receptor
(touch)

Pacinian corpuscle
(vibration)

Ruffini's ending
(stretch)

Epidermis

Dermis

Hypodermis

8.4 Receptors in Skin   The main receptors found in human skin are Pacinian corpuscles, Meissner's corpuscles, Merkel's discs, Ruffini's endings, and free nerve endings. The different functions of several of these receptors are compared in Figure 8.13.

membrane. Changing the signal in this way is called **sensory transduction** (devices that convert energy from one form to another are known as *transducers*, and the process is called *transduction*). Receptor cells are transducers that convert energy around us into neural activity that leads to sensory perception. **Figure 8.4** shows some different receptor cells in skin. We will look at these types in more detail later in the chapter.

Some receptor cells have axons to transmit information. Other receptor cells have no axons of their own but stimulate an associated nerve ending, either mechanically or chemically. For example, various kinds of energy-detecting corpuscles are associated with nerve endings in the skin. The eye has specialized receptor cells that convert light energy into electrical changes that cause neurotransmitter to be released on nearby neurons. The inner ear has specialized hair cells that transduce mechanical energy into electrical signals that stimulate the fibers of the auditory nerve.

The initial stage of sensory processing is a change in electrical potential in receptor cells

The structure of a receptor determines the forms of energy to which it will respond. The steps between the arrival of energy at a receptor cell and the initiation of action potentials in a nerve fiber involve local changes of membrane potential called **generator potentials**. (In most instances, the generator potential resembles the excitatory postsynaptic potentials discussed in Chapter 3.)

One example of the generator potential can be studied in a receptor called the **Pacinian corpuscle** (Loewenstein, 1971). This receptor, which detects vibration, is found throughout the body in skin and muscle. It consists of an axon surrounded by a structure that resembles a tiny onion because it has concentric layers of tissue (**Figure 8.5a**).

Mechanical stimuli (in this case vibration) delivered to the corpuscle produce a graded electrical potential with an amplitude that is directly proportional to the strength of the stimulus. When this generator potential gets big enough, an action potential is generated and we say that the receptor has reached **threshold**. Careful dissection of the corpuscle, leaving the bared axon intact, shows that this graded potential—the generator potential—is initiated in the axon terminal itself. The sequence of excitatory events is as follows:

sensory transduction   The process in which a receptor cell converts the energy in a stimulus into a change in the electrical potential across its membrane.

generator potential   A local change in the resting potential of a receptor cell that mediates between the impact of stimuli and the initiation of action potentials.

Pacinian corpuscle   A skin receptor cell type that detects vibration.

threshold   The stimulus intensity that is just adequate to trigger an action potential at the axon hillock.

8.5 The Structure and Function of the Pacinian Corpuscle (*a*) The Pacinian corpuscle surrounds an afferent nerve fiber ending. (*b*) When the nerve membrane is at rest (*left*), the ion channels are too narrow to admit sodium ions (Na⁺). Vibration applied to the corpuscle (*right*) stretches part of the neuronal membrane, enlarging the ion channels and permitting the entry of Na⁺, which initiates an action potential (Lumpkin and Caterina, 2007). (*c*) The neuron shows increasing response to stimuli of increasing intensity until it reaches threshold, triggering an action potential.

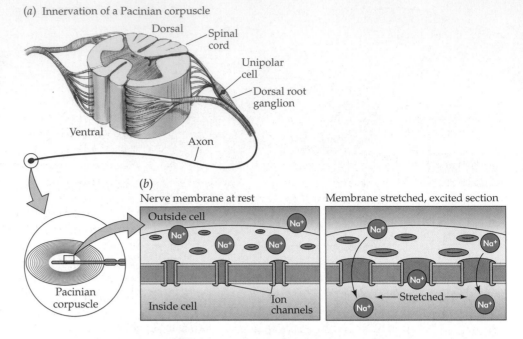

(*a*) Innervation of a Pacinian corpuscle

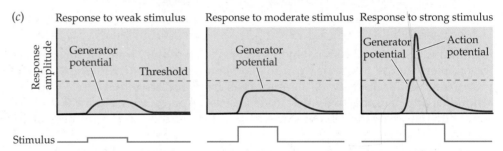

1. Mechanical stimulation deforms the corpuscle.
2. Deformation of the corpuscle stretches the tip of the axon.
3. Stretching the axon opens mechanically gated ion channels in the membrane, allowing sodium ions to enter (**Figure 8.5*b***).
4. When the generator potential reaches threshold amplitude, the axon produces one or more action potentials (**Figure 8.5*c***).

Sensory Information Processing Is Selective and Analytical

Thinkers in ancient Greece believed that nerves were tubes through which tiny bits of stimulus objects traveled to the brain, to be analyzed and recognized there. (Imagine the nerves in your tongue sending minuscule chunks of garlic to your brain for analysis.) Even after learning about neural conduction in the twentieth century, many investigators thought that the sensory nerves simply transmitted accurate information about stimulation to the brain centers. Now, however, it is clear that the sensory organs and peripheral sensory pathways convey only limited—*even distorted*—information to the brain. A good deal of selection and analysis takes place along sensory pathways. In the discussion that follows we will examine six aspects of sensory processing: coding, adaptation, pathways, suppression, receptive fields, and attention.

Coding: Sensory events are represented by action potentials

Information about the world is represented in the nervous system by electrical potentials in cells. We have already considered the first steps in this process—the transduction of energy at receptors, the generator potential, and the creation of action potentials in sensory neurons. But how does this neural activity "stand for" (or *represent*) the stimuli impinging on the organism? Through some form of **coding**, the pattern of electrical activity in the sensory system must convey information about the original stimulus. Neural codes are limited in that each action potential is always the same size and duration, so sensory information is encoded by other features of neural activity, such as the number and frequency of the action potentials, the rhythm in which clusters of action potentials occur, and so on. Let's examine neural representations of the intensity and location of stimuli.

coding The rules by which action potentials in a sensory system reflect a physical stimulus.

STIMULUS INTENSITY We respond to sensory stimuli over a wide range of intensities. Furthermore, within this range we can detect small differences of intensity. How are different intensities of a stimulus represented in the nervous system? A single nerve cell could represent the intensity of the stimulus by changing the frequency of action potentials transmitted (**Figure 8.6a**). However, only a limited range of different sensory intensities can be represented in this manner, because neurons can fire only so fast.

As we noted in Chapter 3, the maximal rate of firing for a single nerve cell is about 1200 action potentials per second, and most sensory fibers do not fire more than a few hundred action potentials per second. But the number of differences in

(*a*) Response rate versus stimulus intensity for three neurons with different thresholds

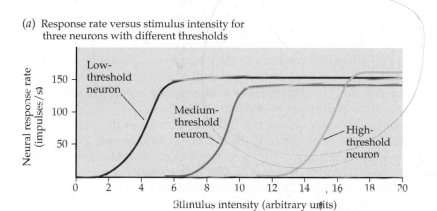

(*b*) Simulation of responses for the three neurons

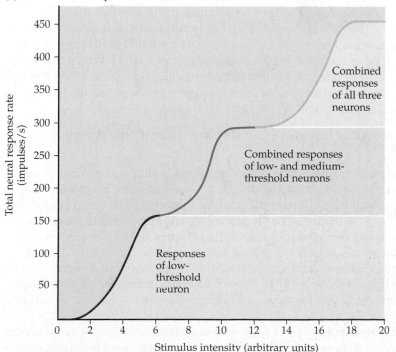

8.6 Intensity Coding (*a*) Each of the three nerve cells represented here has a different threshold—low, medium, or high—and thus a different response to stimuli. Each cell varies its response over a *fraction* of the total *range* of stimulus intensities. (*b*) Although none of these nerve cells can respond faster than 150 times per second, the *sum* of all three can vary in response rate from 0 to 450 action potentials per second, accurately indicating the intensity of the stimulus—an example of range fractionation.

intensity that can be detected in vision and hearing is much, much greater than this basic encoding can offer. For example, we can see both in very dim light and when the light is 10 billion–fold brighter. A *single* receptor that could change activity only a few hundred–fold could never represent that entire range.

Multiple receptor cells acting in a parallel manner provide a broader range for coding the intensity of a stimulus. As the strength of a stimulus increases, new nerve cells are "recruited"; thus, intensity can be represented by the number of active cells. **Range fractionation** takes place when different receptor cells are "specialists" in particular segments, or *fractions*, of an intensity scale (**Figure 8.6*b***). This mode of stimulus coding requires an array of receptors and nerve cells that differ in threshold to fire. Some sensory neurons have a very low threshold (so they are highly sensitive); others have a much higher threshold (so they are less sensitive). Thus, one clue to the intensity of a stimulus is whether it activated only low-threshold receptors, or both low- and high-threshold receptors.

STIMULUS LOCATION   The position of an object or event, either outside or inside the body, is an important piece of information. Did something just poke my foot or my hand? Some sensory systems reveal this information by the position of excited receptors on the sensory surface. This feature is most evident in the **somatosensory** ("body sensation") system.

You know that an object is on your back if a receptor in the skin there is stimulated. If a receptor on your palm is stimulated, then the object must be there. Each receptor activates pathways that convey unique positional information. The spatial properties of a stimulus are represented by labeled lines that uniquely convey spatial information. Similarly, in the visual system an object's spatial location determines which receptors in the eye are stimulated.

In both the visual and the touch system, cells at all levels of the nervous system—from the surface sheet of receptors to the cerebral cortex—are arranged in an orderly, maplike manner. The map at each level is not exact, but reflects both position and receptor density. More cells are allocated to the spatial representation of sensitive, densely innervated sites like the skin of the lips or the center of the eye, than to sites that are less sensitive, such as the skin of the back or the periphery of the eye.

With bilateral receptor systems—the two ears or the two nostrils—the relative time of arrival of the stimulus at the two receptors, or the relative intensity, is directly related to the location of the stimulus. For example, the only time when both ears are excited identically is when the sound source is equidistant from the ears, in the median plane of the head. As the stimulus moves to the left or right, receptors of the left and right sides are excited asymmetrically. Specialized neurons that receive inputs from both left and right ears to determine where sounds come from are discussed in Chapter 9.

Adaptation: Receptor response can decline even if the stimulus is maintained

Many receptors show progressive loss of response when stimulation is maintained. This process is called **adaptation**. We can demonstrate adaptation by recording action potentials in a fiber leading from a sensory receptor that is receiving a constant level of stimulation. The frequency of action potentials progressively declines, even though the stimulus is continued (**Figure 8.7**). In terms of adaptation, there are two kinds of receptors: **Tonic receptors** show little or no decrease in the frequency of action potentials as stimulation is maintained; in other words, these receptors show relatively little adaptation. **Phasic receptors** display adaptation, rapidly decreasing the frequency of action potentials when the stimulus is maintained.

Adaptation means that there is a progressive shift in neural activity *away from accurate portrayal* of maintained physical events. Thus, the nervous system may

range fractionation   A hypothesis of stimulus intensity perception stating that a wide range of intensity values can be encoded by a group of cells, each of which is a specialist for a particular range of stimulus intensities.

somatosensory   Referring to body sensation, particularly touch and pain sensation.

adaptation   The progressive loss of receptor sensitivity as stimulation is maintained.

tonic receptor   A receptor in which the frequency of action potentials declines slowly or not at all as stimulation is maintained.

phasic receptor   A receptor in which the frequency of action potentials drops rapidly as stimulation is maintained.

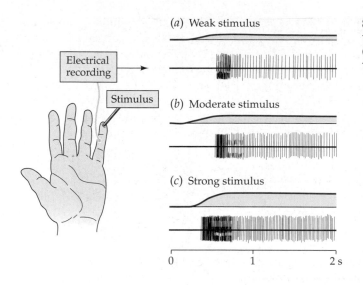

(a) Weak stimulus

(b) Moderate stimulus

(c) Strong stimulus

0   1   2 s

8.7 Sensory Adaptation   The neuron represented here responds to a touch on the fifth finger. It fires rapidly when the stimulus—whether weak (a), moderate (b), or strong (c)—is first applied, but then it adapts, slowing to a steady rate. (After Knibestol and Valbo, 1970.)

fail to register neural activity even though the stimulus continues. Such a striking discrepancy is no accident; sensory systems emphasize *change* in stimuli because changes are more likely to be significant for survival. Sensory adaptation prevents the nervous system from becoming overwhelmed by stimuli that offer very little "news" about the world. For example, your pants may press a hair on your leg continually, but you're saved from a constant neural barrage from this stimulus by several mechanisms, including adaptation.

The basis of adaptation includes both neural and nonneural events. For example, in some mechanical receptors, adaptation develops from the elasticity of the receptor cell itself. This situation is especially evident in the Pacinian corpuscle, which detects vibration (see Figure 8.5). Maintained vibration on the receptor results in an initial burst of neural activity and a rapid decrease to almost nothing. But when the corpuscle (which is a separate, accessory cell) is removed, the same constant stimulus applied to the uncovered sensory nerve fiber produces a continuing discharge of action potentials. So for this receptor, at least some adaptation is due to mechanical properties of the nonneural component, the corpuscle rather than the axon.

Suppression: Sometimes we need receptors to be quiet

We have noted that successful survival does not depend on exact reporting of stimuli. Rather, our success as a species demands that our sensory systems accentuate, from among the many things happening about us, the important *changes* of stimuli. We just discussed how sensory receptor adaptation can suppress a constant stimulus, but two other suppression strategies are also available.

In many sensory systems, accessory structures can reduce the level of input in the sensory pathway. For example, closing the eyelids reduces the amount of light that reaches the retina. In the auditory system, contraction of the middle-ear muscles reduces the intensity of sounds that reach the inner ear. In this form of sensory control, the relevant mechanisms change the intensity of the stimulus before it reaches the receptors.

In a second form of information control, neural connections descend from the brain to lower stations in the sensory pathway, in some cases as far as the receptor surface. For example, higher centers in the pain system (discussed later in this chapter) send axons down the spinal cord, where they can inhibit incoming pain signals. This **central modulation of sensory information** is also evident in the auditory system, where a small group of cells in the brainstem sends axons along the auditory nerve to connect with the base of the receptor cells to dampen sounds selectively.

central modulation of sensory information   The process in which higher brain centers, such as the cortex and thalamus, suppress some sources of sensory information and amplify others.

8.8 Levels of Sensory Processing Sensory information enters the CNS through the brainstem or spinal cord and then reaches the thalamus. The thalamus shares the information with the cerebral cortex; the cortex directs the thalamus to suppress some sensations. Primary sensory cortex swaps information with nonprimary sensory cortex. This organization is present in all sensory systems except smell (see Chapter 9).

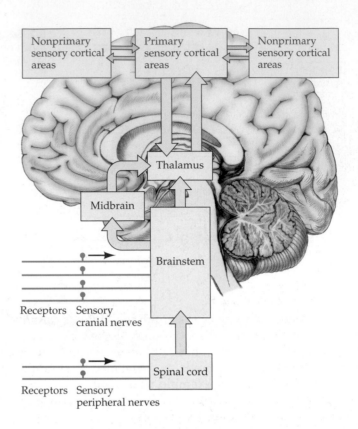

Pathways: Successive levels of the CNS process sensory information

Sensory information travels from the sensory surface to the highest levels of the brain, and each sensory system has its own distinctive pathway. Pathways from receptors lead into the spinal cord or brainstem, where they connect to distinct clusters of neurons. These cells, in turn, have axons that connect to other groups of neurons. Each sensory modality—such as touch, vision, or hearing—has a distinct hierarchy of tracts and stations in the brain that are collectively known as the **sensory pathway** for that modality.

Each station in the pathway accomplishes a basic aspect of information processing. For example, painful stimulation of the finger leads to reflex withdrawal of the hand, which is mediated by spinal circuits. At the brainstem level, other circuits can turn the head toward the source of pain. Eventually, sensory pathways terminate in the cerebral cortex, where the most complex aspects of sensory processing take place. For most senses, information reaches the **thalamus** before being relayed to the cortex (**Figure 8.8**). Information about each sensory modality is sent to a separate division of the thalamus. One way for the brain to suppress particular stimuli is for the cortex to direct the thalamus to emphasize some sensory information and suppress other information.

Receptive fields: What turns on this particular receptor cell?

The **receptive field** of a sensory neuron consists of a region of space in which a stimulus will alter that neuron's firing rate. To determine this receptive field, investigators record the neuron's electrical responses to a variety of stimuli to see what makes the activity of the cell change from its resting rate (**Figure 8.9**). For example, which patch of skin must we vibrate to change the activity of a particular Pacinian corpuscle? Such experiments show that somatosensory receptive fields have either an excitatory center and an inhibitory surround, or an inhibitory center and an excitatory surround. These receptive fields make it easier to detect edges and discontinuities on the objects we feel.

sensory pathway The chain of neural connections from sensory receptor cells to the cortex.

thalamus The brain regions at the top of the brainstem that trade information with the cortex.

receptive field The stimulus region and features that affect the activity of a cell in a sensory system.

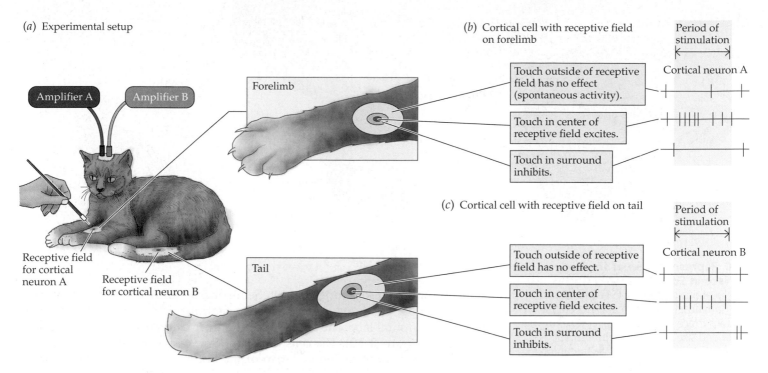

(a) Experimental setup

Amplifier A   Amplifier B

Receptive field for cortical neuron A

Receptive field for cortical neuron B

(b) Cortical cell with receptive field on forelimb

Forelimb

Period of stimulation

Cortical neuron A

Touch outside of receptive field has no effect (spontaneous activity).

Touch in center of receptive field excites.

Touch in surround inhibits.

(c) Cortical cell with receptive field on tail

Tail

Period of stimulation

Cortical neuron B

Touch outside of receptive field has no effect.

Touch in center of receptive field excites.

Touch in surround inhibits.

8.9 Identifying Somatosensory Receptive Fields   The procedures illustrated here are used to record from somatosensory neurons of the cerebral cortex. Changes in the position of the stimulus affect the rate of action potentials. Neuron A responds to touch on a region of the forepaw; neuron B, only a few centimeters away in the somatosensory cortex, responds to stimulation of the tail. The receptive fields of these neurons include an excitatory center and an inhibitory surround, but other neurons have receptive fields with the reverse organization: inhibitory centers and excitatory surrounds.

Receptive fields differ also in size and shape, and in the quality of stimulation that activates them. For example, some neurons respond preferentially to light touch, while others fire most rapidly in response to painful stimuli, and still others respond to cooling.

Following sensory information from the receptor cell in the periphery into the brain shows that neurons all along the pathway will respond to particular stimuli, so each of these cells has a receptive field too. But as each successive neuron combines information from prior cells in the pathway, the receptive fields change considerably. Receptive fields have been studied for cells at all levels, from the periphery to the brain, and we will see many examples of receptive fields later in this chapter and in the next two chapters.

RECEPTIVE FIELDS IN THE CEREBRAL CORTEX   For a given sensory modality we can find several different regions of cortex that receive information about that sense. Each of these cortical regions has a separate map of the same receptive surface, but the different cortical regions process the information differently and make different contributions to perceptual experiences (Miyashita, 1993; Zeki, 1993).

By convention, one of the cortical maps is designated as **primary sensory cortex** for that particular modality. Thus, there is primary somatosensory cortex, primary auditory cortex, and so on. The other cortical maps for a given modality are said to be **secondary sensory cortex**, or **nonprimary sensory cortex** (see Figure 8.8). The primary cortical area is the main source of input to the other fields for the same modality, even though these other fields also have direct thalamic inputs. Information is sent back and forth between the primary and nonprimary sensory cortex through subcortical loops (see Figure 8.8).

primary sensory cortex   For a given sensory modality, the region of cortex that receives most of the information about that modality from the thalamus or, in the case of olfaction, directly from the secondary sensory neurons.

secondary sensory cortex or nonprimary sensory cortex   For a given sensory modality, the cortical regions receiving direct projections from primary sensory cortex for that modality.

(a)

Central sulcus | Postcentral sulcus

Primary somatosensory cortex (S1)

Secondary somatosensory cortex (S2)

(b)

Trunk
Neck
Head
Shoulder
Arm
Elbow
Forearm

Hand

Digit 5
4
3
2
Thumb
Eyes
Nose
Face
Upper lip
Lower lip
Chin

Leg
Foot
Toes
Genitalia

Throat

Tongue

Teeth, jaw, gums

(c)

8.10 Representation of the Body Surface in Somatosensory Cortex (a) The locations of primary (S1) and secondary (S2) somatosensory cortical areas on the lateral surface of the parietal cortex. (b) The order and size of cortical representations of different regions of skin. Note that information from the various parts of the hand and fingers take up much more room than does information from the shoulder. (c) The *homunculus* (literally, "little man") depicts the body surface with each area drawn in proportion to the size of its representation in the primary somatosensory cortex.

Primary somatosensory cortex of each hemisphere—known as **somatosensory 1** or **S1**—lies in parietal cortex just behind the central sulcus dividing the parietal lobe from the frontal lobe, and receives touch information from the opposite side of the body (**Figure 8.10**). The cells in S1 are arranged according to the plan of the body surface. Each region is a map of the body in which the relative areas devoted to body regions reflect the density of body innervation. Thus, parts of the body where we are especially sensitive to touch (like the hand and fingers) send information to a greater portion of S1 than do less sensitive body regions (like the shoulder). **Secondary somatosensory cortex** (**somatosensory 2**, or **S2**) maps both sides of the body in registered overlay; that is, the left-arm and right-arm representations occupy the same part of the map, and so forth.

Some mammals have a very different pattern of representation in somatosensory cortex. For example, the nose of the star-nosed mole is a very sensitive organ for touch, and a considerable portion of its somatosensory cortex is devoted to responding to each of the 11 rays of the "star" (**Figure 8.11**) (Catania, 2001). For information about the organization of sensory information within a column of somatosensory cortex, see **A Step Further: Cortical Columns Show Specificity for Modality and Location** on the website.

primary somatosensory cortex (S1) or somatosensory 1 The gyrus just posterior to the central sulcus where sensory receptors on the body surface are mapped. Primary cortex for receiving touch and pain information, in the parietal lobe.

secondary somatosensory cortex (S2) or somatosensory 2 The region of cortex that receives direct projections from primary somatosensory cortex.

(a)

(b)

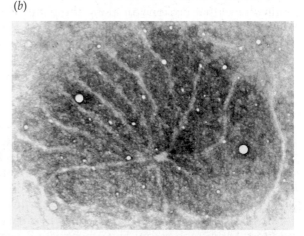

8.11 Hey There, You with the Star on Your Nose (a) The tip of the star-nosed mole's nose is a very delicate organ for touch. (b) In this section from the somatosensory cortex of a star-nosed mole, we can see how each of the 11 rays from one-half of the star-shaped nose projects to its own patch of cortex. The two bottom-most rays, which are the most sensitive, each innervate a larger piece of cortex than do the other rays. (From Catania, 2001; photographs courtesy of Ken Catania.)

Attention: How do we notice some stimuli but not others?

In 1890, William James wrote, "Everyone knows what attention is. It is the taking possession by the mind in clear and vivid form one out of what seem several simultaneous objects or trains of thought." In fact, however, not everyone agrees about the definition of **attention**. This important aspect of sensory processing has a multiplicity of meanings.

One view emphasizes the state of alertness or vigilance that enables animals to detect signals. In this view, attention is a generalized activation that attunes us to all inputs. According to another view, attention is the process that allows the *selection* of some sensory inputs from among many competing ones. Other investigators view attention as a "mental spotlight" that focuses on some stimuli, casting others in a "shadow." Obviously this "self-evident" notion has considerable complexity.

One cortical region that appears to play a special role in attention is a part of the *posterior parietal lobe*. Many cells here are especially responsive in a trained monkey that is expecting the appearance of a stimulus (Mountcastle et al., 1981), whether auditory or visual. Lesions of this area in monkeys result in inattention, or neglect of stimuli, on the opposite side. (In Chapter 18 we will see that this symptom is especially severe in people with lesions of the right parietal lobe.) A portion of the frontal cortex, called the *frontal eye field*, seems to be involved in attentive visual exploration of space. The *cingulate cortex* (the portion of cortex along and just above the corpus callosum; see Figure 2.15) has been implicated in motivational aspects of attention. **Figure 8.12** shows activation in the cingulate and posterior parietal cortex during a task involving a shift in spatial orientation (Gitelman et al., 1996; Nobre et al., 1997). We will discuss attention in more detail in Chapter 18.

Sensory systems influence one another

Often the use of one sensory system influences perception derived from another sensory system. For example, cats may not respond to birds unless they can both see and hear the birds; neither sense alone is sufficient to elicit a response (B. Stein and Meredith, 1993). Similarly, humans detect a visual signal more accurately if it is accompanied by a sound from the same part of space (McDonald et al., 2000).

Many sensory areas in the brain—so-called *association areas*—do not represent exclusively a single modality, but show a mixture of inputs from different modalities. Some "visual" cells, for instance, also respond to auditory or touch stimuli. Perhaps loss of input from one modality allows these cells to analyze input from the remaining senses better, as happens, for example, in cases of people who become blind early in life and are better than sighted people at localizing auditory stimuli (Gougoux et al., 2005). The normal stimulus convergence on such **polymodal** cells provides a mechanism for intersensory interactions (B. E. Stein and Stanford, 2008). For a few people, a stimulus in one modality may evoke an additional perception

attention A state or condition of selective awareness or perceptual receptivity, by which specific stimuli are selected for enhanced processing.

polymodal Involving several sensory modalities.

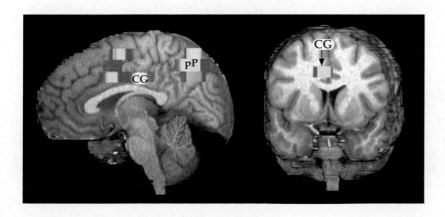

8.12 Brain Regions Activated When We Are Attending Functional-MRI images of a subject cued to expect a stimulus in a particular portion of the visual field show right-hemisphere activation in posterior parietal cortex (pP) and cingulate cortex (CG) in midsagittal (*left*) and frontal (*right*) views. Areas of highest activation are shown in yellow. (Courtesy of Darren Gitelman.)

BOX 8.1 Synesthesia

For a few people, stimuli in one modality evoke the involuntary experience of an additional sensation in another modality—a condition known as **synesthesia** (from the Greek *syn*, "union," and *aesthesis*, "sensation"). For example, a person with synesthesia (a "synesthete") may perceive different colors when seeing different letters of the alphabet ("*D* looks green, but *E* is red") or words for days of the week ("*Tuesday* is a yellow word"). In one documented example, a musician experienced a particular taste whenever she heard a specific musical tone interval (Beeli et al., 2005). Discordant tones evoked unpleasant tastes.

How common synesthesia is depends to some extent on how it's defined, but it is estimated that as much as 2%–4% of the population displays some form of synesthesia, and as much as 1% reports experiencing a color along with particular days of the week or numbers (Simner et al., 2006). Synesthesia

is more commonly reported among artists and poets than in the general population, so it may be associated with creativity (Cytowic and Eagleman, 2009). Brain imaging shows that synesthetes who see letters in color have more axonal connections across cortex, especially in the temporal lobe (Rouw and Scholte, 2007), suggesting that the experience of color is due to excessive connections between brain regions.

Since you probably do not have this experience, you may doubt whether other people really do, if the basis for knowing that they do is self-report alone. For some

forms of synesthesia, however, a clever test may confirm whether, for example, "2 is red but 5 is green." To someone who reported having this experience, Ramachandran and Hubbard (2001) showed a page like that in Figure A and asked the person to quickly point to all of the 2s. Because the shapes of 2 and 5 are so similar, it takes a certain amount of time for most people (nonsynesthetes) to pick out each 2 among all those 5s. But this subject found them much faster than that. For such a synesthete, the numbers look colored, as in Figure B; and with the addition of colors, it's certainly much easier to pick out the 2s.

You can test whether *you* have synesthesia online at http://synesthete.org (Eagleman et al., 2007).

(A)

(B)

synesthesia A condition in which stimuli in one modality evoke the involuntary experience of an additional sensation in another modality.

in another modality, as when seeing a number evokes a color, or hearing different tones evokes different flavors—a situation that is described further in **Box 8.1**.

Touch: Many Sensations Blended Together

The skin that envelops our bodies is a delicate yet durable boundary that separates us from our surroundings. It also presents to the world a massive array of sensory receptors monitoring many types of stimuli. Among primates, an important aspect of skin sensations is the active manipulation of objects by the hands, which enables the identification of various shapes. But touch is not just touch. Careful studies of skin sensations reveal qualitatively different sensory experiences: pressure, vibration, tickle, "pins and needles," and more-complex dimensions, such as smoothness or wetness—all recorded by the receptors in the skin.

Skin Is a Complex Organ That Contains a Variety of Sensory Receptors

Because the average person has about 1–2 m² (10–20 square feet) of skin, skin is sometimes considered the largest human organ. Skin is made up of three separate layers; the relative thickness of each varies over the body surface. The outermost layer—the **epidermis**—is the thinnest. The middle layer—the **dermis**—contains a rich web of nerve fibers in a network of connective tissue and blood vessels. The

epidermis The outermost layer of skin, over the dermis.

dermis The middle layer of skin, between the epidermis and the hypodermis.

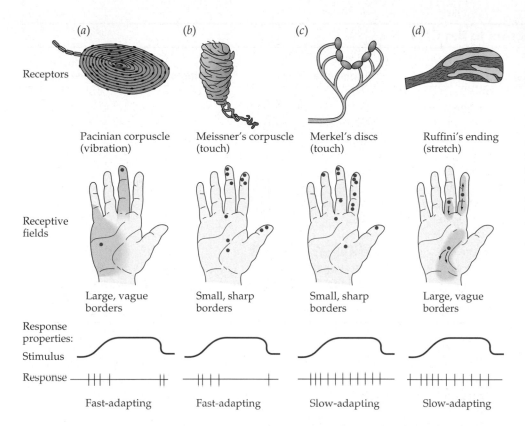

(a) Pacinian corpuscle (vibration) (b) Meissner's corpuscle (touch) (c) Merkel's discs (touch) (d) Ruffini's ending (stretch)

Receptors

Receptive fields

Large, vague borders   Small, sharp borders   Small, sharp borders   Large, vague borders

Response properties:

Stimulus

Response

Fast-adapting   Fast-adapting   Slow-adapting   Slow-adapting

8.13 Properties of Skin Receptors Related to Touch   Shown here for each skin receptor is the type of receptor (*top*), the size and type of the receptive field (*middle*), and the electrophysiological response (*bottom*). (*a*) Pacinian corpuscles activate fast-adapting fibers with large receptive fields. (*b*) Meissner's corpuscles are fast-adapting mechanoreceptors with small receptive fields. (*c*) Merkel's discs are slow-adapting receptors with small receptive fields. (*d*) Ruffini's endings are slow-adapting receptors with large receptive fields. The locations of these receptors in the skin are illustrated in Figure 8.4. (After Johansson and Flanagan, 2009.)

innermost layer—the **hypodermis** (or *subcutaneous tissue*)—provides an anchor for muscles, contains Pacinian corpuscles, and helps shape the body (see Figure 8.4).

Pain, heat, and cold at the skin are detected by free nerve endings (see Figure 8.4), which are described later in this chapter. In contrast, light touch is detected by four highly sensitive touch receptors (**Figure 8.13**). We mentioned earlier the Pacinian corpuscles, which are found in the hypodermis. The onionlike outer portion of the corpuscle acts as a filter, shielding the underlying nerve fiber from most stimulation. Only vibrating stimuli of more than 200 Hz will pass through the corpuscle and stretch the nerve fiber to reach threshold. Normally, the skin receives this sort of rapid *vibration* when it is moving across the *texture* of an object's surface. The ridges provided by fingerprints mechanically filter out vibrations of some frequencies and amplify others, apparently optimizing the stimulation of Pacinian corpuscles (Scheibert et al., 2009). Pacinian corpuscles are fast-responding and fast-adapting receptors (**Figure 8.13a**).

The **tactile** (touch) receptors that mediate most of our ability to perceive the form of objects we touch are the fast-adapting **Meissner's corpuscles** (**Figure 8.13b**) and the slow-adapting, oval **Merkel's discs** (**Figure 8.13c**). These receptors are densely distributed in skin regions where we can discriminate fine details by touch (fingertips, tongue, and lips).

The receptive fields of Merkel's discs usually have an inhibitory surround, which increases their spatial resolution. This field also makes them especially responsive to edges and to isolated *points* on a surface (such as the dots for Braille characters). Genetically modified mice that lack Merkel's discs no longer respond to light touch (Maricich et al., 2009).

Meissner's corpuscles are more numerous than Merkel's discs but offer less spatial resolution. Meissner's corpuscles seem specialized to respond to *changes* in stimuli (as one would expect from rapidly adapting receptors) to detect localized movement between the skin and a surface. This sensitivity to change in stimuli provides detailed information about *texture* (K. O. Johnson and Hsiao, 1992).

hypodermis   Also called *subcutaneous tissue*. The innermost layer of skin, under the dermis.

tactile   Of or relating to touch.

Meissner's corpuscle   A skin receptor cell type that detects light touch.

Merkel's disc   A skin receptor cell type that detects light touch.

TABLE 8.2 Fibers That Link Receptors to the CNS

Sensory function(s)	Receptor type(s)	Axon type	Diameter (μm)	Conduction speed (m/s)
Proprioception (see Chapter 11)	Muscle spindle	Aα (A alpha)	13–20	80–120
Touch (see Figures 8.13 and 8.14)	Pacinian corpuscle, Ruffini's ending, Merkel's discs, Meissner's corpuscle	Aβ (A beta)	6–12	35–75
Pain, temperature	Free nerve endings; TRP2	Aδ (A delta)	1–5	5–30
Temperature, pain, itch	Free nerve endings; TRPV1, CMR1	C	0.02–1.5	0.5–2

Ruffini's ending   A skin receptor cell type that detects stretching of the skin.

8.14 Various Touch Receptors Responding to Braille (After J. R. Phillips et al., 1990.)

The final touch receptors are the slow-adapting **Ruffini's endings**, which detect *stretching* of the skin when we move fingers or limbs (**Figure 8.13d**). The very few Ruffini's endings (Pare et al., 2003) have large receptive fields (Johansson and Flanagan, 2009).

Figure 8.14 compares how the four touch receptors respond when a finger is moved across the raised dots of Braille. All four of these light-touch receptors utilize moderately large (so-called Aβ) myelinated fibers (**Table 8.2**). Recall from Chapter 3 that large axons conduct action potentials faster than small axons do, and that myelination speeds conduction even more. So the light-touch receptors

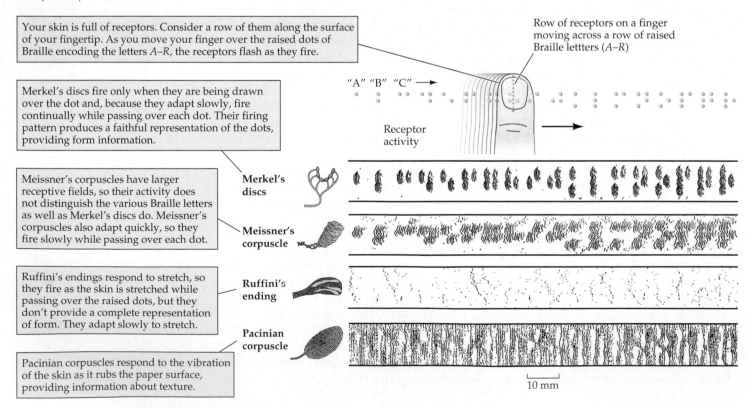

Your skin is full of receptors. Consider a row of them along the surface of your fingertip. As you move your finger over the raised dots of Braille encoding the letters *A–R*, the receptors flash as they fire.

Merkel's discs fire only when they are being drawn over the dot and, because they adapt slowly, fire continually while passing over each dot. Their firing pattern produces a faithful representation of the dots, providing form information.

Meissner's corpuscles have larger receptive fields, so their activity does not distinguish the various Braille letters as well as Merkel's discs do. Meissner's corpuscles also adapt quickly, so they fire slowly while passing over each dot.

Ruffini's endings respond to stretch, so they fire as the skin is stretched while passing over the raised dots, but they don't provide a complete representation of form. They adapt slowly to stretch.

Pacinian corpuscles respond to the vibration of the skin as it rubs the paper surface, providing information about texture.

Row of receptors on a finger moving across a row of raised Braille lettters (*A–R*)

"A" "B" "C" →

Receptor activity

Merkel's discs

Meissner's corpuscle

Ruffini's ending

Pacinian corpuscle

10 mm

send information very rapidly to the CNS. Later in this chapter we'll learn that some pain fibers are large and conduct rapidly, while others are small and conduct slowly. In Chapter 11 we'll meet a man whose large fibers were destroyed by a virus, so he can no longer feel light touch. He can still feel pain, coolness, and warmth on his skin, however, because those smaller axons were spared.

The Dorsal Column System Carries Somatosensory Information from the Skin to the Brain

The touch receptors that we have described (Pacinian corpuscles, Merkel's discs, Meissner's corpuscles, and Ruffini's endings) send their axons to the spinal cord, where they enter the dorsal horn and turn upward, traveling to the brain along the spinal cord's dorsal column of white matter, which is why this is called the **dorsal column system**. These axons go all the way up to the brainstem, where they synapse on neurons of the *dorsal column nuclei* in the medulla (**Figure 8.15**). The axons of these medullary neurons then cross the midline to the opposite side and ascend to a group of nuclei of the thalamus. Outputs of the thalamus are directed to primary somatosensory cortex (S1).

The skin surface can be divided into bands corresponding to the spinal nerves that carry the axons from each region (**Figure 8.16a**). A **dermatome** (from the

dorsal column system A somatosensory system that delivers most touch stimuli via the dorsal columns of spinal white matter to the brain.

dermatome A strip of skin innervated by a particular spinal root.

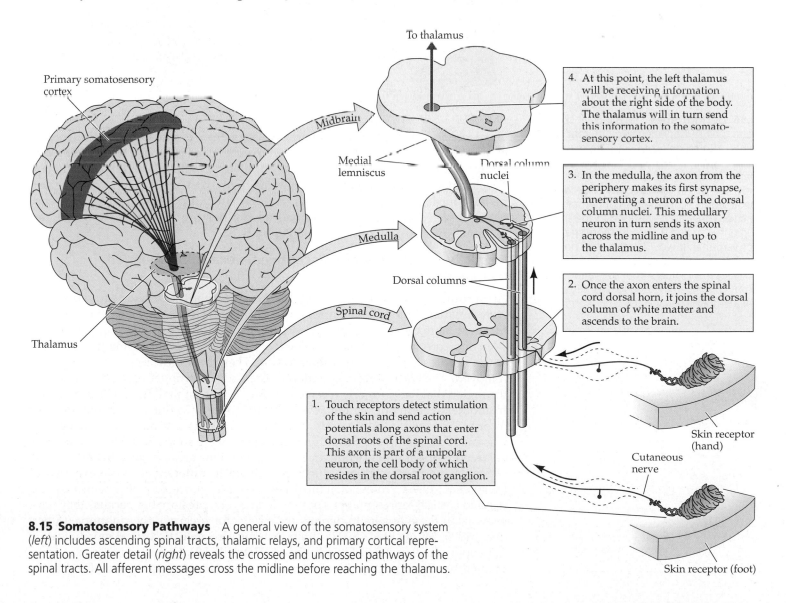

8.15 Somatosensory Pathways A general view of the somatosensory system (*left*) includes ascending spinal tracts, thalamic relays, and primary cortical representation. Greater detail (*right*) reveals the crossed and uncrossed pathways of the spinal tracts. All afferent messages cross the midline before reaching the thalamus.

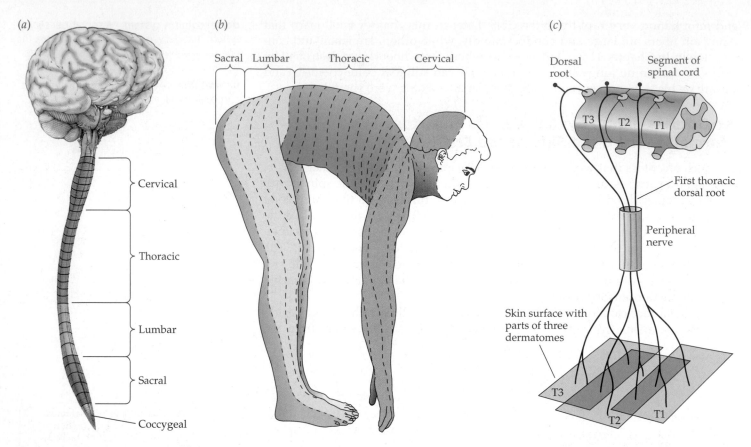

(a) Cervical
Thoracic
Lumbar
Sacral
Coccygeal

(b) Sacral Lumbar Thoracic Cervical

(c) Dorsal root   Segment of spinal cord
T3 T2 T1
First thoracic dorsal root
Peripheral nerve
Skin surface with parts of three dermatomes
T3 T2 T1

8.16 Dermatomes (a) Bands of skin send their sensory inputs to different dorsal roots of the spinal cord. Each dermatome is the section of skin that is innervated primarily by a given dorsal root. (b) In this side view of the human body in quadrupedal position, the pattern of dermatomes is color-coded to correspond to the spinal regions in a, and it appears more straightforward than it would in the erect posture. (c) Adjacent dorsal roots of the spinal cord collect sensory fibers from overlapping strips of skin, so the boundaries between the dermatomes overlap.

Greek *derma*, "skin," and *tome*, "part" or "segment") is a strip of skin innervated by a particular spinal nerve. The pattern of dermatomes is hard to understand in an upright human, but remember that our erect posture is a recent evolutionary development. The mammalian dermatomal pattern evolved among our quadrupedal (four-legged) ancestors. Thus, the dermatomal pattern makes more sense when depicted on a person in a quadrupedal posture (**Figure 8.16b**). The dermatomes overlap a modest amount (**Figure 8.16c**).

Plasticity in cortical maps: Receptive fields can be changed by experience

At one time, most researchers thought that cortical maps were fixed early in life and were invariant among all members of the same species. Now, however, we know that cortical maps can change with experience (Merzenich and Jenkins, 1993).

In one experiment, the receptive field of a monkey's hand was mapped in detail in the somatosensory cortex (**Figure 8.17a**). Then the middle finger was surgically removed. The cortical representation of each adjacent finger expanded, filling in the region that had formerly received information from that finger (**Figure 8.17b**). In another experiment, a monkey was trained to rest two fingers on a rotating disk in order to obtain food rewards. After several weeks of training, the hand area was mapped again, and the stimulated fingers were found to have considerably enlarged representations compared to their previous areas (**Figure 8.17c**).

Similar findings were noted in rats exposed to differential tactile experiences (Xerri et al., 1996). Professional musicians who play stringed instruments have expanded cortical representations of their left fingers, presumably because they have been using these fingers to depress the strings for precisely the right note (Elbert et al., 1995; Münte et al., 2002). Brain imaging also reveals cortical reorganization in people who lose a hand in adulthood (**Figure 8.18**). One man received a transplanted hand (from an accident victim) 35 years after losing his own. Despite the

(a) Representation of the left hand in primary somatosensory cortex in right hemisphere of monkey brain

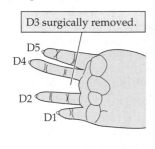

Digit 5
Digit 4
Digit 3
Digit 2
Digit 1 (thumb)

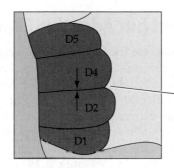

Details of cortical map (D5 = digit 5, etc.)

(b) Experiment 1

D3 surgically removed.

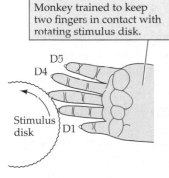

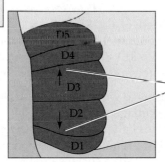

Several weeks later, areas representing D2 and D4 have expanded, replacing the representation of D3.

(c) Experiment 2

Monkey trained to keep two fingers in contact with rotating stimulus disk.

Stimulus disk

Areas representing stimulated digits expand and replace part of the areas that formerly represented adjacent digits.

8.17 The Plasticity of Somatosensory Representations These experiments demonstrate that the adult brains of monkeys can be altered by experience. (After Merzenich and Jenkins, 1993.)

(a) Normal somatosensory cortex

Arm
Hand
Face
Central sulcus

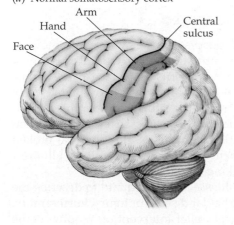

(b) Somatosensory cortex reorganized after loss of hand

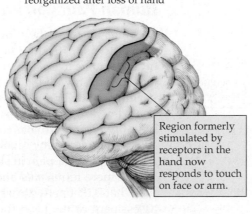

Region formerly stimulated by receptors in the hand now responds to touch on face or arm.

8.18 Normal and Reorganized Somatosensory Cortex (a) Normally, the region of S1 receiving information from the hand is interposed between the regions representing the upper arm and the face. In humans we can map S1 using functional brain imaging to determine which parts of cortex are activated by touch on different parts of the body. (b) In a person who, as an adult, loses one hand, the cortical regions representing the upper arm and face expand, taking over the cortical region previously representing the missing hand. Presumably the loss of sensory input from the lost hand allows those cortical neurons to become innervated by neighboring cortical neurons. (After T. T. Yang et al., 1994.) One man lost his right hand at age 19 but received a transplanted hand from an accident victim 35 years later. A few months later, the map of his S1 showed a return of the hand region as in a.

THE HUMAN PINCUSHION WHO INCURS CONSTANT RISKS OF BLOOD POISONING.

8.19 Doesn't That Hurt? The earliest scientific report of a person with congenital insensitivity to pain was of a man working in the theater, like the man shown here, as a "human pincushion." (Photograph by Culver Pictures, Inc.)

length of time that had passed, his brain reorganized in just a few months to receive sensation from the hand in the appropriate part of S1 (S. H. Frey et al., 2008).

Some changes in cortical maps occur after weeks or months of use or disuse; they may arise from the production of new synapses and dendrites (Florence et al., 1998; Hickmott and Steen, 2005) or the loss of others. As described on the website in **A Step Further: Somatosensory Perception of Objects**, we must actively manipulate objects in order for the somatosensory cortex to perceive them. Having dealt with the pleasant aspects of touch, we turn now to the mixed blessing of pain.

Pain: An Unpleasant but Adaptive Experience

The International Association for the Study of Pain defines **pain** as "an unpleasant sensory and emotional experience associated with actual or potential tissue damage, or described in terms of such damage." Because pain is unpleasant and causes great suffering, it may be difficult to imagine a biological role for it. But clues to the adaptive significance of pain can be gleaned from the study of rare individuals with **congenital insensitivity to pain**, who never experience pain (Hirsch et al., 1995).

The first clinically reported person with congenital insensitivity to pain worked on the stage as a "human pincushion" (**Figure 8.19**) (Dearborn, 1932). A little later in this chapter we'll learn how studies of these individuals provided a breakthrough in understanding pain. People who display pain insensitivity can discriminate between the touch of the point or head of a pin, but they experience no pain when pricked with the point. Such people show extensive scarring from injuries to fingers, hands, and legs (Manfredi et al., 1981); and they tend to die young of injuries, suggesting that pain guides adaptive behavior by signaling harm to our bodies.

The experience of pain vividly teaches us how to avoid injury. Dennis and Melzack (1983) list three more ways that pain helps us:

1. Short-lasting pain causes us to withdraw from the source, often reflexively, thus preventing further damage.
2. Long-lasting pain promotes behaviors, such as sleep, inactivity, grooming, feeding, and drinking, that promote recuperation.
3. The expression of pain serves as a social signal to other animals. For example, screeching after a painful stimulus signals the potential harm to genetically related individuals and elicits caregiving behavior from them, such as grooming, defending, and feeding.

pain The discomfort normally associated with tissue damage.

congenital insensitivity to pain The condition of being born without the ability to perceive pain.

Human Pain Can Be Measured

In some parts of the world people endure, with stoic indifference, rituals (including body mutilation) that would cause most other humans to cry out in pain. Incisions of the face, hands, arms, legs, or chest; walking on hot coals; and other treatments clearly harmful to the body can be part of the ritual. Comparable experiences are also seen in more ordinary circumstances, such as when a highly excited athlete continues to play a game with a broken arm or leg. Learning, experience, emotion, and culture all affect the perception of pain in striking ways.

The mere terms *mild* and *intense* are inadequate to describe the pain that is distinctive to a particular disease or injury. Furthermore, assessment of the need for pain relief intervention requires some

8.20 The Multifaceted Character of Pain

Pain perception
- Cognitive system
- Motivational-affective system
- Sensory-discriminative system

Peripheral input → Spinal cord processing → Motivational-affective system → Motor response mechanism

kind of quantitative measurement (Chapman et al., 1985). For example, Melzack (1984) has provided a detailed quantitative rating scale for pain. This rating scale—called the *McGill Pain Questionnaire*—consists of a list of words arranged into classes that describe three different aspects of pain:

1. The *sensory-discriminative* quality (e.g., throbbing, gnawing, shooting)
2. The *motivational-affective* (emotional) quality (e.g., tiring, sickening, fearful)
3. An overall *cognitive* evaluative quality (e.g., no pain, mild, excruciating)

Patients are asked to select the set of words that best describes their pain. These three components reflect different aspects of pain perception (**Figure 8.20**).

One of the interesting aspects of the McGill scale is that it can distinguish among pain syndromes, meaning that patients use a distinctive constellation of words to describe a particular pain experience. For example, tooth pain is described differently from arthritic pain, which in turn is described differently from menstrual pain. The physician's simple query "Is the pain still there?" has been replaced by a more detailed analysis that provides better clues about how to control pain.

A Specific Pathway Transmits Pain Information

Contemporary studies of pain mechanisms have revealed receptors in the skin that transmit pain information to the central nervous system. In this section we will discuss some features of peripheral and CNS pathways that mediate pain.

Peripheral receptors get the initial message

In most cases the initial stimulus for pain is the destruction or injury of tissue adjacent to certain nerve fibers. The damaged tissue releases chemicals that activate pain fibers in the skin. Various substances have been suggested as the chemical mediators of pain, including neuropeptides, serotonin, histamine, various proteolytic (protein-metabolizing) enzymes, prostaglandins (a group of widespread hormones), and nerve growth factor (**Figure 8.21**).

Some peripheral receptors and nerve fibers are specialized for pain. Receptors that respond to noxious stimulation are called **nociceptors**. **Free nerve endings** in the dermis display no specialized structures (they look like naked nerve endings), but they have specialized receptor proteins on the cell membrane that respond to

nociceptor A receptor that responds to stimuli that produce tissue damage or pose the threat of damage.

free nerve ending An axon that terminates in the skin without any specialized cell associated with it and that detects pain and/or changes in temperature.

8.21 Peripheral Mediation of Pain When the skin is injured, activity of the peripheral nervous system causes the local release of various substances.

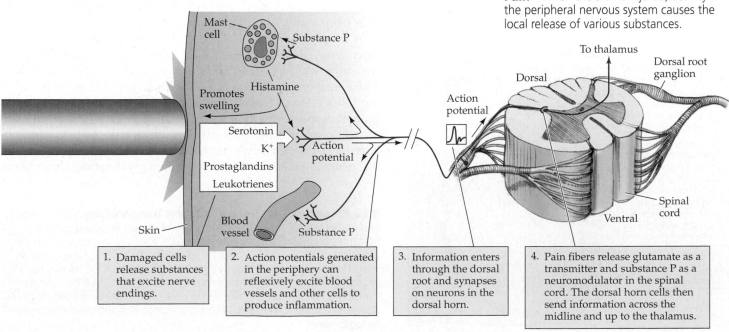

1. Damaged cells release substances that excite nerve endings.

2. Action potentials generated in the periphery can reflexively excite blood vessels and other cells to produce inflammation.

3. Information enters through the dorsal root and synapses on neurons in the dorsal horn.

4. Pain fibers release glutamate as a transmitter and substance P as a neuromodulator in the spinal cord. The dorsal horn cells then send information across the midline and up to the thalamus.

capsaicin A compound synthesized by various plants to deter predators by mimicking the experience of burning.

transient receptor potential vanilloid type 1 (TRPV1) Also called *vanilloid receptor 1*. A receptor that binds capsaicin to transmit the burning sensation from chili peppers and normally detects sudden increases in temperature.

transient receptor potential 2 (TRP2) A receptor, found in some free nerve endings, that opens its channel in response to rising temperatures.

various signals. Different free nerve endings produce different receptor proteins, so they report different stimuli, such as pain and/or changes in temperature.

HOT, COLD, OR COOL? The best evidence for specialized pain fibers in the periphery came from studies of **capsaicin**, the chemical that makes chili peppers spicy hot. Investigators isolated a receptor found in some free nerve endings that binds capsaicin, and they found that the receptor also responds to sudden increases in temperature (Caterina et al., 1997). The receptor was cloned and found to be a member of a family of proteins called *transient receptor potential* (*TRP*) ion channels. They named the capsaicin receptor **transient receptor potential vanilloid type 1** (**TRPV1**), or *vanilloid receptor 1*, because the crucial component of the capsaicin molecule is a chemical known as *vanilloid*. Mice lacking the gene for this receptor still responded to *mechanosensory* pain, but not to mild heat or capsaicin (Caterina et al., 2000). So the reason that chili peppers taste "hot" is that the capsaicin in the peppers activates TRPV1 receptors in the body that normally detect noxious heat. The venom of a Caribbean tarantula contains three different peptides that all activate this receptor, causing an intense burning sensation (Siemens et al., 2006).

TRPV1's normal job is to report a rise in temperature to warn us of danger. Chili peppers evolved the chemical capsaicin to ward off mammalian predators, as its ability to deter deer from eating prized flower bushes, which we learned about at the start of the chapter, suggests. Capsaicin molecules have the perfect shape to bind to TRPV1 and open its ion channel, which is normally opened by heat. Because the brain interprets action potentials from that nerve as signaling painful heat, we (and the deer) experience painful heat.

Why, though, aren't birds discouraged by capsaicin? The answer is that the *bird* version of TRPV1 is *not* affected by capsaicin (Tewksbury and Nabhan, 2001). In this case both the animal and the plant are benefited by capsaicin: the birds are able to get food from the plants—food that might be gone if mammals were able to eat it—and then fly off to spread the seeds of the plants far and wide. Clever, clever chili plants.

Why do our lips swell when we have overindulged in capsaicin? As Figure 8.21 illustrates, the action potentials generated by the chemical travel back out other branches of the axon to affect blood vessels and mast cells, triggering the swelling. Paradoxically, rubbing capsaicin into the skin overlying arthritic joints brings some pain relief, perhaps because overactivated pain fibers temporarily run out of transmitter.

A related receptor, **TRP2**, detects even higher temperatures than does TRPV1 (**Figure 8.22a**). TRP2 differs from TRPV1 in two other ways as well: TRP2 does *not* respond to capsaicin, and TRP2 receptors are found on nerve fibers larger than those carrying TRPV1. Recall from Chapter 3 that large axons conduct action potentials more rapidly than do small axons. TRP2 receptors are found on relatively large axons known as type **Aδ** ("A delta") **fibers**: large-diameter, myelinated axons (**Figure 8.22b**). Because of the relatively large axon diameter and myelination, these fibers

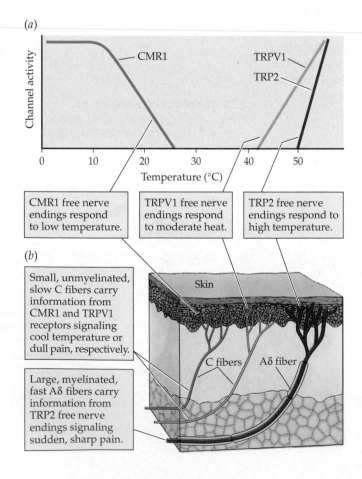

(*a*)

CMR1 free nerve endings respond to low temperature.

TRPV1 free nerve endings respond to moderate heat.

TRP2 free nerve endings respond to high temperature.

(*b*)

Small, unmyelinated, slow C fibers carry information from CMR1 and TRPV1 receptors signaling cool temperature or dull pain, respectively.

Large, myelinated, fast Aδ fibers carry information from TRP2 free nerve endings signaling sudden, sharp pain.

8.22 Receptors That Detect Pain and Temperature (*a*) Free nerve endings with cool-menthol receptor 1 (CMR1) are activated by temperatures below normal body temperature. Free nerve endings with the capsaicin receptor (TRPV1) respond to moderate heat and the capsaicin found in chili peppers. Other free nerve endings, with the related receptor protein TRP2, detect high temperatures. (*b*) The TRP2 free nerve endings transmit a fast action potential along large, myelinated Aδ fibers to the spinal cord. CMR1 and TRPV1 receptors transmit along slower, unmyelinated C fibers.

report to the spinal cord very quickly. When you burn your finger on a hot skillet, the first, sharp pain you feel is conducted by these fat Aδ fibers that detected the heat with TRP2 receptors. In contrast, the nerve fibers that possess TRPV1 receptors consist of thin, unmyelinated fibers called **C fibers** (see Figure 8.22*b*). These C fibers conduct slowly, and TRPV1 adapts slowly, providing the second wave of pain—the dull, lasting ache in that darned finger.

This is the reason for the slight delay between licking the cut surface of a chili pepper and feeling the burn. Only the TRPV1 fibers, with their slowly conducting C fibers, have been activated, not the fast Aδ fibers using TRP2. Table 8.2 compares these different fibers.

Taking a cue from the success with capsaicin, another group of investigators tried looking for the "coolness" receptor, reasoning that it should respond to the chemical menthol. They found and named **cool-menthol receptor 1** (**CMR1**). CMR1 is also a member of the TRP family (so it is sometimes called *TRP8*), but it responds to *cool* temperatures and is found on small C fibers (Bautista et al., 2007), so it transmits information about cool temperatures rather slowly (see Figure 8.22*a*). Another member of the TRP family is expressed by other free nerve endings to make them responsive to the spices oregano, thyme, and clove (H. Xu et al., 2006), while another receptor responds to garlic and onion (Salazar et al., 2008), and yet another receptor from this family responds to the mustard oils that are found in wasabi (Jordt et al., 2004). Spices add so much to our experience of food because they stimulate these various receptors in our mouth (in addition to the olfactory receptors we discuss in the next chapter).

Yet other free nerve endings provide us with the sensation of itch (gee, thanks!). These fibers respond to histamine that is released from mast cells in the skin (see Figure 8.21) and send their slowly conducting C fibers to the spinal cord, where they use **gastrin-releasing peptide** (**GRP**) to stimulate neurons in the dorsal horn (Y. G. Sun and Chen, 2007). Scratching the affected area of skin provides temporary relief by silencing those spinal neurons, which normally report itch sensation to the thalamus (S. Davidson et al., 2009). But sometimes scratching leads to infections and other problems, and some cases of chronic itch do not respond to current medications like antihistamines (Gawande, 2008). So someday it may be possible to use GRP antagonists to block itch sensation as it arrives in the spinal cord.

THE PAIN RECEPTOR? The search for the protein receptor used by free nerve endings to detect *mechanical* damage was hindered by the fact that so many chemicals are released by damaged tissue. It was unclear which chemical was crucial for activating those particular nociceptors. But a family in northern Pakistan may have solved the question of the "pure" pain receptor protein for us. A 10-year-old boy there was giving street performances of piercing his arms with knives and walking on coals without pain. Before scientists could study him, he died after jumping off a roof to impress his friends.

This boy's apparent fearlessness, which cost him his life, reminds us that pain, and fear derived from pain, really can be our friend. Six of the boy's surviving relatives also felt no pain. They could detect light touch, coolness, warmth, and other sensations just fine. Scientists isolated the gene (called *SCN9A*) responsible for pain insensitivity in this family and found that it encodes a sodium channel expressed in many free nerve endings (Cox et al., 2006). There is great excitement that this sodium channel may represent the specific pain receptor protein, and that drugs targeted at this protein may provide new ways to relieve pain.

Special CNS pathways mediate pain

In the central nervous system, special pathways mediate pain and temperature information. Earlier we discussed the dorsal column system that carries touch information to the brain (see Figure 8.15). The sensations of pain and temperature are transmitted separately by the **anterolateral**, or **spinothalamic**, **system**. Free nerve

Aδ fiber A moderately large, myelinated, and therefore fast-conducting, axon, usually transmitting pain information.

C fiber A small, unmyelinated axon that conducts pain information slowly and adapts slowly.

cool-menthol receptor 1 (CMR1) Also called *TRP8*. A sensory receptor, found in some free nerve endings, that opens an ion channel in response to a mild temperature drop or exposure to menthol.

gastrin-releasing peptide (GRP) A neuropeptide that stimulates neurons in the dorsal horn to provide the sensation of itch.

anterolateral system or spinothalamic system A somatosensory system that carries most of the pain information from the body to the brain.

8.23 Ascending Pain Pathways in the CNS Pain sensation travels from its origin to the brain via the spinothalamic system, crossing the midline in the spinal cord.

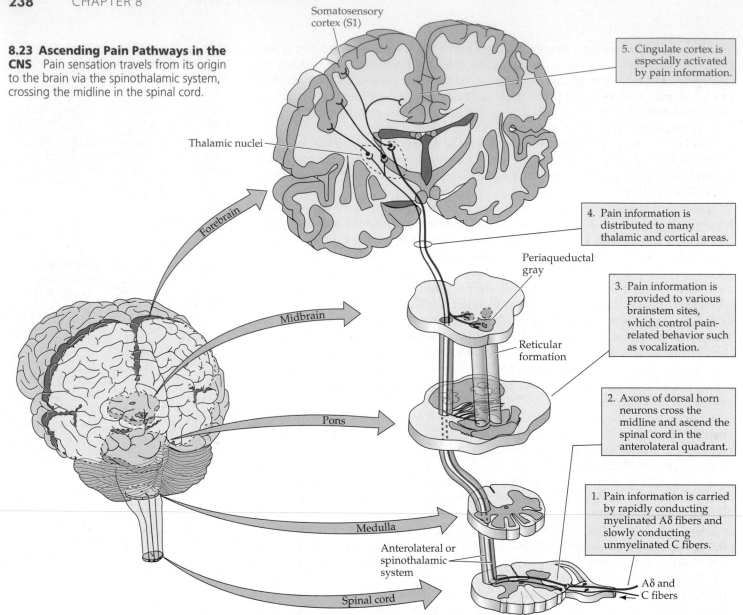

Somatosensory cortex (S1)

Thalamic nuclei

5. Cingulate cortex is especially activated by pain information.

4. Pain information is distributed to many thalamic and cortical areas.

Periaqueductal gray

3. Pain information is provided to various brainstem sites, which control pain-related behavior such as vocalization.

Reticular formation

2. Axons of dorsal horn neurons cross the midline and ascend the spinal cord in the anterolateral quadrant.

1. Pain information is carried by rapidly conducting myelinated Aδ fibers and slowly conducting unmyelinated C fibers.

Forebrain

Midbrain

Pons

Medulla

Anterolateral or spinothalamic system

Spinal cord

Aδ and C fibers

glutamate An amino acid transmitter, the most common excitatory transmitter.

substance P A peptide transmitter implicated in pain transmission.

endings in the skin send their axons to synapse on neurons in the dorsal horn of the spinal cord. These spinal cord neurons send their axons across the midline to the opposite side and up the anterolateral column of the spinal cord to the thalamus (hence the term *spinothalamic*). So, in the spinothalamic system pain information crosses the midline in the spinal cord before ascending to the brain (**Figure 8.23**); recall that touch information, in contrast, first ascends to the brainstem and then crosses the midline (see Figure 8.15). Either way, sensory information from one side of the body ends up in the opposite side of the brain.

The afferent fibers from the periphery that carry nociceptive information probably use **glutamate** as a neurotransmitter to excite spinal cells in the dorsal horn (S. Li and Tator, 2000), but they also release the neuromodulator **substance P**, which is a neuropeptide (the *P* stands for *peptide*). Injection of capsaicin into the skin provides a specific painful stimulus that leads to the release of substance P in the dorsal horn. There, the postsynaptic neurons take up the substance P and begin remodeling their dendrites; investigators have speculated that this neural plasticity later affects pain perception, as we'll see shortly (Mantyh et al., 1997).

Further evidence that substance P plays a role in pain comes from experiments with knockout mice that lack either the gene for the precursor to substance P

(Cao et al., 1998) or a gene for the substance P receptor (De Felipe et al., 1998). These mice are unresponsive to certain kinds of intense pain. Interestingly, they still respond to mildly painful stimuli, suggesting that other signals, perhaps the glutamate neurotransmitter, can carry that information.

Sometimes pain persists long after the injury that gave rise to it has healed. The most dramatic example is a person's continued perception of chronic pain coming from a missing limb after loss of an arm or leg. Called *phantom limb pain*, this sensation is an example of **neuropathic pain**, so called because the pain seems to be due to inappropriate signaling of pain by neurons (rather than to tissue damage). Such cases can be seen as a disagreeable example of neural plasticity, because the nervous system seems to have amplified its response to the pain signal (Woolf and Salter, 2000). Some of this amplification is taking place in the cortex (Flor et al., 2006), but changes in the spinal cord also contribute. After peripheral nerve injury (such as a damaged back or lost limb), microglial cells surround the synapses between pain fibers and neurons in the dorsal horn of the spinal cord (see Figure 8.23). These microglial cells release brain-derived neurotrophic factor (BDNF; see Chapter 7), which makes the dorsal horn neurons hyperexcitable: although GABA from other synapses had inhibited these neurons before, now GABA excites them (Milligan and Watkins, 2009). Thus, the dorsal horn neurons become chronically active, flooding the thalamus with action potentials signaling pain.

Chronic pain can have dramatic effects on the brain. One study found that the gray matter in the dorsolateral prefrontal cortex of people with chronic back pain shrinks faster than in normal aging, averaging 1.3 mm^3 more per year of pain (Apkarian et al., 2004). This shrinkage is equivalent to 10–20 years of normal aging.

Cases of phantom limb pain are notoriously difficult to treat. In one type, the patient perceives that a missing limb is twisted and therefore hurts. Vilayanur Ramachandran has proposed a treatment for this condition: the patient looks at himself in a mirror, positioned in such a way that the reflection of the intact limb seems to have filled in for the missing limb (**Figure 8.24**). The patient then repeatedly moves "both limbs" (by moving the remaining one), watching closely the whole while, and sometimes reports that the phantom limb feels as though it has straightened out and no longer hurts (Ramachandran and Rogers-Ramachandran, 2000). This result suggests that the brain interprets the signals coming from the limb stump as painful, but visual stimuli may lead to a reinterpretation.

Pain information is eventually integrated in the **cingulate cortex**. Recall from Chapter 1 that the cingulate cortex is much more activated by a stimulus if people are led to believe that the stimulus will be painful (see Figure 1.4) (Rainville et al., 1997). The extent of activation in the cingulate (as well as in somatosensory cortex) also correlates with how much discomfort different people report in response to the same mildly painful stimulus (Coghill et al., 2003). Studies suggest that the emotional and sensory components of pain are associated with different subregions of the cingulate cortex (Vogt, 2005). In people experiencing pain, both rostral and caudal cingulate were activated; but when they were *empathizing* with a loved one who was experiencing pain, only the rostral cingulate was activated (T. Singer et al., 2004).

The cingulate cortex is also activated in people experiencing illusory pain (Craig et al., 1996): placing your hand over alternating pipes of cool and warm (not hot) water produces the sensation of pain, as though the pipes were hot. Presumably this illusory pain sensation is produced by the unusual circumstance of neighboring CMR1 and TRPV1 receptors being stimulated at the same time. Since no tissue is actually being damaged, this is a wonderful illustration that "pain is in the brain."

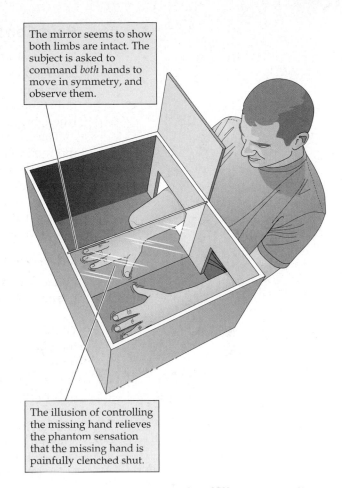

The mirror seems to show both limbs are intact. The subject is asked to command *both* hands to move in symmetry, and observe them.

The illusion of controlling the missing hand relieves the phantom sensation that the missing hand is painfully clenched shut.

8.24 Using a Visual Illusion to Relieve Phantom Limb Pain (After Ramachandran and Rogers-Ramachandran, 2000).

neuropathic pain Pain caused by damage to peripheral nerves; often difficult to treat.

cingulate cortex Also called *cingulum*. A region of medial cerebral cortex that lies dorsal to the corpus callosum.

Pain Control Can Be Difficult

Relief from the suffering of pain has long been a dominant concern of humans. Throughout history, different remedies have been offered. One frustrating, puzzling aspect of pain pathways is that cutting the pathway reduces pain perception only temporarily. After a pathway in the spinal cord is cut, pain is initially diminished, but it returns in a few weeks or months.

The usual way that these data are interpreted is that nociceptive input from the remaining intact pathways becomes abnormally effective. In an enormously influential paper, Melzack and Wall (1965) suggested that pain is subject to many modulating influences, including some that can close spinal "gates" controlling the flow of pain information from the spinal cord to the brain. Maybe the spinal gates get stuck open in some people, sending pain signals continuously, and maybe we could find strategies to close those gates to alleviate pain.

Different strategies can alleviate pain

In the sections that follow, we will discuss some of these strategies, which are prime examples of the interaction between basic research and application.

OPIATE DRUGS Opium has been used for **analgesia** (loss of pain sensation; from the Greek *an-*, "not," and *algesis*, "feeling of pain") for centuries. In attempts to determine how **opiates** (drugs, such as morphine, that are derived from or related to opium) control pain, modern researchers found that the brain contains natural opiate-like substances, or **opioids**. In effect, the brain modulates pain in a manner akin to how exogenous opioids such as morphine do. Three classes of **endogenous opioids**—**endorphins**, **enkephalins**, and **dynorphins**—have been discovered (see Chapter 4), and several classes of **opioid receptors** have been identified and designated by Greek letters. Of these, the mu (μ) receptor seems to be most affected by morphine. There are interesting individual differences in opioid receptor function. For example, analgesics that act on μ receptors are more effective in men than in women, while drugs that act on the kappa (κ) receptor are more effective in women than in men (Mogil and Chanda, 2005). Furthermore, the κ receptor–specific drugs are especially effective in redheaded women (Mogil et al., 2003).

Early observations showed that electrical stimulation of the **periaqueductal gray** area (see Figure 8.23) of the brainstem in rats produces potent analgesia. Injection of opiates into this area also relieves pain, suggesting that the region contains synaptic receptors for opiate-like substances. The periaqueductal gray area receives strong input from the spinal cord delivering nociceptive information.

According to one model, the brainstem controls pain transmission in the spinal cord. Periaqueductal gray neurons send endorphin-containing axons to stimulate neurons in the medulla. These medullary neurons send axons to the spinal cord, eventually stimulating neurons to release opioids there. In this way, pain information is blocked by a direct gating action in the spinal cord (**Figure 8.25**). Electrical stimulation of the descending tract inhibits the response of spinal cord sensory relay cells to noxious stimulation of the skin. Morphine provides analgesia by stimulating the opioid receptors in this descending pain control system, in both the brainstem and the spinal cord.

In addition to their beneficial pain-relieving effects, opiates and other analgesics (painkillers) often produce side effects such as confusion, drowsiness, vomiting, constipation, and depression of the respiratory system. Now that we know the circuitry of the pain relief system, why give large doses of the drug systemically (i.e., throughout the body)? Instead, physicians can administer very small doses of opiates directly to the spinal cord to relieve pain, thus avoiding many of the side effects. The drugs can be administered *epidurally* (just outside the spinal cord's dura mater) or *intrathecally* (between the dura mater and the spinal cord). Both

analgesia Absence of or reduction in pain.

opiates A class of compounds that exert an effect like that of opium, including reduced pain sensitivity.

opioids A class of peptides produced in various regions of the brain that bind to opioid receptors and act like opiates.

endogenous opioids A family of peptide transmitters that have been called the body's own narcotics. The three kinds are enkephalins, endorphins, and dynorphins.

endorphins One of three kinds of endogenous opioids.

enkephalins One of three kinds of endogenous opioids.

dynorphins One of three kinds of endogenous opioids.

opioid receptor A receptor that responds to endogenous and/or exogenous opioids.

periaqueductal gray The neuronal body–rich region of the midbrain surrounding the cerebral aqueduct that connects the third and fourth ventricles; involved in pain perception.

(*a*) Ascending pain communication pathways

(*b*) Descending pain modulation pathways

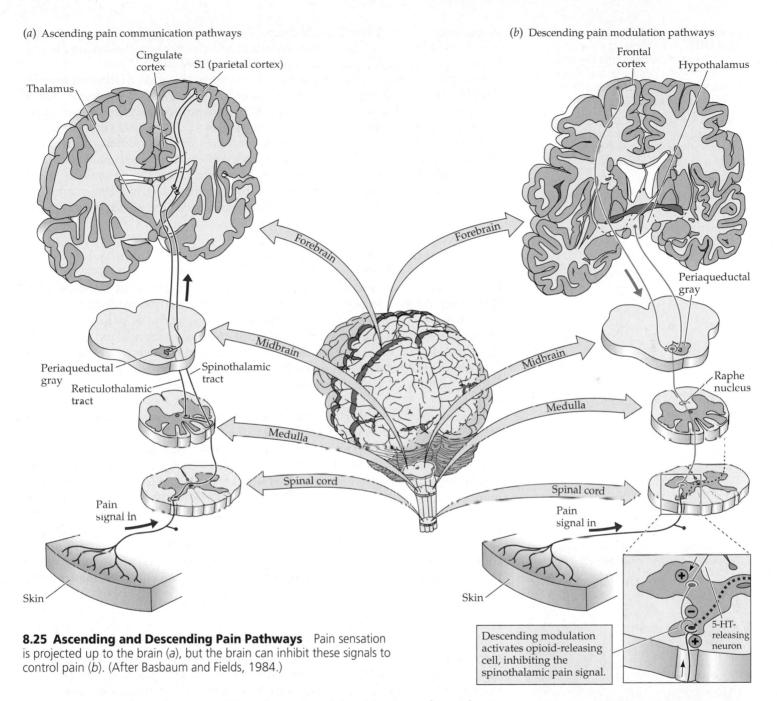

8.25 Ascending and Descending Pain Pathways   Pain sensation is projected up to the brain (*a*), but the brain can inhibit these signals to control pain (*b*). (After Basbaum and Fields, 1984.)

routes are somewhat invasive and therefore are restricted to surgical anesthesia, childbirth, or the management of severe chronic pain (Landau and Levy, 1993).

Because of long-standing concerns about the addictive potential of morphine and other opiates, the traditional standard for using them to relieve pain was to prescribe them only infrequently and in low doses. However, the Agency for Healthcare Research and Quality urges swift use of painkillers after surgery. Once chronic pain develops, it is extremely difficult to overcome, so the best approach is to prevent the onset of chronic pain by early, aggressive treatment. The danger of addiction from the use of morphine to relieve surgical pain has been vastly overexaggerated (Melzack, 1990); it is no more than 0.04% (Brownlee and Schrof, 1997). In the media, people addicted to painkillers are often said to have "gotten hooked" when given a prescription for pain. But further investigations reveal that almost all of these people had been drug abusers *before* they were given a prescription for pain (Szalavitz, 2004). Unfortunately, the myth that opiate treatment leads

transcutaneous electrical nerve stimulation (TENS) The delivery of electrical pulses through electrodes attached to the skin, which excite nerves that supply the region to which pain is referred. TENS can relieve the pain in some instances.

naloxone A potent antagonist of opiates that is often administered to people who have taken drug overdoses. It binds to receptors for endogenous opioids.

placebo A substance, given to a patient, that is known to be ineffective or inert but that sometimes brings relief.

acupuncture The insertion of needles at designated points on the skin to alleviate pain or neurological malfunction.

to addiction results in millions of people being undertreated for pain each year (Quill and Meier, 2006). So we will conclude this chapter by considering alternative means of controlling pain, as summarized in **Table 8.3**.

Marijuana's analgesic effect has been known for centuries. Marijuana reduces pain by stimulating endogenous cannabinoid receptors (CB_1 receptors), both in the spinal cord (Pernía-Andrade et al., 2009) and, surprisingly, in the free nerve endings of the nociceptors themselves (Agarwal et al., 2007). This latter discovery suggests it may be possible to devise topical creams that provide cannabinoid stimulation through the skin to relieve pain. Other, non-opioid analgesics may be available soon. The evidence that nerve growth factor (NGF; see Chapter 7) is one of the chemicals released by mechanical damage to trigger nociceptors is prompting the search for NGF receptor blockers that might alleviate pain (Summer et al., 2006).

STIMULATION OF THE SKIN Humans have tried some strange techniques to relieve pain. Centuries ago, for example, electric fishes or eels were applied to sites of pain. A modern version of such treatment, called **transcutaneous electrical nerve stimulation** (**TENS**), can suppress certain types of pain that are difficult to control. For some reason, stimulating the nerves around the source of pain provides relief, perhaps by closing the spinal "gate" for pain that Melzack and Wall (1965) described. Recall, for example, the last time you stubbed your toe. In addition to expelling a string of expletives, you may have vigorously rubbed the injured area, bringing a little relief. TENS is a more efficient way of stimulating those adjacent nerves.

In TENS treatment, electrical pulses delivered through electrodes attached to the skin excite nerves supplying the region that hurts. The stimulation itself produces a sense of tingling rather than pain. In some cases, dramatic relief of pain can outlast the stimulation by a factor of hours. TENS has been especially successful in the treatment of patients whose pain is derived from peripheral nerve injuries such as arthritis or surgical incisions. We know that TENS acts at least in part by releasing endogenous opioids, because administration of **naloxone**, an opioid antagonist, partially blocks this analgesic action. Cool temperatures can also soothe peripheral pain, and some investigators are trying to develop synthetic chemicals that are even better than menthol at stimulating the cool-menthol receptors described earlier to relieve pain (Proudfoot et al., 2006). Recall that rubbing capsaicin on aching joints also sometimes provides pain relief.

8.26 Placebo Affects Opioid Systems in the Brain Volunteers were subjected to a painful procedure and given a placebo for the pain. Some subjects seemed to respond to the placebo, but others did not. This difference image shows brain regions that were more activated in responders than in nonresponders. These regions are rich in receptors for endogenous opioids (D. J. Scott et al., 2008). (From Wager et al., 2007; Courtesy Jon-Kar Zubieta.)

PLACEBOS The search for pain relief has led people to consume many unusual substances; even chemically inert pills alleviate pain in many patients. The term **placebo** (Latin for "I shall please") refers to an inert substance (such as a sugar pill) or other treatment that has no obvious direct physiological effect. In one example, volunteer subjects who had just had their wisdom teeth extracted were told that they were being given an analgesic but were not told what kind (J. D. Levine et al., 1978). Some of these patients received morphine-based drugs, and some were given saline solutions—the placebo. One out of three patients given the placebo experienced pain relief. (Morphine produced relief in most, but not all, patients.)

The researchers gave the opioid antagonist naloxone to other patients, who were also administered the placebo. Patients given the placebo *and* naloxone did not experience pain relief; this result implies that placebo relieves pain by causing the release of endogenous opioids. Functional brain imaging indicates that opioids and placebos activate the same brain regions (Petrovic et al., 2002), and that both treatments reduce the activity of brain regions responding to pain, including cingulate cortex (Wager et al., 2004). A consistent finding is that some people experience relief from a placebo and others do not. People who respond to placebo show a greater activation of brain regions with opioid receptors than do nonresponders (**Figure 8.26**), further implicating endogenous opioids in the placebo effect.

ACUPUNCTURE The earliest description of pain relief from **acupuncture** is at least 3000 years old. In some acupuncture procedures the needles are manipulated once they are in position; in others, electrical or heat stimulation is delivered through the inserted needles. Acupuncture has gained popularity, but only some people achieve continued relief from chronic pain. At least part of the pain-blocking character of acupuncture appears to be mediated by the release of endorphins, because administering opioid antagonists such as naloxone prior to acupuncture blocks or reduces its pain control effects (N. M. Tang et al., 1997).

Pain relief from acupuncture is also at least partly due to placebo effect. Thousands of years of acupuncture tradition indicate that the points at which needles are inserted must be chosen carefully to match the type of pain and its location on the body (**Figure 8.27**). But one report that acupuncture relieves headaches in many people also found that *where* the needles were inserted *made no difference* (Linde et al., 2009). The expectation that the needles will relieve pain appears to release endogenous opioids, which indeed relieve pain.

8.27 Acupuncture for Controlling Pain In some cases, acupuncture controls pain. Opioid antagonists block this analgesia, indicating that acupuncture, like placebo, activates endogenous opioids.

TABLE 8.3 Types of Pain Relief Intervention

Measure	Mechanism	Limitations/comments
PSYCHOGENIC		
Placebo	May activate endorphin-mediated pain control system	Ethical concerns of deceiving patient
Hypnosis	Alters brain's perception of pain	Control unaffected by opiate antagonists
Stress	Both opioid and non-opioid mechanisms	Clinically impractical and inappropriate
Cognitive (learning, coping strategies)	May activate endorphin-mediated pain control system	Limited usefulness for severe pain
PHARMACOLOGICAL		
Opiates	Bind to opioid receptors in periaqueductal gray and spinal cord	Severe side effects due to binding in other brain regions
Spinal block	Drugs block pain signals in spinal cord	Avoids side effects of systemic administration
Anti-inflammatory drugs	Block prostaglandin and/or leukotriene synthesis at site of injury (see Figure 8.21)	Major side effects
Cannabinoids	Act in spinal cord and on nociceptor endings	Illegal in some regions; smoke damages lungs
STIMULATION		
TENS/mechanical	Tactile or electrical stimulation of large fibers blocks or alters pain signal to brain	Segmental control; must be applied at site of pain
Acupuncture	Seems similar to TENS	Sometimes affected by opiate antagonists
Central gray	Electrical stimulation activates endorphin-mediated pain control systems, blocking pain signal in spinal cord	Control inhibited by opiate antagonists; invasive surgery to implant electrodes
SURGICAL		
Cut peripheral nerve cord		
Rhizotomy (cutting dorsal root)	Create physical break in pain pathway	Considerable risk of failure or return of pain
Cord hemisection		
Frontal lobotomy	Disrupts affective response to pain	Irreversible; risky; severe effects on behavior

STRESS   A deer fleeing an encounter with a mountain lion would do well to ignore any pain from injuries for the moment. Similarly, sometimes people badly hurt in traumatic circumstances report little or no immediate pain. Laboratory studies demonstrate the existence of pain control circuitry, but they don't tell us how the inhibitory systems are normally activated.

To answer this question, researchers have examined pain inhibition that arises in stressful circumstances. It appears that brain systems produce analgesia when pain threatens to overwhelm effective coping strategies. For example, exposing rats to several different kinds of inescapable foot shock induces analgesia (Terman et al., 1984). Stress analgesia may be blocked by the opiate antagonist naltrexone or not, depending on the type of stress, indicating that stress activates both an opioid-sensitive analgesic system and a pain control system that does *not* involve opioids. In some cases, the non-opioid analgesia is caused by the release of cannabinoids (Hohmann et al., 2005). As we mentioned earlier, cannabinoids seem to block pain by acting both in the spinal cord and on the nociceptor nerve endings themselves.

The many types of pain relief strategies, including surgical and pharmacological strategies, psychological treatments, brain and spinal cord stimulation, and sensory stimulation reflect how powerfully pain affects us. The elusive nature of pain is also evident in this range of potential interventions, some of which reflect desperation in the face of great anguish. As we learn more about how the brain controls pain, we can hope for better, safer analgesics in the future.

SUMMARY

SENSORY PROCESSING

Sensory Receptor Organs Detect Energy or Substances

■ A sensory system furnishes selected information to the brain about internal and external events and conditions. It captures and processes only information that is significant for the particular organism. **Review Table 8.1**

What Type of Stimulus Was That?

■ Some **stimuli** are detected readily by some species but have no effect on species that lack the necessary **sensory receptor organs**.

Sensory Processing Begins in Receptor Cells

■ Some **receptors** are simple free nerve endings, but most include cells that are specialized to transduce particular kinds of energy. **Review Figures 8.4 and 8.13**, **Web Activity 8.1**

■ Energy is transduced at sensory receptors by the production of a **generator potential** that stimulates the sensory neurons. **Review Figure 8.5**

Sensory Information Processing Is Selective and Analytical

■ **Coding** translates receptor information into patterns of neural activity. The frequency and pattern of action potentials signal the intensity and type of stimulus encountered. **Review Figure 8.6**

■ In **adaptation**, the rate of action potentials progressively decreases as the same stimulation is maintained. This decline is slow in the case of **tonic receptors** but rapid for **phasic receptors**. Adaptation protects the nervous system from redundant stimulation. **Review Figure 8.7**

■ Other mechanisms of information suppression include accessory structures that reduce the level of sensory input, and descending pathways that modulate sensory information centrally.

■ The succession of levels in a **sensory pathway** allows for increasingly elaborate kinds of processing. **Review Figure 8.8**

■ The **receptive field** of a neuron is the region in space where a stimulus will change the firing of that cell. The receptive fields of neurons may be very different at successive levels of the sensory pathway. **Review Figure 8.9**, **Web Activity 8.2**

■ **Attention** is the temporary enhancement of certain sensory messages during particular states. Attention is modulated at higher levels of the sensory pathway. **Review Figure 8.12**

TOUCH: MANY SENSATIONS BLENDED TOGETHER

Skin Is a Complex Organ That Contains a Variety of Sensory Receptors

■ The skin contains several distinct types of receptors that have specific sensitivities and use large, myelinated axons to transmit information rapidly. Inputs from the skin course through a distinct spinal pathway, the **dorsal column system**. **Review Figure 8.15**, **Web Activity 8.3**

- **Merkel's discs** and **Meissner's corpuscles** detect fine touch, while **Pacinian corpuscles** and **Ruffini's endings** respond to vibration and stretch, providing information about textures. **Review Table 8.2**

The Dorsal Column System Carries Somatosensory Information from the Skin to the Brain

- The surface of the body is represented at each level of the somatosensory system, and at the level of the cerebral cortex there are multiple maps of the body surface. **Review Figure 8.16**

- Touch information enters the spinal cord and ascends the **dorsal column system** to the medulla, synapsing on neurons in the dorsal column nuclei. These neurons in turn send their axons across the midline and to the thalamus.

PAIN: AN UNPLEASANT BUT ADAPTIVE EXPERIENCE

Human Pain Can Be Measured

- **Pain** guides adaptive behavior by providing indications of harmful stimuli. Pain is a complex state that is strongly influenced by cultural factors and emotional state.

A Specific Pathway Transmits Pain Information

- **Free nerve endings** detect mechanical damage or temperature changes because they have specialized receptor proteins that detect these conditions (such as **transient receptor potential vanilloid 1 [TRPV1]**, which detects heat and is activated by chili peppers), opening up ion channels to trigger action potentials. Some peripheral pain fibers have fairly large, myelinated axons to transmit sharp pain rapidly; others use small, unmyelinated axons to transmit dull, aching pain after injury. **Review Figure 8.22**

- Pain, temperature, and itch information enters the spinal cord, crosses the midline, and ascends through the **anterolateral (spinothalamic) system** to the brain. **Review Figure 8.23**, **Web Activity 8.4**

Pain Control Can Be Difficult

- Pain sensation is subject to many controlling or modulating conditions, including circuitry within the brain and spinal cord that employs **opioid** synapses. One component in the modulation of pain is made up of the descending pathways arising in the brain that inhibit incoming neural activity at synapses within the spinal cord. **Review Figure 8.25**, **Web Activity 8.5**

- Pain control has been achieved by the administration of drugs (including **placebos**), electrical and mechanical stimulation of the skin, **acupuncture**, and surgery, among other methods. **Review Table 8.3**

Go to www.biopsychology.com for study questions, quizzes, key terms, and other resources.

Recommended Reading

Ballantyne, J. C., and Fishman, S. M. (Eds.). (2010). *Bonica's management of pain* (4th ed.). Philadelphia: Lippincott.

Basbaum, A. I., and Julius, D. (2006). Toward better pain control. *Scientific American*, 294(6), 60–67.

Cytowic, R. E., and Eagleman, D. M. (2009). *Wednesday is indigo blue.* Cambridge: MIT Press.

Lumpkin, E. A., and Caterina, M. J. (2007). Mechanisms of sensory transduction in the skin. *Nature, 445*, 858–865.

Melzack, R., and Wall, P. D. (2002). *The challenge of pain* (2nd ed.). London: Penguin Global.

Merskey, H., Loeser, J. D., and Dubner, R. (2005). *The paths of pain: 1975–2005.* Seattle, WA: IASP Press.

Wolfe, J. M., Kluender, J. R., Levi, D. M., Bartoshuk, L. M., et al. (2008). *Sensation and perception* (2nd ed.). Sunderland, MA: Sinauer.

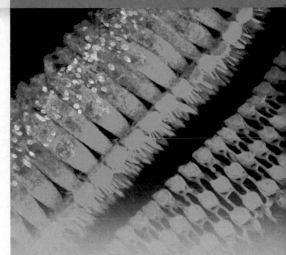

Hearing, Vestibular Perception, Taste, and Smell

CHAPTER 9

No Ear for Music

Given the category "wedding music," you will probably immediately think of a tune or two that you can hear in your head—perhaps "The Wedding March" or, less fortunately, "The Chicken Dance." The same goes for Beethoven's Fifth Symphony, or the theme from *Star Wars*. These pieces of music, and others like them, are tunes that most people can identify right away, after hearing just a few bars. But Tony is different.

Tony is completely flummoxed by music. His ability to understand pitch, and the relationships between chords, is nearly at chance levels. Although he is happy to try to belt out a song, he is unable to sing in tune and doesn't even recognize that he is singing off-key unless he is told so by a (grimacing) friend. He cannot identify the tune to "Happy Birthday" unless he also hears the lyrics, in which case he can identify it immediately. Yet he has no problem with nonmusical uses of pitch, such as the rising tone at the end of a question.

Tony is a man of better-than-average intelligence, with perfectly normal cognitive functioning, except for his lifelong inability to appreciate music despite years of childhood music lessons. This highly specific difficulty with music is an affliction that Tony has in common with many other people; revolutionary Che Guevara and Nobel Prize–winning economist Milton Friedman are two noted examples.

What is the nature of this mysterious problem? Is it a kind of hearing problem? A learning disability?

You exist only because your ancestors had keen senses that enabled them to find food and to avoid predators and other dangers. In this chapter we turn to systems that allow us to sense signals from distant sources, particularly sounds (audition) and smells (olfaction). We also discuss related systems for detecting position and movement of the body (the vestibular system, related to the auditory system) and tastes of foods (the gustatory or taste sense, which, like olfaction, is a chemical sense). We begin with hearing because audition evolved from special mechanical receptors related to the somatosensory elements that we discussed in Chapter 8.

Hearing

Hearing is vital for the survival of many animals. For humans, the sounds of speech form the basic elements of languages and therefore of social relations. Helen Keller, who was both blind and deaf, said, "Blindness deprives you of contact with things; deafness deprives you of contact with people."

The sounds of any single language are only a small subset of the enormous variety of sounds that can be produced by the human vocal cavity. The sounds produced by animals—from insects to whales—also have a wide range of complexity, in keeping with their adaptive significance. For example, the melodic songs of male birds and the chirps of male crickets attract females of their species. The grunts, screeches,

transduction The conversion of one form of energy to another.

external ear The part of the ear that we readily see (the pinna) and the canal that leads to the eardrum.

pinna The external part of the ear.

and burbly sounds of primates signal danger or the need for comfort or satisfaction. Elephants can recognize individuals by their calls (McComb et al., 2000). Owls and bats exploit the directional property of sound to locate prey and avoid obstacles in the dark, and whales employ sounds that can travel hundreds of miles in the ocean. Unlike visual stimuli, sounds can go around obstacles, and they work as well in the dark as in the light.

Your auditory system detects rapid changes of sound *intensity* (measured in decibels, dB) and *frequency* (measured in cycles per second or hertz, Hz). Your ear is so sensitive to sounds in the middle of the hearing range that, if it were any more sensitive, you would be distracted by the noise of air molecules bouncing against each other in your ear canal! **Box 9.1** describes some basic properties of sound.

Each Part of the Ear Performs a Specific Function in Hearing

How do small vibrations of air molecules become the speech, music, and other sounds we hear? The outer parts of the auditory system have been shaped through evolution to capture biologically important sound vibrations and direct them toward the highly specialized auditory organs where the mechanical force of sound is **transduced** into neural activity.

The external ear captures, focuses, and filters sound

Sound waves are collected by the **external ear**, which consists of the part we readily see, called the **pinna** (plural *pinnae*; Latin for "wing"), and a canal that leads to the eardrum. The pinna is a distinctly mammalian characteristic, and mammals show a wide array of ear shapes and sizes.

The "hills and valleys" of the pinna modify the character of sound that reaches the middle ear. Some frequencies of sound are enhanced; others are suppressed. For example, the shape of the human ear especially increases the reception of sounds between 2000 and 5000 Hz—a frequency range that is important for speech perception. The shape of the external ear is also important in identifying the direction and distance of the source of a sound (discussed later in this chapter).

Although (some) humans can move their ears only enough to entertain children, many other mammals deftly shape and swivel their pinnae to help determine the source of a sound (**Figure 9.1**). Animals with exceptional auditory localization abilities, such as bats, may have especially mobile ears. Of course, animals with mobile ears have to take into account the position of the pinnae when interpreting sounds around them. Receptors in the pinnae, as well as the muscles attached to them, provide information to the auditory pathways about the position of the external ears.

9.1 The Ears Have It The external ears, or pinnae, of mammals come in a variety of shapes, each adapted to a particular niche. Many mammals can move their ears to direct them toward a particular sound. In such cases, the brain must account for the position of the ear in judging where a particular sound came from.

BOX 9.1 The Basics of Sound

We perceive a repetitive pattern of local increases and decreases in air pressure as sound. Usually this oscillation is caused by a vibrating object, such as a tuning fork or a person's larynx during speaking. A single alternation of compression and expansion of air is called one *cycle*.

Figure A illustrates the changes in pressure produced by a vibrating tuning fork. Because the sound produced by a tuning fork has only one frequency of vibration, it is called a **pure tone** and can be represented by a sine wave. A pure tone is described physically in terms of two measures:

1. **Amplitude**, or intensity—usually measured as sound pressure, or force per unit area, in dynes per square centimeter (dyn/cm²). Our perception of amplitude is termed **loudness**.
2. **Frequency**, or the number of cycles per second, measured in **hertz** (**Hz**). For example, middle A on a piano has a frequency of 440 Hz. Our perception of frequency is termed **pitch**.

Most sounds are more complicated than a pure tone. For example, a sound made by a musical instrument contains a fundamental frequency and harmonics. The **fundamental** is the basic frequency, and the **harmonics** are multiples of the fundamental. Thus, if the fundamental is 440 Hz, the harmonics are 880, 1320, 1760, and so on. When different instruments play the same note, the notes differ in the relative intensities of the various harmonics; this difference is what gives each instrument its characteristic sound quality, or **timbre**.

Any complex sound can be decomposed into a sum of simple sine waves, through a mathematical process called **Fourier analysis**. (We will see in Chapter 10 that Fourier analysis can also be applied to visual patterns.) Figure B shows how several pure-tone sine waves can be summed to produce a complex waveform.

Because the ear is sensitive to a huge range of sound pressures, sound intensity (a measure of the difference between two pressures) is usually expressed in **decibels** (**dB**), a logarithmic scale. The common reference level for human hearing is

0.0002 dyn/cm², the smallest amplitude at which an average human ear can detect a 1000-Hz tone. A faint whisper is about ten times as intense, and a jet airliner 500 feet overhead is about a million times as intense. The whisper is about 20 dB above threshold, and the jetliner is about 120 dB above threshold. Normal conversation is about 60 dB above the reference level.

pure tone   A tone with a single frequency of vibration.

amplitude   The force sound exerts per unit area, usually measured as dynes per square centimeter.

loudness   The subjective experience of the pressure level of a sound.

frequency   The number of cycles per second in a sound wave; measured in hertz (Hz).

hertz (Hz)   Cycles per second, as of an auditory stimulus.

pitch   A dimension of auditory experience in which sounds vary from low to high.

fundamental   The predominant frequency of an auditory tone or a visual scene.

harmonics   Multiples of a particular frequency called the *fundamental*.

timbre   The characteristic sound quality of a musical instrument, as determined by the relative intensities of its various harmonics.

Fourier analysis   The analysis of a complex pattern into the sum of sine waves.

decibel (dB)   A measure of sound intensity.

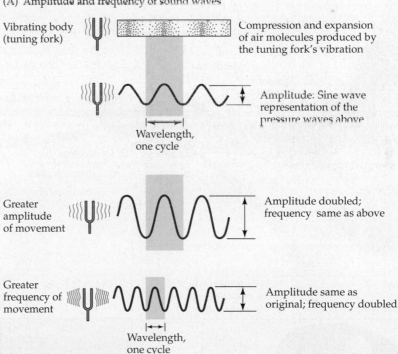

(A) Amplitude and frequency of sound waves

Vibrating body (tuning fork) — Compression and expansion of air molecules produced by the tuning fork's vibration

Amplitude: Sine wave representation of the pressure waves above

Wavelength, one cycle

Greater amplitude of movement — Amplitude doubled; frequency same as above

Greater frequency of movement — Amplitude same as original; frequency doubled

Wavelength, one cycle

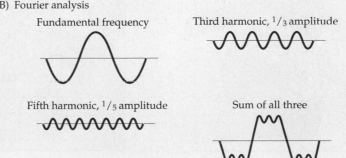

(B) Fourier analysis

Fundamental frequency

Third harmonic, ¹/₃ amplitude

Fifth harmonic, ¹/₅ amplitude

Sum of all three

middle ear The cavity between the tympanic membrane and the cochlea.

ossicles Three small bones (incus, malleus, and stapes) that transmit sound across the middle ear, from the tympanic membrane to the oval window.

tympanic membrane Also called *eardrum*. The partition between the external ear and the middle ear.

oval window The opening from the middle ear to the inner ear.

malleus Latin for "hammer." A middle-ear bone that is connected to the tympanic membrane.

The middle ear concentrates sound energies

Between the external ear and the receptor cells of the inner ear (**Figure 9.2a**) is a group of structures, including bones and muscles, that constitute the **middle ear** (**Figure 9.2b**). A chain of three tiny bones, or **ossicles**, connects the **tympanic membrane** (eardrum) at the end of the ear canal to an opening of the inner ear called the **oval window**. These ossicles, the smallest bones in the body, are called the **malleus** (Latin for "hammer"), the **incus** (Latin for "anvil"), and the **stapes** (Latin for "stirrup").

Small displacements of the tympanic membrane move the chain of ossicles. These bones help concentrate the tiny mechanical forces of vibrating air particles, focusing the pressures from the relatively large tympanic membrane onto the small oval window. This arrangement vastly amplifies sound pressure so that it can produce movement in the fluid of the inner ear, as we'll see.

Two muscles vary the mechanical linkage between the ossicles to improve auditory perception and protect the delicate inner ear from loud, potentially damaging sounds. One of these muscles, the **tensor tympani** (see Figure 9.2b), is attached to the malleus, which is connected to the tympanic membrane. The other muscle of the middle ear is attached to

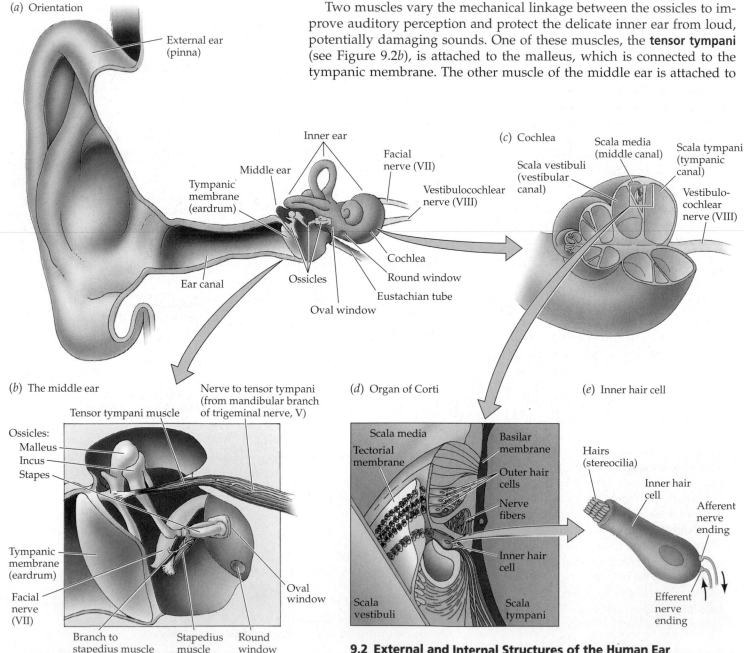

9.2 External and Internal Structures of the Human Ear

the stapes and thus is called the **stapedius**. When activated, these muscles stiffen the linkages of the middle-ear bones, thereby reducing the effectiveness of sounds. When a loud sound reaches the ear, the stapedius muscle starts to contract about 200 ms later. The middle-ear muscles also attenuate self-made sounds; without this system, body movement, swallowing, vocalizations, and other internally produced sounds would be distractingly loud. Species that produce especially loud calls, such as bats, rely on this system to protect their auditory receptors from physical damage (Avan et al., 1992). Interestingly, the middle-ear muscles contract just *before* the self-made sound occurs, in anticipation of a cough, for example. People whose middle-ear muscles have been damaged by disease complain about the annoying loudness of such sounds, which they formerly ignored.

The cochlea converts vibrational energy into waves of fluid

The complex structures of the **inner ear** ultimately convert sound into neural activity. In mammals the auditory portion of the inner ear is a coiled, fluid-filled structure called the **cochlea** (from the Greek *kochlos*, "snail") (**Figure 9.2c and d**). Embedded in the temporal bone of the skull, the human cochlea is a marvel of miniaturization. In an adult, the cochlea measures only about 4 mm in diameter—about the size of a pea. Unrolled, the cochlea would measure about 35–40 mm in length.

The region nearest the oval-window membrane is the *base* of the spiral; the other end is referred to as the *apex*. The cochlea is a coil of three parallel canals: (1) the **scala vestibuli** (*vestibular canal*), (2) the **scala media** (*middle canal*), and (3) the **scala tympani** (*tympanic canal*) (see Figure 9.2c). Because these canals are filled with noncompressible fluid, movement inside the cochlea in response to a push on the oval window requires a second membrane-covered window that can bulge outward a bit. This membrane is the **round window**, which separates the scala tympani from the middle ear (see Figure 9.2b).

The principal components that do the work of converting sounds into neural activity, collectively known as the **organ of Corti** (see Figure 9.2d), consist of three main structures: (1) the sensory cells (**hair cells**) (**Figure 9.2a**), (2) an elaborate framework of supporting cells, and (3) the terminations of the auditory fibers. The base of the organ of Corti is the **basilar membrane**. This flexible membrane separates the scala tympani from the scala media and, importantly, vibrates in response to sound. The basilar membrane is about five times wider at the apex of the cochlea than at the base, even though the cochlea itself narrows toward its apex.

When the stapes moves in and out as a result of acoustic vibrations, it exerts varying pressure on the fluid of the scala vestibuli, which in turn causes oscillating movements of the basilar membrane. Different parts of the basilar membrane are affected by different frequencies of sound (**Figure 9.3**). High frequencies cause maximal displacement of the basilar membrane near the base, where the membrane is narrow. For low-frequency stimuli, displacement of the basilar membrane is greatest where the membrane is wider—toward the apex (Ashmore, 1994).

The hair cells transduce movements of the basilar membrane into electrical signals

Each human ear contains two sets of hair cells within the organ of Corti: a single row of about 3500 **inner hair cells** (**IHCs**; called *inner* because they are closer to the central axis of the coiled cochlea) and about 12,000 **outer hair cells** (**OHCs**) in three rows (see Figure 9.2d).

From the upper end of each hair cell protrude tiny hairs that range from 2 to 6 μm in length (see Figure 9.2e). Each hair cell has 50–200 of these relatively stiff hairs, called **stereocilia** (singular *stereocilium*; from the Greek *stereos*, "solid," and the Latin *cilium*, "eyelid") or simply *cilia*. The heights of the stereocilia increase progressively across the hair cell, so the tops form a slope. Atop the organ of Corti is the **tectorial membrane** (see Figure 9.2d). The stereocilia of the OHCs extend into indentations in the bottom of this membrane.

incus Latin for "anvil." A middle-ear bone situated between the malleus and the stapes.

stapes Latin for "stirrup." A middle-ear bone that is connected to the oval window.

tensor tympani The muscle attached to the malleus that modulates mechanical linkage to protect the delicate receptor cells of the inner ear from damaging sounds.

stapedius A middle-ear muscle that is attached to the stapes.

inner ear The cochlea and vestibular apparatus.

cochlea A snail-shaped structure in the inner ear that contains the primary receptor cells for hearing.

scala vestibuli Also called *vestibular canal*. One of three principal canals running along the length of the cochlea.

scala media Also called *middle canal*. The central of the three spiraling canals inside the cochlea, situated between the scala vestibuli and the scala tympani.

scala tympani Also called *tympanic canal*. One of three principal canals running along the length of the cochlea.

round window A membrane separating the cochlear duct from the middle-ear cavity.

organ of Corti A structure in the inner ear that lies on the basilar membrane of the cochlea and contains the hair cells and terminations of the auditory nerve.

hair cell One of the receptor cells for hearing in the cochlea.

basilar membrane A membrane in the cochlea that contains the principal structures involved in auditory transduction.

inner hair cell (IHC) One of the two types of receptor cells for hearing in the cochlea.

outer hair cell (OHC) One of the two types of receptor cells for hearing in the cochlea.

stereocilium A relatively stiff hair that protrudes from a hair cell in the auditory or vestibular system.

tectorial membrane A membrane that sits atop the organ of Corti in the cochlear duct.

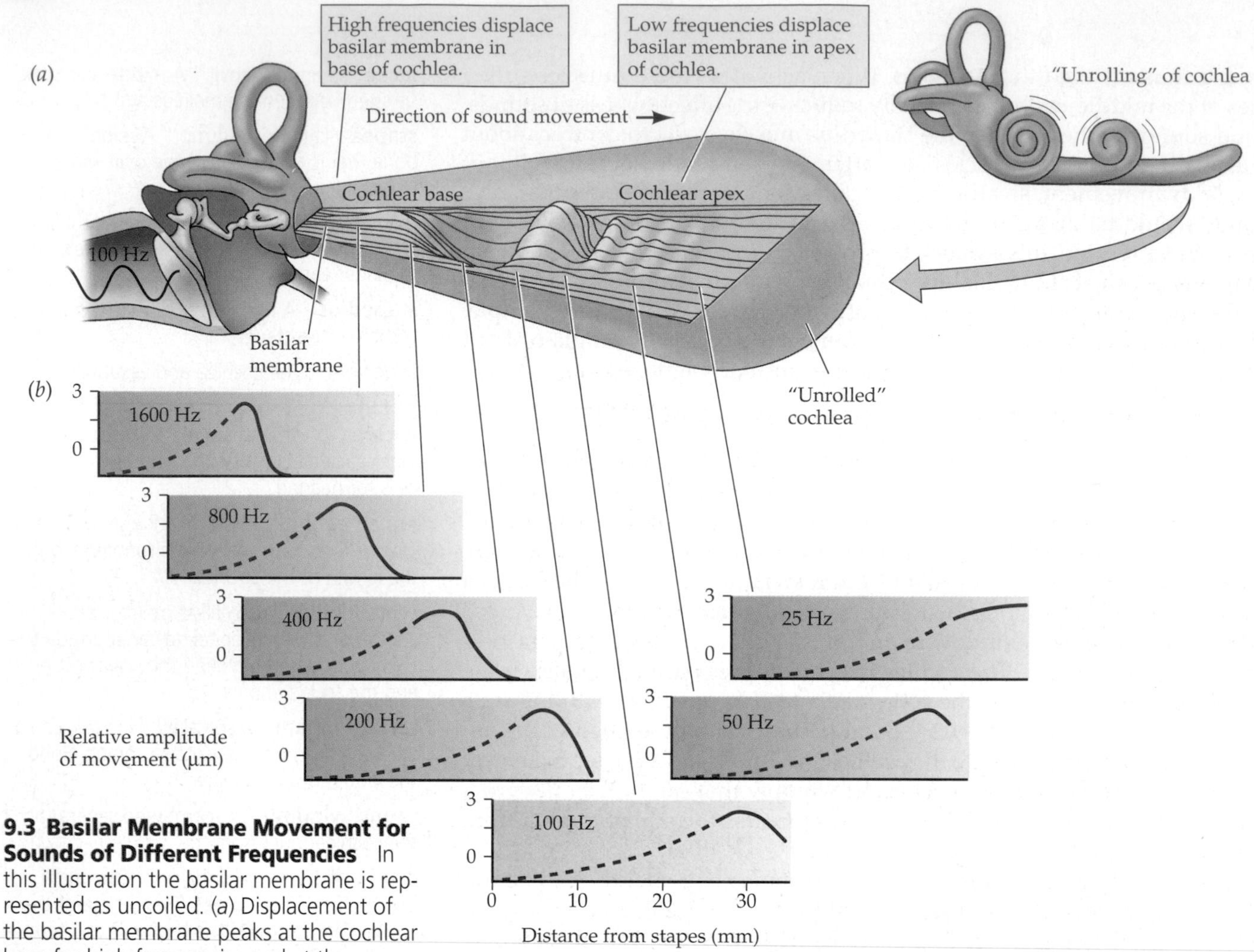

(a)

High frequencies displace basilar membrane in base of cochlea.

Low frequencies displace basilar membrane in apex of cochlea.

"Unrolling" of cochlea

Direction of sound movement →

Cochlear base

Cochlear apex

100 Hz

Basilar membrane

"Unrolled" cochlea

(b)

1600 Hz

800 Hz

400 Hz

Relative amplitude of movement (µm)

200 Hz

25 Hz

50 Hz

9.3 Basilar Membrane Movement for Sounds of Different Frequencies In this illustration the basilar membrane is represented as uncoiled. (a) Displacement of the basilar membrane peaks at the cochlear base for high frequencies and at the apex for low frequencies. (b) As the frequency of stimulation—measured in hertz (Hz), or cycles per second—decreases, the peak of membrane movement is displaced progressively toward the apex of the cochlea.

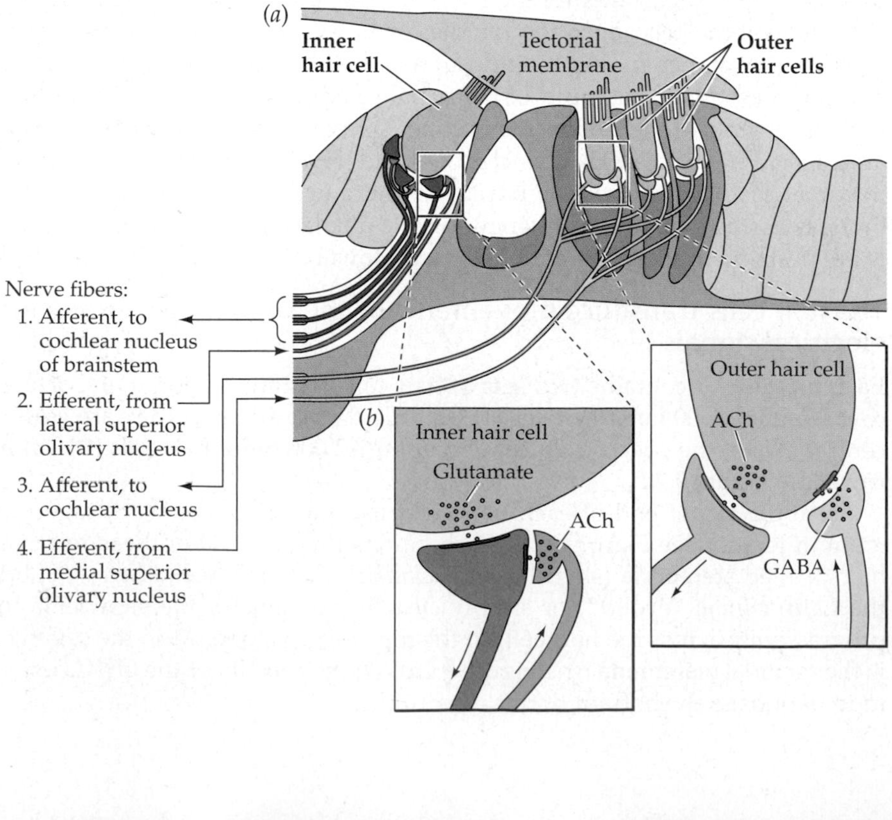

100 Hz

Distance from stapes (mm)

(a)

Inner hair cell

Tectorial membrane

Outer hair cells

Nerve fibers:
1. Afferent, to cochlear nucleus of brainstem

2. Efferent, from lateral superior olivary nucleus

3. Afferent, to cochlear nucleus

4. Efferent, from medial superior olivary nucleus

Outer hair cell

ACh

(b)

Inner hair cell

Glutamate

ACh

GABA

9.4 Auditory Nerve Fibers and Synapses in the Organ of Corti (a) The inner and outer hair cells form synaptic connections to and from the brain. (b) Different synaptic transmitters are hypothesized to be active at the synapses of inner and outer hair cells in the organ of Corti.

Auditory nerve fibers contact the base of the hair cells (see Figure 9.2*e*). The organ of Corti has four kinds of synapses and nerve fibers. Two of these (1 and 3 in **Figure 9.4*a***) are *afferents* that convey messages from the hair cells to the brain; the other two (2 and 4 in Figure 9.4*a*) are *efferents* that convey messages from the brain to the hair cells. Different synaptic transmitters are active at each type of synapse (**Figure 9.4*b***) (Eybalin, 1993). Each IHC is associated with 16–20 auditory nerve fibers; relatively few nerve fibers contact the many OHCs. In fact, the afferent nerve fibers running from the IHCs account for 90%–95% of the afferent auditory fibers, and give rise to the perception of sound. Thus, mutant mice that lack IHCs but have normal OHCs are deaf (Deol and Glueksohn-Waelsch, 1979).

The OHCs don't detect sound; they push on the tectorial membrane in response to commands from the brain via the efferent nerve fibers. The OHCs change their length (Zheng et al., 2000), thereby fine-tuning the organ of Corti, as we'll discuss shortly. The IHCs also receive efferent messages (blue fibers in 9.4*b*), probably to inhibit afferent responses to loud sounds.

How do IHCs turn movement into neural activity? As sounds induce vibrations of the basilar membrane, the vibrations bend the hair cell stereocilia that are inserted into the tectorial membrane (see Figure 9.2*d*). Very small displacements of hair bundles cause rapid changes in ionic channels of the stereocilia. These electrical changes excite IHCs, which release neurotransmitter to trigger action potentials in afferent axons (**Figure 9.5**). The action potentials reach the brain via the vestibulocochlear nerve (cranial nerve VIII), as we discuss shortly.

Each hair cell has only about 100 ion channels, about one or two per stereocilium, located toward the tops of the cilia. Fine, threadlike fibers called **tip links**

tip link   A fine, threadlike fiber that runs along and connects the tips of stereocilia.

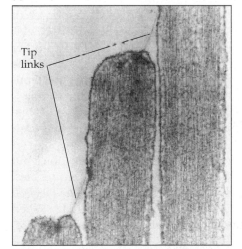

9.5 How Auditory Stimulation Affects the Stereocilia on Cochlear Hair Cells
(*a*) This micrograph of stereocilia shows the threadlike tip links. (*b*) Hudspeth (1992) proposed the model of hair cell stimulation illustrated here. Displacement of the stereocilia (*right*) opens large, nonselective ion channels, allowing K^+ and Ca^{2+} to enter the stereocilia. The resulting depolarization opens Ca^{2+} channels in the cell's base, causing the release of neurotransmitter to excite afferent nerves. Here we depict the channels near the top of each tip link, but they may be near the bottom (Beurg et al., 2009). (Micrograph courtesy of A. J. Hudspeth.)

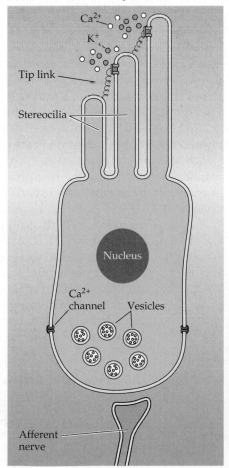

(*b*) Before stereocilia displacement

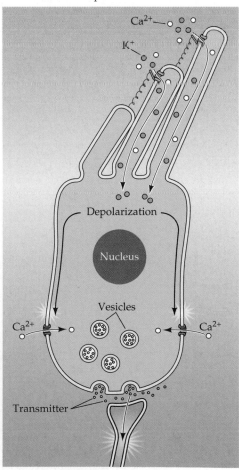

After stereocilia displacement

cochlear amplifier   The mechanism by which the cochlea is physically distorted by outer hair cells in order to "tune" the cochlea to be particularly sensitive to some frequencies more than others.

otoacoustic emission   A sound produced by the cochlea itself, either spontaneously or in response to an environmental noise.

tuning curve   A graph of the responses of a single auditory nerve fiber or neuron to sounds that vary in frequency and intensity.

run along the tips of the stereocilia. These tip links play a key role in the generation of hair cell potentials. Sounds that cause the stereocilia to sway, even only very slightly, increase the tension on the elastic tip links and pop open the ion channels to which they are attached (Hudspeth, 1997; Hudspeth et al., 2000). The channels snap shut again in a fraction of a millisecond as the hair cell sways back. The ion channels of stereocilia resemble trapdoors or portholes and appear to consist of a channel protein, called TRPA1 (for *transient receptor potential type A1*) (Corey et al., 2004), that contains a springlike component—so in a real sense, a stereocilium ion channel is spring-loaded with a hair trigger.

Opening of the channels allows an inrush of potassium (K^+) and calcium (Ca^{2+}) ions and rapid depolarization of the entire hair cell. This initial depolarization leads to a rapid influx of Ca^{2+} at the *base* of the hair cell, which causes synaptic vesicles there to fuse with the presynaptic membrane and release their transmitter contents—probably glutamate—from the base of the hair cell, and stimulate the afferent nerve fiber (see Figure 9.5*b*).

Active electromechanical processes in the cochlea enhance frequency discrimination

Humans can discriminate between sounds that differ in frequency by just 2 Hz. The basic physical characteristics of the basilar membrane cannot account for such sharp discrimination of sounds, so an additional sharpening process must be at work. It turns out that the OHCs fine-tune the cochlea to permit finer discrimination of frequencies. We mentioned earlier that OHCs show the surprising property of changing length when their membrane potential changes (Brownell et al., 1985). Hyperpolarization causes the OHCs to lengthen; depolarization causes them to shorten. These changes, which affect the length of the cell by as much as 4%, can stiffen or relax segments of the basilar membrane and thus actively sharpen its tuning to different frequencies (Ashmore, 1994). These mechanical responses of the OHCs serve as a **cochlear amplifier**, amplifying the movements of the basilar membrane in some regions and damping basilar membrane movements in other regions. This active, ongoing modulation of the basilar membrane sharpens the tuning of the cochlea (Hubbard, 1993). A surprising consequence of this mechanical movement of the basilar membrane is that the cochlea itself produces sounds—called **otoacoustic emissions**—by pushing back on the eardrum. (Otoacoustic emissions are discussed in more detail on the website in **A Step Further: The Ears Emit Sounds as Part of the Hearing Process**.)

Each auditory neuron responds to a very precise frequency at its threshold, but for more-intense stimuli the neuron responds to a broader range of frequencies. For example, the fiber whose responses are shown in red in **Figure 9.6** has its *best frequency* at 1200 Hz; that is, it responds to a very weak tone at 1200 Hz. When sounds are 20 dB stronger, however, the fiber responds to any frequency from 500 to 1800 Hz. We call this the **tuning curve** of that cell's response to sounds of various frequencies. Thus, although an auditory nerve fiber transmits exclusively auditory information, it does not respond to just one frequency of stimulation. If the brain received a signal from only one such fiber, it would not be able to tell whether the stimulus was a weak tone of 1200 Hz or a stronger tone of 500 or 1800 Hz, or any frequency in between. Instead, the

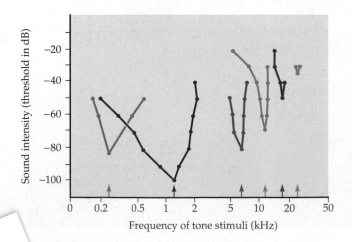

9.6 Examples of Tuning Curves of Auditory Nerve Cells   These curves were obtained from measuring the responses of six different neurons to sounds of different intensities and frequencies. Because they represent threshold measurements, the *lowest* point on each curve (indicated by arrows on the *x*-axis for six cells) corresponds to that neuron's preferred frequency. These six neural units were recorded from the auditory nerve of the cat. (After Kiang, 1965.)

brain analyzes signals from thousands of such units to calculate the intensity and frequency of each sound.

Auditory System Pathways Run from the Brainstem to the Cortex

On each side of your head, about 30,000–50,000 auditory fibers from the cochlea make up the auditory part of the **vestibulocochlear nerve** (cranial nerve VIII). Recall that most of these afferent fibers are carrying messages from the IHCs, each of which stimulates several nerve fibers. Input from the auditory nerve is distributed in a complex manner to both sides of the brain, as depicted in **Figure 9.7**. Each auditory nerve fiber divides into two main branches as it enters the brainstem. Each branch then goes to separate groups of cells in the dorsal and ventral **cochlear nuclei**.

The output of the cochlear nuclei also travels via multiple paths. One path goes to the **superior olivary nuclei**, which receive inputs from both right and left cochlear nuclei. This bilateral input is the first stage in the CNS at which *binaural* (two-ear) effects are processed; as you might expect, this mechanism plays a key role in localizing sounds by comparing the two ears, as we'll discuss shortly. Several other parallel paths converge on the **inferior colliculi**, which are the primary auditory centers of the midbrain. Outputs of the inferior colliculi go to the **medial geniculate nuclei** of the thalamus. At least two different pathways from the medial geniculate extend to several auditory cortical areas.

Throughout the auditory pathways, neuronal response is frequency-sensitive, as with the vestibulocochlear nerve fibers that we discussed earlier (see Figure 9.5). This ability to discriminate frequencies is even sharper at higher stations of the auditory nervous system. At the medial geniculate nucleus and the auditory cortex, not only are neurons excited by certain frequencies, but they are also *inhibited* by neigh-

vestibulocochlear nerve Cranial nerve VIII, which runs from the cochlea to the brainstem auditory nuclei.

cochlear nuclei Brainstem nuclei that receive input from auditory hair cells and send output to the superior olivary complex.

superior olivary nuclei Brainstem nuclei that receive input from both right and left cochlear nuclei, and provide the first binaural analysis of auditory information.

inferior colliculi Paired gray matter structures of the dorsal midbrain that receive auditory information.

medial geniculate nuclei Nuclei in the thalamus that receive input from the inferior colliculi and send output to the auditory cortex.

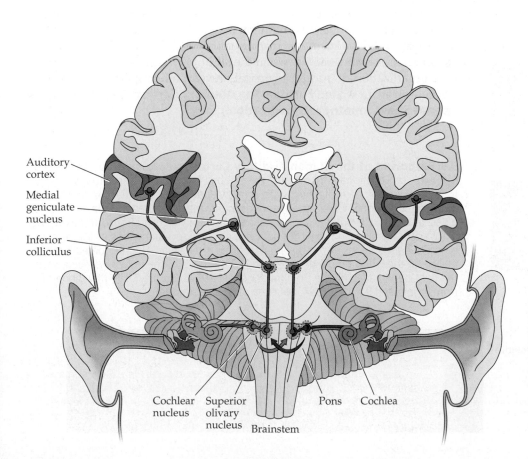

Auditory cortex

Medial geniculate nucleus

Inferior colliculus

Cochlear nucleus   Superior olivary nucleus   Pons   Cochlea
Brainstem

9.7 Auditory Pathways of the Human Brain This view from the front of the head shows the first binaural (two-ear) interactions in the brainstem superior olivary nucleus. Most (but not all) of the information from each ear projects to the cortex on the opposite side of the brain, as illustrated here by the colors of the projections to the medial geniculate of the thalamus and then the cortex.

9.8 Mapping Auditory Frequencies in the Cat Inferior Colliculus (a) This lateral view of the cat brain shows the plane of the transverse section through the inferior colliculus shown in part b. (c, d) Locations of the cells labeled with 2-DG via (c) 2000-Hz stimulation and (d) 21,000-Hz stimulation are indicated here by blue and red, respectively. (e) Complete tonotopic mapping shows the range of frequencies that can stimulate the cat's auditory system. (After Serviere et al., 1984.)

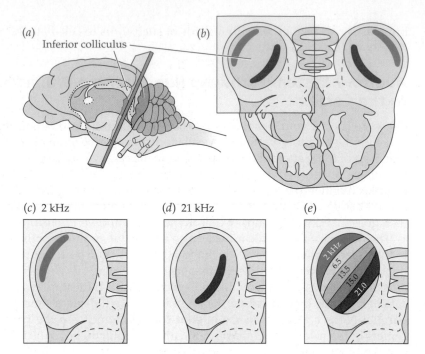

(a) Inferior colliculus (b)

(c) 2 kHz   (d) 21 kHz   (e)

tonotopic organization A major organizational feature in auditory systems in which neurons are arranged as an orderly map of stimulus frequency, with cells responsive to high frequencies located at a distance from those responsive to low frequencies.

boring frequencies. This interplay of excitation and inhibition further sharpens the frequency responses, allowing us to discriminate very small frequency differences.

At every level of the auditory system, from cochlea to auditory cortex, auditory pathways display **tonotopic organization**; that is, they are spatially arranged in an orderly map according to the auditory frequencies to which they respond. Tonotopic organization can be demonstrated by the mapping of auditory brain regions using 2-deoxyglucose (2-DG), as shown in **Figure 9.8**. Following 2-DG injection, an animal is exposed to a tone of a particular frequency. Because 2-DG is taken up like glucose by neurons, but not metabolized, the most-active neurons take up the most 2-DG. Postmortem processing of 2-DG distribution reveals which cells were most active when the stimulus frequency was presented. (The organization of auditory cortical areas in other species is described on the website in **A Step Further: The Auditory Cortical Regions of Many Species Show Tonotopic Organization**.)

(a) Noise

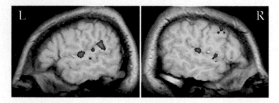

Speech sounds

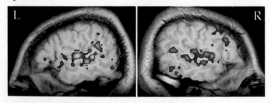

9.9 Responses of the Human Auditory Cortex to Random Sounds versus Speech (a) Functional-MRI scans of the cerebral hemispheres show that pure tones or noise (left) activate chiefly the primary auditory area on the superior aspect of the temporal lobe, while speech sounds (right) activate other auditory cortical regions, as well as the primary auditory area. (b) Lateral (left) and horizontal (right) PET scans show that listening to words activates not only several regions of the cerebral cortex but also regions of the thalamus and the cerebellum. The numbered horizontal lines in the left-hand panel correspond to the levels of the horizontal sections in the right-hand panel. (Part a from Binder et al., 1994, courtesy of Jeffrey Binder; b from Posner and Raichle, 1994, courtesy of Marcus Raichle.)

(b) Listening to words

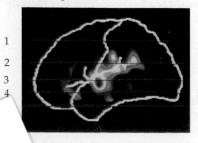

Anterior

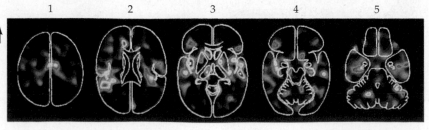

In humans, PET and fMRI studies show that stimulation with pure tones or noise activates chiefly the primary auditory cortex on the superior temporal lobe (**Figure 9.9a**). Speech activates this and other, more specialized auditory areas (**Figure 9.9b**). Interestingly, at least some of these regions are activated when normal subjects try to lip-read—that is, to understand someone by watching that person's lips without auditory cues (L. E. Bernstein et al., 2002; Calvert et al., 1997); this result suggests that the auditory cortex integrates other, nonauditory, information with sounds.

Two Main Theories Describe How We Discriminate Pitch

Most of us can discriminate very small differences in frequency of sound over the entire audible range—from 20 Hz to 15,000 or even 20,000 Hz. The ability to detect a change in frequency is usually measured as the **minimal discriminable frequency difference** between two tones. The detectable difference is about 2 Hz for sounds up to 2000 Hz; above these frequencies it grows larger.

Note that *frequency* and *pitch* are not synonymous terms. *Frequency* describes a physical property of sounds; *pitch* relates solely to the subjective sensory experience of sounds (see Box 9.1). This is an important distinction because frequency is not the sole determinant of perceived pitch (at some frequencies, higher-intensity sounds may seem higher-pitched), and changes in pitch do not precisely parallel changes in frequency.

How do we account for the ability to discriminate pitches? Two main theories have been offered. One, described as **place theory**, argues that pitch is encoded in the physical location of the activated receptors along the length of the basilar membrane: activation of receptors near the base of the cochlea (which is narrow and responds to high frequencies) signals *treble*, and activation of receptors nearer the apex (which is wide and responds to low frequencies) signals *bass*. The alternative idea, **volley theory**, proposes that the frequency of auditory stimuli is directly encoded in the firing pattern of auditory neurons: for example, a 500-Hz sound might cause some neurons to fire 500 action potentials per second. In such cases the firing of the action potential is *phase-locked* to the stimulus; that is, it occurs at a particular portion of the cycle. Such a phase-locked representation can be accomplished more accurately by several cells than by a single cell—hence the term *volley*, as in a volley of action potentials.

Are these views—place and volley theories—necessarily antagonistic? No. In fact, the contemporary view of pitch perception incorporates both perspectives:

1. As *place theory* predicts, a change in frequency is accompanied by a change in the region of maximal disturbance of the basilar membrane, as well as activation of the auditory receptors found there. For complex sounds with components at several different frequencies, the cochlea accomplishes a sort of Fourier analysis (see Box 9.1), with the different frequencies mapped as peaks of vibration at different places along the basilar membrane.

2. As *volley theory* predicts, temporal patterns of neural discharges appear to encode auditory frequencies. Direct recordings indicate that, for lower-frequency sounds, the frequency of action potentials often encodes the auditory frequency on a one-to-one basis. For higher-frequency sounds, the frequency of action potentials may instead encode an auditory frequency that is an integer multiple. Encoding a multiple, rather than one-to-one, frequency allows the auditory system to overcome the maximal neuronal firing rate of about 1000 action potentials per second. In general, volley coding is emphasized at the lower end of the hearing range, up to about 4000 Hz.

Thus, the frequency properties of a sound are coded in two ways: (1) according to the distribution of excitation among cells—that is, place coding or tonotopic representation; and (2) according to the temporal pattern (volley) of discharge in cells projecting to the auditory cortex.

minimal discriminable frequency difference The smallest change in frequency that can be detected reliably between two tones.

place theory A theory of frequency discrimination stating that pitch perception depends on the place of maximal displacement of the basilar membrane produced by a sound.

volley theory A theory of frequency discrimination that emphasizes the relation between sound frequency and the firing pattern of nerve cells.

ultrasound High-frequency sound; in general, above the threshold for human hearing, at about 20,000 Hz.

infrasound Very low frequency sound; in general, below the threshold for human hearing, at about 20 Hz.

binaural Pertaining to two ears.

intensity differences Perceived differences in loudness between the two ears, which can be used to localize a sound source.

latency differences Differences between the two ears in the time of arrival of a sound, which can be employed by the nervous system to localize sound sources.

duplex theory A theory that we localize sound by combining information about intensity differences and latency differences between the two ears.

9.10 Cues for Binaural Hearing The two ears receive somewhat different information from sound sources located to one side or the other of the observer's midline. (a) The head casts a sound shadow, producing binaural differences in sound intensity. (b) The resulting differences in perceived intensity are greater at higher frequencies. (c) Sounds also take longer to reach the more distant ear, resulting in binaural differences in time of arrival. *Onset disparity* is the latency difference between the two ears for the beginning of a sound. *Ongoing phase disparity* is the difference between the ears for arrival of the peaks and troughs of the sound wave.

Some species are sensitive to sounds with very high frequencies (**ultrasound**) or very low frequencies (**infrasound**), and make use of them in special ways. For example, many species of bats produce loud vocalizations, in the range of 50,000–100,000 Hz, and listen to the echoes reflected back from objects in order to navigate and hunt in the dark. Their extraordinary sensitivity and accuracy is conferred by elaborate adaptations of their bodies and brains.

At the other end of the spectrum, homing-pigeon races are severely disrupted if the birds encounter the sonic-boom shock wave of a supersonic jet (an infrasound pulse that can travel hundreds of miles), suggesting that the pigeons use infrasound cues to establish a navigational map (Hagstrum, 2000). Tigers may use infrasound to add impact to their roars (Walsh et al., 2003), and infrasound experimentally inserted into concerts heightens the music's emotional effect on human listeners, but it's not yet known how we detect infrasound.

By Comparing the Ears, We Can Localize Sounds

Normally we can locate the position of a sound source with great accuracy (within about 1°) by analyzing **binaural** (two-ear) differences in the sound. Two kinds of binaural cues signal the location of a sound source.

Intensity differences are differences in *loudness* at the two ears. In humans, intensity differences arise because the head casts a *sound shadow* (**Figure 9.10a**), blocking sounds located to one side (off-axis sounds) from reaching both ears with equal loudness (sound shadow is less of a factor in species such as dogs and cats with pinnae that move). The head shadow is most pronounced for higher-frequency sounds. Low-frequency sounds have longer sound waves that reach around the head (**Figure 9.10b**).

Latency differences are differences between the two ears in the *time of arrival* of sounds. They arise because one ear is always a little closer to an off-axis sound than is the other ear. Two kinds of latency differences are present in a sound: *onset disparity*, which is the difference between the two ears in hearing the beginning of the sound; and *ongoing phase disparity*, which is the continuous mismatch between the two ears in the arrival of all the peaks and troughs that make up the sound wave (these cues are illustrated in **Figure 9.10c**).

We now know that sound localization involves processing of *both* intensity differences and latency differences; this is known as the **duplex theory**. At low frequencies, no matter where sounds are presented horizontally around the head,

(a)

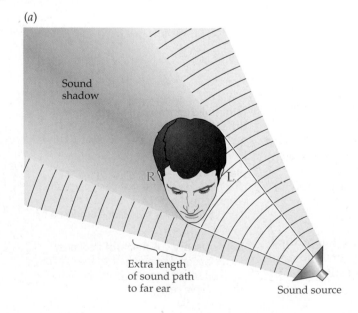

(b)

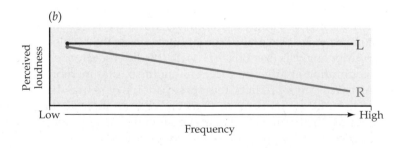

(c)

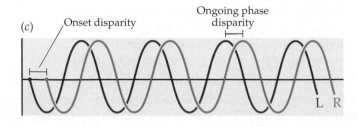

there are virtually no intensity differences between the ears. For these frequencies, differences in times of arrival are the principal cues for sound position (and at very low frequencies, neither cue is much help; this is why you can place the sub-woofer of an audio system anywhere you want). At higher frequencies, however, the sound shadow cast by the head produces significant binaural intensity differences. Of course, you can't perceive which types of processing you're relying on for any given sound; in general, we are aware of the *results* of neural processing but not the processing itself.

What brain systems analyze binaural cues? Both birds and mammals have highly specialized brainstem mechanisms that receive information from the two ears, and they use arrays of bipolar neurons to derive sound location from the left and right auditory signals. These bipolar neurons are capable of making very precise timing calculations by comparing the inputs to their two dendrites (Agmon-Snir et al., 1998).

In birds, the organization of neurons within the primary sound localization nucleus (called the *nucleus laminaris*) constitutes an auditory map of space. In this model, originally proposed by Lloyd Jeffress (1948), each binaural neuron of the nucleus laminaris functions as a **coincidence detector** and is maximally excited by a particular latency difference between inputs from the two ears, corresponding to a particular place in space (**Figure 9.11**). This map is further developed at higher levels, especially the *tectum* (equivalent to the mammalian inferior colliculus), which contains a complete map of space.

coincidence detector   A device that senses the co-occurrence of two events.

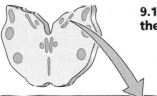

9.11 The Classic (Jeffress) Model of Sound Localization in the Auditory Brainstem of Birds

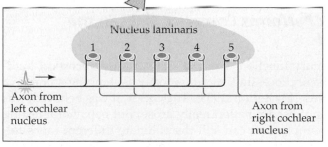

1. A sound occurring to the left of the owl's midline is detected by the left cochlea slightly earlier than the right cochlea.

2. Monaural neurons of the left cochlear nucleus of the brainstem become active, sending action potentials along their axons toward the nucleus laminaris.

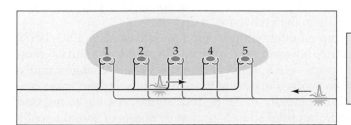

3. Shortly thereafter, the monaural neurons of the right cochlear nucleus send their own action potentials toward the nucleus laminaris. Because they were fired earlier, the action potentials from the left side have traveled farther along their axons…

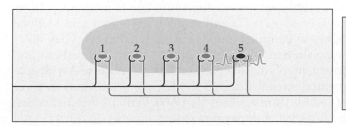

4. …with the result that the action potential from the left side and the one from the right side arrive simultaneously at neuron 5, but not at any other binaural neuron. Neuron 5 is thus a coincidence detector that signals a particular location to the left of midline. For simplicity, only 5 neurons are shown; in reality, thousands of such neurons make up a detailed map of space.

9.12 All Ears   Like other mammals, including humans, the ridges and valleys of this bat's outer ear produce precise changes, called *spectral filtering*, in the sounds being funneled into the ear. This process provides additional cues about the location of a sound source. Some moths produce ultrasonic clicks that interfere with these signals (Corcoran et al., 2009), confusing the bat about where to find that tasty moth.

Mammals apparently do things quite differently. The superior olivary nucleus is the primary sound localization nucleus in the mammalian brain, and its two main divisions serve different functions. The *lateral superior olive* processes intensity differences. The *medial superior olive (MSO)* processes latency differences, but in contrast to birds the MSO does not appear to contain a map of auditory space. Instead, sound location is encoded by the relative activity of the *entire* left MSO compared with the *entire* right MSO (Grothe, 2003; McAlpine et al., 2001). So, for example, a sound on the midline would activate the left and right MSO equally, and the two signals would effectively cancel each other out. But a sound on the right would produce more excitation of the left MSO than the right MSO, and the converse would be true for sounds on the left. The bigger the difference between the left and right MSO is, the farther the sound source is from the midline. This disparity is passed along for further processing at other levels of the auditory system.

The structure of the external ear provides yet another sort of localization cue. As we mentioned earlier, the hills and valleys of the external ear selectively reinforce some frequencies in a complex sound and diminish others (**Figure 9.12**). This process is known as **spectral filtering**, and the frequencies that are affected depend on where the sound originates (Kulkarni and Colburn, 1998).

The relationship between spectral cues and location is learned and calibrated during development. Spectral cues provide critical information about *elevation* (vertical localization) and are especially important for sounds located on the midline, where there are no intensity or latency differences between the ears. In fact, people who are deaf in one ear can utilize **monaural** (one-ear) spectral cues to localize sounds to some extent. Similarly, researchers can place a speaker directly in the ear canal and, by varying the spectral filtering of natural sounds, fool a person or animal into believing that the sound came from a particular point in space (L. Xu et al., 1999). Orchestra conductors are especially good at identifying the spatial location of sound sources (Münte et al., 2001), presumably because of extensive practice ("Mr. Watson, could you *please* play in tune?").

The Auditory Cortex Performs Complex Tasks in the Perception of Sound

The historical view of auditory function was that the various subcortical auditory areas performed only basic processing, serving mostly as stepping-stones in a pathway to the auditory cortex (Masterton, 1993). The cortex, it was believed, was where auditory sensation and discrimination really arose. But behavioral testing suggested otherwise; for example, cats can still discriminate different tones following surgical removal of auditory cortex (M. R. Rosenzweig, 1946; for a review, see Neff and Casseday, 1977). If the auditory cortex is not involved in these basic kinds of auditory discrimination, then what *does* it do?

Early studies relied on simple, but unnatural, pure tones (Masterton, 1993, 1997). Most of the sounds in nature, however—such as vocalizations of animals, footsteps, snaps, crackles, and pops—contain many frequencies and change rapidly. The auditory nervous system evolved to deal with such sounds. Indeed, most central auditory neurons habituate rapidly to continuous sound, ceasing to respond after only a few milliseconds; but brief sounds or abrupt onsets of sound usually evoke responses from many neurons, from the cochlear nuclei to the auditory cortex. Ablation of the auditory cortex does impair discrimination of temporal *patterns* of sound in cats (Neff and Casseday, 1977) and monkeys (Heffner and Heffner, 1989). So auditory cortex analyzes complex sounds encountered in everyday life.

There seem to be two main streams of auditory processing in cortex (Kaas and Hackett, 1999): a dorsal stream, involving the parietal lobe, is concerned with spatial *location* of sounds; a ventral stream through the temporal lobe may analyze the various components of sounds (Romanski et al., 1999). Perhaps this distinction forms the basis of the *where* and *what* auditory processing streams (Recanzone and

spectral filtering   Alteration of the amplitude of some, but not all, frequencies in a sound.

monaural   Pertaining to one ear.

Cohen, 2010); a similar processing scheme has been proposed for visual processing too (see Chapter 10).

Experience affects auditory perception and the auditory pathways

Aspects of auditory discrimination, and the neural circuits involved in hearing, change as we grow. Studies in animals demonstrate that the tonotopic organization of auditory circuits in the developing brain is fine-tuned by experience (Kandler et al., 2009). At birth, human infants have diverse hearing abilities, but as they grow they become better and better at perceiving complex sounds, such as speech. They become particularly adept at discriminating different sounds in whatever language they hear.

Another demonstration of the role of early auditory experience comes from studies of musicians (Pantev et al., 1998). In these studies the evoked brain activity from musicians and nonmusicians was identical in response to pure tones. But if, instead of pure tones, the more complex and musically relevant sounds from a piano were used, musicians displayed a greater brain response than did nonmusicians. Now, maybe these people became musicians because their brains were more responsive to complex tones to begin with. However, there was a significant correlation between the magnitude of brain response to piano tones and the age at which the musicians had begun studying music. The earlier the musician had begun her studies, the greater was her brain response to piano tones, suggesting that early exposure to musical training affects auditory responsiveness of the brain.

Certainly there are big differences by adulthood: the portion of primary auditory cortex where music is first processed, called *Heschl's gyrus*, is more than twice as large in professional musicians as in nonmusicians, and more than twice as strongly activated by music (P. Schneider et al., 2002). Debate continues about whether musical ability is a specific and hardwired human trait, or just a happy by-product of systems that evolved for other purposes (Balter, 2004), but the existence of disorders in which people cannot accurately discern tunes (called **amusia**; from the Greek *amousia*, "want of harmony") suggests that at least the rudiments of a musical sense are innate (Münte, 2002).

Tone-deaf Tony, whom we described at the beginning of the chapter, exemplifies this dyslexia-like problem. Whereas most infants clearly understand the basics of musical relationships almost from birth, people with congenital amusia never develop that ability (Peretz and Hyde, 2003). This seems to be a problem in recognizing pitch, not the timing aspects of music (*rhythm*), since that facet of music sensation may be unaffected in amusia (K. L. Hyde and Peretz, 2004). Brain imaging suggests that the right inferior frontal gyrus is abnormal in amusia, containing less white matter than people with normal music perception have (K. L. Hyde et al., 2006); and this finding agrees with earlier studies indicating that the right frontal region is active during pitch perception.

A special use of MRI called **diffusion tensor imaging** (**DTI**) takes advantage of the differences in how water molecules are constrained in myelin to reveal axonal tracts connecting brain regions. DTI images of tone-deaf people indicate that they have fewer connections between frontal cortex and the temporal lobe (Loui et al., 2009), where auditory processing takes place (**Figure 9.13**). We assume Tony was born with a problem that severely limited the ability of some part(s) of his brain to comprehend music (especially pitch), such as Heschl's gyrus, right inferior frontal cortex, or connections between frontal cortex and the temporal lobe.

The role of auditory experience in the development of sound localization is illustrated by observations in bilaterally deaf children who were fitted with different types of hearing aids (Beggs and Foreman, 1980). The children in one group were given a hearing aid that delivered the same sounds to both ears. In a second group, children were fitted with a separate hearing aid for each ear so that they experienced binaural stimuli. When examined years later, the children who had been fitted with binaural hearing aids were able to localize sounds with significantly

amusia   A disorder characterized by the inability to discern tunes accurately.

diffusion tensor imaging (DTI)   A special use of MRI that takes advantage of the differences in how water molecules are constrained in myelin to reveal axonal tracts connecting brain regions.

(a) Control   (b) Tone-deaf

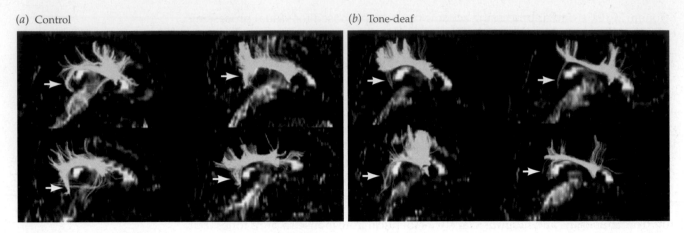

9.13 Brain Connections in Tone-Deaf Subjects Diffusion tensor imaging (DTI) reveals myelinated tracts in these midsagittal images of subjects facing to the right. The fibers connecting the frontal cortex, which is active during pitch discrimination, to the temporal lobe, where auditory processing begins, is called the arcuate fasciculus because it is arc-shaped (arrow). The arcuate fasciculus is much more prominent in four control subjects (a) than in four people who are tone-deaf (b). (Courtesy of Psyche Loui; from Loui et al., 2009.)

greater accuracy than were the children who had experienced comparable overall levels of sounds but had been deprived of binaural stimuli.

We can also see evidence that experience affects auditory processing in animals. For example, training a guinea pig to detect tones of a particular frequency caused cortical neurons to shift their response to favor that frequency (**Figure 9.14**) (N. M. Weinberger, 1998). This remodeling can occur very quickly, on the order of just a few minutes (Fritz et al., 2003), reflecting an adaptive ability to continually tune and retune the auditory cortex to detect biologically significant sounds. You can learn about the role of experience in auditory localization in owls on the website in **A Step Further: Auditory Systems Are Calibrated through Polymodal Integration**.

Deafness Is a Major Disorder of the Nervous System

In the United States, about 11 million people (over 3% of the population) are categorized as either hard of hearing or profoundly deaf (Mitchell, 2006); the prevalence in other developed countries is probably similar. Auditory problems, which

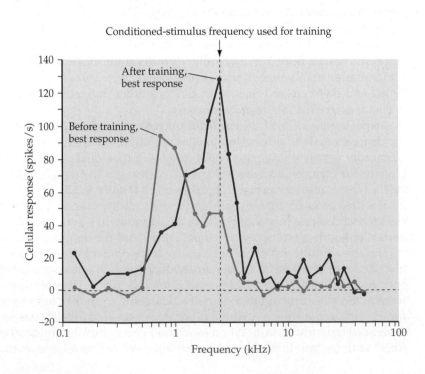

9.14 Long-Term Retention of a Trained Shift in Tuning of an Auditory Receptive Field Before training, the best frequency of the auditory cortex cell of an adult guinea pig that is represented on this graph was about 0.7 kHz. After training with a 1.1-kHz tone, the best frequency shifted to 1.1 kHz. After 2 and 4 weeks, the shift had remained stable. (From N. M. Weinberger, 1998.)

range in severity from occasional difficulties in speech perception to a complete inability to hear, can come about in several different ways.

There are three main causes of deafness

Many severe hearing impairments arise early in life and impair language acquisition. Others occur later in life as a consequence of environmental factors, such as exposure to loud sounds, infections, or side effects of certain drugs. Of the three general categories of deafness—conduction, sensorineural, and central—the latter two involve compromised neural function.

CONDUCTION DEAFNESS **Conduction deafness** arises when disorders of the outer or middle ear prevent vibrations produced by auditory stimuli from reaching the cochlea. In one common form of conduction deafness, the ossicles become fused and can no longer transmit sound vibrations effectively. Surgery to free up the ossicular chain is helpful in some cases. The nervous system is generally not involved in conduction deafness.

SENSORINEURAL DEAFNESS Metabolic dysfunctions, infections, exposure to toxic substances, trauma, exposure to loud sounds, and hundreds of hereditary disorders are all causes of **sensorineural deafness**, a condition in which auditory nerve fibers are unable to become excited in a normal manner. This hearing loss is usually permanent. Defects in certain genes affecting hair cell structure and function are prominent causes of sensorineural deafness that is present from birth (Petit and Richardson, 2009). Mutations in a gene named *GJB2* may be responsible for as much as 50% of congenital or early-onset hearing impairment (Cryns and Van Camp, 2004); this gene encodes the protein connexin-26, which is involved in the formation of electrical synapses (*gap junctions*; see Chapter 3).

Drug-induced deafness sometimes results from the toxic properties of a group of antibiotics that includes streptomycin and gentamicin. The **ototoxic** (ear-damaging) properties of streptomycin were discovered when many patients that received it as treatment for tuberculosis subsequently developed cochlear damage. In severe cases the hair cells of the cochlea were completely destroyed, producing total, irreversible loss of hearing.

Noise pollution and loud sounds—industrial noise, loud engines, the firing of guns—can severely damage the cochlea in a short period of time. Once again, the hair cells suffer the brunt of the damage: in the affected part of the cochlea, the stereocilia appear shattered and broken, like a flattened forest. There is growing concern about hearing loss caused by listening to personal music players over headphones, which can produce sounds above 100 dB (louder than a nearby airplane at takeoff). Anyone listening for more than 5 hours per week at 89 dB or louder is exceeding workplace limits, so they are exposing themselves to levels known to induce permanent hearing loss (SCENIHR, 2008). Loud sounds coupled with the use of some over-the-counter drugs, such as aspirin, can also have profound cumulative effects on hearing (McFadden and Champlin, 1990), reducing sensitivity to certain tones by up to 40 dB and/or leading to the development of **tinnitus**, a sensation of noises or ringing in the ears (Brien, 1993).

Can damaged hair cells be regrown? Although fishes and amphibians produce new hair cells throughout life, mammals traditionally have been viewed as incapable of regenerating hair cells. This conclusion may have been too hasty, however (Brigande and Heller, 2009). Through manipulation of certain genes, tissue cultures from the organ of Corti of young rats have been induced to produce new hair cells (Zheng and Gao, 2000). As in fishes and birds, the supporting cells packed around the hair cells of the mammalian organ of Corti do remain capable of dividing and differentiating into hair cells in adulthood (P. M. White et al., 2006). Insertion of a gene called *Atoh1* (also known as *Math1*) into the cochlea of deafened guinea pigs, resulted in new hair cells and some restoration of hearing after about 8 weeks (Izu-

conduction deafness A hearing impairment that is associated with pathology of the external-ear or middle-ear cavities.

sensorineural deafness A hearing impairment that originates from cochlear or auditory nerve lesions.

ototoxic Toxic to the ears, especially the middle or inner ear.

tinnitus A sensation of noises or ringing in the ears.

central deafness A hearing impairment that is related to lesions in auditory pathways or centers, including sites in the brainstem, thalamus, or cortex.

word deafness The specific inability to hear words, although other sounds can be detected.

cortical deafness A hearing impairment that is caused by a fault or defect in the cortex.

cochlear implant An electromechanical device that detects sounds and selectively stimulates nerves in different regions of the cochlea via surgically implanted electrodes.

mikawa et al., 2005). Alternatively, deletion of a gene called *Rb1* enables hair cells themselves to divide, providing new, functional hair cells in a deafened cochlea (Sage et al., 2006). There is thus good reason to hope that a combination of these approaches may provide an effective gene therapy for deaf people, someday.

CENTRAL DEAFNESS **Central deafness** (hearing loss caused by brain lesions such as stroke) is seldom a simple loss of auditory sensitivity. An example illustrating the complexity of changes in auditory perception following cerebral cortical damage is **word deafness**, a disorder in which people show normal speech and hearing for simple sounds but cannot recognize spoken words. Word deafness may be due to an abnormally slow analysis of auditory inputs. Another example of central deafness is **cortical deafness**, in which patients have difficulty recognizing both verbal and nonverbal auditory stimuli. Cortical deafness is a rare syndrome because it requires bilateral damage to the auditory cortex.

Strokes that interrupt all of the projection fibers from the medial geniculate nucleus to the various auditory cortical regions also cause deafness (Y. Tanaka et al., 1991). Patients who suffer from stroke-induced deafness still show various acoustic reflexes mediated by the brainstem—such as bodily responses to environmental sounds—although they deny hearing the sounds to which they are reacting. In contrast, patients with bilateral destruction of only the *primary* auditory cortex often have less-severe hearing loss, presumably because other auditory cortical regions contribute to hearing, as discussed earlier.

Electrical stimulation of the auditory pathway can alleviate deafness

As described already, many cases of sensorineural hearing loss involve damaged hair cells. Although the hair cells may be completely destroyed, the electrical excitability of the auditory nerve often remains unchanged. So one practical approach for circumventing deafness due to hair cell loss involves directly stimulating the auditory nerve with electrical currents (Loeb, 1990; J. M. Miller and Spelman, 1990). Progress in the development of **cochlear implants** that deliver such electrical stimulation has been rapid (**Figure 9.15**). Although some advocates of deaf culture oppose the use of such prostheses (Crouch, 1997), studies confirm an increase in speech perception with continued use of cochlear implants (Skinner et al., 1997).

Cochlear implants can provide only a limited range of frequencies and loudness, but the auditory information that they deliver can nonetheless greatly facilitate acoustically mediated behaviors. For example, this treatment makes it possible to distinguish voiced and unvoiced

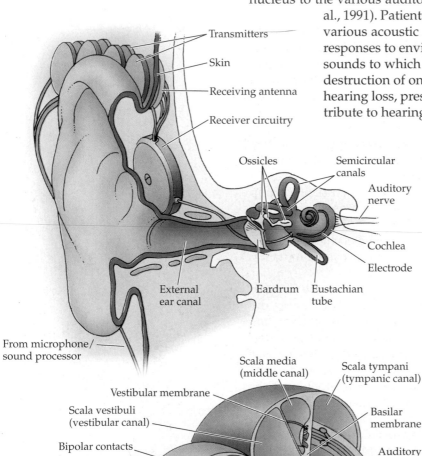

Transmitters
Skin
Receiving antenna
Receiver circuitry
Ossicles
Semicircular canals
Auditory nerve
Cochlea
Electrode
External ear canal
Eardrum
Eustachian tube
From microphone/ sound processor

Scala media (middle canal)
Scala tympani (tympanic canal)
Vestibular membrane
Scala vestibuli (vestibular canal)
Basilar membrane
Bipolar contacts
Auditory nerve
Organ of Corti
Electrode

9.15 Cochlear Implants Provide Hearing in Some Deaf People A microphone detects sound and directs the cochlear implant circuitry to stimulate the auditory nerve. Although this apparatus provides only a crude simulation of ordinary auditory nerve activity, the brain can learn to use the information to decipher speech.

speech sounds (e.g., "v" and "f"), which cannot be distinguished in lip-reading. When a cochlear implant is turned on, functional imaging shows that the auditory cortex is activated (Klinke et al., 1999), and tonotopic organization of the activation is evident (Lazeyras et al., 2002), indicating that this region is processing the information. Furthermore, the earlier the implants are provided, the better the eventual performance is (Grieco-Calub et al., 2009). The success of these implants is due mainly to the cleverness of the brain, not the implant.

A new generation of implantable aids, called **auditory brainstem implants** (**ABIs**), produce auditory sensations by directly stimulating the cochlear nuclei of the brainstem. By bypassing the ear altogether, ABI devices offer hope of hearing restoration even for people who lack a functional auditory nerve (Rauschecker and Shannon, 2002). Preliminary work suggests that direct stimulation of the auditory midbrain (the inferior colliculi) may provide an additional option for restoring hearing in such cases (Lenarz et al., 2006).

Vestibular Perception

The vestibular system provides information about the force of gravity on the body and the acceleration of the head. When you go up in an elevator, you feel the acceleration clearly. When you turn your head or ride in a car going around a tight curve, you feel the change of direction. If you are not used to these kinds of stimulation, sensitivity to motion can make you queasy. The receptors of the vestibular system inform the brain about mechanical forces that act on the body.

The Receptor Mechanisms for the Vestibular System Are in the Inner Ear

The receptors of the vestibular system lie within the inner ear next to the cochlea. (The term *vestibular* comes from the Latin *vestibulum*, "entrance hall," and reflects the fact that the system lies in hollow spaces in the temporal bone.) In mammals, one portion of the vestibular system consists of three **semicircular canals**, fluid-filled tubes that are each oriented in a different plane (**Figure 9.16a**). The three canals are connected at their ends to a saclike structure called the **utricle** (literally, "little uterus"). Lying below the utricle is another small fluid-filled sac, the **saccule** ("little sac").

Receptors in these structures, just like those of the auditory system, are groups of hair cells whose bending leads to the excitation of nerve fibers. In each semicircular canal, the hair cells are in an enlarged region, the **ampulla** (plural *ampullae*), that lies at the junction between each canal and the utricle (**Figure 9.16b**). Here the cilia of the hair cells are embedded in a gelatinous mass. The orientation of the hairs is quite precise and determines the kind of mechanical force to which they are especially sensitive.

The three semicircular canals are at right angles to each other, so one or another detects rotational acceleration in any direction. The receptors in the saccule and utricle respond to vertical and horizontal linear forces, and thus signal static position as well (see Figure 9.16b). Small, bony crystals on the gelatinous membrane, called **otoliths** (from the Greek *ot-*, "ear," and *lithos*, "stone"), increase the sensitivity of these receptors to movement. At the base of the hair cells in these receptors are nerve fibers connected much like those that connect auditory hair cells.

Evolution Has Shaped the Auditory and Vestibular End Organs

The long evolutionary history of the auditory-vestibular system is better known than that of other sensory systems because the receptors are encased in bone, which can fossilize (E. G. Wever, 1974). It is generally accepted that the auditory organ evolved

auditory brainstem implant (ABI) A type of auditory prosthesis in which implanted microphones directly stimulate the auditory nuclei of the brainstem rather than the cochlea.

semicircular canal One of the three fluid-filled tubes in the inner ear that are part of the vestibular system. Each of the tubes, which are at right angles to each other, detects angular acceleration.

utricle A small, fluid-filled sac in the vestibular system above the saccule that responds to static positions of the head.

saccule A small, fluid-filled sac under the utricle in the vestibular system that responds to static positions of the head.

ampulla An enlarged region of each semicircular canal that contains the receptor cells (hair cells) of the vestibular system.

otolith A small crystal on the gelatinous membrane in the vestibular system.

CHAPTER 9

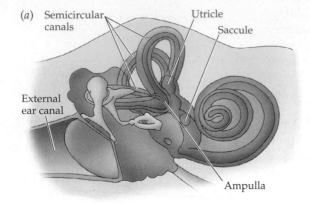

(a) Semicircular canals · Utricle · Saccule · External ear canal · Ampulla

9.16 Structures of the Vestibular System
(a) The vestibular apparatus is located in the temporal bone, continuous with the cochlea. The semicircular canals are connected through ampullae to the utricle, which connects to the saccule. (b) The semicircular canals detect rotation in three planes; hair cells in the ampullae detect flow of endolymph in the canals when the head is rotated. The utricle and saccule detect linear acceleration and static position, aided by tiny crystals, called *otoliths*, that overlie the hair cells in these structures and maximize the deflection of hair cells in response to movement.

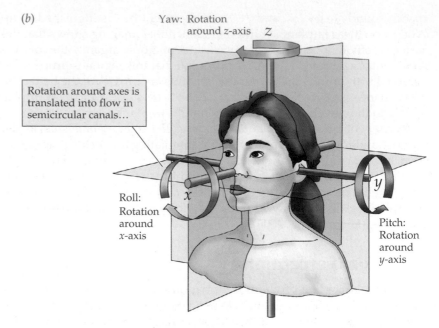

(b) Yaw: Rotation around z-axis · Rotation around axes is translated into flow in semicircular canals… · Roll: Rotation around x-axis · Pitch: Rotation around y-axis

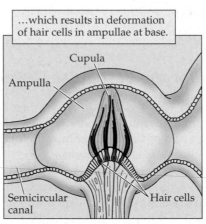

…which results in deformation of hair cells in ampullae at base.
Cupula · Ampulla · Semicircular canal · Hair cells

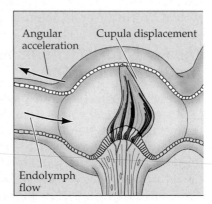

Angular acceleration · Cupula displacement · Endolymph flow

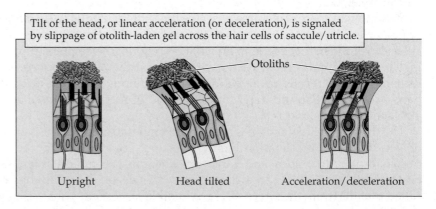

Tilt of the head, or linear acceleration (or deceleration), is signaled by slippage of otolith-laden gel across the hair cells of saccule/utricle.
Otoliths · Upright · Head tilted · Acceleration/deceleration

lateral-line system A sensory system, found in many kinds of fishes and some amphibians, that informs the animal of water motion in relation to the body surface.

cupula A small gelatinous column that forms part of the lateral-line system of aquatic animals and also occurs within the vestibular system of mammals.

from the vestibular system, although the ossicles probably evolved from parts of the jaw. Before that, the vestibular system evolved from the **lateral-line system**, a sensory system found in many kinds of fishes and some amphibians. The lateral-line system consists of an array of receptors along the side of the body. Tiny hairs that emerge from sensory cells in the skin are embedded in small gelatinous columns called **cupulae** (singular *cupula*), like those in mammals (see Figure 9.16b).

In aquatic animals with lateral-line systems, movements of water in relation to the body surface stimulate these receptors so that the animal can detect currents of

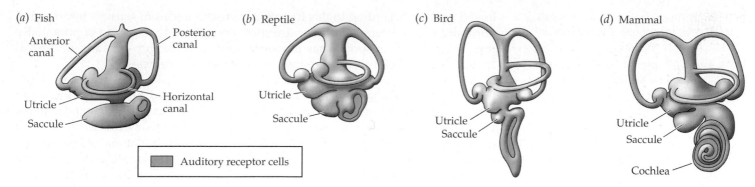

9.17 Evolution of the Vestibular and Auditory End Organs

water and movements of other animals, prey, or predators. It is speculated that the first semicircular canals developed from a stretch of lateral-line canal that migrated inside the body. This development gave the animal a sensor for turns to the right or left; and this receptor, being away from the surface of the body, was free of effects of stimulation of the skin. Sensitivity to change of direction was optimized when the canal developed into a roughly circular form. From the vestibular system that arose out of the lateral-line system evolved the auditory system (**Figure 9.17**).

Nerve Fibers from the Vestibular Portion of the Vestibulocochlear Nerve (VIII) Synapse in the Brainstem

The brain pathways carrying vestibular system information reflect its importance to motor control and posture. Nerve fibers from the vestibular receptors enter lower levels of the brainstem and synapse in the **vestibular nuclei**. Some of the fibers bypass this structure and go directly to the cerebellum, contributing to its motor functions. The outputs of the vestibular nuclei are complex, as is appropriate, considering their influences on the motor system. These outputs go to the motor nuclei of the eye muscles, the thalamus, and the cerebral cortex, among others.

One of the many important functions of the vestibular system is the precise control of eye movements. Try moving your head around while staring at a particular spot on the wall. It seems almost effortless to maintain your gaze on the fixation point, but in reality it is a very complex processing problem; the six muscles that control the movement of each eye must rapidly and precisely counter the movements of the head as they occur. This function is called the **vestibulo-ocular reflex** (**VOR**), involving a high-speed network within the brainstem that uses vestibular information about head rotations to move the eyes in compensation. The VOR functions accurately even when the eyes are closed, showing that vestibular inputs—rather than visual ones—control the accuracy of gaze as we move through the world.

Some Forms of Vestibular Excitation Produce Motion Sickness

There is one aspect of vestibular activation that many of us would gladly do without. Certain types of body acceleration—as when riding in a boat, car, plane, or roller coaster—can produce the misery of **motion sickness**. Motion sickness is caused especially by movements of the body that we cannot control. For example, passengers in a car are more likely to suffer from motion sickness than is the driver.

Why do we experience motion sickness? The **sensory conflict theory** argues that we feel bad when we receive contradictory sensory messages, especially a discrepancy between vestibular and visual information. When an airplane bounces around in turbulence, for instance, the vestibular system signals that various accelerations are occurring, but as far as the visual system is concerned, nothing is happening; the plane's interior is a constant. Michel Treisman (1977) hypothesized that such sensory conflict sets off responses that evolved to rid the body of swal-

vestibular nuclei   Brainstem nuclei that receive information from the vestibular organs through cranial nerve VIII (the vestibulocochlear nerve).

vestibulo-ocular reflex (VOR)   The brainstem mechanism that maintains gaze on a visual object despite movements of the head.

motion sickness   The experience of nausea brought on by unnatural passive movement, as in a car or boat.

sensory conflict theory   A theory of motion sickness suggesting that discrepancies between vestibular information and visual information simulate food poisoning and therefore trigger nausea.

papilla   A small bump that projects from the surface of the tongue. Papillae contain most of the taste receptor cells.

taste bud   A cluster of 50–150 cells that detects tastes. Taste buds are found in papillae.

lowed poison. According to this hypothesis, discrepancies in sensory information normally signal danger and cause dizziness and vomiting to get rid of potentially toxic food. Such a response has obvious significance for preservation of life, although it is not helpful as a response to movements of vehicles.

A different type of vestibular disorientation can strike airplane pilots. Note from Figure 9.16b that linear acceleration and an upward head tilt produce the same stimulation of the otolith organs (the saccule and utricle). So in conditions of very low visibility, an acceleration of the plane may be misinterpreted as a climb (an upward tilt of the plane) (P. R. MacNeilage et al., 2007). This *false-climb illusion* can be very compelling, leading pilots to force their planes into a dive because they mistakenly believe they are climbing. Because the dive itself produces further acceleration, heightening the illusion of climbing, an even steeper dive may be adopted, with tragic consequences. Fortunately, pilots of modern aircraft making landings in low-visibility conditions learn to rely on a variety of instruments rather than on their vestibular systems.

The Chemical Senses: Taste and Smell

Detecting chemicals in the environment is vital for the survival of organisms throughout the animal kingdom. The sense of taste provides an immediate assessment of foods (Lindemann, 1995): sweet indicates high-calorie foods; savory tastes signal a protein source; salty and sour relate to important aspects of homeostasis; bitter warns of toxic constituents. The sense of smell is critical for appreciating the rich and complex flavors of individual foods but has additional important functions as well, such as signaling the presence of prey, predators, or potential mates. This section will explore the many roles of the chemical senses—taste and smell—in guiding behavior.

Chemicals in Tastants Elicit Taste Sensations

We'll start our review of the chemical senses with taste, which is somewhat simpler than smell and in some ways has been more thoroughly investigated.

Humans detect five basic tastes

Most people derive great pleasure from eating delicious food, and because we recognize many substances by their distinct flavor, we tend to think that we can discriminate many tastes. In reality, though, humans detect only five basic tastes: salty, sour, sweet, bitter, and umami. (*Umami*, Japanese for "delicious taste," is the savory, meaty taste that is characteristic of broth).

The sensations uniquely aroused by an apple, a steak, or an olive are *flavors* rather than simple tastes; they involve smell as well as taste. Block your nose, and a raw potato tastes the same as an apple. Our ability to respond to many odors—it is estimated that humans can detect more than 10,000 different odors and can discriminate as many as 5000 (Ressler et al., 1994)—is what produces the complex array of flavors that we normally think of as tastes. Ordinarily, smell and taste work together, such that detecting certain tastes makes it easier to detect certain odors (P. Dalton et al., 2000). Although the taste system is very similar across different species of mammals, there is some variability; for example, cats are not sensitive to sweet.

Tastes excite specialized receptor cells on the tongue

In mammals, most taste receptor cells are located on small projections from the surface of the tongue; these little bumps are called **papillae** (singular *papilla*; Latin for "nipples") (**Figure 9.18**). Each papilla holds one or more **taste buds**, and each taste bud consists of a cluster

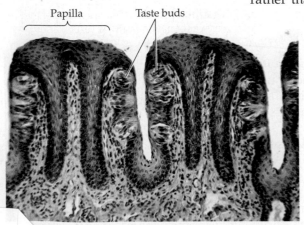
Papilla   Taste buds

Cross Section of the Tongue

of 50–150 taste receptor cells (**Figure 9.19a**). At the surface end of the taste bud is an opening called the **taste pore** (**Figure 9.19b**). The taste cells extend fine cilia into the taste pore, which come into contact with **tastants** (substances that can be tasted). As we'll discuss a little later, each taste receptor cell appears to specifically sense just one of the five basic tastes.

With a life span of only 10–14 days, taste cells are constantly being replaced. A single taste bud has receptor cells that are at many different stages of development (see Figure 9.19b). Not all of the sensory cells in taste buds signal taste sensations; some are pain receptors responding to stimuli such as "hot" red pepper, and others are touch receptors.

There are three kinds of taste papillae, distributed on the tongue as shown in **Figure 9.19c**. Each of the relatively few **circumvallate papillae** and **foliate papillae** contains many taste buds in its sides. **Fungiform papillae**, which contain only about six taste buds each, resemble button mushrooms in shape (*fungus* is Latin for "mushroom"). The tongue contains hundreds of fungiform papillae, but we'll see that the numbers vary greatly among individuals.

Many books show a map of the tongue indicating that each taste is perceived mainly in one region (sweet at the tip of the tongue, bitter at the back, and so on), but this map is erroneous. This scientific myth was first published in 1942 by a textbook author who (unintentionally) misrepresented someone else's research, and was then repeated by other textbooks! All five basic tastes can be perceived *anywhere* on the tongue where there are taste receptors (Chandrashekar, 2006; Collings, 1974; Yanagisawa et al., 1992). The areas do not differ greatly in the strength of taste sensations that they mediate (**Figure 9.19d**).

taste pore The small aperture through which tastant molecules are able to access the sensory receptors of the taste bud.

tastant A substance that can be tasted.

circumvallate papillae One of three types of small structures on the tongue, located in the back, that contain taste receptors.

foliate papillae One of three types of small structures on the tongue, located along the sides, that contain taste receptors.

fungiform papillae One of three types of small structures on the tongue, located in the front, that contain taste receptors.

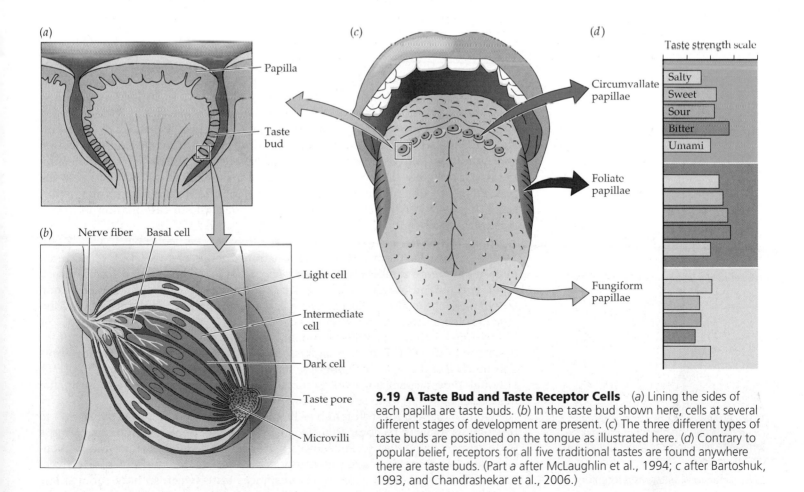

9.19 A Taste Bud and Taste Receptor Cells (a) Lining the sides of each papilla are taste buds. (b) In the taste bud shown here, cells at several different stages of development are present. (c) The three different types of taste buds are positioned on the tongue as illustrated here. (d) Contrary to popular belief, receptors for all five traditional tastes are found anywhere there are taste buds. (Part a after McLaughlin et al., 1994; c after Bartoshuk, 1993, and Chandrashekar et al., 2006.)

The ability to taste many substances is already well developed in humans at birth. Even premature infants show characteristic responses to different tastes, sucking in response to a sweet substance but trying to spit out a bitter substance. Newborns seem to be relatively insensitive to salty tastes, but a preference for mildly salty substances develops in the first few months. This preference does not seem to be related to experience with salty tastes; rather it probably indicates maturation of the mechanisms of salt perception (Beauchamp et al., 1994).

Different cellular processes transduce the basic tastes

The tastes salty and sour are evoked when taste cells are stimulated by simple ions acting on ion channels in the membranes of the taste cells. Sweet and bitter tastes are perceived by specialized receptor molecules and communicated by second messengers. At least two types of receptors may be involved in the perception of umami.

SALTY   Sodium ions (Na^+) are transported across the membranes of taste cells by sodium ion channels. Blocking these channels with a drug greatly reduces the salty taste of sodium chloride in both humans and rats; facilitating the passage of Na^+ across the membrane with another drug intensifies salty tastes (Schiffman et al., 1986). The entry of sodium ions partially depolarizes the taste cells and causes them to release neurotransmitters that stimulate the afferent neurons that relay the information to the brain. Blockade of sodium channels does not completely eradicate salt taste, however. A second salt receptor, a variant of a receptor called *TRPV1* (*transient receptor potential vanilloid type 1*), provides this additional sensitivity to Na^+, as well as other cations from salts (such as K^+ and Ca^{2+}) (Treesukosol et al., 2007). Transient receptor potential (TRP) proteins form a large family of receptors that are sensitive to external stimuli of many kinds, including temperature detectors in skin, as we discussed in Chapter 8.

SOUR   An acid tastes sour, whether it is a simple inorganic compound, such as hydrogen chloride, or a more complex organic compound, such as lactic acid. The property that all acids share is that they release hydrogen ions (H^+). A number of mechanisms have been proposed for sour detection, especially acid-sensing ion channels. For example, one type of potassium channel is blocked by H^+, preventing the release of potassium ions (K^+) from taste cells and causing depolarization and neurotransmitter release. Although the exact mechanisms of sour detection are not completely understood, sour-specific taste cells all appear to need one particular type of ion channel (called PKD2LI) in order to function (Huang et al., 2006). Interestingly, this same receptor detects the taste of carbonation in drinks (Chandrashekar et al., 2009).

SWEET   The molecular mechanisms in the transduction of sweet, bitter, and umami tastes are more complex than those responsible for salty and sour tastes. Sweet, bitter, and umami tastants appear to stimulate specialized receptor molecules on membranes of the taste cells, causing a cascade of internal cellular events involving G proteins and second messengers.

Investigators have identified two families of G protein–coupled taste receptors, designated **T1R** and **T2R**, that are expressed by some taste cells. These receptors function much like the slow metabotropic receptors that we considered in Chapter 3, although they may employ a unique G protein alpha subunit, called *gustducin*, that has been isolated in taste cells (McLaughlin et al., 1994).

Two members of the T1R family—T1R2 and T1R3—combine (*heterodimerize*) to function as a sweet receptor in taste cells (G. Nelson et al., 2001), recognizing a wide array of sweet-tasting substances. Mice lacking T1R2 or T1R3—and particularly knockout mice that lack both components—are rendered insensitive to sweet tastes (Zhao et al., 2003). Dozens of substances taste sweet, so how can a single

T1R   A family of taste receptor proteins that, when particular members heterodimerize, form taste receptors for sweet flavors and umami flavors.

T2R   A family of bitter taste receptors.

receptor be sensitive to sweet molecules that are as different as, for example, sugar, aspartame, and saccharin? Different sweet tastants appear to interact with different recognition sites within the T1R2+T1R3 receptor complex (Cui et al., 2006).

If you've spent any time around cats, you may be aware that they couldn't care less about sweets. It turns out that all cats, from house cats to leopards, share a mutation in the gene that encodes T1R2; their sweet receptors don't work (X. Li et al., 2009).

BITTER Bitter sensations are evoked by many different tastants. The association of bitter tastes with many toxic substances—such as nicotine, caffeine, strychnine, and morphine—provided strong evolutionary pressure to develop a high sensitivity to bitterness. The fact that different bitter substances can be discriminated—as determined by psychophysical work with human tasters (McBurney et al., 1972) and with animal subjects (Lush, 1989)—suggested that there is more than one receptor protein for bitterness.

Members of the T2R family of G protein–coupled receptors appear to be bitter receptors (E. Adler et al., 2000; Chandrashekar et al., 2000). The T2R family has about 30 members, and this large number may reflect the wide variety of bitter substances encountered in the environment, as well as the adaptive importance of being able to detect and avoid them. Interestingly, each bitter-sensing taste cell produces most or all of the different types of T2R bitter receptors (E. Adler et al., 2000). This means that these taste cells serve as broadly tuned bitter sensors: the cells are sensitive to any of a wide variety of bitter substances but not very good at encoding qualitative distinctions *between* different types of bitterness. This inability to discriminate makes sense from an evolutionary point of view: if bitterness signals toxicity, then being able to sensitively detect *any* bitterness is far more important than being able to evaluate the qualities of specific bitter tastes. The observation that rats and mice have only limited abilities to distinguish between different kinds of bitter substances (Brasser et al., 2005) buttresses this idea.

About 25% of people in the United States cannot taste the chemical phenylthiocarbamide (PTC) and the related compound 6-*n*-propylthiouracil (PROP), even though they can taste other bitter substances. Family studies indicate that tasters and nontasters are genetically different. Furthermore, some people, referred to as *supertasters*, exhibit heightened sensitivity to some bitter tastes, suggesting that they are genetically different as well (Bartoshuk and Beauchamp, 1994). In fact, supertasters also enjoy stronger sweet sensations from some substances. Nontasters of PROP have the fewest fungiform papillae (averaging 96 per square centimeter) on the tongue tip, medium tasters have an intermediate number (184), and supertasters have the most (425) (**Figure 9.20**).

UMAMI The fifth basic taste, **umami**, is described as a meaty, savory flavor. For most of the twentieth century, researchers argued about whether a distinct umami taste existed, but at least two types of receptors appear to be specialized to respond to exactly this sort of tastant. One of these, a variant of the metabotropic glutamate receptor, is expressed in certain taste buds (Chaudhari et al., 2000; Maruyama et al., 2006) and likely responds to the amino acid glutamate. Monosodium glutamate (MSG), which is used widely in cooking, stimulates this taste receptor.

Foods rich in protein will, of course, also be rich in amino acids, and this seems like useful information for an animal to detect. It turns out that a second probable

umami One of the five basic tastes (along with salty, sour, sweet, and bitter), probably mediated by amino acids in foods.

(a) Nontaster

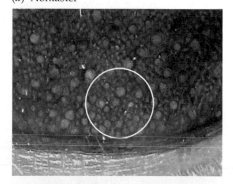

(b) Supertaster

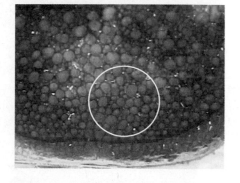

9.20 There's No Disputing Taste Buds We can count the number of fungiform papillae (larger blue-green circles) in a unit area (the white circle is about the size of a hole made by a paper punch). (a) The tongue from this person has only about 22 papillae in the defined area. (b) This "supertaster's" tongue has about twice as many. Some individuals have as few as 5 papillae in this space, while others pack in as many as 60. (Courtesy of Linda Bartoshuk and the Bartoshuk Lab.)

gustatory system The taste system.

pattern coding Coding of information in sensory systems based on the temporal pattern of action potentials.

labeled lines The concept that each nerve input to the brain reports only a particular type of information.

anosmia The inability to smell.

olfactory epithelium A sheet of cells, including olfactory receptors, that lines the dorsal portion of the nasal cavities and adjacent regions, including the septum that separates the left and right nasal cavities.

umami receptor is a heterodimer of T1R1 and T1R3 receptors. Despite the similarity to the T1R2+T1R3 sweet receptor described already, the T1R1+T1R3 receptor selectively responds to most of the 20 standard amino acids that might be encountered in the diet (G. Nelson et al., 2002).

In mice lacking the gene that encodes the T1R3 receptor, sensitivity to sweet and umami tastants is greatly reduced but not abolished (Damak et al., 2003), implying that there must be additional receptor systems for these tastes that are T1R3-independent. It also suggests that the especially attractive tastes—sweet and umami—may have shared evolutionary origins. The hunt for other types of taste receptors continues.

Taste information is transmitted to several parts of the brain

The **gustatory system** (from the Latin *gustare*, "to taste") extends from the taste receptor cells through brainstem nuclei and the thalamus to the cerebral cortex (**Figure 9.21**). Each taste cell transmits information to several afferent fibers, and each afferent fiber receives information from several taste cells. The afferent fibers run along three different cranial nerves—the facial (VII), glossopharyngeal (IX), and vagus (X) nerves (see Figure 2.9). The gustatory fibers in each of these nerves run to the brainstem. Here they synapse with second-order gustatory neurons that project to the ventral posterior medial nucleus of the thalamus. After another synapse, third-order gustatory fibers extend to the cortical taste areas in the somatosensory cortex.

For several decades it has been thought that individual taste cells express receptors for more than one of the five kinds of tastes, and that the brain extrapolates taste information from **pattern coding**, the relative activity across ensembles of axons from different taste receptor cells. However, selectively inactivating taste cells that express receptors for just one of the five tastes tends to completely eradicate sensitivity to that one taste while leaving the other four tastes unaffected (Huang et al., 2006). These effects suggest that taste is actually a simple system of **labeled lines**, in which there are five classes of taste receptor cells—one type for each taste (plus the sensors for heat, pain, and so on that we discussed earlier). Taste perception is thus determined by the specific axons that are active rather than by the pattern of activity across groups (Chandrashekar et al., 2006).

9.21 Anatomy and Main Pathways of the Human Gustatory System

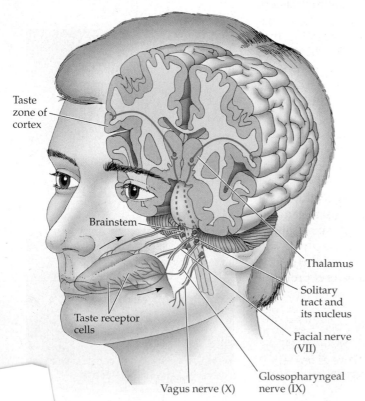

Taste zone of cortex

Brainstem

Taste receptor cells

Thalamus

Solitary tract and its nucleus

Facial nerve (VII)

Glossopharyngeal nerve (IX)

Vagus nerve (X)

Chemicals in the Air Elicit Odor Sensations

Many aspects of an animal's world are determined by chemicals carried in the air. Olfactory sensitivity varies widely across species of mammals: cats and mice, dogs and rabbits—all have a sharper sense of smell than humans. In the 1980s, a large survey of olfaction revealed widespread partial **anosmia** (odor blindness) among humans, with men exhibiting slightly worse olfaction than women (Gilbert and Wysocki, 1987). Dolphins don't have olfactory receptors at all (Freitag et al., 1998). These differences evolved because of variability in the importance of smell for survival and reproduction. Nevertheless, different species of mammals, including humans, accomplish olfaction in much the same way, as we will describe next.

The sense of smell starts with receptor neurons in the nose

In humans, a sheet of cells called the **olfactory epithelium** (**Figure 9.22**) lines the dorsal portion of the nasal cavities and adjacent regions, including the septum that separates the left and right nasal cavities. Within the olfactory epithelium of the

9.22 Anatomy and Main Pathways of the Human Olfactory System
The schematic at lower right indicates the main olfactory pathways in the brain.

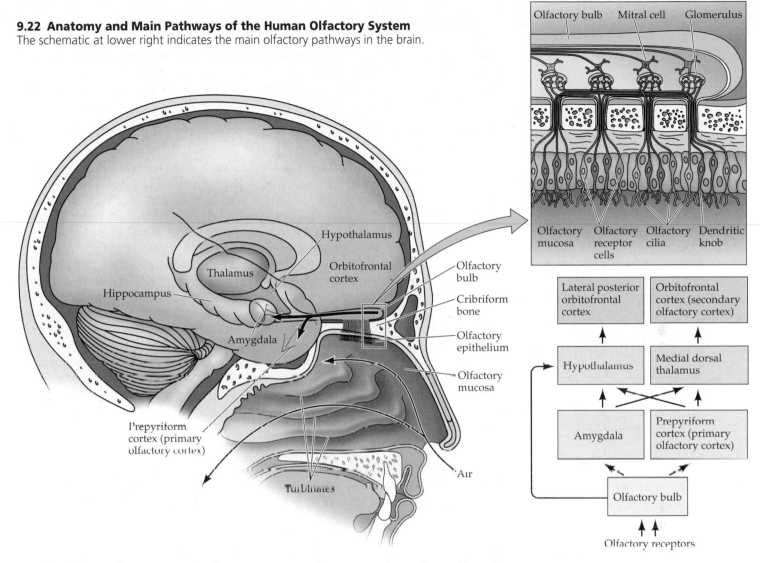

nasal cavity are three types of cells: receptor neurons, supporting cells, and basal cells. At least 6 million olfactory receptor neurons are found in the 2-cm^2 area of human olfactory epithelium on each side. In many other mammals this number is an order of magnitude greater; for example, bloodhounds have over 200 million receptor neurons in the olfactory epithelium. This is one reason why they can follow an odor trail better than we can, although, interestingly, people can learn to do this pretty well (J. Porter et al., 2007).

Each receptor cell has a long, slender apical dendrite that extends to the outermost layer of the epithelium, the mucosal surface. There, numerous **cilia** (singular *cilium*) emerge from the **dendritic knob** and extend along the mucosal surface. At the opposite end of each bipolar olfactory receptor cell, a fine, unmyelinated axon, which is among the smallest-diameter axons in the nervous system, runs to the olfactory bulb (to be discussed shortly).

In contrast with many other receptor neurons in the body, olfactory receptor neurons can be replaced in adulthood (Costanzo, 1991). One theory is that these receptor neurons normally degenerate after a few weeks because they are in direct contact with external irritants, such as chemicals and viruses, so they must constantly be replaced. It's clear that, if destroyed, an olfactory receptor cell will be replaced as an adjacent basal cell differentiates into a neuron and extends dendrites to the mucosal surface and an axon into the brain (C. T. Leung et al., 2007). What's not clear is whether receptor cells are *normally* "disposable," subject to constant turnover even in the absence of a particular trauma.

cilium   A hairlike extension.

dendritic knob   A portion of olfactory receptor cells present in the olfactory epithelium.

turbinates Complex shapes underlying the olfactory mucosa that direct inspired air over receptor cells.

If the olfactory epithelium is damaged, it can be regenerated and will properly reconnect to the olfactory bulb. The functional capability of these new connections has been clearly demonstrated in both behavioral and electrophysiological studies of animals with completely regenerated olfactory epithelium. Investigators are trying to determine how these neurons can regenerate while those in most other parts of the nervous system cannot.

Odorants excite specialized receptor molecules on olfactory receptor cells

Odorants enter the nasal cavity during inhalation and especially during periods of sniffing; they also rise to the nasal cavity from the mouth when we chew food. The direction of airflow in the nose is determined by complex curved surfaces called **turbinates** that form the nasal cavity (see Figure 9.22). Airborne molecules initially encounter the fluids of the mucosal layer, which contain binding proteins that transport odorants to receptor surfaces (Farbman, 1994).

The odorant stimulus then interacts with receptor proteins located on the surface of the olfactory cilia and the dendritic knob of the receptor cells. These receptor proteins are members of a superfamily of G protein–linked receptors (Buck and Axel, 1991). Interactions of odorants with their receptors trigger the synthesis of second messengers, including cyclic AMP (cAMP) and inositol trisphosphate (IP_3). Cyclic AMP opens cation channels (Brunet et al., 1996), resulting in depolarization of the olfactory receptor cell, which in turn leads to the generation of action potentials.

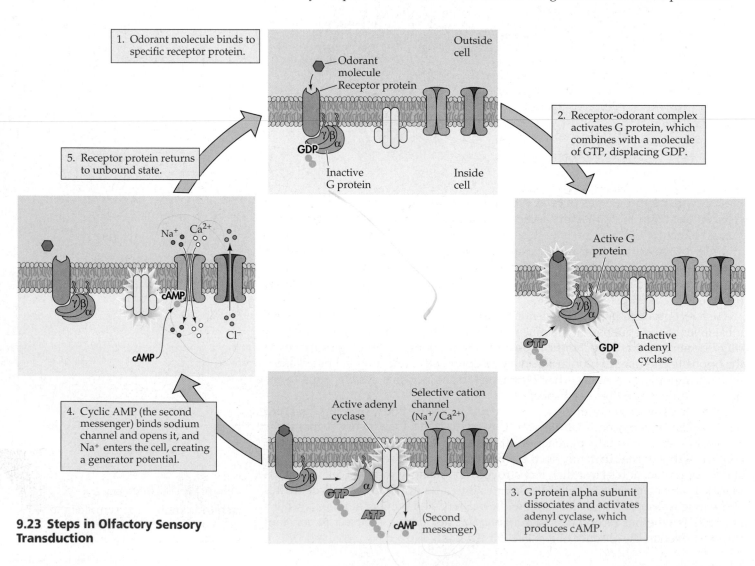

1. Odorant molecule binds to specific receptor protein.

Outside cell

Odorant molecule

Receptor protein

Inactive G protein

GDP

Inside cell

2. Receptor-odorant complex activates G protein, which combines with a molecule of GTP, displacing GDP.

5. Receptor protein returns to unbound state.

Active G protein

GTP → GDP

Inactive adenyl cyclase

Na^+ Ca^{2+}

cAMP

cAMP

Cl^-

4. Cyclic AMP (the second messenger) binds sodium channel and opens it, and Na^+ enters the cell, creating a generator potential.

Active adenyl cyclase

Selective cation channel (Na^+/Ca^{2+})

GTP

ATP

cAMP

(Second messenger)

3. G protein alpha subunit dissociates and activates adenyl cyclase, which produces cAMP.

9.23 Steps in Olfactory Sensory Transduction

This sensory transduction process, portrayed in **Figure 9.23**, is similar to the activation of other sensory systems, such as those for sweet and bitter tastes, and those in the eye (see Chapter 10). A specific G protein, named G_{olf} in recognition of its importance in olfaction, must be used by all the olfactory receptors because mice in which the gene that encodes G_{olf} is knocked out are generally anosmic (Belluscio et al., 1998).

Mice have about 2 million olfactory receptor cells, each of which expresses only one of about 1000 different receptor proteins. These receptor proteins can be divided into four different subfamilies of about 250 receptors each (Mori et al., 1999). Within each subfamily, members have a very similar structure and presumably recognize similar odorants. Each subfamily of receptors is synthesized in a separate band of the epithelium (**Figure 9.24**) (Vassar et al., 1993).

Now that it has been fully mapped, we know that the human genome also contains about 1000 apparent olfactory receptor genes, but only about 350 of these appear to be fully functional (Crasto et al., 2001; Glusman et al., 2001). The rest have apparently accumulated mutations and become nonfunctional during the course of evolution, implying that whatever they detected ceased to be important to our ancestors' survival and reproduction.

Since humans can discriminate about 5000 odors, each of the 350 functional odorant receptors must interact with a number of different odorants. Although some odorants may be "recognized" by a single kind of receptor molecule, most odorants probably are recognized by their activation of a characteristic combination of a few different kinds of receptor molecules (Duchamp-Viret et al., 1999)

Olfactory axons connect with the olfactory bulb, which sends its output to several brain regions

The numerous axons of the olfactory nerve terminate in a complex structure at the anterior end of the brain called the **olfactory bulb** (see Figures 9.22 and 9.24). The olfactory bulb is organized into many roughly spherically shaped neural circuits called **glomeruli** (singular *glomerulus*; from the Latin *glomus*, "ball"), within which the axon terminals of olfactory neurons synapse on the dendrites of the specialized **mitral cells** of the olfactory bulb (see Figure 9.22). The intrinsic circuitry within and between these glomeruli contributes to an elaborate system for modulating, tuning, and sharpening olfactory bulb activity (Aungst et al., 2003).

olfactory bulb   An anterior projection of the brain that terminates in the upper nasal passages and, through small openings in the skull, provides receptors for smell.

glomerulus   A complex arbor of dendrites from a group of olfactory cells.

mitral cell   A type of cell in the olfactory bulb that conducts smell information from the glomeruli to the rest of the brain.

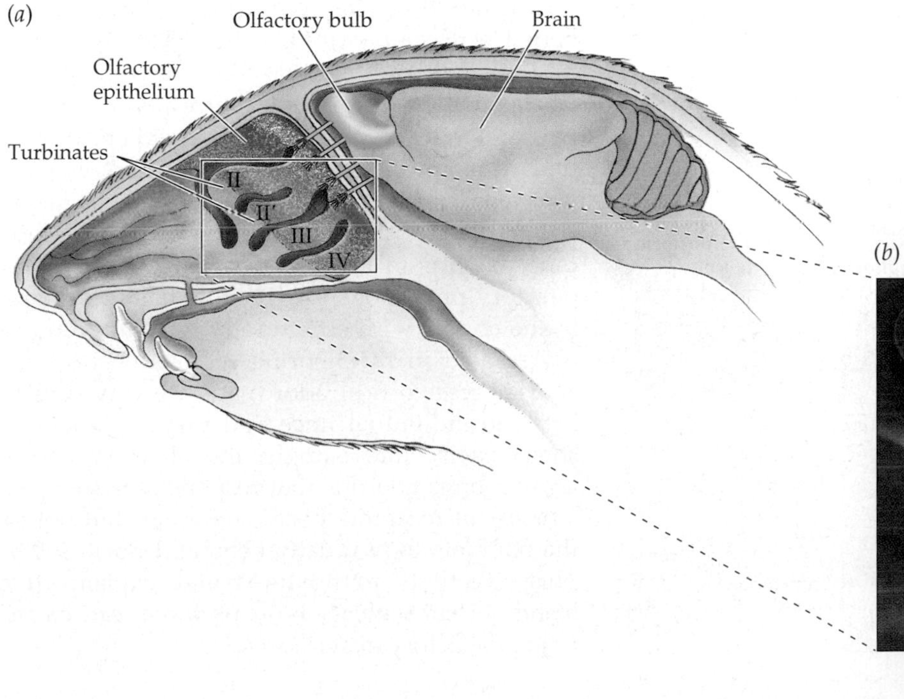

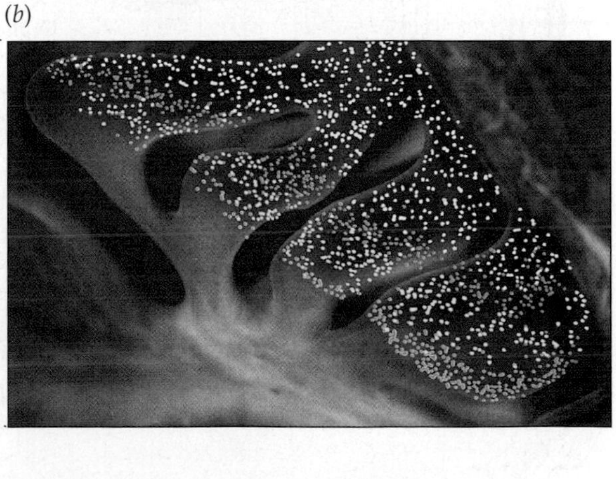

9.24 Different Kinds of Olfactory Receptor Molecules on the Olfactory Epithelium   (a) In this diagram showing the anatomy of the rat olfactory organ, the Roman numerals designate different turbinates. (b) The different colors in this photograph of rat olfactory epithelium show receptor locations for four receptor subfamilies (and also correspond to those on the olfactory bulb, which illustrate the probable topographic innervation of that structure). The different receptor types have distinct but overlapping spatial distributions. (After Vassar et al., 1993; b courtesy of Robert Vassar.)

(a)

(b)

Mice have about 1800 glomeruli. Each one receives inputs exclusively from olfactory neurons that are expressing the same type of olfactory receptor, and the glomeruli are organized in functional zones according to the four receptor protein subfamilies described in the previous section (Mori et al., 1999). So there appears to be a topographic distribution of smells in the bulb, and within each functional zone, neighboring glomeruli tend to receive inputs from receptors that are closely related.

Perhaps surprisingly, olfactory receptors are found in the axon terminals of olfactory neurons, as well as in their dendrites (Barnea et al., 2004). Experiments with knockout mice (see Box 7.3) suggest that olfactory receptor proteins help guide the innervating axons to their corresponding glomeruli (Imai et al., 2009). Disruptions of the receptor protein prevent newly generated olfactory receptor axons from reaching their normal targets (F. Wang et al., 1998). The olfactory bulb, in relation to the rest of the brain, is much smaller in humans than in animals, such as rats, that depend extensively on olfaction (compare Figures 9.22 and 9.24).

Output from the olfactory bulb consists of the axons from mitral cells, which extend to a variety of brain regions. These include the prepyriform and entorhinal cortex (note that smell is the only sensory modality that can synapse directly in the cortex rather than having to pass through the thalamus), the amygdala, and the hypothalamus.

9.25 Organization of Odor Projections in the Brain (a) Projections from two different types of olfactory receptors that were labeled with a barley lectin gene knock-in. Note that all of the olfactory neurons expressing one type of receptor terminate on the same glomerulus; all neurons expressing the other receptor terminate on a different glomerulus. This segregation is maintained largely in projections from the olfactory bulb to the cortex, terminating in a map of slightly overlapping fields. (b) Schematic of the organization of the olfactory projections from the two types of receptors. (After Zou et al., 2001.)

The olfactory map of receptor subtypes is maintained throughout the olfactory projections to the cortex. In a "knock-in" mouse model, the gene for a substance called *barley lectin* was inserted right next to a particular gene encoding one type of olfactory receptor. In other mice, the barley lectin gene was knocked in beside a different olfactory receptor gene belonging to a different subfamily (Zou et al., 2001). Because of the proximity of the genes, any neuron that expressed the targeted olfactory receptor gene also made barley lectin. Barley lectin is a transsynaptic marker, meaning that it is transferred across synapses, from the originating receptor neuron to the connecting neurons, all the way to the cortex.

Tracing these connections by following the barley lectin marker in their mice (**Figure 9.25a**), researchers found that two discrete glomeruli are labeled in the olfactory bulb, corresponding to the two different receptor types. Subsequent projections from these glomeruli to olfactory cortical sites maintained their high degree of segregation and terminated in stereotyped, partially overlapping patterns in the cortex (**Figure 9.25b**). The olfactory projections form highly complex maps in the cortex, with structurally related receptors represented in neighboring regions (Zou et al., 2005). These cortical odor maps are very similar between individual mice and may be innate to some extent. Interestingly, the olfactory cortex also contains neurons that respond selectively to *mixtures* of receptor-specific odorants, but not to the odorants individually (Zou and Buck, 2006). This sensitivity to mixtures may explain why blends of substances, as in perfume, can create unique olfactory experiences.

(a)

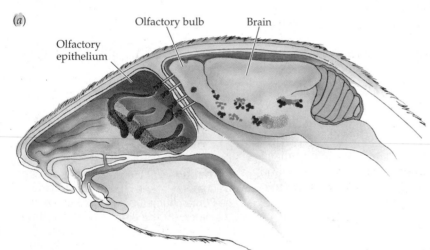

Olfactory epithelium   Olfactory bulb   Brain

(b)

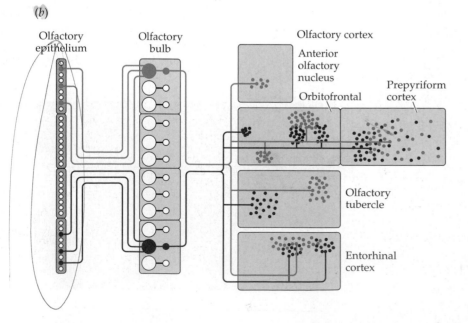

Olfactory epithelium   Olfactory bulb   Olfactory cortex

Anterior olfactory nucleus

Orbitofrontal   Prepyriform cortex

Olfactory tubercle

Entorhinal cortex

Functional-MRI studies suggest that the human prepyriform cortex is activated during sniffing, whether or not an odor is present, because the airflow induced by sniffing provides somatosensory stimulation. When an odor is present, primary olfactory cortex (prepyriform cortex) and secondary olfactory cortex (orbitofrontal cortex) are both activated during a sniff (Sobel et al., 2000). Furthermore, the same chemical mix may produce a different odor perception, depending on how fast the air enters during a sniff (Sobel et al., 1999). So the brain gauges the airflow rate during a sniff in order to interpret olfactory information properly. In addition, the size of the sniff appears to reflect attentional processes: larger sniffs occur during *imagined* sampling of pleasant odors, even though no odor is present (Bensafi et al., 2003).

Many vertebrates possess a vomeronasal system

Many vertebrates have a second chemical detection system that appears to specialize in detecting **pheromones**, the odor signals or trails that many animals secrete (see Chapter 5). This **vomeronasal system** (**Figure 9.26**), as it is called, is present in most terrestrial mammals, amphibians, and reptiles. The receptors for the system are found in a **vomeronasal organ** (**VNO**) of epithelial cells near the olfactory epithelium.

Rodents express two major families of vomeronasal receptors—V1R and V2R—that encode hundreds of different types of receptors (Dulac and Torello, 2003). Although both are families of G protein–coupled receptors, they are quite different from each other; in fact, the V1Rs are more similar to the T2R bitter taste receptors (discussed earlier) than they are to the receptors of the main olfactory system. Interestingly, the distribution of certain V2Rs differs between male and female rats, in keeping with the critical role of pheromones in organizing rodent reproductive behavior (Herrada and Dulac, 1997). V2Rs are also sensitive to certain major histocompatibility complex (MHC) molecules (Loconto et al., 2003); detection of MHCs is thought to be one of the main ways in which animals can assess their degree of relatedness to other animals, which has implications for mating strategies (see Chapter 6). A VNO-specific ion channel called TRP2 (*transient receptor potential 2*)—a member of the TRP family of sensory receptors that we mentioned earlier—is also essential for VNO function (Stowers et al., 2002).

VNO receptors are remarkably sensitive, detecting extremely low concentrations of pheromone molecules (Leinders-Zufall et al., 2000). The receptors send their information to the accessory olfactory bulb (adjacent to the main olfactory bulb), which projects to the medial amygdala, which in turn projects to the hypothalamus. Relying in part on MHCs, hamsters (Mateo and Johnston, 2000) and mice (Isles et al., 2001) can distinguish relatives from nonrelatives just by smell, even if they were raised by foster parents. Presumably these animals compare whether other animals smell like themselves, perhaps to avoid mating with kin.

In humans, molecular and anatomical evidence for a functional VNO is scanty at best. Although humans have a structure that resembles a VNO, analysis of the genome indicates that almost all of the human variants of the genes that encode the V1R and V2R vomeronasal receptors are nonfunctional, as is the gene that encodes the TRP2 ion channel.

Despite our apparent lack of a functional VNO, some behavioral evidence indicates that humans are sensitive to certain pheromones. For example, applying

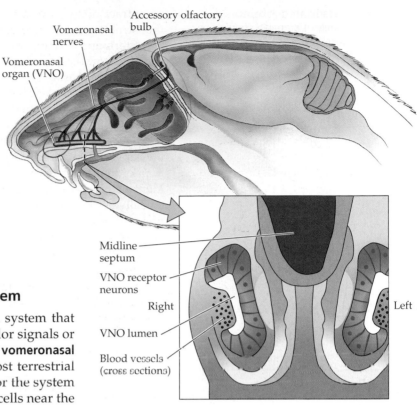

9.26 The Vomeronasal System

pheromone A chemical signal that is released outside the body of an animal and affects other members of the same species.

vomeronasal system A specialized chemical detection system that detects pheromones and transmits information to the brain.

vomeronasal organ (VNO) A collection of specialized receptor cells, near to but separate from the olfactory epithelium, that detect pheromones and send electrical signals to the accessory olfactory bulb in the brain.

trace amine–associated receptors (TAARs) A family of probable pheromone receptors produced by neurons in the main olfactory epithelium.

an extract of sweat to a woman's upper lip produces systematic changes in the menstrual cycle of the recipient that reflect the menstrual phase of the sweat *donor* (Stern and McClintock, 1998). Other studies have suggested that humans are sensitive to MHCs and may alter their social behavior and attraction to potential mates on this basis.

The recent discovery of a new class of olfactory receptors within the main olfactory epithelium (Liberles and Buck, 2006) may finally resolve the question of human pheromone sensitivity. Called **TAARs** (for **trace amine–associated receptors**), these receptors are expressed in specific olfactory neurons within the main olfactory epithelium, just like the regular olfactory receptors, but they seem to respond to pheromones instead of odorants. In mice, five of the nine TAARs that have been identified respond to volatile substances found in mouse urine; one of these is specifically activated by urine from adult males, but not urine from females or juvenile males. Other studies have shown that the secretion of gonadotropins (crucial for sexual behavior) is regulated primarily by projections from the main olfactory epithelium, not the vomeronasal organ (Yoon et al., 2005).

These and other observations indicate that the old notion that the olfactory epithelium detects odors while the VNO detects pheromones is an oversimplification, even in rodents. So the ability of humans to respond to pheromones, despite a vestigial or absent VNO, no longer presents a paradox. If rodents can detect pheromones through the olfactory epithelium, perhaps we can too.

SUMMARY

HEARING

Each Part of the Ear Performs a Specific Function in Hearing

- The **external ear** captures, focuses, and filters sound. The sound arriving at the **tympanic membrane** (eardrum) is focused by the three **ossicles** of the **middle ear** onto the **oval window** to stimulate the fluid-filled inner ear (**cochlea**). **Review Figure 9.2**, **Web Activity 9.1**

- Sound arriving at the oval window causes traveling waves to sweep along the **basilar membrane** of the cochlea. For high-frequency sounds, the largest displacement of the basilar membrane is at the base of the cochlea, near the oval window; for low-frequency sounds, the largest **amplitude** is near the apex of the cochlea. **Review Figure 9.3**, **Web Activity 9.2**

- The **organ of Corti** has both **inner hair cells** (about 3500 in humans) and **outer hair cells** (about 12,000 in humans). The inner hair cells convey most of the information about sounds. The outer hair cells change their length under the control of the brain, amplifying the movements of the basilar membrane in response to sound and sharpening the frequency tuning of the cochlea. **Review Figure 9.4**

- Movement of the **stereocilia** of the hair cells causes the opening and closing of ion channels, thereby **transducing** mechanical movement into changes in electrical potential. These changes in potential stimulate the nerve cell endings that contact the hair cells. **Review Figure 9.5**

- Efferents from the brainstem activate the outer hair cells, causing them to move and thereby fine-tune the cochlea to detect particular frequencies, a mechanism known as the **cochlear amplifier**. **Review Figure 9.6**

Auditory System Pathways Run from the Brainstem to the Cortex

- Afferents from the inner hair cells transmit auditory information into the **cochlear nuclei** of the brainstem. Cochlear neurons project bilaterally to the **superior olive**, which in turn innervates the **inferior colliculus**. From there auditory information is relayed to the **medial geniculate** and then **primary auditory cortex** in the temporal lobe. **Review Figure 9.7**, **Web Activity 9.3**

- At each level of the auditory system, sound frequencies are mapped in an orderly succession called **tonotopic organization**. **Review Figure 9.8**

Two Main Theories Describe How We Discriminate Pitch

- Two theories explain the discrimination of auditory frequency. According to **place theory**, our perception of **pitch** depends on where the sound causes maximal displacement of the basilar membrane. **Volley theory** argues that frequencies of auditory stimuli are reflected in the pattern or timing of neural discharges to allow pitch discrimination. In practice, we appear to use both of these encoding systems to determine pitch.

By Comparing the Ears, We Can Localize Sounds

■ Auditory localization depends on differences in the sounds arriving at the two ears. For low-frequency sounds, differences in time of arrival at the two ears (**latency differences**) are especially important. For high-frequency sounds, **intensity differences** are especially important. **Review Figure 9.10**

■ Birds and mammals evolved different neural mechanisms for localizing sounds; in mammals the lateral **superior olivary nucleus** of the brainstem processes differences in intensity, and the medial superior olivary nucleus processes differences in time of arrival. **Review Figure 9.11**

■ **Spectral filtering** performed by the external ear provides elevation cues.

The Auditory Cortex Performs Complex Tasks in the Perception of Sound

■ Primary auditory cortex is specialized for processing complex, biologically important sounds, rather than pure tones.

■ Experiences with sound early in life can influence later auditory localization and the responses of neurons in auditory pathways. Experiences later in life can also lead to changes in responses of auditory neurons. **Review Figure 9.14**

Deafness Is a Major Disorder of the Nervous System

■ Deafness can be caused by changes at any level of the auditory system. **Conduction deafness** consists of impairments in the transmission of sound through the external or middle ear to the cochlea. **Sensorineural deafness** arises in the cochlea, often because of the destruction of hair cells, or in the auditory nerve. **Central deafness** stems from brain damage.

■ Some forms of deafness may be alleviated by direct electrical stimulation of the auditory nerve (by a **cochlear implant**) or the brainstem cochlear nuclei (by an **auditory brainstem implant**). Genetic manipulations can induce new hair cell growth in laboratory animals, raising hope of a gene therapy for sensorineural deafness. **Review Figure 9.15, Web Activity 9.4**

VESTIBULAR PERCEPTION

The Receptor Mechanisms for the Vestibular System Are in the Inner Ear

■ The receptors of the vestibular system lie within the inner ear next to the cochlea. In mammals the vestibular system consists of three **semicircular canals**, plus the **utricle** and the **saccule**. **Review Figure 9.16**

■ Within these structures, the receptors, like those of the auditory system, are groups of hair cells whose bending leads to the excitation of nerve fibers. The semicircular canals detect rotation of the body in three planes, and the utricle and saccule sense static positions and linear accelerations. **Review Figure 9.17**

Evolution Has Shaped the Auditory and Vestibular End Organs

■ From the **lateral-line system** of fishes and some amphibians evolved the vestibular system, followed by the auditory system. **Review Figure 9.17**

Nerve Fibers from the Vestibular Portion of the Vestibulocochlear Nerve (VIII) Synapse in the Brainstem

■ Nerve fibers from the vestibular receptors enter the brainstem and synapse in the **vestibular nuclei**, which send their outputs to the motor nuclei of numerous structures, including the eye muscles, the thalamus, and the cerebral cortex.

■ One important function of the vestibular system is the **vestibulo-ocular reflex** (**VOR**), which uses vestibular information about head rotations to precisely move the eyes to keep our gaze fixed.

Some Forms of Vestibular Excitation Produce Motion Sickness

■ The vestibular system provides extensive information to brain motor systems, offering valuable feedback about body movement to coordinate our behavior.

■ The **sensory conflict theory** argues that contradictory sensory messages are the cause of **motion sickness**.

THE CHEMICAL SENSES: TASTE AND SMELL

Chemicals in Tastants Elicit Taste Sensations

■ Humans detect only five main tastes: salty, sour, sweet, bitter, and **umami**.

■ In mammals, most taste receptor cells are located in clusters of cells called **taste buds**. Taste cells extend fine cilia into the **taste pore** of each bud, where **tastants** come into contact with them. The taste buds are situated on small projections from the surface of the tongue called **papillae**. **Review Figure 9.19, Web Activity 9.5**

■ The tastes of salty and sour are evoked primarily by the action of simple ions on ion channels in the membranes of taste cells. Sweet and bitter tastes are perceived by specialized receptor molecules belonging to the **T1R** and **T2R** families, which are coupled to G proteins. A heterodimer of T1R proteins functions as a sweet receptor. Umami is detected by a specialized glutamate receptor and another T1R heterodimer that responds to most amino acids. About 25 different T2R receptors act as bitter receptors.

■ Each taste cell transmits information to several afferent fibers, and each afferent fiber receives information from several taste cells. The afferent fibers run along cranial nerves to brainstem nuclei. The **gustatory system** extends from the taste receptor cells through brainstem nuclei to the thalamus and then to the cerebral cortex. **Review Figure 9.21, Web Activity 9.6**

■ Each taste axon responds most strongly to one category of tastes, providing a **labeled line** to the brain.

Chemicals in the Air Elicit Odor Sensations

■ In contrast to being able to detect only a few tastes, humans can detect thousands of different odors. Yet many species depend more on smell than humans do and thus have even more olfactory receptor cells and larger **olfactory bulbs**.

■ Each olfactory receptor cell is a small bipolar cell whose dendrites extend to the **olfactory epithelium** in the nose. The fine, unmyelinated axon runs to the olfactory bulb and synapses on the dendrites of mitral cells, within **glomeruli**. If an olfactory receptor cell dies, an adjacent cell will replace it. **Review Figure 9.22**

■ There is a large family of odor receptor molecules, each of which utilizes G proteins and second messengers. **Review Figure 9.23**

■ Neurons that express the same olfactory receptor gene are not closely clustered in the olfactory epithelium; rather they are limited to distinct regions of the epithelium. Each sub-family of receptors is synthesized in a different band of the epithelium.

■ All olfactory neurons expressing a particular receptor synapse in the same glomerulus in the olfactory bulb. The projection from the epithelium to the bulb maintains a zonal distribution for different kinds of receptor molecules.

■ Outputs from the olfactory bulb extend to prepyriform cortex, entorhinal cortex, amygdala, and hypothalamus, among other brain regions. Olfactory projections to the cortex maintain a stereotyped olfactory map of slightly overlapping projections from the glomeruli.

■ The **vomeronasal organ** contains receptors to detect **pheromones** released from other individuals of the species. These receptors transmit signals to the accessory olfactory bulb, which in turn communicates with the amygdala. Pheromones can also be detected by specialized receptors in the main olfactory epithelium. **Review Figure 9.24**

Go to **www.biopsychology.com** for study questions, quizzes, key terms, and other resources.

Recommended Reading

Bartoshuk, L. M., and Beauchamp, G. K. (2005). *Tasting and smelling* (2nd ed.). New York: Academic Press.

Doty, R. L. (2003). *Handbook of gustation and olfaction* (2nd ed.). New York: Dekker.

Finger, T. E., Silver, W. L., and Restrepo, D. (Eds.). (2000). *The neurobiology of taste and smell* (2nd ed.). New York: Wiley-Liss.

Menini, A. (2009). *The neurobiology of olfaction.* Boca Raton, FL: CRC Press.

Musiek, F. E., and Baran, J. A. (2007). *The auditory system: Anatomy, physiology, and clinical correlates.* Boston: Pearson.

Palmer, A., and Rees, A. (2010). *Oxford handbook of auditory science.* Oxford, England: Oxford University Press.

Wilson, D. A., and Stevenson, R. J. (2006). *Learning to smell: Olfactory perception from neurobiology to behavior.* Baltimore: Johns Hopkins University Press.

Yost, W. A. (2006). *Fundamentals of hearing* (5th ed.). San Diego, CA: Academic Press.

CHAPTER 10

Vision: From Eye to Brain

When Seeing Isn't Seeing

It was cold in the bathroom, so the young woman turned on a small heater before she got in the shower. She didn't know that the heater was malfunctioning, filling the room with deadly, odorless carbon monoxide gas. Her husband found her unconscious on the floor and called for an ambulance to rush her to the emergency room. When she regained consciousness, "D.F." seemed to have gotten off lightly, avoiding what could have been a fatal accident. She could understand the doctors' questions and reply sensibly, move all her limbs, and perceive touch on her skin. But something was wrong with her sight.

D.F. couldn't recognize faces, even her husband's, nor could she name any objects presented to her view. D.F. still cannot recognize objects today, more than 15 years after her accident. Yet she is not entirely blind. Show her a flashlight and she can tell you that it's made of shiny aluminum with some red plastic, but she doesn't recognize it ("Is it a kitchen utensil?"). Without telling her what it is, if you ask her to pick it up, D.F.'s hand goes directly to the flashlight and holds it exactly as one normally holds a flashlight. Show D.F. a slot in a piece of plastic and she cannot tell you whether the slot is oriented vertically, horizontally, or diagonally; but if you hand her a disk and ask her to put it through the hole, D.F. invariably turns the disk so that it goes smoothly through the slot (Goodale et al., 1991).

Can D.F. see or not?

Vision offers tremendous benefits for vital behaviors such as finding food, avoiding predators, finding a mate, and locating shelter, so a variety of visual systems—different in some respects but similar in others—have evolved. Beyond serving basic needs, vision affords most of us the pleasures of nature and art, reading and writing, and watching films and TV. Because vision is so important, much effort is expended to improve it, to prevent its deterioration, and even to restore vision to the blind.

However, the sheer volume of visual information poses a serious problem. Seeing the surrounding world has been compared to drinking from a waterfall. How does the visual system avoid being overwhelmed by the flood of information entering the eyes? The answer seems to be that the visual perceptions of each species depend on how their eyes and brains evolved to process information about light and attend to the aspects likely to be important for their survival.

Different kinds of processing allow us to see the form, color, position, and distance of objects in the visual field and to recognize objects. Research on vision is one of the most active fields of biological psychology and neuroscience, as it should be, since about one-third of the human cerebral cortex is devoted to visual analysis and perception.

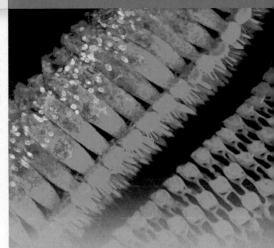

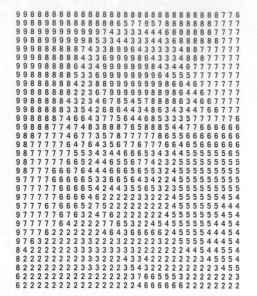

```
99888888888888888888888888888776
99889898888888886577957888888887777
99899999999974333344468888887777
99889999998533443334436888888777
99988888874338996433334887777777
99988888843369999864333488877777
99998888643499999984344677777777
99888888533699999999645557777777
99888888423889999999988664677777
99888888223679999999889864467777
99888884323467845457888863467777
99888883354268644386343447766777
99888874664377564468533357777776
99887774748388876588854477666666
98877774673578777778656566666666
98777776476435677677766465666666
98777775534346665343445555555565
98777776652446556774232555555555
98777776664446665556532455555555
97777666665336656434224555555555
97777766665424435565323555555555
97777666466222223322245555555555
97776766652752222222245555555444
97777767632476222224555555555454
97777764222277653224554555555454
97776222222246436666624555544454
97632222233223222223225555544454
84222222333333333222222244544554
82222222233322243342222222345554
82222222233322235432222222223455
62222222222222223766555532222223
62222222222222224666666622222222
```

10.1 Can You Identify the Subject?
This array of numbers represents the point-to-point illumination of a picture, with each number representing a particular shade of gray from darkest (2) to lightest (9).

visual field   The whole area that you can see without moving your head or eyes.

visual acuity   Sharpness of vision.

photoreceptors   Neural cells in the retina that respond to light.

10.2 The Subject of Figure 10.1

Vision Provides Information about the Form, Color, Location, Movement, and Identity of Objects

Although we're familiar with vision because we use it every day, some features of visual perception are not immediately apparent. For one thing, it's easy to overlook how much information has to be analyzed in the fraction of a second we need to recognize a scene or a face. In addition, you might think that the visual system simply gives a faithful report of whatever light reaches our eyes, but that is not so. Rather, neurons in the eye and brain select out certain important features and construct a visual experience that emphasizes those features, such as context and movement. So let's begin by getting an idea of the scope of the problem of visual perception, and then look at some examples of how the visual system constructs our perceptions.

Perception of form and identification of objects are complex accomplishments

The whole area that you can see without moving your head or eyes is called your **visual field**. In a single glance, you perceive the details of objects accurately only in the center of your visual field. We are usually not aware of this phenomenon, because we move our gaze rapidly as we scan a scene or read text (Rucci et al., 2007). Thus, we build up a sort of collage of detailed views. But try keeping your eyes fixed on a letter in the center of a line and then attempt to read a word on the opposite page. You'll find this task difficult because **visual acuity** (the sharpness of vision) falls off rapidly from the center of the visual field toward the periphery. This difference in acuity across the visual field is the reason your gaze has to jump from place to place in a line as you read.

If a stimulus suddenly appears away from the center of the visual field, we shift our view, placing the new stimulus in the center of the visual field, where we can see it clearly. When we examine the circuitry of the retina and of higher stations of the visual system a little later, we will learn why vision is so much more acute in the center of the visual field.

We perceive a simple form like a triangle or recognize the face of a friend so rapidly and easily that we do not appreciate that these are exceedingly complex events requiring processing in several parts of the brain. Most of the forms we see are embedded in complicated fields of objects; extracting a particular form for attention and identification requires practice and skill. It has been very difficult for artificial systems to achieve even primitive recognition of objects. Furthermore, recognition requires more than the accurate perception of objects. For example, some people with brain damage, like D.F., lose their ability to recognize familiar faces or objects, even though they can still describe them accurately.

Consider the complexity of visual perception at the level of the nervous system. The retina, a sheet of tissue covering the inside of the eye, contains about 100 million light-sensitive receptor cells (called **photoreceptors**). At any given moment, each retinal receptor is in a particular state of excitation that can be represented numerically. About three times per second, the nervous system surveys the values of all the millions of photoreceptors. It then faces the stupendous task of trying to figure out what in the outside world could have produced that particular array of values.

Figure 10.1 illustrates a simple example of such a task. The numbers in this array represent shades of gray from darkest (2) to lightest (9). As you inspect this grid, you may notice that the numbers representing lighter shades appear mainly in the upper half of the array, but you don't perceive a familiar form. Now look at **Figure 10.2**, which shows the shades of gray that correspond to the numbers in the array in Figure 10.1; the form and identity leap out. Your nervous system processes data such as those in Figure 10.1 to achieve the perception of the form in Figure 10.2 in an instant. How the nervous system processes so much data so

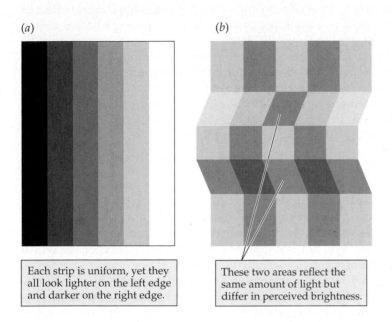

(a) (b)

Each strip is uniform, yet they all look lighter on the left edge and darker on the right edge.

These two areas reflect the same amount of light but differ in perceived brightness.

10.3 The Effect of Context on the Perception of Brightness (a) Although each of the four central bars shown here is uniform in color, each appears lighter on the left edge and darker on the right. (b) Shading around a patch of light affects the perception of brightness. For example, even though the two indicated patches are the same shade of gray, one appears darker than the other. If you don't believe this, punch two holes 17 mm apart on a piece of white paper, put the holes over the two areas, and compare them again. (Part b from Adelson, 1993.)

quickly is the staggering problem that confronts anyone who tries to understand vision.

It appears we have to *learn* how to recognize faces and objects. In fact, as we'll see, object recognition, color, brightness, motion, and other aspects of visual perception do not come directly from the retinal image. Rather, the retinal stimuli trigger responses determined by the consequences of our prior experiences. That is, "the observer sees the probability distribution of the possible sources of the visual stimulus" (Purves and Lotto, 2003, p. 227).

Brightness is created by the visual system

The brightness dimension of visual perception is created in part by the visual system, not simply by the amount of light reflected. Figure 10.3 presents two examples. The enhancement of the boundaries of the bars in **Figure 10.3a**, each of which is uniformly gray but looks as though it varies in brightness, is based on a neural process called **lateral inhibition**.

Lateral inhibition occurs where the neurons in a region—in this case, retinal cells—are interconnected, either through their own axons or by means of intermediary neurons (interneurons), and each neuron tends to inhibit its neighbors (**Figure 10.4**). The photoreceptors stimulated by the right-hand edge of each dark band are inhibited by the neighboring photoreceptors stimulated by the lighter band next door. Thus, photoreceptors on the right edge report receiving less light than they actually do (i.e., that edge looks darker to us).

Again in **Figure 10.3b**, two patches that clearly differ in brightness *reflect the same amount of light*. If you use your hands to cover the surrounding pattern to the left and right of the two patches, they appear

lateral inhibition The phenomenon by which interconnected neurons inhibit their neighbors, producing contrast at the edges of regions.

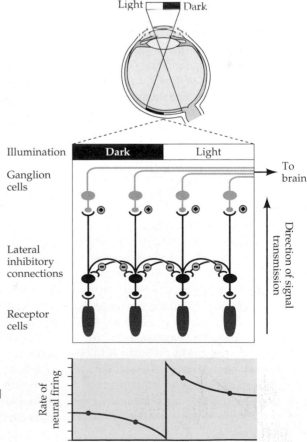

10.4 Lateral Inhibition in the Retina As the graph shows, because of lateral inhibitory connections, the two central receptor cells differ more in their rates of firing than do either the two left-hand cells or the two right-hand cells. This is a simplified view; in fact, each blue cell inhibits many of its neighbors and not just those directly adjacent.

the same. How are such puzzling effects produced? Although the contrast effect in Figure 10.3*a* is determined, at least in part, by interactions among adjacent retinal cells, the two areas indicated in Figure 10.3*b* are not adjacent, so the effect must be produced higher in the visual system (Adelson, 1993). The important point is that our visual experience is not a simple reporting of the physical properties of light (reviewed in **Box 10.1**). Rather, our experience of light versus dark is created by the brain in response to many factors, including surrounding stimuli. Later in the chapter we'll find that our experience of color is also created by the visual system, and not a simple reporting of the wavelengths of light.

Motion can enhance the perception of objects

Movement enhances the visibility of objects, which is an important adaptation because predators and prey alike must be sensitive to moving objects in order to survive. In the periphery of our visual field, we may not be able to see stationary objects, but we can detect motion. Again, our visual system is not simply reporting the light that reaches our eye, but is highlighting important aspects of the world around us, like movement.

We detect motion only within a range of speed that is appropriate to the locomotion of animals. Anything that moves faster is a blur or may be invisible, as is a bullet speeding by. Anything that moves too slowly—such as the hour hand of a clock—is not seen as moving, although we can note from time to time that it has changed position. A succession of still pictures, presented at the proper rate, can cause apparent motion, as in motion pictures. Perception of motion is analyzed by special areas of the brain, as we will see later in this chapter.

BOX 10.1 The Basics of Light

The physical energy to which our visual system responds is a band of electromagnetic radiation. This radiation comes in very small packets of energy called **quanta** (singular *quantum*). Each quantum can be described by a single number, representing its **wavelength** (the distance between two adjacent crests of vibratory activity).

The human visual system responds only to quanta whose wavelengths lie within a very narrow section of the total electromagnetic range, from about 400 to 700 nm, as the figure shows. Such quanta of light energy are called **photons** (from the Greek *phos*, "light"). The band of radiant energy visible to animals may be narrow, but it provides for accurate reflection from the surface of objects in the size range that matters for survival. Radio waves are good for imaging objects of astronomical size; X-rays penetrate below the surfaces of objects. Each photon has a very small amount of energy; the exact amount depends on the wavelength. A single photon of wavelength 560 nm contains only a tiny amount

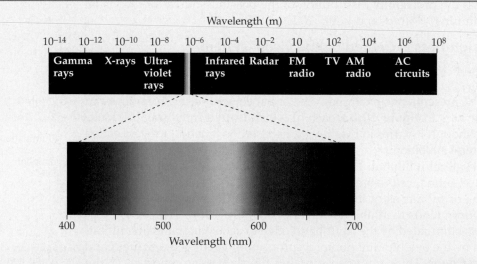

of energy. A 100-watt (W) lightbulb gives off only about 3 W of visible light; the rest is heat. But even the 3 W of light amounts to 8 quintillion (8×10^{18}) photons per second.

When quanta within the visible spectrum enter the eye, they can evoke visual sensations. The exact nature of such sensations depends both on the wavelengths of

the quanta and on the number of quanta per second.

quantum (pl. quanta) A unit of radiant energy.

wavelength The length between two peaks in a repeated stimulus such as a wave, light, or sound.

photon A quantum of light energy.

The Visual System Extends from the Eye to the Brain

To understand how the visual system constructs our vision, let's follow the path of information triggered by light as we explore the visual system, starting with the optical properties of the eye and then the neural processes in the retina, including two types of photoreceptors and the mechanisms that allow them to work in an astonishingly wide range of light intensities. Then we'll examine different parts of the retina and trace the information flowing from retina to cortex.

The vertebrate eye acts in some ways like a camera

The eye is an elaborate structure with optical functions (capturing light and forming detailed spatial images) and neural functions (transducing light into neural signals and processing those signals). Accurate optical images are a prerequisite for discerning the shapes of objects; that is, light from a point on a target object must end up as a point—rather than a blur—in the retinal image. Without optical images, light-sensitive cells would be able to detect only the presence or absence of light and would not be able to see forms, just as a camera without a lens would be unable to produce a picture.

To produce optical images, the eye has many of the features of a camera, starting with the **cornea** and **lens** to focus light (**Figure 10.5**). Light travels in a straight line until it encounters a change in the density of the medium, which causes light rays to bend. This bending of light rays, called **refraction**, is the basis of such instruments as eyeglasses, telescopes, and microscopes. The cornea of the eye—the curvature of which is fixed—bends light rays and is primarily responsible for forming the image on the retina.

In a camera, the lens moves nearer to or farther from the film to adjust focus, and the same system is used in the eyes of fishes, amphibians, and reptiles. In mammals and birds, however, focus is adjusted by changes in the *shape* of the lens, which is controlled by the **ciliary muscles** inside the eye. As the degree of contraction of the ciliary muscles varies, the lens focuses images of nearer or farther objects so that they form sharp images on the retina; this process of focusing is called **accommodation**. As mammals age, their lenses become less elastic and therefore less able to change curvature to bring nearby objects into focus. Aging humans correct this problem by wearing reading glasses.

The amount of light that enters the eye is controlled by the size of the **pupil**, which is an opening in the colorful disc called the **iris** (see Figure 10.5). In Chapter 2 we mentioned that dilation of the pupils is controlled by the sympathetic division of the autonomic system, and constriction by the parasympathetic division. Because usually both divisions are active, pupil size reflects a balance of influences.

cornea The transparent outer layer of the eye, whose curvature is fixed. It bends light rays and is primarily responsible for forming the image on the retina.

lens A structure in the eye that helps focus an image on the retina.

refraction The bending of light rays by a change in the density of a medium, such as the cornea and the lens of the eyes.

ciliary muscle One of the muscles that controls the shape of the lens inside the eye, focusing an image on the retina.

accommodation The process of focusing by the ciliary muscles and the lens to form a sharp image on the retina.

pupil The aperture, formed by the iris, that allows light to enter the eye.

iris The circular structure of the eye that provides an opening to form the pupil.

10.5 Structures of the Human Eye
Here the right eye is viewed in cross section from above. The visual image focused on the retina is inverted top to bottom and reversed right to left. The gap in the retina where the optic nerve leaves the eyeball is called the *optic disc*.

extraocular muscle   One of the muscles attached to the eyeball that control its position and movements.

retina   The receptive surface inside the eye that contains photoreceptors and other neurons.

rods   A class of light-sensitive receptor cells (photoreceptors) in the retina that are most active at low levels of light.

cones   A class of photoreceptor cells in the retina that are responsible for color vision.

bipolar cells   A class of interneurons of the retina that receive information from rods and cones and pass the information to retinal ganglion cells.

ganglion cells   A class of cells in the retina whose axons form the optic nerve.

optic nerve   Cranial nerve II; the collection of ganglion cell axons that extend from the retina to the optic chiasm.

During an eye examination, the doctor may use a drug to block acetylcholine transmission in the parasympathetic synapses of your iris; this drug relaxes the sphincter muscle fibers and permits the pupil to open widely. One drug that has this effect—*belladonna* (Italian for "beautiful lady")—got its name because it was thought to make a woman more beautiful by giving her the wide-open pupils of an attentive person. Other drugs, such as morphine, constrict the pupils.

The movement of the eyes is controlled by the **extraocular muscles**, three pairs of muscles that extend from the outside of the eyeball to the bony socket of the eye. Fixating still or moving targets requires delicate control of these muscles.

Visual processing begins in the retina

The first stages of visual-information processing occur in the **retina**, the receptive surface inside the back of the eye (**Figure 10.6a**). The retina is only 200–300 μm thick—not much thicker than the edge of a razor blade—but it contains several types of cells in distinct layers (**Figure 10.6b**). The photoreceptor cells are modified neurons; some are called **rods** because of their relatively long, narrow form; others are called **cones** (**Figure 10.6c**). There are several different types of cones, which respond differently to light of varying wavelengths, providing us with color vision as described later in the chapter. Both rod and cone photoreceptors release neurotransmitter molecules that control the activity of the **bipolar cells** that synapse with them (see Figure 10.6b). The bipolar cells, in turn, connect with **ganglion cells**. The axons of the ganglion cells form the **optic nerve**, which carries information to the brain.

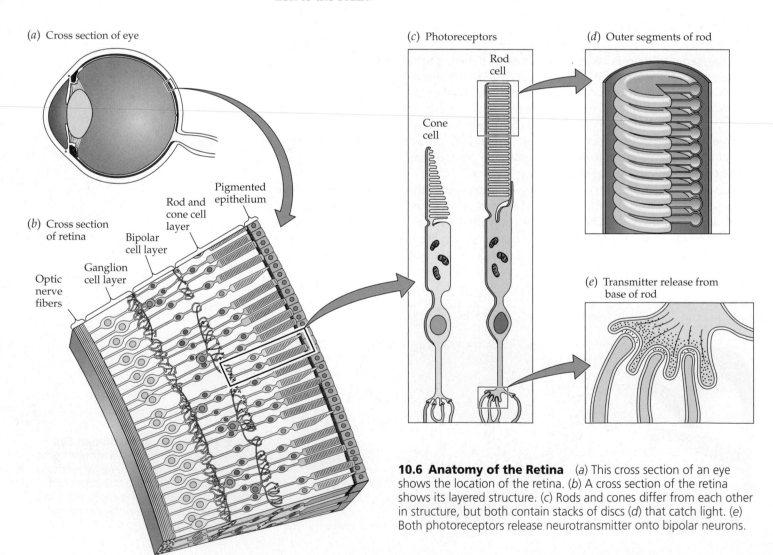

(a) Cross section of eye

(b) Cross section of retina

Optic nerve fibers
Ganglion cell layer
Bipolar cell layer
Rod and cone cell layer
Pigmented epithelium

(c) Photoreceptors
Rod cell
Cone cell

(d) Outer segments of rod

(e) Transmitter release from base of rod

10.6 Anatomy of the Retina   (a) This cross section of an eye shows the location of the retina. (b) A cross section of the retina shows its layered structure. (c) Rods and cones differ from each other in structure, but both contain stacks of discs (d) that catch light. (e) Both photoreceptors release neurotransmitter onto bipolar neurons.

Horizontal cells and **amacrine cells** are especially significant in interactions within the retina, such as lateral inhibition. The horizontal cells make contacts among the receptor cells and bipolar cells; the amacrine cells contact both the bipolar and the ganglion cells.

Interestingly, the rods, cones, bipolar cells, and horizontal cells generate only graded local potentials; they do not produce action potentials. These cells affect each other through the graded release of neurotransmitters in response to graded changes in electrical potentials. The ganglion cells, on the other hand, do conduct action potentials. Because the ganglion cells have action potentials and are relatively large, they were the first retinal cells to have their electrical activity recorded. From the receptor cells to the ganglion cells, enormous amounts of data converge and are compressed; the human eye contains about 100 million rods and 4 million cones, but there are only 1 million ganglion cells to transmit that information to the brain. Thus, a great deal of information processing is done in the eye.

Two different functional systems correspond to the two different populations of receptors (rods and cones) in the retina. One system involves the rods and works in dim light, so it is called the **scotopic system** (from the Greek *skotos*, "darkness," and *ops*, "eye"). The scotopic system has only one receptor type (rods) and therefore does not respond differentially to different wavelengths, which is the basis for the saying "at night, all cats are gray." There is a lot of convergence in the scotopic cell, as many rods provide information to each ganglion cell.

The other system requires more light and, in some species, shows differential sensitivity to wavelengths, enabling color vision. This system involves the cones and is called the **photopic system** (which, like the term *photon*, comes from the Greek *phos*, "light"). Compared to the scotopic system, the photopic system has less convergence, as some ganglion cells report information from only a single cone.

At moderate levels of illumination, both the rods and the cones function, and some ganglion cells receive input from both types of receptors. **Table 10.1** summarizes the characteristics of the photopic and scotopic systems.

Photoreceptors transduce light into chemical reactions

The extraordinary sensitivity of rods and cones is the result of their unusual structure and biochemistry. A portion of their structure, when magnified, looks like a large stack of pancakes or discs (**Figure 10.6d**). The stacking of discs increases the probability of capturing light particles. This is an especially important function because light is reflected in many directions by the surface of the eyeball, the lens, and the fluid inside the eye, so only a fraction of the light that strikes the cornea actually reaches the retina.

horizontal cells Specialized retinal cells that contact both the receptor cells and the bipolar cells.

amacrine cells Specialized retinal cells that contact both the bipolar cells and the ganglion cells, and are especially significant in inhibitory interactions within the retina.

scotopic system A system in the retina that operates at low levels of light and involves the rods.

photopic system A system in the retina that operates at high levels of light, shows sensitivity to color, and involves the cones.

TABLE 10.1 Properties of the Human Photopic and Scotopic Visual Systems

Property	Photopic system	Scotopic system
Receptors[a]	Cones	Rods
Approximate number of receptors per eye	4 million	100 million
Photopigments[b]	Three classes of cone opsins; the basis of color vision	Rhodopsin
Sensitivity	Low; needs relatively strong stimulation; used for day vision	High; can be stimulated by weak light intensity; used for night vision
Location in retina[c]	Concentrated in and near fovea; present less densely throughout retina	Outside fovea
Receptive field size and visual acuity	Small in fovea, so acuity is high; larger outside fovea	Larger, so acuity is lower
Temporal responses	Relatively rapid	Slow

[a]Cones and rods are illustrated in Figure 10.6c.
[b]Figure 10.24 shows the spectral sensitivities of the photopigments.
[c]See Figure 10.9.

rhodopsin The photopigment in rods that responds to light.

RETINAL One of the two components of photopigments in the retina.

opsin One of the two components of photopigments in the retina.

The quanta of light that strike the discs are captured by special photopigment receptor molecules. In the rods this photopigment is **rhodopsin** (from the Greek *rhodon*, "rose," and *opsis*, "vision"). Cones use similar photopigments, as we will see later. The rod and cone photopigments in the eye consist of two parts: RETINAL (an abbreviated name for *retinaldehyde*, which is vitamin A aldehyde) and **opsin**. (In this book the noun RETINAL, standing for the molecule, is printed in small capital letters to distinguish it from the adjective *retinal*, meaning "pertaining to the retina.") The visual receptor molecules span the membranes of receptor discs and

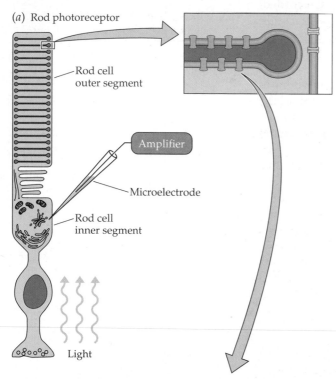

(a) Rod photoreceptor

Rod cell outer segment

Amplifier

Microelectrode

Rod cell inner segment

Light

10.7 Hyperpolarization of Photoreceptors A rod photoreceptor (*a*) is hyperpolarized when stimulated by light (*b*). (*c*) The hyperpolarization is caused by a cascade of neurochemical events that enormously multiply the effect of each photon captured by a receptor cell.

(b) Stimulation hyperpolarizes receptor

Light flash

Electrical potential (mV)

Dim light

Medium light

Bright light

−35

−45

−55

0   100   200

Time (ms)

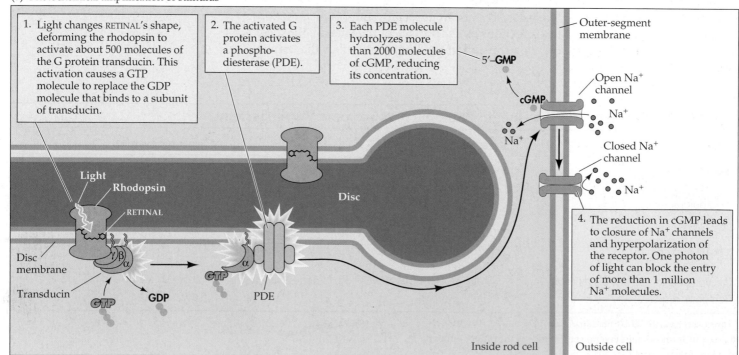

(c) Photochemical amplification of stimulus

1. Light changes RETINAL's shape, deforming the rhodopsin to activate about 500 molecules of the G protein transducin. This activation causes a GTP molecule to replace the GDP molecule that binds to a subunit of transducin.

2. The activated G protein activates a phosphodiesterase (PDE).

3. Each PDE molecule hydrolyzes more than 2000 molecules of cGMP, reducing its concentration.

Outer-segment membrane

5′-GMP

cGMP

Na^+

Open Na^+ channel

Na^+

Closed Na^+ channel

Na^+

4. The reduction in cGMP leads to closure of Na^+ channels and hyperpolarization of the receptor. One photon of light can block the entry of more than 1 million Na^+ molecules.

Light

Rhodopsin

RETINAL

Disc

Disc membrane

Transducin

GTP

GDP

GTP

PDE

Inside rod cell

Outside cell

have structures that are similar to those of the G protein–coupled neurotransmitter receptors that we discussed in Chapter 3.

When hit by light, RETINAL dissociates rapidly from the opsin molecule (**Figure 10.7**), to reveal an enzymatic site. This activated opsin combines rapidly with many molecules of the G protein transducin (**Figure 10.7c**). Transducin, in turn, acts through an enzyme, phosphodiesterase (PDE), to transform cyclic GMP (cyclic guanosine monophosphate) to 5'-GMP. Cyclic GMP holds channels for sodium ions (Na^+) open; stimulation by light initiates a cascade of events that *closes* these channels. Capture of a single quantum of light can lead to the closing of hundreds of sodium channels in the photoreceptor membrane, thereby blocking the entry of more than a million Na^+ ions (Schnapf and Baylor, 1987). Closing the Na^+ channels creates a hyperpolarizing generator potential (**Figure 10.7b**).

This change of potential represents the initial electrical signal activating the visual pathway. Stimulation of rhodopsin by light hyperpolarizes the rods, just as stimulation of the cone pigments by light hyperpolarizes the cones. For both rods and cones, the size of the hyperpolarizing photoreceptor potential determines the magnitude of the reduction in the release of synaptic transmitter (**Figure 10.6e**).

It may seem puzzling at first that stimulation by light *hyper*polarizes vertebrate retinal photoreceptors and causes them to release *less* neurotransmitter, since sensory stimulation depolarizes most other receptor cells. But remember that the visual system responds to *changes* in light. Either an increase or a decrease in the intensity of light can stimulate the visual system, and hyperpolarization is just as much a neural signal as depolarization.

The cascade of processes required to stimulate the visual receptors helps account for three major characteristics of the visual system:

1. Its *sensitivity*, because weak stimuli are amplified to produce physiological effects
2. The *integration* of the stimulus over time, which makes vision relatively slow (compared, for example, to audition) but increases its sensitivity
3. The *adaptation* of the visual system to a wide range of light intensities, as we will discuss next

Different mechanisms enable the eyes to work over a wide range of light intensities

Many sensory systems have to work over wide ranges of stimulus intensity, as we learned in Chapter 8. This is certainly true of the visual system: a very bright light is about 10 billion times as intense as the weakest lights we can see. At any given time, however, we can discriminate over only a small fraction of this range of light intensity. Let's discuss the mechanisms by which the eye adapts to the prevailing level of illumination.

One way the visual system deals with a large range of intensities is by adjusting the size of the pupil. In bright light the pupil contracts quickly to admit only about one-sixteenth as much light as when illumination is dim. Although rapid, this pupil response cannot account for the billionfold range of visual sensitivity (**Figure 10.8**). Another mechanism for handling different light intensities is **range fractionation**, the handling of different intensities by different receptors—some with low thresholds (rods) and others with high thresholds (cones) (see Table 10.1). Figure 8.6 illustrated range fractionation for the somatosensory system.

Additional range fractionation would carry an unacceptable cost: If, at a particular light level, several sets of receptors were not responding, acuity would be impaired. If only a fraction of the receptors responded to the small changes in the intensity of light around a given level, the active receptors would be spaced apart from each other in the retina, and the "grain" of the retina would be coarse. The

range fractionation A hypothesis of stimulus intensity perception stating that a wide range of intensity values can be encoded by a group of cells, each of which is a specialist for a particular range of stimulus intensities.

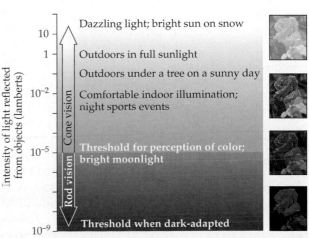

10.8 The Wide Range of Sensitivity to Light Intensity

(figure labels)

Intensity of light reflected from objects (lamberts)

Cone vision
Rod vision

10
1
10^{-2}
10^{-5}
10^{-9}

Dazzling light; bright sun on snow
Outdoors in full sunlight
Outdoors under a tree on a sunny day
Comfortable indoor illumination; night sports events
Threshold for perception of color; bright moonlight
Threshold when dark-adapted

eye solves this problem by giving photoreceptors a great range of adaptation; that is, each photoreceptor adjusts its sensitivity to match the average level of ambient illumination. This tremendous range of **photoreceptor adaptation** is the main reason we can see over such wide ranges of light. Thus, the visual system is concerned with differences, or changes, in brightness—not with the absolute level of illumination.

At any given time, a photoreceptor operates over a range of intensities of about a hundredfold; that is, it is completely depolarized by a stimulus about one-tenth the ambient level of illumination, and a light ten times as intense as the ambient level will completely hyperpolarize it. The receptors constantly shift their whole range of response to work around the prevailing level of illumination. Further adaptation occurs in the ganglion cells and the lateral geniculate nucleus, and probably at higher levels too.

Three main factors help account for receptor adaptation in the visual system:

1. *The role of calcium.* Probably the most important factor is one shared by other sensory modalities: varying the concentration of calcium (Ca^{2+}) ions (E. N. Pugh and Lamb, 1990). The photoreceptors regulate the release and storage of intracellular Ca^{2+} ions to control their sensitivity to light.
2. *The level of photopigment.* When the photoreceptor pigment is split apart by light, its two components—RETINAL and opsin—slowly recombine, so the balance between the rate of breakdown of the pigment and its rate of recombination determines how much photopigment is available at any given time to respond to stimulation by light. If you go from bright daylight into a dark theater, it takes several minutes until enough rhodopsin becomes available to restore your dark vision.
3. *The availability of retinal chemicals for transduction.* Several retinal chemicals are required for transduction. They tend to be abundant at low levels of illumination but increasingly rare at higher levels of illumination, so increasing numbers of photons are required to activate them and hyperpolarize the receptors (E. N. Pugh and Lamb, 1993).

Acuity is best in foveal vision

Early in this chapter we noted that acuity is especially fine in the center of the visual field and falls off rapidly toward the periphery. Reasons for this difference have been found in the retina and successive levels of the visual system.

Figure 10.9a shows a photograph of the back of the eye seen through the pupil. The central region, called the **fovea** (Latin for "pit"), has a dense concentration of cones, and in this region light reaches the cones without having to pass through other layers of cells and blood vessels (**Figure 10.10**). The **optic disc**, to the nasal side of the fovea, is where blood vessels and ganglion cell axons leave the eye. There are no photoreceptors at the optic disc, so there is a **blind spot** here that we normally do not notice. To locate your blind spot and experience firsthand some of its interesting features, see **A Step Further: The Blind Spot** on the website.

The high concentration of cones in the fovea provides high visual acuity in this region (**Figure 10.9b**). People differ in their concentrations of cones (Curcio et al., 1987), and this variation may be related to individual differences in visual acuity. Species differences in visual acuity also reflect the density of cones in the fovea. For example, hawks, whose acuity is much greater than that of humans, have much narrower and more densely packed cones in the fovea than humans have. In the human retina, both cones and rods are larger toward the periphery. Therefore, our acuity falls off about as rapidly in the horizontal direction as in the vertical direction. But species that live in open, flat environments (such as the cheetah and the rabbit) have fields of acute vision that extend farther horizontally than vertically.

The rods show a different distribution from the cones: they are absent in the fovea but more numerous than cones in the periphery of the retina (see Figure 10.9a). They are the most concentrated in a ring about 20° away from the center of the

photoreceptor adaptation   The tendency of rods and cones to adjust their light sensitivity to match ambient levels of illumination.

fovea   The central portion of the retina, packed with the most photoreceptors and therefore the center of our gaze.

optic disc   The region of the retina devoid of receptor cells because ganglion cell axons and blood vessels exit the eyeball there.

blind spot   The portion of the visual field from which light falls on the optic disc. Because there are no receptors in this region, light striking it cannot be seen.

(*a*) Distributions of rods and cones across the retina

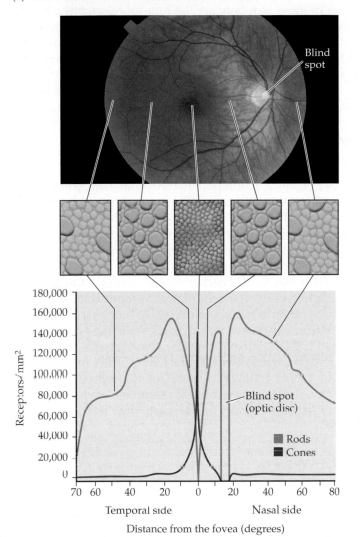

(*b*) Variation of visual acuity across the retina

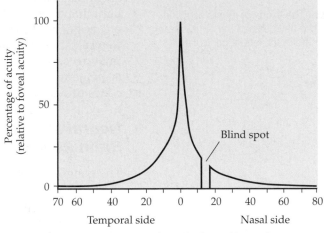

10.9 Densities of Retinal Receptors and Visual Acuity (*a*) The photograph of the retina was taken through the pupil. The rods and cones vary in size *(middle panel)* and density *(bottom graph)* across the retina. (*b*) The variation of visual acuity across the retina reflects the distribution of cones.

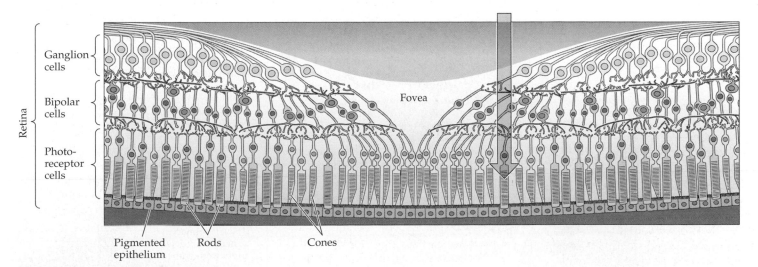

10.10 An Unobstructed View In the fovea, light reaches the cones without having to pass through blood vessels and other layers of cells.

optic chiasm The point at which the two optic nerves meet.

optic tract The axons of retinal ganglion cells after they have passed the optic chiasm; most terminate in the lateral geniculate nucleus.

retina. This is why, if you want to see a dim star, you do best to search for it a little off to the side of your center of gaze. Not only are the rods more sensitive to dim light than the cones but, as we mentioned earlier, input from many rods converges on ganglion cells in the scotopic system, further increasing the system's sensitivity to weak stimuli. On the other hand, that greater convergence of information from photoreceptors to ganglion cells in rods than in cones is another reason why acuity is greater in the cone-rich fovea. Rods provide high sensitivity with limited acuity; cones provide high acuity with limited sensitivity.

Neural Signals Travel from the Retina to Several Brain Regions

The ganglion cells in each eye produce action potentials that are conducted along their axons to send visual information to the brain. These axons make up the optic nerve (also known as cranial nerve II) that brings visual information into the brain on each side, eventually reaching visual cortex in the occipital lobe at the back of the brain (**Figure 10.11**). Primary visual cortex passes along the information to other visual cortical regions, as we discuss shortly.

In all vertebrates, some or all of the axons of each optic nerve cross to the opposite cerebral hemisphere. The optic nerves cross the midline at the **optic chiasm** (named for the Greek letter X [chi] because of its crossover shape). In humans, axons from the half of the retina toward the nose (the *nasal retina*) cross over to the opposite side of the brain (step 3 in Figure 10.11). The half of the retina toward the side of the head (the *temporal retina*) projects its axons to its own side of the head. After they pass the optic chiasm, the axons of the retinal ganglion cells are known collectively as the **optic tract**. Proportionally more axons cross the midline in animals, such as rodents, that have laterally placed eyes with little binocular overlap in their fields of vision.

10.11 Visual Pathways in the Human Brain Visual fields are represented on the retinas and project to the cerebral hemispheres. The right visual field, which falls on parts of both retinas, projects to the left cerebral hemisphere. Similarly, the left visual field projects to both eyes and then to the right cerebral hemisphere.

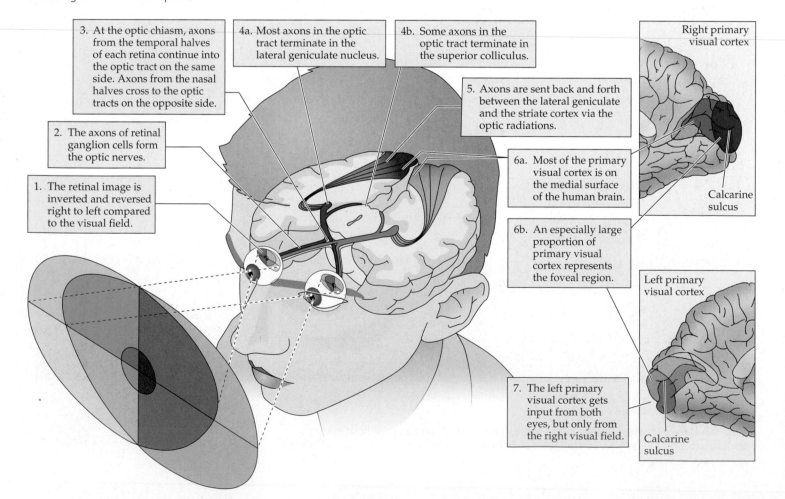

3. At the optic chiasm, axons from the temporal halves of each retina continue into the optic tract on the same side. Axons from the nasal halves cross to the optic tracts on the opposite side.

4a. Most axons in the optic tract terminate in the lateral geniculate nucleus.

4b. Some axons in the optic tract terminate in the superior colliculus.

5. Axons are sent back and forth between the lateral geniculate and the striate cortex via the optic radiations.

2. The axons of retinal ganglion cells form the optic nerves.

1. The retinal image is inverted and reversed right to left compared to the visual field.

6a. Most of the primary visual cortex is on the medial surface of the human brain.

6b. An especially large proportion of primary visual cortex represents the foveal region.

Right primary visual cortex

Calcarine sulcus

Left primary visual cortex

7. The left primary visual cortex gets input from both eyes, but only from the right visual field.

Calcarine sulcus

Most axons of the optic tract terminate on cells in the **lateral geniculate nucleus** (**LGN**; step 4a in Figure 10.11), which is the visual part of the thalamus. Axons of postsynaptic cells in the LGN form the **optic radiations** (step 5), which terminate in **primary visual cortex** (**V1**) of the **occipital cortex** at the back of the brain (step 6). The primary visual cortex is often called **striate cortex** because a broad stripe, or *striation*, is visible in anatomical sections through this region; the stripe represents layer IV of the cortex, where the optic-radiation fibers arrive. Information from the two eyes converges on cells beyond layer IV of the primary visual cortex, making binocular (three-dimensional) vision possible.

As Figure 10.11 shows, the visual cortex in the right cerebral hemisphere receives its input from the left half of the visual field, and the visual cortex in the left hemisphere receives its input from the right half of the visual field. The figure shows that some retinal ganglion cells send their optic-tract axons to the superior colliculus in the midbrain (step 4b). The superior colliculus helps coordinate rapid movements of the eyes toward a target.

In addition to the primary visual cortex (V1) shown in Figure 10.11, numerous surrounding regions of the cortex are also largely visual in function. These visual cortical areas outside the striate cortex are sometimes called **extrastriate cortex**. Together, these different cortical regions work in parallel to process different aspects of visual perception, such as form, color, location, and movement, as we will discuss later in this chapter. In striate cortex, as well as most extrastriate regions, there is a topographic projection of the retina, which means there's a topographic projection of the visual field, discussed next.

The retina projects to the brain in a topographic fashion

The retina represents a two-dimensional map of visual space. As this information courses through the brain, the point-to-point correspondence between neighboring parts of visual space is maintained, forming a maplike projection (see Figure 10.11). Much of this topographic projection of visual space is devoted to the foveal region (**Figure 10.12a**) (Tootell et al., 1982). Although the monkey V1 is located on

lateral geniculate nucleus (LGN) The part of the thalamus that receives information from the optic tract and sends it to visual areas in the occipital cortex.

optic radiation Axons from the lateral geniculate nucleus that terminate in the primary visual areas of the occipital cortex.

primary visual cortex (V1) or striate cortex Also called *area 17*. The region of the occipital cortex where most visual information first arrives.

occipital cortex Also called *visual cortex*. The cortex of the occipital lobe of the brain.

extrastriate cortex Visual cortex outside of the primary visual (striate) cortex.

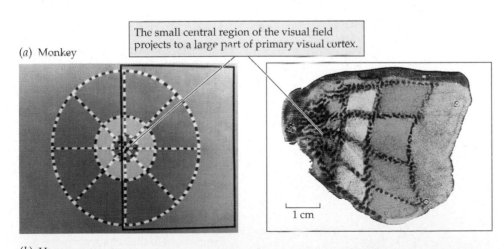

(a) Monkey

The small central region of the visual field projects to a large part of primary visual cortex.

1 cm

(b) Human

10.12 Location of the Primary Visual Cortex (a) A pattern of flickering lights (*left*) was shown in a monkey's visual field, and a map of the visual field (*right*) was revealed by autoradiography in a flattened portion of the primary visual cortex. (b) Maps of human visual cortex derived from functional-MRI measurements show primary visual cortex as the innermost yellow region on each of these medial views. (Part *a* from Tootell et al., 1988; *b* from Tootell et al., 1998; both courtesy of Roger Tootell.)

the lateral surface of the occipital area, human V1 is located mainly on the medial surface of the cortex (**Figure 10.12***b*; see also Figure 10.19*d*). The fact that, as in monkeys, about half of the human V1 is devoted to the fovea and the retinal region just around the fovea does not mean that our spatial perception is distorted. Rather, this representation makes possible the great acuity of spatial discrimination in the central part of the visual field.

Because of the orderly mapping of the visual field (known as *retinotopic mapping*) at the various levels of the visual system, damage to parts of the visual system can be diagnosed from defects in perception of the visual field. If we know the site of injury in the visual pathway, we can predict the location of such a perceptual gap,

BOX 10.2 Eyes with Lenses Have Evolved in Several Phyla

Phylogenetic studies indicate that the evolution of eyes with lenses, like those of a mammal or an octopus, included the following steps (Fernald, 2000), as illustrated in the figure:

1. *Concentrating light-sensitive cells* into localized groups that serve as photoreceptor organs. Animals with such photoreceptor organs have better chances of surviving and reproducing than do similar animals with scattered receptor cells, because photoreceptor organs facilitate an ability to respond differently to stimuli that strike different parts of the body surface.

2. *Clustering light receptors* at the bottom of pitlike or cuplike depressions in the skin. Animals with this adaptation can discriminate better among stimuli that come from different directions. They also perceive increased contrast of stimuli against a background of ambient light.

3. *Narrowing the top of the cup* into a small aperture so that, like a pinhole camera, the eye can focus well.

4. *Closing the opening with transparent skin or filling the cup with a transparent substance.* This covering protects the eye against the entry of foreign substances that might injure the receptor cells or block vision.

5. *Forming a lens* either by thickening the transparent skin or by modifying

other tissue in the eye. This adaptation improves the focusing of the eye while allowing the aperture to be relatively large to let in more light; thus, vision can be acute even when light is not intense.

The only requirement for the evolution of eyes to begin appears to be the existence of light-sensitive cells. Natural selection then favors the development of auxiliary mechanisms to improve vision.

Phylogenetic studies of the structure and development of eyes led investigators to conclude that eyes evolved independently in many different phyla (Salvini-Plawen and Mayr, 1977)—an example of convergent evolution. The fact that the cephalopods (such as squid and octopuses) evolved a visual system that in many ways resembles that of vertebrates (from fishes to humans) suggests that major constraints limit the development of a visual system for a large, rapidly moving animal. In both cephalopods and vertebrates, the eyes are relatively large, allowing for many receptors and the ability to gather large amounts of light. The incoming light is regulated by a pupil and focused by a lens. In both cephalopods and vertebrates, three sets of extraocular muscles move the eyeballs.

However, it is still uncertain whether eyes of all species evolved from a single progenitor or have arisen more than once during evolution (Fernald, 2000). The eyes of all seeing animals share at least two important genetic features: First, they all use opsin pigments. Second, the compound eye of the fruit fly *Drosophila*, the vertebrate eye, and the cephalopod eye all develop through genes of the *Pax* family. The finding that homologous molecules are key regulators of eye development in different phyla argues that eyes in all phyla share a common origin. On the other hand, it is possible that mutations in these genes arose independently in more than one line to give rise to eyes. In that case the convergent evolution is the more remarkable, as natural selection not only arrived at similar structures in the several lines, but utilized some of the same genetic building blocks to construct them.

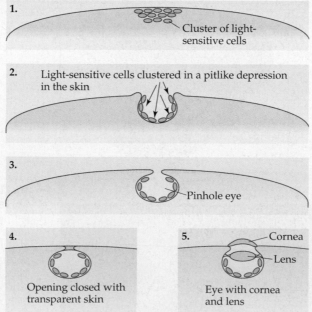

1. Cluster of light-sensitive cells

2. Light-sensitive cells clustered in a pitlike depression in the skin

3. Pinhole eye

4. Opening closed with transparent skin

5. Cornea
Lens
Eye with cornea and lens

or **scotoma** (plural *scotomas* or *scotomata*), in the visual field. Although the word *scotoma* comes from the Greek *skotos*, meaning "darkness," a scotoma is not perceived as a dark patch in the visual field; rather, it is a spot where nothing can be perceived, and usually rigorous testing is required to demonstrate its existence.

Within a scotoma, a person cannot consciously perceive visual cues, but some visual discrimination in this region may still be possible; this paradoxical phenomenon has been called *blindsight*. In other cases, stimuli that cannot be seen within a scotoma affect judgments of stimuli outside it (Stoerig and Cowey, 1997). Blindsight may also be related to the phenomenon of *hemispatial neglect*—neglect of the side opposite to an injured cerebral hemisphere—which we will discuss in Chapter 18.

Before ending our discussion of the retina, we should mention that some retinal ganglion cells possess a special photopigment that makes them sensitive to light (Güler et al., 2008). We will see in Chapter 14 that these ganglion cells help control daily cycles of behavior called *circadian rhythms*, and they also inform the brain about the level of ambient light to control pupil diameter (Lucas et al., 2003).

When we look at a complex organ like the eye of a mammal, an octopus, or a fly, it is hard at first to understand how it could have evolved. But inspection of different living species reveals a gradation from very simple light-sensitive cells to increasingly complex organs with focusing devices (**Box 10.2**), and each kind of photoreceptor confers benefits on the animal that possesses it.

Neurons at Different Levels of the Visual System Have Very Different Receptive Fields

As we noted in Chapter 8, the **receptive field** of a sensory cell consists of the stimulus region and the features that excite or inhibit the cell. The nature of the receptive field of a cell gives us good clues about its function(s) in perception. Cells in the retina or LGN can be activated by simple spots of light, but many cells in the visual cortex are more demanding and respond only to more-complicated stimuli. In the next sections we will see that neurons at lower levels in the visual system seem to account for some perceptual phenomena while neurons at higher levels account for others.

Photoreceptors excite some retinal neurons and inhibit others

At their resting potentials, both rod and cone photoreceptors steadily release the synaptic neurotransmitter glutamate. Light always hyperpolarizes the photoreceptors, causing them to release less glutamate. But the response of the bipolar cells that receive this glutamate differs, depending on what type of glutamate receptor they possess. Glutamate depolarizes one group of bipolar cells but hyperpolarizes another group. These groups differ in their receptive fields.

One group of bipolar cells are **on-center bipolar cells**: turning *on* a light in the center of an on-center bipolar cell's receptive field excites the cell because it receives less glutamate, which otherwise inhibits on-center bipolar cells. (**Figure 10.13**, *left*). The second group are **off-center bipolar cells**: turning *off* light in the center of an off-center bipolar cell's receptive field excites the cell because it receives more glutamate, which depolarizes off-center bipolar cells (**Figure 10.13**, *right*).

scotoma   A region of blindness caused by injury to the visual pathway or brain.

receptive field   The stimulus region and features that affect the activity of a cell in a sensory system.

on-center bipolar cell   A retinal bipolar cell that is excited by light in the center of its receptive field.

off-center bipolar cell   A retinal bipolar cell that is inhibited by light in the center of its receptive field.

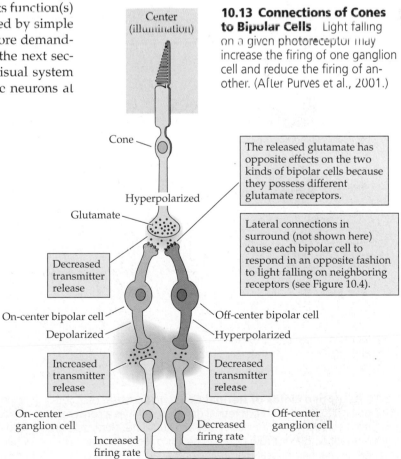

10.13 Connections of Cones to Bipolar Cells   Light falling on a given photoreceptor may increase the firing of one ganglion cell and reduce the firing of another. (After Purves et al., 2001.)

The released glutamate has opposite effects on the two kinds of bipolar cells because they possess different glutamate receptors.

Lateral connections in surround (not shown here) cause each bipolar cell to respond in an opposite fashion to light falling on neighboring receptors (see Figure 10.4).

on-center ganglion cell A retinal ganglion cell that is activated when light is presented to the center, rather than the periphery, of the cell's receptive field.

off-center ganglion cell A retinal ganglion cell that is activated when light is presented to the periphery, rather than the center, of the cell's receptive field.

Bipolar cells also *release* glutamate, and glutamate always depolarizes the ganglion cells. Therefore, when light is turned on, on-center bipolar cells depolarize (excite) **on-center ganglion cells**; and when light is turned off, off-center bipolar cells depolarize (excite) **off-center ganglion cells** (see Figure 10.13). The stimulated on-center and off-center ganglion cells then fire nerve impulses and report "light" or "dark" to higher visual centers.

Neurons in the retina and the LGN have concentric receptive fields

The pattern of connections of photoreceptors to bipolar cells shapes the receptive fields of the ganglion cell. Scientists can record from single ganglion cells while moving a small spot of light across the visual field, keeping the animal's eye still. These studies show that the receptive fields of retinal ganglion cells are concentric, consisting of a roughly circular central area and a ring around it. Through various retinal connections, including the lateral inhibition we discussed earlier (see Fig-

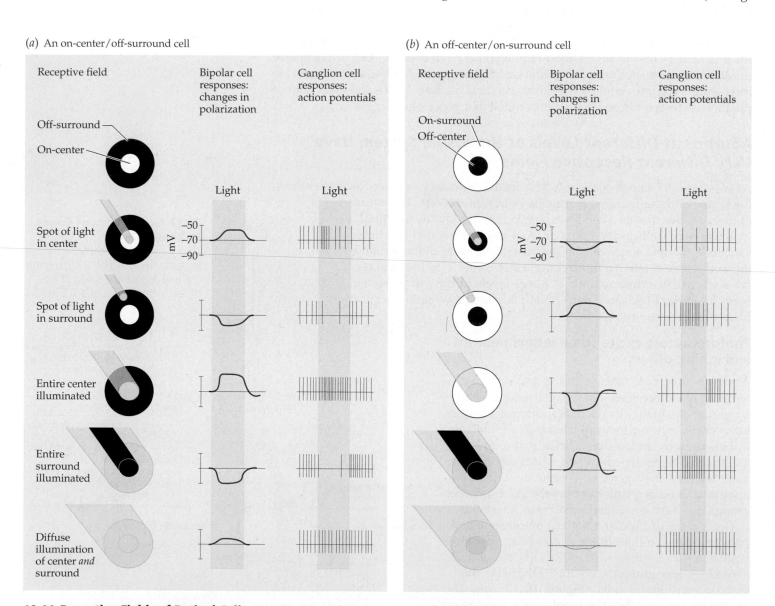

10.14 Receptive Fields of Retinal Cells In primates, each retinal bipolar cell, as well as each retinal ganglion cell, has a concentric receptive field, with antagonistic center and surround. Here, cells are shown responding to narrow or broad beams of light. Bipolar cells respond by changes in local membrane potentials; ganglion cells respond with action potentials. (*a*) An on-center/off-surround cell is excited by an increase of illumination in the center of its receptive field and inhibited by an increase of illumination in the surround. (*b*) Changes in illumination have the opposite effects on an off-center/on-surround cell.

ure 10.4), the photoreceptors in the central area and those in the ring around it tend to have the opposite effects on the next cells in the circuit. Thus, both bipolar cells and ganglion cells have two basic types of retinal receptive fields: **on-center/off-surround** (**Figure 10.14a**) and **off-center/on-surround** (**Figure 10.14b**). These antagonistic effects of the center and its surround explain why uniform illumination of the visual field is less effective in activating a ganglion cell than is a well-placed small spot or a line or edge passing through the center of the cell's receptive field.

We told you earlier that most ganglion cell axons synapse in the lateral geniculate nucleus (LGN) of the thalamus in mammals. The primate LGN has six main layers and some smaller layers in between (**Figure 10.15**). The structure is called *geniculate* because the layers are bent like a knee, which in Latin is *genu*. The smaller layers are called *koniocellular layers* because they contain very small neurons (the Greek root *koni* means "dust").

The four dorsal, or outer, layers of the primate LGN are called **parvocellular** (from the Latin *parvus*, "small") because their cells are relatively small. The two ventral, or inner, layers are called **magnocellular** (from the Latin *magnus*, "large") because their cells are large. The LGN cells of all six layers have concentric receptive fields. For most neurons in the magnocellular layers these concentric receptive fields are relatively large, receiving input from large ganglion cells, which receive their input from retinal bipolar cells that contact many neighboring receptor cells. Most magnocellular neurons do not show differential wavelength responses; that is, they cannot be involved in color discrimination. In contrast, the neurons of the parvocellular layers have relatively small receptive fields, whose input can be traced back

on-center/off-surround Referring to a concentric receptive field in which the center excites the cell of interest while the surround inhibits it.

off-center/on-surround Referring to a concentric receptive field in which the center inhibits the cell of interest while the surround excites it.

parvocellular Of or consisting of relatively small cells.

magnocellular Of or consisting of relatively large cells.

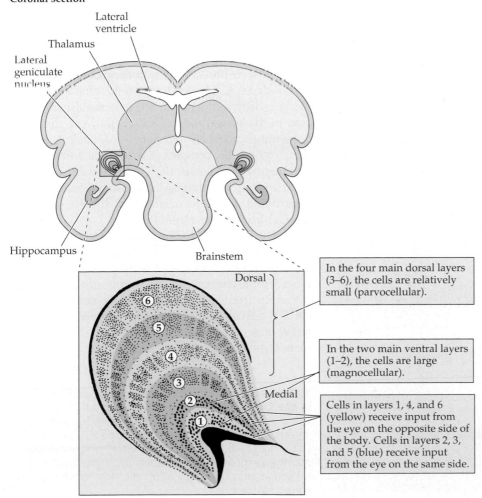

Coronal section

Lateral ventricle

Thalamus

Lateral geniculate nucleus

Hippocampus

Brainstem

Dorsal

Medial

In the four main dorsal layers (3–6), the cells are relatively small (parvocellular).

In the two main ventral layers (1–2), the cells are large (magnocellular).

Cells in layers 1, 4, and 6 (yellow) receive input from the eye on the opposite side of the body. Cells in layers 2, 3, and 5 (blue) receive input from the eye on the same side.

10.15 The Lateral Geniculate Nucleus
This cross section shows the layered structure of the LGN in primates.

simple cortical cell Also called *bar detector* or *edge detector*. A cell in the visual cortex that responds best to an edge or a bar that has a particular width, as well as a particular orientation and location in the visual field.

complex cortical cell A cell in the visual cortex that responds best to a bar of a particular size and orientation anywhere within a particular area of the visual field.

to small ganglion cells, which receive their input from bipolar cells driven (in the central retina) by single cones. These neurons discriminate wavelengths.

We can also classify retinal ganglion cells (Leventhal, 1979; Perry et al., 1984) as *M* or *P* ganglion cells depending on whether they project their axons, respectively, to the magnocellular or parvocellular layers of the LGN. The M and P systems roughly correspond to the scotopic and photopic systems we described earlier, since M cells respond primarily to rods and P cells respond primarily to cones (see Table 10.1). The few konio cells in the LGN seem to respond to a particular class of cones (described later) that respond to light of short wavelengths.

Neurons in the visual cortex have varied and complicated receptive fields

The next level of the visual system, the primary visual cortex, provided a puzzle. Neurons from the LGN send their axons to cells in the primary visual cortex (V1), but the spots of light that are effective stimuli for LGN cells (**Figure 10.16a**) are not very effective for cortical cells. In 1959, David Hubel and Torsten Wiesel reported that visual cortical cells require more-specific, elongated stimuli than those that activate LGN cells. Most cells in area V1 respond best to lines or bars in a particular position and at a particular orientation in the visual field (**Figure 10.16b**). Some cortical cells also require movement of the stimulus to make them respond actively. For some of these cells, any movement in their field is sufficient; others are more demanding, requiring motion in a specific direction (**Figure 10.16c**). For this and related research, Hubel and Wiesel were awarded the Nobel Prize in Physiology or Medicine in 1981.

Hubel and Wiesel categorized cortical cells according to the types of stimuli required to produce maximum responses. So-called **simple cortical cells** responded best to an edge or a bar that had a particular width and a particular orientation and location in the visual field. These cells were therefore sometimes called *bar detectors* or *edge detectors*. Like the simple cells, **complex cortical cells** had elongated receptive fields, but they also showed some latitude for location; that is, they responded to a bar of a particular size and orientation anywhere within a larger area of the visual field.

Hubel and Wiesel's theoretical model can be described as hierarchical; that is, more-complex events are built up from inputs of simpler ones. For example, a simple cortical cell can be thought of as receiving input from a row of LGN cells, and a complex cortical cell can be thought of as receiving input from a row of simple cortical cells. Other theorists extrapolated from this model, suggesting that higher-order

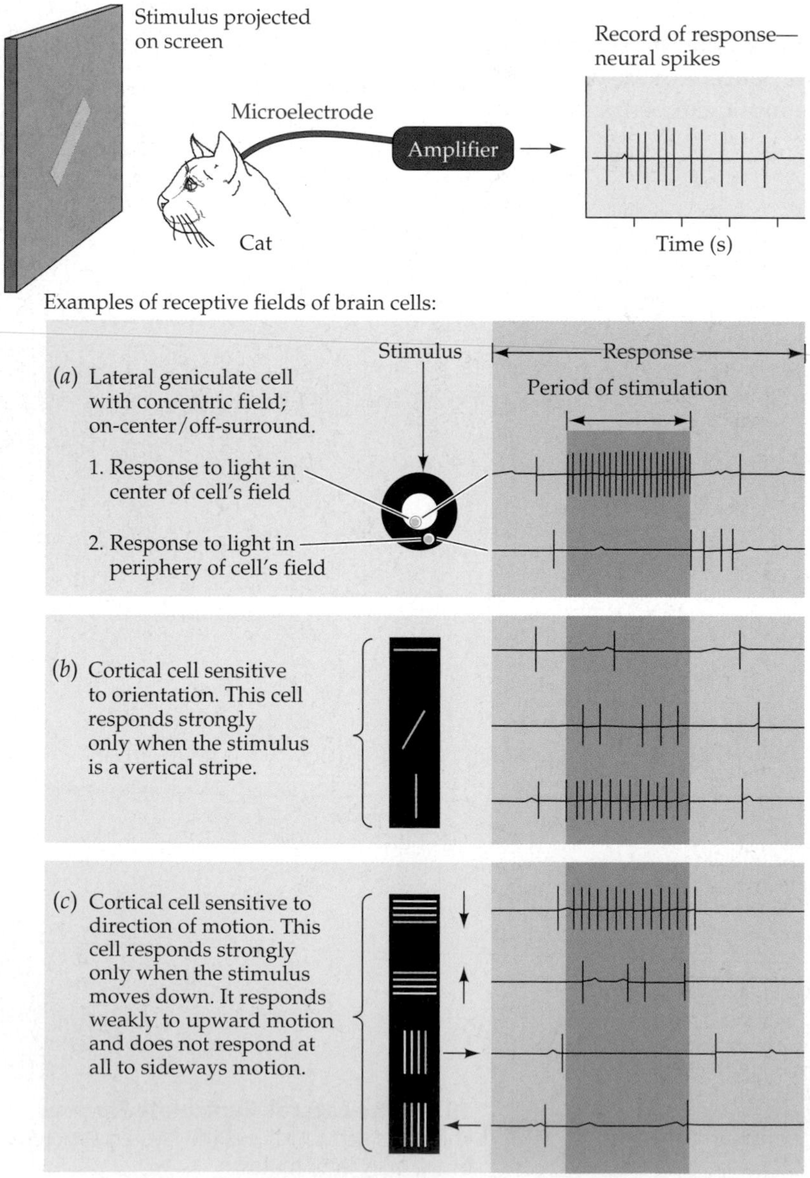

10.16 Receptive Fields of Cells at Various Levels in the Cat Visual System Microelectrode recordings reveal that cells differ greatly in their receptive fields. (a) Visual cells in the lateral geniculate nucleus (LGN) have concentric receptive fields. (b) Visual cells in the cerebral cortex may show orientation specificity or respond only to motion, or (c) they may respond only to motion in a particular direction.

circuits of cells could detect any possible form. Thus it was suggested that, by integration of enough successive levels of analysis, a unit could be constructed that would enable a person to recognize his or her grandmother, and such hypothetical "grandmother cells" were frequently mentioned in the literature. According to this view, whenever such a cell was excited, up would pop a picture of one's grandmother. This hypothesis was given as a possible explanation for facial recognition.

Critics soon pointed out both theoretical and empirical problems with the hierarchical model. For one thing, a hierarchical system like this would require a vast number of cells—perhaps more neurons than the cortex possesses—in order to account for all the visual objects that one may encounter. Although some neurons are activated by the sight of very specific faces (for example, "Halle Berry neurons" are some neurons that were activated by photos of that actress) in both humans (Pedreira et al., 2010) and monkeys (Freiwald et al., 2009), these neurons do not respond to specific features of the face, as you would expect if they were feature detectors. Rather, they respond only when the whole face or most of the face is presented (Freiwald et al., 2009). Thus, we need an alternative model of vision, which we describe next.

Most cells in the primary visual cortex are tuned to particular spatial frequencies

Concepts of pattern analysis in terms of lines and edges have largely given way to what is known as the **spatial-frequency filter model**. To discuss this model, we must become familiar with a way of regarding vision that is not at all intuitive (F. W. Campbell and Robson, 1968; R. L. De Valois and De Valois, 1988). By *spatial frequency of a visual stimulus*, we mean the number of light-dark (or color) cycles that the stimulus shows per degree of visual space. For example, Figure 10.17a and b differ in the spacing of the bars: **Figure 10.17a** has twice as many bars in the same

spatial-frequency filter model   A model of pattern analysis that emphasizes Fourier analysis of visual stimuli.

10.17 Spatial Frequencies   (a, b) The spacing between dark and light stripes shows that the grating in part a has double the spatial frequency of the grating in part b. (c, d) These visual grids show sinusoidal modulation of intensity: (c) high contrast; (d) low contrast. (e–y) A photograph of two penguins subjected to spatial filtering: (e) normal photograph; (f) high spatial frequencies filtered out; (g) low spatial frequencies filtered out.

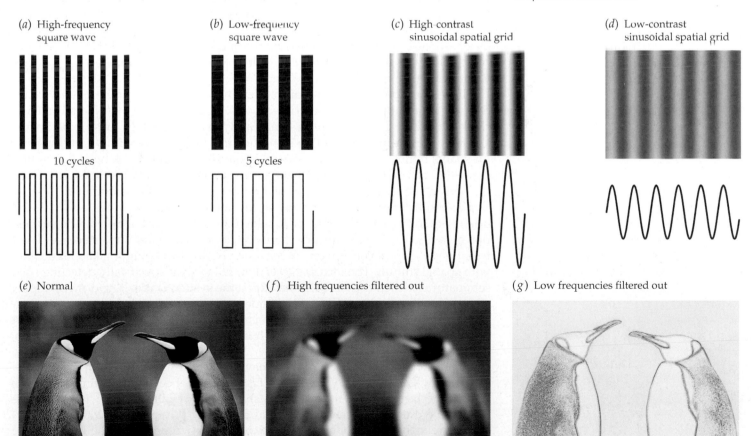

(a) High-frequency square wave

(b) Low-frequency square wave

(c) High-contrast sinusoidal spatial grid

(d) Low-contrast sinusoidal spatial grid

10 cycles

5 cycles

(e) Normal

(f) High frequencies filtered out

(g) Low frequencies filtered out

horizontal space and is therefore said to have double the spatial frequency of **Figure 10.17b**. The spatial-frequency technique applies Fourier analysis (see Box 9.1) or linear systems theory, rather than analyzing visual patterns into bars and angles.

In Box 9.1 we saw that we can produce any complex, repeating auditory stimulus by adding together simple sine waves. Conversely, using Fourier analysis, we can determine which combination of sine waves would be needed to make any particular complex waveform. The same principle of Fourier analysis can be applied to visual patterns. If the dimension from dark to light varies according to a sine wave function, visual patterns like the ones in **Figure 10.17c and d** result. Any series of dark and light stripes, like those in Figure 10.17a and b, can be analyzed into the sum of a visual sine wave and its odd harmonics (multiples of the basic frequency).

A complex visual pattern or scene can also be analyzed by the Fourier technique; in this case, frequency components at different angles of orientation are also used. A given spatial frequency can exist at any level of contrast; Figure 10.17c and d show examples of high and low contrast, respectively. To reproduce or perceive a complex pattern or scene accurately, the system has to handle all the spatial frequencies present. If the high frequencies are filtered out, the small details and sharp contrasts are lost; if the low frequencies are filtered out, the large uniform areas and gradual transitions are lost. **Figure 10.17e–g** show how the filtering of spatial frequencies affects a photograph. The photograph is still recognizable after either the high visual frequencies (10.17f) or low frequencies (10.17g) are filtered out. (Similarly, speech is still recognizable, although it sounds distorted, after either the high audio frequencies or the low frequencies are filtered out.)

F. W. Campbell and J. G. Robson (1968) suggested that the visual system includes many channels tuned to different spatial frequencies, just as the auditory system has channels for different acoustic frequencies. The term *channel* is used here to mean a mechanism that accepts or deals with only a particular band or class of information. This concept is analogous to the transmission of information by a particular radio or television station, which uses an assigned channel, or band of wavelengths; to receive this information, you must tune your receiving device to the particular channel.

The suggestion that the nervous system has different spatial-frequency channels was soon supported by experiments on selective adaptation to spatial patterns (Blakemore and Campbell, 1969; Pantle and Sekuler, 1968). In these experiments a person spent a minute or more inspecting a visual grating with a given spacing (or spatial frequency), such as those in Figure 10.17a and b. Looking at the grating made the cells that are tuned to that frequency adapt (become less sensitive). Then the person's sensitivity to gratings of different spacings was determined.

The results showed that sensitivity to the subsequent gratings was reduced briefly at the particular frequency to which the person had adapted. The suggestion of multiple spatial-frequency channels had revolutionary impact because it led to entirely different conceptions of how the visual system might go about dealing with spatial stimuli. The idea suggests that, rather than specifically detecting such seminaturalistic features as bars and edges, the system is breaking down complex stimuli into their individual spatial-frequency components in a kind of crude Fourier analysis (R. L. De Valois and De Valois, 1988, p. 320). In such a system, we might require a view of the whole face, which includes the low-frequency components, for recognition. This could explain why "Halle Berry neurons" do not respond to small portions of a face, because those have only high-frequency components.

Similarly, Leonardo da Vinci's *Mona Lisa* is famous because sometimes the model seems to be smiling but other times she doesn't (**Figure 10.18**). That ambiguity may be due to differences in spatial frequency (Livingstone, 2000). The low-spatial-frequency components of the picture (left two panels in the figure) make it look as if she is smiling, but the high-spatial-frequency components (right) give her a rueful, almost sad expression. As we run our eyes over the original, views

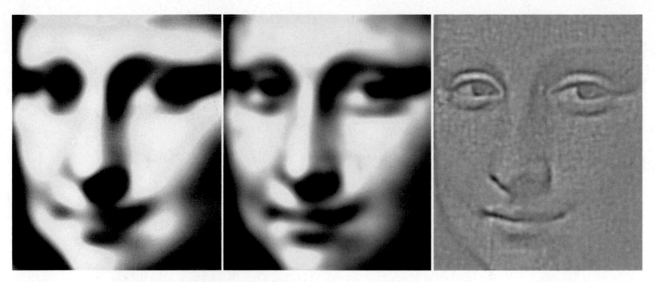

10.18 Mona Lisa's Ambiguous Smile   Leonardo da Vinci's Mona Lisa sometimes seems to be smiling, but other times she doesn't. Filtering that reveals very low spatial frequencies (*left panel*) or moderately low spatial frequencies (*middle*) makes it look as if she is smiling, but the high-spatial-frequency components (*right*) make her look almost sad. (Courtesy of Margaret Livingstone, Harvard University.)

from the fovea report the sad, high-frequency components; but views from the peripheral vision, with large receptor fields that can detect only low-frequency components, emphasize the smile. The spatial-frequency approach has proven useful in the analysis of many aspects of human pattern vision (K. K. De Valois et al., 1979), and it provides the basis of high-definition television (HDTV).

Area V1 is involved in the formation of mental images

Neurons of V1 (the primary visual cortex) appear to be involved not only in perceiving objects and events, but also in forming mental images. For example, imagined objects activate regions that correspond to the retinotopic mapping of V1; when people imagined small letters, PET recording showed activation of the foveal representation; when they imagined large letters, the parafoveal representation was activated (Kosslyn et al., 1993).

To obtain convergent evidence about the role of V1 in forming mental images, Kosslyn et al. (1999) also studied how impairing the function of V1 affected mental images. To impair function, they administered repetitive transcranial magnetic stimulation (rTMS) directed to V1. Before each set of trials in which subjects formed and inspected mental images, rTMS was administered for 10 minutes. This stimulation did not prevent the formation of images, but it significantly impaired the process, thus adding further evidence of the necessity of V1 for the formation of images.

Neurons in the visual cortex beyond area V1 have complex receptive fields and contribute to the identification of forms

Area V1 is only a small part of the portion of cortex that is devoted to vision. Area V1 sends axons to other visual cortical areas, including areas that appear to be involved in the perception of form: V2, V4, and the inferior temporal area (see Figure 10.19*c*). Some of these extrastriate areas also receive direct input from the LGN. The receptive fields of the cells in many of these extrastriate visual areas are even more complex than those in cells of area V1. Van Essen and Drury (1997) reviewed anatomical, physiological and behavioral investigations with macaque monkeys to identify at least 32 distinct cortical areas that are directly involved in visual function (**Figure 10.19*a–c***).

(a) Macaque brain, lateral view

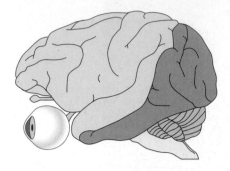

(b) Macaque brain, medial view

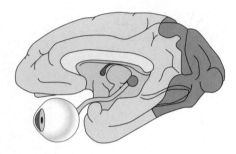

(d) Visual areas in the human occipital cortex, "flattened" by computational techniques

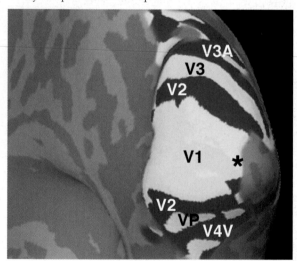

(c) Visual areas in the macaque cortex, unfolded view

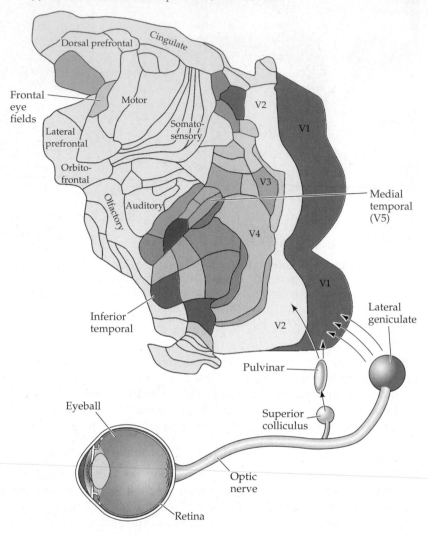

10.19 Main Visual Areas in Monkey and Human Brains (a, b) Macaque visual areas in occipital and temporal cortex are shown in pink. (c) All the known visual areas of the macaque on a flattened cortex in color. (d) Through computational techniques, the occipital regions of human brain shown in Figure 10.12b were "inflated," flattening the brain and bringing sulci in the cortex to the surface, and thus revealing the relative size and extent of various cortical visual areas. The asterisk identifies the representation of the center of the fovea. (Parts a–c after Van Essen and Drury, 1997; d from Tootell et al., 1998, courtesy of Roger Tootell.)

The visual areas of the human brain (**Figure 10.19d**) have been less thoroughly mapped than those of the monkey brain, and mainly by neuroimaging (the spatial resolution of which is not as fine as that of the electrophysiological recording used in the monkey brain), but the general layout appears to be similar in the two species, especially for V1 (Tootell et al., 2003).

An astonishing proportion of primate cortex analyzes visual information. The areas that are largely or entirely visual in function occupy about 55% of the surface of the macaque cortex, and about 30% of human cortex (Tootell et al., 2003). We will discuss only a few of the main visual cortical areas and their functions.

Area V2 is adjacent to V1, and many of its cells show properties similar to those of V1 cells. Many V2 cells can respond to illusory contours, which may help explain how we perceive contours such as the boundaries of the upright triangle in

Figure 10.20 (Peterhans and von der Heydt, 1989). Clearly, such cells respond to complex relations among the parts of their receptive fields. Some V1 cells can also respond to illusory contours (Grosof et al., 1993), but this feature is more common in area V2.

Area V4 receives axons from V2 and has cells that give their strongest responses to the sinusoidal frequency gratings that we discussed earlier (see Figure 10.17*c* and *d*). However, many V4 cells give even stronger responses to concentric and radial stimuli, such as those in **Figure 10.21*a*** (Gallant et al., 1993). Investigators have suggested that these V4 cells show an intermediate stage between the spatial-frequency processing in V1 and V2 cells and the recognition of pattern and form in cells of the inferior temporal area. Area V4 also has many cells that respond most strongly to wavelength differences, as we will see later when we discuss color vision. Area V5, also called the *medial temporal* (*MT*) *area*, appears to be specialized for the perception of motion, as we will also discuss later in the chapter.

The inferior temporal (IT) visual cortex has many cells that respond best to particular complex forms, including forms that the subject has learned to recognize. Since many cells in IT cortex have highly specific receptive fields, it is hard to find the exact stimuli that can activate a particular cell. Investigators start by presenting many three-dimensional animal and plant objects (Desimone et al., 1984; K. Tanaka, 1993). When a stimulus elicits a strong response, the experimenters then simplify the image by sequentially removing parts of the features to determine the necessary and sufficient features for maximal activation of the cell.

Most cells in IT cortex do not require a natural object such as a face to activate them; instead, they require moderately complex shapes, sometimes combined with color or texture, such as those in **Figure 10.21*b***. The complex receptive fields in IT cortex probably develop through experience and learning. After a monkey was trained for a year to discriminate a set of 28 moderately complex shapes, 39% of the cells in its anterior IT cortex responded significantly to some of these shapes. In control monkeys, on the other hand, only 9% of the cells responded strongly to these forms (Kobatake and Tanaka, 1994).

The prefrontal cortex also contains a restricted region of neurons that are activated by faces but not by other visual stimuli, as found both by noninvasive recording of human subjects (Ungerleider et al., 1998) and by electrical recording of neurons in the monkey brain (Scalaidhe et al., 1997). These neurons receive connections from the superior temporal sulcus and adjacent cortex on the inferior

10.20 A Geometric Figure with "Illusory" or "Subjective" Contours Cells have been found in visual cortical areas that respond to illusory contours such as those of the upright triangle shown here. These contours thus have neurophysiological meaning.

10.21 Complex Stimuli Evoke Strong Responses in Visual Cortex (*a*) These concentric and radial stimuli evoke maximal responses from some cells in visual cortical area V4. The stimuli that evoked the highest response rates (see scale bar) are shown in red and orange. (*b*) These 12 examples illustrate the critical features of stimuli that evoke maximal responses from cells in the anterior inferior temporal area. (Part *a* from Gallant et al., 1993, courtesy of Jack Gallant; *b* from K. Tanaka, 1993, courtesy of Keiji Tanaka.)

(a) *(b)*

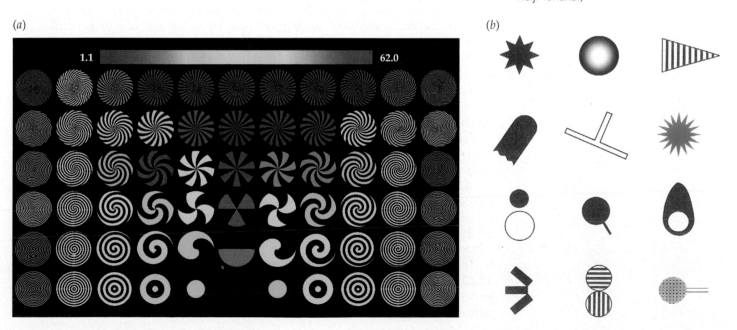

ocular dominance column   A region of cortex in which one eye or the other provides a greater degree of synaptic input.

ocular dominance slab   A slab of visual cortex, about 0.5 mm wide, in which the neurons of all layers respond preferentially to stimulation of one eye.

orientation column   A column of visual cortex that responds to rod-shaped stimuli of a particular orientation.

temporal gyrus. These findings indicate that a visual pathway that processes visual recognition extends from the primary visual cortex through temporal cortical regions to the prefrontal cortex. Later we'll see that this is the ventral pathway that was damaged in D.F., the woman we described at the start of the chapter.

Area V1 Is Organized in Columns and Slabs

The primary visual cortex has separate representations for at least four dimensions of the visual stimulus: (1) location in the visual field, with larger, finer mapping of the central region of the visual field than of the periphery; (2) ocular dominance; (3) orientation; and (4) color.

Ocular dominance columns were first discovered by electrophysiological recording. Although the receptive field of an individual neuron is the same for vision through either eye, some cells are equally activated by the two eyes but other cells respond preferentially (i.e., more strongly) to stimulation of one eye. However, all the cells in a vertical column of cells have the same ocular dominance. The vertical columns are arranged into ocular dominance slabs about 0.5 mm wide, all cells of which respond preferentially to stimulation of one eye. A given point in the visual field elicits responses in cells in adjacent left-eye-preferring and right-eye-preferring ocular dominance slabs. Ocular dominance is especially clear in the broad layer IV, where each cell is monocular, responding to only one eye. Above and below the (monocular) ocular dominance stripes in layer IV, most of the cells respond to stimulation of both eyes but still prefer one eye over the other.

Optical imaging of cortical activity (T. Bonhoeffer and Grinvald, 1991; Ts'o et al., 1990) allows us to see the ocular dominance stripes in the primary visual cortex of an awake monkey (**Figure 10.22a and b**). The imaging is based on small changes in the light reflected from the cortex during activity. These changes are of two types: (1) changes in blood volume, probably in the capillaries of the activated area; and (2) changes in cortical tissue, such as the movement of ions and water or the expansion and contraction of extracellular spaces. Experimenters can combine optical imaging with electrophysiological recording to place microelectrodes in particular parts of ocular dominance slabs. Figure 10.22b shows the ocular dominance columns that were activated when one eye was stimulated. This recording technique may prove useful as a mapping tool in human neurosurgery.

Ocular dominance columns develop during the first 4 months of life in the cat and during the first 6 months in the macaque monkey. As we saw in Chapter 7, both eyes must be exposed to the visual environment if each eye is to obtain its own cortical representation (see Figure 7.22). Up to the age of 3 or 4 months, human infants are unimpressed by stereograms (pairs of pictures showing somewhat different left-eye and right-eye views that most adult observers perceive as a three-dimensional view). Beginning at the age of 3 or 4 months, however, most infants are captivated by stereograms (Held, 1993). Presumably, before that age the cortex is unable to separate the information from the two eyes because the information reaches the same cortical neurons.

Primary visual cortex has a columnar organization for stimulus orientation as well: a microelectrode that follows a path perpendicular to the surface records cells that all prefer the same stimulus orientation within the visual field (**Figure 10.22c and d**). As the recording electrode is moved from one orientation column to the next, the preferred axis of orientation shifts by a few degrees. That is, in one column all the cells may be "tuned" to upright stimuli (at an orientation of 0°); in an adjacent column, all cells may respond best to another orientation, perhaps at 10° from the vertical; in the next column, perhaps at 25°; and so forth.

These columns are organized parallel to the surface of the cortex, as Figure 10.22d shows. In this figure, optical recordings show the regions of primary visual cortex that respond best to stimuli of four different orientations. The orientation columns run perpendicular to the borders of ocular dominance slabs. However,

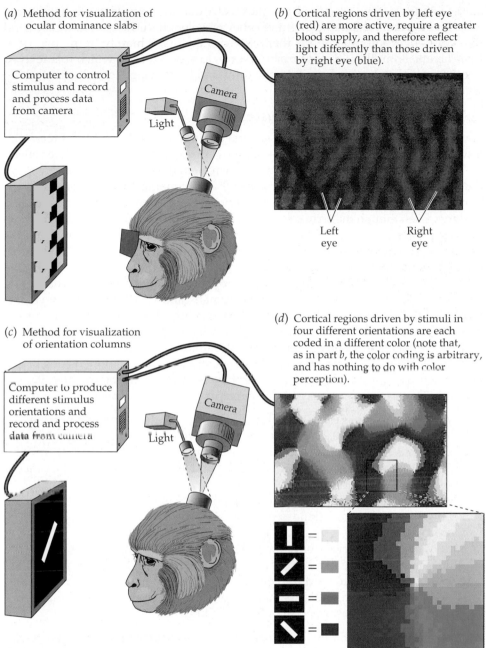

(a) Method for visualization of ocular dominance slabs

Computer to control stimulus and record and process data from camera

Light

Camera

(b) Cortical regions driven by left eye (red) are more active, require a greater blood supply, and therefore reflect light differently than those driven by right eye (blue).

Left eye   Right eye

(c) Method for visualization of orientation columns

Computer to produce different stimulus orientations and record and process data from camera

Light

Camera

(d) Cortical regions driven by stimuli in four different orientations are each coded in a different color (note that, as in part b, the color coding is arbitrary, and has nothing to do with color perception).

10.22 Visualization of Ocular Dominance Columns and Orientation Columns by Optical Imaging (a) In this method for visualization of ocular dominance, a camera records changes in light reflected from the cortex when the monkey views a twinkling checkerboard with one eye. Small differences in reflected light are amplified, and intensity is coded by color (red for strong intensity, blue for weak). (b) After the recording is processed, regions activated by the active eye are seen as red stripes. (c) In this method for visualization of orientation preference, stimuli at different orientations (vertical, horizontal, diagonal) are presented to reveal groups of neurons that respond most strongly to a particular orientation. The stimuli are usually black or white, but here they are color-coded to correspond to color-coded responses to four different orientations combined into a single pattern. (d) Although the pattern at first seems disorderly, closer inspection reveals several regions where four orientations converge in a pinwheel pattern (*inset*). Note that the foci of pinwheels occur at regular intervals, that each orientation is represented only once within a pinwheel, and that the sequence of orientations is consistent across pinwheels. (After T. Bonhoeffer and Grinvald, 1991; b and d courtesy of A. Grinvald.)

the orientation columns stretch only from the center of one ocular stripe to the center of the adjacent stripe. Along the center of the ocular dominance stripes, preferred orientation shifts by 90°, creating regularly spaced "pinwheels" in which responses to the different stimulus orientations pivot around a center. You can read more about the organization of receptive fields in visual cortex in **A Step Further: Slabs and Blobs in Striate Cortex** on the website.

Color Vision Depends on Special Channels from the Retinal Cones through Cortical Area V4

For most people, color is a striking aspect of vision. We will discuss four stages of color perception. In the first stage the cones—the retinal receptor cells that are specialized to respond to certain wavelengths of light—receive visual information. In the second stage this information is processed by neurons in the local circuits

brightness   One of three basic dimensions of light perception, varying from dark to light.

hue   One of three basic dimensions of light perception, varying around the color circle through blue, green, yellow, orange, and red.

saturation   One of three basic dimensions of light perception, varying from rich to pale.

of the retina, leading to retinal ganglion cells that are excited by light of some wavelengths and inhibited by light of other wavelengths. The ganglion cells send the wavelength information via their axons to the LGN, mainly in the parvocellular layers. From there this information goes to area V1, from which it is relayed to other visual cortical areas, where the third and fourth stages of color perception take place.

Color is created by the visual system

For most of us, the visible world has several distinguishable hues: blue, green, yellow, red, and their intermediates. These hues appear different because the reflected light that reaches our eyes can vary in wavelength (see Box 10.1), and we can detect some of these differences. For about 8% of human males and about 0.5% of females, however, some of these color distinctions are either absent or at least less striking. Even though the term *color blindness* is commonly used, most people with impaired color vision are able to distinguish some hues. Complete color blindness can be caused by brain lesions or by the congenital absence of specialized receptors, but in humans it is extremely rare.

Animals exhibit different degrees of color vision. Many species of birds, fishes, and insects have excellent color vision. Humans and Old World monkeys also have an excellent ability to discriminate wavelengths, but many other mammals (e.g., cats) cannot discriminate wavelengths very well. We'll see more about the distribution of color vision among mammals later in this chapter.

The color solid shown in **Figure 10.23** illustrates the basic dimensions of our perception of light; the figure is deliberately asymmetrical, for reasons we will explain. The three dimensions of color perception are

1. **Brightness**, which varies from dark to light. It is represented by the vertical dimension in Figure 10.23, and planes are shown intersecting the figure at different levels of brightness. The planes are tipped up for yellow and down for blue because yellow is perceived as lighter and blue as darker than the other hues.
2. **Hue**, which varies continuously around the color circle through blue, green, yellow, orange, and red. (Hue is what most people mean when they use the term color.)
3. **Saturation**, which varies from rich, full colors at the periphery of the color solid to gray at the center. For example, starting with red at the periphery, the colors become paler toward the center, going through pink to gray. Yellow is shown closer to the central axis than the other saturated hues because yellow is perceived as less saturated than the other hues.

It is important not to equate perception of a particular hue with a particular stimulus (a wavelength of light), because a patch illuminated by a particular wavelength is seen as various different hues, depending on factors such as the intensity of illumination, the surrounding field, and prior exposure to a different stimulus. As illumination fades, the blues in a painting or a rug appear more prominent and the reds appear duller, even though the wavelength distribution in the light has not changed. In addition, the hue perceived at a particular point is strongly affected by the pattern of wavelengths and intensities in other parts of the visual field. To understand how the visual system creates our experience of color, we must understand how cone photoreceptors work.

Color perception requires receptor cells that differ in their sensitivities to different wavelengths

Artists have long known that all the hues can be obtained from a small number of primary colors. On the basis of observations of mixing pigments and lights, scientists at the start of the nineteenth century hypothesized that three separate kinds of receptors in the retina provide the basis for color vision. Endorsed in 1852

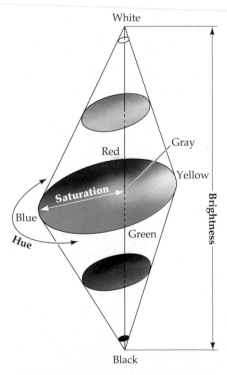

10.23 The Color Solid   The three basic dimensions of the perception of light are brightness (dark to light), hue (color), and saturation (rich to pale).

by the great physiologist-physicist-psychologist Hermann von Helmholtz, this **trichromatic hypothesis** (from the Greek *tri-*, "three," and *chroma*, "color") became the dominant position.

Helmholtz predicted that blue-sensitive, green-sensitive, and red-sensitive receptors would be found, that each would be sharply tuned to its part of the spectrum, and that each type would have a separate path to the brain. The color of an object would be recognized, then, on the basis of which color receptor(s) were activated. This system would be like the mechanisms for discriminating touch and temperature on the basis of which skin receptors and labeled neural lines are activated (see Chapter 8).

Later in the nineteenth century, physiologist Ewald Hering proposed a different explanation. He argued, on the basis of visual experience, that there are four unique hues and three opposed pairs of colors—blue versus yellow, green versus red, and black versus white—and that three physiological processes with opposed positive and negative values must therefore be the basis of color vision. As we will see, both this **opponent-process hypothesis** and the trichromatic hypothesis are encompassed in current color vision theory, but neither of the old hypotheses is sufficient by itself.

Measurements of photopigments in cones have borne out the trichromatic hypothesis in part. Each cone of the human retina has one of three classes of pigments. These pigments do not, however, have the narrow spectral distributions that Helmholtz predicted. The color system that Helmholtz postulated would have given rather poor color vision and poor visual acuity. Color vision would be poor because only a few different hues would be discriminable; within the long-wavelength region of the spectrum there would be only red, not all the range of hues that we see. Acuity would be poor because the grain of the retinal mosaic would be coarse; a red stimulus would be able to affect only one-third of the receptors. (In reality, though, acuity is as good in red light as it is in white light.)

The human visual system does not have receptors that are sensitive to only a narrow part of the visible spectrum. Two of the three retinal cone pigments show some response to light of almost *any* wavelength. The pigments have different *peaks* of sensitivity, but the peaks are not as far apart as Helmholtz predicted. As **Figure 10.24** shows, the cone pigment peaks occur at about 420 nm (in the part of the spectrum where we usually see violet under photopic conditions), about 530 nm (where most of us see green), and about 560 nm (where most of us see yellow-green). Despite Helmholtz's prediction, none of the curves peak in the long-wavelength part of the spectrum, where most of us see red (about 630 nm).

Under ordinary conditions, almost any visual object stimulates at least two kinds of cones, thus ensuring high visual acuity and good perception of form. The spectral sensitivities of the three cone types differ from each other, and the nervous system detects and processes these differences to extract the color information. Thus, certain ganglion cells and certain cells at higher stations in the visual system are color-specific, even though the receptor cells are not. Similarly, photoreceptors are not form-specific (they respond to single points of light), but form is detected later in the system by comparison of the outputs of different receptors.

Because the cones are not color detectors, the most appropriate brief names for them can be taken from their peak areas of wavelength sensitivity: *short* (S) for the receptor with peak sensitivity at about 420 nm, *medium* (M) for 530 nm, and *long* (L) for 560 nm (see Figure 10.24). There are typically twice as many L as M receptors, but far fewer S receptors (Brainard et al., 2000; Carroll et al., 2000; Hagstrom et al., 1998); this difference explains why acuity is much lower with short-wavelength illumination (blue light) than in the other parts of the visible spectrum.

trichromatic hypothesis   A hypothesis of color perception stating that there are three different types of cones, each excited by a different region of the spectrum and each having a separate pathway to the brain.

opponent-process hypothesis   The theory that color vision depends on systems that produce opposite responses to light of different wavelengths.

10.24 Spectral Sensitivities of Human Photopigments   Each pigment has a peak sensitivity but responds to a wide range of wavelengths. S, short-wavelength; M, medium-wavelength; L, long-wavelength. Knowing only that an M cone is active, you cannot tell whether it was stimulated by weak light at 530 nm ("green"), or by strong light anywhere from 450 nm ("blue") to 620 nm ("red"). Only by *comparing* responses of *different* cones can the brain extract color information.

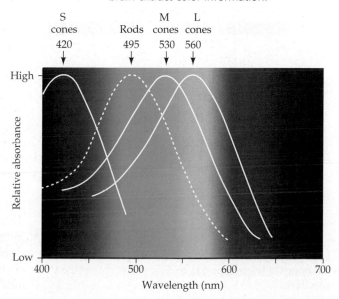

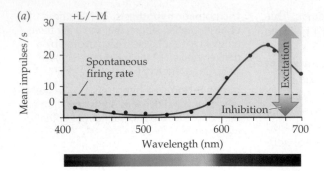

(a) +L/–M

Spontaneous
firing rate

Excitation

Inhibition

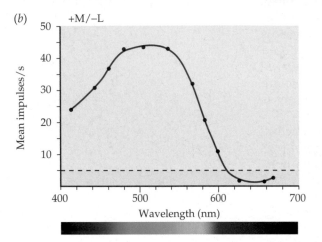

(b) +M/–L

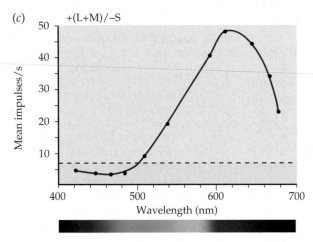

(c) +(L+M)/–S

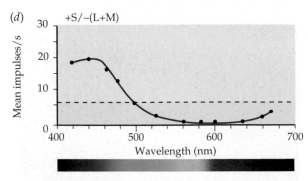

(d) +S/–(L+M)

spectrally opponent cell A visual receptor cell that has opposite firing responses to different regions of the spectrum.

10.25 Responses of the Four Main Types of Spectrally Opponent Cells in Monkey LGN The four main types of spectrally opponent cells are (a) +L/–M, (b) +M/–L, (c) +(L+M)/–S, and (d) +S/–(L+M). Each type is excited by one band of wavelengths and inhibited by another.

The genes for wavelength-sensitive pigments in the retina have been analyzed, and the similarities in structure of the three genes suggest that they are all derived from a common ancestral gene (Nathans, 1987). In addition, the genes for the medium- and long-wavelength pigments occupy adjacent positions on the X chromosome and are much more similar to each other than either is to the gene for the short-wavelength pigment on chromosome 6. Probably our primate ancestors had only one photopigment gene on the X chromosome, which became duplicated. Then, mutations caused the two genes to become more and more different until their response to various wavelengths of light was no longer the same. Thus, our ancestors went from having only two cone pigments (one on the X chromosome and the S pigment on chromosome 6) to three.

This evolution of a third photopigment may have happened recently (in evolutionary terms), because most New World monkeys have only a single longer-wavelength pigment. Furthermore, the genes for the M and L pigments vary among individuals, and particular variants in these pigment genes correspond to variants in color vision: so-called color blindness.

The fact that the genes for the M and L pigments are on the X chromosome also explains why defects of red-green color vision are much more frequent in human males than in human females. Because males have only one X chromosome, a mutation in the genes for the M or L pigments can impair color vision. But if a female has a defective photopigment gene in one of her two X chromosomes, a normal copy of the gene on the other X chromosome can compensate.

Some retinal ganglion cells and parvocellular LGN cells show spectral opponency

Recordings made from retinal ganglion cells in Old World monkeys, which can discriminate colors as humans do, reveal the second stage of processing of color vision. Most ganglion cells and cells in the parvocellular layers of the LGN fire in response to some wavelengths and are inhibited by other wavelengths.

Figure 10.25a shows the response of a parvocellular LGN cell as a large spot of light centered on its receptive field changes from one wavelength to another. Firing is stimulated by wavelengths above 600 nm, where the L cones are most sensitive, and then inhibited at shorter wavelengths, where the L cones are less sensitive than the M cones. A cell exhibiting this response pattern is therefore called a *plus L/minus M cell* (+L/–M). This is an example of a **spectrally opponent cell** because two regions of the spectrum have opposite effects on the cell's rate of firing. Figure 10.25 shows examples of responses of the four main kinds of spectrally opponent cells.

Each spectrally opponent ganglion cell receives input from two or three different kinds of cones through bipolar cells. The connections from at least one type of cone are excitatory, and those from at least one other type are inhibitory. The spectrally opponent ganglion cells thus record the *difference* in stimulation of different populations of cones. For example, a +M/–L cell responds to the difference in the excitation of M and L cones.

The peaks of the sensitivity curves of the M and L cones are not very different (see Figure 10.24). However, whereas the M-minus-L *difference* curve (**Figure 10.25b**) shows a clear peak at about 500 nm (in the green part of the spectrum), the L-minus-M difference function (see Figure 10.25a) shows a peak at about 650 nm (in the red part of the spectrum). Thus, +M/–L and +L/–M cells yield distinctly different neural response curves. LGN cells excited by the L and M cells, but inhibited by S cells—that is, +(L+M)/–S cells—peak in the red range (**Figure 10.25c**); while cells excited by S but inhibited by L and M—that is, +S/–(L+M) cells—peak in the blue-violet range (**Figure 10.25d**).

Spectrally opponent neurons are the second stage in the system for color perception, but they still cannot be called *color cells*, for the following reasons: (1) they send their outputs into many higher circuits—for detection of form, depth, and movement, as well as hue; and (2) their peak wavelength sensitivities do not correspond precisely to the wavelengths that we see as the principal hues.

Figure 10.26 diagrams the presumed inputs to not only the four kinds of spectrally opponent ganglion cells, but also the ganglion cells that detect brightness and darkness. The brightness detectors receive stimulation from both M and L cones (+M/+L); the darkness detectors are inhibited by both M and L cones (–M/–L).

In the monkey LGN, 70%–80% of the cells are spectrally opponent; in the cat, very few spectrally opponent cells are found—only about 1%. This difference explains the ease with which monkeys discriminate wavelengths and the difficulty in training cats to discriminate even large differences in wavelength.

Some visual cortical cells and regions appear to be specialized for color perception

In the cortex, spectral information appears to be used for various kinds of information processing. Forms are segregated from their background by differences in color or intensity (or both). The most important role that color plays in our perception is to denote which parts of a complex image belong to one object and which belong to another. Some animals use displays of brightly colored body parts to call attention to themselves, but color can also be used as camouflage.

Some *spectrally opponent cortical cells* contribute to the perception of color, providing the third stage of the color vision system. Russell De Valois (1926–2003) and Karen De Valois suggested ways in which adding and subtracting the outputs of spectrally opponent ganglion cells could yield cortical cells that are perceptually opponent: red versus green, blue versus yellow, and black versus white (R. L. De Valois and De Valois, 1993). The spectral responses of these cells correspond to the wavelengths of the principal hues specified by human observers, and their characteristics also help explain other color phenomena.

Visual cortical region V4 is particularly rich in color-sensitive cells. V4 cells respond best if the color outside the receptive field is different from the color preferred in the receptive field (Schein and Desimone, 1990). These cells provide a fourth stage of color perception that may be important for color constancy and for discrimination between a figure and background. Area V4 is also activated when humans view colored stimuli but not when they view black-and-white stimuli (Zeki et al., 1991).

10.26 A Model of the Connections of Wavelength Discrimination Systems in the Primate Retina The connections from the cones yield four kinds of spectrally opponent ganglion cells, as well as ganglion cells that detect brightness or darkness. (After R. L. De Valois and De Valois, 1980.)

It would probably be wrong to think of area V4 as devoted exclusively to color perception. Cells in V4 are also tuned in the spatial domain, for orientation and for spatial frequency (Desimone and Schein, 1987). Schiller (1993) lesioned V4 in monkeys and found color vision relatively unaffected. V4 probably serves several aspects of visual perception.

Most mammalian species have some color vision

In 1942, Gordon Walls concluded from a survey that, among mammals, color vision is by no means widespread, and this conclusion has been repeated in many books and articles. A much more extensive survey by Gerald Jacobs (1993), however, indicates that most mammals have at least some degree of color vision. Although only certain primates have good trichromatic color vision (vision based on three classes of cone photopigments), many mammalian species have dichromatic color vision (based on two classes of cone pigments). Most so-called color-blind humans (actually color-*deficient* humans) have dichromatic vision and can distinguish short-wavelength stimuli (blue) from long-wavelength stimuli (not blue). When a gene carrying a third photopigment was introduced into photoreceptors of adult male squirrel monkeys with such dichromatic vision, they soon displayed excellent trichromatic vision (Mancuso et al., 2009), so it may be possible to correct dichromatic vision in humans. Likewise, introducing photopigment genes in mice enabled them to discriminate colors they normally cannot see (G. H. Jacobs et al., 2007).

On the basis of his survey, Jacobs (1993) suggested that it is better to think of a continuum of color capabilities than to use an all-or-none criterion, and he proposed that four categories cover all mammalian species:

1. *Excellent trichromatic color vision* is found in diurnal primates such as humans and the rhesus monkey (*Macaca mulatta*).
2. *Robust dichromatic color vision* is found in species that have two kinds of cone photopigments and a reasonably large population of cones. Examples of such species include the dog, the pig, and many male New World monkeys, such as the squirrel monkey (*Saimiri sciureus*) and the marmoset monkey (*Callithrix jaccus*). (The females may be trichromatic, as a result of having genes that encode differing long-wavelength cones on their two X chromosomes.)
3. *Feeble dichromatic color vision* occurs in species that have two kinds of cone pigments but very few cones. Examples include the domestic cat and the coati (*Nasua nasua*).
4. *Minimal color vision* is possessed by species that have only a single kind of cone pigment and that must rely on interactions between rods and cones to discriminate wavelength. Examples include the owl monkey (*Aotes trivirgatus*) and the raccoon (*Procyon lotor*).

When both diurnal and nocturnal species of a given taxonomic family have been tested for color vision (e.g., the coati and the raccoon), the diurnal species (in this case the coati) usually has been shown to have the better color vision.

Perception of Visual Motion Is Analyzed by a Special System That Includes Cortical Area V5

Some retinal ganglion cells respond preferentially to a certain direction of motion of objects; for example, they may respond to stimuli that move to the left but not to stimuli that move to the right (Barlow and Levick, 1965). Investigators have hypothesized that the direction-selective responses require retinal circuits involving both excitation and inhibition: whereas movement in the preferred direction stimulates excitatory units before inhibitory units, movement in the nonpreferred direction reaches inhibitory units first.

Motion is analyzed by the cortex, partly in regions close to those that control eye movements. All the neurons in area V5 (also called the *medial temporal area* or *MT*;

see Figure 10.19*c*) in the monkey respond to moving visual stimuli, indicating that they are specialized for the perception of motion and its direction. As mentioned previously, PET studies show that moving stimuli also evoke responses in human area V5.

Experimental lesions of area V5 in monkeys trained to report the direction of perceived motion impaired their performance, at least temporarily (Newsome et al., 1985). Electrically stimulating an area of V5 that normally responds to stimuli moving up in other monkeys caused them to report that dots on the screen were moving up even when they were actually moving to the right.

One striking report described a woman who had lost the ability to perceive motion after a stroke damaged her area V5 (Zihl et al., 1983). The woman was unable to perceive continuous motion and saw only separate, successive static images. This impairment led to many problems in her daily life. She had difficulty crossing streets because she could not follow the positions of automobiles in motion: "When I'm looking at the car at first, it seems far away. But then when I want to cross the road, suddenly the car is very near." She also complained of difficulties in following conversations because she could not see the movements of speakers' lips. Except for her inability to perceive motion, this woman's visual perception appeared normal.

The Many Cortical Visual Areas Are Organized into Two Major Streams

Many investigators have wondered why primate visual systems contain so many distinct regions. Certain regions specialize in processing different attributes of visual experience (such as shape, location, color, motion, and orientation). But the number of visual fields—over 30—is larger than the number of basic attributes. Perhaps the reason that so many separate visual regions have been found is simply that investigators, being visually oriented primates themselves, have lavished special attention on the visual system.

Earlier work with hamsters led to the hypothesis that there are two visual systems: one, for *identification* of objects, involves especially the visual cortex; the other, for *location* of objects, involves especially the superior colliculus (G. E. Schneider, 1969). Mortimer Mishkin and Leslie Ungerleider (1982) proposed that primates also have two main cortical processing streams, both originating in primary visual cortex: a ventral processing stream responsible for visually *identifying* objects, and a dorsal stream responsible for appreciating the spatial *location* of objects and visual guidance of movement toward objects (**Figure 10.27**). These processing streams were called, respectively, the *what* and *where* streams.

PET studies, as well as brain lesions in patients, indicate that the human brain possesses *what* and *where* visual processing streams similar to those that have been found in monkeys (Ungerleider et al., 1998). The two streams are not completely separate, because there are normally many cross-connections between them. In the ventral stream, including regions of the occipitotemporal, inferior temporal, and inferior frontal areas, information about faces becomes more specific as one proceeds farther forward. PET studies show that, whereas general information about facial features and gender is extracted more posteriorly, the more anterior parts of the stream provide representations of individual faces (Courtney et al., 1996).

Discovery of these separate visual cortical streams helps us understand the case of patient D.F., described at the start of this chapter. Recall that, after carbon monoxide poisoning, she lost the ability to perceive faces and objects while retaining the ability to reach and grasp under visual control. The investigators who studied her (A. D. Milner et al., 1991) hypothesized that D.F.'s ventral visual stream had been devastated but that her dorsal stream was unimpaired. An opposite kind of dissociation had already been reported: damage to the posterior parietal cortex often results in optic **ataxia** in which patients have difficulty using vision to reach

ataxia An impairment in the direction, extent, and rate of muscular movement.

Dorsal stream:
vision for movement, location

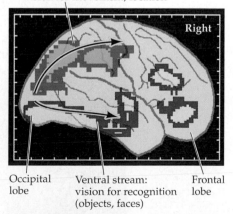

Right

Occipital lobe   Ventral stream:
vision for recognition   Frontal lobe
(objects, faces)

10.27 Parallel Processing Pathways in the Visual System The ventral (*what*) pathway shown in yellow and red, and the dorsal (*where*) pathway shown in green and blue, serve different functions. (Courtesy of Leslie Ungerleider.)

mirror neuron   A neuron that is active both when an individual makes a particular movement and when that individual sees another individual make that same movement.

for and grasp objects, yet some of these patients can still identify objects correctly (Perenin and Vighetto, 1988).

MRI with D.F. supports the interpretation of impairment in her ventral stream but a relatively normal dorsal stream (T. W. James et al., 2003). High-resolution MRI of D.F.'s brain (**Figure 10.28a**) reveals diffuse damage with a concentration in the ventrolateral occipital cortex. Throughout the brain, there is evidence of atrophy, indicated by shrunken gyri and enlarged sulci. **Figure 10.28b** shows the area activated in fMRI recordings when normal subjects viewed pictures of objects; it corresponds to D.F.'s lateral occipital lesion. When D.F. reached for and grasped objects, her fMRI activation in the parietal lobe was similar to that of normal subjects, indicating that D.F.'s dorsal stream is largely intact. D.F.'s intact dorsal pathway not only tells her where objects are but also guides her movements to use these objects properly.

It is still puzzling that one part of D.F. knows exactly how to grasp a pencil while another part of her—the part that talks to you—has no idea whether it's a pencil, a ruler, or a bouquet of flowers. Imagining what this disjointed visual experience must be like for D.F. allows us to appreciate how effortlessly our brains usually bind together information to give us the marvelous sense of sight.

The anterior part of the dorsal stream includes "mirror neurons"

The anterior part of the dorsal visual stream merges with the motor cortex and includes neurons that have both visual and motor functions. These neurons were discovered by investigators who were recording with electrodes implanted in the motor cortex of monkeys. To their surprise, the investigators found cells that fired not only when the monkey grasped and moved an object but also when the monkey observed another monkey or a person grasping and moving an object.

It took the investigators several years to believe and publish their finding (Di Pelligrino et al., 1992). They proposed that these **mirror neurons** mediate the understanding of actions performed by others: when an individual sees an action performed by another, neurons that represent that action are activated in the observer's premotor cortex (see Figure 11.17). This automatically induced motor representation of the observed action corresponds to activation that is generated during motor activity and that has an outcome known to the observer. Thus, the mirror system transforms visual information into knowledge (Rizzolatti and Craighero, 2004).

10.28 Object Recognition Centers in the Brain   (a) In this reconstruction from MRI images, the brain region that was damaged in patient D.F. (blue) is seen from lateral views and from below (outlined in orange on the right). (b) In neurologically intact subjects, this same brain region is activated (yellow) when the subjects are looking at recognizably intact pictures of various objects rather than scrambled pictures. D.F.'s inability to recognize the objects she sees appears to be due to the damage to this region on the border of the occipital and temporal cortex. (From T. W. James et al., 2003; courtesy Thomas James.)

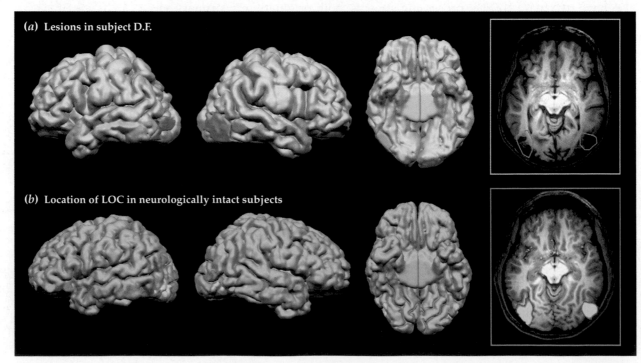

(a) Lesions in subject D.F.

(b) Location of LOC in neurologically intact subjects

Several studies provide data for the existence of a mirror neuron system in humans. For example, it has long been known that EEG activation occurs in the motor region not only during active movement but also when a person observes actions performed by others (Gastaut and Bert, 1954). Further evidence came from studies using functional MRI while the subject watched actions performed by another human or by an animal (e.g., Buccino et al., 2004). Watching was found to evoke cortical activity in the appropriate region of the motor cortex.

The human mirror neuron system possesses some important properties not observed in the monkey system. First, meaningless movements activate the mirror neuron system in humans but not in monkeys. Second, the temporal characteristics suggest that the human systems code for the component movements of an action, whereas the monkey systems code only for the total action. The investigators suggest that these differences should favor the ability of humans to imitate the actions of others (Rizzolatti and Craighero, 2004, p. 176).

The discovery of mirror neurons has stimulated much research and speculation, so you are likely to see more about them in the future. The mirror neuron system has been related to topics as varied as empathy, learning by imitation, and the evolution of language; damage to the mirror neuron system has been proposed as a cause of autism, which is characterized by impairments in understanding other people's behavior. We will consider additional aspects of mirror neurons in Chapter 11 in the context of the motor system.

Visual Neuroscience Can Be Applied to Alleviate Some Visual Deficiencies

Vision is so important that many investigators have sought ways to prevent impairment, to improve inadequate vision, and to restore sight to the blind. In the United States, half a million people are blind. Recent medical advances have reduced some causes of blindness but have increased blindness from other causes. For example, medical advances permit people with diabetes to live longer, but because we don't know how to prevent blindness associated with diabetes, there are more people alive today with diabetes-induced blindness. In the discussion that follows we will first consider ways of avoiding impairment of vision. Then we will take up ways of exercising and training that are designed to improve an impaired visual system.

Impairment of vision often can be prevented or reduced

Studies of the development of vision in children and other animals show that the incidence of **myopia** (nearsightedness) (from the Greek *myein*, "to be closed," and *ops*, "eye") can be reduced. Myopia develops if the eyeball is too long, forcing the eye to focus objects in front of the retina rather than on the retina (**Figure 10.29**). As a result, distant objects appear blurred. Considerable evidence suggests that myopia develops when children spend a lot of time looking at targets close up rather than at objects far away (Marzani and Wallman, 1997).

Before civilization, most people spent the bulk of their time looking at objects far away, such as predators, prey, sources of water, and so on. Thus, they kept the eye relaxed most of the time. Now, however, people spend long periods of time gazing at objects close at hand, such as books and computer screens. This constant close focusing requires that the lens be kept thick (unrelaxed). The developing eyeball compensates by elongating to make focusing easier, thus causing progressive myopia. The following preventive steps can be taken, especially during childhood and adolescence:

- Read only in adequate light—enough that you can hold the book as far away as possible and still discern the words.
- Avoid small type.
- If you already have a prescription for myopia but you can read without using glasses, do so, because reading with glasses forces you to thicken your lens more, thus accelerating the problem.

myopia Nearsightedness; the inability to focus the retinal image of objects that are far away.

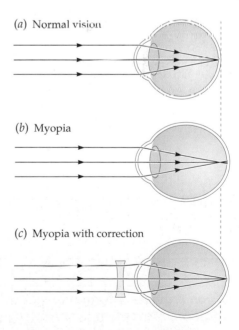

(a) Normal vision

(b) Myopia

(c) Myopia with correction

10.29 Focusing Images on the Retina *(a)* Normally, the cornea and lens refract light to focus a sharp image of the outside world on the retina. *(b)* In myopia, the eyeball is too long, so the image is in focus in front of the retina. In this case, the image that actually reaches the retina is blurred. *(c)* Eyeglasses refract the light before it reaches the cornea to bring the image into sharp focus on the retina.

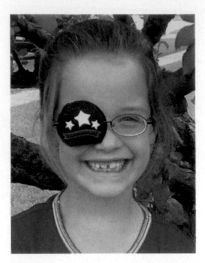

10.30 Hey There, You With the Stars in Your Eye As a treatment for amblyopia, this girl is wearing a patch over her "good" eye—the one she has been relying on while ignoring information from her other, "weak" eye. Visual experience through the weak eye will strengthen its influence on the cortex.

amblyopia Reduced visual acuity that is not caused by optical or retinal impairments.

Increased exercise can restore function to a previously deprived or neglected eye

In Chapter 7 we considered the misalignment of the two eyes (*lazy eye*), which can lead to the condition called **amblyopia** (from the Greek *amblys*, "dull" or "blunt," and *ops*, "eye"), in which acuity is poor in one eye, even though the eye and retina are normal. If the two eyes are not aligned properly during the first few years of life, the primary visual cortex of the child tends to suppress the information that arrives in the cortex from one eye, and that eye becomes functionally blind. Studies of the development of vision in children and other animals also show that most cases of amblyopia are avoidable.

The balance of the eye muscles can be surgically adjusted to bring the two eyes into better alignment. Alternatively, if the weak eye is given regular practice, with the good eye covered, then vision can be preserved in both eyes. Attempts to alleviate amblyopia by training, however, have produced mixed results and a great deal of controversy. In a study sponsored by the American Academy of Ophthalmology, 507 patients, aged 7–17, were assigned at random to one of two groups. The participants in one group were given optimal optical correction. Those in the other group were given not only optical correction but also a patch covering the good eye (**Figure 10.30**), and they participated in visual exercises for 26 weeks. Patients were considered to have improved if, after treatment, they could read two or more lines farther down on a standard eye chart. One-fourth of those who received only optical correction showed improvement, but among those who had eye patches and engaged in visual exercises, half improved (Pediatric Eye Disease Investigator Group, 2005).

Other studies have reported considerable improvement, even with adults, if the eye is exercised sufficiently and if the amblyopia is not too severe. In Chapter 7 we saw that Michael May, who was blind from the age of 3 to 43, regained some aspects of vision quickly following surgery to let light back into one of his eyes. Other aspects, such as the perception of faces and objects, remain severely impaired—but nevertheless show improvement with practice.

Frequent causes of visual impairment, especially with age, are diseases such as macular degeneration that damage the rods and cones. These diseases leave the ganglion cells and the higher neural pathways largely intact. Scientists are working on arrays of electrodes to be placed within the eye in contact with the ganglion cells. These electrodes would be stimulated by a small camera and radio frequency transmitter lodged in the patient's eyeglasses. "The aim is to bring a blind person to the point where he or she can read, move around objects in the house, and do basic household chores," says project leader Kurt Wessendork. "They won't be able to drive cars, at least in the near future … But people who are blind will see" (N. Singer, 2002, p. 1).

SUMMARY

Vision Provides Information about the Form, Color, Location, Movement, and Identity of Objects

■ The perception of forms and the recognition of objects are complex accomplishments that require processing in many parts of the visual system.

■ Each **photoreceptor** reports only how strongly it has been excited, so at any given instant the visual nervous system receives an enormous array of quantitative information and

has to determine what patterns in the outside world could have produced a particular set of "numbers." About one-third of the human cortex is devoted to this computation. **Review Figures 10.1 and 10.2**

■ Circuitry in the eye itself causes photoreceptors to have an inhibitory effect on the report of their neighbors, an instance of **lateral inhibition** that underlies simple illusions in **brightness. Review Figures 10.3*a* and 10.4**

The Visual System Extends from the Eye to the Brain

■ The vertebrate eye is an elaborate structure that forms detailed and accurate optical images on the receptive cells of the **retina. Review Figure 10.5, Web Activity 10.1**

■ Visual-information processing begins in the retina, where cells that contain photopigments capture light and initiate neural activity. Two kinds of retinal receptor cells—**rods** and **cones**—represent the initial stages of two systems: the **scotopic system** (dim light) and **photopic system** (bright light), respectively. **Review Figure 10.6 and Table 10.1**

■ Visual acuity is greatest in the **fovea**, where photoreceptors are most densely packed, there is relatively little convergence of photoreceptors onto **ganglion cells**, and there are fewer overlying blood vessels to impede light. **Review Figure 10.9 and 10.10**

Neural Signals Travel from the Retina to Several Brain Regions

■ Brain pathways of the visual system include the **lateral geniculate nucleus** (**LGN**) in the thalamus, the **primary visual cortex** (**striate cortex**, or **V1**), and other cortical regions. Some axons of retinal ganglion cells extend to the superior colliculus in the midbrain. **Review Figure 10.11, Web Activity 10.2**

■ The cortex contains several visual areas, each presenting a topographic map of the **visual field**, but each somewhat specialized for processing one or more different aspects of visual information, such as form, color, or movement. **Review Figure 10.12**

■ Many different phyla have independently evolved photoreceptor organs; several have evolved eyes with lenses to focus light. **Review Box 10.2**

Neurons at Different Levels of the Visual System Have Very Different Receptive Fields

■ The **receptive fields** of bipolar cells and ganglion cells consist of a circular center and a surround that have opposing effects: either **on-center/off surround** or **off-center/on-surround. Review Figures 10.13 and 10.14, Web Activity 10.3**

■ Recordings from cells at successively higher levels in the visual system reveal that the receptive fields change in two main ways: (1) they become larger (occupy larger parts of the visual field), and (2) they require increasingly specific stimuli to evoke responses. **Review Figures 10.14 and 10.16**

■ For the perception of visual patterns and forms, the stimulus pattern is analyzed at the primary visual cortex according to the orientation and spatial frequency of stimuli, but further analysis at specialized cortical areas is required for the recognition of objects, faces, and three-dimensional forms. **Review Figures 10.17 and 10.19–10.21, Web Activity 10.4**

Area V1 Is Organized in Columns and Slabs

■ The ability to locate visual stimuli in space is aided by detailed spatial maps in some regions of the visual system. **Review Figure 10.22**

Color Vision Depends on Special Channels from the Retinal Cones through Cortical Area V4

■ The discrimination of hue in Old World primates and in humans depends on the existence of three different cone photopigments and on the fact that retinal connections yield four different kinds of **spectrally opponent** retinal ganglion cells. **Review Figures 10.24–10.26**

Perception of Visual Motion Is Analyzed by a Special System That Includes Cortical Area V5

■ In cortical area V5, most neurons respond preferentially to objects that move in a particular direction in the visual field.

The Many Cortical Visual Areas Are Organized into Two Major Streams

■ Visual cortical areas are organized into two main streams: a ventral *what* stream that serves in the recognition of faces and objects, and a dorsal *where* stream that serves in location and visuomotor skills. **Review Figure 10.27**

■ The anterior part of the dorsal visual stream includes **mirror neurons** that respond to the sight of another individual's actions.

Visual Neuroscience Can Be Applied to Alleviate Some Visual Deficiencies

■ Attempts to treat **amblyopia** work best when retraining starts early in life, but success with some older patients demonstrates that the visual nervous system remains plastic even in adults.

Go to **www.biopsychology.com** for study questions, quizzes, key terms, and other resources.

Recommended Reading

De Valois, R. L., and De Valois, K. K. (1988). *Spatial vision.* New York: Oxford University Press.

Ings, S. (2008). *A natural history of seeing: The art and science of vision.* New York: W. W. Norton.

Purves, D., and Lotto, R. B. (2003). *Why we see what we do.* Sunderland, MA: Sinauer.

Rodieck, R. W. (1998). *The first steps in seeing.* Sunderland, MA: Sinauer.

Wandell, B. A. (1995). *Foundations of vision.* Sunderland, MA: Sinauer.

Wolfe, J. M., Kluender, K. R., Levi, D. M., Bartoshuk, L. M., et al. (2008). *Sensation & Perception* (2nd ed.). Sunderland, MA: Sinauer.

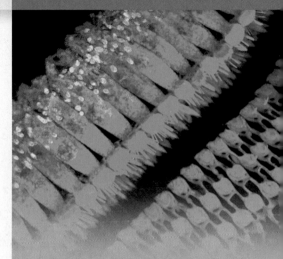

Motor Control and Plasticity

CHAPTER 11

What You See Is What You Get

Ian Waterman had a perfectly ordinary life until he caught a viral infection at age 19. For reasons that no one understands, the infection targeted a very specific set of nerves sending information from his body to his brain. Ian can still feel pain or deep pressure, as well as warm and cool surfaces on his skin, but he has no sensation of light touch below his neck. What's more, although Ian can still move all of his muscles, he receives no information about muscle activity or body position (Cole, 1995). You might think this deficiency wouldn't cause any problem, because you've probably never thought much about your "body sense"; it's not even one of the five senses that people talk about, is it?

In fact, however, the loss of this information was devastating. Ian couldn't walk across a room without falling down, and he couldn't walk up or down stairs. The few other people suffering a loss like this have spent the rest of their lives in wheelchairs. But Ian was a young and determined person, so he started teaching himself how to walk using another source of feedback about his body: his vision. Now, as long as the lights are on, Ian can carefully watch his moving body and gauge what motor commands to send out to keep walking. If the lights go out, however, he collapses; and he has learned that in that circumstance he just has to lie where he is until the lights come on again. He has so finely honed this ability to guide movements with vision that if asked to point repeatedly to the same location in the air, he does so more accurately than control subjects do. Still, it's a mental drain to have to watch and attend constantly to his body just to do everyday tasks.

Today Ian has a good job and an active, independent life, but he is always vigilant. Lying in bed, he has to be very careful to remain calm, tethering his limbs with the covers to prevent them from flailing about.

And the lights are always on at Ian's house.

O ur emphasis in this chapter shifts to the motor system as we complete the circuit from sensory input to behavior. It is important to consider sensory and motor functions together. Just as we saw in Chapters 8–10 that motor activities are important for sensory and perceptual functions—movements of the fingers in active touch perception, sniffing in smell, and movements of the eyes and head in vision—so we will see in this chapter that sensory and perceptual processes guide and correct our actions.

In addition, just as our apparently effortless perception turns out to depend on intricate sensory mechanisms and perceptual processes, so, too, our apparently effortless adult motor abilities—such as reaching out and picking up an object, walking across the room, sipping a cup of coffee—require complex muscular systems with constant feedback from the body, as Ian's case shows. After examining movements and their coordination from the behavioral view and the control systems view, in this chapter we'll integrate these into the neuroscience view.

The Behavioral View

By the early nineteenth century, scientists knew that the dorsal roots of the spinal cord serve sensory functions and that the ventral roots contain motor fibers; connections between the two seemed to provide the basis for simple movements. Research with **spinal animals** (animals in which the spinal cord has been disconnected from the brain) led British physiologist Charles Sherrington to argue that the basic units of behavior are **reflexes**: simple, unvarying, and unlearned responses to sensory stimuli such as touch, pressure, and pain. We analyzed the famous knee jerk reflex in Figure 3.17.

Sherrington's work inspired a rush to identify various reflexes and their pathways in the nervous system, particularly in the spinal cord. These studies showed that some reflexes involve only short pathways in the spinal cord linking dorsal and ventral roots; others involve longer loops connecting spinal cord segments to each other, or to brain regions.

Simple reflexes include brief, unitary activities of muscle called **movements**. Movements are discrete, in many cases limited to a single part of the body, such as a limb. In contrast, complex, sequential behaviors such as putting on a jacket are considered **acts**, or *action patterns*. Different movements of several body parts might be included in such behaviors. You can think of an act as being made up of a particular sequence of movements.

So, are acts simply the connecting together of different reflexes, the sensation from one reflex triggering the next? The limitations of this perspective are apparent when we think about complex sequences of behavior, such as speech. A speaker has a *plan* in which several units (speech sounds and words) are placed in a larger pattern (the intended complete statement). Sometimes the units are misplaced, although the pattern is preserved: "Our queer old dean," said history professor William Spooner, when he meant, "Our dear old queen." Or "You hissed all my mystery lectures." (Spooner was so prone to mixing up the order of sounds in his sentences that this type of error is called a *spoonerism*.) Such mistakes reveal the overall plan: the speaker is *anticipating* a later sound and executing it too soon. A chain of reflexes, each one triggering the next, could not generate such an error.

The **motor plan**, or *motor program*, is a complex set of commands to muscles that is completely established before an act occurs. Feedback from movements informs and fine-tunes the motor program as the execution is unfolding, but the basic sequence of movements is planned. Examples of behaviors that exhibit this kind of internal plan range from highly skilled acts, such as piano playing, to the simple escape behaviors of animals such as crayfish.

Movements and acts can be analyzed and measured in a variety of ways

We can readily analyze movements and acts using high-speed video, which provides an intimate frame-by-frame portrait of even the most rapid events. To deal with the large amounts of data produced by image processing, methods of simplification or numerical analysis have been devised. For example, sports trainers use detailed analyses of athletic acts based on time-lapse photographs or information derived from sensors attached at joints. Computer programs process images to help quantify the performance, enabling detailed measurement of the positions of different body parts in successive instants. Other devices record the direction, strength, and speed of motions. **Figure 11.1** illustrates the paths of normal and impaired reaching movements, a kind of movement considered at several points in this chapter.

Another approach to the fine-grained analysis of movements is to record the electrical activity of muscles—a procedure called **electromyography** (**EMG**). Like neurons, muscles produce action potentials when they contract, as we'll see later in this chapter. Therefore, fine needle electrodes placed in a muscle, or electrodes

spinal animal An animal whose spinal cord has been surgically disconnected from the brain to enable the study of behaviors that do not require brain control.

reflex A simple, highly stereotyped, and unlearned response to a particular stimulus (e.g., an eye blink in response to a puff of air).

movement A brief, unitary activity of a muscle or body part; less complex than an act.

act Also called *action pattern*. Complex behavior, as distinct from a simple movement.

motor plan Also called *motor program*. A plan for action in the nervous system.

electromyography (EMG) The electrical recording of muscle activity.

(*a*) Visually guided reaching task

(*b*) Examples of arm movements after 200 practice trials

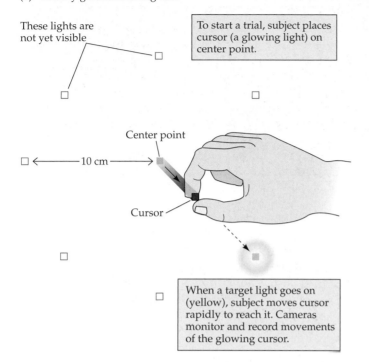

These lights are not yet visible

To start a trial, subject places cursor (a glowing light) on center point.

Center point

□ ←——10 cm——→

Cursor

When a target light goes on (yellow), subject moves cursor rapidly to reach it. Cameras monitor and record movements of the glowing cursor.

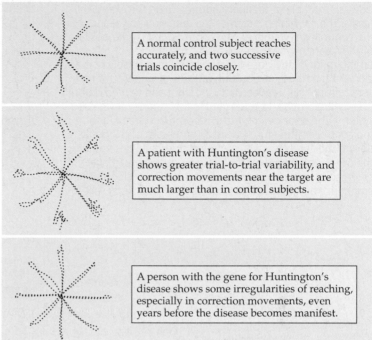

A normal control subject reaches accurately, and two successive trials coincide closely.

A patient with Huntington's disease shows greater trial-to-trial variability, and correction movements near the target are much larger than in control subjects.

A person with the gene for Huntington's disease shows some irregularities of reaching, especially in correction movements, even years before the disease becomes manifest.

11.1 Measurement of Reaching Movements (*a*) An experimental setup to study reaching movements. (*b*) Recorded movement trajectories of a normal subject (*top*), a patient with Huntington's disease (*middle*), and a carrier of the gene for Huntington's disease (*bottom*). We'll discuss this disorder in detail later in this chapter. (Part *b* courtesy of Maurice R. Smith.)

placed on the skin over a muscle, can detect electrical indications of muscle activity (**Figure 11.2**). If electrodes are placed over several different muscles, we get a record of the contraction of the muscles involved in an act, including the progressive buildup and decay of their activity (Hanakawa et al., 2003). The EMGs in Figure 11.2 show that a person pulling a knob will adjust his legs just before moving his arm—another example of motor planning.

The Control Systems View

One way to look at the mechanisms that regulate and control our movements employs the language of engineering. In designing machines, engineers commonly have two goals: (1) accuracy, to prevent or minimize error; and (2) speed, to complete a task quickly and efficiently. It is difficult to accomplish simultaneous improvements in both goals; usually there is a trade-off between the two. Two forms of control mechanisms—closed-loop and open-loop—are commonly employed to optimize performance in each domain.

11.2 Electromyography For these recordings made from biceps and gastrocnemius (calf) muscles, the subject was instructed to pull the handle as soon as a tone sounded. (After Purves et al., 2001.)

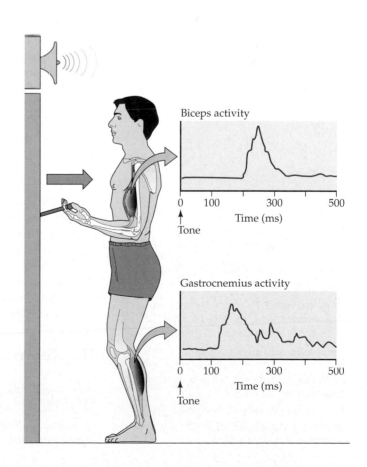

Biceps activity

Time (ms)

Tone

Gastrocnemius activity

Time (ms)

Tone

11.3 A Closed-Loop System (*a*) Automobile driving provides an example of feedback control. (*b*) In the example in part *a*, the *controlled system* is the automobile. The input to the controlled system (i.e., the *control signal*) is the position of the steering wheel; the *output* is the position of the car on the road. In any closed-loop system, the transducer is an element that measures output, and the error detector measures differences between actual output and desired output (the control signal). In this example the *transducer* (the visual system), the *error detector* (the perceptual system), and the *controller* (the muscles) are all properties of the person driving the car. The driver compares the actual position of the car on the road with the desired position and makes corrections to minimize the discrepancy. Closed-loop systems emphasize accuracy and flexibility at the expense of speed.

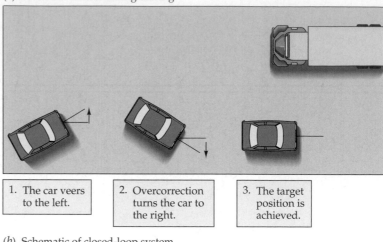

(*a*) Feedback control during driving

| 1. The car veers to the left. | 2. Overcorrection turns the car to the right. | 3. The target position is achieved. |

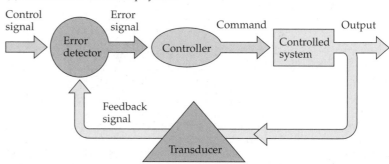

(*b*) Schematic of closed-loop system

closed-loop control mechanism A control mechanism that provides a flow of information from whatever is being controlled to the device that controls it.

ramp movement Also called *smooth movement*. A slow, sustained motion that is often controlled by the basal ganglia.

open-loop control mechanism A control mechanism in which feedback from the output of the system is not provided to the input control.

ballistic movement A rapid muscular movement that is often organized or programmed in the cerebellum.

Closed-loop control mechanisms maximize *accuracy*: information from whatever is being controlled flows back to the device that controls it. Driving a car is an example of a closed-loop motor system; in this case the variable being controlled is the position of an automobile on the road (**Figure 11.3**). Continual information is provided by the driver's visual system, which guides corrections. Slow, sustained movements, sometimes called **ramp movements** (or *smooth movements*) are usually closed-loop in character, continually guided by feedback.

Open-loop control mechanisms maximize *speed*; there are no external forms of feedback, and the activity is preprogrammed. Open-loop controls are needed in systems that must respond so rapidly that there is no time to wait for a feedback pathway. For example, once a baseball pitcher begins throwing a fastball, the pitch will be completed no matter what sensory feedback is received. Such open-loop movements are called **ballistic movements**. Because there is no feedback, open-loop systems need other ways to reduce error and variability. They must anticipate potential error. As living systems, we learn to anticipate and avoid error, so (for example) we can learn to rapidly type our name with our eyes shut. But that's no way to drive a car.

Most of our movements represent a blending of these two types of systems: preprogrammed sequences of movements (open-loop) that are fine-tuned by sensory feedback (closed-loop).

The Neuroscience View

We can distinguish several different levels of hierarchically organized motor control systems:

• The *skeletal system* and the muscles attached to it determine which movements are possible.

- The *spinal cord* controls skeletal muscles in response to sensory information. In the simplest case, the response may be a reflex. The spinal cord also implements motor commands from the brain.
- The *brainstem* integrates motor commands from higher levels of the brain and transmits them to the spinal cord. It also relays sensory information about the body from the spinal cord to the forebrain.
- Some of the main commands for action are initiated in the *primary motor cortex*.
- Areas adjacent to the primary motor cortex, *nonprimary motor cortex*, provide an additional source of motor commands, acting indirectly via primary motor cortex and through direct connections to lower levels of the motor hierarchy.
- Other brain regions—the *cerebellum* and *basal ganglia*—modulate the activities of these hierarchically organized control systems. Some of their contributions are routed via the *thalamus* in a loop back to the cortex.

We will examine each of these levels of control in more detail. This organizational scheme, outlined in **Figure 11.4**, will guide the discussion.

The skeletal system enables particular movements and precludes others

Some properties of behavior arise from physical characteristics of the skeleton. For example, the length, form, and weight of the limbs shape an animal's stride. The primary sites for bending are the joints, where bones meet. **Figure 11.5** illustrates the human skeleton and shows examples of joints and their possible movements.

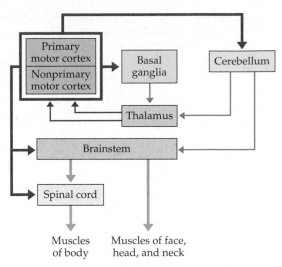

11.4 The Hierarchy of Movement Control The motor cortex receives information from other cortical areas and sends commands to the thalamus and brainstem, which pass commands to the spinal cord. Both the cerebellum and the basal ganglia adjust these commands.

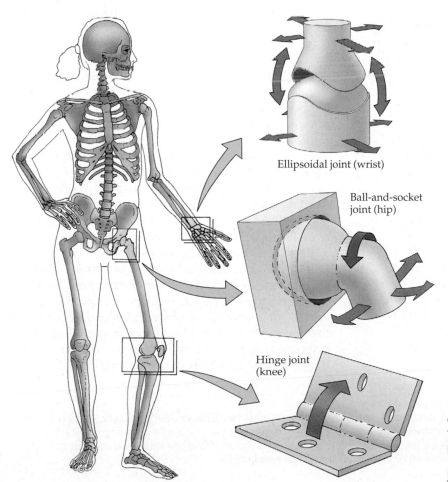

11.5 Joints and Movements Enlarged mechanical models indicate the kinds of movements that each type of joint can perform. The wrist joint moves in two principal planes: lateral and vertical. The hip joint is a "universal" joint, moving in all three planes. The knee joint has a single plane of motion.

smooth muscle   A type of muscle fiber, as in the heart, that is controlled by the autonomic nervous system rather than by voluntary control.

tendon   Strong tissue that connects muscles to bone.

antagonist   A muscle that counteracts the effect of another muscle.

synergist   A muscle that acts together with another muscle.

muscle fiber   A collection of large cylindrical cells, making up most of a muscle, that can contract in response to neurotransmitter released from a motoneuron.

striated muscle   A type of muscle with a striped appearance, generally under voluntary control.

myosin   A protein that, along with actin, mediates the contraction of muscle fibers.

actin   A protein that, along with myosin, mediates the contraction of muscle fibers.

Some joints, such as the hip, are almost "universal" joints, permitting movement in many planes. Others, like the elbow or knee, are more limited and swing mostly in one direction. Interestingly, the octopus has no bones or joints, yet when it grabs food with a tentacle the octopus will place "bends" in the tentacle as if it had an elbow and wrist to bring the food to its mouth (Sumbre et al., 2005), suggesting that joints may be the optimal solution for precise movements.

Muscles control the actions of the skeletal system

Our bare skeleton must now be clothed with muscles. Muscles work solely through contraction (shortening), so the skeletal connections of a muscle give us clues about the particular movements it causes. However, some muscles do not act directly on the skeleton; examples include the muscles that move the eyes, face, and tongue. Muscles have springlike properties that influence the timing of behavior and the forces that can be generated; the rate and force of muscular contractions limit some responses. A variety of visceral organs and blood vessels also employ a type of muscle, called **smooth muscle** (because of its appearance), but since its functions and control are very different from those of the skeletal muscles and smooth muscle is not generally involved in voluntary behavior, we will not concern ourselves with smooth muscle in this chapter.

Muscles are connected to bone by **tendons**. Around a joint, different muscles are arranged in a reciprocal fashion: when one muscle group contracts, it stretches the other group; that is, the muscles are **antagonists**. Muscles that act together are said to be **synergists**. For example, several synergistic muscles act together to extend the arm at the elbow. Another set of muscles that flex the arm are antagonists to those that extend it. Movement around a joint requires one set of motoneurons to be excited while the antagonistic set of motoneurons is inhibited (**Figure 11.6**). We can lock a limb in position by contracting opposing muscles simultaneously.

THE MOLECULAR MACHINERY OF MUSCLES   A skeletal muscle is composed of thousands of individual **muscle fibers** working together under voluntary control. Each muscle fiber contains many filaments of two kinds arranged in a regular manner (**Figure 11.7**), giving the fibers a striped, or "striated," appearance. In this **striated muscle** the thick and thin filaments (made up of the complex proteins **myosin** and **actin**, respectively) overlap. Contraction of the muscle increases the overlap: the filaments slide past each other, shortening the overall length of the muscle fiber (see Figure 11.7).

Because of the varying tasks they perform, different muscles require different speeds, precision, strength, and endurance. So there are two main types of striated muscle fibers: fast-twitch and slow-twitch. Eye movements, for example, must be quick and accurate so that we can follow moving objects and shift our gaze from one target to another. But fibers in the extraocular muscles, which control eye movements, do not have to

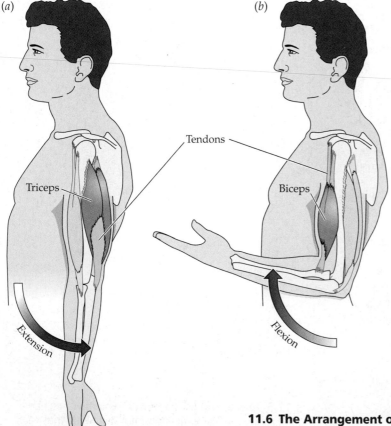

11.6 The Arrangement of Muscles around the Elbow   Because muscles exert force only by contracting, muscle attachments determine the resulting movement. (a) The biceps muscle flexes the arm. (b) The triceps extends the arm. Because these two muscles mediate opposite movements, they are known as *antagonists*.

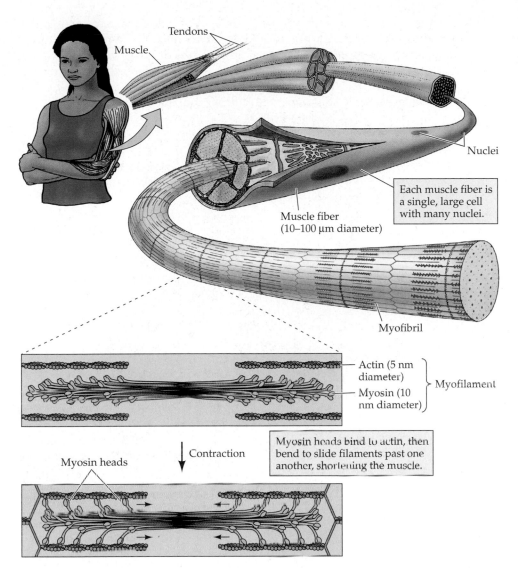

11.7 The Composition of Muscles and the Mechanism of Muscle Contraction   Muscle fibers are shown here at progressively greater magnifications, from life size to 2 million times life size. The actions of myosin and actin cause muscle contraction.

Tendons

Muscle

Nuclei

Each muscle fiber is a single, large cell with many nuclei.

Muscle fiber (10–100 μm diameter)

Myofibril

Actin (5 nm diameter)

Myosin (10 nm diameter)

Myofilament

Contraction

Myosin heads

Myosin heads bind to actin, then bend to slide filaments past one another, shortening the muscle.

maintain tension for long periods of time; accordingly, they are mostly **fast-twitch muscle fibers**. In leg muscles, fast-twitch fibers react promptly and strongly but tire rapidly; they are used mainly for activities in which muscle tension changes frequently, as in walking or running. Mixed in with the fast-twitch muscle fibers are **slow-twitch muscle fibers**, which are not as fast but have greater resistance to fatigue; they are used chiefly to maintain posture.

If you eat chicken or turkey, you've already contrasted fast-twitch and slow-twitch muscles. The "white meat" of the breast was fast-twitch muscle for the rapid wing beats needed for flight. These birds fly only for short periods, so there's no need for these muscles to resist fatigue. In contrast, the "dark meat" of the leg was slow-twitch muscle, which continually supported the animals as they walked about. These muscles contracted slowly but had lots of endurance. Most muscles consist of a mixture of slow-twitch and fast-twitch muscle fibers.

Neural messages reach muscle fibers at the neuromuscular junction

Recall that neurons that send their axons to innervate muscles are called **motoneurons**. As each motoneuron integrates the information bombarding it through hundreds or thousands of synapses, it may produce an action potential. The action potential will travel down the axon, which splits into many branches near the

fast-twitch muscle fiber   A type of striated muscle that contracts rapidly but fatigues readily.

slow-twitch muscle fiber   A type of striated muscle fiber that contracts slowly but does not fatigue readily.

motoneuron   Also called *motor neuron*. A nerve cell in the spinal cord that transmits motor messages from the spinal cord to muscles.

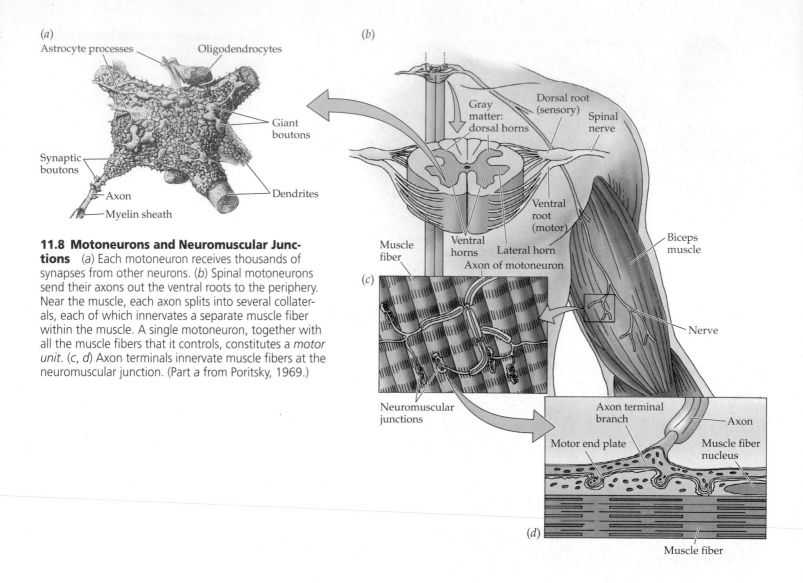

(a)

Astrocyte processes Oligodendrocytes

Giant boutons

Synaptic boutons

Axon

Myelin sheath

Dendrites

(b)

Gray matter: dorsal horns

Dorsal root (sensory)

Spinal nerve

Ventral root (motor)

Biceps muscle

Muscle fiber

Ventral horns Lateral horn

Axon of motoneuron

Nerve

(c)

Neuromuscular junctions

Axon terminal branch

Axon

Motor end plate

Muscle fiber nucleus

(d)

Muscle fiber

11.8 Motoneurons and Neuromuscular Junctions (a) Each motoneuron receives thousands of synapses from other neurons. (b) Spinal motoneurons send their axons out the ventral roots to the periphery. Near the muscle, each axon splits into several collaterals, each of which innervates a separate muscle fiber within the muscle. A single motoneuron, together with all the muscle fibers that it controls, constitutes a *motor unit*. (c, d) Axon terminals innervate muscle fibers at the neuromuscular junction. (Part a from Poritsky, 1969.)

acetylcholine (ACh) A neurotransmitter produced and released by parasympathetic postganglionic neurons, by motoneurons, and by neurons throughout the brain.

neuromuscular junction (NMJ) The region where the motoneuron terminal and the adjoining muscle fiber meet; the point where the nerve transmits its message to the muscle fiber.

motor unit A single motor axon and all the muscle fibers that it innervates.

innervation ratio The ratio expressing the number of muscle fibers innervated by a single motor axon.

target muscle (**Figure 11.8a and b**). Each axonal branch carries an action potential to its axon terminal, which then (in vertebrates) releases the neurotransmitter **acetylcholine** (**ACh**). All the muscle fibers innervated by that motoneuron respond to the ACh by producing action potentials of their own. The action potentials travel along each muscle fiber, permitting sodium (Na^+) and calcium (Ca^{2+}) ions to enter and then trigger the molecular changes in actin and myosin that produce contraction.

The region where the motoneuron terminal and the adjoining muscle fiber meet is called the **neuromuscular junction** (**NMJ**) (**Figure 11.8c and d**). The NMJ is large and very effective: normally every action potential that reaches an axon terminal releases enough ACh to trigger an action potential and contraction in the innervated muscle fiber.

The **motor unit** consists of a single motoneuron's axon and all the muscle fibers innervated by its various branches (see Figure 11.8b). When the motoneuron fires, each of the muscle fibers that it innervates is stimulated. The **innervation ratio** is the number of muscle fibers innervated by one motor axon. Low innervation ratios characterize delicate muscles involved in fine movements, like those that move the eye—which have one motoneuron for every three fibers (a 1:3 ratio). Motor units of massive muscles such as those of the leg have high innervation ratios, with each motoneuron innervating hundreds of muscle fibers, so a single motoneuron contracts many muscle fibers at once and produces a lot of force.

Motoneurons integrate information from the brain and spinal cord

Muscles contract because motoneurons of the spinal cord and cranial nerve nuclei send action potentials along their axons to muscles (see Figures 2.9 and 2.10 for the anatomy of the cranial nerves and spinal cord). Thus, motoneurons are the **final common pathway**: the sole route through which the spinal cord and brain can control our many muscles. Because they respond to inputs from so many sources (see Figure 11.8a), motoneurons often have very widespread dendritic fields, and they are the largest cells in the spinal cord. Furthermore, while motoneurons *release* only ACh, they must respond to a tremendous variety of synaptic transmitters, both excitatory and inhibitory, released by the diverse inputs that each motoneuron receives. Virtually all motoneuron axons are myelinated (Kaar and Fraher, 1985), so their action potentials are conducted quickly.

In general, small motoneurons innervate slow-twitch muscle fibers and are more easily excited by synaptic currents; therefore, they are activated before large motoneurons are (K. E. Jones et al., 1994). Large motoneurons innervate fast-twitch muscle fibers and tend to respond after small cells do because, being large, they are less readily excited by synaptic currents.

As we steadily increase the contraction in a muscle, we activate more and more motoneurons (Henneman, 1991). In doing so, we recruit motoneurons in fixed order according to their size. Weak contraction activates only small, low-threshold neurons for the slow-twitch muscle fibers defined earlier. Stronger stimulation excites larger, higher-threshold neurons that control fast-twitch muscle fibers. This systematic, orderly recruitment of motoneurons based on their size is known as the **size principle**.

Sensory feedback from muscles, tendons, and joints monitors movements

To produce rapid coordinated movements of the body, the brain and spinal cord must continually monitor the state of the muscles, the positions of the limbs, and the instructions being issued by the motor centers. This collecting of information about body movements and positions is called **proprioception** (from the Latin *proprius*, "own," and *recipere*, "to receive"). Because it is crucial for coordinating movement, this information is transmitted to the brain by large, myelinated axons, which conduct action potentials swiftly (see Chapter 3). For some reason, the virus that attacked Ian, whom we met at the start of this chapter, killed only these large axons, leaving him without proprioception below the neck. His predicament illustrates how important this "sixth sense" is for movement.

Two major kinds of proprioceptive receptors that report the state of muscles and joints to the brain are muscle spindles, which monitor muscle *length*; and Golgi tendon organs, which monitor muscle *tension*. We'll discuss each in turn.

THE MUSCLE SPINDLE The **muscle spindle** of vertebrates is a complicated structure consisting of both afferent and efferent elements. Each spindle (a tapered cylinder) contains small muscle fibers called **intrafusal fibers** (from the Latin *intra*, "within," and *fusus*, "spindle"); the ordinary muscle fibers that lie outside the spindles are called **extrafusal fibers** (**Figure 11.9a and c**).

The muscle spindle contains two kinds of receptor endings: **primary sensory endings** (also called *annulospiral endings*) and **secondary sensory endings** (also called *flower spray endings*). These endings are related to different parts of the spindle (see Figure 11.9c). The primary ending wraps in a spiral fashion around the central region of the intrafusal fiber. The secondary endings terminate toward the thin ends of the spindle.

How do these elements become excited? Suppose a muscle is stretched, as when a load is placed on it. For example, imagine that you hold out your hand and someone hands you a heavy book. The additional load would move your arm

final common pathway The information-processing pathway consisting of all the motoneurons in the body. Motoneurons are known by this collective term because they receive and integrate all motor signals from the brain and then direct movement accordingly.

size principle The idea that, as increasing numbers of motor neurons are recruited to produce muscle responses of increasing strength, small, low-threshold neurons are recruited first, followed by large, high-threshold neurons.

proprioception Body sense; information about the position and movement of the body that is sent to the brain.

muscle spindle A muscle receptor that lies parallel to a muscle and sends impulses to the central nervous system when the muscle is stretched.

intrafusal fiber One of the small muscle fibers that lie within each muscle spindle.

extrafusal fiber One of the ordinary muscle fibers that lie outside the spindles and provide most of the force for muscle contraction.

primary sensory ending Also called *annulospiral ending*. The axon that transmits information from the central portion of a muscle spindle.

secondary sensory ending Also called *flower spray ending*. The axon that transmits information from the ends of a muscle spindle.

11.9 Muscle Receptors   (*a*) The receptors in the body of the muscle are muscle spindles; those in the tendons are Golgi tendon organs. (*b*) This sensory ending is typical of a Golgi tendon organ. (*c*) A typical muscle spindle has two types of receptor endings: primary and secondary. Gamma motor fibers control a contractile portion of the spindle. (*d*) When a load is imposed on the muscle, muscle receptors are excited as shown here.

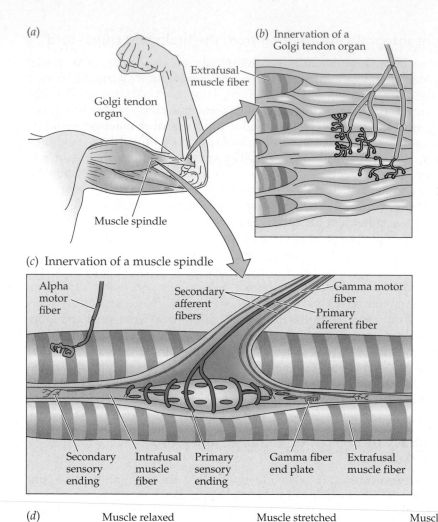

(*a*)

(*b*) Innervation of a Golgi tendon organ

Extrafusal muscle fiber

Golgi tendon organ

Muscle spindle

(*c*)   Innervation of a muscle spindle

Alpha motor fiber

Secondary afferent fibers

Gamma motor fiber

Primary afferent fiber

Secondary sensory ending

Intrafusal muscle fiber

Primary sensory ending

Gamma fiber end plate

Extrafusal muscle fiber

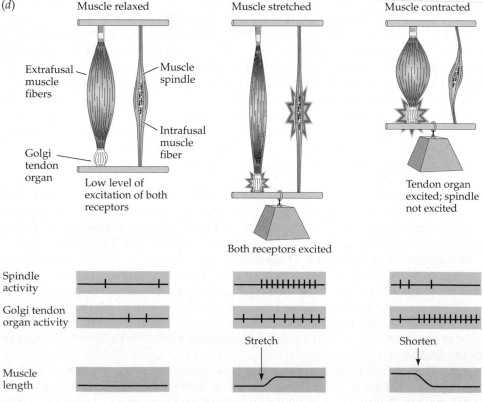

(*d*)

Muscle relaxed

Muscle stretched

Muscle contracted

Extrafusal muscle fibers

Muscle spindle

Golgi tendon organ

Intrafusal muscle fiber

Low level of excitation of both receptors

Both receptors excited

Tendon organ excited; spindle not excited

Spindle activity

Golgi tendon organ activity

Stretch

Shorten

Muscle length

downward, stretching the biceps muscle and the spindles it contains. The resulting deformation of the endings on the spindle would trigger action potentials in the afferent fibers. These afferents would inform the spinal cord, and the spinal cord would tell the brain about the muscle stretch and therefore the load imposed (**Figure 11.9d**).

The different receptor elements of the muscle spindle are differentially sensitive to two aspects of changes in muscle length. The primary (central) endings show a maximum discharge early in stretch and then adapt to a lower discharge rate. This property makes them especially sensitive to changes, or *dynamic* muscle length. In contrast, the secondary endings are slow to change their rate during the early phase of stretch and are maximally sensitive to maintained, or *static*, muscle length. A spindle is informed of planned and ongoing actions through innervation by a special motoneuron that alters the tension within the spindle and thus controls the sensitivity of its receptors. These motoneurons are called **gamma motoneurons**, or *gamma efferents*, to distinguish them from the faster-conducting **alpha motoneurons**, which go to the extrafusal muscle fibers that do all the work (see Figure 11.9c).

The gamma motoneuron axon fibers connect to a contractile region of the spindle. Activity in the gamma fibers causes the spindle to shorten, which modifies its sensitivity to changes in the length of adjacent extrafusal muscle fibers. Hence, the number of action potentials elicited in the spindle afferents is a function of two factors: (1) muscle stretch and (2) the tension in the muscle spindle.

Imagine pulling your hand (and book) up toward your shoulder. As the biceps muscle moves your arm, both the extrafusal and the intrafusal fibers shorten. But in order to ensure that the spindles are operating within their sensitive range, an optimal degree of tension in the intrafusal fibers must be maintained. Therefore, the gamma efferents shorten the intrafusal fibers to prevent them from going slack. One reflection of the importance of the gamma efferent system is the fact that about 30% of all efferent fibers are gamma motoneurons (the rest are alpha motoneurons).

THE GOLGI TENDON ORGAN   While muscle spindles respond primarily to stretch, the other proprioceptive receptors in muscle—Golgi tendon organs—are especially sensitive to muscle *tension*. Structurally, Golgi tendon organs consist of sensory nerve endings interwoven through fibrils of *collagen*, the tough protein that gives tendons their strength and elasticity. Because they are part of a robust structure, **Golgi tendon organs** are relatively insensitive to passive muscle lengthening (see Figure 11.9a, b, and d), such as simply extending an arm. But strong loads (contractions) are able to stretch the collagen of the tendon organ and stimulate the nerve endings to fire. Thus, the Golgi tendon organs monitor the force of muscle contractions, providing a second source of sensory information about the muscles that aids in precisely controlling movement. This arrangement makes the tendon organs useful in another important way: they detect overloads that threaten to tear muscles and tendons. Strong stimulation of the Golgi tendon organs inhibits the motoneurons supplying the muscles that pull on the tendon and thus, by relaxing the tension, prevents mechanical damage.

Classic studies in physiology emphasized the importance of information from muscle spindles and Golgi tendon organs for controlling movement. Mott (1895) and Sherrington (1898) showed that, after they cut the afferent fibers from muscles in monkeys, the monkeys failed to use the deafferented limb, even if the efferent connections from motoneurons to muscles were preserved. The deafferented limb is not paralyzed, since it can be activated (the motoneurons still innervate the muscles), but lack of information from the muscle leads to relative disuse. The arm dangles, apparently useless. If the good arm is restrained (by a ball placed around the hand), however, the animal soon learns to use the deafferented arm and can become quite dexterous (Taub, 1976). Monkeys manage to do this the way Ian

gamma motoneuron   Also called *gamma efferent*. A motor neuron that innervates the contractile tissue in a muscle spindle.

alpha motoneuron   A motoneuron that controls the main contractile fibers (extrafusal fibers) of a muscle.

Golgi tendon organ   One of the receptors located in tendons that send impulses to the central nervous system when a muscle contracts.

stretch reflex The contraction of a muscle in response to stretch of that muscle.

does, guiding their movements by using vision for feedback about how the arm is moving.

Probably all of us use channels of visual information to guide the motor system without being aware that we're doing so. Remember the young woman D.F. from Chapter 10? She could not report whether a slot was vertical or horizontal; yet when she was asked to insert a disk in the slot, she consistently rotated her hand to put it in smoothly. This finding suggests that even neurologically intact people unknowingly use visual cues to guide their movements (Goodale and Haffenden, 1998). These are the only cues available for Ian.

Movements Are Controlled at Several Nervous System Levels

The firing patterns of motoneurons are what determine the onset, coordination, and termination of muscle activity, but to really understand the physiology of movement, we need to know the source of the inputs to motoneurons. How do descending projections from the brain and spinal cord organize the activity of this final common pathway?

Spinal reflexes mediate "automatic" responses

One way to study spinal mechanisms is to sever the connections between the brain and the spinal cord, and then observe the forms of behavior that can be elicited below the level of the cut. (All voluntary movements that depend on brain mechanisms are lost, of course, as is sensation from the regions below the cut.)

A good example of automatic control at the spinal level is the **stretch reflex**—the contraction that results when a muscle stretches. In **Figure 11.10**, a weight added to the hand imposes sudden stretch on muscle A (M_A). The circuit that keeps us from dropping the load is one that links muscle spindles and the relevant muscles:

1. Weight is added, pulling the hand down.
2. The muscle is stretched.
3. Afferents from the muscle spindle are excited (SN_A in Figure 11.10).

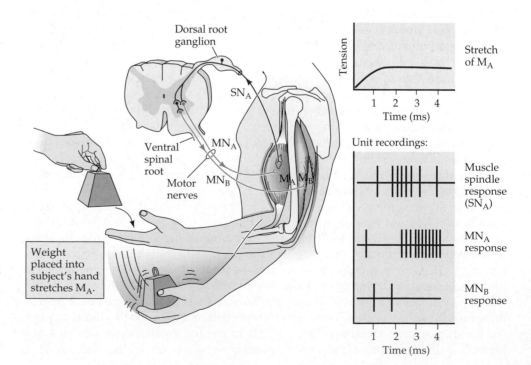

11.10 The Stretch Reflex Circuit MN_A is the motor nerve to muscle A (M_A); MN_B is the motor nerve to muscle B (M_B), an antagonist to M_A. SN_A is the sensory nerve from the muscle spindle of M_A. Characteristic responses at different stages in the circuit are shown at right.

4. The spindle afferents connect directly—that is, monosynaptically—to the motoneurons that control the stretched muscle, exciting them.
5. The motoneurons stimulate the muscle to oppose muscle stretch.

This sequence describes a simple negative feedback system that tends to restore the limb to its "desired" position. Muscle spindle afferents also inhibit the motoneurons that supply the antagonistic muscle (M_B in Figure 11.10). Two synapses are required to inhibit the antagonistic motoneuron. Spindle information terminates on an interneuron, which inhibits the motoneuron that supplies M_B. The relaxation of antagonistic muscles ensures that they do not become injured by the sudden movement. A familiar example of the stretch reflex is the knee jerk used in medical examinations (see Figure 3.17). (Recall from Chapter 5 that the knee jerk reflex was abnormally slow in Chuck, who suffered from hypothyroidism.) Spinal reflexes are integrated and modulated by activity of the brain.

Other spinal circuits can generate more-complex movements. However it is accomplished, most locomotion is rhythmic, consisting of repetitive cycles of the same act, whether the beating of wings or the swinging of legs. Many such rhythmic movements are generated by mechanisms within the spinal cord. These endogenous rhythms are normally modulated by sensory feedback, but they can function independently of brain influences or afferents. The term **central pattern generator** is used to refer to the neural circuitry responsible for generating rhythmic patterns of behavior as seen in walking. Electromyographic records of hindlimb muscles of cats with spinal cord section and dorsal root cuts reveal a "walking" pattern that lasts for seconds when a single dorsal root is briefly stimulated electrically (P. Grillner et al., 1991; S. Grillner, 1985). Thus, the essential rhythm of walking is generated by spinal cord mechanisms, which the brain activates and corrects as needed.

Pathways from the brain control different aspects of movements

Some muscles are controlled directly by the brain. The cranial motor nuclei of the brainstem send their axons to innervate muscles of the head and neck (**Figure 11.11**; see also Figure 2.9). But for all the other muscles, the brain has to send commands to the spinal cord and then the spinal cord controls the muscles. The brain sends these commands to the spinal cord through two major pathways: the pyramidal system (which we discuss next) and extrapyramidal motor system (described later in this chapter).

central pattern generator Neural circuitry that is responsible for generating the rhythmic pattern of a behavior such as walking.

11.11 Motor Nuclei in the Brainstem Shown here from the rear, motor nuclei in the brainstem control muscles of the head and neck. The cranial nerves corresponding to these muscles are shown in Figure 2.9.

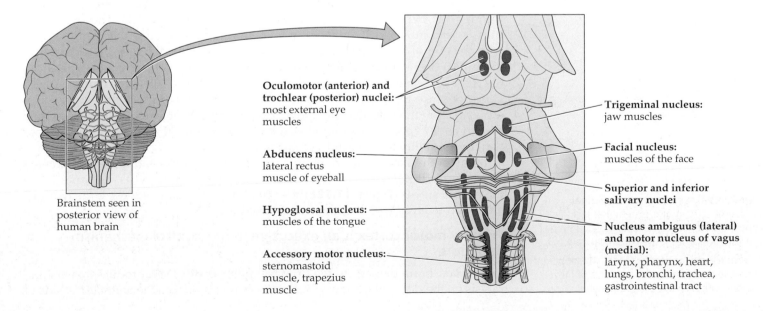

Brainstem seen in posterior view of human brain

Oculomotor (anterior) and trochlear (posterior) nuclei: most external eye muscles

Abducens nucleus: lateral rectus muscle of eyeball

Hypoglossal nucleus: muscles of the tongue

Accessory motor nucleus: sternomastoid muscle, trapezius muscle

Trigeminal nucleus: jaw muscles

Facial nucleus: muscles of the face

Superior and inferior salivary nuclei

Nucleus ambiguus (lateral) and motor nucleus of vagus (medial): larynx, pharynx, heart, lungs, bronchi, trachea, gastrointestinal tract

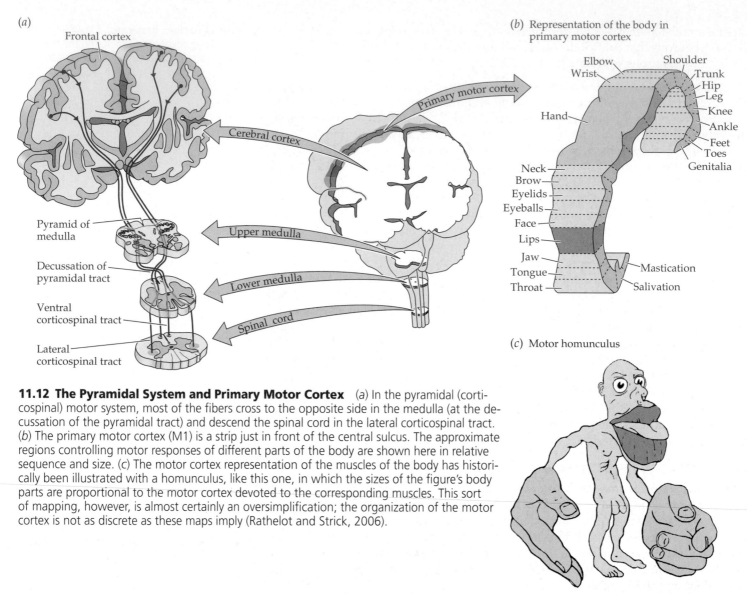

(a)

Frontal cortex

Cerebral cortex

Primary motor cortex

Pyramid of medulla

Upper medulla

Decussation of pyramidal tract

Lower medulla

Ventral corticospinal tract

Spinal cord

Lateral corticospinal tract

(b) Representation of the body in primary motor cortex

Elbow   Shoulder
Wrist   Trunk
   Hip
   Leg
Hand   Knee
   Ankle
   Feet
   Toes
Neck   Genitalia
Brow
Eyelids
Eyeballs
Face
Lips
Jaw   Mastication
Tongue
Throat   Salivation

(c) Motor homunculus

11.12 The Pyramidal System and Primary Motor Cortex   (a) In the pyramidal (corticospinal) motor system, most of the fibers cross to the opposite side in the medulla (at the decussation of the pyramidal tract) and descend the spinal cord in the lateral corticospinal tract. (b) The primary motor cortex (M1) is a strip just in front of the central sulcus. The approximate regions controlling motor responses of different parts of the body are shown here in relative sequence and size. (c) The motor cortex representation of the muscles of the body has historically been illustrated with a homunculus, like this one, in which the sizes of the figure's body parts are proportional to the motor cortex devoted to the corresponding muscles. This sort of mapping, however, is almost certainly an oversimplification; the organization of the motor cortex is not as discrete as these maps imply (Rathelot and Strick, 2006).

pyramidal system or corticospinal system   The motor system that includes neurons within the cerebral cortex and their axons, which form the pyramidal tract.

primary motor cortex (M1)   The apparent executive region for the initiation of movement; primarily the precentral gyrus.

The **pyramidal system** (or **corticospinal system**) consists of neuronal cell bodies within the cerebral cortex and their axons, which pass through the brainstem, forming the pyramidal tract to the spinal cord (**Figure 11.12a**). The pyramidal tract is seen most clearly where it passes through the floor of the medulla. In a cross section of the medulla, the tract is a wedge-shaped anterior protuberance (pyramid) on each side of the midline. In the medulla the pyramidal tract from the right hemisphere crosses the midline to innervate the left spinal cord, and vice versa. Because the pyramidal tract crosses the midline (technically known as a *decussation*) in the medulla, the right cortex controls the left side of the body while the left cortex controls the right. Lesions of the pyramidal system deprive the patient of the ability to move individual joints and limbs.

Many of the axons of the pyramidal tract originate from neurons in the **primary motor cortex (M1)**, which consists mainly of the precentral gyrus, just anterior to the central sulcus (**Figure 11.12b**). The cell bodies of many of these large neurons are found in layer V of the primary motor cortex.

Primary motor cortex is an executive motor control mechanism— and more

In humans, brain damage to the primary motor cortex (M1) produces partial paralysis on the side of the body opposite the brain lesion (i.e., the *contralateral* side of

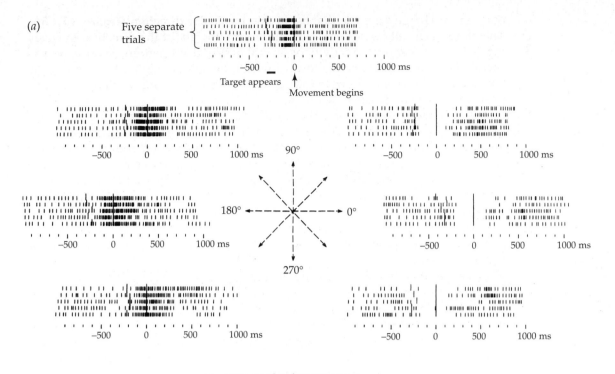

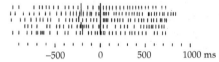

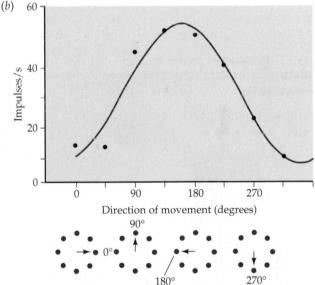

the body). The disturbance is greatest in distal muscles, such as those of the hand. Humans with these lesions are generally disinclined to use the affected limb.

Early-twentieth-century researchers like Wilder Penfield, whom we discussed at the start of Chapter 2, used electrical stimulation to develop functional maps of human primary motor cortex. Disproportionately large regions in the maps of M1 are devoted to the body parts involved in the most elaborate and complex movements. For example, humans and other primates have extremely large cortical fields concerned with hand movements. The representation of the body in motor cortex is often portrayed graphically, as in Figure 11.12b and c, but more modern work suggests that such maps are oversimplifications (Schieber and Hibbard, 1993).

Using nonhuman primates, it is possible to trace motor pathways in a retrograde manner from specific muscles back to corresponding regions of motor cortex, using a type of virus that can jump backward across synapses. This research shows that the organization of M1 is far less discrete than was originally thought; for example, the neurons controlling the individual fingers are extensively intermingled and arise from a variety of locations (Rathelot and Strick, 2006). This arrangement likely aids the coordination of movements that involve multiple muscles. In primates the pyramidal tract has some monosynaptic connections with spinal motoneurons, but most pyramidal-tract neurons influence spinal motoneurons through polysynaptic routes and share control of these motor cells with other descending influences.

By recording from M1 neurons of monkeys that were trained to make free arm movements in eight possible target directions (Georgopoulos et al., 1993), we can eavesdrop on the commands originating there (**Figure 11.13a**). Many M1 cells change their firing rates according to the direction of the movement, but for any

11.13 Directional Tuning of Motor Cortex Cells (a) Shown here is the activity of a single neuron during arm movement toward a target in eight different directions. Each horizontal record in the eight blocks of data represents one of five trials. Note that this cell consistently fires before the arm moves in the direction from 90° to 180° to 270°, and it is silent before movements in the other directions. (b) The average frequency of discharge during the interval before movement changed depending on the direction. (From Georgopoulos et al., 1982.)

one cell, discharge rates are highest in one particular direction (**Figure 11.13b**). Therefore, each cell carries only partial information about the direction of reaching. When we average the activity of several hundred M1 neurons at once, we can predict fairly well the direction toward which the animal will reach with its arm. Given the millions of neurons in this region, a larger sampling would presumably provide an even more accurate prediction.

A long-standing controversy has raged over whether *muscles* or *movements* are represented in M1. That is, does activity of a cortical motor neuron encode a relatively simple parameter, such as contraction of a particular muscle; or does it encode a more abstract parameter, such as a particular movement of the hand through space? To address this controversy, experimenters trained a monkey to perform rapid tracking movements using the hand and wrist (Kakei et al., 1999). As **Figure 11.14** shows, the animal grasped a handle that could be rotated along the two axes of wrist motion. Movement of the handle controlled the position of a cursor on a computer screen. After much training (over 8 years!), the monkey performed well.

The experimenters then recorded the activity of single cells in M1 as the monkey performed from different starting positions. A substantial group of M1 neurons (32%) displayed changes in activity that corresponded to *muscle contractions*, but an even larger group of neurons (50%) showed activity that corresponded to *particular movements*, regardless of hand posture. In other words, these cells were active whenever the monkey moved its hand in a particular direction, no matter which muscles were needed to accomplish that movement. Thus, *both* movements and, to a lesser extent, muscles are represented in M1. In theory, if we can record the activity of motor cortex to predict what movement the person is calling for, we might be able to use that information to guide a robotic arm—the subject of **Box 11.1**.

11.14 Do Neurons in the Primary Motor Cortex Represent Muscles or Movements? (After Kakei et al., 1999.)

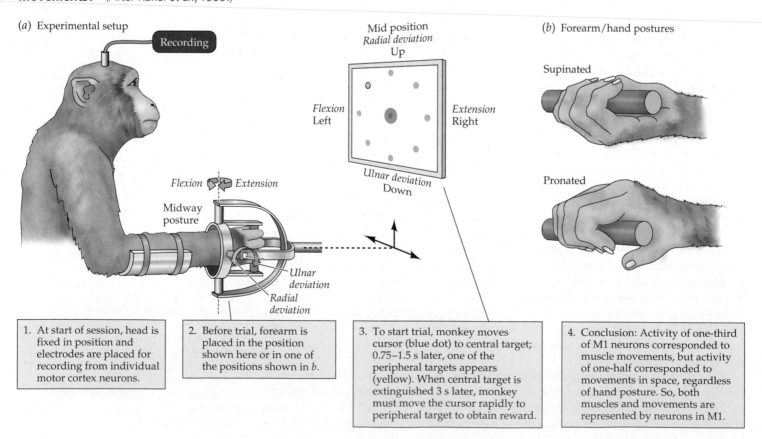

(a) Experimental setup

Recording

Flexion ⟷ Extension

Midway posture

Ulnar deviation

Radial deviation

Mid position
Radial deviation
Up

Flexion
Left

Extension
Right

Ulnar deviation
Down

(b) Forearm/hand postures

Supinated

Pronated

1. At start of session, head is fixed in position and electrodes are placed for recording from individual motor cortex neurons.

2. Before trial, forearm is placed in the position shown here or in one of the positions shown in *b*.

3. To start trial, monkey moves cursor (blue dot) to central target; 0.75–1.5 s later, one of the peripheral targets appears (yellow). When central target is extinguished 3 s later, monkey must move the cursor rapidly to peripheral target to obtain reward.

4. Conclusion: Activity of one-third of M1 neurons corresponded to muscle movements, but activity of one-half corresponded to movements in space, regardless of hand posture. So, both muscles and movements are represented by neurons in M1.

BOX 11.1 Cortical Neurons Control Movements of a Robotic Arm

Signals from rat motor cortex can be used to control one-dimensional movements of a robotic arm, paralleling the movement of the rat's own arm (Chapin et al., 1999). If the rats receive visual feedback and are rewarded for successful movements of the robotic arm, they progressively cease to produce overt arm movements and let the robotic arm accomplish the task. Investigators have also used microwires implanted in the cortex of owl monkeys (Figure A) to control a robotic arm in three dimensions, reproducing movements to reach for pieces of food placed in different positions, pick them up, carry them to the mouth, and return to the start position (Wessberg et al., 2000). The results of these studies suggested that paralyzed patients might learn to operate a robotic arm by cortical activity, even though they can't move their own limbs.

Matthew Nagle was an innocent bystander when a brawl broke out on the beach one night, but it was he who was stabbed in the neck and left paralyzed from the neck down. A former football player, Matt was determined to regain control of his life. He had a surgical team implant 96 microwires into his primary motor cortex to record the activity of neurons there. The firing pattern of the neurons was recorded by a computer. As Matt imagined moving his arm to hit various targets on the screen, the computer eavesdropped on the neuronal firing and a program tried to figure out which firing pattern corresponded to movement in each direction. After this "calibration," the program used the firing pattern to move the cursor in the direction that Matt was imagining his arm to be moving.

With just 4 days of training, Matt learned to move the cursor on the computer so that he could open e-mail and play a simple video game (Figure B). When the computer was interfaced with a prosthetic limb, Matt was able to flex the prosthetic hand and make rudimentary actions with a jointed robotic arm (Hochberg et al., 2006). But he was never able to make really smooth movements of even the computer cursor, and each day's calibration took about a half hour before he could even begin. Furthermore, after a few months the ability of the electrodes to detect neural firing began to degrade, for reasons that are not understood. So after about a year, Matt had the implant removed while researchers worked toward an improved system.

Matt's implants were connected by a wire passing through a hole drilled in his skull, but it may be possible to make an implant that uses radio waves to tell

(A) Owl monkey perched atop a robotic arm

the computer which neurons are firing. Animal work indicates that recording more neurons should give an even better idea of the intended direction of movement, as well as providing the data needed to control grip strength and other more subtle aspects of reaching and grasping (Velliste et al., 2008).

Another possibility is to implant the electrodes in premotor cortex, with the idea that these are the neurons that call on primary motor cortex, so the neuronal signals for the intent to move the arm can be detected sooner. Again, the neuronal activity would be detected by a computer and used to move the computer cursor or a robotic limb. Monkeys given such an implant became very proficient at moving a cursor on a computer screen (Santhanam et al., 2006).

Sadly, Matt Nagle died of an unrelated infection without realizing his dream of effortlessly putting thoughts into action. His legacy is a new generation of work on neural prosthetics. (Photograph A courtesy of Miguel Nicolelis; B © Rick Friedman.)

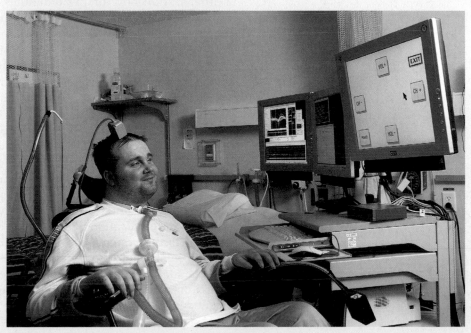

(B) Using only thought conveyed through an implant, Matt Nagle was able to control cursor movement on a computer.

11.15 Motor Learning Causes Remapping of Motor Cortex (*a*) A map of forelimb control in rat motor cortex, prior to training (green areas: digits and wrist; blue areas: shoulder and elbow). (*b*) The same rat's motor cortex, following 10 days of training on a task requiring precise reaching and grasping. The representation of the digits and wrist (green) has expanded into areas previously associated with the shoulder and elbow. The black line indicates the position of a skull landmark. (Courtesy of J. Kleim.)

(*a*) Pretraining

(*b*) Posttraining

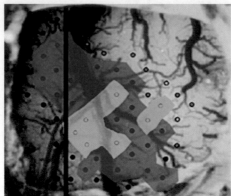
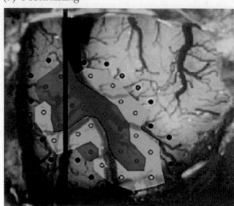

PRIMARY CORTEX AND LEARNING Several studies with both experimental animals and humans demonstrated that motor representations in M1 change as a result of training. Maps prepared from electrical stimulation in M1 show changes as an animal learns new skills—for example, a visually guided tracking movement with the arm (J. N. Sanes and Donoghue, 2000) or a precision grasping task (Nudo et al., 1996).

In humans, the width of the precentral gyrus as seen with MRI offers an estimate of the size of M1. The gyrus is significantly wider in piano players, especially in the hand representation area (see Figure 11.12*b* and *c*), than in nonmusician control subjects. The younger the musician was at the start of musical training, the larger the gyrus is in adulthood (Amunts et al., 1997), so this expansion of M1 seems to be in response to the experience of musical training.

Transcranial magnetic stimulation (*TMS*) uses a brief magnetic field to stimulate cortical neurons beneath the skin and skull (see Chapter 2). In one study (Classen et al., 1998), focal TMS was used in human volunteers to evoke isolated thumb movements in a particular direction. Then the subjects practiced moving the thumb in a different direction for 15–30 minutes. The same TMS was then found to evoke thumb movement in the *new* direction for several minutes before the response reverted to the original direction. (This rapid change seems similar to the retuning of auditory cortical receptors during stimulation at another frequency, as noted in Chapter 9.) It seems likely that the change in response to TMS reflected at least the beginning of plastic changes in motor cortex in response to practice. In rats, cortical remodeling due to motor learning has been directly observed by means of sophisticated mapping of the motor cortex before and after long-duration training of a new skill (Monfils et al., 2005) (**Figure 11.15**).

Nonprimary motor cortex aids complex behaviors

Just anterior to M1 are cortical regions that are also important for motor control. Because they are not primary motor cortex, they are called **nonprimary motor cortex**. Despite the name, nonprimary motor systems can contribute to behavior directly, through communication with lower levels of the motor hierarchy in the brainstem and spinal cord systems, as well as indirectly, through M1. The traditional account of nonprimary motor cortex emphasizes two main regions: the **supplementary motor area** (**SMA**), which lies mainly on the medial aspect of the hemisphere; and the **premotor cortex**, which is anterior to the primary motor cortex (**Figure 11.16**).

Patients with bilateral damage to the SMA are unable to move voluntarily (only some automatic and reflex movements remain), suggesting that this region initiates movement sequences (Tanji, 2001). Experimental data are generally consistent with this view. In one example, cerebral blood flow was measured during simple tasks, such as keeping a spring compressed between two fingers of one hand (P. E.

nonprimary motor cortex Frontal lobe regions adjacent to the primary motor cortex that contribute to motor control and modulate the activity of the primary motor cortex.

supplementary motor area (SMA) A region of nonprimary motor cortex that receives input from the basal ganglia and modulates the activity of the primary motor cortex.

premotor cortex A region of nonprimary motor cortex just anterior to the primary motor cortex.

(a) Lateral view (b) Medial view

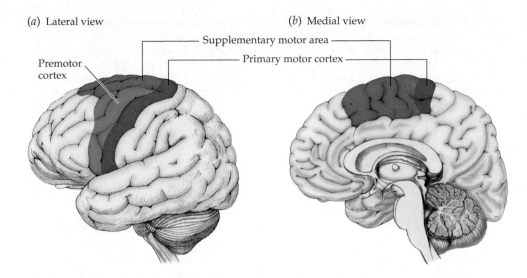

11.16 Human Motor Cortical Areas
(a) The primary motor cortex (M1) lies just anterior to the central sulcus. Anterior to the primary motor cortex are the premotor cortex and the supplementary motor area (SMA), which together make up the nonprimary motor cortex. Although we show it here as a unitary structure for the sake of clarity, recent evidence from nonhuman primates indicates that the premotor cortex is a mosaic of subareas with distinct properties. (b) The SMA lies mainly on the medial surface of the cerebral hemispheres.

Roland, 1980, 1984). As you might expect, this task produced a marked increase in blood flow to the contralateral M1, and increasing the complexity of the tasks to form a sequence of behaviors extended the area of increased blood flow to include the SMA. Interestingly, when subjects simply mentally *rehearse* the complex movement sequence without actually doing it, the enhanced blood flow is seen only in the SMA, not in M1.

In contrast to the observations from the SMA, the premotor cortex is activated when motor sequences are guided externally by stimuli (Halsband et al., 1994; Larsson et al., 1996) rather than generated internally. Various impairments have been associated with premotor lesions, such as problems with stance, gait, and coordination, but recent evidence suggests that our view of premotor cortex has been oversimplified (Graziano, 2006; Graziano and Aflalo, 2007). This work indicates that premotor cortex is not a single system, but really a mosaic of different units, serving separate but overlapping functions in organizing complex motor behavior. These behaviors cluster together in major categories: defensive movements, feeding behavior, and so on. For example, a subset of premotor neurons is activated when objects are brought close to a monkey's face or hand. If the lights are then turned off, some of these neurons continue to fire even if the object is silently moved, suggesting that the cells are coding for where the monkey thinks the object is (Graziano et al., 1997). When the lights are turned back on and the monkey sees that the object is gone, the neurons cease firing. Such neurons may help us reach out for objects that are no longer visible.

In general, evidence is mounting that we should think of the organization of motor and premotor areas in terms of the mapping of behaviors, rather than the mapping of specific movements (Graziano and Aflalo, 2007). It's an idea that is nicely illustrated by recent discoveries about a unique population of premotor neurons, called *mirror neurons*, which we discuss next.

Mirror neurons in premotor cortex track movements in others

One of the subregions making up the mosaic of premotor cortex, an area known as *F5*, contains a population of remarkable neurons that seem to fulfill two functions. These neurons fire shortly before a monkey makes a very particular movement of the hand and arm to reach for an object; different neurons fire during different reaching movements. These results suggest that these neurons trigger specific movements. But these neurons also fire whenever the monkey sees *another* monkey (or a human) make that same movement. These cells are called **mirror neurons** because they fire as though the monkey were imitating the movements of the other

mirror neuron A neuron that is active both when an individual makes a particular movement and when an individual sees another individual make that same movement.

(a)

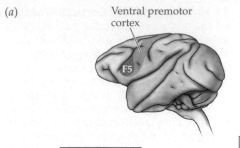

Ventral premotor cortex

F5

11.17 Mirror Neurons (a) In the ventral portion of premotor cortex known as *area F5*, many mirror neurons are found. (b) These neurons fire just before a monkey reaches for an object, such as a raisin (*left*), or when the monkey sees a human experimenter reach for that object in the same manner (*right*). (c) This mirror neuron fired when the monkey reached for a box or, as here, it observed a human reaching for a box (*top*). The mirror neuron also fires, but much less vigorously, if there is no box for the human to grasp (*bottom*) (Umilta et al., 2001). (After Rizzolatti et al., 2006.)

(b)

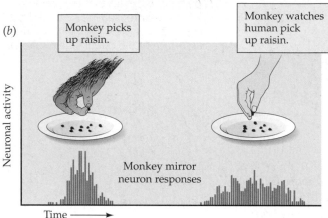

Monkey picks up raisin.

Monkey watches human pick up raisin.

Neuronal activity

Monkey mirror neuron responses

Time ⟶

(c)

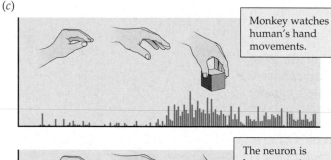

Monkey watches human's hand movements.

The neuron is less responsive if there is no object to be picked up.

individual (**Figure 11.17**). They are matching the observed behavior with an internal motor representation of that behavior, as if the observer were imagining doing the same thing as the observed monkey.

MRI and EEG studies indicate that mirror neurons are also found in adult humans (Buccino et al., 2004) and children (J. F. Lepage and Theoret, 2006). In the classic "mirror game," in which one person moves slowly and the other tries to imitate the first person as closely as possible, these neurons are probably at work. They have also been seen in other areas of frontal cortex (Nelissen et al., 2005) and parietal cortex (Fogassi et al., 2005). The activity of these neurons suggests that they are important in the understanding of other individuals' actions and in attempts to imitate those actions (Rizzolatti and Craighero, 2004). However, some populations of mirror neurons seem to be more active in executing actions that are *complementary* to the observed action, rather than imitative (Newman-Norlund et al., 2007). It's possible that this function of mirror neurons is the basis for acting jointly with others to accomplish a cooperative task.

It is intriguing to think that mirror neurons may help us understand what other people are doing, because the idea suggests a neural basis for empathy. Thus, there has been a great deal of speculation about the function of mirror neurons in the imitating behavior of human infants, the evolution of language, and other behavior. Some have speculated that people with autism, which is characterized by a failure to anticipate other people's thinking and actions, may have a deficit in mirror neuron activity (J. H. Williams et al., 2006).

Extrapyramidal Systems Also Modulate Motor Commands

extrapyramidal system A motor system that includes the basal ganglia and some closely related brainstem structures.

reticular formation An extensive region of the brainstem (extending from the medulla through the thalamus) that is involved in arousal (waking).

reticulospinal tract A tract of axons arising from the brainstem reticular formation and descending to the spinal cord to modulate movement.

red nucleus A brainstem structure related to motor control.

rubrospinal tract A tract of axons arising from the red nucleus in the midbrain and innervating neurons of the spinal cord.

In addition to the corticospinal outflow through the pyramidal tract, many other motor tracts run from the forebrain to the brainstem and spinal cord. Because these tracts are outside the pyramids of the medulla, they and their connections are called the **extrapyramidal system**. In general, lesions of the extrapyramidal system do not prevent the movement of individual joints and limbs, but they do interfere with spinal reflexes, usually exaggerating them.

The extrapyramidal system communicates to the spinal cord through two principal pathways: the reticulospinal and rubrospinal tracts. The extensive pool of interconnected neurons called the **reticular formation** modulates various aspects of movements. Some zones of the reticular formation facilitate movements; other zones are inhibitory. These effects are transmitted in descending tracts known as **reticulospinal tracts** that arise from the reticular formation and connect to spinal interneurons, where they influence spinal motor circuitry. The second extrapyramidal outflow originates from the midbrain's **red nucleus** and so is called the **rubrospinal tract** (the Latin *ruber* means "red"), terminating in the spinal cord to regulate motor output.

The basal ganglia modulate movements

The **basal ganglia** include a group of interconnected forebrain nuclei: the caudate nucleus, putamen, and globus pallidus. Closely associated with these structures are two nuclei in the midbrain: the substantia nigra and the subthalamic nucleus. **Figure 11.18** shows the locations of these structures. The caudate nucleus and putamen together are referred to as the **striatum**.

Each of these structures receives input from wide areas of the cerebral cortex and sends much of its output back to the cortex via the thalamus, forming a loop from the cortex through the basal ganglia and thalamus and back to the cortex. Lesions of basal ganglia in humans produce movement impairments that seem quite different from those that follow interruption of the pyramidal system. Two disorders described later in the chapter—Parkinson's disease and Huntington's disease—are caused by degeneration of the basal ganglia.

Lesions and recordings of single neurons during motor responses indicate that each structure of the basal ganglia contains a topographic representation of body musculature (DeLong et al., 1984). The basal ganglia play a role in determining the amplitude and direction of movement, and changes in activity in regions of the basal ganglia appear to be important for the initiation of movement. Much of the motor function of the basal ganglia appears to be accomplished through the modulation of activity initiated by other brain circuits, such as the motor pathways of the cortex (see Figure 11.4). The basal ganglia are especially important in the performance of movements influenced by memories, in contrast to those guided by sensory control (Graybiel et al., 1994).

The cerebellum affects programs, coordination, and learning of acts

Across vertebrate groups, the size of the cerebellum varies according to the range and complexity of movements. For example, the cerebellum is much larger in fishes with extensive locomotor behavior than it is in less-active fishes; it is also larger in flying birds than in bird species that do not fly.

Recall from Chapter 2 that the outer layers of the cerebellum are called the *cerebellar cortex* and are dominated by a sheet of large multipolar cells called *Purkinje cells* (see Figure 2.16). All output of the cerebellar cortex travels via the axons of Purkinje cells, all of which synapse with the deep cerebellar nuclei. At these synapses, Purkinje cells produce only inhibitory postsynaptic potentials. Hence, all

basal ganglia   A group of forebrain nuclei, including caudate nucleus, globus pallidus, and putamen, found deep within the cerebral hemispheres.

striatum   The caudate nucleus and putamen together.

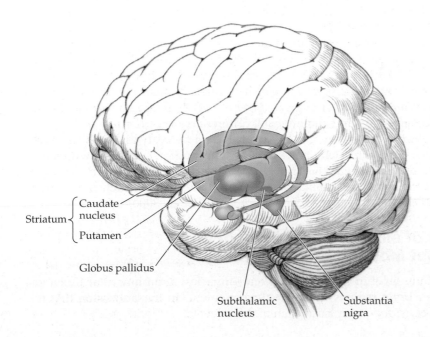

Striatum { Caudate nucleus / Putamen }

Globus pallidus

Subthalamic nucleus

Substantia nigra

11.18 Basal Ganglia Involved in Movement   Several structures within the basal ganglia are involved in modulating and tuning the movements programmed by other systems.

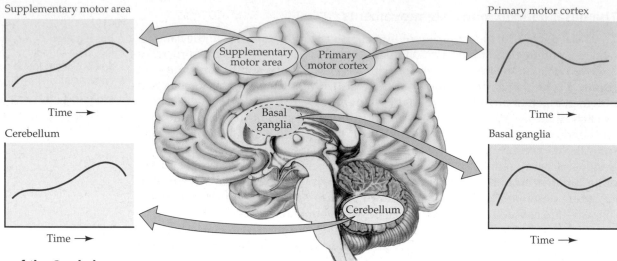

Supplementary motor area

Time →

Cerebellum

Time →

Primary motor cortex

Time →

Basal ganglia

Time →

11.19 Contributions of the Cerebellum and Basal Ganglia to the Modulation of Movements Cerebellar activity correlates with that of the supplementary motor area; basal ganglia activity correlates with that of primary motor cortex. (After Y. Liu et al., 1999.)

the circuitry of the extensive cortical portion of the cerebellum, which also includes 10–20 billion granule cells in humans, guides movement by *inhibiting* neurons.

Inputs to the cerebellar cortex come both from sensory sources and from other brain motor systems. Sensory inputs include the muscle and joint receptors, and the vestibular, somatosensory, visual, and auditory systems. Both pyramidal and nonpyramidal pathways contribute inputs to the cerebellum and in turn receive outputs from the deep nuclei of the cerebellum. It has been suggested that the cerebellum elaborates neural "programs" for the control of skilled movements, particularly rapid, repeated movements that become automatic. In fact, we now know that the cerebellum is crucial for a wide variety of motor and nonmotor learning (Katz and Steinmetz, 2002); this topic is discussed in more detail in Chapter 17.

The cerebellum and the basal ganglia contribute differently to the modulation of motor functions

The foregoing discussion and Figure 11.4 indicate that the cerebellum and the basal ganglia occupy rather similar positions in modulating motor functions. However, Yijun Liu et al. (1999) found differences in the activity of these brain regions when they examined fMRI responses of people performing a tactile discrimination task. The subjects were given two similarly shaped objects—one in each hand—and they had to decide by active touching whether the objects were the same or different.

Changing patterns of activity during this task were found in M1, the SMA, the cerebellum, and the basal ganglia. Cerebellar activity correlated significantly with activity of the SMA but not M1, whereas basal ganglia activity correlated more strongly with activity of M1 than of the SMA. Thus, although the task appears to require the activity of five brain regions (**Figure 11.19**), the cerebellum and basal ganglia show temporally and anatomically different contributions.

The cerebellum and basal ganglia also contribute differently to the task of reaching. As we saw in Figure 11.1*b*, patients with Huntington's disease, who suffer from damage to the basal ganglia, show impairment especially toward the end of a reach, when corrections are made. In contrast, patients with cerebellar damage show errors at the beginning of a reach (M. A. Smith et al., 2000).

Disorders of Muscle, Spinal Cord, or Brain Can Disrupt Movement

Disorders at any level in the motor system—muscles, neuromuscular junctions, spinal cord, or brain regions—can impair movement. In the discussion that follows we will consider examples at each of these levels.

In muscular dystrophy, biochemical abnormalities cause muscles to waste away

Numerous muscle diseases are characterized by biochemical abnormalities that lead to structural changes in muscle; collectively, these disorders are referred to as **muscular dystrophy (MD)** (from the Greek *dys*, "bad," and *trophe*, "nourishment"). As the name implies, in various muscular dystrophies the muscles waste away (Blake et al., 2002).

Duchenne's muscular dystrophy, the most prevalent form of MD, strikes almost exclusively boys, beginning at the age of about 4 to 6 years and usually leading to death in early adulthood. Studies of family pedigrees show that the disorder is a simple Mendelian trait—caused by a single gene, carried on the X chromosome. When the gene was identified, it was named *dystrophin*. In some ways the name is unfortunate because the dystrophin protein, when normal, does *not* lead to dystrophy. **Dystrophin** is normally produced in muscle cells and is part of a vital structural component of muscle fibers. Because females have two X chromosomes, even if one carries the defective copy of the dystrophin gene, the other X chromosome can still produce sufficient normal dystrophin. But about half the sons of such females will receive the defective gene and, because they have only the one X chromosome, will be afflicted with the disease. In the hope of halting the loss of muscle fibers in Duchenne's, scientists are trying to use gene therapy to induce the muscles of boys with this disease to produce normal dystrophin.

The immune system may impair motor function by attacking neuromuscular junctions

Several poisons affect neuromuscular junctions. For example, snake bites can cause neuromuscular blocks because the venom of some highly poisonous snakes contains substances (such as bungarotoxin) that block postsynaptic acetylcholine receptors. If the neuromuscular junctions of the muscles for breathing are blocked, the victim suffocates.

Studies of bungarotoxin led to an understanding of a debilitating neuromuscular disorder, **myasthenia gravis** (from the Greek *mys*, "muscle," and *asthenes*, "weak"; and the Latin *gravis*, "grave" or "serious"). This disorder is characterized by a profound weakness of skeletal muscles. The disease often first affects the muscles of the head, producing symptoms such as drooping of the eyelids, double vision, and slowing of speech. In later stages, paralysis of the muscles that control swallowing and respiration becomes life-threatening.

Myasthenia gravis is an **autoimmune disorder**: most cases result when antibodies develop and attack a patient's own acetylcholine receptors, disrupting neuromuscular junctions. In other cases the antibodies are directed toward other proteins that are associated with the acetylcholine receptor. Treatment often consists of prescribing drugs to suppress the immune system (Richman and Agius, 2003).

Motoneuron pathology leads to motor impairments and death

Virus-induced destruction of motoneurons—for example, by the disease polio—was once a frightening prospect around the world. **Polioviruses** destroy motoneurons of the spinal cord and, in more severe types of the disease, cranial motoneurons of the brainstem. Because the muscles are no longer called on to contract, they atrophy. If the muscles controlling breathing deteriorate sufficiently, the person must rely on a ventilator to stay alive.

Sometimes, for reasons that remain elusive, the motoneurons of the brainstem and spinal cord spontaneously start to die and their target muscles waste away. In this disease, called **amyotrophic lateral sclerosis** (**ALS**; sometimes called *Lou Gehrig's disease* after the 1930s baseball player who lost his life to the disorder), the afflicted person experiences gradually worsening paralysis until most skeletal muscle ceases to function. Although premature death is the usual outcome, some people with

muscular dystrophy (MD) A disease that leads to degeneration of and functional changes in muscles.

dystrophin A protein that is needed for normal muscle function.

myasthenia gravis A disorder characterized by a profound weakness of skeletal muscles; caused by a loss of acetylcholine receptors.

autoimmune disorder A disorder caused when the immune system mistakenly attacks a person's own body, thereby interfering with normal functioning.

polioviruses A class of viruses that destroy motoneurons of the spinal cord and brainstem.

amyotrophic lateral sclerosis (ALS) Also called *Lou Gehrig's disease*. A disease in which motoneurons and their target muscles waste away.

flaccid paralysis   A loss of reflexes below the level of transection of the spinal cord.

ALS can survive for long periods; celebrated British physicist Stephen Hawking, who was diagnosed with ALS in the early 1960s, is an example. A wide range of possible causal factors are under investigation, including premature aging, toxic minerals, viruses, immune responses, and endocrine dysfunction.

About 10% of ALS cases are hereditary. The pedigrees of several afflicted families indicate that mutation in a single gene, called *SOD1*, account for about 20% of the heritable cases of ALS. This gene has been isolated (P. M. Andersen et al., 1995) and found to encode an enzyme: copper/zinc superoxide dismutase. When scientists produced transgenic mice that, in addition to their own normal copies of the enzyme, carried a copy of the defective human *SOD1* gene, these animals displayed an ALS-like syndrome (Gurney et al., 1994). Their muscles wasted away and their motoneurons died, leading to an early death. Because the mice still had their own *SOD1* genes to produce the normal enzyme, these findings suggest that the familial ALS resulted not from the loss of enzyme action but rather from a *toxic gain of function*—a harmful new action of the protein produced by the defective gene.

Studies of this mouse model of ALS suggest that motoneurons die because their mitochondria are being damaged (J. Liu et al., 2004). However, the gene may have multiple effects. In animals expressing the *SOD1* mutation, for example, the blood vessels of the spinal cord are leaky, potentially exposing motoneurons to toxic blood components (Zhong et al., 2008). Furthermore, a study of afflicted British families found that a mutation in an entirely different gene, encoding an RNA-processing protein called FUS, can also cause ALS (Vance et al., 2009).

Spinal cord injuries cause some motor impairments

Vehicular accidents, violence, falls, and sports injuries cause many human spinal injuries that result in motor impairment. Injuries to the human spinal cord commonly develop from force to the neck or back, breaking a bone that compresses the spinal cord. If the spinal cord is severed completely, immediate paralysis results, and reflexes below the level of injury are lost—a condition known as **flaccid paralysis**. Flaccid paralysis generally results only when a considerable stretch of the spinal cord has been destroyed. When the injury severs the spinal cord without causing widespread destruction of tissue, reflexes below the level of injury may become abnormally strong because the intact tissue lacks the dampening influence of brain inhibitory pathways.

An estimated 250,000–400,000 individuals in the United States have spinal cord injuries, and about 10,000 new traumatic spinal injuries occur each year. Tragically, most traumatic spinal injuries occur in young people, with automobile accidents and sports injuries accounting for the majority of cases. Although much remains to be discovered, the hope of reconnecting the injured spinal cord no longer seems far-fetched. Months after the spinal cord is severed in lampreys, the fish can swim again without any therapeutic intervention (A. H. Cohen et al., 1989), but they seem unique among vertebrates in this regard. Four main strategies for reconnecting the brain and spinal cord in humans are being investigated (**Figure 11.20**):

1. Providing stem cells that might differentiate into new neurons to send new axons across the break (Okano et al., 2003).
2. Transplanting glial cells that promote regeneration in the CNS. Recall from Chapter 9 that olfactory receptor neurons are continually produced, and somehow the axons of the new neurons find the way to their proper targets. Specialized glial cells called olfactory *ensheathing cells* appear to play a central role in guiding this axon growth, so researchers tried transplanting ensheathing cells from the olfactory bulbs into spinal cord cuts in rats. In most cases, and for various forms of spinal cord damage, at least some function is restored (Raisman and Li, 2007). Efforts are under way to perfect the use of ensheathing cells to bridge across spinal cord lesions.

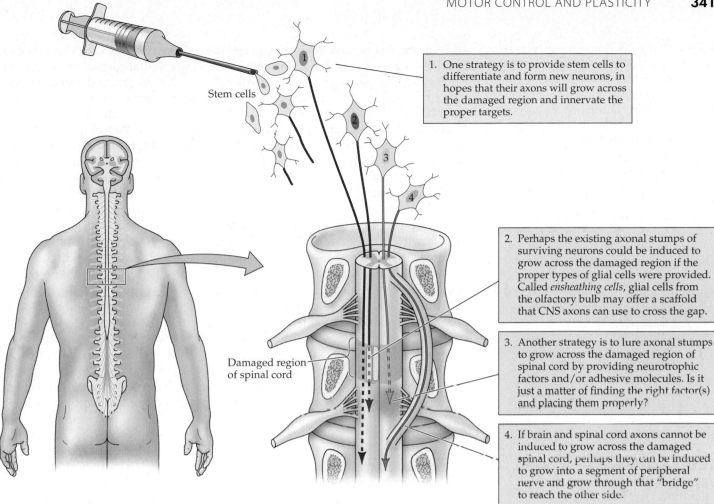

1. One strategy is to provide stem cells to differentiate and form new neurons, in hopes that their axons will grow across the damaged region and innervate the proper targets.

Stem cells

Damaged region of spinal cord

2. Perhaps the existing axonal stumps of surviving neurons could be induced to grow across the damaged region if the proper types of glial cells were provided. Called *ensheathing cells*, glial cells from the olfactory bulb may offer a scaffold that CNS axons can use to cross the gap.

3. Another strategy is to lure axonal stumps to grow across the damaged region of spinal cord by providing neurotrophic factors and/or adhesive molecules. Is it just a matter of finding the right factor(s) and placing them properly?

4. If brain and spinal cord axons cannot be induced to grow across the damaged spinal cord, perhaps they can be induced to grow into a segment of peripheral nerve and grow through that "bridge" to reach the other side.

11.20 Research Strategies for Reconnecting the Brain and Spinal Cord

3. Using neurotrophic factors and/or adhesive molecules (see Chapter 7) to entice the axons of surviving neurons to grow across the damaged region of spinal cord (Hendriks et al., 2004) and reconnect to their targets (Harel and Strittmatter, 2006). In dogs, a nonspecific polymer, polyethylene glycol, seems to repair broken membranes when injected into spinal cord within a few days of injury. Dogs given this treatment were more than twice as likely to walk again (Laverty et al., 2004).

4. Transplanting "regeneration-friendly" peripheral nerves to connect the brain and lower spinal cord by forming a "bridge" around the injured spinal cord (Bernstein-Goral and Bregman, 1993). This approach centers on the observation that axons in peripheral nerves, when cut by injury, will regrow and reconnect to their targets; yet cut axons in the CNS almost never accomplish this feat. No one really knows why peripheral and central axons differ in this regard, but it might be possible to exploit regeneration-friendly peripheral nerves to reconnect the spinal cord.

Cerebral cortex pathology causes some motor impairments

The most common motor impairments that follow strokes or injury to the human cerebral cortex are paralysis (**plegia**) or weakness (**paresis**) of voluntary movements, usually on one side of the body (*hemiplegia* or *hemiparesis*). Generally the paralysis appears on the side of the body opposite the injured hemisphere. In addition, affected patients show some **spasticity**: increased rigidity in response to forced movement of the limbs.

Spasticity reflects the exaggeration of stretch reflexes that have been released from the inhibition they usually receive from the cortex. Abnormal reflexes occur,

plegia   Paralysis, the loss of the ability to move.

paresis   Partial paralysis.

spasticity   Markedly increased rigidity in response to forced movement of the limbs.

apraxia An impairment in the ability to begin and execute skilled voluntary movements, even though there is no muscle paralysis.

ideomotor apraxia The inability to carry out a simple motor activity in response to a verbal command, even though this same activity is readily performed spontaneously.

ideational apraxia An impairment in the ability to carry out a sequence of actions, even though each element or step can be done correctly.

Parkinson's disease A degenerative neurological disorder, characterized by tremors at rest, muscular rigidity, and reduction in voluntary movement, that involves dopaminergic neurons of the substantia nigra.

substantia nigra A brainstem structure in humans that innervates the basal ganglia and is named for its dark pigmentation.

11.21 A Leader in the Campaign against Parkinson's Disease Parkinson's disease can strike at any point in adulthood. Actor Michael J. Fox was just 30 years old when he was diagnosed with Parkinson's, in 1991. Shown here testifying before a U.S. Senate health committee with fellow Parkinson's sufferer, Muhammad Ali, Fox heads a research foundation (www.michaeljfox.org) that provides funding and advocacy for Parkinson's disease research.

such as the flaring and extension of the toes elicited by stroking the sole of the foot (the Babinski reflex). In the months following cerebral cortical injury, the clinical picture changes. The initial paralysis slowly diminishes, and some voluntary movements of the limbs return, although fine motor control of fingers is seldom regained. In humans the symptoms are more severe than in many other mammals.

Damage to nonmotor zones of the cerebral cortex, such as some regions of parietal or frontal association cortex, produces more-complicated changes in motor control. One condition characterized by such damage is **apraxia** (from the Greek *a-*, "not," and *praxis*, "action"), the inability to carry out complex movements even though paralysis or weakness is not evident and language comprehension and motivation are intact. Apraxia is illustrated in the following example: When asked to smile, a patient is unable to do so, although he certainly attempts to. If asked to use a comb placed in front of him, he seems unable to figure out what to do. But things aren't as simple as they might appear. At one point in the discussion the patient spontaneously smiles, and at another point he retrieves a comb from his pocket and combs his hair with ease and accuracy.

Apraxia was first described by the nineteenth-century neurologist John Hughlings Jackson, who noted that some patients could not extend the tongue on command, even though they could use it in a variety of spontaneous acts, such as speech, licking their lips, and eating. Apraxia is a symptom of a variety of disorders, including stroke, Alzheimer's disease, and developmental disorders of children.

Neurologists studying patients who have suffered strokes have discovered several different types of apraxia. **Ideomotor apraxia** is characterized by the inability to carry out a *simple* motor activity, either in response to a verbal command ("smile" or "use this comb") or copying someone else's gesture, even though this same activity is readily performed spontaneously. **Ideational apraxia** is an impairment in carrying out a *sequence* of actions, although each step can be done correctly (Zadikoff and Lang, 2005). Patients with ideational apraxia have difficulty carrying out instructions for a sequence of acts—"push the button, then pull the handle, then depress the switch"—but they can do each of these tasks in isolation. Apraxia may be somewhat independent of language deficits; the patients may be perfectly good at naming objects (Rosci et al., 2003), yet unable to perform the requested sequence of actions with those objects.

In Parkinson's disease the death of dopaminergic neurons alters activity of the basal ganglia

About 200 years ago, physician James Parkinson noted people in London who moved quite slowly, showed regular tremors of the hands and face while at rest, and walked with a rigid bearing. Another feature of what is now known as **Parkinson's disease** is a loss of facial muscle tone, which gives the face a masklike appearance. Patients who suffer from Parkinson's also show few spontaneous actions and have great difficulty in all motor efforts, no matter how routine. The hands may display tremors while at rest but move smoothly while performing a task. Parkinson's disease afflicts almost 1% of the U.S. population aged 65 and older, but it sometimes unaccountably occurs in younger people, such as actor Michael J. Fox (**Figure 11.21**).

Patients with Parkinson's show progressive degeneration of dopamine-containing cells in the **substantia nigra** that project to the basal ganglia, particularly the caudate nucleus and putamen. The loss of cells in this area is continual, but symptoms begin to appear only after extensive cell death. The discovery of a form of the disorder induced by illicit drugs (described in **Box 11.2**) has suggested that exposure to toxins over a prolonged period underlie the development of the disorder.

Most cases of Parkinson's disease are probably not inherited, but in one large Italian family, Parkinson's disease develops in members who inherit a defective copy of the gene that encodes **α-synuclein** (Polymeropoulos et al., 1997), a protein normally expressed in the basal ganglia. Another family with inherited Parkinson's disease turned out to have a defective copy of another gene, named *parkin*, which encodes the protein **parkin** (Lucking et al., 2000).

The two proteins α-synuclein and parkin normally interact with each other (Shimura et al., 2001). One theory is that defects in either protein can lead to abnormal accumulation of the α-synuclein into clumps called *Lewy bodies* in the dopaminergic cells. In the noninherited cases of Parkinson's, other factors, such as toxins or brain injury, may accelerate the formation of Lewy bodies that are associated with the death of the dopaminergic cells. Thus, it might be possible someday to prevent Parkinson's by developing drugs to stop or reverse the accumulation of α-synuclein (T. M. Dawson and Dawson, 2003).

α-synuclein A protein that has been implicated in Parkinson's disease.

parkin A protein that has been implicated in Parkinson's disease.

BOX 11.2 A Tragic Mistake

Parkinson's disease has been problematic to study because of difficulties in producing suitable models of the disorder in laboratory animals. One useful lead began in a hospital in California in 1982. Here, several people in their 20s were admitted with the sudden onset of symptoms that—despite their youth—presented an unmistakable portrait of Parkinson's disease. The movements of these young patients were slow, they had tremors of the hands, their faces were frozen without expression and, confirming the diagnosis, their symptoms were alleviated by treatment with l-dopa.

Researchers eventually pieced together what had gone wrong. All of the young Parkinson's disease cases had recently used a "home-brewed" synthetic form of heroin. Mistakes made during the synthesis of this drug had contaminated it with a neurotoxin that produced brain damage typical of Parkinson's disease (Kopin and Markey, 1988; Langston, 1985). Chemical studies led to the identification of a substance known as *MPTP* (an abbreviation of a much longer chemical name). Patients with symptoms resulting from exposure to MPTP show a decline in dopamine concentrations in the brain, mirroring the situation in "normal" Parkinson's.

The injection of MPTP into various research animals yielded a startling result: although rats and rabbits showed only minimal and transient motor impairments, monkeys were as sensitive to the toxin as humans are, developing a permanent set of motor changes identical to those of humans with Parkinson's disease. Furthermore, the sites of damage in the brain were identical to those in the frozen addicts and in patients suffering from Parkinson's.

MPTP accumulates in the substantia nigra and caudate nucleus because it binds selectively to a form of the enzyme *monoamine oxidase* (MAO), which is plentiful in these regions. MPTP interacts with this enzyme to form a highly toxic metabolite: MPP+. Researchers have suggested that the natural pigment neuromelanin, found in the substantia nigra, accounts for the selectivity of damage produced by MPTP (S. H. Snyder and D'Amato, 1985). They have shown that MPP+ binds with special affinity to this pigment. Thus, cells with neuromelanin accumulate MPP+ to toxic levels, and because cells of the substantia nigra contain large amounts of the pigment, they are particularly vulnerable to the destructive impact of MPP+.

The observed differences among species might be a consequence of the fact that nigral cells of monkeys and humans have pigment but those of rodents are unpigmented.

Discovering a primate model of this disease opened an exciting set of research opportunities for probing the cellular and molecular bases of Parkinson's disease. Experiments with primates have also provided an opportunity to test other therapies, such as neural transplants. This research has led to successful implants in human patients (see Figure 11.22), including some of the original frozen addicts.

Some researchers have speculated that Parkinson's disease in humans arises from exposure to an unknown toxin or toxins. In two cases involving laboratory workers, MPTP-induced disease arose from either inhalation of or skin contact with MPTP, suggesting that brief and almost trivial contact with MPTP is sufficient to begin the disease. Animal experiments indicate that some environmental toxins, such as certain herbicides (Betarbet et al., 2000) or combinations of herbicides (Thiruchelvam et al., 2000), may cause Parkinson's disease.

L-dopa The immediate precursor of the transmitter dopamine.

A third gene was implicated in Parkinson's when it was found that a single mutation in this gene might account for 20% of all cases of Parkinson's among Arabs, North Africans, and Jews (Ozelius et al., 2006). The mutated protein encoded by this gene seems to be overly active at adding phosphate groups to many proteins, including α-synuclein and parkin, which may aggravate the accumulation of abnormal clumps in dopaminergic neurons (L. Chen and Feany, 2005).

There was no treatment for Parkinson's disease until the late 1960s, when administration of a precursor to dopamine was found to enhance the dopamine levels of surviving cells. The precursor, called **L-dopa**, markedly reduces symptoms in patients with Parkinson's; notably, it decreases tremors and increases the speed of movements. Although L-dopa can reverse some symptoms of Parkinson's disease, nerve cell degeneration in the substantia nigra is relentless. Because the cell bodies in the brainstem degenerate, dopamine-containing terminals in the caudate nucleus and putamen also disappear. Eventually, too few dopamine-containing neurons remain in the substantia nigra, and L-dopa stops being effective.

Electrical stimulation of sites within the basal ganglia can reduce the symptoms of Parkinson's disease, and it appears to extend the effectiveness of L-dopa therapy (Nutt et al., 2001). However, this "deep brain stimulation" technique requires the surgical implantation of electrodes into the brain, and it carries the risk of cognitive side effects such as impulsivity and difficulty making decisions (M. J. Frank et al., 2007). Another approach is to deliver a neurotrophic factor (*glial-derived neurotrophic factor*) to maintain and revive ailing dopaminergic neurons, but here the trick is to deliver these factors to the right part of the brain (Kirik et al., 2004).

A more permanent way to compensate for the loss of neurons might be to replace them with new ones. In several experimental treatments, fetal neurons or stem cells have been transplanted into the brains of people with severe Parkinson's in the hope that enough of the cells will establish dopaminergic synaptic connections in the basal ganglia to alleviate the symptoms of the disease (**Figure 11.22**). Although significant symptom relief has been reported in some people with Parkinson's (Isacson et al., 2001; Peschanski et al., 1994), there is room to doubt that these transplants will become a viable treatment option. For one thing, evidence suggests that the transplanted cells may somehow go on to develop Par-

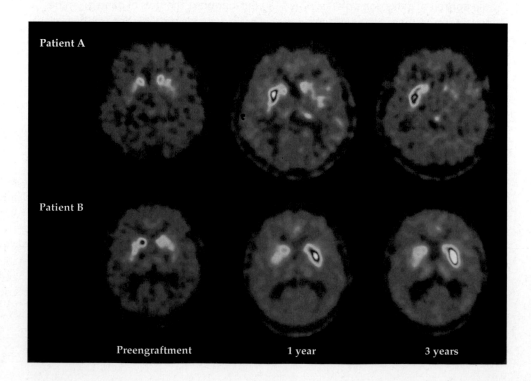

11.22 Brain Implants to Treat Parkinson's Disease The injection of human fetal cells into patients with Parkinson's disease led to increased dopamine receptors (coded in yellow and red) in the striatum 1 and 3 years later, as these PET scans reveal. (From Lindvall et al., 1994.)

kinson's disease themselves (Kordower et al., 2008; J. Y. Li, Englund, et al., 2008). And although the graft of fetal cells clearly improves the condition of some patients, other patients with grafts become afflicted with severe involuntary movements (Freed et al., 2001), in alarmingly high proportions (Olanow et al., 2003). Debate about this procedure will continue for the foreseeable future.

An aspect of Parkinson's disease that may be independent of the degree of motor impairment is the appearance of cognitive and emotional changes. Some patients show marked cognitive decline during the course of their illness (J. L. Cummings, 1995). Depression in patients with Parkinson's is also common; some researchers have attributed such depression to the consequences of reduced mobility and the general stress of such incapacity. However, reports that dopaminergic agonists to treat Parkinson's disease sometimes produce impulsive behaviors such as gambling (Szarfman et al., 2006) indicate that dopamine also plays a role in mood. So depression may be a direct effect of depleted dopamine in Parkinson's.

Huntington's disease is characterized by excessive movement caused by deterioration of the basal ganglia

Whereas damage to the basal ganglia in Parkinson's disease *slows* movement, other kinds of basal ganglia disorders cause *excessive* movement. An example of the latter type was reported by George Huntington, a physician whose only publication (1872) described a strange motor affliction. The first symptoms of **Huntington's disease** are subtle behavioral changes: clumsiness, and twitches in the fingers and face. Subtlety is rapidly lost as the illness progresses; a continuing stream of involuntary jerks engulfs the entire body. Aimless movements of the eyes, jerky leg movements, and writhing of the body turn the routine activities of the day into insurmountable obstacles. Worse yet, as the disease progresses, marked behavioral changes include intellectual deterioration, depression, and, in a minority of patients, a psychotic state that resembles schizophrenia. In some patients, cognitive and emotional changes may appear many years before obvious motor impairments do (Wexler et al., 1991). Huntington's disease usually develops over a period of 15–20 years.

The neuroanatomical basis of this disorder is the profound, progressive destruction of the basal ganglia, especially the caudate nucleus and the putamen (**Figure 11.23**), as well as impairment of the cerebral cortex. Several types of cells are particularly vulnerable, including neurons that contain the transmitter GABA. Acetylcholine-containing neurons are relatively spared.

George Huntington correctly deduced that the disorder is inherited, passed from generation to generation. Careful analysis of family pedigrees eventually revealed that Huntington's disease is transmitted by a single dominant gene on chromosome 4 (Gusella and MacDonald, 1993). Because we have two copies of every gene but pass only one of them on to our children, each child of a person with Huntington's has a 50% chance of inheriting the bad gene and eventually developing the disease. The affected gene, *HTT*, normally encodes a protein called

Huntington's disease Also called *Huntington's chorea*. A progressive genetic disorder characterized by abrupt, involuntary movements and profound changes in mental functioning.

(*a*) Control

Caudate nucleus   Putamen

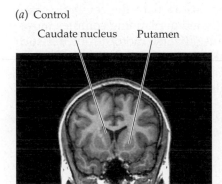

(*b*) Patient with Huntington's disease

Lateral ventricles

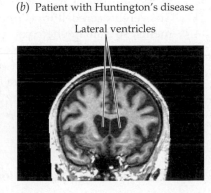

11.23 Neuropathology in Huntington's Disease Compared with the control (*a*), a coronal MRI section through the brain of a patient suffering from Huntington's disease (*b*) shows marked enlargement of the lateral ventricles, caused by atrophy of the neighboring caudate nucleus and putamen. Note also the shrunken cortical gyri and enlarged sulci of the patient compared with those of the brain of a healthy person. (MRI images courtesy of Terry L. Jernigan and C. Fennema Notestine.)

huntingtin A protein produced by a gene (called *HTT*) that, when containing too many trinucleotide repeats, results in Huntington's disease in a carrier.

trinucleotide repeat Repetition of the same three nucleotides within a gene, which can lead to dysfunction, as in the cases of Huntington's disease and fragile X syndrome (see Chapter 7).

spinocerebellum The uppermost part of the cerebellum, consisting mostly of the vermis and anterior lobe.

ataxia An impairment in the direction, extent, and rate of muscular movement; often caused by cerebellar pathology.

cerebrocerebellum The lowermost part of the cerebellum, consisting especially of the lateral parts of each cerebellar hemisphere.

decomposition of movement Difficulty of movement in which gestures are broken up into individual segments instead of being executed smoothly; a symptom of cerebellar lesions.

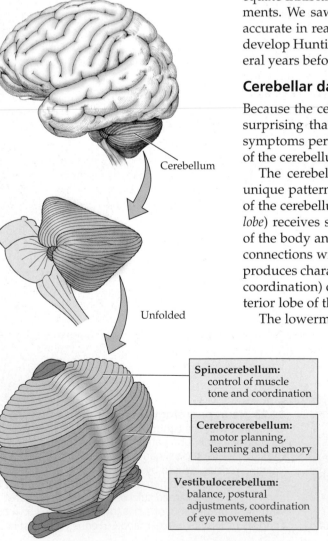

Cerebellum

Unfolded

Spinocerebellum: control of muscle tone and coordination

Cerebrocerebellum: motor planning, learning and memory

Vestibulocerebellum: balance, postural adjustments, coordination of eye movements

huntingtin. In Huntington's disease, the huntingtin protein that is produced is abnormally lengthened because of a series of three nucleotides (CAG; see the Appendix) that is repeated over and over in the *HTT* gene. If the gene contains fewer than 30 of these **trinucleotide repeats**, no symptoms appear, but if there are 38 or more CAG trinucleotide repeats in the *HTT* gene, the person will develop Huntington's disease (A. B. Young, 1993).

We don't yet know what the function of the normal huntingtin protein is, or how the abnormal version of the protein causes the symptoms of Huntington's disease. It's possible that the elongated protein binds inappropriately to other molecules, somehow gumming up important cellular processes (Dunah et al., 2002; Panov et al., 2002). It's also possible that, as the mutant huntingtin protein breaks down, some toxic metabolites form. Preventing cleavage of the huntingtin protein at one particular point seems to prevent motor impairments in transgenic mice (R. K. Graham et al., 2006). Another mystery concerns the tissue specificity of Huntington's disease: Why does the mutant huntingtin protein selectively damage the basal ganglia, when it is also being expressed in neurons and glial cells throughout the brain, as well as in cells in muscle, liver, and testes (A. B. Young, 1993)? By inserting the defective *HTT* gene into the genome of rhesus monkeys, researchers are attempting to create a primate model of Huntington's disease in which to study the specific neurobiological abnormalities of the disease (S. H. Yang et al., 2008).

The example of Huntington's disease, with its increased movements, demonstrates the major role that inhibition plays in normal motor control. Without adequate inhibition, a person is compelled to perform a variety of unwanted movements. We saw in Figure 11.1*b* that patients with Huntington's disease are less accurate in reaching for a target. People whose genetic tests reveal that they will develop Huntington's disease show some impairment in accuracy of reaching several years before apparent onset of the disease (M. A. Smith et al., 2000).

Cerebellar damage causes many types of impairment

Because the cerebellum modulates many aspects of motor performance, it is not surprising that its impairment leads to many abnormalities of behavior. These symptoms permit an examiner to identify with considerable accuracy which part of the cerebellum is damaged (Dichgans, 1984).

The cerebellum has three major functional divisions (**Figure 11.24**), and a unique pattern of impairment results from damage to each. The uppermost part of the cerebellum, or **spinocerebellum** (consisting mostly of the *vermis* and *anterior lobe*) receives sensory information about the current spatial location of the parts of the body and anticipates subsequent movement. The spinocerebellum has rich connections with descending motor pathways, which it modulates. Damage here produces characteristic abnormalities of gait and posture, especially **ataxia** (loss of coordination) of the legs. Long-term alcoholism can cause degeneration of the anterior lobe of the cerebellum, resulting in characteristic weaving and erratic gait.

The lowermost part of the cerebellum (consisting especially of the lateral parts of each cerebellar hemisphere) is called the **cerebrocerebellum** in recognition of its close relationship with the cerebral cortex. The cerebrocerebellum is implicated in planning complex movements, so damage here can cause diverse motor problems, such as **decomposition of movement**, in which gestures are broken up into individual segments instead of being executed smoothly. Because the cerebrocerebellum also functions in higher-level cognition, such as motor learning, damage here can also cause cognitive deficits.

11.24 Functional Organization of the Cerebellum

Sandwiched between the two major divisions of the cerebellum is the **vestibulo-cerebellum**, made up of small and somewhat primitive structures called the *nodule* and *flocculus*. As its name suggests, the vestibulocerebellum has close connections with the vestibular nuclei of the brainstem, through which it receives information about body orientation. Its outputs help the motor systems to maintain posture and appropriate orientation toward the external world; for example, damage to this system produces errors in gaze and difficulty with tracking visual objects as the head moves.

With more research, we are coming to realize that the cerebellum plays a crucial role in an astonishingly wide variety of behaviors. So maybe we shouldn't be too surprised by the report that this compact structure contains more than half of all the neurons in the human nervous system (Andersen et al., 1992).

As we learn more about the cerebellum and other motor centers in the brain, we can look forward to new and better treatments for a wide variety of movement disorders.

vestibulocerebellum The middle portion of the cerebellum, sandwiched between the spinocerebellum and the cerebrocerebellum and consisting of the nodule and the flocculus.

SUMMARY

The Behavioral View

■ There are two broad categories of motor activity: **movements** and **acts**. Reflexes are simple movements; more-complex motor behaviors are acts. Complex acts indicate the existence of a motor plan.

■ **Reflexes** are patterns of relatively simple and stereotyped movements elicited by the stimulation of sensory receptors.

The Control Systems View

■ In **closed-loop control**, movements may be corrected while they are being produced on the basis of feedback from sensory systems. Some behaviors are so rapid, however, that they are controlled by **open-loop** systems; that is, the pattern is preset and not modified by feedback once it has started. **Review Figure 11.3**

The Neuroscience View

■ Motor control systems are organized into a hierarchy that consists of the skeletal system and associated muscles, the spinal cord, the brainstem, and various parts of the brain, including the primary and nonprimary motor cortices, the cerebellum, and the basal ganglia.

■ Muscles around a joint work in pairs. **Antagonists** work in opposition; **synergists** work together. **Review Figure 11.6**

■ **Smooth muscles**, such as those in the stomach, are under involuntary control; **striated muscles** are under voluntary control.

■ Action potentials travel over motor nerve fibers (axons from motoneurons) and reach **muscle fibers** at the **neuromuscular junction**, releasing **acetylcholine** to trigger muscle contraction. **Review Figure 11.7**, **Web Activity 11.1**

■ The final common pathway for action potentials to skeletal muscles consists of **motoneurons** whose cell bodies in vertebrates are located in the ventral horn of the spinal cord and within the brainstem. The motoneurons receive information from a variety of sources, including sensory input from the dorsal spinal roots, other spinal cord neurons, and descending fibers from the brain. **Review Figure 11.8**

■ **Muscle spindles** and **Golgi tendon organs**—sensory receptors in the muscles and tendons, respectively—transmit crucial information about muscle activities to the central nervous system. The sensitivity of the muscle spindle can be adjusted by efferent impulses that control the length of the spindle. This adjustment enables flexible control of posture and movement. **Review Figure 11.9**

Movements Are Controlled at Several Nervous Systems Levels

■ When a muscle is stretched, a reflex circuit often causes contraction, which works to restore the muscle to its original length; this response is called the **stretch reflex**. The stretch of the muscle is detected by muscle spindles. **Review Figure 11.10**, **Web Activity 11.2**

■ The fibers of the **pyramidal (corticospinal)** tract originate mainly in the **primary motor cortex (M1)** and adjacent regions, and they run directly to spinal motoneurons or to interneurons in the spinal cord. **Nonprimary motor cortex** helps control the sequence of movements. **Premotor cortex** contains **mirror neurons** that are active when an individual is moving an object in a particular fashion, or when the individual sees someone else moving an object in that manner. **Review Figures 11.2 and 11.17**

■ Although the primary motor cortex (M1) is organized in the form of a map of the body, the subregional organization is broadly distributed and highly overlapping, in order to efficiently control the multiple muscles that make up a movement. M1 is involved in learning motor responses and is a highly plastic region; the cortical map is continually remodeled as a consequence of motor learning. **Review Figure 11.15**

Extrapyramidal Systems Also Modulate Motor Commands

■ **Extrapyramidal** brain regions that modulate movement include the **basal ganglia** (caudate nucleus, putamen, and globus pallidus), some major brainstem nuclei (**substantia nigra**, thalamic nuclei, **reticular formation**, and **red nucleus**), and the cerebellum. **Review Figures 11.18 and 11.19, Web Activity 11.3**

Disorders of Muscle, Spinal Cord, or Brain Can Disrupt Movement

■ Movement disorders, such as **muscular dystrophy**, **amyotrophic lateral sclerosis (ALS)**, **Parkinson's** and **Huntington's** **diseases**, and others, can result from impairment at any of several levels of the motor system: muscles, neuromuscular junctions, motoneurons, spinal cord, brainstem, cerebral cortex, basal ganglia, or cerebellum. The characteristics of these disorders depend on and permit diagnosis of the locus of impairment.

■ The cerebellum is made up of three major functional divisions: **spinocerebellum**, **cerebrocerebellum**, and **vestibulocerebellum**. Damage in each division is associated with specific motor impairments. **Review Figure 11.24**

Go to www.biopsychology.com for study questions, quizzes, key terms, and other resources.

Recommended Reading

Brundin, P., and Olanow, C. W. (2006). *Restorative therapies in Parkinson's disease.* New York: Springer.

Graziano, M. (2006). The organization of behavioral repertoire in motor cortex. *Annual Review of Neuroscience, 29,* 105–134.

Merchant, H., and Georgopoulos, A. P. (2006). Neurophysiology of perceptual and motor aspects of interception. *Journal of Neurophysiology, 95,* 1–13.

Purves, D., Augustine, G. J., Fitzpatrick, D., Hall, W., et al. (Eds.). (2008). *Neuroscience* (4th ed.). Sunderland, MA: Sinauer. (See Unit III: Movement and Its Central Control, Chapters 16–21.)

Sanes, J. N., and Donoghue, J. P. (2000). Plasticity and primary motor cortex. *Annual Review of Neuroscience, 23,* 393–415.

Vogel, S. (2002). *Prime mover: A natural history of muscle.* New York: Norton.

Regulation and Behavior

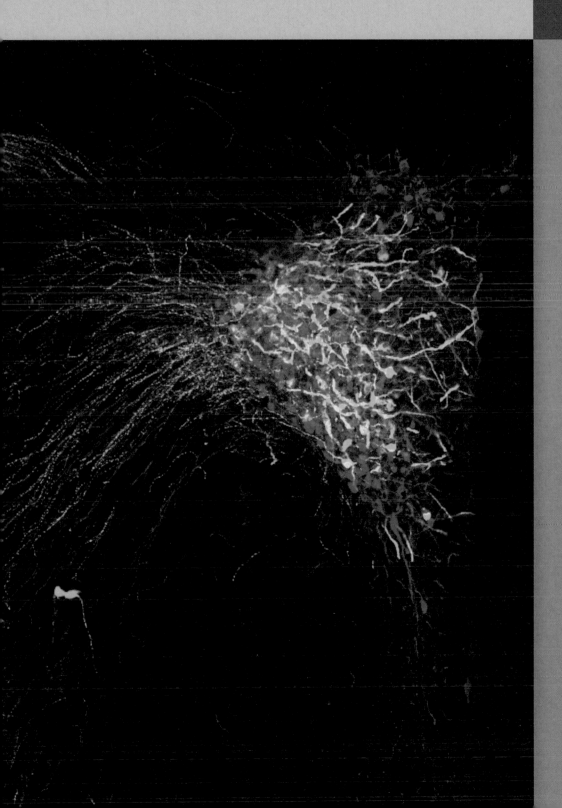

Previous page   **Peptide hormones in the hypothalamus**   In this confocal microscope image, immunolabeling reveals cells containing oxytocin (red) and vasopressin (green) in the paraventricular nucleus of the rat hypothalamus. These hormones have been implicated in diverse behaviors, including sex, memory, and social bonding, in addition to roles in homeostasis. (Image by Vicky Tobin and Mike Ludwig, Centre for Integrative Physiology, University of Edinburgh.)

CHAPTER 12

Sex: Evolutionary, Hormonal, and Neural Bases

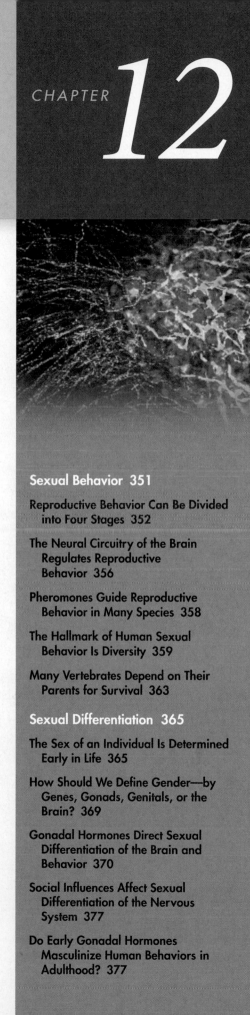

Genitals and Gender: What Makes Us Male and Female?

Few aspects of human biology are as impressive and humbling as the making of a baby; it is a developmental ballet of staggering complexity and critical timing. Given the innumerable processes that must unfold perfectly and in precisely the right order, it is a marvel that, in the great majority of cases, gestation proceeds without a hitch. Inevitably, though, there are times when a crucial part of the program is derailed along the way and a baby is born with a heartbreaking congenital deformity.

Such is the case with cloacal exstrophy, a developmental defect that affects about one in 400,000 live births. As a consequence of abnormal development of the pelvic organs, a genetic male with this condition is typically born with normal testes but lacking a penis. The parents of such an infant are faced with a terrible dilemma: Is it better to leave the child as it is and try to raise it as a boy without a penis, despite the emotional costs of the deformity? Or would the outcome be better if the child were unambiguously assigned to the female gender, underwent early surgery to remove the testes and fashion female-looking genitals, and were raised as a girl? Arguments for each course of action boil down to different opinions about the extent to which our gender identity is shaped through nurturing and socialization, rather than biological factors. What is the best choice?

Sexual behaviors are almost as diverse as the species that employ them. But in every case, males and females must produce a specific set of behaviors, in a precise and intricately coordinated sequence, in order to reproduce successfully. In this chapter we discuss our knowledge of these behaviors and their physiological underpinnings in two main sections. First we review sexual behaviors, which include the sex act itself—copulation—as well as the parental behaviors that are required for the newborns of so many species to survive. Then we consider sexual differentiation, the process by which an individual's body and brain develop in a male or female fashion. For humans, an important aspect of sexual differentiation is the emergence of sexual orientation. Do we *decide* to be attracted to men or to women, are we *taught* whom we should find attractive, or does *nature* have a say?

Sexual Behavior

We wish we could explain exactly why and how humans and other animals engage in the three Cs—courting, copulating, and cohabiting—but very little practical knowledge of such matters exists. Two barriers have blocked our understanding of sexual behavior: (1) a deep-seated reluctance within our culture to disseminate knowledge about sexual behavior and (2) the remarkable variety of sexual behaviors in existence.

Reproductive Behavior Can Be Divided into Four Stages

sexual attraction The first step in the mating behavior of many animals, in which animals emit stimuli that attract members of the opposite sex.

appetitive behavior The second stage of mating behavior; helps establish or maintain sexual interaction.

proceptive Referring to a state in which an animal advertises its readiness to mate through species-typical behaviors, such as ear wiggling in the female rat.

copulation Also called *coitus*. The sexual act.

There are four easily identifiable stages of reproductive behavior: (1) sexual attraction, (2) appetitive behavior, (3) copulation, and (4) postcopulatory behavior.

Sexual attraction is the first stage in bringing males and females together (**Figure 12.1**). In many species, sexual attraction is closely synchronized with physiological readiness to reproduce. Attraction and sexual response are also strongly shaped by learned associations, varying from one individual to the next on the basis of experience (Pfaus et al., 2001).

In experiments we gauge an individual's attractiveness by observing the responses of potential mates: how rapidly they approach, how hard they work to gain access, and so on. By manipulating the appearance of individuals, we can deduce which special features are most attractive. For example, males of many primate species are strongly attracted to the "sex skin," which swells on a female's rump when her ovaries are secreting estrogenic hormones. Most male mammals are attracted by particular female odors, which also tend to reflect estrogen levels.

Because estrogen secretion is associated with the release of eggs, these mechanisms tend to synchronize female sexual attractiveness with peak fertility. Of course, the female may find a particular male to be unattractive and refuse to mate with him. Although apparent rape has been described in some nonhuman species, including such close relatives of ours as orangutans (Maggioncalda and Sapolsky, 2002), for most species copulation is not possible without the female's active cooperation.

If the animals are mutually attracted, they may progress to the next stage: **appetitive behaviors**—species-specific behaviors that establish, maintain, or promote sexual interaction. A female displaying these behaviors is said to be **proceptive**: she may approach males, remain close to them, or show alternating approach and retreat behavior. Proceptive female rats typically exhibit "ear wiggling" and a hopping and darting gait in order to induce a male to mount. Male appetitive behaviors usually consist of staying near the female. In many mammals the male may sniff around the female's face and vagina. Male birds may engage in elaborate songs or nest-building behaviors.

If both animals display appetitive behaviors, they may progress to the third stage of reproduction: **copulation**, also known as *coitus*. In many vertebrates, including all mammals, copulation involves one or

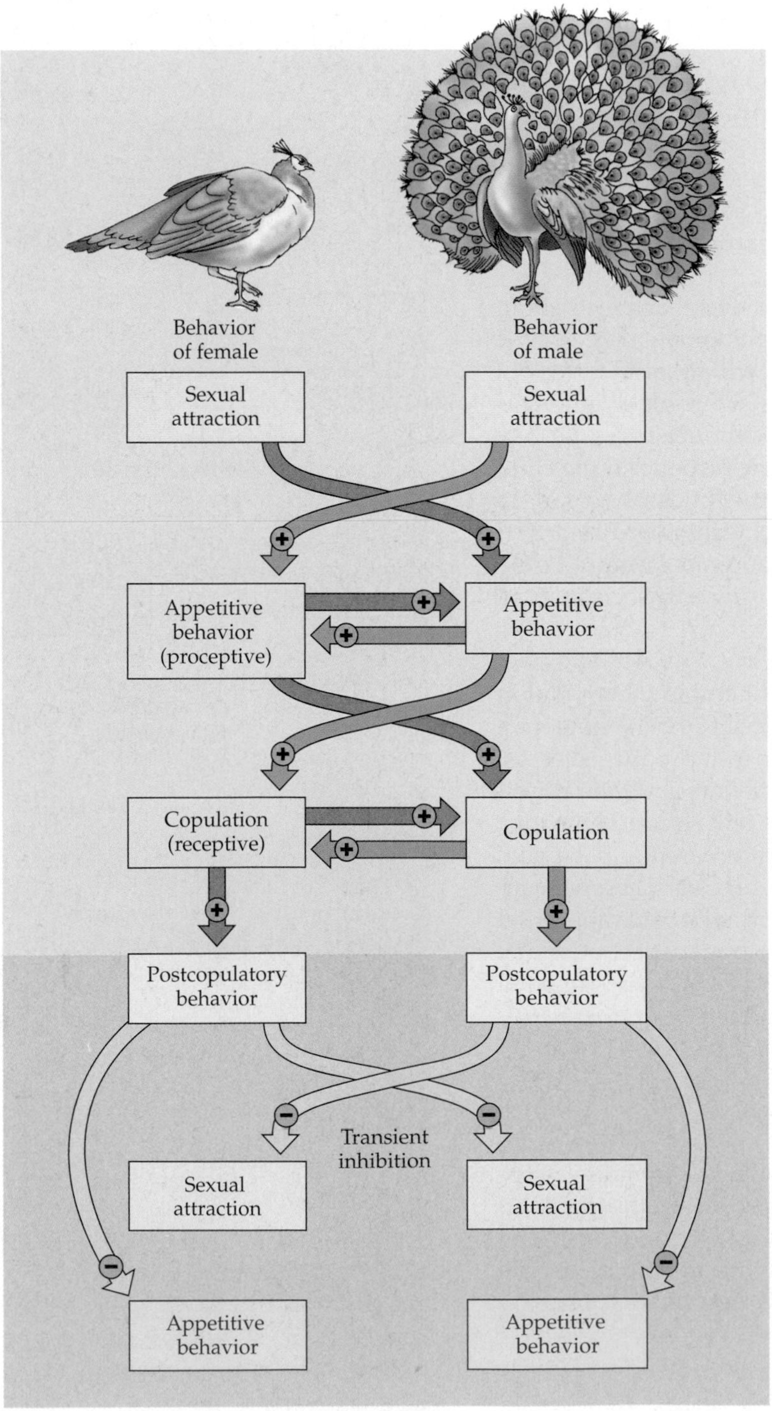

12.1 Stages of Reproductive Behavior Interaction between male and female partners in sexual reproduction is extensive, progressing in four stages: sexual attraction, appetitive behavior, copulation, and postcopulatory behavior. The postcopulatory phase (pink background) includes a temporary decrease in the sexual attractiveness of the partner and inhibition of appetitive behavior. (After Beach, 1977.)

Guinea pig Don Juan sires 43 offspring in 2 nights

PONTYPRIDD, WALES, 1 DECEMBER 2000

HAVING ESCAPED from captivity at Little Friend's Farm earlier this year, a male guinea pig named Sooty chose to re-enter captivity immediately—in the nearby cage housing 24 females. Two months later he is now the father of 43 offspring.

According to his owner, Carol Feehan, Sooty was missing for two whole days before the staff checked the females' pen. "We did a head count and found 25 guinea pigs," she told the press. "Sooty was fast asleep in the corner.

"He was absolutely shattered. We put him back in his cage and he slept for two days."

Sooty enjoyed two nights of passion among 24 females.

more **intromissions**, in which the male inserts his penis into the female's vagina, followed by a variable amount of copulatory stimulation, usually through pelvic thrusting. When stimulation reaches a threshold level, the male **ejaculates** sperm-bearing **semen** into the female; the length of time and quantity of stimulation that are required vary greatly between species and between individuals.

After one bout of copulation the animals will not mate again for a period of time, which is called the **refractory phase**. The refractory phase varies from minutes to months, depending on the species and circumstances. Many animals will resume mating sooner if they are provided with a new partner—a phenomenon known as the **Coolidge effect** (**Figure 12.2**).

The female often appears to be the one to choose whether copulation will take place; when she is willing to copulate, she is said to be **sexually receptive**, in heat, or in **estrus**. In some species the female may show proceptive behaviors days before she will participate in copulation itself. In most (but not all) species, females are receptive only when mating is likely to produce offspring. Most species are seasonal breeders, with females that are receptive only during the breeding season; and some—such as salmon, octopuses, and cicadas—reproduce only once, at the end of life.

Finally, the fourth stage of reproductive behavior consists of **postcopulatory behaviors**. These behaviors are especially varied across species. In some mammals—dogs and southern grasshopper mice, for example—the male's penis swells so much after ejaculation that he can't remove it from the female for a while (10–15 minutes in dogs), and the animals are said to be in a **copulatory lock** (Dewsbury, 1972)—just one of the many strategies employed by males of different species to try and ensure their paternity. (Despite wild stories you may have heard or read, humans never experience copulatory lock; that urban myth started in 1884 when a physician submitted a fake report as a practical joke on a journal editor [Nation, 1973].) For mammals and birds, postcopulatory behavior includes extensive **parental behaviors** to nurture the offspring, as we describe later in this chapter.

Copulation brings gametes together

All mammals, birds, and reptiles employ **internal fertilization**: the fusion of **sperm** and **ovum** (plural *ova*)—their **gametes**—within the female's body to form a **zygote**. Although there is room for only one or a few zygotes to grow, the safe and stable

12.2 The Coolidge Effect By reducing the refractory phase when a sexually exhausted male encounters an unfamiliar female, the Coolidge effect permits him to take advantage of a new reproductive opportunity and sire more offspring. (Of course, encountering 24 lovelorn females at once is a situation few males—guinea pig or otherwise—could even dream of.)

intromission Insertion of the erect penis into the vagina during copulation.

ejaculation The forceful expulsion of semen from the penis.

semen A mixture of fluid, including sperm, that is released during ejaculation.

refractory phase A period following copulation during which an individual cannot recommence copulation.

Coolidge effect The propensity of an animal that has appeared sexually satiated with a present partner to resume sexual activity when provided with a novel partner.

sexually receptive Referring to the state in which an individual (in mammals, typically the female) is willing to copulate.

estrus The period during which female animals are sexually receptive.

postcopulatory behavior The final stage in mating behavior. Species-specific postcopulatory behaviors include rolling (in the cat) and grooming (in the rat).

copulatory lock Reproductive behavior in which the male's penis swells after ejaculation so that the male and female are forced to remain joined for 5–10 minutes; occurs in dogs and some rodents, but not in humans.

parental behavior Behavior of adult animals with the goal of enhancing the well-being of their own offspring, often at some cost to the parents.

internal fertilization The process by which sperm fertilize eggs inside of the female's body, as in all mammals, birds, and reptiles.

sperm The gamete produced by males for fertilization of eggs (ova).

ovum An egg, the female gamete.

gamete A sex cell (sperm or ovum) that contains only unpaired chromosomes and therefore has only half of the usual number of chromosomes.

zygote The fertilized egg.

TABLE 12.1 Types of Sexual Reproduction in Animals

Type	Strategy	Example
EXTERNAL FERTILIZATION		
Aquatic species	Many gametes are released into the environment	Many invertebrates, fishes, amphibians
INTERNAL FERTILIZATION		
Oviparous species	Female lays a few eggs	Insects, all birds, many reptiles
Viviparous species	Female nourishes embryos in her body, giving birth to a few relatively mature young	Some fishes, some reptiles, all mammals except monotremes (echidna and platypus)
Ovoviviparous species	Female gives birth to live young that developed from eggs carried internally	Some fishes, some reptiles

external fertilization The process by which eggs are fertilized outside of the female's body, as in many fishes and amphibians.

ovulation The production and release of an egg (ovum).

lordosis A female receptive posture in quadrupeds in which the hindquarter is raised and the tail is turned to one side, facilitating intromission by the male.

internal environment maximizes the probability that each of these balls of cells will eventually develop into a new individual. Other vertebrates—aquatic species including some fishes and amphibians—employ **external fertilization**, releasing their gametes into the outside world in a reproductive gamble that pits sheer numbers against a high rate of loss. Of course, the particulars of each species' reproductive behaviors reflect evolutionary adaptation to a specific ecological niche, resulting in the impressive diversity we observe between different groups of animals. **Table 12.1** summarizes the different types of sexual reproduction.

Most of what we know about the copulatory behavior of mammals derives from studies of lab animals, especially rats. Like most other rodents, rats do not engage in lengthy courtship, nor do the partners tend to remain together after copulation. Rats are attracted to each other largely through odors. Females are spontaneous ovulators; that is, even when left alone they **ovulate** (release eggs from the ovary) every 4–5 days. For those few hours around the time of ovulation, the female seeks out a male and displays proceptive behaviors, and both animals produce vocalizations at frequencies too high for humans to detect but audible to each other.

These behaviors prompt the male to mount the female from the rear, grasp her flanks with his forelegs, and rhythmically thrust his hips against her rump. If she is receptive, the female adopts a stereotyped posture called **lordosis** (**Figure 12.3**), elevating her rump and moving her tail to one side, allowing intromission. Once intromission has been achieved, the male rat makes a single deep thrust and then springs back off the female. During the next 6–7 minutes the male and female orchestrate seven to nine such intromissions; then, instead of springing away, the male raises the front half of his body up for a second or two while he ejaculates. Finally, he falls backward off the female.

After copulation, the male and female separately engage in grooming their genitalia, and the male pays little attention to the female for the next 5 minutes or

12.3 Copulation in Rats The raised rump and deflected tail of the female (the lordosis posture) make intromission possible in rats.

so, until, often in response to the female's proceptive behaviors, the two engage in another bout of intromissions and ejaculation. This pattern of multiple intromissions before ejaculation is an obligatory part of rat fertility: only after repeated mechanical stimulation of the cervix and vagina will the female's brain cause the release of hormones to support pregnancy. In this instance, then, the behavior of the male rat directly affects the hormonal secretions of his mate.

In other rodent species, intromission may be accompanied by more prolonged thrusting, or the penis may swell to form a copulatory lock. The northern pygmy mouse has only a single ejaculation during a mating session (talk about pressure!). In some rodent species, such as the prairie voles we discuss later in this chapter, a male and a female live together before and long after copulation; such animals are said to form **pair bonds**. Interestingly, there is growing evidence of a distinction between social pair bonds and sexual (or genetic) pair bonds. In the case of voles, the formation of exclusive social pair bonds leads to the greatest reproductive success, even though the partners may occasionally engage in extrapair copulation (Ophir et al., 2008). They are *socially* monogamous (having one partner), but not quite *sexually* monogamous.

Hormones play an important role in rat mating behaviors. Testosterone mediates the male's interest in copulation: if he is **castrated** (his testes removed), he will stop ejaculating within a few weeks and will eventually stop mounting receptive females. Although testosterone disappears from the bloodstream within a few hours after castration, the hormone's effects on the nervous system take days or weeks to dissipate. Treating a castrated male with testosterone eventually restores mating behavior; if testosterone treatment is stopped, the mating behavior fades again. This is an example of a hormone exerting an **activational effect**: the hormone transiently promotes certain behaviors. In normal development, the rise of androgen secretion at puberty activates masculine behavior in males.

Although individual male rats and guinea pigs differ considerably in how eagerly they will mate, blood levels of testosterone clearly are *not* responsible for these differences. For one thing, animals displaying different levels of sexual vigor do not show reliable differences in blood levels of testosterone. Furthermore, when these males are castrated and subsequently all treated with exactly the same doses of testosterone, their precastration differences in sexual activity persist (**Figure 12.4**). Not only that, but it also turns out that a very small amount of testosterone—one-tenth the amount normally produced by the animals—is enough to fully maintain the mating behavior of male rats. Thus, since all male rats make more testosterone than is required to maintain their copulatory behavior, some other factor, which we can call "drive," must differ across individual males.

Estrogens secreted at the beginning of the 4- to 5-day **ovulatory cycle** facilitate the proceptive behavior of the female rat, and the subsequent production of pro-

pair bond   A durable and exclusive relationship between a male and a female.

castration   Removal of the gonads, usually the testes.

activational effect   A temporary change in behavior resulting from the administration of a hormone to an adult animal.

ovulatory cycle   The periodic occurrence of ovulation.

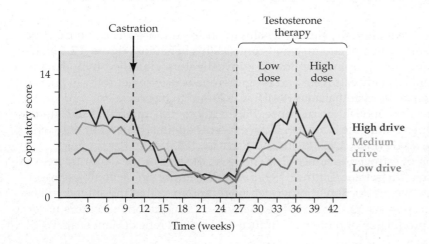

12.4 Androgens Permit Male Copulatory Behavior Although androgens—especially testosterone—are important for normal male sexual function, individual differences in sexual activity are not determined by differences in androgen levels. In this experiment, castration caused the sexual activity of male guinea pigs to gradually decrease, over a number of weeks. At week 26, all of the animals started receiving identical testosterone replacement treatments. Even though testosterone levels were now uniform in all animals, the male guinea pigs returned to the individual levels of sexual activity that they had exhibited prior to castration. Even doubling the amount of hormone at week 36 did not increase the mating activity of any group. Presumably Sooty from Figure 12.2 would have fallen into the "high drive" group. (After Grunt and Young, 1953.)

12.5 The Ovulatory Cycle of Rats   Changes in hormone levels indicate when the female rat will display lordosis. This behavioral receptivity, or estrus, occurs after the animal has been exposed first to estrogens and then to progesterone. In spontaneous ovulators such as rats, the cycle of hormone secretion repeats unless eggs are fertilized. In that case, the embryos secrete hormones to interrupt the cycle and maintain pregnancy.

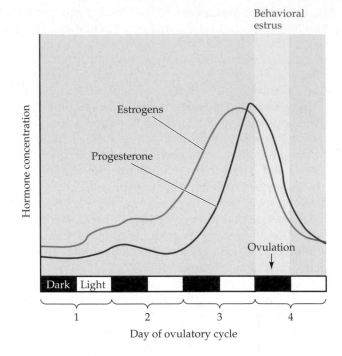

gesterone increases proceptive behavior and activates receptivity (**Figure 12.5**). An adult female whose ovaries have been removed will show neither proceptive nor receptive behaviors. However, 2 days of estrogen treatment followed by a single injection of progesterone will, about 6 hours later, make the female rat proceptive and receptive for a few hours. Only the correct combination of estrogens and progesterone will fully activate copulatory behaviors in female rats—another example of activational effects of gonadal steroids.

The Neural Circuitry of the Brain Regulates Reproductive Behavior

Although most of what we know about the neural circuitry of sexual behavior comes from studies of rats, steroid receptors are found in the same specific brain regions across a wide variety of vertebrate species. Steroid-sensitive regions include the cortex, brainstem nuclei, medial amygdala, hippocampus, and many others. And as we'll see, the hypothalamus plays a particularly important role in regulating copulatory behavior.

Ovarian steroids act on a lordosis circuit that spans from brain to muscle

Scientists have exploited the steroid sensitivity of the rat lordosis response to develop a map of the neural circuitry that controls this behavior (**Figure 12.6b**). Using steroid autoradiography (see Box 5.1), investigators identified hypothalamic nuclei containing many estrogen- and progesterone-sensitive neurons. In particular, the **ventromedial hypothalamus** (**VMH**) was found to be crucial for lordosis because lesions there abolish the response. Furthermore, tiny quantities of estradiol implanted directly into the brain can induce receptivity in females, but only when placed in the VMH (Lisk, 1962; Pleim and Barfield, 1988).

One action of estrogen treatment is to increase the size of the dendritic trees of VMH neurons (Meisel and Luttrell, 1990). Another important action of estrogens is to stimulate the production of progesterone receptors so that the animal will become more responsive to that hormone. Activated progesterone receptors in turn increase the production of proteins to induce the lordosis reflex (Mani et al., 2000).

ventromedial hypothalamus (VMH)   A hypothalamic region involved in eating and sexual behaviors.

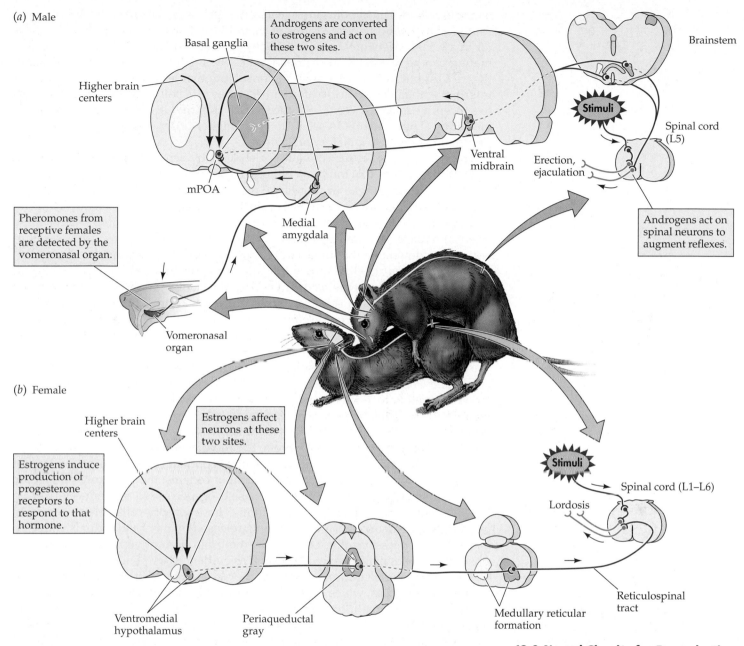

(a) Male

Basal ganglia

Androgens are converted to estrogens and act on these two sites.

Brainstem

Higher brain centers

Stimuli

Spinal cord (L5)

Ventral midbrain

Erection, ejaculation

mPOA

Androgens act on spinal neurons to augment reflexes.

Pheromones from receptive females are detected by the vomeronasal organ.

Medial amygdala

Vomeronasal organ

(b) Female

Higher brain centers

Estrogens affect neurons at these two sites.

Estrogens induce production of progesterone receptors to respond to that hormone.

Stimuli

Spinal cord (L1–L6)

Lordosis

Ventromedial hypothalamus

Periaqueductal gray

Medullary reticular formation

Reticulospinal tract

12.6 Neural Circuits for Reproduction in Rodents (Part *b* after Pfaff, 1980.)

The VMH sends axons to the **periaqueductal gray** region of the midbrain, where again, lesions greatly diminish lordosis. The periaqueductal gray neurons project to the **medullary reticular formation**, which in turn projects to the spinal cord via the **reticulospinal tract**. In the spinal cord the sensory information provided by the mounting male will now evoke the motor response of lordosis. Thus, the role of the VMH is to monitor steroid hormone concentrations and, at the right time in the ovulatory cycle, activate a multisynaptic pathway that induces the spinal cord to contract back muscles, producing a lordosis response to mounting males (Pfaff, 1997). Figure 12.6*b* schematically represents this neural pathway and its steroid-responsive components.

Androgens activate a neural system for male reproductive behavior

Steroid hormones also activate male copulatory behavior in rodents (**Figure 12.6*a***), and again the sites of steroid action provide important clues about the neural cir-

periaqueductal gray The neuronal body–rich region of the midbrain surrounding the cerebral aqueduct that connects the third and fourth ventricles; involved in pain perception.

medullary reticular formation The hindmost portion of the brainstem reticular formation, implicated in motor control and copulatory behavior.

reticulospinal tract A tract of axons arising from the brainstem reticular formation and descending to the spinal cord to modulate movement.

cuitry involved. The hypothalamic **medial preoptic area** (**mPOA**) is chock-full of steroid-sensitive neurons, and lesions of the mPOA abolish male copulatory behavior in a wide variety of vertebrate species (Meisel and Sachs, 1994). Furthermore, mating can be reinstated in castrated males by small implants of testosterone in the mPOA, but not in other brain regions. Note that lesions of the mPOA do not interfere with males' *motivation* for females; they will still press a bar to gain access to a receptive female (Everitt and Stacey, 1987), but they seem unable to commence mounting. Thus, the mPOA seems to be a "higher-order" center that controls the production of male copulatory behaviors.

The mPOA coordinates copulatory behavior by sending axons to the ventral midbrain via the medial forebrain bundle. From the ventral midbrain, information goes to the basal ganglia to coordinate mounting behaviors and, via a multisynaptic pathway that involves several brainstem nuclei, to the spinal cord (Hamson and Watson, 2004), which mediates various reflexes of copulation. One of these brainstem nuclei, the **paragigantocellular nucleus** (**PGN**) in the pons, sends serotonergic fibers down into the spinal cord, where they inhibit the penile erection reflex circuit (McKenna, 1999). So the mPOA must inhibit this "inhibitory nucleus" to permit erection. Antidepressant drugs that augment serotonergic activity in the brain—for example, the selective serotonin reuptake inhibitors like Prozac (see Chapter 16)—can produce side effects including difficulty achieving erection, ejaculation, and/or orgasm, probably by enhancing the effectiveness of PGN-released serotonin in the spinal cord.

A specialized set of lumbar spinal cord neurons acts as an ejaculation generator (Truitt and Coolen, 2002; B. Young et al., 2009). Because the reflex circuits and ejaculation generator are in the lumbar spinal cord, men with damage at higher levels of the spinal cord often remain capable of copulation and ejaculation. (If you're wondering, the famous drug sildenafil, better known as Viagra, acts directly on tissue in the penis, not in the spinal cord or brain, to promote erection [Boolell et al., 1996].)

We can also gather information about male copulatory mechanisms by tracing a sensory system that activates male arousal in rodents: the vomeronasal system. The **vomeronasal organ** (see Chapter 9) consists of specialized receptor cells near to but separate from the olfactory epithelium. These sensory cells detect chemicals, called **pheromones** (see Chapters 5 and 9), released by other individuals and send axons to the accessory olfactory bulb in the brain. Receptive female rats release pheromones that male rats find arousing, as evidenced by penile erections.

The vomeronasal information from the accessory olfactory bulb projects to the **medial amygdala**, which depends on adult circulating levels of sex steroids to maintain a masculine form and function (Cooke et al., 1999, 2003). Lesions here will abolish the penile erections that normally occur around receptive females (Kondo et al., 1997). The medial amygdala, in turn, sends axons to the mPOA. So the mPOA appears to integrate hormonal and sensory information such as pheromones, and to coordinate the motor patterns of copulation. Figure 12.6*a* summarizes the neural circuitry for male rat copulatory behavior.

We will see later that testosterone activates sexual arousal in humans as well, possibly acting on the hypothalamus and medial amygdala.

Pheromones Guide Reproductive Behavior in Many Species

When steroid hormones from the gonads affect the brain to activate mating behavior, the activation is not absolute; individuals are simply *more likely* to engage in mating behaviors when steroid levels are adequate. This activation can be thought of as communication between the gonads and the brain: by producing steroids to make gametes, the gonads also inform the brain that the body is ready to mate. This signaling takes place inside the individual, while pheromones are chemical signals that communicate information *between* animals to help coordinate their reproductive activities.

medial preoptic area (mPOA) A region of the anterior hypothalamus implicated in the control of many behaviors, including thermoregulation, sexual behavior, and gonadotropin secretion.

paragigantocellular nucleus (PGN) A region of the brainstem reticular formation implicated in sleep and modulation of spinal reflexes.

vomeronasal organ (VNO) A collection of specialized receptor cells, near to but separate from the olfactory epithelium, that detect pheromones and send electrical signals to the accessory olfactory bulb in the brain.

pheromone A chemical signal that is released outside the body of an animal and affects other members of the same species.

medial amygdala A portion of the amygdala that receives olfactory and pheromonal information.

For example, female goldfish produce a hormone called *F prostaglandin* that is required for ovulation. But some F prostaglandin also escapes the female's body and passes into her watery surroundings, where it is detectable by male goldfish, which are then stimulated to commence mating behaviors (Sorensen and Goetz, 1993). The most likely scenario for the evolution of this relationship is that long ago, females released F prostaglandin only as a by-product of ovulation, but because the presence of the hormone conveyed important information about the female's condition, natural selection favored males who detected the hormone and began courting in response to the signal. Even very simple unicellular organisms, such as yeasts, prepare each other for mating by releasing and detecting pheromones (S. Fields, 1990).

Pheromones in the urine of male mice can also accelerate puberty in young females (Drickamer, 1992; Price and Vandenbergh, 1992) and can halt pregnancy in mature females (Brennan et al., 1990). Female mice can even identify an individual male by the particular mix of pheromones in his urine, and if the pheromones come from a dominant male—but not a subordinate male—they can induce the birth of new neurons in the olfactory bulbs and hippocampus of the female mouse (Mak et al., 2007). When prairie voles mate (**Figure 12.7**), the female is exposed to pheromones from her mate's mouth and urine. If she is then isolated and has urine from that male or any other male applied to her snout, pregnancy will be blocked; the fetuses are resorbed by the female, and she is soon ready to mate again. So when the female remains with her original mate, she is careful not to apply her mate's urine to her vomeronasal organ; otherwise she would lose their offspring (Smale, 1988). Terminating pregnancy and absorbing the fetuses in the presence of a new male may be an attempt to make the best of a bad situation: if her original mate is gone, a female may be better off beginning a new litter with a different male.

Pheromones can also convey important information about reproductive status between individuals of the same sex. During **musth**, an annual period of increased sexual activity and intermale aggression, male elephants secrete a pheromone-laden liquid from specialized glands located on their temples, just behind their eyes. Among pubescent males, these secretions have a honeylike odor; in fact, they contain substances chemically similar to bee pheromones and sometimes even attract bees. As male elephants mature, they produce a liquid that is more malodorous (to us), containing increasing concentrations of a pheromone named *frontalin* (curiously, frontalin is also an important pheromone in insects). By broadcasting their low rank and avoiding mature-smelling males, the honey-scented juveniles avoid aggressive encounters. The secretions of the older bulls not only signal their rank to each other, but also attract females that are ready to ovulate (Rasmussen and Greenwood, 2003; Rasmussen et al., 2002).

The Hallmark of Human Sexual Behavior Is Diversity

How much of what we've described so far about sexual behavior in animals is relevant to human sexuality? Until the 1940s, when biology professor Alfred Kinsey began to ask friends and colleagues about their sexual histories, there was virtually no scientific study of human sexual behavior. Kinsey constructed a standardized set of questions and procedures to obtain information for samples of the U.S. population categorized by sex, age, religion, and education. Eventually he and his collaborators published extensive surveys (based on tens of thousands of respondents) of the sexual behavior of American males (Kinsey et al., 1948) and females (Kinsey et al., 1953).

Controversial in their time, these surveys indicated that nearly all men masturbated, that college-educated people were more likely to engage in oral sex than were non-college-educated people, that many people had at one time or another engaged in homosexual behaviors, and that as much as 10% of the population pre-

12.7 Prairie Voles

musth An annual period of heightened aggressiveness and sexual activity in male elephants.

(a) Female

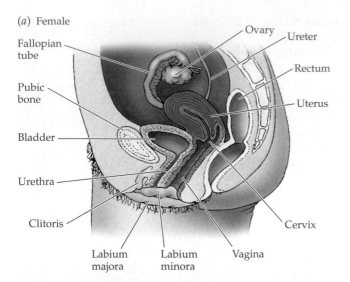

(b) Male

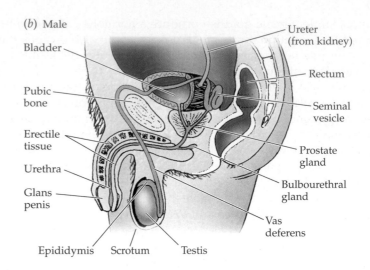

12.8 Adult Human Reproductive Anatomy

Although some of the functional details vary, most of the anatomical structures of the reproductive tract are common across mammalian species. (a) Every 28 days or so, the human ovaries release an ovum into the fallopian tube, where it must be fertilized if pregnancy is to occur. The fertilized zygote implants in the wall of the uterus, and a placenta develops. In some species, if no pregnancy occurs, the uterine wall (endometrium) sloughs off during menstruation (but most mammalian species lose less tissue than humans do and thus do not menstruate). (b) In males, sperm originate in the testes, mature in the adjacent epididymis, and are expelled via the muscular vas deferens. Along the way, structures such as the seminal vesicles and prostate gland add their secretions, forming semen. In ejaculation, the semen is rhythmically expelled via the urethra, which also connects to the bladder and conducts urine outside the body.

orgasm   The climax of sexual experience, marked by extremely pleasurable sensations.

phallus   The clitoris or penis.

ferred homosexual sex. Although it has since been shown that the last figure is an overestimate, these surveys opened our eyes about human sexual behavior.

Another way to investigate human sexual behavior is to make behavioral and physiological observations of people engaged in sexual intercourse or masturbation, but the squeamishness of the general public impeded such research for many years. Finally, after Kinsey's surveys were published, physician William Masters and psychologist Virginia Johnson began a large, famous project of this kind (Masters and Johnson 1966, 1970; Masters et al., 1994), documenting the impressively diverse sexuality of humans.

Among most mammalian species, including most nonhuman primates, the male mounts the female from the rear; but among humans, face-to-face postures are most common. A great variety of coital positions have been described, and many couples vary their positions from session to session or even within a session. It is this variety in reproductive behaviors, rather than differences in reproductive anatomy (**Figure 12.8**), that distinguishes human sexuality from that of most other species.

Another difference between species is that, unlike other animals, humans can report their subjective reactions to sexual behavior—specifically **orgasm**, the brief, extremely pleasurable sensations experienced by most men during ejaculation and by most women during copulation. In the original conceptual model of human sexuality, Masters and Johnson (1966) summarized the typical response patterns of both men and women as consisting of four phases: increasing excitement, plateau, orgasm, and resolution (**Figure 12.9**). During the excitement phase, the **phallus** (the penis in men, the clitoris in women) becomes engorged with blood, making it erect.

In women, parasympathetic activity during the excitement phase causes changes in vaginal blood vessels, resulting in the production of lubricating fluids that facilitate intromission. Stimulation of the penis, clitoris, and vagina during rhythmic thrusting accompanying intromission may lead to orgasm. In both men and women, orgasm is accompanied by waves of contractions of genital muscles (mediating ejaculation in men and contractions of the uterus and vagina in women).

In spite of some basic similarities, the sexual responses of men and women differ in important ways. For one thing, women show a much greater variety of commonly observed copulatory sequences. Whereas men have only one basic pattern, captured by the linear model of Masters and Johnson (Figure 12.9a) women have at least three typical patterns (see Figure 12.9b). Another important aspect of human sexuality is that most men, but not most women, have an absolute refractory phase following orgasm (see Figure 12.9a). That is, most men cannot achieve

(a) Male

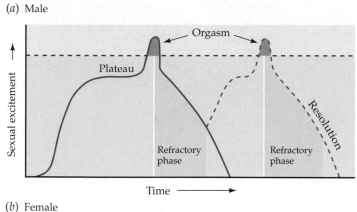

(b) Female

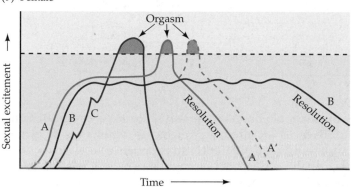

12.9 Human Sexual Response Cycles   (a) The typical male pattern includes an absolute refractory phase after orgasm. (b) These three patterns (A, B, C) are often observed in women. These diagrams are schematic and do not represent a particular physiological measure, although heart rate varies in roughly this manner. The patterns vary considerably from one individual to another. (After Masters and Johnson, 1966.)

full erection and another orgasm until some time has elapsed—the length of time varying from minutes to hours, depending on individual differences and other factors. Many women, on the other hand, can have multiple orgasms in rapid succession. Functional imaging of the brains of men and women during sexual activity suggests that, although the brain circuitry associated with orgasm itself is quite similar between the sexes, substantially different networks are active in men's and women's brains during sexual activity *prior* to orgasm (Georgiadis et al., 2009).

Taking a broader perspective on sexuality reveals additional distinctions between men and women (Peplau, 2003). Research has generally found that basic sex drive is greater in men, reflected in more frequent masturbation, sexual fantasies, and pursuit of sexual contacts. There are closer links between sexuality and aggression in men than in women, ranging from differences in sexual assertiveness to the most extreme manifestation: rape.

In women's sex lives, emotional components and cognitive factors play a stronger role than in men. In addition to a somewhat flexible sexuality that adapts to new experiences and situations over time, women place more emphasis on sexual intimacy within the context of committed relationships. These observations and others have led sex researchers to adopt a more nuanced view of female sexuality. While Masters and Johnson simply adapted the linear model of male sexuality to accommodate their observations in women, the more modern perspective views women's sexuality as a cycle, governed in large measure by emotional factors (Basson, 2001, 2008). According to this model, emotional intimacy and desire (more than physiological arousal) are crucial in the initiation of sexual responses, and following a sexual encounter, a combination of both emotional and physical satisfaction affects the likelihood of subsequent sexual activity (**Figure 12.10**).

Although male and female sexuality may bear the imprint of our evolutionary history, on an individual basis it is also shaped by sociocultural pressures and experience. The similarities and differences in sexual responses thus exemplify the generalization of Chapter 1 that each person is in some ways like all other people,

12.10 Women's Sexual/Emotional Response According to the current model of female sexual responses (Basson, 2008), a willingness to become receptive (top left) interacts with innate sexual drive (red arrows). A combination of sexual stimuli (top) and biological factors result in feelings of arousal and desire (bottom right). A variety of factors, including rewarding nonsexual intimacy, and/or sexual gratification from this encounter, provide feedback that affects levels of motivation (left) for subsequent sexual behavior.

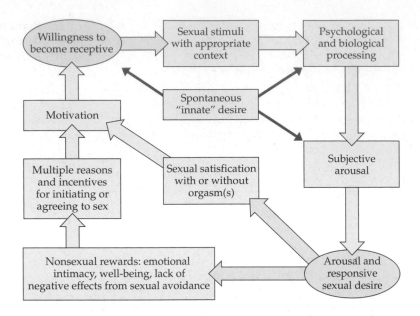

in some ways like some other people, and in some ways like no other person. Some individual behavioral differences are probably related to differences in genetic makeup. But some are certainly due to differences in experience and learning; sexual therapy, for example, usually consists of helping the person to relax, to recognize the sensations associated with coitus, and to learn the behaviors that produce the desired effects in both partners. Masturbation during adolescence, rather than being harmful as suggested in previous times, may help avoid sexual problems in adulthood. As with other behaviors, practice, practice, practice helps.

Sexual behavior may also aid overall health; epidemiological studies indicate that men who have frequent sex tend to live longer than men who do not (Davey-Smith et al., 1997). Of course, it is also important to one's health to take precautions (such as using condoms) to avoid contracting sexually transmitted infections.

Hormones play only a permissive role in human sexual behavior

We saw that a little bit of testosterone must be in circulation to activate male-typical mating behavior in rodents. The same relation seems to hold for human males. For example, boys who fail to produce testosterone at puberty show little interest in sex unless they receive androgen treatments. These males, as well as men who have lost their testes as a result of cancer or accident, have made it possible to conduct double-blind tests demonstrating that testosterone indeed stimulates sexual interest and activity in men. (In **double-blind tests**, neither the subjects nor the investigators know which subjects are receiving the drug and which are receiving a placebo, until after the treatment is over.) Despite the double-blind design of the experiment, men sometimes know when they're getting the testosterone treatment, because they feel more energetic (J. M. Davidson et al., 1979).

Recall that, in rats, additional testosterone has no effect on the vigor of mating. Consequently, there is no correlation between the amount of androgens produced by an individual male rat and his tendency to copulate. In humans, too, just a little testosterone is sufficient to restore behavior, and there is no correlation between systemic androgen levels and sexual activity among men who have at least *some* androgen. In men over 60 years old, testosterone levels gradually decline as gonadotropin levels rise, indicating that the testes become less responsive to pituitary hormones.

Some women experience sexual dysfunction after menopause, reporting decreased sexual desire and difficulty achieving comfortable coitus. There are many possible reasons for such a change, including several hormonal changes. Although

double-blind test A test of a drug or treatment in which neither the subjects nor the attending researchers know which subjects are receiving the drug (treatment) and which are receiving the placebo (control).

we don't yet have a clear picture of the psychosexual consequences of decreased hormone secretion in menopause, evidence is accumulating that providing post-menopausal women with low doses of both estrogens and androgens can have beneficial effects on the genital experience of sex and also on women's sexual interest (Basson, 2008; Sherwin, 1998, 2002). An important but untested possibility is that the synthesis of androgens and estrogens in the brain, rather than circulating levels of these steroids from the gonads, may be crucial for normal sexual functioning in women (Basson, 2008). If true, this idea could help explain why blood tests of hormones sometimes fail to correlate with measures of sexual functioning.

There have been several attempts to determine whether women's interest or participation in sexual behavior varies with the menstrual cycle. Some researchers have found a slight increase in sexual behavior around the time of ovulation, but the effect is small, and several studies have failed to see any significant change in interest in sex across the menstrual cycle.

Do pheromones affect human reproductive function?

Nearly 40 years ago, a report that women residing together in a college dormitory were more likely to have their menstrual cycles in synchrony triggered speculation that pheromones passing between women serve as a signal of the ovulatory cycle, enabling synchronization (McClintock, 1971). This idea has been difficult to confirm (Weller and Weller, 1993), and some researchers argue that it is simply a measurement artifact (Schank, 2001, 2002). If menstrual synchrony indeed exists, the question of whether the synchronization relies on social signals or pheromone signals between the women is even more difficult to determine. However, women who have extracts of sweat from other women applied to their upper lip do display an acceleration or delay of their menstrual cycles, depending on where the donors are in their cycle (Stern and McClintock, 1998).

There is also some evidence that the body odors of men affect women's mate choices (and not just in the obvious way!). The **major histocompatibility complex (MHC)** is a group of immune-related genes that come in so many different forms, or **alleles**, that they encode millions of different overall combinations. The MHC is also a source of unique body odors, which therefore signal the individual's genotype. In general, a woman prefers the smell of a man with MHCs that are not too similar to her own (Wedekind et al., 1995), but also not too dissimilar, and preferably containing some MHC alleles that are the same as those that she inherited from her father (but not from her mother) (Jacob et al., 2002). This sensitivity to a man's scent may be an evolved mechanism for striking a balance between inbreeding and outbreeding. Whether or not MHC sensitivity requires a vomeronasal system is uncertain. Recall from Chapter 9 that the vomeronasal organ appears to be a nonfunctional vestige in humans, but there's growing evidence that the main olfactory system can detect MHC-related odors and pheromones (Liberles and Buck, 2006).

Many Vertebrates Depend on Their Parents for Survival

In many vertebrate species, copulation is not enough to ensure reproduction. Many young vertebrates, and all newborn mammals, need parental attention to survive. Animals that are born or hatched with well-developed sensory and motor systems (e.g., reptiles, chickens, horses) are said to be **precocial**. Species in which the young start life with poorly developed motor or sensory systems (e.g., songbirds, cats, humans) are **altricial**. Among birds, both the male and the female usually feed and care for the eggs and young. Among mammals, whose newborns must receive milk by nursing, often the female alone raises the offspring.

In Chapter 5 we discussed the milk letdown reflex, when the infant's suckling on the nipple triggers the secretion of oxytocin to promote the release of milk (see Figure 5.12). In rats, the pregnant female prepares for her pups by licking all of her nipples. Doing so probably helps clean the nipples before the pups arrive, but

major histocompatibility complex (MHC) A large family of genes that identify an individual's tissues (to aid in immune responses against foreign proteins).

allele Any particular version of a gene.

precocial Referring to animals that are born in a relatively developed state and that are able to survive without maternal care.

altricial Referring to animals that are born in an undeveloped state and depend on maternal care, as human infants do.

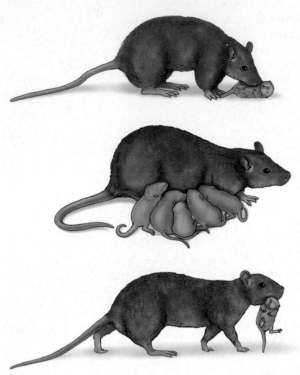

12.11 Parental Behavior in Rats

it also makes them more sensitive to touch. This self-grooming actually expands the amount of sensory cortex that responds to skin surrounding the nipples (Xerri et al., 1994), which probably sets the stage for the letdown reflex. This is a wonderful example of an animal's behavior altering its own brain and therefore changing its future behavior.

Rat mothers (called *dams*) show four easily measured maternal behaviors: nest building, crouching over pups, retrieving pups, and nursing (**Figure 12.11**). A virgin female or male rat won't normally show these behaviors toward rat pups. In fact, a virgin female finds the smell of newborn pups aversive. If exposed to newborn pups a few hours a day for several days in a row, however, she (or almost any adult rat, male or female) will start building a nest, crouching over pups, and retrieving them. As the rat gradually habituates to the smell of the pups, it starts taking care of them. But the rat dam that gives birth to her first litter will instantly show these behaviors. It turns out that the rather complicated pattern of hormones during pregnancy shapes her brain to display maternal behaviors before she is exposed to the pups.

The effect of hormones on a rat's maternal behaviors is demonstrated by a **parabiotic** preparation in which two female rats are surgically joined, sharing a single blood supply, such that each is exposed to any hormones secreted by the other (**Figure 12.12**). If one of those females is pregnant, then at the end of her pregnancy the other female, who was never pregnant but was exposed to the pregnant rat's hormones, will also immediately show maternal behavior (Terkel and Rosenblatt, 1972). Which hormone is responsible for promoting maternal behavior? No single hormone alone can do it; the combination of several hormones, including estrogens, progesterone, and prolactin, is required. There is ample evidence that the hormones of pregnancy also prepare human mothers to nurture their newborns (Fleming et al., 2002).

The network of brain regions that controls maternal behavior shows considerable overlap with the circuitry for sexual behavior. It's not too surprising that the same brain regions are involved in mating and maternal behavior, when you consider that these behaviors are simply two stages in the process of reproduction. Two prominent examples are the mPOA and the periaqueductal gray. The mPOA is sensitive to many steroid hormones, and lesions there severely reduce or eliminate oral maternal behaviors such as licking and pup retrieval, but they have relatively little effect on crouching or nursing. Lesioning the periaqueductal gray, conversely, has no effect on the oral maternal behaviors, but virtually eliminates the crouching position for nursing pups (Lonstein and Stern, 1997).

There is also a brain network that selectively inhibits maternal behavior. The fact that virgin female rats find the smell of pups aversive may be why they don't show maternal behavior at first. This olfactory information projects via the olfac-

parabiotic Referring to a surgical preparation that joins two animals to share a single blood supply.

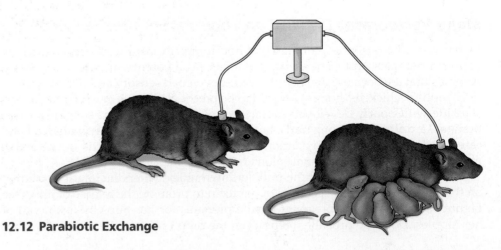

12.12 Parabiotic Exchange

tory bulb to the medial amygdala and on to the VMH (see Figure 9.26). Lesions anywhere along that path will cause virgin rats to show maternal behavior right away (Numan and Numan, 1991). It seems that rats find the smell of pups aversive unless they are exposed to the pups repeatedly or experience the hormones of pregnancy. Once adult rats stop disliking the smell of pups, they display parental behaviors.

Sexual Differentiation

For species such as our own, in which the only kind of reproduction is sexual reproduction (so far), each individual must become either a male or a female to reproduce. **Sexual differentiation** is the process by which individuals develop either male or female bodies and behaviors. In mammals this process begins before birth and continues into adulthood. As we'll see, some people may be very malelike (masculine) in some parts of the body and very femalelike (feminine) in others, so that we sometimes can't say that a person is either male or female, but may be a blend of the two sexes.

The Sex of an Individual Is Determined Early in Life

In mammals, every egg carries an X chromosome from the mother; the penetration of the egg by a sperm carrying either a second X or a Y chromosome is the key event in **sex determination**, the developmentally early event that decides whether the new individual will develop as a male or a female. Mammals that receive an X chromosome from the father will become females with an XX sex chromosome complement; those that receive the father's Y chromosome will become XY males. From that point on, the path of sexual differentiation is set, with only occasional exceptions.

In vertebrates the first major consequence of sexual determination is in the gonads. Very early in development each individual has a pair of **indifferent gonads**, glands that vaguely resemble both testes and ovaries. During the first month of gestation in humans, the indifferent gonads begin changing into either ovaries or testes.

Sex chromosomes direct sexual differentiation of the gonads

In mammals, the Y chromosome contains a gene called the **SRY gene** (for sex-determining *region* on the **Y** chromosome) that is responsible for the development of testes. If an individual has a Y chromosome, the cells of the indifferent gonad begin making the Sry protein. The Sry protein causes the cells in the core of the indifferent gonad to proliferate at the expense of the outer layers, and the indifferent gonad develops into a testis.

If the individual has no Y chromosome (or if it has a Y chromosome but the *SRY* gene is defective), no Sry protein is produced, and the indifferent gonad takes a different course: cells of the outer layers of the gonad proliferate more than those of the inner core, and an ovary forms. This early decision of whether to form testes or ovaries has a domino effect, setting off a chain of events that usually results in either a male or a female.

Gonadal hormones direct sexual differentiation of the body

For all mammals, including humans, the gonads secrete hormones to direct sexual differentiation of the body. Whereas developing testes produce several hormones, early ovaries produce very little hormone. If other cells of the embryo receive the testicular hormones, they begin developing masculine characters; if the cells are not exposed to testicular hormones, they develop feminine characters. Gene mapping has revealed that thousands of genes, in tissues throughout the body, are expressed differently in males and females because of differential exposure to sex steroids (van Nas et al., 2009).

sexual differentiation The process by which individuals develop either malelike or femalelike bodies and behavior.

sex determination The process by which the decision is made for a fetus to develop as a male or a female.

indifferent gonads The undifferentiated gonads of the early mammalian fetus, which will eventually develop into either testes or ovaries.

SRY gene A gene on the Y chromosome that directs the developing gonads to become testes. The name *SRY* stands for **s**ex-determining **r**egion on the **Y** chromosome.

wolffian duct A duct system in the embryo that will develop into male structures (the epididymis, vas deferens, and seminal vesicles) if testes are present in the embryo.

müllerian duct A duct system in the embryo that will develop into female reproductive structures (fallopian tubes, uterus, and upper vagina) if testes are not present.

anti-müllerian hormone (AMH) Also called *müllerian regression hormone*. A protein hormone secreted by the fetal testis that inhibits müllerian duct development.

We can chart masculine or feminine development by examining the structures that connect the gonads to the outside of the body. The conduits between the gametes and the exterior are quite different in adult males and females (see Figure 12.8), but at the embryonic stage all individuals have the precursor tissues of both systems. The early fetus has a genital tubercle that can form either a clitoris or a penis, as well as two sets of ducts that connect the indifferent gonads to the outer body wall: the **wolffian ducts** and the **müllerian ducts** (**Figure 12.13***a*). In females, the müllerian ducts develop into the fallopian tubes (or oviduct), uterus, and inner vagina (**Figure 12.13***b* **and** *c*, right), and only a remnant of the wolffian ducts remains. In males, hormones secreted by the testes orchestrate the converse outcome: the wolffian ducts develop into epididymis, vas deferens, and seminal vesicles (Figure 12.13*b* and *c*, left), while the müllerian ducts shrink to mere remnants.

The system is masculinized by two testicular secretions: testosterone, which promotes the development of the wolffian system, and **anti-müllerian hormone (AMH)**, which induces regression of the müllerian system. In the absence of testes to produce testosterone and AMH, the genital tract develops in a feminine pattern, in which the wolffian ducts regress and the müllerian ducts develop into components of the female internal reproductive tract.

Testosterone also masculinizes other, non-wolffian-derived structures. Testosterone acts on the fetal genitalia to form a scrotum and penis. These effects are

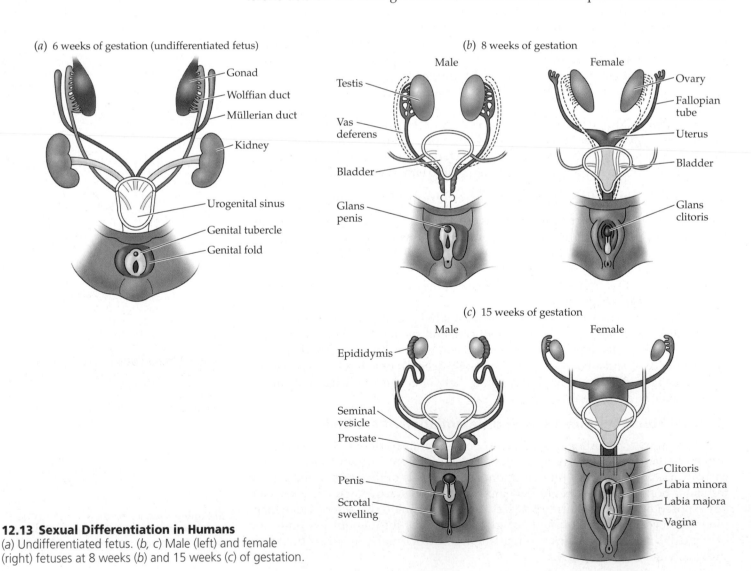

12.13 Sexual Differentiation in Humans
(*a*) Undifferentiated fetus. (*b, c*) Male (left) and female (right) fetuses at 8 weeks (*b*) and 15 weeks (*c*) of gestation.

aided by the local conversion of testosterone into a more potent androgen, **dihy-drotestosterone** (**DHT**), accomplished by an enzyme that is found in the genital skin, **5α-reductase**. We'll see later that without the local production of DHT, testosterone alone is able to masculinize the genitalia only partially. If androgens are absent altogether, the genital tissues grow into the female labia and clitoris.

Departures from the orderly sequence of sexual differentiation result in predictable changes in development

Some people have only one sex chromosome: a single X (embryos containing only single Y chromosomes do not survive). This genetic makeup results in **Turner's syndrome**, in which an apparent female has underdeveloped but recognizable ovaries, as you might expect because no *SRY* gene is available. In general, unless the indifferent gonad becomes a testis and begins secreting hormones, an immature mammal develops as a female in most respects. Immature ovaries, in Turner's syndrome, as in normal females, produce few hormones. So the sex chromosomes determine the sex of the gonad, and gonadal hormones then drive sexual differentiation of the rest of the body (**Figure 12.14a**). Later in life, both hormones and experience guide sexual differentiation and the development of gender identity (**Figure 12.14b**).

Sometimes XX individuals with well-formed ovaries are exposed to androgens in utero and, depending on the degree of exposure, they may be masculinized. For example, most fetal rats develop in the uterus sandwiched between two siblings. If a female is surrounded by brothers, some of the androgen from the siblings must reach the female because, although her gross appearance will be feminine at

dihydrotestosterone (DHT)   The 5α-reduced metabolite of testosterone; a potent androgen that is principally responsible for the masculinization of the external genitalia in mammalian sexual differentiation.

5α-reductase   An enzyme that converts testosterone into dihydrotestosterone (DHT).

Turner's syndrome   A condition seen in individuals carrying a single X chromosome but no other sex chromosome.

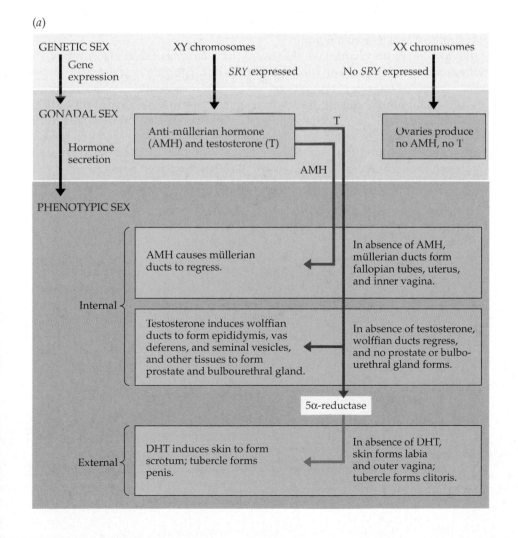

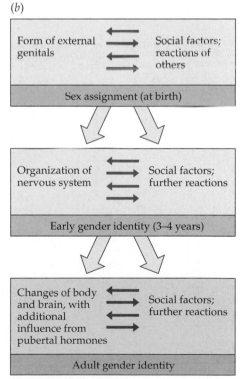

12.14 Sexual Differentiation and Gender Identity   (a) Genetic and hormonal mechanisms of embryonic sexual differentiation. (b) Steps toward adult gender identity in humans.

congenital adrenal hyperplasia (CAH)
Any of several genetic mutations that can result in exposure of a female fetus to adrenal androgens, which results in a clitoris that is larger than normal at birth.

intersex Referring to an individual with atypical genital development and sexual differentiation that generally resembles a form intermediate between typical male and typical female genitals.

cloacal exstrophy A rare medical condition in which XY individuals are born completely lacking a penis.

birth, her anogenital distance (the distance from the tip of the clitoris [or penis in a male] to the anus) will be slightly greater (i.e., more malelike) than that of a female developing between two sisters (Clemens et al., 1978).

In humans, **congenital adrenal hyperplasia** (**CAH**) can cause a developing female to be exposed to excess androgens before birth. In CAH, the adrenal glands fail to produce sufficient corticosteroids, producing instead considerable amounts of androgens. In XX individuals with this condition, the androgen levels produced are usually intermediate between those of normal females and males, and the newborn often has an **intersex** appearance: a phallus that is intermediate in size between a normal clitoris and a normal penis, and skin folds that resemble both labia and scrotum (**Figure 12.15**). Such individuals are readily recognizable at birth because, even in severe cases in which penis and scrotum appear well formed, no testes are present in the "scrotum"; instead, these individuals have normal abdominal ovaries, as you would expect. Once they're born, CAH children are given corticosteroid treatment to prevent further androgen production.

There is controversy over whether the best course of action for the parents of CAH girls is to opt for immediate surgical correction of the genitalia, or to wait until adulthood, when the CAH-affected individuals can decide for themselves whether to have surgery and what gender role to follow. CAH females are much more likely to be described by their parents (and themselves) as tomboys than are other girls, and they exhibit enhanced spatial abilities on cognitive tests that usually favor males (Berenbaum, 2001). In adulthood, most CAH females describe themselves as heterosexual, but they are more likely to report a homosexual orientation than are other women. Interestingly, as females with CAH grow older, the percentage who report homosexual attractions increases to as much as 40% (Dittmann et al., 1992), suggesting that they start off trying to follow the socially approved role of heterosexual female.

At the opening of the chapter we discussed the dilemma of **cloacal exstrophy**, in which genetic boys are born with functional testes but without penises. Historically in these cases, neonatal sex reassignment has been recommended on the assumption that unambiguously raising these children as girls, and surgically providing them with the appropriate external genitalia, could produce a more satisfactory psychosexual outcome. In a long-term follow-up of 14 such cases, however, Reiner and Gearhart (2004) found that 8 of these "girls" eventually declared themselves to be boys, even though several were unaware that they had ever been operated on. Although this finding indicates that prenatal exposure to androgens strongly pre-

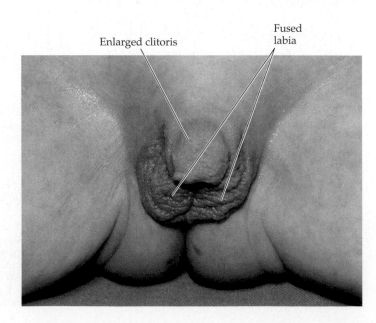

Enlarged clitoris

Fused labia

12.15 An Intersex Phenotype The partially masculinized genitalia of this CAH girl are the result of excessive androgen production by the adrenals.

disposes subsequent male gender identity, 5 of the remaining 6 cases were apparently content with their female identities, suggesting that socialization can also play a strong role. In most people, gender identity is presumably established by nature and nurture working in conjunction.

A dysfunctional androgen receptor can block the masculinization of males

An interesting demonstration of the influence of androgens on sexual differentiation is provided by the condition known as **androgen insensitivity syndrome** (**AIS**). The gene for the androgen receptor is found on the X chromosome. An XY individual whose X chromosome has a dysfunctional androgen receptor gene is thus incapable of producing normal androgen receptors, so their tissues cannot respond to androgenic hormones. The gonads of such people develop as normal testes (as directed by Sry), and the testes produce AMH (which inhibits müllerian duct structures) and plenty of testosterone.

In the absence of working androgen receptors, however, the wolffian ducts fail to develop and the external tissue forms labia and a clitoris. Such individuals look like other females at birth, and at puberty they develop breasts. (Breast development in humans appears to depend on the ratio of estrogenic to androgenic stimulation at puberty, and since androgen-insensitive individuals receive little androgenic *stimulation*, the functional estrogen-to-androgen ratio is high.)

12.16 Androgen-Insensitive Women Although these women have Y chromosomes and were born with testes, they also have complete androgen insensitivity. Therefore their bodies developed in a feminine fashion, and their behavior is feminine too. (Photos courtesy of Jane Goto and Cindy Stone.)

Women with AIS may be recognized when their menstrual cycles fail to commence because neither ovaries nor uterus are present to produce menstruation. Such women are infertile and, lacking a müllerian contribution, have a shallow vagina, but otherwise they look like other women (**Figure 12.16**) and, as we'll see in the next section, behave like other women. At the end of this chapter we will describe another mutation that causes some people to appear to change their sex (without surgery) at adolescence.

How Should We Define Gender—by Genes, Gonads, Genitals, or the Brain?

Most humans are either male or female, and whether we examine their chromosomes, gonads, external genitalia, or internal structures, we see a consistent pattern: each one is either feminine or masculine in character. Compared to physical features, behavior is much more difficult to define as feminine or masculine. The only behavior displayed *exclusively* by one sex is childbirth. Even behaviors that are very rarely displayed by members of one sex or the other (e.g., sexual assault by women or breast-feeding by men) occur sometimes in the unexpected sex. For behaviors that can be measured and studied experimentally in humans or other animals, we have to resort to group means and statistical tests to see the differences. Almost all individuals display some behaviors that are more common in the opposite sex.

Androgen-insensitive individuals show us that even physical features can be confusing criteria by which to judge sex (see Figure 12.16). Androgen-insensitive humans have male XY sex chromosomes and internal testes, and like most males they do not have fallopian tubes or a uterus. But they do have a vagina and

androgen insensitivity syndrome (AIS) A syndrome caused by a mutation of the androgen receptor gene that renders tissues insensitive to androgenic hormones like testosterone. Affected XY individuals are phenotypic females, but they have internal testes and regressed internal genital structures.

breasts, and in most respects their behavior is typical of females: they dress like females, they are attracted to and marry males, and perhaps most important, even after they learn the details of their condition they strongly identify themselves as women (Money and Ehrhardt, 1972). They are males in some respects, but females in others. If laws define marriage as only between a man and a woman, whom should these individuals, carrying a Y chromosome and born with testes, be allowed to marry?

As we will see next, there are also structural sex differences in parts of the central nervous system in humans and other animals. In androgen-insensitive rats, some brain regions are masculine and others are feminine. Thus, from a scientific standpoint we cannot regard an animal, especially a human, as simply masculine or feminine. Rather we must specify which structure or behavior we mean when we say it is typical of females or of males.

Gonadal Hormones Direct Sexual Differentiation of the Brain and Behavior

As scientists began discovering that testicular hormones direct masculine development of the body, behavioral researchers found evidence for a similar influence on the brain. A female guinea pig, like most other rodents, normally displays the lordosis posture in response to male mounting for only a short period around the time of ovulation, when her fertility is highest. If a male mounts her at other times, she does not show lordosis. An experimenter can induce the female to display lordosis by injecting ovarian steroids in the sequence they normally follow during ovulation—giving her estrogens for a few days and then progesterone. A few hours after the progesterone injection, the female will display lordosis in response to male mounting.

Phoenix et al. (1959) exposed female guinea pigs to testosterone in utero. As adults, these females did *not* show lordosis. Even if their ovaries were removed and they were given the steroidal regimen that reliably activated lordosis in normal females, these fetally androgenized females did not show lordosis. On the basis of these data, the researchers inferred that the same testicular steroids that masculinize the genitalia during early development also masculinize the developing brain. This type of lasting change due to steroid exposure is known as an **organizational effect**.

A steroid has an organizational effect only when present during a specific **sensitive period**, generally in early development. Unlike the transient nature of activational effects of hormones, which we discussed earlier, the organizational effects of hormones tend to be permanent. The exact boundaries of the sensitive period of development depend on which behavior and which species are being studied. For rats, androgens given just after birth (the **neonatal** period) can affect later behavior. Guinea pigs, however, must be exposed to androgens *before* birth for adult lordosis behavior to be affected. In mammals, puberty can be viewed as a second sensitive period; for example, steroid exposure during puberty causes the addition of new cells (an organizational effect) to sex-related brain regions of mice (Ahmed et al., 2008).

Early testicular secretions result in masculine behavior in adulthood

The organizational hypothesis provides a unitary explanation for sexual differentiation: a single steroid signal (androgen) masculinizes the body, the brain, and behavior. From this point of view the nervous system is just another type of tissue listening for the androgenic signal that will instruct it to organize itself in a masculine fashion. If the nervous system does not detect androgens, it will organize itself in a mostly feminine fashion. With their capacity to infiltrate the entire body, steroids have a unique ability to communicate a single message to disparate parts of the body to coordinate an integrated response.

organizational effect   A permanent alteration of the nervous system, and thus permanent change in behavior, resulting from the action of a steroid hormone on an animal early in its development.

sensitive period   The period during development in which an organism can be permanently altered by a particular experience or treatment.

neonatal   Referring to newborns.

What was demonstrated originally for the lordosis behavior of guinea pigs has been observed in a variety of vertebrate species and for many behaviors. Exposing female rat pups to testosterone either just before birth or during the first 10 days after birth greatly reduces their lordosis responsiveness as adults. This explains the observation that adult male rats show very little lordosis even when given estrogens and progesterone. However, male rats that are castrated during the first week of life display excellent lordosis responses in adulthood if injected with estrogens and progesterone. In rats, many behaviors are now known to be consistent with the organizational hypothesis: animals exposed to either endogenous or exogenous androgens early in life behave like males, whereas animals not exposed to androgens early in life behave like females.

In most cases, full masculine behavior requires androgens both in development (to organize the nervous system to enable the later behavior) and in adulthood (to activate that behavior). For example, the copulatory behavior of male rats can be quantified in terms of how often they mount a receptive female and how often such mounting results in intromission. Androgens must be present in adulthood to activate this behavior: adult males that have been castrated stop mounting in a few weeks; injecting them with testosterone eventually restores masculine copulatory behavior. Such androgen treatment has some effect on adult female rats as well, causing them to mount other females more often, but they rarely manage intromission of their phallus (the clitoris) into the stimulus female's vagina. Only animals exposed to androgen both in development and in adulthood show fully masculine behavior.

The estrogenic metabolites of testosterone masculinize the nervous system and behavior of rodents

Soon after the organizational hypothesis was published, researchers reported a paradoxical finding: when newborn female rats were treated with estrogens, they failed to show lordosis behavior in adulthood (Feder and Whalen, 1965). Researchers were very puzzled to find that neonatal treatment with a very small dose of estradiol, regarded at that time as a *female* hormone, could permanently *masculinize* these behaviors. The results were especially strange because during development, all rat fetuses are exposed to high levels of estrogens that originate in the mother and cross the placenta. If estrogens masculinize the developing brain, why aren't all females masculinized by maternal estrogens?

A closer look at the synthesis of steroid hormones reveals the answer. Testosterone and estradiol molecules are very closely related in structure. In fact, testosterone is the precursor for the manufacture of estradiol in the ovary. In a single chemical reaction, called **aromatization**, the enzyme **aromatase** converts testosterone to estradiol (and other androgens to other estrogens). The ovaries normally contain a great deal of aromatase, and the brain was found to have high levels of aromatase as well. From this evidence arose the **aromatization hypothesis**, which suggests that testicular androgens enter the brain and are converted there into estrogens, and that these estrogens are what masculinize the developing rodent nervous system.

Why, then, aren't the brains of females masculinized by maternal estrogens? A blood protein called **α-fetoprotein** binds estrogens and prevents them from entering the brain (Bakker et al., 2006). Although both male and female fetuses produce α-fetoprotein, this protein does not bind testosterone. The male rat's brain is masculinized when testosterone from his testes is conveyed by the bloodstream (unimpeded by α-fetoprotein) to his brain, where it is aromatized to an estrogen within individual neurons. This newly synthesized estrogen binds to local estrogen receptors, and the steroid-receptor complex regulates gene expression to cause the brain to develop in a masculine fashion (**Figure 12.17**). If no androgens are present, there can be no estrogenic action in the brain (because α-fetoprotein has blocked estrogens of peripheral origin), so the fetus develops in a feminine fashion. A lack of aromatase seems to play a role in the unusual sexual differentia-

aromatization The chemical reaction that converts testosterone to estradiol, and other androgens to other estrogens.

aromatase An enzyme that converts many androgens into estrogens.

aromatization hypothesis The hypothesis that testicular androgens enter the brain and are converted there into estrogens to masculinize the developing nervous system of some rodents.

α-fetoprotein A protein found in the plasma of fetuses. In rodents, α-fetoprotein binds estrogens and prevents them from entering the brain.

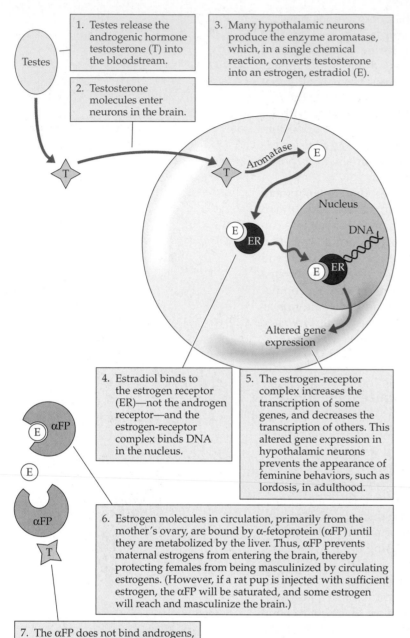

1. Testes release the androgenic hormone testosterone (T) into the bloodstream.

2. Testosterone molecules enter neurons in the brain.

3. Many hypothalamic neurons produce the enzyme aromatase, which, in a single chemical reaction, converts testosterone into an estrogen, estradiol (E).

4. Estradiol binds to the estrogen receptor (ER)—not the androgen receptor—and the estrogen-receptor complex binds DNA in the nucleus.

5. The estrogen-receptor complex increases the transcription of some genes, and decreases the transcription of others. This altered gene expression in hypothalamic neurons prevents the appearance of feminine behaviors, such as lordosis, in adulthood.

6. Estrogen molecules in circulation, primarily from the mother's ovary, are bound by α-fetoprotein (αFP) until they are metabolized by the liver. Thus, αFP prevents maternal estrogens from entering the brain, thereby protecting females from being masculinized by circulating estrogens. (However, if a rat pup is injected with sufficient estrogen, the αFP will be saturated, and some estrogen will reach and masculinize the brain.)

7. The αFP does not bind androgens, so testosterone is free to reach and masculinize the brain in male rats.

12.17 The Aromatization Hypothesis

sexual dimorphism The condition in which males and females show pronounced sex differences in appearance.

tion of the spotted hyena (**Box 12.1**). You may wonder why, if α-fetoprotein binds up estrogens, injecting rat pups with estrogen affects lordosis. The answer is that estrogen injections quickly flood the bloodstream with hormone molecules, saturating the α-fetoprotein, allowing many estrogen molecules to enter the brain.

The aromatization hypothesis was soon shown to be fully applicable to masculine copulatory behavior in rats. If a male rat was castrated at birth, it grew up to have a small penis and show few intromissions, even when given replacement testosterone in adulthood. If a male was castrated at birth and given the androgen dihydrotestosterone (DHT), which cannot be aromatized into an estrogen, it grew up to have a penis of normal size but still showed few or no intromissions when given testosterone. On the other hand, males castrated and treated with estrogens as newborns were able to achieve intromissions regularly when treated with androgens as adults, despite having very small penises (no larger than in untreated castrated males). Thus, it is hormonal masculinization of the *brain*, not the genitalia, that organizes male rat copulatory behavior.

In primates, including humans, aromatization does not seem to play an important role in masculinization of the nervous system (Grumbach and Auchus, 1999). The human brain produces significant quantities of aromatase, but men who have mutations in the aromatase gene—and are thus unable to produce aromatase—nonetheless have masculine gender identities and sexual development. Estrogen resistance caused by mutations in the gene encoding the α-estrogen receptor (one of the two known isoforms of estrogen receptors) similarly does not affect the development of masculine gender behavior in men. Finally, recall that people with AIS display feminine behavior, even though they produce lots of testosterone and have functional estrogen receptors. The details of the masculinization of the primate nervous system remain to be worked out, but hormonal masculinization must be accomplished through the androgen receptor rather than the estrogen receptor. Whichever specific steroid receptor is involved, many vertebrate species display distinct sex differences in the brain.

Several regions of the nervous system display prominent sexual dimorphism

The fact that male and female rats behave differently means that their brains must be different in some way, and according to the organizational hypothesis this difference results primarily from androgenic masculinization of the developing brain. The exact form of these neural sex differences can be very subtle; the same basic circuit of neurons will produce very different behavior if the pattern of synapses varies. Sex differences in the number of synapses were identified in the preoptic area (POA) of the hypothalamus as early as 1971 (Raisman and Field, 1971). But scientists soon found that there are much more obvious sex differences in the brain, in a wide variety of species, including humans. Darwin coined a term, **sexual dimorphism**, to describe the condition in which males and females show pronounced sex differences in appearance. Many examples of sexual dimorphism

BOX 12.1 The Paradoxical Sexual Differentiation of the Spotted Hyena

Scientists of antiquity believed that spotted hyenas were **hermaphrodites** (both male and female). The mistake is understandable because from birth the female hyena has a clitoris that is as large as the penis of males (as the photo shows), through which she urinates, receives semen, and gives birth. Female hyenas are also larger, more aggressive, and socially dominant over males.

What difference in the hyena's prenatal development causes this sexual monomorphism? In other mammals the placenta rapidly aromatizes androgens into estrogens; this conversion may be a way to protect the mother and fetal females from androgens produced by fetal males. But the spotted-hyena placenta is remarkably deficient in the aromatase enzyme (Licht et al., 1992).

Because the hyena mother produces large amounts of the androgen androstenedione (Glickman et al., 1987), and the placenta fails to convert the androstenedione to estrogens, all the fetuses receive considerable amounts of androgens, which may help account for

their masculine appearance. (However, female hyenas treated prenatally with androgen-blocking drugs still develop masculinized exteriors (Drea et al., 1998), suggesting that an additional mechanism must be involved.) One remarkable observation is that female pups, which are born with teeth, fight viciously with siblings immediately from birth. Sisters fight particularly violently, and in wild populations it is common for one pup to kill its sibling (L. G. Frank et al., 1991), at least during periods

when food is scarce (Smale et al., 1999). It remains to be established whether this extreme aggression is due to prenatal stimulation of the brain with androgens.

Even if the extreme aggressiveness of the female hyena is due to fetal androgens, females do mate with males, so their brains have not been made permanently unreceptive (as would happen in prenatally androgenized rats). Indeed, female hyenas seem to have a typically feminine SDN-POA (Fenstemaker et al., 1999) and SNB (Forger et al., 1996) (see the text). Just the same, mating in the spotted hyena is a tense affair: the female seems to just barely tolerate the male's proximity, and the male alternates between approaching and retreating from his alluring but dangerous mate. (Photograph courtesy of Stephen Glickman.)

hermaphrodite An individual possessing the reproductive organs of both sexes, either simultaneously or at different points in time.

---

in the nervous system were found, including differences in the number, size, and shape of neurons. Let's discuss a few well-known models.

SONG CONTROL REGIONS IN MALE SONGBIRDS   While studying the brain regions involved in singing in canaries and zebra finches (see Chapter 19 for details of the song system), Nottebohm and Arnold (1976) noticed that the nuclei controlling song are much larger in males than in females. In fact, the nuclei are five to six times larger in volume in males (which produce elaborate songs) than in females (which produce only simple calls).

Birds produce song through a specialized muscular organ called the **syrinx**, which controls the frequency of sounds produced by changing the tension of membranes around the air passage. The syrinx is controlled by the twelfth cranial nerve, which in turn is innervated primarily by a brain nucleus called the *robustus archistriatum* (*RA*). Literally and figuratively higher still, the *high vocal center* (*HVC*) exerts control over RA. As we would expect, lesions of RA or HVC disrupt singing, and electrical stimulation can elicit song snippets.

As the organizational hypothesis would suggest, steroid hormone masculinizes the brains of newly hatched zebra finches: exposing a hatchling female to either testosterone or estradiol causes HVC and RA to be larger in adulthood. If such a female is also given testosterone as an adult, the nuclei become larger still, and she sings much like a male zebra finch does (Gurney and Konishi, 1979).

syrinx The vocal organ in birds.

sexually dimorphic nucleus of the pre-optic area (SDN-POA) A region of the preoptic area that is five to six times larger in volume in male rats than in females.

spinal nucleus of the bulbocavernosus (SNB) A group of motoneurons in the spinal cord of rats that innervate striated muscles controlling the penis.

Because female zebra finches treated with androgens *only* in adulthood do not sing, we know that in zebra finches early hormone organizes a masculine song system and adult hormone activates the system to produce song. Singing in canaries, in contrast, relies only on *adult* effects of androgens; early exposure is unimportant. Female canaries start singing after a few weeks of androgen treatment in adulthood. The androgens cause HVC and RA to become larger, and their neurons grow and form new synaptic connections.

The difference in the hormonal control of song in zebra finches and canaries may be related to the ecological niche occupied by each. Zebra finches are ready to breed at any time of the year, awaiting only sufficient rainfall to provide the necessary food. Canaries, however, are seasonal breeders whose reproductive tracts shut down in the fall. The male canary song system tracks this ebb and flow: HVC and RA grow large in the spring, when the birds are singing and their testosterone levels are high, and shrink again in the fall, as testosterone levels and singing decline.

THE PREOPTIC AREA OF RATS Where else might there be neural sex differences? Roger Gorski et al. (1978) examined the preoptic area (POA) of the hypothalamus in rats because of earlier reports that the number of synapses in this region was different in males and females, and because lesions of the POA disrupt ovulatory cycles in female rats and reduce copulatory behavior in males. Sure enough, the investigators found a nucleus within the POA that has a much larger volume in males than in females.

This nucleus, dubbed the **sexually dimorphic nucleus of the POA (SDN-POA)**, is much more evident in male rats than in females (**Figure 12.18**). Like the song control nuclei in zebra finches, the SDN-POA conformed beautifully to the organizational hypothesis: males castrated at birth had much smaller SDN-POAs in adulthood, while females androgenized at birth had large, malelike SDN-POAs as adults. Castrating male rats in adulthood, however, did not alter the size of the SDN-POA. Thus, testicular androgens somehow alter the development of the SDN-POA, resulting in a nucleus permanently larger in males than in females (**Figure 12.19**).

In addition to fitting the organizational hypothesis, the rat SDN-POA conforms to the aromatization hypothesis: testosterone is converted to an estrogen in the brain and binds estrogen receptors to masculinize the nucleus. For example, XY rats that are androgen-insensitive (like the people with AIS discussed earlier), have testes but a feminine exterior. These rats have a masculine SDN-POA because their estrogen receptors are normal. Androgen-insensitive rats also do not display lordosis in response to estrogens and progesterone, because the testosterone that they secreted early in life was converted to an *estrogen* in the brain and masculinized their behavior (K. L. Olsen, 1979). Instead, the androgen-insensitive rats show normal male attraction to receptive females, with whom they may attempt to mate despite the lack of a penis (Hamson et al., 2009).

12.18 A Sex Difference in the Hypothalamus The sexually dimorphic nucleus of the preoptic area (SDN-POA) is much larger in male rats than in females. (Courtesy of Roger Gorski.)

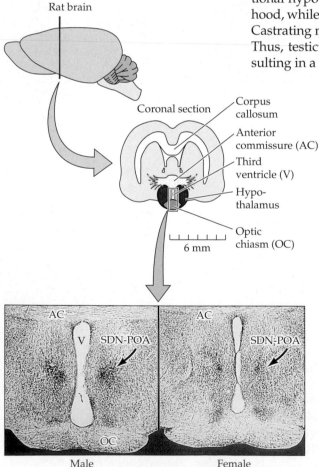

THE SPINAL CORD IN MAMMALS The birdsong work inspired a search for sexual dimorphism in the spinal cord, where neural elements controlling sexual responses should be different for males and females. In rats, the bulbocavernosus (BC) muscles that surround the base of the penis are innervated by motoneurons in the **spinal nucleus of the bulbocavernosus (SNB)**. Male rats have about 200 SNB cells, but females have far fewer motoneurons in this region of the spinal cord.

On the day before birth, female rats have BC muscles attached to the base of the clitoris that are nearly as large as those of males

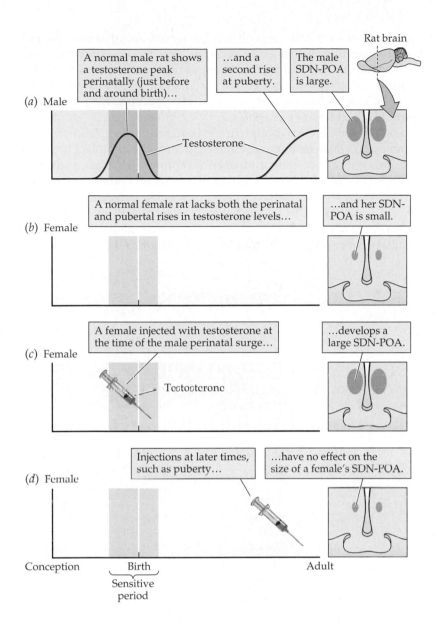

Rat brain

12.19 Sexually Dimorphic Nucleus of the Preoptic Area (SDN-POA) Testosterone can permanently enlarge the SDN-POA in rats, but only if given during a "sensitive period" early in life.

(a) Male

A normal male rat shows a testosterone peak perinatally (just before and around birth)…

…and a second rise at puberty.

The male SDN-POA is large.

Testosterone

(b) Female

A normal female rat lacks both the perinatal and pubertal rises in testosterone levels…

…and her SDN-POA is small.

(c) Female

A female injected with testosterone at the time of the male perinatal surge…

…develops a large SDN-POA.

Testosterone

(d) Female

Injections at later times, such as puberty…

…have no effect on the size of a female's SDN-POA.

Conception   Birth   Adult

Sensitive period

and that are innervated by motoneurons in the SNB region (Rand and Breedlove, 1987). In the days just before and after birth, however, many SNB cells die, especially in females (Nordeen et al., 1985), and the BC muscles of females die.

A single injection of androgens delivered to a newborn female rat permanently spares some SNB motoneurons and their muscles. Castration of newborn males, accompanied by prenatal blockade of androgen receptors, causes the BC muscles and SNB motoneurons to die as in females. Similarly, androgen-insensitive rats have very few SNB cells and no BC muscle, so aromatization seems to be unimportant for masculine development of this system.

Androgens act on the BC muscles to prevent their demise, and this sparing of the muscles causes the innervating SNB motoneurons to survive (Fishman et al., 1990; C. L. Jordan et al., 1991). The exact site within the BC muscle at which androgen has its effects is still unknown, as muscles consist of several different cell types. However, there is evidence that muscle fibers are *not* the cells responding to androgen; in transgenic male rats that express functional androgen receptors in muscle fibers but not in any other cell types, the BC muscle and SNB still die shortly after birth (Niel et al., 2009).

Recall from Chapter 7 that about half of all the spinal motoneurons produced early in development normally die, that the death of the motoneurons can be prevented if they are provided with enough muscle target, and that muscles are thought to provide a neurotrophic factor to keep the appropriate number of motoneurons alive into adulthood. For SNB motoneurons, the neurotrophic factor may resemble ciliary neurotrophic factor (CNTF) because in mice with the receptor for CNTF knocked out, SNB motoneurons die in males, despite the presence of androgens (**Figure 12.20**) (Forger et al., 1997).

The developmental rescue of SNB motoneurons is accomplished indirectly as a consequence of actions on muscle, but androgens can also directly affect the neurons themselves. SNB neurons contain androgen receptors and retain androgen sensitivity throughout life. In adulthood, androgen acts directly on the neurons to cause them to grow (Watson et al., 2001) and start producing substances to aid in the formation of new connections. For example, androgens directly stimulate SNB neurons to produce N-cadherin, a cell adhesion molecule that mediates the formation of new contacts between cells (D. A. Monks and Watson, 2001).

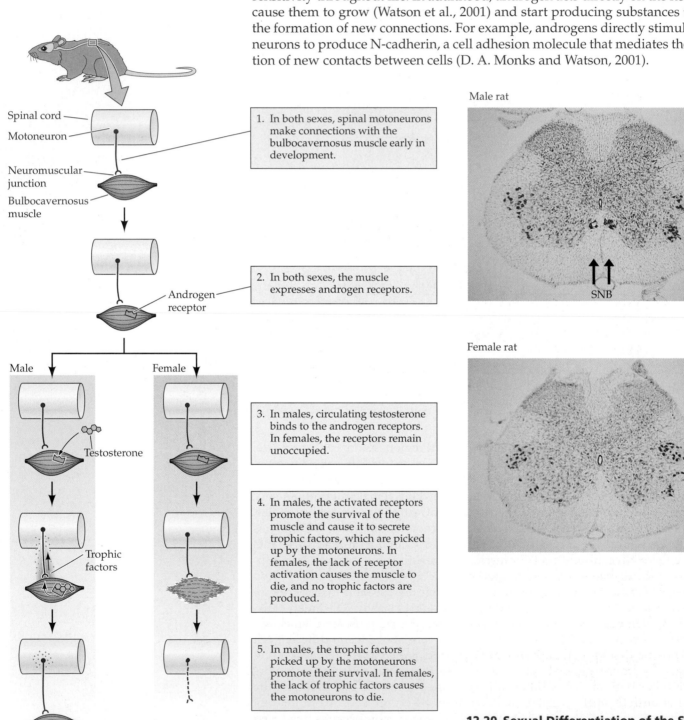

Spinal cord
Motoneuron

1. In both sexes, spinal motoneurons make connections with the bulbocavernosus muscle early in development.

Neuromuscular junction
Bulbocavernosus muscle

2. In both sexes, the muscle expresses androgen receptors.

Androgen receptor

Male   Female

Testosterone

3. In males, circulating testosterone binds to the androgen receptors. In females, the receptors remain unoccupied.

Trophic factors

4. In males, the activated receptors promote the survival of the muscle and cause it to secrete trophic factors, which are picked up by the motoneurons. In females, the lack of receptor activation causes the muscle to die, and no trophic factors are produced.

5. In males, the trophic factors picked up by the motoneurons promote their survival. In females, the lack of trophic factors causes the motoneurons to die.

Male rat

SNB

Female rat

12.20 Sexual Differentiation of the Spinal Nucleus of the Bulbocavernosus (SNB)

All male mammals have BC muscles, but in nonrodents the BC motoneurons are found in a slightly different spinal location and are known as **Onuf's nucleus**. Surprisingly, most female mammals retain a BC muscle into adulthood; in women, for example, the BC (or *constrictor vestibule*) helps constrict the vaginal opening. But, as in rodents, the system is profoundly sexually dimorphic. Men have larger BC muscles and more numerous Onuf's motoneurons, most likely determined by androgen exposure during fetal development (Forger and Breedlove, 1986, 1987).

Onuf's nucleus The human homolog of the spinal nucleus of the bulbocavernosus (SNB) in rats.

Social Influences Affect Sexual Differentiation of the Nervous System

Environmental factors of many sorts, ranging from the temperature and chemical composition of the environment to the social contacts that an individual receives, can potently modulate the masculinization produced by steroids. The development of the SNB offers a clear example. Newborn rat pups can neither urinate nor defecate on their own; the mother (dam) must lick the anogenital region of each pup to elicit a spinal reflex to empty the bladder and colon. (Incidentally, the dam ingests at least some of the wastes and thereby receives pheromones from the pups that adjust the composition of her milk as the pups mature. Another reason not to be a rat!)

Celia Moore et al. (1992) noticed that dams spend more time licking the anogenital regions of male pups than of females. If the dam is anosmic (unable to smell), she licks all the pups less and does not distinguish between males and females. Males raised by anosmic mothers thus receive less anogenital licking, and remarkably, fewer of their SNB cells survive the period around birth. The dam's stimulation of a male's anogenital region helps to masculinize his spinal cord.

On the one hand, this masculinization is still an effect of androgens because the dam identifies male pups by detecting androgen metabolites in their urine. On the other hand, this effect is clearly the result of a social influence: the dam treats a pup differently because he's a male and thereby masculinizes his developing nervous system. Perhaps this example illustrates the futility of trying to distinguish "biological" and "social" influences.

Attention from the dam has a different organizing effect on female rat pups. In adulthood, females who were licked frequently as pups show enhanced estrogen and oxytocin sensitivity in brain regions associated with maternal behavior, and they tend to be attentive mothers themselves. Females who are licked less as pups are less-attentive mothers later (Champagne et al., 2001).

What about humans? (No, no, not the licking part, the social influence part.) Humans are at least as sensitive to social influences as rats are. In every culture, most people treat boys and girls differently, even when they are infants. Such differential treatment undoubtedly has some effect on the developing human brain and contributes to later sex differences in behavior. Of course, this is a social influence, but testosterone instigated the influence when it induced the formation of a penis.

If prenatal androgens have even a very subtle effect on the fetal brain, then older humans interacting with a baby might detect such differences and treat the baby differently. Thus, originally subtle differences might be magnified by social experience, especially early in life. Such interactions of steroidal and social influences are probably the norm in the sexual differentiation of human behavior. Whether hormones or social influences determine human sexual orientation is our final topic.

Do Early Gonadal Hormones Masculinize Human Behaviors in Adulthood?

As with rats and other animals, the fact that men and women behave differently implies that something about them, probably something about their brains, must also be different. Indeed, many parts of the brain are different between men and

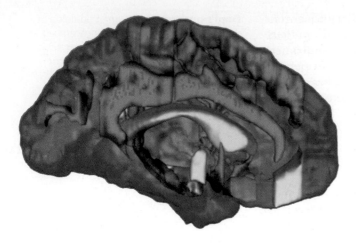

■ Structures that are larger in the healthy female brain, relative to cerebrum size

■ Structures that are larger in the healthy male brain, relative to cerebrum size

women (**Figure 12.21**). But are these sexual dimorphisms in the human brain caused by prenatal hormone exposure, as in other animals, or by social influences? In other words, does prenatal steroid exposure affect the adult behavior of humans? This is a tricky problem because, although prenatal androgens may or may not act on the human brain, they certainly act on the periphery.

If a female fetus is exposed to enough androgen, she will look entirely male on the outside at birth and will be treated by family and society as a male. So if she(?) behaves in a male-typical fashion in adulthood, we won't know whether that behavior is due to a direct effect of androgens on the brain, or is a consequence of what androgens did to the outside of the body and resultant changes in the behavior of others. We saw earlier that CAH females, exposed prenatally to androgens, play more like boys than other females do and are more likely to be lesbians in adulthood. Do they exhibit those behaviors because early androgens partially masculinized their brains? Or did their ambiguous genitalia cause parents and others to treat them differently from infancy? Let's examine another syndrome that presents a similar conundrum.

Some people seem to change sex at puberty

Babies are occasionally born with a rare genetic mutation that disables the enzyme (5α-reductase) that converts testosterone to dihydrotestosterone (DHT). An XY individual with this condition will develop testes and normal male internal reproductive structures (because testosterone and AMH function normally), but the external genitalia will fail to masculinize (**Figure 12.22**). The reason for this failure is that the genital epithelium, which normally possesses 5α-reductase, is unable to amplify the androgenic signal by converting the testosterone to the more active DHT. Consequently, the phallus is only slightly masculinized and resembles

(*a*) Newborn

(*b*) Adolescent

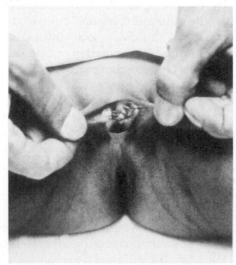
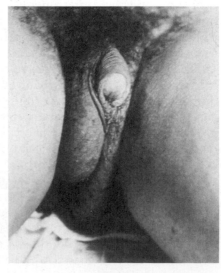

12.22 *Guevedoces*   In the Dominican Republic, some individuals, called *guevedoces*, are born with ambiguous genitalia (*a*) and are raised as girls. At puberty, however, the phallus grows into a recognizable penis (*b*), and the individuals begin acting like young men. (Courtesy of Julianne Imperato-McGinley.)

a large clitoris, and the genital folds resemble labia, although they contain the testes. Usually there is no vaginal opening.

A particular village in the Dominican Republic is home to several families that carry the mutation causing 5α-reductase deficiency. Children born with this appearance seem to be regarded as girls in the way they are dressed and raised (Imperato-McGinley et al., 1974). At puberty, however, the testes increase androgen production, and the external genitalia become more fully masculinized. The phallus grows into a small but recognizable penis; the body develops narrow hips and a muscular build, without breasts; and the individuals begin acting like young men. The villagers have nicknamed such individuals **guevedoces**, meaning "eggs (testes) at 12 (years)." These men never develop facial beards, but they usually have girlfriends, indicating that they are sexually interested in women.

There are two competing explanations for why these people raised as girls later behave as men. First, prenatal testosterone may masculinize their brains; thus, despite being raised as girls, when they reach puberty their brains lead them to seek out females for mates. This explanation suggests that the social influences of growing up—assigning oneself to a gender and mimicking role models of that gender, as well as gender-specific playing and dressing—are unimportant for later behavior and sexual orientation. An alternative explanation is that early hormones have no effect—that this culture simply recognizes and teaches children that some people can start out as girls and change to boys later. If so, then the social influences on gender role development might be completely different in this society from those in ours. Of course, a third option is that both mechanisms contribute to the final outcome; for example, early androgens may affect the brain to masculinize the child's behavior and predispose later sexual orientation toward females, and these masculine qualities of the child could alter the behavior of parents and others in ways that promote the emergence of male gender identity as the child develops.

Seen alone, the studies of people with 5α-reductase deficiency and CAH leave room for doubt about whether prenatal hormones influence sexual orientation in humans. But these are just part of a growing body of evidence that prenatal testosterone masculinizes the fetal brain to influence sexual orientation in humans, as we'll see next.

What determines a person's sexual orientation?

There are two classes of possible influence on human sexual orientation. One class encompasses the sociocultural influences that may instruct developing children about how they should behave when they grow up (think of all those charming princes wooing girls in Disney movies). The other class of influences includes the endogenous factors—especially differences in fetal exposure to testosterone—that could organize developing brains to be attracted to females or males in adulthood. For that great majority of people who are heterosexual, there's no way to distinguish between these two influences, because they both favor the same outcome. However, people who are homosexual provide a test. Given that they seem to have ignored society's prescription, is there evidence that early hormones are responsible for making some people gay? If so, then maybe hormones play a role in heterosexual development too.

Certainly, homosexual behavior is seen in other species—mountain sheep, swans, gulls, and dolphins, to name a few (Bagemihl, 1999). Interestingly, homosexual behavior is more common among anthropoid primates—apes and monkeys—than in prosimian primates like lemurs and lorises (Vasey, 1995), so greater complexity of the brain may make homosexual behavior more likely. In the most studied animal model—sheep—some rams consistently refuse to mount females but prefer to mount other rams. There is growing evidence of differences in the POA (preoptic area) of "gay" versus "straight" rams (Roselli et al., 2004), apparently organized by testosterone acting on the brain via neuronal androgen receptors during fetal development (Roselli and Stormshak, 2009).

guevedoces Literally "eggs at 12" (in Spanish). A nickname for individuals who are raised as girls but at puberty change appearance and begin behaving as boys.

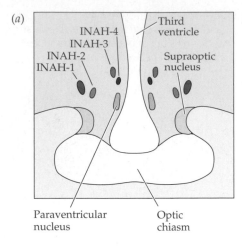

(a)

INAH-4
INAH-3
INAH-2
INAH-1

Third
ventricle

Supraoptic
nucleus

Paraventricular
nucleus

Optic
chiasm

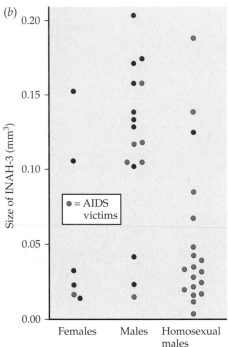

(b)

Size of INAH-3 (mm³)

● = AIDS
victims

0.20
0.15
0.10
0.05
0.00

Females   Males   Homosexual
males

12.23 Interstitial Nuclei of the Anterior Hypothalamus (a) These nuclei in humans are seen in the same part of the hypothalamus where the SDN-POA is found in rats. (b) INAH-3 is larger in men than in women, and larger in straight men than in gay men. Although most of the gay men in this study had died of AIDS, note that heterosexual men who died of AIDS still had a larger INAH-3, indicating that the differences between straight and gay men are not due to AIDS.

Simon LeVay (1991) performed postmortem examinations of the POA in humans and found a nucleus (the third interstitial nucleus of the anterior hypothalamus, or INAH-3) (**Figure 12.23a**) that is larger in men than in women, and larger in heterosexual men than in homosexual men (**Figure 12.23b**). All but one of the gay men in the study had died of AIDS, but the brain differences could not be due to AIDS pathology, because the straight men with AIDS still had a significantly larger INAH-3 than did the gay men. To the press and the public, this finding sounded like strong evidence that sexual orientation is "built in." It's still possible, however, that early social experience affects the development of INAH-3 to determine later sexual orientation. Furthermore, sexual experiences as an adult could affect INAH-3 structure, so the smaller nucleus in some homosexual men may be the *result* of their homosexuality, rather than the *cause*, as LeVay himself was careful to point out.

In women, purported markers of fetal androgen exposure—otoacoustic emissions (McFadden and Pasanen, 1998) (see Chapter 9), finger length patterns (T. J. Williams et al., 2000), patterns of eye blinks (Rahman, 2005), and skeletal features (J. T. Martin and Nguyen, 2004)—all indicate that lesbians, as a group, were exposed to slightly more fetal androgen than were heterosexual women. These findings suggest that fetal exposure to androgen increases the likelihood that a girl will grow up to be gay. These studies indicate considerable overlap between the two groups, so fetal androgens cannot account for all lesbians. Likewise, the finding that homosexual people are more likely to be left-handed than is the general population (Lalumiere et al., 2000) suggests that androgens cannot be the whole story, because there is no known effect of early androgens on handedness. However, handedness does seem to be established early in life, so this correlation, too, indicates that early events influence adult orientation.

Those same markers of fetal androgen do not provide for a consensus about gay versus straight men; some markers suggest that gay men were exposed to less prenatal testosterone, and others suggest that they were exposed to more prenatal testosterone than were straight men. However, another nonsocial factor influences the probability of homosexuality in men: the more older brothers a boy has, the more likely he is to grow up to be gay (Blanchard et al., 2006). Your first guess might be that this is a social influence of older brothers, but it turns out that older stepbrothers that are raised with the boy have no effect, while biological brothers (sharing the same mother) increase the probability of the boy's being gay *even if they are raised apart* (Bogaert, 2006). Furthermore, this "fraternal birth order effect" is seen in boys who are moderately right-handed, but not in left-handed or extremely right-handed boys (Blanchard et al., 2006; Bogaert, 2007), providing another indication of differences in early development between the two sexual orientation groups. Statistically, the birth order effect is strong enough to estimate that about one in every seven homosexual men in North America—about a million people—are gay because their mother had sons before them (Cantor et al., 2002).

Genetic studies in fruit flies (*Drosophila melanogaster*) have identified genes that control whether courtship behaviors are directed toward same- or opposite-sex individuals (Grosjean et al., 2008; S. D. Zhang and Odenwald, 1995), although no one knows the extent to which similar mechanisms are operational in mammals, including humans. Still, there is good evidence that human sexual orientation is at least partly heritable, reinforcing the notion that both biological and social factors have a say. About 50% of variability in human sexual orientation is accounted for by genetic factors, leaving ample room for early social influences. Monozygotic twins, who have exactly the same genes, do not always have the same sexual orientation (J. M. Bailey et al., 1993). In the unusual case of two nontwin brothers who are both homosexual, genetic evidence suggests that they are much more likely than chance would dictate to have both inherited the same X chromosome region (called Xq28) from their mother (Hamer et al., 1993); but again the genetic explanation accounts for only some, not all, of the cases. It seems clear that there are several different pathways to homosexuality.

From a political viewpoint, the controversy—whether sexual orientation is determined before birth or determined by early social influences—is irrelevant. Laws and prejudices against homosexuality are based primarily on religious views that homosexuality is a sin that some people "choose." But almost all homosexual and heterosexual men report that, from the beginning, their interests and romantic attachments matched their adult orientation. So any social influence would have to be acting very early in life and without any conscious awareness (do you remember "choosing" whom to find attractive?). Furthermore, despite extensive efforts, no one has come up with a reliable way to change sexual orientation (LeVay, 1996). These findings, added to evidence that older brothers and prenatal androgens affect the probability of being gay, have convinced most scientists that we do not choose our sexual orientation.

SUMMARY

SEXUAL BEHAVIOR

Reproductive Behavior Can Be Divided into Four Stages

- Reproductive behaviors are divided into four stages: **sexual attraction, appetitive behavior, copulation**, and **postcopulatory behavior**, including parental behaviors in some species. **Review Figure 12.1**

- Although reproductive behaviors vary widely in form between species, their ultimate goal is the successful fusion of male and female **gametes**, and the generation of a maximal number of viable offspring.

The Neural Circuitry of the Brain Regulates Reproductive Behavior

- In the female rat, a steroid-sensitive **lordosis** circuit extends from the **ventromedial hypothalamus** (**VMH**) to the spinal cord, via the **periaqueductal gray** and **medullary reticular formation**.

- In the male rat, neurons of the **medial preoptic area** (**MPOA**) exert descending control of sexual behavior, integrating inputs from the **medial amygdala** and **vomeronasal organ** (**VNO**). These projections, via ventral midbrain and brainstem nuclei, terminate on motoneurons involved in copulation. **Review Figure 12.6**

Pheromones Guide Reproductive Behavior in Many Species

- Sex steroids act on circuits within the nervous system to coordinate reproductive behaviors with gonadal functions such

as **ovulation**. In many species, **pheromone** signals between partners coordinate reproductive behavior.

The Hallmark of Human Sexual Behavior Is Diversity

- Human copulatory behavior is remarkably varied. Most men show a single copulatory pattern; women show much more varied sexual responses. The classic model of sexuality emphasizes four stages: (1) increasing excitement, (2) plateau, (3) **orgasm**, and (4) resolution. Modern models identify emotional factors and desire as crucial aspects of female sexuality, whereas male sexuality may involve feelings of power. However, male and female sexuality overlap and are heavily influenced by sociocultural factors. **Review Figure 12.9, Web Activities 12.1 and 12.2**

- In humans, very low levels of testosterone are required for either men or women to display a full interest in sex, but additional testosterone has no additional effect. Therefore, there is no correlation between circulating androgen levels and reproductive behaviors in men. Nor is there any strong correlation between copulatory behavior and stage of the menstrual cycle in women.

- There is evidence both for and against the idea that humans respond to pheromonal cues, so pheromones play only a subtle role, if any, in human sexuality.

Many Vertebrates Depend on Their Parents for Survival

- Parental behavior is a crucial aspect of reproduction and is significantly influenced by hormones. Brain mechanisms for parental behavior show considerable overlap with mechanisms implicated in sexual behavior. **Review Figures 12.11 and 12.12**

SEXUAL DIFFERENTIATION

The Sex of an Individual Is Determined Early in Life

■ In birds and mammals, genetic sex determines whether testes or ovaries develop, and hormonal secretions from the gonads determine whether the rest of the body, including the brain, develops in a feminine or masculine fashion. In the presence of testicular secretions, a male develops; in the absence of testicular secretions, a female develops. **Review Figures 12.13 and 12.14**

How Should We Define Gender—by Genes, Gonads, Genitals, or the Brain?

■ People can be classified on the basis of their sex chromosomes, their genitalia, or the gender they identify with. The options within each of these categories are complex and sometimes overlap, so attempts to classify all individuals into just two gender groups oversimplify the real situation.

Gonadal Hormones Direct Sexual Differentiation of the Brain and Behavior

■ The brains of vertebrates are masculinized by the presence of testicular steroids during early development. Such organizational effects of steroids permanently alter the structure and function of the brain and therefore permanently alter the behavior of the individual. **Review Figure 12.17, Web Activity 12.3**

■ Among the prominent examples of **sexual dimorphism** in the nervous system, gonadal steroids have been shown to alter characteristics such as neuronal survival, structure, and synaptic connections. **Review Figures 12.18–12.20**

Social Influences Affect Sexual Differentiation of the Nervous System

■ Several regions of the human brain are sexually dimorphic. However, we do not know whether these dimorphisms are generated by fetal steroid levels or by sex differences in the early social environment.

Do Early Gonadal Hormones Masculinize Human Behaviors in Adulthood?

■ Although no perfect animal model of sexual orientation has been developed, all research indicates that sexual orientation is determined early in life and, especially in men, is not a matter of individual choice. **Review Figure 12.23**

Go to **www.biopsychology.com** for study questions, quizzes, key terms, and other resources.

Recommended Reading

Adkins-Regan, E. (2005). *Hormones and animal social behavior.* Princeton, NJ: Princeton University Press.

Becker, J. B., Berkeley, K. J., Geary, N., Hampson, E., and Herman, J. P. (2007). *Sex differences in the brain: From genes to behavior.* Oxford: Oxford University Press.

Becker, J. B., Breedlove, S. M., Crews, D., and McCarthy, M. M. (2002). *Behavioral endocrinology* (2nd ed.). Cambridge, MA: MIT Press.

Fausto-Sterling, A. (2000). *Sexing the body.* New York: Basic Books.

LeVay, S., and Baldwin, J. (2008). *Human sexuality* (3rd ed.). Sunderland, MA: Sinauer.

Miller, G. (2000). *The mating mind: How sexual choice shaped the evolution of human nature.* New York: Doubleday.

Nelson, R. J. (2005). *An introduction to behavioral endocrinology* (3rd ed.). Sunderland, MA: Sinauer.

CHAPTER 13

Homeostasis: Active Regulation of Internal States

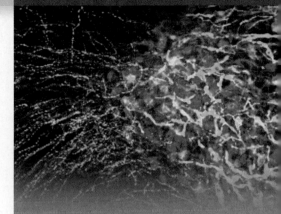

A Love-Hate Relationship with Food

Six-hundred ninety calories—that's what this milkshake represented to me.

But to Kitty it was the object of her deepest fear and loathing. "You're trying to make me fat," she said in a high-pitched, distorted voice that made the hairs on the back of my neck stand up. She rocked, clutching her stomach, chanting over and over: "I'm a fat pig. I'm so fat."

— *Harriet Brown, "One Spoonful at a Time,"*
New York Times Magazine, November 6, 2006

How does food become an object of fear and loathing for some people? In her article, Harriet Brown paints a harrowing portrait of the "demon" of anorexia nervosa that seemed to possess her daughter, Kitty. This disorder completely deranges the sufferer's relationship with food. Obsession with food, lost appetite, starvation, fear, and distorted self-perception are hallmarks of anorexia nervosa. In Kitty's case, these symptoms developed like a gathering storm, from the first hints of unusual fascination with food, poring over *Gourmet* magazine, to the loss of appetite and relentless exercising, until the day when 14-year-old Kitty lay in bed a mere 71 pounds, every bone sharply evident beneath her skin, her hair falling out in clumps, her breath laden with the pearlike scent of ketones as her body metabolized itself for fuel. Still, Kitty considered herself "a fat pig," sobbing and terrified at the prospect of drinking a milkshake or eating a piece of birthday cake. Kitty's parents faced uncertainty and difficult decisions.

What was the best way to strike back at the demon?

Millions of years of evolution have endowed our bodies with complex physiological mechanisms, and multiple backup systems, devoted to producing a stable internal environment. Food energy, body temperature, fluid balance, fat storage, nutrients—all of the conditions required for optimal cellular functioning—are carefully regulated, and although we may be unaware of some of these processes, the nervous system is intimately involved in every stage.

Placed in the context of modern society, some of these ancient systems are creating new challenges for humans. For example, the current epidemic of obesity—and associated diseases like diabetes, cardiovascular disease, and cancer—presents a heavy burden for the health care systems of many nations. Identifying the cultural and physiological roots of obesity, and developing safe and effective methods for controlling it, is an urgent concern. The physiological and behavioral processes governing the internal environment, and their role when things go wrong, are our topic in this chapter.

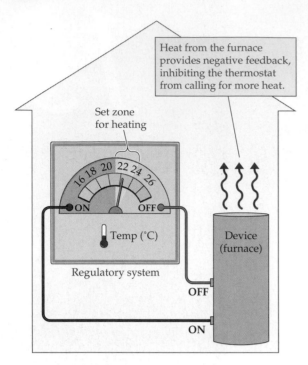

Heat from the furnace provides negative feedback, inhibiting the thermostat from calling for more heat.

Set zone for heating

16 18 20 22 24 26

ON   OFF

Temp (°C)

Device (furnace)

Regulatory system

OFF

ON

13.1 Negative Feedback   The thermostatically controlled heating system found in homes is an example of a negative feedback system. All such systems have a sensor (in this example a thermometer) to monitor the variable (temperature), and a device (the furnace) to change the variable (e.g., by heating the room). The changed variable (heat) provides a negative feedback signal to the sensor, turning the system off.

redundancy   The property of having a particular process, usually an important one, monitored and regulated by more than one mechanism.

homeostatic   Referring to the active process of maintaining a particular physiological parameter relatively constant.

negative feedback   The property by which some of the output of a system feeds back to reduce the effect of input signals.

set point   The point of reference in a feedback system. An example is the setting of a thermostat.

set zone   The range of a variable that a feedback system tries to maintain.

Homeostasis Maintains Internal States within a Critical Range

Because warmth, water, and food are vital and scarce, elaborate physiological systems evolved to monitor and maintain them. One hallmark of these systems is **redundancy**: just as human engineers equip critical equipment with several failsafe backup systems, our bodies tend to have multiple parallel mechanisms for monitoring our stores, conserving remaining supplies, obtaining new resources, and shedding excesses. Loss of function in one part of the system usually can be compensated for by the remaining parts. This redundancy attests to the importance of maintaining our inner environment, but it also makes it difficult for us to figure out exactly how the body regulates temperature, water balance, and food intake under normal conditions. Another hallmark of these regulatory, or **homeostatic**, systems is that they rely on the organism's behavior to regulate and to acquire more heat, water, or food. The nervous system coordinates these actions.

The homeostatic mechanisms that regulate temperature, body fluids, and metabolism are primarily **negative feedback** systems. In each case, deviation from a desired value, called the **set point**, triggers a compensatory action of the system. A simple analogy is the setting of a household thermostat (**Figure 13.1**): a temperature drop below the set point activates the thermostat, which turns on the heating system. (We already discussed negative feedback systems in connection with the regulation of hormone secretion in Chapter 5.) In general, there is a degree of tolerance in the feedback system equivalent to a small range between the "turn on" and "turn off" signals. Without this tolerance the system would be going on and off too frequently. So for most systems there is really a **set zone** rather than a set point.

The setting of the thermostat in your home can be changed; for example, it can be turned down at night to save energy. Similarly, although the body temperature for most mammals is usually held within a narrow range—about 36°C–38°C (97°F–100°F)—most mammals reduce their temperature during sleep. Our bodies also integrate the demands for nutrients and water to result in a set range of body weight that is often remarkably narrow. Later in the chapter we will see examples of animals defending their body weight—that is, maintaining a particular weight in the face of physiological challenges.

The regulation of our internal resources is complicated by the fact that staying alive requires us to use up some of them. Our homeostatic mechanisms are continually challenged by these unavoidable losses (sometimes called *obligatory losses*), which require us to gain and conserve heat, water, and food constantly.

Temperature Regulation

Why do we feel so uncomfortable when we're hot or cold? That's nature's way of telling us that body temperature is a vital concern.

Body Temperature Is a Critical Condition for All Biological Processes

The rate of chemical reactions is temperature-dependent. The enzyme systems of mammals and birds are most efficient within a narrow range around 37°C. At lower temperatures, reactions slow down, and some stop altogether. At higher temperatures, protein molecules fold improperly and thus do not function as they should. At very high temperatures, tissue proteins break down and then fuse again in a haphazard manner; and if the tissue in question happens to be tasty, we say it is *cooked*. Brain cells are especially sensitive to high temperatures. A prolonged

(a)

(b)
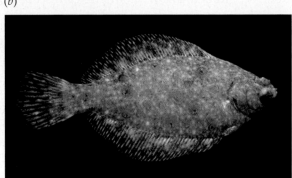

(c)

13.2 Braving the Cold Mealworm beetles (a) and winter flounder (b) are two species that sometimes have body temperatures below 0°C. These animals produce an "antifreeze" protein in body fluids to prevent ice crystals from forming in their cell membranes. Through mechanisms not yet understood, the arctic ground squirrel (c) is also able to withstand subzero temperatures during hibernation.

high fever can cause brain centers that regulate heart rate and breathing to die, killing the rest of the patient too.

At very low temperatures, the lipid bilayers that make up cellular membranes become so disrupted by the formation of ice molecules that they cannot re-form when thawed. Some animals that cannot avoid subfreezing temperatures—for example, some species of fishes and beetles (**Figure 13.2**)—produce "antifreeze" consisting of special protein molecules that suppress the formation of ice crystals and prevent damage to membranes (Harding et al., 2003; Liou et al., 2000; C. B. Marshall et al., 2004).

Some Animals Generate Heat; Others Must Obtain Heat from the Environment

Although popular terminology distinguishes between *warm-blooded* animals (mainly mammals and birds) and *cold-blooded* animals (all the others), this description is inaccurate. Instead, scientists favor a distinction between **endotherms** (from the Greek *endon*, "within"), which generate most of their own heat through internal processes; and **ectotherms** (from the Greek *ektos*, "outside"), which get most of their heat from the environment. Contrary to popular belief, ectotherms do not just passively adopt the local ambient temperature. Like endotherms, ectotherms actively regulate their body temperature, but they do so through behavioral means, such as by moving to warmer or cooler locations. And both endotherms and ectotherms will seek out a preferred environmental temperature, which varies from species to species.

The advantages of endothermy come at a cost

No one knows whether endothermy arose in a common ancestor of the birds and mammals or arose separately in these two lines. What we do know is that endotherms pay substantial costs for maintaining a high body temperature and keeping it within narrow limits. Much food energy is used up in the production of heat, and elaborate regulatory systems are required.

Why evolve such a complicated and costly system, compared to the more economical system of ectotherms? One obvious advantage is greater independence from environmental conditions, allowing endothermic animals to forage in a wider variety of settings. A second advantage of endothermy involves the use of oxygen. Ectotherms rely on bursts of intense *anaerobic* muscular activity—activity stoked by chemical reactions that postpone the requirement for oxygen—so after a few minutes, the animal must rest and repay the oxygen debt. But because they need to constantly stoke the chemical reactions through which they generate heat (discussed next), endotherms evolved a greater capacity for oxygen utilization. This improved oxygen capacity enables intense *aerobic* muscular activity—activity without an oxygen debt—over much longer periods of time (A. F. Bennett and

endotherm An animal whose body temperature is regulated chiefly by internal metabolic processes. Examples include mammals and birds.

ectotherm An animal whose body temperature is regulated by, and whose heat comes mainly from, the environment. Examples include snakes and bees.

metabolism The breakdown of complex molecules into smaller molecules.

kilocalorie (kcal) A measure of energy commonly applied to food; formally defined as the quantity of heat required to raise the temperature of 1 kg of water by 1°C.

brown fat Also called *brown adipose tissue*. A specialized type of fat tissue that generates heat through intense metabolism.

shivering Rapid involuntary muscle contractions that generate heat in hypothermic animals.

Ruben, 1979). Ectotherms can escape from and sometimes even pursue endotherms over short distances, but in a long-distance race the endotherm will always win.

Endotherms generate heat through metabolism

The utilization of food by the body is known as **metabolism**. The breaking of chemical bonds in food releases energy as heat; this food energy is measured in **kilocalories** (**kcal**) (1 kcal, often but incorrectly called a *calorie*, is enough heat to raise the temperature of a liter of water 1°C). An adult human may generate 600 kcal per hour when exercising strenuously, but only 60 kcal per hour when resting.

When the human body is at rest, about a third of the heat it generates is produced by the brain. As body activity increases, the heat production of the brain does not rise much, but that of the muscles can increase nearly tenfold; so when we are active, our bodies produce a much higher percentage of our body heat. Muscles and gasoline engines have about the same efficiency; each produces about four or five times as much heat as mechanical work. Some of the main ways the human body gains, conserves, and dissipates heat are shown in **Figure 13.3**.

The rate of heat production can be adjusted to suit conditions, by altering the metabolic rate of *thermogenic* ("heat-making") tissues. Located in the back and around organs of the trunk, **brown fat** (adipose tissue that looks brown because it is full of mitochondria) breaks down molecules to produce large amounts of heat, under the control of the sympathetic nervous system. A more familiar thermogenic tissue is the skeletal muscle that cloaks your body: when your body temperature drops below about 36°C, the nervous system instructs muscles to commence **shivering**. The fivefold increase in oxygen uptake that accompanies extreme shivering shows how metabolically intense this response is.

The rate at which an animal loses heat is directly proportional to the ratio of its surface area to its volume or weight (**Table 13.1**). Small animals with large surface-to-volume ratios, such as the shrew, must eat nearly constantly and maintain high

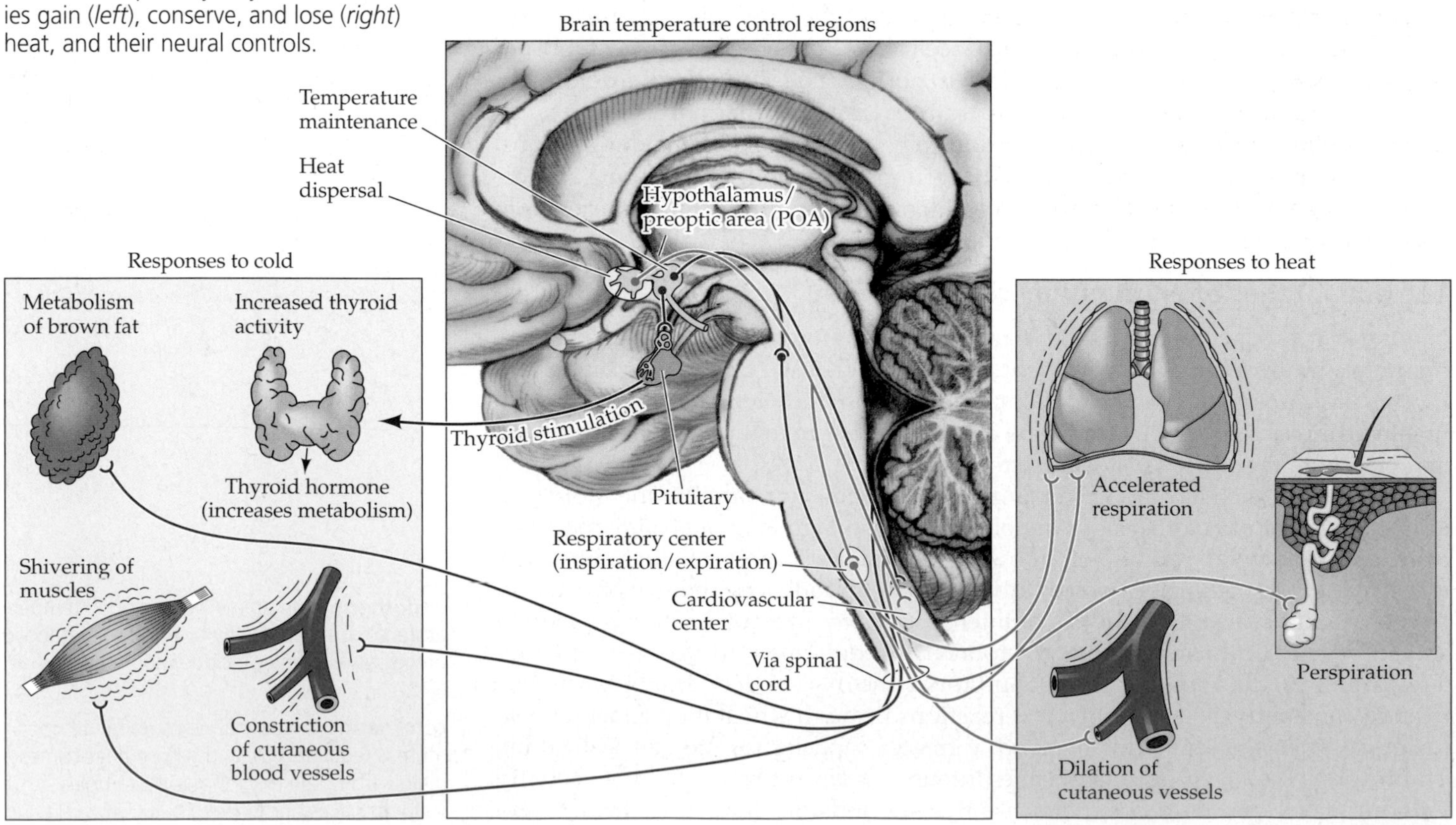

13.3 Thermoregulation in Humans
Some of the primary ways that our bodies gain (*left*), conserve, and lose (*right*) heat, and their neural controls.

Brain temperature control regions

Temperature maintenance

Heat dispersal

Hypothalamus/ preoptic area (POA)

Responses to cold

Metabolism of brown fat

Increased thyroid activity

Thyroid stimulation

Thyroid hormone (increases metabolism)

Pituitary

Shivering of muscles

Respiratory center (inspiration/expiration)

Cardiovascular center

Via spinal cord

Constriction of cutaneous blood vessels

Responses to heat

Accelerated respiration

Perspiration

Dilation of cutaneous vessels

TABLE 13.1 Body Size and Heat Balance of Some Birds and Mammals

Species	Body weight (kg)	Body surface (m²)	Surface-to-weight ratio (m²/kg)	Energy utilization per day		
				Total (kcal)	Per unit of body weight (kcal/kg)	Per unit of body surface (kcal/m²)
Canary	0.016	0.006	0.375	5	310	760
Rat	0.2	0.03	0.15	25	130	830
Pigeon	0.3	0.04	0.13	30	100	670
Cat	3.0	0.2	0.07	150	50	750
Human	60	1.7	0.03	1,500	25	850
Elephant	3,600	24	0.007	47,000	13	2,000

metabolic rates in order to maintain the target body temperature. A large animal, like an elephant, has a much lower surface-to-volume ratio, and because it loses heat more slowly, it can afford a lower metabolic rate per gram of body weight.

Which Behaviors Can Adjust Body Temperature?

Ectotherms generate little heat through metabolism and therefore must rely heavily on behavioral methods to regulate body temperature. The marine iguana of the Galápagos Islands eats seaweed underwater for an hour or more at a time (occasionally coming up for air) in water that is 10°C–15°C cooler than its preferred body temperature. After feeding, the iguana emerges and lies on a warm rock to restore its temperature. While warming up, it lies broadside to the sun to absorb as much heat as possible (**Figure 13.4a**). When its temperature reaches 37°C, the iguana turns to face the sun and thus absorbs less heat, and it may extend its legs to keep its body away from warm surfaces (**Figure 13.4b**). In the laboratory, iguanas carefully regulate their temperature by moving toward or away from a heat lamp, and when infected by bacteria they even produce a fever through behavioral means (**Figure 13.5**).

Many other ectotherms regulate body temperature in similar ways. Some snakes, for example, adjust their coils to expose more or less surface to the sun and thus keep their internal temperature relatively constant during the day. On cold days, bees crowd into the hive and shiver, thus generating heat; on hot days, the bees fan the hive with their wings instead, thereby keeping it cool. As a result of these behavioral measures, hive temperature is regulated at about 35°C.

13.4 Behavioral Control of Body Temperature (a) A Galápagos marine iguana, upon emerging from the cold sea, raises its body temperature by hugging a warm rock and lying broadside to the sun. (b) Once its temperature is sufficiently high, the iguana reduces its surface contact with the rock and faces the sun to minimize its exposure. These behaviors afford considerable control over body temperature. (Photographs by Mark R. Rosenzweig.)

(a)

(b)

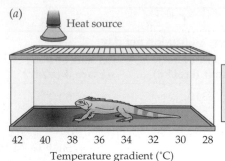

(a)   Heat source

The lizard controls its body temperature by moving around the cage.

42   40   38   36   34   32   30   28
Temperature gradient (°C)

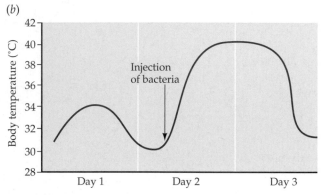

(b)

Body temperature (°C)

Injection of bacteria

Day 1   Day 2   Day 3

13.5 Behavioral Thermoregulation in Bacteria-Challenged Lizards (*a*) By positioning themselves along the temperature gradient between the cool and warm ends of a terrarium, iguanas can exert precise behavioral control over their body temperature. (*b*) Body temperature recorded from iguanas over the course of 3 days is plotted here. Day 1 shows the normal daily cycle of body temperature, averaging 37°C during the day and slightly cooler at night (this is very similar to the daily temperature cycle of endotherms). Early on Day 2, the iguanas were injected with bacteria, to which they reacted by moving closer to the heat source and allowing their body temperature to rise to more than 40°C for about 36 hours. This "behavioral fever" closely resembles the fever that endotherms like humans experience during infection, and it similarly helps fight off infection. (After Kluger, 1978.)

Endotherms such as mammals and birds likewise control their exposure to the sun and to hot or cold surfaces to avoid overtaxing their internal regulatory mechanisms. Throughout history, humans have busily devised adaptations to hot and cold, ranging from the use of fans and swimming pools to the creation of heating systems and highly insulating clothing.

The behavioral thermoregulatory responses of ectotherms and endotherms can be divided into three categories:

1. *Changing exposure of the body surface*—for example, by huddling or extending limbs
2. *Changing external insulation*—for example, by using clothing or nests
3. *Selecting a surrounding that is less thermally stressful*—for example, by moving to the shade or into a burrow

Humans seldom wait to feel cold before putting on a coat. Instead, we *anticipate* homeostatic signals on the basis of experience.

Young birds and mammals need help to regulate body temperature

Fetuses maintained in the mother's body rely on her to provide warmth and regulate temperature. Most birds keep their eggs warm by using a specially vascularized area of skin (the brood patch), which transfers heat efficiently to the eggs. Even after hatching or birth, the young of many species cannot regulate body temperature very well, mainly because they are small (and lose heat quickly) and have limited energy resources. So they must continue to be protected by their parents.

Because rat pups are born without hair, they have a hard time maintaining body temperature when exposed to cold. The rat mother keeps her pups protected in a warm nest, and warms them with her own body heat. Newborn rat pups are able to generate heat by using brown-fat deposits like the one between the shoulder blades, shown in **Figure 13.6a** (Blumberg et al., 1997).

Nonetheless, one problem for newborn rats is insulating their hairless bodies to conserve the heat they generate. To tackle this problem, they huddle together (**Figure 13.6b**). The effectiveness of this strategy is easily demonstrated: placed in a room-temperature environment, an isolated 5-day-old pup will soon cool to less than 30°C, but as part of a group of four, the same pup can maintain a temperature above 30°C for 4 hours or more (Alberts, 1978), while also using less metabolic fuel. Pups frequently change their positions in the huddle, regulating their temperature by moving to the inside or the outside of the clump. All the pups benefit from this cooperative thermoregulation.

The Brain Monitors and Regulates Body Temperature

The crucial role of the brain in controlling body temperature has been apparent since at least the 1880s, when physiologists found that small lesions in the hypothalamus of dogs elevated body temperature. Building on those observations, Barbour (1912) manipulated the temperature of the hypothalamus in dogs by implanting silver wires. When the wires were heated, body temperature fell; when the wires were cooled, body temperature rose. These results suggested that body temperature is monitored in the hypothalamus and that when the local temperature of the hypothalamus departs from normal, the body takes action to compensate. In the 1950s, electrical recording revealed that some neurons change their discharge rate in response to small increases or decreases of brain temperature; these cells are scattered throughout the preoptic area (POA) and the hypothalamus.

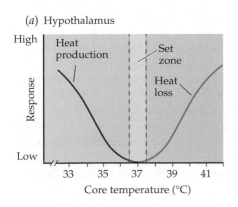

(a)

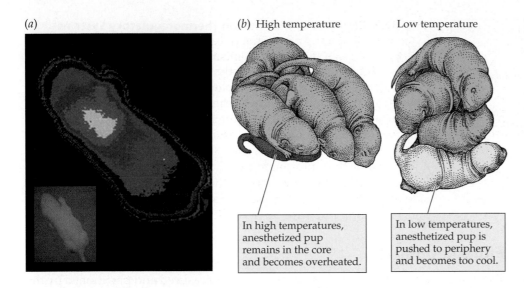

(b) High temperature — Low temperature

In high temperatures, anesthetized pup remains in the core and becomes overheated.

In low temperatures, anesthetized pup is pushed to periphery and becomes too cool.

13.6 Physiological and Social Thermoregulation (a) This infrared thermograph shows the dorsal surface of a 1-week-old rat pup oriented as shown in the inset. Areas of highest heat production are coded in orange and yellow, and the prominent yellow "hot spot" between the shoulder blades overlies a deposit of brown fat, a thermogenic (i.e., heat-producing) organ. When rat pups are placed in a cold environment, they begin producing heat by using brown fat. (b) Rat pups also use behavioral mechanisms to conserve heat. Animals push to the center of a litter to gain heat and move to the periphery to cool off. Thus, an anesthetized pup will be left in the center during high temperatures and pushed to the periphery when temperatures are low. (Part a courtesy of Mark S. Blumberg; b after Alberts, 1978.)

Lesion experiments implicated different hypothalamic sites for the two kinds of thermoregulation—physiological versus behavioral thermoregulation—that we discussed in the previous sections. Lesions in the lateral hypothalamus of rats abolish *behavioral* regulation of temperature but do not affect physiological responses such as shivering and vasoconstriction (Satinoff and Shan, 1971; Van Zoeren and Stricker, 1977). On the other hand, lesions in the POA impaired the *physiological* responses but did not interfere with such behaviors as pressing levers to control heating lamps or cooling fans (Satinoff and Rutstein, 1970; Van Zoeren and Stricker, 1977). This is a clear example of homeostatic redundancy: two different systems for regulating the same variable. But even two distinct thermoregulatory circuits may not be enough to explain all of the ways that we adapt to temperature. For example, sensory receptors in the skin also monitor temperature, and if you enter a cold room, you soon begin to shiver—even before your hypothalamic temperature has changed very much. So the skin must provide information to the central nervous system, which initiates corrective action in *anticipation* of a change in core temperature.

In fact, there seems to be a hierarchy of thermoregulatory circuits, some located at the spinal level, some centered in the brainstem, and others in the forebrain, including the hypothalamus. Even **spinal animals** (in which the brain has been disconnected from the spinal cord) can regulate body temperature somewhat, indicating that systems for temperature detection and thermoregulatory response are present even in the lowest levels of the central nervous system. Such animals cannot survive in extended periods of cold or heat, however, because they do not respond until body temperature deviates too far from normal values.

Evelyn Satinoff (1978) suggested that the thermal set zones are broader in "lower" regions of the nervous system (**Figure 13.7**). The thermoregulatory systems

spinal animal An animal whose spinal cord has been surgically disconnected from the brain to enable the study of behaviors that do not require brain control.

13.7 Multiple Thermostats in the Nervous System The set zones of thermoregulatory systems are narrower at higher levels of the nervous system than at lower levels. (After Satinoff, 1978.)

(a) Hypothalamus — (b) Brainstem — (c) Spinal cord

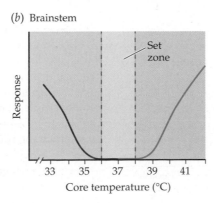
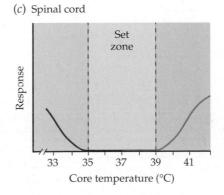

Heat production / Set zone / Heat loss. Response. Core temperature (°C) 33 35 37 39 41

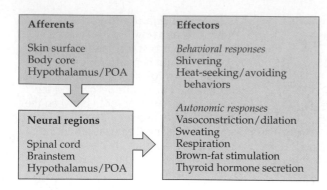

at the "highest" level—the hypothalamus—have the narrowest set zones, and they normally coordinate and adjust the activity of the other systems. This arrangement can give the impression of a single system, although in reality there are multiple interlinked systems.

Figure 13.8 summarizes the basic thermoregulatory system: receptors in the skin, body core, and hypothalamus detect temperature and transmit that information to three neural regions (spinal cord, brainstem, and hypothalamus). If the body temperature moves outside the set zone, each of these neural regions can initiate autonomic and behavioral responses to return it to the set zone.

Fluid Regulation

dehydration   Excessive loss of water.

The water that you drink on a hot day is carefully measured and partitioned by the nervous system. A precise balance of fluids and dissolved salts bathes the cells of the body and enables them to function.

Our Cells Evolved to Function in Seawater

The first living creatures on Earth were unicellular organisms that arose in the sea. It was therefore in this setting—a large body of water with fairly uniform concentrations of salts and minerals—that evolution through natural selection shaped basic cellular activities like gene expression and nutrient metabolism. For these primordial creatures, maintaining the proper concentration of salts in the water was effortless: they simply let seawater inside the cell membrane and let it out again. But when multicellular animals began coming out of the water onto land, they either had to evolve all-new cellular processes to work without water, or they had to bring the water with them. Only the latter solution (no pun intended) was feasible.

Land animals had to prevent **dehydration** (excessive loss of water) so that their cells would work properly. Thus, they needed a more or less watertight outer layer of cells, and they had to maintain the proper concentration of salts and other molecules in body fluids. The composition of the fluid inside your body, once proteins and the like have been removed, is still strikingly similar to that of seawater and, as you can see in **Figure 13.9**, across evolutionary time only very slight differences have arisen among species (Bourque, 2008). Even relatively minor deviation from this optimal concentration of salt in water is generally lethal, with just a few exceptions; the salmon, for example, has unique adaptations that allow it to live in freshwater at hatching, to grow up in salt water, and to return again to freshwater to spawn.

Because we cannot seal our bodies from the outside world, we experience constant obligatory losses of water and salts. Many body functions require that we use up some water (and some salt molecules), as, for example, when we produce urine to rid ourselves of waste molecules. These losses require us to actively replenish the body's water and salts (**Table 13.2**). Let's discuss how the nervous system monitors and controls the precise composition of body fluids that cells require in order to function.

13.9 Sea Inside!   Despite many millions of years of evolution, the concentration of extracellular fluid has remained remarkably constant among different species of animals, with only a few exceptions. (After Bourque, 2008).

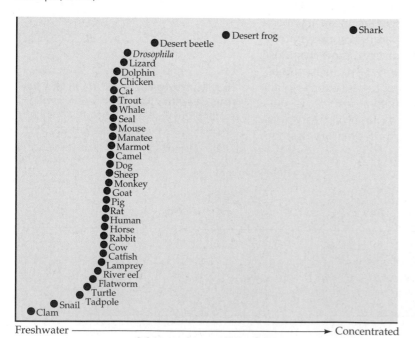

Freshwater ⟶ Concentrated

Saltiness of extracellular fluid

Water in the human body moves back and forth between two major compartments

Most of our water is contained within the trillions of cells that make up the body; this is the **intracellular compartment**. But some fluid is outside of our cells, in the **extracellular compartment**. The extracellular compartment can be subdivided into interstitial fluid (the fluid between cells) and blood plasma (the protein-rich fluid that carries red and white blood cells). Water is continually moving back and forth between these compartments, in and out of cells, via specialized water channels studding the cell membrane. These channels belong to a family of proteins called **aquaporins**: a single aquaporin-1 channel can selectively conduct about 3 *billion* molecules of water per second (Agre et al., 2002)!

To understand the forces driving the movement of water, we must understand osmosis. In **osmosis**, molecules move passively from one place to another. The motive force behind osmosis is the constant vibration and movement of molecules. If we put a drop of food coloring (a **solute**) in a beaker of water (a **solvent**), the molecules of dye meander about because of this jiggling until they are more or less uniformly distributed throughout the beaker.

If we divide a beaker of water with a membrane that is impermeable to water and dye, and we put the dye in the water on one side, the molecules distribute themselves only within that half. If instead the membrane impedes dye molecules only a little, then the dye first distributes itself within the initial half and then slowly invades and distributes itself across both halves. A membrane that is permeable to some molecules but not others is referred to as *selectively permeable* or *semipermeable*. As we saw in Chapter 3, cell membranes are impressively selective in their permeability: for example, neurons normally allow very few sodium ions (Na^+) to pass through their membrane unless the voltage-gated Na^+ channels are opened during the action potential. The osmotic movement of water across a semipermeable membrane is depicted in **Figure 13.10**.

TABLE 13.2 Average Daily Water Balance

Source	Quantity (liters)
Approximate intake	
Fluid water	1.2
Water from food	1.3
TOTAL	**2.5**
Approximate output	
Urine	1.4
Evaporative loss	0.9
Feces	0.2
TOTAL	**2.5**

intracellular compartment The fluid space of the body that is contained within cells.

extracellular compartment The fluid space of the body that exists outside the cells.

aquaporins Channels spanning the cell membrane that are specialized for conducting water molecules into or out of the cell.

osmosis The passive movement of molecules from one place to another.

solute A solid compound that is dissolved in a liquid.

solvent The liquid (often water) in which a compound is dissolved.

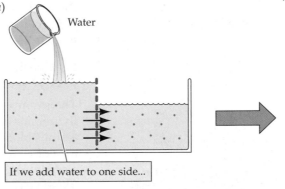

(a) Water

Salt water | Semipermeable membrane

Equal concentration of solute on both sides, so no net change.

If we add water to one side...

...water molecules pass through semipermeable membrane, leading to equal concentration of solute on both sides. Concentration of solute is lower (on both sides) than it was before.

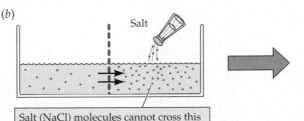

(b) Salt

Salt (NaCl) molecules cannot cross this membrane. If we add salt to one side...

...water molecules on left cross membrane to approach equal solute concentration on both sides, despite the influence of gravity.

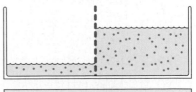

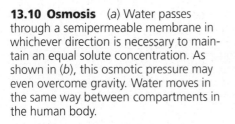

13.10 Osmosis (a) Water passes through a semipermeable membrane in whichever direction is necessary to maintain an equal solute concentration. As shown in (b), this osmotic pressure may even overcome gravity. Water moves in the same way between compartments in the human body.

osmotic pressure   The tendency of a solvent to move through a membrane in order to equalize the concentration of solute.

osmolality   The number of solute particles per unit volume of solvent.

isotonic   Referring to a solution with a concentration of salt that is the same as that found in interstitial fluid and blood plasma (about 0.9% salt).

hypertonic   Referring to a solution with a higher concentration of salt than that found in interstitial fluid and blood plasma (more than about 0.9% salt).

hypotonic   Referring to a solution with a lower concentration of salt than that found in interstitial fluid and blood plasma (less than about 0.9% salt).

hypovolemic thirst   A desire to ingest fluids that is stimulated by a reduced volume of extracellular fluid.

osmotic thirst   A desire to ingest fluids that is stimulated by loss of water from the extracellular compartment.

Molecules have a tendency to spread out—to move *down* concentration gradients (from an area of higher concentration to an area of lower concentration). In the case we have examined here, in which the semipermeable membrane blocks the passage of salt molecules, the water molecules are moving into the compartment where they are less concentrated (because the salt molecules are there). The force that pushes or pulls water across the membrane is called **osmotic pressure**.

We refer to the concentration of solute in a solution as **osmolality**. Normally, the concentration of NaCl in the extracellular fluid of mammals is about 0.9% (weight to volume, which means there's about 0.9 g of NaCl for every 100 mL of water). A solution with this concentration of salt is called *physiological saline* and is described as **isotonic**, having the same concentration of salt that mammalian fluids have. A solution with more salt is **hypertonic**; a solution lower in salt is **hypotonic**.

Drugs injected into the extracellular space of muscles are usually mixed in isotonic solution rather than in pure water because if pure water were injected, it would be pulled inside muscle cells (which are filled with ions) by osmotic pressure and would rupture them. At the other extreme, if hypertonic saline were injected, water would be pulled out of the cells, and that, too, could damage them. These fates could befall any cells bathed in fluid of the wrong tonicity, either too concentrated or too dilute. To prevent such damage, the extracellular fluid serves as a *buffer*, a reservoir of isotonic fluid that provides and accepts water molecules so that cells can maintain proper internal conditions. The nervous system uses two cues to ensure that the extracellular compartment has about the right amount of water and solute to allow cells to absorb or shed water molecules readily, as we'll see next.

Two Internal Cues Trigger Thirst

In addition to acting as a buffer, the extracellular fluid is an indicator of conditions in the intracellular compartment. In fact, the nervous system carefully monitors the extracellular compartment to determine whether we should seek water. Two different states can signal that more water is needed: low extracellular volume (**hypovolemic thirst**) or high extracellular solute concentration (**osmotic thirst**) (**Figure 13.11**). We'll consider each in turn.

Hypovolemic thirst is triggered by a loss of water volume

The example of hypovolemic thirst that is most easily understood is one we hope you never experience: serious blood loss (*hemorrhage*). Any animal that loses a lot of blood has a lowered total blood volume (*hypovolemic* means literally "low volume"). In this condition, blood vessels that would normally be full and slightly

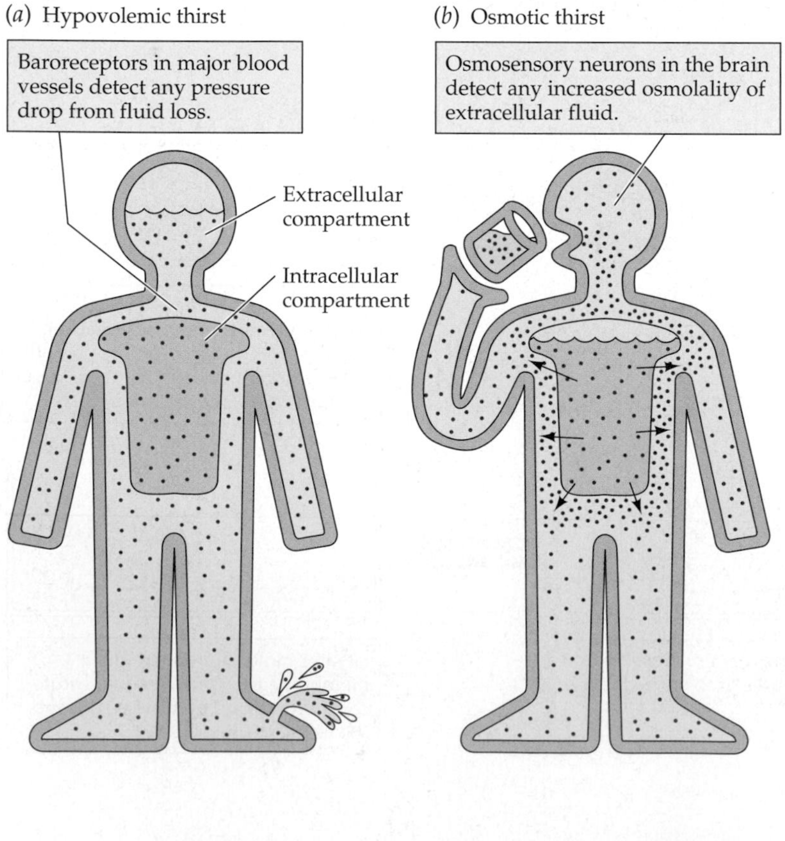

(*a*) Hypovolemic thirst

Baroreceptors in major blood vessels detect any pressure drop from fluid loss.

Extracellular compartment

Intracellular compartment

(*b*) Osmotic thirst

Osmosensory neurons in the brain detect any increased osmolality of extracellular fluid.

13.11 Two Kinds of Thirst   (*a*) Hypovolemic thirst is triggered by the loss of blood or other body fluids (such as through diarrhea or vomiting) that contain both solutes and water. In this case, extracellular fluid is depleted without the solute concentration being changed in either the intracellular or the extracellular compartment, so there is no osmotic pressure to push water from one compartment to the other. (*b*) Osmotic thirst is triggered when the total volume of water is constant but a sudden increase in the amount of solute in the extracellular compartment (as after a very salty meal) exerts osmotic pressure that pulls water out of the intracellular compartment.

stretched no longer contain their full capacity. Blood pressure drops, and the individual becomes thirsty.

Note that losing fluids from blood loss (or from diarrhea or vomiting) does not change the *concentration* of the extracellular fluid, because salts and other ions are lost along with the water. Rather, only the *volume* of the extracellular fluid is affected in these instances (see Figure 13.11*a*). However, continued loss in the extracellular compartment would cause fluid to exit the intracellular compartment. The initial drop in extracellular volume is detected by pressure receptors, called **baroreceptors**, which are located in major blood vessels and in the heart. In response to this drop in pressure, the heart immediately decreases its secretion of the hormone **atrial natriuretic peptide** (**ANP**), which normally reduces blood pressure, inhibits drinking, and promotes the excretion of water and salt at the kidneys. On receiving a signal from the baroreceptors via the autonomic nervous system, the brain also activates several responses, such as thirst (to replace the lost water) and salt hunger (to replace the solutes that have been lost along with the water). Replacing the water without also replacing the salts would result in hypotonic extracellular fluid. The sympathetic portion of the autonomic nervous system also stimulates muscles in the artery walls to constrict, reducing the size of the vessels and partly compensating for the reduced volume.

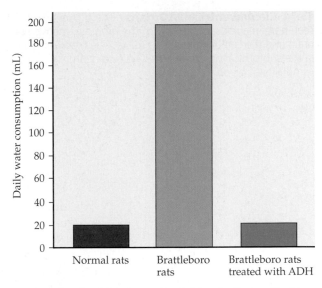

13.12 Inherited Diabetes Insipidus in Rats Unable to produce vasopressin (ADH), Brattleboro rats urinate profusely and so must drink a lot of water. Treatment with vasopressin corrects this condition, which is known as diabetes insipidus

THE ROLE OF VASOPRESSIN An additional response to hypovolemia involves the release of the peptide hormone vasopressin from the posterior pituitary gland. Vasopressin induces additional constriction of blood vessels. Furthermore, vasopressin instructs the kidneys to reduce the flow of water to the bladder. For this reason, vasopressin has also been called *antidiuretic hormone* (*ADH*; *diuresis* is the production of urine), but in light of new knowledge of this hormone's role in love and relationships, perhaps that name is too mundane (L. J. Young, 2009; see Chapter 5).

In the disease **diabetes insipidus** (literally "passing bland"), the production of vasopressin ceases, and the kidneys retain less water; they send more urine to the bladder, and that urine is very pale and dilute (insipid). A consequence of all this urination is chronic thirst. Treatment with vasopressin relieves the symptoms (**Figure 13.12**). (Note that, when people talk about diabetes, they usually do not mean diabetes insipidus, but are referring instead to diabetes mellitus, which we'll discuss later in this chapter.)

THE RENIN-ANGIOTENSIN SYSTEM In response to decreased blood volume, the kidneys release a hormone called *renin* into the circulation, triggering a hormonal cascade (**Figure 13.13**). Renin reacts with a protein called angiotensinogen to form angiotensin I, which is then converted to the active product, **angiotensin II** (from the Greek *angeion*, "blood vessel," and the Latin *tensio*, "tension or pressure").

Angiotensin II has several water-conserving actions. In addition to constricting blood vessels and increasing blood pressure, angiotensin II triggers the release of two hormones: vasopressin (discussed earlier) and aldosterone (to be discussed shortly). However, angiotensin II also directly affects behavior: very low

baroreceptor A pressure receptor in the heart or a major artery that detects a fall in blood pressure.

atrial natriuretic peptide (ANP) A hormone, secreted by the heart, that normally reduces blood pressure, inhibits drinking, and promotes the excretion of water and salt at the kidneys.

diabetes insipidus Excessive urination, caused by the failure of vasopressin to induce the kidneys to conserve water.

angiotensin II A substance that is produced in the blood by the action of renin and that may play a role in the control of thirst.

13.13 The Angiotensin Cascade A drop in blood volume is detected by the kidneys. The kidneys then release renin, which catalyzes the conversion of angiotensinogen (already present in blood) to angiotensin I. Angiotensin I is converted to angiotensin II (the most biologically active of the angiotensins).

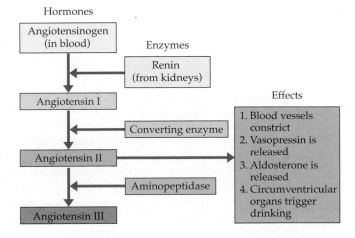

13.14 Circumventricular Organs The circumventricular organs, seen here in a midsagittal view of the rat brain, mediate between the brain and the cerebrospinal fluid (blue). The blood-brain barrier is weak in the subfornical organ and the OVLT, so neurons there can monitor the osmolality of blood.

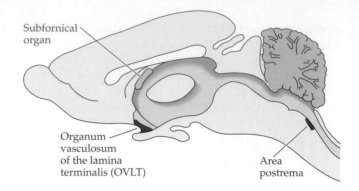

Subfornical organ

Organum vasculosum of the lamina terminalis (OVLT)

Area postrema

doses of angiotensin II injected directly into the preoptic area (POA) are extremely effective in eliciting drinking, even in animals that are not deprived of water (A. N. Epstein et al., 1970; Fitzsimmons, 1998).

Circulating angiotensin II may act via several other brain sites, particularly the **circumventricular organs**. As their name suggests, these organs lie in the walls encircling the cerebral ventricles (**Figure 13.14**). The blood-brain barrier is somewhat "leaky" in these regions, so the neurons here are more easily affected by substances in the bloodstream. Angiotensin II interacts with specific angiotensin receptors on the neurons of the circumventricular organs, producing a neural signal that is passed on to other sites in the brain.

The **subfornical organ** is a circumventricular organ that is particularly sensitive to angiotensin II: when angiotensin II is injected intravenously, neurons of the subfornical organ rapidly increase their activity (Kadekaro et al., 1989) and gene expression (Lebrun et al., 1995). However, the role of angiotensin II in "normal" thirst remains to be established; for example, modest reductions in blood volume can produce thirst independently of circulating angiotensin II levels (Abraham et al., 1975; Stricker, 1977). Perhaps the angiotensin II mechanism is just one of several redundant systems for provoking thirst, and is not active under all conditions (Fitzsimmons, 1998; McKinley and Johnson, 2004).

Osmotic thirst is triggered by a change in the concentration of extracellular fluid

For most of us, hypovolemic thirst is a relatively uncommon event. Thirst is more commonly triggered by obligatory water losses—recall that these include respiration, perspiration, and urination—in which more water is lost than salt. In this case, not only is the *volume* of the extracellular fluid decreased, triggering the responses described in the previous section, but also the solute *concentration* of the extracellular fluid increases. As a result of this increased extracellular saltiness, water is pulled out of cells through osmosis.

Alternatively, the solute concentration of extracellular fluid can be increased without any change in volume—for example, by the consumption of salty food. Once again, water will be drawn out of cells. In general, an increase in solute concentration of the extracellular fluid triggers a thirst that is independent of extracellular volume: *osmotic thirst* (see Figure 13.11b). Osmotic thirst causes us to seek water to return the extracellular fluid to an isotonic state and protect the intracellular compartment from becoming dangerously depleted of water.

In the 1950s it was shown that injecting a small amount of hypertonic (salty) solution into the hypothalamus causes animals to start drinking. This observation suggested that some hypothalamic cells might be **osmosensory neurons**—that is, cells that respond to changes in osmotic pressure. Electrical recordings from single nerve cells have revealed osmotically responsive neurons spread widely throughout the preoptic area, the anterior hypothalamus, the supraoptic nucleus, and the organum vasculosum of the lamina terminalis (OVLT), a circumventricular organ (see Figure 13.14).

circumventricular organ An organ that lies in the wall of a cerebral ventricle and monitors the composition of the cerebrospinal fluid.

subfornical organ One of the circumventricular organs.

osmosensory neuron A specialized neuron that measures the movement of water into and out of the intracellular compartment.

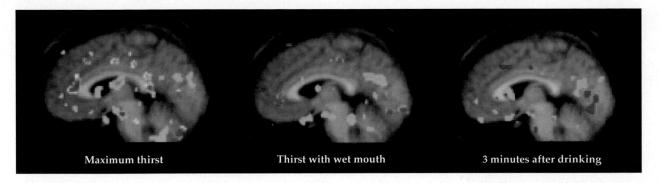

Maximum thirst   Thirst with wet mouth   3 minutes after drinking

13.15 Ahhhhhh! The experience of strong thirst, induced by injection of hypertonic saline, is associated with activity in several brain regions, especially the cingulate cortex and cerebellum (*left*). Wetting the mouth reduces this activation only slightly (*middle*), but drinking a glass of water (*right*) reduces activation in these brain regions dramatically. (From Denton et al., 1999.)

Osmosensory neurons have several key features that let them detect the concentration of extracellular fluid (Z. Zhang and Bourque, 2003). First, they are stretchy. Most cells actively maintain a constant volume in the face of osmotic challenges. Osmosensory neurons don't do this, and they will balloon or shrink to a greater extent than non-osmosensory neurons when the concentration of the extracellular fluid changes. Second, the cell membranes of osmosensory neurons are studded with mechanically gated ion channels—channels that open or close when the cell membrane is physically deformed. The stretching and shrinking of the cell membrane opens and closes the mechanically gated channels, causing changes in cell membrane potentials that track the changes in extracellular concentration. This information is then relayed to other parts of the brain.

Thirst is a homeostatic signal that intrudes forcefully into consciousness, with associated strong activation of certain brain regions, particularly in the limbic system (**Figure 13.15**) (Denton et al., 1999). The two types of thirst (hypovolemic and osmotic), the two fluid compartments (extracellular and intracellular), and the multiple redundant methods to conserve water make for a fairly complicated system that is not yet fully understood. The current conceptualization of this system is depicted in **Figure 13.16**.

We don't stop drinking just because the throat and mouth are wet

Although plausible, the most obvious explanation of why we stop drinking—that a previously dry throat and mouth are now wet—is quite wrong. In one test of this hypothesis, thirsty animals were allowed to drink water, but the water they consumed was diverted out of the esophagus through a small tube. They remained thirsty and continued drinking.

Furthermore, we stop drinking before water has left the gastrointestinal tract and entered the extracellular compartment. Somehow we monitor how much water we have ingested and stop in *anticipation* of correcting the extracellular volume and/or osmolality. Experience may teach us and other animals how to gauge accurately whether we've ingested enough to counteract our thirst (hypovolemic or osmotic). Normally, all the signals—blood vol-

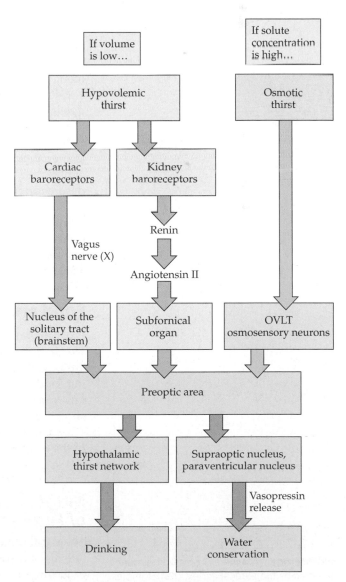

13.16 An Overview of Fluid Regulation

13.17 Excretion of Excess Salt   Marine birds, such as this giant petrel, have only seawater to drink for long periods of time. To compensate, they have salt glands that pull excess salt out of plasma and release it out the nostrils.

ume, osmolality, moisture in the mouth, estimates of the amount of water we have ingested that's "on the way"—register agreement, but the cessation of one signal alone will not stop thirst; in this way, animals ensure against dehydration.

Homeostatic Regulation of Salt Is Required for Effective Regulation of Water

Animals may travel great distances to eat salt (NaCl), and the sodium ion (Na$^+$) is particularly important to fluid balance. We cannot maintain water in the extracellular compartment without solutes; if the extracellular compartment contained pure water, osmotic pressure would drive it into the cells, killing them. The amount of water that we can retain is determined primarily by the number of Na$^+$ ions we possess. That's why thirst is quenched more effectively by very slightly salty drinks (as long as they are hypotonic, like sports drinks) than by pure water. Some Na$^+$ loss is inevitable, as during urination. But when water is at a premium, the body tries to conserve Na$^+$ in order to retain water.

In addition to its effects on thirst and vasopressin secretion, angiotensin II stimulates the release of **aldosterone** from the adrenal glands (see Figure 13.13). Aldosterone, a *mineralocorticoid* steroid hormone, is crucial to Na$^+$ conservation. Aldosterone directly stimulates the kidneys to conserve Na$^+$, thereby aiding water retention. Nonetheless, animals must find additional salt in their environments in order to survive.

Because some Na$^+$ aids water retention, you might think that seawater would quench thirst, but it doesn't. Seawater is hypertonic, so just like eating salty food, drinking seawater causes ever-worsening osmotic thirst. We simply can't get rid of the excess salt fast enough. But some species have evolved special adaptations that enable them to survive on seawater. The kidneys of marine mammals have evolved to dump excess sodium by producing very concentrated urine. Some desert rodents can also produce highly concentrated urine to help conserve water, and a rare variety of Bactrian camel found in Mongolia can meet its water requirements by drinking salt water, unlike its domesticated cousins, which require freshwater. Some seabirds, including gulls and petrels, have specialized salt glands near the nostrils that can excrete highly concentrated salt solutions (**Figure 13.17**) (Schmidt-Nielsen, 1960), so they can drink seawater.

Food and Energy Regulation

Feast or famine—these are poles of human experience. Hunger for the food that we need to build, maintain, and fuel our bodies is a compelling drive; and flavors are powerful reinforcements. The behaviors involved in obtaining and consuming food shape our daily schedules, and our mass media feed us a steady diet of information about food: crop reports, stories about famines and droughts, cooking shows, and restaurant ads.

Our reliance on food for energy and nutrition is shared with all other animals. In the remainder of this chapter we will look at the regulation of feeding and energy expenditure, as well as some species-specific aspects of food-related behavior.

Nutrient Regulation Requires the Anticipation of Future Needs

The regulation of eating and of body energy involves numerous redundant mechanisms and complex homeostatic mechanisms. Overall, the system for controlling food intake and energy balance is significantly more complex than those controlling thermoregulation and fluid balance. One important reason for this greater

aldosterone   A mineralocorticoid hormone, secreted by the adrenal cortex, that promotes conservation of sodium by the kidneys.

complexity is that we need food to supply not only energy, but also crucial **nutrients** (chemicals required for the effective functioning, growth, and maintenance of the body). We do not know all the nutritional requirements of the body—even for humans. Of the 20 amino acids found in our bodies, 9 are difficult or impossible for us to manufacture, so we must find these *essential amino acids* in our diet. From food we must also obtain a few fatty acids, as well as about 15 vitamins and a variety of minerals.

No animal can afford to run out of energy or nutrients; there must be a reserve on hand at all times. If the reserves are too large, though, mobility (for avoiding predators or securing prey) will be compromised. For this reason, the nervous system not only monitors nutrient and energy levels and controls **digestion** (the process of breaking down ingested food), but also has complex mechanisms for *anticipating* future requirements.

Most of our food is used to provide us with energy

All the energy that we need to move, think, breathe, and maintain body temperature is derived in the same way: it is released when the chemical bonds of complex molecules are broken and smaller, simpler compounds form as a result. In a sense we "burn" food for energy just as a car burns gasoline. To raise body temperature, we release chemical-bond energy as heat. For other bodily processes, such as those in the brain, the energy is utilized by more-sophisticated biochemical processes.

Metabolic studies indicate that lab animals lose about 33% of the energy in food during digestion (through excretion of indigestible material or the digestive process itself). Another 55% of food energy in a meal is consumed by **basal metabolism**—processes such as heat production, maintenance of membrane potentials, and all the other basic life-sustaining functions of the body. The remainder, only about 12% of the total, is utilized for active behavioral processes, although this proportion is increased in more-complex environments or during intense activity.

In general, the rate of basal metabolism follows a rule, devised by Max Kleiber (1947), that relates energy expenditure to body weight:

$$\text{kcal/day} = 70 \times \text{weight}^{0.75}$$

where weight is expressed in kilograms. This relationship applies across a vast range of body sizes (**Figure 13.18**). However, although Kleiber's equation fits nicely at the population level, it is not very accurate for *individuals* within a species, because body weight is only one factor affecting metabolic rate. For example, food-deprived people experience a significant decrease in basal metabolism. In fact, severe food restriction affects metabolic rate much more than it affects body weight (Keesey and Corbett, 1984), presumably reflecting the operation of an evolved homeostatic mechanism for conserving energy when food is scarce (Keesey and Powley, 1986).

Because people and animals adjust their metabolism in response to under- or overnutrition, they tend to resist either losing or gaining weight (**Figure 13.19**). To the frustration of dieters everywhere, many studies have now shown that a calorie-reduced diet prompts a reduction in basal metabolic rate in order to *prevent* losing weight, regardless of whether the dieter is initially normal weight or obese (Bray, 1969; C. K. Martin et al., 2007).

nutrient   A chemical that is needed for growth, maintenance, and repair of the body but is not used as a source of energy.

digestion   The process by which food is broken down to provide energy and nutrients.

basal metabolism   The consumption of energy to fuel processes such as heat production, maintenance of membrane potentials, and all the other basic life-sustaining functions of the body.

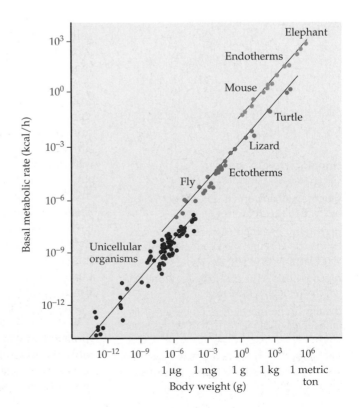

13.18 The Relation between Body Size and Metabolism   Basal metabolic rate increases in a very regular, predictable fashion over a wide range of body weights. However, endotherms have a higher metabolic rate than ectotherms of a similar body weight. (After Hemmingsen, 1960.)

13.19 Why Losing Weight Is So Difficult After 7 days on a diet of 3500 kcal/day, the intake of six obese subjects was restricted to a measly 450 kcal/day—a drop of 87%. However, basal metabolism also declined by 15%; so after 3 weeks, body weight had declined by only 6%. (After Bray, 1969.)

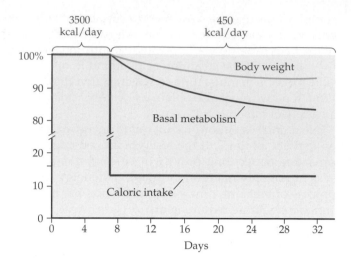

Mice whose basal metabolic rate has been increased (by a transgenic increase in the energy used by mitochondria) eat more and weigh less than normal mice, without increased locomotor activity (Clapham et al., 2000). Perhaps someday a drug will be developed to exert this effect on human mitochondria and produce such wonderful results in humans as well.

However difficult dieting might be, the only known way to cause animals to live longer is to reduce their calorie intake to levels about 50%–75% of what they would eat if food were always available (Weindruch and Walford, 1988). This benefit from reducing calorie intake may be related to the decrease in basal metabolism that is induced by food restriction. Both the body and the brain give evidence of slower aging under such circumstances (C.-K. Lee et al., 1999, 2000). No one knows exactly how food deprivation enhances longevity, but research in invertebrates has identified a pair of genes for transcription factors (substances that control other genes) that are involved (Bishop and Guarente, 2007; Panowski et al., 2007). These genes, which are conserved across many species of animals, may in turn control production of hormones and **trophic factors** (substances that promote cell growth and survival) important for longevity.

During caloric restriction, production of a ubiquitous protein called SIRT1, a marker for increased longevity in various vertebrates and invertebrates, is increased (Anson et al., 2003; Holzenberger et al., 2003). Although no one is likely to do full studies on human longevity (because they would take a century or so to complete), evidence that caloric restriction also increases SIRT1 production in humans raises the possibility that restricting intake—while maintaining healthy nutrition—could have the same life-span benefits in humans as it has in lab animals (Allard et al., 2008).

We can store energy for future needs

The most immediate source of energy for the body is the collection of complex carbohydrates in our diet that are rapidly broken down into the simple sugars that cells can use. **Glucose** is the principal sugar used by the body for energy, and it is especially important for fueling the brain. Because we need a steady supply of glucose between meals and may also experience elevated demand for fuel at other times—for example, during intense physical activity—several mechanisms have evolved to store excess fuel for later use.

For shorter-term storage, glucose can be converted into a more complicated molecule called **glycogen** and stored as reserve fuel in several locations, most notably the liver and skeletal muscles. This process, called **glycogenesis**, is promoted by the pancreatic hormone **insulin** (see Chapter 5). A second pancreatic hormone, **glucagon**, mediates the conversion of glycogen back into glucose, a process known

trophic factor A substance that promotes cell growth and survival.

glucose An important sugar molecule used by the body and brain for energy.

glycogen A complex carbohydrate made by the combining of glucose molecules for a short-term store of energy.

glycogenesis The physiological process by which glycogen is produced.

insulin A hormone, released by beta cells in the islets of Langerhans, that lowers blood glucose.

glucagon A hormone, released by alpha cells in the islets of Langerhans, that increases blood glucose

13.20 The Role of Insulin in Energy Utilization The body can make use of either fatty acids or glucose for energy. The brain, however, can make ready use of only glucose; so the brain requires a constant supply of glucose, which it can use without the aid of insulin. On the other hand, the body can make use of glucose only with the aid of insulin; so, in the absence of insulin the body must use fatty acids for energy.

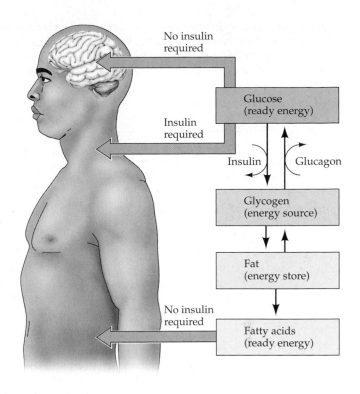

as **glycogenolysis** (**Figure 13.20**), which is triggered when blood concentrations of glucose drop too low.

For longer-term storage, fat (or **lipids**, large molecules consisting of fatty acids and glycerol that are insoluble in water) is deposited in the fat-storing cells that form **adipose tissue**. Some stored fats come directly from our food, but others are synthesized in the body from surplus sugars and other nutrients. Under conditions of prolonged food deprivation, fat can be converted into glucose (a process called **gluconeogenesis**) and a secondary form of fuel, called **ketones**, which can similarly be utilized by the body and brain.

The debate about the most effective ways to decrease fat deposition through dieting is an endlessly popular topic in the mass media. Although it is counterintuitive, some evidence has accumulated to suggest that diets low in carbohydrates, and correspondingly high in proteins and fats, are effective in helping people lose weight and also may increase serum levels of "good" cholesterol while decreasing fats (G. D. Foster et al., 2003; Samaha et al., 2003). However, long-term studies will be required to establish the overall safety of low-carbohydrate diets; after all, plenty of evidence already indicates that people with diets high in fat have more heart disease. For now, the only certain way to lose weight is to decrease the number of calories eaten and/or increase the calories spent in physical activity. For the weight loss to be permanent, these changes in diet and activity must be permanent too.

Insulin Is Crucial for the Regulation of Body Metabolism

We have already mentioned the importance of insulin for converting glucose into glycogen. Another important role of insulin is enabling the body to use glucose. Most cells regulate the import of glucose molecules via **glucose transporters** that span the cell membrane and bring glucose molecules from outside the cell into the cell for use. The glucose transporters must interact with insulin in order to function. (Brain cells are an important exception; they can use glucose without the aid of insulin.)

Each time you eat a meal, the foods are broken down and glucose is released into the bloodstream. Most of your body requires insulin to make use of that glucose, so three different, sequential mechanisms stimulate insulin release:

1. The sensory stimuli from food (sight, smell, and taste) evoke a conditioned release of insulin in anticipation of glucose arrival in the blood. This release, because it is mediated by the brain, is called the *cephalic phase* of insulin release (recall that *cephalic* means "head").

2. During the *digestive phase*, food entering the stomach and intestines causes them to release gut hormones, some of which stimulate the pancreas to release insulin.

3. During the *absorptive phase*, special cells in the liver (called **glucodetectors**) detect the glucose entering the bloodstream and signal the pancreas to release insulin.

glycogenolysis The conversion of glycogen back into glucose, triggered when blood concentrations of glucose drop too low.

lipids Large molecules (commonly called fats) consisting of fatty acids and glycerol that are insoluble in water.

adipose tissue Tissue made up of fat cells.

gluconeogenesis The metabolism of body fats and proteins to create glucose.

ketones A metabolic fuel source liberated by the breakdown of body fats and proteins.

glucose transporter A molecule that spans the external membrane of a cell and transports glucose molecules from outside the cell to inside for use.

glucodetector A cell that detects and informs the nervous system about levels of circulating glucose.

vagus nerve   Cranial nerve X, which provides extensive innervation of the viscera (organs). The vagus both regulates visceral activity and transmits signals from the viscera to the brain.

nucleus of the solitary tract (NST)   A complicated brainstem nucleus that receives visceral and taste information via several cranial nerves.

diabetes mellitus   Excessive glucose in the urine, caused by the failure of insulin to induce glucose absorption by the body.

satiety   A feeling of fulfillment or satisfaction.

hunger   The internal state of an animal seeking food.

The newly released insulin enables the body to make use of some of the glucose immediately, and other glucose is converted into glycogen and stored in the liver and muscles. The liver communicates with the pancreas via the nervous system. Information from glucodetectors in the liver travels via the **vagus nerve** to the **nucleus of the solitary tract** (**NST**) in the brainstem and is relayed to the hypothalamus (Powley, 2000). This system informs the brain of circulating glucose levels and contributes to hunger, as we'll discuss later. Efferent fibers carry signals from the brainstem back out the vagus nerve to the pancreas. These efferent fibers modulate insulin release from the pancreas.

Lack of insulin causes the disease **diabetes mellitus**. In *Type I* (or *juvenile-onset*) *diabetes*, the pancreas stops producing insulin. Although the brain can still make use of glucose from the diet, the rest of the body cannot and is forced to use energy from fatty acids. The result is that lots of glucose is left in the bloodstream because the brain cannot use it all, and the lack of insulin means there is no way to convert that glucose into glycogen for storage. Some of the glucose is secreted into the urine, making the urine sweet, which is how we get the name *diabetes mellitus* (literally "passing honey").

An untreated person with diabetes eats a great deal and yet loses weight because the body cannot make efficient use of the ingested food, and the reliance on fatty acids for energy causes damage to some tissues. People suffering from diabetes also drink and urinate copiously in an attempt to rid the body of the excess circulating glucose. Replacement of the missing insulin (via injection) allows the glucose to be utilized. Another, more common type of diabetes mellitus, called *Type II* (or *adult-onset*) *diabetes*, is primarily a consequence of reduced *sensitivity* to insulin. Particularly associated with obesity, Type II diabetes often leads to further health problems.

Despite their importance, neither insulin nor glucose is the sole signal for either hunger or satiety

Given the crucial role of insulin in mobilizing and distributing food energy, you might think that the brain monitors circulating insulin levels to decide when it's time to eat and when it's time to stop eating. For example, high levels of insulin, secreted because there is food in the pipeline, might signal the brain to produce the sensation of **satiety** (feeling "full"). Conversely, low levels of insulin between meals could signal the brain to make us feel **hunger**, impelling us to find food and eat. Indeed, lowering an animal's blood insulin levels causes it to become hungry and eat a large meal. If moderate levels of insulin are injected, the animal eats much less. These results suggest that insulin is a satiety signal.

Investigators tested this simple hypothesis by injecting a large amount of insulin into animals. But rather than appearing satiated, the animals responded by eating a large meal! High insulin levels direct much of the glucose into storage, which means that there is less glucose in circulation. The brain learns of this functional glucose deficit from its own glucodetectors (probably in one or more of the circumventricular organs; see Figure 13.14) and those of the liver (which communicates to the NST via the vagus nerve). Is circulating glucose signaling satiety and hunger to the brain? Certainly this information plays a role normally, but circulating glucose can't be the only source of information, because people with untreated diabetes have very high levels of circulating glucose, yet they are constantly hungry.

Studies of diabetic rats provide more evidence that insulin is not the only satiety signal. Like untreated humans with diabetes, these rats eat a great deal. But if the rats are fed a high-fat diet, they eat normal amounts (M. I. Friedman, 1978), probably because their bodies can make immediate use of the fatty acids without the aid of insulin. Thus, circulating levels of insulin and glucose contribute to hunger and satiety, but they are not sufficient to explain those states entirely. Somehow the brain integrates insulin and glucose levels with other sources of information to decide whether to initiate eating. This has become a central theme in research on appetite control—that the brain integrates many different signals rather than relying exclusively on any single signal to trigger hunger.

The Hypothalamus Coordinates Multiple Systems That Control Hunger

Although it appears that no single brain region has exclusive control of appetite, many findings demonstrate that the hypothalamus is critically important to the regulation of metabolic rate, food intake, and body weight. For example, the hypothalamus contains glucodetector neurons that directly monitor blood levels of glucose (Parton et al., 2007), and functional-MRI studies show that elevations in circulating glucose after a period of fasting produce large changes in the activity of the human hypothalamus (**Figure 13.21**) (Y. Liu et al., 2000). Hypothalamic control of feeding appears to be quite complicated and, like other homeostatic systems, exhibits redundancy as a safety measure.

Early lesion studies implicated hypothalamic nuclei in the control of appetite

Initial experiments involving hypothalamic lesions led researchers to propose a *dual-center hypothesis* for the control of eating. This simple model proposed two appetite centers: one for signaling hunger and the other, acting in opposition, to signal satiety. Information regarding feeding status originating elsewhere in the body (hormones, signals from the gut, information from other brain regions) was presumed to be integrated through this hypothalamic system.

Early research found that bilateral lesions of the **ventromedial hypothalamus (VMH)** (**Figure 13.22**) could cause obesity in rats (Hetherington and Ranson, 1940); indeed, lesions in this vicinity provoked excess feeding and weight gain in many species, including dogs, monkeys, and humans. Because animals lacking the VMH seemed to have lost the inhibitory control on feeding, the VMH was identified as the *satiety center*.

Lesions placed in the **lateral hypothalamus (LH)** (see Figure 13.22) were found to have the converse effect: LH-lesioned animals displayed **aphagia** (refusal to eat) resulting in rapid weight loss and, in some cases, death from starvation (Anand and Brobeck, 1951). This observation led researchers to identify the LH as the *hunger center*. So, according to the dual-center hypothesis, moment-to-moment appetite

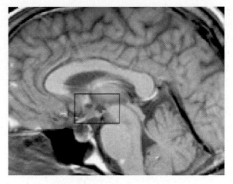

13.21 Sweet Spot Following glucose ingestion, changes in activity in the hypothalamus (inside the black rectangle) are evident in this midsagittal fMRI image. Blue indicates a significant decrease in activity; yellow indicates a significant increase. (From Y. Liu et al., 2000).

ventromedial hypothalamus (VMH) A hypothalamic region involved in eating and sexual behaviors.

lateral hypothalamus (LH) A hypothalamic region involved in the control of appetite and other functions.

aphagia Refusal to eat.

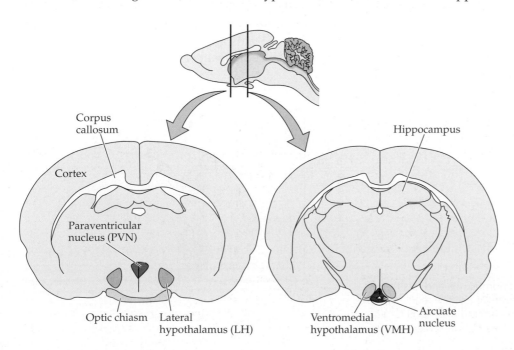

13.22 Brain Regions Implicated in the Regulation of Eating

13.23 Lesion-Induced Obesity Rats in which the ventromedial hypothalamus (VMH) has been lesioned overeat and gain weight until they reach a new, higher body weight, which they defend in the face of either forced feeding or food deprivation. Thus, they continue to regulate body weight, but at a higher set point. (After Sclafani et al., 1976.)

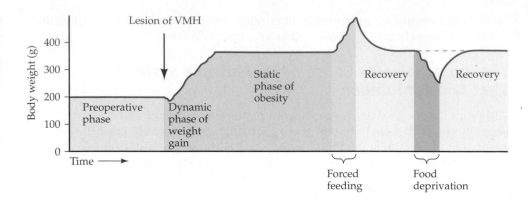

hyperphagia Excessive eating.

arcuate nucleus An arc-shaped hypothalamic nucleus implicated in appetite control.

could be viewed as a balancing act between the LH hunger center and VMH satiety center, with the VMH normally putting a brake on feeding by inhibiting the LH.

Over time, the dual-center hypothesis of appetite control proved to be too simple to account for the regulation of feeding. For one thing, although the VMH was identified as a satiety center, its destruction does not create out-of-control feeding machines. Instead, VMH-lesioned animals exhibit a *dynamic phase of obesity*, characterized by voracious feeding (**hyperphagia**) until they become obese, but their body weight then stabilizes at a new, higher level. In this *static phase of obesity*, food intake and apparent satiety are near normal. When obese VMH-lesioned animals are forced to either gain or lose weight through dietary manipulations, they return to their new "normal" weight as soon as they are allowed to eat freely again (**Figure 13.23**). Furthermore, VMH-lesioned animals are finicky eaters: they won't exhibit hyperphagia and weight gain unless supplied with highly palatable food (Sclafani et al., 1976). So, because VMH-lesioned rats experience satiety, it seems that the VMH cannot be the sole satiety controller.

Similarly, the LH can't be the sole hunger center. Although they initially stop eating, LH-lesioned rats that are kept alive with a feeding tube will soon resume eating and drinking, and eventually stabilize their body weight at a new, lower level. As with the VMH-lesioned animals, LH-lesioned animals can be forced to lose or gain weight, but when returned to their standard diet, they will precisely regulate their body weight at the new lower set point (**Figure 13.24**) (Keesey, 1980).

Peripheral peptide hormones drive a hypothalamic appetite controller

A spate of discoveries has greatly improved our understanding of the hypothalamic control of appetite. This evidence indicates that the **arcuate nucleus** of the hypothalamus contains a highly specialized appetite controller that is governed by

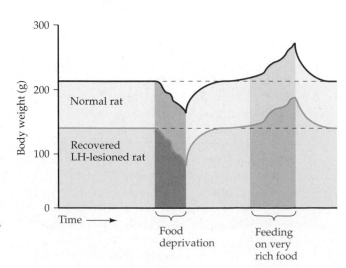

13.24 Lesion-Induced Weight Loss Both normal rats and rats that have recovered from lesions of the lateral hypothalamus (LH) regulate body weight quite well. The LH-lesioned rats regulate around a lowered target weight, but in parallel with normal rats. (After Keesey and Boyle, 1973.)

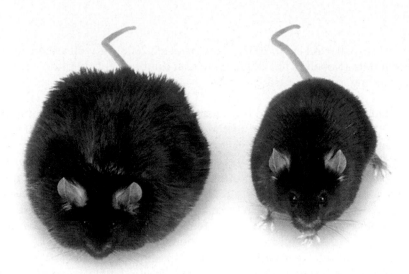

13.25 Inherited Obesity Both of these mice have two copies of the *obese* gene, which impairs the production of leptin by fat cells. The mouse on the left weighs about 67 g; a normal (wild-type) mouse at this age weighs about 25 g. The mouse on the right has been treated with leptin, and weighs about 35 g.

circulating levels of a variety of hormones. One of these hormones is insulin, which we have already discussed. Additional hormones that are believed to participate include some recently discovered peptides: leptin, ghrelin, and a hormone with the cumbersome name *peptide YY$_{3-36}$* (*PYY$_{3-36}$*). We will discuss each in turn, and then look at the probable organization of the hypothalamic appetite controller.

LEPTIN Mice that receive two copies of the gene called *obese* (abbreviated *ob*) regulate their body weight at a high level (**Figure 13.25**), as you might have guessed from the gene's name. These mice have larger and more numerous fat cells than their heterozygous littermates (*ob/+*; the plus sign indicates the wild-type, normal allele). The fat mice (*ob/ob*) maintain their obesity even when given an unpalatable diet or when required to work hard to obtain food (Cruce et al., 1974).

The *ob/ob* mice have defective genes for the peptide **leptin** (from the Greek *leptos*, "thin"). Fat cells produce leptin and then secrete the protein into the bloodstream (Y. Zhang et al., 1994). Leptin receptors (known as ObR because they are receptors to the *obese* gene product, leptin) have been identified in the choroid plexus, the cortex, and several hypothalamic nuclei (Hâkansson et al., 1998), to be discussed shortly. Animals with defects in the gene that encodes ObR, such as Zucker rats (al-Barazanji et al., 1997; L. M. Zucker and Zucker, 1961) and diabetic mice (Coleman and Hummel, 1973), also become obese.

Thus, the brain seems to monitor circulating leptin levels to measure and regulate the body's energy reserves in the form of fat. Defects in leptin production or leptin sensitivity cause a false underreporting of body fat, leading the animals to overeat, especially high-fat or sugary foods.

GHRELIN Ghrelin, released into the bloodstream by endocrine cells of the stomach (Kojima et al., 1999), was named in recognition of its effects on growth hormone secretion (*GH-rel*easing). But we now know that ghrelin is a powerful appetite *stimulant* (Nakazato et al., 2001). Circulating levels of ghrelin rise during fasting and immediately drop after a meal is eaten. Treating either rats or humans with exogenous ghrelin produces a rapid and large increase in appetite (Wren et al., 2000, 2001).

Curiously, obese subjects reportedly have lower baseline levels of ghrelin than do lean subjects prior to eating, but following a meal their circulating levels of ghrelin do not drop (their leptin levels remain high too). So, one mechanism of obesity may involve a ghrelin system that is unresponsive to feeding and thus always slightly elevated, prompting continual hunger (English et al., 2002).

Under some circumstances, the ghrelin gene encodes a second peptide, named *obestatin* in recognition of evidence that it could act as an appetite suppressant (J. V. Zhang et al., 2005). However, controversies over the type and distribution of

leptin A peptide hormone released by fat cells.

ghrelin A peptide hormone emanating from the gut.

PYY$_{3-36}$ A peptide hormone, secreted by the intestines, that probably acts on hypothalamic appetite control mechanisms to suppress appetite.

neuropeptide Y (NPY) A peptide neurotransmitter that may carry some of the signals for feeding.

agouti-related peptide (AgRP) A peptide that is a naturally occurring antagonist to α-melanocyte-stimulating hormone at melanocortin receptors.

NPY/AgRP neurons Neurons involved in the hypothalamic appetite control system, so named because they produce both neuropeptide Y and agouti-related peptide.

POMC/CART neurons Neurons involved in the hypothalamic appetite control system, so named because they produce both pro-opiomelanocortin and cocaine- and amphetamine-related transcript.

pro-opiomelanocortin (POMC) A prohormone that can be cleaved to produce the melanocortins, which also participate in feeding control.

cocaine- and amphetamine-regulated transcript (CART) A peptide produced in the brain when an animal is injected with either cocaine or amphetamine. It is also associated with the appetite control circuitry of the hypothalamus.

obestatin receptors (Chartrel et al., 2007; Lauwers et al., 2006), as well as contradictory behavioral data (Kobelt et al., 2008), have cast doubt on this peptide's role in appetite and feeding, pending further study.

PYY$_{3-36}$ Secreted into the circulation by cells of the small and large intestine, the small peptide **PYY$_{3-36}$** is at a low level in the blood prior to eating, but that level rises rapidly on ingestion of a meal. Systemic injections of PYY$_{3-36}$ curb appetite in both rats and humans, as do injections directly into the arcuate nucleus of the hypothalamus of rats (Batterham and Bloom, 2003; Baynes et al., 2006; Chelikani et al., 2005). Interestingly, lower-than-average levels of circulating PYY$_{3-36}$ are associated with a tendency toward obesity in mice and humans, and postmeal increases in this peptide have been closely linked to feelings of satiety in normal-weight people (see Karra et al., 2009, for a review). It therefore appears that PYY$_{3-36}$ may act in opposition to ghrelin, providing a potent appetite-*suppressing* stimulus to the hypothalamus. The discoveries of PYY$_{3-36}$ and ghrelin have provided important clues about the appetite control mystery, and there is growing evidence that these hormones converge on the arcuate nucleus of the hypothalamus, which we describe next.

THE ARCUATE APPETITE CONTROLLER The current model of the organization of appetite control neurons in the arcuate nucleus is sketched in **Figure 13.26**. The appetite controller relies on two sets of arcuate neurons with opposing effects, which are named according to the types of neurotransmitters and hormones they produce. One set of neurons produces the peptides **neuropeptide Y** (**NPY**) and **agouti-related peptide** (**AgRP**), and so are known as **NPY/AgRP neurons**. When activated, these NPY/AgRP neurons *stimulate* appetite while also reducing metabolism; both actions lead to weight gain. In contrast, activation of the other set of neurons—called **POMC/CART neurons** because they produce **pro-opiomelanocortin** (**POMC**) and **cocaine- and amphetamine-regulated transcript** (**CART**)—*inhibit* appetite and increase metabolism, actions that promote weight loss.

Projections from the POMC/CART neurons and NPY/AgRP neurons have two main functions. Some projections stay within the arcuate, allowing the two sets of neurons to influence each other's activity through reciprocal connections (see Figure 13.26*b*). Other projections leave the arcuate and make contact with neurons in other hypothalamic sites. It is through these projections that the arcuate system ultimately modulates food intake.

Now let's consider how the peripheral hormones interact with this appetite controller. First, because it is made by fat cells, leptin (and to a lesser extent, insulin) conveys information about the body's energy reserves. Both types of neurons in the arcuate appetite controller have leptin receptors, but leptin affects them in opposite ways. High circulating levels of leptin *activate* the appetite-suppressing POMC/CART neurons but *inhibit* the appetite-increasing NPY/AgRP neurons, so in both systems leptin is working to suppress hunger. In keeping with its role as an indicator of the body's current composition, leptin seems to have a long-term effect on the appetite controller, perhaps by promoting the remodeling of neurons in the arcuate nucleus (Bouret et al., 2004).

In contrast to leptin, ghrelin and PYY$_{3-36}$ provide more-acute, rapidly changing hour-to-hour hunger signals from the gut. Both peptides act primarily on the appetite-stimulating NPY/AgRP neurons of the arcuate. Ghrelin stimulates these cells, leading to a corresponding increase in appetite. PYY$_{3-36}$ works in opposition, inhibiting the same cells to *reduce* appetite. Short-term control of appetite thus reflects a balance between ghrelin and PYY$_{3-36}$ concentrations in circulation.

Although much progress has been made in understanding the control of appetite, the story is not yet complete. Further research will clarify the role of additional newly discovered satiety signals from the gut, such as oxyntomodulin and glucagon-like peptide-1 (Neary and Batterham, 2009), along with additional

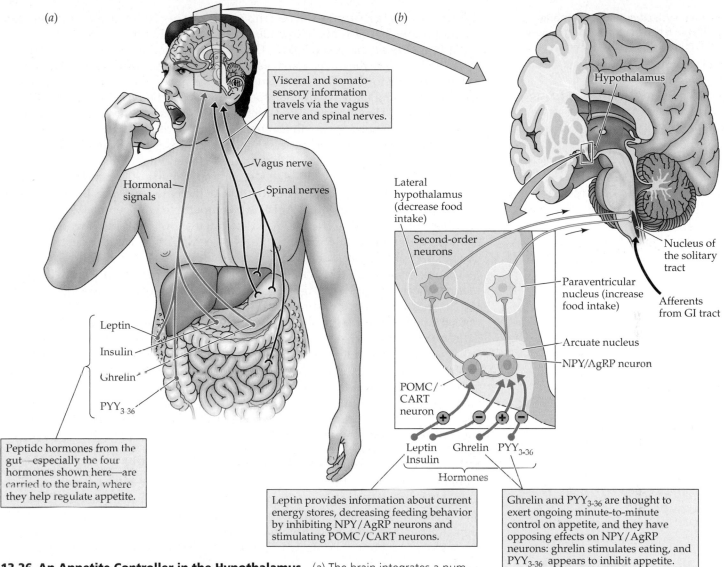

(a)
Visceral and somato-sensory information travels via the vagus nerve and spinal nerves.

(b)

Hypothalamus

Vagus nerve

Spinal nerves

Hormonal signals

Leptin

Insulin

Ghrelin

PYY$_{3-36}$

Peptide hormones from the gut—especially the four hormones shown here—are carried to the brain, where they help regulate appetite.

Lateral hypothalamus (decrease food intake)

Second-order neurons

Paraventricular nucleus (increase food intake)

Nucleus of the solitary tract

Afferents from GI tract

Arcuate nucleus

NPY/AgRP neuron

POMC/CART neuron

Leptin Ghrelin PYY$_{3-36}$
Insulin

Hormones

Leptin provides information about current energy stores, decreasing feeding behavior by inhibiting NPY/AgRP neurons and stimulating POMC/CART neurons.

Ghrelin and PYY$_{3-36}$ are thought to exert ongoing minute-to-minute control on appetite, and they have opposing effects on NPY/AgRP neurons: ghrelin stimulates eating, and PYY$_{3-36}$ appears to inhibit appetite.

13.26 An Appetite Controller in the Hypothalamus (*a*) The brain integrates a number of peripheral signals to determine appetite. Among these are numerous gut peptides secreted into the bloodstream, especially (1) leptin, secreted by fat cells; (2) insulin, secreted by the pancreas; (3) ghrelin, secreted by the stomach; and (4) PYY$_{3-36}$, secreted by the intestines. In addition, visceral and somatosensory information is transmitted via spinal nerves and the vagus. (*b*) Two types of neurons in the arcuate nucleus are sensitive to peptides from the periphery: POMC/CART-synthesizing neurons signal a decrease in food intake; NPY/AgRP-synthesizing neurons promote increased feeding. Both types of arcuate neurons exert their effects via second-order neurons in the paraventricular nucleus and lateral hypothalamus. POMC/CART neurons signal satiety by releasing α-melanocyte-stimulating hormone (α-MSH). NPY/AgRP neurons stimulate appetite through the release of NPY, but also by releasing AgRP, which directly competes for the melanocortin receptors, reducing the effectiveness of α-MSH in suppressing appetite.

components of the hypothalamic appetite controller, like nesfatin-1 (Oh-I et al., 2006). The arcuate appetite controller exerts its effects on feeding behavior via other brain sites, which we discuss in the next section.

Second-order hypothalamic mechanisms integrate appetite signals

Having identified the main components of the arcuate appetite controller, we can turn to the functional connections of these cells to "downstream" sites involved in feeding. Two hypothalamic sites—the **paraventricular nucleus** (**PVN**) and the lateral

paraventricular nucleus (PVN) A nucleus of the hypothalamus.

α-melanocyte stimulating hormone (α-MSH) A peptide that binds the melanocortin receptor.

melanocortins One category of endogenous opioid peptides.

melanocortin type-4 receptors (MC4Rs) A specific subtype of melanocortin receptor.

orexins Also called *hypocretins*. Neuropeptides produced in the hypothalamus that are involved in switching between sleep states, in narcolepsy, and in the control of appetite.

cholecystokinin (CCK) A peptide hormone that is released by the gut after ingestion of food high in protein and/or fat.

endocannabinoid An endogenous ligand of cannabinoid receptors; thus, an analog of marijuana that is produced by the brain.

hypothalamus (LH)—appear to be primary targets of projections from the arcuate (refer to Figure 13.26b for help in understanding this circuit).

The appetite-suppressing POMC/CART neurons of the arcuate project primarily to the LH. Here they release **α-melanocyte-stimulating hormone (α-MSH)**, a peptide hormone belonging to a small family of substances, called **melanocortins**, that are derived from POMC. Acting via specific **melanocortin type-4 receptors** (**MC4Rs**) located on the LH neurons, α-MSH decreases the LH's appetite-stimulating activity, resulting in a net decrease in feeding.

The NPY/AgRP neurons are essential for increases in feeding (Gropp et al., 2005), exerting their effects through both the PVN and the LH (see Figure 13.26b). Injecting NPY into the PVN stimulates feeding (Leibowitz, 1991), and NPY released by the NPY/AgRP neurons appears to provoke increased appetite. But what about that AgRP? We now know that AgRP is a competitive endogenous MC4R ligand. So when it is released in the LH, AgRP competes for MC4R binding. AgRP thus counters the appetite-suppressing effects of α-MSH that we just described and instead provokes an *increase* in feeding behavior via the LH.

The net result of all this is a constant balancing act between the appetite-stimulating effects of the NPY/AgRP system and the appetite-suppressing effects of the POMC/CART system, spread across both the PVN and the LH. Of particular note, the peptide **orexin** (from the Greek *oregein*, "to desire") (**Figure 13.27**), which is produced by neurons in the lateral hypothalamus, appears to participate in the subsequent control of feeding. Direct injection of orexin into the hypothalamus of rats causes up to a sixfold increase in feeding (Sakurai et al., 1998), and evidence is emerging that hypothalamic orexin is regulated to some extent by circulating leptin (Ohno and Sakurai, 2008). Orexins (which are also known as *hypocretins*) are also involved in the sleep disorder narcolepsy (see Chapter 14), but how that function relates to hunger is unknown.

Other systems also play a role in hunger and satiety

Appetite signals from the hypothalamus converge on the nucleus of the solitary tract (NST) in the brainstem (see Figure 13.26b). The NST can be viewed as part of a common pathway for feeding behavior, and it receives and integrates appetite signals from a variety of sources in addition to the hypothalamus. For example, the sensation of hunger is affected by a wide variety of peripheral sensory inputs, such as oral stimulation and the feeling of stomach distension, transmitted via spinal and cranial nerves. The liver detects glucose levels and circulating levels of fatty acids, and it communicates both kinds of information through the vagus nerve to the NST. Cutting the vagus nerve disrupts feeding responses to circulating glucose and fatty acids (Tordoff et al., 1991). The vagus also provides an alternate route by which gut peptides can affect appetite. For example, **cholecystokinin** (**CCK**) is released by the gut after ingestion of food high in protein and/or fat. Administration of exogenous CCK suppresses appetite primarily by acting on receptors of the vagus nerve, and cutting the vagus blocks this action (for a review of CCK's actions, see H. Fink et al., 1998).

A variety of other brain locations also participate in feeding behavior, either directly or through indirect effects on other processes. For example, as you might expect, the brain's reward system appears to be intimately involved with feeding. Activity of a circuit including the amygdaloid nuclei and the dopamine-mediated reward system in the nucleus accumbens (see Chapter 4) is hypothesized to mediate pleasurable aspects of feeding (Ahn and Phillips, 2002; Volkow and Wise, 2005).

The **endocannabinoid** system is also emerging as a major regulator of appetite and feeding. Endocannabinoids, such as *anandamide*, are endogenous substances that act much like the active ingredient in marijuana (*Cannabis sativa*) and, like marijuana, can potently stimu-

13.27 Neuropeptides That Induce Hunger? In situ hybridization indicates that orexin mRNA (white spots) is made only in the lateral hypothalamus. Infusion of orexin into this region causes rats to eat more food. (Courtesy of Masashi Yanagisawa.)

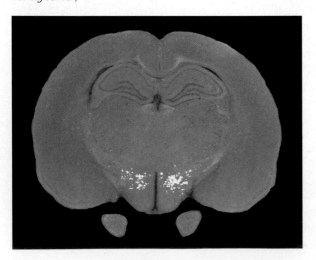

late hunger. Acting both in the brain and in the periphery, endocannabinoids are thought to stimulate feeding by affecting the mesolimbic dopamine reward system, as well as hypothalamic appetite mechanisms, while also inhibiting satiety signals from the gut (Di Marzo and Matias, 2005). Similarly, lesion studies indicate that feeding is impaired following the destruction of regions within the amygdaloid nuclei, the frontal cortex, and the substantia nigra, to name but a few.

Hypothalamic feeding control must be strongly influenced by inputs from higher brain centers, but little is known about these mechanisms. During development, for example, our feeding patterns cease to be determined solely by biological hunger and increasingly are influenced by social factors such as parental and peer group pressures (Birch et al., 2003). Understanding the nature of cortical influences on feeding mechanisms is a major challenge for the future.

The list of participants in appetite regulation is long and growing longer each day (**Table 13.3**), revealing overlapping and complex controls with a high degree of redundancy, as befits a behavioral function of such critical importance to the health and survival of the individual. With each new discovery, we draw nearer to finally developing safe and effective treatments for eating disorders, as we discuss next.

Obesity Is Difficult to Treat

Unfortunately, effective interventions for reversing obesity have been elusive, in part because the multiple redundant adaptations that we have been discussing tend to work against weight loss (**Box 13.1**). Like it or not, our evolutionary history has optimized our bodies for obtaining and storing energy, and protecting against accumulating *too much* energy was not much of a concern for our distant forebears. The tendency to accumulate excess energy is exacerbated by our ever more sedentary lifestyles. The current epidemic of obesity is certainly a major health problem: almost 65% of the adults in the United States are overweight, and about 31% qualify as obese (Flegal et al., 2002). These categories are based on body mass index (BMI), which is defined in **Table 13.4**. The higher incidence of cardiovascular disease, diabetes, and other disorders that accompany obesity will be an increasingly heavy burden on health care services in the future.

In Lewis Carroll's *Alice's Adventures in Wonderland*, Alice quaffs the contents of a small bottle in order to shrink. The quest for a real-life shrinking potion—but one that makes you thin rather than short—is the subject of intense scientific activity, and several major strategies or targets are emerging.

APPETITE CONTROL Hopes are high that drugs designed to modify the functioning of the hypothalamic appetite system will be safe and potent obesity treatments. Unfortunately, despite initial excitement, modifications of leptin signals have not proven to be very effective; only a tiny minority of obese people have abnormal leptin levels, and most have *higher* levels of circulating leptin than do thin people (Montague et al., 1997).

TABLE 13.3 Hormones and Neurotransmitters Involved in Regulating Feeding and Body Weight

Increased feeding and weight gain	Decreased feeding and weight loss
Agouti-related peptide (AgRP)	α-Melanocyte stimulating hormone (α-MSH)
β-Endorphin	Brain-derived neurotrophic factor (BDNF)
Corticosterone/cortisol	Cholecystokinin (CCK)
Dopamine	Cocaine- and amphetamine-regulated transcript (CART)
Dynorphin	Corticotropin-releasing hormone (CRH)
Endocannabinoids	Estrogen
Ghrelin	Glucagon-like peptide-1 (GLP-1)
Melanin-concentrating hormone	Histamine
Neuropeptide Y	Insulin
Norepinephrine	Leptin
Orexin/hypocretin	Nesfatin-1
Testosterone	Oxyntomodulin
	PYY_{3-36}
	Serotonin

Note: Many of the members of this partial list are targets for anti-obesity drug development.

TABLE 13.4 Body Mass Index (BMI)

BMI value	Body weight category
<15	Starvation
15–18.5	Underweight
18.5–25	Ideal weight
25–30	Overweight
30–40	Obese
>40	Morbidly obese

Note:

$$BMI = \frac{weight\ (kg)}{height \times height\ (m \times m)}\ or$$

$$BMI = 703\frac{weight\ (lb)}{height \times height\ (in. \times in.)}$$

BOX 13.1 Body Fat Stores Are Tightly Regulated, Even after Surgical Removal of Fat

As any dieter will attest, the body seems to know how much it wants to weigh, and it defies our efforts to change that value. As in other mammals, our homeostatic mechanisms defend a set value for weight. Perhaps the most striking demonstration of this phenomenon is exhibited by golden-mantled ground squirrels, which show an extreme seasonal variation in body weight, greatly fattening up in the spring.

When these squirrels are brought into the laboratory, they continue to show an annual rhythm in body weight, even when food is always available (Figure A) (I. Zucker, 1988). Force-feeding the squirrels or depriving them of food will cause a temporary increase or decrease in body weight, but as soon as food access returns to normal, body weight returns to the value that is normal for the season.

Even more impressive is the fact that, if body fat is surgically removed, the animals will eat until they regain—with remarkable precision—the amount of fat that would be normal for the season (Figure B) (Dark et al., 1984). Needless to say, these results are not encouraging to humans considering liposuction. Usually the fat simply returns after the procedure.

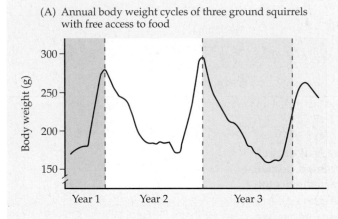

(A) Annual body weight cycles of three ground squirrels with free access to food

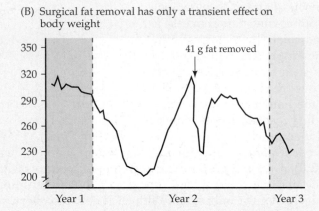

(B) Surgical fat removal has only a transient effect on body weight

Interestingly, leptin appears to regulate endogenous cannabinoid levels in the hypothalamus (Di Marzo and Matias, 2005; Di Marzo et al., 2001). Therefore, drugs that are cannabinoid antagonists might effectively suppress appetite by causing "anti-munchies"—the reverse of the hunger experienced by marijuana users. As predicted, a selective CB_1 cannabinoid receptor blocker (rimonabant) effectively reduces appetite and feeding behavior, leading to weight loss (Thornton-Jones et al., 2006; Van Gaal et al., 2005). Unfortunately, rimonabant reportedly causes significant mood problems (an "anti-high"?), so its use has been suspended while more research is conducted.

Drugs also can be designed to target some of the signaling systems integral to the arcuate appetite controller. For instance, given the efficacy of α-MSH transmission in reducing hunger, agonists of the MC4R melanocortin receptor are presently attractive targets for drug development. Another promising treatment under development is a PYY_{3-36}-based nasal spray. Recall that PYY_{3-36}, from the gut, acts on arcuate neurons to reduce appetite (see Figure 13.26), ultimately resulting in weight loss (Batterham et al., 2003; Chelikani et al., 2005; Sileno et al., 2006). Other newly discovered satiety signals, such as nesfatin-1, oxyntomodulin, and glucagon-like peptide-1, similarly provide excellent targets for drug development; and numerous compounds targeting these systems are in clinical trials (Neary and Batterham, 2009).

INCREASED METABOLISM An alternative approach to treating obesity involves treatments that cause the body's metabolic rate to increase and thus expend extra calories in the form of heat. As we discussed in Chapter 5, metabolic rate is controlled by the thyroid hormones, especially thyroxine; but treating people with thyroxine has undesirable side effects, such as dangerously increased heart rate. The increase in heart rate may be avoided with compounds that selectively activate the thyroid hormone receptors (TRb's) associated with metabolism, but not the thyroid hormone receptors associated with cardiovascular changes (TRa's) (Grover et al., 2003).

INHIBITION OF FAT TISSUE   A third approach to treating obesity involves attempts to interfere with the formation of new fat tissue. For example, in order for fat tissue to grow, it must be able to recruit and develop new blood vessels—a process called *angiogenesis*. Selectively blocking one type of receptor for vascular endothelial growth factor (VEGF)—a signaling protein that normally stimulates angiogenesis—effectively inhibits the growth of fat tissue in mice fed a diet that usually produces obesity (Tam et al., 2009). This finding supports the idea that angiogenesis inhibitors may be useful drugs for treating obesity (Rupnick et al., 2002).

REDUCED ABSORPTION   Only a few drugs are currently approved for the treatment of obesity; most are still in development. One current obesity medication—orlistat (Xenical)—works by interfering with the digestion of fat. However, this approach has generally produced only modest weight loss, and it often causes intestinal discomfort.

REDUCED REWARD   A different perspective on treating obesity focuses on the rewarding properties of food. Not only is food delicious, but "comfort foods" also directly reduce circulating stress hormones, thereby providing another reward. Chronic food restriction makes rewarding brain stimulations even more rewarding than usual, and this effect is reversed by treatment with leptin (Fulton et al., 2000). Drugs that affect the brain's reward circuitry (see Chapter 4), reducing the rewarding properties of food, may prove beneficial for weight loss (Volkow and Wise, 2005).

ANTI-OBESITY SURGERY   The surgical removal of fat tissue, particularly through liposuction, is a popular approach to controlling weight, but it is generally only moderately successful and temporary (see Box 13.1). Because of the propensity of fat tissue to regrow after excision, some people are turning to more invasive weight loss surgeries: **bariatric** procedures that bypass part of the intestinal tract or stomach in order to reduce the volume and absorptive capacity of the digestive system (**Figure 13.28**). Although gastric bypass surgery doesn't directly target appetite-controlling mechanisms, alterations in appetite hormones such as ghrelin reportedly accompany the surgery (Baynes et al., 2006; D. E. Cummings, 2006). As the only current intervention that produces significant and lasting weight loss, gastric bypass surgery can offer hope of substantial weight loss and reversal of co-morbid conditions like Type II diabetes and hypertension, but it is accompanied by significant complications and risks. Although gastric bypass techniques are being improved all the time, mortality and illness remain real threats (Flum et al., 2005).

Less invasive surgical procedures are under study, such as the use of gastric stimulators that activate the gut's satiety signals to reduce appetite. Curiously, simply implanting inert weights into the abdominal cavities of mice causes them to lose a proportionate

bariatric   Having to do with obesity.

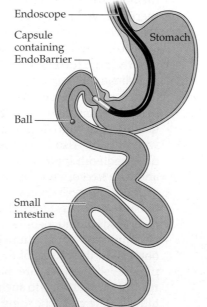

The EndoBarrier is inserted through the mouth via an endoscope and is guided into position by use of a ball and catheter.

Endoscope

Capsule containing EndoBarrier

Stomach

Ball

Small intestine

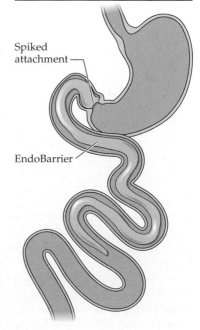

The sleeve lines the small intestine and is held in place with a spiked attachment. It alters the gut's physiology, promoting weight loss.

Spiked attachment

EndoBarrier

13.28 Fat-Busting Liner for the Intestine

amount of weight, apparently by fooling the body into thinking it is fatter than it actually is (Adams et al., 2003). Perhaps some of us, someday, will be able to lose weight simply by taking on extra ballast!

Eating Disorders Are Life-Threatening

Sometimes people shun food, despite having no apparent aversion to it. Like Kitty, whom we met at the opening of the chapter, these people are usually young, become obsessed with their body weight, and become extremely thin—generally by eating very little and sometimes also by regurgitating food, taking laxatives, overexercising, or drinking large amounts of water to suppress appetite. This condition, which is more common in adolescent girls and women than in males, is called **anorexia nervosa**. The name of the disorder indicates (1) that the patients have no appetite (*anorexia*) and (2) that the disorder originates in the nervous system (*nervosa*).

People who suffer from anorexia nervosa tend to think about food a good deal, and physiological evidence suggests that they respond even *more* than normal subjects to the presentation of food (Broberg and Bernstein, 1989); for example, food stimuli provoke a large release of insulin, despite cognitive denial of any feelings of hunger. So, in a physiological sense their hunger may be normal or even exaggerated, but this hunger is somehow absent from the conscious perceptions of these individuals and they refuse to eat. The idea that anorexia nervosa is primarily a nervous system disorder stems from this mismatch between physiology and cognition, and from the distorted body image of the patients (they may consider themselves fat when others see them as emaciated). The observation that agouti-related peptide (AgRP) levels are abnormal in women with anorexia nervosa (Moriya et al., 2006) suggests that the hypothalamic appetite controller described earlier may also be functioning abnormally in this condition. Studies of the incidence of eating disorders in twins indicate that a predisposition toward anorexia is heritable (Klump et al., 2001), and leading candidates for underlying physiological causes include abnormalities in serotonergic neurotransmission and alterations in the functioning of the dopamine-based reward system (see Chapter 4) that persist even after recovery (Kaye et al., 2009).

Anorexia nervosa is notoriously difficult to treat because it appears to involve an unfortunate combination of genetic, endocrine, personality, cognitive, and environmental variables. One approach that is successful in some cases is a family-centered therapy that de-emphasizes the identification of causal factors and instead focuses on intensive, parent-led "refeeding" of the anorexic person (Le Grange, 2005). This approach, termed *Maudsley therapy* after the hospital where it was introduced, was effective in returning Kitty to her normal weight (H. Brown, 2006).

Bulimia (or *bulimia nervosa*, from the Greek *boulimia*, "great hunger") is a related disorder. Like those who suffer from anorexia nervosa, people with bulimia may believe themselves fatter than they are, but they periodically gorge themselves, usually with "junk food," and then either vomit the food or take laxatives to avoid weight gain. Also like sufferers of anorexia nervosa, people with bulimia may be obsessed with food and body weight, but not all of them become emaciated. Both anorexia nervosa and bulimia can be fatal because in each case the patient's lack of nutrient reserves damages various organ systems and/or leaves the body unable to battle otherwise mild diseases.

In **binge eating**, people spontaneously gorge themselves with far more food than is required to satisfy hunger, often to the point of illness. Such people are often obese, and the causes of the bingeing are not fully understood. In susceptible people, the strong pleasure associated with food activates opiate and dopaminergic reward mechanisms to such an extent that bingeing resembles drug addiction. Mutation of the gene encoding the MC4R receptor is also associated with binge eating (Branson et al., 2003). Recall that α-MSH acts on MC4R to signal satiety, so people with the mutation may be failing to receive the signal to stop eating.

anorexia nervosa A syndrome in which individuals severely deprive themselves of food.

bulimia Also called *bulimia nervosa*. A syndrome in which individuals periodically gorge themselves, usually with "junk food," and then either vomit or take laxatives to avoid weight gain.

binge eating The paroxysmal intake of large quantities of food, often of poor nutritional value and high calories.

13.29 Changing Ideals of Female Beauty (a) Actress Keira Knightley provides an extreme example of modern society's emphasis on thinness as an aspect of beauty. (b) In contrast, Helena Fourment, wife of Flemish painter Peter Paul Rubens and pictured here in *Helena Fourment as Aphrodite* (circa 1630), exemplifies the very different ideal for the feminine form during her era. Some people have suggested that our modern weight-conscious notions of female beauty are responsible for some cases of anorexia nervosa and bulimia.

(a)

(b)

Despite the epidemic of obesity in our society, or perhaps because of it, our present culture emphasizes that women, especially young women, must be thin to be attractive (**Figure 13.29a**). This cultural pressure is widely perceived as one of the causes of eating disorders. In earlier times, however, when plump women were considered the most beautiful (witness Renaissance paintings, such as the one shown in **Figure 13.29b**), some women still fasted severely and may have suffered from anorexia nervosa. The origins of these disorders remain elusive, and to date, the available therapies help only a minority of patients like Kitty.

SUMMARY

Homeostasis Maintains Internal States within a Critical Range

- The nervous system plays a crucial role in maintaining the **homeostasis** that the body requires for proper functioning. Temperature, fluid concentration, chemical energy, and nutrients must all be maintained within a critical range.

- The redundancy of homeostatic mechanisms reflects the fundamental importance of a stable internal environment. These mechanisms generally are **negative feedback** systems. **Review Figure 13.1, Web Activity 13.1**

TEMPERATURE REGULATION

Body Temperature Is a Critical Condition for All Biological Processes

- Because the speed of biochemical reactions is temperature dependent, precise control of body temperature is essential. Ice crystals are extremely damaging to many cells, and must be avoided through the production of antifreeze proteins.

Some Animals Generate Heat; Others Must Obtain Heat from the Environment

- Both **endotherms** and **ectotherms** regulate body temperature, but ectotherms depend more on behaviors to capture heat from the environment, while endotherms generate most of their body heat through the **metabolism** of food. **Review Web Activity 13.2**

- Endotherms can remain active longer than ectotherms can, but endotherms are also obliged to gather more food than

ectotherms do to generate their body warmth.

- Body size and shape drastically affect the rate of heat loss. Small endotherms have a higher metabolic rate, using more energy (per gram of body weight) than large endotherms use. **Review Table 13.1**

Which Behaviors Can Adjust Body Temperature?

- Both endotherms and ectotherms use behavioral methods to help regulate body temperature at optimal levels. Young animals particularly depend on this form of thermoregulation.

The Brain Monitors and Regulates Body Temperature

- The preoptic area of the hypothalamus, the brainstem, and the spinal cord monitor and help regulate body temperature. **Review Figures 13.3 and 13.7**

FLUID REGULATION

Our Cells Evolved to Function in Seawater

- Our cells function properly only when the concentration of salts and other ions (the **osmolality**) of the intracellular compartment of the body is within a critical range. The extracellular compartment is a source of replacement water and a buffer between the intracellular compartment and the outside world. **Review Figure 13.10**

Two Internal Cues Trigger Thirst

- Thirst can be triggered either by a drop in the volume of the extracellular compartment (**hypovolemic thirst**) or by an increase in the osmolality of the extracellular compartment (**osmotic thirst**). Either signal indicates that the volume or osmolality of the intracellular compartment may fall outside the critical range. Because of the importance of osmolality, we must regulate salt intake in order to regulate water balance effectively. **Review Figure 13.11**

■ A drop in blood volume triggers at least three responses: (a) **Baroreceptors** in the major blood vessels detect the drop and signal the brain via the autonomic nervous system. (b) The brain in turn releases vasopressin from the posterior pituitary, and the vasopressin reduces blood vessel volume and the amount of water lost through urination. (c) The kidneys release renin, providing circulating **angiotensin II**, which reduces blood vessel volume to maintain blood pressure and may also signal the brain that the blood volume has dropped. **Review Figure 13.1**

■ The hypothalamus contains **osmosensory neurons** that detect the concentration of extracellular fluid. Increased **solute** concentration of the extracellular fluid triggers an intake of water. **Review Figures 13.15 and 13.16**

■ The conscious perception of thirst involves activation of a network of limbic system sites, and is a powerful motivator.

Homeostatic Regulation of Salt Is Required for Effective Regulation of Water

■ The amount of water that the body can retain is determined by salt balance. In the absence of salt, extracellular fluid becomes too dilute and excess water must be eliminated. The adrenal steroid aldosterone performs the vital function of conserving salt.

FOOD AND ENERGY REGULATION

Nutrient Regulation Requires the Anticipation of Future Needs

■ Our digestive system breaks down food and uses most of it for energy, especially because we are endotherms.

Insulin Is Crucial for the Regulation of Body Metabolism

■ Although brain cells can use **glucose** directly, body cells can import glucose only with the assistance of **insulin** secreted by the pancreas. Insulin also promotes the storage of glucose as **glycogen**. Another pancreatic hormone, **glucagon**, helps convert glycogen back into glucose. **Review Figure 13.20**

■ Manipulations of either glucose or insulin can affect whether an animal experiences **hunger**, but experimental studies have indicated that neither glucose nor insulin alone can be the single indicator of hunger or **satiety**. There also seems to be no single brain center for either satiety or hunger.

The Hypothalamus Coordinates Multiple Systems That Control Hunger

■ An appetite controller located in the **arcuate nucleus** of the hypothalamus responds to levels of several peptide gut hormones. **Leptin**, providing a chronic signal about fat levels, stimulates arcuate **POMC/CART neurons** to release α-**MSH** in the lateral hypothalamus to activate **MC4R** receptors to decrease appetite. Leptin inhibits arcuate **NPY/AgRP neurons**, decreasing their release of NPY and AgRP to suppress appetite further. **Review Figure 13.26**

■ **Ghrelin** and **PYY$_{3-36}$** provide more-acute signals from the gut. Ghrelin stimulates and PYY$_{3-36}$ inhibits the arcuate appetite control system. **Review Figure 13.26**

Obesity Is Difficult to Treat

■ Obesity is a pervasive problem that is difficult to treat through diet, drugs, or surgery. The only long-lasting medical intervention for obesity is **bariatric** surgery, but several drug strategies based on a new understanding of appetite control offer promise. **Review Figure 13.28**

Eating Disorders Are Life-Threatening

■ The major eating disorders are **anorexia nervosa**, **bulimia**, and **binge eating**. Although several cultural and physiological correlates of eating disorders have been identified, the fundamental causes of these disorders remain a mystery.

Go to **www.biopsychology.com** for study questions, quizzes, key terms, and other resources.

Recommended Reading

Flouris, A. (2009). *On the functional architecture of the human thermoregulatory system: A guide to the biological principles and mechanisms of human thermoregulation.* Berlin: VDM Verlag.

Jessen, C. (2001). *Temperature regulation in humans and other mammals.* Berlin: Telos.

Kirkham, T., and Cooper, S. J. (Eds.). (2006). *Appetite and body weight: Integrative systems and the development of anti-obesity drugs.* Burlington, MA: Academic Press.

Schulkin, J. (2003). *Rethinking homeostasis: Physiology and pathophysiology.* Cambridge, MA: MIT Press.

Thompson, J. K. (2003). *Handbook of eating disorders and obesity.* New York: Wiley.

Biological Rhythms, Sleep, and Dreaming

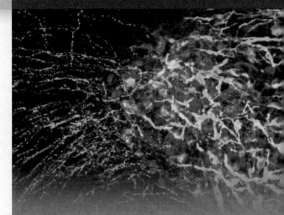

CHAPTER 14

When Sleep Gets Out of Control

Starting college always brings its share of new experiences and adjustments, but "Barry" knew something was wrong freshman year when he seemed to be sleepy all the time (S. Smith, 1997). Barry napped so often that his friends called him the hibernating bear. Of course, college can be exhausting, and many students seek refuge in long snooze sessions. But one day while Barry was camping with his pals, an even odder thing happened: "I laughed really hard, and I kind of fell on my knees … After that, about every week I'd have two or three episodes where if I'd laugh … my arm would fall down or my muscles in my face would get weak. Or if I was running around playing catch and someone said something, I would get weak in the knees. And there was a time there that my friends kinda used it as a joke. If they're going to throw me the ball and they didn't want me to catch it, they'd tell me a joke and I'd fall down and miss it."

It was as if any big surge in emotion in Barry might trigger a sudden paralysis lasting anywhere from a few seconds to a few minutes, affecting either a body part or his whole body. Sex became something of a challenge because sometimes during foreplay, Barry's body would just collapse. "Luckily, you're probably laying down, so it's not that big a deal. But it just puts a damper on the whole thing."

What was happening to Barry?

A ll living systems show repeating, predictable changes over time. These rhythms vary from rapid (e.g., brain potentials) to slow (e.g., annual changes like hibernation). Daily rhythms, the first topic of this chapter, have an intriguing clocklike regularity. The second topic of the chapter is that familiar daily rhythm known as the sleep-waking cycle. By age 60, most humans have spent 20 years asleep (some, alas, on one side or the other of the classroom podium). We'll find that sleep is not a passive state of "nonwaking," but rather the interlocking of several different states orchestrated by the activity of many brain regions.

Biological Rhythms

Biological rhythms range in length from minutes to seconds, and some extend from months to years. We discuss daily rhythms first because they have been studied the most.

Many Animals Show Daily Rhythms in Activity

Most functions of any living system display a rhythm of approximately 24 hours. Because these rhythms last about a day, they are called **circadian rhythms** (from the Latin *circa*, "about," and *dies*, "day"). Circadian rhythms have been studied in a host of creatures at behavioral, physiological, and biochemical levels.

Humans and most other primates are **diurnal**—active during the day. Most rodents, including hamsters, are **nocturnal**—active during dark periods. In either

circadian rhythm A pattern of behavioral, biochemical, or physiological fluctuation that has a 24-hour period.

diurnal Active during the light periods of the daily cycle.

nocturnal Active during the dark periods of the daily cycle.

free-running Referring to a rhythm of behavior shown by an animal deprived of external cues about time of day.

period The interval of time between two similar points of successive cycles, such as sunset to sunset.

case, almost all physiological measures—hormone levels, body temperature, drug sensitivity—change over the course of the day. A favorite way to study circadian rhythms exploits rodents' love of running wheels. A switch attached to the wheel connects to a computer that registers each turn, revealing an activity rhythm as in **Figure 14.1a**.

These circadian activities show extraordinary precision: the beginning of activity may vary only a few minutes from one day to another. For humans who attend to watches and clocks, this regularity may seem uninteresting, but other animals display such remarkable regularity by attending to a *biological clock*.

Circadian rhythms are generated by an endogenous clock

A hamster placed in a dimly lit room continues to show a daily rhythm in wheel running despite the absence of day versus night, suggesting that the animal has an internal clock. But even if the light is always dim, the animal may detect other external cues (e.g., outside noises, temperature, barometric pressure) that signal the time of day. Arguing for an internal clock, however, is the fact that in constant light or dark the circadian cycle is not *exactly* 24 hours: activity starts a few minutes later each day, so eventually the hamster is active while it is daytime outside (**Figure 14.1b**, bottom). The animal is said to be **free-running**, maintaining its own cycle, which, in the absence of external cues, is not exactly 24 hours long.

The free-running period is the animal's natural rhythm. (A **period** is the time between two similar points of successive cycles, such as sunset to sunset.) Because the free-running period does not *quite* match the period of Earth's rotation, and because it differs slightly among individual hamsters in the same room, the free-running period cannot simply be

14.1 How Activity Rhythms Are Measured
(*a*) A running wheel in a hamster's cage is monitored by an event recorder or a computer-linked device. Each revolution of the wheel is displayed as a dark mark that can be printed out on paper. The paper strips are cut apart, and each subsequent day's activity is aligned underneath. Nowadays, computers record the activity and print out plots. (*b*) This hamster's activity record shows that it becomes active shortly *before* the start of the dark phase of the daily cycle and remains active during the dark period (top). When the timing of the light was shifted, so that the lights came on later and went off later each day, the hamster also showed a phase shift of activity. When placed in constant dim light (bottom), the hamster became active a few minutes later each day. This *free-running* activity rhythm indicates that the hamster has an endogenous clock that has a period slightly greater than 24 hours. (After I. Zucker, 1976; based on Rusak and Zucker, 1979.)

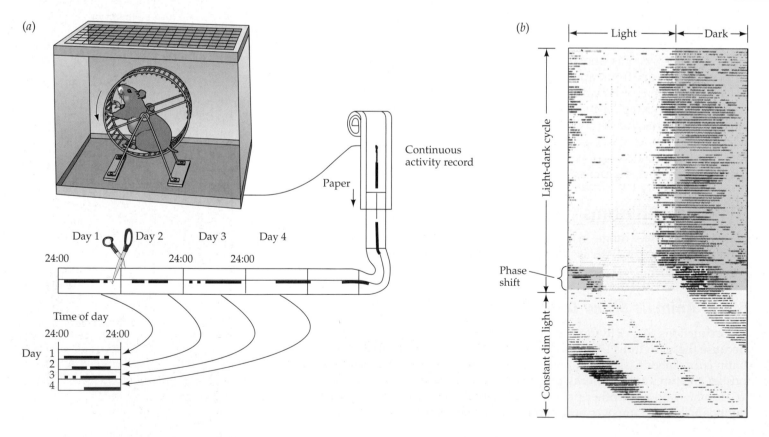

reflecting an external cue. So the animal has some sort of endogenous clock, and in hamsters this clock runs a bit slow.

Normally the internal clock is set by light. If we expose a free-running nocturnal animal to periods of light and dark, it soon synchronizes its wheel running to the beginning of the dark period. The shift of activity produced by a synchronizing stimulus is referred to as a **phase shift** (see Figure 14.1*b*, middle), and the process of shifting the rhythm is called **entrainment**. Any cue that an animal uses to synchronize its activity with the environment is called a **zeitgeber** (German for "time giver"). Light acts as a powerful zeitgeber, and we can easily manipulate it in the laboratory. Because light stimuli can entrain circadian rhythms, the endogenous clock must have inputs from the visual system, as we'll confirm shortly. We humans experience phase shifts when we fly from one time zone to another. Flying three time zones east (say, from California to New York) means that sunlight awakens us 3 hours sooner than the brain expects. In addition to light, the availability of food can serve as a cue to entrain the circadian clock (Fuller et al., 2008; Mistlberger and Skene, 2004).

Circadian rhythms allow animals to anticipate changes in the environment

The major value of circadian rhythms is that they synchronize behavior and body states to changes in the environment. Day and night have great significance for survival. The endogenous clock enables animals to *anticipate* an event, such as darkness, and to begin physiological and behavioral preparations before that event (in this case, before it gets dark). A snack in the den at the end of the day may prepare the animal for a long night of foraging. In other words, circadian rhythms provide the temporal organization of an animal's behavior. Diurnal animals are adapted for obtaining food during the daytime; thus they do not compete with nocturnal animals, whose adaptations favor activity during the night.

The Hypothalamus Houses a Circadian Clock

Where is the endogenous clock that drives circadian rhythms, and how does it work? Early work showed that while removing various endocrine glands has little effect on the free-running rhythm of rats, large lesions of the hypothalamus interfere with circadian rhythms (Richter, 1967). It was subsequently discovered that a tiny subregion of the hypothalamus—the **suprachiasmatic nucleus (SCN)**, named for its location above the optic chiasm—serves as the biological clock. Lesions confined to the SCN portion of the hypothalamus interfere with circadian rhythms of drinking and locomotor behavior (**Figure 14.2**) (F. K. Stephan and Zucker, 1972), and hormone secretion (R. Y. Moore and Eichler, 1972).

The clocklike activity of the SCN is also evident in the metabolic activity of this nucleus. If we take SCN cells out of the brain and put them in a dish (Earnest et al., 1999; Yamazaki et al., 2000), their electrical activity is synchronized to the light-dark cycle that the animal had previously experienced. This striking evidence supports the idea that the SCN contains an endogenous clock (**Figure 14.3**). And as we'll see next, transplants of the SCN from one animal to another provide even stronger proof that the SCN generates a circadian rhythm.

Transplants prove that the SCN produces a circadian rhythm

Ralph and Menaker (1988) found a male hamster that exhibited an unusually short free-running activity rhythm in constant conditions. Normally, hamsters free-run at a period slightly longer than 24 hours, but this male showed a period of 22 hours. Half of the offspring of this male also had a shorter circadian

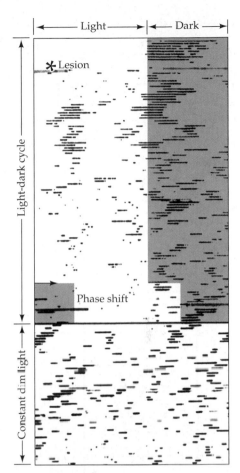

14.2 The Effects of Lesions in the SCN   Circadian rhythms in the animal whose activity is plotted here were normal and synchronized to the light-dark period before an SCN lesion was made (asterisk). After the lesion the animal showed some daily rhythms in activity that were synchronous with the light-dark cycle, but when placed in continuous (dim) light, the animal's activity became completely random, indicating that the lesion had eliminated the endogenous rhythm. The lesioned animal does not show a free-running rhythm of activity but is arrhythmic, running at very different times each day. (From I. Zucker, 1976; based on Rusak and Zucker, 1979.)

phase shift   A shift in the activity of a biological rhythm, typically provided by a synchronizing environmental stimulus.

entrainment   The process of synchronizing a biological rhythm to an environmental stimulus.

zeitgeber   Literally "time-giver" (in German). The stimulus (usually the light-dark cycle) that entrains circadian rhythms.

suprachiasmatic nucleus (SCN)   A small region of the hypothalamus above the optic chiasm that is the location of a circadian oscillator.

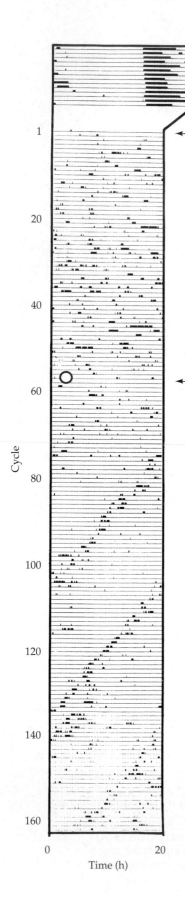

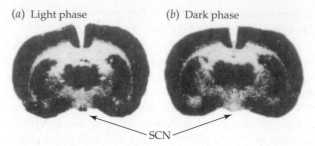

(a) Light phase   (b) Dark phase

SCN

14.3 The Circadian Rhythm of Metabolic Activity of the SCN   These autoradiograms are from coronal sections of rat brains. (a) In a section taken from an animal during a light phase, greater metabolic activity in the SCN is represented by the dark circles at the base of the brain. (b) The SCN has a lower metabolic rate in a section taken from an animal during a dark phase. (From W. J. Schwartz et al., 1979.)

rhythm, so the researchers concluded that he had a genetic mutation affecting the endogenous clock. Animals with two copies of this mutation had an even shorter period: 20 hours. The mutation was named *tau*, after the Greek symbol used by scientists to represent the period of a rhythm. These animals entrained to a normal 24-hour light-dark period just fine; their abnormal endogenous circadian rhythm was revealed only in constant conditions.

Dramatic evidence that this endogenous period is produced in the SCN was provided by transplant experiments. Nonmutant hamsters with lesions of the SCN were placed in constant conditions and, as expected, their circadian activity rhythms were abolished (**Figure 14.4**) (Ralph et al., 1990). The hamsters then received a transplant SCN taken from a fetal hamster with two copies of the mutant *tau* gene. About a week later the hamsters that had received the transplants began showing a free-running activity rhythm again, but the new rhythm matched that of the *donor* SCN: it was about 20 hours rather than the original 24.05.

Reciprocal transplants gave comparable results: the endogenous rhythm following the transplant was always that of the *donor* SCN, not the recipient, so the SCN must be the source of endogenous circadian rhythms. This is the only known case of transplanting brain tissue from one individual to another in which the recipient displays the donor's behavior!

In mammals, light information from the eyes reaches the SCN directly

The pathway that entrains circadian rhythms to light-dark cycles varies depending on the species (Rusak and Zucker, 1979). Most vertebrates have photoreceptors outside the eye that are part of the mechanism of light entrainment. For example, the **pineal gland** of some amphibians is itself sensitive to light (Jamieson and Roberts, 2000) and helps entrain circadian rhythms to light. Because the skull over the pineal is especially thin in some amphibian species, we can think of them as having a primitive "third eye" in the back of the head (some elementary school teachers also seem to have an eye in the back of the head, but this has not been proven to be the pineal gland). In

14.4 Brain Transplants Prove That the SCN Contains a Clock   A wild-type hamster, when kept in constant dim light, displayed an endogenous circadian rhythm 24.05 hours in duration (top). After the SCN was lesioned, the animal became arrhythmic. Later, an SCN from a fetal hamster with two copies of the *tau* mutation was transplanted into the adult hamster (circle). Soon thereafter, the adult hamster began showing a free-running activity rhythm of 19.5 hours, matching the SCN of the donor animal. This response to the transplant showed that the period of the clock is determined within the SCN. (From Ralph et al., 1990.)

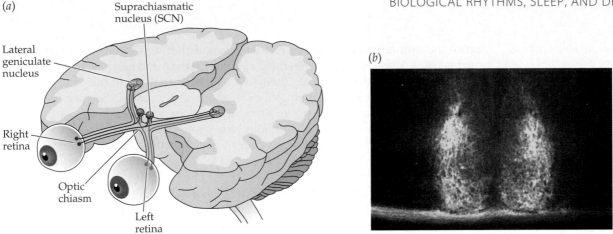

(a)

Suprachiasmatic
nucleus (SCN)

Lateral
geniculate
nucleus

Right
retina

Optic
chiasm

Left
retina

(b)

14.5 The Retinohypothalamic Pathway in Mammals (*a*) This pathway carries information about the light-dark cycle in the environment to the SCN. For clarity of synaptic connections, the SCNs are shown proportionally larger than other features. (*b*) In this image, axons (seen at the bottom) are labeled green from the left eye and red from the right. Both eyes project so diffusely to the two overlying SCNs that they are outlined in yellow. (Photograph courtesy of Andrew D. Huberman.)

birds, too, the pineal possesses photoreceptors that can detect daylight through the skull. In mammals, however, cells in the eye tell the SCN when it is light out.

Certain retinal ganglion cells send their axons along the **retinohypothalamic pathway** veering out of the optic chiasm to synapse directly within the SCN (**Figure 14.5**). This tiny pathway carries information about light to the hypothalamus to entrain behavior (R. Y. Moore, 1983). Most of the retinal ganglion cells that extend their axons to the SCN do not rely on the traditional photoreceptors—rods and cones—to learn about light. Rather, these retinal ganglion cells themselves contain a special photopigment, called **melanopsin**, that makes them sensitive to light (Do et al., 2009). Even transgenic mice that lack rods and cones, and thus cannot detect images on the retina and are blind in every other respect, still entrain their behavior to light (Freedman et al., 1999), because the specialized melanopsin-containing ganglion cells still function. These melanopsin-containing retinal ganglion cells also inform the brain about light to control pupil diameter (Lucas et al., 2003).

Figure 14.6 provides a schematic outline of the mammalian circadian system, including entrainment by light.

pineal gland A secretory gland in the brain midline; the source of melatonin release.

retinohypothalamic pathway The projection of retinal ganglion cells to the suprachiasmatic nuclei.

melanopsin A photopigment found within particular retinal ganglion cells that project to the suprachiasmatic nucleus.

Circadian rhythms have been genetically dissected in flies and mice

The fruit fly *Drosophila melanogaster* displays diurnal circadian rhythms in activity. Flies with a mutation that disabled the gene called *period* (*per*) were arrhythmic when transferred to constant dim light, indicating that their internal clock wasn't running. Subtle mutations of *per* could, depending on the exact change in the gene,

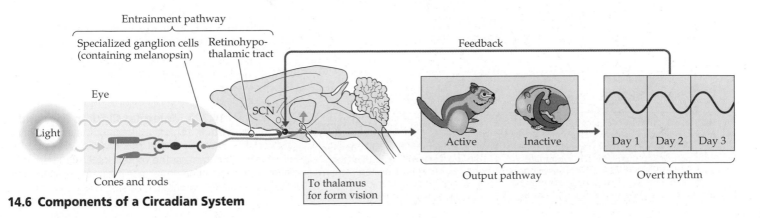

14.6 Components of a Circadian System

dimer   A complex of two proteins that have bound together.

cause the animals to have a free-running period that was longer or shorter than normal (R. J. Konopka and Benzer, 1971). Eventually, more genes were discovered that affect the circadian cycle in *Drosophila*, and mammals were found to have one or more versions of each of them. Work in the fruit fly paved the way for understanding the molecular basis of the circadian clock in mammals.

Cells in the mammalian SCN make two proteins, named Clock and Cycle, that bind together to form a **dimer** (a pair of proteins attached to each other). The Clock/Cycle dimer then binds to the cell's DNA to promote the transcription of *per* and another gene, called *cryptochrome* (*cry*). The resulting Per and Cry proteins then bind to each other and to a third protein, Tau (it was a mutation of the gene for Tau that resulted in hamsters with a shortened period for the brain transplants that we discussed earlier).

Once formed, the Per/Cry/Tau protein complex enters the nucleus to inhibit the transcription of *per* and *cry*. This means that no new Per or Cry proteins are made for a while. But because the Per and Cry proteins degrade with time, eventually the inhibition will be lifted, starting the whole cycle over again (**Figure 14.7**). The entire cycle takes about 24 hours to complete, and it is this 24-hour molecular cycle that drives the 24-hour activity cycle of SCN cells. Each SCN neuron uses this mechanism to keep time approximately, and then they communicate with each other through electrical synapses (see Chapter 3), synchronizing their activity to produce a very consistent period of about 24 hours (M. A. Long et al., 2005), which then drives circadian processes throughout the body.

How does light entrain the molecular clock to the light-dark cycle? In fruit flies, one of the molecules involved in the clock is degraded by exposure to light. So

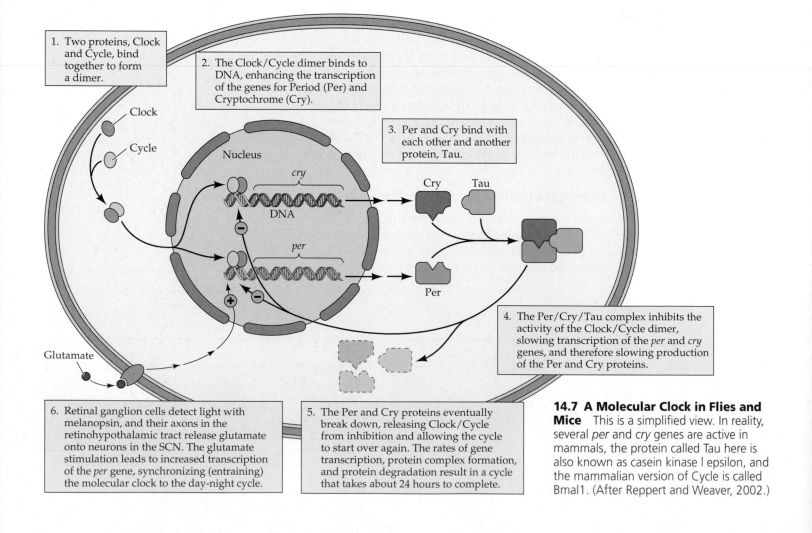

1. Two proteins, Clock and Cycle, bind together to form a dimer.

2. The Clock/Cycle dimer binds to DNA, enhancing the transcription of the genes for Period (Per) and Cryptochrome (Cry).

3. Per and Cry bind with each other and another protein, Tau.

Clock

Cycle

Nucleus

cry

DNA

per

Cry   Tau

Per

Glutamate

4. The Per/Cry/Tau complex inhibits the activity of the Clock/Cycle dimer, slowing transcription of the *per* and *cry* genes, and therefore slowing production of the Per and Cry proteins.

6. Retinal ganglion cells detect light with melanopsin, and their axons in the retinohypothalamic tract release glutamate onto neurons in the SCN. The glutamate stimulation leads to increased transcription of the *per* gene, synchronizing (entraining) the molecular clock to the day-night cycle.

5. The Per and Cry proteins eventually break down, releasing Clock/Cycle from inhibition and allowing the cycle to start over again. The rates of gene transcription, protein complex formation, and protein degradation result in a cycle that takes about 24 hours to complete.

14.7 A Molecular Clock in Flies and Mice   This is a simplified view. In reality, several *per* and *cry* genes are active in mammals, the protein called Tau here is also known as casein kinase I epsilon, and the mammalian version of Cycle is called Bmal1. (After Reppert and Weaver, 2002.)

outside light passes through the fly's body into brain cells to degrade the protein and synchronize the molecular clock. But things are different in thick-headed mammals like us. We use the retinohypothalamic tract to get light information to the SCN. The retinal ganglion cells containing melanopsin detect light and release the neurotransmitter glutamate in the SCN. Glutamate triggers a chain of events in SCN cells that promotes the production of Per protein. When the animal's photoperiod is shifted, this light-mediated boosting of Per production shifts the phase of the molecular clock and therefore the animal's behavior.

One indication of how important the molecular clock is to circadian behavior is the effect of mutations in the genes involved in the clock. We've already seen that hamsters with a mutation in *tau* have a shorter free-running rhythm than normal hamsters have. Mice in which both copies of the *Clock* gene are disrupted show severe arrhythmicity in constant conditions (**Figure 14.8**). People who feel energetic in the morning ("larks") are likely to carry a different version of the *Clock* gene than "night owls" have (Katzenberg et al., 1998). Different alleles of the *per* gene are also associated with being a lark versus a night owl (Carpen et al., 2005).

Many biological rhythms have periods shorter than a day. Such rhythms are referred to as **ultradian** (designating a frequency greater than once per day; the Latin *ultra* means "beyond"), and their periods are usually from several minutes to hours. Ultradian rhythms are seen in such behaviors as bouts of activity, feeding, and hormone release. These ultradian rhythms may be superimposed on a circadian rhythm. For example, humans show a 90-minute cycle of daydreaming that is characterized by vivid sensory imagery (P. Lavie and Kripke, 1981). Ultradian rhythms in performance on various boring tasks reflect fluctuations in alertness (Broughton, 1985).

Animals Use Circannual Rhythms to Anticipate Seasonal Changes

Recall that many animals display a seasonal cycle in body weight (see Box 13.1). Many animal behaviors are also characterized by annual rhythms; for example, most animals breed only during a particular season. Some of these rhythms are driven by exogenous factors, such as food availability and temperature. But in the laboratory, seasonal animals exposed to short days and long nights (mimicking winter) will often change to the nonbreeding condition (**Figure 14.9**). Furthermore, many annual rhythms, including body weight, persist under constant con-

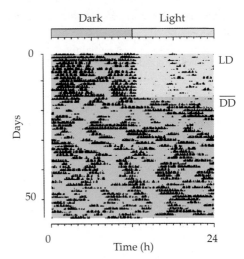

14.8 When the Endogenous Clock Goes Kaput   The homozygous *Clock/Clock* mouse whose activity is plotted here showed a normal circadian rhythm when given light cues (LD). When put in constant dim light (DD), it maintained an activity period of 27.1 hours for the first 10 days but then lost circadian rhythmicity. Note, however, that an ultradian rhythm (i.e., a rhythm that has a frequency of more than once a day) with a period of just over 5 hours remains. (From J. S. Takahashi, 1995.)

ultradian   Referring to a rhythmic biological event whose period is shorter than that of a circadian rhythm, usually from several minutes to several hours long.

14.9 A Hamster for All Seasons   Siberian hamsters in the wild suppress their reproductive systems and develop a silvery fur coat (left) for camouflage in the snow each fall. In the laboratory, they will undergo identical changes, despite warm temperatures and abundant food, if the lights are on only 10 hours per day. They seem to interpret these short days as an indication that winter is coming. (Photo by Carol D. Hegstrom.)

circannual   Occurring on a roughly annual basis.

infradian   Referring to a rhythmic biological event whose period is longer than that of a circadian rhythm—that is, longer than a day.

electroencephalography (EEG)   The recording and study of gross electrical activity of the brain recorded from large electrodes placed on the scalp.

electro-oculography (EOG)   The electrical recording of eye movements.

electromyography (EMG)   The electrical recording of muscle activity.

slow-wave sleep (SWS)   Sleep, divided into stages 1–4, that is defined by the presence of slow-wave EEG activity.

rapid-eye-movement (REM) sleep   Also called *paradoxical sleep*. A stage of sleep characterized by small-amplitude, fast-EEG waves, no postural tension, and rapid eye movements. REM rhymes with "gem."

ditions in the lab. As with circadian rhythms in constant light, animals in isolation show free-running annual rhythms of a period not quite equal to 365 days. Thus, there also seems to be an endogenous **circannual** clock.

This realm of research obviously requires a lot of patience. Such rhythms are called **infradian** because their frequency is less than once per day (the Latin *infra* means "below"). A familiar infradian rhythm is the 28-day human menstrual cycle. The relevance of annual rhythms to human behavior is becoming evident in seasonal disorders of behavior (see Chapter 16).

How does an animal know that a year has passed? Does it simply count the days being measured by the SCN until 365 have gone by? No. Irving Zucker et al. (1983) measured activity rhythms, reproductive cycles, and body weight cycles of animals that were free-running in both their circadian and their circannual rhythms. SCN lesions clearly disrupted circadian activity cycles, but in at least some animals these lesions did *not* affect circannual changes in body weight and reproductive status. Circannual cycles, then, do not arise from the circadian clock, and they seem to involve a mechanism that is separate from the SCN. We do know that light cycles can entrain the circannual rhythm by affecting how long the nightly bout of melatonin secretion lasts (see Figure 5.20).

Sleeping and Waking

Most of us enjoy a single period of sleep starting late in the evening and lasting until morning. The beginning and end of sleep are synchronized to many external events, including light and dark. What happens when all the customary synchronizing or entraining stimuli are removed? To investigate this question, volunteers spent weeks in a dark cave with all cues to external time removed (R. A. Wever, 1979). They displayed a circadian rhythm of the sleep-waking cycle, but the rhythm slowly shifted from 24 to 25 hours. In other words, people in constant conditions free-run just as a hamster does (**Figure 14.10**). Because the free-running period is greater than 24 hours, some people in these studies are surprised when they're told that the experiment has ended. The subject may have experienced only 19 sleep-waking cycles during a 21-day study.

The free-running period of a little more than 24 hours (Czeisler et al., 1999) indicates that humans have an endogenous circadian clock that is very similar to the 24-hour clock in hamsters. External cues (lights, meals, jobs, alarm clocks) entrain our clock to a 24-hour period, and this circadian clock encourages the brain to sleep at some times of the day and to remain awake at others (Mistlberger, 2005).

Human Sleep Exhibits Different Stages

In the 1930s, experimenters found that brain potentials recorded from electrodes on the scalp (by **electroencephalography**, or **EEG**; see Figure 3.19*a*) provided a way to define, describe, and classify levels of arousal and states of sleep. This measure of brain activity is usually supplemented with recordings of eye movements (**electro-oculography**, or **EOG**) and of muscle tension (**electromyography**, or **EMG**). Electrophysiological measurement led to the groundbreaking discovery that there are two distinct classes of sleep: **slow-wave sleep** (**SWS**) and **rapid-eye-movement sleep**, or **REM sleep** (Aserinsky and Kleitman, 1953). In humans, slow-wave sleep can be divided further into four distinct stages, which we'll discuss next.

14.10 Humans Free-Run Too   These sleep-waking patterns were recorded in a subject who, after 5 days, was isolated from cues about the time of day. During this period the subject displayed a free-running rhythm that was a bit longer than 24 hours, getting the equivalent of 74 "nights" of sleep over the 77 days. (From Weitzman et al., 1981.)

What are the electrophysiological distinctions that define different sleep states? To begin, the pattern of electrical activity in a fully awake, vigilant person is a mixture of many frequencies dominated by waves of relatively fast frequencies (greater than 15–20 cycles per second, or hertz [Hz]) and low amplitude, sometimes referred to as *beta activity* or a **desynchronized EEG** (**Figure 14.11a**).

When you relax and close your eyes, a distinctive EEG rhythm appears, consisting of a regular oscillation at a frequency of 8–12 Hz, known as the **alpha rhythm**. As drowsiness sets in, the time spent in the alpha rhythm decreases, and the EEG shows events of much smaller amplitude and irregular frequency, as well as sharp waves called **vertex spikes**. This is the beginning of SWS, called **stage 1 sleep** (**Figure 14.11b**), which is accompanied by a slowing of heart rate and a reduction of muscle tension; in addition, under the closed eyelids the eyes may roll about slowly. Stage 1 sleep usually lasts several minutes and gives way to **stage 2 sleep** (**Figure 14.11c**), which is defined by waves of 12–14 Hz called **sleep spindles** that occur in periodic bursts, and **K complexes**. If awakened during these first two stages of sleep, many subjects deny that they have been asleep, even though they failed to respond to signals while in those stages.

Stage 2 sleep leads to (can you guess?) **stage 3 sleep** (**Figure 14.11d**), which is defined by the appearance of large-amplitude, *very* slow waves (so-called **delta waves**, about one per second). **Stage 4 sleep** (**Figure 14.11e**) is defined as the condition in which delta waves are present at least half the time. Because stages 3 and 4 are so similar, many researchers lump them together as *stage 3/4*. The

desynchronized EEG   Also called *beta activity*. A pattern of EEG activity comprising a mix of many different high frequencies with low amplitude.

alpha rhythm   A brain potential of 8 to 12 Hz that occurs during relaxed wakefulness.

vertex spike   A sharp-wave EEG pattern that is seen during stage 1 slow-wave sleep.

stage 1 sleep   The initial stage of slow-wave sleep, which is characterized by small-amplitude EEG waves of irregular frequency, slow heart rate, and reduced muscle tension.

stage 2 sleep   A stage of slow-wave sleep that is defined by bursts of regular 14- to 18-Hz EEG waves called sleep spindles.

sleep spindle   A characteristic 14- to 18-Hz wave in the EEG of a person said to be in stage 2 sleep.

K complex   A sharp negative EEG potential that is seen in stage 2 sleep.

stage 3 sleep   A stage of slow-wave sleep that is defined by the spindles seen in stage 2 sleep, mixed with larger-amplitude slow waves.

delta wave   The slowest type of EEG wave, characteristic of stages 3 and 4 slow-wave sleep.

stage 4 sleep   A stage of slow-wave sleep that is defined by the presence of delta waves at least half the time.

(a) Waking
Low amplitude, mix of high frequencies

(b) Stage 1 SWS
Alpha rhythm
Vertex spike

(c) Stage 2 SWS
Sleep spindles
K complexes

(d) Stage 3 SWS
Delta waves

(e) Stage 4 SWS
Delta waves

200 μV
1 s

(f) REM sleep

14.11 Electrophysiological Correlates of Sleep and Waking   These are the characteristic EEG patterns seen during different stages of sleep in humans. The sharp wave called a vertex spike appears during stage 1 sleep. Brief periods of sleep spindles are characteristic of stage 2 sleep. Deeper stages of slow-wave sleep show progressively more of the large, slow delta waves. Note the similarity of EEG activity during waking, stage 1 sleep, and REM sleep. (After Rechtschaffen and Kales, 1968.)

slow waves of electrical potential that give SWS its name represent a widespread synchronization of cortical activity that has been likened to a room of people who are all chanting the same phrase over and over. From a distance you would be able to hear the rise and fall of the cadence of speech in a slow rhythm. But if each person were saying something different, you would hear only a buzz—the rapid frequencies of many desynchronized speakers, which is like the desynchronized EEG of wakefulness when many parts of the cortex are saying different things to different target brain regions. During SWS, neighboring cortical neurons tend to have synchronized activity (Poulet and Petersen, 2008), as if they were all "chanting" together rather than fulfilling different functions as they do in waking.

After about an hour—the time usually required for progression through these stages, with a brief return to stage 2—something totally different occurs. Quite abruptly, scalp recordings display a pattern of small-amplitude, high-frequency activity similar in many ways to the pattern of an awake individual (**Figure 14.11f**), but the postural neck muscles and all the other skeletal muscles are completely relaxed and limp. The active-looking EEG coupled with deeply relaxed muscles is typical of REM sleep. If you see a cat sleeping in the sitting, sphinx position, it cannot be in REM sleep; in REM, it will be sprawled limply on the floor.

As we'll see later, this flaccid muscle state appears despite intense brain activity because during this stage of sleep, brainstem regions are profoundly inhibiting motoneurons. Because of this seeming contradiction—the brain waves look awake, but the musculature is flaccid and unresponsive—another name for this state is *paradoxical sleep*. In addition to the rapid eye movements under closed lids that give REM sleep its name, breathing and pulse rates become irregular. It is also during REM sleep that we experience vivid dreams, as we'll discuss in the next section.

TABLE 14.1 Properties of Slow-Wave and REM Sleep

Property	Slow-wave sleep	REM sleep
AUTONOMIC ACTIVITIES		
Heart rate	Slow decline	Variable with high bursts
Respiration	Slow decline	Variable with high bursts
Thermoregulation	Maintained	Impaired
Brain temperature	Decreased	Increased
Cerebral blood flow	Reduced	High
SKELETAL MUSCULAR SYSTEM		
Postural tension	Progressively reduced	Eliminated
Knee jerk reflex	Normal	Suppressed
Phasic twitches	Reduced	Increased
Eye movements	Infrequent, slow, uncoordinated	Rapid, coordinated
COGNITIVE STATE	Vague thoughts	Vivid dreams, well organized
HORMONE SECRETION		
Growth hormone secretion	High	Low
NEURAL FIRING RATES		
Cerebral cortex activity	Many cells reduced and more phasic	Increased firing rates; tonic (sustained)
EVENT-RELATED POTENTIALS		
Sensory-evoked	Large	Reduced

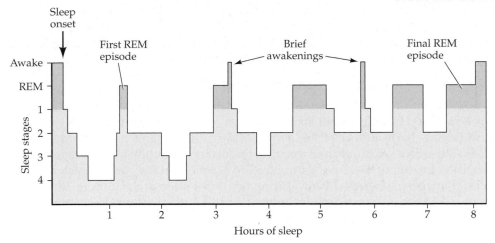

14.12 A Typical Night of Sleep in a Young Adult Note the progressive lengthening of REM episodes (blue) and the loss of stage 3/4 sleep as the night goes on. (After Kales and Kales, 1970.)

The EEG portrait in Figure 14.11 shows that sleep consists of a complex series of brain states, not just an "inactive" period. **Table 14.1** compares the properties of slow-wave sleep and REM sleep. The total sleep time of young adults usually ranges from 7 to 8 hours, about half in stage 2 sleep. REM sleep accounts for about 20% of total sleep. A typical night of adult human sleep shows repeating cycles about 90–110 minutes long, recurring four or five times in a night. These cycles change in a subtle but regular manner through the night. Cycles early in the night are characterized by greater amounts of stage 3/4 SWS (**Figure 14.12**). The latter half of the night has less stage 3/4 sleep. In contrast, REM sleep is typically more prominent in the later cycles of sleep. The first REM period is the shortest, while the last REM period, just before waking, may last up to 40 minutes.

Brief arousals (yellow bars in Figure 14.13) occasionally occur immediately after a REM period, and the sleeper may shift posture at this time (Aaronson et al., 1982). The sleep cycle of 90–110 minutes has been viewed as the manifestation of a basic ultradian rest-activity cycle (Kleitman, 1969); cycles of similar duration occur during waking periods, such as the cycles of daydreaming we mentioned earlier (P. Lavie and Kripke, 1981).

At puberty, most people shift their circadian rhythm of sleep so that they get up later in the day (**Figure 14.13**), but many school systems require students to come to school *earlier* in the day when they hit adolescence. One group of high schools shifted their start from 7:15 to 8:40 and noted improved student attendance and enrollment, with reduced depression and sleeping in class (Wahlstrom, 2002). You may think of sleep as a simple event in your life, but for biological psychologists

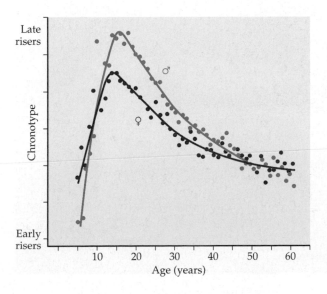

14.13 Oh, How I Hate to Get Out of Bed in the Morning By comparing the time of day that people of differing ages wake up each day, Roenneberg et al. (2004) confirmed the tendency for humans to become late risers at puberty.

nightmare A long, frightening dream that awakens the sleeper from REM sleep.

night terror A sudden arousal from stage 3 or stage 4 slow-wave sleep that is marked by intense fear and autonomic activation.

sleep is a remarkably complex, multifaceted set of behaviors. As one example, let's consider a fascinating aspect of REM sleep: dreaming.

We do our most vivid dreaming during REM sleep

We can record the EEGs of subjects, awaken them at a particular stage—1, 2, 3, 4, or REM—and question them about thoughts or perceptions immediately prior to awakening. Early studies of this sort suggested that dreams happen only during REM sleep, but we now know that dreams also occur in other sleep stages. What is distinctive about the dreams during REM sleep is that they are characterized by visual imagery, whereas dreams during non-REM sleep are of a more "thinking" type. REM dreams are apt to include a story that involves odd perceptions and the sense that the dreamer "is there" experiencing sights, sounds, smells, and acts. Subjects awakened from non-REM sleep report thinking about problems rather than seeing themselves in a stage presentation. Cartwright (1979) found that the dreams of these two states are so different that she could train people to predict accurately whether a described dream occurred during REM sleep or SWS.

Almost everyone has terrifying dreams on occasion (Hartmann, 1984). **Nightmares** are defined as long, frightening dreams that awaken the sleeper from REM sleep. They are occasionally confused with **night terror**, which is a sudden arousal from stage 3/4 SWS marked by intense fear and autonomic activation. In night terror the sleeper does not recall a vivid dream but may remember a sense of a crushing feeling on the chest, as though being suffocated (**Figure 14.14**). Night terrors, common in children during the early part of an evening's sleep, seem to be a disorder of arousal.

Many medications make nightmares more frequent (Pagel and Helfter, 2003), but they are quite prevalent even without such influences. At least 25% of college students report having one or more nightmares per month. Have you had the common one, which Sigmund Freud had, of suddenly remembering that you must take a final exam that is already in progress?

14.14 Night Terror This 1781 painting by Henry Fuseli is called *The Nightmare*. It also aptly illustrates night terror, or even sleep paralysis, discussed later in the chapter, as the demon crushes the breath from his victim.

Different Species Provide Clues about the Evolution of Sleep

With the aid of precise behavioral and EEG techniques, sleep has been studied in a wide assortment of mammals and, to a lesser extent, in reptiles, birds, and amphibians (S. S. Campbell and Tobler, 1984). We don't know why the brain produces slow waves of electrical potential during SWS, but slow waves are also produced in the brains of crayfish (Ramon et al., 2004) and fruit flies (Nitz et al., 2002) when they are inactive, so SWS was probably already present in the common ancestor of invertebrates and vertebrates. Sleep is an ancient adaptation.

REM sleep evolved in some vertebrates

REM sleep does not seem quite as ancient as SWS. Nearly all mammalian species that have been investigated thus far, including the platypus (J. M. Siegel, Manger, et al., 1999), display both REM and SWS (**Figure 14.15**). Among the other vertebrates, only birds display clear signs of both SWS and REM sleep. These comparisons suggest that either REM sleep was present in an ancestor common to birds and mammals, or that REM evolved independently in mammals and birds.

Dolphins don't display REM sleep, but the lack of REM sleep is probably a late adaptation that evolved when their land-dwelling ancestors took to the water, because they must come to the surface of the water to breathe. That requirement may be incompatible with the deep relaxation of muscles during REM sleep. Another dolphin adaptation to living in water is that only one side of the dolphin brain engages in SWS at a time (Mukhametov, 1984). It's as if one whole hemisphere is asleep while the other is awake (**Figure 14.16**). During these periods of "unilateral sleep," the animals continue to come up to the surface occasionally to breathe. Birds can also display unilateral sleep—one hemisphere sleeping while the other

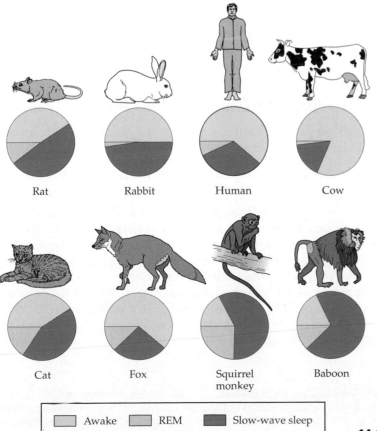

Rat   Rabbit   Human   Cow

Cat   Fox   Squirrel monkey   Baboon

☐ Awake   ☐ REM   ■ Slow-wave sleep

14.15 Amounts of Different Sleep States in Various Mammals

14.16 Sleep in Marine Mammals EEG patterns in right (R) and left (L) brain hemispheres in a porpoise from recordings of the parietal cortex suggest that the two cerebral hemispheres take turns sleeping. (From Mukhametov, 1984.)

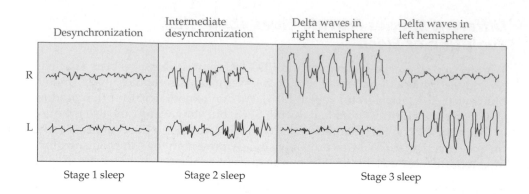

| Desynchronization | Intermediate desynchronization | Delta waves in right hemisphere | Delta waves in left hemisphere |

Stage 1 sleep   Stage 2 sleep   Stage 3 sleep

sleep cycle A period of slow-wave sleep followed by a period of REM sleep. In humans, a sleep cycle lasts 90–110 minutes.

hemisphere watches for predators (Rattenborg, 2006; Rattenborg et al., 2001). Unilateral sleep while gliding may also enable birds to fly long distances without stopping; for example, a bar-tailed godwit flew nonstop more than 10,000 miles, from Alaska to Australia, in a week (Gill et al., 2009).

Vertebrate species differ in their patterns and types of sleep

A **sleep cycle** is a period of one episode of SWS followed by an episode of REM sleep. For laboratory rats, one sleep cycle lasts an average of 10–11 minutes; for humans, one cycle lasts 90–110 minutes, as we said earlier. Across species, cycle duration is inversely related to metabolic rate; that is, small animals, which tend to have high metabolic rates (see Chapter 13), have short sleep cycles, and large species have long sleep cycles.

Except for birds when they are migrating, all vertebrates appear to show a circadian distribution of activity, a prolonged phase of inactivity, raised thresholds to external stimuli during inactivity, and a characteristic posture during inactivity. Many invertebrates also have clear periods of behavioral quiescence that include heightened arousal thresholds and distinctive postures (B. A. Klein, 2003; Koh et al., 2008). Although almost everybody sleeps, the quantity and quality of sleep are not the same throughout life, as we'll see in the next section.

Our Sleep Patterns Change across the Life Span

How much sleep and what kind of sleep we get changes across our lifetime. These changes are most evident during early development.

Mammals sleep more during infancy than in adulthood

A clear cycle of sleeping and waking takes several weeks to become established in human infants (**Figure 14.17**). A 24-hour rhythm is generally evident by 16 weeks of age. Infant sleep is characterized by shorter sleep cycles than those of adults, probably reflecting the relative immaturity of the brain. For example, sleep cycles in premature infants are even shorter than in full-term babies.

Infant mammals also show a large percentage of REM sleep. In humans, for example, 50% of sleep in the first 2 weeks of life is REM sleep. The prominence of REM sleep is even greater in premature infants, accounting for up to 80% of total sleep. Unlike normal adults,

Weeks after birth / Sleeping time (percentage of 24 h)

Week	%
3	64
4	64
5	65
6	64
7	63
8	63
9	63
10	62
11	63
12	59
13	60
14	63
15	62
16	62
17	60
18	58
19	58
20	57
21	57
22	56
23	57
24	57
25	57
26	57

24 2 4 6 8 10 12 14 16 18 20 22 24
Time of day

14.17 The Trouble with Babies A stable pattern of sleep at night does not appear to be consolidated until about 16 weeks of age. The dark portions here indicate time asleep; the blank portions, time awake. (From Kleitman and Engelmann, 1953.)

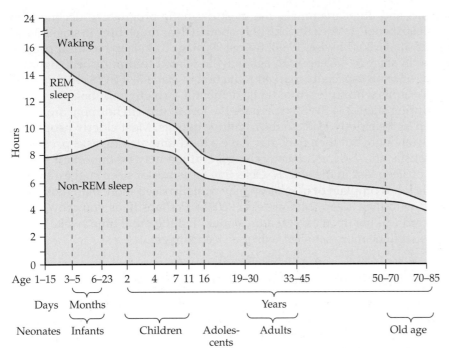

14.18 Human Sleep Patterns Change with Age
Early in life we sleep a great deal, and about half of sleep time is spent in REM sleep. By adulthood, we average about 8 hours of sleep a night, 20% of which is REM sleep. (After Roffwarg et al., 1966.)

human infants can move directly from an awake state to REM sleep for the first few months of life. The REM sleep of infants is quite active, accompanied by muscle twitching, smiles, grimaces, and vocalizations. The preponderance of REM sleep early in life (**Figure 14.18**) suggests that this state provides stimulation that is essential to maturation of the nervous system. On the other hand, killer whales and bottlenose dolphins appear to spend little or no time sleeping for the first month of life (Lyamin et al., 2005), presumably because they have to surface often to breathe. So either REM sleep does not fill a crucial need in mammalian infants, or dolphin and whale infants have found a different way to fill that need.

Most people sleep appreciably less as they age

The parameters of sleep change more slowly in old age than in early development. **Figure 14.19** shows the pattern of a typical night of sleep in an elderly person. The total amount of sleep declines, while the number of awakenings increases (compare with Figure 14.13). Lack of sleep, or insomnia (which we will discuss at the end of this chapter), is a common complaint of the elderly (Miles and Dement, 1980), although daytime naps may contribute to nighttime sleep difficulties.

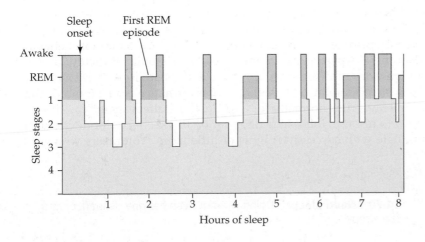

14.19 The Typical Pattern of Sleep in an Elderly Person Recordings of sleep in the elderly are characterized by frequent awakenings (yellow bars), and a severe reduction in stage 3/4 sleep. Compare this recording with the young-adult sleep pattern shown in Figure 14.12. (After Kales and Kales, 1974.)

sleep deprivation The partial or total prevention of sleep.

sleep recovery The process of sleeping more than normally after a period of sleep deprivation, as though in compensation.

In humans and other mammals, the most dramatic progressive decline is in stage 3/4 sleep; people at age 60 spend only about half as much time in stages 3 and 4 as they did at age 20 (Bliwise, 1989). By age 90, stage 3/4 sleep has disappeared. This decline in stage 3/4 sleep with age may be related to diminished cognitive capabilities, since an especially marked reduction of stage 3/4 SWS characterizes the sleep of people who suffer from senile dementia. Growth hormone is secreted primarily during stage 3/4 SWS, so perhaps the loss of growth hormone from disrupted sleep in the elderly leads to the cognitive deficits. Most elderly people fall asleep easily enough, but then they may have a hard time staying asleep, causing sleep "dissatisfaction." As in so many things, attitude may be important for the experience of sleep loss in the elderly. Objective measures of sleep suggest that elderly people who complain of poor sleep may actually sleep more than those who are satisfied with their sleep (McCrae et al., 2005). Perhaps if, as you grow older, you can regard waking up at 3:00 AM as a "bonus" (a little more time awake before you die), you will be more satisfied with the sleep you get.

Manipulating Sleep Reveals an Underlying Structure

Sleep is affected by many environmental, social, and biological influences. From one viewpoint, though, sleep is an amazingly stable state: major changes in our waking behavior have only a minor impact on subsequent sleep. The effects of sleep deprivation are especially interesting because they give insight into the underlying mechanisms of sleep.

Sleep deprivation drastically alters sleep patterns

Most of us at one time or another have been willing or not-so-willing participants in informal **sleep deprivation** experiments. Thus, most of us are aware of the effect of partial or total sleep deprivation: it makes us sleepy (**Figure 14.20**). The study of sleep deprivation is also a way to explore the potential regulatory mechanisms of sleeping and waking. Studies of **sleep recovery** ask questions such as, Does a sleep-deprived organism somehow keep track of the amounts and types of lost sleep? When the organism is given the opportunity to compensate, is recovery partial or complete? Can you pay off sleep debts?

THE EFFECTS OF SLEEP DEPRIVATION Early reports from sleep deprivation studies emphasized a similarity between "bizarre" behavior provoked by sleep deprivation and schizophrenia. A frequent theme in this work was the functional role of dreams as a "guardian of sanity." But examination of patients suffering from schizophrenia does not confirm this view. For example, these patients can show sleep-waking cycles similar to those of normal adults, and sleep deprivation does not exacerbate their symptoms.

The behavioral effects of prolonged, total sleep deprivation vary appreciably and may depend on some general personality factors and on age. In several studies employing prolonged total deprivation—205 hours (8.5 days)—a few subjects showed occasional episodes of hallucinations. But the most common behavior changes noted in these experiments are increases in irritability, difficulty in concentrating, and episodes of disorientation. The subject's ability to perform tasks was summarized by L. C. Johnson (1969): "His performance is like a motor that after much use misfires, runs normally for a while, then falters again" (p. 216).

You don't need to resort to total sleep deprivation to see effects. Moderate sleep debt can accumulate with successive nights of little sleep. Volunteers who got 6

14.20 I Need Sleep! Doing without sleep has one clear effect: you feel sleepy.

BOX 14.1 Sleep Deprivation Can Be Fatal

Sleep that knits up the ravell'd
sleave of care.

— *William Shakespeare,
Macbeth, Act II, Scene 2*

Although some people seem to need very little sleep, most of us feel the need to sleep 7–8 hours a night. In fact, sustained sleep deprivation in rats causes them to increase their metabolic rate, lose weight, and, within an average of 19 days, die (Everson et al., 1989). Allowing them to sleep prevents their death.

After the fatal effect of sleep deprivation had been shown, researchers undertook studies in which they terminated the sleep deprivation before the fatal end point and looked for pathological changes in different organ systems (Rechtschaffen and Bergmann, 1995). No single organ system seems affected in chronically sleep-deprived animals, but early in the deprivation they develop sores on their bodies. These sores mark the beginning of the end; shortly thereafter, blood tests reveal infections from a host of bacteria, which probably enter through the sores (Everson, 1993).

These bacteria are not normally fatal, because the rat's immune system and body defenses keep the bacteria in check; but severely sleep-deprived rats fail to develop a fever in response to these infections. (Fever helps the body fight infection.) In fact, the sleep-deprived animals show a *drop* in body temperature, which probably speeds bacterial infections, which in turn leads to diffuse organ damage. The decline of these severely sleep-deprived rats is complicated, but it seems clear that getting sleep improves immune system function (Bryant et al., 2004). So perhaps Shakespeare's folk theory of the function of sleep, quoted above, isn't so far from the truth.

What about the rare humans who sleep only 1 or 2 hours a night? Why aren't their immune systems and inflammatory responses compromised? We don't know, but since the distinguishing trait of these people is that they don't need much sleep, perhaps their immune systems and inflammatory responses don't need much sleep either. Or perhaps the small amount of sleep they have almost every night is more efficient at doing whatever sleep does.

Some unfortunate humans inherit a defect in the gene for the prion protein (which can transmit mad cow disease, discussed in Chapter 16), and although they sleep normally at the beginning of life, in midlife they simply stop sleeping—with fatal effect. People with this disease, called **fatal familial insomnia**, die 7–24 months after the insomnia begins (Mastrianni et al., 1999; Medori et al., 1992). Autopsy reveals degeneration of the thalamus, which may cause the insomnia (Manetto et al., 1992). (Electrical stimulation of the thalamus can induce sleep in animals.) Like sleep-deprived rats, sleep-deprived humans with this disorder don't have obvious damage to any single organ system, but suffer from diffuse bacterial infections. Apparently these patients die because they are chronically sleep-deprived, and these results, combined with research on rats, certainly support the idea that prolonged insomnia is fatal.

fatal familial insomnia An inherited disorder in which humans sleep normally at the beginning of their life but in midlife stop sleeping, and 7–24 months later die.

---

or 4 hours sleep per night for 2 weeks showed ever-mounting deficits in attention tasks and in speed of reaction compared to those sleeping 8 hours per night (Van Dongen et al., 2003). Interestingly, the sleep-deprived subjects often reported not feeling sleepy, yet they still exhibited behavioral deficits. By the end of the study, the subjects getting less than 8 hours of sleep per night had cognitive deficits equivalent to subjects who had been totally sleep-deprived for 3 days!

Airline employees who had worked for 5 years on schedules that gave them little time to adapt to new time zones showed deficits in cognitive tasks of spatial memory and reduced volume of the brain's temporal lobe compared to employees on a schedule that permitted more time to recover from jet lag (Cho, 2001). Was it the disruption of circadian rhythms or accumulated sleep debt that caused the difference? We don't know.

Finally, it is clear that prolonged, total sleep deprivation in mammals compromises the immune system and leads to death (**Box 14.1**). Even fruit flies need sleep, as evidenced by the fact that a particular mutation of the *Cycle* gene (which is part of the circadian molecular clock; see Figure 14.7) causes the flies to die after only 10 hours of sleep deprivation (P. J. Shaw et al., 2002).

SLEEP RECOVERY Figure 14.21 provides data on sleep recovery in a young man following 11 days of sleep deprivation. No evidence of a psychotic state was noted, and the incentive for this unusually long act of not sleeping was simply the subject's own curiosity. Researchers became involved only after he had started

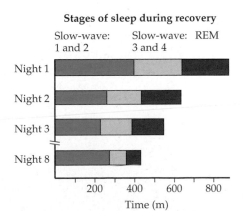

14.21 Sleep Recovery after 11 Days Awake (After Gulevich et al., 1966.)

his deprivation schedule, which is the reason for the absence of predeprivation sleep data.

In the first night of sleep recovery, stage 3/4 sleep shows the greatest relative difference from normal. This increase in stage 3/4 sleep is usually at the expense of stage 2 sleep. However, the rise in stage 3/4 sleep during recovery never completely makes up for the deficit accumulated over the deprivation period. In fact, the amount is no greater than for deprivation periods half as long. REM sleep after prolonged sleep deprivation shows its greatest recovery during the second postdeprivation night. REM recovery may also involve another form of compensation—greater intensity: REM sleep in recovery nights is more "intense" than normal, with a greater number of rapid eye movements per period of time. So you never recover all lost sleep time, but you may make up for the loss by having more intense sleep for a while. The sooner you get to sleep, the sooner you recover.

What Are the Biological Functions of Sleep?

Why do most of us spend one-third of our lifetime asleep? The functions of sleep are a subject of great debate. Keep in mind that the proposed functions, or biological roles, of sleep are not mutually exclusive; sleep may have acquired more than one function during evolution. The four functions most often ascribed to sleep are

1. Energy conservation
2. Niche adaptation
3. Body restoration
4. Memory consolidation

Sleep conserves energy

We use up less energy when we sleep than when we're awake. For example, slow-wave sleep is marked by reduced muscular tension, lowered heart rate, reduced blood pressure, reduced body temperature, and slower respiration. This diminished metabolic activity during sleep suggests that one role of sleep is to conserve energy. From this perspective, sleep imposes rest on animals at a time of day when they would not be very efficient at gathering food (**Figure 14.22**).

We can see the importance of this function by looking at the world from the perspective of small animals. Small animals have very high metabolic rates (see Chapter 13), so activity for them is metabolically expensive. Demand can easily outstrip supply. Reduced activity can be especially valuable if food is scarce. There is also a high correlation between total amount of sleep per day and waking metabolic rate: small animals sleep more than large species, at least among plant-eating species (**Figure 14.23a**). Since smaller mammals lose heat faster (see Chapter 13), they burn more energy per gram of body weight just to maintain body temperature, and so perhaps they sleep more to conserve more energy. Interestingly, predatory species show no such correlation, perhaps because meat eaters tend to get more sleep than prey species do (see **Figure 14.23b**).

Sleep enforces niche adaptation

Almost all animals are either nocturnal or diurnal. This specialization for either nighttime or daytime activity is part of each species' **ecological niche**, that unique assortment of environmental opportunities and challenges to which each organism is adapted. Thanks to these adaptations, each species is better at gathering food either at night or in the daytime, and each species is also better at avoiding predators either during the day or at night. If you're a nocturnal mammal, like a mouse, you are adept at sneaking around in the dark, using acute hearing and smell to navigate and find food. The rest of the time, during daylight, you should spend holed up somewhere safe to stay away from diurnal predators. So, one important function of sleep is to force the individual to conform to a particular eco-

14.22 Sleep Helps Animals to Adapt an Ecological Niche   These bats sleep together in a large leaf each day, waiting until dusk, when they can use their many nocturnal adaptations, to feed. They chew a line along the leaf to create a flap to cover them while they sleep.

ecological niche   The unique assortment of environmental opportunities and challenges to which each organism is adapted.

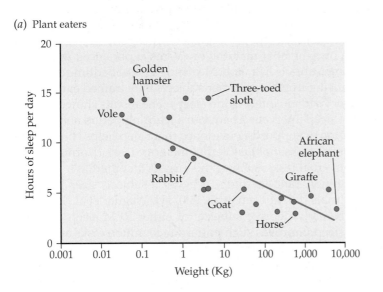

(a) Plant eaters

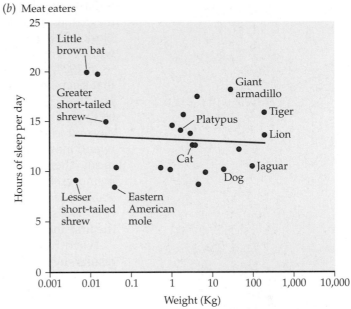

(b) Meat eaters

14.23 Relationship between Body Size and Sleep Time (a) Among plant eaters, the larger the body is, the less time is spent asleep. (b) Meat eaters sleep a lot, no matter what their body size—presumably because they are more secure when asleep. (From J. M. Siegel, 2005.)

logical niche for which it is well adapted (Meddis, 1975). From this perspective, sleep debt and the unpleasant feelings of sleepiness are simply tools that natural selection has evolved to enforce a circadian rhythm in activity. This certainly is a function of sleep, and it must have played an important role in the evolution of sleep, but is it the only function?

Sleep restores the body

If someone asked you why you sleep, chances are you would answer that you sleep because you're tired. Indeed, one of the proposed functions of sleep is simply the rebuilding or restoration of materials used during waking, such as proteins (Moruzzi, 1972). Maybe this is why most growth hormone release happens during SWS.

If simple wear and tear from activity triggered the need for sleep, then you'd expect exercise to result in more sleep. But while exercise often causes people to fall asleep more quickly, it generally does *not* help them sleep longer. We've seen that prolonged and total sleep deprivation—either forced on rats or, in humans, as a result of inherited pathology—interferes with the immune system and leads to death (see Box 14.1). Even relatively mild deprivation, having sleep shortened or disrupted (e.g., by a nurse taking vital signs every hour), makes people more sensitive to pain the following day (R. R. Edwards et al., 2009). A study of over a million Americans found that those sleeping less than 6 hours per night were more likely to die, although interestingly, people who slept *more than 8* hours per night were also at greater risk (Kripke et al., 2002). People who sleep less than 5 hours per night are more likely to develop diabetes (Gangwisch et al., 2007). Perhaps the most impressive link between sleep and health are findings that people who work at night and sleep in the daytime are more likely to develop cancer (Erren et al., 2009). So the widespread belief that sleep helps us ward off illness is well supported by research (S. Cohen et al., 2009; Imeri and Opp, 2009).

Does sleep aid memory consolidation?

A peculiar property of dreams is that, unless we tell them to someone or write them down soon after waking, we tend to forget them (Dement, 1974), as though the brain refuses to consolidate information presented during REM sleep. It is probably beneficial that most dreams are not stored in long-term memory, because it would be counterproductive to squander permanent memory storage space on events that never happened.

How about learning during sleep? Despite ads you might read in the backs of magazines, you cannot learn new material while you're sleeping (Druckman and Bjork, 1994). Putting a speaker under your pillow to recite material for a final exam will not work unless you stay awake to listen (J. M. Wood et al., 1992).

In 1924, however, Jenkins and Dallenbach reported an experiment suggesting that sleep helps you learn or remember material or events experienced *before* you go to bed. They trained some subjects in a verbal learning task at bedtime and tested them 8 hours later on arising from sleep; other subjects they trained early in the day and tested 8 hours later (with no intervening sleep). The results showed better retention when a period of sleep intervened between a learning period and tests of recall. There has been a surge of supporting evidence that sleep helps consolidate memories in a wide variety of tasks, not just verbal memory tasks (Korman et al., 2007). Performance on nonverbal tasks, such as the insight that there is a "hidden rule" in a sequence of seemingly random digits, is better if subjects sleep between the first and second set of trials (Ellenbogen et al., 2007; U. Wagner et al., 2004).

When researchers deliberately deprive subjects of either REM sleep or SWS, results suggest that REM sleep improves such pattern recognition tasks and "perceptual" learning tasks. For example, humans learning to discriminate different visual textures show little improvement in a single training session but show considerable improvement 8–10 hours after the session. If deprived of REM sleep after a training session, however, people fail to show the later improvement (Karni et al., 1994; C. Smith, 1995). In contrast, consolidation of "declarative" memory tasks (see Chapter 17), such as in the original Jenkins and Dallenbach (1924) study, and of complicated motor skills, seems to benefit from SWS (Nishida and Walker, 2007). In fact, researchers were able to improve consolidation of a declarative memory task even more if they electrically stimulated electrodes over the skull to boost cortical slow voltage oscillations during SWS (L. Marshall et al., 2006).

There is also growing evidence that patterns of brain activation seen while learning a task during wakefulness are re-created during subsequent sleep, as if the brain were "rehearsing" the material (Euston et al., 2007). Humans learning a reaction-time task that activated certain brain regions showed, in a following REM period, increased activation of exactly those brain regions that had been exercised (Maquet et al., 2000). Similarly, the patterned activity of neurons in birdsong nuclei while male zebra finches are learning to sing appears to be repeated during subsequent bouts of sleep (Shank and Margoliash, 2009).

Jerome Siegel (2001) remains skeptical, however, that REM sleep is essential for learning. He points out that any sleep deprivation is necessarily accompanied by stress, which might be the cause of memory disruption. He also notes that there is no correlation across species between time spent in REM sleep and obvious learning capacity. In humans, there is no correlation between the amount of REM sleep and either IQ or academic achievement (Borrow et al., 1980). Finally, one man who had brainstem injuries that seemed to eliminate REM sleep could still learn, and he completed his education (P. Lavie, 1996). So even if REM sleep *aids* learning, clearly it is not absolutely *necessary* for learning.

Some humans sleep remarkably little, yet function normally

One challenge to all the theories about the function of sleep is the existence of a few people who seem perfectly normal and healthy, yet sleep hardly at all. These cases are more than just folktales. William Dement (1974) described a Stanford University professor who slept only 3–4 hours a night for more than 50 years and died at age 80. Sleep researcher Ray Meddis (1977) found a cheerful 70-year-old retired nurse who said she had slept little since childhood. She was a busy person who easily filled up her 23 hours of daily wakefulness. During the night she sat in bed reading or writing, and at about 2:00 AM she fell asleep for an hour or so, after which she readily awakened.

For her first 2 days in Meddis's laboratory, she did not sleep at all, because it was all so interesting to her. On the third night she slept a total of 99 minutes, and her sleep contained both SWS and REM sleep periods. Later her sleep was recorded for 5 days. On the first night she did not sleep at all, but on subsequent nights she slept an average of 67 minutes. She never complained about not sleeping more, and she did not feel drowsy during either the day or the night (**Figure 14.24**). Meddis described several other people who sleep only an hour or two per night. Some of these people report having parents who slept little. Whatever the function of sleep is, these people possess some way of fulfilling it with a brief nap. They show less stages 1 and 2 sleep, so perhaps they are more efficient sleepers. Importantly, though, no healthy person has ever been found who does not sleep at all.

At Least Four Interacting Neural Systems Underlie Sleep

At one time sleep was regarded as a passive state, as though most of the brain simply stopped working while we slept, leaving us unaware of events around us. We now know that sleep is an active state mediated by at least four interacting neural systems:

1. A *forebrain* system that by itself can display SWS
2. A *brainstem* system that activates the forebrain into wakefulness
3. A *pontine* system that triggers REM sleep
4. A *hypothalamic* system that affects the other three brain regions to determine whether the brain will be awake or asleep

The forebrain generates slow-wave sleep

General anesthetics—drugs such as barbiturates and anesthetic gases that render people unconscious during surgery—produce slow waves in the EEG that resemble those seen in SWS (Franks, 2008). This finding suggests that general anesthetics tap into existing brain networks promoting sleep. While some general anesthetics are glutamate antagonists and therefore block neuronal excitation throughout the brain, virtually *all* general anesthetics are noncompetitive agonists at $GABA_A$ receptors (**Figure 14.25**). Because they boost $GABA_A$ receptors' inhibitory effect on neurons, these anesthetics suggest that some brain system normally uses GABA to inhibit neuronal activity and promote SWS. Where is the brain system that promotes SWS?

Some of the earliest studies of sleep indicated that the system promoting SWS is in the forebrain. These are experiments in which the brain is transected—literally

14.24 A Nonsleeper When Ray Meddis brought this 70-year-old nurse into the lab for sleep recording, he confirmed that she slept only about an hour per night. Yet she was a healthy and energetic person. Here she's touring a garden with Meddis's son.

general anesthetic A drug that renders an individual unconscious.

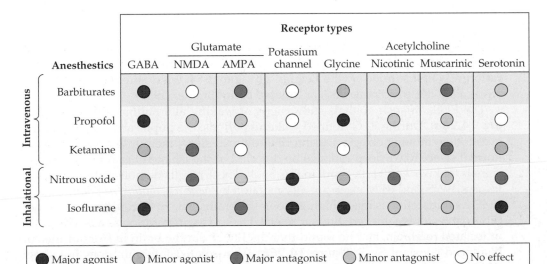

	Receptor types							
		Glutamate		Potassium		Acetylcholine		
Anesthestics	GABA	NMDA	AMPA	channel	Glycine	Nicotinic	Muscarinic	Serotonin
Intravenous Barbiturates	Major agonist	No effect	Major antagonist	No effect	Minor antagonist	Minor antagonist	Minor agonist	Minor antagonist
Propofol	Major agonist	Minor antagonist	Minor antagonist	No effect	Major agonist	Minor antagonist	Minor antagonist	No effect
Ketamine	Minor agonist	Minor agonist	No effect		No effect	Minor antagonist	Minor agonist	Minor antagonist
Inhalational Nitrous oxide	Minor agonist	Minor agonist	Minor antagonist	Major agonist	Minor antagonist	Major antagonist	Minor antagonist	Major agonist
Isoflurane	Major agonist	Minor antagonist	Minor agonist	Major antagonist	Major agonist	Minor antagonist	Minor antagonist	Major agonist

● Major agonist ◉ Minor agonist ● Major antagonist ◉ Minor antagonist ○ No effect

14.25 Neurotransmitter Systems Affected by General Anesthetics Note that all general anesthetics increase $GABA_A$ receptor signaling—a clue that these receptors, which tend to inhibit neural activity, may play a role in sleep. Some anesthetics also inhibit glutamate receptors, which usually excite neurons; and stimulate glycine receptors, which usually inhibit neurons. Singer Michael Jackson died of an overdose of propofol, which was given to him to induce sleep, but the drug does not provide the normal stages of sleep (After Alkire et al., 2008.)

14.26 Transecting the Brain at Different Levels

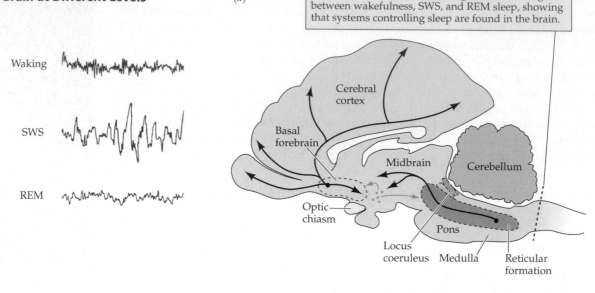

(a)

Transection of the lower brainstem produces an isolated brain, which exhibits signs of alternating between wakefulness, SWS, and REM sleep, showing that systems controlling sleep are found in the brain.

Waking

SWS

REM

Cerebral cortex

Basal forebrain

Midbrain

Cerebellum

Optic chiasm

Pons

Locus coeruleus   Medulla   Reticular formation

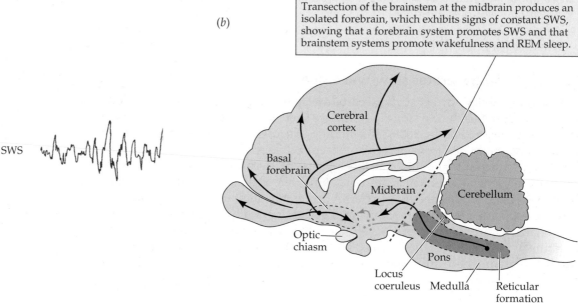

(b)

Transection of the brainstem at the midbrain produces an isolated forebrain, which exhibits signs of constant SWS, showing that a forebrain system promotes SWS and that brainstem systems promote wakefulness and REM sleep.

SWS

Cerebral cortex

Basal forebrain

Midbrain

Cerebellum

Optic chiasm

Pons

Locus coeruleus   Medulla   Reticular formation

isolated brain   Sometimes referred to by the French term, *encéphale isolé*. An experimental preparation in which an animal's brainstem has been separated from the spinal cord by a cut below the medulla.

isolated forebrain   Sometimes referred to by the French term, *cerveau isolé*. An experimental preparation in which an animal's nervous system has been cut in the upper midbrain, dividing the forebrain from the brainstem.

cut into two parts: an upper part and a lower part. The entire brain can be isolated from the body by an incision between the medulla and the spinal cord. This preparation was first studied by the Belgian physiologist Frédéric Bremer (1892–1982), who called it the *encéphale isolé*, or **isolated brain** (Bremer, 1938).

The EEGs of such animals show signs of waking alternating with sleep (**Figure 14.26a**). During EEG-defined wakeful periods, the pupils are dilated and the eyes follow moving objects. During EEG-defined sleep, the pupils are small, as in normal sleep. REM sleep can also be detected in the isolated brain by other EEG signals that we won't talk about in this book. These results demonstrate that wakefulness, SWS, and REM sleep are all mediated by *networks within the brain*.

If the transection is made higher along the brainstem—in the midbrain—a very different result is achieved. Bremer referred to such a preparation as a *cerveau isolé*, or **isolated forebrain**, and he found that the EEG from the brain in front of the cut displayed constant SWS (**Figure 14.26b**). The isolated forebrain does not show REM sleep, so it appears that the forebrain alone can generate SWS, with no contributions from the lower brain regions.

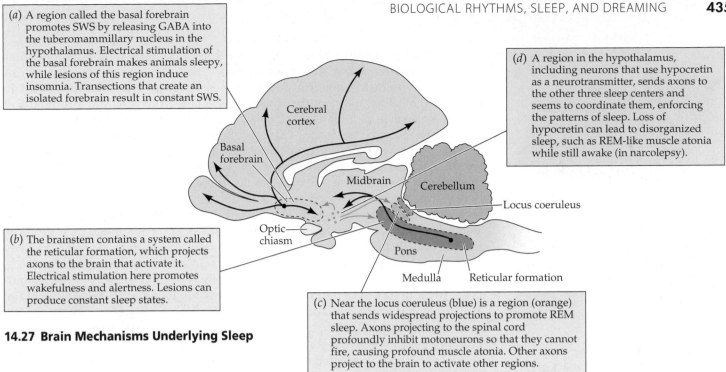

(*a*) A region called the basal forebrain promotes SWS by releasing GABA into the tuberomammillary nucleus in the hypothalamus. Electrical stimulation of the basal forebrain makes animals sleepy, while lesions of this region induce insomnia. Transections that create an isolated forebrain result in constant SWS.

(*d*) A region in the hypothalamus, including neurons that use hypocretin as a neurotransmitter, sends axons to the other three sleep centers and seems to coordinate them, enforcing the patterns of sleep. Loss of hypocretin can lead to disorganized sleep, such as REM-like muscle atonia while still awake (in narcolepsy).

(*b*) The brainstem contains a system called the reticular formation, which projects axons to the brain that activate it. Electrical stimulation here promotes wakefulness and alertness. Lesions can produce constant sleep states.

(*c*) Near the locus coeruleus (blue) is a region (orange) that sends widespread projections to promote REM sleep. Axons projecting to the spinal cord profoundly inhibit motoneurons so that they cannot fire, causing profound muscle atonia. Other axons project to the brain to activate other regions.

14.27 Brain Mechanisms Underlying Sleep

The constant SWS seen in the cortex of the isolated forebrain appears to be generated by the **basal forebrain** in the ventral frontal lobe and anterior hypothalamus (**Figure 14.27a**). Electrical stimulation of the basal forebrain can induce SWS activity (Clemente and Sterman, 1967), while lesions there suppress sleep (McGinty and Sterman, 1968). Neurons in this region become active at sleep onset and release GABA (Gallopin et al., 2000) to stimulate $GABA_A$ receptors in the nearby **tuberomammillary nucleus** in the posterior hypothalamus. These seem to be the $GABA_A$ receptors that general anesthetics act on to make us unconscious and induce slow waves in the EEG (see Figure 14.25). So the basal forebrain promotes SWS by releasing GABA into the nearby tuberomammillary nucleus and, left alone, this system would keep the cortex asleep forever. But as we'll see next, there is a brainstem system that arouses the forebrain from slumber.

The reticular formation wakes up the forebrain

In the late 1940s, electrical stimulation of an extensive region of the brainstem known as the **reticular formation** was shown to activate the cortex (**Figure 14.27b**). The reticular formation consists of a diffuse group of cells whose axons and dendrites course in many directions, extending from the medulla through the thalamus. Giuseppe Moruzzi (1920–1986) and Horace Magoun (1907–1991), pioneers in the study of the reticular formation, found that they could wake sleeping animals by electrically stimulating the reticular formation; the animals showed rapid awakening (Moruzzi and Magoun, 1949). Lesions of these regions produced persistent sleep in the animals. As mentioned already, the basal forebrain region actively imposes SWS on the brain. So the forebrain system and the brainstem reticular formation seem to push the brain back and forth from SWS to wakefulness.

The pons triggers REM sleep

Several methods have pinpointed the region of the pons that is important for REM sleep. Lesions of a region just ventral to the locus coeruleus abolish REM sleep (**Figure 14.27c**) (L. Friedman and Jones, 1984). Electrical stimulation of the same region, or pharmacological stimulation of this region with cholinergic agonists, can induce or prolong REM sleep. Finally, monitoring of neuronal activity in this region reveals some neurons that seem to be active only during REM sleep (J. M. Siegel, 1994). So the pons has a REM sleep center near the locus coeruleus.

basal forebrain   A ventral region in the forebrain that has been implicated in sleep.

tuberomammillary nucleus   A region of the basal hypothalamus, near the pituitary stalk, that plays a role in generating SWS.

reticular formation   An extensive region of the brainstem (extending from the medulla through the thalamus) that is involved in arousal (waking).

(a)

(b)

14.28 Sleep Stage Postures The kitten in (a) is enjoying slow-wave sleep, with enough muscle tone to maintain a sphinxlike posture. The kitten in (b), with a profoundly relaxed muscle tone, may be in REM sleep. Presumably this kitten is dreaming, much as we do. If you want to see what cats in REM sleep dream about, see the video on the book's website.

narcolepsy A disorder that involves frequent, intense episodes of sleep, which last from 5 to 30 minutes and can occur anytime during the usual waking hours.

cataplexy Sudden loss of muscle tone, leading to collapse of the body without loss of consciousness.

hypocretins Also called *orexins*. Neuropeptides produced in the hypothalamus that are involved in switching between sleep states, in narcolepsy, and in the control of appetite.

One job of the pontine REM sleep center is to profoundly inhibit motoneurons to keep them from firing. During REM sleep, the inhibitory transmitters GABA and glycine produce powerful inhibitory postsynaptic potentials (discussed in Chapter 3) in spinal motoneurons that prevent them from reaching threshold and producing an action potential (Kodama et al., 2003). Thus, the dreamer's muscles are not just relaxed, but flaccid. This loss of muscle tone during REM sleep can be abolished by small lesions ventral to the locus coeruleus, suggesting that this is the region that disables the motor system during sleep (A. R. Morrison, 1983).

Cats with such lesions seem to act out their dreams. They enter SWS like a normal cat, but as they begin to display the desynchronized EEG of REM sleep, instead of becoming completely limp as normal cats do (**Figure 14.28**), these cats stagger to their feet. Are they awake or in REM sleep? They move their heads as though visually tracking moving objects (that aren't there), bat with their forepaws at nothing, and ignore objects that are present. In addition, the cat's *inner eyelids*, the translucent nictitating membranes, partially cover the eyes. Thus, the cat appears to be in REM sleep, but motor activity is not being inhibited by the brain. You can watch one of these cats acting out its dream on the website for this book.

So far we've described three interacting brain systems controlling sleep: an SWS-promoting region in the forebrain, an arousing reticular formation in the brainstem, and a system in the pons that triggers paralysis of the body during REM. There is a fourth important system, which seems to act as a "switch" among these three centers, in the hypothalamus. To understand how we learned about this fourth system, we need to consider the rare but fascinating condition called *narcolepsy*.

A hypothalamic sleep center was revealed by the study of narcolepsy

You might not consider getting lots of sleep an affliction, but many people are either drowsy all the time or suffer sudden attacks of sleep. At the extreme of such tendencies is **narcolepsy**, an unusual disorder in which the patient is afflicted by frequent, intense attacks of sleep that last 5–30 minutes and can occur at any time during usual waking hours. These sleep attacks occur several times a day—usually about every 90 minutes (Dantz et al., 1994).

Most people display SWS for an hour or more before entering REM; individuals who suffer from narcolepsy, however, tend to enter REM in the first few minutes of sleep. People with this disorder exhibit an otherwise normal sleep pattern at night, but they suffer abrupt, overwhelming sleepiness during the day. Many people with narcolepsy also show **cataplexy**, a sudden loss of muscle tone, leading to collapse of the body without loss of consciousness. Cataplexy can be triggered by sudden, intense emotional stimuli, including both laughter and anger. Narcolepsy usually manifests itself between the ages of 15 and 25 years and continues throughout life. Remember Barry from the start of this chapter? His narcolepsy symptoms began in his freshman year of college, when he started showing the classic signs of excessive daytime sleepiness and cataplexy.

Several strains of dogs exhibit narcolepsy (Aldrich, 1993), complete with sudden collapse and very short latencies to sleep onset (**Figure 14.29**). (You can watch these dogs displaying cataplexy on the website for this book.) Just like humans who suffer from narcolepsy, they often show REM immediately upon falling asleep. Abrupt collapsing in these dogs is suppressed by the same drugs (discussed shortly) that are used to treat human cataplexy.

The mutant gene responsible for one of these narcoleptic strains of dogs was found to be a receptor for the neuropeptide **hypocretin** (a type of orexin) (L. Lin et al., 1999). Mice with the *hypocretin* gene knocked out also display narcolepsy (Chemelli et al., 1999). Genetically normal rats can be made narcoleptic if injected with a toxin that destroys neurons that possess hypocretin receptors (Gerashchenko et al., 2001). No one knows why interfering with hypocretin signaling leads to narcolepsy, but the narcoleptic dogs show signs of neural degeneration in the amygdala and nearby forebrain structures (J. M. Siegel, Nienhuis, et al., 1999). This

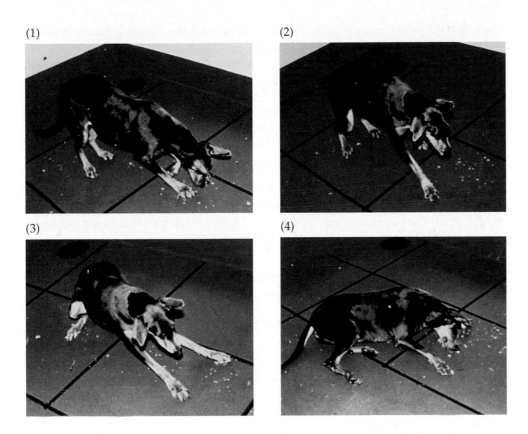

14.29 Narcolepsy in Dogs A narcoleptic dog that suffers cataplexy when excited is offered a food treat (1), becomes wobbly (2), lies down (3), and finally falls limply to the floor (4). (Courtesy of Seiji Nishino.)

degeneration occurs at about the time in development when symptoms of narcolepsy appear.

Similarly, humans with narcolepsy have lost about 90% of their hypocretin neurons (**Figure 14.30**) (Thannickal et al., 2000). This degeneration of hypocretin neurons seems to cause inappropriate activation of the cataplexy pathway that is normally at work during REM sleep. So hypocretin normally keeps sleep at bay and prevents the transition from wakefulness directly into REM sleep.

The neurons that normally produce hypocretin are found almost exclusively in the hypothalamus. Where do these neurons send their axons to release the hypocretin? Not so coincidentally, they send their axons to each of the three brain centers that we mentioned before: basal forebrain, reticular formation, and locus coeruleus (Sutcliffe and de Lecea, 2002). The hypocretin neurons also project axons to the hypothalamic tuberomammillary nucleus that is inhibited by the basal forebrain to induce SWS. So, it looks as if the hypothalamus contains a hypocretin-based sleep center that controls whether we are awake, in SWS sleep, or in REM sleep (see **Figure 14.27d**).

The traditional treatment for narcolepsy was the use of amphetamines in the daytime. The drug GHB (γ-hydroxybutyrate, trade name Xyrem), also known as a "date rape" drug, helps some narcoleptics (although there are concerns about potential abuse of this drug [Tuller, 2002]). A newer drug, modafinil (Provigil), is sometimes effective for preventing narcoleptic attacks and has been proposed as an "alertness drug" for people with attention deficit disorder. There is also debate about whether modafinil should be available to anyone who feels sleepy or needs to stay awake

(*a*) Normal

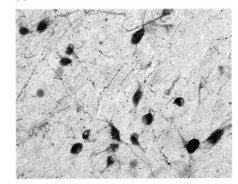

(*b*) Narcoleptic

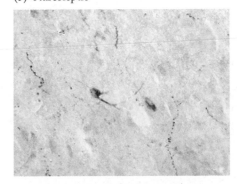

14.30 Neural Degeneration in Humans with Narcolepsy (*a*) Immunocytochemistry reveals hypocretin-containing neurons in the lateral hypothalamus of a person who did not have narcolepsy. (*b*) This same region of the brain from someone who suffered from narcolepsy has far fewer hypocretin neurons. (Courtesy of Jerome Siegel.)

sleep paralysis A state during the transition to or from sleep, in which the ability to move or talk is temporarily lost.

(Pack, 2003), but at least one study found the drug no more effective than caffeine in this regard (Wesensten et al., 2002). Barry eventually found a combination of mild stimulants that worked for him, and he recently earned his MD degree. Now that narcolepsy is known to be caused by a loss of hypocretin signaling, there is hope of developing synthetic drugs to stimulate hypocretin receptors, both for the relief of symptoms in narcolepsy and to combat sleepiness in people without narcolepsy.

One common symptom of narcolepsy is experienced by many people (whether or not they suffer from narcolepsy) on occasion (Fukuda et al., 1998). **Sleep paralysis** is the (temporary) inability to move or talk either just before dropping off to sleep, or, more often, just after waking. In this state people may experience sudden sensory hallucinations (Cheyne, 2002). Sleep paralysis never lasts more than a few minutes, so it's best to relax and avoid panic. One hypothesis is that sleep paralysis results when the pontine center (see Figure 14.27c) continues to impose paralysis for a short while after awakening from a REM episode.

Sleep Disorders Can Be Serious, Even Life-Threatening

Narcolepsy is just one of several sleep disorders (**Table 14.2**) that have made sleep disorder clinics common in major medical centers. For some people, the peace and

---

TABLE 14.2 Classification of Sleep Disorders

DISORDERS OF INITIATING AND MAINTAINING SLEEP (INSOMNIA)
Ordinary, uncomplicated insomnia
  Transient
  Persistent
Drug-related insomnia caused by
  Use of stimulants
  Withdrawal of depressants
  Chronic alcoholism
Insomnia associated with psychiatric disorders
Insomnia associated with sleep-induced respiratory impairment (sleep apnea)

DISORDERS OF EXCESSIVE DROWSINESS
Narcolepsy
Drowsiness associated with psychiatric problems
Drug-related drowsiness
Drowsiness associated with sleep-induced respiratory impairment (sleep apnea)

DISORDERS OF SLEEP-WAKING SCHEDULE
Transient disruption caused by
  Time zone change by airplane flight (jet lag)
  Shift work, especially night work
Persistent disruption (irregular rhythm)

DYSFUNCTIONS ASSOCIATED WITH SLEEP, SLEEP STAGES, OR PARTIAL AROUSALS
Sleepwalking (somnambulism)
Sleep enuresis (bed-wetting)
Night terror
Nightmares
Sleep-related seizures
Teeth grinding
REM behavior disorder (RBD)

Source: After Weitzman, 1981.

comfort of regular, uninterrupted sleep is routinely disturbed by the inability to fall asleep, by prolonged sleep, or by unusual awakenings.

Some minor dysfunctions are associated with sleep

Some dysfunctions associated with sleep are much more common in children than in adults. Two sleep disorders in children—night terrors (described earlier) and **sleep enuresis** (bed-wetting)—are associated with SWS. Most people grow out of these conditions without intervention, but pharmacological approaches can be used to reduce the amount of stage 3/4 sleep (as well as REM time) while increasing stage 2 sleep. For sleep enuresis, some doctors prescribe a nasal spray of the hormone vasopressin (antidiuretic hormone) before bedtime, which decreases urine production.

Somnambulism (sleepwalking) consists of getting out of bed, walking around the room, and appearing awake. Although more common in childhood, it sometimes persists into adulthood. These episodes last a few seconds to minutes, and the person usually does not remember the experience. Because such episodes occur during stage 3/4 SWS, they are more common in the first half of the night (when those stages predominate).

Most sleepwalkers are not acting out a dream (Parkes, 1985). The main problem is the inability of sleepwalkers to wake into full contact with their surroundings. At least one person was acquitted of murder after suggesting that he had suffered from "homicidal somnambulism," but such claims are difficult to evaluate (Broughton et al., 1994). Some people, however, do seem to be acting out their dreams during REM sleep. **REM behavior disorder** (**RBD**) is characterized by organized behavior—such as fighting an imaginary foe, eating a meal, acting like a wild animal—from a person who appears to be asleep (Schenck and Mahowald, 2002). Sometimes the person remembers a dream that fits well with his behavior (C. Brown, 2003). This disorder usually begins after the age of 50 and is more common in men than in women. Individuals with RBD are reminiscent of the cats with a lesion near the locus coeruleus (mentioned earlier) that were no longer paralyzed during REM and so acted out their dreams. The onset of RBD is often followed by the early symptoms of Parkinson's disease and dementia (Postuma et al., 2009), suggesting that the disorder is the beginning of a widespread neurodegeneration. RBD is usually well controlled by antianxiety drugs (benzodiazepines) at bedtime.

Insomniacs have trouble falling asleep or staying asleep

Almost all of us experience an occasional inability to fall asleep, and a very few individuals die apparently because they stop sleeping altogether (see Box 14.1). But many people persistently find it difficult to fall asleep and/or stay asleep as long as they would like. Estimates of the prevalence of insomnia range from 15% to 30% of the adult population (Parkes, 1985). Insomnia is commonly reported by people who are older, female, or users of drugs like tobacco, caffeine, and alcohol. Insomnia seems to be the final common outcome for various situational, neurological, psychiatric, and medical conditions. It is not a trivial disorder; recall that adults who regularly sleep for short periods show a higher mortality rate than those who regularly sleep 7–8 hours each night (Kripke et al., 2002). People with **sleep state misperception** (McCall and Edinger, 1992) report that they didn't sleep even when an EEG showed signs of sleep and they failed to respond to stimuli. They are sleeping without knowing it. But there are also many people who really have a hard time sleeping.

Situational factors that contribute to insomnia include shift work, time zone changes, and environmental conditions such as novelty (that hard motel bed). Usually these conditions produce transient **sleep-onset insomnia**, a difficulty in falling asleep. Drugs, as well as neurological and psychiatric factors, seem to cause **sleep-maintenance insomnia**, a difficulty in remaining asleep. In this type

sleep enuresis   Bed-wetting.

somnambulism   Sleepwalking.

REM behavior disorder (RBD)   A sleep disorder in which a person physically acts out a dream.

sleep state misperception   Commonly, a person's perception that he has not been asleep when in fact he was. Typically occurs at the start of a sleep episode.

sleep-onset insomnia   Difficulty in falling asleep.

sleep-maintenance insomnia   Difficulty in staying asleep.

14.31 A Machine That Prevents Sleep Apnea By supplying continuous positive airway pressure (CPAP), this machine prevents the collapse of the airway that otherwise causes this man to stop breathing for a while several times each night. It also stops his snoring. (Photograph by Christopher Breedlove.)

sleep apnea A sleep disorder in which respiration slows or stops periodically, waking the patient. Excessive daytime somnolence results from the frequent nocturnal awakening.

sudden infant death syndrome (SIDS) Also called *crib death*. The sudden, unexpected death of an apparently healthy human infant who simply stops breathing, usually during sleep.

of insomnia, sleep is punctuated by frequent nighttime arousals. This form of insomnia is especially evident in disorders of the respiratory system.

In some people, respiration becomes unreliable during sleep. Breathing may cease for a minute or so, or it may slow alarmingly; blood levels of oxygen drop markedly. This syndrome, called **sleep apnea**, arises either from the progressive relaxation of muscles of the chest, diaphragm, and throat cavity (*obstructive apnea*) or from changes in the pacemaker respiratory neurons of the brainstem (*central apnea*). In the former instance, relaxation of the throat obstructs the airway—a kind of self-choking. This mode of sleep apnea is common in very obese people, but it also occurs, often undiagnosed, in nonobese people. Sleep apnea is frequently accompanied by loud, interrupted snoring, so loud snorers should consult a physician about the possibility that they suffer from sleep apnea.

Each episode of apnea arouses the person enough to restore breathing, but in rats, such interruptions in oxygen kill neurons in the hippocampus and impair learning ability (Row et al., 2007), so apnea may lead to brain damage. What's more, the frequent nighttime arousals make such people sleepy in the daytime. For some people, breathing through a special machine (called a *continuous positive airway pressure*, or *CPAP*, machine) maintains air pressure in their airways and prevents the collapse of those airways (**Figure 14.31**). Untreated sleep apnea may lead to any of several cardiovascular disorders, including hypertension and diabetes (Rakel, 2009).

Investigators have speculated that **sudden infant death syndrome** (**SIDS**, or *crib death*) arises from sleep apnea as a result of immature systems that normally pace respiration. Autopsies of SIDS victims reveal abnormalities in brainstem serotonin systems (Kinney, 2009), and interfering with this system in mice renders them unable to regulate respiration effectively. What's more, some of these young mice spontaneously stopped breathing and died (Audero et al., 2008). The incidence of SIDS has been cut almost in half by the "Back to Sleep" campaign, which urges parents to place infants on their backs to sleep rather than on their stomachs (**Figure 14.32**). Placing the baby face down may lead to suffocation if the baby cannot regulate breathing or arouse properly.

Although many drugs affect sleep, there is no perfect sleeping pill

Throughout recorded history, humans have reached for substances to enhance the prospects of sleep. Ancient Greeks used the juice of the poppy to obtain opium and used products of the mandrake plant that we recognize today as the anticholinergic drugs scopolamine and atropine (Hartmann, 1978). The preparation of barbituric acid in the mid–nineteenth century by the discoverer of aspirin, Adolph von Bayer, started the development of many drugs—*barbiturates*—that continue to be used for sleep dysfunctions. Unfortunately, none of these substances can provide a completely normal night of sleep in terms of time spent in various sleep states, such as REM sleep, and none of them remain effective when used repeatedly.

Most modern sleeping pills—including the benzodiazepine triazolam (Halcion), and its mimics Ambien, Sonata, and Lunesta—bind to GABA receptors, inhibiting

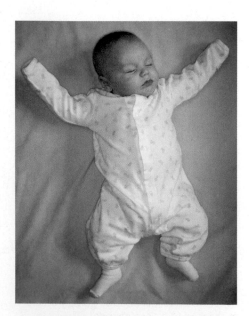

14.32 Back to Sleep Placing infants on their backs for sleep reduces the risk of sudden infant death syndrome (SIDS) by half. Exposure to cigarette smoke increases the risk of crib death.

broad regions of the brain. But reliance on sleeping pills poses many problems (Rothschild, 1992). Viewed solely as a way to deal with sleep problems, current drugs fall far short of being a suitable remedy, for several reasons.

First, continued use of sleeping pills causes them to lose effectiveness, and this declining ability to induce sleep often leads to increased self-prescribed dosages that can be dangerous. A second major drawback is that sleeping pills produce marked changes in the pattern of sleep, both while the drug is being used and for days afterward.

Use of sleeping pills may lead to a persistent "sleep drunkenness," coupled with drowsiness, that impairs waking activity; or to memory gaps about daily activity. Police report cases of "the Ambien driver," a person who took a sleeping pill and then got up a few hours later to go for a spin, with sometimes disastrous results, while apparently asleep (Saul, 2006). In other cases, people taking such medicines eat snacks, shop over the Internet, or even have sex, with no memory of these events the next day (Dolder and Nelson, 2008).

Because the hormone melatonin is normally released from the pineal gland at night (see Figure 5.20), the administration of exogenous melatonin has been suggested to aid the onset of sleep. In fact, melatonin does have a weak hypnotic effect soon after administration (Chase and Gidal, 1997), perhaps because it lowers body temperature, reducing arousal and causing drowsiness (D. Dawson and Encel, 1993).

Certainly, the treatment for insomnia that has the fewest side effects, and that is very effective for many people, is not to use any drug, but to develop a regular routine to exploit the body's circadian clock. The best advice for insomniacs is to use an alarm clock to wake up faithfully at the same time each day (weekends included) and then simply go to bed once they feel sleepy (Webb, 1992). They should also avoid daytime naps and having caffeine at night. Going through a bedtime routine in a quiet, dark environment can also help to condition sleep onset. An important adjunct to this strategy is to ignore preconceived notions about how much sleep you "need." If you get out of bed every day at 6:00 AM and don't feel sleepy until midnight, then your body is telling you that you need only 6 hours of sleep, no matter what $600 million in annual pharmaceutical advertising might say

SUMMARY

BIOLOGICAL RHYTHMS

Many Animals Show Daily Rhythms in Activity

■ Many living systems show **circadian rhythms** that can be **entrained** by environmental stimuli, especially light. These rhythms synchronize behavior and body states to changes in the environment. **Review Figure 14.1**, **Web Activity 14.1**

The Hypothalamus Houses a Circadian Clock

■ Neural pacemakers in the **suprachiasmatic nucleus (SCN)** of the hypothalamus are the basis of many circadian rhythms. The basis of light entrainment is a specialized pathway from the retina to the SCN. **Review Figures 14.2 and 14.6**

■ **Ultradian** rhythms (shorter than 24 hours) and **infradian** rhythms (longer than 24 hours) are evident in both behavior and biological processes. **Review Figures 14.8 and 14.10**

■ Several proteins, including, clock, cycle, and period interact in a cyclic fashion, increasing and decreasing in a cyclic fashion

that takes about 24 hours. Thousands of SCN neurons, each keeping time through this molecular clock, pool this information to provide the circadian biological clock. **Review Figure 14.7**, **Web Activity 14.2**

Animals Use Circannual Rhythms to Anticipate Seasonal Changes

■ Seasonally breeding animals will continue to show annual cycles in body physiology and fur composition, even when kept in constant conditions in the laboratory. The brain region mediating this **circannual rhythm** has not been determined, but it is not the SCN.

SLEEPING AND WAKING

Human Sleep Exhibits Different Stages

■ During sleep, almost all mammals alternate between two main states: **slow-wave sleep (SWS)** and **rapid-eye-movement (REM) sleep**. **Review Figures 14.11, 14.12, and 14.15**

- Human SWS shows four stages defined by **electroencephalography (EEG)** criteria that include bursts of **sleep spindles** and persistent trains of large, slow **delta waves**. During SWS, muscle tension, heart rate, respiratory rate, and temperature decline progressively. **Review Figure 14.11 and Table 14.2**

- REM sleep is characterized by a rapid EEG of low amplitude— almost like the EEG during active waking behavior—and intense autonomic activation, but the postural muscles are flaccid because of profound inhibition of motoneurons.

- In adult humans, SWS and REM sleep alternate every 90–110 minutes. Smaller animals have shorter sleep cycles and spend more overall time asleep. **Review Figures 14.12 and 14.15, Web Activity 14.3**

- Mental activity does not cease during sleep. Subjects awakened from REM sleep frequently report vivid perceptual experiences (dreams); subjects awakened from SWS often report ideas or thinking. **Review Web Activities 14.4 and 14.5**

Different Species Provide Clues about the Evolution of Sleep

- SWS seems widespread among animal species, but REM sleep appears restricted to mammals and birds. It is unknown whether REM was inherited from a common ancestor of birds and mammals, or evolved independently in the two groups.

Our Sleep Patterns Change across the Life Span

- The characteristics of sleep-waking cycles change during the course of life. Mature animals sleep less than the young, and REM sleep accounts for a smaller fraction of their sleep. **Review Figures 14.12, 14.18, and 14.19**

- The prominence of REM sleep in infants suggests that REM sleep contributes to development of the brain and to learning. **Review Figure 14.18**

Manipulating Sleep Reveals an Underlying Structure

- Deprivation of sleep for a few nights in a row leads to impairment in tasks that require sustained vigilance. During recovery nights following deprivation, the lost SWS and REM sleep are partially restored over several nights. **Review Figure 14.21**

What Are the Biological Functions of Sleep?

- Researchers have suggested several biological roles for sleep, including conservation of energy, niche adaptation, restoration of the body, and consolidation of memory. **Review Figure 14.23**

- The fact that prolonged **sleep deprivation** can lead to death suggests that sleep promotes health. No pill can guarantee a normal night of sleep. **Review Box 14.1**

At Least Four Interacting Neural Systems Underlie Sleep

- **General anesthetics**, which seem to mimic slow wave sleep, act as non-competitive agonists to boost the inhibitory activity of $GABA_A$ receptors. **Review Figure 14.25**

- Four brain structures are involved in the initiation and maintenance of sleep. A **basal forebrain** system promotes SWS, the brainstem **reticular formation** promotes arousal, a pontine system appears to trigger REM sleep, and a hypothalamic system of **hypocretin**-releasing neurons regulates these three centers to control the sleep-waking cycle. **Review Web Activity 14.6**

- **Narcolepsy** is the sudden, uncontrollable intrusion of sleep, which may be accompanied by **cataplexy**, during wakefulness. Disruption of hypocretin signaling, brought about by the lack of either hypocretin or hypocretin receptors, causes narcolepsy. **Review Web Activity 14.7**

Sleep Disorders Can Be Serious, Even Life-Threatening

- Sleep disorders fall into four major categories: disorders of initiation and maintenance of sleep (e.g., insomnia); disorders of excessive drowsiness (e.g., narcolepsy); disorders of the sleep-waking schedule; and dysfunctions associated with sleep, sleep stages, or partial arousals (e.g., sleepwalking). **Review Table 14.2**

Go to **www.biopsychology.com** for study questions, quizzes, key terms, and other resources.

Recommended Reading

Dunlap, J. C., Loros, J. J., and DeCoursey, P. J. (2003). *Chronobiology: Biological timekeeping.* Sunderland, MA: Sinauer.

Kryger, M. K., Roth, T., and Dement, W. C. (Eds.). (2005). *Principles and practice of sleep medicine* (4th ed.). New York: Saunders.

Lavie, P. (2003). *Restless nights: Understanding snoring and sleep apnea.* New Haven, CT: Yale University Press.

Max, D. T. (2007). *The family that couldn't sleep: A medical mystery.* New York: Random House.

Refenetti, R. (2005). *Circadian physiology* (2nd ed.). Boca Raton, FL: CRC Press.

Schenk, C. H. (2008). *Sleep: A groundbreaking guide to the mysteries, the problems and the solutions.* New York: Avery.

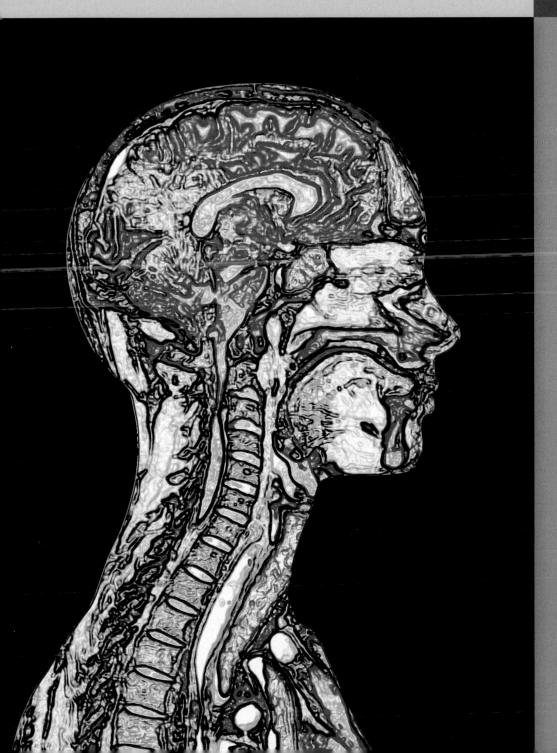

Emotions and Mental Disorders

PART **V**

Previous page **Mid-sagittal view of the human brain and spinal cord** This pseudocolor magnetic resonance imaging (MRI) scan of a healthy brain and upper spinal cord provides a vivid portrait of the source of our feelings and behaviors. (Image © Mehau Kulyk/Photo Researchers, Inc.)

Emotions, Aggression, and Stress

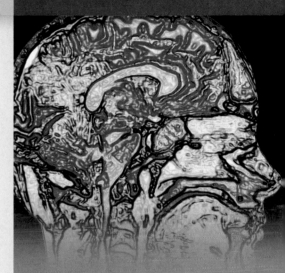

CHAPTER 15

Too Embarrassed to Work

Christine Drury had a great start on a career that was her dream: being anchorwoman of a television news program. At only 26, she was already doing late-night news bulletins for an NBC affiliate in Indianapolis, and she was good at the job—not just being pretty and articulate in front of the camera, but writing the news scripts to make them direct and clear. Still, she had a big problem: blushing. She had always blushed easily, and she had been teased about it often, sometimes by strangers.

Something about her job—perhaps the anxiety or concentration—started causing her to blush on camera, and because of her pale skin the blush was very visible to viewers. When Christine became self-conscious about it, the problem grew even worse, until she was blushing during almost every broadcast (Gawande, 2002). Wearing turtlenecks and really heavy makeup made the blushing harder to see, but she still experienced the blush, and she would visibly stiffen, her voice rising in pitch. A colleague said she looked like a deer caught in the headlights when this happened. Christine was never going to be promoted unless she could look more relaxed on-screen.

Breathing control and giving up caffeine didn't help. Neither did a variety of medicines: antianxiety drugs, antidepressants, sympathetic blockers. It looked like her young career was already over, when Christine learned of a clinic in Sweden that claimed to eliminate blushing—through surgery. The procedure would be expensive and, like all surgery, involved some risks.

Should she go through with it?

The sound of unexpected footsteps in the eerie quiet of the night brings fear to many of us. But the sound of music we enjoy and the voice of someone we love summons feelings of warmth. For some of us, feelings and emotions can become vastly exaggerated; fears, for example, can become paralyzing attacks of anxiety and panic. No story about our behavior is complete without considering the everyday events that involve feelings.

The psychobiological study of emotions has progressed in several directions. One traditional area focuses on bodily responses during emotional states, especially changes in facial expression and visceral responses such as changes in heart rate. The study of brain mechanisms related to emotional states has especially emphasized fear and aggression because both are important for survival and they are readily studied in animals. But today's research reveals a more nuanced view of emotional states, including humor, perceptions of fairness, and empathy.

Strong negative emotion is often associated with stress, and stress, in turn, is associated with a variety of health problems. Stress involves and affects not only the nervous and endocrine systems but also the immune system, so we also discuss the immune system in this chapter. We'll find that the nervous, endocrine, and immune systems interact extensively.

What Are Emotions?

The complicated world of emotions includes a wide range of observable behaviors, expressed feelings, and physiological changes. This diversity—that is, the many meanings of the word *emotion*—has made the subject hard to study. For many of us emotions are very personal states, difficult to define or identify except in the most obvious instances. Is the hissing cat afraid, angry, or just enjoying our startled reaction? Moreover, many aspects of our emotions seem unconscious. For these reasons, emotions were neglected as a field of study for many years, but there has been a significant renaissance in this fascinating subject.

Emotions have four different aspects

There are at least four aspects to emotion:

1. *Feelings.* In many cases, emotions are feelings that are private and subjective. Humans report an extraordinary range of states that they say they feel or experience.
2. *Actions.* Emotions may involve actions commonly deemed "emotional," such as defending or attacking in response to a threat, or laughing out loud at a good joke.
3. *Physiological arousal.* The strength of the emotions we experience is correlated with our physiological arousal: the distinctive somatic and autonomic responses that integrate ongoing behaviors. Because this constellation of bodily responses can be objectively studied, measures of physiological arousal also give us a starting place for studying emotion in nonhuman animals.
4. *Motivation.* Emotions are motivational programs that coordinate responses to solve specific adaptive problems. We are motivated to seek pleasure and avoid pain.

Broad Theories of Emotion Emphasize Bodily Responses

In many emotional states the heart races, the hands and face become warm, the palms sweat, and the stomach feels queasy. Strong emotions are nearly inseparable from activation of these events. Common expressions capture this association: "with all my heart," "my hair standing on end," "a sinking feeling in my stomach."

Several theories have tried to explain the close ties between the subjective psychological phenomena that we know as emotions and the activity of visceral organs controlled by the autonomic nervous system, which we described in Chapter 2 (see Figure 2.11). Folk wisdom suggests that the autonomic reactions are caused by the emotion—"I was so angry my stomach was churning"—as though the anger produced the churning (**Figure 15.1a**). Yet research indicates that the relationship between emotion and physiological arousal is more subtle than that.

The James-Lange theory considers emotions to be the perception of bodily changes

William James (1842–1910), the leading figure in American psychology at the start of the twentieth century, turned the folk notion on its head, suggesting that the emotions we experience are caused by the bodily changes. About the same time, Danish physician Carl G. Lange (1834–1900) proposed a similar view, emphasizing peripheral physiological events—regulated by the autonomic nervous system—in the perception of emotion. From this perspective, we experience fear because we perceive the body activity triggered by particular stimuli (**Figure 15.1b**). Different emotions thus feel different because they are generated by a different constellation of physiological responses.

The James-Lange theory initiated many attempts to link emotions to bodily responses—a focus of lasting interest in the field. Questions such as "What are the

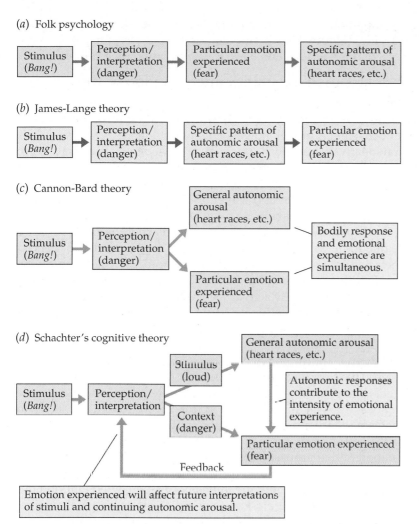

(a) Folk psychology

(b) James-Lange theory

(c) Cannon-Bard theory

(d) Schachter's cognitive theory

15.1 Different Views of the Chain of Events in Emotional Responses (a) Informal observation suggested that emotions cause the body to react. (b) James and Lange argued that the bodily response evokes the emotional experience. (c) Cannon and Bard insisted that the brain must interpret the situation to decide which emotion is appropriate. (d) Schachter attempted to reconcile these views by suggesting that the intensity of emotion can be affected by the bodily responses and that the brain continually assesses the situation.

responses of the heart in love, anger, fear?" continue to form a prominent part of the biological study of emotions. Although research eventually showed that the James-Lange theory does not provide a complete account of emotion, it contributed an important idea: that the experience of emotions may involve "reading" the state of one's own body. For example, people with spinal cord injuries reportedly experience less intense emotions, presumably because sensory signals from the body are absent (Hohmann, 1966).

The Cannon-Bard theory emphasizes central processes

In criticizing the James-Lange theory, physiologists Walter Cannon (1871–1945) and Philip Bard (1898–1977) argued that the experience of emotion most likely starts well before the autonomic changes can occur, because the latter are relatively slow. In addition, autonomic changes accompanying strong emotions seemed very much the same, whether the emotion experienced was anger, fear, or great surprise. Cannon emphasized that these bodily reactions (increased heart rate, glucose mobilization, and other effects) are an emergency response of an organism to a sudden threat, producing maximal activation of the sympathetic nervous system and thereby readying the organism for "fight or flight" (W. B. Cannon, 1929). So the function of emotion is to help us deal with a changing environment.

In Cannon and Bard's view, however, it is the brain's job to decide what particular emotion is an appropriate response to the stimuli. According to this view, the cerebral cortex simultaneously decides on the appropriate emotional response

polygraph   Popularly known as a *lie detector*. A device that measures several bodily responses, such as heart rate and blood pressure.

and activates the sympathetic system so that the body is ready for appropriate action, as the brain decides (**Figure 15.1c**). The Cannon-Bard theory provoked many studies of the effects of brain lesions and electrical stimulation on emotion.

Stanley Schachter proposed a cognitive interpretation of stimuli and visceral states

Like Cannon and Bard, Stanley Schachter (1975) emphasized cognitive mechanisms in emotion. Under Schachter's model, however, emotional labels (e.g., *anger*, *fear*, *joy*) are attributed to relatively nonspecific feelings of physiological arousal. These attributions are arrived at by internal cognitive systems that interpret our current social, physical, and cognitive situation to appropriately label the emotion.

In a famous experiment (Schachter and Singer, 1962), people were injected with epinephrine (adrenaline) and told either that there would be no effect or that their heart would race. Participants who were warned of the reaction reported no emotional experience, but some participants who were not forewarned experienced emotions when their bodies responded to the drug, as would be predicted by the James-Lange theory (bodily reactions are experienced as emotion) but not the Cannon-Bard theory (the cortex separately activates emotion and the bodily reaction).

However, which emotion was experienced could be affected by whether a confederate in the room acted angry or happy. The unsuspecting subjects injected with epinephrine were much more likely to report feeling angry when in the presence of an "angry" confederate, and more likely to report feeling elated when with a "happy" confederate. These findings are at odds with the James-Lange prediction that feelings of anger or happiness should each be associated with a unique profile of autonomic reactions. Subjects injected with placebo were much less likely to report an emotional experience, no matter how the confederate behaved. Thus, an emotional state is the result of an interaction between physiological arousal and cognitive interpretation of that arousal (**Figure 15.1d**).

Schachter's theory has its critics. For example, the theory asserts that physiological arousal is nonspecific, affecting only the intensity of a perceived emotion but not its quality. Yet when subjects were asked to adopt facial expressions distinctive for particular emotions, autonomic patterns of the subjects were different for several emotions, such as fear and sadness (Levenson et al., 1990). Indeed, positive emotions elicit a different array of autonomic responses than do negative emotions (Cacioppo et al., 2000), although, within those categories, different emotions elicit approximately the same autonomic profile. The fact that all negative emotions involve the same physiological responses is one reason why the **polygraph**—which measures various aspects of autonomic arousal, such as heart rate, blood pressure, sweating, and so on—is so poor at distinguishing liars from, say, anxious innocents (**Box 15.1**).

How Many Emotions Do We Experience?

Research suggests that there may be a basic core set of emotions underlying the more varied and delicate nuances of our world of feelings. One popular formulation (Plutchik, 1994) posits that there are eight basic emotions, grouped in four pairs of opposites—joy/sadness, affection/disgust, anger/fear, and expectation/surprise—with all other emotions arising from combinations of this basic array (**Figure 15.2**). But investigators do not yet agree about the number of basic emotions (six, seven, eight?). Although there is no way to determine once and for all

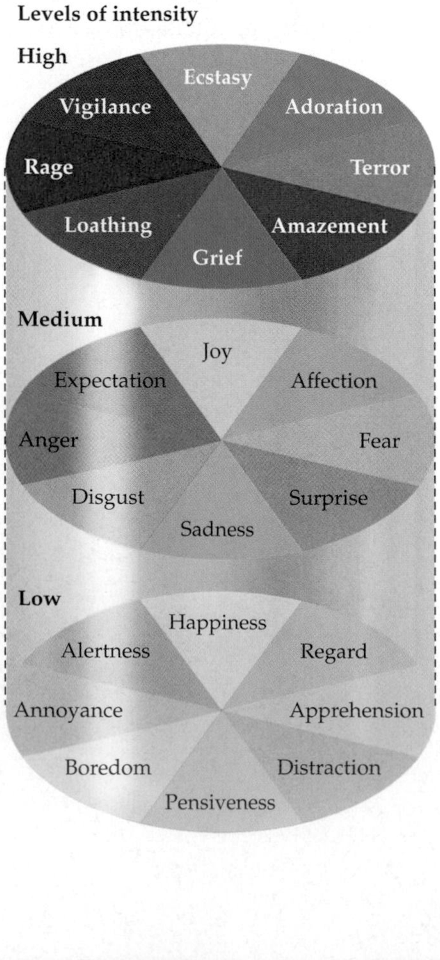

Levels of intensity

15.2 Basic Emotions   According to one popular scheme, the eight basic emotions are arrayed as four pairs of opposite emotions. Lower- and higher-intensity forms of each basic emotion appear at the bottom and top levels, respectively. (Modified from Plutchik, 1994.)

BOX 15.1 Lie Detector?

One of the most controversial attempts to apply biomedical science is the so-called lie detector test. In this procedure, properly known as a *polygraph* test (from the Greek *polys*, "many," and *graphein*, "to write"), multiple physiological measures are recorded in an attempt to detect lying during a carefully structured interview. The test is based on the assumption that people have emotional responses when lying because they fear detection and/or feel guilt about lying. Emotions are usually accompanied by bodily responses that are difficult to control, such as changes in respiratory rate, heart rate, blood pressure, skin conductance (a measure of sweating), and so on. In polygraph recordings like Figure A, each wiggly line, or *trace*, provides a measurement of one of these physiological variables, and taken together the measures are assumed to track the subject's physiological arousal over time. When subjects lie in response to a direct question (arrows) momentary changes in several of the measured variables may occur.

Proponents of polygraph examinations claim that they are accurate in 95% of tests, but the estimate from impartial research is an overall accuracy of about 65% (Nietzel, 2000). Even if the higher figure were correct, the fact that these tests are widely used means that thousands of truthful people could be branded as liars and fired, disciplined, or not hired. On the other hand, many criminals and spies have been able to pass the tests without detection. For example, long-time CIA agent Aldrich Ames, who was sentenced in 1995 to life in prison for espionage, successfully passed polygraph tests after becoming a spy. In the wake of the terrorist attacks of 2001, the National Research Council (2003) took up the question again and confirmed that the polygraph test's "accuracy in distinguishing actual or potential security violators from innocent test takers is insufficient to justify reliance on its use in employee security screening."

It is difficult to do convincing research on lie detection because most studies focus on only trivial attempts at deception that do not necessarily involve subjects emotionally. Paul Ekman, a leading expert on behavioral displays of emotions, argues that such research won't yield solid results unless the subjects are playing for "high stakes," such as loss of a job (Holden, 2001).

"Because of the controversies that surround the polygraph, most [American] courts do not allow testimony about it in trials. However, it is widely used in the initial stages of criminal investigations, often to convince suspects that they should confess" (Nietzel, 2000, p. 225). Unfortunately, even innocent people may display emotional arousal when being questioned by the police. Polygraph testing was also widely used for employee screening in U.S. businesses in the 1970s and 1980s; but in 1988, Congress passed the Employee Polygraph Protection Act, which, with some exceptions, prohibits the use of lie detectors by private businesses involved in interstate commerce. Even where such tests are permitted, employees are granted several rights (such as seeing the questions in advance), and the results of a lie detector test cannot be the sole basis for action against an employee.

Some scientists believe that modern neuroscience may provide new methods of lie detection someday. Conscious lying may involve unusual activation of executive control mechanisms of the prefrontal cortex (Figure B) (Abe et al., 2007). Fear results in activation of the amygdala (as we'll discuss later in this chapter) that also might be visible with functional MRI (see Chapter 2) in the case of deception. Daniel Langleben et al. (2002) used fMRI to show that the anterior cingulate cortex (another region associated with executive control) became more active when subjects were lying. Although initial results from brain-imaging studies of deception are intriguing, much more work will be required to establish that brain imaging can detect lies with enough reliability to be useful in making important decisions about individual people. And of course, even if they are validated, such lie detectors would be more costly and less widely available than polygraphs. (Figure B from Abe et al., 2007.)

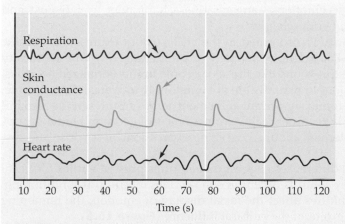

(A) The polygraph measures signs of arousal

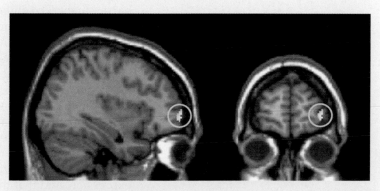

(B) **Your cheatin' brain** PET images reveal selective activation of prefrontal cortex in a subject engaged in lying (relative to a control scan). (Courtesy of Nobuhito Abe.)

Anger Sadness Happiness Fear

Disgust Surprise Contempt Embarrassment

15.3 Universal Facial Expressions of Emotion According to Paul Ekman and colleagues, the seven basic emotional facial expressions shown here are displayed in all cultures. Embarrassment has recently been proposed to be an eighth basic emotion. (C. R. Harris, 2006.)

the number of basic emotions, one clue comes from examining the number of different kinds of facial expressions that we produce and can recognize in others.

Facial expressions have complex functions in communication

How many different emotions can be detected in facial expressions? According to Paul Ekman and collaborators, there are distinctive expressions for anger, sadness, happiness, fear, disgust, surprise, contempt, and embarrassment (**Figure 15.3**) (Keltner and Ekman, 2000). Facial expressions of these emotions are interpreted similarly across many cultures without explicit training. (In case you're keeping track, whereas Plutchik included affection and expectation in his eight basic emotions, Keltner and Ekman include, instead, facial expressions of contempt and embarrassment. The other six emotions—anger, sadness, happiness, fear, disgust, and surprise—are the same in both schemes.)

Cross-cultural similarity is also noted in the *production* of expressions specific to particular emotions. For example, people in a preliterate New Guinea society show emotional facial expressions like those of people in industrialized societies. However, facial expressions apparently are not unfailingly universal. For example, although Russell (1994) found significant agreement across cultures in the recognition of most emotional states from facial expressions, isolated nonliterate groups did not agree with Westerners about recognizing expressions of surprise and disgust (**Figure 15.4**).

These subtle cultural differences suggest that cultures prescribe rules for facial expression, and that they control and enforce those rules by cultural conditioning. Everyone agrees that cultures affect the facial display of emotion; the remaining controversy is over the extent of the cultural influence (**Figure 15.5**).

According to Fridlund (1994), a major role of facial expression is paralinguistic; that is, the face is accessory to verbal communication, providing emphasis and

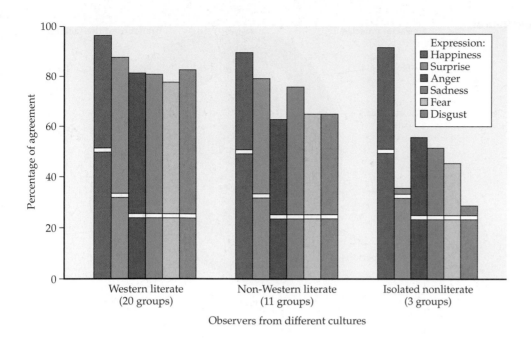

15.4 Cultural Differences in Recognizing Facial Expressions of Emotion   Within Western and non-Western literate groups (*left and middle*), there is widespread agreement about the emotions represented by photographs of basic facial expressions. But people from isolated nonliterate groups (*right*) are much less likely to agree with literate people's judgments of some facial expressions, especially those of surprise and disgust. The white horizontal bars indicate the percentage of agreement that would be expected by chance alone. (From Russell, 1994.)

direction in conversation. For example, Gilbert et al. (1986) showed that subjects display few facial responses to odor when smelling alone, but significantly more in a social setting. Similarly, bowlers tend to smile after making a strike only after they turn around to meet the faces of onlookers (Kraut and Johnston, 1979). Sometimes we communicate our emotions too well, as we saw at the start of the chapter with Christine's tendency to blush when she didn't want to.

Facial expressions are mediated by muscles, cranial nerves, and CNS pathways

How are facial expressions produced? Within the human face is an elaborate network of finely innervated muscles whose functional roles, in addition to facial expression, include speech production, eating, and respiration, among others. Facial muscles can be divided into two categories:

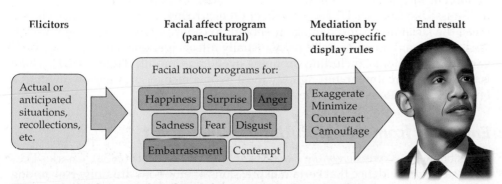

15.5 A Model for Emotional Facial Expressions across Cultures

15.6 Superficial Facial Muscles and Their Neural Control

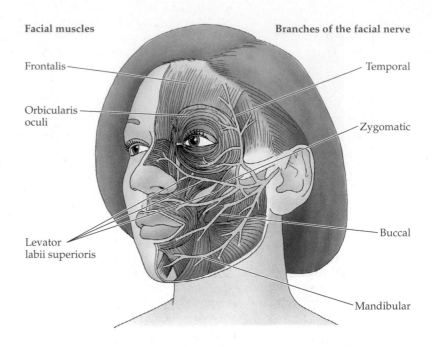

Facial muscles

Frontalis

Orbicularis oculi

Levator labii superioris

Branches of the facial nerve

Temporal

Zygomatic

Buccal

Mandibular

Bell's palsy   A disorder, usually caused by viral infection, in which the facial nerve on one side stops conducting action potentials, resulting in paralysis on one side of the face.

1. *Superficial facial muscles* that attach only to facial skin (**Figure 15.6**). On contraction they change the shape of the mouth, eyes, or nose, for example; or they pull on their attachment to the skin. One such muscle, the frontalis, wrinkles the forehead and raises the eyebrow.
2. *Deep facial muscles* that attach to bone. These muscles enable movements such as chewing and large movements of the face. An example of a deep muscle is the masseter, a powerful jaw muscle.

Human facial muscles are innervated by two cranial nerves: (1) the facial nerve (VII), which innervates the superficial muscles of facial expression; and (2) the motor branch of the trigeminal nerve (V), which innervates muscles that move the jaw (see Figure 2.9). Studies of the facial nerve reveal that the right and left sides are completely independent. As Figure 15.6 shows, the main trunk of the facial nerve divides into upper and lower divisions shortly after entering the face. These nerve fibers originate in the brainstem in the nucleus of the facial nerve.

The cerebral cortex innervates the facial nucleus both bilaterally and unilaterally: the lower two-thirds of the face receives input only from the opposite side of the cortex; the upper third receives input from *both* sides. This is why most of us find it easier to sneer (drawing back the lips on one side) than to arch one eyebrow. A lot of the human motor cortex is devoted to the face (see Figure 11.12), probably reflecting the ecological importance of emotional expression in our species.

Impaired facial expression may affect social interactions. Chronic selective inhibition of the facial musculature is one symptom of Parkinson's disease (which is discussed in Chapter 11) and of schizophrenia (Kring, 1999). Sometimes viruses infect the facial nerve and damage it enough to cause paralysis of facial muscles. This condition, known as **Bell's palsy**, usually affects just one side, resulting in a variety of symptoms, including drooping eyelid and mouth (**Figure 15.7**). There is no standard treatment, but happily most people recover on their own within a few weeks, and almost everyone recovers within 6 months.

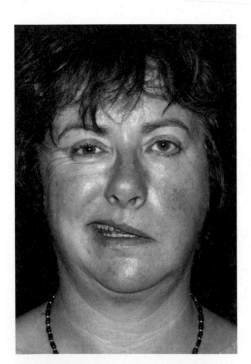

15.7 Bell's Palsy Leaves Half of the Face Paralyzed   This woman is smiling, but only the muscles on the right side of her face (left half of photograph) respond to her commands.

Emotions from the Evolutionary Viewpoint

In his book *The Expression of the Emotions in Man and Animals* (1872), Charles Darwin presented evidence that certain expressions of emotions are universal among people of all regions of the world, anticipating by more than a century the studies of facial expressions that we reviewed earlier (see Figure 15.4). Furthermore, Darwin asked whether nonhuman animals show comparable expressions of some emotions and argued that aspects of emotional expression may have originated in a common ancestor.

Darwin's perspective encompassed behavioral phenomena—the apparent emotional expressions of various mammals (**Figure 15.8**)—as well as the physiological mechanisms of emotional display, such as facial muscles and their innervation. Earlier scholars had believed the facial muscles were given uniquely to humans so that they could express their feelings, but Darwin emphasized that nonhuman primates have the same facial muscles that humans have. A century later, Redican (1982) noted distinct facial expressions in nonhuman primates: (1) *grimace*, perhaps analogous to human expressions of fear or surprise; (2) *tense mouth*, akin to human expressions of anger; and (3) *play face*, homologous to the human laugh. Different facial expressions may represent different emotions across primate species (**Figure 15.9**). This connection may even extend beyond primates: for example, tickling and playing with rats can elicit ultrasonic vocalizations that may be analogous to laughter. Expression of positive emotions of this sort, across species, may facilitate social contact and learning (Burgdorf et al., 2008; Panksepp, 2007).

How may emotion and emotional displays have evolved?

How do emotions and their expression help individuals survive and reproduce? Darwin (1872) offered several suggestions:

> The movements of expression in the face and body .., are ... of much importance for our welfare. They serve as the first means of communication between the mother and her infant; she smiles approval, and thus encourages her child on the right path, or frowns disapproval. We readily perceive sympathy in others by their expression; our sufferings are thus mitigated and our pleasure increased; and mutual good feeling is thus strengthened. The movements of expression give vividness and energy to our spoken words. They reveal the thoughts and intentions of others more truly than do words, which may be falsified. (p. 365)

Current proponents of **evolutionary psychology** point to additional ways in which emotions are adaptive and could have developed through natural selection (Cosmides and Tooby, 2000). They suggest that emotions are broad motivational programs that coordinate various responses to solve specific adaptive problems,

15.8 Emotional Expression in Animals (a) Crested black macaque monkey "in a placid condition." (b) "The same when pleased by being caressed." (From Darwin, 1872, p. 136.)

evolutionary psychology A field devoted to asking how natural selection has shaped behavior in humans and other animals.

15.9 Facial Expression of Emotions in Nonhuman Primates (a) An adult female chimpanzee screams at another female, who is pulling at her food. Screaming is used in submission and protest. (b) A juvenile chimpanzee shows a play face while being tickled. He also makes a guttural laughing sound. (c) A Tibetan macaque bares his teeth, grinning to signal submission to a dominant animal. In other primates, including humans, teeth baring has gained a different, friendlier meaning. (Photographs by Frans de Waal, from de Waal, 2003.)

including maintaining cooperative relations with other members of your group, choosing a mate, avoiding predators, finding food sources, and so forth.

For example, most of us have experienced the frightening nighttime perception of being stalked by a predator: real or imagined, human or nonhuman. The intensity of the experience may be a legacy of the ancestral environment in which our behavioral systems evolved, where the presence of an unseen predator would be a situation of utmost urgency. Back then, as with most kinds of behavior, individuals differed in their responses to this life-threatening situation. Some individuals made poor choices resulting in reduced reproductive success. Others made more-effective choices, and to the extent that this behavior was heritable, their descendants were also more likely to survive in similar situations. Thus, through natural selection, an effective program for dealing with this situation evolved: fear. The emotion of fear calls forth shifts in perception, attention, cognition, and action that focus on avoiding danger and seeking safety, as well as physiologically preparing for fighting or flight. Other activities, such as seeking food, sleep, or mates, are suppressed. From an evolutionary perspective, in the face of an imminent threat to life it is better to be afraid, calling on this recipe for action, developed and tested over the ages, than to ad-lib something.

Viewed in this way, emotions can be seen as evolved preprogramming that helps deal quickly and effectively with a wide variety of situations. To give you another example, feelings of disgust for body fluids may help us avoid exposure to germs (Curtis et al., 2004), so it may be wise to recognize disgust in others. It is possible that our human tendency to make snap judgments about other people, based on their appearance and facial expressions, is an overgeneralization of mechanisms that evolved to help us recognize signs of threat or danger in others (Todorov et al., 2008).

Emotions develop in early childhood

Children show some emotions from the time of birth, and during the first 3 years of life they become capable of showing most of the emotions that adults display (M. Lewis, 2000). At birth, infants show both general distress and contentment or pleasure, and some people suggest that newborns also show a third emotion: interest or attention. By the age of 3 months, infants also show evidence of joy: they start to smile and appear to show excitement and/or happiness in response to familiar faces. Sadness also emerges at this time, especially caused by the withdrawal of positive events. Disgust also appears, in the primitive form of spitting out distasteful objects placed in the mouth. Anger has been reported to appear between 4 and 6 months when babies are frustrated or restrained. Surprise first appears at about 6 months in response to violation of an expectation or to a discovery. Fear first emerges at about 7 or 8 months. Thus, what some have called the primary or basic emotions are all present by 8–9 months after birth.

Between 18 and 24 months, the emergence of self-consciousness or self-awareness allows an additional group of emotions to develop, including embarrassment, empathy, and envy. Another milestone occurs sometime between 2 and 3 years of age when children become capable of evaluating their behavior against a standard. This ability allows the emergence of "self-conscious evaluative emotions" (pride, guilt, regret, shame), followed by the development of altruistic sharing (of candy, toys, and so on) through age 7 or 8 years (Fehr et al., 2008). This sort of self-consciousness and self-evaluation was viewed by Darwin (1872) as unique to our species. Mark Twain (1897) agreed, saying, "Man is the only animal that blushes … Or needs to."

Blushing is caused by activation of sympathetic fibers that innervate the fine blood vessels of the skin, causing them to dilate. Remember Christine at the start of the chapter? She elected to have the surgery to cut two nerves exiting from the sympathetic chain on each side of her face (see Figure 2.11 *left*), losing sympathetic control of her entire face except for her pupils. Christine no longer blushes (and her ability to move and feel her face was not altered). She has no regrets and is working toward her dream. An interesting aspect of blushing is that it can be self-reinforcing: Christine's awareness of the problem made it happen more often. For the same reason, it's sometimes possible to trick people into blushing. Just look at someone closely and say, "Hey, you're blushing!"

Individuals differ in their emotional responsiveness

Even as newborns, people differ in their emotional reactivity and physiological responses to emotional situations—a characteristic known as **individual response stereotypy** (Lacey and Lacey, 1970). In longitudinal studies (extending over many years), researchers have tracked the emotional reactivity of people from early childhood through adulthood, using stimuli that provoke autonomic responses such as immersion of the hand in ice-cold water, performance of rapidly paced arithmetic calculations, and intense stimulation of the skin. Across these conditions, investigators observed individual profiles of response that are evident even in newborns. For example, some newborns respond vigorously with heart rate changes, others with gastric contractions, and still others with blood pressure responses.

The response patterns remain remarkably consistent throughout life. When newborns were classified on the basis of their behavioral responses to being swabbed with rubbing alcohol (the sudden cold sensation surprises and sometimes upsets babies), about 20% of the infants were classified as "*high reactives*" because they gave especially strong reactions to the stimuli (Kagan, 1997). Many of these high reactives went on to become extremely shy children, and by the time they were old enough for school, about a third of them displayed extreme phobias (compared to fewer than 10% of the other children). In adulthood, high reactives show an exaggerated activation of the amygdala in response to photographs of strangers' faces (C. E. Schwartz et al., 2003). Because the amygdala has been implicated in fear (as we'll see later in this chapter), high reactives may have a lifelong aversion to new acquaintances, which would certainly affect many aspects of life.

Do Distinct Brain Circuits Mediate Emotions?

This question has been explored in studies involving either localized brain lesions or electrical stimulation. Taken together, these studies make it clear that particular brain regions are involved in emotions, but often the same regions seem to be involved in many emotions.

Electrical stimulation of the brain can produce emotional effects

One way to study the neuroanatomy of emotion is to electrically stimulate sites in the brains of awake, freely moving animals and then observe the effects on behavior. Such stimulation can have either rewarding or aversive effects, or it may elicit sequences of emotional behavior.

Experiments with electrical stimulation in the 1950s produced an intriguing finding: rats will readily press a lever in order to receive a brief burst of electrical stimulation in a brain region called the *septum* (Olds and Milner, 1954) (**Figure 15.10**). This phenomenon, called **brain self-stimulation**, can also happen in humans. Patients receiving electrical stimulation in this region feel a sense of pleasure or warmth, and in some instances stimulation in this region provokes sexual excitation (Heath, 1972).

The discovery of brain self-stimulation was one of those rare scientific moments that launch a new field; many investigators have since employed similar stimulation techniques, mapping the distribution of brain sites that yield self-stimulation responses. Animals will work to receive electrical stimulation of many different subcortical sites, but cerebral cortical stimulation usually does not

individual response stereotypy   The tendency of individuals to show the same response pattern to particular situations throughout their life span.

brain self-stimulation   The process in which animals will work to provide electrical stimulation to particular brain sites, presumably because the experience is very rewarding.

15.10 Self-Stimulation Sites in the Rodent Brain   Animals will work very hard pressing a bar to receive mild electrical stimulation at any of the sites indicated here by large, red circles.

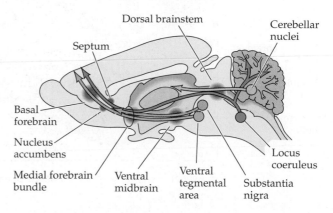

medial forebrain bundle A collection of axons traveling in the midline region of the forebrain.

decorticate rage Also called *sham rage*. Sudden intense rage characterized by actions (such as snarling and biting in dogs) that lack clear direction.

Papez circuit A group of brain regions within the limbic system.

limbic system A loosely defined, widespread group of brain nuclei that innervate each other to form a network. These nuclei are implicated in emotions.

Klüver-Bucy syndrome A condition, brought about by bilateral amygdala damage, that is characterized by dramatic emotional changes including reduction in fear and anxiety.

have positive reinforcement properties. Positive brain sites are concentrated in the hypothalamus and extend into the brainstem. A large tract that ascends from the midbrain through the hypothalamus—the **medial forebrain bundle**—contains many sites that yield strong self-stimulation behavior. This bundle of axons is characterized by widespread origins and innervates an extensive set of forebrain regions. One important target for the axons is the nucleus accumbens, which we discussed in Chapter 4. Dopaminergic stimulation of this site appears to be very pleasurable.

One theory is that electrical stimulation taps into the circuits mediating more-customary rewards, such as the presentation of food to a hungry animal or water to a thirsty animal (N. M. White and Milner, 1992). As we discussed in Chapter 4, there is a growing belief that drugs of abuse are addictive because they activate these same neural circuits (Ranaldi and Beninger, 1994; Wise et al., 1992).

Brain lesions affect emotions

Early in the twentieth century, decorticate dogs (dogs from which the cortex has been removed) were found to respond to routine handling with sudden intense **decorticate rage**—snarling, biting, and so on—sometimes referred to as *sham rage* because it lacks well-directed attack. Clearly, then, emotional behaviors of this type must be organized at a subcortical level, with the cerebral cortex normally providing *inhibition of* emotional responsiveness. On the basis of studies of the spread of rabies virus in the brains of cats, combined with observations from brain autopsies of humans with emotional disorders, James W. Papez (1937) proposed a subcortical circuit of emotion. Papez (which rhymes with "capes") noted associations between emotional changes and specific sites of brain damage, and concluded that destruction of a set of interconnected pathways in the brain would impair emotional processes.

These interconnected regions, known as the **Papez circuit**, include the mammillary bodies of the hypothalamus, the anterior thalamus, the cingulate cortex, the hippocampus, and the fornix. The arrows in **Figure 15.11** schematically depict this circuit. Later, Paul MacLean (1949) suggested that the amygdala and several other regions also interacted with the components of this circuit, and he proposed that the entire system be called the **limbic system**.

A report of an unusual emotional syndrome in primates with temporal lobe lesions provided early support for the limbic model of emotion (Klüver and Bucy, 1938). During studies on the cortical mechanisms of perception, the researchers removed large portions of the temporal lobes of monkeys. The animals' behavior changed dramatically after surgery; the highlight of what is now known as the **Klüver-Bucy syndrome** was an extraordinary taming effect. Animals that had been wild and fearful of humans prior to surgery became tame and showed neither fear nor aggression afterward. In addition, they showed strong oral tendencies, eating a variety of objects, including some that were indigestible. Frequent mounting behavior was observed and was described as hypersexuality.

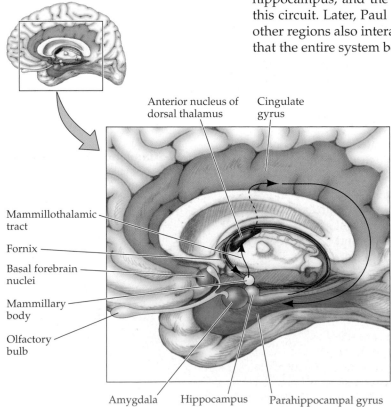

Anterior nucleus of dorsal thalamus

Cingulate gyrus

Mammillothalamic tract

Fornix

Basal forebrain nuclei

Mammillary body

Olfactory bulb

Amygdala   Hippocampus   Parahippocampal gyrus

15.11 Medial Regions of the Brain Involved in Emotions Brain regions included in the Papez circuit are overlaid with arrows and are shown with structures included in MacLean's later conception of the limbic system.

Because lesions restricted to the cerebral cortex did not produce these results, deeper regions of the temporal lobe, including sites within the limbic system (see Figure 15.11), were implicated, and more-detailed investigation focused on the amygdala. In the earlier studies, attempts to surgically lesion the amygdala had injured adjacent structures and interrupted fibers passing through the region, making it difficult to interpret results. In a more modern study, researchers managed to destroy the amygdala bilaterally in monkeys without harming adjacent tissue or fibers of passage (Emery et al., 2001). The amygdalectomized monkeys demonstrated increased social affiliation, decreased anxiety, and increased confidence compared to control animals. The amygdala lesions led to a decrease in the usual reluctance of adult monkeys to engage a strange monkey in social behavior. In other words, the animals with amygdala lesions appeared to be much less fearful than control monkeys. Next we'll expand on this role of the amygdala in fear.

Fear is mediated by circuitry that includes the amygdala

There is nothing subtle about fear. Many animals display similar behavior under conditions that provoke fear, such as danger to one's life posed by a predator. This lack of subtlety and the similarity of fear-related behavior across species may explain why we know much more about the neural circuitry of fear than of any other emotion (LeDoux, 1995). For example, it is very easy to reliably elicit fear by using classical conditioning (see Box 17.1), in which the person or animal is presented with a stimulus such as light or sound that is paired with a brief aversive stimulus such as mild electrical shock. After several such pairings, the response to the sound or light itself is the typical fear portrait, including freezing and autonomic signs such as cardiac and respiratory changes (**Figure 15.12a**).

Studies of such fear conditioning have provided a map of the neural circuitry that implicates the **amygdala** as a key structure in the mediation of fear (**Figure 15.12b**). Located at the anterior medial portion of each temporal lobe, the amygdala is composed of about a dozen different nuclei, each with a distinctive set of connections. Recall that lesions of the entire amygdala seemed to abolish fear in monkeys with Klüver-Bucy syndrome. Lesioning just the central nucleus of the amygdala has the same effect, preventing blood pressure increases and freezing behavior in response to a conditioned fear stimulus.

On its way to the amygdala, via various sensory channels, information about fear-provoking stimuli reaches a fork in the road at the level of the thalamus (recall from Chapter 2 that the thalamus acts like a switchboard, directing sensory information to specific brain regions). A direct projection from the thalamus to the amygdala, nicknamed the "low road" for fear responses, bypasses conscious processing and allows for immediate reactions to fearful stimuli (LeDoux, 1996). An alternate "high road" pathway routes the incoming information through sensory cortex, allowing for processing that, while slower, is conscious, fine-grained, and integrated with higher-level cognitive processes, such as memory (see Figure 15.12b). Contributions from prefrontal cortex and anterior cingulate offer an additional level of fear conditioning: *observational fear learning*, in which fear of potentially harmful stimuli is learned through social transmission (Olsson and Phelps, 2007). So, to extend our example, an individual can learn to fear scorpions by observing signs of fear and pain in others, without personally experiencing a scorpion attack. Given the considerable adaptive benefits that it confers, it's not surprising that observational fear learning is seen in species as diverse as mice, cats, cows, and primates, including humans.

Interconnections within the amygdala also form an important part of the story. Information about the stimulus (the sound in Figure 15.12a) from several brain regions, including sensory cortex, reaches the lateral portion of the amygdala first; and evidence suggests that neurons here encode the association between specific stimuli and aversive events like electrical shock (Maren and Quirk,

amygdala A group of nuclei in the medial anterior part of the temporal lobe.

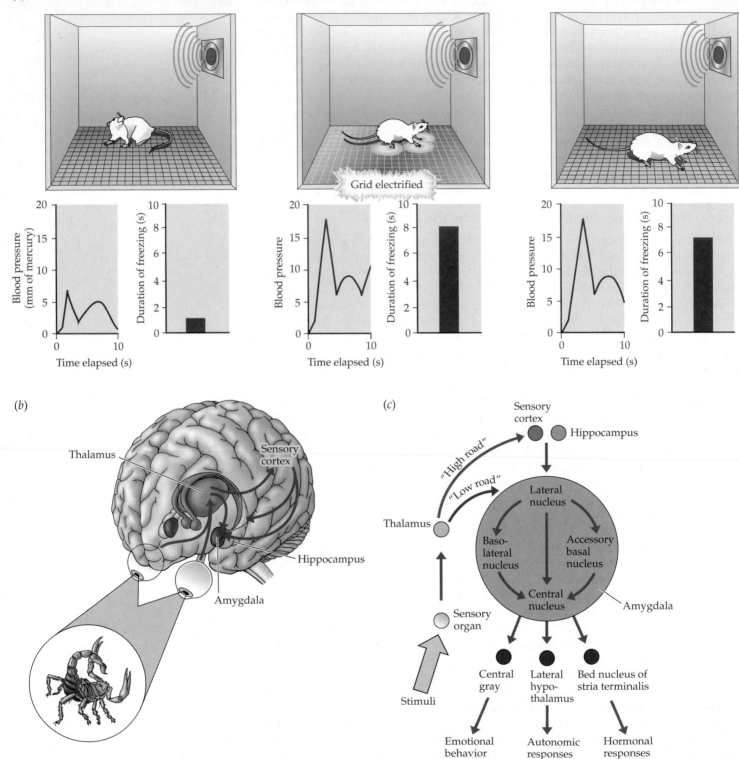

15.12 The Circuitry of Fear (a) In one classical-conditioning procedure to study fear, a tone is associated with a mild electrical shock, which causes increased blood pressure and "freezing" (*left* and *middle*); eventually the tone alone elicits these responses (*right*). (b) Proposed circuitry for the mediation of conditioned fear responses. (c) A fear-inducing stimulus reaches the thalamus and is relayed either directly to the lateral nucleus of the amygdala (the "low road" for unconscious reactions to threat) or via the cortex and hippocampus (the "high road," involving more detailed and conscious processing of stimuli). The information ultimately reaches the amygdala's central nucleus, which projects to three different brain nuclei (central gray, lateral hypothalamus, and bed nucleus of stria terminalis), each of which seems to produce a different component of the fear response. (After LeDoux, 1994, 1996.)

2004). The lateral amygdala triggers a network within the amygdala, ultimately activating the central nucleus. The central nucleus then transmits information to various brainstem centers to evoke three different aspects of emotional responses (see Figure 15.12b): pathways through the central gray (or periaqueductal gray) evoke emotional behaviors, those through the lateral hypothalamus evoke autonomic responses, and those through the bed nucleus of stria terminalis evoke hormonal responses.

Learned fears are notoriously slow to extinguish; in our example (see Figure 15.12a), once the shock and the sound have been paired, the auditory tone must be presented without shock many times before animals stop freezing in response. Mice missing one of the two types of cannabinoid receptors (see Chapter 4) have an even harder time unlearning their fearful reaction to a tone (Marsicano et al., 2002), suggesting that stimulation of these receptors normally extinguishes learned fears. If so, then it may be possible to develop cannabinoid drugs to treat phobias in humans.

The data from rats and mice fit well with observations in humans. People who suffer from temporal lobe seizures that include the amygdala commonly report that intense fear heralds the start of a seizure (Engel, 1992). Likewise, presurgical stimulation of temporal lobe sites may elicit feelings of fear in patients (Bancaud et al., 1994). Conversely, patients with damaged amygdalas do poorly at recognizing fear in human facial expressions (Adolphs et al., 1994, 2005; A. W. Young et al., 1996). When normal humans are shown visual stimuli associated with pain or fear, blood flow to the amygdala increases (LaBar et al., 1998), even in the absence of conscious perception of the stimuli (Pegna et al., 2005).

Neural circuitry has also been studied for other emotions

Disgust has been studied only in humans, where fMRI suggests that a cortical region called the *insula* and the nearby putamen (part of the basal ganglia; see Figure 2.15), but not the amygdala, are activated when we see or hear someone expressing disgust (M. L. Phillips et al., 1998). Confirming this idea is the report of a man whose head injury damaged these two regions: he was very poor at recognizing disgust in other people but was normal in recognizing other emotions (Calder et al., 2000).

The feeling of mirth leading to laughter has also been studied only in humans so far (but note that Panksepp [2007] argues that rats also laugh). People with stroke damage to the right frontal lobe often stop finding anything funny (Shammi and Stuss, 1999), suggesting a cerebral asymmetry in humor. But fMRI studies of people exposed to different kinds of humor suggest that prefrontal cortex of *both* hemispheres is active when we experience mirth (Goel and Dolan, 2001). Electrical stimulation of prefrontal cortex also lifts mood even in people with depression that have not responded to other treatments (Mayberg et al., 2005), so there's good evidence that prefrontal cortex, either on the right or bilaterally, is activated when we laugh.

Considerable progress has been made in identifying the neural circuits of other emotions in addition to fear (Panksepp, 1998, 2000). **Figure 15.13** presents an overview of some of this information. Note that, in general, there is no one-to-one correspondence between an emotion and a brain region; that is, each emotion involves activity of more than one brain region, and some brain regions are involved in more than one emotion.

The two cerebral hemispheres process emotion differently

The fact that the two cerebral hemispheres play different roles in cognitive processes in humans is well established by many experimental and clinical observations (see Chapter 19). Researchers have investigated the possibility that there are similar hemispheric differences in emotion processing.

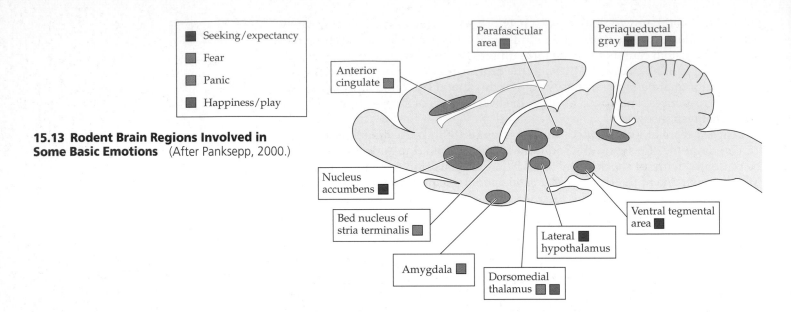

15.13 Rodent Brain Regions Involved in Some Basic Emotions   (After Panksepp, 2000.)

Seeking/expectancy
Fear
Panic
Happiness/play

Parafascicular area
Periaqueductal gray
Anterior cingulate
Nucleus accumbens
Bed nucleus of stria terminalis
Amygdala
Dorsomedial thalamus
Lateral hypothalamus
Ventral tegmental area

EMOTIONAL SYNDROMES   A major theme to emerge from studies of patients who have sustained injury or disease confined to one hemisphere is that the hemispheres differ in emotional tone. Patients who have suffered strokes involving the left cerebral hemisphere have the highest frequency of depressive symptoms. In these patients, injury-produced language deficits are not correlated with severity of depression (Starkstein and Robinson, 1994). In contrast, patients with lesions of the right parietal or temporal cortex are described as unduly cheerful and indifferent to their loss. **Table 15.1** lists some of the clinical syndromes that include emotional changes following cerebrovascular disorders.

Unilateral injection of the anesthetic sodium amytal into the left or right carotid artery (the Wada test, described in Box 19.1), causes the entire ipsilateral cerebral hemisphere to go to sleep for a short time. Consistent with the data from brain-injured people, injection of sodium amytal into the left hemisphere reportedly produces a depressive aftereffect, whereas right-sided injections elicit smiling and a feeling of euphoria (Terzian, 1964).

PROCESSING OF EMOTIONAL STIMULI   Dichotic listening techniques (see Chapter 19) have shown that the cerebral hemispheres may function differently in how they recognize emotional stimuli. Ley and Bryden (1982) presented normal subjects with brief sentences spoken in happy, sad, angry, and neutral voices. The sentences were presented through headsets—a different sentence in each ear. Subjects were instructed to attend to one ear and report both the content of the message and its emotional tone.

Subjects showed a distinct left-ear advantage for identifying the *emotional tone* of the voice and a right-ear advantage for understanding the *meaning* of the brief message. Because each ear projects more strongly to the opposite hemisphere (see Chapter 9), these results indicate that the right hemisphere is better than the left at interpreting emotional aspects of vocal messages.

The visual presentation of different stimuli to the left versus right hemisphere similarly reveals hemispheric differences in the visual perception of emotional expressions. In a variety of tasks that emphasize either reaction time or identification, the common finding is that emotional stimuli presented to the left visual field (projecting to the right hemisphere) result in faster reaction times and more-accurate identification of emotional states (Bryden, 1982). Likewise, in one split-brain patient, in whom the corpus callosum connecting the two hemispheres had been surgically cut (see Chapter 19), the right cerebral hemisphere was much better than

TABLE 15.1　Some Clinical Syndromes Associated with Cerebrovascular Disease

Syndrome	Clinical symptoms	Location of associated lesion
Indifference reaction	Undue cheerfulness or joking; loss of interest	Right parietal or temporal lobe
Major depression	Depressed mood; loss of energy; anxiety; restlessness; worry; social withdrawal	Left frontal lobe; left basal ganglia
Pathological laughing and crying	Frequent, usually brief laughing and/or crying; social withdrawal secondary to emotional outbursts	Bilateral hemispheric lesions, with almost any location
Mania	Elevated mood; increased energy; increased appetite; decreased sleep; feeling of well-being; flight of ideas	Right inferior temporal or right orbitofrontal region

the left at discriminating emotional facial expressions (Stone et al., 1996). Babies with cataracts that block vision in the left visual field, and are therefore deprived of stimulation to the right hemisphere, are impaired at processing facial information even years after the cataracts are removed (Le Grand et al., 2003), compared to people who, as babies, had cataracts in the right visual field. So, apparently visual experience teaches the right hemisphere to become expert at deciphering facial expressions.

ASYMMETRY OF EMOTIONAL FACIAL EXPRESSIONS　By cutting a photograph of the face of a person who is displaying an emotion down the exact middle of the face, we can create two new composite photos—one that combines two left sides of the face (one of which is printed in mirror image), and another that combines two right sides. The results reveal that facial expressions are not symmetrical (**Figure 15.14**). Most observers judge the left-sides photos as more emotional than the right-sides photos. Because the left side of the face is controlled by the right hemisphere (and vice versa), this observation again suggests that the right hemisphere is especially important for emotional processing. A review of 49 experiments on facial asymmetry in emotional expression (Borod et al., 1997) concluded that the right cerebral hemisphere is dominant for the facial expression of emotion, and this is true for both posed and spontaneous faces, for pleasant and unpleasant emotions, and for both sexes and all ages.

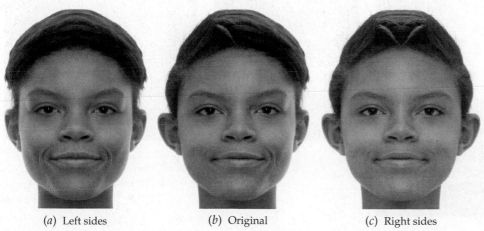

(a) Left sides　　　(b) Original　　　(c) Right sides

15.14 Emotions and Facial Asymmetry　Composite faces reveal differences between left and right in the level of intensity of emotional expression. Photographs constructed from only the left side of the face (a) are judged to be more emotional than either the original face (b) or a composite based on just the right side of the face (c).

Different emotions activate different regions of the human brain

What regions of the human brain are active during different emotions? As we'll see, several forebrain areas are consistently implicated in varying emotions (**Figure 15.15**; for research examples, see Canli et al., 2001; A. R. Damasio et al., 2000; Lane et al., 1999; Maddock, 1999; M. L. Phillips et al., 1998, 2000; H. Takahashi et al., 2009; Teasdale et al., 1999).

In Chapter 1 we mentioned a study by Bartels and Zeki (2000) in which they recruited volunteers who professed to be "truly, deeply, and madly in love." Each participant furnished four color photographs: one of his or her boy- or girlfriend, and three of friends who were the same sex as the loved partner and were similar in age and length of friendship. Functional-MRI brain scans were taken while each participant was shown counterbalanced sequences of the four photographs. Brain activity elicited by viewing the loved person was compared with that elicited by viewing friends (see Figure 1.6a).

Love, compared with friendship, involved increased activity in the *insula* and *anterior cingulate cortex* (see Figure 15.15a and c) and, subcortically, in the caudate and putamen—all bilaterally (see Figure 1.6). It also led to *reduced* activity in the *posterior cingulate* and *amygdala*, and in the right *prefrontal cortex* (see Figure 15.15a–c). This combination of sites differs from those found in other emotional states, suggesting that a unique network of brain areas is responsible for the emotion of love. In contrast, feelings of envy reportedly involve increased activity of anterior cingulate cortex activity; and the feeling of schadenfreude (literally, "dark joy" in German), experienced when an envied rival falls from grace, is associated with activation of reward-related regions of the ventral forebrain, including the nucleus accumbens (H. Takahashi et al., 2009).

Antonio Damasio et al. (2000) compared brain activation during four different kinds of emotion, and again the insula, cingulate cortex, and prefrontal cortex (see Figure 15.15) were among the regions implicated. In a screening session, adults were asked to recall and attempt to reexperience episodes involving sadness, happiness, anger, or fear, as well as an equally specific but emotionally neutral episode. Measures were taken of skin conductance and heart rate, and subjects provided subjec-

15.15 The Emotional Brain   Brain regions implicated in emotions are depicted here in midsagittal (a), anterior coronal (b), and posterior coronal (c) sections. (From Dolan, 2002.)

(a) Orbitofrontal region of prefrontal cortex   Anterior cingulate cortex   Posterior cingulate cortex

(b) Orbitofrontal region of prefrontal cortex

(c) Anterior cingulate cortex   Amygdala

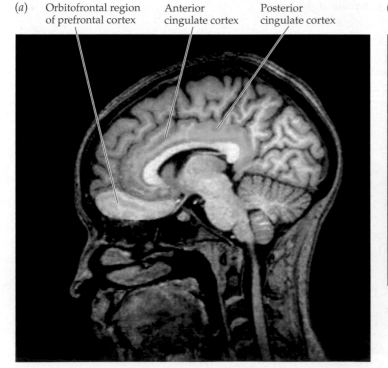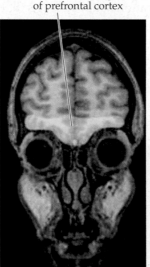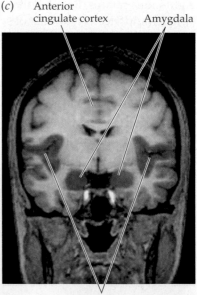

Insula

tive intensity ratings of the experience. During the experimental session, the subject was asked to signal as soon as the desired emotion was experienced, and PET images of brain activity were made. Interestingly, the physiological responses (skin conductance response and change in heart rate) *preceded* the signal, supporting the idea that at least some physiological responses precede the feeling of emotion (as the James-Lange theory would predict). The PET images were averaged for all subjects experiencing a given emotion, and activity during the neutral state was subtracted from activity during the emotion (see Box 2.3). Results showed that activity was altered in many brain regions during emotional experience, and even though we don't understand what role each region plays, it does appear that the four emotions were accompanied by significantly different patterns of brain activity (**Figure 15.16**).

(*a*) Sadness

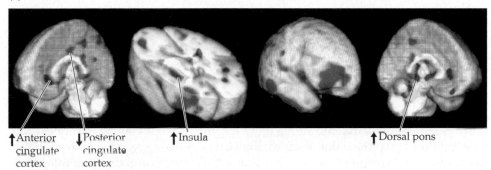

↑Anterior cingulate cortex   ↓Posterior cingulate cortex   ↑Insula   ↑Dorsal pons

(*b*) Happiness

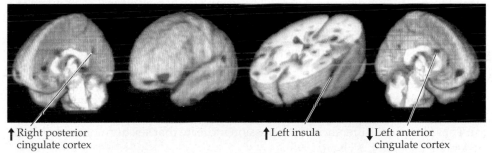

↑Right posterior cingulate cortex   ↑Left insula   ↓Left anterior cingulate cortex

(*c*) Fear

↑Midbrain   ↓Orbitofrontal region of prefrontal cortex

(*d*) Sadness

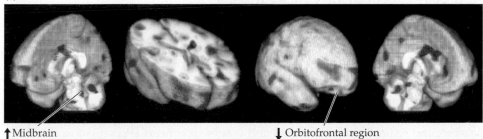

↑Pons   ↑Left anterior cingulate cortex

15.16 Brain Regions Involved in Four Emotions   Red and yellow indicate areas of increased activity; purple indicates areas of decreased activity. For the identified sites, an upward arrow indicates increased activity; a downward arrow, decreased activity. (Courtesy of Antonio Damasio.)

These studies confirm that, as we saw for rats in Figure 15.13, there is no simple, one-to-one relation between a specific emotion and changed activity of a brain region. There is no "happy center" or "sad center." Instead, each emotion involves differential patterns of activation across a network of brain regions associated with emotion. For example, activity of the cingulate cortex is altered in sadness, happiness, and anger; the left somatosensory cortex is deactivated in both anger and fear. Feelings of regret over costly decisions (a topic we return to in Chapter 18) apparently involve activation of the amygdala and orbitofrontal cortex (see Figure 18.30). Although different emotions are associated with different patterns of activation, there is a good deal of overlap among patterns for different emotions.

Neural Circuitry, Hormones, and Synaptic Transmitters Mediate Violence and Aggression

Violence, assaults, and homicide exact a high toll in many human societies; for example, homicide is a prominent cause of death among young adults in the United States. Many different approaches have been used to investigate the psychological, anthropological, and biological dimensions of aggression.

What is aggression?

The all-too-familiar term *aggression* has many different meanings. We commonly use it in a general sense to refer to strong inner feelings, often involving hate or a desire to inflict harm on others. But when we limit our view of aggression to overt, objectively observable forms of aggressive behavior, we see several different categories, ranging from physical attack, to verbal jousting, to the behavior of corporations and armed forces. In this discussion we will focus primarily on physical aggression and violence between individuals, excluding the aggression of predators toward their prey, which is perhaps better viewed as *feeding behavior* (Glickman, 1977).

Intermale aggression (aggression between males of the same species) is observed in most vertebrates. The relevance to humans may be reflected in the fact that males are 5 times as likely as females to be arrested on charges of murder in the United States. Further, aggressive behavior between boys, in contrast to that between girls, is evident early, in the form of vigorous and destructive play behavior. These large sex differences in aggression indicate that sex hormones play a role (J. Archer, 2006; R. J. Nelson, 1995).

Androgens seem to increase aggression

Whatever we may think about aggression, it seems clear that in many species aggressive behavior in males is adaptive for gaining access to food and mates, so it makes sense that the same hormone that prepares males for reproduction would also make them more aggressive. For example, at sexual maturity, when levels of circulating androgens such as testosterone rise, intermale aggression markedly increases in many species (McKinney and Desjardins, 1973). In seasonally breeding species as diverse as birds and primates, levels of testosterone change with the seasons and male aggression waxes and wanes in concert (Wingfield et al., 1987). In spotted hyenas, the females are more aggressive than the males (see Box 12.1), and the more androgen a female is exposed to before birth, the more aggressive she will be growing up (Dloniak et al., 2006). In more-typical mammals, such as mice or rats, decreasing circulating androgens by castration usually reduces intermale aggressive behavior profoundly. Treating castrated males with testosterone restores fighting behavior (**Figure 15.17**). Fruit flies don't make testosterone, but the same genes that trigger male courtship and copulatory behavior also promote intermale aggression (Vrontou et al., 2006), so the link between reproduction and intermale aggression seems to extend throughout the animal kingdom.

The relationship between testosterone and aggression in humans is less clear-cut (J. Archer, 2006). Treating adult volunteers with extra testosterone does not

intermale aggression   Aggression between males of the same species.

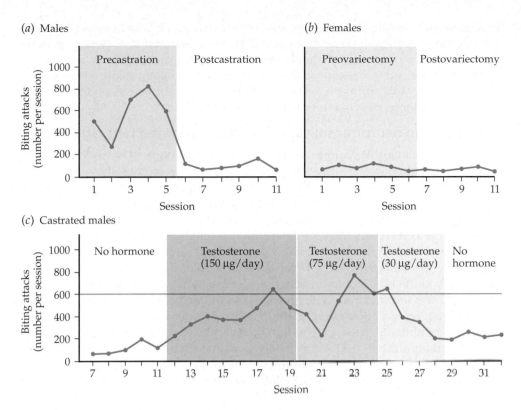

15.17 The Effects of Androgens on the Aggressive Behavior of Mice Counts of the number of biting attacks initiated by males before and after castration (a) and by females before and after removal of the ovaries (b) reveal significantly higher aggression in males before castration. When castrated males are treated with testosterone (c), aggressive behavior is reinstated. (After G. C. Wagner et al., 1980.)

increase their aggression (O'Connor et al., 2004). Similarly, young men going through puberty experience a sudden large increase in circulating testosterone, and yet do not show a correlated increase in aggressive behavior (Archer, 2006; Halpern, 1993). Nevertheless, some human studies have shown a positive correlation between testosterone levels and the magnitude of hostility, as measured by behavior rating scales. Comprehensive studies of military veterans suggest that testosterone *is* related to antisocial behavior (Dabbs and Morris, 1990). Nonaggressive tendencies in males are associated with satisfaction in family functioning and with lower levels of serum testosterone (Julian and McKenry, 1979). Among female convicts, testosterone concentrations are highest in women convicted of unprovoked violence and lowest among women convicted of defensive violent crimes (Dabbs and Hargrove, 1997; Dabbs et al., 1988).

At least two variables seem to confound the correlations between testosterone and aggression. First is the observation that experience can affect testosterone levels. In mice and monkeys, the loser in aggressive encounters shows reduced androgen levels (I. S. Bernstein and Gordon, 1974; Lloyd, 1971), so measured levels of testosterone sometimes may be a result, rather than a cause, of behavior. In men, testosterone levels rise in the winners and fall in the losers after competitions ranging from wrestling to chess. Male sports fans even show a vicarious competition effect in response to simply watching "their" team win or lose a sporting event (Bernhardt, 1997), and as poll results rolled in during the 2008 U.S. presidential election, male McCain voters experienced a sharp drop in circulating testosterone, compared to Obama backers (Stanton et al., 2009).

These observations suggest that a second confounding variable between testosterone and aggression is dominance (Mazur and Booth, 1998), since most chess players could hardly be said to be aggressive, at least not physically. According to this model, testosterone levels should be associated with behaviors that confer or protect the individual's social status (and thus reproductive fitness). These behaviors may *sometimes*, but not always, involve overt aggression. Despite the lack of a close relationship between aggression and androgens, people have tried to modify the behavior of male criminals by manipulating sex hormones, through surgical castration or "chemical" castration with drugs that block androgen receptors or testosterone production. Results suggest that while lowered testosterone may reduce violence in some sex offenders (Brain, 1994), the main effect is a reduction in sexual drive and interest more than a direct effect on aggression. Many ethical issues raised by this approach to the rehabilitation of sex offenders and the intricacies of such intervention have yet to be worked out.

Alterations in neurotransmitter levels are associated with aggression

Aggressive behavior in various animals, including humans, is modulated by activity in several neurotransmitter systems. In particular, studies show a negative correlation between brain serotonin activity and aggression. For example, Higley et al. (1992) used observations of aggressive behavior and fight injuries in 28 monkeys from a large, free-ranging colony to rank the animals from least to most aggressive. The researchers then gauged serotonin activity by measuring a serotonin metabolite, 5-HIAA (5-hydroxyindoleacetic acid), in cerebrospinal fluid. The most aggressive monkeys had the lowest levels of serotonin metabolites, suggesting that they had the least serotonin being released at synapses in the brain. In agreement with this finding, mice with one of the serotonin receptor genes knocked out are hyperaggressive (Bouwknecht et al., 2001), as one would expect if serotonin normally inhibits aggression. This inhibitory role of serotonin in aggression is probably evolutionarily ancient, as it is evident even in invertebrates: for example, enhanced serotonergic activity prompts solitary locusts to overcome their usual aversion to one another and form the huge swarms that decimate broad swaths of cropland (Anstey et al., 2009).

Diminished serotonin activity (as measured by low concentrations of 5-HIAA in cerebrospinal fluid) is seen in humans who become violent with alcohol use (Virkkunen and Linnoila, 1993), in U.S. marines expelled for excessive violence (G. L. Brown et al., 1979), in children who torture animals (Kruesi, 1979), and in children whose poor impulse control produces disruptive behavior. Taken together, the evidence suggests that serotonin is a key participant in cortical networks—particularly portions of prefrontal and anterior cingulate cortex—that are responsible for high-level control of aggressive behavior (Siever, 2008).

However, serotonin is not the only neurotransmitter involved in aggression. Other substances have been implicated in various forms of aggression in both humans and other animals. For example, the balance between the inhibitory neurotransmitter GABA and the excitatory neurotransmitter glutamate appears to be important in aggressive responses to stimuli. Enhancement of GABA transmission (using the drug tiagabine) significantly reduces aggressive behavior in human subjects (Lieving et al., 2008). Likewise, a variety of peptide hormones, including vasopressin, oxytocin, and the endogenous opioids, have all been implicated in the control of aggression (Siever, 2008). Increased aggression is often seen in knockout mice (see Box 7.3), no matter which of several genes is deleted (R. J. Nelson et al., 1995). So it's clear that aggression is regulated by many systems. Development of antiaggression treatments based on these mechanisms is an active area of research.

The biopsychology of human violence is a topic of controversy

Some forms of human violence are characterized by sudden, intense physical assaults. A long-standing controversy surrounds the idea that some forms of intense human violence are derived from temporal lobe disorders (Mark and Ervin, 1970). Aggression is sometimes a prominent symptom in patients with temporal lobe seizures, and a significant percentage of people arrested for violent crimes have abnormal EEGs or other forms of neuropathology, often associated with temporal lobe function (D. O. Lewis, 1990; D. O. Lewis et al., 1979; D. Williams, 1969).

These abnormalities may contribute to a behavioral disorder sometimes labeled **emotional dyscontrol syndrome**. Devinsky and Bear (1984) examined a group of patients with seizures involving the limbic system, especially the temporal lobes.

emotional dyscontrol syndrome A condition consisting of temporal lobe disorders that may underlie some forms of human violence.

15.18 Psychopathic Impulsivity   Serial killer Theodore Bundy displayed many characteristics of a psychopath. He was superficially charming and, as shown here acting out in the courtroom when the judge was away, impulsive in nature. This scene also hints that, like other psychopaths, Bundy felt little or no remorse for his actions.

These patients showed aggressive behavior that occurred after an epileptic focus (the neural abnormality that spawns seizure discharges) developed within this system. None of these patients had a history that included traditional sociological factors linked to aggression, such as parental abuse, poverty, or use of drugs (Delgado-Escueta et al., 1981). In another case, a babysitter's violent murder of a child happened during a temporal lobe seizure provoked by the child's laughter, which was a specific seizure-eliciting stimulus for this person (Engel, 1992).

Psychopaths are intelligent individuals with superficial charm who have poor self-control, a grandiose sense of self-worth, and little or no feelings of remorse (Hare et al., 1990), and who sometimes commit very violent acts (**Figure 15.18**). Compared to controls, psychopaths do not react as negatively to words about violence (Gray et al., 2003). PET studies suggest that psychopaths have reduced activity in the prefrontal cortex (Raine et al., 1998), and it is hypothesized that this lower activity may impair their ability to control impulsive behavior. An MRI follow-up indicated that the prefrontal cortex of psychopaths is smaller than in controls (Raine et al., 2000)—another finding that is consistent with this hypothesis.

Undoubtedly, human violence and aggression stem from many sources. Biological studies of aggression have been vigorously criticized by both politicians and social scientists. These critics argue that, as a result of emphasizing biological factors such as genetics or brain mechanisms, the most evident origins of human violence and aggression might be overlooked, and odious forms of biological controls of social dysfunction might be instituted. However, the quality of life of some violent persons might be significantly improved if biological problems could be identified and addressed. For example, treatments that enhance serotonin activity in the brain may be an important addition to a social-environmental or psychotherapeutic intervention (Coccaro and Siever, 1995; Hollander, 1999).

Stress Activates Many Bodily Responses

We all experience stress, but what is it? Attempts to define *stress* have not overcome a certain vagueness implicit in this term. Hans Selye (1907–1982), whose work launched the modern field of stress research, broadly defined stress as "the rate of all the wear and tear caused by life" (Selye, 1956). Nowadays, researchers try to sharpen their focus by treating **stress** as a multidimensional concept that encompasses stressful stimuli, the stress-processing system (including cognitive assessment of the stimuli), and responses to stress.

On the basis of his many studies of the impact of "stressors" on different organ systems of the body, Selye emphasized a close connection between stress and disease that he termed "general adaptation syndrome." According to this scheme, the initial response to stress (called the **alarm reaction**) is followed by a second stage (the **adaptation stage**), which includes the successful activation of appropriate response systems and the reestablishment of homeostatic balance. Prolonged or frequently repeated stress leads to the **exhaustion stage**, which is characterized by increased susceptibility to disease. Uncertainty or unpredictability about how to gain positive outcomes when confronted with stressful situations, or poor coping strategies, may exacerbate the health consequences of stress (S. Levine and Ursin, 1980).

Ursin et al. (1978) studied a group of young recruits in the Norwegian military both before and during the early phase of parachute training. In the training period, subjects were propelled down a long, sloping cable suspended from a tower 12

psychopath   An individual incapable of experiencing remorse

stress   Any circumstance that upsets homeostatic balance.

alarm reaction   The initial response to stress.

adaptation stage   The second stage in the stress response, including successful activation of the appropriate response systems and the reestablishment of homeostatic balance.

exhaustion stage   A stage in the response to stress that is caused by prolonged or frequently repeated stress and is characterized by increased susceptibility to disease.

(a) Response systems affected in jump situation

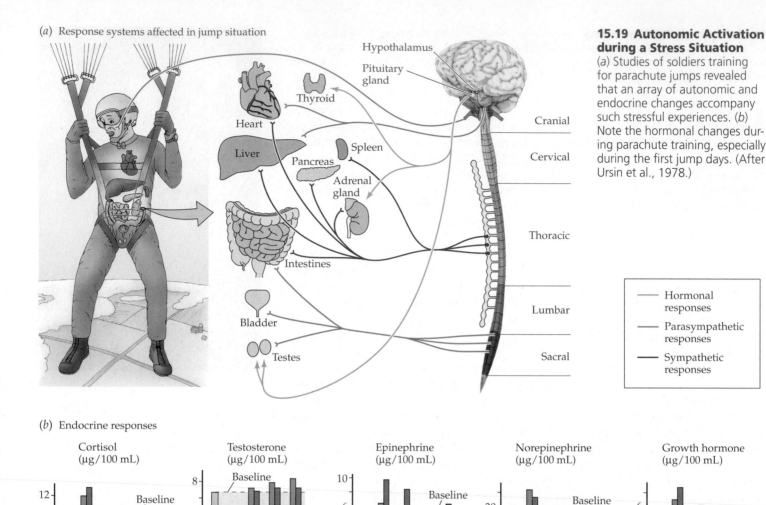

15.19 Autonomic Activation during a Stress Situation (a) Studies of soldiers training for parachute jumps revealed that an array of autonomic and endocrine changes accompany such stressful experiences. (b) Note the hormonal changes during parachute training, especially during the first jump days. (After Ursin et al., 1978.)

Hypothalamus
Pituitary gland
Thyroid
Heart
Liver
Spleen
Pancreas
Adrenal gland
Intestines
Bladder
Testes

Cranial
Cervical
Thoracic
Lumbar
Sacral

— Hormonal responses
— Parasympathetic responses
— Sympathetic responses

(b) Endocrine responses

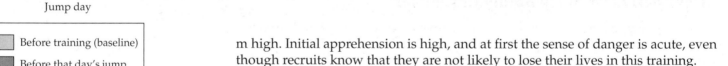

Cortisol (μg/100 mL)
Testosterone (μg/100 mL)
Epinephrine (μg/100 mL)
Norepinephrine (μg/100 mL)
Growth hormone (μg/100 mL)

Jump day

Before training (baseline)
Before that day's jump
After that day's jump

m high. Initial apprehension is high, and at first the sense of danger is acute, even though recruits know that they are not likely to lose their lives in this training.

On each jump day in this study, samples of blood revealed enhanced release of hormones from the anterior pituitary, as well as activation of both the sympathetic and parasympathetic systems (**Figure 15.19**). Under stressful conditions the hypothalamus produces corticotropin-releasing hormone (CRH), which, as we saw in Chapter 5 (see Figure 5.15), causes the release of adrenocorticotropic hormone (ACTH) from the anterior pituitary. ACTH causes the release of corticosteroid hormones such as cortisol from the adrenal cortex.

Initially, cortisol levels were elevated in the blood, but successful jumps during training quickly led to a decrease in the pituitary-adrenal response. On the first jump, testosterone levels in the plasma fell below those of controls, but these levels returned to normal with subsequent jumps. Other substances that showed marked increases in concentration at the initial jump included growth hormone, which is also released by the anterior pituitary; and epinephrine and norepinephrine from the adrenal medulla (see Figure 15.19b), whose release is mediated by the sympathetic nervous system.

Less-dramatic real-life situations also evoke clear endocrine responses (Frankenhaeuser, 1978). For example, riding in a commuter train was found to provoke the release of epinephrine; the longer the ride and the more crowded the train, the

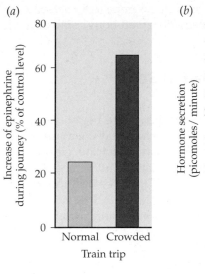

(a)

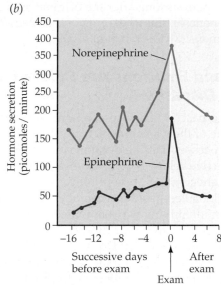

(b)

15.20 Hormonal Changes in Humans in Response to Social Stresses (a) Small changes in crowding on a morning commuter train ride affect hormone levels in humans. A 10% increase in the number of passengers during a period of gasoline rationing (*right*) resulted in a much higher level of epinephrine secretion. (b) Levels of epinephrine and norepinephrine in a graduate student during a 2-week period before, during, and after a thesis exam reflect levels of stress. (After Frankenhaeuser, 1978.)

greater the hormonal response (**Figure 15.20a**). Factory work also leads to the release of epinephrine; the shorter the work cycle—that is, the more frequently the person has to repeat the same operations—the higher the levels of epinephrine. The stress of a PhD oral exam was shown to lead to a dramatic increase in both epinephrine and norepinephrine (**Figure 15.20b**).

Robert Sapolsky (2001) studied baboons living freely in a natural reserve in Kenya. At first appearance, these animals seem to have a good life: food is abundant, predators are rare. Instead, the main source of stress in a baboon's life is other baboons. For males, this stress is the vigorous competition that surrounds courtship and the establishment of dominance hierarchies. An animal's place in the dominance hierarchy influences the physiology of the stress response, as revealed by how the animal responds to anesthesia produced by a dart gun syringe. In general, the testosterone levels of dominant males recover more rapidly after a stressful event than do those of subordinate males. Likewise, the subordinates display a more prolonged increase in levels of circulating cortisol.

Why do individuals differ in their response to stress? One hypothesis focuses on early experience. Rat pups clearly find it stressful to have a human experimenter pick them up and handle them. Yet Seymour Levine et al. (1967) found that rats that had been briefly handled as pups were less susceptible to adult stress than were rats that had been left alone as pups. For example, the previously handled rats secreted less corticosteroid in response to a wide variety of adult stressors. This effect was termed **stress immunization** because a little stress early in life seemed to make the animals more resilient to later stress.

Follow-up research suggests that there is more to the story. When pups are returned to their mother after a separation, she spends considerable time licking and grooming them. In fact, she will lick the pups much longer if they were handled by humans during the separation. Michael Meaney and colleagues suggest that this gentle tactile stimulation from Mom is crucial for the stress immunization effect. They found that, even among undisturbed litters, the offspring of mother rats that exhibited more licking and grooming behavior were more resilient in their response to adult stress than other rats were (D. Liu et al., 1997). Repeated bouts of *prolonged* maternal deprivation has a negative effect on rat pups: as adults, these deprived rats show a greater stress response to novel stimuli, difficulty learning mazes, and reduced neurogenesis in the hippocampus (Mirescu et al., 2004). These early life experiences appear to exert their negative effects on adult stress responses by causing long-lasting changes in the expression of glucocorticoid receptors in the brain. Termed *epigenetic regulation* in recognition of the fact that the change in gene

stress immunization The concept that mild stress early in life makes an individual better able to handle stress later in life.

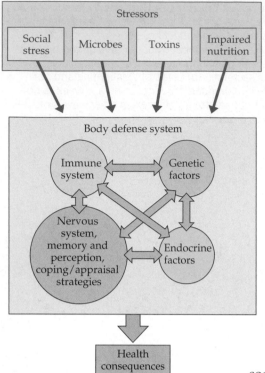

15.21 Factors That Interact during the Development and Progression of Disease

psychosomatic medicine   A field of study that emphasizes the role of psychological factors in disease.

health psychology   Also called *behavioral medicine*. A field that studies psychological influences on health-related processes, such as why people become ill or how they remain healthy.

psychoneuroimmunology   The study of the immune system and its interaction with the nervous system and behavior.

phagocyte   An immune system cell that engulfs invading molecules or microbes.

B lymphocyte   Also called *B cell*. An immune system cell, formed in the bone marrow (hence the *B*), that mediates humoral immunity.

antibody   Also called *immunoglobulin*. A large protein that recognizes and permanently binds to particular shapes, normally as part of the immune system attack on foreign particles.

T lymphocyte   Also called *T cell*. An immune system cell, formed in the thymus (hence the *T*), that attacks foreign microbes or tissue; "killer cell."

cytokine   A protein that induces the proliferation of other cells, as in the immune system.

expression persists long after the original stimulus is gone (*epigenetic* means "above genetics"), this phenomenon has been observed both in lab animals and in humans (McGowan et al., 2009).

Stress and Emotions Are Related to Some Human Diseases

During the past 50 years, researchers and clinicians have begun to understand some of the ways in which psychological factors play a central role in disease processes. This field, known as **psychosomatic medicine**, emphasizes that distinctive behaviors, psychological characteristics, and personality factors may affect either susceptibility or resistance to diverse illnesses. The related field called **health psychology** (or *behavioral medicine*) has developed to focus on identifying ways in which specific emotions and social contexts affect health outcomes and disease processes (Baum and Posluszny, 1999; Schwartzer and Gutiérrez-Doña, 2000). **Figure 15.21** shows how several factors interact to affect human health and disease.

Although many methodological problems complicate this approach, some consistent correlations between stressful events and illness have been found (N. Adler and Matthews, 1994). For example, men who report frequent and severe stress in a period of 1–5 years prior to interviews are more likely to experience heart disease during a 12-year period following the interview than are those who report little stress (Rosengren et al., 1991). The social network within which stress occurs may be a more important determinant of disease outcome than is stress itself (N. Adler and Matthews, 1994).

Emotions and stress influence the immune system

Researchers once viewed the immune system as an automatic mechanism: a pathogen, such as a virus, arrived on the scene, and soon the defense mechanisms of the immune system went to work, usually prevailing with their armory of antibodies and other immunological devices. Few investigators thought of the nervous system as having an important role in this process.

In the 1980s there appeared a new field, **psychoneuroimmunology**, emphasizing that the immune system—with its collection of cells that recognize and attack intruders—interacts with other organs, especially hormone systems and the nervous system (Ader, 2001). Studies of both human and nonhuman subjects now clearly show psychological and neurological influences on the immune system. For example, people with happy social lives are less likely to develop a cold when exposed to the virus (S. Cohen et al., 2006). Likewise, people who tend to feel positive emotions will also produce more antibodies in response to a flu vaccination (Rosenkranz et al., 2003), which should help them fight off sickness. These interactions go in both directions: the brain influences responses of the immune system, and immune cells and their products affect brain activities.

THE IMMUNE SYSTEM   To understand this intriguing story, we need to note some of the main features of the immune system. In your blood are different classes of white blood cells (leukocytes). The **phagocytes** ("eating" cells) are specialized to engulf and destroy invading germs. But phagocytes rely on other white blood cells (the lymphocytes) to tell them what to attack. **B lymphocytes** (or *B cells*, because they form in the *b*one marrow), produce proteins called **antibodies** (or *immunoglobulins*). Antibodies latch onto foreign molecules such as viruses or bacteria and summon phagocytes and circulating proteins to destroy the invaders. **T lymphocytes** (*T cells*), so called because they form in the *t*hymus gland, can act as *killer cells*, forming a strong part of the body's attack against foreign substances. In addition, special T lymphocytes called *helper T cells* secrete **cytokines**, cell signaling proteins that regulate the activity of B lymphocytes and phagocytes.

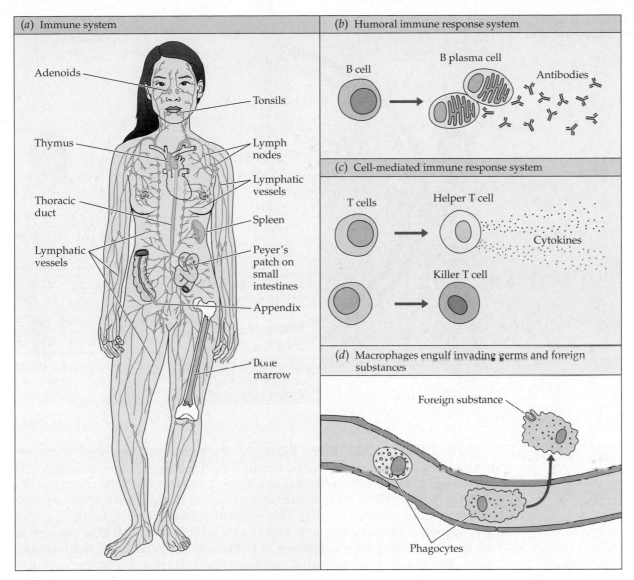

(a) Immune system

- Adenoids
- Tonsils
- Thymus
- Lymph nodes
- Lymphatic vessels
- Thoracic duct
- Spleen
- Lymphatic vessels
- Peyer's patch on small intestines
- Appendix
- Bone marrow

(b) Humoral immune response system

B cell → B plasma cell → Antibodies

(c) Cell-mediated immune response system

T cells → Helper T cell → Cytokines

Killer T cell

(d) Macrophages engulf invading germs and foreign substances

Foreign substance

Phagocytes

15.22 Main Components of the Human Immune System (a) The various components of the immune system protect us by means of three classes of white blood cells: B lymphocytes (b) produce antibodies to attack invading microbes. T lymphocytes (c) form helper cells that release cytokines to regulate B cells to divide or die. T cells also form killer cells that, together with phagocytes ("eating" cells) (d), directly attack foreign tissues or microbes.

These immune system cells form in the thymus gland, bone marrow, spleen, and lymph nodes (**Figure 15.22**), which release the cells into the bloodstream.

COMMUNICATION AMONG THE NERVOUS, IMMUNE, AND ENDOCRINE SYSTEMS The brain affects the immune system through autonomic nerve fibers that innervate immune system organs such as the spleen and thymus gland. These fibers are usually noradrenergic, sympathetic postganglionic axons that affect antibody production and immune cell proliferation (Bellinger et al., 1992).

The brain also carefully monitors immune reactions to make sure they are not too extreme and ultimately harmful to the body. For example, peripheral axons of the vagus nerve have receptors to detect high levels of cytokines and relay the information to the brain. Then, brainstem neurons with axons that lead back out the vagus nerve release acetylcholine, which inhibits cytokine release from immune cells (H. Wang et al., 2003). Hypothalamic neurons and neurons located in the walls of cerebral ventricles also monitor cytokines in circulation (Bartfai, 2001; Dantzer et al., 2008; Samad et al., 2001). Thus, the brain is directly informed about the actions of the immune system, which serves as an early-warning sensory system to alert the brain when microbes invade the body (Besedovsky and del Rey, 1992).

15.23 Examples of Reciprocal Relations of the Nervous, Endocrine, and Immune Systems

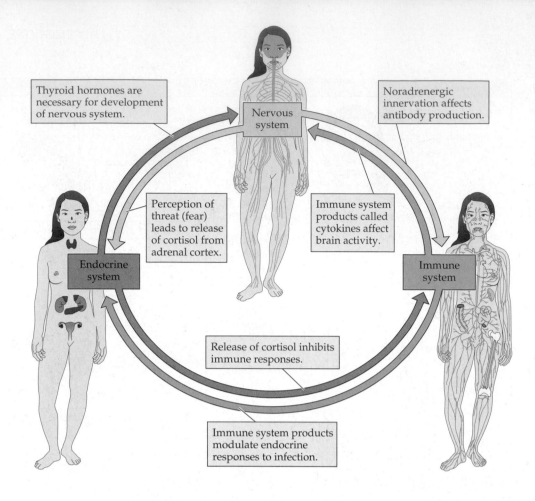

Thyroid hormones are necessary for development of nervous system.

Noradrenergic innervation affects antibody production.

Nervous system

Perception of threat (fear) leads to release of cortisol from adrenal cortex.

Immune system products called cytokines affect brain activity.

Endocrine system

Immune system

Release of cortisol inhibits immune responses.

Immune system products modulate endocrine responses to infection.

There is an interesting theory about why our brains monitor the immune system so closely. Although that achy, lethargic feeling that we have with the flu is unpleasant, it is also adaptive because it forces us to rest and keep out of trouble until we recover (Hart, 1988). Perhaps high levels of cytokines are what cause the brain to enforce that sick feeling. This suggestion has given rise to the idea that some people's depression may be due to a broad set of physiological changes in the brain, including large alterations in availability of several neurotransmitters, that is brought about by excessive quantities of cytokines in circulation and penetrating the brain. Indeed, one action of antidepressant drugs is to reduce cytokine production (Dantzer et al., 2008; Kenis and Maes, 2002; Maes et al., 1991).

The immune system and nervous system also interact extensively with the endocrine system. **Figure 15.23** shows some examples of these relationships. All three systems interact reciprocally, so there is a constant state of flux, carefully tuning the immune system so that it vigorously attacks foreign cells but leaves the body's own cells alone.

IMMUNOSUPPRESSION AS A DEFENSE MECHANISM Under stressful conditions, as noted earlier, a chain of processes starting with the production of corticotropin-releasing hormone causes the release of corticosteroid hormones from the adrenal cortex. One effect of these hormones is to suppress immunological responses by inhibiting the proliferation of some lymphocytes and triggering the death of others. If adrenal steroids suppress the immune system, you might ask why the brain causes them to be released during times of stress. Modern evolutionary theory offers some possible explanations for this seemingly maladaptive situation (for a very readable account, see Sapolsky, 2004).

To the extent that stress might be a sudden emergency, the temporary suppression of immune responses makes some sense because the stress response demands a rapid mobilization of energy. Slow and long-lasting immune responses consume energy that otherwise could be used for dealing with the emergency at hand. A

TABLE 15.2 The Stress Response and Consequences of Prolonged Stress

Principal components of the stress response	Common pathological consequences of prolonged stress
Mobilization of energy at the cost of energy storage	Fatigue, muscle wasting, steroid diabetes
Increased cardiovascular and cardiopulmonary tone	Hypertension (high blood pressure)
Suppression of digestion	Ulcers
Suppression of growth	Psychogenic dwarfism, bone decalcification
Suppression of reproduction	Suppression of ovulation, impotency, loss of libido
Suppression of immunity and of inflammatory response	Impaired disease resistance
Analgesia	Apathy
Neural responses, including altered cognition and sensory thresholds	Accelerated neural degeneration during aging

Source: Sapolsky, 1992.

zebra wounded by a lion must first escape and hide, and only then does infection of the wound pose a threat. So the stress of the encounter first suppresses the immune system, saving resources until a safe haven is found. Later the animal can afford to mobilize the immune system to heal the wound. The adrenal steroids also suppress swelling (inflammation) of injuries, especially of joints, to help the animal remain mobile long enough to find refuge.

In the wild, animals are under stress for only a short while; an animal stressed for a prolonged period dies. So natural selection favored stress reactions as a drastic effort to deal with a short-term problem. What makes humans unique is that, with our highly social lives and keen analytical minds, we are capable of experiencing stress for prolonged periods—months or even years. The bodily reactions to stress, which evolved to deal with short-term problems, become a handicap when extended too long (Sapolsky, 2004). For example, long-term stress (lasting over a month) affects the probability that a person will catch a cold (S. Cohen et al., 1998). **Table 15.2** lists a variety of stress responses that are beneficial in the short term but detrimental in the long term.

PSYCHOLOGICAL STRESS AND IMMUNITY   The anatomical and physiological systems described in the previous sections give us some hints about ways in which psychological factors can alter immune system responses. For example, several lines of evidence indicate that the immune system is compromised during depression (M. Stein et al., 1991)—a situation that, if sustained, could increase susceptibility to infectious diseases, cancer, and autoimmune disorders. Altered immune function is also observed in people who are grieving the death of a relative, especially a spouse (M. Stein and Miller, 1993).

Stressful exam periods usually produce a decline in the number of immune cells and in levels of cytokines (Glaser et al., 1986). Most important, some studies have noted that the student's *perception* of the stress of the academic program is a predictor of the level of circulating antibody: those who perceived the program as stressful showed the lowest levels. One experiment considered the effects of university examinations on wound healing in dental students (Marucha et al., 1998). Two small wounds were placed on the roof of the mouth of 11 dental students (sounds like revenge, doesn't it?). The first wound was timed during summer vacation; the second was inflicted 3 days before the first major examination of the term. Two independent daily measures showed that no student healed as rapidly during the exam period, when healing took 40% longer. A measure of immunological response declined 68% during the exam period. The experimenters concluded that even something as transient, predictable, and relatively benign (do students agree with this description?) as examination stress can have significant consequences for wound healing.

Another connection between the nervous and immune systems was described in Chapter 14, where we learned that sleep deprivation impairs the responsiveness of the immune system.

Emotions and stress influence cardiac function

"Calm down before you blow a fuse!" People have long understood that there's a link between strong emotions and heart attacks. An important development in understanding this relationship was the identification of two general behavior patterns—type A and type B personalities—in the development and maintenance of heart disease (M. Friedman and Rosenman, 1974). *Type A* behavior is characterized by excessive competitive drive, impatience, hostility, and accelerated speech and movements; in short, life is hectic and demanding for such individuals. In contrast, *type B* behavior patterns are more relaxed, with little evidence of aggressive drive or emphasis on getting things done fast. Of course, this is a crude dichotomy—many individuals have some of each pattern in their characteristic style (Steptoe, 1993)—but it has been a useful starting point for research on personality factors in disease. A more recent refinement is the identification of type D personality: a constellation of traits centered on a tendency toward negative feelings coupled with strong social inhibition. Type D personality is more closely associated with poor outcomes in heart disease than is the traditional type A personality (Kupper and Denollet, 2007).

A strong association between hostility and heart disease has also been noted (Almada et al., 1991). This link may ultimately be a consequence of social isolation, possibly caused by personality factors. For example, people—especially men—who go through separation or divorce and then remain separated or divorced through subsequent decades are at much more risk of dying from heart disease than are people in other at-risk groups (Sbarra and Nietert, 2009). In normal young subjects, the presence of a friend during a demanding task lessens the magnitude of cardiovascular responses to this type of stress. So perhaps one of the best ways to deal with stress is to build strong friendships and a happy family.

SUMMARY

What Are Emotions?

■ The four main aspects of emotions are feelings, actions, physiological arousal, and motivational programs.

Broad Theories of Emotion Emphasize Bodily Responses

■ Whereas the James-Lange theory considered emotions to be the perceptions of stimulus-induced bodily changes, the Cannon-Bard theory emphasized the integration of emotional experiences and responses in the brain. A cognitive theory of emotions argues that the key feature in emotion is the cognitive attribution of visceral arousal to specific emotions on the basis of context. **Review Figure 15.1**

How Many Emotions Do We Experience?

■ Distinct facial expressions represent anger, sadness, happiness, fear, disgust, surprise, contempt, and embarrassment, and these expressions are interpreted similarly across many cultures. **Review Figure 15.3**

■ Facial expressions are controlled by distinct sets of facial muscles that, in turn, are controlled by the facial and trigeminal nerves. **Review Figure 15.6**

Emotions from the Evolutionary Viewpoint

■ Emotions may have evolved as coordinated motivational programs that are useful in solving specific adaptive problems.

■ Emotions emerge during early development in a predictable order. By age 3, the rudiments of most of the basic emotions are evident.

Do Distinct Brain Circuits Mediate Emotions?

- Electrical stimulation, including **self-stimulation**, of some brain regions is rewarding. **Review Figure 15.10**

- Brain lesions have revealed that particular brain circuits and interconnected regions mediate and control emotions. Relevant regions include **limbic system** sites described in the **Papez circuit** and other related regions, including the amygdala. **Review Figure 15.11**

- Fear is mediated by circuitry that involves the **amygdala**, which receives information both through a rapid direct route and via cortical sensory regions, allowing for both immediate responses and cognitive processing. **Review Figure 15.12, Web Activity 15.1**

- The left and right cerebral hemispheres process emotions differently. In normal people the right hemisphere is better at interpreting emotional states or stimuli.

Neural Circuitry, Hormones, and Synaptic Transmitters Mediate Violence and Aggression

- Aggressive behavior is increased by androgens. Brain regions of the limbic system and related sites differ in their relationship to aggressive behavior: Stimulation of some regions elicits a full, species-typical pattern of aggression.

- Serotonin levels are negatively correlated with aggression, and other transmitter and hormone systems also make important contributions to the control of aggression. **Review Figure 15.17**

Stress Activates Many Bodily Responses

- Assessment of **stress** in real-life situations shows that stress elevates the levels of several hormones (including cortisol, epinephrine, and norepinephrine) and suppresses other hormones (such as testosterone). **Review Figure 15.19**

Stress and Emotions Are Related to Some Human Diseases

- Stress affects human health and influences the outcome of disease. Incidence of illness tends to be higher in people who sustain prolonged stress, although constitutional factors, as well as strategies for coping with stress, are also important.

- The nervous, endocrine, and immune systems interact reciprocally to monitor and maintain health. **Review Figure 15.23**

- Stress tends to decrease immune system competence, possibly to conserve energy In ancestral environments, but chronic stress increases risk of disease. Other emotional traits, such as aggressive and depressive characteristics, can increase the risk of heart attack. **Review Web Activity 15.2**

Go to **www.biopsychology.com** for study questions, quizzes, key terms, and other resources.

Recommended Reading

Davidson, R. J., Scherer, K. R., and Goldsmith, H. H. (Eds.). (2002). *Handbook of affective sciences.* New York: Oxford University Press.

Ekman, P. (2007). *Emotions revealed: Recognizing faces and feelings to improve communication and emotional life.* New York: Owl Books.

Hodgins, S., Viding, E., and Plodowski, A. (2009). *The neurobiological basis of violence: Science and rehabilitation.* New York: Oxford University Press.

LeDoux, J. (2003). *The synaptic self: How our brains become who we are.* New York: Penguin.

Nelson, R. J. (2006). *The biology of aggression.* New York: Oxford University Press.

Nettle, D. (2006). *Happiness: The science behind your smile.* New York: Oxford University Press.

Oatley, K., Keltner, D., and Jenkins, J. M. (2006). *Understanding emotions* (2nd ed.). Oxford: Blackwell.

Sapolsky, R. (2004). *Why zebras don't get ulcers* (3rd ed.). New York: Holt.

CHAPTER 16

Psychopathology: Biological Basis of Behavioral Disorders

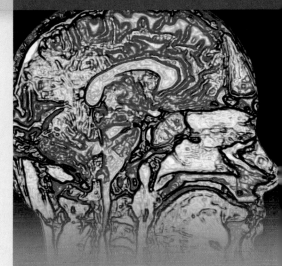

Twist and Shout

Sometimes his limbs would fling about unpredictably. Sometimes he would take to grunting or shouting for no apparent reason. Every movement he attempted was a chaos of twitches, tics, and jerks so severe that he had to use a sippy cup to drink anything. At the age of 6, Jeff Matovic had been diagnosed with Tourette's syndrome, a disease characterized by uncontrollable movements and vocalizations, or tics. He had struggled valiantly with Tourette's for 25 years, overcoming ridicule, graduating from college, and marrying, but the drugs that had given him partial relief from his symptoms had lost their effectiveness. Now that he was 31, Jeff's disorder had progressed to the point that daily life was exceptionally difficult. In desperation, Jeff was ready to try anything, no matter how experimental or extreme.

Sufferers of Tourette's syndrome tend to be of normal or above-normal intelligence and have normal cognitive and behavioral functioning—aside from their tics—making their plight all the more painful. People with this disorder often sense the buildup of an urge to emit tics; they report that only performing these acts can relieve this powerful need. Tics can take a wide variety of forms, ranging from shouted obscenities to repeated movements or compulsions.

Professionals have long argued about whether this collection of symptoms is a psychiatric disturbance derived from the stresses of life or emerges from a fundamental disturbance in the brain. The same sort of discourse has informed the study of all the major categories of psychiatric disorders, but for Tourette's syndrome and many other disorders, major strides in neurobiological research are paving the way to improved understanding and treatment.

How can an understanding of the brain help people like Jeff? What combinations of therapies, drugs, and even surgery can offer hope?

Debilitating mental afflictions have plagued humankind throughout history, plunging their victims into an abyss of disordered thought and emotional chaos. Despite rapid advances in our understanding of the causes and treatment of illnesses such as schizophrenia, depression, and anxiety disorders, the need to reduce the emotional and economic costs of psychiatric illness remains great. Psychopathology affects hundreds of millions of people worldwide, not just an exotic few.

Our aim in this chapter is to survey the major categories of psychiatric disorders and explore their biological underpinnings. Although no single remedy has been found that cures all who suffer from these disorders, modern discoveries have restored millions of people to normal life.

The Toll of Psychiatric Disorders Is Huge

The classification of psychiatric disorders is an evolving science and subject to periodic revision, but we know from **epidemiology** (the scientific study of disease incidence) that psychiatric disorders are startlingly prevalent in modern society.

About one-third of the U.S. population at some point in life reports symptoms that match the defining features of a major psychiatric disorder (Robins and Regier, 1991). Total rates for mental disorders in men and women are comparable, although depression is more prevalent in females, and drug dependency and alcoholism are more frequent in males.

Certain psychiatric disorders—for example, schizophrenia—tend to appear in adolescence and young adulthood. Peaks for depression and antisocial personality appear in 25- to 44-year-olds, whereas cognitive impairment occurs especially in people older than 65. In a single year, as much as 19% of the adult population experiences psychiatric symptoms (Narrow et al., 2002). Clearly, mental disorders exact an enormous toll on our lives.

The seeds for a biological perspective in psychiatry were sown at the start of the twentieth century. At that time, almost a quarter of the patient population in mental hospitals suffered from a psychosis called *paralytic dementia*. It was characterized by the sudden onset of **delusions** (false beliefs strongly held in spite of contrary evidence), grandiosity (boastful self-importance), euphoria, poor judgment, impulsive and capricious behavior, and fundamental changes in thought structure. One sign of the disease was the "Argyll-Robertson pupil": the pupil in the eye did not constrict in response to light (as pupils normally do), but would still constrict when the patient tried to look at something close up (Argyll-Robertson, 1869). This disorder had been noted in all societies of the world for centuries. Many people believed it was derived from the stresses and strains of personal and social interactions, and from "weak character."

In 1911, however, microbiologist Hideyo Noguchi (1876–1928) discovered that the brains of people suffering from this disorder had been extensively damaged by syphilis, a sexually transmitted disease. The disease got a new name, *syphilitic psychosis*, and the subsequent discovery of antibiotics to combat the bacterium that causes syphilis soon made syphilitic psychosis (and the Argyll-Robertson pupil) a rarity. This success encouraged researchers to study other forms of psychopathology with renewed vigor and hopes for finding effective treatments.

Schizophrenia Is the Major Neurobiological Challenge in Psychiatry

Throughout the world, some persons are recognized as unusual because they hear voices that others don't, feel intensely frightened, sense persecution from unseen enemies, and act strangely. People with **schizophrenia** seem to have been a part of all the cultures of the world for centuries, although the historical origins of this disorder continue to be debated (Bark, 2002; Heinrichs, 2003). For many, this state lasts a lifetime; for others, it appears and disappears unpredictably. Schizophrenia is also a "public" disorder because many people who suffer from it become homeless on our streets. Epidemiological surveys of schizophrenia reveal a prevalence of 1%–2% of the population—about 2.2 million people in the United States (**Table 16.1**). This disorder consumes a disproportionate share of community health resources because of its chronic and overwhelming character.

Schizophrenia is characterized by an unusual array of symptoms

The term *schizophrenia* (from the Greek *schizein*, "to split," and *phren*, "mind") was introduced by Eugen Bleuler (1857–1939) in his monograph *Dementia Praecox; or, The Group of Schizophrenias* (Bleuler, 1950), which was originally published in 1911. Bleuler closely examined the underlying psychological processes of schizophrenia. He identified the key symptom as **dissociative thinking**, a major impairment in the logical structure of thought. Bleuler also described a mix of accompanying symptoms, including loosened associations, emotional disturbance, delusions, and hallucinations.

epidemiology   The statistical study of patterns of disease in a population.

delusion   A false belief strongly held in spite of contrary evidence.

schizophrenia   A severe psychopathology characterized by negative symptoms such as emotional withdrawal and impoverished thought, and by positive symptoms such as hallucinations and delusions.

dissociative thinking   A condition, seen in schizophrenia, that is characterized by disturbances of thought and difficulty relating events properly.

TABLE 16.1 Standardized 6-Month and Lifetime Prevalence of DIS/DSM-IV[a] Disorders in Persons 18 Years and Older

Disorders	Rate (%)	
	Previous 6 months	Lifetime
Any psychiatric disorder covered	19.1	32.2
Substance use disorders	6.0	16.4
Alcohol abuse or dependence	4.7	13.3
Drug abuse or dependence	2.0	5.9
Schizophrenia	0.9	1.5
Affective disorders	5.8	8.3
Manic episode	0.5	0.8
Major depressive episode	3.0	5.8
Minor depression	—	3.3
Anxiety disorders	8.9	14.6
Phobia	7.7	12.5
Panic	0.8	1.6
Obsessive-compulsive disorder	1.5	2.5

Note: The rates are standardized to the age, sex, and race distribution of the 1980 noninstitutionalized population of the United States aged 18 years and older.

[a]DIS, Diagnostic Interview Schedule; DSM-IV, *Diagnostic and Statistical Manual of Mental Disorders* (4th ed.).

German psychiatrist Emil Kraepelin (1856–1926) described schizophrenia in modern terms in his book *Dementia Praecox and Paraphrenia* (1919). Kraepelin described numerous clinical features common to the varied forms of schizophrenia: paranoia, grandiose delusions, abnormal emotional regulation, bizarre disturbances of thought, and auditory hallucinations (**Figure 16.1**). The term *dementia praecox* refers to the fact that schizophrenia usually begins during adolescence (*praecox* comes from the Latin for "early") and may move relentlessly to a chronic state of cognitive impairment (*dementia* comes from the Latin *de*, "away from," and *mens*, "mind"). Kraepelin believed the cause of the disease to be partly genetic.

16.1 Not So Beautiful Voices Mathematician John Nash's struggle with schizophrenia is depicted in the Academy Award–winning movie *A Beautiful Mind*. The movie portrays him having elaborate visual hallucinations, but in fact his hallucinations were exclusively auditory, consisting of taunting voices that fueled his paranoid thinking. Auditory hallucinations are common in schizophrenia; visual hallucinations are quite rare.

TABLE 16.2 Symptoms of Schizophrenia

Positive symptoms	Negative symptoms
Hallucinations, most often auditory	Social withdrawal
Delusions of grandeur, persecution, etc.	Flat affect (blunted emotional responses)
Disordered thought processes	Anhedonia (loss of pleasurable feelings)
Bizarre behaviors	Reduced motivation, poor focus on tasks
	Alogia (reduced speech output)
	Catatonia (reduced movement)

positive symptom In psychiatry, an abnormal state. Examples include hallucinations, delusions, and excited motor behavior.

negative symptom In psychiatry, a symptom that reflects insufficient functioning. Examples include emotional and social withdrawal, blunted affect, and slowness and impoverishment of thought and speech.

Modern researchers have worked toward more-objective and reliable definitions of the symptoms of schizophrenia (K. Schneider, 1959), and have focused on first-rank symptoms, including (1) auditory hallucinations, (2) highly personalized delusions, and (3) changes in affect (emotion). Some investigators have proposed a major division of schizophrenic symptoms into two separate groups: positive and negative (**Table 16.2**) (Andreasen, 1991). The term **positive symptoms** refers to abnormal behavioral states that have been *gained*; examples include hallucinations, delusions, and excited motor behavior. The term **negative symptoms** refers to abnormality that results from normal functions that have been *lost*—for example, slow and impoverished thought and speech, emotional and social withdrawal, or blunted affect. Since people who suffer from schizophrenia report experiencing very strong emotions, the blunted emotions that are thought to characterize schizophrenia may be limited to emotional *expression*—facial and body signals (Kring, 1999). The fact that positive and negative symptoms respond differently to drug treatments suggests that they arise from different neural abnormalities. Likewise, there are probably several different kinds of schizophrenia, which vary in the relative degree of paranoia, blunted affect, or cognitive impairment.

Schizophrenia has a heritable component

For many years, genetic studies of schizophrenia were controversial because some early researchers failed to understand that genes need not act in an all-or-none fashion. For any genotype there is often a large range of alternative outcomes determined by both developmental and environmental factors, as we will see.

FAMILY STUDIES If schizophrenia is inherited, relatives of people with schizophrenia should show a higher incidence of the disorder than is found in the general population. In addition, the risk of schizophrenia among relatives should increase with the closeness of the relationship because closer relatives share a greater number of genes. Indeed, parents and siblings of people with schizophrenia have a higher risk of becoming schizophrenic than do individuals in the general population (**Figure 16.2**) (Gottesman, 1991). However, the mode of inheritance of schizophrenia is not simple; that is, it does not involve a single recessive or dominant gene (Tamminga and Schulz, 1991). Rather, multiple genes play a role in the emergence of schizophrenia.

ADOPTION STUDIES It is easy to find fault with family studies. They confuse hereditary and experiential factors because members of a family share both. But what about children who are not raised with their biological parents? In fact, studies of adopted persons confirm the significance of genetic factors in schizophrenia. The biological parents of adoptees who suffer from schizophrenia are far more likely than the adopting parents to have suffered from this disorder (Kety et al., 1975, 1994).

TWIN STUDIES In twins, nature provides researchers with what seem to be the perfect conditions for a genetic experiment. Human twins from the same fertilized

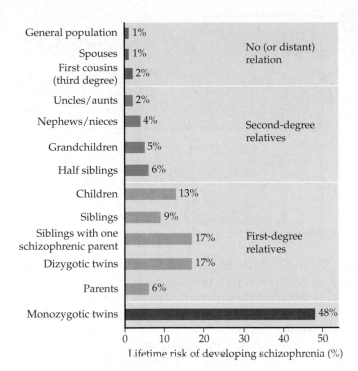

16.2 The Heritability of Schizophrenia   The more closely related a person is to a patient with schizophrenia, the greater are that person's chances of also developing schizophrenia. (After Gottesman, 1991.)

egg—called **monozygotic** (*identical*) twins—share an identical set of genes. Twins from two different eggs—**dizygotic** (*fraternal*) twins—like other full siblings, have only half of their genes in common. When both individuals of a twin pair suffer from schizophrenia, they are described as being **concordant** for this trait. If only one member of the pair exhibits the disorder, the pair is described as **discordant**. Whereas about half of the monozygotic twins of people with schizophrenia are concordant for the disorder, the rate of concordance for dizygotic twins is only about 17% (see Figure 16.2) (Cardno and Gottesman, 2000; Gottesman, 1991). The significantly higher concordance rate among monozygotic twins (who are twice as closely related genetically as dizygotic twins are) is strong evidence of a genetic factor. After all, environmental variables like family structure and socioeconomic stress would presumably be comparable for the two kinds of twins.

Even with identical twins, however, the concordance rate for schizophrenia is only about 50% (see Figure 16.2), so genes alone cannot fully explain whether a person will develop schizophrenia. What accounts for the discordance of the other 50% of monozygotic twins? The answer to this question could provide crucial clues about the environmental and developmental determinants of schizophrenia, and factors that protect against its emergence in susceptible people. In studying discordant cases, E. Fuller Torrey noted that the twin who went on to develop schizophrenia tended to be the one who was more abnormal throughout life. The symptomatic twin frequently weighed less at birth and had an early developmental history that included more instances of physiological distress (Torrey et al., 1994; Wahl, 1976). During development, this twin was more submissive, tearful, and sensitive than the identical sibling, and often was viewed by the twins' parents as being more vulnerable.

During childhood the developmental difficulties of twins who later suffer from schizophrenia are reflected in behavioral, cognitive, and other neurological signs, such as impairments in motor coordination (Torrey et al., 1994). Elaine Walker (1991) found that these early signs are sufficiently evident that observers watching home films of children can, with uncanny accuracy, pick out the child who went on to suffer from schizophrenia in adulthood.

These sorts of behavioral distinctions can be objectively measured by various neuropsychological tests. For example, eye-tracking measurements, in which eye

monozygotic   Referring to twins derived from a single fertilized egg (*identical* twins). Such individuals have the same genotype.

dizygotic   Referring to twins derived from separate eggs (*fraternal* twins). Such twins are no more closely related genetically than are other full siblings.

concordant   Referring to any trait that is seen in both individuals of a pair of twins.

discordant   Referring to any trait that is seen in only one individual of a pair of twins.

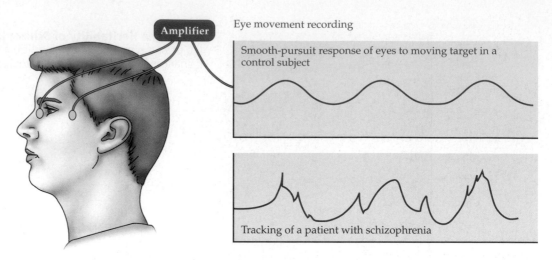

Eye movement recording

Smooth-pursuit response of eyes to moving target in a control subject

Tracking of a patient with schizophrenia

Amplifier

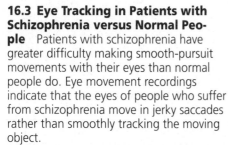

16.3 Eye Tracking in Patients with Schizophrenia versus Normal People Patients with schizophrenia have greater difficulty making smooth-pursuit movements with their eyes than normal people do. Eye movement recordings indicate that the eyes of people who suffer from schizophrenia move in jerky saccades rather than smoothly tracking the moving object.

movements are recorded while the eyes follow a moving target on a computer screen, are abnormal in patients with schizophrenia (Levy et al., 1993; Stuve et al., 1997). These patients tend to be unable to use normal smooth movements of the eyes to follow the moving target, and instead show an intrusion of the rapid, jerky eye movements called *saccades* (**Figure 16.3**).

While studies of twins indicate that genes alone cannot account for the development of schizophrenia, they make it clear that genetics contributes to the incidence of schizophrenia. But which genes are related to this disorder, and what processes do they control?

INDIVIDUAL GENES It has proven difficult to identify any single gene that causes schizophrenia to develop or increases susceptibility (Levinson et al., 2002; Mowry et al., 2004). In fact, genetic analyses suggest that genes influencing the development of schizophrenia are scattered across many different human chromosomes (Stefansson et al., 2009). Nonetheless, a few genes have been identified that appear to be abnormal in a substantial proportion of schizophrenia cases. These include the genes encoding neuregulin 1, which participates in NMDA (*N*-methyl-D-aspartate), GABA (gamma-aminobutyric acid), and ACh (acetylcholine) receptor regulation (Mei and Xiong, 2008); dysbindin, which is implicated in synaptic plasticity; catechol-O-methyltransferase (COMT), which is involved in metabolizing dopamine; and G72, which is thought to contribute to glutamatergic activity (Kennedy et al., 2003). In one large Scottish family, the several members who had schizophrenia also carried a mutant, disabled version of a gene, which was therefore named *disrupted in schizophrenia 1* (*DISC1*). We'll discuss *DISC1* further in the next section.

An interesting epigenetic factor (see Chapter 7) in schizophrenia is paternal age: older fathers are more likely than younger men to have children with schizophrenia (Rosenfield et al., 2010). It is thought that, because the sperm of older men are the product of more cell divisions than the sperm of younger men, they have thus had more opportunity to accumulate mutations caused by errors in copying the chromosomes; these mutations may contribute to the development of schizophrenia in some cases.

The brains of some patients with schizophrenia show structural changes

Because the symptoms of schizophrenia can be so marked and persistent, investigators hypothesized early in the twentieth century that the brains of people with this illness would show distinctive and measurable structural anomalies (Trimble, 1991). Only with the advent of CT and MRI scans, however, has it become possible to study brain anatomy in living patients at all stages of their illness (T. M. Hyde and Weinberger, 1990). Such studies reveal the presence of significant, consistent anatomical differences in the brains of many patients with schizophrenia.

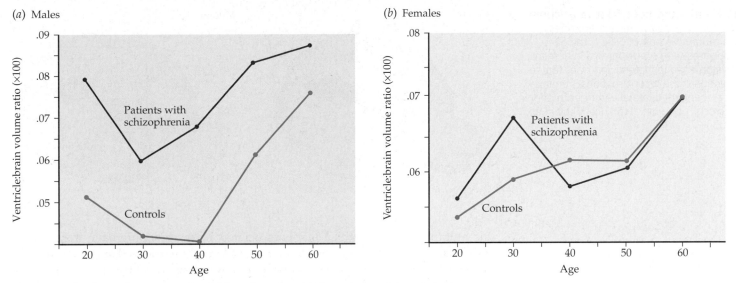

(a) Males

(b) Females

16.4 Ventricular Enlargement in Schizophrenia (a) The volume of the cerebral ventricles, relative to overall brain volume, is greater in male patients with schizophrenia than in control subjects. (b) This difference is also seen in some female patients. (After T. M. Hyde and Weinberger, 1990.)

VENTRICULAR ABNORMALITIES Many patients with schizophrenia have enlarged cerebral ventricles, especially the lateral ventricles (**Figure 16.4**) (T. M. Hyde and Weinberger, 1990). Ventricular enlargement is not related to length of illness or to duration of hospitalization. Patients with this anatomical characteristic form a distinct subgroup in which the extent of ventricular enlargement predicts responsiveness to antipsychotic drugs (Garver et al., 2000; D. R. Weinberger et al., 1980): patients with more-enlarged ventricles tend to show poorer response to these drugs.

Enlargement of the ventricles appears to be a stable trait in patients, remaining for many years after the initial onset of the disease (Andreasen, 1994). Studies of identical twins discordant for schizophrenia have yielded startlingly clear results: twins with schizophrenia have decidedly enlarged lateral ventricles compared to their well counterparts, whose ventricles are normal size (**Figure 16.5**; also see Figure 1.8) (Torrey et al., 1994).

Recall that a disabled version of the gene *DISC1* is associated with schizophrenia in one large family. The DISC1 protein normally interacts with a bewildering array of neuronal proteins, but one function seems to be the regulation of synaptic spines at glutamatergic synapses (Hayashi-Takagi et al., 2010). Creating mice that express

MRI brain images of twins discordant for schizophrenia

35-year-old female identical twins

28-year-old male identical twins

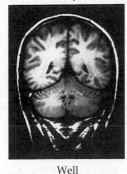 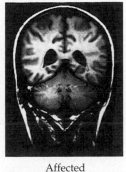

Well   Affected   Well   Affected

16.5 Identical Genes, Different Fates Although the two members of each set of monozygotic twins shown here have the same genes, only one of the twins (the one with larger ventricles) developed schizophrenia. (After Torrey et al., 1994; MRIs courtesy of E. Fuller Torrey.)

16.6 Enlarged Ventricles in a Mouse Model Transgenic mice that express the mutant version of *DISC1*, the gene associated with schizophrenia in humans, develop enlarged lateral ventricles (green region in these reconstructions), reminiscent of enlarged lateral ventricles in people with schizophrenia. (From Pletnikov et al., 2008.)

Control

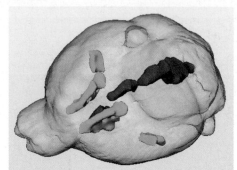

Mutant

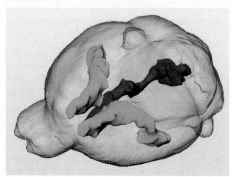

the mutant version of *DISC1* that is associated with schizophrenia in humans has a dramatic effect: the mice develop enlarged lateral ventricles (**Figure 16.6**) (Pletnikov et al., 2008) that are very reminiscent of the enlarged ventricles in people with schizophrenia.

What is the significance of enlarged ventricles? Because overall brain size does not seem to be affected in people with schizophrenia or mice expressing mutant *DISC1*, the enlarged ventricles must come at the expense of brain tissue. Therefore, interest has centered on brain structures that run alongside the lateral ventricles, as we discuss next.

LIMBIC SYSTEM ABNORMALITIES Because the hippocampus and amygdala help form some of the walls of the lateral ventricles, ventricular enlargement in patients with schizophrenia might arise from atrophy or destruction of these adjacent regions. Indeed, comparing twins who are discordant for schizophrenia reveals that the hippocampus and the amygdala are smaller in the twin with schizophrenia.

Postmortem studies of patients with schizophrenia have revealed cellular abnormalities in several parts of the limbic system, including the hippocampus, amygdala, and parahippocampal regions. Kovelman and Scheibel (1984), comparing the brains of chronic sufferers of schizophrenia with those of medical patients of the same age that did not exhibit brain pathology, especially noted changes in the hippocampus. **Figure 16.7** shows an example of these cellular differences. The hippocampal pyramidal cells of chronic sufferers of schizophrenia exhibit a characteristic disorganization (see Figure 16.7*e*), possibly resulting from abnormal synaptic arrangements of both the inputs and outputs of these cells. The degree of cellular disorientation reportedly reflects the severity of the disorder: the most-impaired individuals exhibit the greatest disorganization (A. J. Conrad et al., 1991). Abnormalities are also evident in other limbic system structures, including the entorhinal cortex, parahippocampal cortex, and cingulate cortex (R. M. Shapiro, 1993).

The cellular derangement of schizophrenia probably arises during early cell development (Mednick et al., 1994). These abnormalities of cellular arrangement in the hippocampus also resemble those of mutant mice that show disordered neurogenesis in the hippocampus (A. B. Scheibel and Conrad, 1993). Since we now know that humans make new neurons throughout life, especially in the hippocampus (see Chapter 7), abnormal neurogenesis or disordered integration of newly born cells could be a contributing factor in the development of schizophrenia in humans.

CORTICAL ABNORMALITIES Chronic sufferers of schizophrenia whose disorder started early in life have a thicker corpus callosum, both in anatomical preparations and in some CT scans (Bigelow et al., 1983). One study of postmortem materials found evidence that neuronal migration during the fetal period had been abnormal in the frontal cortex of patients with schizophrenia (Akbarian et al.,

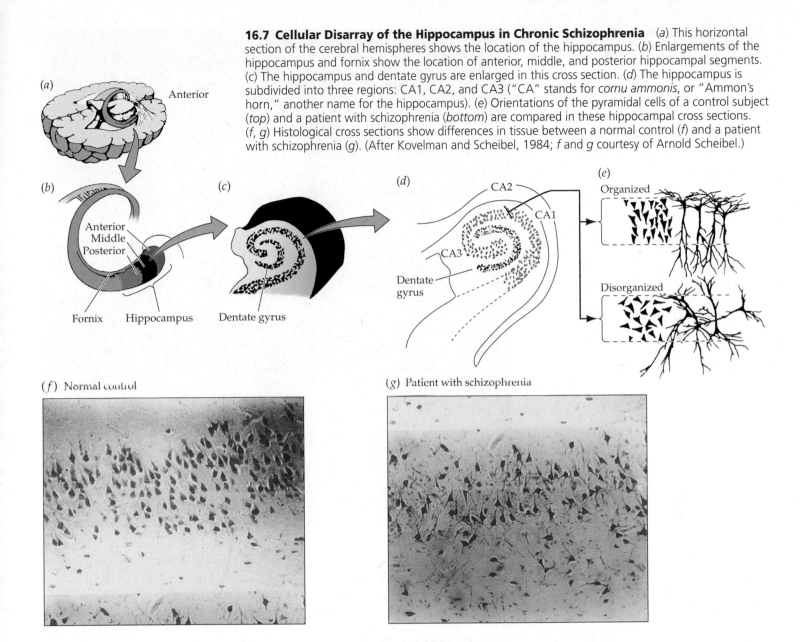

16.7 Cellular Disarray of the Hippocampus in Chronic Schizophrenia (a) This horizontal section of the cerebral hemispheres shows the location of the hippocampus. (b) Enlargements of the hippocampus and fornix show the location of anterior, middle, and posterior hippocampal segments. (c) The hippocampus and dentate gyrus are enlarged in this cross section. (d) The hippocampus is subdivided into three regions: CA1, CA2, and CA3 ("CA" stands for *cornu ammonis*, or "Ammon's horn," another name for the hippocampus). (e) Orientations of the pyramidal cells of a control subject (*top*) and a patient with schizophrenia (*bottom*) are compared in these hippocampal cross sections. (f, g) Histological cross sections show differences in tissue between a normal control (f) and a patient with schizophrenia (g). (After Kovelman and Scheibel, 1984; f and g courtesy of Arnold Scheibel.)

1996). Several studies have reported a loss of gray matter in schizophrenia patients (M. Suzuki et al., 2002; P. M. Thompson et al., 2001), with a wave of cortical gray matter loss occurring during adolescence in the case of early-onset schizophrenia (**Figure 16.8**).

Although some researchers have claimed that the frontal lobes are especially affected, other studies have failed to find major abnormalities of the frontal cortex (Highley et al., 2001; Wible et al., 1995), suggesting that structural differences in the frontal lobes, if present at all, must be quite subtle. So if the frontal lobes of people suffering from schizophrenia are not very different in their *structure*, what about the *activity* of the frontal cortex?

Functional maps reveal differences in schizophrenic brains

People with schizophrenia tend to be impaired on neuropsychological tests that are sensitive to frontal cortical lesions. These findings raise the possibility of frontal cortical abnormality as an important component of schizophrenia. Early observations using PET indicated that patients with schizophrenia show relatively less

16.8 Accelerated Loss of Gray Matter in Adolescents with Schizophrenia

Although neuron loss is a normal part of development, adolescents with schizophrenia (*right*) lose gray matter over wide regions at a faster rate than do unaffected adolescents (*left*). (From P. M. Thompson et al., 2001; courtesy of Paul Thompson.)

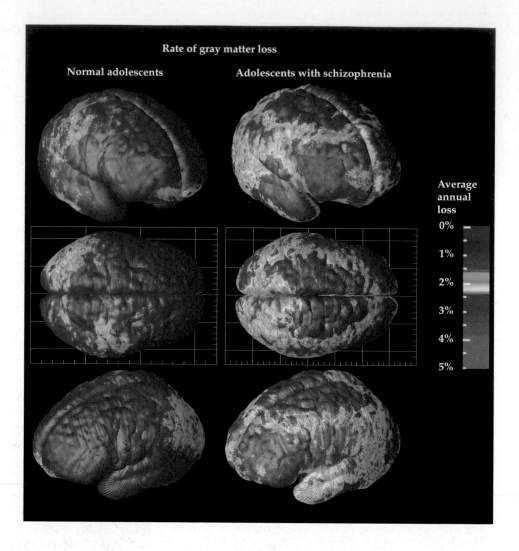

Rate of gray matter loss

Normal adolescents   Adolescents with schizophrenia

Average annual loss
0%
1%
2%
3%
4%
5%

hypofrontality hypothesis   The hypothesis that schizophrenia may reflect underactivation of the frontal lobes.

metabolic activity in the frontal lobes (compared with their posterior lobes), while control subjects have more equal activation of frontal and posterior cortex (Buchsbaum et al., 1984). This observation, referred to as the **hypofrontality hypothesis**, fueled interest in the role of the frontal lobes in schizophrenia (Minzenberg et al., 2009; D. R. Weinberger et al., 1994).

In discordant identical twins, frontal blood flow levels are low only in the twin who suffers from schizophrenia (Andreasen et al., 1986; Morihisa and McAnulty, 1985). Furthermore, the functional lateralization of the cerebral hemispheres may be altered in schizophrenia, with the left hemisphere showing more activity than the right during resting states (Gur et al., 1987), at least in the frontal lobe (Berman and Weinberger, 1990).

Some experiments show the hypofrontality effect only during difficult cognitive tasks that particularly depend on the frontal lobes for accurate performance, such as the Wisconsin Card Sorting Task (**Figure 16.9**). Unlike control subjects, subjects with schizophrenia show no increase in their prefrontal activation above resting levels during the task (D. R. Weinberger et al., 1994). Treatment with drugs that alleviate symptoms of schizophrenia, discussed in the next section, is associated with increased activation of frontal cortex (Honey et al., 1999). Neurons in the frontal cortex of patients with schizophrenia have dendrites with a reduced density of synaptic spines compared to control subjects (L. A. Glantz and Lewis, 2000), which may contribute to a less active frontal cortex.

(a) At rest

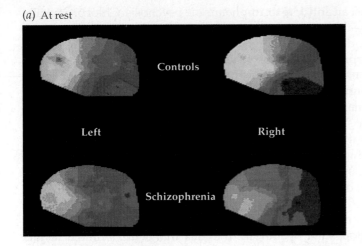

(b) During card-sorting task

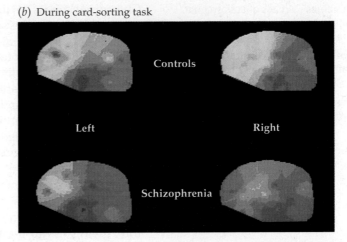

The brains of patients with schizophrenia show neurochemical changes

It is difficult to separate the neurochemical events that are primary causes of a psychiatric disorder from those that are secondary effects. Some secondary effects arise from the profound impairments of social behavior and may range from dietary limitations to prolonged stress. Treatment variables, especially the long-term use of antipsychotic drugs, can mask or distort primary causes because they frequently produce marked changes in the physiology and biochemistry of brain and body. Another major problem in the neurochemical research of schizophrenia is the definition of schizophrenia itself. Is it a single disorder, or many disorders with different origins and outcomes?

Although drugs such as LSD and mescaline produce some perceptual, cognitive, and emotional changes that resemble psychosis in some ways, the resemblance is superficial at best. For instance, drug-induced psychoses often involve confusion, disorientation, and outright delirium; these are not typical symptoms of schizophrenia. And the hallucinations produced by these drugs are usually visual, in contrast to the predominantly auditory hallucinations of schizophrenia. Patients with schizophrenia who are given LSD report that the experience produced by the drug is very different from the experiences of their disorder. But high doses of one drug—amphetamine—come much closer than the rest to replicating the schizophrenic state, suggesting a hypothesis about the basis of schizophrenia.

THE DOPAMINE HYPOTHESIS As a consequence of the development of drug tolerance (see Chapter 4), some daily users of amphetamine reach a point at which they are taking astonishingly high doses—as much as 3000 mg per day—in order to experience the drug's euphoriant and stimulant effects. (Compare this with the normal 5-mg dose used to prolong wakefulness.) Many individuals taking these large doses of amphetamine develop symptoms of paranoia, often involving delusions of persecution with auditory hallucinations, and exhibit suspiciousness and bizarre motor behavior. These phenomena bear a striking resemblance to the symptoms of schizophrenia and are referred to as **amphetamine psychosis**. Amphetamine also exacerbates the symptoms of schizophrenia. What does amphetamine do to the brain that might cause these effects?

Neurochemically, amphetamine promotes the release of catecholamines, particularly dopamine, and prolongs the action of the released transmitter by blocking reuptake (see Chapter 4). Rapid relief from amphetamine psychosis is provided by injection of the dopamine antagonist **chlorpromazine** (trade name Thorazine), a substance that brings us to the second part of the story of the dopamine hypothesis.

16.9 Hypofrontality in Schizophrenia The frontal cortex (left side of each brain profile) is less activated in patients with schizophrenia compared to their twins who don't have schizophrenia ("controls") both at rest (a) and during the Wisconsin Card Sorting Task (b), a task that is very difficult for people with damage to the frontal lobes. Areas of high activation are shown in red and yellow. (Courtesy of Karen Berman.)

amphetamine psychosis A delusional and psychotic state, closely resembling acute schizophrenia, that is brought on by repeated use of high doses of amphetamine.

chlorpromazine An antipsychotic drug, one of the class of phenothiazines.

phenothiazines A class of antipsychotic drugs that reduce the positive symptoms of schizophrenia.

neuroleptics or antipsychotics A class of drugs that alleviate symptoms of schizophrenia, typically by blocking dopamine receptors.

typical neuroleptics A major class of antischizophrenic drugs that share an antagonist activity at dopamine D_2 receptors.

dopamine hypothesis The hypothesis that schizophrenia results from either excessive levels of synaptic dopamine or excessive postsynaptic sensitivity to dopamine.

16.10 Antipsychotic Drugs That Affect Dopamine Receptors Drugs vary widely in the affinity with which they bind to various neurotransmitter receptors. Drugs that block dopamine receptors, specifically the D_2 variety (purple), are more effective at combating symptoms of schizophrenia. Atypical neuroleptics such as clozapine tend to block $5HT_2$ receptors (green) more effectively than they block D_2 receptors. (After Seeman, 1990.)

Chlorpromazine is not just an antidote to amphetamine psychosis. Chlorpromazine and its family members—the **phenothiazines**—were the first identified class of effective antischizophrenic drugs (also known as **neuroleptic** or **antipsychotic** drugs). The introduction of chlorpromazine in the 1950s revolutionized psychiatry, relieving symptoms for millions of sufferers and freeing them from long-term beds in psychiatric hospitals around the world. In the intervening years, researchers have learned that the phenothiazines exert their specific antipsychotic effects by blocking postsynaptic receptor sites for dopamine—specifically the dopamine D_2 receptor subtype—associated with the terminals of the mesolimbic dopamine system (see Chapter 4 for a review of the major dopaminergic projections of the brain).

All of the various antipsychotic drugs that are now classified as **typical neuroleptics**—the phenothiazines, butyrophenones like haloperidol (Haldol), and others—feature this antagonist activity at D_2 receptors (**Figure 16.10**). In fact, the clinical potency of a typical neuroleptic can be predicted from its affinity for D_2 receptors, giving rise to the **dopamine hypothesis**: the idea that schizophrenia results either from excessive levels of synaptic dopamine, or from excessive postsynaptic sensitivity to dopamine. Over the years, other clinical and experimental findings have bolstered the dopamine hypothesis; for example, treating patients who suffer from Parkinson's disease with L-dopa (the metabolic precursor of dopamine) may induce schizophrenia-like symptoms, presumably by boosting the synaptic availability of dopamine.

There are several problems with the dopamine hypothesis of schizophrenia. Studies of dopamine metabolites in blood, cerebrospinal fluid, and urine provide inconsistent results. For example, many patients with schizophrenia have normal levels of dopamine metabolites in cerebrospinal fluid. Some postmortem and PET studies of schizophrenic brains reveal an increase in dopamine receptors, especially the D_2 type (Breier, Su, et al., 1997), even in patients who have been off neu-

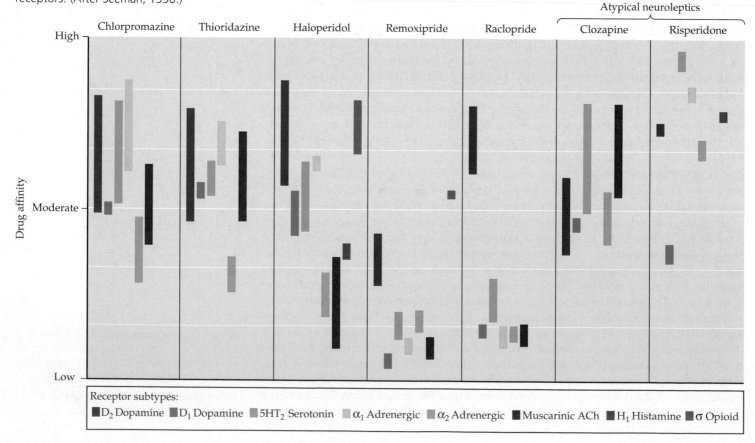

BOX 16.1 Long-Term Effects of Antipsychotic Drugs

Few people would deny that neuroleptic drugs have revolutionized the treatment of schizophrenia. With such treatment, many people who might otherwise have been in mental hospitals their whole lives can take care of themselves in nonhospital settings. Drugs of this class can justly be regarded as "miracle drugs."

Unfortunately, traditional antipsychotic drugs can have other, undesirable effects. Soon after beginning to take these drugs, some people develop maladaptive motor symptoms (**dyskinesia**, from the Greek *dys*, "bad," and *kinesis*, "motion"). Although many of these symptoms are transient and disappear when the dosage of drug is reduced, some drug-induced motor changes emerge only after prolonged drug treatment—after months, sometimes years—and are effectively permanent. The condition, called **tardive dyskinesia** (the Latin *tardus* means "slow"), is characterized by repetitive, involuntary movements, especially involving the face, mouth, lips, and tongue. Elaborate, uncontrollable movements of the tongue are particularly prominent, including incessant rolling movements and sucking or smacking of the lips. Some patients show twisting and

sudden jerking movements of the arms or legs (D. E. Casey, 1989).

The underlying mechanism for tardive dyskinesia continues to be a puzzle. Some researchers claim that it arises from the chronic blocking of dopamine receptors, which results in receptor site supersensitivity. Critics of this view, however, point out that tardive dyskinesia frequently takes a long time to develop and tends to be irreversible—a time course that is different from dopamine receptor supersensitivity. In addition, there is no difference in D_1 or D_2 receptor binding between patients with tardive dyskinesia and those without these symptoms.

Fibiger and Lloyd (1984) offer a GABA deficiency hypothesis of tardive dyskinesia: that it is caused by drug-induced destruction of GABA neurons in the corpus striatum. Neuroleptics induce changes in GABA-related enzymes in animals. A noradrenergic hypothesis of this disorder has also been presented, because the concentration of norepinephrine in cerebrospinal fluid is correlated with tardive dyskinesia (Kaufmann et al., 1986).

Long-term treatment with traditional antipsychotic drugs has another unusual

effect: Prolonged blockage of dopamine receptors seems to increase the number of dopamine receptors and lead to receptor supersensitivity. In some patients, discontinuation of the drugs or a lowering of dosage results in a sudden, marked increase in positive symptoms of schizophrenia, such as delusions or hallucinations. This **supersensitivity psychosis** can often be reversed by administration of increased dosages of dopamine receptor–blocking agents. The atypical neuroleptics discussed in the text, have fewer dyskinesia side effects than traditional neuroleptics have, but unfortunately they are more likely to lead to weight gain.

dyskinesia Difficulty or distortion in voluntary movement.

tardive dyskinesia A disorder characterized by involuntary movements, especially involving the face, mouth, lips, and tongue; related to prolonged use of antipsychotic drugs, such as chlorpromazine.

supersensitivity psychosis An exaggerated psychosis that may emerge when doses of antipsychotic medication are reduced, probably as a consequence of the up-regulation of receptors that occurred during drug treatment.

roleptic drugs for some time (Okubo et al., 1997). But PET studies of D_2 receptor density in people who suffer from schizophrenia are inconsistent, as are efforts to relate a D_2 receptor gene to schizophrenia.

Another problem with the dopamine hypothesis is the lack of correspondence between the speed with which drugs block dopamine receptors (quite rapidly—within hours) and how long it takes for the symptoms to diminish (usually on the order of weeks). Thus, the relation of dopamine to schizophrenia is more complex than is envisioned by the simple model of hyperactive dopaminergic synapses.

Another weakness of the dopamine model of schizophrenia is that some patients show no changes when treated with dopamine antagonists (Alpert and Friedhoff, 1980). The search for new neuroleptics to avoid motor side effects (**Box 16.1**) raised additional problems for the dopamine hypothesis. Called **atypical neuroleptics**, these drugs generally don't have the selective high affinity for dopamine receptors that is the hallmark of the typical neuroleptics. Atypical neuroleptic drugs such as **clozapine** selectively block serotonin receptors (especially $5HT_{2A}$ receptors), as well as other receptor types, including D_2 dopamine receptors (see Figure 16.10).

Atypical neuroleptics are just as effective as the older generation of drugs for relieving the symptoms of schizophrenia. So, if the problem is as simple as overstimulation of dopamine receptors, why are the atypical neuroleptics effective? For example, clozapine can *increase* dopamine release in frontal cortex (Hertel et al., 1999)—hardly what we would expect if excess dopaminergic activity lies at the

atypical neuroleptics A class of antischizophrenic drugs that have actions other than the dopamine D_2 receptor antagonism that characterizes the typical neuroleptics.

clozapine An atypical neuroleptic.

phencyclidine (PCP) Also called *angel dust*. An anesthetic agent that is also a psychedelic drug. PCP makes many people feel dissociated from themselves and their environment.

psychotomimetic A drug that induces a state resembling schizophrenia.

root of schizophrenia. In fact, it seems that supplementing neuroleptic treatments with L-dopa (thereby increasing dopaminergic activity) actually has a beneficial effect on symptoms of schizophrenia (Jaskiw and Popli, 2004).

Until recently, almost all clinicians believed that atypical antipsychotics were more effective than typical antipsychotics for treating schizophrenia, especially for relieving negative symptoms. But a large British study comparing the outcome for patients given the two types of drugs found no difference (P. B. Jones et al., 2006), even though the newer drugs may cost 10 times as much. Although the atypical antipsychotics are less likely than older antipsychotics to cause side effects in motor function (see Box 16.1), they are more likely to cause weight gain, alarmingly so in teenagers and young adults (Sikich et al., 2008). So the overall outcome for quality of life appears equivalent for the two types of drugs. Why were psychiatrists so certain the newer drugs were better if they really weren't? One problem is that company-sponsored clinical trials appear to be biased. One team of psychiatrists remarked that to accept the trials as valid you would have to conclude that "whichever company sponsors the trial produces the better antipsychotic drug" (Heres et al., 2006).

THE GLUTAMATE HYPOTHESIS Initially developed to produce a *dissociative* anesthetic state (one in which an animal is insensitive to pain but shows some types of arousal or responsiveness), **phencyclidine (PCP)** was soon found to be a potent **psychotomimetic**; that is, PCP produces phenomena strongly resembling both the positive and negative symptoms of schizophrenia. Users of PCP often experience auditory hallucinations, strange depersonalization, and disorientation; and they may become violent as a consequence of their drug-induced delusions. Prolonged psychotic states can develop with chronic use of PCP.

As illustrated in **Figure 16.11**, PCP acts as a noncompetitive NMDA receptor antagonist. PCP blocks the NMDA receptor's central calcium channel, thereby preventing the endogenous ligand—glutamate—from having its usual effects. Treating monkeys with PCP for 2 weeks produces a schizophrenia-like syndrome, including poor performance on a test that is sensitive to prefrontal damage (J. D. Jentsch et al., 1997). Other antagonists of NMDA receptors, such as ketamine, have similar effects. These and other observations therefore have prompted research-

16.11 The Effects of PCP on the NMDA Receptor (a) The serum concentrations of PCP that elicit clinical effects are the same concentrations that result in PCP binding of the NMDA receptor. (b) PCP acts as a noncompetitive antagonist at NMDA receptors (see Chapter 4). This means that, as long as PCP is bound to the receptor, the endogenous ligands may bind but can have no effect, rendering the receptor nonfunctional. The resemblance of PCP-induced psychosis to schizophrenia has prompted the development of a glutamate hypothesis of schizophrenia.

(a) Effects of PCP on various receptors

Serum PCP concentration (μM)	Mechanisms affected by PCP	Clinical effects
0.01		
0.1	NMDA receptor	Psychosis
	NE/DA/5-HT reuptake	Anesthesia
1.0	σ Opioid receptor	Coma
	K⁺ channel Na⁺ channel Nicotinic ACh receptor	
10.0	μ Opioid receptor	
	Muscarinic ACh receptor Acetylcholinesterase	
100.0		
	GABA receptors	
1000.0		

(b) A model of PCP action on the NMDA receptor

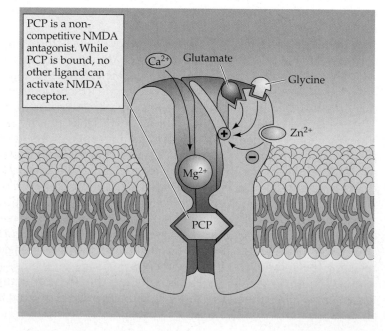

PCP is a noncompetitive NMDA antagonist. While PCP is bound, no other ligand can activate NMDA receptor.

ers to advance a **glutamate hypothesis** of schizophrenia (Moghaddam and Adams, 1998), proposing that schizophrenia results from an underactivation of glutamate receptors (Coyle et al., 2003).

Glutamate's role in schizophrenia might also help explain the effectiveness of the atypical neuroleptics, which act on $5HT_{2A}$ serotonin receptors. There is evidence that some metabotropic glutamate (mGlu) receptors form complexes with $5HT_{2A}$ receptors, and examination of postmortem brain tissue from people with schizophrenia suggests mGlu expression is reduced while $5HT_{2A}$ receptors are increased compared to controls (González-Maeso et al., 2008).

If blocked or reduced activity of NMDA receptors is part of the cause of schizophrenia, you might ask whether compounds that increase glutamatergic activity would be effective antischizophrenic drugs. Although selective NMDA receptor agonists tend to produce seizures, other glutamatergic candidates are in development. In particular, drugs that modulate the activity of the mGlu receptors may prove useful in schizophrenia (Moghaddam, 2004). There are at least eight different subtypes of metabotropic receptors for glutamate, providing several promising targets for drug development (Mueller et al., 2004). Several drug companies are testing glutamatergic agonists for schizophrenia, so a third generation of antipsychotics may soon supplant the typical and atypical neuroleptics.

An integrative psychobiological model of schizophrenia emphasizes the interaction of multiple factors

In some ways, research on schizophrenia has given us many pieces of a large puzzle whose overall appearance is still unknown. One influential model, presented by Mirsky and Duncan (1986), views schizophrenia as an outcome of the interaction of genetic, developmental, and stress factors; each life stage thus has its own specific features that increase vulnerability to schizophrenia. From this perspective, the emergence of schizophrenia and related disorders depends on whether a person who is genetically susceptible to schizophrenia is subjected to environmental stressors (**Figure 16.12**).

A host of environmental stressors have been associated with schizophrenia. One example is city life, which is considered more stressful than rural life. People raised in a city are more likely to develop schizophrenia than are rural dwellers (Mortensen et al., 1999). For another example, if a pregnant woman contracts influenza in the first trimester of pregnancy, her baby is 7 times as likely to develop schizophrenia (A. S. Brown et al., 2004; P. H. Patterson, 2007). This correlation may be why people born in late winter and early spring are more likely to develop schizophrenia (Messias et al., 2004): their mothers may be more likely to have gotten sick during the winter before, when the fetus was vulnerable. Likewise, if the mother and baby have incompatible blood types, the baby is more likely to develop schizophrenia. Birth complications that deprive the baby of oxygen also increase the probability of schizophrenia (Rosso et al., 2000). Because we know that some people are genetically more susceptible than others, these findings suggest that relatively minor stress during development can make the difference in whether they become schizophrenic. It is fascinating to think that events in the womb can affect the outcome 16 or 20 years later when the schizophrenia appears.

The models of genes interacting with environmental stressors also suggest the possibility of decreasing the likelihood of schizophrenia in a child at risk (Häfner, 1998). New biological aids, such as functional brain imaging and genetic tools, might help us identify and understand the at-risk child at a stage early in life, when interventions to reduce stress might avert schizophrenia later in life.

glutamate hypothesis The hypothesis that schizophrenia may be caused, in part, by understimulation of glutamate receptors.

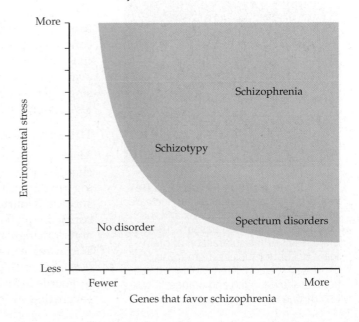

16.12 A Model of the Interaction between Stress and Genetic Influences in Schizophrenia Environmental stress and genetic susceptibility may combine to produce a schizophrenic disorder. Disorders ranging from more mild to more severe are called, respectively, *spectrum disorders*, *schizotypy*, and *schizophrenia*. (After Mirsky and Duncan, 1986.)

depression A psychiatric condition characterized by such symptoms as an unhappy mood; loss of interests, energy, and appetite; and difficulty concentrating.

unipolar depression Depression that alternates with normal emotional states.

Mood Disorders Are a Major Psychiatric Category

Disturbances of mood are a fact of life for humans; most of us experience periods of unhappiness that we commonly describe as depression. But for some people, an unhappy mood state is more than a passing malaise and occurs over and over with cyclical regularity. This condition is most common in people over 40 years of age, especially women, but it can affect people of any age.

Depression is the most prevalent mood disorder

Clinically, **depression** is characterized not by sadness, but by an unhappy mood; loss of interests, energy, and appetite; difficulty in concentration; and restless agitation. Pessimism seems to seep into every act (Solomon, 2001). Periods of such **unipolar depression** (i.e., depression that alternates with normal emotional states) can occur with no readily apparent stress. Without treatment, the depression often lasts several months. Depressive illnesses of this sort are estimated to afflict 13%–20% of the population at any one time (Cassens et al., 1990). A second major type of mood disorder is bipolar disorder (formerly known as *manic-depressive illness*), characterized by repeated fluctuation between depressive periods and episodes of euphoric, sometimes grandiose, positive mood (or *mania*), which we will discuss a little later.

Depression can be lethal, as it may lead to suicide. Most estimates indicate that about 80% of all suicide victims are profoundly depressed. Whether or not the person is depressed, many suicides appear to be impulsive acts. For example, one classic study found that of over 500 people who were prevented from jumping off the Golden Gate Bridge in San Francisco, only 6% later went on to commit suicide (Seiden, 1978). Similarly, suicide rates went down by a third in Britain when that country switched from using coal gas, which contains lots of deadly carbon monoxide, to natural gas for heating. The suicide rate has remained at that reduced level in the 40+ years since. Apparently those thousands of Britons who would have found it easy to follow a suicidal impulse by turning on the kitchen oven, did not kill themselves when more planning was required. Thus, it is important for society to erect barriers, either literally (e.g., on bridges) or metaphorically, to make it difficult for people suffering from depression to kill themselves.

Inheritance is an important determinant of depression

Genetic studies of depressive disorders reveal strong hereditary contributions. The concordance rate for monozygotic twins (about 60%) is substantially higher than the concordance rate for dizygotic twins (about 20%) (Kendler et al., 1999). The concordance rates for monozygotic twins are similar whether the twins are reared apart or together. Adoption studies show high rates of affective illness in biological parents compared to foster parents. Although several early studies implicated specific chromosomes, subsequent linkage studies have failed to identify the locus of any relevant gene (Risch et al., 2009). As is the case for schizophrenia, there probably is no single gene for depression. Rather, many genes contribute to make a person more or less susceptible, and environmental factors determine whether depression results.

The brain changes with depression

Most reports of differences in the brains of depressed people focus on functional changes. PET scans of depressed patients show increases in blood flow, suggesting greater activity, in the prefrontal cortex and the amygdala compared to control subjects (**Figure 16.13**) (Drevets, 1998). In addition to increasing in the prefrontal cortex, blood flow decreases in the parietal and posterior temporal cortex and in the anterior cingulate, systems that have been implicated in attention (see Chapter 18). The increase in blood flow in the amygdala—a structure involved in mediating fear (see Chapter 15)—persists even after the alleviation of depression over time.

People at risk for depression (because they are descendants of someone with severe depression) also have a thinner cortex across large swaths of the right hemi-

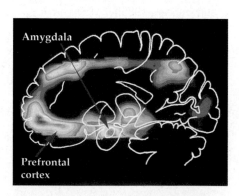

16.13 Brain Activity Patterns in Depression This PET scan reveals increased activity in the prefrontal cortex and the amygdala of depressed patients. The image is the result of the subtraction of brain scans of control subjects from those of depressed subjects. Areas of highest activation are shown in red and orange. (Courtesy of Wayne C. Drevets.)

sphere than do control subjects (B. S. Peterson et al., 2009), which might make them vulnerable to depression. Let's consider some of the treatments for depression.

A wide variety of treatments are available for depression

Electroconvulsive shock therapy (**ECT**)—the intentional induction of a large-scale seizure (Weiner, 1994)—was originally deployed during the 1930s in a desperate and unsuccessful attempt to relieve the symptoms of schizophrenia. Despite its failure at helping sufferers of schizophrenia, however, clinical observations soon revealed that ECT *could* rapidly reverse severe depression. The advent of antidepressant drugs has made ECT less common, but it remains an important tool for treating severe, drug-resistant depression (M. Fink and Taylor, 2007). A more modern technique for altering cortical electrical activity, called *transcranial magnetic stimulation* (*TMS*; see Chapter 2), is also being explored as a treatment for depression (Gershon et al., 2003; D. R. Kim et al., 2009).

Today, the most common treatment for depression is the use of drugs that affect monoamine transmitters. The monoamine hypothesis (Schildkraut and Kety, 1967) was suggested by the first antidepressants, which were inhibitors of **monoamine oxidase** (**MAO**), the enzyme that normally inactivates the monoamines: norepinephrine, dopamine, and serotonin. The fact that MAO inhibitors raise the level of monoamines present in synapses suggests that depressed people do not get enough stimulation at those synapses. This would also explain why the drug **reserpine**, which reduces norepinephrine and serotonin release in the brain, can cause profound depression. Inducing the release of monoamines may be the way ECT helps depression. A second generation of antidepressants, called tricyclics, conformed to the monoamine hypothesis because they inhibit the reuptake of monoamines, boosting their synaptic activity.

Among the monoamines, serotonin seems the most likely to play a role in depression. For example, suicide victims show lower concentrations of serotonin or its metabolites in the brain (Asberg et al., 1986). Suicide attempters who show lower levels of serotonin metabolites are 10 times as likely to die of suicide later in their lives as suicide attempters who show higher levels. In addition, a variant version of the gene for the $5HT_{2A}$ receptor is more common in suicide victims than in controls (L. Du et al., 2000), and altering $5HT_{1B}$ receptors in mice can induce a depression-like state (Svenningsson et al., 2006).

This focus on serotonin has yielded the most recently developed class of antidepressants—**selective serotonin reuptake inhibitors** (**SSRIs**), such as Prozac (**Table 16.3**) (see Chapter 4). These drugs are more effective than MAO inhibitors and tricyclics and have fewer side effects. In rats, SSRIs increase neurogenesis in the hippocampus (Sahay and Hen, 2007), which may mediate some of the mood effects of the drugs. SSRI treatment also increases the production of brain steroids (Griffin and Mellon, 1999), such as allopregnanolone, which may contribute to the effectiveness of SSRIs by stimulating GABA receptors and reducing anxiety.

electroconvulsive shock therapy (ECT)   A last-resort treatment for intractable depression in which a strong electrical current is passed through the brain, causing a seizure.

monoamine oxidase (MAO)   An enzyme that breaks down and thereby inactivates monoamine transmitters.

reserpine   A drug that causes the depletion of monoamines and can lead to depression.

selective serotonin reuptake inhibitor (SSRI)   A drug that blocks the reuptake of transmitter at serotonergic synapses; commonly used to treat depression.

TABLE 16.3 Drugs Used to Treat Depression

Drug class	Mechanism of action	Examples[a]
Monoamine oxidase (MAO) inhibitors	Inhibit the enzyme monoamine oxidase, which breaks down serotonin, norephinephrine, and dopamine	Marplan, Nardil, Parnate
Tricyclics and heterocyclics	Inhibit the reuptake of norepinephrine, serotonin, and/or dopamine	Elavil, Wellbutrin, Aventyl, Ludiomil, Norpramin
Selective serotonin reuptake inhibitors (SSRIs)	Block the reuptake of serotonin, having little effect on norepinephrine or dopamine synapses	Prozac, Paxil, Zoloft

[a]We give here the more commonly used trade names rather than chemical names.

There is a problem with the theory that reduced serotonin stimulation causes depression. We know that SSRI drugs increase synaptic serotonin within hours of administration. Yet it typically takes several weeks of SSRI treatment before people feel better. This paradox suggests that it is the brain's *response* to increased synaptic serotonin that relieves the symptoms, and that this response takes time. So even though boosting serotonin helps some people, their depression may originally have been caused by other factors in the brain.

While SSRIs help many people who are depressed, they do not help everyone. In placebo-controlled trials, although a slightly higher proportion of people report relief among those taking the drug (Turner et al., 2008), about a third of the people taking the placebo also feel better. This result suggests that some people helped by SSRI treatment are actually benefiting from a placebo effect (Berton and Nestler, 2006). One review concluded that only a minority of depressed patients, the 13% constituting the most severe cases, responded significantly better to SSRIs than to placebos (Fournier et al., 2010). Furthermore, only about half of the people getting the drug are completely "cured," and about 20% show no improvement at all. Finally, there is no evidence that SSRIs or any other antidepressant drugs do better than placebos when given to children or teenagers (Bower, 2006), yet millions of American children have been given prescriptions for SSRIs. This is unfortunate, because evidence suggests that SSRIs actually increase the risk of suicide in children and adolescents (Olfson et al., 2006), and that drug companies have concealed these troubling data (Ramchandani, 2004). Other drugs being studied as potential antidepressants are the glutamate receptor antagonist ketamine (see Chapter 4), which relieves depression almost instantly (Machado-Viera et al., 2009); and leptin (X. Y. Lu, 2007), the hormone normally secreted by fat cells (see Chapter 13).

An unusual treatment for depression is vagal nerve stimulation. In this treatment, electrodes are surgically wrapped around the vagus nerve (see Chapter 2) in the neck and a pacemaker provides mild electrical stimulation at intervals. The treatment is offered for people who have not experienced relief from drugs or ECT, but it is an expensive procedure and there is little evidence that it actually works (Boodman, 2006; Grimm and Bajbouj, 2010). Because the electrodes, once implanted, cannot be safely removed, it is also an irreversible step. Likewise, **deep brain stimulation (DBS)**, mild electrical stimulation of brain sites through a surgically implanted electrode, is being directed at the cingulate cortex to treat depression that resists other treatments (Kringelbach et al., 2007). The effectiveness of DBS or vagal nerve stimulation for depression is difficult to evaluate because trials have few subjects and most have no placebo control (R. Robinson, 2009). The lack of such controls is unfortunate because we know depression is very susceptible to placebo effects. Patients may be reluctant to have a wire permanently implanted in their neck or head if there's a chance that they will be receiving only sham stimulation.

Despite the overwhelming popularity of SSRIs for treating depression, 20 or so sessions of **cognitive behavioral therapy (CBT)**, psychotherapy aimed at correcting negative thinking and improving interpersonal relationships, is about as effective as SSRI treatment (Butler et al., 2006). Furthermore, the rate of relapse is lower for CBT than for SSRI treatment (DeRubeis et al., 2008). Interestingly, CBT and SSRI treatment together are more effective in combating depression than either one is alone (March et al., 2004).

The hypothalamic-pituitary-adrenal axis is involved in depression

It has been known for some time that people who have very high levels of circulating glucocorticoids such as cortisol are prone to depression. This condition, called **Cushing's syndrome**, may have several different causes, including hormone-secreting tumors or therapeutic treatments with synthetic glucocorticoids. In more than 85% of patients with Cushing's syndrome, depression appears quite early in the disorder, even before other typical signs, such as obesity or unusual growth and distribution of body hair (Haskett, 1985; Krystal et al., 1990). These observations

deep brain stimulation Mild electrical stimulation through an electrode that is surgically implanted deep in the brain.

cognitive behavioral therapy (CBT) Psychotherapy aimed at correcting negative thinking and improving interpersonal relationships.

Cushing's syndrome A condition in which levels of adrenal glucocorticoids are abnormally high.

16.14 The Hypothalamic-Pituitary-Adrenal Axis in Depression (a) Evidence shows that the hypothalamic-pituitary-adrenal system is involved in depression. ACTH, adrenocorticotropic hormone; CRH, corticotropin-releasing hormone. (b) Circulating cortisol levels are usually higher in depressed subjects than in psychiatric or normal controls. In this plot, each dot represents an individual case. (c) The normal circadian rhythm in the secretion of cortisol (day 1) is abolished by treatment with the synthetic glucocorticoid dexamethasone (day 2). (d) The same dose of dexamethasone is far less effective in patients with depression.

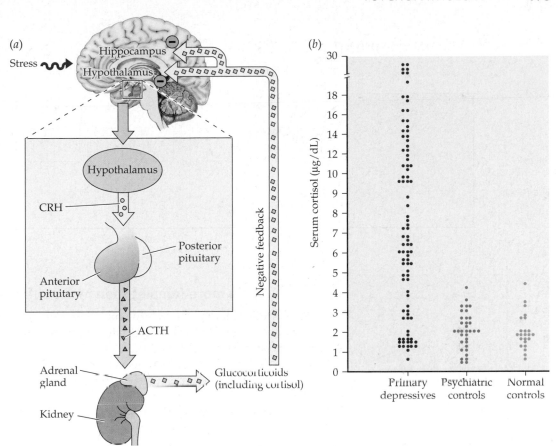

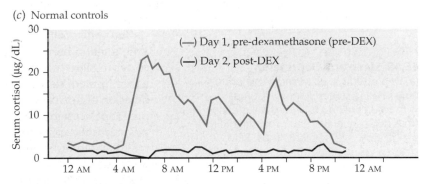

(c) Normal controls

(d) Patients with depression

suggest that dysfunction of the hypothalamic-pituitary-adrenal axis (**Figure 16.14a**) may be involved in depression, perhaps as part of a depression-inducing stress reaction (Heit et al., 1997).

Suicide victims show very high levels of circulating cortisol (Roy, 1992), and hospitalized patients with depression show elevated cortisol levels (**Figure 16.14b**). These findings suggest that adrenocorticotropic hormone (ACTH) is released in excessive amounts by the anterior pituitary. A standard method for assessing hypothalamic-pituitary-adrenal function—the **dexamethasone suppression test**—can reveal a tendency to release excess cortisol.

Dexamethasone is a potent synthetic glucocorticoid that ordinarily suppresses the early-morning rise in ACTH that is typical in normal people. When given late at night, dexamethasone seems to "fool" the hypothalamus into believing that there is a high level of circulating cortisol. In normal individuals, dexamethasone suppresses cortisol release the next day (**Figure 16.14c**), but in many individuals suffering from depression it fails to have this effect (**Figure 16.14d**). As depression is relieved, dexamethasone again suppresses cortisol normally, no matter what caused the relief—passage of time, psychotherapy, pharmacotherapy, or electroconvulsive shock therapy.

dexamethasone suppression test A test of pituitary-adrenal function in which the subject is given dexamethasone, a synthetic glucocorticoid hormone, which should cause a decline in the production of adrenal corticosteroids.

(a) Sleep pattern of a patient with depression

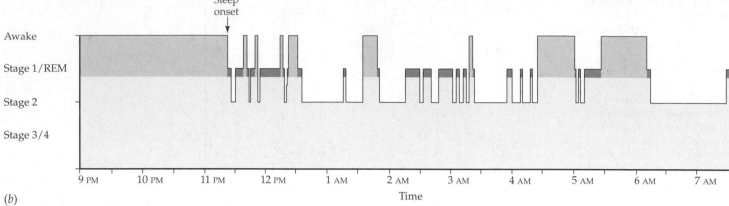

(b)

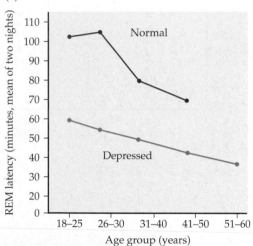

16.15 Sleep and Depression
(a) Depressed subjects spend little or no time in sleep stages 3 and 4. (Compare with Figure 14.13.) (b) Patients suffering from depression also enter their first REM period earlier in the night. Thus, REM sleep seems to be distributed differently in people with depression.

Why do more females than males suffer from depression?

Studies all over the world show that more women than men suffer from major depression. In the United States, women are twice as likely as men to suffer major depression (Robins and Regier, 1991). Some researchers suggest that the apparent sex difference reflects patterns of help-seeking by males and females—notably, that women use health facilities more than men do. But sex differences in the incidence of depression also are evident in door-to-door surveys (Robins and Regier, 1991), which would appear to rule out the simple explanation that women seek treatment more often than men do.

Some researchers have emphasized gender differences in endocrine physiology. The occurrence of clinical depression often is related to events in the female reproductive cycle—for example, before menstruation, during use of contraceptive pills, following childbirth, and during menopause. Although there is little relation between circulating levels of individual hormones and measures of depression, the phenomenon of **postpartum depression**, a bout of depression either immediately preceding or following childbirth, suggests that some combination of hormones can precipitate depression. About one out of every seven pregnant women will show symptoms of depression (Dietz et al., 2007). Because postpartum depression may affect the mother's relationship with her child and may have long-lasting deleterious effects on the child's behavior (Tronick and Reck, 2009), there is growing alarm about this problem. No one knows how SSRIs and other antidepressants taken by the mother would affect breast-fed infants, so CBT is the preferred treatment for postpartum depression.

Sleep characteristics change in affective disorders

Difficulty falling asleep and inability to maintain sleep are common in depression. In addition, EEG sleep studies of depressed patients show certain abnormalities that go beyond difficulty falling asleep. The sleep of patients with major depressive disorders is marked by a striking reduction in stages 3 and 4 of slow-wave sleep (SWS) and a corresponding increase in stages 1 and 2 (**Figure 16.15a**). Alterations of REM sleep patterns seem to have a special relationship with depression. Depressed patients enter REM sleep much sooner after sleep onset (**Figure 16.15b**)—the latency to REM sleep correlates with the severity of depression—and their REM sleep is unusually vigorous. Furthermore, the temporal distribution of REM sleep is altered, with an increased amount of REM sleep occurring during the first half of sleep, as though REM sleep were displaced toward an earlier period in the night (Wehr et al., 1985). In addition to these links between the daily rhythm of sleep and depression, seasonal rhythms have been implicated in a particular depressive condition known as *seasonal affective disorder* (*SAD*), which is described in **Box 16.2**.

postpartum depression   A bout of depression that afflicts a woman either immediately before or after giving birth.

BOX 16.2 The Season to Be Depressed

Seasonal rhythms characterize the behavior and physiology of many animals, including humans. For some unfortunate people, winter brings a low period that may become a profound depression. Sometimes the winter depression alternates with summertime mania (Blehar and Rosenthal, 1989). In wintertime, affected people feel depressed, slow down, generally sleep a lot, and overeat. Come summer, they are elated, energetic, and active, and they become thinner. This syndrome—called **seasonal affective disorder** (**SAD**)—appears predominantly in women and generally starts in early adulthood.

Some early reports suggested a positive correlation between latitude and the frequency of SAD: the farther from the equator, the more cases of SAD. But a study in a country at a far northern latitude—Iceland—where a relatively high rate of SAD would be expected, failed to confirm this relationship (Magnusson and Stefansson, 1993); and in general, a relationship between latitude and SAD has not been very evident (Mersch et al., 1999). Nevertheless, seasonal rhythms are controlled by the length of the day, so researchers asked if seasonal changes in exposure to sunlight might cause SAD.

To examine that prospect, some investigators have treated SAD sufferers with doses of bright light, to see if it acts as an antidepressant. The efficacy of light

therapy, or *phototherapy*, in SAD is fairly well established (Golden et al., 2005), and in many ways light therapy resembles treatment with traditional antidepressant drugs (A. Moscovitch et al., 2004); there is even a dose-response relationship for light therapy. Light therapy may be most effective when administered immediately upon awakening in the morning (Lewy et al., 1998). A person receiving phototherapy is shown in the figure.

One important biological effect of light is that it suppresses melatonin, a hormone

that is normally released from the pineal gland at night (see Figure 5.20). Hypothesizing that SAD may result from a misalignment of melatonin secretion with sleep, one group administered melatonin as a treatment. Most patients benefited only if the melatonin was taken in the afternoon (Lewy et al., 2007). (Photo courtesy of Uplift Technologies.)

seasonal affective disorder (SAD) A depression putatively brought about by the short days of winter.

Light therapy for SAD

Animal models aid research on depression

Because a monkey or a cat or a rat can't tell us if it has delusions of persecution or if it hears voices telling it what to do, animal models of schizophrenia are limited. But many of the signs of depression—such as decreased social contact, problems with eating, and changes in activity—are behaviorally overt. An animal model for the study of depression can provide the ability to evaluate proposed neurobiological mechanisms, a convenient way to screen potential treatments, and the opportunity to explore possible causes experimentally (Lachman et al., 1993).

In one type of stress model—**learned helplessness**—an animal is exposed to a repetitive stressful stimulus, such as an electrical shock, that it cannot escape. Like depression, learned helplessness has been linked to a decrease in serotonin function (Petty et al., 1994). Removing the olfactory bulb from rodents also creates a model of depression: the animals display irritability, preferences for alcohol, and elevated levels of corticosteroids—all of which are reversed by many antidepressants. A strain of rats created through selective breeding—the Flinders-sensitive line—has been proposed as a model of depression because these animals show

learned helplessness A learning paradigm in which individuals are subjected to inescapable, unpleasant conditions.

(a) Manic

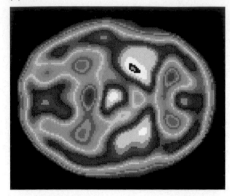

(b) Depressive

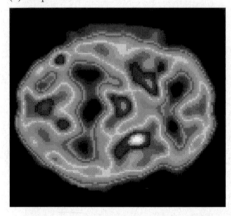

16.16 Functional Images of Bipolar Disorder Dramatic differences in brain activity are evident between the manic (a) and depressive (b) phases of this patient's bipolar illness. (Courtesy of Dr. Robert G. Kohn, Brain-Spect.com.)

bipolar disorder Also called *manic-depressive illness*. A psychiatric disorder characterized by periods of depression that alternate with excessive, expansive moods.

lithium An element that, administered to patients, often relieves the symptoms of bipolar disorder.

reduced locomotor activity, reduced body weight, increased REM sleep, learning difficulties, and exaggerated immobility in response to chronic stress (Overstreet, 1993). These varied animal models may be useful in finding the essential mechanisms that cause and maintain depression in humans.

People with bipolar disorder show repeating mood cycles

Bipolar disorder is characterized by periods of depression alternating with periods of excessively expansive mood (or *mania*) that includes sustained overactivity, talkativeness, strange grandiosity, and increased energy (**Figure 16.16**). The rate at which the alternation occurs varies between individuals: Some patients exhibit *rapid-cycling* bipolar disorder, defined as consisting of four or more distinct cycles in one year (and some individuals have many more cycles than that; some may even show several cycles per *day*). Other people experience a milder, subclinical, related state called *cyclothymia*, in which the patient experiences less-extreme moods, cycling between *dysthymia* (poor mood or mild depression) and *hypomania* (a state of increased energy and positive mood that lacks some of the bizarre aspects of frank *mania*).

Men and women are equally affected by bipolar disorder, and the age of onset is usually much earlier than that of unipolar depression. Bipolar disorder has a complex heritability: several different genes affect the probability of the disorder (Smoller and Finn, 2003). Interestingly, the age of onset of bipolar disorder also appears to be partly heritable, governed by at least three different genes (Faraone et al., 2004). One specific gene implicated in bipolar disorder is the gene that encodes brain-derived neurotrophic factor (BDNF) (E. Green and Craddock, 2003; Neves-Pereira et al., 2002), which we discussed in Chapter 7.

The neural basis of bipolar disorder is not fully understood, but since the 1980s it has been known that patients with bipolar disorder exhibit enlarged ventricles on brain scans. As in schizophrenia (see Figures 16.4 and 16.5), this enlargement probably indicates reduced gray matter, although the specific regions affected may differ (Arnone et al., 2009). The more manic episodes the person has experienced, the greater the reduction in gray matter, suggesting an accumulation of brain loss over time. These changes probably include subcortical limbic structures, such as the amygdala (DelBello et al., 2004) and hippocampus (Moorhead et al., 2007).

Most people suffering from bipolar disorder benefit from treatment with mood-stabilizing drugs, such as the element **lithium** (Kingsbury and Garver, 1998). The benefits of lithium for bipolar disorder were discovered by accident when it was intended as an inert "control" for another drug, so the mechanism of action is not understood. Lithium has wide-ranging effects on the brain, including interacting with a protein that is part of the circadian molecular clock (L. Yin et al., 2006) (see Chapter 14), and also boosting BDNF activity (Rowe and Chuang, 2004). Recall that the gene for BDNF has also been implicated in the heritability of bipolar disorder. Increasing BDNF activity may combat the disorder by reducing the neuronal cell death underlying shrinking gray matter. Because lithium has a narrow therapeutic index (the range of safe doses; see Chapter 4), care must be taken to avoid toxic side effects of an overdose. Nevertheless, well-managed lithium treatment produces marked relief for many patients and even has been reported to increase the volume of gray matter in the human brain (G. J. Moore et al., 2000).

Perhaps the fact that the manic phases blocked by lithium are so exhilarating is the reason that some bipolar clients stop taking the medication. Unfortunately, doing so means that the depressive episodes return as well. But other drug treatments are available; and, as in unipolar depression, it appears that transcranial magnetic stimulation may provide a nonpharmacological treatment alternative in difficult cases of bipolar disorder (Michael and Erfurth, 2004). Furthermore, evidence has accumulated suggesting that, in both unipolar and bipolar depressive disorders, some forms of CBT can be as effective as drug treatments (Hollon et al., 2002) and perhaps can be beneficially combined with other forms of treatment.

There Are Several Types of Anxiety Disorders

All of us have at times felt apprehensive and fearful. Some people experience this state with an intensity that is overwhelming and includes irrational fears, a sense of terror, unusual body sensations such as dizziness, difficulty breathing, trembling, shaking, and a feeling of loss of control. For some, anxiety comes in sudden attacks of panic that are unpredictable and last for minutes or hours. Anxiety can be lethal: a follow-up of patients with panic disorder revealed an increased mortality in men with this disorder resulting from cardiovascular disease and suicide (Coryell et al., 1986).

The American Psychiatric Association distinguishes several major types of anxiety disorders. **Phobic disorders** are intense, irrational fears that become centered on a specific object, activity, or situation that the person feels compelled to avoid. **Anxiety disorders** include *panic disorder*, characterized by recurrent transient attacks of intense fearfulness, as well as *generalized anxiety disorder*, in which persistent, excessive anxiety and worry are experienced for months. Other anxiety disorders that we'll consider are posttraumatic stress disorder and obsessive-compulsive disorder. There is a strong genetic contribution to each of these disorders (Shih et al., 2004).

Panic disorders are characterized by structural and functional changes in the temporal lobes

Some patients who suffer from recurrent panic attacks have temporal lobe abnormalities, according to MRI studies. Ontiveros et al. (1989) found temporal lobe abnormalities—including small lesions in white matter and dilation of the lateral ventricles—in 40% of patients with panic disorder. Overall temporal lobe volumes tend to be lower in patients with panic disorder (Vythilingam et al., 2000), but hippocampal volumes tend to be normal. Instead, given the special role of the amygdala in mediating fear, changes may be especially evident in the amygdala and associated circuitry (Rauch et al., 2003). The role of the amygdala in fear is discussed in detail in Chapter 15.

Functional-imaging technologies such as PET and fMRI (discussed in Chapter 2) provide a vivid portrait of the anatomy of anxiety. Metabolic abnormalities of the brain are present in people with panic disorder even in the resting, nonpanic state, especially in the temporal lobes. People with panic disorder show increased activity of the parahippocampal gyrus, and decreased activity of the anterior temporal cortex and amygdala, especially on the right side (Boshuisen et al., 2002; H. Fischer et al., 1998), as well as changes in activity of the anterior cingulate gyrus and frontal cortex.

Drug treatment of anxiety provides clues to the mechanisms of this disorder

Throughout history, people have consumed all sorts of substances in the hopes of controlling anxiety. The list includes alcohol, bromides, scopolamine, opiates, and barbiturates. In the 1960s the tranquilizing agent meprobamate (Miltown) was introduced and became an instant best seller, ushering in the modern age of anxiety pharmacotherapy. Spurred on by the promise of enormous profits, researchers discovered a new class of drugs called **benzodiazepines**, which quickly became the favored drugs for treating anxiety. One type of benzodiazepine—diazepam (trade name Valium)—is one of the most prescribed drugs in history. Drugs that combat anxiety are commonly described as **anxiolytic** ("anxiety-dissolving"), although at high doses they also have anticonvulsant and sleep-inducing properties. The anxiolytic drugs are also discussed in Chapter 4.

Anxiolytic benzodiazepines bind to GABA receptors, where they act as noncompetitive agonists (recall from Chapter 4 that GABA is the most common inhibitory transmitter in the brain). This interaction with GABA receptors results in

phobic disorder An intense, irrational fear that becomes centered on a specific object, activity, or situation that a person feels compelled to avoid.

anxiety disorder Any of a class of psychological disorders that include recurrent panic states, generalized persistent anxiety disorders, and posttraumatic stress disorders.

benzodiazepines A class of antianxiety drugs that bind with high affinity to receptor molecules in the central nervous system. One example is diazepam (Valium).

anxiolytics A class of substances that are used to combat anxiety. Examples include alcohol, opiates, barbiturates, and the benzodiazepines.

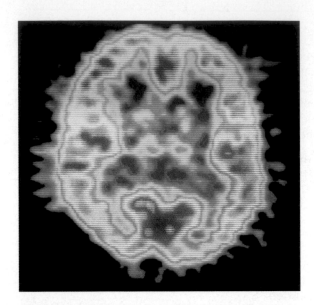

16.17 The Distribution of Benzodiazepine Receptors in the Human Brain This PET scan of benzodiazepine receptors shows their wide distribution in the brain, especially the cortex. Highest concentrations are in orange and red. (Courtesy of Goran Sedvall.)

the enhancement of GABA's action at inhibitory synapses in the brain. In other words, GABA-mediated postsynaptic inhibition is facilitated by benzodiazepines. Benzodiazepines preferentially bind to the many GABA$_A$ receptors that are widely distributed throughout the brain, especially in the cerebral cortex (**Figure 16.17**) and some subcortical areas, such as the hippocampus and the amygdala.

The ultimate function of the benzodiazepine-GABA$_A$ receptor complex is to regulate the permeability of neural membranes to chloride ions (Cl$^-$). When GABA is released from a presynaptic terminal and activates postsynaptic receptors, chloride ions are allowed to move from the outside to the inside of the nerve cell, creating a local hyperpolarization (an inhibitory postsynaptic potential, or IPSP) and therefore inhibiting the neuron from firing. Benzodiazepines alone do little to change chloride conductance, but in the presence of GABA they markedly enhance GABA-provoked increases in chloride permeability and thus potentiate the inhibitory effect of GABA. Interestingly, the brain probably makes its own anxiety-relieving substances that interact with the benzodiazepine-binding site; the neurosteroid allopregnanolone is a prime candidate for this function (see Chapter 4). Drugs developed to act at this site are effective anxiolytics in both rats and humans (Rupprecht et al., 2009).

Although the benzodiazepines remain an important category of anxiolytics, other types of anxiety-relieving drugs have been developed. A notable example is the drug buspirone (Buspar), an agonist at serotonin 5HT$_{1A}$ receptors that has been shown to provide relief from anxiety. This observation is consistent with findings from functional-imaging research confirming that 5HT$_{1A}$ receptor density is abnormal in anxiety disorders (Neumeister et al., 2004). SSRI antidepressants, such as paroxetine (Paxil) and fluoxetine (Prozac), which increase stimulation of serotonin receptors, are also sometimes effective for the treatment of anxiety disorders.

In posttraumatic stress disorder, horrible memories won't go away

Some people experience especially awful moments in life that seem indelible, resulting in vivid impressions that persist the rest of their lives. The kind of event that seems particularly likely to produce subsequent stress disorders is one that is intense and usually associated with witnessing abusive violence and/or death. Examples include the sudden loss of a close friend, rape, torture, kidnapping, or profound social dislocation, such as in forced migration. In these cases, memories of horrible events intrude into consciousness and produce the same intense visceral arousal—the fear and trembling and general autonomic activation—that the original event caused. These traumatic memories are easily reawakened by stressful circumstances and even by seemingly benign stimuli that somehow prompt recollection of the original event. An ever-watchful and fearful stance becomes the portrait of individuals afflicted with what is called **posttraumatic stress disorder** (**PTSD**, formerly called *combat fatigue*, *war neurosis*, or *shell shock*).

Analysis of a random sample of Vietnam War veterans indicates that 19% had PTSD at some point after service. This was the rate for all Vietnam veterans; of those exposed to high war-zone stressors, more than 35% developed PTSD at some point and most of them were still suffering from the disorder decades later (Dohrenwend et al., 2006). Familial factors affect vulnerability, as shown in twin studies of Vietnam veterans who had seen combat. Monozygotic twins were more similar than dizygotic twins, and the specific contribution of inheritance to PTSD may account for one-third of the variance. People who display combat-related PTSD show (1) memory changes such as amnesia for some war experiences, (2) flashbacks, and (3) deficits in short-term memory (Bremner et al., 1993). These memory disturbances suggest involvement of the hippocampus, and indeed the volume of

posttraumatic stress disorder (PTSD)
Formerly called *combat fatigue*, *war neurosis*, or *shell shock*. A disorder in which memories of an unpleasant episode repeatedly plague the victim.

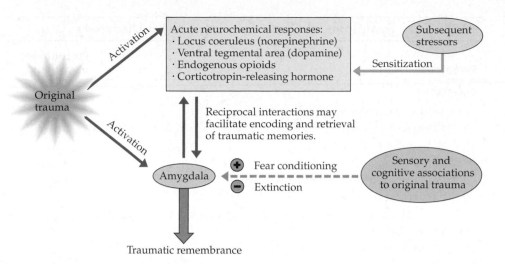

16.18 A Neural Model of Posttraumatic Stress Disorder The original trauma activates two systems: one in the brainstem, which sensitizes the subject to related stimuli in the future; and another in the amygdala, which conditions a long-lasting fearful reaction.

the right hippocampus is smaller in combat veterans with PTSD than in controls, with no differences in other brain regions (Bremner et al., 1995). It was once widely assumed that the stressful episode caused the hippocampus to shrink, but some veterans suffering PTSD left a monozygotic twin at home, and it turns out that the nonstressed twins without PTSD also tend to have a smaller hippocampus (Gilbertson et al., 2002). So an inherited tendency to have a small hippocampus may be what makes a person more susceptible to PTSD if exposed to stress.

A comprehensive psychobiological model of the development of PTSD draws connections among the symptoms and the neural mechanisms of fear conditioning, behavioral sensitization, and extinction. Charney et al. (1993) argue that patients learn to avoid a large range of stimuli associated with the original trauma. Work in animals has revealed that this type of memory—**fear conditioning**—is very persistent and involves the amygdala and some brainstem pathways that are part of a circuit of startle response behavior (see Chapter 15).

Finally, the persistence of memory and fear in PTSD may depend on the failure or fragility of mechanisms to *forget*. In experimental animals, NMDA antagonists delivered to the amygdala prevent the extinction of fear-mediated startle. Sites projecting to the amygdala, such as the hippocampus and prefrontal cortex, may also lose their effectiveness in suppressing learned fear responses (**Figure 16.18**). There is also a hormonal link, because PTSD sufferers exhibit a paradoxical long-term *reduction* in cortisol levels (Yehuda, 2002; Yehuda et al., 1995). One possibility is that patients with PTSD have persistent increases in *sensitivity* to cortisol. If, as a result, they feel the effect of stress hormones more strongly than other people do, it might be harder for them to forget stressful events. In Chapter 17 we will discuss research-based methods that have been proposed to help people forget traumatic life events.

In obsessive-compulsive disorder, thoughts and acts keep repeating

Neatness, orderliness, and similar traits are attributes we tend to admire, especially during those chaotic moments when we realize we have created another tottering pile of papers, bills, or the like. But when does orderliness and routine cross the line into pathology? People with **obsessive-compulsive disorder** (**OCD**) lead lives riddled with repetitive rituals and persistent thoughts that they are powerless to control or stop, despite recognizing that the behaviors are abnormal. In OCD patients, routine acts that we all engage in, such as checking whether the door is locked when we leave our home, become *compulsions* that are repeated over and over. Recurrent thoughts, or *obsessions*, such as fears of germs or other potential harms in the world, invade the consciousness. These symptoms progressively isolate a person from ordinary social engagement with the world. For many patients,

fear conditioning A form of learning in which fear comes to be associated with a previously neutral stimulus.

obsessive-compulsive disorder (OCD) A syndrome in which the affected individual engages in recurring, repetitive acts that are carried out without rhyme, reason, or the ability to stop.

TABLE 16.4 Symptoms of Obsessive-Compulsive Disorders

Symptoms	Percentage of patients
OBSESSIONS	
Dirt, germs, or environmental toxins	40
Something terrible happening (fire, death or illness of self or loved one)	24
Symmetry, order, or exactness	17
Religious obsessions	13
Body wastes or secretions (urine, stool, saliva)	8
Lucky or unlucky numbers	8
Forbidden, aggressive, or perverse sexual thoughts, images, or impulses	4
Fear of harming self or others	4
Household items	3
Intrusive nonsense sounds, words, or music	1
COMPULSIONS	
Performing excessive or ritualized hand washing, showering, bathing, tooth brushing, or grooming	85
Repeating rituals (going in or out of a door, getting up from or sitting down on a chair)	51
Checking (doors, locks, stove, appliances, emergency brake on car, paper route, homework)	46
Engaging in miscellaneous rituals (such as writing, moving, speaking)	26
Removing contaminants from contacts	23
Touching	20
Counting	18
Ordering or arranging	17
Preventing harm to self or others	16
Hoarding or collecting	11
Cleaning household or inanimate objects	6

hours of each day are consumed by compulsive acts such as repetitive hand washing. **Table 16.4** summarizes some of the symptoms of OCD.

Determining the number of persons afflicted with OCD is difficult, especially because many people with this disorder tend to hide their symptoms. It is estimated that more than 4 million people are affected by OCD in the United States (Rapoport, 1989). In many cases, the initial symptoms of this disorder appear in childhood; the peak age group for onset of OCD, however, is 25–44 years. PET scan studies of patients with OCD consistently report increased metabolic rates in the orbitofrontal cortex, cingulate cortex, and caudate nuclei (Chamberlain et al., 2008; Rauch et al., 1994; Saxena and Rauch, 2000).

Happily, OCD responds to drug treatment in most cases. What do effective OCD drugs—like fluoxetine (Prozac), fluvoxamine (Luvox), and clomipramine (Anafranil)—tend to have in common? They share the ability to inhibit the reuptake of serotonin at serotonergic synapses, thereby increasing the synaptic availability of serotonin. This observation suggests that dysfunction of serotonergic neurotransmission plays a central role in OCD. Recall that we already discussed SSRIs like Prozac that inhibit the reuptake of serotonin when we discussed treatments for depression. How can the same drug help two disorders that seem so different? For one thing, depression often accompanies OCD, so the two disorders may be related. Furthermore, functional brain imaging suggests that the same SSRI drugs alter the activity of the orbitofrontal prefrontal cortex in people with OCD (Saxena et al., 2001), while affecting primarily ventrolateral prefrontal cortex in people with depression (see Figure 16.13).

Many researchers also believe that OCD and another disease involving repetitive behaviors, *Tourette's syndrome*, are part of a spectrum of related disorders (Olson, 2004). Jeff, the young man we described at the opening of the chapter, suffers from Tourette's. OCD and Tourette's are often **co-morbid** (occurring together), and both disorders involve abnormalities of the basal ganglia. However, drug therapy in Tourette's syndrome has typically focused on modifying the actions of dopamine rather than of serotonin (**Box 16.3**).

There is a heritable genetic component to OCD; again, several genes may contribute to susceptibility to this disorder (Grados et al., 2003). For example, the gene that encodes BDNF, which we already discussed in the context of bipolar depression, appears to be involved in OCD (Hall et al., 2003). The gene encoding the serotonin $5HT_{2A}$ receptor has also been implicated (Enoch et al., 1998). There is evidence that OCD can be triggered by infections. Upon observing that numerous children exhibiting OCD symptoms had recently been treated for strep throat, R. C. Dale et al. (2005) found that many children with OCD are producing anti-

co-morbid   Referring to the tendency of certain diseases or disorders to occur together in individuals.

BOX 16.3   Tics, Twitches, and Snorts: The Unusual Character of Tourette's Syndrome

Their faces twitch in an insistent way, and every now and then, out of nowhere, they blurt out an odd sound. At times they fling their arms, kick their legs, or make violent shoulder movements. Sufferers of **Tourette's syndrome** also exhibit heightened sensitivity to tactile, auditory, and visual stimuli (A. J. Cohen and Leckman, 1992). Many patients report that an urge to emit verbal or phonic tics builds up and that giving in to the urge brings relief. Although popular media often portray people with Tourette's shouting out insults and curse words (coprolalia), verbal tics of that sort are rare.

Tourette's syndrome begins early in life; the mean age of diagnosis is 6–7 years (de Groot et al., 1995), and the syndrome is 3–4 times more common in males than in females. Figure A draws a portrait of the chronology of symptoms. Often people with Tourette's also exhibit attention deficit hyperactivity disorder (ADHD) or obsessive-compulsive disorder (OCD) (S. Park et al., 1993). Children with Tourette's display a thinning of primary somatosensory and motor cortex representing facial, oral, and laryngeal structures (Sowell et al., 2008), suggesting that the tics mediated by these regions may be underinhibited by cortex.

Family studies indicate that genetics plays an important role in this disorder.

(A) The chronology of Tourette's symptoms

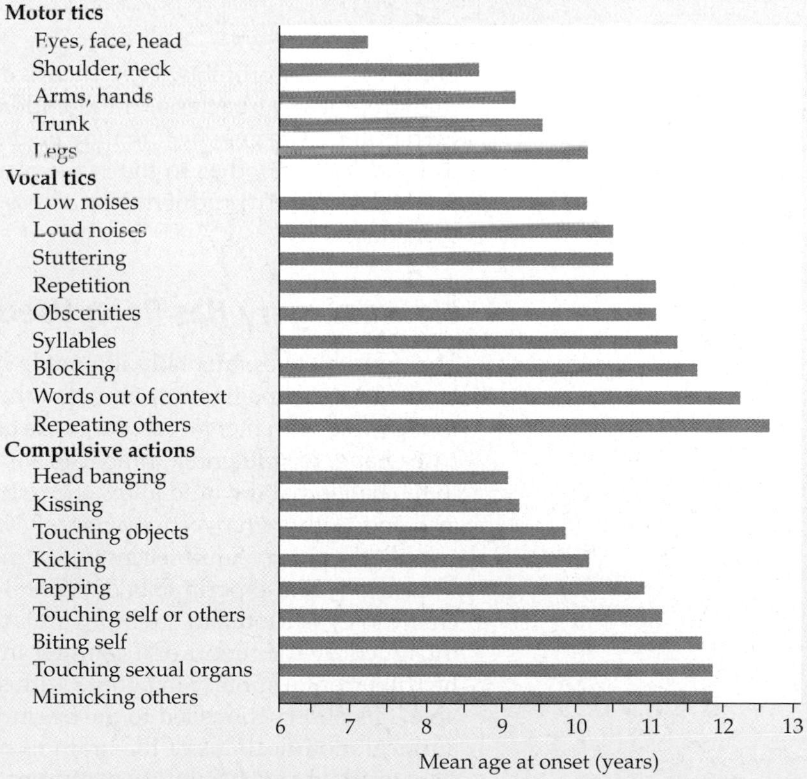

Twin studies of the disorder reveal a concordance rate among monozygotic twins of 53%–77%, contrasted with a concordance rate among dizygotic twins of 8%–23% (T. M. Hyde et al., 1992). Among discordant monozygotic twin pairs, the twin with Tourette's has a greater density of dopamine D_2 receptors in the caudate nucleus of the basal ganglia than the

(Continued on next page)

BOX 16.3 *(continued)*

unaffected twin has (Wolf et al., 1996). This observation suggests that differences in the dopaminergic system, especially in the basal ganglia, may be important (D_2 receptor binding in an affected twin is illustrated in Figure B). The contemporary view is that Tourette's syndrome is mediated in a complex manner by more than one gene, but the precise genes that are involved remain unidentified (Abelson et al., 2005; Pauls, 2003).

Administration of haloperidol, a dopamine D_2 receptor antagonist that is better known as an effective antischizophrenic drug, significantly reduces tic frequency and is a primary treatment for Tourette's syndrome. Unfortunately, this treatment has the side effects we mentioned when discussing schizophrenia and, as with people who suffer from schizophrenia,

(B) D_2 receptor binding in Tourette's syndrome. (*Left*) PET scan of D_2 binding. (*Right*) MRI scan illustrating the location of the caudate nuclei.

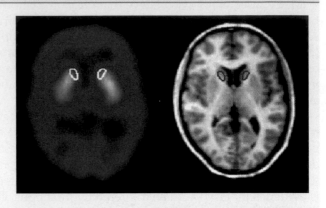

some people with Tourette's respond well to the atypical antipsychotics, which bring fewer side effects. Behavior modification techniques that aim at reducing the frequency of some symptoms, especially tics, help some patients learn to substitute more-subtle or more socially acceptable behaviors in place of the more obvious tics (Himle et al., 2006). As detailed in the text, some people with Tourette's that did not respond to medication reported relief

from electrical stimulation of their own thalamus via implants (Porta et al., 2009). (Figure B courtesy of Steven Wolf.)

Tourette's syndrome A heightened sensitivity to tactile, auditory, and visual stimuli that may be accompanied by the buildup of an urge to emit verbal or phonic tics.

---

bodies to brain proteins. They theorize that, in mounting an immune response to the streptococcal bacteria, these children also make antibodies that attack their own brains. The genetic link may be that some people are more likely than others to produce antibodies to the brain proteins. This theory suggests that measures to block antibody production or access to the brain might relieve OCD symptoms someday.

Neurosurgery Has Been Used to Treat Psychiatric Disorders

Through the ages, mentally ill people have been treated by methods limited only by the human imagination. Some methods have been gruesome, inspired by views that people with mental disorders are controlled by demonic forces. Disparate cultures have, for millennia, practiced *trephination* (drilling a hole through the skull) in the belief that it would allow the unhealthy spirit to escape from the brain of the afflicted. Although psychiatry largely was purged of such magical thinking by the twentieth century, until recently treatment was a trial-and-error affair.

In the 1930s, experiments on frontal lobe lesions in chimpanzees inspired psychiatrist Egas Moniz to attempt similar operations in human patients. Moniz was intrigued by the report of a calming influence in nonhuman primates, and when he tried frontal surgery in people with severe mental illnesses, little else was available. His observations led to the beginning of **psychosurgery**, defined as the use of surgical modifications of the brain to treat severe psychiatric disorders. Vigorous debate about psychosurgery continues (Valenstein, 1986).

During the 1940s, **lobotomy** (disconnecting parts of the frontal lobes from the rest of the brain) was forcefully advocated by some neurosurgeons and psychiatrists. A presidential commission on psychosurgery estimated that during this period, 10,000–50,000 U.S. patients underwent such surgery (National Commission for the Protection of Human Subjects of Biomedical and Behavioral Research, 1978). During the most intense period of enthusiasm, patients of all diagnostic types were operated on, and different varieties of surgery were employed.

psychosurgery Surgery in which brain lesions are produced to modify severe psychiatric disorders.

lobotomy The detachment of a portion of the frontal lobe from the rest of the brain, once used as a treatment for schizophrenia and many other ailments.

Follow-up assessments of the value of frontal lobe surgery revealed that outcomes were much less positive than originally claimed, and the procedure was widely abolished, except in cases of intractable pain. However, William Sweet (1973) and others argued that much more localized brain lesions—in contrast to the widespread damage caused by frontal lobotomy—might significantly relieve particular psychiatric disorders. Since the 1970s, a variety of experimental focal brain surgeries have been performed in severe cases of psychiatric illness, when all else has failed.

Positive results have been reported for several procedures. For example, Ballantine et al. (1987), reported beneficial effects of *cingulotomy* (lesions that interrupt pathways in the cingulate cortex) in the treatment of depression and anxiety disorders. About one-third of severely disabled OCD patients who underwent cingulotomy (**Figure 16.19**) benefited substantially from this intervention (Jenike et al., 1991; Martuza et al., 1990). Patients who received ventromedial frontal lesions as a last-resort therapy for OCD also showed significant improvement in obsessive-compulsive symptoms (Irle et al., 1998). This clinical improvement was sustained in some patients for 20 years. A different type of surgery, called *capsulotomy*, in which small, discrete lesions are placed in the anterior part of the internal capsule (the white matter projections underlying the cortex), reportedly is of long-lasting benefit in some cases of severe anxiety disorders (Ruck et al., 2003).

In epilepsy (discussed in Chapter 3), waves of electrical activity in the brain can disrupt behavior or induce seizures. Some people with epilepsy do not respond to pharmacological treatment, and in some cases physicians may track down the part of the brain where the discharges begin and surgically remove that portion. Although this technique is often effective at stopping the seizures, there may be consequences from removing that part of the brain, and sometimes the consequences can be quite unexpected, as we'll learn in Chapter 17.

Deep brain stimulation (DBS), which we mentioned earlier as a treatment for depression, may also benefit people with other disorders. Jeff Matovic, whose situation we described at the opening of the chapter, turned to DBS in a desperate attempt to gain relief from the symptoms of his Tourette's syndrome. In Jeff's operation, neurosurgeons implanted bilateral stimulating electrodes within the thalamus, in regions associated with the control of movement. The stimulators are controlled by pacemakers and batteries implanted near Jeff's collarbone. Within hours after the stimulators were activated, Jeff's symptoms completely abated; and for the first time in 25 years he was free of the motor and vocal tics that had threatened to ruin his life. Jeff reports being 100% tic-free more than 4 years later. A group of 15 people with Tourette's who, like Jeff, did not respond to medication, received thalamic implants and reported reduced symptoms 24 months later (Porta et al., 2009).

(*a*) Horizontal view

(*b*) Sagittal view

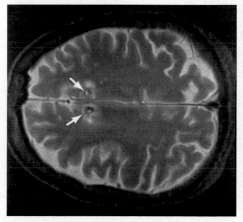
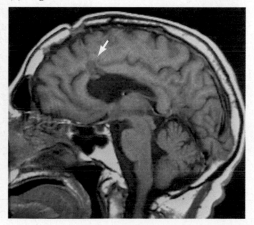

16.19 Neurosurgery to Treat Obsessive-Compulsive Disorder These horizontal (*a*) and sagittal (*b*) MRIs show the brain of a patient who underwent a cingulotomy—the disruption of cingulate cortex connections (arrows)—in an attempt to treat OCD. (From Martuza et al., 1990; courtesy of Robert L. Martuza.)

prion A protein that can become improperly folded and thereby can induce other proteins to follow suit, leading to long protein chains that impair neural function.

bovine spongiform encephalopathy (BSE) Mad cow disease, a disorder caused by improperly formed prion proteins, leading to dementia and death.

Creutzfeldt-Jakob disease (CJD) A brain disorder in humans, leading to dementia and death, that is caused by improperly folded prion proteins; the human equivalent of mad cow disease.

Despite some apparently dramatic successes like Jeff Matovic's, psychosurgery remains a very uncommon treatment, limited to the most severe and unresponsive cases. The use of drugs has overshadowed psychosurgery, especially because most neurosurgical interventions are not reversible.

Abnormal Prion Proteins Destroy the Brain

Over two centuries ago, shepherds in Europe recognized a fatal disease in sheep that was called *scrapie* because the animals "scraped" their skin, presumably in an attempt to relieve itching. The shepherds learned that the only way they could stop an outbreak was to kill all the sheep, burn the carcasses and the fields they had used, and keep new sheep away from those fields for years. These drastic measures were needed because the disease is not transmitted by a virus or bacterium, which would rely on relatively fragile DNA or RNA for reproduction. Rather, scrapie arises when a particular endogenous protein that normally takes one shape takes on a new, abnormal shape. Once one protein molecule does this, it induces the other molecules of that protein to fold abnormally around it. The accumulation of abnormally folded proteins leads to brain degeneration. These infectious protein particles were named **prions** (pronounced "PREE-ons"). There is increasing speculation that such misfolding of other proteins, leading to clumping and toxicity, might underlie other diseases, including Alzheimer's (Frost et al., 2009).

At some point, feed that contained protein derived from sheep with scrapie was fed to some cows in England and caused the cow version of the prion protein to fold abnormally. The result was a bovine version of scrapie called **bovine spongiform encephalopathy** (**BSE**, or *mad cow disease*) because the massive brain degeneration leaves the brain "spongy" (**Figure 16.20**). Unfortunately, before BSE was detected, infected cows provided beef for Britons and caused a similar disorder called **Creutzfeldt-Jakob disease** (**CJD**) in humans. CJD is fatal, causing widespread brain degeneration and therefore dementia, sleep disorders (see Chapter 14), schizophrenia-like symptoms, and death. Although a few cases of BSE have now been detected in North American cattle, currently they are believed to pose little risk to human health because of changes in screening and feed production procedures. On the other hand, wild deer herds in North America suffer from a similar, prion-induced disease (Tamgüney et al., 2009), raising the specter of people contracting CJD from eating venison.

16.20 The Culprits of Mad Cow Disease Proteins that transmit disease, called *prions*, are the cause of bovine spongiform encephalopathy (mad cow disease).

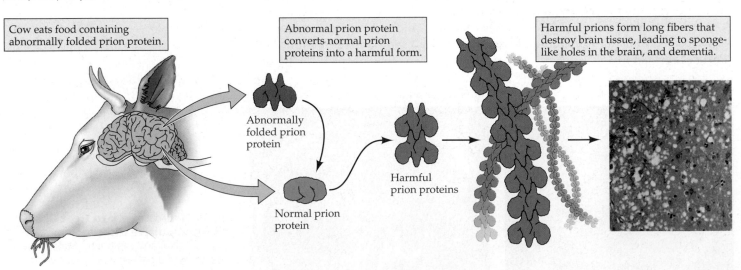

Cow eats food containing abnormally folded prion protein.

Abnormal prion protein converts normal prion proteins into a harmful form.

Harmful prions form long fibers that destroy brain tissue, leading to sponge-like holes in the brain, and dementia.

Abnormally folded prion protein

Normal prion protein

Harmful prion proteins

SUMMARY

The Toll of Psychiatric Disorders Is Huge

- **Epidemiology** reveals that psychiatric disorders are startlingly prevalent in modern society. **Review Table 16.1**

Schizophrenia Is the Major Neurobiological Challenge in Psychiatry

- There is strong evidence for a genetic factor in the origin of **schizophrenia**. Consistent evidence comes from studies of the incidence of schizophrenia in families, twins, and adoptees. Several genes that may contribute to schizophrenia have been identified. **Review Table 16.2 and Figure 16.2**

- Structural changes in the brains of patients with schizophrenia—including enlarged ventricles, limbic system abnormalities, loss of gray matter in the cortex, and abnormalities of other brain regions—may arise from early developmental problems. Functional-imaging studies indicate that, in schizophrenia, the frontal lobes are less active than normal. **Review Figures 16.4–16.9**

- Biochemical theories of schizophrenia especially emphasize the importance of the transmitters dopamine, glutamate, and serotonin. **Typical neuroleptics** block D_2 receptors, while **atypical neuroleptics** block $5HT_{2A}$ receptors. Despite pharmaceutical marketing, the two appear to be equally effective. **Review Figures 16.10 and 16.11**

- According to an integrative psychobiological model, the emergence of schizophrenia depends on the interaction of a vulnerable biological substrate and environmental stressors. **Review Figure 16.12**

Mood Disorders Are a Major Psychiatric Category

- Biological studies of **depression** reveal a strong genetic factor and the importance of levels of various neurotransmitters, including serotonin.

- People suffering from depression show increased blood flow in the frontal cortex and the amygdala, and decreased blood flow in the parietal and posterior temporal cortex. **Review Figure 16.13**

- The most effective approach to treating depression may be a combination of **cognitive behavioral therapy** (**CBT**) and treatment with a **selective serotonin reuptake inhibitor** (**SSRI**).

- Dysregulation of the hypothalamic-pituitary-adrenal axis is often associated with depression. **Review Figure 16.14**

- In the general population, females are more likely than males to suffer from depression.

- Changes in REM sleep that accompany depression include shortened onset to REM sleep and larger percentages of REM sleep in overall amounts of sleep. **Review Figure 16.15**

- **Bipolar disorder** is characterized by extreme mood swings and subtle changes in the brain, and it has a complex genetic component. The disorder is commonly treated with **lithium**. **Review Figure 16.16**

There Are Several Types of Anxiety Disorders

- Anxiety states are characterized by functional changes in the temporal lobes that can be revealed by PET scans and functional MRI.

- **Benzodiazepine** antianxiety drugs (**anxiolytics**) affect receptors for the transmitter GABA, enhancing its inhibitory influence. Drugs that affect serotonergic transmission may also reduce anxiety. **Review Figure 16.17**

- **Posttraumatic stress disorder** (**PTSD**) is characterized by an inability to forget horrible experiences. Temporal lobe atrophy in this disorder is common and may be caused by exposure to glucocorticoids, but long-term PTSD sufferers have paradoxically low levels of glucocorticoids. **Review Figure 16.18**

- **Obsessive-compulsive disorder** (**OCD**) is characterized by changes in basal ganglia and frontal structures and strongly linked to serotonin activities. It bears many similarities to **Tourette's syndrome**, in which people display motor and verbal tics and compulsions. **Review Table 16.4 and Box 16.3**

Neurosurgery Has Been Used to Treat Psychiatric Disorders

- Though once a common approach to psychiatric treatment, today neurosurgery is used to treat only the most severe and unresponsive cases.

Abnormal Prion Proteins Destroy the Brain

- Infectious proteins (**prions**) become concentrated in brain tissues, leading to damage and dementia in **bovine spongiform encephalopathy** (**BSE**) and, in humans, **Creutzfeldt-Jakob disease**. **Review Figure 16.20**

Review Web Activity 16.1 for a concept review.

Go to **www.biopsychology.com** for study questions, quizzes, key terms, and other resources.

Recommended Reading

Charney, D., and Nestler E. J. (Eds.). (2005). *Neurobiology of mental illness* (2nd ed.). New York: Oxford University Press.

Cichetti, D., and Walker, E. F. (Eds.). (2003). *Neurodevelopmental mechanisms in psychopathology*. Cambridge, England: Cambridge University Press.

Hersen, M., Turner, S. M., and Beidel, D. C. (2007). *Adult psychopathology and diagnosis* (2nd ed.). New York: Wiley.

Huettel, S. A., Song, A. W., and McCarthy, G. (2004). *Functional magnetic resonance imaging.* Sunderland, MA: Sinauer.

Meyer, J. S., and Quenzer, L. F. (2004). *Psychopharmacology: Drugs, the brain, and behavior.* Sunderland, MA: Sinauer.

Solomon, A. (2001). *The noonday demon: An atlas of depression.* New York: Scribner.

Walkup, J. T., Mink, J. W., and Hollenbeck, P. J. (2006). *Tourette syndrome.* New York: Lippincott Williams and Wilkins.

Cognitive Neuroscience

PART VI

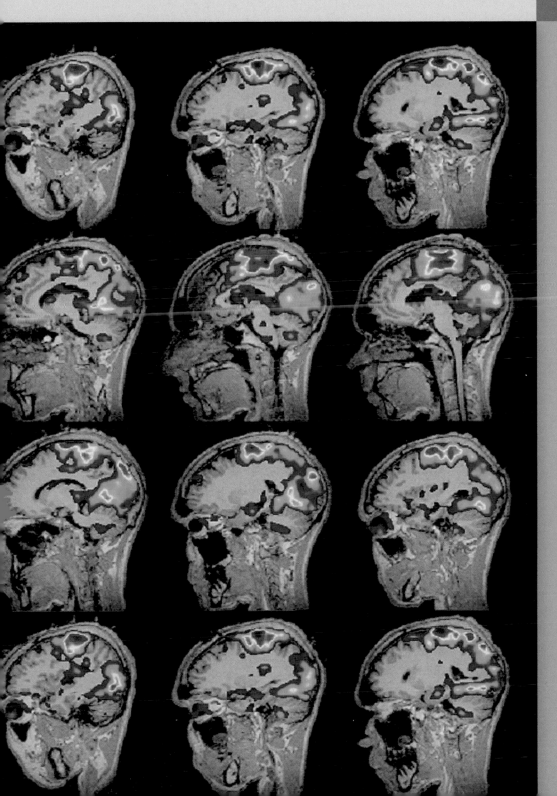

Previous page   **Simultanenous registration maps of EEG and functional MRI**   In this technique the excellent spatial resolution of fMRI and the excellent temporal resolution of EEG are combined to provide an improved method for tracking brain activation associated with complex cognitive processing. (Image by Jan C. De Munck V, VU University Medical Center, Amsterdam.)

CHAPTER 17

Learning and Memory

Trapped in the Eternal Now

Henry Molaison, known to the world as "patient H.M." in a classic series of research articles, was probably the most famous research subject in the history of brain science. Henry started to suffer seizures during adolescence, and by his late 20s, in 1953, Henry's epilepsy was out of control. Because tests showed that his seizures began in both temporal lobes, a neurosurgeon removed most of the anterior temporal lobe, including much of the amygdala and hippocampus, on both sides.

After Henry recovered from the operation, his seizures were milder, and they could be controlled by medication. But this relief came at a terrible, unforeseen price: Henry had lost the ability to form new memories (Scoville and Milner, 1957). For more than 50 years after the surgery, until his death in 2008, Henry could retain any new fact only briefly; as soon as he was distracted, the newly acquired information vanished. Long after the surgery, he didn't know his age or the current date, and he didn't know that his parents (with whom he lived well into adulthood) had died years previously. His IQ remained a little above average (Corkin et al., 1997) because most IQ tests monitor problem solving that doesn't require remembering new facts for more than a few minutes. Henry knew that something was wrong with him, because he had no memories from the years since his surgery, or even memories from earlier the same day.

> Every day is alone in itself, whatever enjoyment I've had, and whatever sorrow I've had. … Right now, I'm wondering, have I done or said anything amiss? You see, at this moment everything looks clear to me, but what happened just before? That's what worries me. It's like waking from a dream. I just don't remember. (B. Milner, 1970, p. 37)

Henry's inability to form new memories meant that he couldn't construct a lasting relationship with anybody new. No matter what experiences he might share with someone he met, Henry would have to start the acquaintance anew the following day, because he would have no recollection of ever meeting the person before.

What happened to Henry, and what does his experience teach us about learning and memory?

All the distinctively human aspects of our behavior are learned: the languages we speak, how we dress, the foods we eat and how we eat them, our skills and the ways we reach our goals. So much of our own individuality depends on **learning**, the process of acquiring new information; and **memory**, the ability to store and retrieve that information.

Functional Perspectives on Memory

Conditions that impair memory are particularly frightening; they can make it impossible to take part in normal social life and can rob us of our identity. We can discover a great deal about learning and memory by examining how they fail.

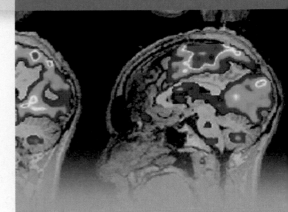

learning The process of acquiring new and relatively enduring information, behavior patterns, or abilities, characterized by modifications of behavior as a result of practice, study, or experience.

memory 1. The ability to retain information, based on the mental process of learning or encoding, retention across some interval of time, and retrieval or reactivation of the memory. 2. The specific information that is stored in the brain.

patient H.M. A patient who, because of damage to medial temporal lobe structures, was unable to encode new declarative memories. Upon his death we learned his name was Henry Molaison.

amnesia Severe impairment of memory.

retrograde amnesia Difficulty in retrieving memories formed before the onset of amnesia.

anterograde amnesia The inability to form new memories beginning with the onset of a disorder.

Clinical case studies show that memory can fail in very different ways, indicating that there are different forms of learning and memory, and that multiple brain regions are involved. The clinical research has provided guidance for further studies employing animal models and brain-imaging technology; together, these diverse approaches are generating a comprehensive picture of the brain's mechanisms of learning and memory.

There Are Several Kinds of Memory and Learning

The terms *learning* and *memory* are so often paired that it sometimes seems as if one necessarily implies the other. We cannot be sure that learning has occurred unless a memory can be elicited later. Many kinds of brain damage, caused by disease or accident, impair learning and memory, and specific cases continue to provide powerful lessons. We'll start by looking at some of these cases before progressing to newer brain-imaging techniques that provide novel information about brain regions involved in learning and memory. Study of different types of memory impairment has revealed different classes of learning and memory, which we will discuss later in the chapter. First, let's look at a few cases of memory impairment that have posed puzzles and have generated a great deal of controversy.

For patient H.M., the present vanished into oblivion

Patient H.M.—Henry Molaison, whom we met at the start of the chapter—suffered from **amnesia** (Greek for "forgetfulness"), a severe impairment of memory. In Henry's case, most old memories remained intact, but he had difficulty recollecting any events after his surgery. Loss of memories formed prior to an event (such as surgery or trauma) is called **retrograde amnesia** (from the Latin *retro-*, "backward," and *gradi*, "to go"), and is not uncommon. What was striking about Henry was a far more unusual symptom: his apparent inability to retain *new* material for more than a brief period. The inability to form new memories *after* an event is called **anterograde amnesia** (the Latin *antero-* means "forward").

Over the very short term, Henry's memory was normal. If given a series of six or seven digits, he could immediately repeat the list back without error. But if he was given a list of words to study and then tested on them after other tasks had intervened, he could not repeat the list or even recall that there *was* a list. So Henry's case provided clear neuroanatomical evidence that *short-term memory* differs from *long-term memory*—a distinction long recognized by biological psychologists on behavioral grounds (W. James, 1890). We will discuss long- and short-term memory in more depth later in this chapter.

Henry's surgery removed the amygdala, most of the hippocampus, and some surrounding cortex from both temporal lobes (**Figure 17.1**). The memory deficit seemed to be caused by loss of the hippocampus, because other surgical patients who had received the same type of damage to the amygdala, but less damage to the hippocampus, did not exhibit memory impairment. But to the puzzlement of researchers, it soon became evident that experimental bilateral hippocampal lesions in laboratory animals

17.1 Brain Tissue Removed from Henry Molaison (Patient H.M.) (a) MRI scans of a normal subject (*left*) and Henry (*right*) show that Henry's hippocampus (H) and entorhinal cortex (EC) were extensively damaged, bilaterally. (b) Henry had a small amount of posterior hippocampus left (see drawing for orientation), but the parahippocampal cortex (PH) was totally gone, and the cerebellum (Cer) was dramatically shrunken. (From Corkin et al., 1997; courtesy of Suzanne Corkin.)

seemed not to produce widespread memory deficits (Isaacson, 1972). What might account for this discrepancy between humans and lab animals?

An interesting early finding suggested that Henry's memory deficit might involve verbal function. Brenda Milner (1965) gave Henry a mirror-tracing task (**Figure 17.2a**) and found that he improved considerably over ten trials. The next day the test was presented again. When asked if he remembered it, Henry said no, yet his performance was better than at the start of the first day (**Figure 17.2b**). Over three successive days, Henry never recognized the task, but his improved tracings showed evidence of memory, in the form of motor skill. If an animal subject with comparable brain damage showed similar improvement on a task, we would probably conclude that the animal had normal memory, because we cannot ask animal subjects to tell us if they *recognize* the test.

However, further research showed that difficulty with verbal material could not be the sole cause of Henry's memory problems. First, patients like Henry have difficulty reproducing or recognizing pictures and spatial designs that are not recalled in verbal terms. Second, although the patients have difficulty with the specific content of verbal material, they can learn some kinds of information *about* verbal material (N. J. Cohen and Squire, 1980). For example, several kinds of patients with amnesia can learn the *skill* of reading mirror-reversed text but show impaired learning of specific words.

Thus, the important distinction is probably not between motor and verbal performances but between two kinds of memory:

1. **Declarative memory** is what we usually think of as memory: facts and information acquired through learning. It is memory we are aware of accessing, which we can declare to others. This is the type of memory so profoundly impaired by Henry's surgery. Tests of declarative memory take the form of requests for specific information that has been learned previously, such as a story or word list.
2. **Nondeclarative memory**, or **procedural memory**—that is, memory about perceptual or motor procedures—is shown by *performance* rather than by conscious recollection. Examples of procedural memory include memory for the mirror-tracing task and for the skill of mirror reading, as we just described.

Put another way, declarative memory deals with *what*, and nondeclarative memory deals with *how* (summarized in **Figure 17.3**). So, an animal's inability to speak is probably not what accounts for its apparent immunity to the effects of medial temporal lesions on memory storage. Rather, the culprit is the difficulty of measuring declarative memory in animals.

(a) The mirror-tracing task

(b) Performance of H.M. on mirror-tracing task

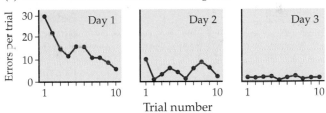

17.2 Henry's Performance on a Mirror-Tracing Task (a) Henry was given this mirror-tracing task to test motor skill. (b) His performance on this task progressively improved over three successive days, demonstrating a type of long-term memory. (After B. Milner, 1965.)

declarative memory   A memory that can be stated or described.

nondeclarative memory or procedural memory   A memory that is shown by performance rather than by conscious recollection.

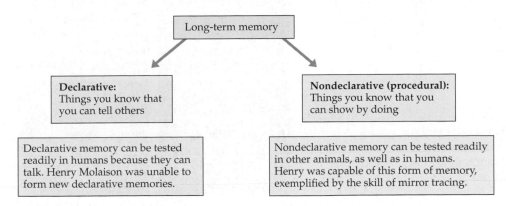

17.3 Two Main Kinds of Memory: Declarative and Nondeclarative

Long-term memory

Declarative: Things you know that you can tell others

Nondeclarative (procedural): Things you know that you can show by doing

Declarative memory can be tested readily in humans because they can talk. Henry Molaison was unable to form new declarative memories.

Nondeclarative memory can be tested readily in other animals, as well as in humans. Henry was capable of this form of memory, exemplified by the skill of mirror tracing.

Damage to the medial diencephalon can also cause amnesia

The medial temporal lobe is not the only brain region involved in the formation of declarative memories. For example, the case of **patient N.A.** indicates that damage to the dorsomedial thalamus can also impair memory formation (Squire and Moore, 1979; Teuber et al., 1968). N.A. acquired amnesia as the result of a bizarre accident in which a miniature fencing foil injured his brain after entering through his nostril. N.A. has a striking case of anterograde amnesia, primarily for verbal material, and he can give little information about events since his accident in 1960, but he shows almost normal recall for earlier events (Kaushall et al., 1981).

MRI study of N.A. (**Figure 17.4**) shows damage to several diencephalic structures: clear damage to the left dorsal thalamus, bilateral damage to the mammillary bodies (limbic structures contiguous with the hypothalamus), and probable damage to the mammillothalamic tract (Squire et al., 1989). Like Henry Molaison, N.A. shows normal short-term memory but is impaired in forming declarative (but not nondeclarative/procedural) long-term memories. The similarity in symptoms suggests that the medial temporal region damaged in Henry's brain and the midline diencephalic region damaged in N.A. are normally parts of a larger memory system.

Patients with Korsakoff's syndrome show damage to medial diencephalic structures and to the frontal cortex

People with **Korsakoff's syndrome**—named for its nineteenth-century discoverer, Russian neurologist Sergei Korsakoff—fail to recall many past events, and may fail to recognize or sense any familiarity with some items even when presented repeatedly. People with Korsakoff's syndrome frequently deny that anything is wrong with them, and they often **confabulate**—that is, fill a gap in memory with a falsification that they seem to accept as true.

The main cause of Korsakoff's syndrome is lack of the vitamin thiamine. Alcoholics who obtain most of their calories from alcohol and neglect their diet often exhibit this deficiency. Treating them with thiamine can prevent further deterioration of memory functions but will not reverse the damage already done.

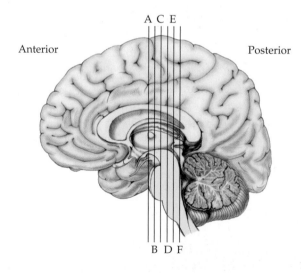

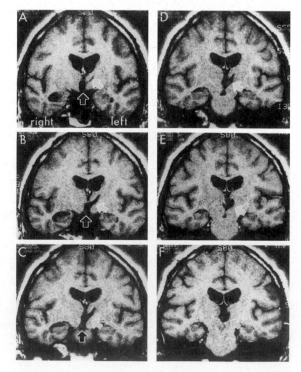

17.4 The Brain Damage in Patient N.A. Successive MRI scans show a prominent diencephalic lesion on the left side of the brain (yellow arrows), as well as a lesion on the floor of the third ventricle (red arrows). The mammillary bodies should be present in B and C, but they are totally absent. (From Squire et al., 1989; MRI scans courtesy of Larry Squire.)

Mair et al. (1979) examined the brains of two Korsakoff's patients whose behavior had been studied for several years. Temporal lobe structures, including the hippocampus, were normal in these patients. But their brains showed shrunken, diseased mammillary bodies, as well as some damage in the dorsomedial thalamus. This damage is similar to that seen in N.A. The mammillary bodies may serve as a processing system connecting medial temporal regions (such as those removed from Henry Molaison) to the thalamus via the mammillothalamic tract and, from there, to other cortical sites (Vann and Aggleton, 2004). Damage to the basal frontal cortex, also found in patients suffering from Korsakoff's syndrome, probably causes the denial and confabulation that differentiates them from other patients who have amnesia, such as Henry.

Brain damage can destroy autobiographical memories while sparing general memories

One striking case study illustrates an important distinction between two subtypes of declarative memory. **Patient K.C.**, who sustained brain damage in a motorcycle accident at age 30, can no longer retrieve any personal memory of his past, although his general knowledge remains good. He converses easily and plays a good game of chess, but he cannot remember where he learned to play chess or who taught him the game. Detailed autobiographical declarative memory of this sort is known as **episodic memory**: you show episodic memory when you recall a specific episode in your life or relate an event to a particular time and place. In contrast, **semantic memory** is generalized declarative memory, such as knowing the meaning of a word without knowing where or when you learned that word (Tulving, 1972). If care is taken to space out the trials to prevent interference among items, K.C. can acquire new *semantic* knowledge (Tulving et al., 1991). But even with this method, K.C. cannot acquire new *episodic* knowledge.

Brain scans of K.C. reveal extensive damage to the left frontoparietal and the right parieto-occipital cerebral cortex, and severe shrinkage of the hippocampus and parahippocampal cortex (Rosenbaum et al., 2005). As with Henry, the bilateral hippocampal damage probably accounts for K.C.'s anterograde declarative amnesia, but not for the selective loss of nearly his entire autobiographical memory (i.e., retrograde episodic amnesia), because other patients with restricted hippocampal damage apparently lack this symptom. K.C.'s inability to recall any autobiographical details of his life, even personal memories from many years before his accident, may instead be a consequence of his cortical injuries (Tulving, 1989).

Different forms of nondeclarative memory serve varying functions

In discussing the distinctions between nondeclarative (procedural) memory and declarative memory, we have seen that there are two different kinds of declarative memory: semantic and episodic. There are several different types of nondeclarative memory too.

In **skill learning**, subjects perform a challenging task on repeated trials in one or more sessions. The mirror-tracing task performed by Henry Molaison (see Figure 17.2) is an example. Learning to read mirror-reversed text, also mentioned earlier, is a type of perceptual skill learning.

Priming, also called *repetition priming*, is a change in the processing of a stimulus, usually a word or a picture, as a result of prior exposure to the same stimulus or related stimuli. For example, if a person is shown the word *stamp* in a list and later is asked to complete the word stem *STA-*, he or she is more likely to reply "stamp" than is a person who was not exposed to that word. Even patients like Henry, who do not recall being shown the list of words, nevertheless show the effect of priming.

Conditioning is learning simple associations between stimuli. The various forms of conditioning and other learning terms are defined in **Box 17.1**. Different brain areas are responsible for conditioning, depending on the complexity of the conditioning circumstances.

patient K.C.   A patient who sustained damage to the cortex that renders him unable to form and retrieve new episodic memories, especially autobiographical memories.

episodic memory   Memory of a particular incident or a particular time and place.

semantic memory   Generalized memory— for instance, knowing the meaning of a word without knowing where or when you learned that word.

skill learning   Learning to perform a task that requires motor coordination.

priming   Also called *repetition priming*. The phenomenon by which exposure to a stimulus facilitates subsequent responses to the same or a similar stimulus.

conditioning   A form of learning in which an organism comes to associate two stimuli, or a stimulus and a response.

BOX 17.1 Learning and Memory: Some Basic Concepts and Definitions

Because you have probably studied learning and memory in one or more psychology courses, here we only briefly review some of the basic concepts and definitions. Basic experiments on learning and memory compare individuals' behavior before exposure to a particular experience—a sensory stimulus or another opportunity to learn—to behavior after the exposure. Trained animals are usually contrasted against "control" animals that didn't receive the training experience, in order to determine whether the experience produced a lasting change.

In **nonassociative learning**—habituation, dishabituation, and sensitization—only a single stimulus is presented once or repeatedly. **Habituation** is a decrease in response to a stimulus as the stimulus is repeated (when the decrement cannot be attributed to sensory adaptation or motor fatigue). Sitting in a café, you may stop noticing the door chime when someone enters; in this case you have habituated to the chime. Once habituation has occurred, a strong stimulus (of the same sort, or even in another sensory modality) will often cause the response to the habituated stimulus to increase sharply; it may become even larger than the original response. The increase in response amplitude is called **dishabituation**. So, if a loud firecracker is set off behind you, the next ring of the door chime may startle you; in this case you have become temporarily dishabituated to the chime. Even a response that has not been habituated may increase in amplitude after a strong stimulus. This effect is known as **sensitization**: the response is greater than the baseline level because of prior stimulation. After the firecracker, for example, you may overreact to someone standing up nearby. That horrible firecracker has sensitized you to many stimuli.

Learning that involves relations between events—for example, between two or more stimuli, between a stimulus and a response, or between a response and its consequence—is called **associative learning**. In one form, **classical condition-**

(A) Pavlov and spectators in his laboratory

nonassociative learning   A type of learning in which presentation of a particular stimulus alters the strength or probability of a response according to the strength and temporal spacing of that stimulus; includes habituation and sensitization.

habituation   A form of nonassociative learning in which an organism becomes less responsive following repeated presentations of a stimulus.

dishabituation   The restoration of response amplitude following habituation.

sensitization   A form of nonassociative learning in which an organism becomes more responsive to most stimuli after being exposed to unusually strong or painful stimulation.

associative learning   A type of learning in which an association is formed between two stimuli or between a stimulus and a response; includes both classical and instrumental conditioning.

The taxonomy of memory we presented in Figure 17.3 is updated in **Figure 17.5**, where we have added the subtypes of declarative and nondeclarative memory described in this section, along with some examples.

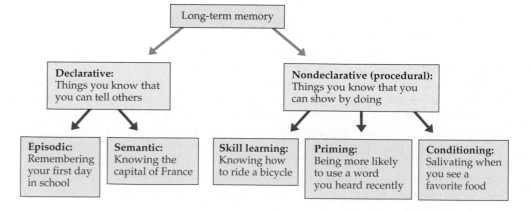

17.5 Subtypes of Declarative and Nondeclarative Memory

BOX 17.1 *(continued)*

ing (also called *Pavlovian conditioning*), an initially neutral stimulus comes to predict an event. At the end of the nineteenth century, Ivan Pavlov (1849–1936) (Figure A) found that a dog would salivate when presented with an auditory or visual stimulus if the stimulus came to predict an event that normally caused salivation. If the experimenter rang a bell just before putting meat powder in the dog's mouth, repeating this sequence a few times would

(B) A Skinner box

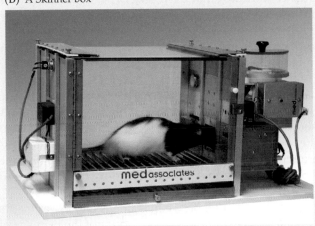

cause the dog to respond to the bell itself by salivating. In this case the meat powder in the mouth is the *unconditioned stimulus* (*US*), which already evokes an unconditioned response (UR). The sound is the *conditioned stimulus* (*CS*), and the learned response to the CS alone (salivation in response to the bell in this example) is called the conditioned response (CR).

In **instrumental conditioning** (also called **operant conditioning**), an association is formed between the animal's behavior and the consequence(s) of that behavior. An example of an apparatus designed to study instrumental learning is an operant conditioning apparatus (Figure B), often called a *Skinner box* after its originator, B. F. Skinner. Here, the conditioned instrumental response is pressing a bar to gain the reward of a food pellet.

Typical learning events have multiple dimensions or attributes. For example, Pavlov's dogs learned the relation between the conditioned auditory stimulus (the bell) and not only the meat powder, but also the location of the test and the rewarding features of the situation. So whenever they entered the test room, they would eagerly leap onto the test stand.

classical conditioning Also called *Pavlovian conditioning*. A type of associative learning in which an originally neutral stimulus (the *conditioned stimulus*, or *CS*)—through pairing with another stimulus (the *unconditioned stimulus*, or *US*) that elicits a particular response—acquires the power to elicit that response when presented alone. A response elicited by the US is called an *unconditioned response* (*UR*); a response elicited by the CS alone is called a *conditioned response* (*CR*).

instrumental conditioning or operant conditioning A form of associative learning in which the likelihood that an act (instrumental response) will be performed depends on the consequences (reinforcing stimuli) that follow it.

Memory Has Temporal Stages: Short, Intermediate, and Long

The span of time that a piece of information will be retained in the brain varies. Although investigators often contrast short-term and long-term memories, this dichotomy is an oversimplification. Evidence suggests at least four different duration categories for memory. The briefest memories are called **iconic memories** (from the Greek *eikon*, "image"); an example is the fleeting impression of a glimpsed scene that vanishes from memory seconds later. These brief memories are thought to be residual sensory neural activity—the so-called sensory buffers.

Somewhat longer than iconic memories are **short-term memories** (**STMs**). If you look up a phone number and keep it in mind (perhaps through rehearsal) just until you make the phone call, you are using STM. In the absence of rehearsal, STMs last only about 30 seconds (J. Brown, 1958; L. R. Peterson and Peterson, 1959). With rehearsal, you may be able to retain an STM until you turn to a new task a few minutes later; but when the STM is gone, it's gone for good. Many researchers now refer to this form of memory as **working memory**, in recognition of the way we use it; this is where we hold information while we are working with it to solve a problem or are otherwise actively manipulating the information. One influential model (Baddeley, 2003) subdivides working memory into three complementary components:

1. A *phonological loop* that contains auditory information (such as speech); this is what you use to rehearse that phone number.

2. A so-called *visuospatial sketch pad* that holds visual impressions of stimuli; you use this to imagine the route back to your car in a parking building.

iconic memory A very brief type of memory that stores the sensory impression of a scene.

short-term memory (STM) A form of memory that usually lasts only for seconds, or as long as rehearsal continues.

working memory A buffer that holds memories available for ready access during performance of a task.

intermediate-term memory (ITM) A form of memory that lasts longer than short-term memory, but not as long as long-term memory.

long-term memory (LTM) An enduring form of memory that lasts days, weeks, months, or years and has a very large capacity.

primacy effect The superior performance seen in a memory task for items at the start of a list; usually attributed to long-term memory.

recency effect The superior performance seen in a memory task for items at the end of a list; attributed to short-term memory.

3. An *episodic buffer* that contains more integrated information, spanning across sensory modalities, sort of like movie clips.

According to this model, the flow of information into and out of working memory is supervised by a fourth module, the *central executive*, which we will discuss in more detail in Chapter 18.

Some memories last beyond the short term but fall short of long-term memories. Chances are good that you can remember what you had for lunch today or yesterday, but not most of your lunches last week. You may recall today's weather forecast, but not that of a few days ago. These are examples of what some (but not all) memory researchers identify as **intermediate-term memory (ITM)**—that is, a memory that outlasts STM but is far from being permanent (McGaugh, 1966; M. R. Rosenzweig et al., 1993). The really long-lasting memories—the address of your childhood home, how to ride a bike, your first love—are called **long-term memories (LTMs)**, lasting from days to years.

A substantial body of evidence indicates that STM and LTM, in particular, rely on different processes to store information. A classic demonstration involves learning lists of words or numbers. If you hear a list of ten words and then try to repeat them back after a 30-second delay, you will probably do especially well with the earliest few words, termed a **primacy effect**, and with the last few words, termed a **recency effect**, and less well with words in the middle of the list. **Figure 17.6** shows typical results from such an experiment: a U-shaped *serial position curve*. If the delay prior to recall is a few minutes instead of a few seconds, there is no recency effect; the recency effect is short-lived and thus attributed to working memory (or STM). The primacy effect, however, lasts longer and is usually attributed to LTM. Like humans, various experimental animals show U-shaped serial position functions (A. A. Wright et al., 1985)—a finding that strengthens our confidence about the basic distinction between working memory and LTM.

Brain lesion studies corroborate the parallel between humans and experimental animals: Rats with hippocampal lesions exhibit the recency but not the primacy effect, as though, like Henry, they cannot form new LTMs (Kesner and Novak, 1982). Similarly, patients with amnesia caused by impairment of the hippocampus show a reduced primacy effect but retain the recency effect (see Figure 17.6). Pharmacological manipulations also indicate that the different stages of memory rely on separable physiological mechanisms, as reviewed in **A Step Further: Memories of Different Durations Form by Different Neurochemical Mechanisms** on the website.

Long-term memory is vast but subject to distortion

You might think it would be wonderful to effortlessly recall almost everything from your past, but studies of real-life cases reveal that perfect recall—for example, being able to remember in detail what you did on a specific date for each of the last 10 years—is a great burden. Without the usual process of pruning out unimportant memories, continual perfect recall can become uncontrollable, distracting, and exhausting (Luria, 1987; Parker et al., 2006). These cases also illustrate that the brain's memory systems—even the more fallible versions found in most of us—have the capability to retain vast amounts of information. We take this capacity for granted and barely notice, for example, that knowledge of a language involves remembering at least 100,000 pieces of information. Most of us also store a huge assortment of information about faces, tunes, odors, skills, stories, and so on.

Our memories are acquired rapidly and retained well. In one classic experiment, subjects viewed long sequences of color photos of various scenes; several days later, the subjects were shown pairs of images—in each case a new image plus one from the

17.6 Serial Position Curves from Immediate-Recall Experiments These curves show the percentage of correct responses for immediate recall of a list of ten words. The patients with amnesia performed as well on the most recent items (8–10) as the normal adults did, but they performed significantly worse on earlier items. (After Baddeley and Warrington, 1970.)

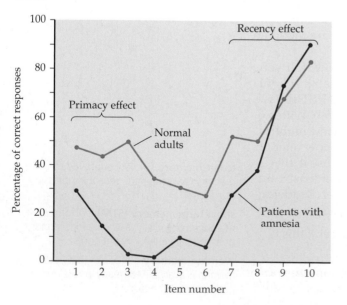

previous session—and asked to identify the images seen previously. Astonishingly, subjects performed with a high degree of accuracy for series of up to 10,000 different stimuli, prompting the researcher to conclude that for all practical purposes, "there is no upper bound to memory capacity" (Standing, 1973). Similar impressive feats of memory in our distant relatives, such as pigeons (Vaughan and Greene, 1984), illustrate that a great capacity for information storage is a general property of nervous systems across the animal kingdom.

Despite the vast capacity of LTM, we all normally forget information, or have inaccurate recollections. The discomfort felt by those rare people with perfect recall shows us that forgetting is a normal aspect of memory, helping to filter out unimportant information and freeing up needed cognitive resources (Kuhl et al., 2007). Interestingly, research indicates that the **memory trace** (the record laid down in memory by a learning experience) doesn't simply deteriorate from disuse and the passage of time; instead, memories tend to suffer interference from events before or after their formation.

For example, experiments show that each time a memory trace is activated during recall, it is subject to changes and fluctuations, so with successive activations it may deviate more and more from its original form. Furthermore, new information that is provided at the time of recall can add new aspects to the memory trace, so evoking the memory later is likely to reactivate the newer traces along with the older, and to produce distorted memories (Estes, 1997; Nader and Hardt, 2009).

Sometimes people can "remember" events that never happened. We can create false memories by asking leading questions—"Did you see the broken headlight?" rather than "Was the headlight broken?"—or by providing misinformation via trusted channels (Loftus, 2003). For example, by burying false details among biographical details provided to some subjects, researchers found it relatively easy to plant a memory of meeting a Bugs Bunny character at a Disney resort (Braun et al., 2002)—something that could never happen in real life (because Bugs is a Warner Brothers character).

This possibility of planting false memories clouds the issue of "recovered memories" of childhood sexual or physical abuse. Controversial therapeutic methods such as hypnosis or guided imagery (in which the patient is encouraged to imagine hypothetical abuse scenarios) can inadvertently plant false memories. Indeed, one study found that people who had "recovered" memories of childhood sexual abuse, when brought to the laboratory and asked to remember lists of words, were more easily manipulated into falsely remembering a word than were control subjects or people who had always remembered their childhood abuse (McNally, 2003).

Successive Processes Capture, Store, and Retrieve Information in the Brain

A functional memory system must incorporate three aspects of information processing: (1) **encoding** of raw information from sensory channels into short-term memory, (2) **consolidation** of the volatile short-term traces into more durable long-term memory, and (3) eventual **retrieval** of the stored information for use in future behavior (**Figure 17.7**). A problem with any of these processes can cause us to forget information.

Multiple brain regions are involved in encoding

A special "event-related" fMRI procedure has been used to study the encoding process (Rosen et al., 1998). First the brain was repeatedly and rapidly scanned while a series of stimulus items was presented. Then the fMRI activations elicited by individual items were classified according to whether subjects successfully recognized them later (indicating that successful encoding must have occurred) or failed to recognize them (no encoding). The analysis showed that although the stimuli activated many brain areas, only a few brain areas predicted which stimuli

memory trace A persistent change in the brain that reflects the storage of memory.

encoding A stage of memory formation in which the information entering sensory channels is passed into short-term memory.

consolidation A stage of memory formation in which information in short-term or intermediate-term memory is transferred to long-term memory.

retrieval A process in memory during which a stored memory is used by an organism.

17.7 Hypothesized Memory Processes: Encoding, Consolidation, and Retrieval

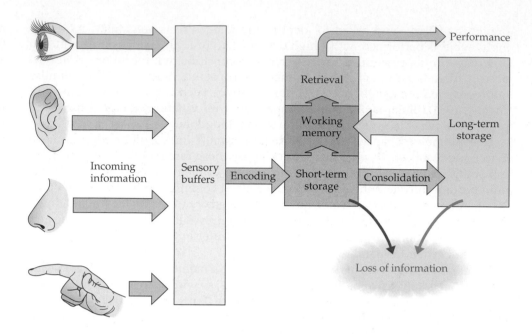

would later be recognized. When the stimuli were pictures (Brewer et al., 1998), the critical areas showing greater activation to correctly recalled stimuli were the right prefrontal cortex and the parahippocampal cortex in both hemispheres. In the case of words (A. D. Wagner et al., 1998), the critical areas were the *left* prefrontal cortex and the *left* parahippocampal cortex. The results thus indicate that parahippocampal and prefrontal cortex are crucial for consolidation, and these mechanisms reflect the hemispheric specializations (left hemisphere for language and right hemisphere for spatial ability) that we discuss in Chapter 19.

Different mechanisms are used for consolidating and retrieving declarative information

Studies of patients with brain injuries, like Henry Molaison, suggested that consolidation of declarative long-term memories takes considerable time and involves the hippocampus. Numerous additional studies using functional-imaging technology in normal subjects have confirmed the importance of the hippocampus for forming declarative memories, and further revealed that the formation and retrieval of memories rely on somewhat different parts of the hippocampal system (i.e., the hippocampus plus adjacent medial temporal cortex) (M. Lepage et al., 1998). But where are the new long-term memories actually being stored? Because Henry could recall events before his surgery, those memories must have been stored somewhere other than the hippocampus.

In laboratory studies investigating this question, animals received lesions of the hippocampal formation at various intervals after learning trials (J. J. Kim and Fanselow, 1992; Winocur, 1990; Zola-Morgan and Squire, 1990). Although some species differences emerged, in general the surgery impaired memory for items learned most recently before the surgery. Material learned a little bit earlier was unaffected. These results show that the hippocampal system cannot be a repository of long-term memory. In each of the animal experiments, it was possible to identify a time after learning when damage to the hippocampal system no longer affected the memory. Instead, although the hippocampus is important over the shorter term for *consolidation* of a memory, after that period the memory is *stored* in the cortex. An important principle that has emerged from this area of research is that *permanent storage of information tends to be in the regions of the cortex where the information was first processed and held in short-term memory*. For example, visual cortex is crucial for visual object recognition memory (López-Aranda et al., 2009).

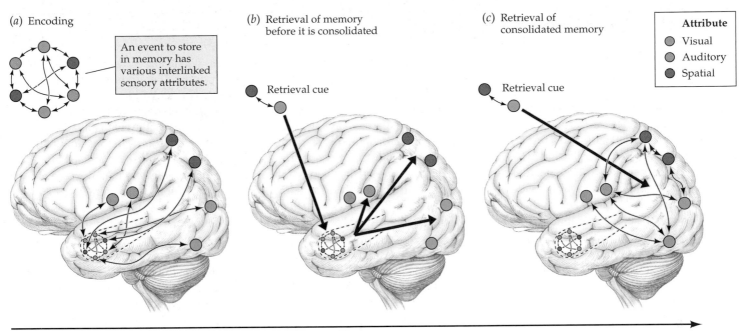

(a) Encoding

An event to store in memory has various interlinked sensory attributes.

(b) Retrieval of memory before it is consolidated

Retrieval cue

(c) Retrieval of consolidated memory

Retrieval cue

Attribute
- Visual
- Auditory
- Spatial

Time

17.8 Encoding, Consolidation, and Retrieval of Declarative Memories (a) According to this model, medial temporal lobe processes distribute the various sensory attributes of an event, and linkages between them, in corresponding regions of cortex. (b) Before consolidation is complete, retrieval involves the hippocampus and other medial temporal structures. (c) After consolidation, retrieval may occur independent of the medial temporal system.

After further processing that involves the medial temporal region, the permanent memory storage becomes independent and memories can be retrieved directly for use by other cognitive processes. This schema is illustrated in **Figure 17.8**.

Not all memories are created equal. We all know from firsthand experience that emotion can powerfully enhance our memory for past events. For example, an emotionally arousing story is remembered significantly better than a closely matched but emotionally neutral story (Reisberg and Heuer, 1995). But if people are treated with propranolol (a beta-adrenergic antagonist, or "beta-blocker," that blocks the effects of epinephrine) this emotional enhancement of memory vanishes. It's not that treated subjects perceive the story as being any less emotional; in fact, treated subjects rate the emotional content of the stories just the same as untreated subjects do. Instead, the evidence indicates that propranolol directly interferes with the ability of adrenal stress hormones to act on brain substrates to enhance memory (Cahill et al., 1994). **Box 17.2** delves further into this topic.

Physiological mechanisms of memory *retrieval* have received much less attention than mechanisms of memory *formation*. However, several studies have found that the process of retrieving information from LTM causes the memories to become temporarily unstable, and susceptible to disruption or alteration before undergoing **reconsolidation** and returning to stable status (Nader and Hardt, 2009). It thus seems that using memories makes them plastic again, and amenable to updating; this is especially true for memories that most potently control ongoing behavior (Debiec et al., 2002; Eisenberg et al., 2003).

This finding agrees with the observation that a dialogue between cortical and hippocampal sites directs the consolidation process (Remondes and Schuman, 2004). LTM updating and reconsolidation are specifically limited to memory traces directly activated by the task being performed; associated memories and other aspects of the memory network, although they may be activated through indirect means, do not become labile again (Debiec et al., 2006). So perhaps it's not surprising that one of the best ways to improve learning is simply repeated retrieval (and thus, repeated reconsolidation) of the stored information (Karpicke and Roediger, 2008). For your next exam, try making up some practice tests for yourself, or have a friend quiz you, instead of simply "cramming."

reconsolidation The return of a memory trace to stable long-term storage after it has been temporarily made volatile during the process of recall.

BOX 17.2 Emotions and Memory

Almost everyone knows from personal experience that strong emotions can potently enhance memory formation and retrieval. Examples of memories enhanced in this way might include a strong association between special music and a first kiss, or uncomfortably vivid recollection of the morning of September 11, 2001. A large-scale research effort in many labs has identified a suite of biochemical agents that participate in the emotional enhancement of memory. These compounds include acetylcholine, epinephrine, norepinephrine, vasopressin, the opioids, and GABA (gamma-aminobutyric acid), as well as drugs that act as agonists and antagonists of these agents.

Epinephrine (adrenaline), released in large quantities during times of stress and strong emotion, appears to affect memory formation by influencing the amygdala, especially the basolateral part. Electrical stimulation or lesions of the amygdala potently alter the memory-enhancing effects of injections of epinephrine (Cahill and McGaugh, 1991), and tiny doses of epinephrine injected directly into the amygdala enhance memory formation in the same way that systemic injections do. This treatment appears to cause the release of norepinephrine within the amygdala, as do emotional experiences. Injecting propranolol, a blocker of beta-adrenergic receptors, into the amygdala blocks the memory-enhancing effects. Opioid peptides also block the release of norepinephrine (NE) in the amygdala and elsewhere in the brain.

A functional model of the basolateral amygdala (BLA), and the endogenous and exogenous compounds that affect this memory system, is presented in the figure. In this model (McGaugh, 2003), activity in four main hormone/transmitter systems that signal aspects of memory—adrenergic, opioid, GABA-ergic and cholinergic inputs—converge on and are integrated in the BLA. Outputs of the BLA, in turn, project widely to brain regions including the hippocampus, caudate, and cortex, influencing memory formation in these locations (McGaugh, 2003; McIntyre et

al., 2005). Drugs that alter the biochemical messages to the BLA may potently alter the effect of emotion on memory. For example, if people who have just had a traumatic experience are given the beta-adrenergic antagonist propranolol, which blocks the effects of epinephrine, their memory for the event is significantly reduced when tested months later (Pitman et al., 2002). Alternatively, manipulations of the stress hormone cortisol have been reported to reduce symptoms caused by the memories of posttraumatic stress (de Quervain, 2006), and knocking out BLA neurons that are overexpressing CREB (cAMP responsive element–binding protein) can selectively erase fear memories in mice (J. H. Han et al., 2009). So, can we develop pharmacological treatments to weaken or erase unwanted memories?

People who have had life-threatening or other catastrophic experiences often develop **posttraumatic stress disorder (PTSD)**, characterized as "reliving experiences such as intrusive thoughts, nightmares, dissociative flashbacks to elements of the original traumatic event, and … preoccupation with that event" (Keane, 1998, p. 398). In PTSD, each recurrence of the strong emotions and memories of the traumatic event may reactivate memories that, when reconsolidated in the presence

of stress signals like epinephrine, become even stronger. Therefore, one strategy to prevent PTSD formation could be to block the effects of epinephrine in the BLA system by treating victims with antiadrenergic drugs either shortly before a traumatic experience (e.g., in rescue workers) or as quickly as possible after it (in the case of victims of violence, for example) (Cahill, 1997). This treatment would not delete memories of the event but might diminish the traumatic aspects, and it might also be useful for weakening existing traumatic memories. A study with rats found that, when a previously formed memory is reactivated, it can be weakened by administration of propranolol up to 2 hours after reactivation of the memory (Przybyslawski et al., 1999; Sara, 2000).

Perhaps one day it will be possible to selectively interfere with several of the neurotransmitters at work in the amygdala (see the figure) to provide more-specific and more-complete relief from traumatic memories. Even so, the treatment would probably have to be administered soon after the accident to effectively dull the painful memories.

posttraumatic stress disorder (PTSD) A disorder in which memories of an unpleasant episode repeatedly plague the victim.

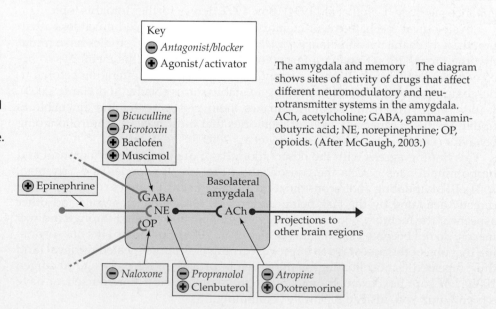

The amygdala and memory   The diagram shows sites of activity of drugs that affect different neuromodulatory and neurotransmitter systems in the amygdala. ACh, acetylcholine; GABA, gamma-aminobutyric acid; NE, norepinephrine; OP, opioids. (After McGaugh, 2003.)

Different Brain Regions Process Different Aspects of Memory

In this section we will first consider the roles of different parts of the medial temporal lobe in the formation of declarative memory, and then take up how other parts of the brain are involved in the formation of memories for specific aspects of experience.

Medial temporal lobe structures are crucial for declarative memory

Publication of Henry Molaison's case prompted an intensive effort to develop methods for systematically studying declarative memory in monkeys and other lab animals. For example, in the **delayed non-matching-to-sample task** (**Figure 17.9**)—a test of *object recognition memory*—monkeys must identify which of two objects was *not* seen previously, with delays ranging from 8 seconds to 2 minutes (Spiegler and Mishkin, 1981). Monkeys with extensive damage to the medial temporal lobe, and thus similar to Henry, are severely impaired on this task, especially with the longer delays. But which specific temporal lobe structures are most important?

Selective removal of specific parts of the medial temporal lobes of monkeys revealed that the amygdala—one of the structures removed in Henry's surgery—was not crucial for performance on tests of declarative memory. However, removal of the adjacent hippocampus significantly impaired performance on these tests and, as shown in **Figure 17.10**, the deficit was even more pronounced when the hippocampal damage was paired with lesions of the nearby entorhinal and parahippocampal cortex, and much worse when lesions of perirhinal cortex were added (Zola-Morgan et al., 1994). Human patients similarly show larger impairments when both the hippocampus and medial temporal cortex are damaged (Rempel-Clower et al., 1996; Zola-Morgan and Squire, 1986).

Overall, the performance of experimental animals on tests of declarative memory suggests that the hippocampus acts as the final stage of convergence for combining operations of the adjacent, more specialized regions of cortex (Zola et al., 2000), resulting in storage of information about the relationships between stimuli across different points in time and different sensory modalities. Working as a unit, the hippocampus and perirhinal cortex appear to be crucial for the recollection of facts and events, and also for our sense of familiarity when we recognize something that we have been exposed to previously (Squire et al., 2007).

delayed non-matching-to-sample task A test in which the subject must respond to the unfamiliar stimulus of a pair.

Sample

Test

Food found under the nonmatching object

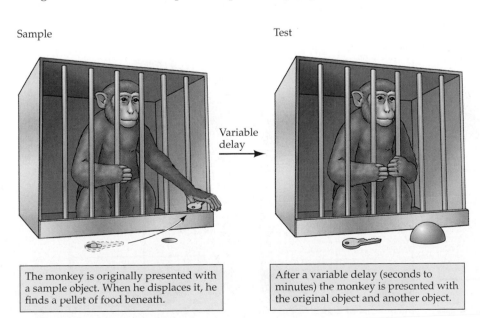

| The monkey is originally presented with a sample object. When he displaces it, he finds a pellet of food beneath. | After a variable delay (seconds to minutes) the monkey is presented with the original object and another object. | Over a series of trials with different pairs of objects, the monkey learns that food is present under the object that differs from the sample. |

Variable delay

17.9 The Delayed Non-Matching-to-Sample Task

(a) Ventral view of monkey brain showing areas of different medial temporal lesions

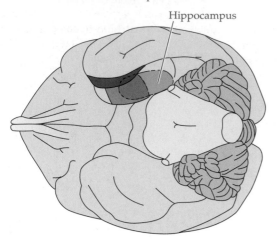

Hippocampus

(b) Scores of groups with different lesions

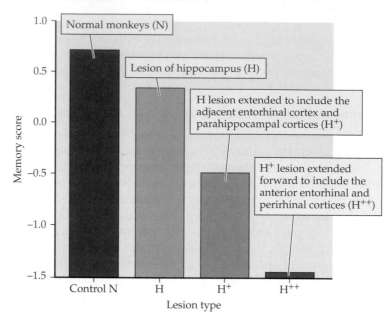

17.10 Memory Performance after Medial Temporal Lobe Lesions (a) In this ventral view of a monkey brain, the hippocampus is embedded beneath (dorsal to) the entorhinal cortex (orange) and perirhinal cortex (yellow). The parahippocampal cortex is shown in green. (b) Different bilateral lesions of the medial temporal lobe yielded different results in tests of memory. (Part a after Squire and Zola-Morgan, 1991).

Imaging studies have revealed much about declarative memory

As expected from the studies of patients with amnesia and of lesioned lab animals already discussed, brain-imaging studies confirm the crucial importance of medial temporal (hippocampal) and diencephalic systems in forming long-term memories. These regions are activated during both encoding of new material and retrieval (Schacter et al., 1996; Tulving et al., 1996). But as we mentioned earlier, long-term storage appears to depend on the cortex.

Some patients with lesions of the cortex seem to lose their memory of specific categories of objects, such as animals, names of different tools, or brands of automobiles. Neuroimaging studies of normal subjects are consistent with the observations in people with cortical damage. For example, asking subjects to name tools or animals activates cortical regions that overlap in some areas but differ in others (A. Martin et al., 1996).

17.11 My Story versus Your Story Autobiographical passages (a) cause greater activation of the right frontal and temporal lobes than do nonautobiographical passages (b). (After G. R. Fink et al., 1996; courtesy of Gereon Fink.)

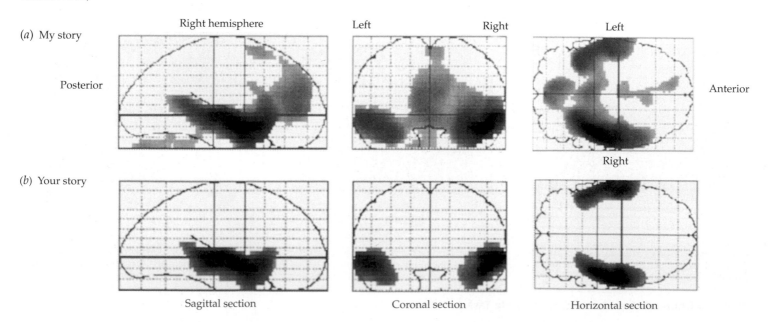

Brain imaging has also been used to study the distinction between *semantic* (general) memory and *episodic* (autobiographical) memory, exemplified by patient K.C., in normal subjects. In one study, subjects listened to autobiographical passages and to passages written by other people (G. R. Fink et al., 1996). The autobiographical passages, relative to the others, caused greater activation of right frontal and temporal lobe regions, as **Figure 17.11** shows. Thus, autobiographical memories and semantic memories appear to be processed in different locations.

Hippocampal mechanisms are important in spatial memory

The caricature of the white-coated biopsychologist watching rats run in mazes, a staple of cartoonists to this day (**Figure 17.12**), has its origins in the intensive memory research of the early twentieth century. The early work indicated that rats and other animals don't just learn a series of turns but instead form a **cognitive map** (an understanding of the *relative* spatial organization of objects and information) in order to solve a maze (Tolman, 1949). Animals apparently learn at least some of these details of their spatial environment simply by moving through it—an example of **latent learning** (Tolman and Honzik, 1930).

We now know that, in parallel with its role in other types of declarative memory, the hippocampus is a crucial neural participant in spatial learning. Within the rat hippocampus are found many neurons that selectively encode spatial location (O'Keefe and Dostrovsky, 1971; Leutgeb et al., 2005). These **place cells** become active when the animal is in—or moving toward—a particular location. If placed in a new environment, place cell activity indicates that the hippocampus remaps to the new locations (Moita et al., 2004).

Two types of cells discovered in nearby entorhinal cortex probably help the animal to learn the local spatial environment. **Grid cells** are entorhinal neurons that fire selectively when the animal crosses the intersection points of an abstract grid map of the local environment, acting like an innate system of latitude and longitude (Hafting et al., 2005). Arrival at the perimeter of the local spatial map is signaled by the activation of entorhinal **border cells** (Solstad et al., 2008).

The monkey hippocampus contains place cells (Rolls and O'Mara, 1995) and also features *spatial view cells* that respond to the part of the environment that the monkey is looking at, perhaps reflecting the importance of vision for primates. This type of connection, between hippocampal features and the ecology of individual species, illustrates how evolution has shaped species-specific memory abilities. As we'll discuss later in the chapter, learning can be demonstrated in almost all animals, possibly even unicellular organisms, indicating that the ability to retain information was an early evolutionary development. The *specific* abilities to learn and remember that each species has evolved are determined by the selective pressures they have experienced within their particular ecological niches (J. L. Gould, 1986; Sherry and Schacter, 1987).

SPATIAL MEMORY AND THE EVOLUTION OF HIPPOCAMPAL SIZE Careful comparisons of natural behavior and brain anatomy have revealed that for many species, their manner of making a living has left an imprint on the hippocampus. For example, species of birds that hide caches of food in spatially scattered locations are reliably found to have larger hippocampi than noncaching species, even when the comparison species are very close relatives that have otherwise similar lifestyles (Krebs et al., 1989; Sherry, 1992; Sherry et al., 1989) (see Figure 6.7). Lesions of the hippocampus impair the ability of these birds to store and retrieve caches of food (Sherry and Vaccarino, 1989). Homing pigeons also have enlarged hippocampi relative to other varieties of pigeons, presumably serving the spatial demands of their prodigious navigational abilities (Rehkamper et al., 1988). A relation-

cognitive map A mental representation of a spatial relationship.

latent learning Learning that has taken place but has not (yet) been demonstrated by performance.

place cell A neuron within the hippocampus that selectively fires when the animal is in a particular location.

grid cell A neuron that selectively fires when the animal crosses the intersection points of an abstract grid map of the local environment.

border cell A neuron that selectively fires when the animal arrives at the perimeter of the local spatial cognitive map.

17.12 Biological Psychologists at Work We don't all like weird hairdos. Or mazes.

(a) Size of home range

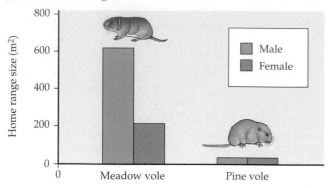

(b) Ranking in spatial learning

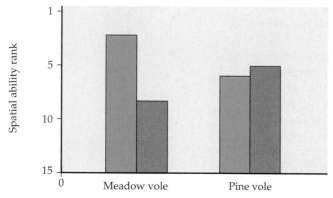

(c) Relative hippocampal size

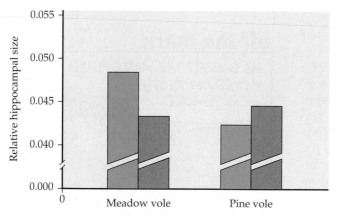

17.13 Sex, Memory, and Hippocampal Size   Males and females of two species of voles were compared on three variables: (a) size of home range, (b) score on a spatial learning task, and (c) hippocampal size divided by brain size. (After L. F. Jacobs et al., 1990.)

ship between spatial cognition and hippocampal size is evident in mammals too. Just as with the food-caching birds, Merriam's kangaroo rat, which stashes food in scattered locations, has a significantly larger hippocampus than its noncaching cousin, the bannertail kangaroo rat (L. F. Jacobs and Spencer, 1994).

In voles, mating strategies and sex differences in spatial behavior, rather than food caching, seem to have shaped the hippocampus. In nature, pine voles and prairie voles are monogamous, and males and females have comparably sized home ranges. But their close relatives, the meadow voles, are polygynous, so meadow vole males' home ranges are much larger and encompass the home ranges of several females. In meadow voles, but not in pine voles, males have larger hippocampi than females (L. F. Jacobs et al., 1990), reflecting this sex-related species difference in spatial processing (**Figure 17.13**). Accordingly, when studied in the laboratory, a significant male-favoring sex difference in spatial ability is found only for the meadow voles (Gaulin and Fitzgerald, 1989). Even within individual life spans, spatial learning can change the anatomy of the hippocampus. For a fascinating example in humans, see **A Step Further: Mastering London Topography Changes Hippocampal Structure in Taxi Drivers** on the website.

Imaging studies help us understand nondeclarative memory

As noted earlier, three major categories of nondeclarative (procedural) memory are skill learning, repetition priming, and conditioning. Each of these types of nondeclarative memory has been investigated with modern functional-imaging technology.

SKILL MEMORY   Imaging studies have investigated learning and memory for different kinds of skills, including *sensorimotor skills* (e.g., mirror tracing; see Figure 17.2), *perceptual skills* (e.g., learning to read mirror-reversed text), and *cognitive skills* (tasks involving planning and problem solving, common in puzzles like the Tower of Hanoi problem, which you can play on the website). All three kinds of skill learning are impaired in people with damage to the basal ganglia; damage to other brain regions, especially the motor cortex and cerebellum, also affects aspects of some skills.

Neuroimaging studies confirm that the basal ganglia, cerebellum, and motor cortex are important for sensorimotor skill learning in normal people (Grafton et al., 1992). For example, learning specific sequences of finger movements is associated with selective activation of motor cortex and the basal ganglia (Doyon et al., 1996; Hazeltine et al., 1997), with the cerebellum possibly providing error correction during learning (Flament et al., 1996). Often the activations shift among brain regions as performance changes during the course of learning, so learning appears to involve a complex set of interacting neural networks.

REPETITION PRIMING   We mentioned earlier that priming is a change in the processing of a stimulus due to prior exposure to the same or a related stimulus. Priming does not require declarative memory of the stimulus—Henry Molaison and other patients with amnesia show priming for words they don't remember having seen. In contrast with skill learning, tests of priming are not impaired by damage to the basal ganglia.

In functional-imaging studies, perceptual priming (priming based on the visual *form* of words) is related to *reduced* activity in bilateral occipitotemporal cortex (Schacter et al., 1996), presumably because the priming makes the task easier. Conceptual priming (priming based on word *meaning*) is associated with reduced activation of the left frontal cortex (Blaxton et al., 1996; Gabrieli et al., 1996; A. D. Wagner et al., 1997).

CONDITIONING Experimental evidence in lab animals, which we will discuss later in the chapter, shows that cerebellar circuits are crucial for simple eye-blink conditioning, in which a tone or other stimulus is associated with eye blinking in response to a puff of air (see Box 17.1 for a discussion of conditioning). A PET study of human eye-blink conditioning (Logan and Grafton, 1995) found that in the course of conditioning, there was a progressive increase in activity in several regions of the brain, including not only the cerebellum, but also the hippocampus, the ventral striatum, and regions of the cerebral cortex. But activity in these other areas may not be *essential* for eye-blink conditioning in the way that the cerebellum is. For example, patients with hippocampal lesions can acquire the conditioned eye-blink response, but patients with unilateral cerebellar damage can acquire a conditioned eye-blink response only on the side where the cerebellum is intact (Papka et al., 1994).

A variety of brain regions are involved in different attributes of working memory

Because they span verbal and nonverbal material, in multiple sensory modalities, for multiple purposes, working memories tend to have unique features or attributes. So, for example, an individual memory may include a mix of information about space, time, sensory perception, response, and/or affect (i.e., emotional factors). Researchers have attempted to devise memory tasks that selectively tap some of these attributes of memory, in order to assess the relative contributions of different regions of the brain.

Figure 17.14 presents some examples of tests used to probe working memory (Kesner, 1998; Kesner et al., 1993). For testing *spatial* location memory, the well-known eight-arm radial maze was used (**Figure 17.14a**). To solve this task correctly and receive a food reward, rats must recognize and enter an arm of the maze that they have been down shortly beforehand. Rats were tested following surgical lesions of the hippocampus, the caudate nucleus, or the extrastriate cortex (visual cortex outside the primary visual area). Only the animals with hippocampal lesions were impaired on this predominantly spatial task—a result that is consistent with the role of the hippocampus in spatial cognition that we discussed earlier. The test shown in **Figure 17.14b** was used to assess the memory of the same rats for their own *motor* behavior. Here the animal must use working memory to remember whether it made a left or right turn a few moments previously, and it receives a food reward only if it makes a turn in the same direction on a follow-up trial. Only the animals with lesions of the caudate nucleus were significantly impaired on this task. Finally, in the test depicted in **Figure 17.14c** the rats were required to hold in working memory the *sensory* attributes of presented stimuli, identifying the novel stimulus in each pair of stimuli presented. Here, only the rats with extrastriate lesions were significantly impaired. This impressive lack of overlap between the symptoms of the different lesions nicely illustrates how memories involving different attributes are parceled out to diverse brain regions for storage.

It's perhaps not surprising that the brain regions that do the initial processing of the stimuli often also act as the memory buffers for holding the stimuli in working memory—visual information in visual cortex, motor information in motor areas, and so on. One additional common attribute of working memory is the passage of time—a delay between stimulus and response during which information must be

(*a*) Spatial-location recognition memory

In the study phase of each trial, the rat can choose any of the eight arms. In the test phase, doors block all but two arms: the arm entered in the study phase and one other. The rat obtains food only if it chooses the arm it entered in the study phase.

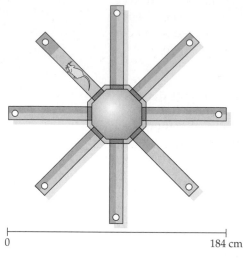

0   184 cm

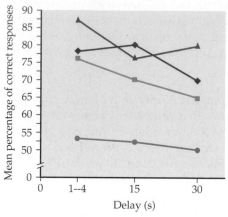

Brain region lesioned
● Hippocampus
■ Control
▲ Caudate nucleus
◆ Extrastriate visual cortex

Only rats with hippo-campal lesions are impaired, relative to controls.

(*b*) Response recognition memory

In the first part of each trial, the rat is placed in the middle compart-ment on one side (2), and it finds food if it enters the compartment to either its right (1) or its left (3). In the second part of the trial, it is placed in the middle compartment on the other side (5), and it finds food only if it turns to the same side of its body as in the first part.

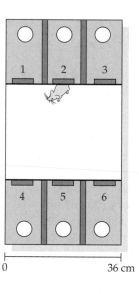

0   36 cm

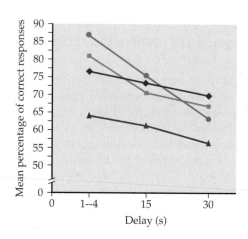

Brain region lesioned
● Hippocampus
■ Control
▲ Caudate nucleus
◆ Extrastriate visual cortex

Only rats with caudate nucleus lesions are impaired, relative to controls.

(*c*) Object recognition memory (non-matching-to-sample)

In the study phase of each trial, the rat obtains food by displacing a sample object over a small food well (top). In the test phase (bottom), the rat chooses between two objects and obtains food only if it chooses the object that does *not* match the sample.

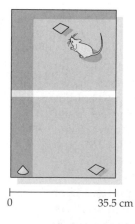

0   35.5 cm

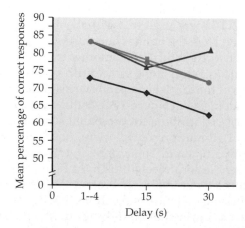

Brain region lesioned
● Hippocampus
■ Control
▲ Caudate nucleus
◆ Extrastriate visual cortex

Only rats with lesions of the extrastriate visual cortex are impaired, relative to controls.

17.14 Tests of Specific Attributes of Memory Brain lesion experiments testing spatial-location recognition (*a*), response recognition (*b*), and object recognition (*c*)—using the setups shown on the left—yielded the results shown on the right. (After Kesner et al., 1993.)

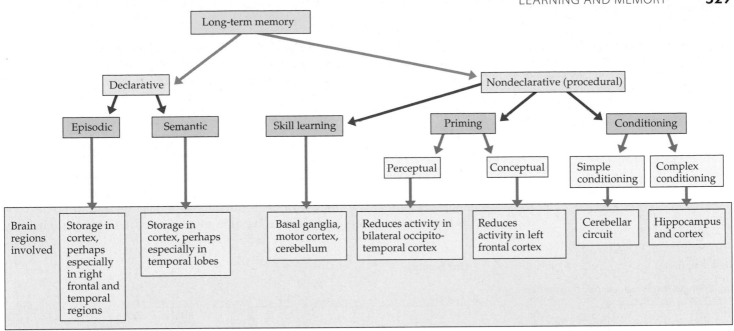

17.15 Brain Regions Involved in Different Kinds of Learning and Memory

held ready for further processing. Delayed-response tasks, which tap this aspect of working memory by varying the delay between presentation and removal of a stimulus and making a response, are especially associated with activity of the prefrontal cortex—particularly the dorsolateral parts—in humans and experimental animals (Funahashi, 2006; H. C. Leung et al., 2002, 2005).

Brain regions involved in learning and memory: An interim summary

Figure 17.15 updates and summarizes the taxonomy of long-term memory that we have been discussing. Several major conclusions should be apparent by now, especially (1) that many regions of the brain are involved in learning and memory; (2) that different forms of memory rely on at least partly different brain mechanisms, which may include several different regions of the brain; and (3) that the same brain structure can be a part of the circuitry for several different forms of learning.

Neural Mechanisms of Memory

What are the basic molecular, synaptic, and cellular events that store information in the nervous system? The remainder of this chapter concerns the cellular and physiological underpinnings of memory. We will look at some of the ways in which new learning involves changes in the strength of existing synapses, and the biochemical signals that may produce those changes. We'll consider how the formation of memories may require the formation of new synapses, or even the birth of new neurons. The observation that **neuroplasticity** (or **neural plasticity**)—the ability of neurons and neural circuits to be remodeled by events—is found in virtually all animals indicates that it is an ancient and vital product of evolution.

Memory Storage Requires Neuronal Remodeling

In introducing the term *synapse,* Charles Sherrington (1897) speculated that synaptic alterations might be the basis of learning, anticipating an area of research that to this day is one of the most intensive efforts in all of neuroscience. Modern ideas about neuroplasticity have their origins in the theories of Donald Hebb (1949), who proposed that when a presynaptic and a postsynaptic neuron are repeatedly activated together, the synaptic connection between them will become stronger and more stable (the oft-repeated maxim "cells that fire together wire together"

neuroplasticity or neural plasticity The ability of the nervous system to change in response to experience or the environment.

cell assembly   A large group of cells that tend to be active at the same time because they have been activated simultaneously or in close succession in the past.

Hebbian synapse   A synapse that is strengthened when it successfully drives the postsynaptic cell.

captures the basic idea). Ensembles of neurons, or **cell assemblies**, linked via synchronized activity of these **Hebbian synapses** (see also Figure 7.22), could then act together to store memory traces. It was an idea that would eventually be confirmed in various brain tissues, including the hippocampus (e.g., Kelso and Brown, 1986). Most current theories of the cellular basis of learning focus on plasticity of the structure and physiological functioning of synapses.

Plastic changes at synapses can be physiological or structural

Synaptic changes that may store information can be measured physiologically. The changes could be presynaptic, postsynaptic, or both (**Figure 17.16a**). Such changes include greater release of neurotransmitter molecules and/or greater effects because the receptor molecules become more numerous or more sensitive.

Before training   **After training**

(*a*) Changes involving synaptic transmitters

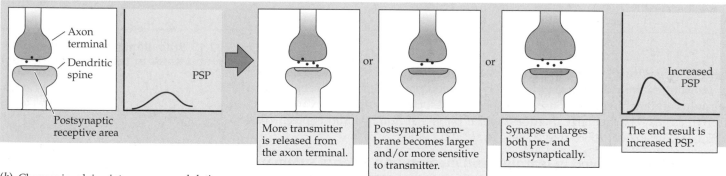

(*b*) Changes involving interneuron modulation

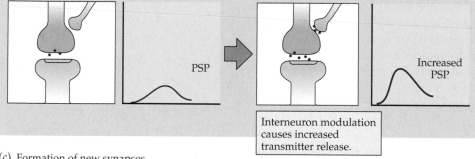

(*c*) Formation of new synapses

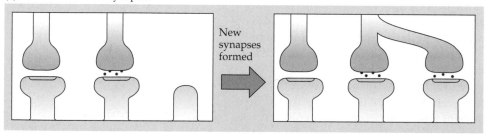

(*d*) Rearrangement of synaptic input

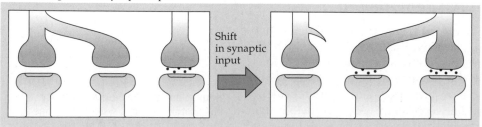

17.16 Synaptic Changes That May Store Memories   After training, each action potential in the relevant neural circuit causes increased release of transmitter molecules (red dots). The postsynaptic potential (PSP) therefore increases in size, as indicated by the graphs in (*a*) and (*b*). (*a*) Several different changes in the synapse each result in an increase in size of the PSP. (*b*) An interneuron modulates polarization of the axon terminal and causes the release of more transmitter molecules per nerve impulse. (*c*) A neural circuit that is used more often increases the number of synaptic contacts. (*d*) A more frequently used neural pathway takes over synaptic sites formerly occupied by a less active competitor.

The result of such changes would be an increase in the size of the postsynaptic potential. Changes in the rate of inactivation of the transmitter (through reuptake or enzymatic degradation) could produce a similar effect.

Synaptic activity could also be modulated by inputs from other neurons (members of the same or other cell assemblies) causing extra depolarization or hyperpolarization of the axon terminals and changes in the amount of neurotransmitter released (**Figure 17.16b**).

Long-term memories may require changes in the nervous system so substantial that they can be directly observed (with the aid of a microscope, of course). Structural changes resulting from use are apparent in other parts of the body. For example, exercise changes the mass and/or shape of muscles and bone. In a similar way, new synapses could form or synapses could be eliminated as a function of training (**Figure 17.16c**).

Training could also lead to reorganization of synaptic connections. For example, it could cause a more used pathway to take over sites formerly occupied by a less active competitor (**Figure 17.16d**).

Varied experiences and learning cause the brain to change and grow

The remarkable plasticity of the brain is not all that difficult to demonstrate. Simply living in a complex environment, with its many opportunities for new learning, produces pronounced biochemical and anatomical changes in the brains of rats (E. L. Bennett et al., 1964, 1969; Renner and Rosenzweig, 1987; M. R. Rosenzweig, 1984; M. R. Rosenzweig et al., 1961). This area of research is covered in more detail in **A Step Further: Cerebral Changes Result from Training** on the website.

In standard studies of environmental enrichment, rats are randomly assigned to three housing conditions:

1. **Standard condition (SC)**. Animals are housed in small groups in standard lab cages (**Figure 17.17a**). This is the typical environment for laboratory animals.

standard condition (SC) The usual environment for laboratory rodents, with a few animals in a cage and adequate food and water, but no complex stimulation.

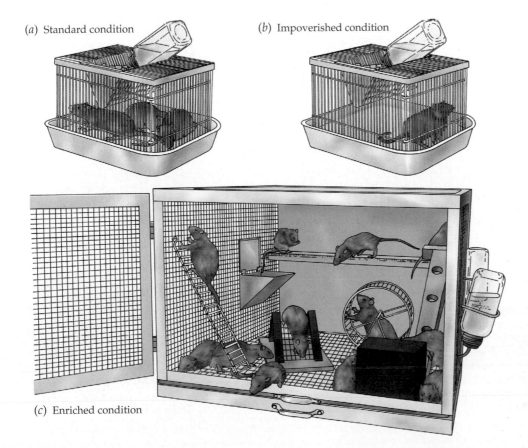

(a) Standard condition

(b) Impoverished condition

(c) Enriched condition

17.17 Experimental Environments to Test the Effects of Enrichment on Learning and Brain Measures Interaction with an enriched environment has measurable effects on the brain, on stress reactions, and on learning.

impoverished condition (IC) Also called *isolated condition*. A condition in which laboratory rodents are housed singly in a small cage without complex stimuli.

enriched condition (EC) Also called *complex environment*. A condition in which laboratory rodents are group-housed with a wide variety of stimulus objects.

2. **Impoverished condition (IC).** Animals are housed individually in standard lab cages (**Figure 17.17***b*).
3. **Enriched condition (EC).** Animals are housed in large social groups in special cages containing various toys and other interesting features (**Figure 17.17***c*). This condition provides enhanced opportunities for learning perceptual and motor skills, social learning, and so on.

In dozens of studies over several decades, a variety of plastic changes in the brain have been linked to such environmental enrichment. For example, compared to IC animals (or SC animals in many cases):

- EC animals have heavier, thicker cortex, especially in somatosensory and visual cortical areas (M. C. Diamond, 1967; M. R. Rosenzweig et al., 1962).
- EC animals show enhanced cholinergic activity throughout the cortex (Rosenzweig et al., 1961).
- EC animals have more dendritic branches, especially on dendrites closer to the cell body (called basal *dendrites*). EC animals also have many more dendritic spines on those branches, suggesting that EC animals have more numerous synapses and more elaborate information-processing circuitry than IC animals have (Globus et al., 1973; Greenough, 1976; Greenough and Volkmar, 1973) (**Figure 17.18**).
- EC animals have *larger* cortical synapses (M. C. Diamond et al., 1975; Greenough and Volkmar, 1973), consistent with the storage of long-term memory in cortical areas through Hebbian changes in synapses and circuits.
- EC animals exhibit altered expression of a variety of genes related to neuronal structure and physiology, and thus possibly involved in memory processes (Rampon, Tang, et al., 2000).

(*a*)

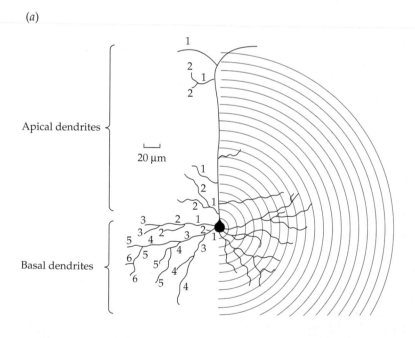

(*b*) Apical dendrites

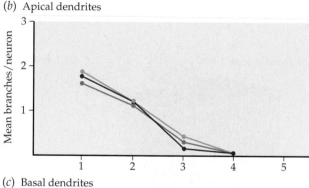

(*c*) Basal dendrites

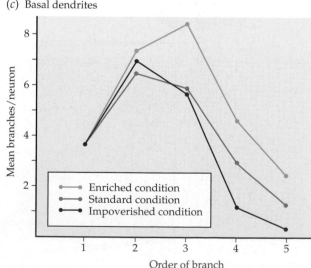

17.18 Measurement of Dendritic Branching (*a*) An enlarged photograph of a neuron is used to quantify branching either by counts of the number of branches of different orders (*left*), or by counts of the number of intersections with concentric rings (*right*). (*b, c*) These results were obtained by counts of the number of branches on apical dendrites (*b*) and basal dendrites (*c*). There are significant differences in branching, especially in the basal dendrites, among rats kept for 30 days in enriched, standard, or impoverished environments. (From Greenough, 1976.)

- EC animals show enhanced recovery from brain damage (Will et al., 2004).

Rats are not the only animals to benefit from environmental enrichment. Similar effects on brain processes and behavior are seen in fishes, birds, mice, cats, and monkeys (Rampon and Tsien, 2000; Renner and Rosenzweig, 1987; van Praag et al., 2000). And the evidence indicates that the human brain is no exception: for example, we saw in Chapter 11 that the hand area of the motor cortex becomes larger in musicians, presumably because of their extensive practice. In another example, 100 children assigned to a 2-year enriched nursery school program showed improvements in tests of orienting and arousal when reassessed at age 11 (Raine et al., 2001). And as we will see later in this chapter, enriched experience also appears to protect against age-related declines in memory, both in laboratory animals and in humans.

Thus, the cerebral effects of experience that were surprising when first reported for rats in the early 1960s are now seen to occur widely in the animal kingdom—from flies to philosophers (Mohammed, 2001). But how can we study the physiology of learning when the mammalian cortex has many billions of neurons, organized in vast networks, and upwards of a billion synapses per cubic centimeter (Merchán-Pérez et al., 2009)? Researchers have made progress by studying simple learning circuits, in various species including mammals, to uncover basic cellular principles of memory formation that may generalize to neurons at all levels of the nervous system.

Invertebrate Nervous Systems Show Plasticity

As we've discussed, neuroplasticity and the ability to learn are ancient adaptations found throughout the animal kingdom. At the neuronal level, even species that are only remotely related likely share the same basic cellular processes for information storage. Consequently, one fruitful research strategy has been to focus on memory mechanisms in the very simple nervous systems of certain invertebrates. Invertebrate nervous systems have relatively few neurons (on the order of hundreds to tens of thousands). Because these neurons are arranged identically in different individuals, it is possible to construct detailed neural circuit diagrams for particular behaviors and study the same few neurons in multiple individuals. An especially successful program of research focused on the sea slug *Aplysia* (Kandel, 2009; Kandel et al., 1987).

If you squirt water at an *Aplysia*'s *siphon*—a tube through which it draws water—the animal protectively retracts its delicate gill (**Figure 17.19**). But with repeated stimulation the animal retracts the gill less and less, as it learns that the stimulation represents no danger to the gill. Kandel and associates demonstrated that this habituation—a form of nonassociative learning (see Box 17.1)—is caused by changes in the synapse between the sensory cell that detects the squirt of water and the motoneuron that retracts the gill. As this synapse releases less and less transmitter, the gill slowly stops retracting in response to the stimulation (**Figure 17.20a**) (M. Klein et al., 1980). So in this case the synaptic plasticity underlying learning is within the reflex circuit itself.

Similarly, both the number and the size of synaptic junctions vary with training in *Aplysia*. For example, if an *Aplysia* is tested in the habituation paradigm over a series of days, each successive day the animal habituates faster than it did the day before. This phenomenon represents long-term habituation (as opposed to the

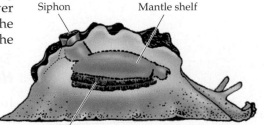

17.19 The Sea Slug *Aplysia* In the usual posture, the siphon is extended and the gill is spread out on the back. Ordinarily only the tip of the siphon would be visible in a lateral view; here, the rest of the siphon and the gill are shown as if the animal were transparent.

17.20 Synaptic Plasticity Underlying Habituation in *Aplysia*

(a) Short-term habituation

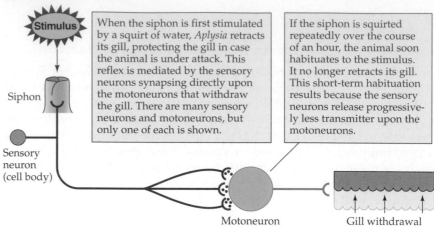

When the siphon is first stimulated by a squirt of water, *Aplysia* retracts its gill, protecting the gill in case the animal is under attack. This reflex is mediated by the sensory neurons synapsing directly upon the motoneurons that withdraw the gill. There are many sensory neurons and motoneurons, but only one of each is shown.

If the siphon is squirted repeatedly over the course of an hour, the animal soon habituates to the stimulus. It no longer retracts its gill. This short-term habituation results because the sensory neurons release progressively less transmitter upon the motoneurons.

(b) Long-term habituation

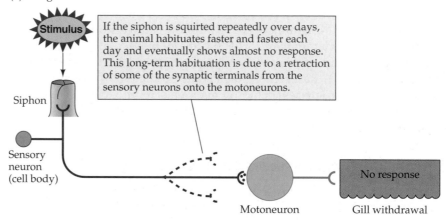

If the siphon is squirted repeatedly over days, the animal habituates faster and faster each day and eventually shows almost no response. This long-term habituation is due to a retraction of some of the synaptic terminals from the sensory neurons onto the motoneurons.

short-term habituation that we've already discussed), and in this case there is a reduction in the number of synapses between the sensory cell and the motoneuron (**Figure 17.20*b***) (C. H. Bailey and Chen, 1983).

Elements of the *Aplysia* gill withdrawal system are similarly capable of sensitization (a different form of nonassociative learning; see Box 17.1) in which strong stimulation anywhere on the skin causes subsequent stimulations of the siphon to produce successively *larger* gill withdrawals (N. Dale et al., 1988). The strong stimulation of the skin activates a facilitating neuron that releases the transmitter serotonin onto the presynaptic nerve terminals in the gill withdrawal reflex circuit shown in Figure 17.20*a*. Serotonin boosts the activity in the circuit by prolonging the activity of the sensory neuron's synapses onto the motoneuron, leading to a longer-lasting response (J. X. Bao et al., 1998).

The comparability of results obtained with diverse species of invertebrates indicates that, over a wide range of species, information can be stored in the nervous system by changes in both strength and number of synaptic contacts, confirming the hypotheses diagrammed in Figure 17.16. (For another example of memory research in invertebrates, see **A Step Further: In *Drosophila*, Each Stage in Memory Formation Depends on a Different Gene** on the website.) Next we'll consider a simple neural circuit in the mammalian brain in which neural activity alters the strength of synaptic connections.

Synaptic Plasticity Can Be Measured in Simple Hippocampal Circuits

In the 1970s, researchers probing the properties of hippocampal circuitry discovered an impressive form of neuroplasticity that appeared to confirm Hebb's theories about synaptic remodeling (Bliss and Lømo, 1973; Schwartzkroin and Wester,

17.21 Long-Term Potentiation Occurs in the Hippocampus (*a*) If axons in the circuit are stimulated only once every second, the size of the response in the postsynaptic neurons is quite stable. However, after a brief tetanus (a burst of electrical stimulation triggering hundreds or thousands of action potentials over 1–2 seconds), the size of the excitatory post-synaptic potential (EPSP) responses increases markedly and remains high throughout the recording period. This greater responsiveness is called *long-term potentiation* (*LTP*). (*b*) (*Top*) This diagram shows the location of the hippocampal formation in whole rat brain and in a horizontal section. (*Bottom*) This diagram of the right hippocampal formation shows various neural pathways found in the hippocampal formation, many of which display LTP. (See the text for an explanation of CA1, CA2, and CA3.)

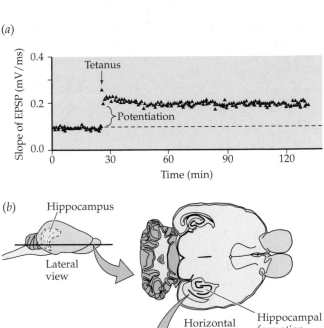

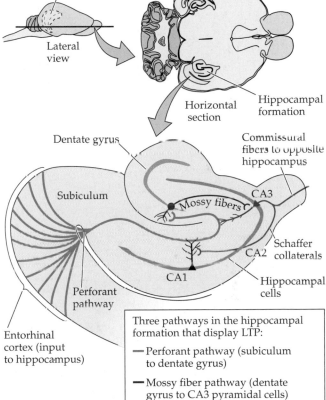

1975). In these experiments, electrodes were placed within the rat hippocampus, positioned so that the researchers could stimulate a group of *presynaptic* axons and immediately record the electrical response of a group of *postsynaptic* neurons. Normal, low-level activation of the presynaptic cells produced stable and predict-able excitatory postsynaptic potentials (EPSPs; see Chapter 3), as expected. But when the researchers applied a brief high-frequen-cy burst of electrical stimuli (called a **tetanus**) to the presynaptic hippocampal neurons, thus inducing high rates of action poten-tials, the response of the postsynaptic neurons changed. Now the postsynaptic cells responded to normal levels of presynap-tic activity by producing much larger EPSPs; in other words, the synapses appeared to have become stronger or more effective. This stable and long-lasting enhancement of synaptic transmis-sion, termed **long-term potentiation** (**LTP**), is illustrated in **Figure 17.21a**. Interestingly, a *weakening* of synaptic efficacy—termed *long-term depression*—can also encode information. This phenom-enon is discussed in **A Step Further: Long-Term Depression Is the Converse of Long-Term Potentiation** on the website.

We now know that LTP can be generated in conscious and freely behaving animals, in anesthetized animals, and in tissue slices, and that LTP is evident in a variety of invertebrate and vertebrate species. LTP also lasts for weeks or more (Bliss and Gardner-Medwin, 1973). So, at least superficially, LTP appears to have the hallmarks of a cellular mechanism of memory. This hint at a cellular origin has prompted an intensive research effort, centered mainly on the rat hippocampus, aimed at understanding the molecular and physiological mechanisms by which learning may induce LTP.

LTP occurs at several sites in the hippocampal formation

The *hippocampal formation* (**Figure 17.21b**) consists of two interlocking C-shaped structures—the **hippocampus** itself and the **dentate gyrus**—along with the adjacent **subiculum** (*subicular complex* or *hippocampal gyrus*). On structural grounds, neuro-scientists distinguish three major divisions within the hippocampus, labeled CA1, CA2, and CA3. It was in the main input pathway to the hippocampal formation (the *perforant* pathway, originating in nearby entorhinal cortex and terminating at synapses in dentate gyrus) that LTP was originally demonstrated. But LTP is also intensively studied in other hippocampal pathways, notably the mossy fiber pathway to CA3, and the *Schaffer collaterals* that synapse in CA1. These pathways are illustrated in Figure 17.21b.

LTP research has focused on the hippocampal CA1 region more than anywhere else in the brain, although evidence is accumulating that LTP may be a property of all excitatory synapses (Malenka and Bear, 2004). In CA1, LTP occurs at synapses

tetanus An intense volley of action potentials.

long-term potentiation (LTP) A stable and enduring increase in the effectiveness of syn-apses following repeated strong stimulation.

hippocampus A medial temporal lobe structure that is important for learning and memory.

dentate gyrus A strip of gray matter in the hippocampal formation.

subiculum Also called *subicular complex* or *hippocampal gyrus*. A region adjacent to the hippocampus that contributes to the hip-pocampal formation.

NMDA receptor   A glutamate receptor that also binds the glutamate agonist NMDA (*N*-methyl-D-aspartate), and that is both ligand-gated and voltage sensitive.

AMPA receptor   A glutamate receptor that also binds the glutamate agonist AMPA.

that use the excitatory neurotransmitter glutamate, and is critically dependent on a glutamate receptor subtype called the **NMDA receptor** (after its selective ligand, *N*-methyl-D-aspartate). Treatment with drugs that selectively block NMDA receptors completely prevents new LTP in the CA1 region, but it does not affect LTP that has already been established. As you might expect, these postsynaptic NMDA receptors—working in conjunction with related glutamate receptors called **AMPA receptors**—have some unique characteristics, which we discuss next.

NMDA receptors and AMPA receptors collaborate in LTP

During normal, low-level activity, the release of glutamate at a CA1 synapse activates only the AMPA receptors. The NMDA receptors cannot respond to the glutamate, because magnesium ions (Mg^{2+}) block the NMDA receptor's integral Ca^{2+} channel (**Figure 17.22a**); thus, few Ca^{2+} ions can enter the neuron. The situation changes, however, if larger quantities of glutamate are released (in response to a barrage of action potentials), thus stimulating the AMPA receptors more strongly. Because AMPA receptors admit Na^+ ions when activated, the increased activation of AMPA receptors depolarizes the postsynaptic membrane, and if a threshold value of about –35 mV or so is reached, the Mg^{2+} plug is driven from the central channels of the NMDA receptors (**Figure 17.22b**). The NMDA receptors are now able to respond to glutamate, admitting large amounts of Ca^{2+} into the postsynap-

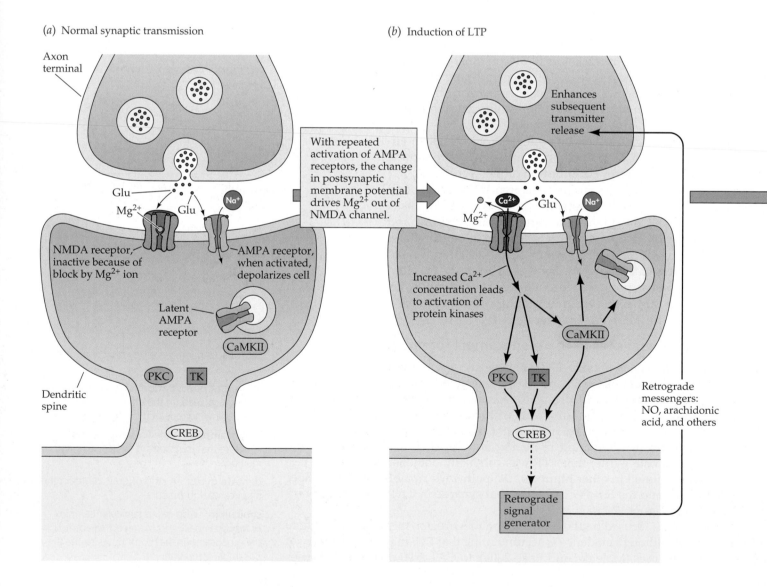

(a) Normal synaptic transmission

(b) Induction of LTP

Axon terminal

With repeated activation of AMPA receptors, the change in postsynaptic membrane potential drives Mg^{2+} out of NMDA channel.

Enhances subsequent transmitter release

Glu
Mg^{2+} Glu Na^+

Ca^{2+} Glu Na^+
Mg^{2+}

NMDA receptor, inactive because of block by Mg^{2+} ion

AMPA receptor, when activated, depolarizes cell

Increased Ca^{2+} concentration leads to activation of protein kinases

Latent AMPA receptor

CaMKII

CaMKII

Dendritic spine

PKC   TK

PKC   TK

Retrograde messengers: NO, arachidonic acid, and others

CREB

CREB

Retrograde signal generator

tic neuron. Thus, NMDA receptors are fully active only when gated by a combination of voltage (depolarization via AMPA receptors) and the ligand (glutamate).

The large influx of Ca^{2+} at NMDA receptors activates intracellular enzymes, called **protein kinases**, that alter or activate a variety of other proteins. One of these protein kinases, named CaMKII (calcium/calmodulin-dependent protein kinase II) then affects AMPA receptors in several important ways (**Figure 17.22*b* and *c***) (Kessels and Malinow, 2009; Lisman et al., 2002). Activated CaMKII causes more AMPA receptors to be produced and inserted into the postsynaptic membrane, and existing nearby AMPA receptors are induced to move to the active synapse (T. Takahashi et al., 2003). The membrane-bound AMPA receptors are also modified to increase their conductance of Na^+ and K^+ ions (Sanderson et al., 2008). The net effect of these changes, therefore, is to enhance the sensitivity of the synapse to released glutamate.

A second major effect of the activated protein kinases involves a substance called **CREB** (*c*AMP *r*esponsive *e*lement–*b*inding protein). CREB is a *transcription factor* (a protein that binds to the promoter region of genes and causes those genes to change their rate of expression) that is activated by protein kinases including CaMKII and chemical cousins like MAPK (mitogen-activated protein kinase), PKC (protein kinase C), and TK (tyrosine kinase). So, as shown in **Figure 17.23**, a direct result of the activation of NMDA receptors is the activation

protein kinase An enzyme that adds phosphate groups (PO_4) to protein molecules.

cAMP responsive element–binding protein (CREB) A protein that is activated by cyclic AMP (cAMP) so that it now binds the promoter region of several genes involved in neural plasticity.

(*c*) Enhanced synapse, after induction of LTP

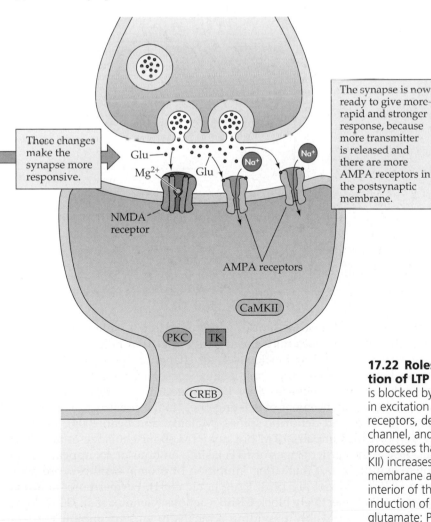

These changes make the synapse more responsive.

Glu
Mg^{2+}
Glu
Na^+
Na^+

NMDA receptor

AMPA receptors

CaMKII

PKC   TK

CREB

The synapse is now ready to give more-rapid and stronger response, because more transmitter is released and there are more AMPA receptors in the postsynaptic membrane.

17.22 Roles of the NMDA and AMPA Receptors in the Induction of LTP in the CA1 Region (a) Normally, the NMDA channel is blocked by a Mg^{2+} molecule and only the AMPA channel functions in excitation of the neuron. (b) With repeated activation of AMPA receptors, depolarization of the neuron drives Mg^{2+} out of the NMDA channel, and Ca^{2+} ions enter. The rapid increase of Ca^{2+} ions triggers processes that lead to LTP. Activation of the protein CaM kinase II (CaMKII) increases the conductance of AMPA receptors already present in the membrane and promotes the movement of AMPA receptors from the interior of the cell into the membrane. (c) The synapse is enhanced after induction of LTP. CREB, cAMP responsive element–binding protein; Glu, glutamate; PKC, protein kinase C; TK, tyrosine kinase.

17.23 Steps in the Neurochemical Cascade during the Induction of LTP This illustration is based on LTP induction in the CA1 region of the hippocampus.

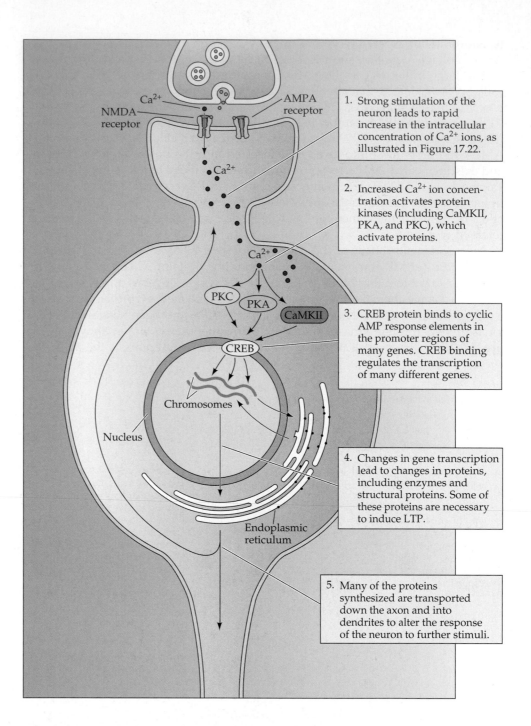

1. Strong stimulation of the neuron leads to rapid increase in the intracellular concentration of Ca^{2+} ions, as illustrated in Figure 17.22.

2. Increased Ca^{2+} ion concentration activates protein kinases (including CaMKII, PKA, and PKC), which activate proteins.

3. CREB protein binds to cyclic AMP response elements in the promoter regions of many genes. CREB binding regulates the transcription of many different genes.

4. Changes in gene transcription lead to changes in proteins, including enzymes and structural proteins. Some of these proteins are necessary to induce LTP.

5. Many of the proteins synthesized are transported down the axon and into dendrites to alter the response of the neuron to further stimuli.

of CREB and changes in the expression of genes encoding a wide range of proteins. Because the affected genes may encode anything from new receptors and kinases to the structural building blocks used for changing the shape of the cell, this action can have profound and long-lasting consequences for the neuron.

The long-term changes in neurons after LTP range from the formation of additional synapses and enhancement of existing ones, to the construction of whole new dendritic branches and dendritic spines (Malenka and Bear, 2004). In mice, genetic deletion of CREB impairs LTM but not STM (Bourtchuladze et al., 1994; Kogan et al., 1997). The earlier stages of LTP, lasting an hour or so, appear not to require protein synthesis, but thereafter, inhibition of protein synthesis prevents longer-lasting LTP (U. Frey et al., 1993; Krug et al., 1984). Furthermore, neurons can make proteins that selectively block CREB's actions (Genoux et al., 2002; Mioduszewska et al., 2003), possibly providing a means to erase or inhibit the formation of unwanted memories. Much remains to be discovered about the many controls on long-lasting components of LTP.

Not all of the changes in LTP are postsynaptic. When the postsynaptic cell is strongly stimulated and its NMDA receptors become active and admit Ca^{2+}, an intracellular process causes the postsynaptic cell to release a **retrograde messenger**—often a diffusible gas—that travels back across the synapse and alters the functioning of the *presynaptic* neuron (see Figure 17.22b). By affecting the presynaptic cell, the retrograde transmitter ensures that more glutamate will be released into the synapse than previously, thereby strengthening the synapse. So, LTP involves active participation on both sides of the synapse. Nitric oxide (NO), carbon monoxide (CO), arachidonic acid, and nerve growth factor are among more than a dozen possible retrograde signals in LTP (J. R. Sanes and Lichtman, 1999).

In other locations in the hippocampus, such as the mossy fiber pathway (see Figure 17.21b), LTP can occur without NMDA receptor activity (E. W. Harris and Cotman, 1986); and some forms of LTP are blocked by drugs with completely different modes of action, such as opiate antagonists (Aroniadou et al., 1993; Derrick and Martinez, 1994). The diversity of mechanisms involved in LTP has complicated one of the central questions in LTP research, which we address next.

Is LTP a mechanism of memory formation?

Even the simplest learning involves circuits of multiple neurons and many synapses, and more-complex declarative and procedural memory traces must involve vast networks of neurons, so we are unlikely to conclude that LTP is the only mechanism of learning. However, LTP may be an important part of a multifaceted system for storing information. Evidence from several research perspectives—as we defined way back in Figure 1.2—implicates LTP in memory:

1. *Correlational observations.* The time course of LTP bears strong similarity to the time course of memory formation (Lynch et al., 1991; Staubli, 1995). Covarying with memory, LTP can be induced within seconds, may last for days or weeks, and shows a labile consolidation period that lasts for several minutes after induction.

2. *Somatic intervention experiments.* In general, pharmacological treatments that interfere with basic physiological processes that contribute to LTP tend to impair learning. So, for example, NMDA receptor blockade interferes with performance in the Morris water maze (a test of spatial memory) and other types of memory tests (R. G. Morris et al., 1989). Drugs that inhibit CaMKII and other protein kinases also generally interfere with aspects of memory formation (M. R. Rosenzweig et al., 1992, 1993; Serrano et al., 1994). Because these same basic physiological processes are at work in many regions of the brain, in earlier research it was difficult to know exactly where and how the drugs were acting to affect memory. But more recently, regional genetic manipulations have enabled researchers to zero in on specific brain regions. Mice with one copy of the CaM kinase II gene knocked out can still form short-term memories (STMs), but they cannot form LTMs (Frankland et al., 2001). And knockout mice that lack functional NMDA receptors only in CA1 appear normal in many respects, but their hippocampi are incapable of LTP and their memory is impaired (Rampon, Tang, et al., 2000). In a clever reversal, researchers have also shown that mice engineered to overexpress NMDA receptors in the hippocampus have enhanced LTP, and better-than-normal long-term memory (Y. P. Tang et al., 1999, 2001). (For the full story of these mice, known as *Doogies*, see **A Step Further: How to Build a Doogie** on the website.)

3. *Behavioral intervention experiments.* In principle, the most convincing evidence for a link between LTP and learning would be "behavioral LTP": a demonstration that training an animal in a memory task can induce LTP in the brain. Such research is difficult because of uncertainty about exactly where

retrograde messenger Transmitter that is released by the postsynaptic region, travels back across the synapse, and alters the functioning of the presynaptic neuron.

to put the recording electrodes in order to detect any induced LTP. Nevertheless, several examples of successful behavioral LTP have been reported. Fear conditioning—for example, the repeated pairing of an aversive stimulus and a tone, eventually resulting in exaggerated reactions to the tone alone—produces clear LTP specifically in fear circuits in the amygdala and not elsewhere (McKernan and Shinnick-Gallagher, 1997; Rogan et al., 1997). And in the CA1 region of the hippocampus, a different form of aversive learning in rats has been shown to produce exactly the same electrophysiological changes, as well as changes in AMPA receptor accumulation, that are seen with conventionally induced LTP (Whitlock et al., 2006).

Taken together, the research findings support the idea that LTP is a kind of synaptic plasticity that underlies (or is very similar to) certain forms of learning and memory.

Some Simple Learning Relies on Circuits in the Mammalian Cerebellum

Although LTP may be a synaptic mechanism of memory, a more complete understanding of memory processes requires analysis of networks of neurons. Describing the complete circuit for even a simple learned behavior is very difficult in mammals because, in contrast to *Aplysia*, mammals have brains containing billions of neurons that are not organized in fixed circuits. Success came when researchers probed a very simple mammalian behavior: the corneal eye-blink reflex (Lavond et al., 1993; R. F. Thompson, 1990; Thompson and Steinmetz, 2009).

When a puff of air is applied to the cornea of a rabbit, the animal reflexively blinks. The eye-blink reflex is quite amenable to classical conditioning: over several trials, if the air puff (US) immediately follows an acoustic tone (CS), a simple conditioned response (CR) develops rapidly: the rabbit comes to blink when the tone is sounded (for the fundaments of conditioning, see Box 17.1). The basic circuit of the eye-blink reflex is also simple, involving cranial nerves and some interneurons that connect their nuclei (**Figure 17.24a**). Sensory fibers from the cornea run along cranial nerve V (the trigeminal nerve) to its nucleus in the brainstem. From there, some interneurons send axons to synapse on other cranial nerve motor nuclei (VI and VII), which in turn activate the muscles of the eyelids, causing them to close.

Early studies showed that destruction of the hippocampus has little effect on the acquisition or retention of the conditioned eye-blink response in rabbits (Lockhart and Moore, 1975). Therefore, the hippocampus is *not* required for this conditioning. (Interestingly, eye-blink training that involves a delay between the CS and US *does* rely on the hippocampus; see **A Step Further: The Hippocampus is Needed for Complex Eye-Blink Conditioning** on the website.) Instead, as we mentioned earlier in the chapter, researchers found that learning-related increases in the activity of individual neurons are specific to the cerebellum and associated structures. A large research effort eventually described a cerebellar circuit that is both necessary and sufficient for eye-blink conditioning.

The trigeminal (V) pathway that carries information about the corneal stimulation (the US) to the cranial motor nuclei also sends axons to the brainstem (specifically a structure called the *inferior olive*). These brainstem neurons, in turn, send axons called *climbing fibers* to synapse on cerebellar neurons, in a region called the interpositus nucleus. The same cells also receive information about the auditory CS by a pathway through the auditory nuclei and other brainstem nuclei (**Figure 17.24b**). So the US and CS converge in the *interpositus nucleus* of the cerebellum. After conditioning, the occurrence of the CS—the tone—has an enhanced effect on the cerebellar neurons, so they now trigger eye blink even in the absence of an air puff (**Figure 17.24c**).

(a) Before

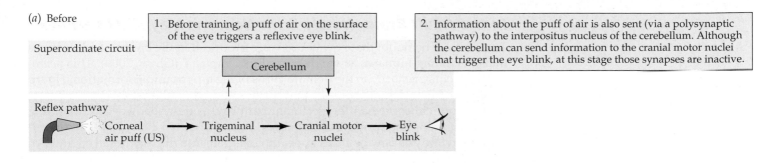

1. Before training, a puff of air on the surface of the eye triggers a reflexive eye blink.

2. Information about the puff of air is also sent (via a polysynaptic pathway) to the interpositus nucleus of the cerebellum. Although the cerebellum can send information to the cranial motor nuclei that trigger the eye blink, at this stage those synapses are inactive.

(b) Training

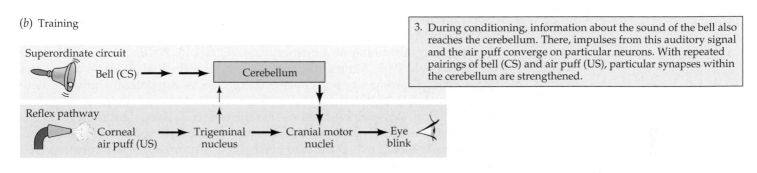

3. During conditioning, information about the sound of the bell also reaches the cerebellum. There, impulses from this auditory signal and the air puff converge on particular neurons. With repeated pairings of bell (CS) and air puff (US), particular synapses within the cerebellum are strengthened.

(c) After

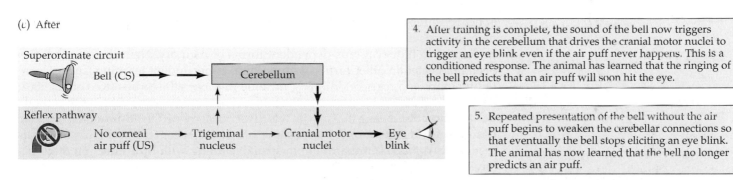

4. After training is complete, the sound of the bell now triggers activity in the cerebellum that drives the cranial motor nuclei to trigger an eye blink even if the air puff never happens. This is a conditioned response. The animal has learned that the ringing of the bell predicts that an air puff will soon hit the eye.

5. Repeated presentation of the bell without the air puff begins to weaken the cerebellar connections so that eventually the bell stops eliciting an eye blink. The animal has now learned that the bell no longer predicts an air puff.

17.24 Functioning of the Neural Circuit for Conditioning of the Eye-Blink Reflex (After R. F. Thompson and Krupa, 1994.)

Local cooling, or drugs that block the neurotransmitter GABA (gamma-aminobutyric acid, the transmitter used at synapses in the cerebellar circuit), have the effect of reversibly shutting down the interpositus nucleus. If this manipulation is performed at the beginning of training, then no conditioning occurs until after the effect wears off. Conversely, if animals are fully trained before treatment, subsequent injection of a GABA antagonist causes the conditioned behavior to disappear, along with its electrophysiological signature, until after the drug effect wears off. On the basis of these and other experiments, the complete eye-blink conditioning circuit is now understood, and the cerebellum's interpositus nucleus appears to be the key location for storing this type of memory (R. F. Thompson and Steinmetz, 2009).

As we discussed earlier, studies on human subjects are consistent with the animal research on eye-blink conditioning. Furthermore, by rapidly stimulating sensory cranial nerves in the circuit during training in human volunteers, researchers have been able to show that LTP probably plays a role in human eye-blink conditioning (Mao and Evinger, 2001). Unsurprisingly, other cases of conditioning also depend on cerebellar mechanisms. For example, conditioned leg flexion (in which the animal learns to withdraw a leg on hearing a tone) is cerebellum-dependent (Donegan et al., 1983; Voneida, 1990). Studies of humans with cerebellar damage indicate that the cerebellum is important for conditioning across several domains, including conditioning of emotions like fear, and aspects of cognitive learning (Timman et al., 2009).

In the Adult Brain, Newly Born Neurons May Aid Learning

There is now no doubt that new neurons are produced in the brains of adult mammals, including humans, as we discussed in Chapter 7 (Gross, 2000). This *neurogenesis* occurs primarily in the dentate gyrus of the hippocampal formation (**Figure 17.25**), and new dentate neurons that survive and grow ultimately receive inputs from entorhinal cortex via the perforant pathway, as described earlier, extending their own axons and forming glutamatergic synapses (Toni et al., 2008). Anatomically, therefore, the new neurons appear to integrate into the functional circuitry of the hippocampus and adjacent cortex (Bruel-Jungerman et al., 2007), which we've seen play a role in forming new memories.

In experimental animals, neurogenesis and the survival of young neurons can be enhanced by a variety of factors, such as exercise, experience in an enriched environment, or training in a memory task (E. Gould, Beylin, et al., 1999; Kempermann et al., 1997; Ming and Song, 2005; Prickaerts et al., 2004; Waddell and Shors, 2008). Reproductive hormones and experiences also potently influence neurogenesis (Galea, 2008; Pawluski and Galea, 2007). Although these observations are tantalizing, clear demonstrations that the new cells have significant functions in behavior—especially learning and memory—have been somewhat elusive.

Rats given a drug that is lethal to newly born neurons are reportedly impaired on tests of conditioning, but only when there is an interval between the CS and the US (Shors et al., 2001). As we discussed earlier, this form of conditioning is believed to rely on hippocampal function, so the finding that it is impaired when neurogenesis is prevented suggests that the role of neurogenesis in memory may be limited to hippocampus-dependent forms of memory. Neurogenesis has also been implicated in other forms of hippocampus-dependent learning, such as spatial memory and fear conditioning in some (but not all) studies (Kee et al., 2007; Saxe et al., 2006; Winocur et al., 2006). In a recent study using mice with a **conditional knockout**—a gene that can be selectively deactivated in adulthood in specific tissues—researchers found that turning off neurogenesis in the brains of adults resulted in a marked impairment in spatial learning with little effect on other behaviors (C. L. Zhang et al., 2008).

Although much remains to be established about the functional significance of adult neurogenesis, on the whole the available evidence indicates that the newly born cells do play a role in learning. Intense research interest centers on the possible therapeutic applications of adult neurogenesis, limited somewhat by the assertion that adult neurogenesis may not occur in other human brain regions—especially the cortex—that are compromised in disorders like Alzheimer's disease (Rakic, 2006).

conditional knockout A gene that can be selectively deactivated in adulthood in specific tissues.

17.25 Neurogenesis in the Dentate Gyrus (a) BrdU (bromo-deoxyuridine) is a label that is selectively incorporated into the DNA of cells that are about to divide. (b) NeuN selectively labels neurons, in order to distinguish them from other nearby cells, such as glial cells. (c) Merging the two images makes it clear that some of the newly born cells are in fact neurons (arrows). (Courtesy of Elodie Bruel-Jungerman and Serge Laroche, from Bruel-Jungerman et al., 2006.)

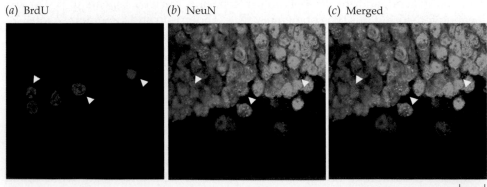

(a) BrdU   (b) NeuN   (c) Merged

20 µm

Learning and Memory Change as We Age

Understanding the impact of aging on cognition is a pressing issue; by 2030, there will be more than twice as many senior citizens alive as there were in 2000. In people and other mammals, normal aging brings a gradual decline in some but not all aspects of learning and memory (N. D. Anderson and Craik, 2000; Gallagher and Rapp, 1997; Lister and Barnes, 2009). For some tasks, differences in motivation, earlier education, and other confounding factors may masquerade as age-related memory problems. So experiments on memory in the elderly must be carefully constructed to control for alternate explanations.

What kinds of tasks reliably show decrements in performance with aging? Normal elderly people tend to show some memory impairment in tasks of conscious recollection that require effort (Hasher and Zacks, 1979) and that rely primarily on internal generation of the memory rather than on external cues (Craik, 1985). Giving elderly subjects easily organized task structures, or cues, can often raise their performance to the level of the young. Although working memory, episodic memory, and declarative memory abilities typically decline with age, other types of memory, such as autobiographical memory and semantic knowledge, tend to remain stable (Hedden and Gabrieli, 2004). If vocabulary is tested in isolation, older adults outperform younger adults (D. C. Park et al., 2002), but on tests of executive function even individuals in their 40s are likely to show age-related decline (Rhodes, 2004).

As we age, we also experience some decreases in spatial memory and navigational skills (Barnes and Penner, 2007; E. S. Rosenzweig and Barnes, 2003). Similarly, aged rats show decrements in the eight-arm radial maze (see Figure 17.14a) compared to younger animals (Mizumori et al., 1996; M. A. Rossi et al., 2005). Along with other memory impairments, spatial-memory problems may become much more severe in dementias like Alzheimer's disease, which is discussed in detail in Chapter 7. In these severe cases of amnesia, memory performance may resemble that of an infant: shown a familiar object in a new location, patients continue to search for it in the old location, even passing over the object in plain sight in the new site. They appear to remember the search procedure and not the object being sought (M. Moscovitch, 1985).

Age-related impairments of memory have several causes

Why do some measures of learning and memory decline with age, while others remain intact? There are a number of ways in which neural changes may affect learning and memory during aging (Craik and Salthouse, 2007; Lister and Barnes, 2009). Some of the major contributors to memory problems in old age include

- *Impairments of encoding and retrieval.* Older subjects show less cortical activation than younger subjects when encoding or retrieval is self-initiated. In **Figure 17.26**, less frontal and temporal activity is seen in the older subjects while learning new faces (Grady et al., 1995), but when recognizing faces (a retrieval task that is not self-initiated, because retrieval is prompted by viewing stimuli) the elders' brain activity is comparable to that of the younger subjects. Some studies find *increased* activation in elderly subjects, possibly due to recruitment of neurons to compensate for difficulty or just more-diffuse or nondifferentiated activity (Grady and Craik, 2000).

- *Loss of neurons and/or neural connections.* The brain gradually loses weight after the age of 30, and some parts of the brain, such as frontal cortex (Raz, 2000), lose a larger proportion of volume or weight than other parts. Although not all investigators agree, age-related memory impairment may involve steady loss of synapses and neurons in the hippocampus and cortex (Geinisman et al., 1995; J. H. Morrison and Hof, 2007; Simic et al., 1997).

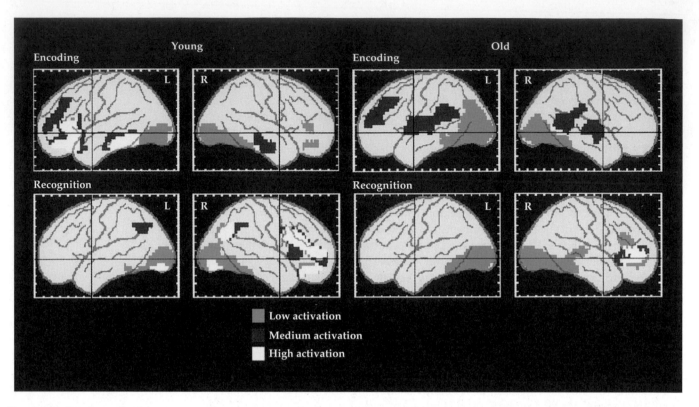

17.26 Active Brain Regions during Encoding and Retrieval Tasks in Young and Old People Lateral views of the cerebral hemispheres show regions of enhanced cerebral blood flow caused by encoding information (*top*) and retrieving it (*bottom*). (Courtesy of Cheryl Grady.)

• *Problems with cholinergic neurotransmission.* Two subcortical regions—the *septal complex* and the *nucleus basalis of Meynert* (*NBM*)—provide profuse cholinergic inputs to the hippocampus and cortex. Age-related deterioration in these pathways appears to be a factor in age-related memory impairment and in Alzheimer's disease (McGeer et al., 1984; Rossor et al., 1982). In experimental animals, lesions of the septum and NBM impair memory (Meck et al., 1987), and stimulation of the NBM to increase acetylcholine release improves aspects of memory performance in animals (McLin et al., 2002). Similarly, drug treatments that enhance acetylcholine transmission improve aspects of memory performance in human subjects (Furey et al., 2000; Ricciardi et al., 2009). Acetylcholine levels are reduced in old rats that show memory impairment in the water maze, when compared to either old rats that perform well or young rats (Gallagher et al., 1995). In general, the evidence indicates that cholinergic projections refine and enhance memory, probably by producing long-lasting changes in the excitability of target neurons, thus making them more susceptible to plastic change (Froemke et al., 2007).

• *Impaired coding by place cells.* In aged rats that show poor spatial learning in behavioral tests, the number of hippocampal place cells (neurons that respond to spatial cues) isn't different from that in young rats, but compared to old rats with normal memory or young rats, the neurons encode a smaller amount of spatial information (Tanila, Shapiro, et al., 1997). Another possibility is that the changes in performance of hippocampal place cells could reflect changes in the cortical inputs to the hippocampus. Inputs to the dorsal hippocampus from the medial entorhinal cortex are spatial in nature, but those from the lateral entorhinal cortex generally serve other functions (Hargreaves et al., 2005); perhaps the balance of these inputs is rearranged with age.

Can the effects of aging on memory be prevented or alleviated?

The search for anti-aging interventions and **nootropics**—drugs that enhance cognitive function—is an area of intense activity. Pharmacological approaches include the use of drugs, such as donepezil (Aricept), that inhibit cholinesterase, the enzyme that breaks down acetylcholine. The resultant increase in cholinergic transmission in the forebrain has a positive effect on memory and cognition in mild to moderate cases (Ringman and Cummings, 2006). Compounds in a different class—*ampakines*—act via glutamate receptors to improve hippocampal LTP (Rex et al., 2006); ampakines are under study as potential memory-enhancing therapeutics. And research shows that one particular protein kinase—PKMζ (the squiggle is the Greek letter zeta)—is needed for long-term maintenance of both hippocampal LTP *and* cortical memory traces (Shema et al., 2007, 2009), raising the possibility that compounds that alter this kinase could be highly selective memory drugs. The list of other possible targets for developing memory-boosting drugs grows longer every day.

Rats raised in enriched conditions show improved handling of stress and associated reduction in glucocorticoid secretion, and lower chronic levels of glucocorticoids may protect hippocampal function during aging (Sapolsky, 1993). Enriched experience also increases the release of nerve growth factor (NGF) in the hippocampus (Mohammed et al., 1993; Ottoson et al., 1995). So lifelong environmental enrichment may have strongly protective effects on cognitive functions, such as memory, later in life. Longitudinal research tracking thousands of people suggests several general lifestyle factors that can help reduce the risk of cognitive decline in old age (Schaie, 1994), including

- *Living in favorable environmental circumstances* (e.g., getting an above-average education, pursuing occupations that involve high complexity and low routine, earning above-average income, and maintaining intact families).
- *Involvement in complex and intellectually stimulating activities* (e.g., extensive reading, travel, attendance at cultural events, continuing-education activities, and participation in clubs and professional associations).
- *Having a spouse/partner with high cognitive status.*

Because so much of the brain is involved in the creation, storage, and retrieval of memories, a full understanding of learning and memory will require an enormous research effort at many levels of analysis, from molecular processes to cognitive studies of special cases like Henry Molaison. As we prepare this book to go to press, it is exactly one year since Henry died and, in a final act of generosity to a field of science that he helped launch, donated his brain for further study. Through webcasting technology, the dissection of Henry's brain was viewed live by thousands of people (see www.thebrainobservatory.ucsd.edu), and a series of more than 2000 sections will eventually be made available. To the end, although he could remember so little of his entire adult life, Henry was courteous and concerned about other people. He remembered the surgeon he had met several times before his operation: "He did medical research on people ... What he learned about me helped others too, and I'm glad about that" (Corkin, 2002, p. 158). Henry never knew how famous he was, or how much his dreadful condition taught us about learning and memory; yet despite being deprived of one of the most important characteristics of a human being, he held fast to his humanity.

nootropics A class of drugs that enhance cognitive function

SUMMARY

FUNCTIONAL PERSPECTIVES ON MEMORY

■ The abilities to learn and remember affect all behaviors that are characteristically human. Because every animal species appears capable of some **learning** and **memory**, the ability to learn must be required for survival.

There Are Several Kinds of Memory and Learning

■ Case studies of individuals with memory impairments have especially implicated hippocampal, diencephalic, and cortical systems in memory formation, storage, and retrieval.

■ **Declarative memory** includes facts (called **semantic memory**) and autobiographical information (called **episodic memory**). **Nondeclarative memory** (**procedural memory**) is memory for perceptual and motor behaviors—acquired through **skill learning**, **priming**, and **conditioning**—that are demonstrated through performance. **Review Figures 17.3 and 17.5, Web Activity 17.1**

■ Learning includes both **nonassociative** forms such as **habituation**, **dishabituation**, and **sensitization**; and **associative** forms such as **classical conditioning** (Pavlovian conditioning) and **instrumental conditioning** (**operant conditioning**). **Review Box 17.1**

Memory Has Temporal Stages: Short, Intermediate, and Long

■ Memories are often classified by how long they last. Frequently used classifications include **iconic memory**, **short-term memory** (sometimes called **working memory**), **intermediate-term memory**, and **long-term memory**.

■ Although the capacity of long-term memory is huge, most of what we experience is not remembered. Attention, reinforcement, and emotional responses help determine what is held in memory beyond the short term.

Successive Processes Capture, Store, and Retrieve Information in the Brain

■ Recall of a past event requires three successive memory processes: **encoding**, **consolidation**, and **retrieval**. **Review Figures 17.7 and 17.8**

■ Strong emotion has a powerful effect on the strength of memories. Compounds that block biochemical signals of strong emotion may be useful for blunting unwanted traumatic memory such as that characterizing **posttraumatic stress disorder** (**PTSD**). **Review Box 17.2**

Different Brain Regions Process Different Aspects of Memory

■ The hippocampal region is required for processing but not for storage of long-term declarative memory. Long-term (permanent) memory is probably stored in the cortex. Specialized hippocampal neurons called **place cells**, **grid cells**, and

border cells play a crucial role in spatial memory. **Review Figures 17.9 and 17.10**

■ Different forms of working memory rely on diverse brain re-gions, including the hippocampus, caudate, and prefrontal cortex. **Review Figures 17.14 and 17.15, Web Activity 17.2**

■ Encoding, consolidation and retrieval are three crucial aspects of memory; failure of any one of these can produce **amnesia**.

■ Long-term memory has enormous capacity, but it is quite inaccurate. Memories are subject to revision during recall and **reconsolidation**.

NEURAL MECHANISMS OF MEMORY

■ Learning and forming new memories require neural changes in nearly all organisms. The near universality of **neuroplasticity** indicates its evolutionary importance.

Memory Storage Requires Neuronal Remodeling

■ Memory storage has long been hypothesized to involve changes in neural circuits. Research since the 1960s has demonstrated both functional and structural synaptic changes related to learning. **Review Figure 17.16**

■ Training or enriched experience in rats leads to structural changes in the cerebral cortex, including alterations in the number and size of synaptic contacts, and in the branching of dendrites. **Review Figure 17.18**

Invertebrate Nervous Systems Show Plasticity

■ Research on the simple nervous systems of invertebrates provides insights into fundamental properties of plasticity and learning that may be generalized to other species. **Review Figure 17.20**

Synaptic Plasticity Can Be Measured in Simple Hippocampal Circuits

■ **Long-term potentiation** of neural responses is a lasting increase in amplitude of the response of neurons caused by brief high-frequency stimulation of their afferents (**tetanus**). **Review Figure 17.21, Web Activity 17.3**

■ In mammalian **hippocampus**, some forms of LTP depend on the activation of **NMDA receptors**, which induces an increase in the number of postsynaptic **AMPA receptors** and greater neurotransmitter release. **Review Figures 17.22 and 17.23, Web Activity 17.4**

■ Although not conclusive yet, the evidence indicates that LTP is probably a cellular mechanism of memory. **Review Web Activities 17.5–17.10**

Some Simple Learning Relies on Circuits in the Mammalian Cerebellum

■ Conditioning of the eye-blink response in the rabbit is crucially dependent on the cerebellum. This simple mammalian system provides a model for understanding the formation of associations in the mammalian brain. **Review Figure 17.24**

In the Adult Brain, Newly Born Neurons May Aid Learning

■ Unlike the cortex, the hippocampus remains capable of producing new neurons throughout life. These new neurons may play a role in certain forms of hippocampus-dependent learning. **Review Figure 17.25**

Learning and Memory Change as We Age

■ Some neurochemical and neuroanatomical measures correlate with specific declines in learning and memory that occur in most elderly subjects. Some biological changes occur only in subjects who show behavioral decline.

■ The incidence of memory impairments in old age can be reduced by pharmacological intervention or by adequate early environment and continuing enriched experience.

Go to www.biopsychology.com for study questions, quizzes, key terms, and other resources.

Recommended Reading

Baddeley, A. D., Eysenck, M., and Anderson, M. C. (2009). *Memory.* London: Psychology Press.

Bontempi, B., Silva, A. J., and Christen, Y. (Eds.). (2007). *Memories: Molecules and circuits.* New York: Springer.

Gluck, M. A., Mercado, E., and Myers, C. E. (2007). *Learning and memory: From brain to behavior.* New York: Worth.

Kesner, R. P., and Martinez, J. L. (Eds.). (2007). *The neurobiology of learning and memory* (2nd ed.). San Diego, CA: Elsevier.

Lieberman, D. A. (2004). *Learning and memory: An integrative approach.* Belmont, CA: Thomson/Wadsworth.

McGaugh, J. L. (2003). *Memory and emotions: The making of lasting memories.* New York: Columbia University Press.

Rudy, J. W. (2008). *The neurobiology of learning and memory.* Sunderland MA: Sinauer.

Squire, L. R., and Kandel, E. R. (2008). *Memory: From mind to molecules.* Greenwood Village, CO: Roberts and Company.

Thompson, R. F., and Madigan, S. A. (2005). *Memory: The key to consciousness.* Washington, DC: Henry.

Tulving, E., and Craik, F. I. M. (Eds.). (2000). *The Oxford handbook of memory.* Oxford, England: Oxford University Press.

Attention and Higher Cognition

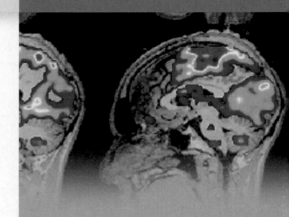

CHAPTER 18

A Change of Mind

Phineas P. Gage was a sober, efficient, capable young man, respected by the workmen he supervised as they blasted rock to clear a path for a new railroad in northwestern Vermont. But one day in 1848, something went wrong. Gage was using an iron tamping rod to tightly pack explosives into a hole that had been drilled into the solid rock. The tamping rod—custom-made for Gage by a local blacksmith—was a cylinder an inch and a quarter in diameter, about three and a half feet long, flat at the bottom to tamp the charge, tapering to a point at the top. It resembled a javelin.

The iron rod must have struck a spark from the surrounding rock because the charge went off unexpectedly, shooting the rod straight at Gage's head. The rod pierced his left cheek and passed behind his left eye and out the top of his skull, landing some 60 feet away. Gage was thrown onto his back, his limbs convulsing. Yet in a minute or two he spoke. With help from his men he walked to a wagon, where he sat for the ride to town. There, Gage walked upstairs, unaided, to a doctor's office to have his wounds cleaned and dressed. No one expected him to live; an undertaker made a coffin for him (Macmillan, 2000).

In fact, however, Gage worked at a series of menial jobs for another 12 years, but he was definitely a changed man. After the accident he was rude and aimless, and his powers of attention and concentration were badly impaired. Despite the miracle of his physical recovery, "his mind was radically changed, so decidedly that his friends and acquaintances said that he was 'no longer Gage.'"

How did his injury so alter Phineas Gage's behavior?

In 1890, brilliantly anticipating the key issues in a field of study that wouldn't fully blossom for another century, the great American psychologist William James wrote,

> Everyone knows what attention is. It is the taking possession by the mind, in clear and vivid form, of one out of what seem several simultaneously possible objects or trains of thought. Focalization, concentration, of consciousness are of its essence. It implies withdrawal from some things in order to deal effectively with others, and is a condition which has a real opposite in the confused, dazed, scatterbrained state.

James understood that attention can be effortful, improves perception, and acts as a filter on the outside world. When we are alert and functioning normally, we are *always* paying attention to something. This continual process of shifting our focus between interesting stimuli, either in our surroundings or in our thoughts, lies at the heart of the experience of consciousness.

Attention Selects Stimuli for Processing

Although she may delight in pretending otherwise, any average 5-year-old understands what it means when an exasperated parent shouts, "Pay attention!" We all share an intuitive understanding of the term *attention*, but to this day scientists

attention   Also called *selective attention*. A state or condition of selective awareness or perceptual receptivity, by which specific stimuli are selected for enhanced processing.

arousal   The global, nonselective level of alertness of an individual.

overt attention   Attention in which the focus coincides with sensory orientation (e.g., you're attending to the same thing you're looking at).

covert attention   Attention in which the focus can be directed independently of sensory orientation (e.g., you're attending to one sensory stimulus while looking at another).

have been unable to agree on a definition that goes much beyond the one provided by James—a testament to the great complexity and scope of the topic. In general, **attention** (or *selective attention*) is the process by which we select or focus on one or more specific stimuli—either sensory phenomena or internal cognitive processes—for enhanced processing and analysis. As we will see, this ability of attention to augment the operation of sensory processing systems in the brain can be directly measured using electrophysiological and brain-imaging techniques. It is the *selective* quality of attention that distinguishes it from the related concept of **arousal**, the global level of alertness of the individual.

Early scientific investigations of attention were performed by renowned German scientist Hermann von Helmholtz (1962; original work published in 1894). Helmholtz knew that most of the time we employ **overt attention**, where the focus of our attention coincides with our sensory orientation. For example, as you read this sentence, it is both the center of your visual gaze and (we hope) the main item that your brain has selected for attention. But in cataloging the capabilities of the human visual system, Helmholtz discovered that the focus of visual attention also could be moved independently of gaze—a phenomenon now known as **covert attention** (**Figure 18.1**). In an experiment with himself as the subject, Helmholtz locked his gaze on the center of a screen and then used a bright electrical spark to project an array of letters on the screen for a very brief moment. He found that he could voluntarily decide in advance which location in the array to attend to, and after the flash he could accurately report the letters from the chosen location, but not from other locations. Because the array was illuminated for less than the roughly 200 ms that we need to shift our gaze from a fixation point to a target location (B. Fischer and Weber, 1993), covert attention must have enhanced the processing of the target location in Helmholtz's peripheral vision.

Selective attention isn't restricted to visual stimuli. Imagine yourself socializing in a crowded and noisy room (like, say, a cocktail party), chatting with an old

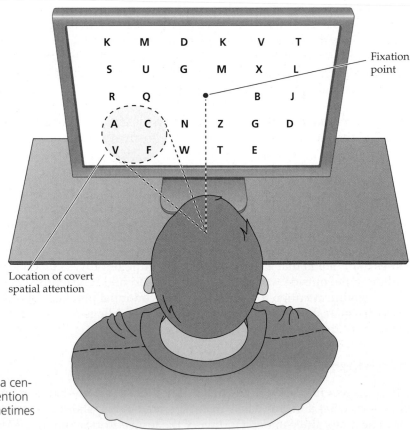

18.1 Covert Attention   While holding our gaze steady on a central fixation point, we can independently center our visual attention on a different spatial location. This selective attention has sometimes been referred to as an *attentional spotlight*.

friend. Despite the high levels of background noise, you would probably find it relatively easy to focus on what she was saying, even if she was speaking quietly, because closely attending to your friend enhances your processing of her speech and helps filter out distracters. This selective enhancement is known as the **cocktail party effect**. Though it may seem effortless, in this scenario you are solving a very difficult information-processing problem: In a room filled with equally loud fragments of speech coming from every direction, how do you know which sounds go together? Solving that problem requires that you maintain the focus of your attention on a single speech source, and if your attention shifts to a different auditory stimulus—for example, if you start eavesdropping on a more interesting conversation—it becomes virtually impossible to simultaneously follow your friend's conversation. And actually having cocktails exacerbates the problem, because alcohol elevates auditory thresholds (thereby lowering sensitivity) for speech-related frequencies, reducing your ability to distinguish your friend's speech from background noise (Upile et al., 2007). Maybe this is one reason that parties get louder as the night wears on.

There are limits on attention

In a cocktail party setting you have a variety of clues, in different sensory modalities, to help you distinguish your friend's speech from all the other conversations going on in the room. The location from which the speech sounds originate, the movements of your friend's face as she speaks, the unique sounds of her voice, and so on, all help you to separate what she is saying from that noisy background. In now-classic experiments on the cocktail party effect (Cherry, 1953), these extra cues were systematically excluded in order to highlight the effects of selective auditory attention on sensory processing. Through headphones, subjects heard recordings of two different streams of dialog, recited by the same person and delivered simultaneously to the left and right ears. This testing technique is known as **dichotic presentation**. Subjects were asked to focus their attention on one ear or the other, and repeat aloud the material as it was presented to that ear. On this demanding task, called **shadowing**, subjects could accurately report what they were hearing in the attended ear, but about the nonattended auditory stream they could report very little beyond simple characteristics, such as the sex of the speaker. If a shadowing task is sufficiently difficult, then even advance warning that they will be quizzed later doesn't help subjects remember and report information from the unattended auditory stream (Moray, 1959). In fact, even when the subject's own name is presented in the unattended ear, it is detected only about a third of the time (Wood and Cowan, 1995).

The cocktail party effect is not limited to speech (or parties!), of course. For example, musicians are better than nonmusicians at focusing attention on target notes and segregating them from multiple simultaneous musical sounds (Zendel and Alain, 2009). A shadowing procedure can be used to study visual attention too. In this case, subjects are asked to attend to just one of two fully overlapping videos being presented simultaneously—imagine two movies being projected onto a single screen. As in the auditory shadowing experiments, subjects are able to focus on one video only at the expense of the other; little of the nonattended video can be reported (Neisser and Becklen, 1975). Furthermore, if the attended visual stream is sufficiently complicated, subjects show **inattentional blindness**: a surprising failure to perceive nonattended stimuli that you'd think would be impossible to miss, like a gorilla strolling across the screen (Simons and Chabris, 1999; Simons and Jensen, 2009).

People are also surprisingly poor at noticing changes—sometimes quite large ones—when comparing two alternating static visual scenes. This **change blindness** (Rensink, 2002; Rensink et al., 1997) generally requires a momentary disruption in viewing the scene, such as a flicker or blank between still images on a computer screen. This requirement suggests that, unlike inattentional blindness, change

cocktail party effect The selective enhancement of attention in order to filter out distracters, such as while listening to one person talking in the midst of a noisy party.

dichotic presentation The simultaneous delivery of different stimuli to both the right and the left ears at the same time.

shadowing A task in which the subject is asked to focus attention on one ear or the other while stimuli are being presented separately to both ears, and to repeat aloud the material presented to the attended ear.

inattentional blindness The failure to perceive nonattended stimuli that seem so obvious as to be impossible to miss.

change blindness A failure to notice changes in comparisons of two alternating static visual scenes.

divided attention task A task in which the subject is asked to simultaneously focus attention on two or more stimuli.

attentional spotlight The shifting of our limited selective attention around the environment to highlight stimuli for enhanced processing.

attentional bottleneck A filter that results from the limits intrinsic to our attentional processes, with the result that only the most important stimuli are selected for special processing.

early-selection model A model of attention postulating that the attentional bottleneck imposed by the nervous system can exert control early in the processing pathway, filtering out stimuli before even preliminary perceptual analysis has occurred.

late-selection model A model of attention postulating that the attentional bottleneck imposed by the nervous system exerts control late in the processing pathway, filtering out stimuli only after substantial analysis has occurred.

blindness uses short-term memory in order to compare the current scene with memory for the one viewed before the brief disruption. Observations from studies of inattentional and change blindness show that focused attention is crucial for the detection of change. (You can try out some examples on the website.)

In general, **divided attention tasks**—in which the subject is asked to process two or more simultaneous stimuli—confirm that attention is a limited resource and that it's very difficult to attend to more than one thing at a time, particularly if the stimuli to be attended to are spatially separated (Bonnel and Prinzmetal, 1998). So, our limited selective attention generally acts like an **attentional spotlight**, which shifts around the environment, highlighting stimuli for enhanced processing. It's an adaptation that we share with many other species because, like us, they are confronted with the problem of extracting important signals from a noisy background (Bee and Micheyl, 2008). Birds, for example, have to be able to isolate the vocalizations of specific individuals from a cacophony of calls and other noises in the environment—an avian version of the cocktail party problem (Benney and Braaten, 2000). Having a single attentional spotlight helps an individual focus cognitive resources and behavioral responses toward the most important things in the environment at any given moment (the smell of smoke, the voice of a potential mate, a glimpse of a big spotty cat), while filtering out extraneous information.

Attention filters information early or late in sensory processing

Because the brain has limited information-processing capacity, attentional processes have to provide a strict filter, sifting through the torrent of information coming in through our senses and selecting only the most important events for special processing. But at what level might this **attentional bottleneck** be found?

One possibility is that a gating mechanism operates near the level of the sensory inputs. According to **early-selection models** of attention (**Figure 18.2a**), higher-order cognitive processes—presumably located in the forebrain—can exert descending control over the gating mechanism to exclude unattended information before even preliminary perceptual processing has occurred (Broadbent, 1958). But this cannot be a complete account of the attentional control of information because, as we noted earlier, some important but unattended stimuli (such as your name) are apparently processed right up to the level of semantic meaning and awareness, at which point they can suddenly capture attention (Wood and Cowan, 1995). Observations of this sort have given rise to **late-selection models** of attention, in which the processing bottleneck imposed by the nervous system is situated later in the processing pathway, filtering out stimuli only after substantial analysis has occurred (**Figure 18.2b**).

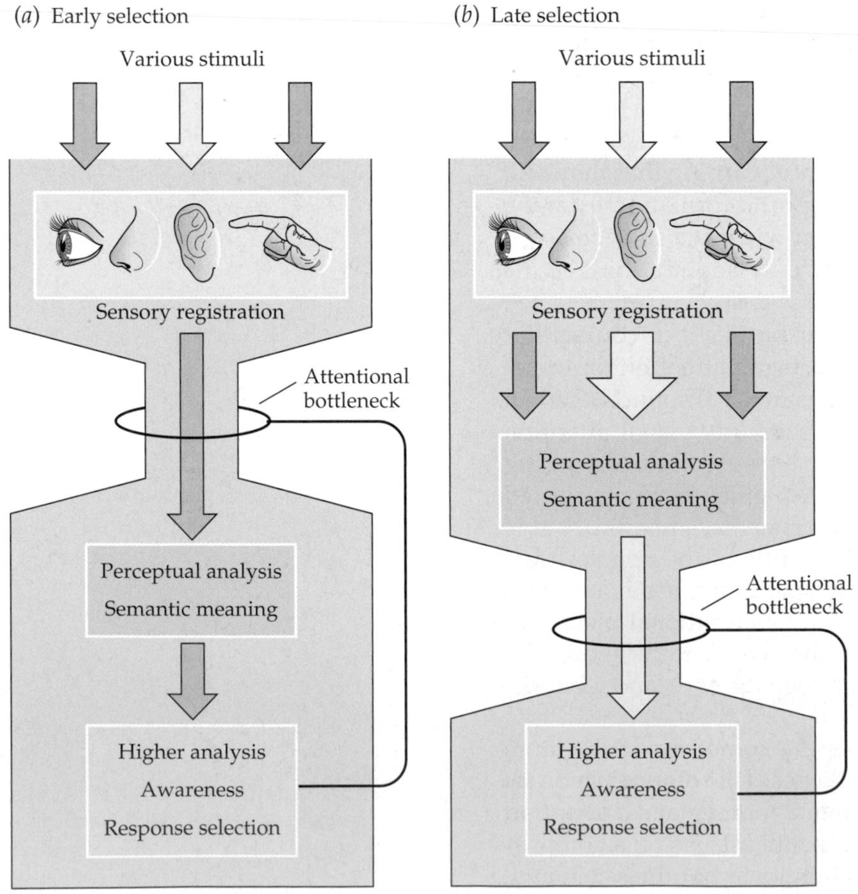

(a) Early selection

Various stimuli

Sensory registration

Attentional bottleneck

Perceptual analysis
Semantic meaning

Higher analysis
Awareness
Response selection

(b) Late selection

Various stimuli

Sensory registration

Perceptual analysis
Semantic meaning

Attentional bottleneck

Higher analysis
Awareness
Response selection

18.2 Bottlenecks in Attention (a) In early-selection models of attention, unattended stimuli are filtered out before much perceptual processing occurs. (b) In late selection, incoming information is not filtered out until after some analysis of the perceptual and semantic features has occurred. Early processing may, however, alter the weighting of the competing stimuli prior to later selection (e.g., emphasizing the stimuli represented by the yellow arrow).

red blue orange purple

orange blue green red

blue purple green red

orange blue red green

purple orange red blue

green red blue purple

18.3 The Stroop Effect Starting at the top and moving from left to right, say the *ink color* of each word. You'll most likely find that the task becomes much slower and more effortful after the first two lines. The later lines are more challenging because the semantic meaning of the words powerfully interferes with the task when the label and ink color mismatch, requiring some degree of late attentional selection to overcome the interference.

In the many variants of the *Stroop task*, irrelevant information interferes with target stimuli at a semantic level (**Figure 18.3**)—the *meaning* of the word makes it hard to name the color of the ink, so we must be processing that word we are trying to ignore. Here accurate attention to the target and exclusion of the interfering information must involve late attentional selection, along with other processes (MacLeod, 1991). Many models of attention contain both early- and late-selection mechanisms (e.g., Wolfe, 1994), and vigorous debate continues over their relative importance. When simple visual stimuli are rapidly presented one after another, subjects are poor at detecting a target stimulus if it follows another target by about 200–450 ms. Known as an **attentional blink** (Raymond et al., 1992), this phenomenon indicates that limitations on attention create a bottleneck at a fairly late point in stimulus processing. Emotional or other important targets can reduce or abolish the attentional blink, consistent with a late-selection process (Raymond and O'Brien, 2009; K. L. Shapiro et al., 1997).

A possible resolution to the debate over early versus late selection involves **perceptual load**—the immediate processing challenge presented by a stimulus. According to this view (N. Lavie, 1995; N. Lavie et al., 2004), when we focus on a complex stimulus that requires a lot of perceptual processing, no perceptual resources remain for use on competing unattended items. So in this case, attention exerts early selection and excludes other stimuli from the outset. But when we focus on simpler stimuli, there is enough perceptual capacity to allow for processing of additional stimuli, right up to the level of semantic meaning, recognition, and awareness (and thus, late selection) (N. Lavie et al., 2009). These studies indicate that attention strikes a precise and dynamic balance between early and late selection, determined by the difficulty of the task at hand.

Attention May Be Endogenous or Exogenous

We've now seen that through an act of willpower we can direct our attention to specific stimulus sources without moving our eyes or otherwise reorienting. Early experiments on this phenomenon, like Helmholtz's, employed **sustained attention tasks**, in which a single stimulus source or location must be held in the attentional spotlight for a protracted period (see Figure 18.1). Although these tasks are useful

attentional blink The reduced ability of subjects to detect a target stimulus if it follows another target stimulus by about 200–450 ms.

perceptual load The immediate processing challenge presented by a stimulus.

sustained attention task A task in which a single stimulus source or location must be held in the attentional spotlight for a protracted period.

stimulus cuing A technique for testing reaction time to sensory stimuli in which a cue to the location in which the stimulus will be presented is provided before the stimulus itself.

endogenous attention Also called *voluntary attention*. The voluntary direction of attention toward specific aspects of the environment, in accordance with our interests and goals.

top-down process A process in which higher-order cognitive processes control lower-order systems, often reflecting conscious control. Endogenous attention is one example.

symbolic cuing task A task that tests endogenous attention by presenting a visual stimulus and asking subjects to respond as soon as the stimulus appears on a screen. Each trial is preceded by a meaningful symbol used as a cue to hint at where the stimulus will appear.

18.4 Measuring the Effects of Endogenous Shifts of Attention (a) In symbolic cuing tasks, subjects are provided with a cue (the arrows) that accurately predicts target location (valid trials), or provides an inaccurate prediction (invalid trials), or provides no prediction (neutral trials). Subjects are instructed to maintain visual fixation on a central point throughout the trial. (b) Whether the target appears to the left or the right of the fixation point, valid cues significantly enhance reaction time to detect the target, and invalid cues significantly impair reaction time. (After Posner, 1980.)

for studying basic phenomena, and for assessing attention problems due to neurological disorders, we need something more powerful to address key questions about attention. For example, how do we shift attention around? How does attention enhance the processing of stimuli, and which brain regions are involved? To answer these questions, researchers have devised various clever tasks that employ **stimulus cuing** to control attention, and they have found that there are two general categories of attention: endogenous and exogenous. Although selective attention can be paid to stimuli in all sensory modalities, the great majority of research on attention employs visual stimuli, as we describe next.

With endogenous attention, we choose stimuli to study

The types of tasks that we have discussed thus far all involve **endogenous** (or *voluntary*) **attention**, the voluntary direction of attention toward specific aspects of the environment, in accordance with our interests and goals. Because endogenous attention comes from within, under conscious control by higher-order cognitive processes, researchers refer to it as a **top-down process**. It is as though the "higher" parts of the brain are directing "lower" brain centers that are conducting the first steps in analysis.

By far the most common experimental procedure for studying voluntary control of attention is the **symbolic cuing task**, originated by Posner (1980). In tasks of this sort, subjects must stare at a fixation point in the center of a computer screen, and they are instructed to press a key as quickly as possible when a specific target appears on the screen (the response being measured is therefore reaction time, described in **Box 18.1**). Each trial is preceded by a cue that gives the subject a hint as to where the stimulus will appear. So in our simple example (**Figure 18.4a**), subjects fixate on the central cross and an arrow pointing left, right, or both directions briefly flashes in a central location. Then, after a delay, the target stimulus flashes on the screen and the subject presses a key if he or she detects it. In most trials where there is a single arrow, it points in the correct direction and thus provides a *valid cue* about which side of the screen the target will appear on, but about once in every five trials there's an *invalid cue*, where the arrow points the opposite direction of where the target subsequently appears. The effects of these cues on reaction time are averaged over many trials and compared with *neutral trials*, in which the cue provides no hint about subsequent target location.

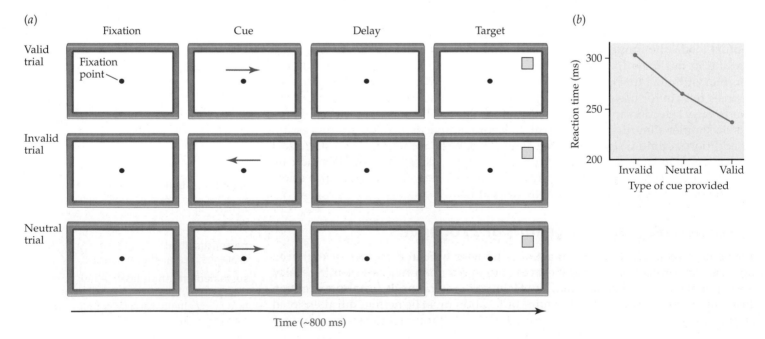

Time (~800 ms)

BOX 18.1 Reaction-Time Responses, from Input to Output

Reaction-time measures are a mainstay of cognitive neuroscience research. In tests of *simple reaction time*, subjects make a single response—for example, pressing a button—in response to experimental stimuli (the appearance of a target, the solution to a problem, a tone, or whatever the experiment is testing). Tests of *choice reaction time* involve a slightly more complicated situation, in which a person is presented with alternatives and has to choose among them (e.g., right versus wrong, same versus different) by pressing one of two or more buttons.

Reaction times in an uncomplicated choice reaction-time test, in which the subject indicates if two stimuli are the same or different, average about 300–350 ms. The delay between stimulus and response varies depending on the amount of neural processing required between input and output. The stations involved in our sample task, and the timing of events, are illustrated in the figure. Activity proceeds from the primary visual cortex through a ventral visual object identification pathway (see Chapter 10) to prefrontal cortex, and then through premotor and primary motor cortex, down to the spinal motoneurons and out to the finger muscles. In the sequence shown in the figure—proceeding from the presentation of visual stimuli to a discrimination response—notice that it takes about 110 ms for the sensory system to recognize the stimulus (somewhere in the inferior temporal lobe), and about 35 ms more for that information to reach the prefrontal cortex, which then

takes about 30 ms to determine which button to push. Then it takes about 75 ms for the movement to be executed (i.e., the time elapsed between the point at which the signal from the prefrontal cortex arrives in the premotor cortex and the point at which the finger pushes the button). It

is fascinating to think that something like this sequence of neural events happens over and over in more-complicated behaviors, such as recognizing a long lost friend or composing an opera.

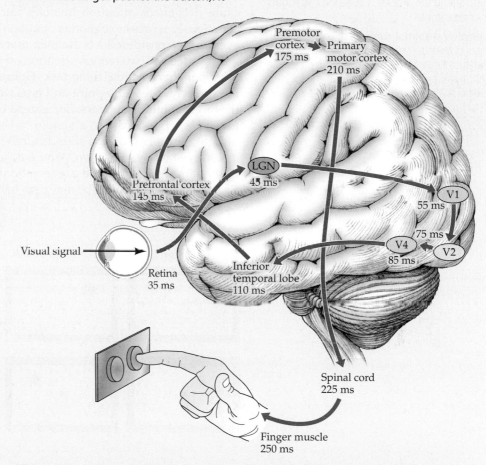

The sequence and timing of brain events that determine reaction time. LGN, lateral geniculate nucleus; V1, primary visual cortex; V2 and V4, extrastriate visual areas. (Timings based on Thorpe and Fabre-Thorpe, 2001.)

As you can see in **Figure 18.4b**, subjects swiftly learn to use the cues to predict stimulus location, shifting their attention in the cued direction—without shifting their gaze—in anticipation of the appearance of the target stimulus. Reaction time is thus significantly faster for validly cued trials, compared to the uncued neutral condition, even when subjects do not move their eyes to the cued location. And subjects clearly pay a price for shifting their attention on the 20% of cued trials in which the cue is invalid, misdirecting attention to the wrong side of the display. Many variants of the symbolic cuing paradigm—changing the timing of the stimuli, altering their complexity, choosing between different responses (as in Box 18.1), and so on—have been employed to study the neurophysiological mechanisms of attention (R. D. Wright and Ward, 2008), as we'll discuss a little later in the chapter.

In exogenous attention, stimuli grab our interest

Everyone knows that paying attention to events in the surrounding environment involves more than just consciously steering your attentional spotlight around. Loud noises, flashes, sudden movements—important changes generally—can potently capture our attention and draw it away from what we are doing, unless we are very focused (every conversation stops and every head swivels when someone drops a plate in a restaurant). Our responses to these sudden or important events provide examples of **exogenous** (or *reflexive*) **attention**, the involuntary reorienting of attention toward a specific stimulus source, cued by an object or event. Because exogenous attention involves unconscious shifts (indeed, it is difficult to consciously repress exogenous attention), and is oriented on the basis of sensory events, it is considered a **bottom-up process**.

The effects of exogenous attention on stimulus processing can be measured using a **peripheral spatial cuing task** (**Figure 18.5a**). As in the symbolic cuing tasks, the subject fixates on a point and is asked to respond as quickly as possible when the target stimulus appears. But instead of a meaningful symbol to direct attention toward a target location, a simple *task-irrelevant* sensory stimulus (often a flash of light, but it could be a sound or other stimulus) is presented *in the location to which attention is to be drawn*. After a delay, the target stimulus is presented, either in the same location as the cue (a valid trial) or somewhere else (an invalid trial). Reaction-time measures for many such trials are averaged for each subject.

exogenous attention Also called *reflexive attention*. The involuntary reorienting of attention toward a specific stimulus source, cued by an unexpected object or event.

bottom-up process A process in which lower-order mechanisms, like sensory inputs, trigger further processing by higher-order systems. There may be no conscious awareness until late in the process. Exogenous attention is one example.

peripheral spatial cuing task A task that tests exogenous attention, using latency to detect a visual stimulus, preceded by a simple task-irrelevant sensory stimulus in the location where the stimulus will appear.

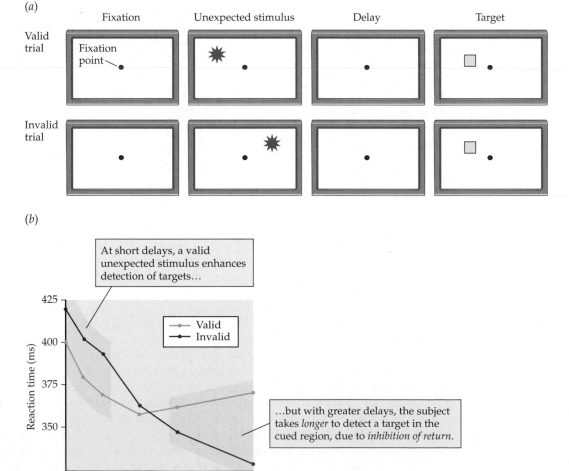

18.5 Exogenous Attention and Inhibition of Return (a) In valid trials, a momentary flash appears in the location where a stimulus will appear moments later. In invalid trials, the flash appears somewhere other than where the stimulus subsequently appears. (b) Reaction times indicate that attention is focused on the cued location for less than about 200 ms. (After R. M. Klein, 2000.)

Two important effects are evident in the results of such an experiment (**Figure 18.5b**). First, a valid exogenous cue enhances processing of subsequent stimuli at the same location, but only when the interval between cue and target is brief— the cue draws attention to a particular location, but after 150 ms or so attention apparently wanders away again and the enhancement of processing is lost. At longer cue-to-target intervals, from about 200 ms onward, a second phenomenon appears: detection of stimuli at the former location of the task-irrelevant cue is increasingly *impaired* (R. M. Klein, 2000; Posner and Cohen, 1984), as though attention has moved on and is reluctant to return to the previously attended location. This effect, termed **inhibition of return**, probably reflects an evolved adaptation to prevent exogenously controlled attention from settling on unimportant stimuli for more than an instant.

Normally, exogenous and endogenous attention work together to control an individual's cognitive activities (**Figure 18.6**), probably relying on somewhat overlapping neural mechanisms. Anyone who has watched a squirrel at work has seen that twitchy interplay: the animal purposefully searches for tasty nuts, and good places to bury them, but frequently pauses to attend to noises and movements. Furthermore, an exogenous attentional cue occurring in one modality (like a sound) can improve detection of a stimulus in another modality (like vision) coming from the same location (R. D. Wright and Ward, 2008). House cats are much better at localizing prey when they have a combination of cues to guide their attention (Schnupp et al., 2005), which may be one reason that squirrels are twitchy.

We use visual search to make sense of a cluttered world

Another familiar use for attention is the systematic scanning of the world in order to find specific objects of interest in a sea of distracters. Sometimes, in what is known as **feature search**, the sought-after item is sufficiently different from all the distracters in one attribute that it immediately "pops out." But more often we must rely on a **conjunction search**: searching for an item on the basis of two or more features (e.g., size and color) that together distinguish the target from distracters that may share some of the same attributes.

Visual search is studied in the laboratory using arrays of stimuli that systematically vary in the number of attributes they share with nearby distracters, and

inhibition of return   The phenomenon, observed in peripheral spatial cuing tasks and occurring when the interval between cue and target stimulus is 200 ms or more, in which detection of stimuli at the former location of the cue is increasingly impaired.

feature search   A search for an item in which the target pops out right away, because it possesses a unique attribute, no matter how many distracters are present.

conjunction search   A search for an item that is based on two or more features (e.g., size and color) that together distinguish the target from distracters that may share some of the same attributes.

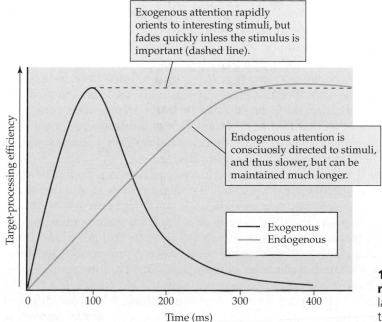

Exogenous attention rapidly orients to interesting stimuli, but fades quickly inless the stimulus is important (dashed line).

Endogenous attention is consciuosly directed to stimuli, and thus slower, but can be maintained much longer.

Exogenous
Endogenous

Target-processing efficiency

0   100   200   300   400

Time (ms)

18.6 Exogenous and Endogenous Attention Are Complementary   Quick-reacting exogenous attention and slower, longer-lasting endogenous attention work together to direct our analysis of the environment.

(*a*) Feature search

Find a green object

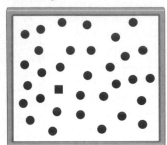

Find a square

(*b*) Conjunction search

Find a red circle

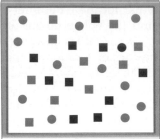

Find a green square

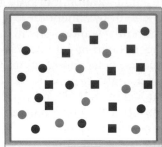

(*c*)

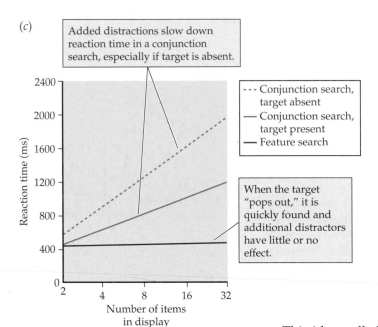

Added distractions slow down reaction time in a conjunction search, especially if target is absent.

- - - Conjunction search, target absent
— Conjunction search, target present
— Feature search

When the target "pops out," it is quickly found and additional distractors have little or no effect.

18.7 Visual Search (*a*) In these two feature search arrays, targets pop out. (*b*) In these two conjunction search arrays, one contains the target and one does not. (*c*) Data for three types of visual search. (After A. M. Treisman and Gelade, 1980.)

also in the number of distracters present. In a simple feature search (**Figure 18.7a**), targets pop out right away, no matter how many distracters are present, with only a few exceptions (Joseph et al., 1997); effortful voluntary attention is not required. In contrast, performance on conjunction searches (**Figure 18.7b**) is directly related to the number of distracters present. The patterns of results obtained from many such experiments (**Figure 18.7c**) suggest that conjunction searches involve sequential shifts of attention that help coordinate multiple cognitive *feature maps*—overlapping representations of the search array based on individual stimulus attributes (color, shape, and so on).

This idea, called **feature integration theory** (A. M. Treisman and Gelade, 1980) remains very influential in attention research and helps us address an issue that has come to be known as the **binding problem** (A. [M.] Treisman, 1996): How does the brain understand which individual attributes blend together into a single object, when these different features are processed by different regions in the brain? According to feature integration theory, simple preattentive stimulus attributes (e.g., color, shape) guide our scanning of the environment, with higher-order processes coordinating the binding of features and, ultimately, conscious perception and selection. This may be why conjunction searches run much faster when you can let your attention be controlled unsystematically by the basic attributes in the stimuli to be scanned (bottom-up process: scan for black things, then cars, then Subarus, and so on) rather than through systematic voluntary steering of the attentional spotlight using all attributes simultaneously (top-down process: search for the black 2002 Subaru Forester) (Wolfe et al., 2000).

To uncover finer details of the brain's attentional mechanisms, neuroscientists employ two general experimental strategies. First, we can look at *consequences of attention* in the brain, asking how selective attention modifies brain activity to enhance processing of stimuli. To do this, we need a brain measurement technique that offers maximal **temporal resolution**, the ability to track changes in the brain that occur very quickly. Electrophysiological measures are commonly used here, because they can track rapid oscillations in brain areas involved in stimulus processing. A second class of questions is concerned with the *mechanisms of attention*, the brain regions that produce and control attention, shifting it between different stimuli in different sensory modalities. Here, we need excellent **spatial resolution**,

feature integration theory The idea that conjunction searches involve sequential shifts of attention that help coordinate multiple cognitive feature maps—overlapping representations of the search array based on individual stimulus attributes.

binding problem The question of how the brain understands which individual attributes blend together into a single object, when these different features are processed by different regions in the brain.

temporal resolution The ability to track changes in the brain that occur very quickly.

spatial resolution The ability to observe the detailed structure of the brain.

the ability to observe the detailed structure of the brain. Single-cell recording, lesion studies, and brain-imaging techniques provide this capability, but they are relatively slow and unable to capture rapid changes in brain activity. So, in engineering terms, there is a *speed-accuracy tradeoff* in the techniques used to study attention. We discuss the two types of questions individually in the following sections.

Electrophysiological Techniques Trace Rapid Changes of Brain Activity

By attaching sensitive recording electrodes to the scalp at standardized locations (**Figure 18.8a**), we can record changes in the electrical activity of the brain, from second to second, in the region of the electrode. As we discussed in Chapter 3, this measurement, called an **electroencephalogram** (**EEG**), necessarily records from huge ensembles of neurons, numbering many millions, located in the region of each recording electrode. Ordinarily, the activity of all these neurons is desynchronized, so the recording looks like a randomly varying line, but sometimes, in seizure disorders, large numbers of neurons start firing together and large-amplitude synchronized waves become evident in the EEG trace (see Box 3.3 for a more complete discussion of epilepsy and EEGs).

Another way to synchronize electrical activity across large numbers of neurons is to get them to work together on a specific task, but this synchronized activity is still hard to see in individual EEGs. So instead, researchers have subjects do the same task over and over again, and they average all the EEGs recorded during the repeated trials (**Figure 18.8b**). Over enough trials, the random variation due to the chance firing of neurons averages out, and what's left is the overall electrical activity specifically associated with task performance (**Figure 18.8c**). This averaged activity is called the **event-related potential** (**ERP**) (Luck, 2005). Several components of the ERP, identified in Figure 18.8c, tend to be highly comparable between sub-

electroencephalogram (EEG) A measurement of gross electrical activity of the brain recorded from large electrodes placed on the scalp.

event-related potential (ERP) Also called *evoked potential*. Averaged EEG recordings measuring brain responses to repeated presentations of a stimulus. Components of the ERP tend to be reliable because the background noise of the cortex has been averaged out.

18.8 Event-Related Potentials

(a) Scalp electrodes record EEG activity during task performance. (b) The task is repeated many times; individual EEG segments for multiple trials show considerable random variation. (c) Averaging many such trials cancels out the random variation, leaving only task-related components, labeled as shown. Note that by convention, negative voltages are charted above the zero-line.

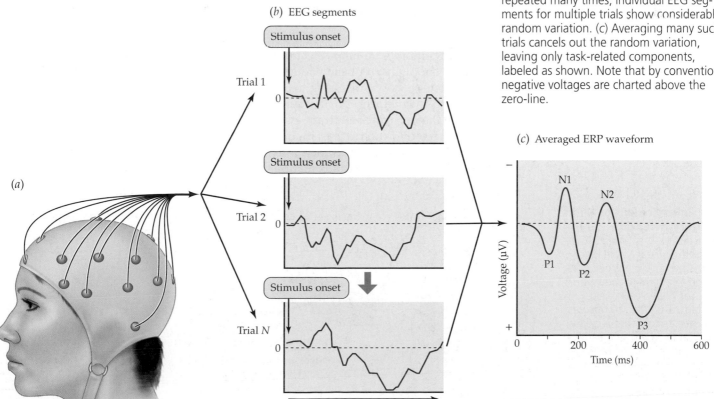

(b) EEG segments

Stimulus onset

Trial 1

Stimulus onset

Trial 2

Stimulus onset

Trial N

Time (ms) after stimulus presentation

(a)

(c) Averaged ERP waveform

N1

N2

P1

P2

P3

Voltage (μV)

0   200   400   600

Time (ms)

N1 effect A negative deflection of the event-related potential, occurring about 100 ms after stimulus presentation, that is enhanced for selectively attended input compared to ignored input.

P20–50 effect A positive deflection of the event-related potential, occurring about 20–50 ms after stimulus presentation, that is enhanced for selectively attended input compared to ignored input.

jects and track changes in processing associated with different brain regions over millisecond time courses. In contrast, MRI images take minutes to assemble, during which time many changes in attention may occur. Therefore, ERP measures have become a mainstay for studying the effects of attention on brain processing in several modalities, as we'll see.

Auditory attention produces a unique pattern of electrical activity

In one classic study of auditory attention (Hillyard et al., 1973), dichotic tones were presented to subjects who were asked to attend to the stimuli arriving at one ear and ignore the other ear. In half the trials subjects attended to the left; in the other half, to the right. EEGs were recorded and averaged into ERPs as already described. Thus, for each ear the researchers were able to compare ERPs for attended stimuli with ERPs for unattended stimuli. Importantly, the stimuli delivered to the ears across trials were identical, the only difference being which ear the person was attending to on each trial. Because the subjects were always attending to one ear or the other, any differences observed in the ERP couldn't be due to subjects simply not paying attention to *any* sounds.

All else being equal, the ERPs for stimuli being attended to were larger in amplitude than for the same stimuli at the same ear when not attended to (**Figure 18.9**). This effect was particularly evident in the ERP component called *N1*, a large negativity occurring about 100 ms after stimulus onset. Because the only thing that changed between conditions was subjects' attention to the stimuli, this auditory **N1 effect** must have been caused by selective attention somehow acting on neural mechanisms to enhance processing of information from that ear.

Later investigations sought to clarify the early electrophysiological events in endogenous auditory attention (Woldorff and Hillyard, 1991), using a special high-fidelity ERP procedure that allowed recording to begin much earlier after stimulus presentation. Not only was the N1 enhancement replicated, but a new phenomenon, called the **P20–50 effect**, was observed. As the *P* in its name suggests, this is a positive ERP deflection, occurring just 20–50 ms after stimulus presentation, that is enhanced for the selectively attended input relative to the ignored input stream. Because they occur so soon after stimulus presentation, the P20–50 effect and subsequent N1 enhancement provide strong physiological evidence of the operation of an *early*-selection mechanism in endogenous auditory attention. There simply hasn't been enough time for the auditory stimuli to have received complete sensory processing to the level of speech cues or semantic meaning.

With magnetoencephalography (MEG; see Chapter 2), a brain-imaging technique that measures electromagnetic emissions from the brain with excellent temporal resolution and at least moderate spatial resolution, the P20–50 effect has been localized to primary auditory and associated regions of superior temporal cortex. This is where auditory information first reaches the cortex, confirming an action of

18.9 Enhancement of N1 in Auditory Attention (*a*) The subject is asked to attend to stimuli in one ear, while ignoring the other. The ear being attended to alternates between trials. (*b*) With all else held constant, attending to one ear produces a significant increase in the amplitude of the early N1 component of the response to sound in that ear, presumably reflecting an effect of attention on neural processing. (After Hillyard et al., 1973.)

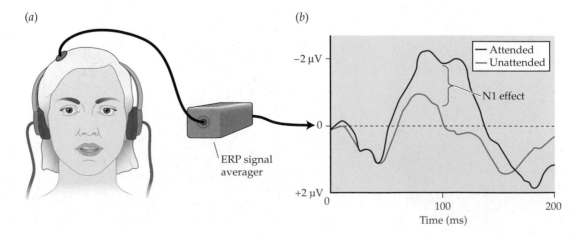

attention at early stages of auditory processing (Woldorff et al., 1993), where it acts as a gain control (like the volume control on a radio).

What about later aspects of auditory processing? Late attentional selection of auditory inputs, based on higher-order processing such as the identity of the person speaking or the semantic meaning of the sounds and so on, is evident in enhancement of long-latency ERP components. For example, an enhancement is seen at about 300 ms after stimulus presentation, in a component called P3 (or *auditory P300*, see Figure 18.8), one of the most prominent ERP markers of stimulus-processing activity (Herrmann and Knight, 2001). The **P3 effect** in auditory testing seems to be roughly located over parietal cortex and is associated with higher-order stimulus processing and late response selection. Abnormal P3 responses are a reliable finding in schizophrenia, and they may be linked to the decrements in attention evident in those patients (Ford, 1999).

Endogenous visual attention can be traced electrophysiologically

As you might expect, given that the sensory pathways and brain mechanisms involved are different, the effects of visual selective attention on the processing of stimuli in the brain leave their own unique imprint in ERP experiments. Typical experiments use symbolic cuing to direct covert attention to one location of the visual field, after which a target stimulus appears in the cued location (on most trials) or elsewhere (**Figure 18.10a**). ERPs are simultaneously recorded from electrodes located on the scalp over occipital cortex contralateral to the visual field in which the stimuli are presented because, as we discussed in Chapter 10, information from the left visual fields is processed in right occipital cortex, and vice versa (see Figure 10.11).

Figure 18.10b presents typical results from this sort of experiment. Notably, at 70–100 ms after stimulus presentation, the effect of attention is evident in an ERP component called *P1*, the first positive wave to appear over the occipital lobes, usually carrying over into an enhancement of the following N1 wave as well. The visual **P1 effect** involves a large increase in the amplitude of P1 for attended stimuli, if compared to ERPs for exactly the same stimulus presentation when attention is being directed elsewhere. The P1 effect apparently reflects a crucial early-selection mechanism: an attentional bottleneck whereby attention selectively boosts the activity of occipital sensory processing mechanisms (Mangun, 1995).

P3 effect Also called *auditory P300*. A positive deflection of the event-related potential, occurring about 300 ms after stimulus presentation, that is associated with higher-order auditory stimulus processing and late attentional selection.

P1 effect A positive deflection of the event-related potential, occurring 70–100 ms after stimulus presentation, that is enhanced for selectively attended visual input compared to ignored input.

18.10 ERP Changes in Endogenous Visual Attention (a) In this example, the subject maintains central fixation and covertly orients (dashed circle) in the direction indicated by a prior cue, pressing a key as soon as a stimulus appears. In most trials the cue is valid (*left*), but sometimes it misdirects attention to a different location (*right*; the dashed box indicates an alternate possible stimulus location). (b) This ERP, collected over the right occipital cortex while a stimulus was presented in the left visual field, shows that directing attention to the correct location significantly enhances neural processing and detection when the stimulus appears, reflected as large enhancements in the P1 and N1 components, starting 70–100 ms after stimulus presentation.

(*a*) Cued visual attention test

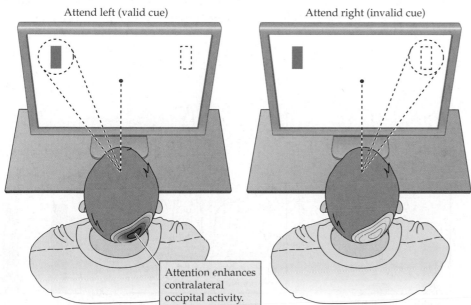

Attend left (valid cue)

Attend right (invalid cue)

Attention enhances contralateral occipital activity.

(*b*) Right occipital ERP

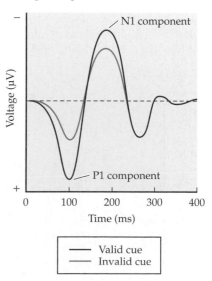

N1 component

P1 component

Voltage (µV)

Time (ms)

—— Valid cue
—— Invalid cue

In ERPs of visual voluntary attention tasks, no homolog of the auditory P20–50 effect is evident, probably because initial visual processing, especially in the retina, is slower than in the auditory system. A mathematical procedure called *dipole source modeling*, which helps identify the approximate points of origin of electrical events in the brain, has localized the P1 effect to extrastriate visual cortex (areas V2, V3, and V4; see Chapter 10) (Herrmann and Knight, 2001). This result suggests that the earliest effects of visual spatial attention on neural processing are at the level of visual cortex, although, as we'll discuss shortly, recent work indicates that attention might also affect subcortical visual components (Lovejoy and Krauzlis, 2010; K. A. Schneider and Kastner, 2009). Interestingly, the P1 effect is evident only in visual tasks involving manipulations of *spatial* attention (where is the target?)—not other features, like color, orientation, or various conjunctions.

Attentional selection based on higher-order complex properties of stimuli—as in late-selection tasks—doesn't generate a P1 effect. Recall that in the attentional blink paradigm that we described earlier, a target stimulus following another target stimulus by about 200–450 ms is poorly processed, indicating that this task involves relatively late selection (to put it another way, at 200–450 ms or so, attention is busy with the first stimulus, so the second stimulus is neglected). ERP studies find that the long-latency component P3 is selectively affected during the attentional blink but, impressively, neither P1 nor N1 shows any effect of attention in this paradigm. The dissociations in the ERP experiments—the P1 effect in cued attention versus the P3 effect in the attentional blink—thus provide electrophysiological evidence of differential consequences of early-selection versus late-selection mechanisms on underlying neural processes.

The neural mechanisms are evidently somewhat plastic: players of fast-paced "first-person shooter" video games—where stimuli are continually streaming toward the player and require rapid and accurate serial identification—show a much smaller attentional blink than do nonplayers. The additional observation that nonplayers show similar effects after they gain some playing experience suggests that the visual experience has a causal effect, improving visual attention capacity (C. S. Green and Bavelier, 2003), although serious gamers may be drawn to gaming because they have other, preexisting visuospatial talents (Boot et al., 2008).

Exogenous visual attention also produces electrophysiological effects

An important topic in attention research has been the extent to which endogenous and exogenous attention may involve overlapping neural substrates. Just how closely related are they? Do the same electrophysiological changes occur when attention is *reflexively* drawn to locations in exogenous attention paradigms?

18.11 ERPs in Exogenous Attention (*a*) With short delays between the appearance of the sensory cue and the appearance of the target stimulus, the P1 component is enhanced in the validly cued condition, where a flash automatically attracted attention to the spot where the stimulus appeared. (*b*) At longer delays between the cue and target, the P1 effect vanishes because of inhibition of return. (After Hopfinger and Mangun, 1998.)

(*a*) Short delay

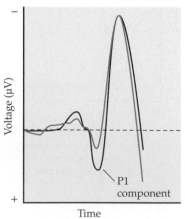

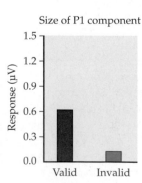

(*b*) Long delay

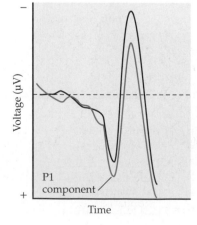

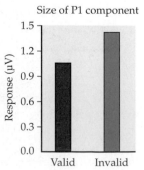

In exogenous spatial cuing tasks, like the one shown in Figure 18.5, occipital ERP data reveal an enhancement of P1 (Hopfinger and Mangun, 1998, 2001), just as with endogenous attention, discussed in the previous section. Exogenous attention studies such as that shown in **Figure 18.11** indicate that exogenous attention augments the processing of visual stimuli at the level of striate and extrastriate cortex, in much the same way that endogenous attention does. But this is true only for short-latency trials, in which the target stimulus follows closely after the sensory cue (recall that in this type of exogenous attention task, the cue is often a simple flash in the location to be attended to). As the delay between the sensory cue and the target lengthens, the P1 enhancement reduces and even inverts (see Figure 18.11*b* and **Figure 18.12**); this is the electrophysiological manifestation of inhibition of return, which we discussed earlier.

Taken together, the visual ERP data indicate that whether attention comes from the bottom up (exogenous) or from the top down (endogenous), it has similar effects on sensory analysis mechanisms, augmenting electrophysiological activity. That doesn't mean that the sources and control of the two types of attention are identical, however, or even overlapping—just that their outcomes are comparable. Probing the anatomical origins of attention requires a different experimental approach, as we will discuss shortly.

Neural processes that are at work when we are searching among an array of objects, and particularly fixing on a pop-out stimulus within an array (see Figure 18.7*a*), have been tracked using ERPs. This form of focused attention generates a unique component called the *N2pc wave*, so named because it is a variant of the second major negative ERP peak, and because it is found over posterior cortex contralateral to the location of the visual search stimulus (Luck and Hillyard, 1994). Considering the nature of the task, N2pc could reflect enhanced processing of the target stimulus, or active rejection of the field of distracters. Recent evidence suggests that the N2pc is a consequence of both actions occurring together (Hickey et al., 2009); perhaps this process is what makes the pop-out effect in visual search so forceful.

Many Brain Regions Are Involved in Processes of Attention

Electrophysiological measures like ERP do an excellent job of tracking the effects of attention on the selection of important sensory information for enhanced processing, and they offer a window into the real-time workings of cognition. However, to understand the anatomical details of attention's effects in the brain, and the mechanisms that originate and direct this mysterious property of consciousness, researchers turn to additional experimental strategies, such as studies of lab animals, human brain-imaging studies, and insights from rare neurological disorders that impair attention.

Neuroimaging confirms that the anatomical foci of attention show augmented processing

Although they operate too slowly to track momentary changes in activity, studies employing PET and fMRI in carefully designed experiments have confirmed that a principal consequence of attention is selective enhancement of neural activity in brain regions important for processing specific aspects of target stimuli. In one such study, subjects participated in a simple spatial cuing task while both fMRI and ERP data were collected (McMains and Somers, 2004). Using ERP data to identify the time points for taking fMRI images, the researchers found anatomically distinct regions of enhanced activity in visual cortex that corresponded very

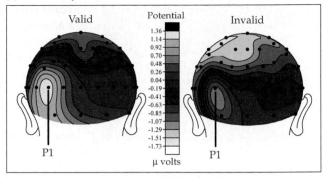

(*a*) Short delay

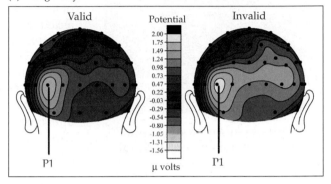

(*b*) Long delay

18.12 ERP Maps in Exogenous Visual Attention These voltage maps illustrate the enhancing effect of exogenous attention on neural processing. The same right-sided stimulus was presented in every case, but in some trials the stimulus was preceded by a flash in the location that the stimulus subsequently appeared (valid trials), whereas in other trials the flash drew attention to a different location (invalid trials). For short delays (*a*), an enhancement in P1 is evident (yellow) over left occipital cortex; but at longer delays (*b*), the P1 response in the cued location is blunted because of inhibition of return. In fact, at long delays the P1 response to the stimulus is larger for invalid cues! (Courtesy of Joe Hopfinger.)

Subject A

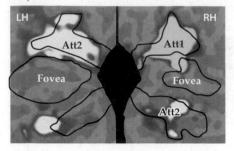

Subject B

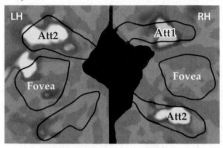

18.13 Effects of Attentional Spotlights on fMRI Activation in Visual Cortex These maps of visual cortex in two subjects are displayed so as to correspond to visual space (in other words, they are retinotopic; see Chapter 10). Covert attention to one location (Att1) produced increased activity on fMRI as targets appeared in that attended location (blue), relative to control conditions. In a second experimental condition, subjects divided their attention between two spatial locations (the two Att2's), and fMRI again showed enhanced activity for targets in the two corresponding regions of visual cortex (red-yellow). (Image courtesy of David Somers.)

closely to the spatial location of covert attention (**Figure 18.13**), consistent with an early selection process. As subjects shifted attention to other locations, the locus of enhanced activity within the retinotopic map of primary visual cortex also shifted (see Chapter 10). And dividing attention between two spatial locations resulted in two corresponding patches of enhancement.

Evidence suggests that an effect of attention on neural activation can even be observed in *subcortical* visual structures (Schneider and Kastner, 2009). Using a sustained attention task, the researchers found fMRI enhancements in the superior colliculi and lateral geniculate nuclei (see Figure 10.11). This finding indicates that some degree of attentional selection may be occurring very early indeed, before visual information has even reached the cortex, in both subcortical visual pathways.

At later stages of the visual system, physiological effects of attention become even more pronounced. In one clever study, researchers devised stimuli composed of faces overlaid on pictures of houses (O'Craven et al., 1999). When subjects were asked to ignore the houses and sustain attention on the faces in the stimuli, attention-related enhancement was seen in a cortical region specifically responsible for face processing, called the fusiform face area (see Figure 19.19). When subjects were instructed to attend to the houses and ignore the faces—using the same stimuli—fMRI enhancement was instead seen in a cortical area responsible for processing location (the parahippocampal place area). This neuroimaging evidence of late attentional selection illustrates once again that the attentional bottleneck can vary, depending on task demands (N. Lavie et al., 2004).

Attention alters the functioning of individual neurons

As you'll recall from Chapter 10, visual neurons have distinctive receptive fields; visual stimuli falling within these fields can excite or inhibit the neurons, reflected in changes in the frequency of action potentials they produce. Single-cell recordings of the effects of visual attention can be accomplished in much the same way, by recording from visual cortex neurons while attention within the visual field is manipulated. In principle, the consequences of attention—its effects on the response of a sensory neuron—could be evident in single-cell recordings in three different ways. One possibility is that selective attention to a cell's receptive field might globally *enhance or suppress* responses, increasing or decreasing the firing rate of the cell (**Figure 18.14a**). Alternatively, attention could *sharpen* the tuning of cortical neurons, causing them to focus more keenly on specific stimuli (**Figure 18.14b**). Or attention might induce a *shift in tuning* of the cell, indicating a change in the cell's preferred stimulus (**Figure 18.14c**).

In an important study (**Figure 18.15**), Moran and Desimone (1985) studied the effects on single-cell activity of shifts in attention *within the cell's receptive field*. Using a system of rewards, the researchers trained macaque monkeys to covertly attend to one spatial location or another (on the basis of symbolic cues) while recordings were made from single extrastriate visual neurons. In one condition, a display was presented that included the cell's most preferred stimulus, as well as a nonpreferred

18.14 Some Ways That Attention Could Modify Single-Cell Activity

(*a*) Enhanced or suppressed response

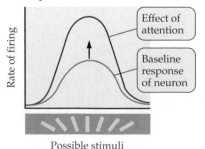

Possible stimuli

(*b*) Sharpened tuning to specific stimuli

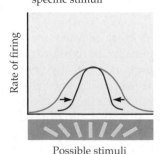

Possible stimuli

(*c*) Cell's tuning shifted to favor a different stimulus

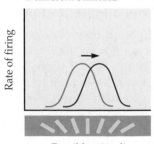

Possible stimuli

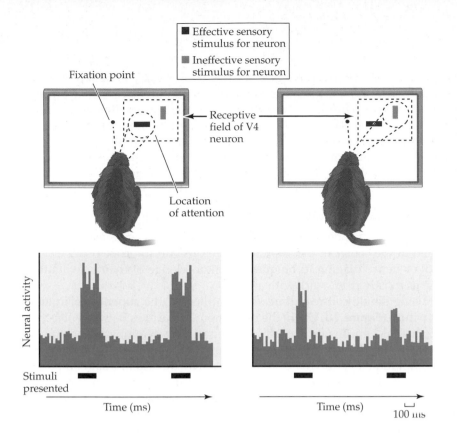

Effective sensory stimulus for neuron

Ineffective sensory stimulus for neuron

Fixation point

Receptive field of V4 neuron

Location of attention

Neural activity

Stimuli presented

Time (ms)

Time (ms)

100 ms

18.15 Effect of Selective Attention on the Activity of Single Visual Neurons Here, a macaque monkey has been trained to maintain central fixation while moving covert attention. Within the receptive field for the particular cortical neuron being recorded, the area being attended to is shown as a dashed circle. In the first condition (*left*) the area of attention within the cell's receptive field includes the effective stimulus (red) and excludes the distracter (green). The only difference in the second condition is that the attentional spotlight has been moved to include the stimulus that is normally less effective in firing the cell. Because (1) both stimuli are present in both conditions, (2) the fixation point hasn't changed, and (3) the same cell is being recorded from in both conditions, attentional mechanisms must have directly altered the cell's preferences and sensitivity. (After Moran and Desimone, 1985.)

stimulus a short distance away but still within the cell's visual field. Counts of action potentials were made while attention was covertly directed at the preferred stimulus and, as expected, a robust response was recorded. In the second condition, exactly the same display was presented and the same neuron was recorded from, but the monkey's covert attention was shifted elsewhere in the receptive field. Because (1) the favored stimulus was present, (2) the same cell was being recorded, and (3) the animal's gaze had not shifted, you might expect that the rate of firing would remain robust, but that was not the result. Instead, rates of firing were significantly diminished in the second condition. Only the shift in attention could account for this change (consistent with the process depicted in Figure 18.14*a*).

Endogenous visual attention can exert continual control over the properties of the receptive fields of extrastriate visual neurons (Womelsdorf et al., 2006). In this work, researchers mapped sensitivity across the receptive field of a single neuron, by presenting the cell's preferred stimulus repeatedly throughout the receptive field. Their efforts produced the type of map shown in **Figure 18.16*a***. The researchers found that when the monkey covertly shifted attention from one cued location (S1 in the figure) to a different cued location but still within the receptive field (S2), the

18.16 Attentional Remodeling of a Neuron's Receptive Field Each panel is a map from the same single neuron in extrastriate cortex, showing sensitivity to its preferred stimulus throughout its receptive field. In (*a*), a region of heightened sensitivity is evident while the animal attends to a location cued by S1 (green diamond). In (*b*), stimuli are identical, except the animal is attending to the position cued by S2 (blue circle). Panel (*c*) is a difference map, showing the net change in receptive-field characteristics as attention shifted from position S1 to position S2. The cell's receptive field has evidently been retuned by attentional processes. (Image courtesy of Thilo Womelsdorf and Stefan Treue.)

(*a*)　　　　　　　(*b*)　　　　　　　(*c*)

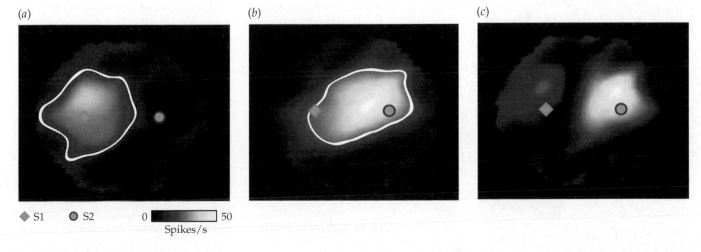

S1　　S2　　0 ▬▬▬ 50

Spikes/s

superior colliculus   A gray matter structure of the dorsal midbrain that receives visual information and is involved in direction of visual gaze and visual attention to intended stimuli.

pulvinar   In humans, the posterior portion of the thalamus, heavily involved in visual processing and direction of attention.

peak sensitivity within the receptive field for this neuron shifted right along with attention (**Figure 18.16*b***). Furthermore, attention can apparently cause the overall size of receptive fields to shrink, as if sharpening a spotlight to exclude neighboring distracters (Mounts, 2000; Womelsdorf et al., 2008). Results of the study are therefore consistent with the process depicted in Figure 18.14*b*. These and other studies have documented effects of attention on single-cell responses throughout extrastriate cortex, including V1, V2, V3, V4, IT (inferior temporal), and MT (medial temporal) regions (see Figure 10.19 for a refresher of extrastriate cortex topography).

The superior colliculus guides attentional eye movements

Subcortical structures can be difficult to study with less invasive techniques because, situated in the center of the brain, they are difficult to probe using electrophysiological or neuroimaging techniques. Our knowledge of their role in attention thus comes mostly from work with animals.

Research using single-cell recordings has implicated the **superior colliculus**, a midbrain structure (**Figure 18.17**), in the movement of the eyes between objects of attention. Collicular neurons increase their firing during eye movements toward a stimulus that is also the focus of attention (Wurtz and Goldberg, 1972; Wurtz et al., 1982). Comparable eye movements made *without* the attentional component are not associated with increased activity. So, cells of the superior colliculus are involved in producing eye movements toward attended objects, during overt attention. Collicular neurons are particularly sensitive to relative motion in any direction (R. M. Davidson and Bender, 1991), perhaps due to visual aspects of moving gaze around. A person with damage to one superior colliculus showed diminished inhibition of return for stimuli on the affected side; the superior colliculus may therefore help us avoid repeatedly returning to previously attended locations (Sapir et al., 1999).

Although implicated primarily in overt attention, the superior colliculus may help control covert attention too—a top-down task generally assigned to cortical mechanisms (as we'll discuss shortly). For example, reversible inactivation of the superior colliculus on one side abolishes monkeys' ability to utilize selective attention cues on the corresponding side of visual space (Lovejoy and Krauzlis, 2010).

The pulvinar drives shifts of attention

Making up about the posterior quarter of the thalamus in humans (see Figure 18.17), the **pulvinar** is heavily involved in visual processing, is organized retinotopically, and shares extensive connections with the superior colliculus, parietal cortex, and cingulate. In attention tasks, the pulvinar has been linked to the orienting and shifting of attention, and to the attentional filtering of stimuli. One innovative approach involved direct injections of GABA agonists and antagonists to reversibly inhibit or activate the pulvinar (recall that GABA is an inhibitory transmitter, so its antagonists tend to increase neural activity). Following injection of a GABA agonist into the pulvinar, monkeys reportedly had great difficulty with orienting covert attention toward targets in the contralateral visual field (D. L. Robinson and Petersen, 1992). Injections of a GABA *antagonist*, however, enhanced covert shifting of attention. In addition, the pulvinar seems to mediate the ability of monkeys to filter out and ignore distracting stimuli while engaged in covert attention tasks. The pulvinar's role in attentional filtering has been observed in fMRI research in humans too, where attention tasks with larger numbers of distracters induce greater activation of the pulvinar nuclei (Buchsbaum et al., 2006).

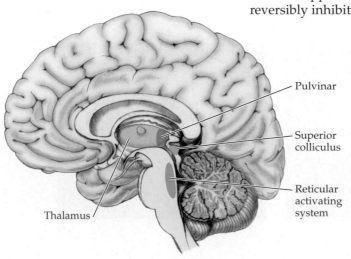

Pulvinar

Superior colliculus

Reticular activating system

Thalamus

18.17 Subcortical Sites Implicated in Visual Attention

Several cortical areas are crucial for generating and directing attention

In addition to cortical regions (mostly sensory) that reveal the consequences of attention, a number of cortical regions are associated with the control or source of attention. The extensive connections of subcortical mechanisms of attention with regions of the parietal lobes, along with observations from clinical cases that we will discuss shortly, point to a special role of the parietal lobes for attentional control. Initial work with single-cell recordings in monkeys showed that certain parietal cells selectively increase their firing rate when the animal identifies a target stimulus to which it will covertly attend, but not when the stimulus is in the same location in the absence of planning for covert attention (Wurtz et al., 1982). In other words, the cells behave as though they are processing details and preparing for a shift of attention.

These and other single-cell studies indicate that a region in the monkey parietal lobe called the **lateral intraparietal area**, or just **LIP**, is especially involved in the voluntary, top-down control of attention. The human homolog of this region is the **intraparietal sulcus** (**IPS**) (**Figure 18.18**). Activity of LIP neurons is correlated with the direction of attention to particular locations, and it is enhanced regardless of whether the attention is directed toward visual or auditory targets (Bisley and Goldberg, 2003; J. Gottlieb, 2007). By comparing LIP cells' responses to targets and distracters across space, researchers have found that the LIP encodes a *salience map* (or *priority map*) which controls the direction of attention between important stimuli from one moment to the next (Bisley and Goldberg, 2006; Ipata et al., 2006).

The human IPS appears to behave much like the monkey LIP. In covert attention tasks that are long enough to allow for fMRI analysis, enhanced activity is evident in the IPS in association with the control of attention (Corbetta and Schulman, 1998). Conversely, interfering with the normal function of IPS through transcranial magnetic stimulation (see Chapter 2) causes humans to have difficulty voluntarily shifting attention (Koch et al., 2005).

In conjunction with the LIP/IPS, an area in the frontal lobes of the brain called the **frontal eye field** (**FEF**) has been intensively studied, in part because of observations in neurological patients: people with damage to the FEF have a very difficult time suppressing unwanted reorientation of the eyes toward peripheral distracters (Paus et al., 1991). Located in the premotor area of the frontal lobes (see Figure 18.18), neurons of the FEF are important for establishing gaze in accordance with cognitive goals (top-down processes) rather than with any characteristics of stimuli (bottom-up processes). This may be why the FEF has rich interconnections with the superior colliculus, which, as we discussed earlier, is important for planned eye movements.

Unlike the dorsal frontoparietal system just described, a region located more posteriorly and ventrally seems to be critically involved in the reorientation of attention to new locations on the basis of stimulus characteristics (i.e., a bottom-up function). As its name implies, the **temporoparietal junction** (**TPJ**) lies at the junction of the parietal and temporal lobes (see Figure 18.18), at about the posterior end of the Sylvian fissure. It includes parts of the temporal lobe (specifically, the superior temporal gyrus) and parts of the inferior parietal lobe (namely, the supramarginal gyrus). Unlike the IPS/LIP, the TPJ plays a role in shifting attention to a new location *after* target onset, especially if the stimulus is unexpected. In one experiment, subjects selectively attending to a specific location showed a significant increase in TPJ activity if a relevant stimulus suddenly appeared in a novel, unexpected loca-

lateral intraparietal area (LIP) A region in the monkey parietal lobe, homologous to the human intraparietal sulcus, that is especially involved in voluntary, top-down control of attention.

intraparietal sulcus (IPS) A region in the human parietal lobe, homologous to the monkey lateral intraparietal area, that is especially involved in voluntary, top-down control of attention.

frontal eye field (FEF) An area in the frontal lobe of the brain containing neurons important for establishing gaze in accordance with cognitive goals (top-down processes) rather than with any characteristics of stimuli (bottom-up processes).

temporoparietal junction (TPJ) The point in the brain where the temporal and parietal lobes meet; plays a role in shifting attention to a new location after target onset.

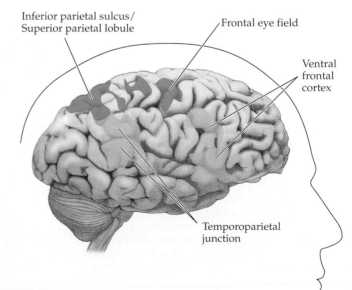

Inferior parietal sulcus/
Superior parietal lobule

Frontal eye field

Ventral frontal cortex

Temporoparietal junction

18.18 Cortical Regions Implicated in the Top-Level Control of Attention

tion (Corbetta and Shulman, 2002). Patients with TPJ damage respond poorly to unanticipated targets (Friedrich et al., 1998). The role of the TPJ has been likened to an alerting signal or "circuit breaker," overriding the current attentional priority in order to redirect to something new. Interestingly, this system is strongly lateralized to the right hemisphere, unlike the more dorsal system involving the IPS and FEF. This right-hemisphere dependence has implications for clinical conditions, which we will discuss a little later.

Two cortical networks collaborate to govern attention

To produce our seamless experience of the world, continually selecting and shifting between objects of interest, the cortical and subcortical mechanisms of attention must all operate as a coordinated network. Projections from executive sources of attentional control extend to sensory cortical areas to modify their function, as we've described in the preceding sections. Convergent evidence suggests that the higher-order attention mechanisms work together within two overall networks—dorsal frontoparietal and right temporoparietal—for controlling attention to the world.

A DORSAL FRONTOPARIETAL SYSTEM FOR TOP-DOWN CONTROL OF ENDOGENOUS ATTENTION   A modified form of fMRI that allows partial tracking of activity during rapid events (called, unsurprisingly, *event-related fMRI*, or *ER-fMRI*) enables us to visualize network activities during top-down attentional processing (Hopfinger et al., 2000; Corbetta et al., 2000). **Figure 18.19** illustrates results from a typical experiment. **Figure 18.19a** shows patterns of activation uniquely evident during the cue presentation phase of the task. Enhanced activity is evident in the vicinity of the frontal eye fields (dorsolateral frontal cortex) and, simultaneously, in the IPS. By comparison, the target-processing phase of the trial (**Figure 18.19b**) was associated with activity of regions around the pre- and postcentral gyrus, reflecting response initiation; and in visual cortex, reflecting stimulus processing. Observations from studies like this confirm that several identified attention-controlling regions work together as a dorsal frontoparietal system for top-down endogenous control of attention.

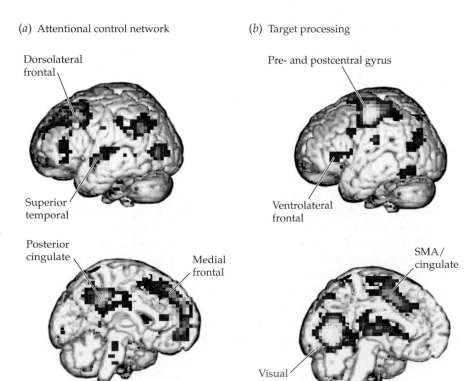

(a) Attentional control network

Dorsolateral frontal

Superior temporal

Posterior cingulate

Medial frontal

(b) Target processing

Pre- and postcentral gyrus

Ventrolateral frontal

SMA/ cingulate

Visual cortex

18.19 A Frontoparietal Attentional Control Network   While subjects performed a spatial cued-attention task, ER-fMRI images were collected, tied to either (a) the cue-processing phase of the trial (thus, the covert direction of attention) or (b) the target-processing phase of the task (corresponding to target processing and selection of motor responses). In part a, the conscious direction of attention is associated with selective activations of the dorso-frontal cortex, corresponding to the frontal eye field, the intraparietal sulcus, and the temporoparietal junction (see text for details). (Image courtesy of Joe Hopfinger and George Mangun.)

18.20 A Right Temporoparietal System Responds to Novel Stimuli   As described in the text, this pathway becomes more active when relevant stimuli appear unexpectedly. IPL, inferior parietal lobule; TPJ, temporoparietal junction. (Image courtesy of Maurizio Corbetta.)

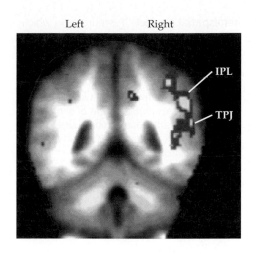

A RIGHT TEMPOROPARIETAL SYSTEM FOR BOTTOM-UP CONTROL AND SHIFTS OF EX-OGENOUS ATTENTION   Results of ER-fMRI studies confirm the involvement of a system in the temporoparietal junction in directing attention to novel or unexpect-ed stimuli (**Figure 18.20**). To investigate this question, researchers synchronized scans to the occasional appearance of novel stimuli in a stream of distracters. As Figure 18.20 indicates, this system shows a strong right-hemisphere lateralization; activity is localized on the right TPJ regardless of whether the stimulus falls in left or right hemispace (Corbetta et al., 2000). The ventral temporoparietal system receives inputs from visual cortex (conveying stimulus properties) and also from ventral frontal cortex (VFC); VFC is implicated in working memory (see Chapter 17) and thus may provide crucial information about novelty by comparing the present state of stimuli with that of the recent past.

Accumulating evidence supports combining the dorsal and ventral attentional control networks into a single interactive model (Corbetta and Shulman, 2002). In this model the network implicated in endogenous attention and the network con-trolling exogenous attention interact extensively (**Figure 18.21**). According to this scheme, the more dorsal stream of processing reflects endogenous attention, pro-jecting from frontal cortex to the IPS region of posterior parietal cortex, ultimately having two effects: attentional modulation of neuronal function in visual areas, as we discussed earlier in the chapter (e.g., McMains and Somers, 2004); and coordina-tion with the subcortical system mediated by the pulvinar and superior colliculus, in order to steer attention. Simul-taneously with these actions, projections from visual cor-tex to the TPJ help the right-sided ventral system scan for novel salient stimuli (drawing exogenous attention), with the help of working memory inputs from the VFC.

The strong connections between IPS and TPJ allow for rapid reassignment of attention and give us the ef-fortless awareness of environmental stimuli that we take for granted as we shift rapidly between intended objects of attention and the other interesting things that pop up around us. And although most research has focused on visuospatial stimuli, the frontoparietal cortical attention network appears to be active in other visual modalities (e.g., color, shape), temporal judgments (Kanwisher and Wojciulik, 2000), and auditory stimuli (Brunetti et al., 2008; Walther et al., 2010). Integration across sensory mo-dalities is an essential aspect of attentional selection—for example, exogenous auditory stimuli enhance visual per-ception and ERPs in visual cortex (McDonald et al., 2000,

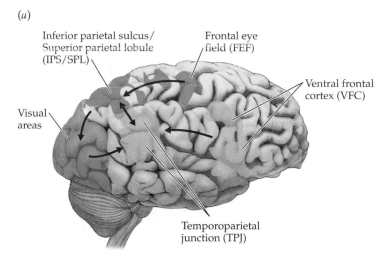

(a)

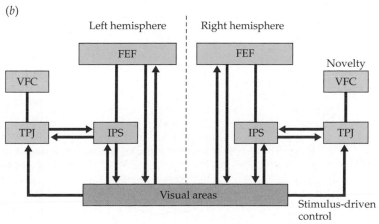

(b)

18.21 The Cortical Attentional Control Network   (a) Regions shaded blue are involved in controlling endogenous at-tention. Regions in yellow are part of a right-hemisphere system for reorienting and exogenous attention. Arrows indicate the presumed direction of control. Extensive interaction between the systems provides integrated control over attention. (b) Schematic of the attentional control network. Connections between the TPJ and IPS provide a means for novel stimuli to interrupt and reorga-nize attentional priorities. (After Corbetta and Shulman, 2002.)

hemispatial neglect A syndrome in which the patient fails to pay any attention to objects presented to one side of the body and may even deny connection with that side.

extinction Short for *extinction of simultaneous double stimulation*, an inability to recognize the double nature of stimuli presented simultaneously to both sides of the body. People experiencing extinction report the stimulus from only one side.

anosognosia Denial of illness.

2003)—and the "supramodal" characteristics of the attention network are the subject of intensive research efforts.

Neurological Disorders Reveal the Anatomy of Attention

A time-honored method for learning about the organization of the human brain is careful analysis of neuropsychological impairments—sometimes subtle, sometimes profound—that accompany injuries and diseases of the brain. By noting the behavioral consequences of damage to discrete neuroanatomical regions, we can make inferences about the affected region's function in the intact brain. It's an approach that has drawn back the curtain on some aspects of attention and awareness as components of human consciousness.

Neglect of one side of the body and space can result from parietal lobe injury

One peculiar syndrome reinforces the notion of the attentional system in the right hemisphere that we just discussed. Brain damage involving the right inferior parietal cortex produces an unusual set of behavioral changes (Rafal, 1994). The key feature is neglect of the left side of both the body and space. People and objects to the left of the patient's midline may be completely ignored, as if unseen, despite the absence of any visual-field defects. For example, the patient may fail to dress the left side of her body, will not notice visitors if they approach from the left, and may fail to eat the food on the left side of her dinner plate. This phenomenon, called **hemispatial neglect**, can also be seen in simple test situations. A common test requires the patient to copy drawings of familiar objects. In a typical result, a patient who is asked to draw the face of a clock draws numbers on only the right side of the clock face (**Figure 18.22**) (Schenkerberg et al., 1980).

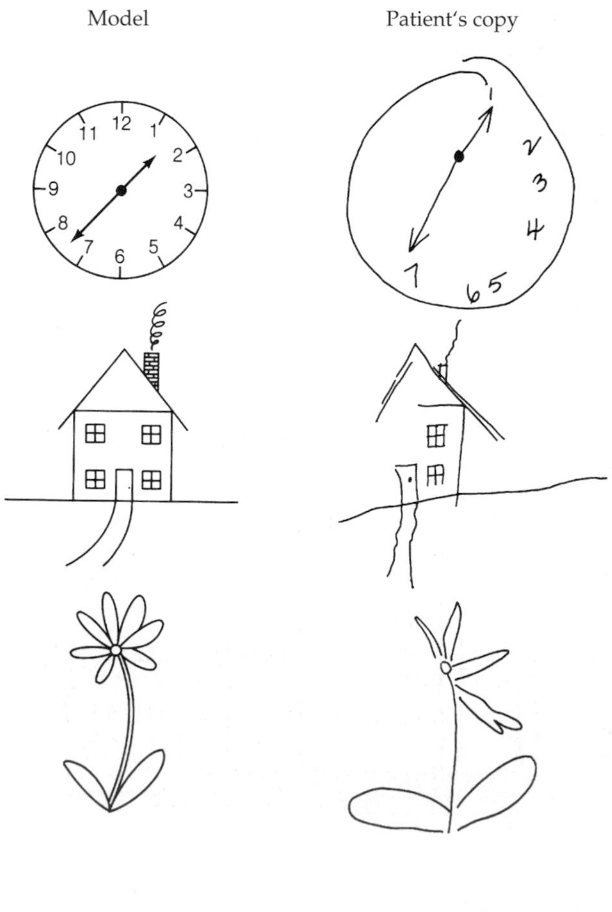

Associated with this dramatic change is a feature called *extinction of simultaneous double stimulation*, or just **extinction**. Most people can readily report the presence of two stimuli when those stimuli are presented simultaneously on both sides of the body. Patients with right inferior parietal lesions, however, are unable to note the double nature of the stimulation and usually report only the stimulus presented to the right side. It is as if the normally balanced competition for attention between the two sides has become skewed, so that the input from the right side now overrules or extinguishes the input from the left. This syndrome extends to visual imagery as well; for example, patients with hemispatial neglect describe events from only one side of dream scenes, consistent with the observation that they make no leftward eye movements during REM sleep (Doricchi et al., 1991). Although many patients with injury to this region show recovery from unilateral neglect, the feature of extinction is quite persistent. And even though neglect and extinction are most dramatically evident in the visual domain, similar problems are reported with stimuli in other sensory modalities (e.g., Funk et al., 2010; Schindler, et al., 2006), indicating that a supramodal attentional control system has been compromised by the damage.

Yet another striking feature of this syndrome is frequent **anosognosia** (denial of illness). Neglect patients may adamantly maintain that they are capable of engaging in their customary activities and do not recognize the impressive signs of unilateral neglect. They may even disclaim "ownership" of their own left arm or leg, rather than accepting that anything unusual is occurring. "Well then, whose left arm is that, there in your bed?" "I don't know. My sister must have left that here. Wasn't that an awful thing to do?!" Remarkably, having these patients wear prisms to shift their visual field 10° to the

18.22 Diagnostic Test for Hemispatial Neglect When asked to duplicate drawings of common symmetrical objects, patients suffering from hemispatial neglect ignore the left side of the model that they're copying. (From Kolb and Whishaw, 1990.)

Model   Patient's copy

Critical areas damaged in spatial neglect

Model of cortical attention control network

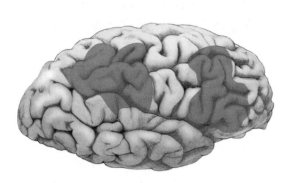

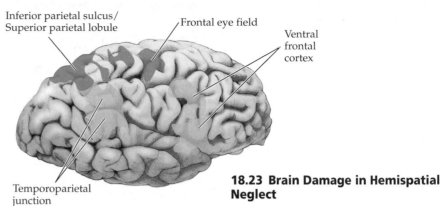

Inferior parietal sulcus/
Superior parietal lobule

Frontal eye field

Ventral
frontal
cortex

Temporoparietal
junction

**18.23 Brain Damage in Hemispatial
Neglect**

right for a few minutes eases their symptoms: for a few hours they are less neglect-
ful of the left visual field (Rossetti et al., 1998).

Many hypotheses have been offered to account for these symptoms. For example, some investigators regard the disorder as a consequence of loss of the ability to analyze spatial patterns, consistent with right-hemisphere specialization for
spatial ability. But most evidence now supports the conclusion that the syndrome
involves important attentional deficits, and disconnections between high-level
cognitive mechanisms (Bartolomeo, 2007; Mesulam, 1985). Lesion maps, averaged
over numerous neglect patients, fit with impressive precision over the model of
the frontoparietal attention network we discussed earlier (**Figure 18.23**).

In Balint's syndrome, narrowed attention combines with spatial disorientation

Bilateral lesions that include those same cortical regions implicated in attention,
specifically the posterior parietal and lateral occipital cortex, can produce an unusual and debilitating combination of symptoms. First described by Hungarian
neurologist Rezs Bálint in the early 1900s, the syndrome consists of three principal
symptoms:

1. **Oculomotor apraxia**, a pronounced difficulty in voluntarily steering visual gaze
   toward specific targets.
2. **Optic ataxia**, a spatial disorientation in which the patient is unable to accurately reach for objects using visual guidance.
3. **Simultagnosia**, a profound restriction of attention, often limited to a single item
   or feature. The cardinal and most debilitating symptom in Balint's syndrome,
   simultagnosia is like a dramatic narrowing of the metaphorical attentional
   spotlight described earlier, to the point that it is impossible to encompass more
   than one object at a time. It's as though the patient is simply unable to see
   more than one thing at once, despite having little or no loss of vision.

Balint's syndrome thus illustrates the coordination of attention and awareness with
mechanisms that orient us within our environment. It also exemplifies the consequences of a severe restriction of attention, to the point that most of the world is
being excluded from processing.

Subcortical mechanisms are compromised in progressive supranuclear palsy

Some people suffer from a rare degenerative disease of the brain that begins with
marked, persistent visual symptoms. **Progressive supranuclear palsy** (**PSP**) gets its
name from an early impairment of gaze control mechanisms that are "supra" to the
brainstem nuclei that control eye movements; specifically, the superior colliculi are

oculomotor apraxia   A severe difficulty in
voluntarily steering visual gaze toward specific
targets.

optic ataxia   A spatial disorientation in
which the patient is unable to accurately
reach for objects using visual guidance.

simultagnosia   A profound restriction of
attention, often limited to a single item or
feature.

progressive supranuclear palsy (PSP)   A
rare, degenerative disease of the brain that
begins with marked, persistent visual symptoms and leads to more widespread intellectual deterioration.

tauopathy Any disease that is associated with abnormal accumulations of the protein Tau, forming neurofibrillary tangles that impair the normal function of neurons.

damaged. In the early phases of the disease, before more widespread intellectual deterioration becomes evident, PSP patients have trouble with visual tasks such as moving the eyes voluntarily, and with the convergence of the eyes that is needed to view close-up objects. But patients with PSP also experience problems with covert attention; they find it increasingly difficult to switch attention between different *attentional* targets, even without eye movements. So damage to the human superior colliculus appears to impair a mechanism for shifting the attentional spotlight (Rafal et al., 1988; R. D. Wright and Ward, 2008), which is in keeping with work in monkeys indicating the superior colliculus plays a role in shifting visual attention.

Like Alzheimer's disease, PSP is a **tauopathy**—it is associated with abnormal accumulations of the protein Tau, forming neurofibrillary tangles that impair the normal function of neurons (see Chapter 7). Although there is no cure for PSP, scientists are seeking drug treatments to help manage the symptoms of PSP and slow its progression. For example, some symptoms of PSP are relieved by medications used to treat Parkinson's disease (Ludolph et al., 2009).

Consciousness Is the Most Mysterious Property of the Nervous System

There can be no denying the close relationship of attention and consciousness. As noted at the outset of the chapter, as long as we are awake and alert we are attending to *something*, be it internal or external. William James (1890), captured the superficial experience of consciousness when he wrote, "*My experience is what I agree to attend to. Only those items which I notice, shape my mind—without selective interest, experience is an utter chaos.*" Attention and awareness are indeed behavioral and experiential manifestations of consciousness, but no one would accept them as synonymous. A more complete description of consciousness is freighted with the notion that we enjoy volitional control over experience—the belief that we can employ *free will* to direct our attention and ultimately make decisions about how to act. Add to this the observation that consciousness involves awareness of the passage of time, integration with memory of past events, and anticipation of future events, and we have a concept of immense scope. So as a rough approximation, we can define consciousness as the state of being *aware* that we are conscious and that we can perceive what is going on in our minds and all around us. This awareness is colored by events that affected our inner selves in the past, and by our sense of what the future might hold.

Despite the definitional complexities, consciousness is an active area of study with many competing theoretical models but not, as yet, much hard physiological data. One practical approach has been to define consciousness by its absence. By studying the brains of people who appear to be unconscious, we might gain some insight into brain mechanisms of consciousness. Such investigation requires great care in identifying disorders or states with effects limited to changes in consciousness; for example, damage to the brainstem (especially the arousal mechanisms of the reticular activating system; see Figure 18.17) may cause the entire cerebrum to shut down, but this is a global loss of brain function, not a selective impairment of consciousness.

Using fMRI to track brain activity in conditions of diminished consciousness ranging from sleep to persistent vegetative states due to head injuries, researchers have devised maps of cortical areas that appear to be deactivated in unconsciousness (Tsuchiya and Adolphs, 2007). The overlap in these maps suggests shared reliance on a frontoparietal network (**Figure 18.24**) that includes much of the attention network we have been discussing, as well as portions of medial frontal cortex and the cingulate. But is clinical unconsciousness really the inverse of consciousness? Surprisingly, some patients in persistent vegetative state (a deep and unresponsive coma) can be instructed to use two different forms of mental imagery to signal yes and no answers to questions (Monti et al., 2010). While in an fMRI scan-

(a)

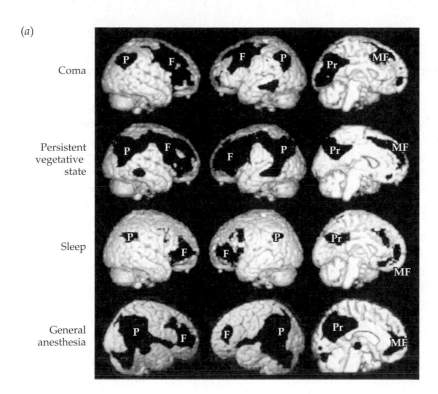

(b)

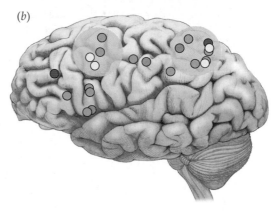

18.24 The Unconscious Brain (a) Functional-imaging studies of people in various states of diminished consciousness show impairment or reduced activity of a frontoparietal network including dorsolateral prefrontal cortex (F), medial frontal cortex (MF), posterior parietal cortex (P), and posterior cingulate (Pr). This general pattern of frontoparietal deactivation agrees well with a model (b) summarizing areas of activation in previous studies (indicated by different-colored dots) of visual awareness and consciousness. (Part a courtesy of Ralph Adolphs; b after Rees et al., 2002.)

ner, the apparently unconscious patients were asked to imagine playing tennis to signal one response (yes), and imagine navigating somewhere familiar to signal the other response (no). Because these mental tasks produce different fMRI activations—determined in advance with normal control subjects (see Figure 2.24)—the researchers could determine that the patients were accurately answering questions about themselves ("Is your father named Alexander?") (**Figure 18.25**). This is an impressive and unsettling finding that raises new questions about consciousness. But as we noted earlier, there seems to be more to consciousness than just being

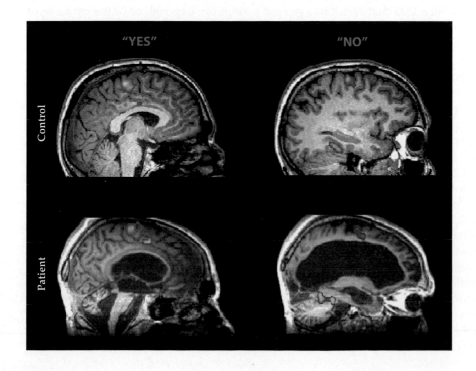

18.25 Communication in "Unconscious" Patients Functional-MRI scans reveal distinctive patterns of brain activity obtained when a control subject (*top*) was asked to use two different mental images (playing tennis versus navigating) to signal yes or no answers to questions. The striking similarity of activation in the brain of a patient in a persistent vegetative state (*bottom*) who received the same instructions raises questions about the definition of unconsciousness. The patient was able to correctly answer a variety of questions using this technique, despite apparently deep unconsciousness due to profound brain damage (black regions on MRI scan) and lack of behavioral responses. (Image courtesy of Adrian Owen.)

awake, aware, and attending. How can we ascertain the additional dimensions of consciousness?

Some aspects of consciousness are easier to study than others

Most of the activity of the central nervous system is unconscious. In scientific language, these functions are said to be **cognitively impenetrable**: data-processing operations that cannot be introspectively experienced. We don't have conscious access to the subordinate components of perceptions—we see whole objects and can't even imagine what the primitive visual precursors of those perceptions could look like. Sweet food tastes sweet, and we can't mentally break it down any further. But those simpler mechanisms, operating below the surface of awareness, are the foundation that conscious experiences are built on. So in principle, we might someday develop technology that would let us directly reconstruct people's conscious experience—read their minds—by amalgamating lower-order brain activity into identifiable patterns.

Philosophers refer to this as the **easy problem of consciousness**: understanding how particular patterns of neural activity create *specific* conscious experiences. Of course, as a practical matter this undertaking is far from "easy," but it is at least tractable. We can reasonably say that, someday, brain-imaging technology may provide the combined temporal and spatial resolution required for the task of eavesdropping on large networks of neurons, in real time (**Figure 18.26a**). In fact, present-day technology offers a glimpse of that possible future. For example, if subjects are repeatedly scanned while viewing several distinctive scenes, a computer can eventually learn to identify which of the scenes the subject is viewing on each trial, solely on the basis of the pattern of brain activation (Kay et al., 2008). Of course, this outcome relies on having the subjects repeatedly view the same static images—hardly a normal state of consciousness. A more difficult problem is so-called *constraint-free* reconstruction of conscious experiences—that is, the ability to "read" what a person is perceiving rather than just identifying items that were previously trained. Although this sort of reconstruction has been accomplished for very simple stimuli, like letters and shapes (**Figure 18.26b**) (Miyawaki et al., 2008), we are still a very long way from directly reconstructing anything like a rich conscious experience. But at least it's conceivable.

Unsurprisingly, there is also the **hard problem of consciousness**: understanding the brain processes that result in a person's *subjective* experience of the contents of consciousness. To use a simple example, every person with normal color vision will identify a ripe tomato as being red because we all learned early on that the particular perceptual information entering our consciousness from the color-processing mechanisms of the visual system is described as "red." We learn to relate labels to patterns of neural activity. But that doesn't mean that your friend's internal *personal* experience of "red" is the same as yours. These purely subjective experiences of perceptions are referred to as **qualia** (singular *quale*). Because they are subjective and impossible to communicate to others—how can your friend know if redness feels the same in your mind as it does in hers?—qualia may prove impossible to study (**Figure 18.26c**). At this point anyway, we are unable to conceive of a technology that would make it possible.

Our subjective experience of consciousness is closely tied up with the notion of free will, or what are sometimes called *feelings of agency*: the perception (real or imagined) that our conscious self is the author of our actions and decisions. Aside from the issue of whether we actually have free will—a matter that won't be resolved anytime soon—there must be a neural substrate for the universal *feeling* of having free will. Conscious manipulations of intentions to act—an exercise in willful control of actions—result in selective fMRI activations of the pre–supplementary motor area (pre-SMA) in the frontal lobes of normal subjects, along with activations of the IPS (which we implicated earlier in top-down attention) and dorsal prefrontal cortex (Lau et al., 2004). However, recent research suggests that *conscious experiences*

---

cognitively impenetrable   Referring to data-processing operations of the central nervous system that are unconscious.

easy problem of consciousness   The problem of how to read current conscious experiences directly from people's brains as they're happening.

hard problem of consciousness   The problem of how to read people's subjective experience of consciousness and determine the qualia that accompany perception.

quale   A purely subjective experience of perception.

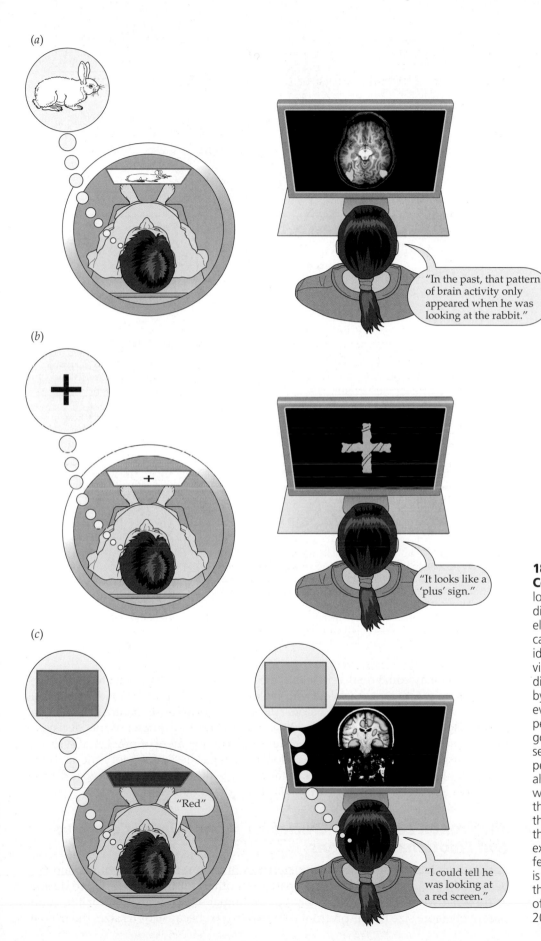

18.26 Easy and Hard Problems of Consciousness (*a*) When a subject is looking at one of 20 photographs, slightly different patterns of brain activity are elicited by different pictures. A computer can learn the patterns and eventually identify the scene being viewed. (*b*) In fact, vision scientists know enough about how different parts of the brain are activated by light striking the retina that they can even predict what sort of simple shapes a person is viewing. (*c*) The "hard" problem goes beyond predicting what a person is seeing or thinking to knowing what that person's *subjective experience* is like. So, although the subject and the researcher would both use the label "red" to describe the color being viewed, how can we know their personal subjective experiences of that stimulus? Maybe the subject's personal experience of red feels the way that blue feels to the researcher, in our example. It is difficult to see how we can ever be sure that we share any subjective experiences of consciousness. (Part *a* after Kay et al., 2008; *b* after Miyawaki et al., 2008.)

18.27 Act First, Think Later Our brain may decide what we'll do before our conscious self is aware of that decision. In this experiment (Soon et al., 2008), subjects decided for themselves when to press a button with either the right hand or the left. Using brain MRI, the scientists found that they could predict beforehand when subjects would "decide" to press the left or right button, and even *whether* they would press the left or the right button, up to 10 seconds before subjects were aware of their own decision.

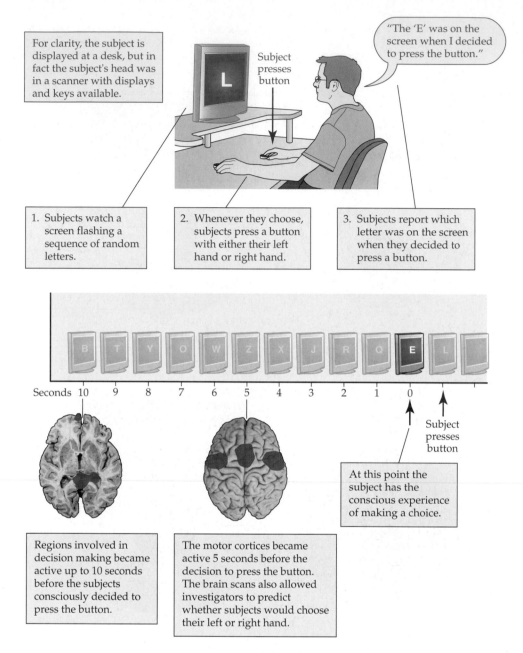

For clarity, the subject is displayed at a desk, but in fact the subject's head was in a scanner with displays and keys available.

Subject presses button

"The 'E' was on the screen when I decided to press the button."

1. Subjects watch a screen flashing a sequence of random letters.

2. Whenever they choose, subjects press a button with either their left hand or right hand.

3. Subjects report which letter was on the screen when they decided to press a button.

Seconds 10 9 8 7 6 5 4 3 2 1 0

Subject presses button

At this point the subject has the conscious experience of making a choice.

Regions involved in decision making became active up to 10 seconds before the subjects consciously decided to press the button.

The motor cortices became active 5 seconds before the decision to press the button. The brain scans also allowed investigators to predict whether subjects would choose their left or right hand.

of intention may come relatively late in the process of deciding what to do. Astonishingly, brain activity associated with making a decision may be evident in fMRI scans as much as 5–10 seconds before subjects are consciously aware of making a choice (**Figure 18.27**) (Soon et al., 2008). The earliest indications of this decision-making process are found in frontal cortex. Such involvement of prefrontal systems in most aspects of attention and consciousness, regardless of sensory modality or emotional tone, suggests that the frontal cortex is the main source of goal-driven behaviors (E. K. Miller and Cohen, 2001), as we discuss next.

The Frontal Lobes Are Crucial for Higher-Order Cognitive and Emotional Functions

Researchers have long sought characteristics of the brain that might explain the behavioral complexity that sets us apart from other animals. How do we decide to do what we do? As noted in Chapter 6, humans are distinctive for the comparatively large size of our prefrontal cortex. In part because of its size, the frontal region has been regarded as the seat of intelligence and abstract thinking. Adding to the mystery of frontal lobe function is the unusual assortment of behavioral changes that follows surgical or accidental lesions of this region.

The human frontal cortex accounts for almost one-third of the entire cerebral cortical surface. The posterior portion of the frontal cortex includes motor and premotor regions (see Chapter 11). The anterior portion, usually referred to as **prefrontal cortex**, is a critical component of a widespread neuronal network, with extensive linkages throughout the brain (Fuster, 1990; Mega and Cummings, 1994). This prefrontal cortex was disconnected from the rest of the brain in frontal lobotomy, the now discredited treatment for psychiatric disorders that we discussed in Chapter 16. The prefrontal cortex is further subdivided into a *dorsolateral* region and an *orbitofrontal* region (**Figure 18.28a**). The prefrontal cortex is especially prominent in humans and apes (Semendeferi et al., 2002), but it is a smaller portion of the cerebral cortex in other mammals (**Figure 18.28b**).

The study of prefrontal cortical function in animals began with Carlyle Jacobsen's work in the 1930s. In his experiments with chimpanzees, Jacobsen employed delayed-response learning. The animals were shown where food was hidden, but

prefrontal cortex The anteriormost region of the frontal lobe.

(*a*) The prefrontal cortex in humans

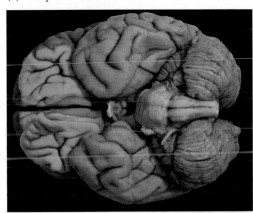
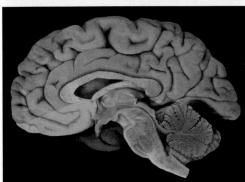
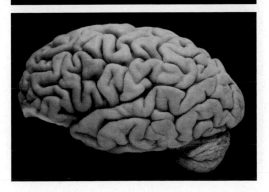

(*b*) Relative prefrontal cortex size in several mammals

Squirrel monkey

Cat

Rhesus monkey

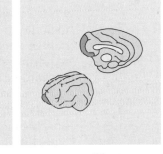
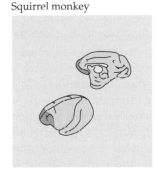
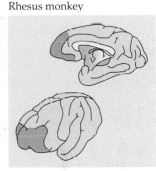

Chimpanzee

Human

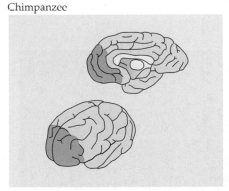
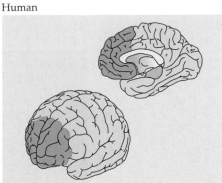

18.28 The Prefrontal Cortex (*a*) The human prefrontal cortex can be subdivided into a dorsolateral region (blue) and an orbitofrontal region (green). Lesions in these different areas of prefrontal cortex have different effects on behavior. (*b*) The relative percentage of prefrontal cortex is greatest in humans and the great apes, such as the chimpanzees, but it decreases successively in monkeys, carnivores (such as cats), and rodents (not shown). The brains here are drawn to different scales. (Photographs courtesy of S. Mark Williams and Dale Purves).

executive function A neural and cognitive system that helps develop plans of action and organizes the activities of other high-level processing systems.

they had to wait before being allowed to reach for it. Chimpanzees with prefrontal lesions showed striking impairment on this simple task, compared to animals that sustained lesions in other brain regions. Jacobsen believed the impairment was attributable to memory problems. But subsequent observations, discussed in the next section, now suggest that the chimps were probably having trouble directing attention to the task and formulating a plan of action.

Frontal lobe injury in humans leads to emotional, motor, and cognitive changes

The complexity of change following prefrontal damage is epitomized by the classic case of Phineas Gage (**Figure 18.29a**), which we discussed at the start of this chapter. What happened to his brain to change his behavior so radically that he was "no longer Gage"? A century and a half after the accident, reconstructions suggest that Gage suffered extensive bilateral frontal lobe damage, especially in orbitofrontal regions (**Figure 18.29b**). The historical descriptions of Gage's syndrome agree with the symptoms of other patients with damage to the same brain region (H. Damasio et al., 1994; Wallis, 2007).

The clinical portrait of humans with frontal lesions reveals an unusual collection of emotional, motor, and cognitive changes. The emotional reactivity of these patients shows a persistent strange apathy, broken by bouts of euphoria (an exalted sense of well-being). Ordinary social conventions are readily cast aside by impulsive behavior. Concern for the past or the future is absent (Duffy and Campbell, 1994; Petrides and Milner, 1982). Frontal patients show shallow emotions, even including reduced responsiveness to pain. Standard IQ test performance shows only slight changes after injury or stroke. Forgetfulness is shown in many tasks requiring sustained attention. In fact, some of these patients even forget their own warnings to "remember."

Clinical examination of patients with frontal lesions also reveals an array of strange impairments in their behavior, especially in the realm of **executive function**, the high-level control of other cognitive functions in order to attend to important stimuli and make suitable "plans" for action. For example, a frontal patient

18.29 Phineas Gage (a) This recently discovered daguerreotype is the only known photograph of Phineas Gage. Gage survived after the tamping rod in his hands was blasted right through his head—but he was a changed man. (b) This computer reconstruction illustrates the tamping rod's trajectory as it passed through Gage's head, severely damaging both frontal lobes. (Part b courtesy of Hanna Damasio.)

(a)

(b)

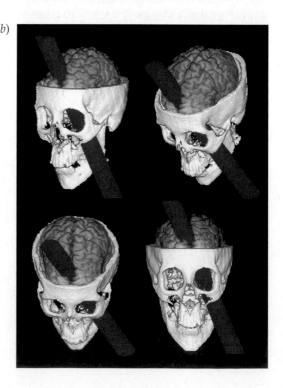

given a simple set of errands may be unable to complete them (if able to do any at all) without numerous false starts, backtracking, and confusion (Shallice and Burgess, 1991). Regions of dorsolateral prefrontal cortex, along with anterior portions of the cingulate, are closely associated with executive control.

Frontal patients struggle with *task shifting* and tend to **perseverate** (continue beyond a reasonable degree) in any activity (Alvarez and Emory, 2006; B. Milner, 1963). Similarly, frontal patients may show motor perseveration, repeating a simple movement over and over. However, the overall level of motor activity—especially ordinary, spontaneous movements—is quite diminished in these patients. Facial expression becomes blank, and head and eye movements are markedly reduced. Sometimes reflexes that normally are evident only very early in life, such as the infantile grasp reflex of the hand, will reappear after frontal lobe damage. Frontal lobe lesions also produce systematic problems with memory.

One explanation for these disparate effects of prefrontal lesions is that this region of cortex may be important for organizing the diverse aspects of goal-directed behavior; crucial components include the capacity for prolonged attention and sensitivity to potential rewards and punishments. Patients with prefrontal lesions, like Phineas Gage, often have an inability to plan acts and use foresight. Their social skills may decline, especially the ability to inhibit inappropriate behaviors, and they may be unable to stay focused on any but short-term projects. They may agonize over even simple decisions. **Table 18.1** lists the main clinical features of patients with lesions of the major subdivisions of the frontal lobes.

Examination of healthy subjects confirms the idea that prefrontal cortex—especially the orbitofrontal region—is important for goal-directed behaviors. In monkeys, prefrontal cortical neurons become especially active when the animal has to make a decision that may provide a reward (Matsumoto et al., 2003), suggesting that prefrontal cortex controls goal-directed behaviors. In general, orbitofrontal cortex seems important for forming associations between hedonic experiences (such as the subjective pleasantness of eating gourmet food) and reward signals from elsewhere in the brain (Kringelbach, 2005). In humans performing a task in which some stimuli have more reward value than others, the level of activation in prefrontal cortex (as measured by fMRI) correlated with how rewarding the stimulus was (Gottfried et al., 2003). In another testing situation that involved gambling, event-related potentials indicated that prefrontal cortex was especially active when people were making choices that could cost them money (Gehring and Willoughby, 2002). In fact, understanding how we make decisions about money has spawned a new field of research, as we discuss next.

perseverate To continue to show a behavior repeatedly.

TABLE 18.1 Core Characteristics of the Regional Prefrontal Syndromes

Syndrome type	Prefrontal region affected	Characteristics
Dysexecutive	Dorsolateral	Diminished judgment, planning, insight, and temporal organization; cognitive impersistence; motor programming deficits (possibly including aphasia and apraxia); diminished self-care
Disinhibited	Orbitofrontal	Stimulus-driven behavior; diminished social insight; distractibility; emotional lability
Apathetic	Mediofrontal	Diminished spontaneity; diminished verbal output (including mutism); diminished motor behavior (including akinesis); urinary incontinence; lower-extremity weakness and sensory loss; diminished spontaneous prosody; increased response latency

Neuroeconomics identifies brain regions active during decision making

A new field has arisen to study what happens in the brain specifically when we are making everyday decisions. In asking people to make decisions in the lab, it is convenient to use monetary transactions because then you can vary how much money is at stake, how great a reward is offered, and so on to really gauge how we make economic decisions. Psychologists and economists have learned that most of us are very risk-averse: we are more sensitive to losing a certain amount of money than we are to gaining that amount. In other words, losing $20 makes us feel a lot worse than gaining $20 makes us feel better.

Neuroeconomics is the study of brain mechanisms at work during economic decision making, and our attention to environmental factors and evaluation of rewards has a tremendous impact on these decisions. For example, in monkeys playing these sorts of economic games (yes, monkeys will gamble for apple juice, which they really, *really* like), neurons in the posterior cingulate cortex become more active when risky choices are being made (McCoy and Platt, 2005). In one study on humans, anterior cingulate cortex became more active when rewards were diminished, signaling that the subjects should change how they played a game (Z. M. Williams et al., 2004). When this brain region was lesioned (cingulotomy as a last-ditch attempt to control obsessive-compulsive disorder; see Figure 16.19), the subjects made more errors, failing to switch strategies as if they did not fully experience the disappointment of a reduced reward.

Although neuroeconomics is a young field, enough data has been amassed for theoretical models of the neural bases of decision making to be advanced. In general, findings suggest that two main systems underlie decision processes (Kable and Glimcher, 2009). The first, consisting of the ventromedial prefrontal cortex (including the anterior cingulate) plus the dopamine-based reward system of the basal forebrain (see Chapter 4), is a *valuation system*, a network that ranks choices on the basis of their perceived worth and potential reward. The second system, involving mostly dorsolateral prefrontal cortex and parietal regions (like LIP/IPS) that we have already discussed in the context of attention and awareness, is thought to be a *choice system*, sifting through the valuated alternatives and producing the conscious decision.

Neuroeconomics research is also confirming that the prefrontal cortex inhibits impulsive decisions, enforcing our loss aversion (Tom et al., 2007). As people are faced with more and more uncertainty, the prefrontal cortex becomes more and more active (Hsu et al., 2005; Huettel et al., 2006). Likewise, when people have made wrong, costly decisions that they regret, activity increases in the amygdala and prefrontal cortex (Coricelli et al., 2005), probably reflecting the subject's perception of diminished reward and increasing aversion to loss (**Figure 18.30**).

As we've seen in this chapter, our higher cognitive processes involve a constellation of mechanisms for attention, awareness, consciousness, and decision making that span most of the brain. Although we may never be able to truly understand the neural basis of the personal, subjective experiences of consciousness, current research on these topics holds the promise of profound insights into brain processes that lie at the heart of human experience.

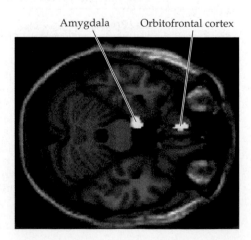

Amygdala   Orbitofrontal cortex

18.30 A Poor Choice A costly decision is associated with activation of the amygdala and orbitofrontal cortex, signaling diminished reward and aversion to loss. (From Coricelli et al., 2005; courtesy of Angela Sirigu.)

SUMMARY

Attention Selects Stimuli for Processing

■ Although we pay mostly **overt attention** to stimuli, we can also pay **covert attention** to stimuli or locations of our choosing. **Attention** helps us distinguish stimuli from distracters. **Review Figure 18.1**

■ We can attend to only a small subset of available stimuli at any time; attention has been likened to a spotlight that picks out stimuli for processing. **Review Web Activity 18.1**

■ Because we have limited processing capabilities, attention imposes a bottleneck on incoming information. The **attentional bottleneck** may occur early in processing or later, when stimuli reach awareness, as determined possibly by the processing load of the stimuli. **Review Figures 18.2 and 18.3**

Attention May Be Endogenous or Exogenous

■ In **endogenous attention** we voluntarily select objects to attend to. It is said to be a **top-down process** and is studied using **symbolic cuing tasks**. **Review Figures 18.4 and 18.6, Web Activity 18.2**

■ **Exogenous attention** is the involuntary capture of attention by stimuli. It is a **bottom-up process**, studied using **peripheral spatial cuing tasks**. **Review Figures 18.5 and 18.6**

■ In visual search, targets may pop out if they are distinctive on a particular feature (**feature search**). More often, we use **conjunction searches**, identifying target stimuli on the basis of two or more features. **Review Figure 18.7**

Electrophysiological Techniques Trace Rapid Changes of Brain Activity

■ **Event-related potentials** (**ERPs**) are created by the averaging of many EEG recordings from repeated experimental trials. ERPs can track neural operations with excellent temporal resolution. **Review Figure 18.8**

■ We can study both the consequences of attention on neural processes, and the source and control of attention.

■ Auditory attention enhances the **N1 effect** and the **P20–50 effect**—components of the ERP. **Review Figure 18.9**

■ Endogenous visual attention enhances the **P1 effect** (the P1 component of the ERP), related to early attentional selection; and the **P3 effect**, related to later attentional selection. **Review Figure 18.10**

■ Exogenous visual attention also enhances P1, but only for short delays between cue and stimulus. **Review Figures 18.11 and 18.12**

Many Brain Regions Are Involved in Processes of Attention

■ Neuroimaging, single-cell recordings, and other anatomical studies provide excellent spatial resolution, helping us identify the brain sites involved in attention.

■ Selective attention causes enhanced activations of discrete regions of sensory cortex, such as primary visual cortex and extrastriate visual areas. **Review Figure 18.13**

■ Single-cell recordings in lab animals confirm that attention affects the responses of individual neurons. **Review Figures 18.14–18.16**

■ Subcortical mechanisms involving the **superior colliculi** and the **pulvinar** are crucial for shifting visual attention and gaze between important objects of attention. **Review Figure 8.17, Web Activity 18.3**

■ A dorsal frontoparietal attention network in the cortex is responsible for directing voluntary, endogenous attention. A right-sided temporoparietal attentional system, centered on the right **temporoparietal junction** (**TPJ**), is responsible for detecting and shifting attention to novel stimuli. The two networks interact extensively. **Review Figures 18.19–18.21, Web Activities 18.4 and 18.5**

Neurological Disorders Reveal the Anatomy of Attention

■ Damage to the right hemisphere involving the right parietal cortex can cause **hemispatial neglect**. Patients with this condition ignore the left side of the world, presumably because of damage to attentional mechanisms. **Review Figures 18.22 and 18.23**

■ **Balint's syndrome** is a rare consequence of bilateral parietal damage. In Balint's syndrome, patients are spatially disoriented and experience a dramatic narrowing of attention, to the point that only one object at a time can be seen (**simultagnosia**).

■ Damage to the superior colliculi, as in **progressive supranuclear palsy** (**PSP**), may make it very difficult for the patient to switch attention between stimuli.

Consciousness Is the Most Mysterious Property of the Nervous System

■ People in various unconscious states show reduced activity of frontoparietal regions. **Review Figure 18.24**

■ The **easy problem of consciousness** is the problem of how to read specific current conscious experiences directly from people's brains as they are happening. Although not currently possible, the needed technology to do this may someday be available. **Review Figure 18.26**

■ The **hard problem of consciousness** is the problem of how to read people's subjective experience of consciousness and determine the **qualia** that accompany perception. No one knows how to approach this problem, or even if a solution is possible. **Review Figure 18.26**

■ Feelings of agency, sometimes referred to as free will, may rely on the activity of specific frontal lobe mechanisms. But even if that's true, it's possible that unconscious mechanisms make many of our decisions well before we consciously realize it. **Review Figure 18.27**

The Frontal Lobes Are Crucial for Higher-Order Cognitive and Emotional Functions

■ **Prefrontal cortex** consists of dorsolateral and orbitofrontal divisions; damage in these regions produces a distinctive set of symptoms. **Review Figure 18.28**

■ Medial aspects of the frontal lobes, including anterior cingulate regions, are associated with **executive function**.

■ Prefrontal cortex appears to be essential for coordinating the resources needed for goal-directed behavior. **Review Table 18.1**

■ A new field, **neuroeconomics**, is concerned with the neural mechanisms responsible for decision making. A current model emphasizes a ventromedial frontal evaluation system and a dorsolateral choice network.

Go to **www.biopsychology.com** for study questions, quizzes, key terms, and other resources.

Recommended Reading

Glimcher, P. W., Camerer, C., Poldrack, R. A., and Fehr, E. (2008). *Neuroeconomics: Decision making and the brain.* San Diego, CA: Academic Press.

Goldberg, E. (2009). *The new executive brain: Frontal lobes in a complex world.* Oxford, England: Oxford University Press.

Itti, L., Rees, G., and Tsotsos, J. K. (2005). *Neurobiology of attention.* Amsterdam: Elsevier.

Koch, C. (2004). *The quest for consciousness: A neurobiological approach.* Englewood, CO: Roberts.

Posner, M. I. (2004). *Cognitive neuroscience of attention.* New York: Guilford.

Stuss, D. T., and Knight, R. T. (2002). *Principles of frontal lobe function.* Oxford, England: Oxford University Press.

Wright, R. D., and Ward, L. M. (2008). *Orienting of attention.* Oxford, England: Oxford University Press.

CHAPTER 19

Language and Hemispheric Asymmetry

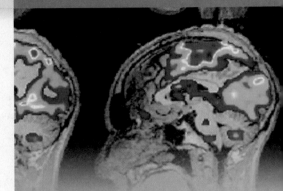

Putting a Name to a Face

Humpty Dumpty, the famously grouchy egg in Lewis Carroll's *Through the Look-ing-Glass, and What Alice Found There*, was grumbling to Alice about his problem distinguishing between people:

> "The face is what one goes by, generally," Alice remarked in a thoughtful tone.

> "That's just what I complain of," said Humpty Dumpty. "Your face is the same as ev-erybody has—the two eyes, so—" (marking their places in the air with his thumb) "nose in the middle, mouth under. It's always the same. Now, if you had the two eyes on the same side of the nose, for instance—or the mouth at the top—that would be of some help."

Barry can relate. Throughout his 54 years of life, Barry has had great difficulty distinguishing between people. He regularly fails to recognize his seven children, his wife, or even himself reflected in a mirror. He relies on name badges to identify colleagues he has worked with for years. Yet Barry has not suffered any neurologi-cal adversities, can make out other people's features perfectly well, and is other-wise just like anyone else.

What might account for Barry's—and Humpty's—difficulty with putting a name to a face?

Although many species are capable of some form of communication, complex language—in common with art and music—is mostly a human trait. Our linguistic and aesthetic perception of the world gives us a mental life that is unique among animal species. Some of the most fascinating findings of twen-tieth-century neuroscience were built on observations that the left hemisphere of the brain is specialized for verbal processing. We now know that there are many ways in which the left and right sides of the human brain perform different but complementary functions. In this chapter we survey the neuroscience of cerebral asymmetry, focusing in particular on left-hemisphere specializations for language processes. We will consider the key functions of the right hemisphere—especially in spatial cognition. And because much of what we know about human brain or-ganization is derived from studies of people who have suffered strokes and other forms of brain injury, we will review evidence that some recovery of function is possible even after severe brain damage.

The Development and Evolution of Speech and Language Are Remarkable

There are an estimated 7000 languages in the world today, about 1000 of which have been studied by linguists (Wuethrich, 2000). All these languages have similar basic elements, and each is composed of a set of sounds and symbols that have distinct meanings. These elements are arranged according to rules characteristic of the particular language. Each language has basic speech sounds, or **phonemes**,

phoneme A sound that is produced for language.

morpheme The smallest grammatical unit of a language; a word or meaningful part of a word.

semantics The meanings or interpretation of words and sentences in a language.

syntax The grammatical rules for constructing phrases and sentences in a language.

grammar All of the rules for usage of a particular language.

sensitive period The period during development in which an organism can be permanently altered by a particular experience or treatment.

that are assembled into simple units of meaning called **morphemes**. Morphemes are assembled into words (the word *unfathomable*, for example, consists of the morphemes *un-*, *fathom*, and *-able*), which have meaning (termed **semantics**), and in turn the words are assembled into meaningful strings (which may be complete sentences or just phrases) according to the language's **syntax** (rules for constructing phrases; an element of **grammar**). Anyone who knows the sounds, symbols, and rules of a particular language can generate sentences that convey information to others who have similar knowledge of the language.

A child's brain is an incredible linguistic machine, rapidly acquiring the phonemes, vocabulary, and grammar of the local language without need of formal instruction. At birth, for example, a baby can distinguish between sounds from Dutch and sounds from Japanese. Because adult monkeys can also make this discrimination (Ramus et al., 2000), this ability may reflect a basic property of the primate auditory system. But by attending to these sounds, the human baby, who begins life babbling nearly all the phonemes known in all human languages, soon comes to use only the subset of phonemes in use around her. The baby's developing language abilities are especially shaped by "motherese," the singsong speech that parents universally use with their babies (Falk, 2004). The lilting qualities of motherese convey emotional tone and reward, helping to attach meaning to previously arbitrary speech sounds.

By 7 months of age, infants pay more attention to sentences with unfamiliar structure than to sentences with familiar structure (Marcus et al., 1999), indicating that they have already acquired a sense of the rules of language being spoken around them and are actively looking out for exceptions. In rare, tragic cases of children rescued from long-term profound isolation (we discussed the case of Genie in Box 5.2), little or no language develops, pointing to the importance of experience during a **sensitive period** early in life. Similarly, when hearing was restored to an adult who had been deaf most of her life, she did not learn to speak (Curtiss, 1989), presumably because the sensitive period for language acquisition had ended many years earlier.

The notion of a sensitive period for language acquisition is also supported by the difficulty that postadolescents experience in learning a second language. Imaging studies indicate that people who learn a second language early in life activate the same brain region when using either language. But people learning a second language later than age 11 seem to use different brain regions for each language (K. H. Kim et al., 1997).

Scholars have suggested that speech and language originally developed from gestures of the face and hands (Corballis, 2002; Hewes, 1973). Even today, hand movements facilitate speech: if people are prevented from gesturing, they make more slips and have more pauses in their speech (Krauss, 1998). Furthermore, people who have been blind from birth, and so have never seen the hand gestures of others, make hand gestures while they speak (Iverson and Goldin-Meadow, 1998). Later we'll see that deaf people who communicate exclusively with gestures use the same part of the brain that hearing people use while speaking and listening. Deaf children raised without access to an established sign language will often invent one of their own, complete with structural features that characterize other spoken and sign languages (Goldin-Meadow, 2006). And in chimpanzees, complementary oral movements accompany precise hand movements (Waters and Fouts, 2002). Studies like these provide additional hints of an ancient association between gestures and speech.

Analysis of a British family with a rare heritable language disorder has led to identification of a gene that appears to be important for the normal acquisition of human language (**Figure 19.1**). Children with a specific mutation of the gene *FOXP2* take a long time to learn to speak, and they display long-lasting difficulties with particular language tasks (such as learning verb tenses) (Lai et al., 2001). The pattern of brain activation in these individuals during performance of a lan-

(a)

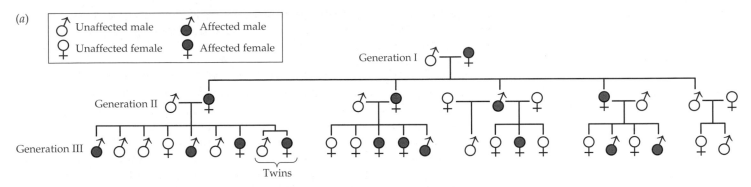

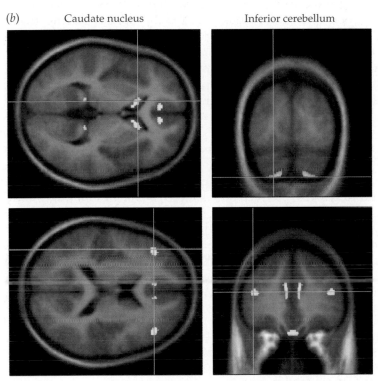

(b)

Caudate nucleus   Inferior cerebellum

Inferior frontal gyrus from two perspectives

19.1 A Heritable Language Disorder (a) Three generations of the KE family, illustrating the transmission of a language disorder caused by mutation of the gene *FOXP2*. (b) Regions of thinned gray matter in the brains of affected members of the KE family. In these brain images, the crossed lines indicate the affected region. (Part b courtesy of Dr. Faraneh Vargha-Khadem.)

guage task is different from that seen in normal speakers (Liégeois et al., 2003). The *FOXP2* gene in the other great apes is quite different from that seen in humans (Enard, Przeworski, et al., 2002), and the human gene has different functions (G. Konopka et al., 2009), suggesting that this gene has been evolving rapidly in humans, presumably because language is so adaptive in our species.

There's a genetic connection in language production too. Most of us have little trouble with *verbal articulation*, the mechanical process of moving the vocal tract to produce speech sounds, but some otherwise normal people tend to produce speech sounds only in fits and starts, tripping over certain syllables or unable to start vocalizing certain words. We call this difficulty *stuttering* or *stammering*. Scientists have long suspected that stuttering is at least partly heritable, and again by analysis of extended families for transmission of the disorder, mutations in members of a set of three specific genes have been implicated (C. Kang et al., 2010). These genes—*GNPTAB*, *GNPTG*, and *NAGPA*—play a part in the normal functioning of lysosomes, organelles involved in the breakdown of cellular waste materials. It remains to be seen why a dysfunction in this basic and ubiquitous system should so specifically affect speech. But recall that, in Chapter 6, we asked how humans and chimpanzees could differ so little in their total genome yet behave so differently. Perhaps major differences in a relatively few genes like *FOXP2* and the lysosomal stuttering genes are enough to explain why we write books and give speeches, and chimps do not.

Many nonhuman species engage in elaborate vocal behavior

Chirps, barks, meows, songs, and other sounds are among the many vocalizations produced by nonhuman animals. Many of these sounds seem to distinguish species, signal readiness to mate, or alert a group to danger. Whales sing and may imitate songs that they hear from distant oceans (Noad et al., 2000), and some seal mothers recognize their pups' vocalizations even after 4 years of separation (Insley, 2000). In fact, many species—from elephants to bats to birds to dolphins—are capable of vocal learning and use their vocalizations to help form social bonds and identify individuals (Poole et al., 2005; Tyack, 2003). In the lab, measurement with special instruments reveals that rats and mice produce complex ultrasonic vocalizations that they use to communicate emotional information (Panksepp, 2005). These ultrasonic vocalizations are impaired in mice with mutations in the *FOXP2* gene (Shu et al., 2005), providing an intriguing parallel to the situation in humans. So, could the vocal behavior of nonhuman animals be related to the evolution of human language?

BIRDSONG   Some birds sing tunes that we find pleasing, and although no one would suggest that birdsong is an evolutionary precursor to human speech, these songs offer intriguing analogies to human language (Marler, 1970). Many birds, such as chickens and ringdoves, produce only simple calls with limited communicative functions, but songbirds like canaries, zebra finches, and song sparrows produce complex vocalizations that are crucial for social behaviors and reproductive success. (For more on the complexity of birdsong and its social roles, see **A Step Further: Birdsong Broadcasts Information about the Singer** on the website.) In these songbirds, only males of the species sing, and the song is *learned*—in much the same way that humans learn language (DeVoogd, 1994). Birdsong learning has several distinct stages:

1. Initial exposure to the song of a male tutor, usually the father, whose song becomes a stored model for the young bird's own singing
2. A trial-and-error period, during which the young bird makes successive approximations of the stored model
3. Fixing, or **crystallization**, of the song into a permanent form

Normally, song learning in birds is complete by the time of sexual maturity (90 days). We have already seen that humans must be exposed to language during an early sensitive period if they are ever to learn to speak. Likewise, male songbirds raised in isolation fail to develop normal song (**Figure 19.2**), but simply exposing the birds to a tape recording of species-typical song during an early sensitive period—but not before or after—will allow them to develop normal song. Alternatively, if developing males are deafened during the second stage of song learning, they will never produce normal song (Konishi, 1985). So the male must first hear himself sing and compare his chirps with the memory of his father's song until he has replicated it. Deafening after the song has crystallized has very little effect on song production, as if the song has become fixed.

When a bird is exposed to synthetic songs, composed of notes of both the same species and another species, it prefers to copy the song of its own species (Baptista, 1996; Marler, 1991; Marler and Peters, 1982; R. G. Morrison and Nottebohm, 1993), indicating a predisposition to learn the appropriate song. And even if socially isolated male canaries learn highly abnormal songs in their youth, their singing is reprogrammed to show normal canary phrasing as they enter adulthood (T. J. Gardner et al., 2005), indicating that an innate system of vocal rules constrains singing behavior.

crystallization   The final stage of birdsong formation, in which fully formed adult song is achieved.

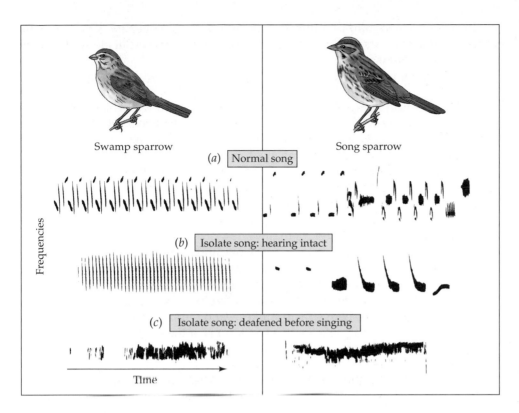

Swamp sparrow

Song sparrow

(a) Normal song

Frequencies

(b) Isolate song: hearing intact

(c) Isolate song: deafened before singing

Time

19.2 Effects of Isolation on Birdsong Development (*a*) These sonograms show the typical adult song patterns of two sparrow species. The songs illustrated in part *b* were produced by males reared in isolation; those in part *c*, by males deafened in infancy. Both early auditory isolation and deafening result in abnormal song, but the two species still produce different patterns. Deafening has a more profound effect because the animal is prevented from hearing its own song production, as well as that of other males. (After Marler and Sherman, 1983, 1985.)

A series of brain nuclei and their connections control the production of song by the vocal organ, the **syrinx** (**Figure 19.3**) (Arnold and Schlinger, 1993; DeVoogd, 1994). First, a direct pathway from the high vocal center (HVC) to the nucleus robustus of the archistriatum (RA), and then on to the brainstem nucleus of the twelfth cranial nerve, controls the vocal organ. Lesions along this direct pathway at any stage of development will disrupt song. A second, less direct pathway from HVC to the brainstem includes several forebrain nuclei that may be involved in aspects of song acquisition. Early lesions of one of its components, the lateral magnocellular nucleus of the anterior neostriatum (LMAN), will stop song development. But LMAN lesions in adulthood do not affect song performance (Bottjer et al., 1984), implying that the LMAN might be involved in some aspects of song learning, but its exact role remains unclear. The LMAN probably is *not* involved in storing the tutor song that the bird uses as a template: exposure to a tutor song during the sensitive period causes increased expression of immediate early genes (IEGs; see Box 2.1) in several auditory regions of the brain, but not in any of the song control nuclei, including the LMAN (Bolhuis and Gahr, 2006; Mello et al.,

syrinx   The vocal organ in birds.

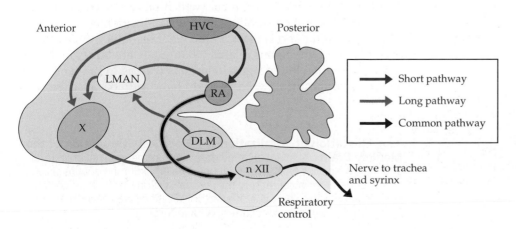

Anterior   HVC   Posterior

LMAN

RA

X

DLM

n XII   Nerve to trachea and syrinx

Respiratory control

Short pathway
Long pathway
Common pathway

19.3 Song Control Nuclei of the Songbird Brain   Two neural pathways control birdsong. A direct route from the high vocal center (HVC) to the nucleus robustus of the archistriatum (RA) to the nucleus of the twelfth cranial nerve (n XII) is crucial for song; lesions of any of these areas will disrupt song. (The nucleus labeled X is called area X of the paraolfactory lobe, and the DLM is the medial dorsolateral nucleus of the thalamus.) The indirect path that includes the lateral magnocellular nucleus of the anterior neostriatum (LMAN) may play a role in song learning, although the memory of the tutor's song is probably stored elsewhere. (After A. P. Arnold, 1980.)

1992). In female songbirds—which do not sing but remember the songs of their fathers as models for selecting mates—the same auditory nuclei store the songs (Terpstra et al., 2006).

Vocal learning is accompanied by the generation in adulthood of new neurons (neurogenesis; see Chapter 7) in a variety of brain regions in songbirds (Scharff et al., 2000). Increased neurogenesis similarly is seen in starlings, which accumulate a large vocal repertoire over the course of their lives (Absil et al., 2003). And what about the *FOXP2* gene, which we've already discussed in the context of mouse vocalization and human language acquisition? The level of expression of *FOXP2* in the brains of birds is greater during song learning than before or after (Haesler et al., 2004). When researchers selectively silenced *FOXP2* expression in part of the song-learning pathway, called area X (see Figure 19.3), adolescent males failed to properly learn and recite the tutor's song, producing errors that resemble those in the humans with abnormal *FOXP2* that we described earlier (Haesler et al., 2007).

Another striking similarity between birdsong and human language involves the different contributions of the left and right cerebral hemispheres. We'll see later in this chapter that the left hemisphere plays a crucial role in human language—left-hemisphere strokes are far more likely to disrupt language than are right-hemisphere strokes—and the same is true for some songbirds: only left-hemisphere lesions of the song control system will impair singing (Nottebohm, 1980).

VOCALIZATION IN NONHUMAN PRIMATES   The calls of nonhuman primates have been examined intensively in both field and laboratory studies (Seyfarth and Cheney, 1997). Many nonhuman primate vocalizations seem preprogrammed, including infant crying and the emotional vocalizations of adults, such as shrieking in pain and moaning. Ploog (1992) cataloged the calls that squirrel monkeys make and the communication properties of those sounds in a social context. The monkeys produce a variety of calls, including shrieking, purring, peeping, growling, and cackling sounds. Many of these calls can penetrate a forest for some distance, communicating alarm, territoriality, and other emotional statements.

Direct electrical stimulation of subcortical regions can elicit some calls (**Figure 19.4**), but stimulation of the cerebral cortex generally fails to elicit vocal behavior. Brain regions where stimulation generates vocalizations tend to be structures that are also involved in defense, attack, feeding, and sexual behaviors. These regions include sites in the limbic system and related structures. Just before vocalizing, however, monkeys display changes in electrical potential in cortical areas homologous to human speech areas (Gemba et al., 1995). Furthermore, monkeys, like people, are more likely to point the right ear (which has preferential connections with the left hemisphere) toward vocalizations from conspecifics (Ghazanfar and Hauser, 1999). We'll see later in this chapter that several brain regions related to language are larger in the left hemisphere than in the right, in apes as well as in humans. Apes tend to favor gesturing with the right hand, and because the right

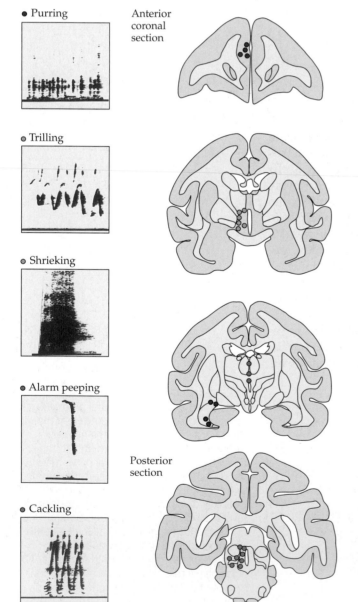

19.4 Elicitation of Vocalizations by Electrical Stimulation of the Monkey Brain   Stimulation at different sites in the monkey brain results in different, species-typical vocalizations. The left column contains spectrograms of different vocalizations; the coronal sections in the right column show brain sites at which the different vocalizations are elicited. (After Ploog, 1992; spectrograms courtesy of Uwe Jürgens.)

hand has preferential connections with the left side of the brain, this observation provides behavioral evidence that the left hemisphere may play a special role in communicative behavior, just as in people (Meguerditchian and Vauclair, 2006; Taglialatela et al., 2006). This behavior suggests selective reliance on the left cerebral hemisphere to decode communication—an idea that has been amply confirmed in humans, as we'll see shortly.

Can nonhuman primates acquire language with training?

People have long tried to communicate with animals, sometimes quite successfully: anyone who has watched a sheepdog at work, responding to commands from its handler, has to acknowledge that the human is transmitting lots of information to a highly intelligent companion. Instilling *language* in a nonhuman is a different matter, however. Every day, you utter sentences that you have never said before, yet the meaning is clear to both you and your listener because you both understand the speech sounds and syntax involved. Animals generally are incapable of similar feats, instead requiring extensive training with each specific utterance (e.g., each voice command to the sheepdog) in order for communication to occur at all. In other words, most animals appear to lack grammar. For this reason, scientists have investigated language capabilities only in our nearest relatives, the great apes.

Because both the vocal tracts and the vocal repertoires of nonhuman primates are different from those of humans, scientists have given up attempting to train animals to produce human speech. But can nonhuman primates be taught other forms of communication that have features similar to those of human language, including the ability to represent objects with symbols and to manipulate those symbols according to rules of order? Can animals other than humans generate a novel string of symbols, such as a new sentence, in a grammatical form? Some researchers argue that language is a uniquely human adaptation that evolved, independently of other cognitive capabilities, in order to solve specific problems in our evolutionary past (Pinker and Jackendoff, 2005).

Our nearest primate relatives, chimpanzees, are capable of learning many of the hand gestures of American Sign Language (ASL), the standardized sign language used by deaf people in most of North America (R. A. Gardner and Gardner, 1969, 1984). Chimps trained in ASL have been reported to use signs spontaneously, and in novel sequences. Gorillas apparently also possess the ability to learn ASL signs numbering in the hundreds (F. Patterson and Linden, 1981). An alternative system involves the use of assorted colored chips (symbols) that can be arranged on a magnetic board. After extensive training with this system, chimps reportedly organize the chips in ways that seem to reflect an acquired ability to form short sentences and to note various logical classifications (Premack, 1971). A third language system, named *Yerkish* after the Yerkes National Primate Research Center, uses computerized keys to represent concepts (**Figure 19.5**); again, apes show some ability to acquire words in this language, which they appear to string together into novel, meaningful chains (Rumbaugh, 1977).

The idea that apes can acquire and use rudiments of language is controversial. According to many linguists, grammar is the essence of language, so investigators look for the ability of chimps to generate meaningful and novel sequences of signs that follow grammatical rules. The work of R. A. Gardner and Gardner (1969, 1984), Premack (1971), and others suggests that chimps do make distinctive series of signs, just as though they were using words in a sentence, including categories and negatives. However, other researchers have argued that these sequences may simply be subtle forms of imitation (Terrace, 1979), perhaps unconsciously cued by the experimenter who is providing the training. Native ASL users dispute the linguistic validity of the signs generated by apes; and Pinker (1994) insists,

19.5 Chimpanzee Using Symbols
Although chimpanzees can learn to use arbitrary signs and/or symbols to communicate, it is questionable whether this usage is equivalent to human language. (Photo courtesy of Sue Savage-Rumbaugh.)

"Even putting aside vocabulary, phonology, morphology, and syntax, what impresses one the most about chimpanzee signing is that fundamentally, deep down, chimps just don't get it" (p. 349).

Nevertheless, considering that apes can comprehend spoken words, produce novel combinations of words, and respond appropriately to sentences arranged according to a syntactic rule, it seems likely that the linguistic capacity of apes was underestimated historically (Savage-Rumbaugh, 1993). For example, a bonobo (or pygmy chimpanzee) named Kanzi, the focus of a long-term research program (Savage-Rumbaugh and Lewin, 1994), reportedly learned numerous symbols and ways to assemble them in novel combinations, entirely through observational learning rather than the usual intensive training. And in natural settings, monkeys combine certain vocalizations into higher-order, more complex calls, suggesting the presence of both syntax and semantic meaning, at least on a rudimentary level (Arnold and Zuberbühler, 2006; Ouattara, et al., 2009). So although the debate is far from settled, the linguistic accomplishments of primates have at least forced investigators to sharpen their criteria of what constitutes language (Fitch and Hauser, 2004).

Language Disorders Result from Region-Specific Brain Injuries

Much of our early understanding of the relationship between brain mechanisms and language was gained through observations of people who experienced language impairment as a consequence of accidents, diseases, or strokes that caused damage to specific regions of the brain.

Several defining signs characterize aphasia

Early Egyptian medical records, written at least 3000 years ago, describe people who lost the ability to speak after blows to the temporal bone (Finger, 1994), and anecdotes from the centuries that followed suggest a folk awareness that focal brain injuries—perhaps especially left-sided ones—could impair language abilities. But it wasn't until 1861 that systematic study of the organization of the brain's language systems began, when French neurologist Paul Broca (1824–1880) examined a man who had lost the ability to utter much more than the single syllable "tan." Postmortem study of this patient revealed damage to the left inferior frontal region—a region now known as **Broca's area** (see Figure 19.6). In approximately 90%–95% of the cases of language impairment due to brain injury—called **aphasia**—the damage is to the left cerebral hemisphere. This critical role of the left hemisphere is confirmed by techniques such as the **Wada test** (**Box 19.1**). We'll expand our discussion of the different functions of the two hemispheres later in this chapter.

Following severe left-hemisphere damage, some people lose the ability to produce any speech whatsoever. Many other patients, usually with more-restricted lesions, retain the ability to produce at least some speech sounds but show pronounced **paraphasia**: the substitution of a word by a sound, an incorrect word, or an unintended word. At times an entirely novel word—called a **neologism**—may be generated by the substitution of a phoneme. Paraphasic speech in aphasic patients is evident both in spontaneous conversation and in attempts to read aloud from a text. Conversation reveals another important aspect of speech: its fluency or ease of production. **Nonfluent speech** is talking with considerable effort, in short sentences, and without the usual melodic character of conversational speech.

Almost all patients with aphasia show some impairment in writing (**agraphia**) and disturbances in reading (**alexia**). Finally, the brain impairments or disorders that produce aphasia also produce a distinctive motor impairment called *apraxia* (see Chapter 11). Apraxia is characterized by impairment in the execution of complex sequential movements that is unrelated to paralysis, coordination problems,

Broca's area   A region of the frontal lobe of the brain that is involved in the production of speech.

aphasia   An impairment in language understanding and/or production that is caused by brain injury.

Wada test   A test in which a short-lasting anesthetic is delivered into one carotid artery to determine which cerebral hemisphere principally mediates language.

paraphasia   A symptom of aphasia that is distinguished by the substitution of a word by a sound, an incorrect word, an unintended word, or a neologism (a meaningless word).

neologism   An entirely novel word, sometimes produced by a patient with aphasia.

nonfluent speech   Talking with considerable effort, short sentences, and the absence of the usual melodic character of conversational speech.

agraphia   The inability to write.

alexia   The inability to read.

BOX 19.1 The Wada Test

Clinical observations of humans with brain injury indicate that about 90%–95% of us show left-hemisphere specialization for verbal activities, but how can we determine which side of the brain mediates language in a person who is not ill? Wada and Rasmussen (1960) developed a technique to temporarily shut down much of one hemisphere without inflicting permanent damage. They injected a short-acting anesthetic (sodium amytal) into the carotid artery—first on one side and then, several minutes later, on the other. Recall from Chapter 2

that the circulation of the anterior two-thirds of the cerebral hemisphere comes from branches of the carotid artery. Most of the anesthetic in the first pass remains on the side of the brain where it was injected. The patient shows arrest of speech for a brief period when the anesthetic is injected in the hemisphere specialized for language processing. After a few minutes the effects wear off, so the injection is much like a reversible brain lesion.

The sodium amytal test (sometimes called the *Wada test*) confirms stroke data

indicating that about 90%–95% of humans have a left-hemisphere specialization for language. The Wada test also confirms that, although most left-handed people show left dominance for language, the reverse pattern (right-hemisphere dominance for language) is more common in left-handed people than in right-handed people. As described in the text, a new variant of the Wada test is to use transcranial magnetic stimulation (TMS) in healthy subjects to disrupt electrical activity in the left hemisphere or the right (Knecht et al., 2002).

---

sensory impairments, or understanding of instructions. Patients suffering from apraxia are unable to imitate arbitrary sequences of movements or some common gestures, such as sticking out the tongue or waving goodbye, although these acts might appear in the patients' spontaneous behavior. Aphasia seems to confer one advantage: patients who suffer from this disorder are better than controls at detecting when someone is lying (Etcoff et al., 2000). This sensitivity to lying may result from a focus on facial features of speakers (as we'll see, the undamaged right hemisphere is important for face processing) and a lack of distraction by the words being spoken.

Three major types of aphasia result from injury to particular brain regions

Linking particular language disorders to specific regions of brain damage has been a major research focus to uncover details of the left-hemisphere language network. **Figure 19.6** shows the main brain regions of the left hemisphere that are related to language abilities. **Table 19.1** summarizes the main features of various types of aphasia that we'll cover in this chapter. The sections that follow discuss the three primary aphasias in more detail.

NONFLUENT APHASIA   Lesions in the left inferior frontal region (Broca's area) produce a type of aphasia known as **nonfluent** (or **Broca's**) **aphasia**. Patients with nonfluent aphasia have considerable difficulty producing speech, talking only in a labored and hesitant manner. Reading and writing are also impaired. The ability to utter automatic speech, however, is often preserved. Such speech includes greetings ("Hello"); short, common expressions ("Oh, my God!"); and swear words. Compared to the difficulty that these patients have expressing themselves, their *comprehension* of language remains relatively good. Because primary and supplementary motor cortex are located in anterior portions of the hemisphere, as we saw in Chapter 11, many people who suffer from nonfluent aphasia

nonfluent aphasia or Broca's aphasia
A language impairment characterized by difficulty with speech production but not with language comprehension; related to damage in Broca's area.

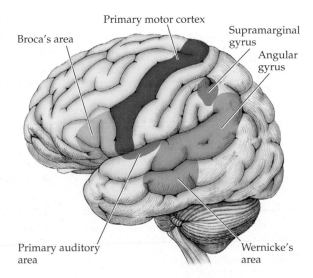

19.6 Cortical Speech and Language Areas in Humans   Lesions in the anterior frontal region called *Broca's area* interfere with speech production; injury to an area of temporoparietal cortex called *Wernicke's area* interferes with language comprehension; injury to the supramarginal gyrus interferes with repetition of heard speech. For most individuals, these language-related systems are found only in the left hemisphere.

TABLE 19.1 Language Symptomatology in Aphasia

Type of aphasia	Brain area affected	Spontaneous speech	Comprehension	Paraphasia	Repetition	Naming
Nonfluent (Broca's) aphasia	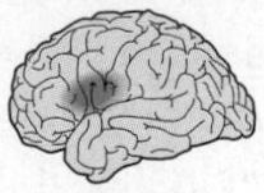	Nonfluent	Good	Uncommon	Poor	Poor
Fluent (Wernicke's) aphasia	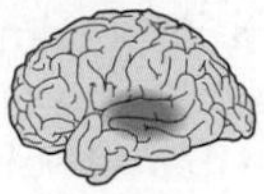	Fluent	Poor	Common	Poor	Poor
Global aphasia	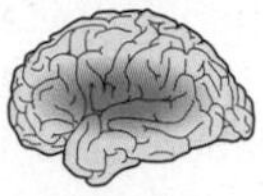	Nonfluent	Poor	Variable	Poor	Poor
Conduction aphasia	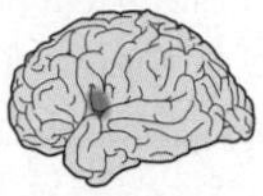	Fluent	Good	Common	Poor	Poor
Subcortical aphasia	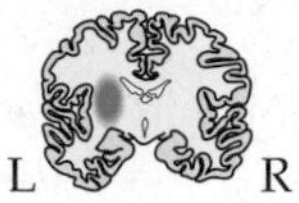 L R	Variable	Variable	Common	Good	Variable

also have **hemiplegia**—paralysis of one side of the body (usually the right side, which is controlled by the left hemisphere). Sometimes there is unilateral weakness, termed **hemiparesis**, rather than full paralysis.

The CT scans in **Figure 19.7a and b** reveal lesion sites in patients with nonfluent aphasia. Seven years after a stroke, one such patient still spoke slowly, used mainly nouns and very few verbs or function words (a selective loss of action words, called *averbia*, sometimes occurs in nonfluent aphasia) and spoke only with great effort. When asked to repeat the phrase "Go ahead and do it if possible," she could say only, "Go to do it," with pauses between each word. Patients who suffer from nonfluent aphasia and have brain lesions as extensive as hers show little recovery of speech with the passing of time.

FLUENT APHASIA   German neurologist Carl Wernicke (1848–1905) described several syndromes of aphasia following brain lesions to a region of the posterior temporal cortex called **Wernicke's area** (see Figure 19.6). The syndrome now known as **fluent** (or **Wernicke's**) **aphasia** includes a complex array of symptoms. People who have fluent aphasia produce plenty of verbal output, but their utterances, although speechlike, tend to contain many paraphasias that make their speech unintelligible. Paraphasias may involve sound substitutions (e.g., "girl" becomes "curl") and/or word substitutions (e.g., *bread* becomes *cake*); neologisms are also common. Some fluent aphasias are marked by difficulty in naming persons or objects—an impairment referred to as **anomia**.

Paraphasias and speech errors occur in a context that preserves syntactic structure, although sentences seem empty of content. The ability to repeat words and sentences is impaired. For this reason, people with fluent aphasia are believed to have difficulty *understanding* what they read or hear. In some cases reading comprehension appears to be more impaired than comprehension of spoken language; in other cases the reverse is true. Naturally, communication with people who have fluent aphasia is difficult, often consisting of gestures and demonstration. This communication is facilitated by the patient's intact understanding of facial expressions.

In fluent aphasia the most prominent brain lesions are in posterior regions of the left superior temporal gyrus and extend partially into adjacent parietal cortex,

hemiplegia   Partial paralysis involving one side of the body.

hemiparesis   Weakness of one side of the body.

Wernicke's area   A region of temporoparietal cortex in the brain that is involved in the perception and production of speech.

fluent aphasia or Wernicke's aphasia   A language impairment characterized by fluent, meaningless speech and little language comprehension; related to damage in Wernicke's area.

anomia   The inability to name persons or objects readily.

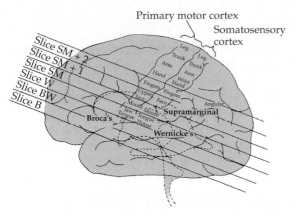

Primary motor cortex
Somatosensory cortex

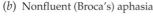

19.7 Brain Lesions That Produce Aphasia Levels of CT scan slices are labeled according to brain language regions shown by that slice: B, Broca's area; SM, supramarginal gyrus; W, Wernicke's area. (a) CT scans for one patient with nonfluent aphasia, aged 51, 7 years after stroke. (b) Lesion sites for four cases of nonfluent aphasia. Large lesions (blue) are located in Broca's area on slices B and BW, and the peak amount of tissue damage occurred in the frontoparietal areas on slices SM and SM + 1. (c) Lesion sites for four cases of fluent aphasia. Lesions are located in Wernicke's area on slice W and in the supramarginal gyrus area on slice SM. (d) Lesion sites for five cases of global aphasia. Large lesions are present in every language area. (After Naeser and Hayward, 1978; CT scans courtesy of Margaret Naeser.)

(*a*) Case of nonfluent (Broca's) aphasia

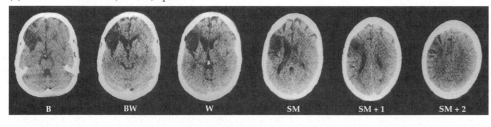

(*b*) Nonfluent (Broca's) aphasia

(*c*) Fluent (Wernicke's) aphasia

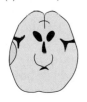

(*d*) Global aphasia

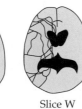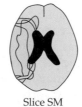

Slice B — Slice BW — Slice W — Slice SM — Slice SM + 1 — Slice SM + 2

including the supramarginal and angular gyri (**Figure 19.7c**) (H. Damasio, 1995). When *word deafness* (the inability to understand spoken words) is more evident than reading impairment, patients show greater involvement of the superior temporal lobe, especially tracts from the auditory cortex. In contrast, when *word blindness* (the inability to understand written words) predominates, greater destruction of the angular gyrus is evident. Because the typical lesion spares the motor cortex of the precentral gyrus, patients with fluent aphasia (unlike those with nonfluent aphasia) usually do not display hemiplegia.

GLOBAL APHASIA In some patients, brain injury or disease results in total loss of the ability to understand or produce language. This syndrome is called **global apha-**

global aphasia The total loss of ability to understand language, or to speak, read, or write.

sia. Patients suffering from global aphasia may retain some ability for automatic speech, especially emotional exclamations. But they can utter very few words, and no semblance of syntax is evident in their vocalizations. Global aphasia generally results from very large left-hemisphere lesions that encompass both anterior and posterior language zones. Frontal, temporal, and parietal cortex—including Broca's area, Wernicke's area, and the supramarginal gyrus—are usually affected (**Figure 19.7d**). The prognosis for language recovery in these patients is quite poor and, because of the extent of their lesions, the aphasia is generally accompanied by other debilitating neurological impairments.

Models of aphasia offer varying accounts of the anatomy of speech and language

Speech and language pervade every aspect of our cognitive lives, from our social transactions with others to our innermost thoughts. Considering how language is intertwined with so many other functions, it is not surprising that a complete description of the brain's language circuitry has been elusive and subject to much debate.

THE WERNICKE-GESCHWIND MODEL OF APHASIA One traditional approach to understanding aphasic disturbances, introduced by Wernicke in the early twentieth century, uses a *connectionist* perspective. According to this view, deficits can be understood as breaks in an interconnected network of components, each of which is involved with a particular feature of language analysis or production.

Norman Geschwind (1926–1984) developed an expanded version of this theory, which is referred to as *disconnection theory* to emphasize the symptoms of language impairment following the loss of connections among brain regions in a network (Geschwind, 1972). According to this perspective, when a word or sentence is heard, the auditory cortex transmits information about the sounds to Wernicke's area, where the sounds are analyzed to decode what they mean. For the word to be spoken, Wernicke's area must transmit this information to Broca's area, where a speech plan is activated. Broca's area then transmits this plan to adjacent motor cortex, which controls the relevant muscles for speech production.

The axons transmitting information from Wernicke's area to Broca's area form a bundle of nerve fibers called the **arcuate fasciculus** (from the Latin *arcuatus*, "bow-shaped," and *fasciculus*, "small bundle"). This network linking anterior and posterior speech zones may be one of the primary adaptations for language in the human brain, since chimpanzees and monkeys appear to lack a homologous pathway (Rilling et al., 2008). Patients with lesions that disrupt the arcuate fasciculus have relatively fluent speech and good comprehension of spoken words because Broca's and Wernicke's areas are intact. But they may display **conduction aphasia**, an impairment in the *repetition* of words and sentences (**Figure 19.8a**). When these patients attempt to repeat words they have heard, they are likely to produce incorrect phonemes substituting for correct sounds.

According to the Wernicke-Geschwind model, saying the name of a *seen* object or word involves the transfer of visual information to the **angular gyrus**, which then arouses the auditory pattern in Wernicke's area. From Wernicke's area the auditory form is transmitted via the arcuate fasciculus to Broca's area. There the template for the spoken form is activated and transmitted to the face area of the motor cortex, and the word is then spoken (**Figure 19.8b**). In this model, lesions affecting the angular gyrus would thus disconnect the systems involved in visual and auditory language; patients with lesions in this region would have difficulty reading aloud but would retain the ability to speak and understand speech.

THE MOTOR THEORY OF LANGUAGE Critics of the Wernicke-Geschwind model argue that it oversimplified the neural mechanisms of language and prematurely attached functional labels to anatomical findings. For one thing, it has long been

arcuate fasciculus A tract connecting Wernicke's speech area to Broca's speech area.

conduction aphasia An impairment in the repetition of words and sentences.

angular gyrus A brain region in which strokes can lead to word blindness.

(*a*) Speaking a *heard* word

1. Information about the sound is analyzed by primary auditory cortex and transmitted to Wernicke's area.

2. Wernicke's area analyzes the sound information to determine the word that was said.

3. This information from Wernicke's area is transmitted through the arcuate fasciculus to Broca's area.

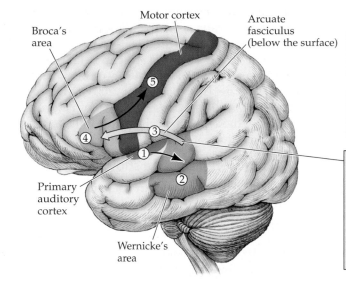

4. Broca's area forms a motor plan to repeat the word and sends that information to motor cortex.

5. Motor cortex implements the plan, manipulating the larynx and related structures to say the word.

Lesions of the arcuate fasciculus disrupt the transfer from Wernicke's area to Broca's area, so the patient has difficulty repeating spoken words (so-called conduction aphasia), but may retain comprehension of spoken language (because of intact Wernicke's area) and may still be able to speak spontaneously (because of intact Broca's area).

(*b*) Speaking a *written* word

1. Visual cortex analyzes the image and transmits the information about the image to the angular gyrus.

2. The angular gyrus decodes the image information to recognize the word and associate this visual form with the spoken form in Wernicke's area.

3. Information about the word is transmitted via the arcuate fasciculus to Broca's area.

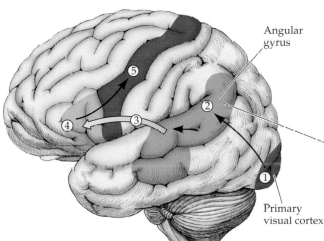

4. Broca's area formulates a motor plan to say the appropriate word and transmits that plan to motor cortex for implementation.

5. Motor cortex implements the plan, manipulating the larynx and related structures to say the word.

A lesion of the angular gyrus disrupts the flow of information from visual cortex, so the person has difficulty saying words he has seen but not words he has heard.

19.8 The Wernicke-Geschwind Connectionist Model of Aphasia   (After Geschwind, 1976.)

clear that, although anterior- and posterior-lesioned people with aphasia differ greatly with regard to fluency (Benson, 1967; Goodglass et al., 1964), the expressive-receptive dichotomy that has been applied to them under the Wernicke-Geschwind model doesn't hold up very well. Anterior aphasics appear to have difficulty comprehending some aspects of speech in addition to their expressive problems, and posterior aphasics make speech selection errors despite their fluency (Kimura, 1993).

An alternative perspective—the **motor theory of language**—proposes that the left-hemisphere language zones are motor control systems that are concerned with both the precise production and the *perception* of the extremely complex movements that go into speech (Kimura, 1993; Lieberman, 1985). According to this view, the anterior left hemisphere programs the simple phonemic units of speech, and the posterior systems are responsible for stringing speech sounds together into long sequences of movements (Kimura and Watson, 1989). Proponents of the motor theory further suggest that when we *listen* to speech we are using elements of this same system to perceive the very rapid sequences of facial, throat, tongue, and respiratory movements that the speaker is making. So, in a way, speech sounds are simply an auditory representation of a series of rapid facial gestures that we perceive using our own gesture-making machinery. From an evolutionary per-

motor theory of language   The theory proposing that the left-hemisphere language zones are motor control systems that are concerned with both the precise production and the perception of the extremely complex movements that go into speech.

spective, this arrangement is economical because we can use the same evolved neural substrate—perhaps building on preexisting systems controlling other movements—to both produce and perceive speech sounds (Lieberman, 2002).

In any event, detailed structural imaging studies have revealed that the left hemisphere contains several speech areas well outside of the classical Broca's and Wernicke's areas (E. Bates et al., 2003; Dronkers et al., 2004), implying greater complexity than was proposed by the Wernicke-Geschwind model. It remains to be seen how the various mechanisms of the left hemisphere collaborate to give us the vocal abilities that seem so effortless.

Users of sign language show aphasia following brain injury

As we have noted, the control of hand and arm gestures seems to be closely related to the production of speech. A formalized set of hand and arm gestures, along with specific rules of arrangement, forms the basis of nonvocal languages of the deaf, such as American Sign Language. ASL consists of an elaborate code and grammar; **Figure 19.9** shows some examples of ASL signs.

Exhaustive analysis of ASL clearly established this gesture-based set of symbols as a full-fledged language, as elaborate as its vocal counterparts (Klima and Bellugi, 1979) and with features as subtle as dialect. During the last 25 years or so, researchers have observed the invention and evolution of a new sign language among deaf children in Nicaragua (Senghas et al., 2004); the form and fluency of this new language gives further support to the idea that the fundamental rules of language are innate. Investigators therefore have been interested in determining whether sign language similarly shares the neural organization of spoken language. Is there hemispheric specialization for a language system based on hand signals, most of which are formed by the right hand?

Meckler et al. (1979) described a young man who had been raised by deaf-mute parents and who began to suffer from aphasia after an accident. Previously he had used both spoken and sign language for communication. After the accident, impairments in his spoken language and sign language were equally severe, as though the damaged brain region had subserved both languages. Intriguingly, we now know that this is precisely how it works in people who are fluently bilingual in two *spoken* languages: provided that they were acquired early in life, both languages will rely on the same neural systems (Perani and Abutalebi, 2005). Chiarello et al. (1982) analyzed sign language deficits in an older deaf-mute person. This person had well-developed sign language skills until, following a stroke in the left temporal cortex (including Wernicke's area), she became unable to generate signs with either hand. In other examples (Bellugi et al., 1983; Kimura, 1981), aphasia in deaf signers was strongly associated with damage limited to the left hemisphere.

19.9 American Sign Language In ASL, letters, words, and concepts are communicated via different configurations (*signs*) of the hands and arms, as these three examples illustrate.

Feeling

Be quiet

Secret

Together, these studies indicate that the same neural mechanisms are used for both spoken and signed languages. Subsequent functional-imaging work has confirmed that hearing and deaf people activate the same areas of the left hemisphere during language tasks (Neville et al., 1998; Petitto et al., 2000). Cerebral injury in these areas interferes with the production of language movements, whether conveyed by speech or by hand. Deaf patients with damage to the *right* hemisphere, like hearing patients, tend to retain nearly normal communication skills. However, some right-hemisphere activity is also evident in signers during language tasks, perhaps because some signs require the use of both hands.

Reading Skills Are Difficult to Acquire and Frequently Impaired

Learning to read and write requires far more effort than learning to speak. This difference reflects the evolutionary heritage of our brains, which are more or less the same as those of the prehistoric humans that lived tens of thousands of years ago, before the advent of written language. Speaking is an ancient human adaptation, old enough that innate speech mechanisms have evolved in the brain. But reading and writing are relatively recent developments, and we have not had enough time to evolve the same sort of innate mechanisms for these behaviors. Presumably, this is why many primitive modern societies lack writing but none lack complex spoken language. Difficulty with reading is called **dyslexia** (from the Greek *dys*, "bad," and *lexis*, "word"). Dyslexia can result from several developmental and neurological causes.

Brain damage may cause specific impairments in reading

Sometimes people who learned to read just fine as children suddenly become dyslexic in adulthood as a result of disease or injury, usually to the left hemisphere. This *acquired dyslexia* (sometimes called *alexia*) reveals hints about how the brain processes written language. One type of acquired dyslexia, known as **deep dyslexia**, is characterized by errors in which patients read a word as another word that is related in meaning; for example, the printed word *cow* is read as *horse*. These patients are also unable to read aloud words that are abstract as opposed to concrete, and they make frequent errors in which they seem to fail to see small differences in words. It's as though they grasp words whole, without noting the details of the letters, so they have a hard time reading nonsense words.

In another form of acquired dyslexia, **surface dyslexia**, the patient makes different types of errors when reading. These patients can read nonsense words just fine, indicating that they know the rules of which letters make which sounds. But they find it difficult to recognize words in which the letter-to-sound rules are irregular. *The Tough Coughs as He Ploughs the Dough* by Dr. Seuss (1987), for example, would utterly confound them. In contrast to patients with deep dyslexia, those with surface dyslexia seem restricted to the details and sounds of letters. Interestingly, surface dyslexia doesn't occur in native speakers of languages that are perfectly phonetic (such as Italian). This finding indicates that what's lost in speakers of nonphonetic languages, like English, is purely a learned aspect of language. In contrast, deep dyslexia probably involves language mechanisms that are more hardwired.

Other aspects of brain damage can also produce acquired difficulty with reading. For example, patients experiencing hemispatial neglect due to a right parietal lobe lesion (discussed in Chapter 18) fail to perceive the left half of a visual world, despite having otherwise normal visual function. Such patients sometimes fail to properly read just the first half of a word, presumably because of a failure to attend to that half. And some cases of acquired dyslexia feature *letter-by-letter reading*, in which the patient must laboriously spell out each word to herself (aloud or silently). Consciously attending to spelling is the only way by which patients can identify words, consequently their reading is significantly slowed.

dyslexia   A reading disorder attributed to brain impairment. *Acquired dyslexia* occurs as a result of injury or disease. *Developmental dyslexia* is associated with brain abnormalities present from birth.

deep dyslexia   Acquired dyslexia in which the patient reads a word as another word that is semantically related.

surface dyslexia   Acquired dyslexia in which the patient seems to attend only to the fine details of reading.

Some people struggle to read throughout their lives

Some children seem to take forever to learn to read. Their efforts are laden with frustration, and prolonged practice produces only small improvements. This *developmental dyslexia* is seen in nearly 5% of children in the general population; it is even more common in boys and in left-handed people. Some children with dyslexia have a high IQ; several have grown up to amass billion-dollar fortunes (B. Morris, 2002). So dyslexia seems to be a specific problem with written language, especially the coordination of reading behavior with brain mechanisms that evolved to serve speech functions, and not a general cognitive deficit.

Albert Galaburda (1994) conducted postmortem investigations of four patients with dyslexia who had died from acute disease or trauma that did not involve the brain. All the brains showed striking anomalies in the arrangement of cortical cells, especially in areas of the frontal and temporal cortical regions. These anomalies consisted of unusual groupings of cells in outer layers of the cerebral cortex that distorted the normal layered arrangements and columnar organization (**Figure 19.10**). Some cells were disoriented, and excessive cortical folding (**micropolygyria**) was observed. Nests of extra cells—**ectopias**—were seen. Similarly, people showing MRI evidence of these abnormalities tend to have reading disorders (Chang et al., 2005). It is likely that anomalies of cerebral cortical cell arrangements arise quite early in development, perhaps during the middle of gestation, a period during which cells are actively migrating in cerebral cortex. Defective neuronal migration thus may be responsible for unusual patterns of connectivity in language-related regions of the temporal cortex (Galaburda et al., 2006).

micropolygyria   A condition of the brain in which small regions are characterized by more gyri than usual.

ectopia   Something out of place—for example, clusters of neurons seen in unusual positions in the cortex of someone suffering from dyslexia.

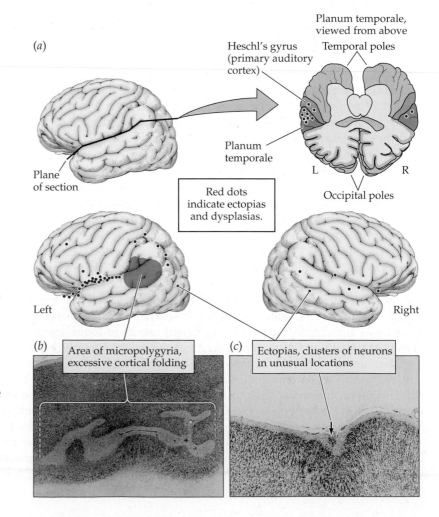

19.10 Neural Disorganization in Dyslexia (*a*) (*Top*) Drawings of the left and right planum temporale (see Figure 19.16) from the brain of a person suffering from dyslexia show these regions as nearly symmetrical; in most people the left planum temporale is considerably larger. The dots and the shaded area represent regions where microscopic anomalies called *ectopias*, *dysplasias*, and *micropolygyria* have been found in the brains of individuals with dyslexia. (*Bottom*) Anomalies in patients with dyslexia are much more common in the left hemisphere, which is primarily responsible for language function. (*b, c*) These micrographs show (*b*) micropolygyria (literally "many tiny gyri") and (*c*) ectopias, clusters of neurons in unusual locations, such as this cluster in cortical layer I (arrow), which is normally devoid of neuronal cell bodies. (After Galaburda, 1994; micrographs courtesy of Albert Galaburda.)

Functional-imaging studies have revealed systematic abnormalities of brain activity in dyslexia. Compared to control subjects, people with dyslexia show diminished activation of left posterior regions that include the superior temporal lobe and angular gyrus (K. R. Pugh et al., 2000; Shaywitz et al., 1998, 2003), as well as the occipital lobe (Demb et al., 1998), while showing a relative overactivation of anterior regions. Abnormality is also seen in the nearby temporoparietal region and has been particularly linked to the phonological (phoneme-processing) aspects of dyslexia (Hoeft et al., 2006). In addition to abnormalities of the temporal *cortex*, brain imaging has revealed subtle changes in the fine structure of the temporoparietal white matter pathways in adult dyslexics (Klingberg et al., 2000). These abnormalities may indicate possible problems with the axonal connections between language-related cortical areas. Furthermore, the white matter changes were evident in both hemispheres, consistent with evidence that the brains of dyslexic people are more bilaterally symmetrical than those of nondyslexic people (Jenner et al., 1999). Researchers also find a consistent relationship between developmental dyslexia and cerebellar dysfunction (Stoodley and Stein, 2010). It is not yet clear exactly what role the cerebellum plays in reading, because cerebellar lesions later in life do not result in acquired dyslexia.

Taken together, imaging and behavioral studies indicate that our brains rely on two different language systems during reading: one focused on the sounds of letters, the other on the meanings of whole words (McCarthy and Warrington, 1990). Presumably, these systems are shaped by training: as with learning any highly skilled behavior, our brains appear to mold themselves to accommodate our acquired expertise with written language. The observation that remedial training in people with dyslexia induces changes in the left-hemisphere systems that are used for reading (Temple et al., 2003) is consistent with this view. And intriguingly, there appears to be a cultural component to dyslexia: the specific brain regions involved may vary depending on the graphical form of the written language being learned. Most research implicates the left temporoparietal cortex as being centrally important in dyslexia, but in readers of Chinese—a language based on logographic symbols rather than an alphabet—dyslexia is especially associated with dysfunction of the left medial frontal cortex (Siok et al., 2004).

Developmental dyslexia appears to have a genetic component. In large studies of familial dyslexia in Finland, disruptions in two genes—*DYXC1* and *ROBO1*—have been linked to reading disorders (Hannula-Jouppi et al., 2005; Taipale et al., 2003). *ROBO1* is known to be involved in guiding growing axons to their destinations. The precise function of *DYXC1* is not yet known, but it is estimated to be abnormal in 9% of individuals suffering from dyslexia in the general population (Taipale et al., 2003), and a large-scale study of families found a significant association between mutations of this gene and behavioral measures of dyslexia (T. C. Bates et al., 2009). In a different sample of people with dyslexic family members, the gene *DCDC2* has been associated with dyslexia (Meng et al., 2005). Estimated to be abnormal in as many as 17% of people with dyslexia, *DCDC2* is believed to participate in the migration of neurons into their positions in the cortex (discussed in Chapter 7). Variation in this gene was associated with reading performance in a large familial analysis, indicating that the gene may be involved in normal reading ability, and that mutations in the gene are a genetic risk factor for dyslexia (Lind et al., 2010). Finally, the gene *KIAA0319*, linked to processes of brain development, is also reported to be associated with developmental dyslexia (Cope et al., 2005; Harold et al., 2006). In rats, inhibition of *KIAA0319* causes ectopias to form in temporal cortex, strongly supporting the idea that an early problem with neuronal migration is a prime cause of dyslexia (Peschansky et al., 2009).

Although more work will be needed before we really understand the genetic basis of the disorder, these discoveries raise the prospect of early identification of dyslexia via genetic screening. Such detection would allow for earlier, and more effective, intervention strategies.

Brain Stimulation Provides Information about the Organization of Language in the Brain

Localized stimulation of the brain can be used to explore language functions of the human cerebral cortex. Although this approach has historically been limited to neurological patients, new technology is allowing stimulation mapping studies of normal people too.

The cortical surface can be mapped using stimulating electrodes

Subjects in these studies are patients undergoing surgery for the relief of seizures. Electrical stimulation during surgery is used to help neurosurgeons locate—and thus avoid damaging—language-related cortical regions. Once the brain has been exposed, small stimulating electrodes are touched to the surface, disrupting the normal functioning of neurons in the immediate vicinity. By observing language interference produced by the electrical stimuli, the surgeon can identify regions serving various behavioral functions. Patients are given only local anesthesia, so that they can continue to respond to neuropsychological tests of language and other cognitive functions during the surgery.

Pioneering work by Penfield and Roberts (1959; discussed at the start of Chapter 2) provided a map of language-related zones of the left hemisphere (**Figure 19.11***a*). Pooled data from many patients showed that stimulation anywhere within a large anterior zone stops speech. Other forms of language interference, such as misnaming or impaired repetition of words, were evident from stimulation of both this region and more-posterior temporoparietal cortex regions.

George Ojemann and collaborators (Calvin and Ojemann, 1994) examined the effects of electrical stimulation within a wide extent of cerebral cortex and found evidence of anatomical compartmentalization of linguistic systems such as naming, reading, speech production, and verbal memory. An interesting example of the effects of cortical stimulation on naming is illustrated in **Figure 19.11***b*, which shows the different loci of naming errors in English and Spanish in a bilingual subject. Presumably the subject being studied learned the two languages sequentially, for if they had been learned simultaneously, a more complete overlap of the English and Spanish language zones would be predicted (Perani and Abutalebi, 2005).

19.11 Electrical Stimulation of Some Brain Sites Can Interfere with Language (*a*) This summary of data obtained from many monolingual patients shows the brain sites where stimulation interferes with speech production. (*b*) This map highlights stimulation sites that affected the speech of a patient who was bilingual—fluent in Spanish and English. Different regions interfere with either one language or the other, but not both. (Part *a* after Penfield and Roberts, 1959; *b* after Ojemann and Mateer, 1979.)

(*a*) Sites where stimulation interferes with speech in monolingual patients

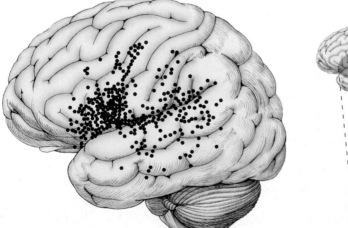

(*b*) Sites where stimulation affects speech in a bilingual patient

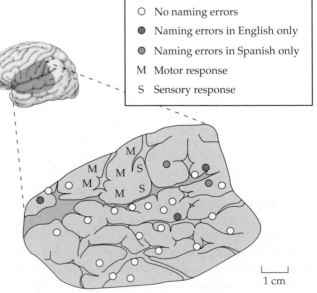

O   No naming errors
●   Naming errors in English only
●   Naming errors in Spanish only
M   Motor response
S   Sensory response

1 cm

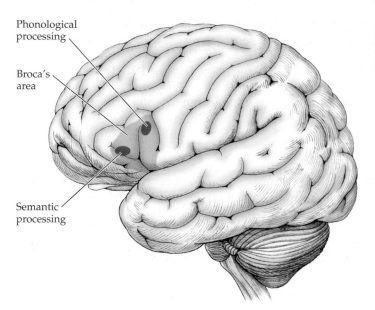

Phonological
processing

Broca's
area

Semantic
processing

19.12 Subregions of Broca's Area Revealed by TMS TMS stimulation affects semantic processing (meaning) when applied to anterior regions of Broca's area, but similar stimulation of posterior regions of Broca's area affects phonological processing (sound patterns). (After Devlin and Watkins, 2007; Gough et al., 2005.)

Transcranial magnetic stimulation provides precise and noninvasive identification of language areas

As we described in Chapter 2, transcranial magnetic stimulation (TMS) provides a noninvasive method for altering the activity of cortical neurons located below the stimulator (see Figure 2.22). By using a structural MRI scan to provide precise coordinates, it is possible to use the TMS effect as a sort of temporary brain lesion, disrupting the activity of selected brain regions and cataloging the resultant changes in behavior. Depending on how it is applied, TMS can disrupt neural function for up to an hour. Alternatively, TMS can be used along with PET or fMRI to precisely localize regions of increased activity.

Studies with TMS mapping have generally replicated and extended the earlier findings regarding the cortical organization of language functions (Devlin and Watkins, 2007). For example, TMS studies have found that speech production activates not only face areas in motor cortex but also hand areas, confirming the linkage and possible evolutionary relationship of hand gestures and speech (Meister et al., 2003). Speech *perception* apparently activates specific regions that TMS shows to be involved with speech *production* (S. K. Scott and Wise, 2004), providing support for the motor theory of speech, which we discussed earlier. And, impressively, the TMS temporary-lesion approach has revealed distinct regional differences within Broca's area (**Figure 19.12**). Specifically, a more anterior and ventral division of Broca's area appears to be important for the semantic *meaning* of words, while a more posterior part of Broca's area is important for phonological processing: the patterning of speech *sounds* (Gough et al., 2005; Devlin and Watkins, 2007). A similar experimental approach has shown that the supramarginal gyrus, within the posterior speech zone, is involved in both semantic and phonological aspects of language (Stoeckel et al., 2009); previously, this structure was thought to be involved in phonological processes only. So the TMS procedure is providing new insights into the fine details of cortical organization of function, especially in conjunction with traditional neuroimaging techniques.

Functional Neuroimaging Portrays the Organization of the Brain for Speech and Language

A series of PET studies, summarized by Posner and Raichle (1994), examined brain activation during different levels of the processing of words. These levels include (1) passive exposure to visually presented words, (2) passive exposure to spoken words, (3) oral repetition of words, and (4) generation of a semantic association to a presented word. The successive levels of these experiments and the accompanying PET scans are shown in **Figure 19.13**. Passive viewing of words activates a posterior area within the left hemisphere (**Figure 19.13a**). Passive hearing of words shifts the focus of maximum brain activation to the temporal lobes (**Figure 19.13b**). Repeating the words orally activates the motor cortex of both sides, the supplementary motor cortex, and a portion of the cerebellum and

(a) Passively viewing words

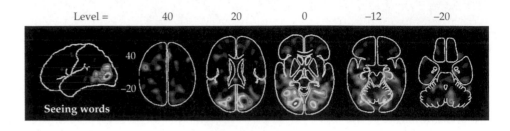

(b) Listening to words

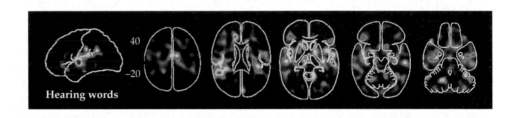

(c) Speaking words

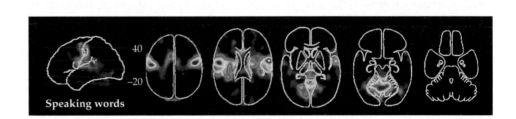

(d) Generating a verb associated with each noun shown

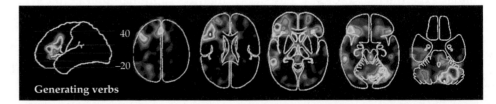

19.13 PET Scans of Brain Activation in Progressively More-Complex Language Tasks (*Left*) For clarity concerning the tasks, the subject is depicted here at a desk, but when the PET scans were made, the subjects reclined with their heads in a PET scanner and viewed a specially mounted display. (*Right*) These PET scans correspond to the tasks at left; see the text for details of these results. (After Posner and Raichle, 1994; PET scans courtesy of Marcus Raichle.)

insular cortex (**Figure 19.13c**). During word repetition or reading aloud, activity was relatively absent in Broca's area. But when subjects were required to provide a verb that was an appropriate semantic association for a presented noun, language-related regions in the left hemisphere, including Broca's area, were markedly activated (**Figure 19.13d**).

Interestingly, slightly different brain regions are activated when native speakers are reading Italian versus English (Paulesu et al., 2000). Perhaps the reason for this difference is one that we mentioned earlier—that the sound associated with each letter is very regular in Italian, whereas in English a given letter may have a very different sound in one word from the sound it has in another (to repeat the earlier example, compare the sounds of "ough" in the words *tough, cough, plough,* and *dough*). But overall, even languages that sound maximally different tend to activate much the same brain regions in native speakers.

Silbo Gomero is a very unusual whistled language of the Canary Islands, used by shepherds (known as *silbadores*) to communicate over long distances. In Silbo, whistled notes serve as the phonemes and morphemes of a stripped-down form of Spanish (for an audio sample of Silbo, with translation, see **A Step Further: Whistling Up Some Brain Activity** on the website). Functional MRI reveals that silbadores process Silbo using the same left-hemisphere mechanisms that they (and nonsilbadore control subjects) use to process spoken language (Carreiras et al., 2005). Nonsilbadore controls, in contrast, process the whistle sounds of Silbo using completely different regions of the brain. The brain's innate language systems appear to be sufficiently plastic to adapt to many types of signals.

Event-related potentials (ERPs; see Chapters 3 and 18) can distinguish how different aspects of language are processed by the brain, from one millisecond to the next. Subjects are asked to read a sentence in which they encounter a word that is grammatically correct but, because of its meaning, doesn't fit—for example, "The man started the car engine and stepped on the pancake." About 400 ms after the patient reads the word *pancake,* a negative wave is detected on the scalp (Kutas and Hillyard, 1980). Such "N400" responses (*N* denotes "negative," and the number represents the response time in milliseconds) to word meanings seem to be centered over the temporal lobe (Neville et al., 1992) and therefore may originate from temporoparietal cortex (including Wernicke's area). But *grammatically* inappropriate words elicit a positive potential about 600 ms after they are encountered (a "P600" response), suggesting that detection of this level of error requires an extra 200 ms of brain processing (Osterhout, 1997).

This propensity for humans to use their left cerebral hemisphere for language processing can be seen quite early. Even 3-month-old infants, when exposed to speech, show more metabolic activity in the left hemisphere than in the right (Dehaene-Lambertz et al., 2002), suggesting that we may be born with a predisposition to use the left brain for language.

Williams Syndrome Offers Clues about Language

Williams syndrome, which occurs in approximately one out of 20,000 births (Bower, 2000), offers a fascinating dissociation between what we normally regard as intelligence and language. Individuals with Williams syndrome speak freely and fluently with a large vocabulary, yet they may be unable to draw simple images, arrange colored blocks to match an example, or tie shoelaces. The individuals are very sociable, ready to strike up conversation and smile. They may also display strong musical talent, either singing or playing an instrument.

The syndrome results from the deletion of about 28 genes from one of the two chromosomes numbered 7 (de Luis et al., 2000). No one understands why the remaining copies of these genes, on the other chromosome 7, do not compensate for the lost copies. The absence of one copy of the gene called *elastin* (which encodes a protein important for connective tissue in skin and ligaments), leads to pixie-

Williams syndrome A disorder characterized by fluent linguistic function, but poor performance on standard IQ tests and great difficulty with spatial processing.

19.14 The Appearance of Williams Syndrome Children with Williams syndrome often have a characteristic facial shape, caused by the loss of a copy of the *elastin* gene. The loss of copies of other nearby genes is thought to cause mild mental disability paired with verbal fluency. (Photo courtesy of the Williams Syndrome Association.)

lateralization The tendency for the right and left halves of a system to differ from one another.

split-brain individual An individual whose corpus callosum has been severed, halting communication between the right and left hemispheres.

like facial features (**Figure 19.14**). Several of the other missing genes are thought to lead to changes in brain development and to the behavioral features of the syndrome.

The psychological development of such individuals is complicated: As infants they may display a greater understanding of numerosity than other infants, but as adults they may show a poor grasp of numbers. Conversely, their language performance is poor in infancy but greatly improved by adulthood (Paterson et al., 1999). These findings suggest that the developmental process is distinctively altered in Williams syndrome. Impressively, possession of extra copies of the identified genes on chromosome 7—rather than deletions of these genes—produces a syndrome that is, in many ways, the converse of Williams syndrome: very poor expressive language accompanied by normal spatial abilities (Somerville et al., 2005).

The Left Brain Is Different from the Right Brain

By the early twentieth century it was firmly established that the cerebral hemispheres are not equivalent in mediating language functions (Finger, 1994). The left hemisphere seemed to control this function and was commonly described as the dominant hemisphere. However, the right hemisphere does not just idly sit within the skull, awaiting an occasional call to duty. In fact, most researchers have abandoned the notion of cerebral *dominance* in favor of models of hemispheric *specialization*, or **lateralization**. This emphasis implies that some functional systems are connected more to one side of the brain than the other—that is, that functions become lateralized—and that each hemisphere is specialized for particular ways of working.

Lateralization of function is not a surprising idea; other body organs also show considerable asymmetry between the right and left sides. For example, in all vertebrates the heart is slightly to the left of the midline and the liver is on the right. Sometimes a person with a defect in one of the genes involved will develop the reverse pattern (B. Casey and Hackett, 2000). Nevertheless, at the level of brain processing in normal individuals, the rich connections between the hemispheres ordinarily mask evidence of hemispheric specialization. But by studying patients whose interhemispheric pathways have been disconnected—**split-brain individuals**—researchers have been able to see cerebral hemispheric specialization in cognitive, perceptual, emotional, and motor activities.

Disconnection of the cerebral hemispheres reveals their individual processing specializations

Starting in the 1940s, a small group of human patients underwent a surgical procedure designed to provide relief from frequent, disabling epileptic seizures. In these patients, epileptic activity that was initiated in one hemisphere spread to the other hemisphere via the corpus callosum, the large white matter tract that connects the two hemispheres. Surgically cutting the corpus callosum appreciably reduced the frequency and severity of such seizures. It is a very rare procedure; some patients had only partial splits, and nowadays there are better medical alternatives, so only about ten split-brain patients have been fully studied (A. M. Gazzaniga, 2008).

Studies at that time seemed to show that this remedy for seizures caused no apparent changes in brain function, as assessed by general behavior tests such as IQ tests. But the human corpus callosum is made up of hundreds of millions of axons passing between the hemispheres; it seemed strange that they could be cut without producing detectable changes in behavior. Subsequent animal research soon confirmed that hemispheric disconnection produces unique alterations in behavior.

In one study on cats, both the corpus callosum and the optic chiasm were sectioned, so that each eye was connected only to the ipsilateral hemisphere. Using the left eye (and hence the left hemisphere, because only the uncrossed axons of the optic nerve remained intact; see Chapter 10), the cats learned that a particular symbol was associated with a reward but that the inverted symbol was not. Using the right eye (and right hemisphere), the same cats simultaneously were able to learn the opposite—that the inverted symbol was rewarded rather than the upright symbol. Thus, each hemisphere was ignorant of what the other had learned (Sperry et al., 1956).

In the 1960s, Roger Sperry began using the behavioral techniques that he had perfected in split-brain cats to study split-brain humans. In this group of patients, as in the cats, stimuli can be directed to either hemisphere. For example, objects that the patient feels with the left hand stimulate activity in nerve cells of the sensory regions in the right hemisphere. Because the corpus callosum is cut in these patients, most of the information sent to one half of the brain cannot travel to the other half. By controlling stimuli in this fashion—selectively presenting them to one hemisphere or the other—the experimenter can test the capabilities of each hemisphere.

In some of Sperry's studies, words were projected to either the left or the right hemisphere; that is, printed stimuli were presented in either the right or the left side of the visual field. The results were dramatic. Split-brain subjects could easily read and verbally communicate words projected to the left hemisphere, but no such linguistic capabilities were evident when the information was directed to the right hemisphere (**Figure 19.15**). In subsequent work, Zaidel (1976) showed that the right hemisphere has a small amount of linguistic ability; for example, it can recognize simple words, and it participates in the emotion content of verbal material. But in most people, vocabulary and grammar are the exclusive domain of the left hemisphere (left-handers occasionally show a reversed asymmetry).

The ability of the "mute" right hemisphere had to be tested by nonverbal means. For example, a picture of a key might be projected to the left visual field and so reach only the right visual cortex. The subject would then be asked to touch several different objects that she could not see and hold up the correct one. Such a

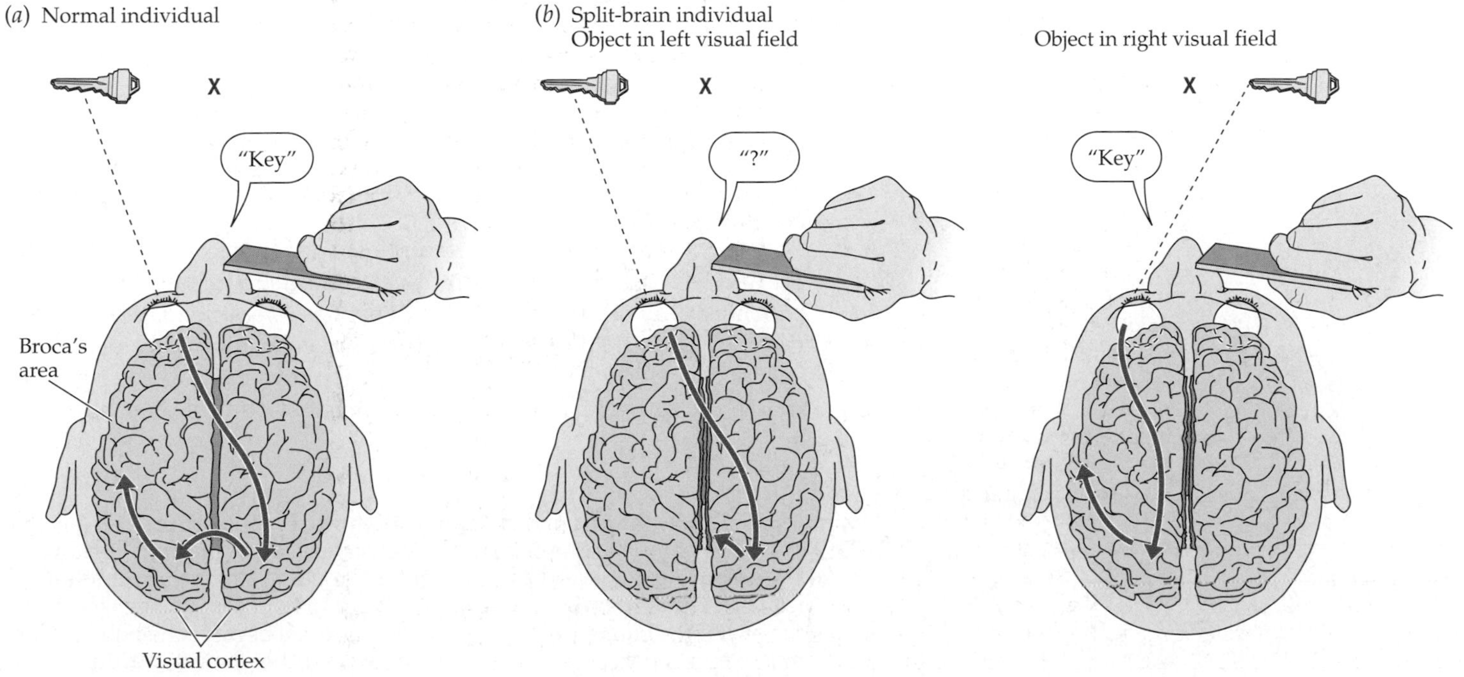

19.15 Testing a Split-Brain Individual Words or pictures projected to the left visual field activate the right visual cortex. (a) In normal individuals, activation of the right visual cortex excites corpus callosum fibers, which transmit verbal information to the left hemisphere, where the information is analyzed and language is produced. (b) In split-brain patients, stimuli from the left visual field reaches the right hemisphere visual cortex via the subcortical visual pathways (they are independent of the corpus callosum). However, the split corpus callosum prevents right hemisphere visual areas from communicating with the language areas of the left hemisphere, so verbal responses to the stimuli are impossible (left). In contrast, split-brain individuals are able to respond verbally to stimuli appearing in the right visual fields, because inter-hemispheric transfer is not required (right).

(a) Normal individual

(b) Split-brain individual
Object in left visual field

Object in right visual field

"Key"

"?"

"Key"

Broca's area

Visual cortex

dichotic presentation The simultaneous delivery of different stimuli to both the right and the left ears at the same time.

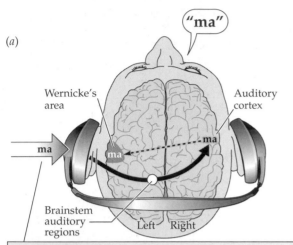

(a)

"ma"

Wernicke's area

Auditory cortex

ma

ma

ma

Brainstem auditory regions

Left   Right

Information to the left ear goes to right auditory cortex and then to Wernicke's area in the left hemisphere. Subject repeats word.

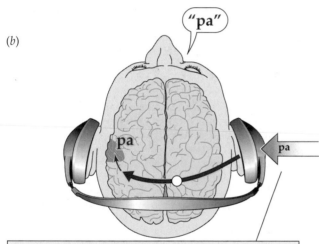

(b)

"pa"

pa

pa

Information to the right ear goes to left auditory cortex and then to Wernicke's area. Subject repeats word.

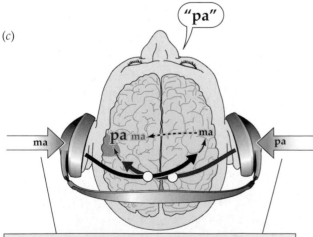

(c)

"pa"

ma

pa ma   ma

pa

When conflicting information goes to both ears, the information to the right ear reaches Wernicke's area first. Subject repeats only the right-ear information.

task could be performed correctly by the left hand (controlled by the right hemisphere) but not by the right hand (controlled by the left hemisphere). So in this case, the left hemisphere literally does not know what the left hand is doing! In general, these and other studies with split-brain individuals provided early evidence that, in most people, the right hemisphere is specialized for processing spatial information. Right-hemisphere mechanisms are also crucial for face perception, for processing emotional aspects of language, and for controlling attention (as we discussed in Chapter 18).

As many as one in 4000 people are born either partially or totally lacking a corpus callosum. Although there may be subtle behavioral consequences of this *callosal agenesis*, these people generally lack the constellation of neuropsychological changes evident in surgical split-brain patients (Paul et al., 2007). Somehow, the nervous system compensates for the loss of the main connection between the hemispheres (compensation is also evident after childhood split-brain surgery), perhaps by strengthening alternative subcortical routes of transmission. This observation again highlights the incredible plasticity of the developing brain.

The two hemispheres process information differently in normal humans

Almost all the research concerning hemispheric differences in how information is processed has concentrated on two sensory modalities: hearing and vision. In each modality, researchers can detect differences in behavioral responses to confirm that, in most people, the left cerebral hemisphere has become specialized to process language.

THE RIGHT-EAR ADVANTAGE Through earphones, we can present different sounds to each ear at the same time; this process is called **dichotic presentation**. The subject hears a particular speech sound in one ear and, at the same time, a different vowel, consonant, or word in the other ear. The task for the subject is to identify or recall both sounds. Although this technique may seem to be a program designed to produce confusion, in general, data from dichotic presentation experiments indicate that right-handed persons identify the verbal stimuli delivered to the right ear more accurately than the stimuli simultaneously presented to the left ear. This result is described as a right-ear "advantage" for verbal information. In contrast, about 50% of left-handed individuals reveal a reverse pattern, showing a left-ear advantage—more-accurate performance for verbal stimuli delivered to the left ear.

As a consequence of the preferential connections between the right ear and left hemisphere, the right-ear advantage for verbal stimuli is probably a reflection of the left hemisphere's specialization for language (**Figure 19.16**). Thus, although we can normally use either ear for processing speech sounds, speech presented to the right ear in dichotic presentation tests exerts stronger control over language

19.16 The Right-Ear Advantage in Dichotic Presentation (a) A word delivered to the left ear results in stronger stimulation of the right auditory cortex. (b) A word delivered to the right ear results in stronger input to the left hemisphere. (c) When words are delivered to both ears simultaneously, the one to the right ear is the one usually perceived because the right ear has more-direct connections to the left hemisphere. (After Kimura, 1973.)

mechanisms in the left hemisphere than does speech simultaneously presented to the left ear (Kimura, 1973).

The right-ear advantage for speech sounds in right-handed individuals is restricted to particular kinds of speech sounds (Tallal and Schwartz, 1980), such as consonants like *b*, *d*, *t*, and *k*, but not vowel sounds. The competition between the left- and right-ear inputs is the key; presentation of speech stimuli to one ear at a time (*monaural* presentation) does not produce a right-ear advantage.

VISUAL PERCEPTION OF LINGUISTIC STIMULI We can study hemispheric specialization in normal humans using **tachistoscope tests**, in which stimuli are very briefly exposed in either the left or right visual half-field (see Figures 10.11 and 19.15). If the stimulus exposure lasts less than 150 ms or so, input is restricted to one hemisphere because there is not enough time for the eyes to shift their direction. In intact humans, of course, further processing may involve the transmission of information through the corpus callosum to the other hemisphere.

Most studies show that verbal stimuli (words and letters) presented to the right visual field (going to the left hemisphere) are better recognized than the same input presented to the left visual field (going to the right hemisphere). On the other hand, nonverbal visual stimuli (such as faces or geometric forms) presented to the left visual field are better recognized than the same stimuli presented to the right visual field. Simpler visual processing, such as detection of light, hue, or simple patterns, is equivalent in the two hemispheres.

Does the left hemisphere hear words and the right hemisphere hear music?

The left and right auditory cortical areas appear to play somewhat different roles in human perception of speech and music. An early clue to this difference came from a study of temporal lobe anatomy in adults (Geschwind and Levitsky, 1968): In 65% of the brains examined, the upper surface of the lobe—a region known as the **planum temporale**—was larger in the left hemisphere than in the right (**Figure 19.17a and b**). In only 11% of adults was the right side larger. Because the planum temporale includes part of Wernicke's area, some researchers have argued that the larger left planum temporale is related to the known left-hemisphere specialization for language. However, direct links between language function and the leftward asymmetry of the planum temporale are lacking. For example, a study using structural MRI to make anatomical measurements failed to find a relationship

tachistoscope test A test in which stimuli are very briefly exposed in either the left or right visual half-field.

planum temporale A region of superior temporal cortex adjacent to the primary auditory area.

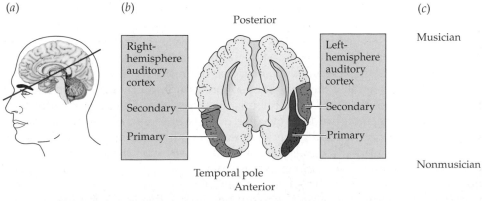

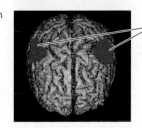

If we view the brain from above as if the overlying cortex were transparent, we see that in the musician with perfect pitch the planum temporale (red) is much larger in the left hemisphere than in the right.

In the nonmusician, the asymmetry of the planum temporale is much less distinct.

19.17 Structural Asymmetry of the Human Planum Temporale (*a*) This diagram shows the orientation of the brain section in part *b*. (*b*) The planum temporale (green and blue) is on the upper surface of the human temporal lobe. (*c*) MRI images from the brain of a musician with perfect pitch (*top*) and the brain of a nonmusician (*bottom*) show some differences: in the musician, the left planum temporale is larger. (After Schlaug et al., 1995; c courtesy of Gottfried Schlaug.)

between asymmetry of the planum temporale and the lateralization of language functions in the brain (Dorsaint-Pierre et al., 2006).

As in right-handers, language is vested in the left hemisphere in the great majority of left-handers. However, in the rare case of right-hemisphere dominance for language, the person is more likely to be left-handed than right-handed. MRI studies show that the asymmetry of the planum temporale is also reduced in left-handed people (Steinmetz et al., 1991), reinforcing the idea that the planum temporale is involved in speech. A similar difference in size of the planum temporale was also found in an extensive series of infant brains (Wada et al., 1975). This difference may be related to the fact that speech activates the left cerebral hemisphere more than the right in infants as young as 3 months (as discussed earlier).

This evidence suggests an innate basis for cerebral specialization for language and speech perception because the asymmetry is established before any experience with speech. In fact, by just 12–14 weeks of gestation, a variety of genes show asymmetrical expression in the embryonic human brain (T. Sun et al., 2005). The planum temporale tends to be larger on the left than on the right in chimpanzees too (Gannon et al., 1998). Similarly, Broca's area is larger on the left than on the right in chimps, bonobos, and gorillas, as well as in humans (Cantalupo and Hopkins, 2001). Furthermore, just as our left hemisphere is more activated than the right when we hear speech rather than other sounds, the left hemisphere of monkeys is more activated than the right when they hear monkey vocalizations rather than human speech (Poremba et al., 2004). These results suggest that other primates already possess a precursor to language, as we discussed at the start of this chapter, and that the same brain regions mediate this communication ability across primate species.

In contrast, the auditory areas of the *right* hemisphere play a major role in the perception of music. Musical perception is impaired particularly by damage to the right hemisphere (Samson and Zatorre, 1994), and music activates the right hemisphere more than the left (Zatorre et al., 1994). But perfect pitch (the ability to identify any musical note without comparing it to a reference note) seems to involve the left rather than the right hemisphere.

Schlaug et al. (1995) made MRI measurements of the planum temporale in three kinds of subjects, all right-handed (because the larger size of the left planum temporale is seen especially in right-handed individuals): (1) musicians with perfect pitch, (2) musicians without perfect pitch, and (3) nonmusicians. The size of the left planum temporale was twice as large in musicians with perfect pitch than in nonmusicians (**Figure 19.17c**). The size of the left planum temporale in musicians without perfect pitch was intermediate, but closer to that of nonmusicians. Because perfect pitch requires both verbal ability (to name the pitch) and musical ability, perhaps it is not surprising to find that, like language, perfect pitch is associated with the left hemisphere.

Despite these data, we cannot assign the perception of speech and pitch entirely to the left hemisphere and the perception of music entirely to the right hemisphere. We have seen that the right hemisphere can play a role in speech perception even in people in whom the left hemisphere is speech-dominant. In addition, the perception of emotional tone-of-voice aspects of language, termed **prosody**, is a *right*-hemisphere specialization. Furthermore, although damage to the right hemisphere can impair the perception of music, it does not abolish it. Damage to *both* sides of the brain can completely wipe out musical perception (Samson and Zatorre, 1991). Thus, even though each hemisphere plays a greater role than the other in different kinds of auditory perception, the two hemispheres appear to collaborate in these functions, as well as in many others.

Are left-handed people different?

Anthropologists speculate that the predominance of right-handedness goes back a long time into prehistory. People portrayed in cave paintings held things in their

prosody The perception of emotional tone-of-voice aspects of language.

right hand, and Stone Age tools seem to be shaped for the right hand. Skull fractures of animals preyed on by ancient humans are usually on the animal's left side, so anthropologists conclude that most attackers held a club in the right hand.

Historically, unusual attributes have been ascribed to the left-handed person—from an evil personality to an "abnormal" cortical organization of language. (Indeed, the Latin word for "left-handed" provides the root of not only the English term *sinistral*, meaning "left-handed," but also the negative word *sinister*.) About 10% of the population is left-handed; surveys of left-handed writing in American college populations reveal an incidence of 13.8% (Spiegler and Yeni-Komshian, 1983). This percentage is viewed as a significant increase over prior generations, perhaps reflecting a continuing decline in the social pressures toward right-handedness and an increase in the general acceptability of left-handedness. Interestingly, other primates also show a preference for using the right hand (P. F. MacNeilage et al., 2009; Westergaard et al., 1998).

Geneticists have established that handedness is influenced by heredity, but it is not a simple, single-gene effect. According to Klar (2003), hair on the back of the scalp forms a clockwise whorl in 93% of right-handers but is a random mix of clockwise or anticlockwise among non-right-handers. Klar suggests that a single gene has a major (but not absolute) influence on asymmetries throughout the body. Other aspects of development presumably account for the remaining variability in hand preference.

Hardyck et al. (1976) examined more than 7000 children in grades 1–6 for school achievement, intellectual ability, motivation, socioeconomic level, and other factors. A detailed analysis showed that left-handed children do not differ from right-handed children on any measure of cognitive performance. However, the idea that left-handed people are "damaged" humans has been common in the past and has even found occasional support in research.

Silva and Satz (1979) noted that several studies show a higher incidence of left-handedness in clinical populations than in the general population. They suggested that brain injury explains the high rate of left-handedness in this population. Early brain injury, these investigators argued, can cause a shift in handedness. Because most people are right-handed, early one-sided brain injury is more likely to cause a change from right-handedness to left-handedness than the reverse. Other, rare circumstances can also cause a change in handedness in adults. Two right-handed people who received double hand transplants after losing their own hands in accidents reportedly both became left-handers after the surgery (Vargas et al., 2009). One possible explanation is that the right hemisphere required less reorganization in order to take control of the contralateral hand, and that reconnection of the left hemisphere to the new right hand was initially hampered by the strong cortical representation of the former right hand. After getting an early start, perhaps the right hemisphere/left hand simply outcompeted the left hemisphere/right hand. Of course, no one yet knows if this process bears any relationship to the normal establishment of hand preference, but it does suggest a surprising degree of flexibility.

How did hemispheric asymmetry and specialization evolve?

Some scientists believe that hemispheric specialization originated in the differential use of the limbs for many routine tasks. Picture early humans hunting. One hand holds the weapon and provides power; the other is used in more-delicate guidance or body balance. One possibility is that powerful throwing, a strongly right-handed behavior in most right-handed people, was a particularly important evolutionary development, providing obvious advantages in hunting and defense. In time, the left-hemisphere neural specializations needed for programming throwing movements may have been co-opted to control language as well (Watson, 2001). However, other vertebrates—including toads (Vallortigara et al., 1999), crows (Hunt et al., 2001), walruses (Levermann et al., 2003), and chimpan-

TABLE 19.2 Proposed Cognitive Modes of the Two Cerebral Hemispheres in Humans

Left hemisphere	Right hemisphere
Phonetic	Nonlinguistic
Sequential	Holistic
Analytical	Synthetic
Propositional	Gestalt
Discrete temporal analysis	Form perception
Linguistic	Spatial

zees (Corp and Byrne, 2004)—have been found to show preferences for using one limb or the other for particular behaviors, suggesting that handedness has additional adaptive advantages. For other examples of the evolution of asymmetry, see **A Step Further: Evolution Favors Asymmetry under Some Conditions** on the website. Some researchers go significantly further, arguing that hemispheric asymmetry reflects a left-right division of labor that, as a matter of processing efficiency, arose in the first vertebrates, hundreds of millions of years ago (P. F. MacNeilage et al., 2009).

One common view of lateralization posits that the left hemisphere provides processing that is analytical and sequential while the right hemisphere offers a more holistic, general analysis of information (**Table 19.2**). Some theorists suggest that hemispheric specialization allows for separate cognitive modes that are mutually incompatible (Ivry and Robertson, 1998). But the notion, now common among members of the public, that the two hemispheres are so different that they need separate instruction, is not supported by the data. For example, although the left hand draws better than the right hand after the corpus callosum is cut, neither hand draws as well as before the surgery. The notion that people can have "left-brain" or "right-brain" personalities is likewise a concept that lacks scientific foundation.

Deficits in Spatial Perception Follow Right-Hemisphere Damage

Normal people studied with procedures such as tachistoscope tests have reliably demonstrated a right-hemisphere advantage for the processing of spatial stimuli. Some examples include processing of geometric shapes and relations, direction sense and navigation, face processing, and the mental rotation of objects held in the mind's eye. Unsurprisingly, then, right-hemisphere lesions—especially more-posterior lesions that involve the temporal and parietal lobes—tend to produce a variety of striking impairments, such as inability to recognize faces, spatial disorientation, inability to recognize objects placed in the hand, or complete neglect of one side of the body, as we discussed in Chapter 18.

The diversity of behavioral changes following injury to the parietal lobe is related partly to its large expanse and its critical position, abutting all three of the other major lobes of the brain. The anterior end of the parietal region includes the postcentral gyrus, which is the primary cortical receiving area for somatic sensation. Brain injury in this area does not produce numbness; rather, it produces sensory deficits on the opposite side that seem to involve complex sensory processing. In one example, objects placed in the hand opposite the injured somatosensory area can be *felt* but cannot be identified by touch and active manipulation. This deficit is called **astereognosis** (from the Greek *a-*, "not"; *stereos*, "solid"; and *gnosis*, "knowledge").

astereognosis The inability to recognize objects by touching and feeling them.

More-extensive injuries in the parietal cortex, beyond the somatosensory cortex, affect interactions between or among sensory modalities, such as visual or tactile matching tasks, which require the subject to visually identify an object that is touched or to reach for an object that is identified visually.

In prosopagnosia, faces are unrecognizable

Suppose one day you look in the mirror and you see someone who is not familiar to you. As incredible as this scenario might seem, some individuals suffer this fate after brain damage. This rare syndrome is called **prosopagnosia** (from the Greek *prosop-*, "face"; *a-*, "not"; and *gnosis*, "knowledge"), or sometimes *face blindness*. People with prosopagnosia fail to recognize not only their own faces but also the faces of relatives and friends. No amount of remedial training restores their ability to recognize anyone's face. In contrast, the ability to recognize *objects* may be retained, and the patient may readily identify familiar people by their voices.

Faces simply lack meaning in the patient's life. No disorientation or confusion accompanies this condition, nor is there evidence of diminished intellectual abilities. Visual acuity is maintained, although the majority of patients have a small visual-field defect—that is, an area of the visual field where they are blind. Most research indicates that the right hemisphere is more important than the left for recognizing faces. For example, using the Wada test (see Box 19.1) to anesthetize the right hemisphere causes patients to have difficulty recognizing faces, whereas anesthetizing the left hemisphere has less effect on facial recognition (**Figure 19.18**). Similarly, split-brain patients do a better job of recognizing faces if those faces are presented to the right hemisphere (M. S. Gazzaniga and Smylie, 1983). However, split-brain patients and functional imaging make it clear that both hemispheres have some capacity for recognizing faces. Thus, although damage restricted to the right hemisphere can impair face processing, the most complete cases of prosopagnosia are caused by *bilateral* damage. The **fusiform gyrus**, a region of

prosopagnosia Also called *face blindness*. A condition characterized by the inability to recognize faces. *Acquired prosopagnosia* is caused by damage to the brain, particularly the fusiform gyrus. *Developmental* (or *congenital*) *prosopagnosia* is the result of brain defects present from birth.

fusiform gyrus A region on the inferior surface of the cortex, at the junction of temporal and occipital lobes, that has been associated with recognition of faces.

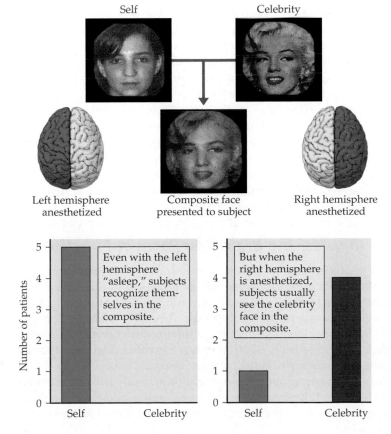

19.18 Use of the Right Hemisphere for Facial Recognition Anesthetizing the left hemisphere in a Wada test (see Box 19.1) does not interfere with a subject's ability to recognize her own face in a picture that is a composite of her face and the face of a celebrity. But when the right hemisphere is anesthetized, the subject interprets the composite face as that of the celebrity. (From Keenan et al., 2001; courtesy of Julian Keenan.)

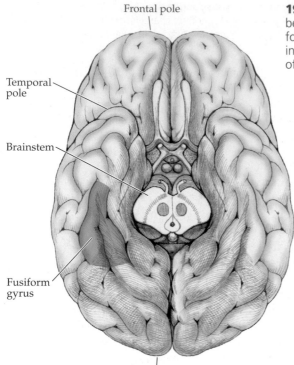

Frontal pole

Temporal pole

Brainstem

Fusiform gyrus

Occipital pole

19.19 The Fusiform Gyrus In this view from below the brain, the cerebellum has been removed to reveal the region of cortex that normally lies opposite to it. The fusiform gyrus, at the juncture of the temporal and occipital lobes, is active during discrimination of objects in a large category, such as faces or birds or cars. Bilateral destruction of this region leads to prosopagnosia, the inability to recognize individual faces.

cortex on the inferior surface of the brain where occipital and temporal cortices meet (**Figure 19.19**), is crucial, and cases of prosopagnosia following brain damage almost always involve damage here. Symptoms may be exacerbated when lesions also include a nearby occipital area that performs initial face-specific visual processing, as well as the superior temporal sulcus, which has been implicated in connecting faces with speech and facial expressions.

Until recently, it was believed that prosopagnosia occurred solely as a result of brain damage (*acquired prosopagnosia*), but a number of cases of *developmental* (or *congenital*) *prosopagnosia* have now been identified. This is apparently the problem that has dogged Barry, whom we met at the beginning of the chapter, and the discovery that he is not alone in this problem has been a huge relief (we can only guess how Humpty Dumpty would feel about it). Unexpectedly, surveys have revealed that about 2.5% of the general population has impaired processing and identification of faces meeting the criteria for congenital prosopagnosia (Duchaine et al., 2007; Kennerknecht et al., 2006). The developmental form of prosopagnosia appears to run in families, indicating that there is a genetic aspect to the disorder (Grüter et al., 2008). Developmental prosopagnosia is associated with diminished activation of the fusiform gyrus and reduced white matter connectivity in the ventral occipitotemporal cortex, in keeping with the anatomical findings in acquired prosopagnosia. (You can learn more, and test yourself for prosopagnosia, at www.faceblind.org/facetests).

Prosopagnosia of both types may be accompanied by additional forms of **agnosia** (an inability to identify items, in the absence of sensory problems) (Gauthier et al., 1999). For example, people with prosopagnosia may also be unable to distinguish between different makes of cars, or to recognize their own. Bird-watchers may lose the ability to distinguish between avian species. Functional-MRI studies of healthy subjects show that the fusiform gyrus is activated when people are identifying faces, birds, or cars (Gauthier et al., 2000). Thus, this region is important for identifying individual members of large categories (e.g., faces or birds or cars) in which all members have many things in common. The fusiform system may contain different subregions that are specialized for one category or another. Of course, specialized fusiform subsystems certainly cannot exist for *every* possible category of visual objects that we discriminate, so the full extent of fusiform subdivision remains to be determined (Haxby, 2006).

Following Some Injuries, the Brain Can Recover Function

In the months following a brain injury, patients may show conspicuous spontaneous improvements, associated with physiological stabilization of the injury site. Language recovery following stroke in adults can be impressive, and the full extent of recovery may not be evident for 1 or 2 years. Amazing examples of language recovery have been described in children following the complete removal of a diseased left cerebral hemisphere. Many theories are offered to describe the mechanisms mediating the **recovery of function** after lesions.

In spite of these encouraging developments, prevention is clearly better than treatment. Motor vehicle accidents, horseback riding, diving, and contact sports such as boxing are major causes of injuries to the brain and spinal cord. **Box 19.2** describes

agnosia The inability to recognize objects, despite being able to describe them in terms of form and color; may occur after localized brain damage.

recovery of function The recovery of behavioral capacity following brain damage from stroke or injury.

BOX 19.2 A Sport That Destroys the Mind

Boxing has a long history, much of it unpleasant. In ancient Greece and Rome, some boxers were admired for their courage and strength, but others, wearing leather wrappings studded with metal nuggets, bludgeoned each other to death for the entertainment of spectators. Although rules were developed during the eighteenth and nineteenth centuries in England, including the requirement of padded gloves and a scoring system, the goal of prizefighting has always been to knock the opponent out.

To achieve that goal, boxers aim relentlessly at the head, which sustains blow after blow. The result of so many blows to the head has been historically called *dementia pugilistica* (the Latin *pugil* means "boxer"), or *punch-drunk* (Erlanger et al., 1999), although nowadays the syndrome is known as **chronic traumatic encephalopathy** (CTE). Punch-drunk boxers have markedly impaired cognitive abilities. Even a boxer as formerly loquacious (and talented at dodging blows) as Muhammad Ali is, today, unable to utter more than a word or two at a time, because of acquired Parkinson's disease. Deaths in the ring are usually due to brain injuries, especially brain hemorrhage (Ryan, 1998). Various medical and neuro-

logical societies have urged the banning of this sport.

Studies of the brain indicate that very few boxers escape unscathed. Casson et al. (1982) studied ten active professional boxers who had been knocked out. The group included those of championship caliber, as well as mediocre and poor boxers. None of the knockouts sustained by the fighters involved a loss of consciousness lasting more than 10 seconds. Yet at least five of the group had definitely abnormal CT scans. One type of abnormality was mild generalized cortical atrophy, which in some cases included ventricular dilation. Only one boxer had a clearly normal brain picture. The age of the boxers was not related to the degree of cortical atrophy.

Ironically, the most successful boxers were the ones with the most profound cortical atrophy. In fact, the total number of professional fights correlated directly with the magnitude of brain changes. During a career of boxing, a fighter accumulates many blows to the head; the most "successful" boxers thus frequently sustain the most punishment (A. H. Roberts, 1969) because they participate in more matches.

A Parkinson's-like syndrome of tremors or paralysis may result from boxing. A large-scale CT study of 338 active boxers showed that scans were abnormal in 7% (showing brain atrophy) and borderline in 12% (B. D. Jordan et al., 1992).

Neuropathological evidence indicates that CTE in athletes is a type of *tauopathy*, the family of dementias, including Alzheimer's disease, that result from inappropriate deposition of the protein Tau within neurons, producing neurofibrillary tangles that interfere with the normal functioning of the neurons (McKee et al., 2009). The photos in the figure show the brain of a former boxer who, by his mid-thirties, was experiencing punch-drunk symptoms including memory loss, confusion, and a tendency to fall. Like other cases of CTE, an excessive amount of Tau (the brown immunolabel in the photos) is evident in the brain, and is found forming tangles within many neurons.

Mild traumatic brain injury (often called *concussion*) is a common athletic injury, especially in sports like soccer, football, and rugby that may involve violent bodily contact. Although uncomplicated concussions generally clear up with time, up to 25% of concussion cases may experience persistent cognitive symptoms (Ponsford, 2005), some of which may not become evident until later in an athlete's life (A. E. Thornton et al., 2008). But only in boxing is head trauma an explicit goal—no small reason that many believe boxing is a sport whose time has passed.

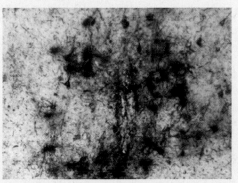

Tau protein in CTE in a boxer   (*Left*) Unmagnified section of cortex. (*Right*) Cortical gray matter magnified 350×. (Courtesy of Ann McKee.)

chronic traumatic encephalopathy (CTE)   Also called *dementia pugilistica* or *punch-drunk*. The dementia that develops in boxers; it is especially prominent in successful boxers because they participate in more bouts.

the devastating effects of boxing on the brain. (Mechanisms of brain damage, and the mitigation of brain injuries, are discussed in **A Step Further: Different Strategies Aim to Reduce Brain Damage following Injury or Stroke** on the website.)

Many patients with aphasia show some recovery

Many people with brain disorders that produce aphasia recover some language abilities. For some people, language recovery may depend on specific forms of

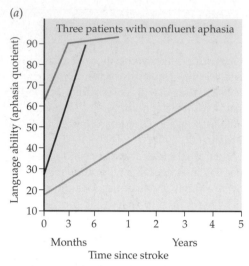

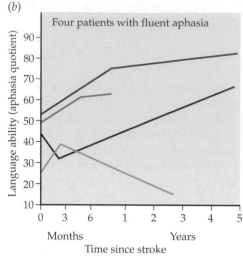

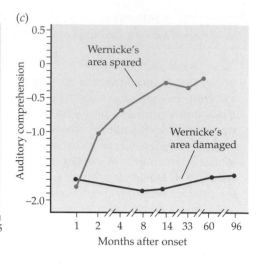

19.20 Courses of Recovery of Patients with Aphasia (*a*, *b*) The course of recovery from nonfluent (Broca's) aphasia (*a*) differs from the course of recovery from fluent (Wernicke's) aphasia (*b*). These graphs depict the aphasia quotient, a score derived from a clinical test battery. Higher scores indicate better language performance. (*c*) Here the course of recovery of the auditory comprehension of speech after a stroke in which Wernicke's area was damaged is compared with the course of recovery after a stroke in which Wernicke's area was spared. (Parts *a* and *b* after Kertesz et al., 1979; *c* after Naeser et al., 1990.)

speech therapy. The relative extent of recovery from aphasia can be predicted from several factors. For example, recovery is better in survivors of brain damage due to trauma, such as a blow to the head, than in those whose brain damage is caused by stroke. Patients with more-severe language loss recover less. Left-handed people show better recovery than those who are right-handed.

Kertesz et al. (1979) reported that the largest amount of recovery usually occurs during the initial 3 months following brain damage (**Figure 19.20**). In many instances, little further improvement is noted after 1–1½ years, although this result may reflect impoverished therapeutic tools rather than a property of neural plasticity. Therapeutic approaches using alternate communication channels, such as singing, can be helpful in some cases (Racette et al., 2006).

Damage to the left hemisphere can also produce aphasia in children, but they often recover language. Language recovery is possible in children even after removal of the entire left hemisphere (**Box 19.3**)! These observations show that the right hemisphere *can* take over the language functions of the left hemisphere if

BOX 19.3 The Comparatively Minor Effects of Childhood Loss of One Hemisphere

During early development the brain is a vulnerable organ—a fact that is especially apparent when we look at the effect of a prolonged, difficult birth involving a period of oxygen loss: some children born under such circumstances sustain lateralized brain injury involving a single cerebral hemisphere. Early in development such a child may show paralysis on one side of the body and frequent seizures. These seizures can be difficult to control with medication, and they may occur so often that they endanger life.

Surgical removal of the malfunctioning hemisphere reduces seizures. Although at first some severe effects of the surgery are

evident, over a long period of time recovery of function may be essentially complete. This result is strikingly illustrated in a case presented by A. Smith and O. Sugar (1975). The boy they described showed paralysis on his right side as an infant, and by 5 years of age he was experiencing 10–12 seizures a day. Although the boy's verbal comprehension was normal, his speech was hard to understand. To treat the problem, doctors removed all the cerebral cortex of the left hemisphere. At first, the boy's language capacity worsened, but then it improved rapidly. Long-term follow-up studies extended to age 26, when the patient had almost completed college.

Tests revealed an above-normal IQ and superior language abilities; thus, the early loss of most of the left hemisphere had not precluded language development. This patient also had remarkable development of nonverbal functions, including visuospatial tasks and manual tasks.

Whereas adult hemispherectomy of the left side usually results in drastic impairment of language, this case shows that childhood hemispherectomy can be followed by extensive functional recovery, demonstrating the additional plasticity of the young brain.

impairment occurs early in life. But as we grow older, the brain slowly loses the ability to compensate for injury.

The brain regrows and reorganizes anatomically after being injured

We now know that the nervous system has much more potential for plasticity and recovery than was previously believed. For example, damaged neurons can regrow their connections under some circumstances, through a process called *collateral sprouting* (for more information on collateral sprouting, see **A Step Further: Some Nerve Fibers Can Be Regrown** on the website). And, as we've discussed in several places in this book, it has become evident that the adult brain is capable of producing new neurons; perhaps we will learn how to bend these new neurons to our will and use them to replace missing cells.

Possibly the most exciting prospect for brain repair following stroke, injury, or many other neurological conditions is the use of **embryonic stem cells** (Lindvall and Kokaia, 2006). Derived from embryos, these cells have not yet differentiated into specific roles and therefore seem to be able to develop, under local chemical cues, into the type of neuron needed. We already know from the research on adult neurogenesis that new neurons can become integrated into functional brain circuits. Such cells even seem to migrate to the site of injury to take on their new roles (Björklund and Lindvall, 2000).

Although not all studies report encouraging results (Freed et al., 2001), in several studies implants of embryonic stem cells have been shown to reduce symptoms of Parkinson's disease (see Chapter 11) and stroke (Kondziolka et al., 2000). However, controversy surrounds the ethics of utilizing human embryos as cell donors, providing impetus to find ways of creating stem cells from other sources. There are also difficulties associated with inducing implanted stem cells to form large functional populations of neurons at injury sites without triggering an immune reaction leading to tissue rejection (J. Y. Li, Christopherson, et al., 2008). Nevertheless, these issues are potentially surmountable, and stem cell grafts offer a very promising direction for future research.

Rehabilitation and retraining can help recovery from brain and spinal cord injury

Cognitive and/or perceptual handicaps that develop from brain impairments can be modified by training; similarly, intensive training may restore some measure of walking ability after certain spinal cord injuries (Barbeau, 1998). But it is important to distinguish restoration of function from compensation. It is well known that practice can significantly reduce the impact of brain injury by fostering compensatory behavior. For example, vigorous eye movements can make up for large scotomata (blind spots in the visual field) that result from injury to the visual pathways. Behavior strategies can be changed after a brain injury to enable successful performance on a variety of tests.

Previous generations may have been too pessimistic about recovery from stroke, for now there's increasing evidence that people can regain considerable use of limbs affected by stroke if they are forced to. **Constraint-induced movement therapy** persuades stroke patients to use the affected arm by simply tying the "good" arm to a splint for up to 90% of waking hours (Taub et al., 2002). But immobilizing the good arm isn't enough; such patients are subjected to rehabilitation therapy 6 hours a day to practice moving the affected limb repeatedly (**Figure 19.21**). In a study conducted by Liepert et al. (2000), most

embryonic stem cell A cell, derived from an embryo, that has the capacity to form any type of tissue that a donor might produce.

constraint-induced movement therapy A therapy for recovery of movement after stroke or injury in which the person's unaffected limb is constrained while he is required to perform tasks with the affected limb.

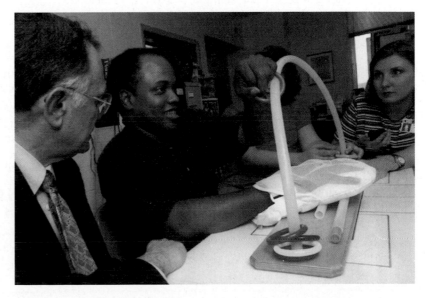

19.21 Constraint-Induced Movement Therapy In this therapy, an unaffected limb is gently restrained (in this case in a white mitten) so that the patient must use the limb that was affected by the stroke in a series of repetitive tasks. (Photo courtesy of Edward Taub.)

patients who received this treatment had regained 75% of normal use of the paralyzed arm after only 2 weeks of therapy, and there was evidence of a remapping of the motor cortex.

Another surprising use of experience for rehabilitation involves a simple mirror. Altschuler et al. (1999) treated stroke patients who had reduced use of one arm by placing them before a mirror with only their "good" arm visible. To the patients, it looked as though they were seeing the entire body, but now both arms were the good arm. The patient was told to make symmetrical fluid motions with both arms. In the mirror, the motions looked perfectly symmetrical (of course), but surprisingly, most of the patients soon learned to use the "weak" arm more extensively. It was as though the visible feedback, indicating that the weak arm was moving perfectly, overcame the brain's reluctance to use that arm. It is likely that the mirror neurons of the brain, discussed in Chapters 10 and 11, mediate some of the beneficial effects of this sort of rehearsal (Buccino et al., 2006).

Brain damage will remain a serious problem for the foreseeable future, one that will touch the lives of most of us as our friends and relations go through their lives. Perhaps the most important message to convey to victims of stroke and other nervous system damage is the encouragement that, with effort and perseverance, their remarkably plastic brains can recover much of the lost behavioral capacity.

SUMMARY

The Development and Evolution of Speech and Language Are Remarkable

- Languages are made up of speech sounds, called **phonemes** and **morphemes**, that are assembled into words and sentences according to **syntax**.

- Humans are distinct in the animal kingdom for their language and associated cognitive abilities. Possible evolutionary origins of human speech may be seen in aspects of gestures.

- Humans are born with an innate mechanism for acquiring language during an early **sensitive period**. Aspects of language acquisition appear to be controlled by genes like *FOXP2*. Other genes appear to be crucial for language articulation. **Review Figure 19.1**

- Studies of communication among nonhumans provide analogies to human speech. For example, the control of birdsong is lateralized in the brains of some species of songbirds, and early experience is essential for proper song development. **Review Figures 19.2 and 19.3**, **Web Activity 19.1**

- Nonhumans lack the peripheral apparatus to produce speech, but nonhuman primates like the chimpanzee can learn to use the signs of American Sign Language. However, controversy surrounds claims that these animals can arrange signs in novel orders to create new sentences.

Language Disorders Result from Region-Specific Brain Injuries

- Language impairment due to brain damage (**aphasia**) is much more likely after injury of the left cerebral hemisphere than the right hemisphere. Left inferior frontal lesions produce an impairment in speech production called **nonfluent** (or **Broca's**) **aphasia**. More-posterior lesions, involving the temporoparietal cortex, cause **fluent** (or **Wernicke's**) **aphasia**. Extensive destruction of the left hemisphere causes a more complete loss of language called **global aphasia**. **Review Figures 19.6 and 19.7 and Table 19.1**, **Web Activity 19.2**

- The Wernicke-Geschwind model of aphasia emphasizes a loop from a posterior speech reception zone to an anterior expressive zone. In contrast, the **motor theory of language** suggests that the entire circuit serves motor control and is used for both production and perception. Nonhuman primates lack this specialization. **Review Figure 19.8**, **Web Activity 19.3**

- Left-hemisphere lesions in users of sign language produce impairments in the use of sign language that are similar to impairments in spoken language shown by nondeaf individuals suffering from aphasia.

Reading Skills Are Difficult to Acquire and Frequently Impaired

- **Acquired dyslexia** is a difficulty with reading resulting from brain damage, usually in the left hemisphere. In **deep dyslexia** there is a disturbance in reading whole words; **surface dyslexia** involves a difficulty with the sounds of words.

- Developmental dyslexia is a congenital difficulty with reading that is associated with brain abnormalities. Several brain systems have been identified in developmental dyslexia. Abnormalities in any of several different genes may predispose an individual to dyslexia. **Review Figure 19.10**

Brain Stimulation Procedures Provide Information about the Organization of Language in the Brain

- Electrical stimulation during brain surgery has confirmed the left-hemisphere organization for language functions. Stimulation within anterior regions causes speech arrest, while

SUMMARY

stimulation in other locations causes misnaming and other speech errors. **Review Figure 19.11**

- Mapping with transcranial magnetic stimulation provides a way to create temporary "virtual lesions" in speech zones. TMS studies are revealing fine divisions within traditional speech zones in the brain. **Review Figure 19.12**

Functional Neuroimaging Portrays the Organization of the Brain for Speech and Language

- Studies using PET and fMRI reveal that distinct regions of the left hemisphere are active during viewing, hearing, repeating, or assembling verbal material. **Review Figure 19.13**

- ERP recordings reveal that the left hemisphere of the brain processes semantic content and grammar.

Williams Syndrome Offers Clues about Language

- In **Williams syndrome**, deletion of a relatively small number of genes from chromosome 7 produces a set of symptoms including excellent verbal function and sociability against a background of impaired general reasoning.

The Left Brain Is Different from the Right Brain

- **Split-brain individuals** show striking examples of hemispheric specialization (**lateralization**). Most words projected only to the right hemisphere, for example, cannot be read, but the same stimuli directed to the left hemisphere can be read. Spatial tasks, however, are performed better by the right hemisphere than by the left. **Review Figure 19.15**

- Normal humans show many forms of cognitive specialization of the cerebral hemispheres, although these specializations are not as striking as those shown by split-brain individuals. For example, most normal humans show an advantage for

verbal stimuli presented to the right ear or right visual field. **Review Figure 19.16**

- Anatomical asymmetry of the hemispheres is seen in some structures in the human brain. Especially striking is the large size difference in the **planum temporale** (which is larger in the left hemisphere than in the right hemisphere of most right-handed individuals). Nevertheless, in most cases mental activity depends on interactions between the cerebral hemispheres. **Review Figure 19.17**

- About 10% of people are left-handed, but most of these nonetheless show left-hemisphere lateralization for language.

Deficits in Spatial Perception Follow Right-Hemisphere Damage

- In most patients, parietal cortical injuries produce perceptual changes, including alterations in sensory and spatial processing.

- Damage including the **fusiform gyrus** can produce acquired **prosopagnosia**, a dramatic inability to recognize the faces of familiar people. A congenital form of prosopagnosia affects about 2.5% of the population. **Review Figures 19.18 and 19.19**

Following Some Injuries, the Brain Can Recover Function

- Much of the damage following brain injury can show at least partial **recovery of function**, especially during the first year or so, as the damaged brain stabilizes.

- Retraining is a significant part of functional recovery and may involve both compensation, by establishing new solutions to adaptive demands, and reorganization of surviving networks. **Review Figure 19.20**

Go to **www.biopsychology.com** for study questions, quizzes, key terms, and other resources.

Recommended Reading

Bradbury, J. W., and Vehrencamp, S. L. (1998). *Principles of animal communication.* Sunderland, MA: Sinauer.

Deutscher, G. (2005). *The unfolding of language: An evolutionary tour of mankind's greatest invention.* New York: Metropolitan Books.

Ellard, C. (2009). *You are here: Why we can find our way to the moon, but get lost in the mall.* New York: Doubleday.

Gazzaniga, M.S. (2008). *Human: The science behind what makes us unique.* New York: HarperCollins.

Hauser, M., and Konishi, M. (Eds.). (2003). *The design of animal communication.* Cambridge, MA: MIT Press.

Kolb, B., and Whishaw, I. Q. (2008). *Fundamentals of human neuropsychology* (6th ed.). New York: Worth.

Maynard-Smith, J., and Harper, D. (2004). *Animal signals.* Oxford, England: Oxford University Press.

McManus, I. C. (2003). *Right hand, left hand: The origins of asymmetry in brains, bodies, atoms, and cultures.* Cambridge, MA: Harvard University Press.

Patel, A. (2007). *Music, language, and the brain.* Oxford, England: Oxford University Press.

Purves, D., Brannon, E. M., Cabeza, R., Huettel, S. A., et al. (2008). *Principles of cognitive neuroscience.* Sunderland, MA: Sinauer.

Zeigler, H. P., and Marler, P. (2008). *Neuroscience of birdsong.* Cambridge, England: Cambridge University Press.

Afterword

As a student, you are no doubt relieved to reach, at last, the final pages of a textbook. As authors, we, too, were relieved to arrive here. But before you go, we would like to have a final word with you to emphasize a theme that runs throughout the book.

Plasticity Is a Defining Feature of the Brain

This book is dedicated to illustrating how behavior, ranging from simple reflexes to complex cognition, is the product of an organic machine—the *brain*—whose parts must obey the laws of a material world. But this machine is unlike any human-made machine because it is continually remodeling itself—rearranging the relationships between its parts—in a manner that (normally) improves its function. As you undoubtedly know from bitter experience, most human-made machines reach their peak performance once they are assembled, and they simply tumble downhill after that. Computer scientists struggle and yearn to develop systems that can truly learn from experience—something that unfolds quite readily when egg and sperm combine.

The study of behavior, and the way it changes over time, is the special domain of psychology. Since the nineteenth century it has been understood that changes in behavior necessarily involve physical changes in the brain. (The only alternatives would require nonphysical explanations of behavior, such as the actions of spirits or demons.) But the complexity of the brain is so daunting that, until recently, few researchers even attempted to find out what part of the brain had been altered when behavior changed.

During the past few decades, however, biological psychologists and other neuroscientists have documented many ways in which brain changes are associated with lasting changes in behavior. Just as important is the now abundant evidence that the relationship between changes in the brain and changes in behavior is bidirectional: experience also can alter neural structure. Indeed, we now realize that this constant remodeling is one of the brain's defining features, from embryonic development until old age.

Plasticity is prominent in neural development

The brain is most malleable early in life, when so much information must be learned, and so many behaviors perfected, to help the developing individual adapt to her environment. That's why infants learn new languages and recover from brain injuries so much more readily than we adults do. In Chapter 7 we reviewed the many changes that occur as the brain puts itself together and showed how cell-cell interactions play a crucial role in all of those processes: the eventual form and function of developing cells is largely determined by the activities of their neighboring cells. This principle is especially clear in studies of the visual system (Chapter 10), but it is evident at every level of the nervous system. The cells of the developing nervous system are in constant communication with one another, and they direct and constrain each other's fates.

Plasticity occurs at the molecular level

Even at the molecular level, plasticity and change are the norm. Remember from Chapters 3 and 4 that the number of neurotransmitter receptors in the postsynaptic region of a given synapse can increase or decrease depending on the amount of activity at that synapse. Usually this action regulates the sensitivity of a particular pathway: For example, cells in the basal ganglia that receive too little dopamine stimulation start making more receptors to compensate, until they become super-sensitive. Conversely, overstimulation leads to "down-regulation" of the receptors so that the signal is attenuated. Because experience clearly can affect which of our brain cells are firing, it must also indirectly affect the number and distribution of neurotransmitter receptors.

Gene expression, too, is governed by environmental inputs. In Chapter 7 we discussed the recent explosion of interest in epigenetics, mechanisms by which experience causes long-lasting changes in gene expression without changing the genes themselves. Discoveries of epigenetic actions are changing our view of the role of the genome in regulating behavior, and showing that even the basic genetic instruction set for the nervous system is subject to plastic change over the life span.

Endocrine regulation shows plasticity

Chapter 5 presented many examples of the complicated feedback loops in the endocrine system that regulate secretion to maintain relatively steady hormone levels. But experience also modulates patterns of hormone secretion: winning an aggressive encounter can elevate testosterone levels; stress can cause chronic elevation of circulating cortisol, to the detriment of the brain; and exposure to pheromones can accelerate or delay puberty. Although no data indicate that pheromones play a role in human puberty, during the past century the average age at which individuals undergo puberty in our society has declined markedly, indicating that some environmental factors—perhaps better nutrition or greater exposure to sexual stimuli—have affected our reproductive systems too.

Sensory and motor systems show plasticity

The effects of experience on brain development and structure are plainly evident in the neural systems that give us our senses of sight, sound, smell, touch, and hearing, and the brain mechanisms that control movement. In Chapter 8 we learned that changes in tactile stimulation, even in adulthood, can alter the projection patterns of information from the skin to the brain. This finding was first demonstrated in monkeys, and new, noninvasive techniques are now confirming that the same effects occur in humans (see Figure 8.18). And in Chapter 11, we saw that new motor learning causes large-scale changes in the organization of cortical motor areas (see Figure 11.15). In Chapter 18 we discussed how attentional mechanisms continually recalibrate the sensitivity of sensory systems and adjust the salience of environmental stimuli in our conscious awareness. The allocation of neural resources for sensory processing and motor control seems to be subject to constant revision, as required for the ever-changing business of surviving and reproducing.

Plasticity contributes to the causes and treatments of psychopathology

Our bodies and brains constantly make adjustments for the time of day and time of year, as detailed in Chapter 14. The waxing and waning of neural activity across these biological rhythms clearly influences behavior; in humans, for example, the short days of winter exacerbate certain forms of depression.

In Chapter 16 we saw that even severe psychopathologies, such as schizophrenia, are not entirely concordant in identical twins, so something other than genes must influence these disorders. The best candidate for that "something" is differential experience.

The injured brain has significant capacity to recover from damage, as we discussed in Chapter 19, and prior to puberty the human brain can almost completely rewire itself to largely overcome enormous lesions, even the loss of a whole hemisphere. Now, hopes are blossoming that more complete recovery from brain accidents may someday be accomplished with grafts of genetically manipulated cells. In order for these transplants to work, the brain must change to integrate the new cells into existing networks. Thus, the underlying plasticity of the brain will prove to be of vital practical importance in this arena.

Memory formation requires plasticity

In Chapter 17 we dealt with the phenomena that most explicitly depend on structural alterations in the adult nervous system: learning and memory. If our adult brains could not change, we would not be able to learn anything at all. But we *can* learn, and scientists have made remarkable progress in finding structural changes that may underlie learning and memory. Recall that, in a synapse that is activated in a particular way, the NMDA receptor allows ions to enter the postsynaptic cell; this action results in lasting changes to the synapse, so that it transmits its signal more forcefully in the future. In other words, "neurons that fire together wire together." Researchers are continuing to find evidence supporting Donald Hebb's (1949) basic idea: that learning causes the number, pattern, and strength of synapses to change.

Neural prostheses exploit plasticity

Because the nervous system is very plastic, sometimes artificial devices—prostheses—can be integrated by the brain to improve functioning in cases of sensory or motor disabilities. For example, in Chapter 9 we found that cochlear implants afford partial hearing to many deaf people, and in Chapter 11 we discussed how specific brain activity can drive computerized systems to control a computer cursor or move a robotic arm. In the future, such devices may help paralyzed people move limbs under the control of brain circuits. But in order to be used successfully, most prostheses require learning. Cochlear implants are limited in the number of auditory frequencies to which they respond, and users have to learn how to interpret this information and to integrate it with other sensory input. The mentally controlled computer cursor and robotic arm similarly require learning for successful use. So behavioral plasticity and underlying neural processes are necessary parts of any prosthetic program.

Temporal Constraints on Plasticity Are Diverse

Not only does neural plasticity take many different forms; it also takes many different time courses. Forms of learning and/or neural plasticity that seem to be similar may in fact follow different time courses over the life span. Let's look more closely at a few examples.

Plasticity can be limited to an early critical or sensitive period

Ocular dominance columns in the visual cortex (see Chapter 10) form early and do not change later in life (Wiesel and Hubel, 1963). In cats, plasticity appears to be maximal at about 1 month of age and then declines over the next 3 months, after which time the visual pathways are virtually immutable (**Figure 1a**). During the sensitive period, every major response property of visual cortical cells (ocular dominance, orientation selectivity, direction selectivity, disparity sensitivity) can be modified by manipulation of the visual environment (Mower et al., 1983). It is not clear what normally terminates plasticity in these aspects of the visual system.

Another example of learning that seems to be limited to an early critical period is learning of a first language with complete mastery. Investigators are not in complete agreement about the age limits, but such learning appears to be possible up

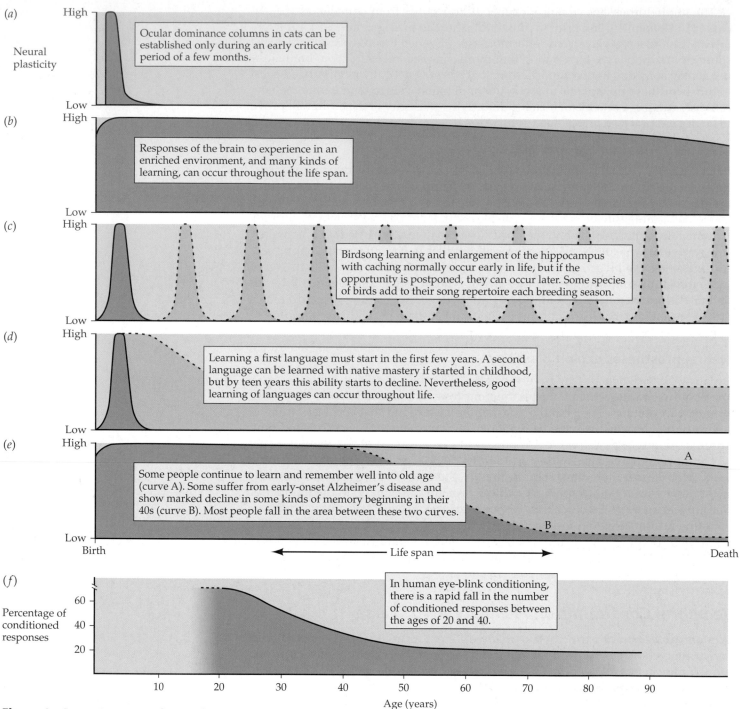

(*a*)

Neural plasticity

High

Low

Ocular dominance columns in cats can be established only during an early critical period of a few months.

(*b*)

High

Low

Responses of the brain to experience in an enriched environment, and many kinds of learning, can occur throughout the life span.

(*c*)

High

Low

Birdsong learning and enlargement of the hippocampus with caching normally occur early in life, but if the opportunity is postponed, they can occur later. Some species of birds add to their song repertoire each breeding season.

(*d*)

High

Low

Learning a first language must start in the first few years. A second language can be learned with native mastery if started in childhood, but by teen years this ability starts to decline. Nevertheless, good learning of languages can occur throughout life.

(*e*)

High

Low

Some people continue to learn and remember well into old age (curve A). Some suffer from early-onset Alzheimer's disease and show marked decline in some kinds of memory beginning in their 40s (curve B). Most people fall in the area between these two curves.

A

B

Birth ⟵———— Life span ————⟶ Death

(*f*)

Percentage of conditioned responses

60

40

20

In human eye-blink conditioning, there is a rapid fall in the number of conditioned responses between the ages of 20 and 40.

10   20   30   40   50   60   70   80   90

Age (years)

Figure 1   Some Patterns of Neural Plasticity across the Life Span

to about 3 years of age, with a gradual falloff thereafter (Morford and Mayberry, 2000). Very few children with normal hearing are deprived of the possibility of acquiring speech in their first years, so most of the research in this area is based on the acquisition of sign language by deaf children.

Plasticity can extend over the life span

Although there is a great deal of interest in plasticity associated with early development of the nervous system, we must not lose sight of the fact that the nervous system remains plastic throughout life. The beneficial effects of environmental enrichment on cortical morphology and function, as discussed in Chapter 17, are evident in juveniles, adults, and aged animals (**Figure 1b**) (E. L. Bennett et al., 1964; M. R. Rosenzweig et al., 1961). Lifelong plasticity is crucial for new learning through out life, such as learning to play a musical instrument as an adult, learning to use another language, and so forth. The remapping of the somatosensory cortex in adults by altering experience (Kaas, 1991; see Chapter 8), remapping of auditory receptive fields (N. M. Weinberger, 1998; see Chapter 9), and remapping of motor cortex in response to motor learning in adulthood (Monfils et al., 2005; see Chapter 11) are additional examples of lifelong plasticity.

Plasticity can occur at the first opportunity

Some kinds of plasticity develop as soon as the opportunity arises. For example, the critical period for plasticity of the visual system can be extended if cats are reared in the dark. Interestingly, however, if dark-reared cats are exposed to light for only 6 hours, the light exposure triggers the developmental process, and once triggered, the process runs to completion in the absence of further input (Mower et al., 1983).

Birdsong learning provides another example in which learning occurs at the first opportunity, as described in Chapter 19. Normally, a male bird learns its song from its father, but if a bird is prevented from hearing song at the usual age, it can still learn later, provided it is given an accurate model (Eales, 1985). For many years it was believed to be impossible for a bird to acquire a normal song after a certain critical period—a conclusion that was based on experiments with a taped song tutor. However, when live tutors or naturalistic taped tutors are used, song can be acquired later. This finding fits well with the observation that some species of songbirds add to their repertoire during each breeding season—a feat that requires recurring periods of neural plasticity (**Figure 1c**).

Learning a second language with native mastery is possible if the learner starts the second language in childhood, provided the first language was begun during the first year or two of life (**Figure 1d**). Furthermore, in people who start their second language in their teens or later, the neural organization of the second language differs from the organization of the first language. Nevertheless, even people who start to learn a second (or third or fourth) language as an adult can gain conversational fluency, provided they work at it hard enough.

The decline in plasticity in later life takes many forms

On many kinds of learning, some older people and animals perform as well as younger conspecifics (**Figure 1e**, curve A). On the other hand, some individuals suffer from early-onset Alzheimer's disease and show a marked decline in the formation of declarative memories in their 40s (curve B). Most people fall into the area between these two curves as they age. In older individuals who show declines in ability with age, some studies show changes in neuroanatomy (such as shrinkage of the hippocampus) or in neurochemistry that may explain the decline. In Chapter 17 we saw that enriched experience early in life and continued throughout the life span helps reduce the risk of cognitive decline in old age.

As we noted in Chapters 7 and 17, abilities to learn and remember generally decline in the latter part of the life span, but the amount of the decline varies with the type of learning. **Figure 1f** is based on an experiment that involved 150 healthy participants with ages ranging from 20 to 89 years (Woodruff-Pak and Jaeger, 1998). The subjects were trained in delayed eye-blink conditioning and were given some other tests as well. Figure 1f shows the percentage of conditioned responses during 72 trials in which a tone (the conditioned stimulus) was paired with an air puff to the eye. Note the rapid fall in the number of conditioned responses over the first three decades (20s–40s). After age 40, there was no further significant decline with age. This decline in conditioning with age parallels declines in other aspects of cerebellar function.

Future Directions

To the extent that certain types of neural plasticity are limited to parts of the life span, it will be important to find the mechanisms that enable plasticity and those that inhibit it. Identifying them will help us find ways to keep our brains malleable and our memory systems accurate well into old age.

The perspective we hope to have imparted is that the brain is enormously changeable and adaptable. So we hope you have learned that the cardinal concern of neuroscience is the systematic investigation of the origins of behavior, because although physiology and anatomy are crucial ingredients, the control of behavior is the principal function of the brain, just as the circulation of blood is the principal function of the heart. We feel that the most impressive aspects of the behavior of both humans and other animals are its variety and adaptedness: individuals use all sorts of different (sometimes bizarre) solutions to accomplish the same goals; they display different sets of behaviors across the span of their lifetimes; they develop unique strategies to solve life's basic problems of survival and reproduction. This diversity is the product of the individual's accumulated experiences, manifested in physical changes in the brain.

The central remaining challenge—and it is a formidable one—is to try to understand exactly how experience molds the nervous system and exactly how neural changes govern subsequent behaviors. It is a challenge that engages us and thousands of other neuroscientists around the world. Perhaps you'll decide to join us. We have every expectation of fascinating and surprising stories yet to come.

Appendix

Molecular Biology:
Basic Concepts and Important Techniques

Genes Carry Information That Encodes the Synthesis of Proteins

The most important thing about **genes** is that they are pieces of information, inherited from parents, that affect the development and function of our cells. Information carried by the genes is a very specific sort: each gene codes for the construction of a specific string of amino acids to form a **protein** molecule. This is *all* that genes do; they do not *directly* encode intelligence, or memories, or any other sort of complex behavior. The various proteins, each encoded by its own gene, make up the physical structure and most of the constituents of cells, such as enzymes. These proteins make complex behavior possible, and in that context they are also the targets upon which the forces of evolution act.

Enzymes are protein molecules that allow particular chemical reactions to occur in our cells. For example, only cells that have liver-typical proteins will look like a liver cell and be able to perform liver functions. Neurons are cells that make neuron-typical proteins so that they can look and act like neurons. The genetic information for making these various proteins is crucial for an animal to live and for a nervous system to work properly.

One thing we hope this book will help you understand is that everyday experience can affect whether and when particular genetic recipes for making various proteins are used. But first let's review how genetic information is stored and how proteins are made. Our discussion will be brief, but many online tutorials can provide you with more detailed information (see **A Step Further: Molecular Biology Online** on the website).

Genetic information is stored in molecules of DNA

The information for making all of our proteins could, in theory, be stored in any sort of format—on sheets of paper, magnetic tape, a DVD, an iPod—but all living creatures on this planet store their genetic information in a chemical called **deoxyribonucleic acid**, or **DNA**. Each molecule of DNA consists of a long strand of chemicals called **nucleotides** strung one after the other. DNA has only four nucleotides: guanine, cytosine, thymine, and adenine (abbreviated G, C, T, and A). The particular sequence of nucleotides (e.g., GCTTACC or TGGTCC or TGA) holds the information that will eventually make a protein. Because many millions of these nucleotides can be joined one after the other, a tremendous amount of information can be stored in very little space—on a single molecule of DNA.

A set of nucleotides that has been strung together can snuggle tightly against another string of nucleotides if it has the proper sequence: T nucleotides preferentially link with A nucleotides, and G nucleotides link with C nucleotides. Thus, T nucleotides are said to be complementary to A nucleotides, and C nucleotides are complementary to G nucleotides. In fact, most of the time our DNA consists not of a single strand of nucleotides, but of two complementary strands of nucleotides wrapped around one another.

The two strands of nucleotides are said to **hybridize** with one another, coiling slightly to form the famous double helix (**Figure A.1**). The double-stranded DNA

gene A length of DNA that encodes the information for constructing a particular protein.

protein A long string of amino acids. The basic building material of organisms.

enzyme A complicated protein whose action increases the probability of a specific chemical reaction.

deoxyribonucleic acid (DNA) A nucleic acid that is present in the chromosomes of cells and codes hereditary information.

nucleotide A portion of a DNA or RNA molecule that is composed of a single base and the adjoining sugar-phosphate unit of the strand.

hybridization The process by which a string of nucleotides becomes linked to a complementary series of nucleotides.

chromosome A complex of condensed strands of DNA and associated protein molecules; found in the nucleus of cells.

A.1 Duplication of DNA   Before cell division, the genome must be duplicated as illustrated here so that each daughter cell has the full complement of genetic information.

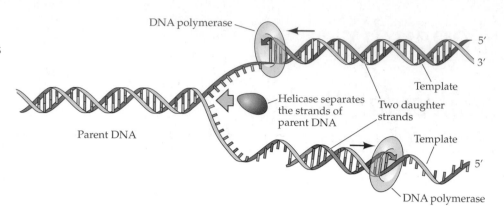

twists and coils further, becoming visible in microscopes as **chromosomes**, which resemble twisted lengths of yarn. Humans and many other organisms are known as **eukaryotes** because we store our chromosomes in a membranous sphere called a **nucleus** (plural *nuclei*) inside each cell. You may remember that the ability of DNA to exist as two complementary strands of nucleotides is crucial for the duplication of the chromosomes, but that story will not concern us here. Just remember that, with very few exceptions, every cell in your body has a faithful copy of all the DNA you received from your parents.

DNA is transcribed to produce messenger RNA

The information from DNA is used to assemble another molecule—**ribonucleic acid**, or **RNA**—that serves as a template for later steps in protein synthesis. Like DNA, RNA is made up of a long string of four different nucleotides. For RNA, those nucleotides are G and C (which, you recall, are complementary to each other), and A and U (uracil), which are also complementary to each other. Note that the T nucleotide is found only in DNA, and the U nucleotide is found only in RNA.

When a particular gene becomes active, the double strand of DNA unwinds enough so that one strand becomes free of the other and becomes available to special cellular machinery (including an enzyme called *transcriptase*) that begins **transcription**—the construction of a specific string of RNA nucleotides that are complementary to the exposed strand of DNA (**Figure A.2**). This length of RNA goes by several names: **messenger RNA** (**mRNA**), **transcript**, or sometimes, *message*. Each DNA nucleotide encodes a specific RNA nucleotide (an RNA G for every DNA C, an RNA C for every DNA G, an RNA U for every DNA A, and an RNA A for every DNA T). This transcript is made in the nucleus where the DNA resides; then the mRNA molecule moves to the cytoplasm, where protein molecules are assembled.

RNA molecules direct the formation of protein molecules

In the cytoplasm are special organelles, called **ribosomes**, that attach themselves to a molecule of RNA, "read" the sequence of RNA nucleotides, and, using that information, begin linking together amino acids to form a protein molecule. The structure and function of a protein molecule depend on which particular amino acids are put together and in what order. The decoding of an RNA transcript to manufacture a particular protein is called **translation** (see Figure A.2), as distinct from *transcription*, the construction of the mRNA molecule.

Each trio of RNA nucleotides, or **codon**, encodes one of 20 or so different amino acids. Special molecules associated with the ribosome recognize the codon and bring a molecule of the appropriate amino acid so that the ribosome can fuse that amino acid to the previous one. If the resulting string of amino acids is short (say, 50 amino acids or so), it is called a **peptide**; if it is long, it is called a *protein*. Thus the ribosome assembles a very particular sequence of amino acids at the behest of a very

eukaryote   Any organism whose cells have the genetic material contained within a nuclear envelope.

cell nucleus   The spherical central structure of a cell that contains the chromosomes.

ribonucleic acid (RNA)   A nucleic acid that implements information found in DNA.

transcription   The process during which mRNA forms bases complementary to a strand of DNA. The resulting message (called a *transcript*) is then used to translate the DNA code into protein molecules.

messenger RNA (mRNA)   A strand of RNA that carries the code of a section of a DNA strand to the cytoplasm.

transcript   The mRNA strand that is produced when a stretch of DNA is "read."

ribosomes   Structures in the cell body where genetic information is translated to produce proteins.

translation   The process by which amino acids are linked together (directed by an mRNA molecule) to form protein molecules.

codon   A set of three nucleotides that uniquely encodes one particular amino acid.

peptide   A short string of amino acids. Longer strings of amino acids are called *proteins*.

particular sequence of RNA nucleotides, which were themselves encoded in the DNA inherited from our parents. In short, the secret of life is that DNA makes RNA, and RNA makes protein.

There are fascinating amendments to this short story. Often the information from separate stretches of DNA is spliced together to make a single transcript; so-called alternative splicing can create different transcripts from the same gene. Sometimes a protein is modified extensively after translation ends; special chemical processes can cleave long proteins to create one or several active peptides.

Keep in mind that each cell has the complete library of genetic information (collectively known as the **genome**) but makes only a fraction of all the proteins encoded in that DNA. In modern biology we say that each cell **expresses** only some genes; that is, the cell transcribes certain genes and makes the corresponding gene products (protein molecules). Thus, each cell must come to express all the genes needed to perform its function. Modern biologists refer to the expression of a particular subset of the genome as **cell differentiation**: the process by which different types of cells acquire their unique appearance and function. During development, individual cells appear to become more and more specialized, expressing progressively fewer genes. Many molecular biologists are striving to understand which cellular and molecular mechanisms "turn on" or "turn off" gene expression, in order to understand development and pathologies such as cancer, or to provide crucial proteins to afflicted organs in a variety of diseases.

Molecular Biologists Have Craftily Enslaved Microorganisms and Enzymes

Many basic methods of molecular biology are not explicitly discussed in the text, so we will not describe them in detail here. However, you should understand what some of the terms *mean*, even if you don't know exactly how the methods are performed.

Molecular biologists have found ways to incorporate DNA from other species into the DNA of microorganisms such as bacteria and viruses. After the foreign DNA is incorporated, the microorganisms are allowed to reproduce rapidly, producing more and more copies of the (foreign) gene of interest. At this point the gene is said to be **cloned** because the researcher can make as many copies as she likes. To ensure that the right gene is being cloned, the researcher generally clones many, many different genes—each into different bacteria—and then "screens" the bacteria rapidly to find the rare one that has incorporated the gene of interest.

When enough copies of the DNA have been made, the microorganisms are ground up and the DNA extracted. If sufficient DNA has been generated, chemical steps can then determine the exact sequence of nucleotides found in that stretch of DNA—a process known as **DNA sequencing**. Once the sequence of nucleotides has been determined, the sequence of complementary nucleotides in the messenger RNA for that gene can be inferred. The sequence of mRNA nucleotides tells the investigator the sequence of amino acids that will be made from that transcript because biologists know which amino acid is encoded by each trio of DNA nucleotides. For example, scientists discovered the amino acid sequence of neurotransmitter receptors by this process.

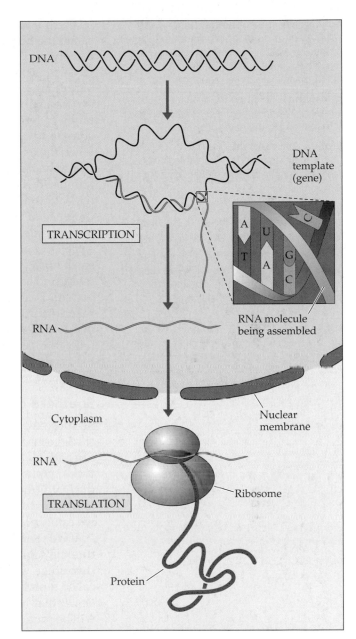

A.2 DNA Makes RNA, and RNA Makes Protein

genome   Also called *genotype*. All the genetic information that one specific individual has inherited.

expression   The process by which a cell makes an mRNA transcript of a particular gene.

cell differentiation   The developmental stage in which cells acquire distinctive characteristics, such as those of neurons, as the result of expressing particular genes.

clones   Asexually produced organisms that are genetically identical.

DNA sequencing   The process by which the order of nucleotides in a gene, or amino acids in a protein, is determined.

polymerase chain reaction (PCR)   Also called *gene amplification*. A method for reproducing a particular RNA or DNA sequence manyfold, allowing amplification for sequencing or manipulating the sequence.

transgenic   Referring to an animal in which a new or altered gene has been deliberately introduced into the genome.

probe   A manufactured sequence of DNA that is made to include a label (a colorful or radioactive molecule) that lets us track its location.

gel electrophoresis   A method of separating molecules of differing size or electrical charge by forcing them to flow through a gel.

blotting   Transferring DNA, RNA, or protein fragments to nitrocellulose following separation via gel electrophoresis. The blotted substance can then be labeled.

The business of obtaining many copies of DNA has been boosted by a technique called the **polymerase chain reaction**, or **PCR**. This technique exploits a special type of polymerase enzyme that, like other such enzymes, induces the formation of a DNA molecule that is complementary to an existing single strand of DNA (see Figure A.1). Because this particular polymerase enzyme (called *Taq polymerase*) evolved in bacteria that inhabit geothermal hot springs, it can function in a broad range of temperatures. By heating double-stranded DNA, we can cause the two strands to separate, making each strand available to polymerase enzymes that, when the temperature is cooled enough, construct a new "mate" for each strand so that they are double-stranded again. The first PCR yields only double the original number of DNA molecules; repeating the process results in four times as many molecules as at first. Repeatedly heating and cooling the DNA of interest in the presence of this heat-resistant polymerase enzyme soon yields millions of copies of the original DNA molecule, which is why this process is also referred to as *gene amplification*. In practice, PCR usually requires the investigator to provide primers: short nucleotide sequences synthesized to hybridize on either side of the gene of interest to amplify that particular gene more than others.

With PCR, sufficient quantities of DNA are produced for chemical analysis or other manipulations, such as introducing DNA into cells. For example, we might inject some of the DNA encoding a protein of interest into a fertilized mouse egg (a zygote) and then return the zygote to a pregnant mouse to grow. Occasionally the injected DNA becomes incorporated into the zygote's genome, resulting in a **transgenic** mouse that carries and expresses the foreign gene (see Box 7.3).

Southern blots identify particular genes

Suppose we want to know whether a particular individual or a particular species carries a certain gene. Because all cells contain a complete copy of the genome, we can gather DNA from just about any kind of cell population: blood, skin, or muscle, for example. After the cells are ground up, a chemical extraction procedure isolates the DNA (discarding the RNA and protein). Finding a particular gene in that DNA just boils down to finding a particular sequence of DNA nucleotides. To do that, we can exploit the tendency of nucleic acids to hybridize with one another.

If we were looking for the DNA sequence GCT, for example, we could manufacture the sequence CGA (there are machines to do that), which would then stick to (hybridize with) any DNA sequence of GCT. The manufactured sequence CGA is called a **probe** because it is made to include a label (a colorful or radioactive molecule) that lets us track its location. Of course, such a short length of nucleotides will be found in many genes. In order for a probe to recognize one particular gene, it has to be about 15 nucleotides long.

When we extract DNA from an individual, it's convenient to let enzymes cut up the very long stretches of DNA into more manageable pieces of 1000 to 20,000 nucleotides each. A process called **gel electrophoresis** uses electrical current to separate these millions of pieces more or less by size (**Figure A.3**). Large pieces move slowly through a tube of gelatin-like material, and small pieces move rapidly. The tube of gel is then sliced and placed on top of a sheet of paperlike material called *nitrocellulose*. When fluid is allowed to flow through the gel and nitrocellulose, DNA molecules are pulled out of the gel and deposited on the waiting nitrocellulose. This process of making a "sandwich" of gel and nitrocellulose and using fluid to move molecules from the former to the latter is called **blotting** (see Figure A.3).

If the gene that we're looking for is among those millions of DNA fragments sitting on the nitrocellulose, our labeled probe should recognize and hybridize to the sequence. The nitrocellulose sheet is soaked in a solution containing our labeled probe; we wait for the probe to find and hybridize with the gene of interest (if it is present), and we rinse the sheet to remove probe molecules that did not find the gene. Then we *visualize* the probe, either by causing the label to show its color or,

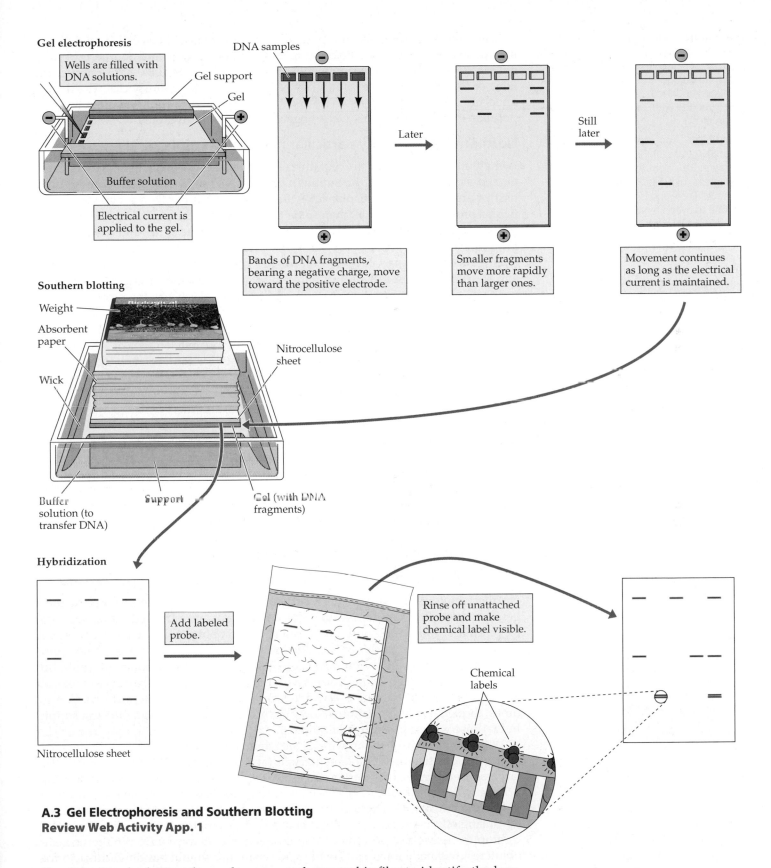

Gel electrophoresis

Wells are filled with DNA solutions.

DNA samples

Gel support

Gel

Electrical current is applied to the gel.

Buffer solution

Bands of DNA fragments, bearing a negative charge, move toward the positive electrode.

Later

Smaller fragments move more rapidly than larger ones.

Still later

Movement continues as long as the electrical current is maintained.

Southern blotting

Weight

Absorbent paper

Wick

Nitrocellulose sheet

Buffer solution (to transfer DNA)

Support

Gel (with DNA fragments)

Hybridization

Add labeled probe.

Rinse off unattached probe and make chemical label visible.

Chemical labels

Nitrocellulose sheet

A.3 Gel Electrophoresis and Southern Blotting
Review Web Activity App. 1

if radioactive, by letting the probe expose photographic film to identify the locations where the probe has accumulated. In either case, if the probe found the gene, a labeled band will be evident, corresponding to the size of DNA fragment that contained the gene (see Figure A.3).

This process of looking for a particular sequence of DNA is called a **Southern blot**, named after the man who developed the technique, Edward Southern. Southern blots are useful for determining whether related individuals share a particular gene or for assessing the evolutionary relatedness of different species. The developed blots, with their lanes of labeled bands (see Figure A.3), are often seen in popular-media accounts of "DNA fingerprinting" of individuals.

Northern blots identify particular mRNA transcripts

A method more relevant for our discussions is the **Northern blot** (whimsically named as the opposite of the Southern blot). A Northern blot can identify which tissues are making a particular RNA transcript. If liver cells are making a particular protein, for example, then some transcripts for the gene that encodes that protein should be present. So we can take the liver, grind it up, and use chemical processes to isolate most of the RNA (discarding the DNA and protein). The resulting mixture consists of RNA molecules of many different sizes: long, medium, and short transcripts. Gel electrophoresis will separate the transcripts by size, and we can blot the size-sorted mRNAs onto nitrocellulose sheets; the process is very similar to the Southern blot procedure.

To see whether the particular transcript that we're looking for is among the mRNAs, we construct a labeled probe (of either DNA nucleotides or RNA nucleotides) that is complementary to the mRNA transcript of interest and long enough that it will hybridize only to that particular transcript. We incubate the nitrocellulose in the probe, allow time for the probe to hybridize with the targeted transcript (if present), rinse off any unused probe molecules, and then visualize the probe as before. If the transcript of interest is present, we should see a band on the film (see Figure A.3). The presence of several bands indicates that the probe has hybridized to more than one transcript and we may need to make a more specific probe or alter chemical conditions to make the probe less likely to bind similar transcripts.

Because different gene transcripts are of different lengths, the transcript of interest should have reached a particular point in the electrophoresis gel: small transcripts should have moved far; large transcripts should have moved only a little. If our probe has found the right transcript, the single band of labeling should be at the point that is appropriate for a transcript of that length.

In situ hybridization localizes mRNA transcripts within specific cells

Northern blots can tell us whether a particular *organ* has transcripts for a particular gene product. For example, Northern blot analyses have indicated that thousands of genes are transcribed only in the brain. Presumably the proteins encoded by these genes are used exclusively in the brain. But such results alone are not very informative, because the brain consists of so many different kinds of glial and neuronal cells. We can refine Northern blot analyses somewhat, by dissecting out a particular part of the brain—say, the hippocampus—to isolate mRNAs. Sometimes, though, it is important to know *exactly which cells* are making the transcript. In that case we use **in situ hybridization**.

With in situ hybridization we use the same sort of labeled probe, constructed of nucleotides that are complementary to (and will therefore hybridize with) the targeted transcript, as in Northern blots. Instead of using the probe to find and hybridize with the transcript on a sheet of nitrocellulose, however, we use the probe to find the transcripts "in place" (*in situ* in Latin)—that is, on a section of tissue. After rinsing off the probe molecules that didn't find a match, we visualize the probe right in the tissue section. Any cells in the section that were transcribing the gene of interest will have transcripts in the cytoplasm that should have hybridized with our labeled probe (**Figure A.4**; see also Box 2.1). In situ hybridization therefore can tell us exactly which cells are expressing a particular gene.

Western blots identify particular proteins

Sometimes we wish to study a particular protein rather than its transcript. In such cases we can use antibodies. **Antibodies** are large, complicated molecules (proteins, in fact) that our immune system adds to the bloodstream to identify and fight invading microbes, thereby arresting and preventing disease (see Figure 15.22). But if we inject a rabbit or mouse with a sample of a protein of interest, we can induce the animal to create antibodies that recognize and attach to that particular protein, just as if it were an invader.

Once these antibodies have been purified and chemically labeled, we can use them to search for the target protein. We grind up an organ, isolate the proteins (discarding the DNA and RNA), and separate them by means of gel electrophoresis. Then we blot these proteins out of the gel and onto nitrocellulose. Next we use the antibodies to tell us whether the targeted protein is among those made by that organ. If the antibodies identify only the protein we care about, there should be a single band of labeling (if there are two or more, then the antibodies recognize more than one protein). Because proteins come in different sizes, the single band of label should be at the position corresponding to the size of the protein that we're studying. Such blots are called **Western blots**.

To review, Southern blots identify particular DNA pieces (genes), Northern blots identify particular RNA pieces (transcripts), and Western blots identify particular proteins (sometimes called *products*).

Antibodies can also tell us which cells possess a particular protein

If we need to know which particular cells within an organ such as the brain are making a particular protein, we can use the same sorts of antibodies that we use in Western blots, but in this case directed at that protein in tissue sections. We slice up the brain, expose the sections to the antibodies, allow time for them to find and attach to the protein, rinse off unattached antibodies, and use chemical treatments to visualize the antibodies. Cells that were making the protein will be labeled from the chemical treatments (see Box 2.1).

Because antibodies from the *immune* system are used to identify *cells* with the aid of *chemical* treatment, this method is called **immunocytochemistry**, or **ICC**. This technique can even tell us where, within the cell, the protein is found. Such information can provide important clues about the function of the protein. For example, if the protein is found in axon terminals, it may be a neurotransmitter.

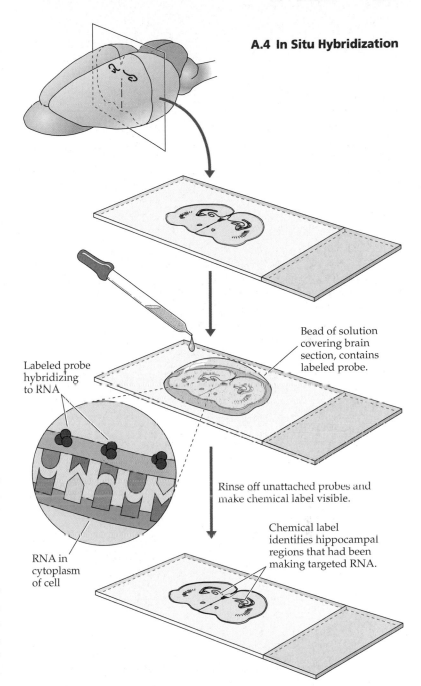

A.4 In Situ Hybridization

Bead of solution covering brain section, contains labeled probe.

Labeled probe hybridizing to RNA

Rinse off unattached probes and make chemical label visible.

RNA in cytoplasm of cell

Chemical label identifies hippocampal regions that had been making targeted RNA.

antibody   Also called *immunoglobulin*. A large protein that recognizes and permanently binds to particular shapes, normally as part of the immune system attack on foreign particles.

Western blot   A method of detecting a particular protein molecule in a tissue or organ, by separating proteins from that source with gel electrophoresis, blotting the separated proteins onto nitrocellulose, and then using an antibody that binds, and highlights, the protein of interest.

immunocytochemistry (ICC)   A method for detecting a particular protein in tissues in which an antibody recognizes and binds to the protein and then chemical methods are used to leave a visible reaction product around each antibody.

Glossary

17β-estradiol See *estradiol*.

5α-reductase An enzyme that converts testosterone into dihydrotestosterone.

5-HT See *serotonin*.

A

ABI See *auditory brainstem implant*.

absence attack See *petit mal seizure*.

absolute refractory phase See *refractory phase* (definition 1).

accommodation The process of focusing by the ciliary muscles and the lens to form a sharp image on the retina.

acetylcholine (ACh) A neurotransmitter produced and released by parasympathetic postganglionic neurons, by motoneurons, and by neurons throughout the brain.

acetylcholinesterase (AChE) An enzyme that inactivates the transmitter acetylcholine both at synaptic sites and elsewhere in the nervous system.

ACh See *acetylcholine*.

AChE See *acetylcholinesterase*.

acid See *LSD*.

acquired dyslexia See *dyslexia*.

acquired prosopagnosia See *prosopagnosia*.

act Also called *action pattern*. Complex behavior, as distinct from a simple movement.

ACTH See *adrenocorticotropic hormone*.

actin A protein that, along with myosin, mediates the contraction of muscle fibers. See Figure 11.7.

action pattern See *act*.

action potential Also called *nerve impulse*. The propagated electrical message of a neuron that travels along the axon to the presynaptic axon terminals. See Figures 3.6, 3.7.

activational effect A temporary change in behavior resulting from the administration of a hormone to an adult animal. Compare *organizational effect*.

acupuncture The insertion of needles at designated points on the skin to alleviate pain or neurological malfunction.

adaptation 1. In the context of evolution, a trait that increases the probability that an individual will leave offspring in subsequent generations. 2. In the context of sensory processing, the progressive loss of receptor sensitivity as stimulation is maintained. See Figure 8.7.

adaptation stage The second stage in the stress response, including successful activation of the appropriate response systems and the reestablishment of homeostatic balance.

addiction See *dependence*.

Aδ fiber A moderately large, myelinated, and therefore fast-conducting axon, usually transmitting pain information. See Table 8.2. Compare *C fiber*.

adenohypophysis See *anterior pituitary*.

adenosine In the context of neural transmission, a neuromodulator that alters synaptic activity. Adenosine receptors are the site of action of caffeine.

adequate stimulus The type of stimulus for which a given sensory organ is particularly adapted. Light energy, for example, is the adequate stimulus for photoreceptors.

ADH See *arginine vasopressin*.

ADHD See *attention deficit hyperactivity disorder*.

adipose tissue Tissue made up of fat cells.

adrenal cortex The outer rind of the adrenal gland. Each of the three cellular layers of the adrenal cortex produces different hormones. See Figures 5.1, 5.16; Table 5.2.

adrenal gland An endocrine gland atop the kidney. See Figures 5.1, 5.16.

adrenal medulla The inner core of the adrenal gland. The adrenal medulla secretes epinephrine and norepinephrine. See Figures 5.1, 5.16.

adrenal steroids See *adrenocorticoids*.

adrenaline See *epinephrine*.

adrenocorticoids Also called *adrenal steroids*. A class of steroid hormones that are secreted by the adrenal cortex.

adrenocorticotropic hormone (ACTH) A tropic hormone secreted by the anterior pituitary gland that controls the production and release of hormones of the adrenal cortex. See Table 5.2; Figure 5.15.

adult neurogenesis The creation of new neurons in the brain of an adult.

affective disorder A disorder of mood, such as depression or bipolar disorder.

afferent In reference to an axon, carrying nerve impulses from a sensory organ to the central nervous system, or from one region to another region of interest. See Box 2.2. Compare *efferent*.

affinity See *binding affinity*.

afterpotential The positive or negative change in membrane potential that may follow an action potential.

agnosia The inability to recognize objects, despite being able to describe them in terms of form and color; may occur after localized brain damage.

agonist 1. A molecule, usually a drug, that binds a receptor molecule and initiates a response like that of another molecule, usually a neurotransmitter. Compare *antagonist* (definition 1). 2. A muscle that moves a body part in the same general way as the muscle of interest; a synergistic muscle. Compare *antagonist* (definition 2). See also *synergist*.

agouti-related peptide (AgRP) A peptide that is a naturally occurring antagonist to α-melanocyte-stimulating hormone at melanocortin receptors.

agraphia The inability to write. Compare *alexia*.

AgRP See *agouti-related peptide*.

AIS See *androgen insensitivity syndrome*.

alarm reaction The initial response to stress.

aldosterone A mineralocorticoid hormone, secreted by the adrenal cortex, that induces the kidneys to conserve sodium ions.

alexia The inability to read. Compare *agraphia*.

all-or-none property The fact that the amplitude of the action potential is independent of the magnitude of the stimulus. See Table 3.1. Compare *postsynaptic potential*.

allele Any particular version of a gene.

allocortex Formerly called *archicortex* or *paleocortex*. Brain tissue with three layers or unlayered organization. Compare *neocortex*.

allomone A chemical signal that is released outside the body by one species and affects the behavior of other species. See Figures 5.3, 5.4. Compare *pheromone*.

allopregnanolone A naturally occurring steroid that modulates GABA receptor activity in much the same way that benzodiazepine anxiolytics do.

α-fetoprotein A protein found in the plasma of fetuses. In rodents, α-fetoprotein binds estrogens and prevents them from entering the brain.

α-melanocyte stimulating hormone (α-MSH) A peptide that binds the melanocortin receptor.

alpha motoneuron A motoneuron that controls the main contractile fibers (extrafusal fibers) of a muscle. See Figure 11.9. Compare *gamma motoneuron*.

α-MSH See *α-melanocyte stimulating hormone*.

alpha rhythm A brain potential of 8–12 Hz that occurs during relaxed wakefulness. See Figure 14.11. Compare *desynchronized EEG*.

α-synuclein A protein that has been implicated in Parkinson's disease.

ALS See *amyotrophic lateral sclerosis*.

altricial Referring to animals that are born in an undeveloped state and depend on maternal care, as human infants do. Compare *precocial*.

Alzheimer's disease A form of dementia that may appear in middle age but is more frequent among the aged.

amacrine cells Specialized retinal cells that contact both the bipolar cells and the ganglion cells, and are especially significant in inhibitory interactions within the retina.

amblyopia Reduced visual acuity that is not caused by optical or retinal impairments.

AMH See *anti-müllerian hormone*.

amine hormones Also called *monoamine hormones*. A class of hormones, each composed of a single amino acid that has been modified into a related molecule, such as melatonin or epinephrine.

amine neurotransmitter A neurotransmitter based on modifications of a single amino acid nucleus. Examples include acetylcholine, serotonin, or dopamine.

amino acid neurotransmitter A neurotransmitter that is itself an amino acid. Examples include GABA, glycine, or glutamate.

amnesia Severe impairment of memory.

AMPA receptor A glutamate receptor that also binds the glutamate agonist AMPA. The AMPA receptor is responsible for most of the activity at glutamatergic synapses. See Figure 17.22.

amphetamine A molecule that resembles the structure of the catecholamine transmitters and enhances their activity.

amphetamine psychosis A delusional and psychotic state, closely resembling acute schizophrenia, that is brought on by repeated use of high doses of amphetamine.

amplitude The maximum extent of a single oscillation in a periodic event, such as a sound wave, measured as the distance from peak to trough in a single cycle. In practical terms, amplitude corresponds to the "volume" of a sound. See Box 9.1.

ampulla (pl. ampullae) An enlarged region of each semicircular canal that contains the receptor cells (hair cells) of the vestibular system. See Figure 9.16.

amusia A disorder characterized by the inability to discern tunes accurately.

amygdala A group of nuclei in the medial anterior part of the temporal lobe. See Figure 2.15.

amyloid plaques See *senile plaques*.

amyloid precursor protein (APP) A protein that, when cleaved by several enzymes, produces β-amyloid. Buildup of β-amyloid is thought to cause Alzheimer's disease.

amyotrophic lateral sclerosis (ALS) Also called *Lou Gehrig's disease*. A disease in which motoneurons and their target muscles waste away.

analgesia Absence of or reduction in pain.

analgesic Referring to painkilling properties.

analogy Similarity of function, although the structures of interest may look different. The human hand and an elephant's trunk are analogous features. Compare *homology*.

anandamide An endogenous substance that binds the cannabinoid receptor molecule.

androgen insensitivity syndrome (AIS) A syndrome caused by a mutation of the androgen receptor gene that renders tissues insensitive to androgenic hormones like testosterone. Affected XY individuals are phenotypic females, but they have internal testes and regressed internal genital structures. See Figure 12.16.

androgens A class of hormones that includes testosterone and other male hormones. See Figure 5.19; Table 5.2.

androstenedione The chief sex hormone secreted by the human adrenal cortex. Androstenedione is responsible for the adult pattern of body hair in men and women.

angel dust See *phencyclidine*.

angiography A brain-imaging technique in which a specialized X-ray image of the head is taken shortly after the cerebral blood vessels have been filled with a radiopaque dye by means of a catheter. This technique allows visualization of the major blood vessels and is used to assess stroke risk and other conditions.

angiotensin II A substance that is produced in the blood by the action of renin and that play a role in the control of thirst.

angular gyrus A brain region in which strokes can lead to word blindness.

anion A negatively charged ion, such as a protein or chloride ion. Compare *cation*.

annulospiral ending See *primary sensory ending*.

anomia The inability to name persons or objects readily.

anorexia nervosa A syndrome in which individuals severely deprive themselves of food.

anosmia The inability to smell.

anosognosia Denial of illness.

ANP See *atrial natriuretic peptide*.

antagonist 1. A molecule, usually a drug, that interferes with or prevents the action of a transmitter. Compare *agonist* (definition 1). 2. A muscle that counteracts the effect of another muscle. Compare *agonist* (definition 2) and *synergist*.

anterior Also called *rostral*. In anatomy, toward the head end of an organism. See Box 2.2. Compare *posterior*.

anterior cerebral arteries Two large arteries, arising from the internal carotids, that provide blood to the anterior poles and medial surfaces of the cerebral hemispheres.

anterior pituitary Also called *adenohypophysis*. The front division of the pituitary gland; secretes tropic hormones. See Figures 5.1, 5.14, 5.15; Table 5.2. Compare *posterior pituitary*.

anterograde amnesia The inability to form new memories beginning with the onset of a disorder. Compare *retrograde amnesia*.

anterograde degeneration Also called *Wallerian degeneration*. The loss of the distal portion of an axon resulting from injury to the axon. See Box 7.1. Compare *retrograde degeneration*.

anterograde transport Movement of cellular substances away from the cell body toward the axon terminals. Compare *retrograde transport*.

anterolateral system Also called *spinothalamic system*. A somatosensory system that carries most of the pain information from the body to the brain. See Figure 8.23. Compare *dorsal column system*.

antibody Also called *immunoglobulin*. A large protein that recognizes and permanently binds to particular shapes, normally as part of the immune system attack on foreign particles.

antidepressants A class of drugs that relieve the symptoms of depression. Major categories include monoamine oxidase inhibitors, tricyclics, and selective serotonin reuptake inhibitors.

antidiuretic hormone (ADH) See *arginine vasopressin*.

anti-müllerian hormone (AMH) Also called *müllerian regression hormone (MRH)*. A protein hormone secreted by the fetal testis that inhibits müllerian duct development.

antipsychotics See *neuroleptics*.

anxiety disorder Any of a class of psychological disorders that include recurrent panic states, generalized persistent anxiety disorders, and posttraumatic stress disorders.

anxiolytics A class of substances that are used to combat anxiety. Examples include alcohol, opiates, barbiturates, and the benzodiazepines.

aphagia Refusal to eat; often related to damage to the lateral hypothalamus. Compare *hyperphagia*.

aphasia An impairment in language understanding and/or production that is caused by brain injury.

apical dendrite The dendrite that extends from a pyramidal cell to the outermost surface of the cortex. Compare *basal dendrite*.

ApoE See *apolipoprotein E*.

apolipoprotein E (ApoE) A protein that may help break down amyloid. Individuals carrying the *ApoE4* allele are more likely to develop Alzheimer's disease.

apoptosis See *cell death*.

APP See *amyloid precursor protein*.

appetitive behavior The second stage of mating behavior; helps establish or maintain sexual interaction. See Figure 12.1.

apraxia An impairment in the ability to begin and execute skilled voluntary movements, even though there is no muscle paralysis. See also *ideational apraxia* and *ideomotor apraxia*.

aquaporins Channels spanning the cell membrane that are specialized for conducting water molecules into or out of the cell.

arachnoid The thin covering (one of the three meninges) of the brain that lies between the *dura mater* and *pia mater*.

arborization The elaborate branching of the dendrites of some neurons.

archicortex See *allocortex*.

arcuate fasciculus A tract connecting Wernicke's speech area to Broca's speech area. See Figure 19.8.

arcuate nucleus An arc-shaped hypothalamic nucleus implicated in appetite control. See Figure 13.22.

area 17 See *primary visual cortex*.

arginine vasopressin (AVP) Also called *antidiuretic hormone (ADH)* or simply *vasopressin*. A peptide hormone from the posterior pituitary that promotes water conservation. See Table 5.2.

aromatase An enzyme that converts many androgens into estrogens.

aromatization The chemical reaction that converts testosterone to estradiol, and other androgens to other estrogens.

aromatization hypothesis The hypothesis that testicular androgens enter the brain and are converted there into estrogens to masculinize the developing nervous system of some rodents.

arousal The global, nonselective level of alertness of an individual.

aspartate An amino acid transmitter that is excitatory at many synapses.

Asperger's syndrome Sometimes called *high-functioning autism*. A syndrome characterized by difficulties in social cognitive processing; usually accompanied by strong language skills.

associative learning A type of learning in which an association is formed between two stimuli or between a stimulus and a response; includes both classical and instrumental conditioning. Compare *nonassociative learning*.

astereognosis The inability to recognize objects by touching and feeling them.

astrocyte A star-shaped glial cell with numerous processes (extensions) that run in all directions. Astrocyte extensions provide structural support for the brain and may isolate receptive surfaces. See Figure 2.6.

ataxia An impairment in the direction, extent, and rate of muscular movement; often caused by cerebellar pathology.

atrial natriuretic peptide (ANP) A hormone, secreted by the heart, that normally reduces blood pressure, inhibits drinking, and promotes the excretion of water and salt at the kidneys.

attention Also called *selective attention*. A state or condition of selective awareness or perceptual receptivity, by which specific stimuli are selected for enhanced processing. See Figure 8.12.

attention deficit hyperactivity disorder (ADHD) Syndrome of distractibility, impulsiveness, and hyperactivity that, in children, interferes with school performance.

attentional blink The reduced ability of subjects to detect a target stimulus if it follows another target stimulus by about 200–450 ms.

attentional bottleneck A filter that results from the limits intrinsic to our attentional processes, with the result that only the most important stimuli are selected for special processing.

attentional spotlight The shifting of our limited selective attention around the environment to highlight stimuli for enhanced processing.

atypical neuroleptics A class of antischizophrenic drugs that have actions other than the dopamine D_2 receptor antagonism that characterizes the *typical neuroleptics*. Atypical neuroleptics often feature selective and high-affinity antagonism of serotonin $5HT_2$ receptors.

auditory brainstem implant (ABI) A type of auditory prosthesis in which implanted microphones directly stimulate the auditory nuclei of the brainstem rather than the cochlea. Compare *cochlear implant*.

auditory P300 See *P3 effect*.

aura In epilepsy, the unusual sensations or premonition that may precede the beginning of a seizure. See Box 3.3.

australopithecine Of or related to *Australopithecus*, a primate genus, known only from the fossil record, thought to be an ancestor to humans. See Figure 6.17.

autism A disorder arising during childhood, characterized by social withdrawal and perseverative behavior.

autocrine Referring to a signal that is secreted by a cell into its environment and that feeds back to the same cell. See Figure 5.3. Compare *paracrine*.

autoimmune disorder A disorder caused when the immune system mistakenly attacks a person's own body, thereby interfering with normal functioning.

autonomic ganglia Collections of nerve cell bodies, belonging to the autonomic division of the peripheral nervous system, that are found in various locations and innervate the major organs.

autonomic nervous system The part of the peripheral nervous system that supplies neural connections to glands and to smooth muscles of internal organs. Its two divisions (sympathetic and parasympathetic) act in opposite fashion. See Figure 2.11.

autoradiography A histological technique that shows the distribution of radioactive chemicals in tissues. See Boxes 2.1, 5.1.

autoreceptor A receptor for a synaptic transmitter that is located in the presynaptic membrane and tells the axon terminal how much transmitter has been released.

AVP See *arginine vasopressin*.

axo-axonic Referring to a synapse in which a presynaptic axon terminal synapses onto another axon's terminal. Compare *axo-dendritic*, *axo-somatic*, and *dendro-dendritic*.

axo-dendritic Referring to a synapse in which a presynaptic axon terminal synapses onto a dendrite of the postsynaptic neuron, either via a dendritic spine or directly onto the dendrite itself. Compare *axo-axonic*, *axo-somatic*, and *dendro-dendritic*.

axo-somatic Referring to a synapse in which a presynaptic axon terminal synapses onto the cell body (soma) of the postsynaptic neuron. Compare *axo-axonic*, *axo-dendritic*, and *dendro-dendritic*.

axon A single extension from the nerve cell that carries nerve impulses from the cell body to other neurons. See Figure 2.2.

axon collateral A branch of an axon from a single neuron.

axon hillock A cone-shaped area from which the axon originates out of the cell body. Functionally, the integration zone of the neuron. See Figure 2.7.

axon terminal The end of an axon or axon collateral, which forms a synapse on a neuron or other target cell.

axonal transport The transportation of materials from the neuronal cell body to distant regions in the dendrites and axons, and from the axon terminals back to the cell body.

B

B cell See *B lymphocyte*.

B lymphocyte Also called *B cell*. An immune system cell, formed in the bone marrow (hence the *B*), that mediates humoral immunity. Compare *T lymphocyte*. See Figure 15.22.

ballistic movement A rapid muscular movement that is often organized or programmed in the cerebellum. Compare *ramp movement*.

bar detector See *simple cortical cell*.

bariatric Having to do with obesity.

baroreceptor A pressure receptor in the heart or a major artery that detects a fall in blood pressure.

basal dendrite One of several dendrites on a pyramidal cell that extend horizontally from the cell body. Compare *apical dendrite*.

basal forebrain A ventral region in the forebrain that has been implicated in sleep and Alzheimer's disease. See Figure 4.2.

basal ganglia A group of forebrain nuclei, including caudate nucleus, globus pallidus, and putamen, found deep within the cerebral hemispheres. See Figures 2.13, 2.15, 11.17.

basal metabolism The consumption of energy to fuel processes such as heat production, maintenance of membrane potentials, and all the other basic life-sustaining functions of the body.

basilar artery An artery, formed by the fusion of the vertebral arteries, that supplies blood to the brainstem and to posterior cerebral arteries. See Figure 2.20.

basilar membrane A membrane in the cochlea that contains the principal structures involved in auditory transduction. See Figures 9.2, 9.3.

batrachotoxin A toxin, produced by poison arrow frogs, that selectively interferes with Na$^+$ channels.

Bcl-2 A family of proteins that regulate apoptosis.

BDNF See *brain-derived neurotrophic factor*.

behavioral intervention An approach to finding relations between body variables and behavioral variables that involves intervening in the behavior of an organism and looking for resultant changes in body structure or function. See Figure 1.2. Compare *somatic intervention*.

behavioral medicine See *health psychology*.

behavioral neuroscience See *biological psychology*.

behavioral teratology The study of impairments in behavior that are produced by embryonic or fetal exposure to toxic substances.

Bell's palsy A disorder, usually caused by viral infection, in which the facial nerve on one side stops conducting action potentials, resulting in paralysis on one side of the face. See Figure 15.7.

benzodiazepine agonists A class of antianxiety drugs that bind to sites on GABA$_A$ receptors.

benzodiazepines A class of antianxiety drugs that bind with high affinity to receptor molecules in the central nervous system; one example is diazepam (Valium).

beta activity See *desynchronized EEG*.

β-amyloid A protein that accumulates in senile plaques in Alzheimer's disease.

β-secretase An enzyme that cleaves amyloid precursor protein, forming β-amyloid, which can lead to Alzheimer's disease. See also *presenilin*.

bigamy A mating system in which an individual has two mates or spouses. Compare *monogamy* and *polygamy*.

binaural Pertaining to two ears. Compare *monaural*.

binding affinity Also called simply *affinity*. The propensity of molecules of a drug (or other ligand) to bind to their corresponding receptors. Drugs with high affinity for their receptors are effective even at low doses.

binding problem The question of how the brain understands which individual attributes blend together into a single object, when these different features are processed by different regions in the brain.

binge eating The paroxysmal intake of large quantities of food, often of poor nutritional value and high calories.

binocular deprivation Depriving both eyes of form vision, as by sealing the eyelids. Compare *monocular deprivation*.

bioavailable Referring to a substance, usually a drug, that is present in the body in a form that is able to interact with physiological mechanisms.

biological psychology Also called *behavioral neuroscience*. The study of the biological bases of psychological processes and behavior.

biotransformation The process in which enzymes convert a drug into a metabolite that is itself active, possibly in ways that are substantially different from the actions of the original substance.

bipolar cells A class of interneurons of the retina that receive information from rods and cones and pass the information to retinal ganglion cells. See Figure 10.6. See also *amacrine cells*.

bipolar disorder Also called *manic-depressive illness*. A psychiatric disorder characterized by periods of depression that alternate with excessive, expansive moods. Compare *unipolar depression*.

bipolar neuron A nerve cell that has a single dendrite at one end and a single axon at the other end; found in some vertebrate sensory systems. See Figure 2.5. Compare *unipolar neuron* and *multipolar neuron*.

blind spot The portion of the visual field from which light falls on the optic disc. Because there are no receptors in this region, light striking it cannot be seen.

blob Also called *peg*. A region of visual cortex distinguished by stains for the enzyme cytochrome oxidase.

blood-brain barrier The mechanisms that make the movement of substances from blood vessels into brain cells more difficult than exchanges in other body organs, thus affording the brain greater protection from exposure to some substances found in the blood.

blotting Transferring DNA, RNA, or protein fragments to nitrocellulose following separation via gel electrophoresis. The blotted substance can then be labeled.

border cell A neuron that selectively fires when the animal arrives at the perimeter of the local spatial cognitive map.

bottom-up process A process in which lower-order mechanisms, like sensory inputs, trigger further processing by higher-order systems. There may be no conscious awareness until late in the process. Exogenous attention is one example. Compare *top-down process*.

bovine spongiform encephalopathy (BSE) Mad cow disease, a disorder caused by improperly formed prion proteins, leading to dementia and death. See also *Creutzfeldt-Jakob disease*.

brain-derived neurotrophic factor (BDNF) A protein purified from the brains of animals that can keep some classes of neurons alive.

brain self-stimulation The process in which animals will work to provide electrical stimulation to particular brain sites, presumably because the experience is very rewarding.

brainstem The region of the brain that consists of the midbrain, the pons, and the medulla.

brightness One of three basic dimensions (along with hue and saturation) of light perception. Brightness varies from dark to light. See Figure 10.23.

Broca's aphasia See *nonfluent aphasia*.

Broca's area A region of the left frontal lobe of the brain that is involved in the production of speech. See Figures 19.6, 19.7, 19.8.

Brodmann's areas A classification of cortical regions based on subtle variations in the relative appearance of the six layers of neocortex.

brown fat Also called *brown adipose tissue*. A specialized type of fat tissue that generates heat through intense metabolism.

BSE See *bovine spongiform encephalopathy*.

bulimia Also called *bulimia nervosa*. A syndrome in which individuals periodically gorge themselves, usually with "junk food," and then either vomit or take laxatives to avoid weight gain.

bungarotoxin A neurotoxin, isolated from the venom of the banded krait, that selectively blocks acetylcholine receptors.

C

C fiber A small, unmyelinated axon that conducts pain information slowly and adapts slowly. See Table 8.2. Compare *Aδ fiber*.

c-fos An immediate early gene commonly used to identify activated neurons. See Box 2.1.

caffeine A stimulant compound found in coffee, cacao, and other plants.

CAH See *congenital adrenal hyperplasia*.

calcium ion (Ca²⁺) A calcium atom that carries a double positive charge because it has lost two electrons.

CAM See *cell adhesion molecule*.

cAMP See *cyclic adenosine monophosphate*.

cAMP responsive element–binding protein See *CREB*.

capsaicin A compound synthesized by various plants to deter predators by mimicking the experience of burning. Capsaicin is responsible for the burning sensation in chili peppers.

carotid arteries The major arteries that ascend the left and right sides of the neck to the brain, supplying blood to the anterior and middle cerebral arteries. The branch that enters the brain is called the *internal carotid artery*. See Figure 2.20.

CART See *cocaine- and amphetamine-regulated transcript*.

caspases A family of proteins that regulate cell death (apoptosis).

castration Removal of the gonads, usually the testes.

CAT or CT scan See *computerized axial tomography*.

cataplexy Sudden loss of muscle tone, leading to collapse of the body without loss of consciousness.

catecholamines A class of monoamines that serve as neurotransmitters, including dopamine and norepinephrine. See Table 4.1.

cation A positively charged ion, such as a potassium or sodium ion. Compare *anion*.

cauda equina Literally "horse's tail" (in Latin). The caudalmost spinal nerves, which extend beyond the spinal cord proper to exit the spinal column.

caudal See *posterior*.

caudate nucleus One of the basal ganglia; it has a long extension or tail. See Figure 2.15.

CBT See *cognitive behavioral therapy*.

CCK See *cholecystokinin*.

cell adhesion molecule (CAM) A protein found on the surface of a cell that guides cell migration and/or axonal pathfinding.

cell assembly A large group of cells that tend to be active at the same time because they have been activated simultaneously or in close succession in the past.

cell-autonomous Referring to cell processes that are directed by the cell itself rather than being under the influence of other cells.

cell body Also called *soma*. The region of a neuron that is defined by the presence of the cell nucleus. See Figure 2.2.

cell-cell interactions The general process during development in which one cell affects the differentiation of other, usually neighboring, cells.

cell death Also called *apoptosis*. The developmental process during which "surplus" cells die. See Figure 7.3.

cell differentiation The developmental stage in which cells acquire distinctive characteristics, such as those of neurons, as the result of expressing particular genes. See Figure 7.3.

cell membrane The lipid bilayer that ensheathes a cell.

cell migration The movement of cells from site of origin to final location. See Figure 7.3.

cell nucleus The spherical central structure of a cell that contains the chromosomes.

central deafness A hearing impairment that is related to lesions in auditory pathways or centers, including sites in the brainstem, thalamus, or cortex. Cortical deafness and word deafness are two examples of central deafness. Compare *conduction deafness* and *sensorineural deafness*.

central modulation of sensory information The process in which higher brain centers, such as the cortex and thalamus, suppress some sources of sensory information and amplify others.

central nervous system (CNS) The portion of the nervous system that includes the brain and the spinal cord. See Figures 2.8, 2.14. Compare *peripheral nervous system*.

central pattern generator Neural circuitry that is responsible for generating the rhythmic pattern of a behavior such as walking.

central sulcus A fissure that divides the frontal lobe from the parietal lobe. See Figure 2.12.

cerebellum A structure located at the back of the brain, dorsal to the pons, that is involved in the central regulation of movement. See Figures 2.12, 2.14, 2.16.

cerebral cortex Often called simply *cortex*. The outer covering of the cerebral hemispheres, which consists largely of nerve cell bodies and their branches. In mammals, the cerebral cortex has the six distinct layers that are typical of neocortex. See Figure 2.17.

cerebral hemispheres The right and left halves of the forebrain. See Figure 2.14.

cerebrocerebellum The lowermost part of the cerebellum, consisting especially of the lateral parts of each cerebellar hemisephere. It is implicated in planning complex movements. Compare *spinocerebellum* and *vestibulocerebellum*.

cerebrospinal fluid (CSF) The fluid that fills the cerebral ventricles. See Figure 2.19.

cerveau isolé See *isolated forebrain*.

cervical Referring to topmost eight segments of the spinal cord, in the neck region. See Figures 2.10, 2.11.

cGMP See *cyclic guanosine monophosphate*.

change blindness A failure to notice changes in comparisons of two alternating static visual scenes.

channelopathy A genetic abnormality of ion channels, causing a variety of symptoms.

ChAT See *choline acetyltransferase*.

chemical neuroanatomy The distribution of key chemicals, such as transmitters and enzymes, within the structure of the nervous system.

chemical transmitter See *neurotransmitter*.

chemically gated ion channel See *ligand-gated ion channel*.

chemoaffinity hypothesis The notion that each cell has a chemical identity that directs it to synapse on the proper target cell during development. See Box 7.2.

chemoattractants Compounds that attract particular classes of growth cones. Compare *chemorepellents*.

chemorepellents Compounds that repel particular classes of growth cones. Compare *chemoattractants*.

chloride ion (Cl⁻) A chlorine atom that carries a negative charge because it has gained one electron.

chlorpromazine An antipsychotic drug, one of the class of phenothiazines.

cholecystokinin (CCK) A peptide hormone that is released by the gut after ingestion of food high in protein and/or fat.

choline acetyltransferase (ChAT) An important enzyme involved in the synthesis of the neurotransmitter acetylcholine.

cholinergic Referring to cells that use acetylcholine as their synaptic transmitter.

choroid plexus A highly vascular portion of the lining of the ventricles that secretes cerebrospinal fluid.

chromosome A complex of condensed strands of DNA and associated protein molecules; found in the nucleus of cells.

chronic traumatic encephalopathy (CTE) Also called *dementia pugilistica* or *punch-drunk*. The dementia that develops in boxers; it is especially prominent in successful boxers because they participate in more bouts.

ciliary muscle One of the muscles that controls the shape of the lens inside the eye, focusing an image on the retina. See Figure 10.5.

cilium (pl. cilia) A hairlike extension. The extensions in the hair cells of the cochlea, for example, are cilia. See Figure 9.2.

cingulate cortex Also called *cingulate gyrus* or *cingulum*. A region of medial cerebral cortex that lies dorsal to the corpus callosum. See Figures 2.15, 16.19.

cingulate gyrus Also called *cingulate cortex* or *cingulum*. A cortical portion of the limbic system, found in the frontal and parietal midline. See Figures 2.12, 2.15.

cingulum (pl. cingula) See *cingulate cortex* or *cingulate gyrus*.

circadian rhythm A pattern of behavioral, biochemical, or physiological fluctuation that has a 24-hour period.

circannual Occurring on a roughly annual basis.

circle of Willis A structure at the base of the brain that is formed by the joining of the carotid and basilar arteries. See Figure 2.20.

circumvallate papillae One of three types of small structures on the tongue, located in the back, that contain taste receptors. See Figure 9.19. Compare *foliate papillae* and *fungiform papillae*.

circumventricular organ An organ that lies in the wall of a cerebral ventricle and monitors the composition of the cerebrospinal fluid. See Figure 13.14.

CJD See *Creutzfeldt-Jakob disease*.

classical conditioning Also called *Pavlovian conditioning*. A type of associative learning in which an originally neutral stimulus (the *conditioned stimulus*, or *CS*)—through pairing with another stimulus (the *unconditioned stimulus*, or *US*) that elicits a particular response—acquires the power to elicit that response when presented alone. A response elicited by the US is called an *unconditioned response* (*UR*); a response elicited by the CS alone is called a *conditioned response* (*CR*). See Box 17.1. Compare *instrumental conditioning*.

cloaca The sex organ in many birds, through which sperm are discharged (in the male) and eggs are laid (in the female). This is the same passage through which wastes are eliminated.

cloacal exstrophy A rare medical condition in which XY individuals are born completely lacking a penis.

clones Asexually produced organisms that are genetically identical.

closed-loop control mechanism A control mechanism that provides a flow of information from whatever is being controlled to the device that controls it. See Figure 11.3. Compare *open-loop control mechanism*.

clozapine An atypical neuroleptic.

CMR1 See *cool-menthol receptor 1*.

CNS See *central nervous system*.

cocaine A drug of abuse, derived from the coca plant, that acts by potentiating catecholamine stimulation.

cocaine- and amphetamine-regulated transcript (CART) A peptide produced in the brain when an animal is injected with either cocaine or amphetamine. It is also associated with the appetite control circuitry of the hypothalamus.

coccygeal Referring to the lowest spinal vertebra (also known as the tailbone). See Figure 2.11.

cochlea A snail-shaped structure in the inner ear that contains the primary receptor cells for hearing. See Figure 9.2.

cochlear amplifier The mechanism by which the cochlea is physically distorted by outer hair cells in order to "tune" the cochlea to be particularly sensitive to some frequencies more than others.

cochlear implant An electromechanical device that detects sounds and selectively stimulates nerves in different regions of the cochlea via surgically implanted electrodes. Compare *auditory brainstem implant*.

cochlear nuclei Brainstem nuclei that receive input from auditory hair cells and send output to the superior olivary complex. See Figure 9.7.

cocktail party effect The selective enhancement of attention in order to filter out distracters, such as while listening to one person talking in the midst of a noisy party.

coding The rules by which action potentials in a sensory system reflect a physical stimulus.

codon A set of three nucleotides that uniquely encodes one particular amino acid. A series of codons determines the structure of a peptide or protein.

cognitive behavioral therapy (CBT) Psychotherapy aimed at correcting negative thinking and improving interpersonal relationships.

cognitive map A mental representation of a spatial relationship.

cognitively impenetrable Referring to data-processing operations of the central nervous system that are unconscious.

coincidence detector A device that senses the co-occurrence of two events.

coitus See *copulation*.

collateral sprouting The formation of a new branch on an axon, usually in response to the uncovering of unoccupied postsynaptic sites.

co-localization Also called *co-release*. Here, the appearance of more than one neurotransmitter in a given presynaptic terminal.

combat fatigue See *posttraumatic stress disorder*.

co-morbid Referring to the tendency of certain diseases or disorders to occur together in individuals.

competitive ligand A substance that directly competes with the endogenous ligand for binding to a receptor molecule. See Figure 4.7. Compare *noncompetitive ligand*.

complex cortical cell A cell in the visual cortex that responds best to a bar of a particular size and orientation anywhere within a particular area of the visual field. Compare *simple cortical cell*.

complex environment See *enriched condition*.

complex partial seizure In epilepsy, a type of seizure that doesn't involve the entire brain, and therefore can cause a wide variety of symptoms. See Box 3.3.

computerized axial tomography (CAT or CT) A noninvasive technique for examining brain structure in humans through computer analysis of X-ray absorption at several positions around the head. CT affords a virtual direct view of the brain. The resulting images are referred to as *CAT scans* or *CT scans*. See Figure 2.21.

concentration gradient Variation of the concentration of a substance within a region. Molecules and ions tend to move down the concentration gradient from areas of high concentration to areas of low concentration. See Figure 3.2.

concordant Referring to any trait that is seen in both individuals of a pair of twins. Compare *discordant*.

conditional knockout A gene that can be selectively deactivated in adulthood in specific tissues.

conditioned response (CR) See *classical conditioning*.

conditioned stimulus (CS) See *classical conditioning*.

conditioning A form of learning in which an organism comes to associate two stimuli, or a stimulus and a response. See Box 17.1. See also *classical conditioning* and *instrumental conditioning*.

conduction aphasia An impairment in the repetition of words and sentences.

conduction deafness A hearing impairment that is associated with pathology of the external-ear or middle-ear cavities. Compare *central deafness* and *sensorineural deafness*.

conduction velocity The speed at which an action potential is propagated along the length of an axon (or section of peripheral nerve).

conduction zone The part of the neuron over which the nerve's electrical signal may be actively propagated. Usually corresponds to the cell's axon.

cones A class of photoreceptor cells in the retina that are responsible for color vision. See Figure 10.6. Compare *rods*.

confabulate To fill in a gap in memory with a falsification; often seen in Korsakoff's syndrome.

congenital adrenal hyperplasia (CAH) Any of several genetic mutations that can result in exposure of a female fetus to adrenal androgens, which results in a clitoris that is larger than normal at birth.

congenital hypothyroidism See *cretinism*.

congenital insensitivity to pain The condition of being born without the ability to perceive pain.

congenital prosopagnosia See *prosopagnosia*.

conjunction search A search for an item that is based on two or more features (e.g., size and color) that together distinguish the target from distracters that may share some of the same attributes. Compare *feature search*.

consciousness The state of awareness of one's own existence and experience.

conserved In the context of evolution, referring to a trait that is passed on from a common ancestor to two or more descendant species.

consolidation A stage of memory formation in which information in short-term or intermediate-term memory is transferred to long-term memory. See Figure 17.7.

constraint-induced movement therapy A therapy for recovery of movement after stroke or injury in which the person's unaffected limb is constrained while he is required to perform tasks with the affected limb.

contralateral In anatomy, pertaining to a location on the opposite side of the body. See Box 2.2. Compare *ipsilateral*.

convergence The phenomenon of neural connections in which many cells send signals to a single cell. Compare *divergence*.

convergent evolution The evolutionary process by which responses to similar ecological features bring about similarities in behavior or structure among animals that are only distantly related (i.e., that differ in genetic heritage).

cool-menthol receptor 1 (CMR1) Also called *TRP8*. A sensory receptor, found in some free nerve endings, that opens an ion channel in response to a mild temperature drop or exposure to menthol. See Figure 8.22.

Coolidge effect The propensity of an animal that has appeared sexually satiated with a present partner to resume sexual activity when provided with a novel partner.

copulation Also called *coitus*. The sexual act.

copulatory lock Reproductive behavior in which the male's penis swells after ejaculation so that the male and female are forced to remain joined for 5–10 minutes; occurs in dogs and some rodents, but not in humans.

co-release See *co-localization*.

cornea The transparent outer layer of the eye, whose curvature is fixed. It bends light rays and is primarily responsible for forming the image on the retina. See Figure 10.5.

coronal plane Also called *frontal plane* or *transverse plane*. The plane that divides the body or brain into front and back parts. See Box 2.2. Compare *horizontal plane* and *sagittal plane*.

corpora lutea (sing. corpus luteum) The structures formed from collapsed ovarian follicles subsequent to ovulation. The corpora lutea are a major source of progesterone.

corpus callosum The main band of axons that connects the two cerebral hemispheres. See Figures 2.12, 2.18.

correlation The covariation of two measures.

cortex (pl. cortices) The outer layer of a structure. See also *cerebral cortex* and *neocortex*.

cortical column One of the vertical columns that constitute the basic organization of the neocortex.

cortical deafness A hearing impairment that is caused by a fault or defect in the cortex.

corticospinal system See *pyramidal system*.

cortisol A glucocorticoid stress hormone of the adrenal cortex.

courtship The period during which two potential sexual partners increase their attractiveness toward each other.

covert attention Attention in which the focus can be directed independently of sensory orientation (e.g., you're attending to one sensory stimulus while looking at another). Compare *overt attention*.

CR See *classical conditioning*.

cranial nerve A nerve that is connected directly to the brain. Composed of a set of pathways concerned mainly with sensory and motor systems associated with the head, the cranial nerves together constitute one of the three main subdivisions of the peripheral nervous system. There are 12 cranial nerves, typically designated by Roman numerals I–XII. See Figure 2.9.

CREB cAMP responsive element–binding protein. A protein that is activated by cyclic AMP (cAMP) so that it now binds the promoter region of several genes involved in neural plasticity. See Figure 17.22.

cretinism Also called *congenital hypothyroidism*. Reduced stature and intellectual disability caused by thyroid deficiency during early development.

Creutzfeldt-Jakob disease (CJD) A brain disorder in humans, leading to dementia and death, that is caused by improperly folded prion proteins. CJD is the human equivalent of bovine spongiform encephalopathy, or mad cow disease.

crib death See *sudden infant death syndrome*.

cross-tolerance A condition in which the development of tolerance for an administered drug causes an individual to develop tolerance for another drug.

crystallization The final stage of birdsong formation, in which fully formed adult song is achieved.

CS See *classical conditioning*.

CSF See *cerebrospinal fluid*.

CT or CAT scan See *computerized axial tomography*.

CTE See *chronic traumatic encephalopathy*.

cue-induced drug use An increased likelihood to use a drug (especially an addictive drug) because of the presence of environmental stimuli that were present during previous use of the same drug.

cupula A small gelatinous column that forms part of the lateral-line system of aquatic animals and also occurs within the vestibular system of mammals. See Figure 9.16.

curare An alkaloid neurotoxin that causes paralysis by blocking acetylcholine receptors in muscle.

Cushing's syndrome A condition in which levels of adrenal glucocorticoids are abnormally high.

cyclic adenosine monophosphate (cyclic AMP, or cAMP) A second messenger activated in target cells in response to synaptic or hormonal stimulation.

cyclic AMP See *cyclic adenosine monophosphate*.

cyclic GMP See *cyclic guanosine monophosphate*.

cyclic guanosine monophosphate (cyclic GMP, or cGMP) A second messenger activated in target cells in response to synaptic or hormonal stimulation.

cytokine A protein that induces the proliferation of other cells, as in the immune system. Examples include interleukins and interferons.

cytoplasm See *intracellular fluid*.

cytoskeleton The lattice of specialized proteins that gives a cell its shape. Changes in the cytoskeleton allow neurons to change their shape and form new connections; therefore the cytoskeleton plays an important role in neural plasticity.

D

DA See *dopamine*.

dB See *decibel*.

DBS See *deep brain stimulation*.

death gene A gene that is expressed only when a cell becomes committed to natural cell death (apoptosis).

decibel (dB) A measure of sound intensity. See Box 9.1.

declarative memory A memory that can be stated or described. See Figures 17.3, 17.5, 17.8. Compare *nondeclarative memory*.

decomposition of movement Difficulty of movement in which gestures are broken up into individual segments instead of being executed smoothly; a symptom of cerebellar lesions.

decorticate rage Also called *sham rage*. Sudden intense rage characterized by actions (such as snarling and biting in dogs) that lack clear direction.

deep brain stimulation (DBS) Mild electrical stimulation through an electrode that is surgically implanted deep in the brain.

deep dyslexia Acquired dyslexia in which the patient reads a word as another word that is semantically related. Compare *surface dyslexia*.

degradation The chemical breakdown of a neurotransmitter into inactive metabolites.

dehydration Excessive loss of water.

delay conditioning A form of conditioning in which only a brief delay separates the conditioned and unconditioned stimuli. Compare *trace conditioning*.

delayed non-matching-to-sample task A test in which the subject must respond to the unfamiliar stimulus of a pair. See Figure 17.9.

delta wave The slowest type of EEG wave, characteristic of stages 3 and 4 slow-wave sleep. See Figure 14.11.

Δ9-tetrahydrocannabinol (THC) The major active ingredient in marijuana.

delusion A false belief strongly held in spite of contrary evidence.

dementia Drastic failure of cognitive ability, including memory failure and loss of orientation.

dementia pugilistica See *chronic traumatic encephalopathy*.

dendrite One of the extensions of the cell body that are the receptive surfaces of the neuron. See Figure 2.5.

dendritic knob A portion of olfactory receptor cells present in the olfactory epithelium. See Figure 9.22.

dendritic spine An outgrowth along the dendrite of a neuron. See Figure 2.7.

dendro-dendritic Referring to a type of synapse in which a synaptic connection forms between the dendrites of two neurons. Compare *axo-axonic*, *axo-dendritic*, and *axo-somatic*.

dentate gyrus A strip of gray matter in the hippocampal formation. See Figure 17.21.

deoxyribonucleic acid (DNA) A nucleic acid that is present in the chromosomes of cells and codes hereditary information. Compare *ribonucleic acid*.

dependence Also called *addiction*. In the context of substance-related disorders, the strong desire to self-administer a drug of abuse.

dependent variable The factor that an experimenter measures to monitor a change in response to changes in an *independent variable*.

depolarization A reduction in membrane potential (the interior of the neuron becomes less negative). See Figure 3.5. Compare *hyperpolarization*.

depressants A class of drugs that act to reduce neural activity.

depression A psychiatric condition characterized by such symptoms as an unhappy mood; loss of interests, energy, and appetite; and difficulty concentrating. See also *bipolar disorder* and *unipolar depression*.

dermatome A strip of skin innervated by a particular spinal root. See Figure 8.16.

dermis The middle layer of skin, between the epidermis and the hypodermis. See Figure 8.4.

desynchronized EEG Also called *beta activity*. A pattern of EEG activity comprising a mix of many different high frequencies with low amplitude. Compare *alpha rhythm*.

developmental dyslexia See *dyslexia*.

developmental prosopagnosia See *prosopagnosia*.

dexamethasone suppression test A test of pituitary-adrenal function in which the subject is given dexamethasone, a synthetic glucocorticoid hormone, which should cause a decline in the production of adrenal corticosteroids.

DHT See *dihydrotestosterone*.

diabetes insipidus Excessive urination, caused by the failure of vasopressin to induce the kidneys to conserve water.

diabetes mellitus Excessive glucose in the urine, caused by the failure of insulin to induce glucose absorption by the body. Two types of diabetes mellitus are known: Type I (juvenile-onset) and Type II (adult-onset).

Diablo A protein released by mitochondria, in response to high calcium levels, that activates apoptosis.

diaschisis A temporary period of generalized impairment following brain injury.

dichotic presentation The simultaneous delivery of different stimuli to both the right and the left ears at the same time. See Figure 19.16.

diencephalon The posterior part of the forebrain, including the thalamus and hypothalamus. See Figure 2.14.

differentiation See *cell differentiation*.

diffusion The spontaneous spread of molecules of one substance among molecules of another substance until a uniform concentration is achieved. See Figure 3.2.

diffusion tensor imaging (DTI) A special use of MRI that takes advantage of the differences in how water molecules are constrained in myelin to reveal axonal tracts connecting brain regions.

digestion The process by which food is broken down to provide energy and nutrients.

dihydrotestosterone (DHT) The 5α-reduced metabolite of testosterone; a potent androgen that is principally responsible for the masculinization of the external genitalia in mammalian sexual differentiation. See Figure 12.14.

dimer A complex of two proteins that have bound together.

dioecious Having distinct male and female sexes that specialize in making just one type of gamete, either ova or sperm.

discordant Referring to any trait that is seen in only one individual of a pair of twins. Compare *concordant*.

dishabituation The restoration of response amplitude following habituation.

dissociative drug A type of drug that produces a dreamlike state in which consciousness is partly separated from sensory inputs.

dissociative thinking A condition, seen in schizophrenia, that is characterized by disturbances of thought and difficulty relating events properly.

distal In anatomy, toward the periphery of an organism or toward the end of a limb. See Box 2.2. Compare *proximal*.

diurnal Active during the light periods of the daily cycle. Compare *nocturnal*.

divergence The phenomenon of neural connections in which one cell sends signals to many other cells. See Figure 3.18. Compare *convergence*.

divided attention task A task in which the subject is asked to simultaneously focus attention on two or more stimuli.

dizygotic Referring to twins derived from separate eggs (*fraternal* twins). Such twins are no more closely related genetically than are other full siblings. Compare *monozygotic*.

DNA See *deoxyribonucleic acid*.

DNA sequencing The process by which the order of nucleotides in a gene, or amino acids in a protein, is determined.

dopamine (DA) A monoamine transmitter found in the midbrain—especially the substantia nigra—and basal forebrain. See Table 4.1; Figure 4.3.

dopamine hypothesis The hypothesis that schizophrenia results from either excessive levels of synaptic dopamine or excessive postsynaptic sensitivity to dopamine.

dorsal In anatomy, toward the back of the body or the top of the brain. See Box 2.2. Compare *ventral*.

dorsal column system A somatosensory system that delivers most touch stimuli via the dorsal columns of spinal white matter to the brain. See Figure 8.15. Compare *anterolateral system*.

dorsal root See *roots*.

dose-response curve (DRC) A formal plot of a drug's effects (on the *y*-axis) versus the dose given (on the *x*-axis). Analysis of dose-response curves can provide a range of information about the drug, such as its efficacy, potency, and safety. See Figure 4.8.

double-blind test A test of a drug or treatment in which neither the subjects nor the attending researchers know which subjects are receiving the drug (treatment) and which are receiving the placebo (control).

down-regulation A compensatory decrease in receptor availability at the synapses of a neuron. Compare *up-regulation*.

Down syndrome Intellectual disability that is associated with an extra copy of chromosome 21. See Figure 7.18.

DRC See *dose-response curve*.

DTI See *diffusion tensor imaging*.

dual dependence Dependence for emergent drug effects that occur only when two drugs are taken simultaneously.

dualism The notion, promoted by René Descartes, that the mind is subject only to spiritual interactions, while the body is subject only to material interactions.

duplex theory A theory that we localize sound by combining information about intensity differences and latency differences between the two ears.

dura mater The outermost of the three meninges that surround the brain and spinal cord. See also *pia mater* and *arachnoid*.

dynein A protein "motor" that moves substances in axonal transport. See also *kinesin*.

dynorphins One of three kinds of endogenous opioids. Enkephalins and endorphins are the other two. See Table 4.1.

dyskinesia Difficulty or distortion in voluntary movement.

dyslexia A reading disorder attributed to brain impairment. *Acquired dyslexia* occurs as a result of injury or disease. *Developmental dyslexia* is associated with brain abnormalities present from birth.

dysphoria Unpleasant feelings; the opposite of euphoria.

dystrophin A protein that is needed for normal muscle function. Dystrophin is defective in some forms of muscular dystrophy.

E

eardrum See *tympanic membrane*.

early-selection model A model of attention postulating that the attentional bottleneck imposed by the nervous system can exert control early in the processing pathway, filtering out stimuli before even preliminary perceptual analysis has occurred. Compare *late-selection model*.

easy problem of consciousness The problem of how to read current conscious experiences directly from people's brains as they're happening. Compare *hard problem of consciousness*.

EC See *enriched condition*.

ecological niche The unique assortment of environmental opportunities and challenges to which each organism is adapted.

Ecstasy See *MDMA*.

ECT See *electroconvulsive shock therapy*.

ectoderm The outer cellular layer of the developing fetus. The ectoderm gives rise to the skin and the nervous system.

ectopia Something out of place—for example, clusters of neurons seen in unusual positions in the cortex of someone suffering from dyslexia. See Figure 19.10.

ectopic transmission Cell-cell communication based on release of neurotransmitter in regions outside traditional synapses.

ectotherm An animal whose body temperature is regulated by, and whose heat comes mainly from, the environment. Examples include snakes and bees. Compare *endotherm*.

ED$_{50}$ Effective dose 50%; the dose of a drug that is required to produce half of its maximal effect. See Figure 4.8.

edema The swelling of tissue, especially in the brain, in response to injury.

edge detector See *simple cortical cell*.

EEG See *electroencephalography*.

efferent In reference to an axon, carrying information from the nervous system to the periphery. See Box 2.2. Compare *afferent*.

efficacy Also called *intrinsic activity*. The extent to which a drug activates a response when it binds to a receptor. Receptor antagonist drugs have low efficacy; receptor agonists have high efficacy. See Figure 4.8.

egg See *ovum*.

ejaculation The forceful expulsion of semen from the penis.

electrical synapse Also called *gap junction*. The region between neurons where the presynaptic and postsynaptic membranes are so close that the action potential can jump to the postsynaptic membrane without first being translated into a chemical message. See Box 3.2.

electroconvulsive shock therapy (ECT) A last-resort treatment for intractable depression in which a strong electrical current is passed through the brain, causing a seizure. Rapid relief from depressive symptoms often results, associated with improved accumulation of monoamine neurotransmitters in the brain.

electroencephalography (EEG) The recording and study of gross electrical activity of the brain recorded from large electrodes placed on the scalp. The abbreviation *EEG* may refer either to the process of encephalography or to its product, the encephalogram. See Figures 3.19, 14.11.

electromyography (EMG) The electrical recording of muscle activity. See Figure 11.2.

electro-oculography (EOG) The electrical recording of eye movements, useful in determining sleep stages.

electrostatic pressure The propensity of charged molecules or ions to move, via diffusion, toward areas with the opposite charge.

embryo The earliest stage in a developing animal. Humans are considered to be embryos until 8–10 weeks after conception.

embryonic stem cell A cell, derived from an embryo, that has the capacity to form any type of tissue that a donor might produce.

EMG See *electromyography*.

emotional dyscontrol syndrome A condition consisting of temporal lobe disorders that may underlie some forms of human violence.

encéphale isolé See *isolated brain*.

encephalization factor A measure of brain size relative to body size.

encoding A stage of memory formation in which the information entering sensory channels is passed into short-term memory. See Figure 17.7.

endocannabinoid An endogenous ligand of cannabinoid receptors; thus, an analog of marijuana that is produced by the brain.

endocast A cast of the cranial cavity of a skull, especially useful for studying fossils of extinct species.

endocrine Referring to glands that release chemicals to the interior of the body. These glands secrete the principal hormones. See Figure 5.3.

endocrine gland A gland that secretes products into the bloodstream to act on distant targets. See Figure 5.1. Compare *exocrine gland*.

endogenous Produced inside the body. Compare *exogenous*.

endogenous attention Also called *voluntary attention*. The voluntary direction of attention toward specific aspects of the environment, in accordance with our interests and goals. Compare *exogenous attention*.

endogenous ligand Any substance, produced within the body, that selectively binds to the type of receptor that is under study. Compare *exogenous ligand*.

endogenous opioids A family of peptide transmitters that have been called the body's own narcotics. The three kinds are enkephalins, endorphins, and dynorphins. See Table 4.1.

endorphins One of three kinds of endogenous opioids. Enkephalins and dynorphins are the other two. See Table 4.1.

endotherm An animal whose body temperature is regulated chiefly by internal metabolic processes. Examples include mammals and birds. Compare *ectotherm*.

enkephalins One of three kinds of endogenous opioids. Endorphins and dynorphins are the other two. See Table 4.1.

enriched condition (EC) Also called *complex environment*. A condition in which laboratory rodents are group-housed with a wide variety of stimulus objects. See Figure 17.17. Compare *impoverished condition* and *standard condition*.

enteric nervous system An extensive meshlike system of neurons that governs the functioning of the gut. This system is semiautonomous but is generally considered to be part of the autonomic nervous system.

entrainment The process of synchronizing a biological rhythm to an environmental stimulus. See Figure 14.1.

enzyme A complicated protein whose action increases the probability of a specific chemical reaction.

EOAE See *evoked otoacoustic emission*.

EOG See *electro-oculography*.

ependymal layer See *ventricular zone*.

epidemiology The statistical study of patterns of disease in a population.

epidermis The outermost layer of skin, over the dermis. See Figure 8.4.

epigenetics The study of factors that affect gene expression without making any changes in the nucleotide sequence of the genes themselves.

epilepsy A brain disorder marked by major sudden changes in the electrophysiological state of the brain that are referred to as seizures. See Box 3.3.

epinephrine Also called *adrenaline*. A compound that acts both as a hormone (secreted by the adrenal medulla under the control of the sympathetic nervous system) and as a synaptic transmitter. See Tables 4.1, 5.1.

episodic memory Memory of a particular incident or a particular time and place.

EPSP See *excitatory postsynaptic potential*.

equilibrium In chemistry, the point at which all ongoing reactions are canceled or balanced by others, resulting in a stable, offset, or unchanging system.

ERK See *extracellular signal–regulated kinase*.

ERP See *event-related potential*.

estradiol Also called *17β-estradiol*. The primary type of estrogen that is secreted by the ovary. See Table 5.2.

estrogens A class of steroid hormones produced by female gonads. See Figures 5.15, 5.19; Table 5.2.

estrus The period during which female animals are sexually receptive.

eukaryote Any organism whose cells have the genetic material contained within a nuclear envelope.

event-related potential (ERP) Also called *evoked potential*. Averaged EEG recordings measuring brain responses to repeated presentations of a stimulus. Components of the ERP tend to be reliable because the background noise of the cortex has been averaged out. See Figures 3.19, 18.8.

evoked otoacoustic emission (EOAE) A sound produced by the cochlea in response to acoustic stimulation. Compare *spontaneous otoacoustic emission*.

evoked potential See *event-related potential*.

evolution The process by which a population of interbreeding individuals changes over time.

evolution by natural selection The Darwinian theory that evolution proceeds by differential success in reproduction.

evolutionary psychology A field devoted to asking how natural selection has shaped behavior in humans.

excitatory postsynaptic potential (EPSP) A depolarizing potential in the postsynaptic neuron that is caused by excitatory presynaptic impulses. EPSPs increase the probability that the postsynaptic neuron will fire an action potential. See Figure 3.9. Compare *inhibitory postsynaptic potential*.

excitotoxicity The property by which neurons die when overstimulated, as with large amounts of glutamate.

executive function A neural and cognitive system that helps develop plans of action and organizes the activities of other high-level processing systems.

exhaustion stage A stage in the response to stress that is caused by prolonged or frequently repeated stress and is characterized by increased susceptibility to disease.

exocrine gland A gland whose secretions exit the body via ducts. Compare *endocrine gland*.

exogenous Arising from outside the body. Compare *endogenous*.

exogenous attention Also called *reflexive attention*. The involuntary reorienting of attention toward a specific stimulus source, cued by an object or event. Compare *endogenous attention*.

exogenous ligand Any substance, originating from outside the body, that selectively binds to the type of receptor that is under study. Compare *endogenous ligand*.

expression In the context of genetics, the process by which a cell makes an mRNA transcript of a particular gene.

external ear The part of the ear that we readily see (the pinna) and the canal that leads to the eardrum. See Figure 9.2.

external fertilization The process by which eggs are fertilized outside of the female's body, as in many fishes and amphibians. Compare *internal fertilization*.

extinction Short for *extinction of simultaneous double stimulation*, an inability to recognize the double nature of stimuli presented simultaneously to both sides of the body. People experiencing extinction report the stimulus from only one side.

extracellular compartment The fluid space of the body that exists outside the cells. See Figure 13.11. Compare *intracellular compartment*.

extracellular fluid The fluid in the spaces between cells (interstitial fluid) and in the vascular system. Compare *intracellular fluid*.

extracellular signal–regulated kinase (ERK) An important intracellular signal transduction system that can be activated by many different events that affect the cell surface.

extrafusal fiber One of the ordinary muscle fibers that lie outside the spindles and provide most of the force for muscle contraction. See Figure 11.9. Compare *intrafusal fiber*.

extraocular muscle One of the muscles attached to the eyeball that control its position and movements.

extrapyramidal system A motor system that includes the basal ganglia and some closely related brainstem structures.

extrastriate cortex Visual cortex outside of the primary visual (striate) cortex.

F

face blindness See *prosopagnosia*.

FAS See *fetal alcohol syndrome*.

fast-twitch muscle fiber A type of striated muscle that contracts rapidly but fatigues readily. Compare *slow-twitch muscle fiber*.

fatal familial insomnia An inherited disorder in which humans sleep normally at the beginning of their life but in midlife stop sleeping, and 7–24 months later die.

fear conditioning A form of learning in which fear comes to be associated with a previously neutral stimulus.

feature detector model A model of visual pattern analysis that emphasizes linear and angular components of the stimulus array. Compare *spatial-frequency filter model*.

feature integration theory The idea that conjunction searches involve sequential shifts of attention that help coordinate multiple cognitive feature maps—overlapping representations of the search array based on individual stimulus attributes.

feature search A search for an item in which the target, because it possesses a unique attribute, pops out right away, no matter how many distracters are present. Compare *conjunction search*.

FEF See *frontal eye field*.

fetal alcohol syndrome (FAS) A disorder, including intellectual disability and characteristic facial anomalies, that affects children exposed to too much alcohol (through maternal ingestion) during fetal development.

fetus A developing individual after the embryo stage. Humans are considered to be fetuses from 10 weeks after fertilization until birth.

filopodia (sing. filopodium) Very fine, tubular outgrowths from a cell. See Figure 7.8.

final common pathway The information-processing pathway consisting of all the motoneurons in the body. Motoneurons are known by this collective term because they receive and integrate all motor signals from the brain and then direct movement accordingly.

fission The process of splitting in two. Some unicellular organisms reproduce by fission; that is, they simply split into two daughter cells.

flaccid paralysis A loss of reflexes below the level of transection of the spinal cord.

flavor neophobia The avoidance of new foods.

flower spray ending See *secondary sensory ending*.

fluent aphasia Also called *Wernicke's aphasia*. A language impairment characterized by fluent, meaningless speech and little language comprehension; related to damage in Wernicke's area. See Figure 19.7. Compare *nonfluent aphasia*.

fMRI See *functional MRI*.

foliate papillae One of three types of small structures on the tongue, located along the sides, that contain taste receptors. See Figure 9.19. Compare *circumvallate papillae* and *fungiform papillae*.

follicle-stimulating hormone (FSH) A gonadotropin, named for its actions on ovarian follicles. See Figures 5.15, 5.19; Table 5.2.

follicles Ovarian structures containing immature ova.

forebrain Also called *prosencephalon*. The frontal division of the neural tube, containing the cerebral hemispheres, the thalamus, and the hypothalamus. See Figure 2.14.

fornix A fiber tract that extends from the hippocampus to the mammillary body. See Figures 2.12, 2.15.

Fourier analysis The analysis of a complex pattern into the sum of sine waves. See Box 9.1.

fourth ventricle The passageway within the pons that receives cerebrospinal fluid from the third ventricle and releases it to surround the brain and spinal cord. See Figure 2.19.

fovea The central portion of the retina, packed with the most photoreceptors and therefore the center of our gaze. See Figure 10.5.

fragile X syndrome A condition that is a frequent cause of inherited intellectual disability; produced by a fragile site on the X chromosome that seems prone to breaking because the DNA there is unstable. See Figure 7.18.

free nerve ending An axon that terminates in the skin without any specialized cell associated with it and that detects pain and/or changes in temperature. See Figure 8.4.

free-running Referring to a rhythm of behavior shown by an animal deprived of external cues about time of day. See Figure 14.1.

frequency The number of cycles per second in a sound wave; measured in hertz (Hz). See Box 9.1.

frontal eye field (FEF) An area in the frontal lobe of the brain containing neurons important for establishing gaze in accordance with cognitive goals (top-down processes) rather than with any characteristics of stimuli (bottom-up processes).

frontal lobe The most anterior portion of the cerebral cortex. See Figure 2.12.

frontal plane See *coronal plane*.

FSH See *follicle-stimulating hormone*.

functional MRI (fMRI) Magnetic resonance imaging that detects changes in blood flow and therefore identifies regions of the brain that are particularly active during a given task.

functional tolerance Decreased responding to a drug after repeated exposures, generally as a consequence of up- or down-regulation of receptors.

fundamental Here, the predominant frequency of an auditory tone or a visual scene. Compare *harmonic*. See Box 9.1.

fungiform papillae One of three types of small structures on the tongue, located in the front, that contain taste receptors. See Figure 9.19. Compare *circumvallate papillae* and *foliate papillae*.

fusiform gyrus A region on the inferior surface of the cortex, at the junction of temporal and occipital lobes, that has been associated with recognition of faces. See Figure 19.19.

G

G proteins A class of proteins that reside next to the intracellular portion of a receptor and that are activated when the receptor binds an appropriate ligand on the extracellular surface.

GABA See *gamma-aminobutyric acid*.

gamete A sex cell (sperm or ovum) that contains only unpaired chromosomes and therefore has only half of the usual total number of chromosomes.

gamma-aminobutyric acid (GABA) A widely distributed amino acid transmitter, and the main inhibitory transmitter in the mammalian nervous system. See Table 4.1.

gamma efferent See *gamma motoneuron*.

gamma motoneuron Also called *gamma efferent*. A motor neuron that innervates the contractile tissue in a muscle spindle. See Figure 11.9. Compare *alpha motoneuron*.

ganglion (pl. ganglia) A collection of nerve cell bodies outside the central nervous system. Compare *nucleus* (definition 1).

ganglion cells A class of cells in the retina whose axons form the optic nerve. See Figure 10.4. See also *amacrine cells* and *bipolar cells*.

gap junction See *electrical synapse*.

gas neurotransmitter A soluble gas, such as nitric oxide or carbon monoxide, that is produced and released by a neuron to alter the functioning of another neuron. Usually gas neurotransmitters act, in a retrograde fashion, on presynaptic neurons.

gastrin-releasing peptide (GRP) A neuropeptide that stimulates neurons in the dorsal horn to provide the sensation of itch.

gated Referring to the property by which an ion channel may be opened or closed by factors such as chemicals, voltage changes, or mechanical actions. See Figure 3.6.

gel electrophoresis A method of separating molecules of differing size or electrical charge by forcing them to flow through a gel. See Appendix Figure A.3.

gene A length of DNA that encodes the information for constructing a particular protein.

gene amplification See *polymerase chain reaction*.

general anesthetic A drug that renders an individual unconscious.

generator potential A local change in the resting potential of a receptor cell that mediates between the impact of stimuli and the initiation of nerve impulses.

genetics The study of inheritance, including the genes encoded in DNA.

genome See *genotype*.

genotype Also called *genome*. All the genetic information that one specific individual has inherited. Compare *phenotype*.

genus (pl. genera) A group of species that resemble each other because of shared inheritance. See Figure 6.3.

GH See *growth hormone*.

ghrelin A peptide hormone emanating from the gut. See Figure 13.26. Compare *obestatin*.

giant axon A large-diameter axon; found in some invertebrates. The size of giant axons facilitates research on the properties of neural membrane structure and function.

glia See *glial cells*.

glial cells Also sometimes called *glia* or *neuroglia*. Nonneuronal brain cells that provide structural, nutritional, and other types of support to the brain. See Figure 2.6.

global aphasia The total loss of ability to understand language, or to speak, read, or write. See Figure 19.7.

globus pallidus One of the basal ganglia. See Figure 2.15.

glomerulus (pl. glomeruli) A complex arbor of dendrites from a group of olfactory cells.

glucagon A hormone, released by alpha cells in the islets of Langerhans, that increases blood glucose. See Table 5.2. Compare *insulin*.

glucocorticoids A class of steroid hormones, released by the adrenal cortex, that affect carbohydrate metabolism and inflammation.

glucodetector A cell that detects and informs the nervous system about levels of circulating glucose.

gluconeogenesis The metabolism of body fats and proteins to create glucose.

glucose An important sugar molecule used by the body and brain for energy.

glucose transporter A molecule that spans the external membrane of a cell and transports glucose molecules from outside the cell to inside for use.

glutamate An amino acid transmitter, the most common excitatory transmitter. See Table 4.1.

glutamate hypothesis The hypothesis that schizophrenia may be caused, in part, by understimulation of glutamate receptors.

glutamatergic Referring to cells that use glutamate as their synaptic transmitter.

glycine An amino acid transmitter, often inhibitory. See Table 4.1.

glycogen A complex carbohydrate made by the combining of glucose molecules for a short-term store of energy.

glycogenesis The physiological process by which glycogen is produced.

glycogenolysis The conversion of glycogen back into glucose, triggered when blood concentrations of glucose drop too low.

GnIH See *gonadotropin-inhibiting hormone*.

GnRH See *gonadotropin-releasing hormone*.

goiter A swelling of the thyroid gland resulting from iodine deficiency.

Golgi stain A histological stain that fills a small proportion of neurons with a dark, silver-based precipitate. See Box 2.1.

Golgi tendon organ One of the receptors located in tendons that send impulses to the central nervous system when a muscle contracts. See Figure 11.9.

gonadotropin An anterior pituitary hormone that selectively stimulates the cells of the gonads to produce sex steroids and gametes. See *luteinizing hormone* and *follicle-stimulating hormone*.

gonadotropin-inhibiting hormone (GnIH) A hypothalamic peptide hormone that reduces gonadotropin secretion by inhibiting the release of gonadotropin-releasing hormone. Compare *kisspeptin*.

gonadotropin-releasing hormone (GnRH) A hypothalamic hormone that controls the release of luteinizing hormone and follicle-stimulating hormone from the pituitary. See Figure 5.19.

gonads The sexual organs (ovaries in females, testes in males), which produce gametes for reproduction. See Figure 5.1; Table 5.2.

graded response A membrane electrical potential that spreads passively across the cell membrane, decreasing in strength with time and distance.

grammar All of the rules for usage of a particular language.

grand mal seizure A type of generalized epileptic seizure in which nerve cells fire in high-frequency bursts. Grand mal seizures cause loss of consciousness and sudden muscle contraction. See Box 3.3. Compare *petit mal seizure*.

granule cell A type of small nerve cell. See Figure 2.16.

gray matter Areas of the brain that are dominated by cell bodies and are devoid of myelin. See Figure 2.13. Compare *white matter*.

grid cell A neuron that selectively fires when the animal crosses the intersection points of an abstract grid map of the local environment.

gross neuroanatomy Anatomical features of the nervous system that are apparent to the naked eye.

growth cone The growing tip of an axon or a dendrite. See Figure 7.8.

growth hormone (GH) Also called *somatotropin* or *somatotropic hormone*. A tropic hormone, secreted by the anterior pituitary, that influences the growth of cells and tissues. See Figure 5.15; Table 5.2.

GRP See *gastrin-releasing peptide*.

guevedoces Literally, "eggs at 12" (in Spanish). A nickname for individuals who are raised as girls but at puberty change appearance and begin behaving as boys.

gustatory system The taste system. See Figure 9.21.

gyrus (pl. gyri) A ridged or raised portion of a convoluted brain surface. See Figure 2.12. Compare *sulcus*.

H

habituation A form of nonassociative learning in which an organism becomes less responsive following repeated presentations of a stimulus. See Box 17.1. Compare *sensitization* (definition 1).

hair cell One of the receptor cells for hearing in the cochlea. Displacement of hair cells by sound waves generates nerve impulses that travel to the brain. See Figure 9.2.

hallucinogens A class of drugs that alter sensory perception and produce peculiar experiences.

hard problem of consciousness The problem of how to read people's subjective experience of consciousness and determine the qualia that accompany perception. Compare *easy problem of consciousness*.

harmonics Multiples of a particular frequency called the *fundamental*. See Box 9.1.

health psychology Also called *behavioral medicine*. A field that studies psychological influences on health-related processes, such as why people become ill or how they remain healthy.

Hebbian synapse A synapse that is strengthened when it successfully drives the postsynaptic cell.

hemiparesis Weakness of one side of the body.

hemiplegia Partial paralysis involving one side of the body.

hemispatial neglect A syndrome in which the patient fails to pay any attention to objects presented to one side of the body and may even deny connection with that side.

hermaphrodite An individual possessing the reproductive organs of both sexes, either simultaneously or at different points in time.

heroin Diacetylmorphine; an artificially modified, very potent form of morphine.

hertz (Hz) Cycles per second, as of an auditory stimulus. See Box 9.1.

high-functioning autism See *Asperger's syndrome*.

hindbrain Also called *rhombencephalon*. The rear division of the brain, which, in the mature vertebrate, contains the cerebellum, pons, and medulla. See Figure 2.14.

hippocampal gyrus See *subiculum*.

hippocampus (pl. hippocampi) A medial temporal lobe structure that is important for learning and memory. See Figures 2.15, 17.1, 17.21.

histology The study of tissue structure.

homeostasis The tendency for the internal environment to remain constant.

homeostatic Referring to the process of maintaining a particular physiological parameter relatively constant.

homology A physical resemblance that is based on common ancestry, such as the similarity in forelimb structures of different mammals. See Figure 6.1. Compare *homoplasy* and *analogy*.

homoplasy A physical resemblance that is due to convergent evolution, such as the similar body form of tuna and dolphins. Compare *homology*.

horizontal cells Specialized retinal cells that contact both the receptor cells and the bipolar cells.

horizontal plane The plane that divides the body or brain into upper and lower parts. See Box 2.2. Compare *coronal plane* and *sagittal plane*.

hormone A chemical secreted by an endocrine gland that is conveyed by the bloodstream and regulates target organs or tissues. See Tables 5.1, 5.2.

horseradish peroxidase (HRP) An enzyme found in horseradish and other plants that is used to determine the cells of origin of a particular set of axons. See Box 2.1.

HRP See *horseradish peroxidase*.

hue One of three basic dimensions (along with brightness and saturation) of light perception. Hue varies around the color circle through blue, green, yellow, orange, and red. See Figure 10.23.

hunger The internal state of an animal seeking food. Compare *satiety*.

huntingtin A protein produced by a gene (called *HTT*) that, when containing too many trinucleotide repeats, results in Huntington's disease in a carrier.

Huntington's disease Also called *Huntington's chorea*. A progressive genetic disorder characterized by abrupt, involuntary movements and profound changes in mental functioning.

hybridization The process by which a string of nucleotides becomes linked to a complementary series of nucleotides.

hyperphagia Excessive eating. Compare *aphagia*.

hyperpolarization An increase in membrane potential (the interior of the neuron becomes even more negative). See Figure 3.5. Compare *depolarization*.

hypertonic Referring to a solution with a higher concentration of salt than that found in interstitial fluid and blood plasma (more than about 0.9% salt). Compare *hypotonic* and *isotonic*.

hypocretins Also called *orexins*. Neuropeptides produced in the hypothalamus that are involved in switching between sleep states, in narcolepsy, and in the control of appetite.

hypodermis Also called *subcutaneous tissue*. The innermost layer of skin, under the dermis.

hypofrontality hypothesis The hypothesis that schizophrenia may reflect underactivation of the frontal lobes.

hypophyseal portal system A duplex system of capillaries spanning between the neurosecretory cells of the hypothalamus and the secretory tissue of the anterior pituitary.

hypophysis See *pituitary gland*.

hypothalamus Part of the diencephalon, lying ventral to the thalamus. See Figures 2.12, 2.14.

hypotonic Referring to a solution with a lower concentration of salt than that found in interstitial fluid and blood plasma (less than about 0.9% salt). Compare *hypertonic* and *isotonic*.

hypovolemic thirst A desire to ingest fluids that is stimulated by a reduced volume of extracellular fluid. Compare *osmotic thirst*.

hypoxia A transient lack of oxygen.

Hz See *hertz*.

I

IAPs See *inhibitors of apoptosis proteins*.

IC See *impoverished condition*.

ICC See *immunocytochemistry*.

iconic memory A very brief type of memory that stores the sensory impression of a scene. Compare *short-term memory*.

ideational apraxia An impairment in the ability to carry out a sequence of actions, even though each element or step

can be done correctly. Compare *ideomotor apraxia*.

identifiable neurons Neurons that are large and similar from one individual to the next, enabling investigators to recognize them and give them names.

ideomotor apraxia The inability to carry out a simple motor activity in response to a verbal command, even though this same activity is readily performed spontaneously. Compare *ideational apraxia*.

IEGs See *immediate early genes*.

IHC See *inner hair cell*.

immediate early genes (IEGs) A class of genes that show rapid but transient increases in expression in cells that have become activated. See Box 2.1.

immunocytochemistry (ICC) A method for detecting a particular protein in tissues in which an antibody recognizes and binds to the protein and then chemical methods are used to leave a visible reaction product around each antibody. See Boxes 2.1, 5.1.

immunoglobulin See *antibody*.

impoverished condition (IC) Also called *isolated condition*. A condition in which laboratory rodents are housed singly in a small cage without complex stimuli. See Figure 17.17. Compare *enriched condition* and *standard condition*.

in situ hybridization A method for detecting particular RNA transcripts in tissue sections by providing a nucleotide probe that is complementary to, and will therefore hybridize with, the transcript of interest. See Box 2.1; Appendix Figure A.4.

in vitro Literally, "in glass" (in Latin). Usually, in a laboratory dish; outside the body.

inattentional blindness The failure to perceive nonattended stimuli that seem so obvious as to be impossible to miss (e.g., a gorilla strolling across the screen).

incus (pl. incudes) Latin for "anvil." A middle-ear bone situated between the malleus (attached to the tympanic membrane) and the stapes (attached to the cochlea); one of the three ossicles that conduct sound across the middle ear. See Figure 9.2.

independent variable The factor that is manipulated by an experimenter. Compare *dependent variable*.

indifferent gonads The undifferentiated gonads of the early mammalian fetus, which will eventually develop into either testes or ovaries. See Figure 12.13. See also *gonads*.

individual response stereotypy The tendency of individuals to show the same response pattern to particular situations throughout their life span.

indoleamines A class of monoamines that serve as neurotransmitters, including serotonin and melatonin. See Table 4.1.

induction The process by which one set of cells influences the fate of neighboring cells, usually by secreting a chemical factor that changes gene expression in the target cells.

inferior colliculi (sing. colliculus) Paired gray matter structures of the dorsal midbrain that receive auditory information. See Figure 2.12. Compare *superior colliculi*.

infradian Referring to a rhythmic biological event whose period is longer than that of a circadian rhythm—that is, longer than a day. Compare *ultradian*.

infrasound Very low frequency sound; in general, below the threshold of human hearing, at about 20 Hz. Compare *ultrasound*.

infundibulum See *pituitary stalk*.

inhibition of return The phenomenon, observed in peripheral spatial cuing tasks and occurring when the interval between cue and target stimulus is 200 ms or more, in which detection of stimuli at the former location of the cue is increasingly impaired.

inhibitors of apoptosis proteins (IAPs) A family of proteins that inhibit caspases and thereby stave off apoptosis.

inhibitory postsynaptic potential (IPSP) A hyperpolarizing potential in the postsynaptic neuron that is caused by inhibitory connections. IPSPs decrease the probability that the postsynaptic neuron will fire an action potential. See Figure 3.9. Compare *excitatory postsynaptic potential*.

inner ear The cochlea and vestibular apparatus. See Figure 9.2.

inner hair cell (IHC) One of the two types of receptor cells for hearing in the cochlea. See Figure 9.2. Compare *outer hair cell*.

innervate To provide neural input.

innervation The supply of neural input to an organ or a region of the nervous system.

innervation ratio The ratio expressing the number of muscle fibers innervated by a single motor axon. The fewer muscle fibers an axon innervates (i.e., the lower the ratio), the finer the control of movements.

input zone The part of a neuron that receives information, from other neurons or from specialized sensory structures. Usually corresponds to the cell's dendrites. See Figure 2.5.

instrumental conditioning Also called *operant conditioning*. A form of associative learning in which the likelihood that an act (instrumental response) will be performed depends on the consequences (reinforcing stimuli) that follow it. See Box 17.1. Compare *classical conditioning*.

instrumental response See *instrumental conditioning*.

insula A region of cortex lying below the surface, within the lateral sulcus, of the frontal, temporal, and parietal lobes.

insulin A hormone, released by beta cells in the islets of Langerhans, that lowers blood glucose. See Table 5.2. Compare *glucagon*.

integration zone The part of the neuron that initiates nerve electrical activity if the sum of all inhibitory and excitatory postsynaptic potentials exceeds a threshold value. Usually corresponds to the neuron's axon hillock.

intensity differences Perceived differences in loudness between the two ears, which can be used to localize a sound source. Compare *latency differences*.

intermale aggression Aggression between males of the same species.

intermediate-term memory (ITM) A form of memory that lasts longer than short-term memory, but not as long as long-term memory.

internal carotid artery See *carotid arteries*.

internal fertilization The process by which sperm fertilize eggs inside of the female's body, as in all mammals, birds, and reptiles. Compare *external fertilization*.

interneuron A neuron that is neither a sensory neuron nor a motoneuron. Interneurons receive input from and send output to other neurons.

intersex Referring to an individual with atypical genital development and sexual differentiation that generally resembles a form intermediate between typical male and typical female genitals.

intracellular compartment The fluid space of the body that is contained within cells. See Figure 13.11. Compare *extracellular compartment*.

intracellular fluid Also called *cytoplasm*. The watery solution found within cells. Compare *extracellular fluid*.

intrafusal fiber One of the small muscle fibers that lie within each muscle spindle. See Figure 11.9. Compare *extrafusal fiber*.

intraparietal sulcus (IPS) A region in the human parietal lobe, homologous to the monkey lateral intraparietal area, that is especially involved in voluntary, top-down control of attention.

intrinsic activity See *efficacy*.

intromission Insertion of the erect penis into the vagina during copulation.

inverse agonist A substance that binds to a receptor and causes it to do the opposite of what the naturally occurring transmitter does.

ion An atom or molecule that has acquired an electrical charge by gaining or losing one or more electrons.

ion channel A pore in the cell membrane that permits the passage of certain ions through the membrane when the channels are open. See Figure 3.4.

ionotropic receptor A receptor protein that includes an ion channel that is opened when the receptor is bound by an appropriate ligand. See Figures 3.15, 4.1. See also *ligand-gated ion channel*. Compare *metabotropic receptor*.

IPS See *intraparietal sulcus*.

ipsilateral In anatomy, pertaining to a location on the same side of the body. See Box 2.2. Compare *contralateral*.

IPSP See *inhibitory postsynaptic potential*.

iris The circular structure of the eye that provides an opening to form the pupil. See Figure 10.5.

islets of Langerhans Clusters of cells in the pancreas that release two hormones (insulin and glucagon) with opposite effects on glucose utilization. See Figure 5.1.

isocortex See *neocortex*.

isolated brain Sometimes referred to by the French term, *encéphale isolé*. An experimental preparation in which an animal's brainstem has been separated from the spinal cord by a cut below the medulla. See Figure 14.26. Compare *isolated forebrain*.

isolated forebrain Sometimes referred to by the French term, *cerveau isolé*. An experimental preparation in which an animal's nervous system has been cut in the upper midbrain, dividing the brain from the brainstem. See Figure 14.26. Compare *isolated brain*.

isolated condition See *impoverished condition*.

isotonic Referring to a solution with a concentration of salt that is the same as that found in interstitial fluid and blood plasma (about 0.9% salt). Compare *hypertonic* and *hypotonic*.

ITM See *intermediate-term memory*.

K

K complex A sharp negative EEG potential that is seen in stage 2 sleep.

kcal See *kilocalorie*.

ketamine A dissociative anesthetic drug, similar to PCP, that acts as an NMDA receptor antagonist.

ketones A metabolic fuel source liberated by the breakdown of body fats and proteins.

khat Also spelled *qat*. An African shrub that, when chewed, acts as a stimulant.

kilocalorie (kcal) A measure of energy commonly applied to food; formally defined as the quantity of heat required to raise the temperature of 1 kg of water by 1°C.

kindling A method of experimentally inducing an epileptic seizure by repeatedly stimulating a brain region. See Box 3.3.

kinesin A protein "motor" that moves substances in axonal transport. See also *dynein*.

kisspeptin A hypothalamic peptide hormone that increases gonadotropin secretion by facilitating the release of gonadotropin-releasing hormone. Compare *gonadotropin-inhibiting hormone*.

Klüver-Bucy syndrome A condition, brought about by bilateral amygdala damage, that is characterized by dramatic emotional changes including reduction in fear and anxiety.

knee jerk reflex A variant of the stretch reflex in which stretching of the tendon beneath the knee leads to an upward kick of the leg. See Figure 3.17.

knockout organism An individual in which a particular gene has been disabled by an experimenter. See Box 7.3.

Korsakoff's syndrome A memory disorder, related to a thiamine deficiency, that is generally associated with chronic alcoholism.

L

L-dopa The immediate precursor of the transmitter dopamine.

labeled lines The concept that each nerve input to the brain reports only a particular type of information.

lamellipodia (pl. lamellipodium) Sheet-like extensions of a growth cone. See Figure 7.8.

late-selection model A model of attention postulating that the attentional bottleneck imposed by the nervous system exerts control late in the processing pathway, filtering out stimuli only after substantial analysis has occurred. Compare *early-selection model*.

latency differences Differences between the two ears in the time of arrival of a sound, which can be employed by the nervous system to localize sound sources. Compare *intensity differences*.

latent learning Learning that has taken place but has not (yet) been demonstrated by performance.

lateral In anatomy, toward the side of the body. See Box 2.2. Compare *medial*.

lateral geniculate nucleus (LGN) The part of the thalamus that receives information from the optic tract and sends it to visual areas in the occipital cortex. See Figure 10.15.

lateral hypothalamus (LH) A hypothalamic region involved in the control of appetite and other functions. See Figure 13.22.

lateral inhibition The phenomenon by which interconnected neurons inhibit their neighbors, producing contrast at the edges of regions. See Figure 10.4.

lateral intraparietal area (LIP) A region in the monkey parietal lobe, homologous to the human intraparietal sulcus, that is especially involved in voluntary, top-down control of attention.

lateral-line system A sensory system, found in many kinds of fishes and some amphibians, that informs the animal of water motion in relation to the body surface.

lateral sulcus See *Sylvian fissure*.

lateral ventricle A complexly shaped lateral portion of the ventricular system within each hemisphere of the brain. See Figure 2.19.

lateralization The tendency for the right and left halves of a system to differ from one another.

LD$_{50}$ Lethal dose 50%; the dose of a drug at which half the treated animals will die. See Figure 4.8.

learned helplessness A learning paradigm in which individuals are subjected to inescapable, unpleasant conditions.

learning The process of acquiring new and relatively enduring information, behavior patterns, or abilities, characterized by modifications of behavior as a result of practice, study, or experience.

lens A structure in the eye that helps focus an image on the retina. The shape of the lens is controlled by the ciliary muscles inside the eye. See Figure 10.5.

leptin A peptide hormone released by fat cells.

lesion momentum The phenomenon in which the brain is impaired more by a lesion that develops quickly than by a lesion that develops slowly.

levels of analysis The scope of experimental approaches. A scientist may try to understand behavior by monitoring molecules, nerve cells, brain regions, or social environments, or some combination of these levels of analysis.

LGN See *lateral geniculate nucleus*.

LH 1. See *lateral hypothalamus*. 2. See *luteinizing hormone*.

lie detector See *polygraph*.

ligand A substance that binds to receptor molecules, such as those at the surface of the cell.

ligand-gated ion channel Also known as *chemically gated ion channel*. An ion channel that opens or closes in response to the presence of a particular chemical; an example is the ionotropic neurotransmitter receptor. Compare *voltage-gated Na$^+$ channel*.

limbic system A loosely defined, widespread group of brain nuclei that innervate each other to form a network. These nuclei are implicated in emotions. See Figure 2.15.

LIP See *lateral intraparietal area*.

lipid bilayer The structure of the neuronal cell membrane, which consists of two layers of lipid molecules, within which float various specialized proteins, such as receptors. See Figure 3.4.

lipids Large molecules (commonly called fats) consisting of fatty acids and glycerol that are insoluble in water.

lithium An element that, administered to patients, often relieves the symptoms of bipolar disorder.

lobotomy The detachment of a portion of the frontal lobe from the rest of the brain, once used as a treatment for schizophrenia and many other ailments.

local anesthetic A drug, such as procaine or lidocaine, that blocks sodium channels to stop neural transmission in pain fibers.

local potential An electrical potential that is initiated by stimulation at a specific site, which is a graded response that spreads passively across the cell membrane, decreasing in strength with time and distance.

locus coeruleus Literally, "blue spot." A small nucleus in the brainstem whose neurons produce norepinephrine and modulate large areas of the forebrain.

long-term depression (LTD) A lasting decrease in the magnitude of responses of neurons after afferent cells have been stimulated with electrical stimuli of relatively low frequency. Compare *long-term potentiation*.

long-term memory (LTM) An enduring form of memory that lasts days, weeks, months, or years and has a very large capacity.

long-term potentiation (LTP) A stable and enduring increase in the effectiveness of synapses following repeated strong stimulation. See Figures 17.21, 17.22, 17.23. Compare *long-term depression*.

lordosis A female receptive posture in quadrupeds in which the hindquarter is raised and the tail is turned to one side, facilitating intromission by the male. See Figures 12.3, 12.6.

Lou Gehrig's disease See *amyotrophic lateral sclerosis*.

loudness The subjective experience of the pressure level of a sound. See Box 9.1.

LSD Also called *acid*. Lysergic acid diethylamide, a hallucinogenic drug.

LTD See *long-term depression*.

LTM See *long-term memory*.

LTP See *long-term potentiation*.

lumbar Referring to the five spinal segments that make up the upper part of the lower back. See Figures 2.10, 2.11.

luteinizing hormone (LH) A gonadotropin, named for its stimulatory effects on the ovarian corpora lutea. See Figures 5.15, 5.19; Table 5.2.

lysergic acid diethylamide See *LSD*.

M

M1 See *primary motor cortex*.

mad cow disease See *bovine spongiform encephalopathy*.

magnetic resonance imaging (MRI) A noninvasive technique that uses magnetic energy to generate images that reveal some structural details in the living brain. See Figures 1.6, 2.21.

magnetoencephalography (MEG) A passive and noninvasive functional brain-imaging technique that measures the tiny magnetic fields produced by active neurons, in order to identify regions of the brain that are particularly active during a given task.

magnocellular Of or consisting of relatively large cells. Compare *parvocellular*.

major histocompatibility complex (MHC) A large family of genes that identify an individual's tissues (to aid in immune responses against foreign proteins).

malleus (pl. mallei) Latin for "hammer." A middle-ear bone that is connected to the tympanic membrane; one of the three ossicles that conduct sound across the middle ear. See Figure 9.2.

mammillary body One of a pair of nuclei at the base of the brain. See Figure 2.12.

manic-depressive illness See *bipolar disorder*.

MAO See *monoamine oxidase*.

marijuana A dried preparation of the *Cannabis sativa* plant, usually smoked to obtain THC.

maximal response In pharmacology, the strongest effect that a drug can have on a particular measured response, no matter how much of the drug is given.

MC4Rs See *melanocortin type-4 receptors*.

MD See *muscular dystrophy*.

MDMA Also called *Ecstasy*. A drug of abuse, 3,4-methylenedioxymethamphetamine.

medial In anatomy, toward the middle of an organ or organism. See Box 2.2. Compare *lateral*.

medial amygdala A portion of the amygdala that receives olfactory and pheromonal information.

medial forebrain bundle A collection of axons traveling in the midline region of the forebrain. See Figure 4.21.

medial geniculate nuclei Nuclei in the thalamus that receive input from the inferior colliculi and send output to the auditory cortex. See Figure 9.7.

medial preoptic area (mPOA) A region of the anterior hypothalamus implicated in the control of many behaviors, including thermoregulation, sexual behavior, and gonadotropin secretion.

median eminence Midline feature on the base of the brain marking the point at which the infundibulum exits the hypothalamus to connect to the pituitary. Contains elements of the hypophyseal portal system.

medulla Also called *myelencephalon*. The posterior part of the hindbrain. See Figures 2.12, 2.14.

medullary reticular formation The hindmost portion of the brainstem reticular formation, implicated in motor control and copulatory behavior. See Figure 12.6.

MEG See *magnetoencephalography*.

Meissner's corpuscle A skin receptor cell type that detects light touch. See Figures 8.4, 8.13.

melanocortin type-4 receptors (MC4Rs) A specific subtype of melanocortin receptor.

melanocortins One category of endogenous opioid peptides.

melanopsin A photopigment found within particular retinal ganglion cells that project to the suprachiasmatic nucleus. See Figure 14.6.

melatonin An amine hormone that is released by the pineal gland. See Tables 4.1, 5.2.

memory 1. The ability to retain information, based on the mental process of learning or encoding, retention across some interval of time, and retrieval or reactivation of the memory. 2. The specific information that is stored in the brain.

memory trace A persistent change in the brain that reflects the storage of memory.

meninges The three protective sheets of tissue—dura mater, pia mater, and arachnoid—that surround the brain and spinal cord. See Figure 2.10.

meningitis An acute inflammation of the membranes covering the central nervous system—the meninges—usually caused by a viral or bacterial infection.

Merkel's disc A skin receptor cell type that detects light touch. See Figures 8.4, 8.13.

mesencephalon See *midbrain*.

mesolimbocortical pathway A set of dopaminergic axons arising in the midbrain and innervating the limbic system and cortex. See Figure 4.3. Compare *mesostriatal pathway*.

mesostriatal pathway A set of dopaminergic axons arising from the midbrain and innervating the basal ganglia, including those from the substantia nigra to the striatum. See Figure 4.3. Compare *mesolimbocortical pathway*.

messenger RNA (mRNA) A strand of RNA that carries the code of a section of a DNA strand to the cytoplasm. See the Appendix.

metabolic tolerance The form of drug tolerance that arises when the metabolic machinery of the body becomes more efficient at clearing the drug, as a consequence of repeated exposure.

metabolism The breakdown of complex molecules into smaller molecules.

metabotropic receptor A receptor protein that does not contain an ion channel but may, when activated, use a G protein system to alter the functioning of the postsynaptic cell. See Figures 3.13, 4.1. Compare *ionotropic receptor*.

metencephalon A subdivision of the hindbrain that includes the cerebellum and the pons. See Figure 2.14.

methylation A chemical modification of DNA that does not affect the nucleotide sequence of a gene but makes that gene less likely to be expressed.

MHC See *major histocompatibility complex*.

microelectrode An especially small electrode used to record electrical potentials from living cells.

microfilament A very small filament (7 nm in diameter) found within all cells. Microfilaments determine cell shape.

microglial cells Also called *microglia*. Extremely small glial cells that remove cellular debris from injured or dead cells.

micropolygyria A condition of the brain in which small regions are characterized by more gyri than usual. See Figure 19.10.

microtubule A small, hollow, cylindrical structure (20–26 nm in diameter) in axons that is involved in axonal transport.

midbrain Also called *mesencephalon*. The middle division of the brain. See Figure 2.14.

middle canal See *scala media*.

middle cerebral arteries Two large arteries, arising from the internal carotids, that provide blood to most of the lateral surfaces of the cerebral hemispheres.

middle ear The cavity between the tympanic membrane and the cochlea. See Figure 9.2.

milk letdown reflex The reflexive release of milk in response to suckling, or to stimuli associated with suckling. The mechanism involves release of the hormone oxytocin. See Figure 5.12.

millivolt (mV) A thousandth of a volt.

mineralocorticoids A class of steroid hormones, released by the adrenal cortex, that affect ion concentrations in body tissues.

minimal discriminable frequency difference The smallest change in frequency that can be detected reliably between two tones.

mirror neuron A neuron that is active both when an individual makes a particular movement and when that individual sees another individual make that same movement.

mitochondrion (pl. mitochondria) A cellular organelle that provides metabolic energy for the cell's processes. See Figure 2.7.

mitosis The process of division of somatic cells that involves duplication of DNA.

mitral cell A type of cell in the olfactory bulb that conducts smell information from the glomeruli to the rest of the brain. See Figure 9.22.

modulatory circuit See *superordinate circuit*.

modulatory site A portion of a receptor that, when bound by a compound, alters the receptor's response to its transmitter.

monaural Pertaining to one ear. Compare *binaural*.

monoamine hormones See *amine hormones*.

monoamine oxidase (MAO) An enzyme that breaks down and thereby inactivates monoamine transmitters.

monocular deprivation Depriving one eye of light. Compare *binocular deprivation*.

monogamy A mating system in which a female and a male form a breeding pair that may last for one breeding period or for a lifetime. A durable and exclusive relationship between a male and a female is called a *pair bond*. Compare *polygamy* and *bigamy*.

monopolar neuron See *unipolar neuron*.

monotreme An egg-laying mammal belonging to an order that contains only the echidnas and the platypus.

monozygotic Referring to twins derived from a single fertilized egg (*identical* twins). Such individuals have the same genotype. Compare *dizygotic*.

morpheme The smallest grammatical unit of a language; a word or meaningful part of a word.

morphine An opiate compound derived from the poppy flower.

motion sickness The experience of nausea brought on by unnatural passive movement, as in a car or boat.

motoneuron Also called *motor neuron*. A nerve cell that transmits motor messages, stimulating a muscle or gland. See Figure 11.8.

motor neuron See *motoneuron*.

motor plan Also called *motor program*. A plan for action in the nervous system.

motor theory of language The theory proposing that the left-hemisphere language zones are motor control systems that are concerned with both the precise production and the perception of the extremely complex movements that go into speech.

motor unit A single motor axon and all the muscle fibers that it innervates.

movement A brief, unitary activity of a muscle or body part; less complex than an act.

mPOA See *medial preoptic area*.

MRH See *anti-müllerian hormone*.

MRI See *magnetic resonance imaging*.

mRNA See *messenger RNA*.

müllerian duct A duct system in the embryo that will develop into female reproductive structures (fallopian tubes, uterus, and upper vagina) if testes are not present. See Figures 12.13, 12.14. Compare *wolffian duct*.

müllerian regression hormone (MRH) See *anti-müllerian hormone*.

multiple sclerosis Literally, "many scars"; a disorder characterized by widespread degeneration of myelin.

multipolar neuron A nerve cell that has many dendrites and a single axon. See Figure 2.5. Compare *bipolar neuron* and *unipolar neuron*.

multisensory See *polymodal*.

muscarinic Referring to cholinergic receptors that respond to the chemical muscarine as well as to acetylcholine. Muscarinic receptors mediate chiefly the inhibitory activities of acetylcholine. Compare *nicotinic*.

muscle fiber A collection large, cylindrical cells, making up most of a muscle, that can contract in response to neurotransmitter released from a motoneuron. See Figure 11.7. See also *extrafusal fiber* and *intrafusal fiber*.

muscle spindle A muscle receptor that lies parallel to a muscle and sends impulses to the central nervous system when the muscle is stretched. See Figure 11.9.

muscular dystrophy (MD) A disease that leads to degeneration of and functional changes in muscles.

musth An annual period of heightened aggressiveness and sexual activity in male elephants.

mutant An animal carrying a gene that differs from the norm or from the alleles carried by its parents.

mutation A change in the nucleotide sequence of a gene as a result of unfaithful replication.

mV See *millivolt*.

myasthenia gravis A disorder characterized by a profound weakness of skeletal muscles; caused by a loss of acetylcholine receptors.

myelencephalon See *medulla*.

myelin The fatty insulation around an axon, formed by glial cells. This myelin sheath improves the speed of conduction of nerve impulses. See Figures 2.6, 3.8.

myelination The process of myelin formation. See Figures 2.6, 7.15.

myopia Nearsightedness; the inability to focus the retinal image of objects that are far away.

myosin A protein that, along with actin, mediates the contraction of muscle fibers. See Figure 11.7.

N

N1 effect A negative deflection of the event-related potential, occurring about 100 ms after stimulus presentation, that is enhanced for selectively attended input compared to ignored input.

naloxone A potent antagonist of opiates that is often administered to people who have taken drug overdoses. Naloxone binds to receptors for endogenous opioids.

narcolepsy A disorder that involves frequent, intense episodes of sleep, which last from 5 to 30 minutes and can occur anytime during the usual waking hours.

natural selection See *evolution by natural selection*.

naturalist A student of animal life and structure.

NE See *norepinephrine*.

negative feedback The property by which some of the output of a system feeds back to reduce the effect of input signals. Compare *positive feedback*.

negative polarity A negative electrical-potential difference relative to a reference electrode. A neuron at rest exhibits a greater concentration of negatively charged ions in its interior than in its immediate surrounds; thus it is said to be negatively polarized. See Figure 3.1.

negative symptom In psychiatry, a symptom that reflects insufficient functioning. Examples include emotional and social withdrawal, blunted affect, and slowness and impoverishment of thought and speech. Compare *positive symptom*.

neocortex Also called *isocortex* or simply *cortex*. Cerebral cortex that is made up of six distinct layers. Compare *allocortex*.

neologism An entirely novel word, sometimes produced by a patient with aphasia.

neonatal Referring to newborns.

Nernst equation An equation predicting the voltage needed to just counterbalance the diffusion force pushing an ion across a semipermeable membrane from the side with a high concentration to the side with a low concentration.

nerve A collection of axons bundled together outside the central nervous system. See Figures 2.8, 2.9. Compare *tract*.

nerve cell See *neuron*.

nerve growth factor (NGF) A substance that markedly affects the growth of neurons in spinal ganglia and in the ganglia of the sympathetic nervous system. See Figure 7.12.

nerve impulse See *action potential*.

neural chain A simple kind of neural circuit in which neurons are attached linearly, end-to-end.

neural groove In the developing embryo, the groove between the neural folds. See Figure 7.1.

neural plasticity See *neuroplasticity*.

neural tube An embryonic structure with subdivisions that correspond to the future forebrain, midbrain, and hindbrain. The cavity of this tube will include the cerebral ventricles and the passages that connect them. See Figure 7.1.

neurochemistry The branch of neuroscience concerned with the fundamental chemical composition and processes of the nervous system.

neurocrine Referring to secretory functions of neurons, especially pertaining to synaptic transmission. See Figure 5.3.

neuroeconomics The study of brain mechanisms at work during economic decision making.

neuroendocrine cell See *neurosecretory cell*.

neurofibrillary tangle An abnormal whorl of neurofilaments within nerve cells. Neurofibrillary tangles are especially apparent in people suffering from dementia. See Figure 7.28.

neurofilament A small, rodlike structure found in axons. Neurofilaments are involved in the transport of materials. See Figure 2.22.

neurogenesis The mitotic division of nonneuronal cells to produce neurons. See Figures 7.2, 7.3.

neuroglia See *glial cells*.

neurohypophysis See *posterior pituitary*.

neuroleptics Also called *antipsychotics*. A class of drugs that alleviate symptoms of schizophrenia, typically by blocking dopamine receptors.

neuromodulator A substance that influences the activity of synaptic transmitters.

neuromuscular junction (NMJ) The region where the motoneuron terminal and the adjoining muscle fiber meet; the point where the nerve transmits its message to the muscle fiber.

neuron Also called *nerve cell*. The basic unit of the nervous system. Each neuron is composed of a cell body, receptive extension(s) (dendrites), and a transmitting extension (axon). See Figures 2.4, 2.5.

neuron doctrine The hypothesis that the brain is composed of separate cells that are distinct structurally, metabolically, and functionally.

neuropathic pain Pain caused by damage to peripheral nerves; often difficult to treat.

neuropeptide See *peptide neurotransmitter*.

neuropeptide Y (NPY) A peptide neurotransmitter that may carry some of the signals for feeding.

neuropharmacology Also called *psychopharmacology*. The scientific field concerned with the discovery and study of compounds that selectively affect the functioning of the nervous system.

neurophysiology The study of the life processes of neurons.

neuropil The conglomeration of dendrites and the synapses upon them.

neuroplasticity Also called *neural plasticity*. The ability of the nervous system to change in response to experience or the environment.

neuroscience The study of the nervous system.

neurosecretory cell Also called *neuroendocrine cell*. A neuron that releases hormones into local or systemic circulation.

neurosteroids Steroids produced in the brain.

neurotransmitter Also called *synaptic transmitter*, *chemical transmitter*, or simply *transmitter*. The chemical released from the presynaptic axon terminal that serves as the basis of communication between neurons. See Figure 3.12; Table 4.1.

neurotrophic factor A target-derived chemical that acts as if it "feeds" certain neurons to help them survive. See also *trophic factor*.

neurotrophin A chemical that prevents neurons from dying.

NGF See *nerve growth factor*.

nicotine A compound found in plants, including tobacco, that acts as an agonist on a large class of cholinergic receptors.

nicotinic Referring to cholinergic receptors that respond to nicotine as well as to acetylcholine. Nicotinic receptors mediate chiefly the excitatory activities of acetylcholine, including at the neuromuscular junction. Compare *muscarinic*.

night terror A sudden arousal from stage 3 or stage 4 slow-wave sleep that is marked by intense fear and autonomic activation. Compare *nightmare*.

nightmare A long, frightening dream that awakens the sleeper from REM sleep. Compare *night terror*.

Nissl stain A histological stain that outlines all cell bodies because the dyes are attracted to RNA, which encircles the nucleus. See Box 2.1.

nitric oxide (NO) A soluble gas that serves as a retrograde gas neurotransmitter in the nervous system.

NMDA receptor A glutamate receptor that also binds the glutamate agonist NMDA (*N*-methyl-D-aspartate). The NMDA receptor is both ligand-gated and voltage-sensitive, so it can participate in a wide variety of information processing. See Figure 17.22.

NMJ See *neuromuscular junction*.

NO See *nitric oxide*.

nociceptor A receptor that responds to stimuli that produce tissue damage or pose the threat of damage.

nocturnal Active during the dark periods of the daily cycle. Compare *diurnal*.

node of Ranvier A gap between successive segments of the myelin sheath where the axon membrane is exposed. See Figures 2.6, 3.8.

nonassociative learning A type of learning in which presentation of a particular stimulus alters the strength or probability of a response according to the strength and temporal spacing of that stimulus; includes habituation and sensitization. See Box 17.1. Compare *associative learning*.

noncompetitive ligand A drug that affects a transmitter receptor while binding at a site other than that bound by the endogenous ligand. See Figure 4.7. Compare *competitive ligand*.

nondeclarative memory Also called *procedural memory*. A memory that is shown by performance rather than by conscious recollection. See Figures 17.3, 17.5. Compare *declarative memory*.

nondirected synapse A type of synapse in which the presynaptic and postsynaptic cells are not in close apposition; instead, neurotransmitter is released by axonal varicosities and diffuses away to affect wide regions of tissue.

nonfluent aphasia Also called *Broca's aphasia*. A language impairment characterized by difficulty with speech production but not with language comprehension; related to damage in Broca's area. See Figure 19.7. Compare *fluent aphasia*.

nonfluent speech Talking with considerable effort, short sentences, and the absence of the usual melodic character of conversational speech.

nongenomic effect An effect of a steroid hormone that is not mediated by direct changes in gene expression.

nonprimary motor cortex Frontal lobe regions adjacent to the primary motor cortex that contribute to motor control and modulate the activity of the primary motor cortex. See Figure 11.15.

nonprimary sensory cortex See *secondary sensory cortex*.

nootropics A class of drugs that enhance cognitive function.

noradrenaline See *norepinephrine*.

noradrenergic Referring to systems using norepinephrine (noradrenaline) as a transmitter.

norepinephrine (NE) Also called *noradrenaline*. A neurotransmitter produced and released by sympathetic postganglionic neurons to accelerate organ activity. Also produced in the brainstem and found in projections throughout the brain. See Table 4.1.

Northern blot A method of detecting a particular RNA transcript in a tissue or organ, by separating RNA from that source with gel electrophoresis, blotting the separated RNAs onto nitrocellulose, and then using a nucleotide probe to hybridize with, and highlight, the transcript of interest. Compare *Southern blot* and *Western blot*.

notochord A midline structure arising early in the embryonic development of vertebrates. See Figure 7.1.

NPY See *neuropeptide Y*.

NPY/AgRP neurons Neurons involved in the hypothalamic appetite control system, so named because they produce both neuropeptide Y and agouti-related peptide. Compare *POMC/CART neurons*.

NST See *nucleus of the solitary tract*.

nucleotide A portion of a DNA or RNA molecule that is composed of a single base and the adjoining sugar-phosphate unit of the strand. See Appendix Figure A.2.

nucleus (pl. nuclei) 1. A collection of neurons within the central nervous system (e.g., the caudate nucleus). Compare *ganglion*. 2. See *cell nucleus*.

nucleus accumbens A region of the forebrain that receives dopaminergic innervation from the ventral tegmental area. Dopamine release in this region may mediate the reinforcing qualities of many activities, including drug abuse.

nucleus of the solitary tract (NST) A complicated brainstem nucleus that receives visceral and taste information via several cranial nerves. See Figure 13.16.

nutrient A chemical that is needed for growth, maintenance, and repair of the body but is not used as a source of energy.

O

obestatin A peptide hormone emanating from the gut that acts probably on the appetite controller of the hypothalamus to decrease appetite. Compare *ghrelin*.

obsessive-compulsive disorder (OCD) A syndrome in which the affected individual engages in recurring, repetitive acts that are carried out without rhyme, reason, or the ability to stop.

occipital cortex Also called *visual cortex*. The cortex of the occipital lobe of the brain. See Figure 10.11.

occipital lobes Large regions of cortex covering much of the posterior part of each cerebral hemisphere, and specialized for visual processing. See Figure 2.12.

OCD See *obsessive-compulsive disorder*.

ocular dominance column A region of cortex in which one eye or the other provides a greater degree of synaptic input. See Figure 10.22.

ocular dominance histogram A graph that portrays the strength of response of a brain neuron to stimuli presented to either the left eye or the right eye. Ocular dominance histograms are used to determine the effects of manipulating visual experience. See Figure 7.21.

ocular dominance slab A slab of visual cortex, about 0.5 mm wide, in which the neurons of all layers respond preferentially to stimulation of one eye. See Figure 10.23.

oculomotor apraxia A severe difficulty in voluntarily steering visual gaze toward specific targets.

off-center bipolar cell A retinal bipolar cell that is inhibited by light in the center of its receptive field. See Figure 10.14. Compare *on-center bipolar cell*.

off-center ganglion cell A retinal ganglion cell that is activated when light is presented to the periphery, rather than the center, of the cell's receptive field.

See Figure 10.14. Compare *on-center ganglion cell*.

off-center/on-surround Referring to a concentric receptive field in which the center inhibits the cell of interest while the surround excites it. See Figure 10.14. Compare *on-center/off-surround*.

OHC See *outer hair cell*.

olfactory bulb An anterior projection of the brain that terminates in the upper nasal passages and, through small openings in the skull, provides receptors for smell. See Figures 2.12, 9.18.

olfactory epithelium (pl. epithelia) A sheet of cells, including olfactory receptors, that lines the dorsal portion of the nasal cavities and adjacent regions, including the septum that separates the left and right nasal cavities. See Figures 9.22, 9.24, 9.25.

oligodendrocyte A type of glial cell that forms myelin in the central nervous system. See Figure 2.6.

on-center bipolar cell A retinal bipolar cell that is excited by light in the center of its receptive field. See Figure 10.14. Compare *off-center bipolar cell*.

on-center ganglion cell A retinal ganglion cell that is activated when light is presented to the center, rather than the periphery, of the cell's receptive field. See Figure 10.15. Compare *off-center ganglion cell*.

on-center/off-surround Referring to a concentric receptive field in which the center excites the cell of interest while the surround inhibits it. See Figure 10.14. Compare *off-center/on-surround*.

ontogeny The process by which an individual changes in the course of its lifetime—that is, grows up and grows old.

Onuf's nucleus The human homolog of the spinal nucleus of the bulbocavernosus (SNB) in rats.

open-loop control mechanism A control mechanism in which feedback from the output of the system is not provided to the input control. Compare *closed-loop control mechanism*.

operant conditioning See *instrumental conditioning*.

opiates A class of compounds that exert an effect like that of opium, including reduced pain sensitivity. See Table 4.1, under "Opioid peptides." Compare *opioids*.

opioid peptide A type of endogenous peptide that mimics the effects of morphine in binding to opioid receptors and producing marked analgesia and reward. See Table 4.1.

opioid receptor A receptor that responds to endogenous and/or exogenous opioids.

opioids A class of peptides produced in various regions of the brain that bind to opioid receptors and act like *opiates*. See Table 4.1.

opium A heterogeneous extract of the seedpod juice of the opium poppy, *Papaver somniferum*.

opponent-process hypothesis The theory that color vision depends on systems that produce opposite responses to light of different wavelengths. See Figures 10.24, 10.25.

opsin One of the two components of photopigments in the retina. The other component is RETINAL.

optic ataxia A spatial disorientation in which the patient is unable to accurately reach for objects using visual guidance.

optic chiasm The point at which the two optic nerves meet. See Figures 2.12, 10.11.

optic disc The region of the retina devoid of receptor cells because ganglion cell axons and blood vessels exit the eyeball there. See Figure 10.7.

optic nerve Cranial nerve II; the collection of ganglion cell axons that extend from the retina to the optic chiasm. See Figures 2.9, 10.7.

optic radiation Axons from the lateral geniculate nucleus that terminate in the primary visual areas of the occipital cortex. See Figure 10.11.

optic tract The axons of retinal ganglion cells after they have passed the optic chiasm; most terminate in the lateral geniculate nucleus. See Figure 10.11.

optical imaging A method for visualizing brain activity in which near-infrared light is passed through the scalp and skull. The reflected light contains information about blood flow and electrical activity of the cortical surface.

oral contraceptive A birth control pill, typically consisting of steroid hormones to prevent ovulation.

orexins Also called *hypocretins*. Neuropeptides produced in the hypothalamus that are involved in switching between sleep states, in narcolepsy, and in the control of appetite.

organ of Corti A structure in the inner ear that lies on the basilar membrane of the cochlea and contains the hair cells and terminations of the auditory nerve. See Figure 9.1.

organizational effect A permanent alteration of the nervous system, and thus permanent change in behavior, resulting from the action of a steroid hormone on an animal early in its development. Compare *activational effect*.

orgasm The climax of sexual experience, marked by extremely pleasurable sensations.

orientation column A column of visual cortex that responds to rod-shaped stimuli of a particular orientation. See Figure 10.22.

orphan receptor Any receptor for which no endogenous ligand has yet been discovered.

oscillator circuit A neural circuit that produces a recurring, repeating pattern of output.

osmolality The number of solute particles per unit volume of solvent.

osmosensory neuron A specialized neuron that measures the movement of water into and out of the intracellular compartment. See Figures 13.11, 13.16.

osmosis The passive movement of molecules from one place to another.

osmotic pressure The tendency of a solvent to move through a membrane in order to equalize the concentration of a solute.

osmotic thirst A desire to ingest fluids that is stimulated by excessive loss of water from the extracellular compartment. Compare *hypovolemic thirst*.

ossicles Three small bones (incus, malleus, and stapes) that transmit sound across the middle ear, from the tympanic membrane to the oval window. See Figure 9.2.

otoacoustic emission A sound produced by the cochlea itself, either spontaneously or in response to an environmental noise.

otolith A small crystal on the gelatinous membrane in the vestibular system. See Figure 9.16.

ototoxic Toxic to the ears, especially the middle or inner ear.

outer hair cell (OHC) One of the two types of receptor cells for hearing in the cochlea. See Figure 9.2. Compare *inner hair cell*.

output zone The part of a neuron, usually corresponding to the axon terminals, at which the cell sends information to another cell. See Figure 2.5.

oval window The opening from the middle ear to the inner ear. See Figure 9.2.

ovaries The female gonads, which produce eggs for reproduction. See Figures 5.1, 12.8, 12.14; Table 5.2.

overt attention Attention in which the focus coincides with sensory orientation (e.g., you're attending to the same thing you're looking at). Compare *covert attention*.

oviparous Of or relating to oviparity, reproduction through egg laying. Compare *viviparous* and *ovoviviparous*.

ovoviviparous Of or relating to ovoviviparity, reproduction in which eggs remain inside the mother's body until they hatch or are about to hatch. Compare *oviparous* and *viviparous*.

ovulation The production and release of an egg (ovum).

ovulatory cycle The periodic occurrence of ovulation. See Figure 12.5.

ovum (pl. ova) An egg, the female gamete.

oxytocin A hormone, released from the posterior pituitary, that triggers milk letdown in the nursing female. See Figures 5.11, 5.12; Table 5.2.

P

P1 effect A positive deflection of the event-related potential, occurring 70–100 ms after stimulus presentation, that is enhanced for selectively attended visual input compared to ignored input.

P20–50 effect A positive deflection of the event-related potential, occurring about 20–50 ms after stimulus presentation, that is enhanced for selectively attended input compared to ignored input.

P3 effect Also called *auditory P300*. A positive deflection of the event-related potential, occurring about 300 ms after stimulus presentation, that is associated with higher-order auditory stimulus processing and late attentional selection.

Pacinian corpuscle A skin receptor cell type that detects vibration. See Figures 8.4, 8.5, 8.13.

pain The discomfort normally associated with tissue damage.

pair bond A durable and exclusive relationship between a male and a female.

paleocortex See *allocortex*.

pancreas An endocrine gland, located near the posterior wall of the abdominal cavity, that secretes insulin and glucagon. See Figure 5.1; Table 5.2.

Papez circuit A group of brain regions within the limbic system.

papilla (pl. papillae) A small bump that projects from the surface of the tongue. Papillae contain most of the taste receptor cells. See Figure 9.18.

parabiotic Referring to a surgical preparation that joins two animals to share a single blood supply.

paracrine Referring to cellular communication in which a chemical signal diffuses to nearby target cells through the intermediate extracellular space. See Figure 5.3. Compare *autocrine*.

paradoxical sleep See *rapid-eye-movement sleep*.

paragigantocellular nucleus (PGN) A region of the brainstem reticular formation implicated in sleep and modulation of spinal reflexes.

parallel fiber One of the axons of the granule cells that form the outermost layer of the cerebellar cortex. See Figure 2.16.

paraphasia A symptom of aphasia that is distinguished by the substitution of a word by a sound, an incorrect word, an unintended word, or a neologism (a meaningless word).

parasympathetic nervous system A component of the autonomic nervous system that arises from both the cranial nerves and the sacral spinal cord. Compare *sympathetic nervous system*. See Figure 2.11.

paraventricular nucleus (PVN) A nucleus of the hypothalamus. See Figures 5.11, 13.22.

parental behavior Behavior of adult animals with the goal of enhancing the well-being of their own offspring, often at some cost to the parents.

paresis Partial paralysis. Compare *plegia*.

parietal lobes Large regions of cortex lying between the frontal and occipital lobes of each cerebral hemisphere. See Figure 2.12.

parkin A protein that has been implicated in Parkinson's disease.

Parkinson's disease A degenerative neurological disorder, characterized by tremors at rest, muscular rigidity, and reduction in voluntary movement, that involves dopaminergic neurons of the substantia nigra.

parthenogenesis Literally, "virgin birth." The production of offspring without the contribution of a male or sperm.

partial agonist A drug that, when bound to a receptor, has less effect than the endogenous ligand would. The term *partial antagonist* is equivalent. See Figure 4.7.

parvocellular Of or consisting of relatively small cells. Compare *magnocellular*.

patient H.M. A patient who, because of damage to medial temporal lobe structures, was unable to encode new declarative memories. Upon his death we learned his name was Henry Molaison. See Figure 17.1.

patient K.C. A patient who sustained damage to the cortex that renders him unable to form and retrieve new episodic memories, especially autobiographical memories.

patient N.A. A patient who is unable to encode new declarative memories, because of damage to the dorsal thalamus and the mammillary bodies.

pattern coding Coding of information in sensory systems based on the temporal pattern of action potentials.

Pavlovian conditioning See *classical conditioning*.

PCP See *phencyclidine*.

PCR See *polymerase chain reaction*.

peg See *blob*.

peptide A short string of amino acids. Longer strings of amino acids are called *proteins*.

peptide hormones See *protein hormones*.

peptide neurotransmitter Also called *neuropeptide*. A neurotransmitter consisting of a short chain of amino acids. See Table 4.1.

perceptual load The immediate processing challenge presented by a stimulus.

periaqueductal gray The neuronal body–rich region of the midbrain surrounding the cerebral aqueduct that connects the third and fourth ventricles; involved in pain perception.

period The interval of time between two similar points of successive cycles, such as sunset to sunset.

peripheral nervous system The portion of the nervous system that includes all the nerves and neurons outside the brain and spinal cord. See Figures 2.8, 2.14. Compare *central nervous system*.

peripheral spatial cuing task A task that tests exogenous attention, using latency to detect a visual stimulus, preceded by a simple task-irrelevant sensory stimulus in the location where the stimulus will appear. Compare *symbolic cuing task*.

perseverate To continue to show a behavior repeatedly.

PET See *positron emission tomography*.

petit mal seizure Also called *absence attack*. A seizure that is characterized by a spike-and-wave EEG and often involves a loss of awareness and inability to recall events surrounding the seizure. See Box 3.3. Compare *grand mal seizure*.

PGN See *paragigantocellular nucleus*.

phagocyte An immune system cell that engulfs invading molecules or microbes.

phallus The clitoris or penis.

pharmacodynamics Collective name for the factors that affect the relationship between a drug and its target receptors, such as affinity and efficacy.

pharmacokinetics Collective name for all the factors that affect the movement of a drug into, through, and out of the body.

phase shift A shift in the activity of a biological rhythm, typically provided by a synchronizing environmental stimulus.

phasic receptor A receptor in which the frequency of action potentials drops rapidly as stimulation is maintained. Compare *tonic receptor*.

phencyclidine (PCP) Also called *angel dust*. An anesthetic agent that is also a psychedelic drug. PCP makes many people feel dissociated from themselves and their environment.

phenothiazines A class of antipsychotic drugs that reduce the positive symptoms of schizophrenia.

phenotype The sum of an individual's physical characteristics at one particular time. Compare *genotype*.

phenotype matching In general, processes by which an individual can assess the genetic relatedness of another individual on the basis of shared traits.

phenylketonuria (PKU) An inherited disorder of protein metabolism in which the absence of an enzyme leads to a toxic buildup of certain compounds, causing intellectual disability.

pheromone A chemical signal that is released outside the body of an animal and affects other members of the same species. See Figure 5.3. Compare *allomone*.

phobic disorder An intense, irrational fear that becomes centered on a specific object, activity, or situation that a person feels compelled to avoid.

phoneme A sound that is produced for language.

phosphoinositides A class of common second-messenger compounds in postsynaptic cells.

photon A quantum of light energy.

photopic system A system in the retina that operates at high levels of light, shows sensitivity to color, and involves the cones. See Table 10.1. Compare *scotopic system*.

photoreceptor adaptation The tendency of rods and cones to adjust their light sensitivity to match ambient levels of illumination.

photoreceptors Neural cells in the retina that respond to light.

phrenology The belief that bumps on the skull reflect enlargements of brain regions responsible for certain behavioral faculties. See Figure 1.11.

phylogeny The evolutionary history of a particular group of organisms. See Figure 6.4.

pia mater The innermost of the three meninges that surround the brain and spinal cord. See also *dura mater* and *arachnoid*.

pineal gland A secretory gland in the brain midline; the source of melatonin release. See Figures 2.12, 5.1; Table 5.2.

pinna (pl. pinnae) The external part of the ear.

pinocytosis The process by which synaptic neurotransmitter is repackaged into synaptic vesicles. See Figure 3.12.

pitch A dimension of auditory experience in which sounds vary from low to high.

pituitary gland Also called *hypophysis*. A small, complex endocrine gland located in a socket at the base of the skull. The anterior pituitary and posterior pituitary are separate in function. See Figures 2.12, 5.11, 5.14, 5.15.

pituitary stalk Also called *infundibulum*. A thin piece of tissue that connects the pituitary gland to the hypothalamus.

PKU See *phenylketonuria*.

place cell A neuron within the hippocampus that selectively fires when the animal is in a particular location.

place theory A theory of frequency discrimination stating that pitch perception depends on the place of maximal displacement of the basilar membrane produced by a sound. Compare *volley theory*.

placebo A substance, given to a patient, that is known to be ineffective or inert but that sometimes brings relief.

planum temporale A region of superior temporal cortex adjacent to the primary auditory area. See Figure 19.17.

plegia Paralysis, the loss of the ability to move. Compare *paresis*.

polioviruses A class of viruses that destroy motoneurons of the spinal cord and brainstem.

polyandry A mating system in which one female mates with more than one male. Compare *polygyny*.

polygamy A mating system in which an individual mates with more than one other animal. Compare *monogamy* and *bigamy*.

polygraph Popularly known as a *lie detector*. A device that measures several bodily responses, such as heart rate and blood pressure.

polygyny A mating system in which one male mates with more than one female. Compare *polyandry*.

polymerase chain reaction (PCR) Also called *gene amplification*. A method for reproducing a particular RNA or DNA sequence manyfold, allowing amplification for sequencing or manipulating the sequence.

polymodal Also called *multisensory*. Involving several sensory modalities.

POMC See *pro-opiomelanocortin*.

POMC/CART neurons Neurons involved in the hypothalamic appetite control system, so named because they produce both pro-opiomelanocortin and cocaine- and amphetamine-related transcript. Compare *NPY/AgRP neurons*.

pons A portion of the metencephalon; part of the brainstem connecting midbrain to medulla. See Figures 2.12, 2.14.

positive feedback The property by which some of the output of a system feeds back to increase the effect of input signals. Positive feedback is rare in biological systems. Compare *negative feedback*.

positive symptom In psychiatry, an abnormal state. Examples include hallucinations, delusions, and excited motor behavior. Compare *negative symptom*.

positron emission tomography (PET) A technique for examining brain function by combining tomography with injections of radioactive substances used by the brain. Analysis of the metabolism of these substances reflects regional differences in brain activity. See Figure 2.21.

postcentral gyrus The strip of parietal cortex, just behind the central sulcus, that receives somatosensory information from the entire body. See Figure 2.12. Compare *precentral gyrus*.

postcopulatory behavior The final stage in mating behavior. Species-specific postcopulatory behaviors include rolling (in the cat) and grooming (in the rat). See Figure 12.1.

posterior Also called *caudal*. In anatomy, toward the tail end of an organism. See Box 2.2. Compare *anterior*.

posterior cerebral arteries Two large arteries, arising from the basilar artery, that provide blood to posterior aspects of the cerebral hemispheres, cerebellum, and brainstem.

posterior pituitary Also called *neurohypophysis*. The rear division of the pituitary gland. See Figures 5.1, 5.11; Table 5.2. Compare *anterior pituitary*.

postganglionic Literally, "after the ganglion." Referring to neurons in the autonomic nervous system that run from the autonomic ganglia to various targets in the body. See Figure 2.11. Compare *preganglionic*.

postpartum depression A bout of depression that afflicts a woman either immediately before or after giving birth.

postsynaptic Referring to the region of a synapse that receives and responds to neurotransmitter. See Figure 2.7. Compare *presynaptic*.

postsynaptic membrane The specialized membrane on the surface of the cell that receives information from a presynaptic neuron. This membrane contains specialized receptor proteins that allow it to respond to neurotransmitter molecules. Compare *presynaptic membrane*. See Figure 2.7.

postsynaptic potential A local potential that is initiated by stimulation at a synapse, can vary in amplitude, and spreads passively across the cell membrane, decreasing in strength with time and distance. Compare *all-or-none property*.

posttraumatic stress disorder (PTSD) Formerly called *combat fatigue*, *war neu-rosis*, or *shell shock*. A disorder in which memories of an unpleasant episode repeatedly plague the victim.

potassium ion (K⁺) A potassium atom that carries a positive charge because it has lost one electron.

precentral gyrus The strip of frontal cortex, just in front of the central sulcus, that is crucial for motor control. See Figure 2.12. Compare *postcentral gyrus*.

precocial Referring to animals that are born in a relatively developed state and that are able to survive without maternal care. Compare *altricial*.

prefrontal cortex The anteriormost region of the frontal lobe.

preganglionic Literally, "before the ganglion." Referring to neurons in the autonomic nervous system that run from the central nervous system to the autonomic ganglia. See Figure 2.11. Compare *postganglionic*.

premotor cortex A region of nonprimary motor cortex just anterior to the primary motor cortex. See Figure 11.16.

presenilin An enzyme that cleaves amyloid precursor protein, forming β-amyloid, which can lead to Alzheimer's disease. See also *β secretase*.

presynaptic Referring to the region of a synapse that releases neurotransmitter. See Figure 2.7. Compare *postsynaptic*.

presynaptic membrane The specialized membrane of the axon terminal of the neuron that transmits information by releasing neurotransmitter. Vesicles bearing neurotransmitter can bind to this membrane and release their contents, thus affecting the *postsynaptic membrane*. See Figure 2.7.

primacy effect The superior performance seen in a memory task for items at the start of a list; usually attributed to long-term memory. Compare *recency effect*.

primary motor cortex (M1) The apparent executive region for the initiation of movement; primarily the precentral gyrus.

primary sensory cortex For a given sensory modality, the region of cortex that receives most of the information about that modality from the thalamus or, in the case of olfaction, directly from the secondary sensory neurons. Compare *secondary sensory cortex*.

primary sensory ending Also called *annulospiral ending*. The axon that transmits information from the central portion of a muscle spindle. See Figure 11.9. Compare *secondary sensory ending*.

primary somatosensory cortex (S1) Also called *somatosensory 1*. The gyrus just posterior to the central sulcus where sensory receptors on the body surface are mapped. Primary cortex for receiv-ing touch and pain information, in the parietal lobe. See Figures 8.10, 8.15. Compare *secondary somatosensory cortex*.

primary visual cortex (V1) Also called *striate cortex* or *area 17*. The region of the occipital cortex where most visual information first arrives. See Figures 10.11, 10.12, 10.19.

priming Also called *repetition priming*. In memory, the phenomenon by which exposure to a stimulus facilitates subsequent responses to the same or a similar stimulus.

prion A protein that can become improperly folded and thereby can induce other proteins to follow suit, leading to long protein chains that impair neural function.

probe Here, a manufactured sequence of DNA that is made to include a label (a colorful or radioactive molecule) that lets us track its location.

procedural memory See *nondeclarative memory*.

proceptive Referring to a state in which an animal advertises its readiness to mate through species-typical behaviors, such as ear wiggling in the female rat.

process outgrowth The extensive growth of axons and dendrites.

progesterone The primary type of progestin secreted by the ovary. See Figure 5.19; Table 5.2.

progestins A major class of steroid hormones that are produced by the ovary, including progesterone. See Figure 5.15, 5.19; Table 5.2.

progressive supranuclear palsy (PSP) A rare, degenerative disease of the brain that begins with marked, persistent visual symptoms and leads to more widespread intellectual deterioration.

prolactin A protein hormone, produced by the anterior pituitary, that promotes mammary development for lactation in female mammals. See Table 5.2; Figure 5.15.

promiscuity A mating system in which animals mate with several members of the opposite sex and do not establish durable associations with sex partners.

pro-opiomelanocortin (POMC) A prohormone that can be cleaved to produce the melanocortins, which also participate in feeding control. See Figure 13.26.

proprioception Body sense; information about the position and movement of the body that is sent to the brain.

prosencephalon See *forebrain*.

prosody The perception of emotional tone-of-voice aspects of language.

prosopagnosia Also called *face blindness*. A condition characterized by the inability to recognize faces. *Acquired* *prosopagnosia* is caused by damage to the brain, particularly the fusiform gyrus. *Developmental* (or *congenital*) *prosopagnosia* is the result of brain defects present from birth.

protein A long string of amino acids. The basic building material of organisms. Compare *peptide*.

protein hormones Also called *peptide hormones*. A class of hormones, molecules of which consist of a string of amino acids.

protein kinase An enzyme that adds phosphate groups (PO_4) to protein molecules.

proximal In anatomy, near the trunk or center of an organism. See Box 2.2. Compare *distal*.

PSP See *progressive supranuclear palsy*.

psychoneuroimmunology The study of the immune system and its interaction with the nervous system and behavior.

psychopath An individual incapable of experiencing remorse.

psychopharmacology See *neuropharmacology*.

psychosocial dwarfism Reduced stature caused by stress early in life that inhibits deep sleep. See Box 5.2.

psychosomatic medicine A field of study that emphasizes the role of psychological factors in disease.

psychosurgery Surgery in which brain lesions are produced to modify severe psychiatric disorders.

psychotomimetic A drug that induces a state resembling schizophrenia.

PTSD See *posttraumatic stress disorder*.

pulvinar In humans, the posterior portion of the thalamus, heavily involved in visual processing and direction of attention.

punch-drunk See *chronic traumatic encephalopathy*.

pupil The aperture, formed by the iris, that allows light to enter the eye. See Figure 10.11.

pure tone A tone with a single frequency of vibration. See Box 9.1.

Purkinje cell A type of large nerve cell in the cerebellar cortex. See Figure 2.16.

putamen One of the basal ganglia. See Figure 2.15.

PVN See *paraventricular nucleus*.

pyramidal cell A type of large nerve cell that has a roughly pyramid-shaped cell body. Pyramidal cells are found in the cerebral cortex. See Figure 2.17.

pyramidal system Also called *corticospinal system*. The motor system that includes neurons within the cerebral cortex and their axons, which form the pyramidal tract. See Figure 11.12.

PYY$_{3-36}$ A peptide hormone, secreted by the intestines, that probably acts on hypothalamic appetite control mechanisms to suppress appetite.

Q

qat See *khat*.

quale (pl. qualia) A purely subjective experience of perception.

quantum (pl. quanta) A unit of radiant energy.

R

radial glial cells Glial cells that form early in development, spanning the width of the emerging cerebral hemispheres, and guide migrating neurons. See Figure 7.5.

radioimmunoassay (RIA) A technique that uses antibodies to measure the concentration of a substance, such as a hormone, in blood. See Box 5.1.

ramp movement Also called *smooth movement*. A slow, sustained motion that is often controlled by the basal ganglia. Compare *ballistic movement*.

range fractionation A hypothesis of stimulus intensity perception stating that a wide range of intensity values can be encoded by a group of cells, each of which is a specialist for a particular range of stimulus intensities. See Figure 8.6.

raphe nuclei A string of nuclei in the midline of the midbrain and brainstem that contain most of the serotonergic neurons of the brain.

rapid-eye-movement (REM) sleep Also called *paradoxical sleep*. A stage of sleep characterized by small-amplitude, fast-EEG waves, no postural tension, and rapid eye movements. REM rhymes with "gem." See Figure 14.11. Compare *slow-wave sleep*.

RBD See *REM behavior disorder*.

recency effect The superior performance seen in a memory task for items at the end of a list; attributed to short-term memory. Compare *primacy effect*.

receptive field The stimulus region and features that affect the activity of a cell in a sensory system. See Figures 8.9, 10.14, 10.16.

receptor 1. The initial element in a sensory system, responsible for stimulus transduction. Examples include the hair cells in the cochlea, and the rods and cones in the retina. 2. Also called *receptor molecule*. A protein that captures and reacts to molecules of a neurotransmitter or hormone.

receptor cell A specialized cell that responds to a particular energy or substance in the internal or external environment, and converts this energy into a change in the electrical potential across its membrane.

receptor isoform A version of a receptor protein (in this context, a hormone receptor) with slight differences in structure that give it different functional properties. Conceptually similar to a receptor subtype.

receptor molecule See *receptor* (definition 2).

receptor subtype Any type of receptor having functional characteristics that distinguish it from other types of receptors for the same neurotransmitter. For example, at least 15 different subtypes of receptor molecules respond to serotonin.

reconsolidation The return of a memory trace to stable long-term storage after it has been temporarily made volatile during the process of recall.

recovery of function The recovery of behavioral capacity following brain damage from stroke or injury.

red nucleus A brainstem structure related to motor control.

reductionism The scientific strategy of breaking a system down into increasingly smaller parts in order to understand it.

redundancy The property of having a particular process, usually an important one, monitored and regulated by more than one mechanism.

reflex A simple, highly stereotyped, and unlearned response to a particular stimulus (e.g., an eye blink in response to a puff of air). See Figures 3.17, 11.10.

reflexive attention See *endogenous attention*.

refraction The bending of light rays by a change in the density of a medium, such as the cornea and the lens of the eyes.

refractory Transiently inactivated or exhausted.

refractory phase 1. A period during and after a nerve impulse in which the responsiveness of the axonal membrane is reduced. A brief period of complete insensitivity to stimuli (*absolute refractory phase*) is followed by a longer period of reduced sensitivity (*relative refractory phase*) during which only strong stimulation produces an action potential. 2. A period following copulation during which an individual cannot recommence copulation. The absolute refractory phase of the male sexual response is illustrated in Figure 12.9.

regulation An adaptive response to early injury, as when developing individuals compensate for missing or injured cells.

reinforcing stimulus See *instrumental conditioning*.

relative refractory phase See *refractory phase* (definition 1).

releasing hormones A class of hormones, produced in the hypothalamus, that traverse the hypothalamic-pituitary portal system to control the pituitary's release of tropic hormones. See Figure 5.15.

REM behavior disorder (RBD) A sleep disorder in which a person physically acts out a dream.

REM sleep See *rapid-eye-movement sleep*.

repetition priming See *priming*.

repetitive transcranial magnetic stimulation (rTMS) See *transcranial magnetic stimulation*.

reserpine A drug that causes the depletion of monoamines and can lead to depression.

resting membrane potential A difference in electrical potential across the membrane of a nerve cell during an inactive period. See Figures 3.1, 3.5.

reticular formation An extensive region of the brainstem (extending from the medulla through the thalamus) that is involved in arousal (waking). See Figure 14.26.

reticulospinal tract A tract of axons arising from the brainstem reticular formation and descending to the spinal cord to modulate movement. Compare *rubrospinal tract*.

retina The receptive surface inside the eye that contains photoreceptors and other neurons. See Figures 10.5, 10.6.

RETINAL One of the two components of photopigments in the retina. The other component is opsin. (The term is printed in small capital letters in this text to distinguish it from the adjective *retinal*, meaning "pertaining to the retina.")

retinohypothalamic pathway The projection of retinal ganglion cells to the suprachiasmatic nuclei.

retrieval A process in memory during which a stored memory is used by an organism. See Figure 17.7.

retrograde amnesia Difficulty in retrieving memories formed before the onset of amnesia. Compare *anterograde amnesia*.

retrograde degeneration Destruction of the nerve cell body following injury to its axon. See Box 7.1. Compare *anterograde degeneration*.

retrograde messenger Transmitter that is released by the postsynaptic region, nd travels back across the synapse, and alters the functioning of the presynaptic neuron.

retrograde synapse A synapse in which a signal (usually a gas neurotransmitter) flows from the postsynaptic neuron to the presynaptic neuron, thus counter

to the usual direction of synaptic communication.

retrograde transmitter A neurotransmitter that diffuses from the postsynaptic neuron back to the presynaptic neuron.

retrograde transport Movement of cellular substances toward the cell body from the axon terminals. Compare *anterograde transport*.

reuptake The process by which released synaptic transmitter molecules are taken up and reused by the presynaptic neuron, thus stopping synaptic activity.

rhodopsin The photopigment in rods that responds to light.

rhombencephalon See *hindbrain*.

RIA See *radioimmunoassay*.

ribonucleic acid (RNA) A nucleic acid that implements information found in DNA. Compare *deoxyribonucleic acid*.

ribosomes Structures in the cell body where genetic information is translated to produce proteins.

RNA See *ribonucleic acid*.

rods A class of light-sensitive receptor cells (photoreceptors) in the retina that are most active at low levels of light. See Figure 10.6. Compare *cones*.

roots The two distinct branches of a spinal nerve, each of which serves a separate function. The *dorsal root* enters the dorsal horn of the spinal cord and carries sensory information from the peripheral nervous system to the spinal cord. The *ventral root* arises from the ventral horn of the spinal cord and carries motor messages from the spinal cord to the peripheral nervous system. See Figure 2.10.

rostral See *anterior*.

round window A membrane separating the cochlear duct from the middle-ear cavity. See Figure 9.2.

rTMS See *transcranial magnetic stimulation*.

rubrospinal tract A tract of axons arising from the red nucleus in the midbrain and innervating neurons of the spinal cord. See Figure 11.17. Compare *reticulospinal tract*.

Ruffini's ending A skin receptor cell type that detects stretching of the skin. See Figures 8.4, 8.13.

S

S1 See *primary somatosensory cortex*.

S2 See *secondary somatosensory cortex*.

saccule A small, fluid-filled sac under the utricle in the vestibular system that responds to static positions of the head. See Figure 9.16.

sacral Referring to the five spinal segments that make up the lower part of the lower back. See Figures 2.10, 2.11.

SAD See *seasonal affective disorder*.

sagittal plane The plane that bisects the body or brain into right and left portions. See Box 2.2. Compare *coronal plane* and *horizontal plane*.

saltatory conduction The form of conduction that is characteristic of myelinated axons, in which the action potential jumps from one node of Ranvier to the next.

satiety A feeling of fulfillment or satisfaction. Compare *hunger*.

saturation One of three basic dimensions (along with brightness and hue) of light perception. Saturation varies from rich to pale (e.g., from red to pink to gray in the color solid of Figure 10.23).

saturated Referring to the condition in which a maximal number of receptors of one type have been bound by molecules of a drug; additional doses of drug cannot produce additional binding.

saxitoxin (STX) An animal toxin that blocks sodium channels when applied to the outer surface of the cell membrane.

SC See *standard condition*.

scala media Also called *middle canal*. The central of the three spiraling canals inside the cochlea, situated between the scala vestibuli and scala tympani. See Figure 9.2.

scala tympani Also called *tympanic canal*. One of three principal canals running along the length of the cochlea. The other two are the scala media and scala vestibuli. See Figure 9.2.

scala vestibuli Also called *vestibular canal*. One of three principal canals running along the length of the cochlea. The other two are the scala media and scala tympani. See Figure 9.2.

schizophrenia A severe psychopathology characterized by negative symptoms such as emotional withdrawal and impoverished thought, and by positive symptoms such as hallucinations and delusions.

Schwann cell The glial cell that forms myelin in the peripheral nervous system.

SCN See *suprachiasmatic nucleus*.

scotoma A region of blindness caused by injury to the visual pathway or brain.

scotopic system A system in the retina that operates at low levels of light and involves the rods. See Table 10.1. Compare *photopic system*.

SDN-POA See *sexually dimorphic nucleus of the preoptic area*.

seasonal affective disorder (SAD) A putative depression brought about by the short days of winter.

second messenger A slow-acting substance in the postsynaptic cell that amplifies the effects of synaptic activity and signals synaptic activity within the postsynaptic cell.

secondary sensory cortex Also called *nonprimary sensory cortex*. For a given sensory modality, the cortical regions receiving direct projections from primary sensory cortex for that modality. Compare *primary sensory cortex*.

secondary sensory ending Also called *flower spray ending*. The axon that transmits information from the ends of a muscle spindle. Compare *primary sensory ending*.

secondary somatosensory cortex (S2) Also called *somatosensory 2*. The region of cortex that receives direct projections from primary somatosensory cortex. See Figure 8.12. Compare *primary somatosensory cortex*.

seizure An epileptic episode. See Box 3.3.

selective attention See *attention*.

selective permeability The property of a membrane that allows some substances to pass through, but not others.

selective serotonin reuptake inhibitor (SSRI) A drug that blocks the reuptake of transmitter at serotonergic synapses; commonly used to treat depression.

semantic memory Generalized memory—for instance, knowing the meaning of a word without knowing where or when you learned that word.

semantics The meanings or interpretation of words and sentences in a language.

semen A mixture of fluid, including sperm, that is released during ejaculation.

semicircular canal One of the three fluid-filled tubes in the inner ear that are part of the vestibular system. Each of the tubes, which are at right angles to each other, detects angular acceleration. See Figure 9.16.

senile dementia A neurological disorder of the aged that is characterized by progressive behavioral deterioration, including personality change and profound intellectual decline. It includes, but is not limited to, Alzheimer's disease.

senile plaques Also called *amyloid plaques*. Senile plaques are small areas of the brain that have abnormal cellular and chemical patterns. Senile plaques correlate with senile dementia. See Figure 7.28.

sensitive period The period during development in which an organism can be permanently altered by a particular experience or treatment.

sensitization 1. A form of nonassociative learning in which an organism becomes more responsive to most stimuli after being exposed to unusually strong or painful stimulation. See Box 17.1. Compare *habituation*. 2. A process in which the body shows an enhanced response to a given drug after repeated doses. Compare *tolerance*.

sensorineural deafness A hearing impairment that originates from cochlear or auditory nerve lesions. Compare *central deafness* and *conduction deafness*.

sensory conflict theory A theory of motion sickness suggesting that discrepancies between vestibular information and visual information simulate food poisoning and therefore trigger nausea.

sensory neuron A neuron that is directly affected by changes in the environment, such as light, odor, or touch.

sensory pathway The chain of neural connections from sensory receptor cells to the cortex.

sensory receptor organ An organ specialized to receive particular stimuli. Examples include the eye and the ear.

sensory transduction The process in which a receptor cell converts the energy in a stimulus into a change in the electrical potential across its membrane.

septal complex A brain region that provides subcortical input to the hippocampal formation.

sequential hermaphrodites Species in which individuals may be exclusively of one sex, and then switch to the other sex. Compare *simultaneous hermaphrodites*.

serotonergic Referring to neurons that use serotonin as their synaptic transmitter.

serotonin (5-HT) A synaptic transmitter that is produced in the raphe nuclei and is active in structures throughout the cerebral hemispheres. See Table 4.1; Figure 4.5.

set point The point of reference in a feedback system. An example is the setting of a thermostat.

set zone The range of a variable that a feedback system tries to maintain.

sex determination The process by which the decision is made for a fetus to develop as a male or a female. In mammals this is under genetic control, but in some groups of animals, environmental variables like incubation temperature determine the sex of the offspring.

sex-determining region on the Y chromosome See *SRY gene*.

sex steroids Steroid hormones secreted by the gonads: androgens, estrogens, and progestins.

sexual attraction The first step in the mating behavior of many animals, in which animals emit stimuli that attract members of the opposite sex. See Figure 12.1.

sexual differentiation The process by which individuals develop either male-like or femalelike bodies and behavior.

sexual dimorphism The condition in which males and females show pronounced sex differences in appearance.

sexual selection Darwin's theoretical mechanism for the evolution of anatomical and behavioral differences between males and females.

sexually dimorphic nucleus of the preoptic area (SDN-POA) A region of the preoptic area that is five to six times larger in volume in male rats than in females. See Figure 12.18.

sexually receptive Referring to the state in which an individual (in mammals, typically the female) is willing to copulate. In many species, no sexual activity is possible other than during the period of sexual receptivity in the female, which generally corresponds to ovulation.

shadowing A task in which the subject is asked to focus attention on one ear or the other while stimuli are being presented separately to both ears, and to repeat aloud the material presented to the attended ear.

sham rage See *decorticate rage*.

shell shock See *posttraumatic stress disorder*.

shivering Rapid involuntary muscle contractions that generate heat in hypothermic animals.

short-term memory (STM) A form of memory that usually lasts only for seconds, or as long as rehearsal continues. Compare *iconic memory*.

SIDS See *sudden infant death syndrome*.

simple cortical cell Also called *bar detector* or *edge detector*. A cell in the visual cortex that responds best to an edge or a bar that has a particular width, as well as a particular orientation and location in the visual field. Compare *complex cortical cell*.

simultagnosia A profound restriction of attention, often limited to a single item or feature.

simultaneous hermaphrodites Species in which individuals have both male and female reproductive organs at the same time. Compare *sequential hermaphrodites*.

site-directed mutagenesis A technique in molecular biology that changes the sequence of nucleotides in an existing gene.

size principle The idea that, as increasing numbers of motor neurons are recruited to produce muscle responses of increasing strength, small, low-threshold neurons are recruited first, followed by large, high-threshold neurons.

skill learning Learning to perform a task that requires motor coordination.

sleep apnea A sleep disorder in which respiration slows or stops periodically, waking the patient. Excessive daytime somnolence results from the frequent nocturnal awakening.

sleep cycle A period of slow-wave sleep followed by a period of REM sleep. In humans, a sleep cycle lasts 90–110 minutes.

sleep deprivation The partial or total prevention of sleep.

sleep enuresis Bed-wetting.

sleep-maintenance insomnia Difficulty in staying asleep. Compare *sleep-onset insomnia*.

sleep-onset insomnia Difficulty in falling sleep. Compare *sleep-maintenance insomnia*.

sleep paralysis A state during the transition to or from sleep, in which the ability to move or talk is temporarily lost.

sleep recovery The process of sleeping more than normally after a period of sleep deprivation, as though in compensation.

sleep spindle A characteristic 14- to 18-Hz wave in the EEG of a person said to be in stage 2 sleep. See Figure 14.11.

sleep state misperception Commonly, a person's perception that he has not been asleep when in fact he was. Typically occurs at the start of a sleep episode.

slow-twitch muscle fiber A type of striated muscle fiber that contracts slowly but does not fatigue readily. Compare *fast-twitch muscle fiber*.

slow-wave sleep (SWS) Sleep, divided into stages 1–4, that is defined by the presence of slow-wave EEG activity. See Figure 14.11. Compare *rapid-eye-movement (REM) sleep*.

SMA See *supplementary motor area*.

smooth movement See *ramp movement*.

smooth muscle A type of muscle fiber, as in the heart, that is controlled by the autonomic nervous system rather than by voluntary control. Compare *striated muscle*.

SNB See *spinal nucleus of the bulbocavernosus*.

SOAE See *spontaneous otoacoustic emission*.

sodium ion (Na⁺) A sodium atom that carries a positive charge because it has lost one electron.

sodium-potassium pump The energetically expensive mechanism that pushes sodium ions out of a cell, and potassium ions in.

solute A solid compound that is dissolved in a liquid. Compare *solvent*.

solvent The liquid (often water) in which a compound is dissolved. Compare *solute*.

soma (pl. somata) See *cell body*.

somatic intervention An approach to finding relations between body variables and behavioral variables that involves manipulating body structure or function and looking for resultant changes in behavior. See Figure 1.2. Compare *behavioral intervention*.

somatic nerve See *spinal nerve*.

somatomedins A group of proteins, released from the liver in response to growth hormone, that aid body growth and maintenance.

somatosensory Referring to body sensation, particularly touch and pain sensation.

somatosensory 1 See *primary somatosensory cortex*.

somatosensory 2 See *secondary somatosensory cortex*.

somatotropic hormone See *growth hormone*.

somatotropin See *growth hormone*.

somnambulism Sleepwalking.

Southern blot A method of detecting a particular DNA sequence in the genome of an organism, by separating DNA with gel electrophoresis, blotting the separated DNAs onto nitrocellulose, and then using a nucleotide probe to hybridize with, and highlight, the gene of interest. See Appendix Figure A.3. Compare *Northern blot* and *Western blot*.

spasticity Markedly increased rigidity in response to forced movement of the limbs.

spatial-frequency filter model A model of pattern analysis that emphasizes Fourier analysis of visual stimuli. Compare *feature detector model*.

spatial resolution The ability to observe the detailed structure of the brain. Compare *temporal resolution*.

spatial summation The summation at the axon hillock of postsynaptic potentials from across the cell body. If this summation reaches threshold, an action potential is triggered. See Figure 3.10. Compare *temporal summation*.

species A group of individuals that can readily interbreed to produce fertile offspring. Individuals of different species produce either no offspring or infertile offspring. See Figure 6.3.

specific nerve energies The doctrine that the receptors and neural channels for the different senses are independent and operate in their own special ways,

and can produce only one particular sensation each.

spectral filtering Alteration of the amplitude of some, but not all, frequencies in a sound. When performed by the irregular shapes of the external ear, this process is a source of information that assists in the localization of sound sources.

spectrally opponent cell A visual receptor cell that has opposite firing responses to different regions of the spectrum. See Figures 10.25, 10.26.

sperm The gamete produced by males for fertilization of eggs (ova).

sperm competition The selective pressure that males of promiscuous species exert on each other to produce gametes that can outcompete the sperm of other males, because sperm from multiple males may be present in the genital tract of a single female.

spinal animal An animal whose spinal cord has been surgically disconnected from the brain to enable the study of behaviors that do not require brain control.

spinal nerve Also called *somatic nerve*. A nerve that emerges from the spinal cord. There are 31 pairs of spinal nerves. See Figure 2.10.

spinal nucleus of the bulbocavernosus (SNB) A group of motoneurons in the spinal cord of rats that innervate striated muscles controlling the penis. See Figure 12.20. See also *Onuf's nucleus*.

spinocerebellum The uppermost part of the cerebellum, consisting mostly of the vermis and anterior lobe. It receives sensory information about the current spatial location of the parts of the body and anticipates subsequent movement. Compare *cerebrocerebellum* and *vestibulocerebellum*.

spinothalamic system See *anterolateral system*.

split-brain individual An individual whose corpus callosum has been severed, halting communication between the right and left hemispheres.

spontaneous otoacoustic emission (SOAE) A sound produced by the ears of many normal people. Compare *evoked otoacoustic emission*.

SRY gene A gene on the Y chromosome that directs the developing gonads to become testes. The name *SRY* stands for *sex-determining region on the Y chromosome*.

SSRI See *selective serotonin reuptake inhibitor*.

stage 1 sleep The initial stage of slow-wave sleep, which is characterized by small-amplitude EEG waves of irregular frequency, slow heart rate, and reduced muscle tension. See Figure 14.11.

stage 2 sleep A stage of slow-wave sleep that is defined by bursts of regular 14- to 18-Hz EEG waves called sleep spindles. See Figure 14.11.

stage 3 sleep A stage of slow-wave sleep that is defined by the spindles seen in stage 2 sleep, mixed with larger-amplitude slow waves. See Figure 14.11.

stage 4 sleep A stage of slow-wave sleep that is defined by the presence of delta waves at least half the time. See Figure 14.11.

standard condition (SC) The usual environment for laboratory rodents, with a few animals in a cage and adequate food and water, but no complex stimulation. See Figure 17.17. Compare *enriched condition* and *impoverished condition*.

stapedius A middle-ear muscle that is attached to the stapes. See Figure 9.2.

stapes Latin for "stirrup." A middle-ear bone that is connected to the oval window; one of the three ossicles that conduct sounds across the middle ear. See Figure 9.2.

stem cell A cell that is undifferentiated and therefore can take on the fate of any cell that a donor organism can produce.

stereocilium (pl. stereocilia) A relatively stiff hair that protrudes from a hair cell in the auditory or vestibular system. See Figure 9.2.

steroid hormones A class of hormones, each of which is composed of four interconnected rings of carbon atoms.

steroid receptor cofactors Proteins that affect the cell's response when a steroid hormone binds its receptor.

stimulus (pl. stimuli) A physical event that triggers a sensory response.

stimulus cuing A technique for testing reaction time to sensory stimuli in which a cue to the location in which the stimulus will be presented is provided before the stimulus itself.

STM See *short-term memory*.

stress Any circumstance that upsets homeostatic balance. Examples include exposure to extreme cold or heat or an array of threatening psychological states.

stress immunization The concept that mild stress early in life makes an individual better able to handle stress later in life.

stretch reflex The contraction of a muscle in response to stretch of that muscle. See Figure 11.10.

striate cortex See *primary visual cortex*.

striated muscle A type of muscle with a striped appearance, generally under voluntary control. Compare *smooth muscle*.

striatum The caudate nucleus and putamen together.

stroke Damage to a region of brain tissue that results from blockage or rupture of vessels that supply blood to that region.

STX See *saxitoxin*.

subcutaneous tissue See *hypodermis*.

subfornical organ One of the circumventricular organs. See Figure 13.14.

subicular complex See *subiculum*.

subiculum (pl. subicula) Also called *subicular complex* or *hippocampal gyrus*. A region adjacent to the hippocampus that contributes to the hippocampal formation. See Figure 17.21.

substance abuse A maladaptive pattern of substance use that has lasted more than a month but does not fully meet the criteria for dependence.

substance P A peptide transmitter implicated in pain transmission.

substantia nigra Literally, "black spot." A group of pigmented neurons in the midbrain that provides dopaminergic projections to areas of the forebrain, especially the basal ganglia.

sudden infant death syndrome (SIDS) Also called *crib death*. The sudden, unexpected death of an apparently healthy human infant who simply stops breathing, usually during sleep. SIDS is not well understood.

sulcus (pl. sulci) A furrow of a convoluted brain surface. See Figure 2.12. Compare *gyrus*.

superior colliculi (sing. colliculus) Paired gray matter structures of the dorsal midbrain that receive visual information and are involved in direction of visual gaze and visual attention to intended stimuli. See Figures 2.12, 10.11. Compare *inferior colliculi*.

superior olivary nuclei Brainstem nuclei that receive input from both right and left cochlear nuclei, and provide the first binaural analysis of auditory information. See Figure 9.7.

superordinate circuit Also called *modulatory circuit*. A neural circuit that is hierarchically superior to other, simple circuits.

supersensitivity psychosis An exaggerated psychosis that may emerge when doses of antipsychotic medication are reduced, probably as a consequence of the up-regulation of receptors that occurred during drug treatment.

supplementary motor area (SMA) A region of nonprimary motor cortex that receives input from the basal ganglia and modulates the activity of the primary motor cortex. See Figure 11.16.

suprachiasmatic nucleus (SCN) A small region of the hypothalamus above the optic chiasm that is the location of a circadian oscillator. See Figure 14.5.

surface dyslexia Acquired dyslexia in which the patient seems to attend only to the fine details of reading. Compare *deep dyslexia*.

sustained attention task A task in which a single stimulus source or location must be held in the attentional spotlight for a protracted period.

SWS See *slow-wave sleep*.

Sylvian fissure Also called *lateral sulcus*. A deep fissure that demarcates the temporal lobe. See Figure 2.12.

symbolic cuing task A task that tests endogenous attention by presenting a visual stimulus and asking subjects to respond as soon as the stimulus appears on a screen. Each trial is preceded by a meaningful symbol used as a cue to hint at where the stimulus will appear. Compare *peripheral spatial cuing task*.

sympathetic chain A chain of ganglia that runs along each side of the spinal column; part of the sympathetic nervous system. See Figure 2.11.

sympathetic nervous system A component of the autonomic nervous system that arises from the thoracic and lumbar spinal cord. Compare *parasympathetic nervous system*. See Figure 2.11.

synapse The cellular location at which information is transmitted from a neuron to another cell. See Figure 2.7.

synapse rearrangement Also called *synaptic remodeling*. The loss of some synapses and the development of others; a refinement of synaptic connections that is often seen in development. See Figure 7.13.

synaptic cleft The space between the presynaptic and postsynaptic elements. This gap measures about 20–40 nm. See Figures 2.7, 3.12.

synaptic delay The brief delay between the arrival of an action potential at the axon terminal and the creation of a postsynaptic potential. The delay is caused by the translation of an electrical event into a secretory event, and back to an electrical event on the postsynaptic side.

synaptic remodeling See *synapse rearrangement*.

synaptic transmitter See *neurotransmitter*.

synaptic vesicle A small, spherical structure that contains molecules of neurotransmitter. See Figure 2.7.

synaptogenesis The establishment of synaptic connections as axons and dendrites grow. See Figure 7.8.

synergist A muscle that acts together with another muscle. See also *agonist* (definition 2). Compare *antagonist* (definition 2).

synesthesia A condition in which stimuli in one modality evoke the involuntary experience of an additional sensation in another modality.

syntax The grammatical rules for constructing phrases and sentences in a language.

syrinx The vocal organ in birds.

T

T cell See *T lymphocyte*.

T lymphocyte Also called *T cell*. An immune system cell, formed in the thymus (hence the *T*), that attacks foreign microbes or tissue; "killer cell." See Figure 15.22. Compare *B lymphocyte*.

T1R A family of taste receptor proteins that, when particular members heterodimerize, form taste receptors for sweet flavors and umami flavors. Compare *T2R*.

T2R A family of bitter taste receptors. Compare *T1R*.

TAARs See *trace amine-associated receptors*.

tachistoscope test A test in which stimuli are very briefly exposed in either the left or right visual half-field.

tactile Of or relating to touch.

tardive dyskinesia A disorder characterized by involuntary movements, especially involving the face, mouth, lips, and tongue; related to prolonged use of antipsychotic drugs, such as chlorpromazine. See Box 16.1.

tastant A substance that can be tasted.

taste aversion The conditioned avoidance of a particular food due to a previous pairing between the taste of that food and physical illness.

taste bud A cluster of 50–150 cells that detects tastes. Taste buds are found in papillae. See Figure 9.19.

taste pore The small aperture through which tastant molecules are able to access the sensory receptors of the taste bud. See Figure 9.19.

tau 1. A protein associated with neurofibrillary tangles in Alzheimer's disease. 2. A mutation (*tau*) in hamsters that causes a shorter circadian period in free-running conditions.

tauopathy Any disease that is associated with abnormal accumulations of the protein Tau, forming neurofibrillary tangles that impair the normal function of neurons. Examples include Alzheimer's disease, progressive supranuclear palsy, and chronic traumatic encephalopathy (punch-drunk).

taxonomy The classification of organisms. See Figure 6.3.

tectorial membrane A membrane that sits atop the organ of Corti in the cochlear duct. See Figure 9.2.

tectum The dorsal portion of the midbrain, including the inferior and superior colliculi.

telencephalon The frontal subdivision of the forebrain that includes the cerebral hemispheres when fully developed. See Figure 2.14.

temporal lobes Large lateral cortical regions of each cerebral hemisphere, continuous with the parietal lobes posteriorly, and separated from the frontal lobe by the Sylvian fissure. The temporal lobes contain the hippocampus and amygdala, and are involved in a variety of functions, including memory, emotional processing, and the olfactory and auditory senses. See Figure 2.12.

temporal resolution The ability to track changes in the brain that occur very quickly. Compare *spatial resolution*.

temporal summation The summation of postsynaptic potentials that reach the axon hillock at different times. The closer in time that the potentials occur, the more complete the summation. Compare *spatial summation*.

temporoparietal junction (TPJ) The point in the brain where the temporal and parietal lobes meet; plays a role in shifting attention to a new location after target onset.

tendon Strong tissue that connects muscles to bone.

TENS See *transcutaneous electrical nerve stimulation*.

tensor tympani The muscle attached to the malleus that modulates mechanical linkage to protect the delicate receptor cells of the inner ear from damaging sounds. See Figure 9.2.

testes (sing. testis) The male gonads, which produce sperm and androgenic steroid hormones. See Figures 5.1, 12.8, 12.13; Table 5.2.

testosterone A hormone, produced by male gonads, that controls a variety of bodily changes that become visible at puberty. See Figures 5.15, 5.19; Table 5.2.

tetanus An intense volley of action potentials. See Figure 17.21.

tetrahydrocannabinol (THC) See *Δ9-tetrahydrocannabinol*.

tetraiodothyronine See *thyroid hormones*.

tetrodotoxin (TTX) A toxin from puffer fish ovaries that blocks the voltage-gated sodium channel, preventing action potential conduction.

thalamus (pl. thalami) The brain regions at the top of the brainstem that trade information with the cortex. See Figures 2.12, 2.14.

THC See *Δ9-tetrahydrocannabinol*.

therapeutic index The margin of safety for a given drug, expressed as the distance between effective doses and toxic doses. See Figure 4.8.

third ventricle The midline ventricle that conducts cerebrospinal fluid from the lateral ventricles to the fourth ventricle. See Figure 2.19.

thoracic Referring to the 12 spinal segments below the cervical (neck) portion of the spinal cord, corresponding to the chest. See Figures 2.10, 2.11.

threshold The stimulus intensity that is just adequate to trigger an action potential at the axon hillock.

thrombolytics A class of substances that are used to unblock blood vessels and restore circulation.

thyroid gland An endocrine gland, located in the throat, that regulates cellular metabolism throughout the body. See Figure 5.1; Table 5.2.

thyroid hormones Two hormones, triiodothyronine and thyroxine (also called tetraiodothyronine), released from the thyroid gland that have widespread effects, including growth and maintenance of the brain.

thyroid-stimulating hormone (TSH) A tropic hormone, released by the anterior pituitary gland, that signals the thyroid gland to secrete its hormones. See Figures 5.10, 5.15.

thyrotropin-releasing hormone (TRH) A hypothalamic hormone that regulates the release of thyroid-stimulating hormone from the anterior pituitary. See Figure 5.10.

thyroxine See *thyroid hormones*.

timbre The characteristic sound quality of a musical instrument, as determined by the relative intensities of its various harmonics.

tinnitus A sensation of noises or ringing in the ears.

tip link A fine, threadlike fiber that runs along and connects the tips of stereocilia. See Figure 9.5.

TMS See *transcranial magnetic stimulation*.

tolerance A condition in which, with repeated exposure to a drug, an individual becomes less responsive to a constant dose. Compare *sensitization* (definition 2).

tonic receptor A receptor in which the frequency of action potentials declines slowly or not at all as stimulation is maintained. Compare *phasic receptor*.

tonotopic organization A major organizational feature in auditory systems in which neurons are arranged as an orderly map of stimulus frequency, with cells responsive to high frequencies located at a distance from those responsive to low frequencies.

top-down process A process in which higher-order cognitive processes control lower-order systems, often reflecting conscious control. Endogenous attention is one example. Compare *bottom-up process*.

torpor The condition in which an animal allows its body temperature to fall drastically. During torpor, animals are unresponsive to most stimuli.

Tourette's syndrome A heightened sensitivity to tactile, auditory, and visual stimuli that may be accompanied by the buildup of an urge to emit verbal or phonic tics. See Box 16.3.

TPJ See *temporoparietal junction*.

trace amine-associated receptors (TAARs) A family of probable pheromone receptors produced by neurons in the main olfactory epithelium. TAARs are candidate pheromone receptors, despite being situated outside the vomeronasal organ.

trace conditioning A form of conditioning in which a longer delay separates the conditioned and unconditioned stimuli. Compare *delay conditioning*.

tract A bundle of axons found within the central nervous system. Compare *nerve*.

transcranial magnetic stimulation (TMS) Localized, noninvasive stimulation of cortical neurons through the application of strong magnetic fields. In *repetitive TMS (rTMS)*, this focal magnetic stimulation of the brain is cycled several times per second, producing transient but measurable changes in behavior that may be of use in clinical settings, as well as in research.

transcript The mRNA strand that is produced when a stretch of DNA is "read."

transcription The process during which mRNA forms bases complementary to a strand of DNA. The resulting message (called a *transcript*) is then used to translate the DNA code into protein molecules. See Appendix Figure A.2.

transcription factor A substance that binds to recognition sites on DNA and alters the rate of expression of particular genes.

transcutaneous electrical nerve stimulation (TENS) The delivery of electrical pulses through electrodes attached to the skin, which excite nerves that supply the region to which pain is referred. TENS can relieve the pain in some instances.

transduction The conversion of one form of energy to another.

transgenic Referring to an animal in which a new or altered gene has been deliberately introduced into the genome. See Box 7.3.

transient receptor potential 2 (TRP2) A receptor, found in some free nerve endings, that opens its channel in response to rising temperatures. See Figure 8.22.

transient receptor potential vanilloid type 1 (TRPV1) Also called *vanilloid receptor 1*. A receptor that binds capsaicin to transmit the burning sensation from chili peppers and normally detects sudden increases in temperature. See Figure 8.22.

translation The process by which amino acids are linked together (directed by an mRNA molecule) to form protein molecules. See Appendix Figure A.2.

transmitter See *neurotransmitter*.

transport vesicle A spheroid intracellular structure that contains molecules of important substances. Transport vesicles are moved between locations within the cell—for example, along the axons of neurons—in order to deliver substances to the locations where they are needed.

transporters Specialized receptors in the presynaptic membrane that recognize transmitter molecules and return them to the presynaptic neuron for reuse.

transverse plane See *coronal plane*.

TRH See *thyrotropin-releasing hormone*.

trichromatic hypothesis A hypothesis of color perception stating that there are three different types of cones, each excited by a different region of the spectrum and each having a separate pathway to the brain.

tricyclic antidepressants A class of drugs that act by increasing the synaptic accumulation of serotonin and norepinephrine.

triiodothyronine See *thyroid hormones*.

trinucleotide repeat Repetition of the same three nucleotides within a gene, which can lead to dysfunction, as in the cases of Huntington's disease and fragile X syndrome.

trophic factor A substance that promotes cell growth and survival. See also *neurotrophic factor*.

tropic hormones A class of anterior pituitary hormones that affect the secretion of other endocrine glands. See Figure 5.15.

TRP2 See *transient receptor potential 2*.

TRP8 See *cool-menthol receptor 1*.

TRPV1 See *transient receptor potential vanilloid type 1*.

TSH See *thyroid-stimulating hormone*.

TTX See *tetrodotoxin*.

tuberomammillary nucleus A region of the basal hypothalamus, near the pituitary stalk, that plays a role in generating SWS.

tuning curve A graph of the responses of a single auditory nerve fiber or neuron to sounds that vary in frequency and intensity.

turbinates Complex shapes underlying the olfactory mucosa that direct inspired air over receptor cells. See Figure 9.22.

Turner's syndrome A condition seen in individuals carrying a single X chromosome but no other sex chromosome.

tympanic canal See *scala tympani*.

tympanic membrane Also called *eardrum*. The partition between the external ear and the middle ear. See Figure 9.2.

typical neuroleptics A major class of antischizophrenic drugs that share antagonist activity at dopamine D_2 receptors. Compare *atypical neuroleptics*.

U

ultradian Referring to a rhythmic biological event whose period is shorter than that of a circadian rhythm, usually from several minutes to several hours long. Compare *infradian*.

ultrasound High-frequency sound; in general, above the threshold for human hearing, at about 20,000 Hz. Compare *infrasound*.

umami One of the five basic tastes (along with salty, sour, sweet, and bitter), probably mediated by amino acids in foods.

unconditioned response (UR) See *classical conditioning*.

unconditioned stimulus (US) See *classical conditioning*.

unipolar depression Depression that alternates with normal emotional states. Compare *bipolar disorder*.

unipolar neuron Also called *monopolar neuron*. A nerve cell with a single branch that leaves the cell body and then extends in two directions; one end is the receptive pole, the other end the output zone. See Figure 2.5. Compare *bipolar neuron* and *multipolar neuron*.

up-regulation A compensatory increase in receptor availability at the synapses of a neuron. Compare *down-regulation*.

UR See *classical conditioning*.

US See *classical conditioning*.

utricle A small, fluid-filled sac in the vestibular system above the saccule that responds to static positions of the head. See Figure 9.16.

V

V1 See *primary visual cortex*.

vagus nerve Cranial nerve X, which provides extensive innervation of the viscera (organs). The vagus both regulates visceral activity and transmits signals from the viscera to the brain. See Figures 2.9, 13.26.

vanilloid receptor 1 See *transient receptor potential vanilloid type 1.*

varicosity The axonal swelling from which neurotransmitter diffuses in a nondirected synapse.

vasopressin See *arginine vasopressin.*

ventral In anatomy, toward the belly or front of the body, or the bottom of the brain. See Box 2.2. Compare *dorsal.*

ventral root See *roots.*

ventral tegmental area (VTA) A portion of the midbrain that projects dopaminergic fibers to the nucleus accumbens.

ventricular system A system of fluid-filled cavities inside the brain. See Figure 2.19.

ventricular zone Also called *ependymal layer.* A region lining the cerebral ventricles that displays mitosis, providing neurons early in development and glial cells throughout life. See Figure 7.5.

ventromedial hypothalamus (VMH) A hypothalamic region involved in eating and sexual behaviors. See Figures 12.6, 13.22.

vertebral arteries Arteries that ascend the vertebrae, enter the base of the skull, and join together to form the basilar artery. See Figure 2.20.

vertex spike An sharp-wave EEG pattern that is seen during stage 1 slow-wave sleep. See Figure 14.11.

vestibular canal See *scala vestibuli.*

vestibular nuclei Brainstem nuclei that receive information from the vestibular organs through cranial nerve VIII (the vestibulocochlear nerve).

vestibulocerebellum The middle portion of the cerebellum, sandwiched between the *spinocerebellum* and the *cerebrocerebellum* and consisting of the nodule and the flocculus. It helps the motor systems to maintain posture and appropriate orientation toward the external world. See Figure 11.24.

vestibulocochlear nerve Cranial nerve VIII, which runs from the cochlea to the brainstem auditory nuclei. See Figures 2.9, 9.1.

vestibulo-ocular reflex (VOR) The brainstem mechanism that maintains gaze on a visual object despite movements of the head.

visual acuity Sharpness of vision.

visual cortex See *occipital cortex.*

visual field The whole area that you can see without moving your head or eyes.

viviparous Of or relating to viviparity (literally, "live birth"), reproduction in which the zygote develops extensively within the female until a well-formed individual emerges. Compare *oviparous* and *ovoviviparous.*

VMH See *ventromedial hypothalamus.*

VNO See *vomeronasal organ.*

volley theory A theory of frequency discrimination that emphasizes the relation between sound frequency and the firing pattern of nerve cells. For example, a 500-Hz tone would produce 500 neural discharges per second by a nerve cell or group of nerve cells. Compare *place theory.*

voltage-gated Na$^+$ channel An Na$^+$-selective channel that opens or closes in response to changes in the voltage of the local membrane potential. Voltage-gated Na$^+$ channels mediate the action potential. Compare *ligand-gated ion channel.*

voluntary attention See *endogenous attention.*

vomeronasal organ (VNO) A collection of specialized receptor cells, near to but separate from the olfactory epithelium, that detect pheromones and send electrical signals to the accessory olfactory bulb in the brain.

vomeronasal system A specialized chemical detection system that detects pheromones and transmits information to the brain.

VOR See *vestibulo-ocular reflex.*

VTA See *ventral tegmental area.*

W

Wada test A test in which a short-lasting anesthetic is delivered into one carotid artery to determine which cerebral hemisphere principally mediates language. See Box 19.1.

Wallerian degeneration See *anterograde degeneration.*

war neurosis See *posttraumatic stress disorder.*

wavelength Here, the length between two peaks in a repeated stimulus such as a wave, light, or sound. See Box 9.1.

Wernicke's aphasia See *fluent aphasia.*

Wernicke's area A region of temporoparietal cortex in the brain that is involved in the perception and production of speech. See Figures 19.6, 19.7, 19.8.

Western blot A method of detecting a particular protein molecule in a tissue or organ, by separating proteins from that source with gel electrophoresis, blotting the separated proteins onto nitrocellulose, and then using an antibody that binds, and highlights, the protein of interest. Compare *Northern blot* and *Southern blot.*

whisker barrel A barrel-shaped column of somatosensory cortex in rodents that receives information from a particular whisker.

white matter A shiny layer underneath the cortex that consists largely of axons with white myelin sheaths. See Figure 2.13. Compare *gray matter.*

Williams syndrome A disorder characterized by fluent linguistic function, but poor performance on standard IQ tests and great difficulty with spatial processing. See Figure 19.14.

withdrawal symptom An uncomfortable symptom that arises when a person stops taking a drug that he or she has used frequently, especially at high doses.

wolffian duct A duct system in the embryo that will develop into male structures (the epididymis, vas deferens, and seminal vesicles) if testes are present in the embryo. See Figure 12.13. Compare *müllerian duct.*

word deafness The specific inability to hear words, although other sounds can be detected.

working memory A buffer that holds memories available for ready access during performance of a task. See Figure 17.17.

Z

zeitgeber Literally, "time-giver" (in German). The stimulus (usually the light-dark cycle) that entrains circadian rhythms.

zygote The fertilized egg.

Illustration Credits

The following figures use elements originally rendered for *Neuroanatomy through Clinical Cases* by Hal Blumenfeld, M.D., Ph.D. (Blumenfeld, 2002): Figures 1.11*b*, 2.3, 2.9, 2.11, 2.15, 2.18, 2.19*a*, 2.20, Box 3.3*a*, 4.2, 4.3, 4.4, 4.5, 5.10, 5.11, 5.12, 5.16, 5.19, 5.20*a*, 6.9, 7.25, 7.26, 8.3, 8.5, 8.8, 8.10*a*, 8.16*a*, 8.18, 8.21, 11.16, 11.19, 13.3, 13.20, 15.11, 15.19, 16.13, 17.1, 17.4, Box 18.1, 19.6, 19.8, 19.10, 19.11, 19.16*a*, 19.18*a*, 19.19.

Chapter 1

1.11*a*: © The Print Collector/Alamy. 1.12: © Roman Sigaev/Istockphoto.com.

Chapter 2

2.7*c*: © Dennis Kunkel Microscopy, Inc. 2.8*b*: From Gray's Anatomy, 35th ed., Figure 2.9, page 807. Reprinted with permission of the publisher, Churchill Livingstone. (Dissection by M. C. E. Hutchinson, photograph by Kevin Fitzpatrick, Guy's Hospital Medical School, London.) 2.21*a*: © Scott Camazine/Alamy. 2.21*b*: © Mark Herreid/istockphoto.com. 2.21*c*: Courtesy of Jamie Eberling.

Chapter 3

3.19: Courtesy of Neuroscan Labs, a division of Neurosoft, Inc. Box 3.1 *scorpion*: © Julie de Leseleuc/istockphoto.com. Box 3.1 *frog*: © John Arnold/istockphoto.com. Box 3.1 *puffer*: © Kerry Werry/istockphoto.com.

Chapter 4

4.13: David McIntyre. 4.15: © Jason Bye/Alamy. 4.18: Art by Wes Black, courtesy of www.blotterart.com.

Chapter 5

5.4: © Tom Vezo/Nature Picture Library. 5.18: © Thomas & Pat Leeson/Photo Researchers, Inc.

Chapter 6

6.5: Cartoon by Dan Piraro, www.bizarro.com, courtesy of King Features Syndicate. 6.20: © Konrad Wothe/Minden Pictures. 6.23: © Jeff Foott/Naturepl.com. Box 6.3: © Ashley Cooper/Alamy.

Chapter 7

7.18*a*: © moodboard/Alamy. 7.18*b*: Courtesy of the National Fragile X Foundation.

Chapter 8

8.1*a*: © The Natural History Museum/Alamy. 8.1*b*: Courtesy of Matthew Haskins and Brianna Matthews. 8.1*c*: © Vitaly Titov/istockphoto.com. 8.1*d*: © Stockbyte/PictureQuest. 8.27: © al wekelo/istockphoto.com.

Chapter 9

9.1 *opossums*: © Stuart Elflett/ShutterStock. 9.1 *elephant*: © Gerry Ellis/DigitalVision. 9.1 *chimp*: © Holger Ehlers/ShutterStock. 9.1 *rabbit*: © Heather Craig/istockphoto.com. 9.12: © Dave Watts/Naturepl.com. 9.18: © J & L Weber/Peter Arnold, Inc.

Chapter 10

10.9: © Paul Parker/SPL/Photo Researchers, Inc. 10.17: © Gerry Ellis/DigitalVision. 10.30: Courtesy of Patch Pals, www.PatchPals.com.

Chapter 11

11.21: © Danita Delimont/Alamy.

Chapter 12

12.2: © Jane Burton/Naturepl.com. 12.7: Courtesy of Lisa Davis and Lowell Getz. 12.15: © The Wellcome Photo Library. Box 12.1: © Laurence Frank, courtesy of Stephen Glickman.

Chapter 13

13.2*a*: David McIntyre. 13.2*b*: © Jeff Rotman/Alamy. 13.2*c*: © Sam Chadwick/Alamy. 13.17: © Rod Planck/Photo Researchers, Inc. 13.25: © John Sholtis/Rockefeller University. 13.29*a*: © Ash Knotek/Zuma Press. 13.29*b*: Kunsthistorisches Museum, Vienna.

Chapter 14

14.20: © petech/istockphoto.com. 14.22: © Jouan & Rius/Naturepl.com. 14.28*a*: © Tomo Jesenicnik/istockphoto.com. 14.28*b*: © Ira Bachinskaya/istockphoto.com. 14.32: Courtesy of Joanne Delphia.

Chapter 15

15.3: © Sinauer Associates. 15.7: © Dr. P. Marazzi/SPL/Photo Researchers, Inc. 15.14: © Sinauer Associates. 15.18: © Bill Frakes/Time & Life Pictures/Getty Images.

Chapter 16

16.1: ©EFE/ZUMA Press. 16.20: Courtesy of the USDA Animal and Plant Health Inspection Service.

Chapter 17

17.12: © Atlantic Feature Syndicate/Mark Parisi. Box 17.1*a*: Bettmann/Corbis. Box 17.1*b*: Courtesy of Med Associates.

Chapter 18

18.29*a*: From the collection of Jack and Beverly Wilgus.

References

A

Aaronson, S. T., Rashed, S., Biber, M. P., and Hobson, J. A. (1982). Brain state and body position. A time-lapse video study of sleep. *Archives of General Psychiatry, 39*, 330–335.

Abe, N., Suzuki, M., Mori, E., Itoh, M., et al. (2007). Deceiving others: Distinct neural responses of the prefrontal cortex and amygdala in simple fabrication and deception with social interactions. *Journal of Cognitive Neuroscience, 19*, 287–295.

Abel, E. L. (1984). Prenatal effects of alcohol. *Drug and Alcohol Dependence, 14*, 1–10.

Abelson, J. F., Kwan, K. Y., O'Roak, B. J., Baek, D. Y., et al. (2005). Sequence variants in *SLITRK1* are associated with Tourette's syndrome. *Science, 310*, 317–320.

Abraham, S. F., Baker, R. M., Blaine, E. H., Denton, D. A., et al. (1975). Water drinking induced in sheep by angiotensin—A physiological or pharmacological effect? *Journal of Comparative and Physiological Psychology, 88*, 503–518.

Absil, P., Pinxten, R., Balthazart, J., and Eens, M. (2003). Effect of age and testosterone on autumnal neurogenesis in male European starlings (*Sturnus vulgaris*). *Behavioural Brain Research, 143*, 15–30.

Adams, C. S., Korytko, A. I., and Blank, J. L. (2003). A novel mechanism of body mass regulation. *Journal of Experimental Biology, 206*, 2535–2536.

Adelson, E. H. (1993). Perceptual organization and the judgment of brightness. *Science, 262*, 2042–2044.

Ader, R. (2001). Psychoneuroimmunology. *Current Directions in Psychological Science, 10*, 94–98.

Adler, E., Hoon, M. A., Mueller, K. L., Chandrashekar, J., et al. (2000). A novel family of mammalian taste receptors. *Cell, 100*, 693–702.

Adler, N., and Matthews, K. (1994). Health psychology: Why do some people get sick and some stay well? *Annual Review of Psychology, 45*, 229–259.

Adolphs, R., Gosselin, F., Buchanan, T. W., Tranel, D., et al. (2005). A mechanism for impaired fear recognition after amygdala damage. *Nature, 433*, 68–72.

Adolphs, R., Tranel, D., Damasio, H., and Damasio, A. (1994). Impaired recognition of emotion in facial expressions following bilateral damage to the human amygdala. *Nature, 372*, 669–672.

Agarwal, N., Pacher, P. Tegeder, I., Amay, F., et al. (2007). Cannabinoids mediate analgesia largely via peripheral type cannabinoid receptors in nociceptors. *Nature Neuroscience, 10*, 870–878.

Agmon-Snir, H., Carr, C. E., and Rinzel, J. (1998). The role of dendrites in auditory coincidence detection. *Nature, 393*, 268–272.

Agre, P., King, L. S., Yasui, M., Guggino, W. B., et al. (2002). Aquaporin water channels— From atomic structure to clinical medicine. *Journal of Physiology, 542*, 3–16.

Ahmed, E. I., Zehr, J. L., Schulz, K. M., Lorenz, B. H., et al. (2008). Pubertal hormones modulate the addition of new cells to sexually dimorphic brain regions. *Nature Neuroscience, 11*, 995–997.

Ahn, S., and Phillips, A. G. (2002). Modulation by central and basolateral amygdalar nuclei of dopaminergic correlates of feeding to satiety in the rat nucleus accumbens and medial prefrontal cortex. *Journal of Neuroscience, 22*, 10958–10965.

Akbarian, S., Kim, J. J., Potkin, S. G., Hetrick, W. P., et al. (1996). Maldistribution of interstitial neurons in prefrontal white matter of the brains of schizophrenic patients. *Archives of General Psychiatry, 53*, 425–436.

Albanese, A., Hamill, G., Jones, J., Skuse, D., et al. (1994). Reversibility of physiological growth hormone secretion in children with psychosocial dwarfism. *Clinical Endocrinology (Oxford), 40*, 687–692.

al-Barazanji, K. A., Buckingham, R. E., Arch, J. R., Haynes, A., et al. (1997). Effects of intracerebroventricular infusion of leptin in obese Zucker rats. *Obesity Research, 5*, 387–394.

Alberts, J. R. (1978). Huddling by rat pups: Multisensory control of contact behavior. *Journal of Comparative and Physiological Psychology, 92*, 220–230.

Aldrich, M. A. (1993). The neurobiology of narcolepsy-cataplexy. *Progress in Neurobiology, 41*, 533–541.

Alkire, M. T., Hudetz, A. G., and Tononi, G. (2008). Consciousness and anesthesia. *Science, 322*, 876–880.

Allard, J. S., Heilbronn, L. K., Smith, C., Hunt, N. D., et al. (2008). In vitro cellular adaptations of indicators of longevity in response to treatment with serum collected from humans on calorie restricted diets. *PLoS One, 15*, e3211.

Almada, S. J., Zonderman, A. B., Shekelle, R. B., Dyer, A. R., et al. (1991). Neuroticism and cynicism and risk of death in middle-aged men: The Western Electric Study. *Psychosomatic Medicine, 53*, 165–175.

Alpert, M., and Friedhoff, A. J. (1980). An un-dopamine hypothesis of schizophrenia. *Schizophrenia Bulletin, 6*, 387–390.

Altman, J. (1969). Autoradiographic and histological studies of postnatal neurogenesis. IV. Cell proliferation and migration in the anterior forebrain, with special reference to persisting neurogenesis in the olfactory bulb. *Journal of Comparative Neurology, 137*, 433–457.

Altschuler, E. L., Wisdom, S. B., Stone, L., Foster, C., et al. (1999). Rehabilitation of hemiparesis after stroke with a mirror. *Lancet, 353*, 2035–2036.

Alvarez, J. A., and Emory, E. (2006). Executive function and the frontal lobes: A meta-analytic review. *Neuropsychology Review, 16*, 17–42.

American Psychiatric Association. (2000). *Diagnostic and statistical manual of mental disorders: DSM IV-TR* (4th ed., text revised). Washington, DC: American Psychiatric Association.

Amos, L. A., and Cross, R. A. (1997). Structure and dynamics of molecular motors. *Current Opinion in Structural Biology, 7*, 239–246.

Amunts, K., Schlaug, G., Jaencke, L., Steinmetz, H., et al. (1997). Motor cortex and hand motor skills: Structural compliance in the human brain. *Human Brain Mapping, 5*, 206–215.

Anand, B. K., and Brobeck, J. R. (1951). Localization of a "feeding center" in the hypothalamus of the rat. *Proceedings of the Society for Experimental Biology and Medicine, 77*, 323–324.

Andersen, B. B., Korbo, L., and Pakkenberg, B. (1992). A quantitative study of the human cerebellum with unbiased stereological techniques. *Journal of Comparative Neurology, 326,* 549–560.

Andersen, P. M., Nilsson, P., Ala-Hurula, V., Keranen, M. L., et al. (1995). Amyotrophic lateral sclerosis associated with homozygosity for an Asp90Ala mutation in CuZn-superoxide dismutase. *Nature Genetics, 10,* 61–66.

Anderson, M. J., and Dixson, A. F. (2002). Sperm competition: Motility and the midpiece in primates. *Nature, 416,* 496.

Anderson, N. D., and Craik, F. I. M. (2000). Memory in the aging brain. In E. Tulving and F. I. M. Craik (Eds.), *The Oxford handbook of memory* (pp. 411–425). Oxford, England: Oxford University Press.

Anderson, S. A., Eisenstat, D. D., Shi, L., and Rubenstein, J. L. (1997). Interneuron migration from basal forebrain to neocortex: Dependence on Dlx genes. *Science, 278,* 474–476.

Andreasen, N. C. (1991). Assessment issues and the cost of schizophrenia. *Schizophrenia Bulletin, 17,* 475–481.

Andreasen, N. C. (1994). Changing concepts of schizophrenia and the ahistorical fallacy. *American Journal of Psychiatry, 151,* 1405–1407.

Andreasen, N. C., Flaum, M., Swayze, V. O. D. S., Alliger, R., et al. (1993). Intelligence and brain structure in normal individuals. *American Journal of Psychiatry, 150,* 130–134.

Andreasen, N., Nassrallah, H. A., Dunn, V., Olson, S. C., et al. (1986). Structural abnormalities in the frontal system in schizophrenia. *Archives of General Psychiatry, 43,* 136–144.

Anson, R. M., Guo, Z., de Cabo, R., Iyun, T., et al. (2003). Intermittent fasting dissociates beneficial effects of dietary restriction on glucose metabolism and neuronal resistance to injury from calorie intake. *Proceedings of the National Academy of Sciences, USA, 100,* 6216–6220.

Anstey, M. L., Rogers, S. M., Ott, S. R., Burrows, M., et al. (2009). Serotonin mediates behavioral gregarization underlying swarm formation in desert locusts. *Science, 323,* 627–630.

Apkarian, A. V., Sosa, Y., Sonty, S., Levy, R. M., et al. (2004). Chronic back pain is associated with decreased prefrontal and thalamic gray matter density. *Journal of Neuroscience, 24,* 10410–10415.

Archer, G. S., Friend, T. H., Piedrahita, J., Nevill, C. H., et al. (2003). Behavioral variation among cloned pigs. *Applied Animal Behaviour Science, 82,* 151–161.

Archer, J. (2006). Testosterone and human aggression: An evaluation of the challenge hypothesis. *Neuroscience and Biobehavioral Reviews, 30,* 319–345.

Argyll-Robertson, D. M. C. L. (1869). On an interesting series of eye symptoms in a case of spinal disease, with remarks on the action of belladonna on the iris. *Edinburgh Medical Journal, 14,* 696–708.

Arnold, A. P. (1980). Sexual differences in the brain. *American Scientist, 68,* 165–173.

Arnold, A. P., and Schlinger, B. A. (1993). Sexual differentiation of brain and behavior: The zebra finch is not just a flying rat. *Brain, Behavior and Evolution, 42,* 231–241.

Arnold, K., and Zuberbühler, K. (2006). Language evolution: Semantic combinations in primate calls. *Nature, 441,* 303.

Arnone, D., Cavanagh, J., Gerber, D., Lawrie, S. M., et al. (2009). Magnetic resonance imaging studies in bipolar disorder and schizophrenia: Meta-analysis. *British Journal of Psychiatry, 195,* 194–201.

Arnsten, A. F. (2006). Fundamentals of attention-deficit/hyperactivity disorder: Circuits and pathways. *Journal of Clinical Psychiatry, 67,* 7–12.

Aroniadou, V. A., Maillis, A., and Stefanis, C. C. (1993). Dihydropyridine-sensitive calcium channels are involved in the induction of N-methyl-D-aspartate receptor-independent long-term potentiation in visual cortex of adult rats. *Neuroscience Letters, 151,* 77–80.

Asberg, M., Nordstrom, P., and Traskman-Bendz, L. (1986). Cerebrospinal fluid studies in suicide. An overview. *Annals of the New York Academy of Sciences, 487,* 243–255.

Aschner, M., and Ceccatelli, S. (2009, September 16). Are neuropathological conditions relevant to ethylmercury exposure? *Neurotoxicity Research.* [Epub ahead of print]

Aserinsky, E., and Kleitman, N. (1953). Regularly occurring periods of eye motility, and concomitant phenomena, during sleep. *Science, 118,* 273–274.

Ashmore, J. F. (1994). The cellular machinery of the cochlea. *Experimental Physiology, 79,* 113–134.

Ashtari, M., Kumra, S., Bhaskar, S. L., Clarke, T., et al. (2005). Attention-deficit/hyperactivity disorder: A preliminary diffusion tensor imaging study. *Biological Psychiatry, 57,* 448–455.

Audero, E., Coppi, E., Mlinar, B., Rossetti, T., et al. (2008). Sporadic autonomic dysregulation and death associated with excessive serotonin autoinhibition. *Science, 321,* 130–133.

Aungst, J. L., Heyward, P. M., Puche, A. C., Karnup, S. V., et al. (2003). Centre-surround inhibition among olfactory bulb glomeruli. *Nature, 426,* 623–629.

Avan, P., Loth, D., Menguy, C., and Teyssou, M. (1992). Hypothetical roles of middle ear muscles in the guinea-pig. *Hearing Research, 59,* 59–69.

B

Baddeley, A. (2003). Working memory: Looking back and looking forward. *Nature Review. Neuroscience, 4,* 829–839.

Baddeley, A. D., and Warrington, E. K. (1970). Amnesia and the distinction between long- and short-term memory.

Journal of Verbal Learning and Verbal Behavior, 9, 176–189.

Bagemihl, B. (1999). *Biological exuberance: Animal homosexuality and natural diversity.* New York: St. Martin's.

Bagni, C., and Greenough, W. T. (2005). From mRNP trafficking to spine dysmorphogenesis: The roots of fragile X syndrome. *Nature Reviews. Neuroscience, 6,* 376–387.

Bailey, C. H., and Chen, M. (1983). Morphological basis of long-term habituation and sensitization in *Aplysia. Science, 220,* 91–93.

Bailey, J. M., Pillard, R. C., Neale, M. C., and Agyei, Y. (1993). Heritable factors influence sexual orientation in women. *Archives of General Psychiatry, 50,* 217–223.

Bakker, J., De Mees, C., Douhard, Q., Balthazart, J., et al. (2006). Alpha-fetoprotein protects the developing female mouse brain from masculinization and defeminization by estrogens. *Nature Neuroscience, 9,* 220–226.

Ball, G. F., and Hulse, S. H. (1998). Birdsong. *American Psychologist, 53,* 37–58.

Ballantine, H. T., Bouckoms, A. J., Thomas, E. K., and Giriunas, I. E. (1987). Treatment of psychiatric illness by stereotactic cingulotomy. *Biological Psychiatry, 22,* 807–820.

Balter, M. (2004). Evolution of behavior: Seeking the key to music. *Science, 306,* 1120–1122.

Bancaud, J., Brunet-Bourgin, F., Chauvel, P., and Halgren, E. (1994). Anatomical origin of deja vu and vivid "memories" in human temporal lobe. *Brain, 117,* 71–90.

Bao, J. X., Kandel, E. R., and Hawkins, R. D. (1998). Involvement of presynaptic and postsynaptic mechanisms in a cellular analog of classical conditioning at *Aplysia* sensory-motor neuron synapses in isolated cell culture. *Journal of Neuroscience, 18,* 458–466.

Bao, S., Chan, V. T., and Merzenich, M. M. (2001). Cortical remodelling induced by activity of ventral tegmental dopamine neurons. *Nature, 412,* 79–83.

Baptista, L. F. (1996). Nature and its nurturing in avian vocal development. In D. E. Kroodsma and E. H. Miller (Eds.), *Ecology and evolution of acoustic communication in birds* (pp. 39–60). Ithaca, NY: Cornell University Press.

Baptista, L., and Petrinovich, L. (1986). Song development in the white-crowned sparrow: Social factors and sex differences. *Animal Behaviour, 34,* 1359–1371.

Barasa, A. (1960). Forma, grandezza e densita dei neuroni della corteccia cerebrale in mammiferi di grandezza corporea differente. *Zeitschrift für Zellforschung, 53,* 69–89.

Barbeau, H., Norman, K., Fung, J., Visintin, M., et al. (1998). Does neurorehabilitation play a role in the recovery of walking in neurological populations? *Annals of the New York Academy of Sciences, 860,* 377–392.

Barbour, H. G. (1912). Die Wirkung unmittelbarer Erwärmung und Abkühlung der Warmenzentren auf die Korpertemperatur. *Archiv für Experimentalle Pathologie und Pharmakologie, 70,* 1–26.

Bark, N. (2002). Did schizophrenia change the course of English history? The mental illness of Henry VI. *Medical Hypotheses, 59,* 416–421.

Barkow, J. H., Cosmides, L., and Tooby, J. (1992). *The adapted mind: Evolutionary psychology and the generation of culture.* New York: Oxford University Press.

Barlow, H. B., and Levick, W. R. (1965). The mechanism of directionally selective units in rabbit's retina. *Journal of Physiology, 178,* 477–504.

Barnea, G., O'Donnell, S., Mancia, F., Sun, X., et al. (2004). Odorant receptors on axon termini in the brain. *Science, 304,* 1468.

Barnes, C. A., and Penner, M. R. (2007). Memory changes with age: Neuorobiological correlates. In R. P. Kesner and J. L. Martinez (Eds.), *Neurobiology of learning and memory* (2nd ed., pp. 483–517). San Diego, CA: Elsevier.

Baron Cohen, S. (2003). *The essential difference: Men, women and the extreme male brain.* London: Allen Lane.

Bartels, A., and Zeki, S. (2000). The neural basis of romantic love. *Neuroreport, 11,* 3829–3834.

Bartfai, T. (2001). Telling the brain about pain. *Nature, 410,* 425–426.

Bartolomeo, P. (2007). Visual neglect. *Current Opinion in Neurology, 20,* 381–386.

Bartoshuk, L. M. (1993). Genetic and pathological taste variation: What can we learn from animal models and human disease? In D. Chadwick, J. Marsh, and J. Goode (Eds.), *The molecular basis of smell and taste transduction* (pp. 251–267). New York: Wiley.

Bartoshuk, L. M., and Beauchamp, G. K. (1994). Chemical senses. *Annual Review of Psychology, 45,* 419–449.

Basbaum, A., and Fields, H. L. (1984). Endogenous pain control systems: Brainstem spinal pathways and endorphin circuitry. *Annual Review of Neuroscience, 7,* 309–339.

Basil, J. A., Kamil, A. C., Balda, R. P., and Fite, K. V. (1996). Differences in hippocampal volume among food storing corvids. *Brain, Behavior and Evolution, 47,* 156–164.

Basson, R. (2001). Human sex-response cycles. *Journal of Sex & Marital Therapy, 27,* 33–43.

Basson, R. (2008).Women's sexual function and dysfunction: Current uncertainties, future directions. *International Journal of Impotence Research, 20,* 466–478.

Bates, E., Wilson, S. M., Saygin, A. P., Dick, F., et al. (2003). Voxel-based lesion-symptom mapping. *Nature Neuroscience, 6,* 448–450.

Bates, T. C., Lind, P. A., Luciano, M., Montgomery, G. W., et al. (2009, November 10). Dyslexia and DYX1C1: Deficits in reading and spelling associated with a missense mutation. *Molecular Psychiatry.* [Epub ahead of print]

Batterham, R. L., and Bloom, S. R. (2003). The gut hormone peptide YY regulates appetite. *Annals of the New York Academy of Sciences, 994,* 162–168.

Batterham, R. L., Cohen, M. A., Ellis, S. M., Le Roux, C. W., et al. (2003). Inhibition of food intake in obese subjects by peptide YY_{3-36}. *New England Journal of Medicine, 349,* 941–948.

Baum, A., and Posluszny, D. M. (1999). Health psychology: Mapping biobehavioral contributions to health and illness. *Annual Review of Psychology, 50,* 137–163.

Baumgardner, T. L., Green, K. E., and Reiss, A. L. (1994). A behavioral neurogenetics approach to developmental disabilities: Gene-brain-behavior associations. *Current Opinion in Neurology, 7,* 172–178.

Bautista, D. M., Siemens, J., Glazer, J. M., Tsuruda, P. R., et al. (2007). The menthol receptor TRPM8 is the principal detector of environmental cold. *Nature, 448,* 204–208.

Daynes, K. C., Dhillo, W. S., and Bloom, S. R. (2006). Regulation of food intake by gastrointestinal hormones. *Current Opinion in Gastroenterology, 22,* 626–631.

Beach, F. A. (1977). *Human sexuality in four perspectives.* Baltimore: Johns Hopkins University Press.

Bear, M. F., and Malenka, R. C. (1994). Synaptic plasticity. *Current Opinion in Neurobiology, 4,* 389–399.

Beauchamp, G. K., Cowart, B. J., Mennella, J. A., and Marsh, R. R. (1994). Infant salt taste: Developmental, methodological, and contextual factors. *Developmental Psychobiology, 27,* 353–365.

Bee, M. A., and Micheyl, C. (2008). The cocktail party problem: What is it? How can it be solved? And why should animal behaviorists study it? *Journal of Comparative Psychology, 122,* 235–251.

Beeli, G., Esslen, M., and Jäncke, L. (2005). When coloured sounds taste sweet. *Nature, 434,* 38.

Beggs, W. D., and Foreman, D. L. (1980). Sound localization and early binaural experience in the deaf. *British Journal of Audiology, 14,* 41–48.

Belelli, D., and Lambert, J. J. (2005). Neurosteroids: Endogenous regulators of the GABA(A) receptor. *Nature Reviews. Neuroscience, 6,* 565–575.

Bellinger, D. L., Ackerman, K. D., Felten, S. Y., and Felten, D. L. (1992). A longitudinal study of age-related loss of noradrenergic nerves and lymphoid cells in the rat spleen. *Experimental Neurology, 116,* 295–311.

Bellugi, U., Poizner, H., and Klima, E. S. (1983). Brain organization for language: Clues from sign aphasia. *Human Neurobiology, 2,* 155–171.

Belluscio, L., Gold, G. H., Nemes, A., and Axel, R. (1998). Mice deficient in G(olf) are anosmic. *Neuron, 20,* 69–81.

Bennett, A. F., and Ruben, J. A. (1979). Endothermy and activity in vertebrates. *Science, 206,* 649–654.

Bennett, E. L., Diamond, M. L., Krech, D., and Rosenzweig, M. R. (1964). Chemical and anatomical plasticity of brain. *Science, 146,* 610–619.

Bennett, E. L., Rosenzweig, M. R., and Diamond, M. C. (1969). Rat brain: Effects of environmental enrichment on wet and dry weights. *Science, 163,* 825–826.

Bennett, M. V. (2000). Electrical synapses, a personal perspective (or history). *Brain Research Reviews, 32,* 16–28.

Bennett, W. (1983). The nicotine fix. *Rhode Island Medical Journal, 66,* 455–458.

Benney, K. S., and Braaten, R. F. (2000). Auditory scene analysis in estrildid finches (*Taeniopygia guttata* and *Lonchura striata domestica*): A species advantage for detection of conspecific song. *Journal of Comparative Psychology, 114,* 174–182.

Bensafi, M., Porter, J., Pouliot, S., Mainland, J., et al. (2003). Olfactomotor activity during imagery mimics that during perception. *Nature Neuroscience, 6,* 1142–1144.

Benson, D. F. (1967). Fluency in aphasia: Correlation with radioactive scan localization. *Cortex, 3,* 373–394.

Benton, M. J., and Ayala, F. J. (2003). Dating the tree of life. *Science, 300,* 1698–1700.

Berenbaum, S. A. (2001). Cognitive function in congenital adrenal hyperplasia. *Endocrinology and Metabolism Clinics of North America, 30,* 173–192.

Berger, T. W., and Orr, W. B. (1983). Hippocampectomy selectively disrupts discrimination reversal conditioning of the rabbit nictitating membrane response. *Behavioural Brain Research, 8,* 49–68.

Berman, K. F., and Weinberger, D. R. (1990). The prefrontal cortex in schizophrenia and other neuropsychiatric diseases: *In vivo* physiological correlates of cognitive deficits. *Progress in Brain Research, 85,* 521–536.

Berneche, S., and Roux, B. (2001). Energetics of ion conduction through the K+ channel. *Nature, 414,* 73–77.

Bernhardt, P. C. (1997). Influences of serotonin and testosterone in aggression and dominance: Convergence with social psychology. *Current Directions in Psychological Science, 2(6),* 44–48.

Bernhardt, P. C., Dabbs, J. M., Jr., Fielden, J. A., and Lutter, C. D. (1998). Testosterone changes during vicarious experiences of winning and losing among fans at sporting events. *Physiology & Behavior, 65,* 59–62.

Bernstein, I. S., and Gordon, T. P. (1974). The function of aggression in primate societies. *American Scientist, 62,* 304–311.

Bernstein, L. E., Auer, E. T., Jr., Moore, J. K., Ponton, C. W., et al. (2002). Visual speech perception without primary auditory cortex activation. *Neuroreport, 13,* 311–315.

Bernstein-Goral, H., and Bregman, B. S. (1993). Spinal cord transplants support the regeneration of axotomized neurons after spinal cord lesions at birth: A quantitative double-labeling study. *Experimental Neurology, 123,* 118–132.

Berton, O., and Nestler, E. J. (2006). New approaches to antidepressant drug discovery: Beyond monoamines. *Neuroscience, 7,* 137–151.

Bertram, L., and Tanzi, R. E. (2008). Thirty years of Alzheimer's disease genetics: The implications of systematic meta-analyses. *Nature Reviews. Neuroscience, 9,* 768–778.

Besedovsky, H. O., and del Rey, A. (1992). Immune-neuroendocrine circuits: Integrative role of cytokines. *Frontiers of Neuroendocrinology, 13,* 61–94.

Betarbet, R., Sherer, T. B., MacKenzie, G., Garcia-Osuna, M., et al. (2000). Chronic systemic pesticide exposure reproduces features of Parkinson's disease. *Nature Neuroscience, 3,* 1301–1306.

Beurg, M., Fettiplace, R., Nam, J.-H., and Ricci, A. J. (2009). Localization of inner hair cell mechanotransducer channels using high-speed calcium imaging. *Nature Neuroscience, 12,* 553–558.

Bigelow, L., Nasrallah, H. A., and Rauscher, F. P. (1983). Corpus callosum thickness in chronic schizophrenia. *British Journal of Psychiatry, 142,* 284–287.

Binder, J. R., Rao, S. M., Hammeke, T. A., Yetkin, F. Z., et al. (1994). Functional magnetic resonance imaging of human auditory cortex. *Annals of Neurology, 35,* 662–672.

Birch, L. L., Fisher, J. O., and Davison, K. K. (2003). Learning to overeat: Maternal use of restrictive feeding practices promotes girls' eating in the absence of hunger. *American Journal of Clinical Nutrition, 78,* 215–220.

Bird, C. D., and Emery, N. J. (2009). Insightful problem solving and creative tool modification by captive nontool-using rooks. *Proceedings of the National Academy of Sciences, USA, 106,* 10370–10375.

Birnbaumer, L., Abramowitz, J., and Brown, A. M. (1990). Receptor-effector coupling by G proteins. *Biochimica et Biophysica Acta, 1031,* 163–224.

Bishop, N. A., and Guarente, L. (2007). Genetic links between diet and lifespan: Shared mechanisms from yeast to humans. *Nature Reviews. Genetics, 8,* 835–844.

Bisley, J. W., and Goldberg, M. E. (2003). Neuronal activity in the lateral intraparietal area and spatial attention. *Science, 299,* 81–86.

Bisley, J. W., and Goldberg, M. E. (2006). Neural correlates of attention and distractibility in the lateral intraparietal area. *Journal of Neurophysiology, 95,* 1696–1717.

Björklund, A., and Lindvall, O. (2000). Cell replacement therapies for central nervous system disorders. *Nature Neuroscience, 3,* 537–544.

Blake, D. J., Weir, A., Newey, S. E., and Davies, K. E. (2002). Function and genetics of dystrophin and dystrophin-related proteins in muscle. *Physiology Review, 82,* 291–329.

Blakemore, C., and Campbell, F. W. (1969). On the existence of neurones in the human visual system selectively sensitive to the orientation and size of retinal images. *Journal of Physiology (London), 203,* 237–260.

Blanchard, R., Cantor, J. M., Bogaert, A. F., Breedlove, S. M., et al. (2006). Interaction of fraternal birth order and handedness in the development of male homosexuality. *Hormones and Behavior, 49,* 405–414.

Blaxton, T. A., Bookheimer, S. Y., Zeffiro, T. A., Figlozzi, C. M., et al. (1996). Functional mapping of human memory using PET: Comparisons of conceptual perceptual tasks. *Canadian Journal of Experimental Psychology, 50,* 42–56.

Blehar, M. C., and Rosenthal, N. E. (1989). Seasonal affective disorders and phototherapy. Report of a National Institute of Mental Health-sponsored workshop. *Archives of General Psychiatry, 46,* 469–474.

Bleuler, E. (1950). *Dementia praecox; or, The group of schizophrenias* (J. Zinkin, Trans.). New York: International Universities Press.

Bliss, T. V. P., and Gardner-Medwin, A. R. (1973). Long-lasting potentiation of synaptic transmission in the dentate area of the unanaesthetized rabbit following stimulation of the perforant path. *Journal of Physiology (London), 232,* 357–374.

Bliss, T. V. P., and Lømo, T. (1973). Long-lasting potentiation of synaptic transmission in the dentate area of the anaesthetized rabbit following stimulation of the perforant path. *Journal of Physiology (London), 232,* 331–356.

Bliwise, D. L. (1989). Neuropsychological function and sleep. *Clinics in Geriatric Medicine, 5,* 381–394.

Blomqvist, D., Andersson, M., Kupper, C., Cuthill, I. C., et al. (2002). Genetic similarity between mates and extra-pair parentage in three species of shorebirds. *Nature, 419,* 613–615.

Blue, M. E., and Parnavelas, J. G. (1983). The formation and maturation of synapses in the visual cortex of the rat. II. Quantitative analysis. *Journal of Neurocytology, 12,* 697–712.

Blumberg, M. S., Sokoloff, G., and Kirby, R. F. (1997). Brown fat thermogenesis and cardiac rate regulation during cold challenge in infant rats. *American Journal of Physiology, 272,* R1308–R1313.

Bogaert, A. F. (2006). Biological versus nonbiological older brothers and men's sexual orientation. *Proceedings of the National Academy of Sciences, USA, 103,* 10771–10774.

Bogaert, A. F. (2007). Extreme right-handedness, older brothers, and sexual orientation in men. *Neuropsychology, 21,* 141–148.

Bolhuis, J. J., and Gahr, M. (2006). Neural mechanisms of birdsong memory. *Nature Reviews. Neuroscience, 7,* 347–357.

Bonhoeffer, F., and Huf, J. (1985). Position-dependent properties of retinal axons and their growth cones. *Nature, 315,* 409–410.

Bonhoeffer, T., and Grinvald, A. (1991). Iso-orientation domains in cat visual cortex are arranged in pinwheel-like patterns. *Nature, 353,* 429–431.

Bonnel, A. M., and Prinzmetal, W. (1998). Dividing attention between the color and the shape of objects. *Perception & Psychophysics, 60,* 113–124.

Boodman, S. G. (2006, March 21). Mood machine: Now there's a device to treat depression. If only there were solid evidence that it works. *Washington Post,* p. HE01.

Boolell, M., Gepi-Attee, S., Gingell, J. C., and Allen, M. J. (1996). Sildenafil, a novel effective oral therapy for male erectile dysfunction. *British Journal of Urology, 78,* 257–261.

Boot, W. R., Kramer, A. F., Simons, D. J., Fabiani, M., et al. (2008). The effects of video game playing on attention, memory, and executive control. *Acta Psychologica, 129,* 387–398.

Borod, J. C., Haywood, C. S., and Koff, E. (1997). Neuropsychological aspects of facial asymmetry during emotional expression: A review of the normal adult literature. *Neuropsychology Review, 7,* 41–60.

Borrow, S. J., Adam, K., Chapman, K., Oswald, I., et al. (1980). REM sleep and normal intelligence. *Biological Psychiatry, 15,* 165–169.

Boshuisen, M. L., Ter Horst, G. J., Paans, A. M., Reinders, A. A., et al. (2002). rCBF differences between panic disorder patients and control subjects during anticipatory anxiety and rest. *Biological Psychiatry, 52,* 126–135.

Bottjer, S. W., Miesner, E. A., and Arnold, A. P. (1984). Forebrain lesions disrupt development but not maintenance of song in passerine birds. *Science, 224,* 901–903.

Bouret, S. G., Draper, S. J., and Simerly, R. B. (2004). Trophic action of leptin on hypothalamic neurons that regulate feeding. *Science, 304,* 108–110.

Bourque, C. W. (2008). Central mechanisms of osmosensation and systemic osmoregulation. *Nature Reviews. Neuroscience, 9,* 519–531.

Bourtchuladze, R., Frenguelli, B., Blendy, J., Cioffi, D., et al. (1994). Deficient long-term memory in mice with a targeted mutation of the cAMP-responsive element-binding protein. *Cell, 79,* 59–68.

Boutrel, B., Franc, B., Hen, R., Hamon, M., et al. (1999). Key role of 5-HT$_{1B}$ receptors in the regulation of paradoxical sleep as evidenced in 5-HT$_{1B}$ knock-out mice. *Journal of Neuroscience, 19*, 3204–3212.

Bouwknecht, J. A., Hijzen, T. H., van der Gugten, J., Maes, R. A., et al. (2001). Absence of 5-HT(1B) receptors is associated with impaired impulse control in male 5-HT(1B) knockout mice. *Biological Psychiatry, 49*, 557–568.

Bower, B. (2000). Genes to grow on. *Science News, 157*(9), 142.

Bower, B. (2003).Vision seekers. *Science News, 164*, 331–333.

Bower, B. (2006). Prescription for controversy: Medications for depressed kids spark scientific dispute. *Science News, 169*, 168–172.

Brain, P. F. (1994). Neurotransmission, the individual and the alcohol/aggression link. Commentary on Miczek et al. "Neuropharmacological characteristics of individual differences in alcohol effects on aggression in rodents and primates." *Behavioural Pharmacology, 5*, 422–424.

Brainard, D. H., Roorda, A., Yamauchi, Y., Calderone, J. B., et al. (2000). Functional consequences of the relative numbers of L and M cones. *Journal of the Optical Society of America. Part A, Optics, Image Science and Vision, 17*, 607–614.

Branson, R., Potoczna, N., Kral, J. G., Lentes, K. U., et al. (2003). Binge eating as a major phenotype of melanocortin 4 receptor gene mutations. *New England Journal of Medicine, 348*, 1096–1103.

Brasser, S. M., Mozhui, K., and Smith, D. V. (2005). Differential covariation in taste responsiveness to bitter stimuli in rats. *Chemical Senses, 30*, 793–799.

Braun, K. A., Ellis, R., and Loftus, E. F. (2002). Make my memory: How advertising can change our memories of the past. *Psychology and Marketing, 19*, 1–23.

Bray, G. A. (1969). Effect of caloric restriction on energy expenditure in obese patients. *Lancet, 2*, 397–398.

Breier, A., Malhotra, A. K., Pinals, D. A., Weisenfeld, N. I., et al. (1997). Association of ketamine-induced psychosis with focal activation of the prefrontal cortex in healthy volunteers. *American Journal of Psychiatry, 154*, 805–811.

Breier, A., Su, T. P., Saunders, R., Carson, R. E., et al. (1997). Schizophrenia is associated with elevated amphetamine-induced synaptic dopamine concentrations: Evidence from a novel positron emission tomography method. *Proceedings of the National Academy of Sciences, USA, 94*, 2569–2574.

Breitner, J. C., Wyse, B. W., Anthony, J. C., Welsh-Bohmer, K. A., et al. (1999). APOE-epsilon4 count predicts age when prevalence of AD increases, then declines: The Cache County Study. *Neurology, 53*, 321–331.

Bremer, F. (1938). L'activité électrique de l'écorce cérébrale. *Actualités Scientifiques et Industrielles, 658*, 3–46.

Bremner, J. D., Randall, P., Scott, T. M., Bronen, R. A., et al. (1995). MRI-based measurement of hippocampal volume in patients with combat-related posttraumatic stress disorder. *American Journal of Psychiatry, 152*, 973–981.

Bremner, J. D., Scott, T. M., Delaney, R. C., Southwick, S. M., et al. (1993). Deficits in short-term memory in posttraumatic stress disorder. *American Journal of Psychiatry, 150*, 1015–1019.

Brennan, P., Kaba, H., and Keverne, E. B. (1990). Olfactory recognition: A simple memory system. *Science, 250*, 1223–1226.

Brewer, J. B., Zhao, Z., Desmond, J. E., Glover, G. H., et al. (1998). Making memories: Brain activity that predicts how well visual experience will be remembered. *Science, 281*, 1185–1187.

Bridgham, J. T., Carroll, S. M., and Thornton, J. W. (2006). Evolution of hormone-receptor complexity by molecular exploitation. *Science, 312*, 97–101.

Brien, J. A. (1993). Ototoxicity associated with salicylates. A brief review. *Drug Safety, 9*, 143–148.

Brigande, J. V., and Heller, S. (2009). Quo vadis, hair cell regeneration? *Nature Neuroscience, 12*, 679–685.

Broadbent, D. A. (1958). *Perception and communication.* New York: Pergamon.

Broberg, D. J., and Bernstein, I. L. (1989). Cephalic insulin release in anorexic women. *Physiology and Behavior, 45*, 871–874.

Brody, A. L., Mandelkern, M. A., London, E. D., Olmstead, R. E., et al. (2006). Cigarette smoking saturates brain alpha 4 beta 2 nicotinic acetylcholine receptors. *Archives of General Psychiatry, 63*, 907–915.

Brody, G. H., Beach, S. R., Philibert, R. A., Chen, Y. F., et al. (2009). Parenting moderates a genetic vulnerability factor in longitudinal increases in youths' substance abuse. *Journal of Consulting and Clinical Psychology, 77*, 1–11.

Brook, J. S., Whiteman, M. M., and Finch, S. (1992). Childhood aggression, adolescent delinquency, and drug use: A longitudinal study. *Journal of Genetic Psychology, 153*, 369–383.

Brooks, R. (2000). Negative genetic correlation between male sexual attractiveness and survival. *Nature, 406*, 67–70.

Brose, K., Bland, K. S., Wang, K. H., Arnott, D., et al. (1999). Slit proteins bind Robo receptors and have an evolutionarily conserved role in repulsive axon guidance. *Cell, 96*, 795–806.

Broughton, R. (1985). Slow-wave sleep awakenings in normal and in pathology: A brief review. In W. P. Koella, E. Ruther, and H. Schulz (Eds.), *Sleep '84* (pp. 164–167). Stuttgart, Germany: Gustav Fischer.

Broughton, R., Billings, R., Cartwright, R., Doucette, D., et al. (1994). Homicidal somnambulism: A case report. *Sleep, 17*, 253–264.

Brown, A. S., Begg, M. D., Gravenstein, S., Schaefer, C. A., et al. (2004). Serologic evidence of prenatal influenza in the etiology of schizophrenia. *Archives of General Psychiatry, 61*, 774–780.

Brown, A. S., and Susser, E. S. (2008). Prenatal nutritional deficiency and risk of adult schizophrenia. *Schizophrenia Bulletin, 34*, 1054–1063.

Brown, C. (2003, February 2). The man who mistook his wife for a deer. *The New York Times*, Section 6, p. 32.

Brown, G. L., Goodwin, F. K., Ballenger, J. C., Goyer, P. F., et al. (1979). Aggression in humans correlates with cerebrospinal fluid amine metabolites. *Psychiatry Research, 1*, 131–139.

Brown, H. (2006, November 26). One spoonful at a time. *New York Times Magazine.*

Brown, J. (1958). Some tests of the decay theory of immediate memory. *Quarterly Journal of Experimental Psychology, 10*, 12–21.

Brownell, W. E., Bader, C. R., Bertrand, D., and de Ribaupierre, Y. (1985). Evoked mechanical responses of isolated cochlear outer hair cells. *Science, 227*, 194–196.

Brownlee, S., and Schrof, J. M. (1997). The quality of mercy. Effective pain treatments already exist. Why aren't doctors using them? *U.S. News & World Report, 122*, 54–67.

Bruel-Jungerman, E., Rampon, C., and Laroche S. (2007). Adult hippocampal neurogenesis, synaptic plasticity and memory: Facts and hypotheses. *Review in the Neurosciences, 18*, 93–114.

Brunet, L. J., Gold, G. H., and Ngai, J. (1996). General anosmia caused by a targeted disruption of the mouse olfactory cyclic nucleotide-gated cation channel. *Neuron, 17*, 681–693.

Brunetti, M., Della Penna, S., Ferretti, A., Del Gratta, C., et al. (2008). A frontoparietal network for spatial attention reorienting in the auditory domain: A human fMRI/MEG study of functional and temporal dynamics. *Cerebral Cortex, 18*, 1139–1147.

Brunjes, P. C. (1994). Unilateral naris closure and olfactory system development. *Brain Research. Brain Research Reviews, 19*, 146–160.

Bryant, P., Trinder, J., and Curtis, N. (2004). Sick and tired: Does sleep have a vital role in the immune system? *Nature Reviews. Immunology, 4*, 457–467.

Bryden, M. P. (1982). *Laterality: Functional asymmetry in the intact brain.* New York: Academic Press.

Bu, G. (2009). Apolipoprotein E and its receptors in Alzheimer's disease: Pathways, pathogenesis and therapy. *Nature Reviews. Neuroscience, 10*, 333–344.

Buccino, G., Lui, F., Canessa, N., Patteri, I., et al. (2004). Neural circuits involved in the recognition of actions performed by nonconspecifics: An fMRI study. *Journal of Cognitive Neuroscience, 16*, 114–126.

Buccino, G., Solodkin, A., and Small, S. L. (2006). Functions of the mirror neuron system: Implications for neurorehabilitation. *Cognitive and Behavioral Neurology, 19*, 55–63.

Buchan, J. C., Alberts, S. C., Silk, J. B., and Altmann, J. (2003). True paternal care in a multi-male primate society. *Nature, 425*, 179–181.

Buchsbaum, M. S., Buchsbaum, B. R., Chokron, S., Tang, C., et al. (2006). Thalamo-cortical circuits: fMRI assessment of the pulvinar and medial dorsal nucleus in normal volunteers. *Neuroscience Letters, 404*, 282–287.

Buchsbaum, M. S., Mirsky, A. F., DeLisi, L. E., Morihisa, J., et al. (1984). The Genain quadruplets: Electrophysiological, positron emission and X-ray tomographic studies. *Psychiatry Research, 13*, 95–108.

Buck, L., and Axel, R. (1991). A novel multigene family may encode odorant receptors: A molecular basis for odor recognition. *Cell, 65*, 175–187.

Bullock, T. H. (1984). Comparative neuroscience holds promise for quiet revolutions. *Science, 225*, 473–478.

Bullock, T. H. (1986). Some principles in the brain analysis of important signals: Mapping and stimulus recognition. *Brain, Behavior and Evolution, 28*, 145–156.

Bullock, T. H., Bennett, M. V. L., Johnston, D., Josephson, R., et al. (2005). Neuroscience: The neuron doctrine, redux. *Science, 310*, 791–793.

Bunce, M., Worthy, T. H., Ford, T., Hoppitt, W., et al. (2003). Extreme reversed sexual size dimorphism in the extinct New Zealand moa *Dinornis. Nature, 425*, 172–175.

Burgdorf, J., Kroes, R. A., Moskal, J. R., Pfaus, J. G., et al. (2008). Ultrasonic vocalizations of rats (*Rattus norvegicus*) during mating, play, and aggression: Behavioral concomitants, relationship to reward, and self-administration of playback. *Journal of Comparative Psychology, 122*, 357–367.

Burnett, A. L. (2006). Nitric oxide in the penis—Science and therapeutic implications from erectile dysfunction to priapism. *Journal of Sexual Medicine, 3*, 578–582.

Burton, S. (2006). Symptom domains of schizophrenia: The role of atypical antipsychotic agents. *Journal of Psychopharmacology, 20*(6 Suppl.), 6–19.

Buss, D. M. (2000). *The dangerous passion: Why jealousy is as necessary as love and sex.* New York: Free Press.

Butler, A. C., Chapman, J. E., Forman, E. M., and Beck, A. T. (2006). The empirical status of cognitive-behavioral therapy: A review of meta-analyses. *Clinical Psychology Review, 26*, 17–31.

C

Cacioppo, J. T., Berntson, G. G., Larsen, J. T., Poehlmann, K. M., et al. (2000). The psychophysiology of emotion. In M. Lewis and J. M. Haviland-Jones (Eds.), *Handbook of emotions* (2nd ed., pp. 173–191). New York: Guilford.

Cadoret, R. J., O'Gorman, T., Troughton, E., and Heywood, E. (1986). An adoption study of genetic and environmental factors in drug abuse. *Archives of General Psychiatry, 43*, 1131–1136.

Cahill, L. (1997). The neurobiology of emotionally influenced memory: Implications for understanding traumatic memory. In R. Yehuda and A. C. McFarlane (Eds.), *Annals of the New York Academy of Sciences: Vol. 41. Psychobiology of traumatic stress disorder* (pp. 238–246). New York: New York Academy of Sciences.

Cahill, L. (2006). Why sex matters for neuroscience. *Nature Reviews. Neuroscience, 7*, 477–484.

Cahill, L., and McGaugh, J. L. (1991). NMDA-induced lesions of the amygdaloid complex block the retention-enhancing effect of posttraining epinephrine. *Psychobiology, 19*, 206–210.

Cahill, L., Prins, B., Weber, M., and McGaugh, J. L. (1994). Beta-adrenergic activation and memory for emotional events. *Nature, 371*, 702–704.

Calder, A. J., Keane, J., Manes, F., Antoun, N., et al. (2000). Impaired recognition and experience of disgust following brain injury. *Nature Neuroscience, 3*, 1077.

Calvert, G. A., Bullmore, E. T., Brammer, M. J., Campbell, R., et al. (1997). Activation of auditory cortex during silent lipreading. *Science, 276*, 593–596.

Calvin, W. H., and Ojemann, G. A. (1994). *Conversations with Neil's brain: The neural nature of thought and language.* Reading, MA: Addison-Wesley.

Campbell, F. W., and Robson, J. G. (1968). Application of Fourier analysis to the visibility of gratings. *Journal of Physiology (London), 197*, 551–566.

Campbell, S. S., and Tobler, I. (1984). Animal sleep: A review of sleep duration across phylogeny. *Neuroscience and Biobehavioral Reviews, 8*, 269–301.

Canli, T., Zhao, Z., Kang, E., Gross, J., et al. (2001). An fMRI study of personality influences on brain reactivity to emotional stimuli. *Behavioral Neuroscience, 115*, 33–42.

Cannon, S. C. (1996). Ion-channel defects and aberrant excitability in myotonia and periodic paralysis. *Trends in Neurosciences, 19*, 3–10.

Cannon, W. B. (1929). *Bodily changes in pain, hunger, fear and rage.* New York: Appleton.

Cantalupo, C., and Hopkins, W. D. (2001). Asymmetric Broca's area in great apes. *Nature, 414*, 505.

Cantor, J. M., Blanchard, R., Paterson, A. D., and Bogaert, A. F. (2002). How many gay men owe their sexual orientation to fraternal birth order? *Archives of Sexual Behavior, 31*, 63–71.

Cao, Y. Q., Mantyh, P. W., Carlson, E. J., Gillespie, A. M., et al. (1998). Primary afferent tachykinins are required to experience moderate to intense pain. *Nature, 392*, 390–394.

Capretta, P. J., Petersik, J. T., and Stewart, D. J. (1975). Acceptance of novel flavours is is increased after early experience of diverse tastes. *Nature, 254*, 689–691.

Cardno, A. G., and Gottesman, I. I. (2000). Twin studies of schizophrenia: From bow-and-arrow concordances to star wars Mx and functional genomics. *American Journal of Medical Genetics, 97*, 12–17.

Carmichael, M. S., Warburton, V. L., Dixen, J., and Davidson, J. M. (1994). Relationships among cardiovascular, muscular, and oxytocin responses during human sexual activity. *Archives of Sexual Behavior, 23*, 59–79.

Carpen, J. D., Archer, S. N., Skene, D. J., Smits, M., et al. (2005). A single-nucleotide polymorphism in the 5′-untranslated region of the *hPER2* gene is associated with diurnal preference. *Journal of Sleep Research, 14*, 293–297.

Carreiras, M., Lopez, J., Rivero, F., and Corina, D. (2005). Linguistic perception: Neural processing of a whistled language. *Nature, 433*, 31–32.

Carroll, J., McMahon, C., Neitz, M., and Neitz, J. (2000). Flicker-photometric electroretinogram estimates of L:M cone photoreceptor ratio in men with photopigment spectra derived from genetics. *Journal of the Optical Society of America. Part A, Optics, Image Science, and Vision, 17*, 499–509.

Carter, C. S. (1992). Oxytocin and sexual behavior. *Neuroscience and Biobehavioral Reviews, 16*, 131–144.

Cartwright, R. D. (1979). The nature and function of repetitive dreams: A survey and speculation. *Psychiatry, 42*, 131–137.

Casey, B., and Hackett, B. P. (2000). Left-right axis malformations in man and mouse. *Current Opinion in Genetics and Development, 10*, 257–261.

Casey, D. E. (1989). Clozapine: Neuroleptic-induced EPS and tardive dyskinesia. *Psychopharmacology (Berlin), 99*, S47–S53.

Caspi, A., Moffitt, T. E., Cannon, M., McClay, J., et al. (2005). Moderation of the effect of adolescent-onset cannabis use on adult psychosis by a functional polymorphism in the catechol-O-methyltransferase gene: Longitudinal evidence of a gene X environment interaction. *Biological Psychiatry, 57*, 1117–1127.

Caspi, A., Sugden, K., Moffitt, T. E., Taylor, A., et al. (2003). Influence of life stress on depression: Moderation by a polymorphism in the 5-HTT gene. *Science, 301*, 386–389.

Cassens, G., Wolfe, L., and Zola, M. (1990). The neuropsychology of depressions. *Journal of Neuropsychiatry and Clinical Neurosciences, 2*, 202–213.

Casson, I. R., Sham, R., Campbell, E. A., Tarlau, M., et al. (1982). Neurological and CT evaluation of knocked-out boxers. *Journal of Neurology, Neurosurgery and Psychiatry, 45*, 170–174.

Castellanos, F. X., Lee, P. P., Sharp, W., Jeffries, N. O., et al. (2002). Developmental trajectories of brain volume abnormalities in children and adolescents with attention-deficit/hyperactivity disorder. *Journal of the American Medical Association, 288*, 1740–1748.

Catania, K. C. (2001). Early development of a somatosensory fovea: A head start in the cortical space race? *Nature Neuroscience, 4*, 353–354.

Caterina, M. J., Leffler, A., Malmberg, A. B., Martin, W. J., et al. (2000). Impaired nociception and pain sensation in mice lacking the capsaicin receptor. *Science, 288*, 306–313.

Caterina, M. J., Schumacher, M. A., Tominaga, M., Rosen, T. A., et al. (1997). The capsaicin receptor: A heat-activated ion channel in the pain pathway. *Nature, 389*, 816–824.

Chamberlain, S. R., Menzies, L., Hampshire, A., Suckling, J., et al. (2008). Orbitofrontal dysfunction in patients with obsessive-compulsive disorder and their unaffected relatives. *Science, 321*, 421–422.

Champagne, F., Diorio, J., Sharma, S., and Meaney, M. J. (2001). Naturally occurring variations in maternal behavior in the rat are associated with differences in estrogen-inducible central oxytocin receptors. *Proceedings of the National Academy of Sciences, USA, 98*, 12736–12741.

Chandrashekar, J., Hoon, M. A., Ryba, N. J., and Zuker, C. S. (2006). The receptors and cells for mammalian taste. *Nature, 444*, 288–294.

Chandrashekar, J., Mueller, K. L., Hoon, M. A., Adler, E., et al. (2000). T2Rs function as bitter taste receptors. *Cell, 100*, 703–711.

Chandrashekar, J., Yarmolinsky, D., von Buchholtz, L., Oka, Y., et al. (2009). The taste of carbonation. *Science, 326*, 443–445.

Chang, B. S., Ly, J., Appignani, B., Bodell, A., et al. (2005). Reading impairment in the neuronal migration disorder of periventricular nodular heterotopia. *Neurology, 64*, 799–803.

Chapin, J. K., Moxon, K. A., Markowitz, R. S., and Nicolelis, M. A. (1999). Real-time control of a robot arm using simultaneously recorded neurons in the motor cortex. *Nature Neuroscience, 2*, 664–670.

Chapman, C. R., Casey, K. L., Dubner, R., Foley, K. M., et al. (1985). Pain measurement: An overview. *Pain, 22*, 1–31.

Charney, D. S., Deutch, A. Y., Krystal, J. H., Southwick, S. M., et al. (1993). Psychobiologic mechanisms of posttraumatic stress disorder. *Archives of General Psychiatry, 50*, 295–305.

Chartrel, N., Alvear-Perez, R., Leprince, J., Iturrioz, X., et al. (2007). Comment on "Obestatin, a peptide encoded by the ghrelin gene, opposes ghrelin's effects on food intake." *Science, 315*, 766.

Chase, J. E., and Gidal, B. E. (1997). Melatonin: Therapeutic use in sleep disorders. *Annals of Pharmacotherapy, 31*, 1218–1226.

Chaudhari, N., Landin, A. M., and Roper, S. D. (2000). A metabotropic glutamate receptor variant functions as a taste receptor. *Nature Neuroscience, 3*, 113–119.

Chelikani, P. K., Haver, A. C., and Reidelberger, R. D. (2005). Intravenous infusion of peptide YY(3-36) potently inhibits food intake in rats. *Endocrinology, 146*, 879–888.

Chemelli, R. M., Willie, J. T., Sinton, C. M., Elmquist, J. K., et al. (1999). Narcolepsy in orexin knockout mice: Molecular genetics of sleep regulation. *Cell, 98*, 437–451.

Chen, L., and Feany, M. B. (2005). α-Synuclein phosphorylation controls neurotoxicity and inclusion formation in a *Drosophila* model of Parkinson disease. *Nature Neuroscience, 8*, 657–663.

Chen, M. S., Huber, A. B., Van Der Haar, M. E., Frank, M., et al. (2000). Nogo-A is a myelin-associated neurite outgrowth inhibitor and an antigen for monoclonal antibody IN-1. *Nature, 403*, 434–439.

Chenn, A., and Walsh, C. A. (2002). Regulation of cerebral cortical size by control of cell cycle exit in neural precursors. *Science, 297*, 365–369.

Cherry, E. C. (1953). Some experiments on the recognition of speech, with one and with two ears. *Journal of the Acoustical Society of America, 25*, 975–979.

Cheyne, J. A. (2002). Situational factors affecting sleep paralysis and associated hallucinations: Position and timing effects. *Journal of Sleep Research, 11*, 169–177.

Chiang, M.-C., Barysheva, M., Shattuck, D. W., Lee, A. D., et al. (2009). Genetics of brain fiber architecture and intellectual performance. *Journal of Neuroscience, 29*, 2212–2224.

Chiarello, C., Knight, R., and Mundel, M. (1982). Aphasia in a prelingually deaf woman. *Brain, 105*, 29–52.

Cho, K. (2001). Chronic "jet lag" produces temporal lobe atrophy and spatial cognitive deficits. *Nature Neuroscience, 4*, 567–568.

Christensen, D. (1999). Designer estrogens: Getting all the benefits, few of the risks. *Science News, 156*, 252–254.

Ciccocioppo, R., Martin-Fardon, R., and Weiss, F. (2004). Stimuli associated with a single cocaine experience elicit long-lasting cocaine-seeking. *Nature Neuroscience, 7*, 495–496.

Clapham, J. C., Arch, J. R. S., Chapman, H., Haynes, A., et al. (2000). Mice overexpressing human uncoupling protein-3 in skeletal muscle are hyperphagic and lean. *Nature, 406*, 415–418.

Classen, J., Liepert, J., Wise, S. P., Hallett, M., et al. (1998). Rapid plasticity of human cortical movement representation induced by practice. *Journal of Neurophysiology, 79*, 1117–1123.

Clemens, L. G., Gladue, B. A., and Coniglio, L. P. (1978). Prenatal endogenous androgenic influences on masculine sexual behavior and genital morphology in male and female rats. *Hormones and Behavior, 10*, 40–53.

Clemente, C. D., and Sterman, M. B. (1967). Limbic and other forebrain mechanisms in sleep induction and behavioral inhibition. *Progress in Brain Research, 27*, 34–37.

Clutton-Brock, T. H., and Harvey, P. H. (1980). Primates, brains and ecology. *Journal of Zoology, 190*, 309–323.

Cnotka, J., Güntürkün, O., Rehkämper, G., Gray, R. D., et al. (2008). Extraordinary large brains in tool-using New Caledonian crows (*Corvus moneduloides*). *Neuroscience Letters, 433*, 241–245.

Coccaro, E. F., and Siever, L. J. (1995). Personality disorders. In F. E. Bloom and D. J. Kupfer (Eds.), *Psychopharmacology: The fourth generation of progress* (pp. 1567–1679). New York: Raven.

Coggan, J. S., Bartol, T. M., Esquenazi, E., Stiles, J. R., et al. (2005). Evidence for ectopic neurotransmission at a neuronal synapse. *Science, 309*, 446–451.

Coghill, R. C., McHaffie, J. G., and Yen, Y.-F. (2003). Neural correlates of interindividual differences in the subjective experience of pain. *Proceedings of the National Academy of Sciences, USA, 100*, 8538–8542.

Cohen, A. H., Baker, M. T., and Dobrov, T. A. (1989). Evidence for functional regeneration in the adult lamprey spinal cord following transection. *Brain Research, 496*, 368–372.

Cohen, A. J., and Leckman, J. F. (1992). Sensory phenomena associated with Gilles de la Tourette's syndrome. *Journal of Clinical Psychiatry, 53*, 319–323.

Cohen, N. J., and Squire, L. R. (1980). Preserved learning and retention of pattern-analyzing skill in amnesia: Dissociation of knowing how and knowing what. *Science, 210*, 207–210.

Cohen, S., Alper, C. M., Doyle, W. H., Treanor, J. J., et al. (2006). Positive emotional style predicts resistance to illness after experimental exposure to Rhinovirus or Influenza A virus. *Psychosomatic Medicine, 68*, 809–815.

Cohen, S., Doyle, W. J., Alper, C. M., Janicki-Deverts, D., et al. (2009). Sleep habits and susceptibility to the common cold. *Archive of Internal Medicine, 169*, 62–67.

Cohen, S., Frank, E., Doyle, W. J., Skoner, D. P., et al. (1998). Types of stressors that increase susceptibility to the common cold in healthy adults. *Health Psychology, 17*, 214–223.

Cohen, S., Lichtenstein, E., Prochaska, J. O., Rossi, J. S., et al. (1989). Debunking myths about quitting: Evidence from 10 perspective studies of persons who attempt to quit smoking by themselves. *American Psychologist, 44,* 1355–1365.

Colangelo, W., and Jones, D. G. (1982). The fetal alcohol syndrome: A review and assessment of the syndrome and its neurological sequelae. *Progress in Neurobiology, 19,* 271–314.

Cole, J. (1995). *Pride and a daily marathon.* Cambridge, MA: MIT Press.

Coleman, D. L., and Hummel, K. P. (1973). The influence of genetic background on the expression of the obese (Ob) gene in the mouse. *Diabetologia, 9,* 287–293.

Collings, V. B. (1974). Human taste response as a function of locus of stimulation on the tongue and soft palate. *Perception and Psychophysics, 16,* 169–174.

Colom, R., Haier, R. J., Head, K., Álvarez-Linera, J., et al. (2009). Gray matter correlates of fluid, crystallized, and spatial intelligence: Testing the P-FIT model. *Intelligence, 37,* 124–135.

Coltman, D. W., O'Donoghue, P., Jorgenson, J. T., Hogg, J. Y., et al. (2003). Undesirable evolutionary consequences of trophy hunting. *Nature, 426,* 655–658.

Conel, J. L. (1939). *The postnatal development of the human cerebral cortex: Vol. 1. The cortex of the newborn.* Cambridge, MA: Harvard University Press.

Conel, J. L. (1947). *The postnatal development of the human cerebral cortex: Vol. 3. The cortex of the three-month infant.* Cambridge, MA: Harvard University Press.

Conel, J. L. (1959). *The postnatal development of the human cerebral cortex: Vol. 6. The cortex of the twenty-four-month infant.* Cambridge, MA: Harvard University Press.

Conn, M. P., and Parker, J. V. (2008). *The animal research war.* New York: Palgrave Macmillan.

Conrad, A. J., Abebe, T., Austin, R., Forsythe, S., et al. (1991). Hippocampal pyramidal cell disarray in schizophrenia as a bilateral phenomenon. *Archives of General Psychiatry, 48,* 413–417.

Conrad, K. L., Tseng, K. Y., Uejima, J. L., Reimers, J. M., et al. (2008). Formation of accumbens GlurR2-lacking AMPA receptors mediates incubation of cocaine craving. *Nature, 454,* 118–121.

Constantine-Paton, M., Cline, H. T., and Debski, E. (1990). Patterned activity, synaptic convergence, and the NMDA receptor in developing visual pathways. *Annual Review of Neuroscience, 13,* 129–154.

Cooke, B. M., Breedlove, S. M., and Jordan, C. L. (2003). Both estrogen receptors and androgen receptors contribute to testosterone-induced changes in the morphology of the medial amygdala and sexual arousal in male rats. *Hormones and Behavior, 43,* 336–346.

Cooke, B. M., Chowanadisai, W., and Breedlove, S. M. (2000). Post-weaning social isolation of male rats reduces the volume of the medial amygdala and leads to deficits in adult sexual behavior. *Behavioural Brain Research, 117,* 107–113.

Cooke, B. M., Tabibnia, G., and Breedlove S. M. (1999). A brain sexual dimorphism controlled by adult circulating androgens. *Proceedings of the National Academy of Sciences, USA, 96,* 7538–7540.

Cope, N., Harold, D., Hill, G., Moskvina, V., et al. (2005). Strong evidence that KIAA0319 on chromosome 6p is a susceptibility gene for developmental dyslexia. *American Journal of Human Genetics, 76,* 581–591.

Corballis, M. C. (2002). *From hand to mouth: The origins of language.* Princeton, NJ: Princeton University Press.

Corbetta, M., Kincade, J. M., Ollinger, J. M., McAvoy, M. P., et al. (2000). Voluntary orienting is dissociated from target detection in human posterior parietal cortex. *Nature Neuroscience, 3,* 292–297.

Corbetta, M., and Shulman, G. L. (1998). Human cortical mechanisms of visual attention during orienting and search. *Philosophical Transactions of the Royal Society of London. Series B: Biological Sciences, 353,* 1353–1362.

Corbetta, M., and Shulman, G. L. (2002). Control of goal-directed and stimulus-driven attention in the brain. *Nature Reviews. Neuroscience, 3,* 201–215.

Corcoran, A. J., Barber, J. R., and Conner, W. E. (2009). Tiger moth jams bat sonar. *Science, 325,* 325–327.

Corey, D. P., Garcia-Anoveros, J., Holt, J. R., Kwan, K. Y., et al. (2004). TRPA1 is a candidate for the mechanosensitive transduction channel of vertebrate hair cells. *Nature, 432,* 723–730.

Coricelli, G., Critchley, H. D., Joffily, M., O'Doherty, J. P., et al. (2005). Regret and its avoidance: A neuroimaging study of choice behavior. *Nature Neuroscience, 8,* 1255–1262.

Corkin, S. (2002). What's new with the amnesic patient H.M.? *Neuroscience, 3,* 153–159.

Corkin, S., Amaral, D. G., Gonzalez, R. G., Johnson, K. A., et al. (1997). H.M.'s medial temporal lobe lesion: Findings from magnetic resonance imaging. *Journal of Neuroscience, 17,* 3964–3979.

Corp, N., and Byrne, R. W. (2004). Sex difference in chimpanzee handedness. *American Journal of Physical Anthropology, 123,* 62–68.

Coryell, W., Noyes, R., Jr., and House, J. D. (1986). Mortality among outpatients with anxiety disorders. *American Journal of Psychiatry, 143,* 508–510.

Cosmides, L., and Tooby, J. (2000). Evolutionary psychology and the emotions. In M. Lewis and J. M. Haviland-Jones (Eds.), *Handbook of emotions* (2nd ed., pp. 91–115). New York: Guilford.

Costanzo, R. M. (1991). Regeneration of olfactory receptor cells. *CIBA Foundation Symposium, 160,* 233–242.

Courtney, S., Ungerleider, L., Keil, K., and Haxby, J. (1996). Object and spatial visual working memory activate separate neural systems in human cortex. *Cerebral Cortex, 6,* 39–49.

Cowan, W. M. (1979). The development of the brain. *Scientific American, 241*(3), 112–133.

Cox, J. J., Reimann, F., Nicholas, A. K., Thornton, G., et al. (2006). An SCN9A channelopathy causes congenital inability to experience pain. *Nature, 444,* 894–898.

Coyle, J. T., Tsai, G., and Goff, D. (2003). Converging evidence of NMDA receptor hypofunction in the pathophysiology of schizophrenia. *Annals of the New York Academy of Sciences, 1003,* 318–327.

Crabbe, J. C., Wahlsten, D., and Dudek, B. C. (1999). Genetics of mouse behavior: Interactions with laboratory environment. *Science, 284,* 1670–1672.

Cragg, B. G. (1975). The development of synapses in the visual system of the cat. *Journal of Comparative Neurology, 160,* 147–166.

Craig, A. D., Reiman, E. M., Evans, A., and Bushnell, M. C. (1996). Functional imaging of an illusion of pain. *Nature, 384,* 258–260.

Craik, F. I. M. (1985). Paradigms in human memory research. In L.-G. Nilsson and T. Archer (Eds.), *Perspectives on learning and memory* (pp. 197–221). Hillsdale, NJ: Erlbaum.

Craik, F. I. M., and Salthouse, T. A. (2007). *The handbook of aging and cognition* (3rd ed.). London: Psychology Press.

Crasto, C., Singer, M. S., and Shepherd, G. M. (2001). The olfactory receptor family album. *Genome Biology, 2,* reviews1027.1–1027.4.

Crews, D. (1994). Temperature, steroids and sex determination. *Journal of Endocrinology, 142,* 1–8.

Crouch, R. (1997). Letting the deaf be deaf. Reconsidering the use of cochlear implants in prelingually deaf children. *Hastings Center Report, 27*(4), 14–21.

Cruce, J. A. F., Greenwood, M. R. C., Johnson, P. R., and Quartermain, D. (1974). Genetic versus hypothalamic obesity: Studies of intake and dietary manipulation in rats. *Journal of Comparative and Physiological Psychology, 87,* 295–301.

Cryns, K., and Van Camp, G. (2004). Deafness genes and their diagnostic applications. *Audiology & Neuro-otology, 9,* 2–22.

Cui, M., Jiang, P., Maillet, E., Max, M., et al. (2006). The heterodimeric sweet taste receptor has multiple potential ligand binding sites. *Current Pharmaceutical Design, 12,* 4591–4600.

Cummings, D. E. (2006). Ghrelin and the short- and long-term regulation of appetite and body weight. *Physiology & Behavior, 89,* 71–84.

Cummings, J. L. (1995). Dementia: The failing brain. *Lancet, 345,* 1481–1484.

Curcio, C. A., Sloan, K. R., Packer, O., Hendrickson, A. E., et al. (1987). Distribution of cones in human and monkey retina: Individual variability and radial asymmetry. *Science, 236*, 579–582.

Curtis, V., Aunger, R., and Rabie, T. (2004). Evidence that disgust evolved to protect from risk of disease. *Proceedings. Biological Sciences, 271*(Suppl. 4), S131–S133.

Curtiss, S. (1989). The independence and task-specificity of language. In M. H. Bornstein and J. S. Bruner (Eds.), *Interaction in human development* (pp. 105–137). Hillsdale, NJ: Erlbaum.

Cytowic, R. E., and Eagleman, D. M. (2009). *Wednesday is indigo blue: Discovering the brain of synaesthesia.* Cambridge, MA: MIT Press.

Czeisler, C. A., Duffy, J. F., Shanahan, T. L., Brown, E. N., et al. (1999). Stability, precision, and near-24-hour period of the human circadian pacemaker. *Science, 284*, 2177–2181.

D

Dabbs, J. M., Jr., and Hargrove, M. F. (1997). Age, testosterone, and behavior among female prison inmates. *Psychosomatic Medicine, 59*, 477–480.

Dabbs, J. M., and Morris, R. (1990). Testosterone, social class, and antisocial behavior in a sample of 4,462 men. *Psychological Science, 1*, 209–211.

Dabbs, J. M., Ruback, R. B., Frady, R. L., Hopper, C. H., et al. (1988). Saliva testosterone and criminal violence among women. *Personality and Individual Differences, 9*, 269–275.

Dale, N., Schacher, S., and Kandel, E. R. (1988). Long-term facilitation in *Aplysia* involves increase in transmitter release. *Science, 239*, 282–285.

Dale, R. C., Heyman, I., Giovannoni, G., and Church, A. W. (2005). Incidence of anti-brain antibodies in children with obsessive-compulsive disorder. *British Journal of Psychiatry, 187*, 314–319.

Dalley, J. W., Fryer, T. D., Brichard, L., Robinson, E. S. J., et al. (2007). Nucleus accumbens D2/3 receptors predict trait impulsivity and cocaine reinforcement. *Science, 315*, 1267–1270.

Dalton, K. M., Nacewicz, B. M., Johnstone, T., Schaefer, H. S., et al. (2005). Gaze fixation and the neural circuitry of face processing in autism. *Nature Neuroscience, 8*, 519–526.

Dalton, P., Doolittle, N., Nagata, H., and Breslin, P. A. (2000). The merging of the senses: Integration of subthreshold taste and smell. *Nature Neuroscience, 3*, 431–432.

Daly, M., and Wilson, M. (1978). *Sex, evolution and behavior.* North Scituate, MA: Duxbury Press.

Damak, S., Rong, M., Yasumatsu, K., Kokrashvili, Z., et al. (2003). Detection of sweet and umami taste in the absence of taste receptor T1r3. *Science, 301*, 850–853.

Damasio, A. R., Grabowski, T. J., Bechara, A., Damasio, H., et al. (2000). Subcortical and cortical brain activity during the feeling of self-generated emotions. *Nature Neuroscience, 3*, 1049–1056.

Damasio, H. (1995). *Human brain anatomy in computerized images.* New York: Oxford University Press.

Damasio, H., Grabowski, T., Frank, R., Galaburda, A. M., et al. (1994). The return of Phineas Gage: Clues about the brain from the skull of a famous patient. *Science, 264*, 1102–1105.

Dantz, B., Edgar, D. M., and Dement, W. C. (1994). Circadian rhythms in narcolepsy: Studies on a 90 minute day. *Electroencephalography and Clinical Neurophysiology, 90*, 24–35.

Dantzer, R., O'Connor, J. C., Freund, G. G., Johnson, R. W., et al. (2008). From inflammation to sickness and depression: When the immune system subjugates the brain. *Nature Reviews. Neuroscience, 9*, 46–56.

Dapretto, M., Davies, M. S., Pfeifer, J. H., Scott, A. A., et al. (2006). Understanding emotions in others: Mirror neuron dysfunction in children with autism spectrum disorders. *Nature Neuroscience, 9*, 28–30.

D'Ardenne, K., McClure, S. M., Nystrom, L. E., and Cohen, J. D. (2008). BOLD responses reflecting dopaminergic signals in the human ventral tegmental area. *Science, 319*, 1264–1267.

Darian-Smith, I., Davidson, I., and Johnson, K. O. (1980). Peripheral neural representations of the two spatial dimensions of a textured surface moving over the monkey's finger pad. *Journal of Physiology (London), 309*, 135–146.

Dark, J., Forger, N. G., and Zucker, I. (1984). Rapid recovery of body mass after surgical removal of adipose tissue in ground squirrels. *Proceedings of the National Academy of Sciences, USA, 81*, 2270–2272.

Dark, J., Miller, D. R., and Zucker, I. (1994). Reduced glucose availability induced torpor in Siberian hamsters. *American Journal of Physiology, 267*, R496–R501.

Darwin, C. (1859). *On the origin of species by means of natural selection, or, The preservation of favoured races in the struggle for life.* London: J. Murray.

Darwin, C. (1871). *The descent of man, and selection in relation to sex.* London: J. Murray.

Darwin, C. (1872). *The expression of the emotions in man and animals.* London: J. Murray.

Davalos, D., Grutzendler, J., Yang, G., Kim, J. V., et al. (2005). ATP mediates rapid microglial response to local brain injury in vivo. *Nature Neuroscience, 8*, 752–758.

Davey-Smith, G., Frankel, S., and Yarnell, J. (1997). Sex and death: Are they related? Findings from the Caerphilly Cohort Study. *British Medical Journal (Clinical Research Edition), 315*, 1641–1644.

Davidson, J. M., Camargo, C. A., and Smith, E. R. (1979). Effects of androgen on sexual behavior in hypogonadal men. *Journal of Clinical Endocrinology and Metabolism, 48*, 955–958.

Davidson, R. M., and Bender, D. B. (1991). Selectivity for relative motion in the monkey superior colliculus. *Journal of Neurophysiology, 65*, 1115–1133.

Davidson, S., Zhang, X., Khasabov, S. G., Simone, D. A., et al. (2009). Relief of itching by scratching: State-dependent inhibition of primate spinothalamic tract neurons. *Nature Neuroscience, 12*, 544–546.

Davies, M. J., Baer, D. J., Judd, J. T., Brown, E. D., et al. (2002). Effects of moderate alcohol intake on fasting insulin and glucose concentrations and insulin sensitivity in postmenopausal women: A randomized controlled trial. *Journal of the American Medical Association, 287*, 2559–2562.

Dawson, D., and Encel, N. (1993). Melatonin and sleep in humans. *Journal of Pineal Research, 15*, 1–12.

Dawson, T. M., and Dawson, V. L. (2003). Molecular pathways of neurodegeneration in Parkinson's disease. *Science, 302*, 819–822.

Day, N. L., Leech, S. L., Richardson, G. A., Cornelius, M. D., et al. (2002). Prenatal alcohol exposure predicts continued deficits in offspring size at 14 years of age. *Alcoholism: Clinical and Experimental Research, 26*, 1584–1591.

Dearborn, G. V. N. (1932). A case of congenital general pure analgesia. *Journal of Nervous and Mental Disease, 75*, 612–615.

Debiec, J., Doyere, V., Nader, K., and LeDoux, J. E. (2006). Directly reactivated, but not indirectly reactivated, memories undergo reconsolidation in the amygdala. *Proceedings of the National Academy of Sciences, USA, 103*, 3428–3433.

Debiec, J., LeDoux, J. E., and Nader, K. (2002). Cellular and systems reconsolidation in the hippocampus. *Neuron, 36*, 527–538.

De Felipe, C., Herrero, J. F., O'Brien, J. A., Palmer, J. A., et al. (1998). Altered nociception, analgesia and aggression in mice lacking the receptor for substance P. *Nature, 392*, 394–397.

De Groot, C. M., Janus, M. D., and Bornstein, R. A. (1995). Clinical predictors of psychopathology in children and adolescents with Tourette syndrome. *Journal of Psychiatric Research, 29*, 59–70.

Dehaene-Lambertz, G., Dehaene, S., and Hertz-Pannier, L. (2002). Functional neuroimaging of speech perception in infants. *Science, 298*, 2013–2015.

DelBello, M. P., Zimmerman, M. E., Mills, N. P., Getz, G. E., et al. (2004). Magnetic resonance imaging analysis of amygdala and other subcortical brain regions in adolescents with bipolar disorder. *Bipolar Disorder, 6*, 43–52.

Delgado-Escueta, A. V., Mattson, R. H., King, L., Goldensohn, E. S., et al. (1981). The nature of aggression during epileptic seizures. *New England Journal of Medicine*, *305*, 711–716.

DeLong, M. R., Georgopoulos, A. P., Crutcher, M. D., Mitchell, S. J., et al. (1984). Functional organization of the basal ganglia: Contributions of single-cell recording studies. *CIBA Foundation Symposium*, *107*, 64–82.

de Luis, O., Valero, M. C., and Jurado, L. A. (2000). WBSCR14, a putative transcription factor gene deleted in Williams-Beuren syndrome: Complete characterisation of the human gene and the mouse ortholog. *European Journal of Human Genetics*, *8*, 215–222.

Demb, J. B., Boynton, G. M., and Heeger, D. J. (1998). Functional magnetic resonance imaging of early visual pathways in dyslexia. *Journal of Neuroscience*, *18*, 6939–6951.

Dement, W. C. (1974). *Some must watch while some must sleep*. San Francisco: Freeman.

Demyttenaere, K., Bruffaerts, R., Posada-Villa, J., Gasquet, I., et al. (2004). Prevalence, severity, and unmet need for treatment of mental disorders in the World Heatlh Organization World Mental Health Surveys. *Journal of American Medical Association*, *291*, 2581–2590.

Dennis, S. G., and Melzack, R. (1983). Perspectives on phylogenetic evolution of pain expression. In R. L. Kitchell, H. H. Erickson, E. Carstens, and L. E. Davis (Eds.), *Animal pain* (pp. 151–161). Bethesda, MD: American Physiological Society.

Denton, D., Shade, R., Zamarippa, F., Egan, G., et al. (1999). Neuroimaging of genesis and satiation of thirst and an interoceptor-driven theory of origins of primary consciousness. *Proceedings of the National Academy of Sciences, USA*, *96*, 5304–5309.

Deol, M. S., and Glueksohn-Waelsch, S. (1979). The role of inner hair cells in hearing. *Nature*, *278*, 250–252.

Depaepe, V., Suarez-Gonzalez, N., Dufour, A., Passante, L., et al. (2005). Ephrin signalling controls brain size by regulating apoptosis of neural progenitors. *Nature*, *435*, 1244–1250.

de Paiva, A., Poulain, B., Lawrence, G. W., Shone, C. C., et al. (1993). A role for the interchain disulfide or its participating thiols in the internalization of botulinum neurotoxin A revealed by a toxin derivative that binds to ecto-acceptors and inhibits transmitter release intracellularly. *Journal of Biological Chemistry*, *268*, 20838–20844.

de Quervain, D. J. (2006). Glucocorticoid-induced inhibition of memory retrieval: Implications for posttraumatic stress disorder. *Annals of the New York Academy of Sciences*, *1071*, 216–220.

Derrick, B. E., and Martinez, J. L. (1994). Frequency-dependent associative long-term potentiation at the hippocampal mossy fiber-CA3 synapse. *Proceedings of the National Academy of Sciences, USA*, *91*, 10290–10294.

DeRubeis, R. J., Siegle, G. J., and Hollon, S. D. (2008). Cognitive therapy versus medication for depression: Treatment outcomes and neural mechanisms. *Nature*, *9*, 788–796.

Descartes, R. (1662). *De homine*. Paris: Petrvm Leffen & Franciscvm Moyardvm.

Desimone, R., Albright, T. D., Gross, C. G., and Bruce, C. (1984). Stimulus-selective properties of inferior temporal neurons in the macaque. *Journal of Neuroscience*, *4*, 2051–2062.

Desimone, R., and Schein, S. J. (1987). Visual properties of neurons in area V4 of the macaque: Sensitivity to stimulus form. *Journal of Neurophysiology*, *57*, 835–868.

De Valois, K. K., De Valois, R. L., and Yund, E. W. (1979). Responses of striate cortex cells to grating and checkerboard patterns. *Journal of Physiology (London)*, *291*, 483– 505.

De Valois, R. L., and De Valois, K. K. (1980). Spatial vision. *Annual Review of Psychology*, *31*, 309–341.

De Valois, R. L., and De Valois, K. K. (1988). *Spatial vision*. New York: Oxford University Press.

De Valois, R. L., and De Valois, K. K. (1993). A multi-stage color model. *Vision Research*, *33*, 1053–1065.

Devane, W. A., Dysarz, F. A., Johnson, M. R., Melvin, L. S., et al. (1988). Determination and characterization of a cannabinoid receptor in rat brain. *Molecular Pharmacology*, *34*, 605–613.

Devane, W. A., Hanus, L., Breuer, A., Pertwee, R. G., et al. (1992). Isolation and structure of a brain constituent that binds the cannabinoid receptor. *Science*, *258*, 1946–1949.

Devinsky, O., and Bear, D. (1984). Varieties of aggressive behavior in temporal lobe epilepsy. *American Journal of Psychiatry*, *141*, 651–656.

Devlin, J. T., and Watkins, K. E. (2007). Stimulating language: Insights from TMS. *Brain*, *130*(Pt. 3), 610–622.

DeVoogd, T. J. (1994). Interactions between endocrinology and learning in the avian song system. *Annals of the New York Academy of Sciences*, *743*, 19–41.

de Vries, H. (1901). *Die Mutationen und die Mutationsperioden bei der Entstehung der Arten: Vortrag, gehalten in der allgemeinen Sitzung der Naturwissenschaftlichen Hauptgruppe der Versammlung Deutscher Naturforscher und Aerzte in Hamburg am 26. September 1901*. Leipzig, Germany: Veit.

de Waal, F. B. M. (2003). Darwin's legacy and the study of primate visual communication. *Annals of the New York Academy of Sciences*, *1000*, 7–31.

Dewsbury, D. A. (1972). Patterns of copulatory behavior in male mammals. *Quarterly Review of Biology*, *47*, 1–33.

Diamond, J., Cooper, E., Turner, C., and Macintyre, L. (1976). Trophic regulation of nerve sprouting. *Science*, *193*, 371–377.

Diamond, M. C. (1967). Extensive cortical depth measurements and neuron size increases in the cortex of environmentally enriched rats. *Journal of Comparative Neurology*, *131*, 357–364.

Diamond, M. C., Lindner, B., Johnson, R., Bennett, E. L., et al. (1975). Differences in occipital cortical synapses from environmentally enriched, impoverished, and standard colony rats. *Journal of Neuroscience Research*, *1*, 109–119.

Dichgans, J. (1984). Clinical symptoms of cerebellar dysfunction and their topodiagnostical significance. *Human Neurobiology*, *2*, 269–279.

Di Chiara, G., Tanda, G., Bassareo, V., Pontieri, F., et al. (1999). Drug addiction as a disorder of associative learning. Role of nucleus accumbens shell/extended amygdala dopamine. *Annals of the New York Academy of Sciences*, *877*, 461–485.

Dietz, P. M., Williams, S. B., Callaghan, W. M., Bachman, D. J., et al. (2007). Clinically identified maternal depression before, during, and after pregnancies ending in live births. *American Journal of Psychiatry*, *164*, 1457–1459.

DiFranza, J. R., Savageau, J. A., Fletcher, K., O'Loughlin, J., et al. (2007). Symptoms of tobacco dependence after brief intermittent use: The Development and Assessment of Nicotine Dependence in Youth-2 study. *Archives of Pediatrics & Adolescent Medicine*, *161*, 704–710.

Di Marzo, V., Goparaju, S. K., Wang, L., Liu, J., et al. (2001). Leptin-regulated endocannabinoids are involved in maintaining food intake. *Nature*, *410*, 822–825.

Di Marzo, V., and Matias, I. (2005). Endocannabinoid control of food intake and energy balance. *Nature Neuroscience*, *8*, 585–589.

Di Pelligrino, G., Fadiga, L., Fogassi, L., Galese, V., et al. (1992). Understanding motor events: A neurophysiological study. *Experimental Brain Research*, *91*, 176–180.

Dittmann, R. W., Kappes, M. E., and Kappes, M. H. (1992). Sexual behavior in adolescent and adult females with congenital adrenal hyperplasia. *Psychoneuroendocrinology*, *17*, 153–170.

Dloniak, S. M., French, J. A., and Holekamp, K. E. (2006). Rank-related maternal effect of androgens on behaviour in wild spotted hyenas. *Nature*, *440*, 1190–1193.

Dlugos, C., and Pentney, R. (1997). Morphometric evidence that the total number of synapses on Purkinje neurons of old f344 rats is reduced after long-term ethanol treatment and restored to control levels after recovery. *Alcohol and Alcoholism*, *32*, 161–172.

Do, M. T. H., Kang, S. H., Zue, T., Zhong, H., et al. (2009). Photon capture and signalling by melanopsin retinal ganglion cells. *Nature, 457,* 281–287.

Dodd, M. L., Klos, K. J., Bower, J. H., Geda, Y. E., et al. (2005). Pathological gambling caused by drugs used to treat Parkinson disease. *Archives of Neurology, 62,* 1377–1381.

Dohanich, G. (2003). Ovarian steroids and cognitive function. *Current Directions in Psychological Science, 12,* 57–61.

Dohrenwend, B. P., Turner, J. B., Turse, N. A., Adams, B. G., et al. (2006). The psychological risks of Vietnam for U.S. veterans: A revisit with new data and methods. *Science, 313,* 979–982.

Dolan, R. J. (2002). Emotion, cognition, and behavior. *Science, 298,* 1191–1194.

Dolder, C. R., and Nelson, M. H. (2008). Hypnosedative-induced complex behaviours: Incidence, mechanisms and management. *CNS Drugs, 22,* 1021–1036.

Domjan, M., and Purdy, J. E. (1995). Animal research in psychology: More than meets the eye of the general psychology student. *American Psychologist, 50,* 496–503.

Donaldson, Z. R., and Young, L. J. (2008). Oxytocin, vasopressin, and the neurogenetics of sociality. *Science, 322,* 900–903.

DonCarlos, L. L., Sarkey, S., Lorenz, B., Azcoitia, I., et al. (2006). Novel cellular phenotypes and subcellular sites for androgen action in the forebrain. *Neuroscience, 138,* 801–807.

Donegan, N. H., Lowery, R. W., and Thompson, R. F. (1983). Effects of lesioning cerebellar nuclei on conditioned leg-flexion responses. *Society for Neuroscience Abstracts, 9,* 331.

Doricchi, F., Guariglia, C., Paolucci, S., and Pizzamiglio, L. (1991). Disappearance of leftward rapid eye movements during sleep in left visual hemi-inattention. *Neuroreport, 2,* 285–288.

Dorsaint-Pierre, R., Penhune, V. B., Watkins, K. E., Neelin, P., et al. (2006). Asymmetries of the planum temporale and Heschl's gyrus: Relationship to language lateralization. *Brain, 129,* 1164–1176.

Doyon, J., Owen, A. M., Petrides, M., Sziklas, V., et al. (1996). Functional anatomy of visuomotor skill learning in human subjects examined with positron emission tomography. *European Journal of Neuroscience, 8,* 637–648.

Drea, C. M., Weldele, M. L., Forger, N. G., Coscia, E. M., et al. (1998). Androgens and masculinization of genitalia in the spotted hyaena (*Crocuta crocuta*). 2. Effects of prenatal anti-androgens. *Journal of Reproduction and Fertility, 113,* 117–127.

Drevets, W. C. (1998). Functional neuroimaging studies of depression: The anatomy of melancholia. *Annual Review of Medicine, 49,* 341–361.

Drickamer, L. C. (1992). Behavioral selection of odor cues by young female mice affects age of puberty. *Developmental Psychobiology, 25,* 461–470.

Dronkers, N. F., Wilkins, D. P., Van Valin, R. D., Jr., Redfern, B. B., et al. (2004). Lesion analysis of the brain areas involved in language comprehension. *Cognition, 92,* 145–177.

Druckman, D., and Bjork, R. A. (1994). *Learning, remembering, believing: Enhancing human performance.* Washington, DC: National Academy Press.

Du, J. L., and Poo, M. M. (2004). Rapid BDNF-induced retrograde synaptic modification in a developing retinotectal system. *Nature, 429,* 878–882.

Du, L., Bakish, D., Lapierre, Y. D., Ravindran, A. V., et al. (2000). Association of polymorphism of serotonin 2A receptor gene with suicidal ideation in major depressive disorder. *American Journal of Medical Genetics, 96,* 56–60.

Duchaine, B., Germine, L., and Nakayama, K. (2007). Family resemblance: Ten family members with prosopagnosia and within-class object agnosia. *Cognitive Neuropsychology, 24,* 419–430.

Duchamp-Viret, P., Chaput, M. A., and Duchamp, A. (1999). Odor response properties of rat olfactory receptor neurons. *Science, 284,* 2171–2174.

Dudai, Y. (1988). Neurogenic dissection of learning and short term memory in *Drosophila. Annual Review of Neuroscience, 11,* 537–563.

Duffy, J. D., and Campbell, J. J. (1994). The regional prefrontal syndromes: A theoretical and clinical overview. *Journal of Neuropsychiatry and Clinical Neurosciences, 6,* 379–387.

Dulac, C., and Torello, A. T. (2003). Molecular detection of pheromone signals in mammals, from genes to behaviour. *Nature Reviews. Neuroscience, 4,* 551–562.

Dunah, A. W., Hyunkyung, J., Griffin, A., Kim, Y.-M., et al. (2002). Sp1 and TAFII130 transcriptional activity disrupted in early Huntington's disease. *Science, 296,* 2238–2242.

Dunbar, R. I. M. (1998). The social brain hypothesis. *Evolutionary Anthropology, 6(5),* 178–190.

Dunbar, R. I. M. (2009). The social brain hypothesis and its implications for social evolution. *Annals of Human Biology, 36,* 562–572.

E

Eagleman, D. M., Kagan, A. D., Nelson, S. S., Sagaram, D., et al. (2007). A standardized test battery for the study of synesthesia. *Journal of Neuroscience Methods, 159,* 139–145.

Eales, L. A. (1985). Song learning in zebra finches (*Taeniopygia gyttata*): Some effects of song model availability on what is learnt and when. *Animal Behaviour, 33,* 1293–1300.

Earnest, D. J., Liang, F. Q., Ratcliff, M., and Cassone, V. M. (1999). Immortal time: Circadian clock properties of rat suprachiasmatic cell lines. *Science, 283,* 693–695.

Earnshaw, W. C., Martins, L. M., and Kaufmann, S. H. (1999). Mammalian caspases: Structure, activation, substrates, and functions during apoptosis. *Annual Review of Biochemistry, 68,* 383–424.

Ebbinghaus, H. (1885). *Memory* (H. A. Ruger and C. E. Bussenius, Trans.). Reprint, New York: Teachers College, Columbia University, 1913.

Eberhard, W. G. (1977). Aggressive chemical mimicry by a bolas spider. *Science, 198,* 1173–1175.

Edelsohn, G. A. (2006). Hallucinations in children and adolescents: Considerations in the emergency setting. *American Journal of Psychiatry, 163,* 781–785.

Edwards, J. S., and Palka, J. (1991). Insect neural evolution—A fugue or an opera? *Seminars in the Neurosciences, 3,* 391–398.

Edwards, R. R., Grace, E., Peterson, S., Klick, B., et al. (2009, January 23). Sleep continuity and architecture. Associations with pain-inhibitory processes in patients with temporomandibular joint disorder. *European Journal of Pain, 13,* 1043–1047.

Egaas, B., Courchesne, E., and Saitoh, O. (1995). Reduced size of corpus callosum in autism. *Archives of Neurology, 52,* 794–801.

Eisenberg, M., Kobilo, T., Berman, D. E., and Dudai, Y. (2003). Stability of retrieved memory: Inverse correlation with trace dominance. *Science, 301,* 1102–1104.

Elbert, T., Pantev, C., Wienbruch, C., Rockstroh, B., et al. (1995). Increased cortical representation of the fingers of the left hand in string players. *Science, 270,* 305–307.

Ellenbogen, J. M., Hu, P. T., Payne, J. D., Titone, D., et al. (2007). Human relational memory requires time and sleep. *Proceedings of the National Academy of Sciences, USA, 104,* 7317–7318.

Elster, A. D., and Burdette, J. H. (2001). *Magnetic resonance imaging.* Philadelphia: Mosby.

Emery, N. J., Capitanio, J. P., Mason, W. A., Machado, C. J., et al. (2001). The effects of bilateral lesions of the amygdala on dyadic social interactions in rhesus monkeys (*Macaca mulatta*). *Behavioral Neuroscience, 115,* 515–544.

Enard, W., Khaitovich, P., Klose, J., Zollner, S., et al. (2002). Intra- and interspecific variation in primate gene expression. *Science, 296,* 340–343.

Enard, W., Przeworski, M., Fisher, S. E., Lai, C. S., et al. (2002). Molecular evolution of FOXP2, a gene involved in speech and language. *Nature, 418,* 869–872.

Engel, J., Jr. (1992). Recent advances in surgical treatment of temporal lobe epilepsy. *Acta Neurologica Scandinavica. Supplementum, 140,* 71–80.

English, P. J., Ghatei, M. A., Malik, I. A., Bloom, S. R., et al. (2002). Food fails to suppress ghrelin levels in obese humans. *Journal of Clinical Endocrinology and Metabolism, 87,* 2984–2987.

Enoch, M. A., Kaye, W. H., Rotondo, A., Greenberg, B. D., et al. (1998). 5-HT2A promoter polymorphism -1438G/A, anorexia nervosa, and obsessive-compulsive disorder. *Lancet, 351,* 1785–1786.

Epstein, A. N., Fitzsimons, J. T., and Rolls, B. J. (1970). Drinking induced by injection of angiotensin into the brain of the rat. *Journal of Physiology (London), 210,* 457–474.

Erhardt, V. R., and Goldman, M. B. (1992). Adverse endocrine effects. In M. S. Keshavan and J. S. Kennedy (Eds.), *Drug-induced dysfunction in psychiatry* (pp. 293–310). New York: Hemisphere.

Erickson, J. T., Conover, J. C., Borday, V., Champagnat, J., et al. (1996). Mice lacking brain-derived neurotrophic factor exhibit visceral sensory neuron losses distinct from mice lacking NT4 and display a severe developmental deficit in control of breathing. *Journal of Neuroscience, 16,* 5361–5371.

Eriksson, P. S., Perfilieva, E., Björk-Eriksson, T., Alborn, A. M., et al. (1998). Neurogenesis in the adult human hippocampus. *Nature Medicine, 4,* 1313–1317.

Erlanger, D. M., Kutner, K. C., Barth, J. T., and Barnes, R. (1999). Neuropsychology of sports-related head injury: Dementia pugilistica to post concussion syndrome. *Clinical Neuropsychologist, 13,* 193–209.

Ernst, T., Chang, L., Leonido-Yee, M., and Speck, O. (2000). Evidence for long-term neurotoxicity associated with methamphetamine abuse: A 1H MRS study. *Neurology, 54,* 1344–1349.

Erren, T. C., Morfeld, P., Stork, J., Knauth, P., et al. (2009). Shift work, chronodisruption and cancer?—The IARC 2007 challenge for research and prevention and 10 theses from the Cologne Colloquium 2008. *Scandinavian Journal of Work, Environment & Health, 35,* 74–79.

Estes, W. K. (1997). Processes of memory loss, recovery, and distortion. *Psychological Review, 104,* 148–169.

Etcoff, N. L., Ekman, P., Magee, J. J., and Frank, M. G. (2000). Lie detection and language comprehension. *Nature, 405,* 139.

Euston, D. R., Tatsuno, M., and McNaughton, B. L. (2007). Fast-forward playback of recent memory sequences in prefrontal cortex during sleep. *Science, 318,* 1147–1150.

Evans, C. J., Keith, D. E., Morrison, H., Magendzo, K., et al. (1992). Cloning of a delta opioid receptor by functional expression. *Science, 258,* 1952–1955.

Evans, P. D., Anderson, J. R., Vallender, E. J., Gilbert, S. L., et al. (2004). Adaptive evolution of *ASPM,* a major determinant of cerebral cortical size in humans. *Human Molecular Genetics, 13,* 489–494.

Everitt, B. J., and Stacey, P. (1987). Studies of instrumental behavior with sexual reinforcement in male rats (*Rattus norvegicus*): II. Effects of preoptic area lesions, castration, and testosterone. *Journal of Comparative Psychology, 101,* 407–419.

Everson, C. A. (1993). Sustained sleep deprivation impairs host defense. *American Journal of Physiology, 265,* R1148–R1154.

Everson, C. A., Bergmann, B. M., and Rechtschaffen A. (1989). Sleep deprivation in the rat: III. Total sleep deprivation. *Sleep, 12,* 13–21.

Eybalin, M. (1993). Neurotransmitters and neuromodulators of the mammalian cochlea. *Physiological Reviews, 73,* 309–373.

F

Falk, D. (1993). Sex differences in visuospatial skills: Implications for hominid evolution. In K. R. Gibson and T. Ingold (Eds.), *Tools, language and cognition in human evolution* (pp. 216–229). Cambridge, England: Cambridge University Press.

Falk, D. (2004). Prelinguistic evolution in early hominins: Whence motherese? *Behavioral and Brain Sciences, 27,* 491–503.

Faraone, S. V., Glatt, S. J., Su, J., and Tsuang, M. T. (2004). Three potential susceptibility loci shown by a genome-wide scan for regions influencing the age at onset of mania. *American Journal of Psychiatry, 161,* 625–630.

Farbman, A. I. (1994). The cellular basis of olfaction. *Endeavour, 18,* 2–8.

Fay, R. R. (1988). *Hearing in vertebrates: A psychophysics databook.* Winnetka, IL: Hill-Fay Associates.

Feder, H. H., and Whalen, R. E. (1965). Feminine behavior in neonatally castrated and estrogen-treated male rats. *Science, 147,* 306–307.

Fehr, E., Bernhard, H., and Rockenbach, B. (2008). Egalitarianism in young children. *Nature, 454,* 1079–1083.

Fenstemaker, S. B., Zup, S. L., Frank, L. G., Glickman, S. E., et al. (1999). A sex difference in the hypothalamus of the spotted hyena. *Nature Neuroscience, 2,* 943–945.

Ferguson, J. N., Young, L. J., Hearn, E. F., Matzuk, M. M., et al. (2000). Social amnesia in mice lacking the oxytocin gene. *Nature Genetics, 25,* 284–288.

Fernald, R. D. (2000). Evolution of eyes. *Current Opinion in Neurobiology, 10,* 444–450.

Fibiger, H. C., and Lloyd, K. G. (1984). The neurobiological substrates of tardive dyskinesia: The GABA hypothesis. *Trends in Neurosciences, 8,* 462.

Fields, R. D., and Stevens-Graham, B. (2002). New insights into neuron-glia communication. *Science, 298,* 556–562.

Fields, S. (1990). Pheromone response in yeast. *Trends in Biochemical Sciences, 15,* 270–273.

Finch, C. E., and Kirkwood, T. B. L. (2000). *Chance, development, and aging.* New York: Oxford University Press.

Finger, S. (Ed.). (1978). *Recovery from brain damage: Research and theory.* New York: Plenum.

Finger, S. (1994). *Origins of neuroscience: A history of explorations into brain function.* New York: Oxford University Press.

Fink, G. R., Markowitsch, H. J., Reinkemeier, M., Bruckbauer, T., et al. (1996). Cerebral representation of one's own past: Neural networks involved in autobiographical memory. *Journal of Neuroscience, 16,* 4275–4282.

Fink, H., Rex, A., Voits, M., and Voigt, J. P. (1998). Major biological actions of CCK—A critical evaluation of research findings. *Experimental Brain Research, 123,* 77–83.

Fink, M., and Taylor, M. A. (2007). Electroconvulsive therapy: Evidence and challenges. *JAMA, 298,* 330–332.

Finlay, B. L., and Darlington, R. B. (1995). Linked regularities in the development and evolution of mammalian brains. *Science, 268,* 1578–1584.

Fischer, B., and Weber, H. (1993). Express saccades and visual attention. *Behavioral and Brain Sciences, 16,* 553–610.

Fischer, C., Hatzidimitriou, G., Wlos, J., Katz, J., et al. (1995). Reorganization of ascending 5-HT axon projections in animals previously exposed to the recreational drug (+/−)3,4-methylenedioxymethamphetamine (MDMA, "ecstasy"). *Journal of Neuroscience, 15,* 5476–5485.

Fischer, H., Andersson, J. L., Furmark, T., and Fredrikson, M. (1998). Brain correlates of an unexpected panic attack: A human positron emission tomographic study. *Neuroscience Letters, 251,* 137–140.

Fishman, R. B., Chism, L., Firestone, G. L., and Breedlove, S. M. (1990). Evidence for androgen receptors in sexually dimorphic perineal muscles of neonatal male rats. Absence of androgen accumulation by the perineal motoneurons. *Journal of Neurobiology, 21,* 694–704.

Fitch, W. T., and Hauser, M. D. (2004). Computational constraints on syntactic processing in a nonhuman primate. *Science, 303,* 377–380.

Fitzsimmons, J. T. (1998). Angiotensin, thirst, and sodium appetite. *Physiological Reviews, 78,* 583–686.

Flament, D., Ellermann, J. M., Kim, S. G., Ugurbil, K., et al. (1996). Functional magnetic resonance imaging of cerebellar activation during the learning of a visuomotor dissociation task. *Human Brain Map, 4,* 210–226.

Flegal, K. M., Carroll, M. D., Ogden, C. L., and Johnson, C. L. (2002). Prevalence and trends in obesity among US adults, 1999–2000. *Journal of the American Medical Association, 288,* 1723–1727.

Fleming, A. S., Kraemer, G. W., Gonzalez, A., Lovic, V., et al. (2002). Mothering begets mothering: The transmission of behavior and its neurobiology across generations.

Pharmacology, Biochemistry, and Behavior, 73, 61–75.

Flor, H., Nikolajsen, L., and Jensen, T. S. (2006). Phantom limb pain: A case of maladaptive CNS plasticity? *Nature Neuroscience, 7*, 873–881.

Florence, S. L., Taub, H. B., and Kaas, J. H. (1998). Large-scale sprouting of cortical connections after peripheral injury in adult macaque monkeys. *Science, 282*, 1117–1121.

Flum, D. R., Salem, L., Elrod, J. A., Dellinger, E. P., et al. (2005). Early mortality among Medicare beneficiaries undergoing bariatric surgical procedures. *JAMA, 294*, 1903–1908.

Fogassi, L., Francesco Ferrari, P., Gesierich, B., Rozzi, S., et al. (2005). Parietal lobe: From action organization to intention understanding. *Science, 308*, 662–666.

Ford, J. M. (1999). Schizophrenia: The broken P300 and beyond. *Psychophysiology, 36*, 667–682.

Forger, N. G., and Breedlove, S. M. (1986). Sexual dimorphism in human and canine spinal cord: Role of early androgen. *Proceedings of the National Academy of Sciences, USA, 83*, 7527–7531.

Forger, N. G., and Breedlove, S. M. (1987). Seasonal variation in mammalian striated muscle mass and motoneuron morphology. *Journal of Neurobiology, 18*, 155–165.

Forger, N. G., Frank, L. G., Breedlove, S. M., and Glickman, S. E. (1996). Sexual dimorphism of perineal muscles and motoneurons in spotted hyenas. *Journal of Comparative Neurology, 375*, 333–343.

Forger, N., Howell, M., Bengston, L., Mackenzie, L., et al. (1997). Sexual dimorphism in the spinal cord is absent in mice lacking the ciliary neurotrophic factor receptor. *Journal of Neuroscience, 17*, 9605–9612.

Foster, G. D., Wyatt, H. R., Hill, J. O., McGuckin, B. G., et al. (2003). A randomized trial of a low-carbohydrate diet for obesity. *New England Journal of Medicine, 348*, 2082–2090.

Foster, N. L., Cahse, T. N., Mansi, L., Brooks, R., et al. (1984). Cortical abnormalities in Alzheimer's disease. *Annals of Neurology, 16*, 649–654.

Foster, R. G., and Soni, B. G. (1998). Extraretinal photoreceptors and their regulation of temporal physiology. *Reproduction, 3*, 145–150.

Fournier, J. C., DeRubeis, R. J., Hollon, S. D., Dimidjian, S., et al. (2010). Antidepressant drug effects and depression severity: A patient-level meta-analysis. *JAMA, 303*, 47–53.

Francis, D. D., Szegda, K., Campbell, G., Martin, W. D., et al. (2003). Epigenetic sources of behavioral differences in mice. *Nature Neuroscience, 6*, 445–446.

Frank, L. G., Glickman, S. E., and Licht, P. (1991). Fatal sibling aggression, precocial development, and androgens in neonatal spotted hyenas. *Science, 252*, 702–704.

Frank, M. J., Samanta, J., Moustafa, A. A., and Sherman, S. J. (2007). Hold your horses: Impulsivity, deep brain stimulation, and medication in parkinsonism. *Science, 318*, 1309–1312.

Frankenhaeuser, M. (1978). Psychoneuroendocrine approaches to the study of emotion as related to stress and coping. *Nebraska Symposium on Motivation, 26*, 123–162.

Frankland, P. W., O'Brien, C., Masuo, O., Kirkwood, A., et al. (2001). α-CaMKII-dependent plasticity in the cortex is required for permanent memory. *Nature, 411*, 309–312.

Franklin, T. R., Acton, P. D., Maldjian, J. A., Gray, J. D., et al. (2002). Decreased gray matter concentration in the insular, orbitofrontal, cingulate, and temporal cortices of cocaine patients. *Biological Psychiatry, 51*, 134–142.

Franks, N. P. (2008). General anaesthesia: From molecular targets to neuronal pathways of sleep and arousal. *Nature, 9*, 370–386.

Franz, S. I. (1902). On the functions of the cerebrum. I. The frontal lobes in relation to the production and retention of simple sensory-motor habits. *American Journal of Physiology, 8*, 1–22.

Fredriksson, R., Lagerstrom, M. C., Lundin, L.-G., and Schioth, H. B. (2003). The G-protein coupled receptors in the human genome form five main families. Phylogenetic analysis, paralogon groups and fingerprints. *Molecular Pharmacology, 63*, 1256–1272.

Freed, C. R., Greene, P. E., Breeze, R. E., Tsai, W.-Y., et al. (2001). Transplantation of embryonic dopamine neurons for severe Parkinson's disease. *New England Journal of Medicine, 344*, 710–719.

Freedman, M. S., Lucas, R. J., Soni, B., von Schantz, M., et al. (1999). Regulation of mammalian circadian behavior by non-rod, non-cone, ocular photoreceptors. *Science, 284*, 502–504.

Freitag, J., Ludwig, G., Andreini, P., Roessler, P., et al. (1998). Olfactory receptors in aquatic and terrestrial vertebrates. *Journal of Comparative Physiology, 183*, 635–650.

Freiwald, W. A., Tsao, D. Y., and Livingstone, M. S. (2009). A face feature space in the macaque temporal lobe. *Nature Neuroscience, 12*, 1187–1196.

Frey, S. H., Bogdanov, S., Smith, J. C., Watrous, S., et al. (2008). Chronically deafferented sensory cortex recovers a grossly typical organization after allogenic hand transplantation. *Current Biology, 18*, 1530–1534.

Frey, U., Huang, Y.-Y., and Kandel, E. R. (1993). Effects of cAMP simulate a late stage of LTP in hippocampal CA1 neurons. *Science, 260*, 1661–1664.

Fridlund, A. J. (1994). *Human facial expression: An evolutionary view.* San Diego, CA: Academic Press.

Fried, I., Wilson, C. L., MacDonald, K. A., and Behnke, E. J. (1998). Electric current stimulates laughter. *Nature, 391*, 650.

Fried, I., Wilson, C. L., Morrow, J. W., Cameron, K. A., et al. (2001). Increased dopamine release in the human amygdala during performance of cognitive tasks. *Nature Neuroscience, 4*, 201–206.

Friedman, L., and Jones, B. E. (1984). Study of sleep-wakefulness states by computer graphics and cluster analysis before and after lesions of the pontine tegmentum in the cat. *Electroencephalography and Clinical Neurophysiology, 57*, 43–56.

Friedman, M., and Rosenman, R. H. (1974). *Type A behavior and your heart.* New York: Knopf.

Friedman, M. I. (1978). Hyperphagia in rats with experimental diabetes mellitus: A response to a decreased supply of utilizable fuels. *Journal of Comparative and Physiological Psychology, 92*, 109–117.

Friedrich, F. J., Egly, R., Rafal, R. D., and Beck, D. (1998). Spatial attention deficits in humans: A comparison of superior parietal and temporal-parietal junction lesions. *Neuropsychology, 12*, 193–207.

Fritz, J., Shamma, S., Elhilali, M., and Klein, D. (2003). Rapid task-related plasticity of spectrotemporal receptive fields in primary auditory cortex. *Nature Neuroscience, 6*, 1216–1223.

Froemke, R. C., Merzenich, M. M., and Schreiner, C. E. (2007). A synaptic memory trace for cortical receptive field plasticity. *Nature, 450*, 425–429.

Frost, B., Jacks, R. L., and Diamond, M. I. (2009). Propagation of Tau misfolding from the outside to the inside of a cell. *Journal of Biological Chemistry, 284*, 12845–12852.

Fukuda, K., Ogilvie, R. D., Chilcott, L., Vendittelli, A.-M., et al. (1998). The prevalence of sleep paralysis among Canadian and Japanese college students. *Dreaming: Journal of the Association for the Study of Dreams, 8*(2), 59–66.

Fuller, P. M., Lu, J., and Saper C. B. (2008). Differential rescue of light- and food-entrainable circadian rhythms. *Science, 320*, 1074–1077.

Fulton, S., Woodside, B., and Shizgal, P. (2000). Modulation of brain reward circuitry by leptin. *Science, 287*, 125–128.

Funahashi, S. (2006). Prefrontal cortex and working memory processes. *Neuroscience, 139*, 251–261.

Funk, J., Finke, K., Müller, H. J., Preger, R., et al. (2010). Systematic biases in the tactile perception of the subjective vertical in patients with unilateral neglect and the influence of upright vs. supine posture. *Neuropsychologia, 48*, 298–308.

Furey, M. L., Pietrini, P., and Haxby, J. V. (2000). Cholinergic enhancement and increased selectivity of perceptual processing during working memory. *Science, 290*, 2315–2319.

Fuster, J. M. (1990). Prefrontal cortex and the bridging of temporal gaps in the perception-action cycle. *Annals of the New York Academy of Sciences, 608,* 318–336.

G

Gabrieli, J. D. E., Sullivan, E. V., Desmond, J. E., Stebbins, G. T., et al. (1996). Behavioral and functional neuroimaging evidence for preserved conceptual implicit memory in global amnesia. *Society for Neuroscience, 22,* 1449.

Gainetdinov, R. R., Wetsel, W. C., Jones, S. R., Levin E. D., et al. (1999). Role of serotonin in the paradoxical calming effect of psychostimulants on hyperactivity. *Science, 283,* 397–401.

Galaburda, A. M. (1994). Developmental dyslexia and animal studies: At the interface between cognition and neurology. *Cognition, 56,* 833–839.

Galaburda, A. M., LoTurco, J., Ramus, F., Fitch, R. H., et al. (2006). From genes to behavior in developmental dyslexia. *Nature Neuroscience, 9,* 1213–1217.

Galea, L. A. (2008). Gonadal hormone modulation of neurogenesis in the dentate gyrus of adult male and female rodents. *Brain Res Reviews, 57,* 332–341.

Gallagher, M., Nagahara, A. H., and Burwell, R. D. (1995). Cognition and hippocampal systems in aging: Animal models. In J. L. McGaugh, N. M. Weinberger, and G. Lynch (Eds.), *Brain and memory: Modulation and mediation of neuroplasticity* (pp. 103–126). New York: Oxford University Press.

Gallagher, M., and Rapp, P. R. (1997). The use of animal models to study the effects of aging on cognition. *Annual Review of Psychology, 48,* 339–370.

Gallant, J. L., Braun, J., and Van Essen, D. C. (1993). Selectivity for polar, hyperbolic, and Cartesian gratings in macaque visual cortex. *Science, 259,* 100–103.

Gallopin, T., Fort, P., Eggermann, E., Cauli, B., et al. (2000). Identification of sleep-promoting neurons *in vitro. Nature, 404,* 992–995.

Gangwisch, J. E., Heymsfield, S. B., Boden-Albala, B., Buijs, R. M., et al. (2007). Sleep duration as a risk factor for diabetes incidence in a large U.S. sample. *Sleep, 30,* 1667–1673.

Gannon, P. J., Holloway, R. L., Broadfield, D. C., and Braun, A. R. (1998). Asymmetry of chimpanzee planum temporale: Humanlike pattern of brain language area homolog. *Science, 279,* 220–222.

Gaoni, Y., and Mechoulam, R. (1964). Isolation, structure, and partial synthesis of an active constituent of hashish. *Journal of the American Chemical Society, 86,* 1646–1647.

Garcia, J., Kimmeldorf, D. J., and Koelling, R. A. (1955). Conditioned aversion to saccharin resulting from exposure to gamma radiation. *Science, 122,* 157–158.

Gardner, L. I. (1972). Deprivation dwarfism. *Scientific American, 227*(1), 76–82.

Gardner, R. A., and Gardner, B. T. (1969). Teaching sign language to a chimpanzee. *Science, 165,* 664–672.

Gardner, R. A., and Gardner, B. T. (1984). A vocabulary test for chimpanzees (*Pan troglodytes*). *Journal of Comparative Psychology, 98,* 381–404.

Gardner, T. J., Naef, F., and Nottebohm, F. (2005). Freedom and rules: The acquisition and reprogramming of a bird's learned song. *Science, 308,* 1046–1049.

Garver, D. L., Holcomb, J. A., and Christensen, J. D. (2000). Heterogeneity of response to antipsychotics from multiple disorders in the schizophrenia spectrum. *Journal of Clinical Psychiatry, 61,* 964–972.

Gastaut, H. J., and Bert, J. (1954). EEG changes during cinematographic presentation. *Electroencephalography and Clinical Neurophysiology, 4,* 433–444.

Gaulin, S. J. C, and Fitzgerald, R. W. (1989). Sexual selection for spatial-learning ability. *Animal Behaviour, 37,* 322–331.

Gauthier, I., Behrmann, M., and Tarr, M. J. (1999). Can face recognition really be dissociated from object recognition? *Journal of Cognitive Neuroscience, 11,* 349–370.

Gauthier, I., Skudlarski, P., Gore, J. C., and Anderson, A. W. (2000). Expertise for cars and birds recruits brain areas involved in face recognition. *Nature Neuroscience, 3,* 191–197.

Gawande, A. (2002). *Complications: A surgeon's notes on an imperfect science.* New York: Metropolitan Books.

Gawande, A. (2008, June 30). The itch. *The New Yorker.*

Gazzaniga, A. M. (2008). *Human: The science behind what makes us unique.* New York: HarperCollins.

Gazzaniga, M. S., and Smylie, C. S. (1983). Facial recognition and brain asymmetries: Clues to underlying mechanisms. *Annals of Neurology, 13,* 536–540.

Gegear, R. J., Casselman, A., Waddell, S., and Reppert, S. M. (2008). Cryptochrome mediates light-dependent magnetosensitivity in *Drosophila. Nature, 454,* 1014–1018.

Gehring, W. J., and Willoughby, A. R. (2002). The medial frontal cortex and the rapid processing of monetary gains and losses. *Science, 295,* 2279–2280.

Geinisman, Y., Detoledo-Morrell, L., Morrell, F., and Heller, R. E. (1995). Hippocampal markers of age-related memory dysfunction: Behavioral, electrophysiological and morphological perspectives. *Progress in Neurobiology, 45,* 223–252.

Gemba, H., Miki, N., and Sasaki, K. (1995). Cortical field potentials preceding vocalization and influences of cerebellar hemispherectomy upon them in monkeys. *Brain Research, 697,* 143–151.

Genoux, D., Haditsch, U., Knobloch, M., Michalon, A., et al. (2002). Protein phosphatase 1 is a molecular constraint on learning and memory. *Nature, 418,* 970–975.

George, A. L., Jr. (2005). Inherited disorders of voltage-gated sodium channels. *Journal of Clinical Investigation, 115,* 1990–1999.

Georgiadis, J. R., Reinders, A. A., Paans, A. M., Renken, R., et al. (2009). Men versus women on sexual brain function: Prominent differences during tactile genital stimulation, but not during orgasm. *Human Brain Mapping, 10,* 3089–3101.

Georgopoulos, A. P., Kalaska, J. F., Caminiti, R., and Massey, J. T. (1982). On the relations between the direction of two-dimensional arm movements and cell discharge in primate motor cortex. *Journal of Neuroscience, 2,* 1527–1537.

Georgopoulos, A. P., Taira, M., and Lukashin, A. (1993). Cognitive neurophysiology of the motor cortex. *Science, 260,* 47–52.

Gerard, C. M., Mollereau, C., Vassart, G., and Parmentier, M. (1991). Molecular cloning of a human cannabinoid receptor which is also expressed in testis. *Biochemical Journal, 279,* 129–134.

Gerashchenko, D., Kohls, M. D., Greco, M. A., Waleh, N. S., et al. (2001). Hypocretin-2-saporin lesions of the lateral hypothalamus produce narcoleptic-like sleep behavior in the rat. *Neuroscience, 21,* 7273–7283.

Gershon, A. A., Dannon, P. N., and Grunhaus, L. (2003). Transcranial magnetic stimulation in the treatment of depression. *American Journal of Psychiatry, 160,* 835–845.

Geschwind, N. (1972). Language and the brain. *Scientific American, 226*(4), 76–83.

Geschwind, N. (1976). Language and cerebral dominance. In T. N. Chase (Ed.), *Nervous system: Vol. 2. The clinical neurosciences* (pp. 433–439). New York: Raven.

Geschwind, N., and Levitsky, W. (1968). Human brain: Left-right asymmetries in temporal speech region. *Science, 161,* 186–187.

Ghazanfar, A. A., and Hauser, M. D. (1999). The neuroethology of primate vocal communication: Substrates for the evolution of speech. *Trends in Cognitive Sciences, 3,* 377–384.

Gilbert, A. N., and Wysocki, C. J. (1987). The smell survey results. *National Geographic, 172,* 514–525.

Gilbert, A. N., Yamazaki, K., Beauchamp, G. K., and Thomas, L. (1986). Olfactory discrimination of mouse strains (*Mus musculus*) and major histocompatibility types by humans (*Homo sapiens*). *Journal of Comparative Psychology, 100,* 262–265.

Gilbertson, M. W., Shenton, M. E., Ciszewski, A., Kasai, K., et al. (2002). Smaller hippocampal volume predicts pathologic vulnerability to psychological trauma. *Nature Neuroscience, 5,* 1242–1247.

Gill, R. E., Tibbitts, T. L., Douglas, D. C., Hanel, C. M., et al. (2009). Extreme endurance flights by landbirds crossing the

Pacific Ocean: Ecological corridor rather than barrier? *Proceedings. Biological Sciences, 276,* 447–457.

Gitelman, D. R., Alpert, N. M., Kosslyn, S., Daffner, K., et al. (1996). Functional imaging of human right hemispheric activation for exploratory movements. *Annals of Neurology, 39,* 174–179.

Glantz, L. A., and Lewis, D. A. (2000). Decreased dendritic spine density on prefrontal cortical pyramidal neurons in schizophrenia. *Archives of General Psychiatry, 57,* 65–73.

Glantz, M., and Pickens, R. (1992). *Vulnerability to drug abuse.* Washington, DC: American Psychological Association.

Glaser, R., Rice, J., Speicher, C. E., Stout, J. C., et al. (1986). Stress depresses interferon production by leukocytes concomitant with a decrease in natural killer cell activity. *Behavioral Neuroscience, 100,* 675–678.

Glickman, S. E. (1977). Comparative psychology. In P. Mussen and M. R. Rosenzweig (Eds.), *Psychology: An introduction* (2nd ed., pp. 625–703). Lexington, MA: Heath.

Glickman, S. E., Frank, L. G., Davidson, J. M., Smith, E. R., et al. (1987). Androstenedione may organize or activate sex-reversed traits in female spotted hyenas. *Proceedings of the National Academy of Sciences, USA, 84,* 344–347.

Globus, A., Rosenzweig, M. R., Bennett, E. L., and Diamond, M. C. (1973). Effects of differential experience on dendritic spine counts in rat cerebral cortex. *Journal of Comparative and Physiological Psychology, 82,* 175–181.

Glusman, G., Yanai, I., Rubin, I., and Lancet D. (2001). The complete human olfactory subgenome. *Genome Research, 11,* 685–702.

Goebel, T. (2007). The missing years for modern humans. *Science, 315,* 194–196.

Goel, V., and Dolan, R. J. (2001). The functional anatomy of humor: Segregating cognitive and affective components. *Nature Neuroscience, 4,* 237–238.

Gogtay, N., Giedd, J. N., Lusk, L., Hayashi, K. M., et al. (2004). Dynamic mapping of human cortical development during childhood through early adulthood. *Proceedings of the National Academy of Sciences, USA, 101,* 8174–8179.

Golden, R. N., Gaynes, B. N., Ekstrom, R. D., Hamer, R. M., et al. (2005). The efficacy of light therapy in the treatment of mood disorders: A review and meta-analysis of the evidence. *American Journal of Psychiatry, 162,* 656–662.

Goldin-Meadow, S. (2006). Talking and thinking with our hands. *Current Directions in Psychological Science, 15,* 34–39.

Goldstein, J. M., Seidman, L. J., Horton, N. J., Makris, N., et al. (2001). Normal sexual dimorphism of the adult human brain assessed by in vivo magnetic resonance imaging. *Cerebral Cortex, 11,* 490–497.

Golomb, J., de Leon, M. J., George, A. E., Kluger, A., et al. (1994). Hippocampal atrophy correlates with severe cognitive impairment in elderly patients with suspected normal pressure hydrocephalus. *Journal of Neurology, Neurosurgery and Psychiatry, 57,* 590–593.

Gonzáles-Maeso, J., Ang, R. L., Yuen, T., Chan, P., et al. (2008). Identification of a serotonin/glutamate receptor complex implicated in psychosis. *Nature, 452,* 93–97.

Goodale, M. A., and Haffenden, A. (1998). Frames of reference for perception and action in the human visual system. *Neuroscience and Biobehavioral Reviews, 22,* 161–172.

Goodale, M. A., Milner, A. D., Jakobson, L. S., and Carey, D. P. (1991). A neurological dissociation between perceiving objects and grasping them. *Nature, 349,* 154–156.

Goodglass, H., Quadfasel, F. A., and Timberlake, W. H. (1964). Phrase length and the type and severity of aphasia. *Cortex, 1,* 133–153.

Goodman, C. (1979). Isogenic grasshoppers: Genetic variability and development of identified neurons. In X. O. Breakefeld (Ed.), *Neurogenetics* (pp. 101–151). New York: Elsevier.

Goodman, C. S. (1996). Mechanisms and molecules that control growth cone guidance. *Annual Review of Neuroscience, 19,* 341–377.

Gordon, N. S., Burke, S., Akil, H., Watson, S. J., et al. (2003). Socially-induced brain "fertilization": Play promotes brain derived neurotrophic factor transcription in the amygdala and dorsolateral frontal cortex in juvenile rats. *Neuroscience Letters, 341,* 17–20.

Gorelick, D. A., and Balster, R. L. (1995). Phencyclidine. In F. E. Bloom and D. J. Kupfer (Eds.), *Psychopharmacology: The fourth generation of progress* (pp. 1767–1776). New York: Raven.

Gorski, R. A., Gordon, J. H., Shryne, J. E., and Southam, A. M. (1978). Evidence for a morphological sex difference within the medial preoptic area of the rat brain. *Brain Research, 148,* 333–346.

Gorzalka, B. B., Mendelson, S. D., and Watson, N. V. (1990). Serotonin receptor subtypes and sexual behavior. *Annals of the New York Academy of Sciences, 600,* 435–444.

Gottesman, I. I. (1991). *Schizophrenia genesis: The origins of madness.* New York: Freeman.

Gottfried, J. A., O'Doherty, J., and Dolan, R. J. (2003). Encoding predictive reward value in human amygdala and orbitofrontal cortex. *Science, 301,* 1104–1107.

Gottlieb, G. (1976). The roles of experience in the development of behavior and the nervous system. In G. Gottlieb (Ed.), *Studies on the development of behavior and the nervous system: Vol. 3. Neural and behavioral specificity* (pp. 25–53). New York: Academic Press.

Gottlieb, J. (2007). From thought to action: The parietal cortex as a bridge between perception, action, and cognition. *Neuron, 53,* 9–16.

Gough, P. M., Nobre, A. C., and Devlin, J. T. (2005). Dissociating linguistic processes in the left inferior frontal cortex with transcranial magnetic stimulation. *Journal of Neuroscience, 25,* 8010–8016.

Gougoux, F., Zatorre, R. J., Lassonde, M., Voss, P., et al. (2005). A functional neuroimaging study of sound localization: Visual cortex activity predicts performance in early-blind individuals. *PLoS Biology, 3,* 324–332.

Gould, E., Beylin, A., Tanapat, P., Reeves, A., et al. (1999). Learning enhances adult neurogenesis in the hippocampal formation. *Nature Neuroscience, 2,* 260–265.

Gould, E., Reeves, A. J., Graziano, M. S., and Gross, C. G. (1999). Neurogenesis in the neocortex of adult primates. *Science, 286,* 548–552.

Gould, J. L. (1986). The biology of learning. *Annual Review of Psychology, 37,* 163–192.

Gould, S. J. (1981). *The mismeasure of man.* New York: Norton.

Grados, M. A., Walkup, J., and Walford, S. (2003). Genetics of obsessive-compulsive disorders: New findings and challenges. *Brain & Development, 25*(Suppl. 1), S55–S61.

Grady, C. L., and Craik, F. I. M. (2000). Changes in memory processing with age. *Current Opinion in Neurobiology, 10,* 224–231.

Grady, C. L., McIntosh, A. R., Horowitz, B., Maisog, J. M., et al. (1995). Age-related reductions in human recognition memory due to impaired encoding. *Science, 269,* 218–221.

Grafton, S. T., Mazziotta, J. C., Presty, S., Friston, K. J., et al. (1992). Functional anatomy of human procedural learning determined with regional cerebral blood flow and PET. *Journal of Neuroscience, 12,* 2542–2548.

Graham, D. L., Edwards, S., Bachtell, R. K., DiLeone, R., et al. (2007). Dynamic BDNF activity in nucleus accumbens with cocaine use increases self-administration and relapse. *Nature Neuroscience, 10,* 1029–1037.

Graham, R. K., Deng, Y., Slow, E. J., Haigh, B., et al. (2006). Cleavage at the caspase-6 site is required for neuronal dysfunction and degeneration due to mutant huntingtin. *Cell, 125,* 1179–1191.

Grant, P. R., and Grant, B. R. (2006). Evolution of character displacement in Darwin's finches. *Science, 313,* 224–226.

Gratton, G., and Fabiani, M. (2001). Shedding light on brain function: The event-related optical signal. *Trends in Cognitive Sciences, 5,* 357–363.

Gray, N. S., MacCulloch, M. J., Smith, J., Morris, M., et al. (2003). Violence viewed by psychopathic murderers. *Nature, 423,* 497.

Graybiel, A. M., Aosaki, T., Flaherty, A. W., and Kimura, M. (1994). The basal ganglia and adaptive motor control. *Science, 265,* 1826–1831.

Graziano, M. (2006). The organization of behavioral repertoire in motor cortex. *Annual Review of Neuroscience, 29,* 105–134.

Graziano, M. S., and Aflalo, T. N. (2007). Mapping behavioral repertoire onto the cortex. *Neuron, 56,* 239–251.

Graziano, M. S., Hu, X. T., and Gross, C. G. (1997). Coding the locations of objects in the dark. *Science, 277,* 239–241.

Green, C. S., and Bavelier, D. (2003). Action video game modifies visual selective attention. *Nature, 423,* 534–537.

Green, E., and Craddock, N. (2003). Brain-derived neurotrophic factor as a potential risk locus for bipolar disorder: Evidence, limitations, and implications. *Current Psychiatry Reports, 5,* 469–476.

Green, W. H., Campbell, M., and David, R. (1984). Psychosocial dwarfism: A critical review of the evidence. *Journal of the American Academy of Child Psychiatry, 23,* 39–48.

Greenewalt, C. H. (1968). *Bird song: Acoustics and physiology.* Washington, DC: Smithsonian Institution Press.

Greenough, W. T. (1976). Enduring brain effects of differential experience and training. In M. R. Rosenzweig and E. L. Bennett (Eds.), *Neural mechanisms of learning and memory* (pp. 255–278). Cambridge, MA: MIT Press.

Greenough, W. T., and Volkmar, F. R. (1973). Pattern of dendritic branching in occipital cortex of rats reared in complex environments. *Experimental Neurology, 40,* 491–504.

Greenspan, R. J., Finn, J. A., Jr., and Hall, J. C. (1980). Acetylcholinesterase mutants in *Drosophila* and their effects on the structure and function of the central nervous system. *Journal of Comparative Neurology, 189,* 741–774.

Grieco-Calub, T. M., Saffran, J. R., and Litovsky, R. Y. (2009). Spoken word recognition in toddlers who use cochlear implants. *Journal of Speech, Language, and Hearing Research, 52,* 1390–1400.

Griffin, L. D., and Mellon, S. H. (1999). Selective serotonin reuptake inhibitors directly alter activity of neurosteroidogenic enzymes. *Proceedings of the National Academy of Sciences, USA, 96,* 13512–13517.

Grillner, P., Hill, R., and Grillner, S. (1991). 7-Chlorokynurenic acid blocks NMDA receptor-induced fictive locomotion in lamprey—Evidence for a physiological role of the glycine site. *Acta Physiologica Scandinavica, 141,* 131–132.

Grillner, S. (1985). Neurobiological bases of rhythmic motor acts in vertebrates. *Science, 228,* 143–149.

Grimm, S., and Bajbouj, M. (2010). Efficacy of vagus nerve stimulation in the treatment of depression. *Expert Review of Neurotherapeutics, 19,* 87–92.

Grosjean, Y., Grillet, M., Augustin, H., Ferveur, J. F., et al. (2008). A glial amino-acid transporter controls synapse strength and courtship in Drosophila. *Nature Neuroscience, 11,* 54–61.

Gropp, E., Shanabrough, M., Borok, E., Xu, A. W., et al. (2005). Agouti-related peptide-expressing neurons are mandatory for feeding. *Nature Neuroscience, 8,* 1289–1291.

Grosof, D. H., Shapley, R. M., and Hawken, M. J. (1993). Macaque V1 neurons can signal "illusory" contours. *Nature, 365,* 550–552.

Gross, C. G. (2000). Neurogenesis in the adult brain: Death of a dogma. *Nature Reviews. Neuroscience, 1,* 67–73.

Grothe, B. (2003). New roles for synaptic inhibition in sound localization. *Nature Reviews. Neuroscience, 4,* 540–550.

Grover, G. J., Mellstrom, K., Ye, L., Malm, J., et al. (2003). Selective thyroid hormone receptor-β activation: A strategy for reduction of weight, cholesterol, and lipoprotein (a) with reduced cardiovascular liability. *Proceedings of the National Academy of Sciences, USA, 100,* 10067–10072.

Grumbach, M. M., and Auchus, R. J. (1999). Estrogen: Consequences and implications of human mutations in synthesis and action. *Journal of Clinical Endocrinology and Metabolism, 84,* 4677–4694.

Grunt, J. A., and Young, W. C. (1953). Consistency of sexual behavior patterns in individual male guinea pigs following castration and androgen therapy. *Journal of Comparative and Physiological Psychology, 46,* 138–144.

Grüter T., Grüter, M., and Carbon, C. C. (2008). Neural and genetic foundations of face recognition and prosopagnosia. *Journal of Neuropsychology, 2,* 79–97.

Grutzendler, J., Kasthuri, N., and Gan, W.-B. (2002). Long-term dendritic spine stability in the adult cortex. *Nature, 420,* 812–816.

Güler, A. D., Ecker, J. L., Lall, G. S., Haq, S., et al. (2008). Melanopsin cells are the principal conduits for rod-cone input to non-image-forming vision. *Nature, 453,* 102–105.

Gulevich, G., Dement, W., and Johnson, L. (1966). Psychiatric and EEG observations on a case of prolonged (264 hours) wakefulness. *Archives of General Psychiatry, 15,* 29–35.

Gur, R. E., Resnick, S. M., Alavi, A., Gur, R. C., et al. (1987). Regional brain function in schizophrenia. I. A positron emission tomography study. *Archives of General Psychiatry, 44,* 119–125.

Gurney, M. E., and Konishi, M. (1979). Hormone induced sexual differentiation of brain and behavior in zebra finches. *Science, 208,* 1380–1382.

Gurney, M. E., Pu, H., Chiu, A. Y., Dal Canto, M. C., et al. (1994). Motor neuron degeneration in mice that express a human Cu,Zn superoxide dismutase mutation. *Science, 264,* 1772–1775.

Gusella, J. F., and MacDonald, M. E. (1993). Hunting for Huntington's disease. *Molecular Genetic Medicine, 3,* 139–158.

H

Hadley, M. E., and Levine, J. E. (2006). *Endocrinology* (6th ed.). Upper Saddle River, NJ: Prentice-Hall.

Haesler, S., Rochefort, C., Georgi, B., Licznerski, P., et al. (2007). Incomplete and inaccurate vocal imitation after knockdown of FoxP2 in songbird basal ganglia nucleus Area X. *PLoS Biology, 5,* e321.

Haesler, S., Wada, K., Nshdejan, A., Morrisey, E. E., et al. (2004). FoxP2 expression in avian vocal learners and non-learners. *Journal of Neuroscience, 24,* 3164–3175.

Häfner, H. (1998). Neurodevelopmental disorder and psychosis: One disease or major risk factor? *Current Opinion in Psychiatry, 11,* 17–18.

Hafting, T., Fyhn, M., Molden, S., Moser, M. B., and Moser, E. I. (2005). Microstructure of a spatial map in the entorhinal cortex. *Nature, 436,* 801–806.

Hagstrom, S. A., Neitz, J., and Neitz, M. (1998). Variations in cone populations for red-green color vision examined by analysis of mRNA. *Neuroreport, 9,* 1963–1967.

Hagstrum, J. T. (2000). Infrasound and the avian navigational map. *Journal of Experimental Biology, 203,* 1103–1111.

Hâkansson, M. L., Brown, H., Ghilardi, N., and Skoda, R. C., et al. (1998). Leptin receptor immunoreactivity in chemically defined target neurons of the hypothalamus. *Journal of Neuroscience, 18,* 559–572.

Hall, D., Dhilla, A., Charalambous, A., Gogos, J. A., et al. (2003). Sequence variants of the brain-derived neurotrophic factor (BDNF) gene are strongly associated with obsessive-compulsive disorder. *American Journal of Human Genetics, 73,* 370–376.

Halpern, C. T., Udry, J. R., Campbell, B., and Suchindran, C. (1993). Relationships between aggression and pubertal increases in testosterone: A panel analysis of adolescent males. *Social Biology, 40,* 8–24.

Halsband, U., Matsuzaka, Y., and Tanji, J. (1994). Neuronal activity in the primate supplementary, pre-supplementary and premotor cortex during externally and internally instructed sequential movements. *Neuroscience Research, 20,* 149–155.

Hamburger, V. (1958). Regression versus peripheral control of differentiation in motor hypoplasia. *American Journal of Anatomy, 102,* 365–410.

Hamburger, V. (1975). Cell death in the development of the lateral motor column of the chick embryo. *Journal of Comparative Neurology, 160,* 535–546.

Hamer, D. H., Hu, S., Magnuson, V. L., Hu, N., et al. (1993). A linkage between DNA markers on the X chromosome and male sexual orientation. *Science, 261,* 321–327.

Hampton, R. R., Sherry, D. F., Shettleworth, S. J., Khurgel, M., et al. (1995). Hippocampal volume and food-storing behavior are related in parids. *Brain, Behavior and Evolution, 45,* 54–61.

Hamson, D. K., Csupity, A. S., Ali, F. M., and Watson, N. V. (2009). Partner preference and mount latency are masculinized in androgen insensitive rats. *Physiology & Behavior, 98,* 25–30.

Hamson, D. K., and Watson, N. V. (2004). Regional brainstem expression of Fos associated with sexual behavior in male rats. *Brain Research, 1006,* 233–240.

Han, J. H., Kushner, S. A., Yiu, A. P., Hsiang, H. L., et al. (2009). Selective erasure of a fear memory. *Science, 323,* 1492–1496.

Han, S. K., Gottsch, M. L., Lee, K. J, Popa, S. M., et al. (2005). Activation of gonadotropin-releasing hormone neurons by kisspeptin as a neuroendocrine switch for the onset of puberty. *Journal of Neuroscience, 25,* 11349–11356.

Hanakawa, T., Immisch, I., Toma, K., Dimyan, M. A., et al. (2003). Functional properties of brain areas associated with motor execution and imagery. *Journal of Neurophysiology, 89,* 989–1002.

Hanaway, J., Woolsey, T. A., Gado, M. H., and Roberts, M. P. (1998). *The brain atlas.* Bethesda, MD: Fitzgerald Science.

Hanchar, H. J., Dodson, P. D., Olsen, R. W., Otis, T. S., et al. (2005). Alcohol-induced motor impairment caused by increased extrasynaptic GABA(A) receptor activity. *Nature Neuroscience, 8,* 339–345.

Hannula-Jouppi, K., Kaminen-Ahola, N., Taipale, M., Eklund, R., et al. (2005). The axon guidance receptor gene ROBO1 is a candidate gene for developmental dyslexia. *PLoS Genetics, 1,* e50.

Harder, B. (2003). Unproven elixir: Hormone therapy tempts aging men, but its risks haven't yet been reckoned. *Science News, 163,* 296–301.

Harding, M. M., Anderberg, P. I., and Haymet, A. D. (2003). "Antifreeze" glycoproteins from polar fish. *European Journal of Biochemistry, 270,* 1381–1392.

Hardyck, C., Petrinovich, L., and Goldman, R. (1976). Left-handedness and cognitive deficit. *Cortex, 12,* 226–279.

Hare, R. D., Harpur, T. J., Hakstian, A. R., Forth, A. E., et al. (1990). The revised psychopathy checklist: Descriptive statistics, reliability, and factor structure. *Psychological Assessment, 2,* 338–341.

Harel, N. Y., and Strittmatter, S. M. (2006). Can generating axons recapitulate developmental guidance during recovery from spinal cord injury? *Nature Reviews. Neuroscience, 7,* 603–616.

Hargreaves, E. L., Rao, G., Lee, I., and Knierim, J. J. (2005). Major dissociation between medial and lateral entorhinal input to dorsal hippocampus. *Science, 308,* 1792–1794.

Harold, D., Paracchini, S., Scerri, T., Dennis, M., et al. (2006). Further evidence that the KIAA0319 gene confers susceptibility to developmental dyslexia. *Molecular Psychiatry, 11,* 1085–1091, 1061.

Harris, C. R. (2006). Embarrassment: A form of social pain. *American Scientist, 94,* 524–533.

Harris, D. S., Everhart, E. T., Mendelson, J., and Jones, R. T. (2003). The pharmacology of cocaethylene in humans following cocaine and ethanol administration. *Drug and Alcohol Dependence, 72,* 169–182.

Harris, E. W., and Cotman, C. W. (1986). Long-term potentiation of guinea pig mossy fiber responses is not blocked by N-methyl D-aspartate antagonists. *Neuroscience Letters, 70,* 132–137.

Hart, B. L. (1988). Biological basis of the behavior of sick animals. *Neuroscience and Biobehavioral Reviews, 12,* 123–137.

Hartmann, E. (1978). *The sleeping pill.* New Haven, CT: Yale University Press.

Hartmann, E. (1984). *The nightmare: The psychology and biology of terrifying dreams.* New York: Basic Books.

Harvey, P. H., and Krebs, J. R. (1990). Comparing brains. *Science, 249,* 140–146.

Hasher, L., and Zacks, R. T. (1979). Automatic and effortful processes in memory. *Journal of Experimental Psychology: General, 108,* 356–358.

Haskett, R. F. (1985). Diagnostic categorization of psychiatric disturbance in Cushing's syndrome. *American Journal of Psychiatry, 142,* 911–916.

Hatten, M. E. (1990). Riding the glial monorail: A common mechanism for glial-guided neuronal migration in different regions of the developing mammalian brain. *Trends in Neurosciences, 13,* 179–184.

Hauser, P., Zametkin, A. J., Martinez, P., Vitiello, B., et al. (1993). Attention deficit-hyperactivity disorder in people with generalized resistance to thyroid hormone. *New England Journal of Medicine, 328,* 997–1001.

Haxby, J. V. (2006). Fine structure in representations of faces and objects. *Nature Neuroscience, 9,* 1084–1086.

Hayashi-Takagi, A., Takaki, M., Graziane, N., Seshadri, S., et al. (2010). Disrupted-in-Schizophrenia 1 (DISC1) regulates spines of the glutamate synapse via Rac1. *Nature Neuroscience, 13,* 327–332.

Haynes, K. F., Gemeno, C., Yeargan, K. V., Millar, J. G., et al. (2002). Aggressive chemical mimicry of moth pheromones by a bolas spider: How does this specialist predator attract more than one species of prey? *Chemoecology, 12,* 99–105.

Hazeltine, E., Grafton, S. T., and Ivry, R. (1997). Attention and stimulus characteristics determine the locus of motor-sequence encoding. A PET study. *Brain, 120,* 123–140.

Heath, R. G. (1972). Pleasure and brain activity in man. *Journal of Nervous and Mental Diseases, 154,* 3–18.

Hebb, D. O. (1949). *The organization of behavior.* New York: Wiley.

Hedden, T., and Gabrieli, J. D. (2004). Insights into the ageing mind: A view from cognitive neuroscience. *Current Opinion in Neurology, 18,* 740–747.

Heffner, H. E., and Heffner, R. S. (1989). Unilateral auditory cortex ablation in macaques results in a contralateral hearing loss. *Journal of Neurophysiology, 62,* 789–801.

Heinrichs, R. W. (2003). Historical origins of schizophrenia: Two early madmen and their illness. *Journal for the History of Behavioral Sciences, 39,* 349–363.

Heit, S., Owens, M. J., Plotsky, P., and Nemeroff, C. B. (1997). Corticotropin-releasing factor, stress, and depression. *Neuroscientist, 3,* 186–194.

Held, R. (1993). Binocular vision—Behavioral and neuronal development. In M. H. Johnson (Ed.), *Brain development and cognition: A reader* (pp. 152–166). Oxford, England: Blackwell.

Heldmaier, G., and Ruf, T. (1992). Body temperature and metabolic rate during natural hypothermia in endotherms. *Journal of Comparative Physiology. B, Biochemical, Systemic, and Environmental Physiology, 162,* 696–706.

Helmholtz, H. von. (1962). *Treatise on physiological optics* (J. P. C. Southall, Trans.). New York: Dover. (Original work published 1894)

Hemmingsen, A. M. (1960). Energy metabolism as related to body size and respiratory surfaces, and its evolution. *Reports of Steno Memorial Hospital, Copenhagen, 9,* 1–110.

Hendrickson, A. (1985). Dots, stripes and columns in monkey visual cortex. *Trends in NeuroSciences, 8,* 406–410.

Hendriks, W. T., Ruitenberg, M. J., Blits, B., Boer, G. J., et al. (2004). Viral vector-mediated gene transfer of neurotrophins to promote regeneration of the injured spinal cord. *Progress in Brain Research, 146,* 451–476.

Henneman, E. (1991). The size principle and its relation to transmission failure in Ia projections to spinal motoneurons. *Annals of the New York Academy of Sciences, 627,* 165–168.

Heres, S., Davis, J., Maino, K., Jetzinger, E., et al. (2006). Why olanzapine beats risperidone, risperidone beats quetiapine, and quetiapine beats olanzapine: An exploratory analysis of head-to-head comparison studies of second-generation antipsychotics. *American Journal of Psychiatry, 163,* 185–194.

Herrada, G., and Dulac, C. (1997). A novel family of putative pheromone receptors in mammals with a topographically organized and sexually dimorphic distribution. *Cell, 90,* 763–773.

Herrmann, C., and Knight, R. (2001). Mechanisms of human attention: Event-related potentials and oscillations. *Neuroscience and Biobehavioral Reviews, 25,* 465–476.

Hertel, P., Fagerquist, M. V., and Svensson, T. H. (1999). Enhanced cortical dopamine output and antipsychotic-like effects of raclopride by alpha-2 adrenoceptor blockade. *Science, 286,* 105–107.

Hetherington, A. W., and Ranson, S. W. (1940). Hypothalamic lesions and adiposity in the rat. *Anatomical Record, 78,* 149–172.

Hewes, G. (1973). Primate communication and the gestural origin of language. *Current Anthropology, 14,* 5–24.

Hickey, C., Di Lollo, V., and McDonald, J. J. (2009). Electrophysiological indices of target and distractor processing in visual search. *Journal of Cognitive Neuroscience, 21,* 760–775.

Hickmott, P. W., and Steen, P. A. (2005). Large-scale changes in dendritic structure during reorganization of adult somatosensory cortex. *Nature Neuroscience, 8,* 140–142.

Highley, J. R., Walker, M. A., Esiri, M. M., McDonald, B., et al. (2001). Schizophrenia and the frontal lobes: Post-mortem stereological study of tissue volume. *British Journal of Psychiatry, 178,* 337–343.

Higley, J. D., Mehlman, P. T., Taub, D. M., Higley, S. B., et al. (1992). Cerebrospinal fluid monoamine and adrenal correlates of aggression in free-ranging rhesus monkeys. *Archives of General Psychiatry, 49,* 436–441.

Hill, R. S., and Walsh, C. A. (2005). Molecular insights into human brain evolution. *Nature, 437,* 64–67.

Hillis, D. M., Moritz, C., and Mable, B. K. (Eds.). (1996). *Molecular systematics* (2nd ed.). Sunderland, MA: Sinauer.

Hillyard, S. A., Hink, R. F., Schwent, V. L., and Picton, T. W. (1973). Electrical signs of selective attention in the human brain. *Science, 182,* 177–180.

Himle, M. B., Woods, D. W., Piacentini, J. C., and Walkup, J. T. (2006). Brief review of habit reversal training for Tourette syndrome. *Journal of Child Neurology, 21,* 719–725.

Hingson, R., Heeren, T., Winter, M., and Weschler, H. (2005). Magnitude of alcohol-related mortality and morbidity among U.S. college students ages 18–24: Changes from 1998 to 2001. *Annual Review of Public Heath, 26,* 259–279.

Hiramoto, M., Hiromi, Y., Giniger, E., and Hotta, Y. (2000). The *Drosophila* Netrin receptor Frazzled guides axons by controlling Netrin distribution. *Nature, 406,* 886–889.

Hirsch, E., Moye, D., and Dimon, J. H. (1995). Congenital indifference to pain: Long-term follow-up of two cases. *Southern Medical Journal, 88,* 851–857.

Hitt, E. (2007). Careers in neuroscience: From protons to poetry. *Science, 318,* 661–665.

Hochberg, L. R., Serruya, M. D., Friehs, G. M., Mukand, J. A., et al. (2006). Neuronal ensemble control of prosthetic devices by a human with tetraplegia. *Nature, 442,* 164–171.

Hodgkin, A. L., and Katz, B. (1949). The effect of sodium ions on the electrical activity of the giant axon of the squid. *Journal of Physiology (London), 108,* 37–77.

Hoeft, F., Hernandez, A., McMillon, G., Taylor-Hill, H., et al. (2006). Neural basis of dyslexia: A comparison between dyslexic and nondyslexic children equated for reading ability. *Journal of Neuroscience, 26,* 10700–10708.

Hofmann, A. (1981). *LSD: My problem child.* New York: McGraw-Hill.

Hohmann, A. G., Suplita, R. L., Bolton, N. M., Neely, M. H., et al. (2005). An endocannabinoid mechanism for stress-induced analgesia. *Nature, 435,* 1108–1112.

Hohmann, G. W. (1966). Some effects of spinal cord lesions on experienced emotional feelings. *Psychophysiology, 3,* 143–156.

Holden, C. (2001). Panel seeks truth in lie detector debate. *Science, 291,* 967.

Holland, R. A., Thorup, K., Vonhof, M. J., Cochran, W. W., et al. (2006). Bat orientation using Earth's magnetic field. *Nature, 444,* 702.

Hollander, E. (1999). Managing aggressive behavior in patients with obsessive-compulsive disorder and borderline personality disorder. *Journal of Clinical Psychiatry, 60*(Suppl.), 38–44.

Hollon, S. D., Thase, M. E., and Markowitz, J. C. (2002). Treatment and prevention of depression. *Psychological Science in the Public Interest, 3,* 39–77.

Holman, B. L., Mendelson, J., Garada, B., Teoh, S. K., et al. (1993). Regional cerebral blood flow improves with treatment in chronic cocaine polydrug users. *Journal of Nuclear Medicine, 34,* 723–727.

Holmes, B. (2005). Evolution: Blink and you'll miss it. *NewScientist, 2507,* 28–31.

Holmes, C., Boche, D., Wilkinson, D., Yadegarfar, G., et al. (2008). Long-term effects of Abeta42 immunisation in Alzheimer's disease: Follow-up of a randomized, placebo-controlled phase I trial. *Lancet, 372,* 216–223.

Holzenberger, M., Dupont, J., Ducos, B., Leneuve, P., et al. (2003). IGF-1 receptor regulates lifespan and resistance to oxidative stress in mice. *Nature, 421,* 182–187.

Honey, G. D., Bullmore, E. T., Soni, W., Varatheesan, M., et al. (1999). Differences in frontal cortical activation by a working memory task after substitution of risperidone for typical antipsychotic drugs in patients with schizophrenia. *Proceedings of the National Academy of Sciences, USA, 96,* 13432–13437.

Hopfinger, J. B., Buonocore, M. H., and Mangun, G. R. (2000). The neural mechanisms of top-down attentional control. *Nature Neuroscience, 3,* 284–291.

Hopfinger, J., and Mangun, G. (1998). Reflexive attention modulates processing of visual stimuli in human extrastriate cortex. *Psychological Science, 6,* 441–447.

Hopfinger, J., and Mangun, G. (2001). Tracking the influence of reflexive attention on sensory and cognitive processing. *Cognitive, Affective & Behavioral Neuroscience, 1,* 56–65.

Horton, J. C., and Adams, D. L. (2005). The cortical column: A structure without a function. *Philosophical Transactions of the Royal Society of London. Series B: Biological Sciences, 360,* 837–862.

Hsu, M., Bhatt, M., Adolphs, R., Tranel, D., et al. (2005). Neural systems responding to degrees of uncertainty in human decision-making. *Science, 310,* 1680–1683.

Huang, A. L., Chen, X., Hoon, M. A., Chandrashekar, J., et al. (2006). The cells and logic for mammalian sour taste detection. *Nature, 442,* 934–938.

Hubbard, A. (1993). A traveling-wave amplifier model of the cochlea. *Science, 259,* 68–71.

Hubel, D. H., and Wiesel, T. N. (1959). Receptive fields of single neurones in the cat's striate cortex. *Journal of Physiology (London), 148,* 573–591.

Hubel, D. H., and Wiesel, T. N. (1965). Binocular interaction in striate cortex kittens reared with artificial squint. *Journal of Neurophysiology, 28,* 1041–1059.

Hubel, D. H., Wiesel, T. N., and LeVay, S. (1977). Plasticity of ocular dominance in monkey striate cortex. *Philosophical Transactions of the Royal Society of London. Series B: Biological Sciences, 278,* 377–409.

Hudspeth, A. J. (1992). Hair-bundle mechanics and a model for mechanoelectrical transduction by hair cells. *Society of General Physiologists Series, 47,* 357–370.

Hudspeth, A. J. (1997). How hearing happens. *Neuron, 19,* 947–950.

Hudspeth, A. J., Choe, Y., Mehta, A. D., and Martin, P. (2000). Putting ion channels to work: Mechanoelectrical transduction, adaptation, and amplification by hair cells. *Proceedings of the National Academy of Sciences, USA, 97,* 11765–11772.

Huettel, S. A., Stowe, C. J., Gordon, E. M., Warner, B. T., et al. (2006). Neural signatures of economic preferences for risk and ambiguity. *Neuron, 49,* 765–775.

Huffman, K. J., Nelson, J., Clarey, J., and Krubitzer, L. (1999). Organization of somatosensory cortex in three species of marsupials, *Dasyurus hallucatus, Dactylopsila trivirgata,* and *Monodelphis domestica*: Neural correlates of morphological specializations. *Journal of Comparative Neurology, 403,* 5–32.

Hughes, J., Smith, T. W., Kosterlitz, H. W., Fothergill, L. A., et al. (1975). Identification of two related pentapeptides from the brain with potent opiate agonist activity. *Nature, 258,* 577–580.

Huizink, A. C., and Mulder, E. J. (2006). Maternal smoking, drinking or cannabis use during pregnancy and neurobehavioral and cognitive functioning in human offspring. *Neuroscience and Biobehavioral Reviews, 30,* 24–41.

Hunt, G. R., Corballis, M. C., and Gray, R. D. (2001). Laterality in tool manufacture by crows. *Nature, 414,* 707.

Huntington, G. (1872). On chorea. *Medical and Surgical Reporter, 26,* 317–321.

Huttenlocher, P. R., deCourten, C., Garey, L. J., and Van der Loos, H. (1982). Synaptogenesis in human visual cortex—Evidence for synapse elimination during normal development. *Neuroscience Letters, 33,* 247–252.

Hyde, K. L., and Peretz I. (2004). Brains that are out of tune but in time. *Psychological Science, 15,* 356–360.

Hyde, K. L., Zatorre, R. J., Griffiths, T. D., Lerch, J. P., et al. (2006). Morphometry of the amusic brain: A two-site study. *Brain, 129,* 2562–2570.

Hyde, T. M., and Weinberger, D. R. (1990). The brain in schizophrenia. *Seminars in Neurology, 10,* 276–286.

Hyde, T. M., Aaronson, B. A., Randolph, C., Rickler, K. C., et al. (1992). Relationship of birth weight to the phenotypic expression of Gilles de la Tourette's syndrome in monozygotic twins. *Neurology, 42,* 652–658.

I

Imai, T., Yamazaki, T., Kobayakawa, R., Kobayakawa, K., et al. (2009). Pre-target axon sorting establishes the neural map topography. *Science, 325,* 585–590.

Imeri, L, and Opp, M. R. (2009). How (and why) the immune system makes us sleep. *Nature Reviews. Neuroscience, 10,* 199–210.

Imperato-McGinley, J., Guerrero, L., Gautier, T., and Peterson, R. E. (1974). Steroid 5α-reductase deficiency in man: An inherited form of male pseudohermaphroditism. *Science, 86,* 1213–1215.

Insley, S. J. (2000). Long-term vocal recognition in the northern fur seal. *Nature, 406,* 404–405.

Institute of Medicine. (1990). *Broadening the base of treatment for alcohol problems.* Washington, DC: National Academy Press.

Ipata, A. E., Gee, A. L., Goldberg, M. E., and Bisley, J. W. (2006). Activity in the lateral intraparietal area predicts the goal and latency of saccades in a free-viewing visual search task. *Journal of Neuroscience, 26,* 3656–3661.

Irle, E., Exner, C., Thielen, K., Weniger, G., et al. (1998). Obsessive-compulsive disorder and ventromedial frontal lesions: Clinical and neuropsychological findings. *American Journal of Psychiatry, 155,* 255–263.

Isaacson, R. L. (1972). Hippocampal destruction in man and other animals. *Neuropsychologia, 10,* 47–64.

Isacson, O., Bjorklund, L., and Sanchez Pernaute, R. (2001). Parkinson's disease: Interpretations of transplantation study erroneous. *Nature Neuroscience, 4,* 533.

Isles, A. R., Baum, M. J., Ma, D., Keverne, E. B., et al. (2001). Urinary odour preferences in mice. *Nature, 409,* 783–784.

Ito, M. (1987). Cerebellar adaptive function in altered vestibular and visual environments. *Physiologist, 30,* S81.

Iverson, J. M., and Goldin-Meadow, S. (1998). Why people gesture when they speak. *Nature, 396,* 228.

Ivry, R. B., and Robertson, L. C. (1998). *The two sides of perception.* Cambridge, MA: MIT Press.

Iwamura, Y., and Tanaka, M. (1978). Postcentral neurons in hand region of area 2: Their possible role in the form discrimination of tactile objects. *Brain Research, 150,* 662–666.

Izumikawa, M., Minoda, R., Kawamoto, K., Abrashkin, K. A., et al. (2005). Auditory hair cell replacement and hearing improvement by *Atoh1* gene therapy in deaf mammals. *Nature Medicine, 11,* 271–276.

J

Jackson, H., and Parks, T. N. (1982). Functional synapse elimination in the developing avian cochlear nucleus with simultaneous reduction in cochlear nerve axon branching. *Journal of Neuroscience, 2,* 1736–1743.

Jacob, S., McClintock, M. K., Zelano, B., and Ober, C. (2002). Paternally inherited HLA alleles are associated with women's choice of male odor. *Nature Genetics, 30,* 175–179.

Jacobs, G. H. (1993). The distribution and nature of colour vision among the mammals. *Biological Reviews of the Cambridge Philosophical Society, 68,* 413–471.

Jacobs, G. H., Williams, G. A., Cahill, H., and Nathans, J. (2007). Emergence of novel color vision in mice engineered to express a human cone photopigment. *Science, 315,* 1723–1725.

Jacobs, L. F., Gaulin, S. J., Sherry, D. F., and Hoffman, G. E. (1990). Evolution of spatial cognition: Sex-specific patterns of spatial behavior predict hippocampal size. *Proceedings of the National Academy of Sciences, USA, 87,* 6349–6352.

Jacobs, L. F., and Spencer, W. D. (1994). Natural space-use patterns and hippocampal size in kangaroo rats. *Brain, Behavior and Evolution, 44,* 125–132.

James, T. W., Culham, J., Humphery, G. K., Milner, A. D., et al. (2003). Ventral occipital lesions impair object recognition but not object-directed grasping: An fMRI study. *Brain, 126,* 2464–2475.

James, W. (1890). *Principles of psychology.* New York: Holt.

Jamieson, D., and Roberts, A. (2000). Responses of young *Xenopus laevis* tadpoles to light dimming: Possible roles for the pineal eye. *Journal of Experimental Biology, 203,* 1857–1867.

Jaskiw, G. E., and Popli, A. P. (2004). A meta-analysis of the response to chronic L-dopa in patients with schizophrenia: Therapeutic and heuristic implications. *Psychopharmacology (Berlin), 171,* 365–374.

Jauhar, S. (2003, July 15). A malady that mimics depression. *The New York Times,* p. F5.

Jeffress, L. A. (1948). A place theory of sound localization. *Journal of Comparative and Physiological Psychology, 41,* 35–39.

Jenike, M. A., Baer, L., Ballantine, T., Martuza, R. L., et al. (1991). Cingulotomy for refractory obsessive-compulsive disorder. A long-term follow-up of 33 patients. *Archives of General Psychiatry, 48,* 548–555.

Jenkins, J., and Dallenbach, K. (1924). Obliviscence during sleep and waking. *American Journal of Psychology, 35,* 605–612.

Jenner, A. R., Rosen, G. D., and Galaburda, A. M. (1999). Neuronal asymmetries in primary visual cortex of dyslexic and nondyslexic brains. *Annals of Neurology, 46,* 189–196.

Jentsch, J. D., Redmond, D. E., Jr., Elsworth, J. D., Taylor, J. R., et al. (1997). Enduring cognitive deficits and cortical dopamine dysfunction in monkeys after long-term administration of phencyclidine. *Science, 277,* 953–955.

Jentsch, T. J., Maritzen, T., and Zdebik, A. A. (2005). Chloride channel diseases resulting from impaired transepithelial transport or vesicular function. *Journal of Clinical Investigation, 115,* 2039–2046.

Jerison, H. J. (1991). *Brain size and the evolution of mind.* New York: American Museum of Natural History.

Jiang, Y., Ruta, V., Chen, J., Lee, A., et al. (2003). The principle of gating charge movement in a voltage-dependent K$^+$ channel. *Nature, 423,* 42–48.

Johansson, R. S., and Flanagan, J. R. (2009). Coding and use of tactile signals from the fingertips in object manipulation tasks. *Nature Reviews. Neuroscience, 10,* 345–358.

Johnsen, A., Andersen, V., Sunding, C., and Lifjeld, J. T. (2000). Female bluethroats enhance offspring immunocompetence through extra-pair copulations. *Nature, 406,* 296–299.

Johnson, K. O., and Hsiao, S. S. (1992). Neural mechanisms of tactual form and texture perception. *Annual Review of Neuroscience, 15,* 227–250.

Johnson, L. C. (1969). Psychological and physiological changes following total sleep deprivation. In A. Kales (Ed.), *Sleep: Physiology and pathology.* Philadelphia: Lippincott.

Jones, K. E., Lyons, M., Bawa, P., and Lemon, R. N. (1994). Recruitment order of motoneurons during functional tasks. *Experimental Brain Research, 100,* 503–508.

Jones, P. B., Barnes, T. R. E., Davies, L., Dunn, G., et al. (2006). Randomized controlled trial of the effect on Quality of Life of second- vs first-generation antipsychotic drugs in schizophrenia. *Archives of General Psychiatry, 39*, 1079–1087.

Jordan, B. D., Jahre, C., Hauser, W. A., Zimmerman, R. D., et al. (1992). CT of 338 active professional boxers. *Radiology, 185*, 509–512.

Jordan, C. L., Breedlove, S. M., and Arnold, A. P. (1991). Ontogeny of steroid accumulation in spinal lumbar motoneurons of the rat: Implications for androgen's site of action during synapse elimination. *Journal of Comparative Neurology, 313*, 441–448.

Jordt, S.-E., Bautista, D. M., Chuang, H., McKemy, D. D., et al. (2004). Mustard oils and cannabinoids excite sensory nerve fibres through the TRP channel ANKTM1. *Nature, 427*, 260–265.

Joseph, J. S., Chun, M. M., and Nakayama, K. (1997). Attentional requirements in a "preattentive" feature search task. *Nature, 387*, 805–807.

Jouvet, M. (1967). Neurophysiology of the states of sleep. In G. C. Quarton, T. Melnechuk, and F. O. Schmitt (Eds.), *The neurosciences* (pp. 529–544). New York: Rockefeller University.

Julian, T., and McKenry, P. C. (1979). Relationship of testosterone to men's family functioning at mid-life: A research note. *Aggressive Behavior, 15*, 281–289.

K

Kaar, G. F., and Fraher, J. P. (1985). The development of alpha and gamma motoneuron fibres in the rat. I. A comparative ultrastructural study of their central and peripheral axon growth. *Journal of Anatomy, 141*, 77–88.

Kaas, J. H. (1991). Plasticity of sensory and motor maps in adult mammals. *Annual Review of Neuroscience, 14*, 137–167.

Kaas, J. H., and Hackett, T. A. (1999). "What" and "where" processing in auditory cortex. *Nature Neuroscience, 2*, 1045–1047.

Kaas, J. H., Nelson, R. J., Sur, M., Lin, C. S., et al. (1979). Multiple representations of the body within the primary somatosensory cortex of primates. *Science, 204*, 521–523.

Kable, J. W., and Glimcher, P. W. (2009). The neurobiology of decision: Consensus and controversy. *Neuron, 63*, 733–745.

Kadekaro, M., Cohen, S., Terrell, M. L., Lekan, H., et al. (1989). Independent activation of subfornical organ and hypothalamo-neurohypophysial system during administration of angiotensin II. *Peptides, 10*, 423–429.

Kafitz, K. W., Rose, C. R., Thoenen, H., and Konnerth, A. (1999). Neurotrophin-evoked rapid excitation through TrkB receptors. *Nature, 401*, 918–921.

Kagan, J. (1997). Temperament and the reactions to unfamiliarity. *Child Development, 68*, 139–143.

Kakei, S., Hoffman, D. S., and Strick, P. L. (1999). Muscle and movement representations in the primary motor cortex. *Science, 285*, 2136–2139.

Kales, A., and Kales, J. (1970). Evaluation, diagnosis and treatment of clinical conditions related to sleep. *JAMA, 213*, 2229–2235.

Kales, A., and Kales, J. D. (1974). Sleep disorders. Recent findings in the diagnosis and treatment of disturbed sleep. *New England Journal of Medicine, 290*, 487–499.

Kandel, E. R. (2009). The biology of memory: A forty-year perspective. *Journal of Neuroscience, 29*, 12748–12756.

Kandel, E. R., Castellucci, V. F., Goelet, P., and Schacher, S. (1987). 1987 cell-biological interrelationships between short-term and long-term memory. *Research Publications—Association for Research in Nervous and Mental Disease, 65*, 111–132.

Kandler, K., Clause, A., and Noh, J. (2009). Tonotopic reorganization of developing auditory brainstem circuits. *Nature Neuroscience, 12*, 711–716.

Kang, C., Riazuddin, S., Mundorff, J., Krasnewich, D., et al. (2010). Mutation in the lysosomal enzyme–targeting pathway and persistent stuttering. *New England Journal of Medicine, 362*, 677–685.

Kang, J.-E., Lim, M. M., Bateman, R. J., Lee, J. J., et al. (2009). Amyloid-β dynamics are regulated by orexin and the sleep-wake cycle. *Science, 326*, 1005–1007.

Kanwisher, N., and Wojciulik, E. (2000). Visual attention: Insights from brain imaging. *Nature Reviews. Neuroscience, 1*, 91–100.

Karasawa, J., Touho, H., Ohnishi, H., and Kawaguchi, M. (1997). Rete mirabile in humans—Case report. *Neurologia Medico-Chirurgica, 37*, 188–192.

Karch, S. B. (2006). *Drug abuse handbook* (2nd ed.). Boca Raton, FL: CRC Press.

Karlin, A. (2002). Emerging structure of the nicotinic acetylcholine receptors. *Nature Reviews. Neuroscience, 3*, 102–114.

Karni, A., Tanne, D., Rubenstein, B. S., Askenasy, J. J., et al. (1994). Dependence on REM sleep of overnight improvement of a perceptual skill. *Science, 265*, 679–682.

Karp, L. E. (1976). *Genetic engineering, threat or promise?* Chicago: Nelson-Hall.

Karpicke, J. D., and Roediger, H. L., III. (2008). The critical importance of retrieval for learning. *Science, 319*, 966–968.

Karra, E., Chandarana, K., and Batterham, R. L. (2009). The role of peptide YY in appetite regulation and obesity. *Journal of Physiology, 587*, 19–25.

Kass, R. S. (2005). The channelopathies: Novel insights into molecular and genetic mechanisms of human disease. *Journal of Clinical Investigation, 115*, 1986–1989.

Katz, D. B., and Steinmetz, J. E. (2002). Psychological functions of the cerebellum. *Behavioral Cognitive Neuroscience Review, 1*, 229–241.

Katzenberg, D., Young, T., Finn, L., Lin, L., et al. (1998). A CLOCK polymorphism associated with human diurnal preference. *Sleep, 21*, 569–576.

Kaufmann, C. A., Jeste, D. V., Shelton, R. C., Linnoila, M., et al. (1986). Noradrenergic and neuroradiological abnormalities in tardive dyskinesia. *Biological Psychiatry, 21*, 799–812.

Kaushall, P. I., Zetin, M., and Squire, L. R. (1981). A psychosocial study of chronic, circumscribed amnesia. *Journal of Nervous and Mental Disease, 169*, 383–389.

Kay, K. N., Naselaris, T., Prenger, R. J., and Gallant, J. L. (2008). Identifying natural images from human brain activity. *Nature, 452*, 352–355.

Kaye, W. H., Fudge, J. L., and Paulus, M. (2009). New insights into symptoms and neurocircuit function of anorexia nervosa. *Nature Reviews. Neuroscience, 10*, 573–584.

Keane, T. M. (1998). Psychological and behavioral treatments of post-traumatic stress disorder. In P. E. Nathan, and J. M. Gorman (Eds.), *A guide to treatments that work* (pp. 398–407). New York: Oxford University Press.

Kee, N., Teixeira, C. M., Wang, A. H., and Frankland, P. W. (2007). Preferential incorporation of adult-generated granule cells into spatial memory networks in the dentate gyrus. *Nature Neuroscience, 10*, 355–362.

Keenan, J. P., Nelson, A., O'Connor, M., and Pascual-Leone, A. (2001). Self-recognition and the right hemisphere. *Nature, 409*, 305.

Keesey, R. E. (1980). A set-point analysis of the regulation of body weight. In A. J. Stunkard (Ed.), *Obesity* (pp. 144–165). Philadelphia: Saunders.

Keesey, R. E., and Boyle, P. C. (1973). Effects of quinine adulteration upon body weight of LH-lesioned and intact male rats. *Journal of Comparative and Physiological Psychology, 84*, 38–46.

Keesey, R. E., and Corbett, S. W. (1984). Metabolic defense of the body weight set-point. *Research Publications—Association for Research in Nervous and Mental Disease, 62*, 87–96.

Keesey, R. E., and Powley, T. L. (1986). The regulation of body weight. *Annual Review of Psychology, 37*, 109–133.

Kelso, S. R., and Brown, T. H. (1986). Differential conditioning of associative synaptic enhancement in hippocampal brain slices. *Science, 232*, 85–87.

Keltner, D., and Ekman, P. (2000). Facial expression of emotion. In M. Lewis and J. M. Haviland-Jones (Eds.), *Handbook of emotions* (2nd ed., pp. 236–250). New York: Guilford.

Kemp, D. T. (1979). The evoked cochlear mechanical responses and the auditory microstructure—Evidence for a new element in cochlear mechanics. *Scandinavian Audiology. Supplementum, 9*, 35–47.

Kemp, J. A., and McKernan, R. M. (2002). NMDA receptor pathways as drug targets. *Nature Neuroscience, 5*(Suppl.): 1039–1042.

Kemp, M. (2001). The harmonious hand. Marin Mersenne and the science of memorized music. *Nature, 409,* 666.

Kempermann, G., Kuhn, H. G., and Gage, F. H. (1997). More hippocampal neurons in adult mice living in an enriched environment. *Nature, 386,* 493–495.

Kendler, K. S., Gardner, C. O., and Prescott, C. A. (1999). Clinical characteristics of major depression that predict risk of depression in relatives. *Archives of General Psychiatry, 56,* 322–327.

Kendler, K. S., Karkowski, L. M., Neale, M. C., and Prescott, C. A. (2000). Illicit psychoactive substance use, heavy use, abuse, and dependence in a US population-based sample of male twins. *Archives of General Psychiatry, 57,* 261–269.

Kenis, G., and Maes, M. (2002). Effects of antidepressants on the production of cytokines. *International Journal of Neuropsychopharmacology, 5,* 401–412.

Kennedy, J. L., Farrer, L. A., Andreasen, N. C., Mayeux, R., et al. (2003). The genetics of adult-onset neuropsychiatric disease: Complexities and conundra? *Science, 302,* 822–826.

Kennerknecht, I., Grueter, T., Welling, B., Wentzek, S., et al. (2006). First report of prevalence of non-syndromic hereditary prosopagnosia (HPA). *American Journal of Medical Genetics. Part A, 140,* 1617–1622.

Kertesz, A., Harlock, W., and Coates, R. (1979). Computer tomographic localization, lesion size, and prognosis in aphasia and nonverbal impairment. *Brain and Language, 8,* 34–50.

Kesner, R. P. (1998). Neurobiological views of memory. In J. L. Martinez, Jr., and R. P. Kesner (Eds.), *Neurobiology of learning and memory* (3rd ed., pp. 361–416). San Diego, CA: Harcourt Brace.

Kesner, R. P., Bolland, B. L., and Dakis, M. (1993). Memory for spatial locations, motor responses, and objects: Triple dissociation among the hippocampus, caudate nucleus, and extrastriate visual cortex. *Experimental Brain Research, 93,* 462–470.

Kesner, R. P., and Novak, J. M. (1982). Serial position curve in rats: Role of the dorsal hippocampus. *Science, 218,* 173–175.

Kessels, H. W., and Malinow, R. (2009). Synaptic AMPA receptor plasticity and behavior. *Neuron, 61,* 340–350.

Kety, S., Rosenthal, D., Wender, P. H., Schulsinger, F., et al. (1975). Mental illness in the biological and adoptive families of adopted individuals who have become schizophrenic. A preliminary report based on psychiatric interviews. In R. R. Fieve, D. Rosenthal, and H. Brill (Eds.), *Genetic research in psychiatry.* Baltimore: Johns Hopkins University.

Kety, S. S., Wender, P. H., Jacobsen, B., Ingraham, L. J., et al. (1994). Mental illness in the biological and adoptive relatives of schizophrenic adoptees. Replication of the Copenhagen Study in the rest of Denmark. *Archives of General Psychiatry, 51,* 442–455.

Keynes, R. J., and Cook, G. M. (1992). Repellent cues in axon guidance. *Current Opinion in Neurobiology, 2,* 55–59.

Kiang, N. Y. S. (1965). *Discharge patterns of single fibers in the cat's auditory nerve.* Cambridge, MA: MIT Press.

Kim, D. R., Pesiridou, A., and O'Reardon, J. P. (2009). Transcranial magnetic stimulation in the treatment of psychiatric disorders. *Current Psychiatry Reports, 11,* 447–452.

Kim, D.-S., Duong, T. Q., and Kim, S.-G. (2000). High-resolution mapping of iso-orientation columns by fMRI. *Nature Neuroscience, 3,* 164–169.

Kim, J. J., and Fanselow, M. S. (1992). Modality-specific retrograde amnesia of fear. *Science, 256,* 675–677.

Kim, K. H., Relkin, N. R., Lee, K. M., and Hirsch, J. (1997). Distinct cortical areas associated with native and second languages. *Nature, 388,* 171–174.

Kimmel, H. L., Gong, W., Vechia, S. D., Hunter, R. G., et al. (2000). Intra-ventral tegmental area injection of rat cocaine and amphetamine-regulated transcript peptide 55–102 induces locomotor activity and promotes conditioned place preference. *Journal of Pharmacology and Experimental Therapeutics, 294,* 784–792.

Kimura, D. (1973). The asymmetry of the human brain. *Scientific American, 228*(3), 70–78.

Kimura, D. (1981). Neural mechanisms in manual signing. *Sign Language Studies, 33,* 291–312.

Kimura, D. (1993). *Neuromotor mechanisms in human communication.* Oxford, England: Oxford University Press.

Kimura, D., and Watson, N. V. (1989). The relation between oral movement control and speech. *Brain and Language, 37,* 565–590.

Kingsbury, S. J., and Garver, D. L. (1998). Lithium and psychosis revisited. *Progress in Neuro-Psychopharmacology & Biological Psychiatry, 22,* 249–263.

Kinney, H. C. (2009). Brainstem mechanisms underlying the sudden infant death syndrome: Evidence from human pathologic studies. *Developmental Psychobiology, 51,* 223–233.

Kinsey, A. C., Pomeroy, W. B., and Martin, C. E. (1948). *Sexual behavior in the human male.* Philadelphia: Saunders.

Kinsey, A. C., Pomeroy, W. B., Martin, C. E., and Gebhard, P. H. (1953). *Sexual behavior in the human female.* Philadelphia: Saunders.

Kirik, D., Georgievska, B., and Björklund, A. (2004). Localized striatal delivery of GDNF as a treatment for Parkinson disease. *Nature Neuroscience, 7,* 105–110.

Klar, A. J. (2003). Human handedness and scalp hair-whorl direction develop from a common genetic mechanism. *Genetics, 165,* 269–276.

Kleiber, M. (1947). Body size and metabolic rate. *Physiological Reviews, 15,* 511–541.

Klein, B. A. (2003). Signatures of sleep in a paper wasp. *Sleep, 26,* A115–A116.

Klein, M., Shapiro, K. M., and Kandel, E. R. (1980). Synaptic plasticity and the modulation of the Ca^{2+} current. *Journal of Experimental Biology, 89,* 117–157.

Klein, R. M. (2000). Inhibition of return. *Trends in Cognitive Science, 4,* 138–147.

Kleitman, N. (1969). Basic rest-activity cycle in relation to sleep and wakefulness. In A. Kales (Ed.), *Sleep: Physiology and pathology.* Philadelphia: Lippincott.

Kleitman, N., and Engelmann, T. (1953). Sleep characteristics of infants. *Journal of Applied Physiology, 6,* 269–282.

Klima, E. S., and Bellugi, U. (1979). *The signs of language.* Cambridge, MA: Harvard University Press.

Klingberg, T., Hedehus, M., Temple, E., Salz, T., et al. (2000). Microstructure of temporo-parietal white matter as a basis for reading ability: Evidence from diffusion tensor magnetic resonance imaging. *Neuron, 25,* 493–500.

Klinke, R., Kral, A., Heid, S., Tillein, J., et al. (1999). Recruitment of the auditory cortex in congenitally deaf cats by long-term cochlear electrostimulation. *Science, 285,* 1729–1733.

Kluger, M. J. (1978). The evolution and adaptive value of fever. *American Scientist, 66,* 38–43.

Klump, K. L., Miller, K. B., Keel, P. K., McGue, M., et al. (2001). Genetic and environmental influences on anorexia nervosa syndromes in a population-based twin sample. *Psychological Medicine, 31,* 737–740.

Klüver, H., and Bucy, P. C. (1938). An analysis of certain effects of bilateral temporal lobectomy in the rhesus monkey, with special reference to "psychic blindness." *Journal of Psychology, 5,* 33–54.

Knecht, S., Flöel, A., Dräger, B., Breitenstein, C., et al. (2002). Degree of language lateralization determines susceptibility to unilateral brain lesions. *Nature Neuroscience, 5,* 695–699.

Knibestol, M., and Valbo, A. B. (1970). Single unit analysis of mechanoreceptor activity from the human glabrous skin. *Acta Physiologica Scandinavica, 80,* 178–195.

Knudsen, E. I. (1982). Auditory and visual maps of space in the optic tectum of the owl. *Journal of Neuroscience, 2,* 1177–1194.

Knudsen, E. I. (1984). The role of auditory experience in the development and maintenance of sound localization. *Trends in Neurosciences, 7,* 326–330.

Knudsen, E. I. (1998). Capacity for plasticity in the adult owl auditory system expanded by juvenile experience. *Science, 279,* 1531–1533.

Knudsen, E., and Knudsen, P. (1985). Vision guides adjustment of auditory localization in young barn owls. *Science, 230,* 545–548.

Knudsen, E. I., Knudsen, P. F., and Esterly, S. D. (1984). A critical period for the recovery of sound localization accuracy following monaural occlusion in the barn owl. *Journal of Neuroscience, 4,* 1012–1020.

Knudsen, E. I., and Konishi, M. (1978). A neural map of auditory space in the owl. *Science, 200,* 795–797.

Kobatake, E., and Tanaka, K. (1994). Neuronal selectivities to complex object features in the ventral visual pathway of the macaque cerebral cortex. *Journal of Neurophysiology, 71,* 856–867.

Kobelt, P., Wisser, A. S., Stengel, A., Goebel, M., et al. (2008). Peripheral obestatin has no effect on feeding behavior and brain Fos expression in rodents. *Peptides, 29,* 1018–1027.

Koch, G., Oliveri, M., Torriero, S., and Caltagirone, C. (2005). Modulation of excitatory and inhibitory circuits for visual awareness in the human right parietal cortex. *Experimental Brain Research, 160,* 510–516.

Kodama, T., Lai, Y. Y., and Siegel, J. M. (2003). Changes in inhibitory amino acid release linked to pontine-induced atonia: An *in vivo* microdialysis study. *Journal of Neuroscience, 23,* 1548–1554.

Kogan, J. H., Frankland, P. W., Blendy, J. A., Coblentz, J., et al. (1997). Spaced training induces normal long-term memory in CREB mutant mice. *Current Biology, 7,* 1–11.

Koh, K., Joiner, W. J., Wu, M. N., Yue, Z., et al. (2008). Identification of SLEEPLESS, a sleep-promoting factor. *Science, 321,* 372–376.

Kojima, M., Hosoda, H., Date, Y., Nakazato, M., et al. (1999). Ghrelin is a growth-hormone-releasing acylated peptide from stomach. *Nature, 402,* 656–660.

Kolb, B., and Whishaw, I. Q. (1990). *Fundamentals of human neuropsychology.* San Francisco: Freeman.

Kondo, Y., Sachs, B. D., and Sakuma, Y. (1997). Importance of the medial amygdala in rat penile erection evoked by remote stimuli from estrous females. *Behavioural Brain Research, 88,* 153–160.

Kondziolka, D., Wechsler, L., Goldstein, S., Meltzer, C., et al. (2000). Transplantation of cultured human neuronal cells for patients with stroke. *Neurology, 55,* 565–569.

Konishi, M. (1985). Birdsong: From behavior to neuron. *Annual Review of Neuroscience, 8,* 125–170.

Konopka, G., Bomar, J. M., Winden, K., Coppola, G., et al. (2009). Human-specific transcriptional regulation of CNS development genes by FOXP2. *Nature, 462,* 213–217.

Konopka, R. J., and Benzer, S. (1971). Clock mutants of *Drosophila melanogaster. Proceedings of the National Academy of Sciences, USA, 68,* 2112–2116.

Koob, G. F. (1995). Animal models of drug addiction. In F. E. Bloom and D. J. Kupfer (Eds.), *Psychopharmacology: The fourth generation of progress* (pp. 759–772). New York: Raven.

Kopin, I. J., and Markey, S. P. (1988). MPTP toxicity: Implications for research in Parkinson's disease. *Annual Review of Neuroscience, 11,* 81–96.

Kordower, J. H., Chu, Y., Hauser, R. A., Freeman, T. B., et al. (2008). Lewy body-like pathology in long-term embryonic nigral transplants in Parkinson's disease. *Nature Medicine, 14,* 504–506.

Korman, M., Doyon, J., Doljansky, J., Carrier, J., et al. (2007). Daytime sleep condenses the time course of motor memory consolidation. *Nature Neuroscience, 10,* 1206–1213

Kosslyn, S. M., Alpert, N. M., Thompson, W. L., Maljkovic, V., et al. (1993). Visual mental imagery activates topographically organized visual cortex. *Journal of Cognitive Neuroscience, 5,* 263–287.

Kosslyn, S. M., Pascual-Leone, A., Felician, O., Camposano, S., et al. (1999). The role of Area 17 in visual imagery: Convergent evidence from PET and RTMS. *Science, 208,* 167–170.

Kosten, T., and Owens, S. M. (2005). Immunotherapy for the treatment of drug abuse. *Pharmacology & Therapeutics, 108,* 76–85.

Kovelman, J. A., and Scheibel, A. B. (1984). A neurohistological correlate of schizophrenia. *Biological Psychiatry, 19,* 1601.

Kraepelin, E. (1919). *Dementia praecox and paraphrenia.* Edinburgh, Scotland: Livingstone.

Krauss, R. M. (1998). Why do we gesture when we speak? *Current Directions in Psychological Science, 7*(2), 54–60.

Kraut, R. E., and Johnston, R. E. (1979). Social and emotional messages of smiling: An ethological approach. *Journal of Personality and Social Psychology, 37,* 1539–1553.

Krebs, J. R., Sherry, D. F., Healy, S. D., Perry, V. H., et al. (1989). Hippocampal specialisation of food-storing birds. *Proceedings of the National Academy of Sciences, USA, 86,* 1388–1392.

Kriegsfeld, L. J. (2006). Driving reproduction: RFamide peptides behind the wheel. *Hormones and Behavior, 50,* 655–666.

Kril, J., Halliday, G., Svoboda, M., and Cartwright, H. (1997). The cerebral cortex is damaged in chronic alcoholics. *Neuroscience, 79,* 983–998.

Kring, A. M. (1999). Emotion in schizophrenia: Old mystery, new understanding. *Current Directions in Psychological Science, 8*(5), 160–163.

Kringelbach, M. L. (2005). The human orbitofrontal cortex: Linking reward to hedonic experience. *Nature Reviews. Neuroscience, 6,* 691–702.

Kringelbach, M. L., Jenkinson, N., Owen, S. L. F., and Aziz, T. Z. (2007). Translational principles of deep brain stimulation. *Nature Reviews. Neuroscience, 8,* 623–634.

Kripke, D. F., Garfinkel, L., Wingard, D. L., Klauber, M. R., et al. (2002). Mortality associated with sleep duration and insomnia. *Archives of General Psychiatry, 59,* 131–136.

Krubitzer, L. A., Manger, P., Pettigrew, J. D., and Calford, M. B. (1995). The organization of neocortex in monotremes: In search of the prototypical plan. *Journal of Comparative Neurology, 348,* 1–45.

Kruesi, M. J. (1979). Cruelty to animals and CSF 5HIAA. *Psychiatry Research, 28,* 115–116.

Krug, M., Lössner, B., and Ott, T. (1984). Anisomycin blocks the late phase of long-term potentiation in the dentate gyrus of freely moving rat. *Brain Research Bulletin, 13,* 39–42.

Krystal, A., Krishnan, K. R., Raitiere, M., Poland, R., et al. (1990). Differential diagnosis and pathophysiology of Cushing's syndrome and primary affective disorder. *Journal of Neuropsychiatry and Clinical Neurosciences, 2,* 34–43.

Kuhl, B. A., Dudukovic, N. M., Kahn, I., and Wagner, A. D. (2007). Decreased demands on cognitive control reveal the neural processing benefits of forgetting. *Nature Neuroscience, 10,* 908–914.

Kuiper, G. G., Enmark, E., Pelto-Huikko. M., Nilsson, S., et al. (1996). Cloning of a novel receptor expressed in rat prostate and ovary. *Proceedings of the National Academy of Sciences, USA, 93,* 5925–5930.

Kulkarni, A., and Colburn, H. S. (1998). Role of spectral detail in sound-source localization. *Nature, 396,* 747–749.

Kupper, N., and Denollet, J. (2007). Type D personality as a prognostic factor in heart disease: Assessment and mediating mechanisms. *Journal of Personality Assessment, 89,* 265–276.

Kurson, R. (2007). *Crashing through: A true story of risk, adventure, and the man who dared to see.* New York: Random House.

Kutas, M., and Hillyard, S. A. (1980). Reading senseless sentences: Brain potentials reflect semantic incongruity. *Science, 207,* 203–205.

L

LaBar, K. S., Gatenby, J. C., Gore, J. C., LeDoux, J. E., et al. (1998). Human amygdala activation during conditioned fear acquisition and extinction: A mixed-trial fMRI study. *Neuron, 20,* 937–945.

Lacey, J. I., and Lacey, B. C. (1970). Some autonomic-central nervous system interrelationships. In P. Black (Ed.), *Physiologi-*

cal correlates of emotion (pp. 205–227). New York: Academic Press.

Lachman, H. M., Papolos, D. F., Boyle, A., Sheftel, G., et al. (1993). Alterations in glucorticoid inducible RNAs in the limbic system of learned helpless rats. *Brain Research, 609,* 110–116.

Lack, D. (1968). *Ecological adaptations for breeding in birds.* London: Methuen.

LaFerla, F. M., Green, K. N., and Oddo, S. (2007). Intracellular amyloid-β in Alzheimer's disease. (2007). *Nature Reviews. Neuroscience, 8,* 499–508.

Lai, C. S. L., Fisher, S. E., Hurst, J. A., Vargha-Khadem, F., et al. (2001). A forkhead-domain gene is mutated in a severe speech and language disorder. *Nature, 413,* 519–523.

Lalumiere, M. L., Blanchard, R., and Zucker, K. J. (2000). Sexual orientation and handedness in men and women: A meta-analysis. *Psychological Bulletin, 126,* 575–592.

Landau, B., and Levy, R. M. (1993). Neuromodulation techniques for medically refractory chronic pain. *Annual Review of Medicine, 44,* 279–287.

Lane, R. D., Chua, P. M., and Dolan, R. J. (1999). Common effects of emotional valence, arousal, and attention on neural activation during visual processing of pictures. *Neuropsychologia, 37,* 989–997.

Langleben, D. D., Schroeder, L., Maldjian, J. A., Gur, R. C., et al. (2002). Brain activity during simulated deception: An event-related functional magnetic resonance study. *Neuroimage, 15,* 727–732.

Langston, J. W. (1985). MPTP and Parkinson's disease. *Trends in Neurosciences, 8,* 79–83.

Larroche, J.-C. (1977). *Developmental pathology of the neonate.* Amsterdam: Excerpta Medica.

Larsson, J., Gulyas, B., and Roland, P. E. (1996). Cortical representation of self-paced finger movement. *Neuroreport, 7,* 463–468.

Lau, H. C., Rogers, R. D., Haggard, P., and Passingham, R. E. (2004). Attention to intention. *Science, 303,* 1208–1210.

Lauwers, E., Landuyt, B., Arckens, L., Schoofs, L., et al. (2006). Obestatin does not activate orphan G protein-coupled receptor GPR39. *Biochemical and Biophysical Research Communications, 351,* 21–25.

Laverty, P. H., Leskovar, A., Breur, G. J., Coates, J. R., et al. (2004). A preliminary study of intravenous surfactants in paraplegic dogs: Polymer therapy in canine clinical SCI. *Journal of Neurotrama, 21,* 1767–1777.

Lavie, N. (1995). Perceptual load as a necessary condition for selective attention. *Journal of Experimental Psychology. Human Perception and Performance, 21,* 451–468.

Lavie, N., Hirst, A., de Fockert, J. W., and Viding, E. (2004). Load theory of selective attention and cognitive control. *Journal of Experimental Psychology. General, 133,* 339–354.

Lavie, N., Lin, Z., Zokaei, N., and Thoma, V. (2009). The role of perceptual load in object recognition. *Journal of Experimental Psychology. Human Perception and Performance, 35,* 1346–1358.

Lavie, P. (1996). *The enchanted world of sleep* (A. Berris, Trans.). New Haven, CT: Yale University Press.

Lavie, P., and Kripke, D. F. (1981). Ultradian circa 1 1/2 hour rhythms: A multioscillatory system. *Life Sciences, 29,* 2445–2450.

Lavond, D. G., Kim, J. J., and Thompson, R. F. (1993). Mammalian brain substrates of aversive classical conditioning. *Annual Review of Psychology, 44,* 317–342.

Laxova, R. (1994). Fragile X syndrome. *Advances in Pediatrics, 41,* 305–342.

Lazeyras F., Boex, C., Sigrist, A., Seghier, M. L., et al. (2002). Functional MRI of auditory cortex activated by multisite electrical stimulation of the cochlea. *Neuroimage, 17,* 1010–1017.

Leber, S. M., Breedlove, S. M., and Sanes, J. R. (1990). Lineage, arrangement, and death of clonally related motoneurons in chick spinal cord. *Journal of Neuroscience, 10,* 2451–2462.

Lebrun, C. J., Blume, A., Herdegen, T., Seifert, K., et al. (1995). Angiotensin II induces a complex activation of transcription factors in the rat brain: Expression of Fos, Jun and Krox proteins. *Neuroscience, 65,* 93–99.

Ledent, C., Valverde, O., Cossu, G., Petitet, F., et al. (1999). Unresponsiveness to cannabinoids and reduced addictive effects of opiates in CB₁ receptor knockout mice. *Science, 283,* 401–404.

LeDoux, J. E. (1994). Emotion, memory and the brain. *Scientific American, 270*(6), 50–57.

LeDoux, J. E. (1995). Emotion: Clues from the brain. *Annual Review of Psychology, 46,* 209–235.

LeDoux, J. E. (1996). *The emotional brain: The mysterious underpinnings of emotional life.* London: Simon & Schuster.

Lee, C.-K., Klopp, R. G., Weindruch, R., and Prolla, T. A. (1999). Gene expression profile of aging and its retardation by caloric restriction. *Science, 285,* 1390–1393.

Lee, C.-K., Weindruch, R., and Prolla, T. A. (2000). Gene-expression profile of the ageing brain in mice. *Nature Genetics, 25,* 294–297.

Lee, H.-K., Barbarosie, M., Kameyama, K., Bear, M. F., et al. (2000). Regulation of distinct AMPA receptor phosphorylation sites during bidirectional synaptic plasticity. *Nature, 405,* 955–959.

Lee, S.-Y., and MacKinnon, R. (2004). A membrane-access mechanism of ion channel inhibition by voltage sensor toxins from spider venom. *Nature, 430,* 232–235.

Lee, T. M., and Chan, C. C. (1999). Dose-response relationship of phototherapy for seasonal affective disorder: A meta-analysis. *Acta Psychiatrica Scandinavia, 99,* 315–323.

Lefebvre, L., Whittle, P., Lascaris, E., and Finkelstein, A. (1997). Feeding innovations and forebrain size in birds. *Animal Behavior, 53,* 549–560.

Leggett, J. D., Aspley, S., Beckett, S. R., D'Antona, A. M., et al. (2004). Oleamide is a selective endogenous agonist of rat and human CB1 cannabinoid receptors. *British Journal of Pharmacology, 141,* 253–262.

Le Grand, R., Mondloch, C. J., Maurer, D., and Brent, H. P. (2001). Early visual experience and face processing. *Nature, 410,* 890.

Le Grand, R., Mondloch, C. J., Maurer, D., and Brent, H. P. (2003). Expert face processing requires visual input to the right hemisphere during infancy. *Nature Neuroscience, 6,* 1108–1112.

Le Grange, D. (2005). The Maudsley family-based treatment for adolescent anorexia nervosa. *World Psychiatry, 4,* 142–146.

Leibowitz, S. F. (1991). Brain neuropeptide Y: An integrator of endocrine, metabolic and behavioral processes. *Brain Research Bulletin, 27,* 333–337.

Leinders-Zufall, T., Lane, A. P., Puche, A. C., Ma, W., et al. (2000). Ultrasensitive pheromone detection by mammalian vomeronasal neurons. *Nature, 405,* 792–796.

Lenarz, T., Lim, H. H., Reuter, G., Patrick, J. F., et al. (2006). The auditory midbrain implant: A new auditory prosthesis for neural deafness-concept and device description. *Otology and Neurotology, 6,* 838–843.

Lennie, P., Krauskopf, J., and Sclar, G. (1990). Chromatic mechanisms in striate cortex of macaque. *Journal of Neuroscience, 10,* 649–669.

Lepage, J. F., and Theoret, H. (2006). EEG evidence for the presence of an action observation-execution matching system in children. *European Journal of Neuroscience, 23,* 2505–2510.

Lepage, M., Habib, R., and Tulving, E. (1998). Hippocampal PET activations of memory encoding and retrieval: The HIPER model. *Hippocampus, 8,* 313–322.

Leroi, I., Sheppard, J. M., and Lyketsos, C. G. (2002). Cognitive function after 11.5 years of alcohol use: Relation to alcohol use. *American Journal of Epidemiology, 156,* 747–752.

LeRoith, D., Shemer, J., and Roberts, C. T., Jr. (1992). Evolutionary origins of intercellular communication systems: Implications for mammalian biology. *Hormone Research, 38,* 1–6.

Lesné, S., Koh, M. T., Kotilinek, L., Kayed, R., et al. (2006). A specific amyloid-β protein assembly in the brain impairs memory. *Nature, 440,* 352–357.

Leung, C. T., Coulombe, P. A., and Reed, R. R. (2007). Contribution of olfactory neural stem cells to tissue maintenance and regeneration. *Nature Neuroscience, 10,* 720–726.

Leung, H. C., Gore, J. C., and Goldman-Rakic, P. S. (2002). Sustained mnemonic response in the human middle frontal gyrus during on-line storage of spatial memoranda. *Journal of Cognitive Neuroscience, 14,* 659–671.

Leung, H. C., Gore, J. C., and Goldman-Rakic, P. S. (2005). Differential anterior prefrontal activation during the recognition stage of a spatial working memory task. *Cerebral Cortex, 15,* 1742–1749.

Leutgeb, S., Leutgeb, J. K., Barnes, C. A., Moser, E. I., et al. (2005). Independent codes for spatial and episodic memory in hippocampal neuronal ensembles. *Science, 309,* 619–623.

LeVay, S. (1991). A difference in hypothalamic structure between heterosexual and homosexual men. *Science, 253,* 1034–1037.

LeVay, S. (1996). *Queer science: The use and abuse of research into homosexuality.* Cambridge, MA: MIT Press.

Levenson, R. W., Ekman, P., and Friesen, W. V. (1990). Voluntary facial action generates emotion-specific autonomic nervous system activity. *Psychophysiology, 27,* 363–384.

Leventhal, A. G. (1979). Evidence that the different classes of relay cells of the cat's lateral geniculate nucleus terminate in different layers of the striate cortex. *Experimental Brain Research, 37,* 349–372.

Leventhal, A. G., Thompson, K. G., Liu, D., Zhou, Y., et al. (1995). Concomitant sensitivity to orientation, direction, and color of cells in layers 2, 3, and 4 of monkey striate cortex. *Journal of Neuroscience, 15,* 1808–1818.

Levermann, N., Galatius, A., Ehlme, G., Rysgaard, S., et al. (2003). Feeding behaviour of free-ranging walruses with notes on apparent dextrality of flipper use. *BMC Ecology, 3,* 9.

Levi-Montalcini, R. (1963). Growth and differentiation in the nervous system. In J. Allen (Ed.), *The nature of biological diversity* (pp. 261–296). New York: McGraw-Hill.

Levi-Montalcini, R. (1982). Developmental neurobiology and the natural history of nerve growth factor. *Annual Review of Neuroscience, 5,* 341–362.

Levine, J. D., Gordon, N. C., and Fields, H. L. (1978). The mechanism of placebo analgesia. *Lancet, 2,* 654–657.

Levine, S., Haltmeyer, G. C., and Karas, G. G. (1967). Physiological and behavioral effects of infantile stimulation. *Physiology & Behavior, 2,* 55–59.

Levine, S., and Ursin, H. (1980). *Coping and health.* New York: Plenum.

Levinson, D. F., Holmans, P. A., Laurent, C., Riley, B., et al. (2002). No major schizophrenia locus detected on chromosome 1q in a large multicenter sample. *Science, 296,* 739–741.

Levy, D. L., Holzman, P. S., Matthysse, S., and Mendell, N. R. (1993). Eye tracking dysfunction and schizophrenia: A critical perspective. *Schizophrenia Bulletin, 19,* 461–536.

Lewin, G. R., and Barde, Y. A. (1996). Physiology of the neurotrophins. *Annual Review of Neuroscience, 19,* 289–317.

Lewis, D. O. (1990). Neuropsychiatric and experiential correlates of violent juvenile delinquency. *Neuropsychology Review, 1,* 125–136.

Lewis, D. O., Shankok, S. S., and Pincus, J. (1979). Juvenile male sexual assaulters. *American Journal of Psychiatry, 136,* 1194–1195.

Lewis, M. (2000). The emergence of human emotions. In M. Lewis and J. M. Haviland-Jones (Eds.), *Handbook of emotions* (2nd ed., pp. 265–280). New York: Guilford.

Lewis, R. (1998). Flies invade human genetics. *Scientist, 12,* 1, 4–5.

Lewy, A. J., Bauer, V. K., Cutler, N. L., Sack, R. L., et al. (1998). Morning vs evening light treatment of patients with winter depression. *Archives of General Psychiatry, 55,* 890–896.

Lewy, A. J., Rough, J. N., Songer, J. B., Mishra, N., et al. (2007). The phase shift hypothesis for the circadian component of winter depression. *Dialogues in Clinical Neuroscience, 9,* 291–300.

Ley, R. G., and Bryden, M. P. (1982). A dissociation of right and left hemispheric effects for recognizing emotional tone and verbal content. *Brain and Cognition, 1,* 3–9.

Li, J. Y., Christophersen, N. S., Hall, V., Soulet, D., et al. (2008). Critical issues of clinical human embryonic stem cell therapy for brain repair. *Trends in Neuroscience, 31,* 146–153.

Li, J. Y., Englund, E., Holton, J. L., Soulet, D., et al. (2008). Lewy bodies in grafted neurons in subjects with Parkinson's disease suggest host-to-graft disease propagation. *Nature Medicine, 14,* 501–503.

Li, S., and Tator, C. H. (2000). Action of locally administered NMDA and AMPA/kainate receptor antagonists in spinal cord injury. *Neurological Research, 22,* 171–180.

Li, X., Glaser, D., Li, W., Johnson, W. E., et al. (2009). Analyses of sweet receptor gene (Tas1r2) and preference for sweet stimuli in species of Carnivora. *Journal of Heredity, 100*(Suppl. 1), S90–S100.

Liberles, S. D., and Buck, L. B. (2006). A second class of chemosensory receptors in the olfactory epithelium. *Nature, 442,* 645–650.

Licht, P., Frank, L. G., Pavgi, S., Yalcinkaya, T. M., et al. (1992). Hormonal correlates of "masculinization" in female spotted hyenas (*Crocuta crocuta*). 2. Maternal and fetal steroids. *Journal of Reproduction and Fertility, 95,* 463–474.

Lichtman, J. W., and Purves, D. (1980). The elimination of redundant preganglionic innervation to hamster sympathetic ganglion cells in early post-natal life. *Journal of Physiology (London), 301,* 213–228.

Liebenthal, E., Ellingson, M. L., Spanaki, M. V., Prieto, T. E., et al. (2003). Simultaneous ERP and fMRI of the auditory cortex in a passive oddball paradigm. *Neuroimage, 19,* 1395–1404.

Lieberman, P. (1985). On the evolution of human syntactic ability: Its pre-adaptive bases—motor control and speech. *Journal of Human Evolution, 14,* 657–668.

Lieberman, P. (2002). On the nature and evolution of the neural bases of human language. *American Journal of Physical Anthropology, Suppl. 35,* 36–62.

Liégeois, F., Baldeweg, T., Connelly, A., Gadian, D. G., et al. (2003). Language fMRI abnormalities associated with FOXP2 gene mutation. *Nature Neuroscience, 6,* 1230–1237.

Liepert, J., Bauder, H., Wolfgang, H. R., Miltner, W. H., et al. (2000). Treatment-induced cortical reorganization after stroke in humans. *Stroke, 31,* 1210–1216.

Lieving, L. M., Cherek, D. R., Lane, S. D., Tcheremissine, O. V., et al. (2008). Effects of acute tiagabine administration on aggressive responses of adult male parolees. *Journal of Psychopharmacology, 22,* 144–152.

Lim, M. M., Wang, Z., Olazabal, D. E., Ren, X., et al. (2004). Enhanced partner preference in a promiscuous species by manipulating the expression of a single gene. *Nature, 429,* 754–757.

Lim, M. M., and Young, L. J. (2006). Neuropeptidergic regulation of affiliative behavior and social bonding in animals. *Hormones and Behavior, 50,* 506–557.

Lin, F. H., Witzel, T., Hamalainen, M. S., Dale, A. M., et al. (2004). Spectral spatiotemporal imaging of cortical oscillations and interactions in the human brain. *Neuroimage, 23,* 582–595.

Lin, L., Faraco, J., Li, R., Kadotani, H., et al. (1999). The sleep disorder canine narcolepsy is caused by a mutation in the hypocretin (orexin) receptor 2 gene. *Cell, 98,* 365–376.

Lind, P. A., Luciano, M., Wright, M. J., Montgomery, G. W., et al. (2010, January 13). Dyslexia and DCDC2: Normal variation in reading and spelling is associated with DCDC2 polymorphisms in an Australian population sample. *European Journal of Human Genetics.* [Epub ahead of print]

Linde, K., Allais, G., Brinkhaus, B., Manheimer, E., et al. (2009). Acupuncture for tension-type headache. *Cochrane Database of Systematic Reviews, 1,* CD007587.

Lindemann, B. (1995). Sweet and salty: Transduction in taste. *News in Physiological Sciences, 10,* 166–170.

Linden, D. J. (1994). Long-term synaptic depression in the mammalian brain. *Neuron, 12,* 457–472.

Lindskog, M., Svenningsson, P., Pozzi, L., Kim, Y., et al. (2002). Involvement of DARPP-32 phosphorylation in the stimulant action of caffeine. *Nature, 418,* 774–778.

Lindvall, O., and Kokaia, Z. (2006). Stem cells for the treatment of neurological disorders. *Nature, 441,* 1094–1096.

Lindvall, O., Sawle, G., Widner, H., Rothwell, J. C., et al. (1994). Evidence for long-term survival and function of dopaminergic grafts in progressive Parkinson's disease. *Annals of Neurology, 35,* 172–180.

Liou, Y.-C., Tocilj, A., Davies, P., and Jia, Z. (2000). Mimicry of ice structure by surface hydroxyls and water of a beta-helix antifreeze protein. *Nature, 406,* 322–324.

Lisk, R. D. (1962). Diencephalic placement of estradiol and sexual receptivity in the female rat. *American Journal of Physiology, 203,* 493–496.

Lisman, J. (1989). A mechanism for the Hebb and the anti-Hebb processes underlying learning and memory. *Proceedings of the National Academy of Sciences, USA, 86,* 9574–9578.

Lisman, J., Schulman, H., and Cline, H. (2002). The molecular basis of CAMKII function in synaptic and behavioural memory. *Nature Reviews. Neuroscience, 3,* 175–190.

Lister, J. P., and Barnes, C. A. (2009). Neurobiological changes in the hippocampus during normative aging. *Archives of Neurology, 66,* 829–833.

Liu, D., Diorio, J., Tannenbaum, B., Caldji, C., et al. (1997). Maternal care, hippocampal glucocorticoid receptors, and hypothalamic-pituitary-adrenal responses to stress. *Science, 277,* 1659–1662.

Liu, J., Lillo, C., Jonsson, P. A., Vande Velde, C., et al. (2004). Toxicity of familial ALS-linked SOD1 mutants from selective recruitment to spinal mitochondria. *Neuron, 42,* 5–17.

Liu, S., Qu, Y., Stewart, T. J., Howard, M. J., et al. (2000). Embryonic stem cells differentiate into oligodendrocytes and myelinate in culture and after spinal cord transplantation. *Proceedings of the National Academy of Sciences, USA, 97,* 6126–6131.

Liu, Y., Gao, J. H., Liotti, M., Pu, Y., et al. (1999). Temporal dissociation of parallel processing in the human subcortical outputs. *Nature, 400,* 364–367.

Liu, Y., Gao, J.-H., Liu, H.-L., and Fox, P. T. (2000). The temporal response of the brain after eating revealed by functional MRI. *Nature, 405,* 1058–1062.

Livet, J. W., Weissman, T. A., Kang, H., Draft, R. W., et al. (2007). Transgenic strategies for combinatorial expression of fluorescent proteins in the nervous system. *Nature, 450,* 56–62.

Livingstone, M. S. (2000). Is it warm? Is it real? Or just low spatial frequency? *Science, 290,* 1299.

Livingstone, M. S., and Hubel, D. (1984). Anatomy and physiology of a color system in the primate visual cortex. *Journal of Neuroscience, 4,* 309–356.

Lloyd, J. A. (1971). Weights of testes, thymi, and accessory reproductive glands in relation to rank in paired and grouped house mice (*Mus musculus*). *Proceedings of the Society for Experimental Biology and Medicine, 137,* 19–22.

Lo, E. H., Dalkara, T., and Moskowitz, M. A. (2003). Mechanisms, challenges and opportunities in stroke. *Nature Reviews. Neuroscience, 4,* 399–415.

Lockhart, M., and Moore, J. W. (1975). Classical differential and operant conditioning in rabbits (*Oryctolagus cuniculus*) with septal lesions. *Journal of Comparative and Physiological Psychology, 88,* 147–154.

Loconto, J., Papes, F., Chang, E., Stowers, L., et al. (2003). Functional expression of murine V2R pheromone receptors involves selective association with the M10 and M1 families of MHC class Ib molecules. *Cell, 112,* 607–618.

Loeb, G. E. (1990). Cochlear prosthetics. *Annual Review of Neuroscience, 13,* 357–371.

Loehlin, J. C., and McFadden, D. (2003). Otoacoustic emissions, auditory evoked potentials, and traits related to sex and sexual orientation. *Archives of Sexual Behavior, 32,* 115–127.

Loewenstein, W. R. (1971). Mechano-electric transduction in the Pacinian corpuscle. Initiation of sensory impulses in mechanoreception. In *Handbook of sensory physiology: Vol. 1. Principles of receptor physiology* (pp. 269–290). Berlin: Springer.

Loftus, E. F. (2003). Make-believe memories. *American Psychologist, 58,* 867–873.

Logan, C. G., and Grafton, S. T. (1995). Functional anatomy of human eyeblink conditioning determined with regional cerebral glucose metabolism and positron emission tomography. *Proceedings of the National Academy of Sciences, USA, 92,* 7500–7504.

Logothetis, N. K. (2008). What we can do and what we cannot do with fMRI. *Nature, 453,* 869–878.

Long, M. A., Jutras, M. J., Connors, B. W., and Burwell, R. D. (2005). Electrical synapses coordinate activity in the suprachiasmatic nucleus. *Nature Neuroscience, 8,* 61–66.

Long, S. B., Campbell, E. B., and MacKinnon, R. (2005). Crystal structure of a mammalian voltage-dependent *Shaker* family K+ channel. *Science, 309,* 897–903.

Lonstein, J. S., and Stern, J. M. (1997). Role of the midbrain periaqueductal gray in maternal nurturance and aggression: *c-fos* and electrolytic lesion studies in lactating rats. *Journal of Neuroscience, 17,* 3364–3378.

López-Aranda, M. F., López-Téllez, J. F., Navarro-Lobato, I., Masmudi-Martín, M., et al. (2009). Role of layer 6 of V2 visual cortex in object-recognition memory. *Science, 325,* 87–89.

Loui, P., Alsop, D., and Schlaug, G. (2009). Tone deafness: A new disconnection syndrome? *Journal of Neuroscience, 29,* 10215–10220.

Lovejoy, L. P., and Krauzlis, R. J. (2010). Inactivation of primate superior colliculus impairs covert selection of signals for perceptual judgments. *Nature Neuroscience, 13,* 261–266.

Lu, L., Hope, B. T., Dempsey, J., Liu, S. Y., et al. (2005). Central amygdala ERK signaling pathway is critical to incubation of cocaine craving. *Nature Neuroscience, 8,* 212–219.

Lu, L., Koya, E., Zhai, H., Hope, B. T., et al. (2006). Role of ERK in cocaine addiction. *Trends in Neurosciences, 29,* 695–703.

Lu, X. Y. (2007). The leptin hypothesis of depression: A potential link between mood disorders and obesity? *Current Opinion in Pharmacology, 7,* 648–652.

Lucas, R. J., Hattar, S., Takao, M., Berson, D. M., et al. (2003). Diminished pupillary light reflex at high irradiances in melanopsin-knockout mice. *Science, 299,* 245–247.

Luck, S. J. (2005). *An introduction to the event-related potential technique.* Cambridge, MA: MIT Press.

Luck, S. J., and Hillyard, S. A. (1994). Electrophysiological correlates of feature analysis during visual search. *Psychophysiology, 31,* 291–300.

Lucking, C. B., Durr, A., Bonifati, V., Vaughan, J., et al. (2000). Association between early-onset Parkinson's disease and mutations in the parkin gene. *New England Journal of Medicine, 342,* 1560–1567.

Ludolph, A. C., Kassubek, J., Landwehrmeyer, B. G., Mandelkow, E., et al. (2009). Tauopathies with Parkinsonism: Clinical spectrum, neuropathologic basis, biological markers, and treatment options. *European Journal of Neurology, 16,* 297–309.

Lumpkin, E. A., and Caterina, M. J. (2007). Mechanisms of sensory transduction in the skin. *Nature, 445,* 858–865.

Luria, A. R. (1987). *The mind of a mnemonist.* Cambridge, MA: Harvard University Press.

Lush, I. E. (1989). The genetics of tasting in mice. VI. Saccharin, acesulfame, dulcin and sucrose. *Genetical Research, 53,* 95–99.

Lyamin, O., Pryaslova, J., Lance, V., and Siegel, J. (2005). Continuous activity in cetaceans after birth: The exceptional wakefulness of newborn whales and dolphins has no ill-effect on their development. *Nature, 435,* 1177.

Lynch, G., Larson, J., Staubli, U., and Granger, R. (1991). Variants of synaptic potentiation and different types of memory operations in hippocampus and related structures. In L. R. Squire, N. M. Weinberger, G. Lynch, and J. L. McGaugh

(Eds.), *Memory: Organization and locus of change* (pp. 330–363). New York: Oxford University Press.

M

Mace, G. M., Gittleman, J. L., and Purvis, A. (2003). Preserving the tree of life. *Science, 300,* 1707–1709.

Mace, G. M., Harvey, P. H., and Clutton-Brock, T. H. (1981). Brain size and ecology in small mammals. *Journal of Zoology, 193,* 333–354.

Machado-Vieira, R., Salvador, G., Diazgranados, N., and Zarate, C. A., Jr. (2009). Ketamine and the next generation of anti-depressants with a rapid onset of action. *Pharmacology & Therapeutics, 123,* 143–150.

MacLean, P. D. (1949). Psychosomatic disease and the "visceral brain": Recent developments bearing on the Papez theory of emotion. *Psychosomatic Medicine, 11,* 338–353.

MacLeod, C. M. (1991). Half a century of research on the Stroop effect: An integrative review. *Psychological Bulletin, 109,* 163–203.

Macmillan, M. (2000). *An odd kind of fame: Stories of Phineas Gage.* Cambridge, MA: MIT Press.

MacNeilage, P. F., Rogers, L. J., and Vallortigara, G. (2009). Origins of the left & right brain. *Scientific American, 301*(1), 60–67.

MacNeilage, P. R., Banks, M. S., Berger, D. R., and Bülthoff, H. H. (2007). A Bayesian model of the disambiguation of gravitoinertial force by visual cues. *Experimental Brain Research, 179,* 263–290.

Madden, J. (2001). Sex, bowers and brains. *Proceedings of the Royal Society of London. Series B: Biological Sciences, 268,* 833–838.

Maddock, R. J. (1999). The retrosplenial cortex and emotion: New insights from functional imaging in the human brain. *Trends in Neurosciences, 22,* 310–316.

Maes, M., Bosmans, E., Suy, E., Vandervorst, C., et al. (1991). Depression-related disturbances in mitogen-induced lymphocyte responses and interleukin-1 beta and soluble interleukin-2 receptor production. *Acta Psychiatrica Scandinavica, 84,* 379–386.

Magavi, S. S., Leavitt, B. R., and Macklis, J. D. (2000). Induction of neurogenesis in the neocortex of adult mice. *Nature, 405,* 951–955.

Maggioncalda, A. N., and Sapolsky, R. M. (2002). Disturbing behaviors of the orangutan. *Scientific American, 286*(6), 60–65.

Magnusson, A., and Stefansson, J. G. (1993). Prevalence of seasonal affective disorder in Iceland. *Archives of General Psychiatry, 50,* 941–946.

Maguire, E. A., Frackowiak, R. S. J., and Frith, C. D. (1997). Recalling routes around London: Activation of the right hippocampus in taxi drivers. *Journal of Neuroscience, 17,* 7103–7110.

Maguire, E. A., Gadian, D. G., Johnsrude, I. S., Good, C. D., et al. (2000). Navigation-related structural change in the hippocampi of taxi drivers. *Proceedings of the National Academy of Sciences, USA, 97,* 4398–4403.

Mair, W. G. P., Warrington, E. K., and Wieskrantz, L. (1979). Memory disorder in Korsakoff's psychosis. *Brain, 102,* 749–783.

Mak, G. K., Enwere, E. K., Gregg, C., Pakarainen, T., et al. (2007). Male pheromone-stimulated neurogenesis in the adult female brain: Possible role in mating behavior. *Nature Neuroscience, 10,* 1003–1011.

Maki, P. M., and Resnick, S. M. (2000). Longitudinal effects of estrogen replacement therapy on pet cerebral blood flow and cognition. *Neurobiology of Aging, 21,* 373–383.

Maldonado, R., and Rodríguez de Fonseca, F. (2002). Cannabinoid addiction: Behavioral models and neural correlates. *Journal of Neuroscience, 22,* 3326–3331.

Malenka, R. C., and Bear, M. F. (2004). LTP and LTD: An embarrassment of riches. *Neuron, 44,* 5–21.

Mancuso, K., Hauswirth, W. W., Li, Q., Connor, T. B., et al. (2009). Gene therapy for red-green colour blindness in adult primates. *Nature, 461,* 784–788.

Manetto, V., Medori, R., Cortelli, P., Montagna, P., et al. (1992). Fatal familial insomnia: Clinical and pathologic study of five new cases. *Neurology, 42,* 312–319.

Manfredi, M., Bini, G., Cruccu, G., Accornero, N., et al. (1981). Congenital absence of pain. *Archives of Neurology, 38,* 507–511.

Manger, P. R., Collins, R., and Pettigrew, J. D. (1998). The development of the electroreceptors of the platypus (*Ornithorhynchus anatinus*). *Philosophical Transactions of the Royal Society of London. Series B: Biological Sciences, 353,* 1171–1186.

Mangun, G. R. (1995). Neural mechanisms of visual selective attention. *Psychophysiology, 32,* 4–18.

Mani, S. K., Fienberg, A. A., O'Callaghan, J. P., Snyder, G. L., et al. (2000). Requirement for DARPP-32 in progesterone-facilitated sexual receptivity in female rats and mice. *Science, 287,* 1053–1056.

Manova, M. G., and Kostadinova, I. I. (2000). Some aspects of the immunotherapy of multiple sclerosis. *Folia Medica, 42*(1), 5–9.

Mantyh, P. W., Rogers, S. D., Honore, P., Allen, B. J., et al. (1997). Inhibition of hyperalgesia by ablation of lamina I spinal neurons expressing the substance P receptor. *Science, 278,* 275–279.

Mao, J. B., and Evinger, C. (2001). Long-term potentiation of the human blink reflex. *Journal of Neuroscience, 21,* RC151.

Maquet, P., Laureys, S., Peigneux, P., Fuchs, S., et al. (2000). Experience-dependent changes in cerebral activation during human REM sleep. *Nature Neuroscience, 3,* 831–836.

March, J., Silva, S., Petrychi, S., Curry, J., et al. (2004). Fluoxetine, cognitive-behavioral therapy, and their combination for adolescents with depression: Treatment for adolescents with depression study (TADS) randomized controlled trial. *Journal of the American Medical Association, 292,* 807–820.

Marcus, G. F., Vijayan, S., Bandi Rao, S., and Vishton, P. M. (1999). Rule learning by seven-month-old infants. *Science, 283,* 77–80.

Maren, S., and Quirk, G. J. (2004). Neuronal signalling of fear memory. *Nature, 5,* 844–852.

Mariani, J., and Changeaux, J.-P. (1981). Ontogenesis of olivocerebellar relationships. I. Studies by intracellular recordings of the multiple innervation of Purkinje cells by climbing fibers in the developing rat cerebellum. *Journal of Neuroscience, 1,* 696–702.

Maricich, S. M., Wellnitz, S. A., Nelson, A. M., and Lesniak, D. R. (2009). Merkel cells are essential for light-touch responses. *Science, 324,* 1580–1582.

Mark, V. H., and Ervin, F. R. (1970). *Violence and the brain.* New York: Harper & Row.

Marler, P. (1970). Birdsong and speech development: Could there be parallels? *American Scientist, 58,* 669–673.

Marler, P. (1991). Song-learning behavior: The interface with neuroethology. *Trends in Neurosciences, 14,* 199–206.

Marler, P., and Peters, S. (1982). Developmental overproduction and selective attrition: New processes in the epigenesis of birdsong. *Developmental Psychobiology, 15,* 369–378.

Marler, P., and Sherman, V. (1983). Song structure without auditory feedback: Emendations of the auditory template hypothesis. *Journal of Neuroscience, 3,* 517–531.

Marler, P., and Sherman, V. (1985). Innate differences in singing behaviour of sparrows reared in isolation from adult conspecific song. *Animal Behavior, 33,* 57–71.

Marshall, C. B., Fletcher, G. L., and Davies, P. L. (2004). Hyperactive antifreeze protein in a fish. *Nature, 429,* 153.

Marshall, L., Helgadóttir, H., Mölle, M., and Born, J. (2006). Boosting slow oscillations during sleep potentiates memory. *Nature, 444,* 610–613.

Marsicano, G., Goodenough, S., Monory, K., Hermann, H., et al. (2003). CB1 cannabinoid receptors and on-demand defense against excitotoxicity. *Science, 302,* 84–88.

Marsicano, G., Wotjak, C. T., Azad, S. C., Bisogno, T., et al. (2002). The endogenous cannabinoid system controls extinction of aversive memories. *Nature, 418,* 530–532.

Martin, A., Wiggs, C. L., Ungerleider, L. G., and Haxby, J. V. (1996). Neural correlates of category-specific knowledge. *Nature, 379,* 649–652.

Martin, C. K., Heilbronn, L., de Jonge, L., Delany, J. P., et al. (2007). Effect of calorie restriction on resting metabolic rate and spontaneous physical activity. *Obesity (Silver Spring)*, 15, 2964–2973.

Martin, J. T., and Nguyen, D. H. (2004). Anthropometric analysis of homosexuals and heterosexuals: Implications for early hormone exposure. *Hormones and Behavior*, 45, 31–39.

Martuza, R. L., Chiocca, E. A., Jenike, M. A., Giriunas, I. E., et al. (1990). Stereotactic radiofrequency thermal cingulotomy for obsessive compulsive disorder. *Journal of Neuropsychiatry and Clinical Neurosciences*, 2, 331–336.

Marucha, P. T., Kiecolt-Glaser, J. K., and Favagehi, M. (1998). Mucosal wound healing is impaired by examination stress. *Psychosomatic Medicine*, 60, 362–365.

Maruyama, Y., Pereira, E., Margolskee, R. F., Chaudhari, N., et al. (2006). Umami responses in mouse taste cells indicate more than one receptor. *Journal of Neuroscience*, 26, 2227–2234.

Marzani, D., and Wallman, J. (1997). Growth of the two layers of the chick sclera is modulated reciprocally by visual conditions. *Investigative Ophthalmology & Visual Science*, 38, 1726–1739.

Maskos, U., Molles, B. E., Pons, S., Besson, M., et al. (2005). Nicotine reinforcement and cognition restored by targeted expression of nicotinic receptors. *Nature*, 436, 103–107.

Masters, W. H., and Johnson, V. E. (1966). *Human sexual response*. Boston: Little, Brown.

Masters, W. H., and Johnson, V. E. (1970). *Human sexual inadequacy*. Boston: Little, Brown.

Masters, W. H., Johnson, V. E., and Kolodny, R. C. (1994). *Heterosexuality*. New York: HarperCollins.

Masterton, R. B. (1993). Central auditory system. *Journal of Oto-Rhino-Laryngology and Its Related Specialties*, 55, 159–163.

Masterton, R. B. (1997). Neurobehavioral studies of the central auditory system. *Annals of Otology Rhinology Laryngology, Supplement*, 168, 31–34.

Mastrianni, J. A., Nixon, R., Layzer, R., Telling, G. C., et al. (1999). Prion protein conformation in a patient with sporadic fatal insomnia. *New England Journal of Medicine*, 340, 1630–1638.

Mateo, J. M., and Johnston, R. E. (2000). Kin recognition and the "armpit effect": Evidence of self-referent phenotype matching. *Proceedings of the Royal Society of London. Series B: Biological Sciences*, 267, 695–700.

Matsumoto, K., Suzuki, W., and Tanaka, K. (2003). Neuronal correlates of goal-based motor selection in the prefrontal cortex. *Science*, 301, 229–232.

Mattson, S. N., Riley, E. P., Gramling, L., Delis, D. C., et al. (1998). Neuropsychological comparison of alcohol-exposed children with or without physical features of fetal alcohol syndrome. *Neuropsychology*, 12, 146–153.

Mauch, D. H., Nägler, K., Schumacher, S., Göritz, C., et al. (2001). CNS synaptogenesis promoted by glia-derived cholesterol. *Science*, 294, 1354–1357.

Maurer, P., and Bachmann, M. F. (2007). Vaccination against nicotine: An emerging therapy for tobacco dependence. *Expert Opinion on Investigational Drugs*, 16, 1775–1783.

Mayberg, H. S., Lozano, A. M., Voon, V., McNeely, H. E., et al. (2005). Deep brain stimulation for treatment-resistant depression. *Neuron*, 45, 651–660.

Mayfield, R. D., Lewohl, J. M., Dodd, P. R., Herlihy, A., et al. (2002). Patterns of gene expression are altered in the frontal and motor cortices of human alcoholics. *Journal of Neurochemistry*, 81, 802–813.

Mazur, A., and Booth, A. (1998). Testosterone and dominance in men. *Behavioral and Brain Sciences*, 21, 353–363.

McAllister, A. K., Katz, L. C., and Lo, D. C. (1997). Opposing roles for endogenous BDNF and NT-3 in regulating cortical dendritic growth. *Neuron*, 18, 767–778.

McAlpine, D., Jiang, D., and Palmer, A. R. (2001). A neural code for low-frequency sound localization in mammals. *Nature Neuroscience*, 4, 396–401.

McBurney, D. H., Smith, D. V., and Shick, T. R. (1972). Gustatory cross adaptation: Sourness and bitterness. *Perception & Psychophysics*, 11, 2228–2232.

McCall, W. V., and Edinger, J. D. (1992). Subjective total insomnia: An example of sleep state misperception. *Sleep*, 15, 71–73.

McCarthy, R. A., and Warrington, E. K. (1990). *Cognitive neuropsychology: A clinical introduction*. San Diego, CA: Academic Press.

McClintock, M. K. (1971). Menstrual synchrony and suppression. *Nature*, 229, 244–245.

McComb, K., Moss, C., Sayialel, S., and Baker, L. (2000). Unusually extensive networks of vocal recognition in African elephants. *Animal Behavior*, 59, 1103–1109.

McCoy, A. N., and Platt, M. L. (2005). Risk-sensitive neurons in macaque posterior cingulate cortex. *Nature Neuroscience*, 8, 1220–1227.

McCrae, C. S., Rowe, M. A., Tierney, C. G., Dautovich, N. D., et al. (2005). Sleep complaints, subjective and objective sleep patterns, health, psychological adjustment, and daytime functioning in community-dwelling older adults. *Journals of Gerontology. Series B, Psychological Sciences and Social Sciences*, 60(4), P182–P189.

McDonald, J. J., Teder-Sälejärvi, W. A., Di Russo, F., and Hillyard, S. A. (2003). Neural substrates of perceptual enhancement by crossmodal spatial attention. *Journal of Cognitive Neuroscience*, 15, 10–19.

McDonald, J. J., Teder-Sälejärvi, W. A., and Hillyard, S. A. (2000). Involuntary orienting to sound improves visual perception. *Nature*, 407, 906–908.

McFadden, D. (1993a). A masculinizing effect on the auditory systems of human females having male co-twins. *Proceedings of the National Academy of Sciences, USA*, 90, 11900–11904.

McFadden, D. (1993b). A speculation about the parallel ear asymmetries and sex differences in hearing sensitivity and otoacoustic emissions. *Hearing Research*, 68, 143–151.

McFadden, D., and Champlin, C. A. (1990). Reductions in overshoot during aspirin use. *Journal of the Acoustical Society of America*, 87, 2634–2642.

McFadden, D., and Pasanen, E. (1998). Comparison of the auditory systems of heterosexuals and homosexuals: Click-evoked otoacoustic emissions. *Proceedings of the National Academy of Sciences, USA*, 95, 2709–2713.

McGaugh, J. L. (1966). Time-dependent processes in memory storage. *Science*, 153, 1351–1358.

McGaugh, J. L. (2003). *Memory and emotions: The making of lasting memories*. New York: Columbia University Press.

McGeer, P., McGeer, E., Suzuki, J., Dolman, C., et al. (1984). Aging, Alzheimer's disease, and the cholinergic system of the basal forebrain. *Neurology*, 34, 741–745.

McGinty, D. J., and Sterman, M. B. (1968). Sleep suppression after basal forebrain lesions in the cat. *Science*, 160, 1253–1255.

McGowan, P. O., Sasaki, A., D'Alessio, A. C., Dymov, S., et al. (2009). Epigenetic regulation of the glucocorticoid receptor in human brain associates with childhood abuse. *Nature Neuroscience*, 12, 342–348.

McGue, M. (1999). The behavioral genetics of alcoholism. *Current Trends in Psychological Science*, 8, 109–115.

McIntyre, C. K., Miyashita, T., Setlow, B., Marjon, K. D., et al. (2005). Memory-influencing intra-basolateral amygdala drug infusions modulate expression of Arc protein in the hippocampus. *Proceedings of the National Academy of Sciences, USA*, 102, 10718–10723.

McKee, A. C., Cantu, R. C., Nowinski, C. J., Hedley-Whyte, E. T., et al. (2009). Chronic traumatic encephalopathy in athletes: Progressive tauopathy after repetitive head injury. *Journal of Neuropathology and Experimental Neurology*, 68, 709–735.

McKenna, K. (1999). The brain is the master organ in sexual function: Central nervous system control of male and female sexual function. *International Journal of Impotence Research*, 11(Suppl. 1), S48–S55.

McKernan, M. G., and Shinnick-Gallagher, P. (1997). Fear conditioning induces a lasting potentiation of synaptic currents in vitro. *Nature*, 390, 607–611.

McKim, W. A. (1991). *Drugs and behavior: An introduction to behavioral pharmacology* (2nd ed.). Englewood Cliffs, NJ: Prentice Hall.

McKinley, M. J., and Johnson, A. K. (2004). The physiological regulation of thirst and fluid intake. *News in Physiological Sciences, 19*, 1–6.

McKinney, T. D., and Desjardins, C. (1973). Postnatal development of the testis, fighting behavior, and fertility in house mice. *Biology of Reproduction, 9*, 279–294.

McLaughlin, S. K., McKinnon, P. J., Spickofsky, N., Danho, W., et al. (1994). Molecular cloning of G proteins and phosphodiesterases from rat taste cells. *Physiology & Behavior, 56*, 1157–1164.

McLin, D. E., III, Miasnikov, A. A., and Weinberger, N. M. (2002). Induction of behavioral associative memory by stimulation of the nucleus basalis. *Proceedings of the National Academy of Sciences, USA, 99*, 4002–4007.

McMahon, H. T., Foran, P., Dolly, J. O., Verhage, M., et al. (1992). Tetanus toxin and botulinum toxins type A and B inhibit glutamate, gamma-aminobutyric acid, aspartate, and met-enkephalin release from synaptosomes. Clues to the locus of action. *Journal of Biological Chemistry, 267*, 21338–21343.

McMains, S., and Somers, D. (2004). Multiple spotlights of attentional selection in human visual cortex. *Neuron, 42*, 677–686.

McNally, R. J. (2003). Recovering memories of trauma: A view from the laboratory. *Current Directions in Psychological Science, 12*, 32–35.

McNamara, J. O. (1984). Role of neurotransmitters in seizure mechanisms in the kindling model of epilepsy. *Federation Proceedings, 43*, 2516–2520.

Meck, W. H., Church, R. M., Wenk, G. L., and Olton, D. S. (1987). Nucleus basalis magnocellularis and medial septal area lesions differentially impair temporal memory. *Journal of Neuroscience, 7*, 3505–3511.

Meckler, R. J., Mack, J. L., and Bennett, R. (1979). Sign language aphasia in a non-deaf mute. *Neurology, 29*, 1037–1040.

Meddis, R. (1975). On the function of sleep. *Animal Behavior, 23*, 676–691.

Meddis, R. (1977). *The sleep instinct.* London: Routledge & Kegan Paul.

Mednick, S. A., Huttunen, M. O., and Machon, R. A. (1994). Prenatal influenza infections and adult schizophrenia. *Schizophrenia Bulletin, 20*, 263–267.

Medori, R., Montagna, P., Tritschler, H. J., LeBlanc, A., et al. (1992). Fatal familial insomnia: A second kindred with mutation of prion protein gene at codon 178. *Neurology, 42*, 669–670.

Mega, M. S., and Cummings, J. L. (1994). Frontal-subcortical circuits and neuropsychiatric disorders. *Journal of Neuropsychiatry and Clinical Neurosciences, 6*, 358–370.

Meguerditchian, A., and Vauclair, J. (2006). Baboons communicate with their right hand. *Behavioural Brain Research, 171*, 170–174.

Mei, L., and Xiong, W.-C. (2008). Neuregulin 1 in neural development, synaptic plasticity and schizophrenia. *Nature Reviews. Neuroscience, 9*, 437–452.

Meisel, R. L., and Luttrell, V. R. (1990). Estradiol increases the dendritic length of ventromedial hypothalamic neurons in female Syrian hamsters. *Brain Research Bulletin, 25*, 165–168.

Meisel, R. L., and Sachs, B. D. (1994). The physiology of male sexual behavior. In E. Knobil and J. D. Neill (Eds.), *The physiology of reproduction* (2nd ed., Vol. 1, pp. 3–105). New York: Raven.

Meister, I. G., Boroojerdi, B., Foltys, H., Sparing, R., et al. (2003). Motor cortex hand area and speech: Implications for the development of language. *Neuropsychologia, 41*, 401–406.

Mellars, P. (2006). A new radiocarbon revolution and the dispersal of modern humans in Eurasia. *Nature, 439*, 931–935.

Mello, C. V., Vicario, D. S., and Clayton, D. F. (1992). Song presentation induces gene expression in the songbird forebrain. *Proceedings of the National Academy of Sciences, USA, 89*, 6818–6822.

Melzack, R. (1984). Neuropsychological basis of pain measurement. *Advances in Pain Research, 6*, 323–341.

Melzack, R. (1990). The tragedy of needless pain. *Scientific American, 262*(2), 27–33.

Melzack, R., and Wall, P. D. (1965). Pain mechanisms: A new history. *Science, 150*, 971–979.

Mendel, G. (1967). *Experiments in plant hybridisation* (Royal Horticultural Society of London, Trans.). Cambridge, MA: Harvard University Press.

Meng, H., Smith, S. D., Hager, K., Held, M., et al. (2005). DCDC2 is associated with reading disability and modulates neuronal development in the brain. *Proceedings of the National Academy of Sciences, USA, 102*, 17053–17058.

Merchán-Pérez, A., Rodriguez, J. R., Alonso-Nanclares, L., Schertel, A., et al. (2009). Counting synapses using FIB/SEM microscopy: A true revolution for ultrastructural volume reconstruction. *Frontiers in Neuroanatomy, 3*, 18.

Mersch, P. P., Middendorp, H. M., Bouhuys, A. L., Beersma, D. G., et al. (1999). Seasonal affective disorder and latitude: A review of the literature. *Journal of Affective Disorders, 53*, 35–48.

Merzenich, M. M., and Jenkins, W. M. (1993). Reorganization of cortical representations of the hand following alterations of skin inputs induced by nerve injury, skin island transfers, and experience. *Journal of Hand Therapy, 6*, 89–104.

Merzenich, M. M., Schreiner, C., Jenkins, W., and Wang, X. (1993). Neural mechanisms underlying temporal integration, segmentation, and input sequence representation: Some implications for the origin of learning disabilities. *Annals of the New York Academy of Sciences, 682*, 1–22.

Meshberger, F. L. (1990). An interpretation of Michelangelo's *Creation of Adam* based on neuroanatomy. *Journal of the American Medical Association, 264*, 1837–1841.

Messias, E., Kirkpatrick, B., Bromet, E., Ross, D., et al. (2004). Summer birth and deficit schizophrenia: A pooled analysis from 6 countries. *Archives of General Psychiatry, 61*, 985–989.

Mesulam, M.-M. (1985). Attention, confusional states and neglect. In M.-M. Mesulam (Ed.), *Principles of behavioral neurology.* Philadelphia: Davis.

Michael, N., and Erfurth, A. (2004). Treatment of bipolar mania with right prefrontal rapid transcranial magnetic stimulation. *Journal of Affective Disorders, 78*, 253–257.

Miczek, K. A., Fish, E. W., De Bold, J. F., and De Almeida, R. M. (2002). Social and neural determinants of aggressive behavior: Pharmacotherapeutic targets at serotonin, dopamine and gamma-aminobutyric acid systems. *Psychopharmacology (Berlin), 163*, 434–458.

Miles, L. E., and Dement, W. C. (1980). Sleep and aging. *Sleep, 3*, 1220.

Miller, E. K., and Cohen, J. D. (2001). An integrative theory of prefrontal cortex function. *Annual Review of Neuroscience, 24*, 167–202.

Miller, G. F. (2000). *The mating mind: How sexual choice shaped the evolution of human nature.* New York: Doubleday.

Miller, J. M., and Spelman, F. A. (1990). *Cochlear implants: Models of the electrically stimulated ear.* New York: Springer.

Milligan, E. R., and Watkins, L. R. (2009). Pathological and protective roles of glia in chronic pain. *Nature Reviews. Neuroscience, 10*, 23–36.

Milner, A. D., Perrett, D. I., Johnston, R. S., Benson, P. J., et al. (1991). Perception and action in "visual form agnosia." *Brain, 114*, 405–428.

Milner, B. (1963). Effect of different brain lesions on card sorting. *Archives of Neurology, 9*, 90–100.

Milner, B. (1965). Memory disturbance after bilateral hippocampal lesions. In P. M. Milner and S. E. Glickman (Eds.), *Cognitive processes and the brain; an enduring problem in psychology* (pp. 97–111). Princeton, NJ: Van Nostrand.

Milner, B. (1970). Memory and the medial temporal regions of the brain. In D. H. Pribram and D. E. Broadbent (Eds.), *Biology of memory* (pp. 29–50). New York: Academic Press.

Milner, P. M. (1993). The mind and Donald O. Hebb. *Scientific American, 268*(1), 124–129.

Ming, G. L., and Song, H. (2005). Adult neurogenesis in the mammalian central nervous system. *Annual Review of Neuroscience, 28*, 223–250.

Minzenberg, M. J., Laird, A. R., Thelen, S., Carter, C. S., et al. (2009). Meta-analysis of 41 functional neuroimaging studies of executive function in schizophrenia. *Archives of General Psychiatry, 66,* 811–822.

Mioduszewska, B., Jaworski, J., and Kaczmarek, L. (2003). Inducible cAMP early repressor (ICER) in the nervous system—A transcriptional regulator of neuronal plasticity and programmed cell death. *Journal of Neurochemistry, 87,* 1313–1320.

Mirescu, C., Peters, J. D., and Gould, E. (2004). Early life experience alters response of adult neurogenesis to stress. *Nature Neuroscience, 7,* 841–846.

Mirsky, A. F., and Duncan, C. C. (1986). Etiology and expression of schizophrenia: Neurobiological and psychosocial factors. *Annual Review of Psychology, 37,* 291–321.

Mishkin, M., and Ungerleider, L. (1982). Contribution of striate inputs to the visuospatial functions of parieto-preoccipital cortex in monkeys. *Behavioural Brain Research, 6,* 57–77.

Mistlberger, R. E. (2005). Circadian regulation of sleep in mammals: Role of the suprachiasmatic nucleus. *Brain Research Reviews, 49,* 429–454.

Mistlberger, R. E., and Skene, D. J. (2004). Social influences on mammalian circadian rhythms: Animal and human studies. *Biological Reviews of the Cambridge Philosophical Society, 79,* 533–556.

Mitchell, R. E. (2006). How many deaf people are there in the United States? Estimates from the Survey of Income and Program Participation. *Journal of Deaf Studies and Deaf Education, 11,* 112–119.

Miyashita, Y. (1993). Inferior temporal cortex: Where visual perception meets memory. *Annual Review of Neuroscience, 16,* 245–263.

Miyawaki, Y., Uchida, H., Yamashita, O., Sato, M. A., et al. (2008). Visual image reconstruction from human brain activity using a combination of multiscale local image decoders. *Neuron, 60,* 915–929.

Mizumori, S. J., Lavoie, A. M., and Kalyani, A. (1996). Redistribution of spatial representation in the hippocampus of aged rats performing a spatial memory task. *Behavioral Neuroscience, 110,* 1006–1016.

Moghaddam, B. (2004). Targeting metabotropic glutamate receptors for treatment of the cognitive symptoms of schizophrenia. *Psychopharmacology (Berlin), 174,* 39–44.

Moghaddam, B., and Adams, B. W. (1998). Reversal of phencyclidine effects by a group II metabotropic glutamate receptor agonist in rats. *Science, 281,* 1349–1352.

Mogil, J. S., and Chanda, M. L. (2005). The case for the inclusion of female subjects in basic science studies of pain. *Pain, 117,* 1–5.

Mogil, J. S., Wilson, S. G., Chesler, E. J., Rankin, A. L., et al. (2003). The melanocortin-1 receptor gene mediates female-specific mechanisms of analgesia in mice

and humans. *Proceedings National Academy of Sciences, USA, 100,* 4867–4872.

Mohammed, A. (2001). *Enrichment and the brain. Plasticity in the adult brain: From genes to neurotherapy.* 22nd International Summer School of Brain Research, Amsterdam, Netherlands.

Mohammed, A., Henriksson, B. G., Soderstrom, S., Ebendal, T., et al. (1993). Environmental influences on the central nervous system and their implications for the aging rat. *Behavioural Brain Research, 23,* 182–191.

Moita, M. A., Rosis, S., Zhou, Y., LeDoux, J. E., et al. (2004). Putting fear in its place: Remapping of hippocampal place cells during fear conditioning. *Journal of Neuroscience, 24,* 7015–7023.

Molenda-Figueira, H. A., Williams, C. A., Griffin, A. L., Rutledge, E. M., et al. (2006). Nuclear receptor coactivators function in estrogen receptor- and progestin receptor-dependent aspects of sexual behavior in female rats. *Hormones and Behavior, 50,* 383–392.

Monakow, C. von. (1914). *Die Lokalisation im Grosshirn und der Abbau der Funktion durch kortikale Herde.* Wiesbaden, Germany: Bergmann.

Money, J., and Ehrhardt, A. A. (1972). *Man and woman, boy and girl.* Baltimore: Johns Hopkins University Press.

Monfils, M. H., Plautz, E. J., and Kleim, J. A. (2005). In search of the motor engram: Motor map plasticity as a mechanism for encoding motor experience. *Neuroscientist, 11,* 471–483.

Monks, D. A., and Watson N. V. (2001). N-cadherin expression in motoneurons is directly regulated by androgens: A genetic mosaic analysis in rats. *Brain Research, 895,* 73–79.

Monks, T. J., Jones, D. C., Bai, F., and Lau, S. S. (2004). The role of metabolism in 3,4-(+)-methylenedioxyamphetamine and 3,4-(+)-methylenedioxymethamphetamine (ecstasy) toxicity. *Therapeutic Drug Monitoring, 26,* 132–136.

Montague, C. T., Farooqi, I. S., Whitehead, J. P., Soos, M. A., et al. (1997). Congenital leptin deficiency is associated with severe early-onset obesity in humans. *Nature, 387,* 903–908.

Monti, M. M., Vanhaudenhuyse, A., Coleman, M. R., Boly, M., et al. (2010). Willful modulation of brain activity in disorders of consciousness. *New England Journal of Medicine, 362,* 579–589.

Moore, C. L., Dou, H., and Juraska, J. M. (1992). Maternal stimulation affects the number of motor neurons in a sexually dimorphic nucleus of the lumbar spinal cord. *Brain Research, 572,* 52–56.

Moore, G. J., Bebchuk, J. M., Wilds, I. B., Chen, G., et al. (2000). Lithium-induced increase in human brain grey matter. *Lancet, 356,* 241–242.

Moore, H., Dvorakova, K., Jenkins, N., and Breed, W. (2002). Exceptional sperm cooperation in the wood mouse. *Nature, 418,* 174–177.

Moore, R. Y. (1983). Organization and function of a central nervous system circadian oscillator: The suprachiasmatic nucleus. *Federation Proceedings, 42,* 2783–2789.

Moore, R. Y., and Eichler, V. B. (1972). Loss of circadian adrenal corticosterone rhythm following suprachiasmatic lesions in the rat. *Brain Research, 42,* 201–206.

Moorhead, T. W., McKirdy, J., Sussmann, J. E., Hall, J., et al. (2007). Progressive gray matter loss in patients with bipolar disorder. *Biological Psychiatry, 62,* 894–900.

Morais-Cabral, J. H., Zhou, Y., and MacKinnon, R. (2001). Energetic optimization of ion conduction rate by the K+ selectivity filter. *Nature, 414,* 37–42.

Moran, J., and Desimone, R. (1985). Selective attention gates visual processing in the extrastriate cortex. *Science, 229,* 782–784.

Moray, N. (1959). Attention in dichotic listening: Affective cues and the influence of instructions. *Quarterly Journal of Experimental Psychology, 11,* 56–60.

Moreno, F. A., Wiegand, C. B., Taitano, E. K., and Delgado, P. L. (2006). Safety, tolerability, and efficacy of psilocybin in 9 patients with obsessive-compulsive disorder. *Journal of Clinical Psychiatry, 67,* 1735–1740.

Morford, J. P., and Mayberry, R. I. (2000). A reexamination of "early exposure" and its implications for language acquisition by eye. In C. Chamberlain, J. P. Morford, and R. I. Mayberry (Eds.), *Language acquisition by eye* (pp. 111–127). Mahwah, NJ: Erlbaum.

Mori, K., Nagao, H., and Yoshihara, Y. (1999). The olfactory bulb: Coding and processing of odor molecule information. *Science, 286,* 711–715.

Morihisa, J., and McAnulty, G. B. (1985). Structure and function: Brain electrical activity mapping and computed tomography in schizophrenia. *Biological Psychiatry, 20,* 3–19.

Moriya, J., Takimoto, Y., Yoshiuchi, K., Shimosawa, T., et al. (2006). Plasma agouti-related protein levels in women with anorexia nervosa. *Psychoneuroendocrinology, 31,* 1057–1061.

Morrell, F. (1991). The role of secondary epileptogenesis in human epilepsy [Editorial]. *Archives of Neurology, 48,* 1221–1224.

Morris, B. (2002). Overcoming dyslexia. *Fortune, 145*(10), 1–7.

Morris, R. G., Halliwell, R. F., and Bowery, N. (1989). Synaptic plasticity and learning. II: Do different kinds of plasticity underlie different kinds of learning? *Neuropsychologia, 27,* 41–59.

Morris, S., Humphreys, D., and Reynolds, D. (2006). Myth, marula, and elephant: An assessment of voluntary ethanol intoxication of the African elephant (*Loxodonta africana*) following feeding on the fruit of the marula tree (*Sclerocarya birrea*). *Physiological and Biochemical Zoology, 79,* 363–369.

Morrison, A. R. (1983). A window on the sleeping brain. *Scientific American, 248*(4), 94–102.

Morrison, J. H., and Hof, P. R. (2007). Life and death of neurons in the aging cerebral cortex. *International Review of Neurobiology, 81,* 41–57.

Morrison, R. G., and Nottebohm, F. (1993). Role of a telencephalic nucleus in the delayed song learning of socially isolated zebra finches. *Journal of Neurobiology, 24,* 1045–1064.

Mortensen, P. B., Pedersen, C. B., Westergaard, T., Wohlfahrt, J., et al. (1999). Effects of family history and place and season of birth on the risk of schizophrenia. *New England Journal of Medicine, 340,* 603–608.

Moruzzi, G. (1972). The sleep-waking cycle. *Ergebnisse der Physiologie, biologischen Chemie und experimentellen Pharmakologie, 64,* 1–165.

Moruzzi, G., and Magoun, H. W. (1949). Brain stem reticular formation and activation of the EEG. *Clinical Neurophysiology, 1,* 455–473.

Moscovitch, A., Blashko, C. A., Eagles, J. M., Darcourt, G., et al. (2004). A placebo-controlled study of sertraline in the treatment of outpatients with seasonal affective disorder. *Psychopharmacology (Berlin), 171,* 390–397.

Moscovitch, M. (1985). Memory from infancy to old age: Implications for theories of normal and pathological memory. *Annals of the New York Academy of Sciences, 444,* 78–96.

Mott, F. W. (1895). Experimental inquiry upon the afferent tracts of the central nervous system of the monkey. *Brain, 18,* 1–20.

Mountcastle, V. B. (1979). An organizing principle for cerebral function: The unit module and the distributed system. In F. O. Schmitt and F. G. Worden (Eds.), *The neurosciences: Fourth study program* (pp. 21–24). Cambridge, MA: MIT Press.

Mountcastle, V. B. (1984). Central nervous mechanisms in mechanoreceptive sensibility. In I. Darian-Smith (Ed.), *Handbook of physiology, Section 1: Vol. 3. Sensory processes* (pp. 789–878). Bethesda, MD: American Physiological Society.

Mountcastle, V. B., Andersen, R. A., and Motter, B. C. (1981). The influence of attentive fixation upon the excitability of the light-sensitive neurons of the posterior parietal cortex. *Journal of Neuroscience, 1,* 1218–1235.

Mounts, J. R. (2000). Attentional capture by abrupt onsets and feature singletons produces inhibitory surrounds. *Perception & Psychophysics, 62,* 1485–1493.

Mower, G. D., Christen, W. G., and Caplan, C. J. (1983). Very brief visual experience eliminates plasticity in the cat visual cortex. *Science, 221,* 178–180.

Mowry, B. J., Holmans, P. A., Pulver, A. E., Gejman, P. V., et al. (2004). Multicenter linkage study of schizophrenia loci on chromosome 22q. *Molecular Psychiatry, 9,* 784–795.

Moyer, J. R., Jr., Deyo, R. A., and Disterhoft, J. F. (1990). Hippocampectomy disrupts trace eye-blink conditioning in rabbits. *Behavioral Neuroscience, 104,* 243–252.

Mueller, H. T., Haroutunian, V., Davis, K. L., and Meador-Woodruff, J. H. (2004). Expression of the ionotropic glutamate receptor subunits and NMDA receptor-associated intracellular proteins in the substantia nigra in schizophrenia. *Brain Research. Molecular Brain Research, 121,* 60–69.

Mukamal, K. J., Conigrave, K. M., Mittleman, M. A., Camargo, C. A., Jr., et al. (2003). Roles of drinking pattern and type of alcohol consumed in coronary heart disease in men. *New England Journal of Medicine, 348,* 109–118.

Mukhametov, L. M. (1984). Sleep in marine mammals. In A. Borbely and J. L. Valatx (Eds.), *Experimental Brain Research. Supplementum: 8. Sleep mechanisms.* Berlin: Springer.

Mulkey, R. M., Herron, C. E., and Malenka, R. C. (1993). An essential role for protein phosphatases in hippocampal long-term depression. *Science, 261,* 1051–1055.

Münte, T. F. (2002). Brains out of tune. *Nature, 415,* 589–590.

Münte, T. F., Altenmüller, E., and Jäncke, L. (2002). The musician's brain as a model of neuroplasticity. *Nature Reviews. Neuroscience, 3,* 473–478.

Münte, T. F., Kohlmetz, C., Nager, W., and Altenmüller, E. (2001). Superior auditory spatial tuning in conductors. *Nature, 409,* 580.

Murray, R. M., Morrison, P. D., Henquet, C., and Di Forti, M. (2007). Cannabis, the mind and society: The hash realities. *Nature Reviews. Neuroscience, 8,* 885–895.

N

Nader, K., and Hardt, O. (2009). A single standard for memory: The case for reconsolidation. *Nature Reviews. Neuroscience, 10,* 224–234.

Naeser, M., Gaddie, A., Palumbo, C., and Stiassny-Eder, D. (1990). Late recovery of auditory comprehension in global aphasia. Improved recovery observed with subcortical temporal isthmus lesion vs. Wernicke's cortical area lesion. *Archives of Neurology, 47,* 425–432.

Naeser, M., and Hayward, R. (1978). Lesion localization in aphasia with cranial computed tomography and the Boston Diagnostic Aphasia Exam. *Neurology, 28,* 545–551.

Nair, K. S., Rizza, R. A., O'Brien, P., Dhatariya, K., et al. (2006). DHEA in elderly women and DHEA or testosterone in elderly men. *New England Journal of Medicine, 355,* 1647–1659.

Nakazato, M., Murakami, N., Date, Y., Kojima, M., et al. (2001). A role for ghrelin in the central regulation of feeding. *Nature, 409,* 194–198.

Naqvi, N. H., Rudrauf, D., Damasio, H., and Bechara, A. (2007). Damage to the insula disrupts addiction to cigarette smoking. *Science, 315,* 531–534.

Narrow, W. E., Rae, D. S., Robins, L. N., and Regier, D. A. (2002). Revised prevalence estimates of mental disorders in the United States: Using a clinical significance criterion to reconcile 2 surveys' estimates. *Archives of General Psychiatry, 59,* 115–123.

Nathans, J. (1987). Molecular biology of visual pigments. *Annual Review of Neuroscience, 10,* 163–194.

Nation, E. F. (1973). William Osler on penis captivus and other urologic topics. *Urology, 2,* 468–470.

National Commission for the Protection of Human Subjects of Biomedical and Behavioral Research. (1978). *Special study, implications of advances in biomedical and behavioral research: Report and recommendations of the National Commission for the Protection of Human Subjects of Biomedical and Behavioral Research* (DHEW Publication No. OS 78-0015). Washington, DC: U.S. Department of Health, Education, and Welfare.

National Research Council. (2003). *The polygraph and lie detection.* Washington, DC: National Academic Press.

Neale, G. (2006, December 3). Peter Singer: Monkey business. *Independent* (http://news.independent.co.uk/people/profiles/article2035119.ece).

Neary, M. T., and Batterham, R. L. (2009). Gut hormones: Implications for the treatment of obesity. *Pharmacology & Therapeutics, 124,* 44–56.

Neff, W. D., and Casseday, J. H. (1977). Effects of unilateral ablation of auditory cortex on monaural cat's ability to localize sound. *Journal of Neurophysiology, 40,* 44–52.

Neisser, U., and Becklen, R. (1975). Selective looking: Attending to visually specified events. *Cognitive Psychology, 7,* 480–494.

Nelissen, K., Luppino, G., Vanduffel, W., Rizzolatti, G., et al. (2005). Observing others: Multiple action representation in the frontal lobe. *Science, 310,* 332–336.

Nelson, G., Chandrashekar, J., Hoon, M. A., Feng, L., et al. (2002). An amino-acid taste receptor. *Nature, 416,* 199–202.

Nelson, G., Hoon, M. A., Chandrashekar, J., Zhang, Y., et al. (2001). Mammalian sweet taste receptors. *Cell, 106,* 381–390.

Nelson, R. J. (1995). *Introduction to behavioral endocrinology.* Sunderland, MA: Sinauer.

Nelson, R. J., Demas, G. E., Huang, P. L., Fishman, M. C., et al. (1995). Behavioural abnormalities in male mice lacking neuronal nitric oxide synthase. *Nature, 378,* 383–386.

Neumeister, A., Bain, E., Nugent, A. C., Carson, R. E., et al. (2004). Reduced serotonin type 1A receptor binding in panic disorder. *Journal of Neuroscience, 24,* 589–591.

Neuroscience: Taxicology. (2000). *Economist, 353,* 125.

Neves-Pereira, M., Mundo, E., Muglia, P., King, N., et al. (2002). The brain-derived neurotrophic factor gene confers susceptibility to bipolar disorder: Evidence from a family-based association study. *American Journal of Human Genetics, 71,* 651–655.

Neville, H. J., Bavelier, D., Corina, D., Rauschecker, J., et al. (1998). Cerebral organization for language in deaf and hearing subjects: Biological constraints and effects of experience. *Proceedings of the National Academy of Sciences, USA, 95,* 922–929.

Neville, H. J., Mills, D. L., and Lawson, D. S. (1992). Fractionating language: Different neural subsystems with different sensitive periods. *Cerebral Cortex, 2,* 244–258.

Newman-Norlund, R. D., van Schie, H. T., van Zuijlen, A. M., and Bekkering, H. (2007). The mirror neuron system is more active during complementary compared with imitative action. *Nature Neuroscience, 10,* 817–818.

Newsome, W. T., Wurtz, R. H., Dursteler, M. R., and Mikami, A. (1985). Deficits in visual motion processing following ibotenic acid lesions of the middle temporal visual area of the macaque monkey. *Journal of Neuroscience, 5,* 825–840.

Nichols, M. J., and Newsome, W. T. (1999). The neurobiology of cognition. *Nature, 402,* C35–C38.

Niel, L., Shah, A. H., Lewis, G. A., Mo, K., et al. (2009). Sexual differentiation of the spinal nucleus of the bulbocavernosus is not mediated solely by androgen receptors in muscle fibers. *Endocrinology, 150,* 3207–3213.

Nieto-Sampedro, M., and Cotman, C. W. (1985). Growth factor induction and temporal order in central nervous system repair. In C. W. Cotman (Ed.), *Synaptic plasticity* (pp. 407–457). New York: Guilford.

Nietzel, M. T. (2000). Police psychology. In A. E. Kazdin (Ed.), *Encyclopedia of psychology* (Vol. 6, pp. 224–226). Washington, DC: American Psychological Association.

Nishida, M., and Walker, M. P. (2007). Daytime naps, motor memory consolidation and regionally specific sleep spindles. *PLoS ONE, 2,* e341.

Nitz, D. A., Van Swinderen, B., Tononi, G., and Greenspan, R. J. (2002). Electrophysiological correlates of rest and activity in *Drosophila melanogaster. Current Biology, 12,* 1934–1940.

Nixon, K., and Crews, F. T. (2002). Binge ethanol exposure decreases neurogenesis in adult rat hippocampus. *Journal of Neurochemistry, 83,* 1087–1093.

Noad, M. J., Cato, D. H., Bryden, M. M., Jenner, M.-N., et al. (2000). Cultural revolution in whale songs. *Nature, 408,* 537–538.

Nobre, A. C., Sebestyen, G. N., Gitelman, D. R., Mesulam, M. M., et al. (1997). Functional localization of the system for visuospatial attention using positron emission tomography. *Brain, 120,* 515–533.

Noguchi, H. (1911). *Serum diagnosis of syphilis and the butyric acid test for syphilis.* Philadelphia: Lippincott.

Noguchi, Y., Watanabe, E., and Sakai, K. L. (2003). An event-related optical topography study of cortical activation induced by single-pulse transcranial magnetic stimulation. *Neuroimage, 19,* 156–162.

Nordeen, E. J., Nordeen, K. W., Sengelaub, D. R., and Arnold, A. P. (1985). Androgens prevent normally occurring cell death in a sexually dimorphic spinal nucleus. *Science, 229,* 671–673.

Norman, A. W., and Litwack, G. (1987). *Hormones.* Orlando, FL: Academic Press.

Norsell, U. (1980). Behavioral studies of the somatosensory system. *Physiological Reviews, 60,* 327–354.

Nottebohm, F. (1980). Brain pathways for vocal learning in birds: A review of the first 10 years. *Progress in Psychobiology and Physiological Psychology, 9,* 85–124.

Nottebohm, F. (1981). A brain for all seasons: Cyclical anatomical changes in song control nuclei of the canary brain. *Science, 214,* 1368–1370.

Nottebohm, F., and Arnold, A. P. (1976). Sexual dimorphism in vocal control areas of the songbird brain. *Science, 194,* 211–213.

NRC Committee on Animals as Monitors of Environmental Hazards. (1991). *Animals as sentinels of environmental health hazards.* Washington, DC: National Academy Press.

Nudo, R. J., Milliken, G. W., Jenkins, W. M., and Merzenich, M. M. (1996). Use-dependent alterations of movement representations in primary motor cortex of adult squirrel monkeys. *Journal of Neuroscience, 16,* 785–807.

Numan, M., and Numan. M. J. (1991). Preoptic-brainstem connections and maternal behavior in rats. *Behavioral Neuroscience, 105,* 1010–1029.

Nutt, J. G., Rufener, S. L., Carter, J. H., Anderson, V. C., et al. (2001). Interactions between deep brain stimulation and levodopa in Parkinson's disease. *Neurology, 57,* 1835–1842.

O

Oades, R. D., and Halliday, G. M. (1987). Ventral tegmental (A10) system: Neurobiology. 1. Anatomy and connectivity. *Brain Research Reviews, 12,* 117–165.

Obernier, J. A., White, A. M., Swartzwelder, H. S., and Crews, F. T. (2002). Cognitive deficits and CNS damage after a 4-day binge ethanol exposure in rats. *Pharmacology, Biochemistry and Behavior, 72,* 521–532.

O'Brien, C. P., Childress, A. R., Ehrman, R., and Robbins, S. J. (1998). Conditioning factors in drug abuse: Can they explain compulsion? *Journal of Psychopharmacology, 12,* 15–22.

O'Connor, D. B., Archer, J., and Wu, F. C. (2004). Effects of testosterone on mood, aggression, and sexual behavior in young men: A double-blind, placebo-controlled, cross-over study. *Journal of Clinical Endocrinology & Metabolism, 89,* 2837–2845.

O'Craven, K. M., Downing, P. E., and Kanwisher, N. (1999). fMRI evidence for objects as the units of attentional selection. *Nature, 401,* 584–587.

O'Doherty, A., Ruf, S., Mulligan, C., Hildreth, V., et al. (2005). An aneuploid mouse strain carrying human chromosome 21 with Down syndrome phenotypes. *Science, 309,* 2033–2037.

Oh-I, S., Shimizu, H., Satoh, T., Okada, S., et al. (2006). Identification of nesfatin-1 as a satiety molecule in the hypothalamus. *Nature, 443,* 709–712.

Ohno, K., and Sakurai, T. (2008). Orexin neuronal circuitry: Role in the regulation of sleep and wakefulness. *Frontiers in Neuroendocrinology, 29,* 70–87.

Ojemann, G., and Mateer, C. (1979). Human language cortex. Localization of memory, syntax, and sequential motor-phoneme identification systems. *Science, 205,* 1401–1403.

Okano, H., Ogawa, Y., Nakamura, M., Kaneko, S., et al. (2003). Transplantation of neural stem cells into the spinal cord after injury. *Seminars in Cell and Developmental Biology, 14,* 191–198.

O'Keefe, J., and Dostrovsky, J. (1971). The hippocampus as a spatial map. Preliminary evidence from unit activity in the freely-moving rat. *Brain Research, 34,* 171–175.

Okubo, Y., Suhara, T., Suzuki, K., Kobayashi, K., et al. (1997). Decreased prefrontal dopamine D1 receptors in schizophrenia revealed by PET. *Nature, 385,* 634–636.

Olanow, C. W., Goetz, C. G., Kordower, J. H., Stoessl, A. J., et al. (2003). A double-blind controlled trial of bilateral fetal nigral transplantation in Parkinson's disease. *Annals of Neurology, 54,* 403–414.

Olds, J., and Milner, P. (1954). Positive reinforcement produced by electrical stimulation of septal area and other regions of the rat brain. *Journal of Comparative and Physiological Psychology, 47,* 419–427.

Olfson, M., Marcus, S. C., and Shaffer, D. (2006). Antidepressant drug therapy and suicide in severely depressed children and adults: A case-control study. *Archives of General Psychiatry, 63,* 865–872.

Olsen, E. M., Heino, M., Lilly, G. R., Morgan, M. J., et al. (2004). Maturation trends indicative of rapid evolution preceded the collapse of northern cod. *Nature, 428,* 899–900.

Olsen, K. L. (1979). Androgen-insensitive rats are defeminised by their testes. *Nature, 279,* 238–239.

Olson, S. (2004). Making sense of Tourette's. *Science, 305,* 1390–1392.

Olsson, A., and Phelps, E. A. (2007). Social learning of fear. *Nature Neuroscience, 10,* 1095–1102.

Ontiveros, A., Fontaine, R., Breton, G., Elie, R., et al. (1989). Correlation of severity of panic disorder and neuroanatomical changes on magnetic resonance imaging. *Journal of Neuropsychiatry and Clinical Neurosciences, 1,* 404–408.

Ophir, A. G., Phelps, S. M., Sorin, A. B., and Wolff, J. O. (2008). Social but not genetic monogamy is associated with greater breeding success in prairie voles. *Animal Behavior, 75,* 1143–1154.

Oppenheim, R. W. (1991). Cell death during development of the nervous system. *Annual Review of Neuroscience, 14,* 453–501.

Oroszi, G., Anton, R. F., O'Malley, S., Swift, R., et al. (2009). OPRM1 Asn40Asp predicts response to naltrexone treatment: A haplotype-based approach. *Alcoholism: Clinical and Experimental Research, 33,* 383–393.

Osterhout, L. (1997). On the brain response to syntactic anomalies: Manipulations of word position and word class reveal individual differences. *Brain and Language, 59,* 494–522.

Ottoson, D., Bartfai, T., Hokfelt, T., and Fuxe, K. (Eds.). (1995). *Wenner-Gren international series: Vol. 66. Challenges and perspectives in neuroscience.* Amsterdam: Elsevier.

Ouattara, K., Lemasson, A., and Zuberbühler, K. (2009). Campbell's monkeys concatenate vocalizations into context-specific call sequences. *Proceedings of the National Academy of Sciences, USA, 22,* 22026–22031.

Overstreet, D. H. (1993). The Flinders sensitive line rats: A genetic animal model of depression. *Neuroscience and Biobehavioral Reviews, 17,* 51–68.

Owen, A. M., Coleman, M. R., Boly, M., Davis, M. H., et al. (2006). Detecting awareness in the vegetative state. *Science, 313,* 1402.

Ozelius, L. J., Senthil, G., Saunders-Pullman, R., Ohmann, E., et al. (2006). *LRRK2* G2019S as a cause of Parkinson's disease in Ashkenazi Jews. *New England Journal of Medicine, 354,* 424–425.

P

Pack, A. I. (2003). Should a pharmaceutical be approved for the broad indication of excessive sleepiness? *American Journal of Respiratory and Critical Care Medicine, 167,* 109–111.

Paddock, R. C., and La Ganga, M. (2008, August 5). Officials decry attacks on UC staff. *Los Angeles Times* (http://articles.latimes.com/2008/aug/05/local/me-attacks5).

Pagel, J. F., and Helfter, P. (2003). Drug induced nightmares—An etiology based review. *Human Psychopharmacology, 18,* 59–67.

Palmer, T. D., Schwartz, P. H., Taupin, P., Kaspar, B., et al. (2001). Progenitor cells from human brain after death. *Nature, 411,* 42–43.

Palmiter, R. D. (2008). Dopamine signaling in the dorsal striatum is essential for motivated behaviors: Lessons from dopamine-deficient mice. *Annals of the New York Academy of Sciences, 1129,* 35–46.

Panksepp, J. (1998). *Affective neuroscience.* New York: Oxford University Press.

Panksepp, J. (2000). Emotions as natural kinds within the mammalian brain. In M. Lewis and J. M. Haviland-Jones (Eds.), *Handbook of emotions* (2nd ed., pp. 137–156). New York: Guilford.

Panksepp, J. (2005). Beyond a joke: From animal laughter to human joy? *Science, 308,* 62–63.

Panksepp, J. (2007). Neuroevolutionary sources of laughter and social joy: Modeling primal human laughter in laboratory rats. *Behavioural Brain Research, 182,* 231–244.

Panov, A. V., Gutekunst, C.-A., Leavitt, B. R., Hayden, M. R., et al. (2002). Early mitochondrial calcium defects in Huntington's disease are a direct effect of polyglutamines. *Nature Neuroscience, 5,* 731–736.

Panowski, S. H., Wolff, S., Aguilaniu, H., Durieux, J., et al. (2007). PHA-4/Foxa mediates diet-restriction-induced longevity of *C. elegans. Nature, 447,* 550–555.

Pantev, C., Oostenveld, R., Engelien, A., Ross, B., et al. (1998). Increased auditory cortical representation in musicians. *Nature, 392,* 811–814.

Pantle, A., and Sekuler, R. (1968). Size-detecting mechanisms in human vision. *Science, 162,* 1146–1148.

Papez, J. W. (1937). A proposed mechanism of emotion. *Archives of Neurology and Psychiatry, 38,* 725–745.

Papka, M., Ivry, R., and Woodruff-Pak, D. S. (1994). Eyeblink classical conditioning and time production in patients with cerebellar damage. *Society of Neuroscience Abstracts, 20,* 360.

Pare, M., Behets, C., and Cornu, O. (2003). Paucity of presumptive ruffini corpuscles in the index finger pad of humans. *Journal of Comparative Neurology, 456,* 260–266.

Park, D. C., Lautenschlager, G., Hedden, T., Davidson, N. S., et al. (2002). Models of visuospatial and verbal memory across the adult life span. *Psychology of Aging, 17,* 299–320.

Park, S., Como, P. G., Cui, L., and Kurlan, R. (1993). The early course of the Tourette's syndrome clinical spectrum. *Neurology, 43,* 1712–1715.

Parker, G., Cahill, L., and McGaugh, J. L. (2006). A case of unusual autobiographical remembering. *Neurocase, 12,* 35–49.

Parkes, J. D. (1985). *Sleep and its disorders.* Philadelphia: Saunders.

Parton, L. E., Ye, C. P., Coppari, R., Enriori, P. J., et al. (2007). Glucose sensing by POMC neurons regulates glucose homeostasis and is impaired in obesity. *Nature, 449,* 228–232.

Paterson, S. J., Brown, J. H., Gsödl, M. K., Johnson, M. H., et al. (1999). Cognitive modularity and genetic disorders. *Science, 286,* 2355–2358.

Patterson, F., and Linden, E. (1981). *The education of Koko.* New York: Holt, Rinehart, and Winston.

Patterson, P. H. (2007). Maternal effects on schizophrenia risk. *Science, 318,* 576–578.

Paul, L. K., Brown, W. S., Adolphs, R., Tyszka, J. M., et al. (2007). Agenesis of the corpus callosum: Genetic, developmental and functional aspects of connectivity. *Nature Reviews. Neuroscience, 8,* 287–299.

Paulesu, E., McCrory, E., Fazio, F., Menoncello, L., et al. (2000). A cultural effect on brain function. *Nature Neuroscience, 3,* 91–96.

Pauls, D. L. (2003). An update on the genetics of Gilles de la Tourette syndrome. *Journal of Psychosomatic Research, 55,* 7–12.

Paulson, H. L., and Fischbeck, K. H. (1996). Trinucleotide repeats in neurogenetic disorders. *Annual Review of Neuroscience, 19,* 79–107.

Paus, T., Kalina, M., Patocková, L., Angerová, Y., et al. (1991). Medial vs lateral frontal lobe lesions and differential impairment of central-gaze fixation maintenance in man. *Brain, 114,* 2051–2067.

Paus, T., Keshavan, M., and Giedd, J. N. (2008). Why do many psychiatric disorders emerge during adolescence? *Nature Reviews. Neuroscience, 9,* 947–956.

Pawluski, J. L., and Galea, L. A. (2007). Reproductive experience alters hippocampal neurogenesis during the postpartum period in the dam. *Neuroscience, 149,* 53–67.

Peck, J. R., and Waxman, D. (2000). Mutation and sex in a competitive world. *Nature, 406,* 399–404.

Pediatric Eye Disease Investigator Group. (2005). Randomized trial of treatment of amblyopia in children aged 7 to 17 years. *Archives of Ophthalmology, 13,* 437–447.

Pedreira, C., Mormann, F., Kraskov, A., Cerf, M., et al. (2010). Responses of human medial temporal lobe neurons are modulated by stimulus repetition. *Journal of Neurophysiology, 103,* 97–107.

Pegna, A. J., Khateb, A., Lazeyras, F., and Seghier, M. L. (2005). Discriminating emotional faces without primary visual cortices involves the right amygdala. *Nature Neuroscience, 8,* 24–25.

Peña, J. L., and Konishi, M. (2000). Cellular mechanisms for resolving phase ambiguity in the owl's inferior colliculus. *Proceedings of the National Academy of Sciences, USA, 97*, 11787–11792.

Penfield, W., and Rasmussen, T. (1950). *The cerebral cortex in man.* New York: Macmillan.

Penfield, W., and Roberts, L. (1959). *Speech and brain-mechanisms.* Princeton, NJ: Princeton University Press.

Pennisi, E. (2003). Systems biology: Tracing life's circuitry. *Science, 302*, 1646–1649.

Peplau, L. A. (2003). Human sexuality: How do men and women differ? *Current Directions in Psychological Science, 12*, 37–40.

Perani, D., and Abutalebi, J. (2005). The neural basis of first and second language processing. *Current Opinion in Neurobiology, 15*, 202–206.

Perenin, M. T., and Vighetto, A. (1988). Optic ataxia: A specific disruption in visuomotor mechanisms. I. Different aspects of the deficit in reaching for objects. *Brain, 111*, 643–674.

Peretz, I., and Hyde, K. L. (2003). What is specific to music processing? Insights from congenital amusia. *Trends in Cognitive Sciences, 7*, 362–367.

Peris, J., Boyson, S. J., Cass, W. A., Curella, P., et al. (1990). Persistence of neurochemical changes in dopamine systems after repeated cocaine administration. *Journal of Pharmacology and Experimental Therapeutics, 253*, 38–44.

Pernía-Andrade, A. J., Kato, A., Witschi, R., Nyilas, R., et al. (2009). Spinal endocannabinoids and CB_1 receptors mediate C-fiber–induced heterosynaptic pain sensitization. *Science, 325*, 760–764.

Perry, V. H., Oehler, R., and Cowey, A. (1984). Retinal ganglion cells that project to the dorsal lateral geniculate nucleus in the macaque monkey. *Neuroscience, 12*, 1101–1123.

Pertwee, R. G. (1997). Pharmacology of cannabinoid CB1 and CB2 receptors. *Pharmacology & Therapeutics, 74*, 129–180.

Peschanski, M., Defer, G., N'Guyen, J. P., Ricolfi, F., et al. (1994). Bilateral motor improvement and alteration of L-dopa effect in two patients with Parkinson's disease following intrastriatal transplantation of foetal ventral mesencephalon. *Brain, 117*, 487–499.

Peschansky, V. J., Burbridge, T. J., Volz, A. J., Fiondella, C., et al. (2009, August 13). The effect of variation in expression of the candidate dyslexia susceptibility gene homolog Kiaa0319 on neuronal migration and dendritic morphology in the rat. *Cerebral Cortex.* [Epub ahead of print]

Peter, M. E., Medema, J. P., and Krammer, P. H. (1997). Does the *Caenorhabditis elegans* protein CED-4 contain a region of homology to the mammalian death effector domain? *Cell Death and Differentiation, 4*, 51–134.

Peterhans, E., and von der Heydt, R. (1989). Mechanisms of contour perception in monkey visual cortex. II. Contours bridging gaps. *Journal of Neuroscience, 9*, 1749–1763.

Peters, A., Palay, S. L., and Webster, H. deF. (1991). *The fine structure of the nervous system: Neurons and their supporting cells* (3rd ed.). New York: Oxford University Press.

Peterson, B. S., Warner, V., Bansal, R., Zhu, H., et al. (2009). Cortical thinning in persons at increased familial risk for major depression. *Proceedings of the National Academy of Sciences, USA, 106*, 6273–6278.

Peterson, L. R., and Peterson, M. J. (1959). Short-term retention of individual verbal items. *Journal of Experimental Psychology, 58*, 193–198.

Petit, C., and Richardson, G. P. (2009). Linking genes underlying deafness to hair-bundle development and function. *Nature Neuroscience, 12*, 703–710.

Petitto, L. A., Zatorre, R. J., Gauna, K., Nikelski, E. J., et al. (2000). Speech-like cerebral activity in profoundly deaf people processing signed languages: Implications for the neural basis of human language. *Proceedings of the National Academy of Sciences, USA, 97*, 13961–13966.

Petrides, M., and Milner, B. (1982). Deficits on subject-ordered tasks after frontal- and temporal-lobe lesions in man. *Neuropsychologia, 20*, 249–262.

Petrovic, P., Kalso, E., Petersson, K. M., and Ingvar, M. (2002). Placebo and opioid analgesia imaging—A shared neuronal network. *Science, 295*, 1737–1740.

Pettit, H. O., and Justice, J. B., Jr. (1991). Effect of dose on cocaine self-administration behavior and dopamine levels in the nucleus accumbens. *Brain Research, 539*, 94–102.

Petty, F., Kramer, G., Wilson, L., and Jordan, S. (1994). In vivo serotonin release and learned helplessness. *Psychiatry Research, 52*, 285–293.

Pfaff, D. W. (1980). *Estrogens and brain function: Neural analysis of a hormone-controlled mammalian reproductive behavior.* New York: Springer.

Pfaff, D. W. (1997). Hormones, genes, and behavior. *Proceedings of the National Academy of Sciences, USA, 94*, 14213–14216.

Pfaus, J. G., Kippin, T. E., and Centeno, S. (2001). Conditioning and sexual behavior: A review. *Hormones and Behavior, 40*, 291–321.

Pfefferbaum, A., Sullivan, E. V., Mathalon, D. H., Shear, P. K., et al. (1995). Longitudinal changes in magnetic resonance imaging brain volumes in abstinent and relapsed alcoholics. *Alcoholism: Clinical and Experimental Research, 19*, 1177–1191.

Pfrieger, F. W., and Barres, B. A. (1997). Synaptic efficacy enhanced by glial cells in vitro. *Science, 277*, 1684–1687.

Phillips, J. R., Johansson, R. S., and Johnson, K. O. (1990). Representation of braille characters in human nerve fibres. *Experimental Brain Research, 81*, 589–592.

Phillips, M. L., Marks, I. M., Senior, C., Lythgoe, D., et al. (2000). A differential neural response in obsessive-compulsive disorder patients with washing compared with checking symptoms to disgust. *Psychological Medicine, 30*, 1037–1050.

Phillips, M. L., Young, A. W., Scott, S. K., Calder, A. J., et al. (1998). Neural responses to facial and vocal expressions of fear and disgust. *Proceedings of the Royal Society of London. Series B: Biological Sciences, 265*, 1809–1817.

Phoenix, C. H., Goy, R. W., Gerall, A. A., and Young, W. C. (1959). Organizing action of prenatally administered testosterone propionate on the tissues mediating mating behavior in the female guinea pig. *Endocrinology, 65*, 369–382.

Pickens, R., and Thompson, T. (1968). Drug use by U.S. Army enlisted men in Vietnam: A followup on their return home. *Journal of Pharmacology and Experimental Therapeutics, 161*, 122–129.

Pierce, K., Muller, R.-A., Ambrose, J., Allen, G., et al. (2001). Face processing occurs outside the fusiform "face area": Evidence from functional MRI. *Brain, 124*, 2059–2073.

Pines, J. (1992). Cell proliferation and control. *Current Opinion in Cell Biology, 4*(2), 144–148.

Pinker, S. (1994). *The language instinct.* New York: Morrow.

Pinker, S., and Jackendoff, R. (2005). The faculty of language: What's special about it? *Cognition, 95*, 201–236.

Pitman, R. K., Sanders, K. M., Zusman, R. M., Healy, A. R., et al. (2002). Pilot study of secondary prevention of posttraumatic stress disorder with propranolol. *Biological Psychiatry, 51*, 189–192.

Pleim, E. T., and Barfield, R. J. (1988). Progesterone versus estrogen facilitation of female sexual behavior by intracranial administration to female rats. *Hormones and Behavior, 22*, 150–159.

Pletnikov, M. V., Ayhan, Y., Nikolskaia, O., Xu, Y., et al. (2008). Inducible expression of mutant human DISC1 in mice is associated with brain and behavioral abnormalities reminiscent of schizophrenia. *Molecular Psychiatry, 13*, 13–186.

Ploog, D. W. (1992). Neuroethological perspectives on the human brain: From the expression of emotions to intentional signing and speech. In A. Harrington (Ed.), *So human a brain: Knowledge and values in the neurosciences* (pp. 3–13). Boston: Birkhauser.

Plutchik, R. (1994). *The psychology and biology of emotion.* New York: HarperCollins.

Polleux, F., Morrow, T., and Ghosh, A. (2000). Semaphorin 3A is a chemoattractant for cortical apical dendrites. *Nature, 404*, 567–573.

Polymeropoulos, M. H., Lavedan, C., Leroy, E., Ide, S. E., et al. (1997). Mutation in the alpha-synuclein gene identified in families with Parkinson's disease. *Science, 276,* 2045–2047.

Ponsford, J. (2005). Rehabilitation interventions after mild head injury. *Current Opinion in Neurology, 18,* 692–697.

Poole, J. H., Tyack, P. L., Stoeger-Horwath, A. S., and Watwood, S. (2005). Animal behaviour: Elephants are capable of vocal learning. *Nature, 434,* 455–456.

Pope, H. G., Jr., Kouri, E. M., and Hudson, J. I. (2000). Effects of supraphysiologic doses of testosterone on mood and aggression in normal men: A randomized controlled trial. *Archives of General Psychiatry, 57,* 133–140.

Poremba, A., Malloy, M., Saunders, R. C., Carson, R. E., et al. (2004). Species-specific calls evoke asymmetric activity in the monkey's temporal poles. *Nature, 427,* 448–451.

Poritsky, R. (1969). Two and three dimensional ultrastructure of boutons and glial cells on the motoneuronal surface in the cat spinal cord. *Journal of Comparative Neurology, 135,* 423–452.

Porta, M., Brambilla, A., Cavanna, A. E., Servello, D., et al. (2009). Thalamic deep brain stimulation for treatment-refractory Tourette syndrome: Two-year outcome. *Neurology, 73,* 1375–1380.

Porter, J., Craven, B., Khan, R. H., Chang, S.-J., et al. (2007). Mechanisms of scent-tracking in humans. *Nature Neuroscience, 10,* 27–29.

Posner, M. I. (1980). Orienting of attention. *Quarterly Journal of Experimental Psychology, 32,* 3–25.

Posner, M. I., and Cohen, Y. (1984). Components of visual orienting. In H. Bouma and D. Bowhuis (Eds.), *Attention and performance: Vol 10. Control of language processes* (pp. 531–556). Hillsdale, NJ: Erlbaum.

Posner, M. I., and Raichle, M. E. (1994). *Images of mind.* New York: Scientific American Library.

Posthuma, D., De Geus, E. J. C., Baaré, W. F. C., Hulshoff Pol, H. E., et al. (2002). The association between brain volume and intelligence is of genetic origin. *Nature Neuroscience, 5,* 83–84.

Postuma, R. B., Gagnon, J. F., Vendette, M., Fantini, M. L., et al. (2009). Quantifying the risk of neurodegenerative disease in idiopathic REM sleep behavior disorder. *Neurology, 72,* 1296–1300.

Poulet, J. F. A., and Petersen, C. C. H. (2008). Internal brain state regulates membrane potential synchrony in barrel cortex of behaving mice. *Nature, 454,* 881–885.

Powley, T. L. (2000). Vagal circuitry mediating cephalic-phase responses to food. *Appetite, 34,* 184–188.

Premack, D. (1971). Language in a chimpanzee? *Science, 172,* 808–822.

Price, M. A., and Vandenbergh, J. G. (1992). Analysis of puberty-accelerating pheromones. *Journal of Experimental Zoology, 264,* 42–45.

Prickaerts, J., Koopmans, G., Blokland, A., and Scheepens, A. (2004). Learning and adult neurogenesis: Survival with or without proliferation? *Neurobiology of Learning and Memory, 81,* 1–11.

Proudfoot, C. J., Garry, E. M., Cottrell, D. F., Rosie, R., et al. (2006). Analgesia mediated by the TRPM8 cold receptor in chronic neuropathic pain. *Current Biology, 16,* 1591–1605.

Przybyslawski, J., Roullet, P., and Sara, S. J. (1999). Attenuation of emotional and nonemotional memories after their reactivation: Role of beta adrenergic receptors. *Journal of Neuroscience, 19,* 6623–6628.

Pugh, E. N., Jr., and Lamb, T. D. (1990). Cyclic GMP and calcium: The internal messengers of excitation and adaptation in vertebrate photoreceptors. *Vision Research, 30,* 1923–1948.

Pugh, E. N., Jr., and Lamb, T. D. (1993). Amplification and kinetics of the activation steps in phototransduction. *Biochimica et Biophysica Acta, 1141,* 111–149.

Pugh, K. R., Mencl, W. E., Shaywitz, B. A., Shaywitz, S. E., et al. (2000). The angular gyrus in developmental dyslexia: Task-specific differences in functional connectivity within posterior cortex. *Psychological Science, 11,* 51–56.

Purves, D., Augustine, G. J., Fitzpatrick, D., Katz, L., et al. (Eds.). (2001). *Neuroscience* (2nd ed.). Sunderland, MA: Sinauer.

Purves, D., and Lotto, R. B. (2003). *Why we see what we do.* Sunderland, MA: Sinauer.

Q

Quill, T. E., and Meier, D. E. (2006). The big chill—Inserting the DEA into end-of-life care. *New England Journal of Medicine, 354,* 1–3.

R

Racette, A., Bard, C., and Peretz, I. (2006). Making non-fluent aphasics speak: Sing along! *Brain, 129,* 2571–2584.

Racine, E., Bar-Ilan, O., and Illes, J. (2005). fMRI in the public eye. *Nature Reviews. Neuroscience, 6,* 159–164.

Rafal, R. D. (1994). Neglect. *Current Opinion in Neurobiology, 4,* 231–236.

Rafal, R. D., Posner, M. I., Friedman, J. H., Inhoff, A. W., et al. (1988). Orienting of visual attention in progressive supranuclear palsy. *Brain, 111,* 267–280.

Rahman, Q. (2005). The neurodevelopment of human sexual orientation. *Neuroscience and Biobehavioral Reviews, 29,* 1057–1066.

Raine, A., Lencz, T., Bihrle, S., LaCasse, L., et al. (2000). Reduced prefrontal gray matter volume and reduced autonomic activity in antisocial personality disorder. *Archives of General Psychiatry, 57,* 119–127.

Raine, A., Meloy, J. R., Bihrle, S., Stoddard, J., et al. (1998). Reduced prefrontal and increased subcortical brain functioning assessed using positron emission tomography in predatory and affective murderers. *Behavioral Sciences & the Law, 16,* 319–332.

Raine, A., Reynolds, C., Venables, P. H., and Mednick, S. A. (2002). Stimulation seeking and intelligence: A prospective longitudinal study. *Journal of Personality and Social Psychology, 82,* 663–674.

Raine, A., Venables, P. H., Dalais, C., Mellingen, K., et al. (2001). Early educational and health enrichment at age 3–5 years is associated with increased autonomic and central nervous system arousal and orienting at age 11 years: Evidence from the Mauritius Child Health Project. *Psychophysiology, 38,* 254–266.

Rainville, P., Duncan, G. H., Price, D. D., Carrier, B., et al. (1997). Pain affect encoded in human anterior cingulate but not somatosensory cortex. *Science, 277,* 968–971.

Raisman, G. (1978). What hope for repair of the brain? *Annals of Neurology, 3,* 101–106.

Raisman, G., and Field, P. M. (1971). Sexual dimorphism in the preoptic area of the rat. *Science, 173,* 731–733.

Raisman, G., and Li, Y. (2007). Repair of neural pathways by olfactory ensheathing cells. *Nature Reviews. Neuroscience, 8,* 312–319.

Rakel, R. E. (2009). Clinical and societal consequences of obstructive sleep apnea and excessive daytime sleepiness. *Postgraduate Medicine, 121,* 86–95.

Rakic, P. (1971). Guidance of neurons migrating to the fetal monkey neocortex. *Brain Research, 33,* 471–476.

Rakic, P. (1985). Mechanisms of neuronal migration in developing cerebellar cortex. In G. M. Edelman, W. M. Cowan, and E. Gull (Eds.), *Molecular basis of neural development* (pp. 139–160). New York: Wiley.

Rakic, P. (2006). Neuroscience: No more cortical neurons for you. *Science, 313,* 928–929.

Ralph, M. R., Foster, R. G., Davis, F. C., and Menaker, M. (1990). Transplanted suprachiasmatic nucleus determines circadian period. *Science, 247,* 975–978.

Ralph, M. R., and Menaker, M. (1988). A mutation of the circadian system in golden hamsters. *Science, 241,* 1225–1227.

Ramachandran, V. S., and Hubbard, E. M. (2001). Psychophysical investigations into the neural basis of synthaesthesia. *Proceedings of the Royal Society of London. Series B: Biological Sciences, 268,* 979–983.

Ramachandran, V. S., and Rogers-Ramachandran D. (2000). Phantom limbs and neural plasticity. *Archives of Neurology, 57,* 317–320.

Ramchandani, P. (2004). A question of balance: How safe are the medicines that are prescribed to children? *Nature, 430,* 401–402.

Ramey, C. T., Campbell, F. A., Burchinal, M., Skinner, M. L., et al. (2000). Persistent effects of early childhood education on high-risk children and their mothers. *Applied Developmental Science, 4*(1), 2–14.

Ramon, F., Hernandex-Falcon, J., Nguyen, B., and Bullock, T. H. (2004). Slow wave sleep in crayfish. *Proceedings of the National Academy of Sciences, USA, 101,* 11857–11861.

Rampon, C., Tang, Y. P., Goodhouse, J., Shimizu, E., et al. (2000). Enrichment induces structural changes and recovery from nonspatial memory deficits in CA1 NMDAR1-knockout mice. *Nature Neuroscience, 3,* 238–244.

Rampon, C., and Tsien, J. Z. (2000). Genetic analysis of learning behavior-induced structural plasticity. *Hippocampus, 10,* 605–609.

Ramus, F., Hauser, M. D., Miller, C., Morris, D., et al. (2000). Language discrimination by human newborns and by cotton-top tamarin monkeys. *Science, 288,* 349–351.

Ranaldi, R., and Beninger, R. J. (1994). The effects of systemic and intracerebral injections of D1 and D2 agonists on brain stimulation reward. *Brain Research, 651,* 283–292.

Rand, M. N., and Breedlove, S. M. (1987). Ontogeny of functional innervation of bulbocavernosus muscles in male and female rats. *Brain Research, 430,* 150–152.

Randolph, M., and Semmes, J. (1974). Behavioral consequences of selective subtotal ablations in the postcentral gyrus of *Macaca mulatta. Brain Research, 70,* 55–70.

Rao, P. D. P., and Finger, T. E. (1984). Asymmetry of the olfactory system in the brain of the winter flounder *Pseudopleuronectes americanus. Journal of Comparative Neurology, 225,* 492–510.

Rapoport, J. L. (1989). The biology of obsessions and compulsions. *Scientific American, 260*(6), 82–89.

Rasmussen, L. E., and Greenwood, D. R. (2003). Frontalin: A chemical message of musth in Asian elephants (*Elephas maximus*). *Chemical Senses, 28,* 433–446.

Rasmussen, L. E., Riddle, H. S., and Krishnamurthy, V. (2002). Chemical communication: Mellifluous matures to malodorous in musth. *Nature, 415,* 975–976.

Rathelot, J. A., and Strick, P. L. (2006). Muscle representation in the macaque motor cortex: An anatomical perspective. *Proceedings of the National Academy of Sciences, USA, 103,* 8257–8262.

Rattenborg, N. C. (2006). Do birds sleep in flight? *Naturwissenschaften, 93,* 413–425.

Rattenborg, N. C., Amlaner, D. J., and Lima, S. L. (2001). Unilateral eye closure and interhemispheric EEG asymmetry during sleep in the pigeon (*Columba livia*). *Brain Behavior and Evolution, 58,* 323–332.

Rauch, S. L., Jenike, M. A., Alpert, N. M., Baer, L., et al. (1994). Regional cerebral blood flow measured during symptom provocation in obsessive-compulsive disorder using oxygen 15-labeled carbon dioxide and positron emission tomography. *Archives of General Psychiatry, 51,* 62–70.

Rauch, S. L., Shin, L. M., and Wright, C. I. (2003). Neuroimaging studies of amygdala function in anxiety disorders. *Annals of the New York Academy of Sciences, 985,* 389–410.

Rauschecker, J. P, and Shannon, R. V. (2002). Sending sound to the brain. *Science, 295,* 1025–1029.

Raymond, J. E., and O'Brien, J. L. (2009). Selective visual attention and motivation: The consequences of value learning in an attentional blink task. *Psychical Science, 20,* 981–988.

Raymond, J. E., Shapiro, K. L., and Arnell, K. M. (1992). Temporary suppression of visual processing in an RSVP task: An attentional blink? *Journal of Experimental Psychology. Human Perception and Performance, 18,* 849–860.

Raz, N. (2000). Aging of the brain and its impact on cognitive performance: Integration of structural and functional findings. In F. I. M. Craik and T. A. Salthouse (Eds.), *The handbook of aging and cognition* (2nd ed., pp. 1–90). Mahwah, NJ: Erlbaum.

Reader, S. M., and Laland, K. N. (2002). Social intelligence, innovation, and enhanced brain size in primates. *Proceedings of the National Academy of Sciences, USA, 99,* 4436–4441.

Recanzone, G. H., and Cohen, Y. E. (2010). Serial and parallel processing in the primate auditory cortex revisited. *Behavioural Brain Research, 206,* 1–7.

Recanzone, G. H., Schreiner, D. E., and Merzenich, M. M. (1993). Plasticity in the frequency representation of primary auditory cortex following discrimination training in adult owl monkeys. *Journal of Neuroscience, 13,* 87–103.

Rechtschaffen, A., and Bergmann, B. M. (1995). Sleep deprivation in the rat by the disk-over-water method. *Behavioural Brain Research, 69,* 55–63.

Rechtschaffen, A., and Kales, A. (1968). *A manual of standardized terminology, techniques and scoring system for sleep stages of human subjects.* Bethesda, MD: U.S. National Institute of Neurological Diseases and Blindness, Neurological Information Network.

Redican, W. K. (1982). An evolutionary perspective on human facial displays. In P. Ekman (Ed.), *Emotion in the human face* (2nd ed., pp. 212–280). Elmsford, NY: Pergamon.

Rees, G., Kreiman, G., and Koch, C. (2002). Neural correlates of consciousness in humans. *Nature Reviews. Neuroscience, 3,* 261–270.

Rehkamper, G., Haase, E., and Frahm, H. D. (1988). Allometric comparison of brain weight and brain structure volumes in different breeds of the domestic pigeon, *Columba livia* f. d. (fantails, homing pigeons, strassers). *Brain, Behavior and Evolution, 31,* 141–149.

Reichardt, L. F., and Tomaselli, K. J. (1991). Extracellular matrix molecules and their receptors: Functions in neural development. *Annual Review of Neuroscience, 14,* 531–570.

Reiner, W. G., and Gearhart, J. P. (2004). Discordant sexual identity in some genetic males with cloacal exstrophy assigned to female sex at birth. *New England Journal of Medicine, 350,* 333–341.

Reisberg, D., and Heuer, F. (1995). Emotion's multiple effects on memory. In J. L. McGaugh, N. M. Weinberger, and G. Lynch (Eds.), *Brain and memory: Modulation and mediation of neuroplasticity* (pp. 84–92). New York: Oxford University Press.

Remondes, M., and Schuman, E. M. (2004). Role for a cortical input to hippocampal area CA1 in the consolidation of a long-term memory. *Nature, 431,* 699–703.

Rempel-Clower, N. L., Zola, S. M., Squire, L. R., and Amaral, D. G. (1996). Three cases of enduring memory impairment after bilateral damage limited to the hippocampal formation. *Journal of Neuroscience, 16,* 5233–5255.

Rende, R., and Plomin, R. (1995). Nature, nurture, and the development of psychopathology. In D. Cicchetti and D. J. Cohen (Eds.), *Developmental psychopathology: Vol. 1. Theory and methods* (pp. 291–314). New York: Wiley.

Renner, M. J., and Rosenzweig, M. R. (1987). *Enriched and impoverished environments: Effects on brain and behavior.* New York: Springer.

Rensink, R. A. (2002). Change detection. *Annual Review of Psychology, 53,* 245–277.

Rensink, R. A., O'Regan, J. K., and Clark, J. J. (1997). To see or not to see: The need for attention to perceive changes in scenes. *Psychological Science, 8,* 368–373.

Reppert, S. M., Perlow, M. J., Tamarkin, L., and Klein, D. C. (1979). A diurnal melatonin rhythm in primate cerebrospinal fluid. *Endocrinology, 104,* 295–301.

Reppert, S. M., and Weaver, D. R. (2002). Coordination of circadian timing in mammals. *Nature, 418,* 935–941.

Ressler, K. J., Sullivan, S. L., and Buck, L. B. (1994). A molecular dissection of spatial patterning in the olfactory system. *Current Opinion in Neurobiology, 4,* 588–596.

Reuter, J., Raedler, T., Rose, M., Hand, I., et al. (2005). Pathological gambling is linked to reduced activation of the mesolimbic reward system. *Nature Neuroscience, 8,* 147–148.

Revel, F. G., Masson-Pévet, M., Pévet, P., Mikkelsen, J. D., et al. (2009). Melatonin controls seasonal breeding by a network of hypothalamic targets. *Neuroendocrinology, 90,* 1–14.

Rex, C. S., Lauterborn, J. C., Lin, C. Y., Kramár, E. A., et al. (2006). Restoration of long-term potentiation in middle-aged hippocampus after induction of brain-derived neurotrophic factor. *Journal of Neurophysiology, 96,* 677–685.

Rhodes, M. G. (2004). Age-related differences in performance on the Wisconsin card sorting test: A meta-analytic review. *Psychology of Aging, 19,* 482–494.

Ribeiro, R. C., Kushner, P. J., and Baxter, J. D. (1995). The nuclear hormone receptor gene superfamily. *Annual Review of Medicine, 46,* 443–453.

Ricciardi, E., Pietrini, P., Schapiro, M. B., Rapoport, S. I., et al. (2009). Cholinergic modulation of visual working memory during aging: A parametric PET study. *Brain Research Bulletin, 79,* 322–332.

Rice, W. R., and Chippindale, A. K. (2001). Sexual recombination and the power of natural selection. *Science, 294,* 555–559.

Richman, D. P., and Agius, M. A. (2003). Treatment of autoimmune myasthenia gravis. *Neurology, 61,* 1652–1661.

Richter, C. (1967). Sleep and activity: Their relation to the 24-hour clock. *Proceedings of the Association for Research in Nervous and Mental Diseases, 45,* 8–27.

Ridley, M. (2003). *Nature via nurture: Genes, experience, and what makes us human.* New York: Harper Collins.

Rilling, J. K., Glasser, M. F., Preuss, T. M., Ma, X., et al. (2008). The evolution of the arcuate fasciculus revealed with comparative DTI. *Nature Neuroscience, 11,* 426–428.

Ringman, J. M., and Cummings, J. L. (2006). Current and emerging pharmacological treatment options for dementia. *Behavioral Neurology, 17,* 5–16.

Risch, N., Herrell, R., Lehner, T., Liang, K. Y., et al. (2009). Interaction between the serotonin transporter gene (5-HT-TLPR), stressful life events, and risk of depression: A meta-analysis. *JAMA, 301,* 2462–2471.

Rizzolatti, G., and Craighero, L. (2004). The mirror-neuron system. *Annual Review of Neuroscience, 27,* 169–192.

Rizzolatti, G., Fogassi, L., and Gallese, V. (2006). Mirrors of the mind. *Scientific American, 295*(5), 54–61.

Roberts, A. H. (1969). *Brain damage in boxers.* London: Pitman.

Roberts, C. G., and Ladenson, P. W. (2004). Hypothyroidism. *Lancet, 363,* 793–803.

Roberts, W. W., and Mooney, R. D. (1974). Brain areas controlling thermoregulatory grooming, prone extension, locomotion, and tail vasodilation in rats. *Journal of Comparative and Physiological Psychology, 86,* 470–480.

Robins, L. N., and Regier, D. A. (1991). *Psychiatric disorders in America: The epidemiologic catchment area study.* New York: Free Press.

Robins, L. N., and Slobodyan, S. (2003). Post-Vietnam heroin use and injection by re-turning US veterans: Clues to preventing injection today. *Addiction, 98,* 1053–1060.

Robinson, D. L., and Petersen, S. E. (1992). The pulvinar and visual salience. *Trends in Neuroscience, 15,* 127–132.

Robinson, R. (2009). Intractable depression responds to deep brain stimulation. *Neurology Today, 9,* 7–10.

Rocca, W. A., Hofman, A., Brayne, C., Breteler, M. M., et al. (1991). The prevalence of vascular dementia in Europe: Facts and fragments from 1980–1990 studies. *Annals of Neurology, 30,* 817–824.

Roelink, H., Augsburger, A., Heemskerk, J., Korzh, V., et al. (1994). Floor plate and motor neuron induction by vhh-1, a vertebrate homolog of hedgehog expressed by the notochord. *Cell, 76,* 761–775.

Roenneberg, T., Kuehnle, T., Pramstaller, P. P., Ricken, J., et al. (2004). A marker for the end of adolescence. *Current Biology, 14,* R1038–R1039.

Roffwarg, H. P., Muzio, J. N., and Dement, W. C. (1966). Ontogenetic development of the human sleep-dream cycle. *Science, 152,* 604–619.

Rogan, M. T., Staubli, U. V., and LeDoux, J. E. (1997). Fear conditioning induces associative long-term potentiation in the amygdala. *Nature, 390,* 604–607.

Rogawski, M. A., and Löscher, W. (2004). The neurobiology of antiepileptic drugs. *Nature Reviews. Neuroscience, 5,* 553–564.

Roland, E., and Larson, B. (1976). Focal increase of cerebral blood flow during stereognostic testing in man. *Archives of Neurology, 33,* 551–558.

Roland, P. E. (1980). Quantitative assessment of cortical motor dysfunction by measurement of the regional cerebral blood flow. *Scandinavian Journal of Rehabilitation Medicine, 7,* 27–41.

Roland, P. E. (1984). Metabolic measurements of the working frontal cortex in man. *Trends in Neurosciences, 7,* 430–436.

Roland, P. E. (1993). *Brain activation.* New York: Wiley-Liss.

Rolls, E. T., and O'Mara, S. M. (1995). View-responsive neurons in the primate hippocampal complex. *Hippocampus, 5,* 409–424.

Romanski, L. M., Tian, B., Fritz, J., Mishkin, M., et al. (1999). Dual streams of auditory afferents target multiple domains in the primate prefrontal cortex. *Nature Neuroscience, 2,* 1131–1136.

Rorabaugh, W. J. (1976). Estimated U.S. alcoholic beverage consumption, 1790–1860. *Journal of Studies on Alcohol, 37,* 357–364.

Rosci, C., Chiesa, V., Laiacona, M., and Capitani, E. (2003). Apraxia is not associated to a disproportionate naming impairment for manipulable objects. *Brain and Cognition, 53,* 412–415.

Roselli, C. E., Larkin, K., Resko, J. A., Stellflug, J. N., et al. (2004). The volume of a sexually dimorphic nucleus in the ovine medial preoptic area/anterior hypothala-mus varies with sexual partner preference. *Endocrinology, 145,* 475–477.

Roselli, C. E., and Stormshak, F. (2009). The neurobiology of sexual partner preferences in rams. *Hormones and Behavior, 55,* 611–620.

Rosen, B. R., Buckner, R. L., and Dale, A. M. (1998). Event-related functional MRI: Past, present, and future. *Proceedings of the National Academy of Sciences, USA, 95,* 773–780.

Rosenbaum, R. S., Köhler, S., Schacter, D. L., Moscovitch, M., et al. (2005). The case of K.C.: Contributions of a memory-impaired person to memory theory. *Neuropsychologia, 43,* 989–1021.

Rosenfield, P. J., Kleinhaus, K., Opler, M., Perrin, M., et al. (2010). Later paternal age and sex differences in schizophrenia symptoms. *Schizophrenia Research, 116,* 191–195.

Rosengren, A., Tibblin, G., and Wilhelmsen, L. (1991). Self-perceived psychological stress and incidence of coronary artery disease in middle-aged men. *American Journal of Cardiology, 68,* 1171–1175.

Rosenkranz, M. A., Jackson, D. C., Dalton, K. M., Dolski, I., et al. (2003). Affective style and in vivo immune response: Neurobehavioral mechanisms. *Proceedings of the National Academy of Sciences, USA, 100,* 11148–11152.

Rosenzweig, E. S., and Barnes, C. A. (2003). Impact of aging on hippocampal function: Plasticity, network dynamics, and cognition. *Progress in Neurobiology, 69,* 143–179.

Rosenzweig, M. R. (1946). Discrimination of auditory intensities in the cat. *American Journal of Psychology, 59,* 127–136.

Rosenzweig, M. R. (1984). Experience, memory, and the brain. *American Psychologist, 39,* 365–376.

Rosenzweig, M. R., and Bennett, E. L. (1977). Effects of environmental enrichment or impoverishment on learning and on brain values in rodents. In A. Oliveno (Ed.), *Genetics, environment, and intelligence* (pp. 1–2). Amsterdam: Elsevier/North-Holland.

Rosenzweig, M. R., and Bennett, E. L. (1978). Experimental influences on brain anatomy and brain chemistry in rodents. In G. Gottlieb (Ed.), *Studies on the development of behavior and the nervous system: Vol. 4. Early influences* (pp. 289–327). New York: Academic Press.

Rosenzweig, M. R., Bennett, E. L., Colombo, P. J., Lee, D. W., et al. (1993). Short-term, intermediate-term, and long-term memory. *Behavioural Brain Research, 57,* 193–198.

Rosenzweig, M. R., Bennett, E. L., and Diamond, M. C. (1972). Brain changes in response to experience. *Scientific American, 226*(2), 22–29.

Rosenzweig, M. R., Bennett, E. L., Martinez, J. L., Colombo, P. J., et al. (1992). Studying stages of memory formation with chicks. In L. R. Squire and N. Butters (Eds.), *Neuropsychology of memory* (2nd ed., pp. 533–546). New York: Guilford.

Rosenzweig, M. R., Krech, D., and Bennett, E. L. (1961). Heredity, environment, brain biochemistry, and learning. In *Current trends in psychological theory* (pp. 87–110). Pittsburgh, PA: University of Pittsburgh Press.

Rosenzweig, M. R., Krech, D., Bennett, E. L., and Diamond, M. C. (1962). Effects of environmental complexity and training on brain chemistry and anatomy: A replication and extension. *Journal of Comparative and Physiological Psychology, 55,* 429–437.

Roses, A. D. (1995). On the metabolism of apolipoprotein E and the Alzheimer diseases. *Experimental Neurology, 132,* 149–156.

Rossetti, Y., Rode, G., Pisella, L., Farné, A., et al. (1998). Prism adaptation to a rightward optical deviation rehabilitates left hemispatial neglect. *Nature, 395,* 166–169.

Rossi, D. J., Oshima, T., and Attwell, D. (2000). Glutamate release in severe brain ischaemia is mainly by reversed uptake. *Nature, 403,* 316–321.

Rossi, M. A., Mash, D. C., and deToledo-Morrell, L. (2005). Spatial memory in aged rats is related to PKCγ-dependent G-protein coupling of the M1 receptor. *Neurobiology of Aging, 26,* 53–68.

Rosso, I. M., Cannon, T. D., Huttunen, T., Huttunen, M. O., et al. (2000). Obstetric risk factors for early-onset schizophrenia in a Finnish birth cohort. *American Journal of Psychiatry, 157,* 801–807.

Rossor, M., Garrett, N., Johnson, A., Mountjoy, C., et al. (1982). A post-mortem study of the cholinergic and GABA systems in senile dementia. *Brain, 105,* 313–330.

Rothschild, A. J. (1992). Disinhibition, amnestic reactions, and other adverse reactions secondary to triazolam: A review of the literature. *Journal of Clinical Psychiatry, 53,* 69–79.

Rothstein, J. D. (2000). Bundling up excitement. *Nature, 407,* 141, 143.

Rouw, R., and Scholter, H. S. (2007). Increased structural connectivity in grapheme-color synesthesia. *Nature Neuroscience, 10,* 792–797.

Row, B. W., Kheirandish, L., Cheng, Y., Rowell, P.P., et al. (2007). Impaired spatial working memory and altered choline acetyltransferase (CHAT) immunoreactivity and nicotinic receptor binding in rats exposed to intermittent hypoxia during sleep. *Behavioural Brain Research, 177,* 308–314.

Rowe, M. K., and Chuang, D. M. (2004). Lithium neuroprotection: Molecular mechanisms and clinical implications. *Expert Reviews in Molecular Medicine, 18,* 1–18.

Roy, A. (1992). Hypothalamic-pituitary-adrenal axis function and suicidal behavior

in depression. *Biological Psychiatry, 32,* 812–816.

Rucci, M., Iovin, R., Poletti, M., and Santini, F. (2007). Miniature eye movements enhance fine spatial detail. *Nature, 447,* 851–854.

Ruck, C., Andreewitch, S., Flyckt, K., Edman, G., et al. (2003). Capsulotomy for refractory anxiety disorders: Long-term follow-up of 26 patients. *American Journal of Psychiatry, 160,* 513–521.

Rumbaugh, D. M. (1977). *Language learning by a chimpanzee: The LANA project.* New York: Academic Press.

Rupnick, M. A., Panigrahy, D., Zhang, C. Y., Dallabrida, S. M., et al. (2002). Adipose tissue mass can be regulated through the vasculature. *Proceedings of the National Academy of Sciences, USA, 99,* 10730–10735.

Rupprecht, R., Rammes, G., Eser, D., Baghai, T. C., et al. (2009). Translocator protein (18 kD) as target for anxiolytics without benzodiazepine-like side effects. *Science, 325,* 490–493.

Rusak, B., and Zucker, I. (1979). Neural regulation of circadian rhythms. *Physiological Reviews, 59,* 449–526.

Russell, J. A. (1994). Is there universal recognition of emotion from facial expressions? A review of the cross-cultural studies. *Psychological Bulletin, 115,* 102–141.

Russo, E. B., Jiang, H. E., Li, X., Sutton, A., et al. (2008). Phytochemical and genetic analyses of ancient cannabis from Central Asia. *Journal of Experimental Botany, 59,* 4171–4182.

Ruthazer, E. S., Akerman, C. J., and Cline, H. T. (2003). Control of axon branch dynamics by correlated activity in vivo. *Science, 301,* 66–70.

Ryan, A. J. (1998). Intracranial injuries resulting from boxing. *Clinics in Sports Medicine, 17*(1), 155–168.

Rymer, R. (1993). *Genie: An abused child's flight from silence.* New York: HarperCollins.

Rypma, B., Berger, J. S., Genova, H. M., Rebbechi, D., et al. (2005). Dissociating age-related changes in cognitive strategy and neural efficiency using event-related fMRI. *Cortex, 41,* 582–594.

S

Sack, R. L., Blood, M. L., and Lewy, A. J. (1992). Melatonin rhythms in night shift workers. *Sleep, 15,* 434–441.

Sage, C., Huang, M., Vollrath, M. A., Brown, M. C., et al. (2006). Essential role of retinoblastoma protein in mammalian hair cell development and hearing. *Proceedings of the National Academy of Sciences, USA, 103,* 7345–7350.

Sahay, A., and Hen, R. (2007). Adult hippocampal neurogenesis in depression. *Nature Neuroscience, 10,* 1110–1114.

Salazar, H., Llorente, I., Jara-Oseguera, A., García-Villegas, R., et al. (2008). A single

N-terminal cysteine in TRPV1 determines activation by pungent compounds from onion and garlic. *Nature Neuroscience, 11,* 255–260.

Salvini-Plawen, L. V., and Mayr, E. (1977). On the evolution of photoreceptors and eyes. *Evolutionary Biology, 10,* 207–263.

Samad, T. A., Moore, K. A., Sapirstein, A., Billet, S., et al. (2001). Interleukin-1β-mediated induction of Cox-2 in the CNS contributes to inflammatory pain hypersensitivity. *Nature, 410,* 471–475.

Samaha, F. F., Iqbal, N., Seshadri, P., Chicano, K. L., et al. (2003). A low-carbohydrate as compared with a low-fat diet in severe obesity. *New England Journal of Medicine, 348,* 2074–2081.

Samson, S., and Zatorre, R. J. (1991). Recognition memory for text and melody of songs after unilateral temporal lobe lesion: Evidence for dual encoding. *Journal of Experimental Psychology. Learning, Memory, and Cognition, 17,* 793–804.

Samson, S., and Zatorre, R. J. (1994). Contribution of the right temporal lobe to musical timbre discrimination. *Neuropsychologia, 32,* 231–240.

Sanderson, D. J., Good, M. A., Seeburg, P. H., Sprengel, R., et al. (2008). The role of the GluR-A (GluR1) AMPA receptor subunit in learning and memory. *Progress in Brain Research, 169,* 159–178.

Sanes, J. N., and Donoghue, J. P. (2000). Plasticity and primary motor cortex. *Annual Review of Neuroscience, 23,* 393–415.

Sanes, J. R., and Lichtman, J. W. (1999). Can molecules explain long-term potentiation? *Nature Neuroscience, 2,* 597–604.

Santhanam, G., Ryu, S. I., Yu, B. M., Afshar, A., et al. (2006) A high-performance brain–computer interface. *Nature, 442,* 195–198.

Sapir, A., Soroker, N., Berger, A., and Henik, A. (1999). Inhibition of return in spatial attention: Direct evidence for collicular generation. *Nature Neuroscience, 2,* 1053–1054.

Sapolsky, R. M. (1992). Neuroendocrinology of the stress-response. In J. B. Becker, S. M. Breedlove, and D. Crews (Eds.), *Behavioral endocrinology* (pp. 287–324). Cambridge, MA: MIT Press.

Sapolsky, R. M. (1993). Potential behavioral modification of glucocorticoid damage to the hippocampus [Special issue: Alzheimer's disease: Animal models and clinical perspectives]. *Behavioural Brain Research, 57,* 175–182.

Sapolsky, R. M. (2001). *A primate's memoir.* New York: Scribner.

Sapolsky, R. M. (2004). *Why zebras don't get ulcers* (3rd ed.). New York: Holt.

Sara, S. J. (2000). Retrieval and reconsolidation: Toward a neurobiology of remembering. *Learning and Memory, 7,* 73–84.

Satinoff, E. (1978). Neural organization and evolution of thermal regulation in mammals. *Science, 201,* 16–22.

Satinoff, E., and Rutstein, J. (1970). Behavioral thermoregulation in rats with anterior hypothalamic lesions. *Journal of Comparative and Physiological Psychology, 71*, 77–82.

Satinoff, E., and Shan, S. Y. (1971). Loss of behavioral thermoregulation after lateral hypothalamic lesions in rats. *Journal of Comparative and Physiological Psychology, 77*, 302–312.

Saul, S. (2006, March 8). Some sleeping pill users range far beyond bed. *The New York Times.*

Savage-Rumbaugh, E. S. (1993). *Language comprehension in ape and child.* Chicago: University of Chicago Press.

Savage-Rumbaugh, [E.] S., and Lewin, R. (1994). *Kanzi: The ape at the brink of the human mind.* New York: Wiley.

Sawamoto, K., Wichterle, H., Gonzalez-Perez, O., Cholfin, J. A., et al. (2006). New neurons follow the flow of cerebrospinal fluid in the adult brain. *Science, 311*, 629–632.

Sawin, C. T. (1996). Arnold Adolph Berthold (1803–1861). *Endocrinologist, 6*, 164–168.

Saxe, M. D., Battaglia, F., Wang, J. W., Malleret, G., et al. (2006). Ablation of hippocampal neurogenesis impairs contextual fear conditioning and synaptic plasticity in the dentate gyrus. *Proceedings of the National Academy of Sciences, USA, 103*, 17501–17506.

Saxena, S., Brody, A. L., Ho, M. L., Alborzian, S., et al. (2001). Cerebral metabolism in major depression and obsessive-compulsive disorder occurring separately and concurrently. *Biological Psychiatry, 50*, 159–170.

Saxena, S., and Rauch, S. L. (2000). Functional neuroimaging and the neuroanatomy of obsessive-compulsive disorder. *Psychiatric Clinics of North America, 23*, 563–586.

Sbarra, D. A., and Nietert, P. J. (2009). Divorce and death: Forty years of the Charleston Heart Study. *Psychological Science, 20*, 107–113.

Scalaidhe, S. P. O., Wilson, F. A. W., and Goldman-Rakic, P. S. (1997). Areal segregation of face-processing neurons in prefrontal cortex. *Science, 278*, 1135–1138.

SCENIHR (Scientific Committee on Emerging and Newly Identified Health Risks). (2008, September 23). Scientific opinion on the potential health risks of exposure to noise from personal music players and mobile phones including a music playing function.

Schachter, S. (1975). Cognition and peripheralist-centralist controversies in motivation and emotion. In M. S. Gazzaniga and C. Blakemore (Eds.), *Handbook of psychobiology* (pp. 529–564). New York: Academic Press.

Schachter, S., and Singer, J. (1962). Cognitive, social, and physiological determinants of emotional state. *Psychological Review, 69*, 379–399.

Schacter, D. L., Alpert, N. M., Savage, C. R., Rauch, S. L., et al. (1996). Conscious recollection and the human hippocampal formation: Evidence from positron emission tomography. *Proceedings of the National Academy of Sciences, USA, 93*, 321–325.

Schaie, K. W. (1994). The course of adult intellectual development. *American Psychologist, 49*, 304–313.

Schank, J. C. (2001). Menstrual-cycle synchrony: Problems and new directions for research. *Journal of Comparative Psychology, 115*, 3–15.

Schank, J. C. (2002). A multitude of errors in menstrual-synchrony research: Replies to Weller and Weller (2002) and Graham (2002). *Journal of Comparative Psychology, 116*, 319–322.

Scharff, C., Kirn, J. R., Grossman, M., Macklis, J. D., et al. (2000). Targeted neuronal death affects neuronal replacement and vocal behavior in adult songbirds. *Neuron, 25*, 481–492.

Scheibel, A. B., and Conrad, A. S. (1993). Hippocampal dysgenesis in mutant mouse and schizophrenic man: Is there a relationship? *Schizophrenia Bulletin, 19*, 21–33.

Scheibel, M. E., Tomiyasu, U., and Scheibel, A. B. (1977). The aging human Betz cells. *Experimental Neurology, 56*, 598–609.

Scheibert, J., Leurent, S., Prevost, A., and Debrégeas, G. (2009). The role of fingerprints in the coding of tactile information probed with a biomimetic sensor. *Science, 323*, 1503–1506.

Schein, S. J., and Desimone, R. (1990). Spectral properties of V4 neurons in the macaque. *Journal of Neuroscience, 10*, 3369–3389.

Schenck, C. H., and Mahowald, M. W. (2002). REM sleep behavior disorder: Clinical, developmental, and neuroscience perspectives 16 years after its formal identification in *Sleep. Sleep, 25*, 120–138.

Schenkerberg, T., Bradford, D. C., and Ajax, E. T. (1980). Line bisection and unilateral visual neglect in patients with neurologic impairment. *Neurology, 30*, 509–518.

Schieber, M. H, and Hibbard, L. S. (1993). How somatotopic is the motor cortex hand area? *Science, 261*, 489–492.

Schiffman, S. S., Simon, S. A., Gill, J. M., and Beeker, T. G. (1986). Bretylium tosylate enhances salt taste. *Physiology & Behavior, 36*, 1129–1137.

Schildkraut, J. J., and Kety, S. S. (1967). Biogenic amines and emotion. *Science, 156*, 21–30.

Schiller, P. H. (1993). The effects of V4 and middle temporal (MT) area lesions on visual performance in the rhesus monkey. *Visual Neuroscience, 10*, 717–746.

Schindler, I., Clavagnier, S., Karnath, H. O., Derex, L., et al. (2006). A common basis for visual and tactile exploration deficits in spatial neglect? *Neuropsychologia, 44*, 1444–1451.

Schlaug, G., Jancke, L., Huang, Y., and Steinmetz, H. (1995). In vivo evidence of structural brain asymmetry in musicians. *Science, 267*, 699–701.

Schlupp, I., Marler, C., and Ryan, M. J. (1994). Benefit to male sailfin mollies of mating with heterospecific females. *Science, 263*, 373–374.

Schmidt-Nielsen, K. (1960). *Animal physiology.* Englewood Cliffs, NJ: Prentice-Hall.

Schmolesky, M. T., Wang, Y., Pu, M., and Leventhal, A. G. (2000). Degradation of stimulus selectivity of visual cortical cells in senescent rhesus monkeys. *Nature Neuroscience, 3*, 384–390.

Schnapf, J. L., and Baylor, D. A. (1987). How photoreceptor cells respond to light. *Scientific American, 256*(4), 40–47.

Schnapp, B. J. (1997). Retroactive motors. *Neuron, 18*, 523–526.

Schneider, G. E. (1969). Two visual systems. *Science, 163*, 895–902.

Schneider, K. (1959). *Clinical psychopathology.* New York: Grune & Stratton.

Schneider, K. A., and Kastner, S. (2009). Effects of sustained spatial attention in the human lateral geniculate nucleus and superior colliculus. *Journal of Neuroscience, 29*, 1784–1795.

Schneider, P., Scherg, M., Dosch, H. G., Specht, H. J., et al. (2002). Morphology of Heschl's gyrus reflects enhanced activation in the auditory cortex of musicians. *Nature Neuroscience, 5*, 688–694.

Schnupp, J. W., Dawe, K. L., and Pollack, G. L. (2005). The detection of multisensory stimuli in an orthogonal sensory space. *Experimental Brain Research, 162*, 181–190.

Schuckit, M. A., and Smith, T. L. (1997). Assessing the risk for alcoholism among sons of alcoholics. *Journal of Studies on Alcohol, 58*, 141–145.

Schumann, C. M., and Amaral, D. G. (2006). Stereological analysis of amygdala neuron number in autism. *Journal of Neuroscience, 26*, 7674–7679.

Schummers, J., Yu, H., and Sur, M. (2008). Tuned responses of astrocytes and their influence on hemodynamic signals in the visual cortex. *Science, 320*, 1638–1643.

Schuster, C. R. (1970). Psychological approaches to opiate dependence and self-administration by laboratory animals. *Federation Proceedings, 29*, 1–5.

Schwartz, C. E., Wright, C. I., Shin, L. M., Kagan, J., et al. (2003). Inhibited and uninhibited infants "grown up": Adult amygdalar response to novelty. *Science, 300*, 1952–1953.

Schwartz, W. J., Smith, C. B., Davidsen, L., Savaki, H., et al. (1979). Metabolic mapping of functional activity in the hypothalamo-neurohypophysial system of the rat. *Science, 205*, 723–725.

Schwartzer, R., and Gutiérrez-Doña, B. (2000). Health psychology. In K. Pawlik and M. R. Rosenzweig (Eds.), *Interna-*

tional handbook of psychology (pp. 452–465). London: Sage.

Schwartzkroin, P. A., and Wester, K. (1975). Long-lasting facilitation of a synaptic potential following tetanization in the in vitro hippocampal slice. *Brain Research, 89*, 107–119.

Sclafani, A., Springer, D., and Kluge, L. (1976). Effects of quinine adulteration on the food intake and body weight of obese and nonobese hypothalamic hyperphagic rats. *Physiology & Behavior, 16*, 631–640.

Scott, D. J., Stohler, C. S., Egnatuk, C. M., Wang, H., et al. (2008). Placebo and nocebo effects are defined by opposite opioid and dopaminergic responses. *Archives of General Psychiatry, 65*, 220–231.

Scott, S. K., and Wise, R. J. (2004). The functional neuroanatomy of prelexical processing in speech perception. *Cognition, 92*, 13–45.

Scoville, W. B., and Milner, B. (1957). Loss of recent memory after bilateral hippocampal lesions. *Journal of Neurology, Neurosurgery and Psychiatry, 20*, 11–21.

Seeman, P. (1990). Atypical neuroleptics: Role of multiple receptors, endogenous dopamine, and receptor linkage. *Acta Psychiatrica Scandinavica. Supplementum, 358*, 14–20.

Seiden, R. H. (1978). Where are they now? A follow-up study of suicide attempters from the Golden Gate Bridge. *Suicide and Life Threatening Behavior, 8*, 203–216.

Seil, F. J., Kelly, J. M., and Leiman, A. L. (1974). Anatomical organization of cerebral neocortex in tissue culture. *Experimental Neurology, 45*, 435–450.

Selkoe, D. J. (1991). Amyloid protein and Alzheimer's disease. *Scientific American, 265*(5), 68–71.

Selye, H. (1956). *The stress of life.* New York: McGraw-Hill.

Semendeferi, K., Lu, A., Schenker, N., and Damasio, H. (2002). Humans and great apes share a large frontal cortex. *Nature Neuroscience, 5*, 272–276.

Semple, D. M., Ebmeier, K. P., Glabus, M. F., O'Carroll, R. E., et al. (1999). Reduced in vivo binding to the serotonin transporter in the cerebral cortex of MDMA ("ecstasy") users. *British Journal of Psychiatry, 175*, 63–69.

Sendtner, M., Holtmann, B., and Hughes, R. A. (1996). The response of motoneurons to neurotrophins. *Neurochemical Research, 21*, 831–841.

Senghas, A., Kita, S., and Ozyurek, A. (2004). Children creating core properties of language: Evidence from an emerging sign language in Nicaragua. *Science, 305*, 1779–1782.

Senju, A., Southgate, V., White, S., and Frith, W. (2009). Mindblind eyes: An absence of spontaneous theory of mind in Asperger syndrome. *Science, 325*, 883–885.

Serrano, P. A., Beniston, D. S., Oxonian, M. G., Rodriguez, W. A., et al. (1994). Differ-

ential effects of protein kinase inhibitors and activators on memory formation in the 2-day-old chick. *Behavioral and Neural Biology, 61*, 60–72.

Serviere, J., Webster, W. R., and Calford, M. B. (1984). Isofrequency labelling revealed by a combined [14C]-2-deoxyglucose, electrophysiological, and horseradish peroxidase study of the inferior colliculus of the cat. *Journal of Comparative Neurology, 228*, 463–477.

Seuss, Dr. (1987). *The tough coughs as he ploughs the dough: Early writings and cartoons by Dr. Seuss.* New York: Morrow.

Seyfarth, R. M., and Cheney, D. L. (1997). Behavioral mechanisms underlying vocal communication in nonhuman primates. *Animal Learning & Behavior, 25*, 249–267.

Shallice, T., and Burgess, P. W. (1991). Deficits in strategy application following frontal lobe damage in man. *Brain, 114*, 727–741.

Shammi, P., and Stuss, D. T. (1999). Humour appreciation: A role of the right frontal lobe. *Brain, 122*, 657–666.

Shank, S. S., and Margoliash, D. (2009). Sleep and sensorimotor integration during early vocal learning in a songbird. *Nature, 458*, 73–77.

Shapiro, K. L., Caldwell, J., and Sorensen, R. E. (1997). Personal names and the attentional blink: A visual "cocktail party" effect. *Journal of Experimental Psychology. Human Perception and Performance, 23*, 504–514.

Shapiro, R. M. (1993). Regional neuropathology in schizophrenia: Where are we? Where are we going? *Schizophrenia Research, 10*, 187–239.

Shaw, P., Eckstrand, K., Sharp, W., Blumenthal, J., et al. (2007). Attention-deficit/hyperactivity disorder is characterized by a delay in cortical maturation. *Proceedings of the National Academy of Sciences, USA, 104*, 19649–19654.

Shaw, P., Greenstein, D., Lerch, J., Clasen, L., et al. (2006). Intellectual ability and cortical development in children and adolescents. *Nature, 440*, 676–679.

Shaw, P. J., Tononi, G., Greenspan, R. J., and Robinson, D. F. (2002). Stress response genes protect against lethal effects of sleep deprivation in *Drosophila. Nature, 417*, 287–291.

Shaywitz, S. E., Shaywitz, B. A., Fulbright, R. K., Skudlarski, P., et al. (2003). Neural systems for compensation and persistence: Young adult outcome of childhood reading disability. *Biological Psychiatry, 54*, 25–33.

Shaywitz, S. E., Shaywitz, B. A., Pugh, K. R., Fulbright, R. K., et al. (1998). Functional disruption in the organization of the brain for reading in dyslexia. *Proceedings of the National Academy of Sciences, USA, 95*, 2636–2641.

Shema, R., Hazvi, S., Sacktor, T. C., and Dudai, Y. (2009). Boundary conditions for the maintenance of memory by PKMzeta

in neocortex. *Learning & Memory, 16*, 122–128.

Shema, R., Sacktor, T. C., and Dudai, Y. (2007). Rapid erasure of long-term memory associations in the cortex by an inhibitor of PKM zeta. *Science, 317*, 951–953.

Sherrington, C. S. (1897). *A textbook of physiology. Part III. The Central Nervous System* (7th ed.), M. Foster (Ed.). London: Macmillan.

Sherrington, C. S. (1898). Experiments in examination of the peripheral distribution of the fibres of the posterior roots of some spinal nerves. *Philosophical Transactions, 190*, 45–186.

Sherry, D. F. (1992). Memory, the hippocampus, and natural selection: Studies of food-storing birds. In L. R. Squire and N. Butters (Eds.), *Neuropsychology of memory* (2nd ed., pp. 521–532). New York: Guilford.

Sherry, D. F., and Schacter, D. L. (1987). The evolution of multiple memory systems. *Psychological Review, 94*, 439–454.

Sherry, D. F., and Vaccarino, A. L. (1989). Hippocampus and memory for food caches in black-capped chickadees. *Behavioral Neuroscience, 103*, 308–318.

Sherry, D. F., Vaccarino, A. L., Buckenham, K., and Herz, R. S. (1989). The hippocampal complex of food-storing birds. *Brain Behavior and Evolution, 34*, 308–317.

Sherwin, B. B. (1998). Use of combined estrogen-androgen preparations in the postmenopause: Evidence from clinical studies. *International Journal of Fertility and Women's Medicine, 43*(2), 98–103.

Sherwin, B. B. (2002). Randomized clinical trials of combined estrogen-androgen preparations: Effects on sexual functioning. *Fertility and Sterility, 77*(Suppl. 4), 49–54.

Shih, R. A., Belmonte, P. L., and Zandi, P. P. (2004). A review of the evidence from family, twin and adoption studies for a genetic contribution to adult psychiatric disorders. *International Review of Psychiatry, 16*, 260–283.

Shimura, H., Schlossmacher, M. G., Hattori, N., Frosch, M. P., et al. (2001). Ubiquitination of a new form of α-synuclein by parkin from human brain: Implications for Parkinson's disease. *Science, 293*, 263–269.

Shingo, T., Gregg, C., Enwere, E., Fujikawa, H., et al. (2003). Pregnancy-stimulated neurogenesis in the adult female forebrain mediated by prolactin. *Science, 299*, 117–120.

Shors, T. J., Miesegaes, G., Beylin, A., Zhao, M., et al. (2001). Neurogenesis in the adult is involved in the formation of trace memories. *Nature, 410*, 372–376.

Shu, W., Cho, J. Y., Jiang, Y., Zhang, M., et al. (2005). Altered ultrasonic vocalization in mice with a disruption in the Foxp2 gene. *Proceedings of the National Academy of Sciences, USA, 102*, 9643–9648.

Siegel, J. M. (1994). Brainstem mechanisms generating REM sleep. In M. H. Kryger, T. Roth, and W. C. Dement (Eds.), *Principles and practice of sleep medicine* (2nd ed., pp. 125–144). Philadelphia: Saunders.

Siegel, J. M. (2001). The REM sleep–memory consolidation hypothesis. *Science, 294,* 1058–1063.

Siegel, J. M. (2005). Clues to the function of mammalian sleep. *Nature, 437,* 1264–1271.

Siegel, J. M., Manger, P. R., Nienhuis, R., Fahringer, H. M., et al. (1999). Sleep in the platypus. *Neuroscience, 91,* 391–400.

Siegel, J. M., Nienhuis, R., Gulyani, S., Ouyang, S., et al. (1999). Neuronal degeneration in canine narcolepsy. *Journal of Neuroscience, 19,* 248–257.

Siegel, R. K. (1989). *Intoxication: Life in pursuit of artificial paradise.* New York: Dutton.

Siemens, J., Zhou, S., Piskorowski, R., Nikai, T., et al. (2006). Spider toxins activate the capsaicin receptor to produce inflammatory pain. *Nature, 444,* 208–212.

Siever, L. J. (2008). Neurobiology of aggression and violence. *American Journal of Psychiatry, 165,* 429–442.

Sikich, L, Frazier, J. A., McClellan, J., Findling, R. L., et al. (2008). Double-blind comparison of first- and second-generation antipsychotics in early-onset schizophrenia and schizo-affective disorder: Findings from the treatment of early-onset schizophrenia spectrum disorders (TEOSS) study. *American Journal of Psychiatry, 165,* 1420–1431.

Sileno, A. P., Brandt, G. C., Spann, B. M., and Quay, S. C. (2006). Lower mean weight after 14 days intravenous administration peptide YY$_{3-36}$ (PYY$_{3-36}$) in rabbits. *International Journal of Obesity, 30,* 68–72.

Silva, D. A., and Satz, P. (1979). Pathological left-handedness. Evaluation of a model. *Brain and Language, 7,* 8–16.

Simic, G., Kostovic, I., Winblad, B., and Bogdanovic, N. (1997). Volume and number of neurons of the human hippocampal formation in normal aging and Alzheimer's disease. *Journal of Comparative Neurology, 379,* 482–494.

Simner, J., Mulvenna, C., Sagiv, N., Tsakanikos, E., et al. (2006). Synaesthesia: The prevalence of atypical cross-modal experiences. *Perception, 35,* 1024–1033.

Simons, D. J., and Chabris, C. F. (1999). Gorillas in our midst: Sustained inattentional blindness for dynamic events. *Perception, 28,* 1059–1074.

Simons, D. J., and Jensen, M. S. (2009). The effects of individual differences and task difficulty on inattentional blindness. *Psychonomic Bulletin & Review, 16,* 398–403.

Singer, N. (2002). Ambitious plan to give sight to the blind. *Sandia Lab News, 54,* 19, 1.

Singer, O., Marr, R. A., Rockenstein, E., Crews, L., et al. (2005). Targeting BACE1 with siRNAs ameliorates Alzheimer disease neuropathology in a transgenic model. *Nature Neuroscience, 8,* 1343–1349.

Singer, P. (1975). *Animal liberation: A new ethics for our treatment of animals.* New York: New York Review.

Singer, T., Seymour, B., O'Doherty, J., Kaube, H., et al. (2004). Empathy for pain involves the affective but not sensory components of pain. *Science, 303,* 1157–1162.

Singh, D. (2002). Female mate value at a glance: Relationship of waist-to-hip ratio to health, fecundity and attractiveness. *Neuroendocrinology Letters, 23*(Suppl. 4), 81–91.

Siok, W. T., Perfetti, C. A., Jin, Z., and Tan, L. H. (2004). Biological abnormality of impaired reading is constrained by culture. *Nature, 431,* 71–76.

Sirotnak, A. P., Grigsby, T., and Krugman, R. D. (2004). Physical abuse of children. *Pediatrics in Review, 25,* 264–277.

Siveter, D. J., Sutton, M. D., Briggs, D. E., and Siveter, D. J. (2003). An ostracode crustacean with soft parts from the Lower Silurian. *Science, 302,* 1749–1751.

Skinner, M., Holden, L., and Holden, T. (1997). Parameter selection to optimize speech recognition with the nucleus implant. *Otolaryngology and Head and Neck Surgery, 117,* 188–195.

Smale, L. (1988). Influence of male gonadal hormones and familiarity on pregnancy interruption in prairie voles. *Biology of Reproduction, 39,* 28–31.

Smale, L., Holekamp, K. E., and White, P. A. (1999). Siblicide revisited in the spotted hyaena: Does it conform to obligate or facultative models? *Animal Behaviour, 58,* 545–551.

Smith, A., and Sugar, O. (1975). Development of above normal language and intelligence 21 years after hemispherectomy. *Neurology, 25,* 813–818.

Smith, C. (1995). Sleep states and memory processes. *Behavioural Brain Research, 69,* 137–145.

Smith, C. M., and Luskin, M. B. (1998). Cell cycle length of olfactory bulb neuronal progenitors in the rostral migratory stream. *Developmental Dynamics, 213,* 220–227.

Smith, D. E., Roberts, J., Gage, F. H., and Tuszynski, M. H. (1999). Age-associated neuronal atrophy occurs in the primate brain and is reversible by growth factor gene therapy. *Proceedings of the National Academy of Sciences, USA, 96,* 10893–10898.

Smith, J. T., Clifton, D. K., amd Steiner, R. A. (2006). Regulation of the neuroendocrine reproductive axis by kisspeptin-GPR54 signaling. *Reproduction, 131,* 623–630.

Smith, M. A., Brandt, J., and Shadmehr, R. (2000). Motor disorder in Huntington's disease begins as a dysfunction in error feedback control. *Nature, 403,* 544–549.

Smith, P. B., Compton, D. R., Welch, S. P., Razdan, R. K., et al. (1994). The pharmacological activity of anandamide, a putative endogenous cannabinoid, in mice. *Journal of Pharmacology and Experimental Therapeutics, 270,* 219–227.

Smith, S. (1997, September 2). Dreaming awake Part 1: Living with narcolepsy. *Minnesota Public Radio News* (http://news.minnesota.publicradio.org/features/199709/02_smiths_narcolepsy/narco_1.shtml).

Smoller, J. W., and Finn, C. T. (2003). Family, twin, and adoption studies of bipolar disorder. *American Journal of Medical Genetics. Part C, Seminars in Medical Genetics, 123,* 48–58.

Smyth, K. A., Pritsch, T., Cook, T. B., McClendon, M. J., et al. (2004). Worker functions and traits associated with occupations and the development of AD. *Neurology, 63,* 498–503.

Snyder, S. H., and D'Amato, R. J. (1985). Predicting Parkinson's disease. *Nature, 317,* 198–199.

Sobel, N., Khan, R. M., Saltman, A., Sullivan, E. V., et al. (1999). The world smells different to each nostril. *Nature, 402,* 35.

Sobel, N., Prabhakaran, V., Zhao, Z., Desmond, J. E., et al. (2000). Time course of odorant-induced activation in the human primary olfactory cortex. *Journal of Neurophysiology, 83,* 537–551.

Sol, D., Duncan, R. P., Blackburn, T. M., Casey, P., et al. (2005). *Proceedings of the National Academy of Sciences, USA, 102,* 5460–5465.

Solomon, A. (2001). *The noonday demon: An atlas of depression.* New York: Scribner.

Solstad, T., Boccara, C. N., Kropff, E., Moser, M. B., et al. (2008). Representation of geometric borders in the entorhinal cortex. *Science, 322,* 1865–1868.

Somerville, M. J., Mervis, C. B., Young, E. J., Seo, E. J., et al. (2005). Severe expressive-language delay related to duplication of the Williams-Beuren locus. *New England Journal of Medicine, 353,* 1694–1701.

Soon, C. S., Brass, M., Heinze, H. J., and Haynes, J. D. (2008). Unconscious determinants of free decisions in the human brain. *Nature Neuroscience, 11,* 543–545.

Sorensen, P. W., and Goetz, F. W. (1993). Pheromonal and reproductive function of F prostaglandins and their metabolites in teleost fish. *Journal of Lipid Mediators, 6,* 385–393.

Sowell, E. R., Kan, E., Yoshii, J., Thompson, P. M., et al. (2008). Thinning of sensorimotor cortices in children with Tourette syndrome. *Nature Neuroscience, 11,* 637–639.

Sperry, R. W., Stamm, J., and Miner, N. (1956). Relearning tests for interocular transfer following division of optic chiasma and corpus callosum in cats. *Journal of Comparative and Physiological Psychology, 49,* 529–533.

Spiegler, B. J., and Mishkin, M. (1981). Evidence for the sequential participation of inferior temporal cortex and amygdala in the acquisition of stimulus-reward associations. *Behavioural Brain Research, 3,* 303–317.

Spiegler, B. J., and Yeni-Komshian, G. H. (1983). Incidence of left-handed writing in a college population with reference to family patterns of hand preference. *Neuropsychologia, 21,* 651–659.

Squire, L. R., Amaral, D. G., Zola-Morgan, S., and Kritchevsky, M. P. G. (1989). Description of brain injury in the amnesic patient N.A. based on magnetic resonance imaging. *Experimental Neurology, 105,* 23–35.

Squire, L. R., and Moore, R. Y. (1979). Dorsal thalamic lesion in a noted case of chronic memory dysfunction. *Annals of Neurology, 6,* 503–506.

Squire, L. R., Wixted, J. T., and Clark, R. E. (2007). Recognition memory and the medial temporal lobe: A new perspective. *Nature Reviews. Neuroscience, 8,* 872–883.

Squire, L. R., and Zola-Morgan, S. (1991). The medial temporal lobe memory system. *Science, 253,* 1380–1386.

Standing, L. G. (1973). Learning 10,000 pictures. *Quarterly Journal of Experimental Psychology, 25,* 207–222.

Stanovich, K. E. (2009). *What intelligence tests miss: The psychology of rational thought.* New Haven, CT: Yale University Press.

Stanton, S. J., Beehner, J. C., Saini, E. K., Kuhn, C. M., et al. (2009). Dominance, politics, and physiology: Voters' testosterone changes on the night of the 2008 United States presidential election. *PLoS ONE, 4,* e7543.

Starkstein, S. E., and Robinson, R. G. (1994). Neuropsychiatric aspects of stroke. In C. E. Coffey, J. L. Cummings, M. R. Lovell, and G. D. Pearlson (Eds.), *The American Psychiatric Press textbook of geriatric neuropsychiatry* (pp. 457–477). Washington, DC: American Psychiatric Press.

Staubli, U. V. (1995). Parallel properties of long-term potentiation and memory. In J. L. McGaugh, N. M. Weinberger, and G. Lynch (Eds.), *Brain and memory: Modulation and mediation of neuroplasticity* (pp. 303–318). New York: Oxford University Press.

Stefansson, H., Ophoff, R. A., Steinberg, S. Andreassen, O. A., et al. (2009). Common variants conferring risk of schizophrenia. *Nature, 460,* 744–747.

Stein, B., and Meredith, M. A. (1993). *The merging of the senses.* Cambridge, MA: MIT Press.

Stein, B. E., and Stanford, T. R. (2008). Multisensory integration: Current issues from the perspective of the single neuron. *Nature Reviews. Neuroscience, 9,* 255–266.

Stein, M., and Miller, A. H. (1993). Stress, the hypothalamic-pituitary-adrenal axis, and immune function. *Advances in Experimental Medicine and Biology, 335,* 1–5.

Stein, M., Miller, A. H., and Trestman, R. L. (1991). Depression, the immune system, and health and illness. Findings in search of meaning. *Archives of General Psychiatry, 48,* 171–177.

Steinlein, O. K. (2004). Genetic mechanisms that underlie epilepsy. *Nature Reviews. Neuroscience, 5,* 400–408.

Steinmetz, H., Volkmann, J., Janckc, L., and Freund, H. J. (1991). Anatomical left-right asymmetry of language-related temporal cortex is different in left- and right-handers. *Annals of Neurology, 29,* 315–319.

Stella, N., Schweitzer, P., and Piomelli, D. (1997). A second endogenous cannabinoid that modulates long-term potentiation. *Nature, 388,* 773–778.

Stephan, F. K., and Zucker, I. (1972). Circadian rhythms in drinking behavior and locomotor activity of rats are eliminated by hypothalamic lesions. *Proceedings of the National Academy of Sciences, USA, 69,* 1583–1586.

Stephan, H., Frahm, H., and Baron, G. (1981). New and revised data on volumes of brain structures in insectivores and primates. *Folia Primatologica, 35,* 1–29.

Steptoe, A. (1993). Stress and the cardiovascular system: A psychosocial perspective. In S. C. Stanford and P. Salmon (Eds.), *Stress: From synapse to syndrome* (pp. 119–141). London: Academic Press.

Stern, K., and McClintock, M. (1998). Regulation of ovulation by human pheromones. *Nature, 392,* 177–179.

Stoeckel, C., Gough, P. M., Watkins, K. E., and Devlin, J. T. (2009). Supramarginal gyrus involvement in visual word recognition. *Cortex, 45,* 1091–1096.

Stoerig, P., and Cowey, A. (1997). Blindsight in man and monkey. *Brain, 120,* 535–559.

Stone, V. E., Nisenson, L., Eliassen, J. C., and Gazzaniga, M. S. (1996). Left hemisphere representations of emotional facial expressions. *Neuropsychologia, 34,* 23–29.

Stoodley, C. J., and Stein, J. F. (2010, January 8). The cerebellum and dyslexia. *Cortex.* [Epub ahead of print]

Stowers, L., Holy, T. E., Meister, M., Dulac, C., et al. (2002). Loss of sex discrimination and male-male aggression in mice deficient for TRP2. *Science, 295,* 1493–1500.

Stranahan, A. M., Khalil, D., and Gould, E. (2006). Social isolation delays the positive effects of running on adult neurogenesis. *Nature Neuroscience, 9,* 526–533.

Stricker, E. M. (1977). The renin-angiotensin system and thirst: A reevaluation. II. Drinking elicited in rats by caval ligation or isoproterenol. *Journal of Comparative and Physiological Psychology, 91,* 1220–1231.

Striedter, G. P. (2005). *Principles of brain evolution.* Sunderland, MA: Sinauer.

Stuve, T. A., Friedman, L., Jesberger, J. A., Gilmore, G. C., et al. (1997). The relationship between smooth pursuit performance, motion perception and sustained visual attention in patients with schizophrenia and normal controls. *Psychological Medicine, 27,* 143–152.

Substance Abuse and Mental Health Services Administration. (2006). *Results from the 2005 National Survey on Drug Use and Health: National findings* (DHHS Publication No. SMA 06-4194, NSDUH Series H-30). Rockville, MD: Substance Abuse and Mental Health Services Administration, Office of Applied Studies.

Sumbre, G., Fiorito, G., Flash, T., and Hochner, B. (2005). Motor control of flexible octopus arms. *Nature, 443,* 595–596.

Summer, G. J., Puntillo, K. A., Miaskowski, C., Dina, O. A., et al. (2006). TrkA and PKC-epsilon in thermal burn-induced mechanical hyperalgesia in the rat. *Journal of Pain, 7,* 884–891.

Sumnall, H. R., and Cole, J. C. (2005). Self-reported depressive symptomatology in community samples of polysubstance misusers who report Ecstasy use: A meta-analysis. *Journal of Psychopharmacology, 19,* 84–92.

Sun, T., Patoine, C., Abu-Khalil, A., Visvader, J., et al. (2005). Early asymmetry of gene transcription in embryonic human left and right cerebral cortex. *Science, 308,* 1794–1798.

Sun, Y. G., and Chen, Z. F. (2007). A gastrin-releasing peptide receptor mediates the itch sensation in the spinal cord. *Nature, 448,* 700–702.

Sunn, N., Egli, M., Burazin, T. C. D., Burns, P., et al. (2002). Circulating relaxin acts on subfornical organ neurons to stimulate water drinking in the rat. *Proceedings of the National Academy of Sciences, USA, 99,* 1701–1706.

Sunstein, C. R., and Nussbaum, M. C. (Eds.) (2004). *Animal rights: Current debates and new directions.* Oxford, England: Oxford University Press.

Sutcliffe, J. G., and de Lecea, L. (2002). The hypocretins: Setting the arousal threshold. *Nature Reviews. Neuroscience, 3,* 339–349.

Suzuki, M., Nohara, S., Hagino, H., Kurokawa, K., et al. (2002). Regional changes in brain gray and white matter in patients with schizophrenia demonstrated with voxel-based analysis of MRI. *Schizophrenia Research, 55,* 41–54.

Suzuki, S., Brown, C. M., and Wise, P. M. (2009). Neuroprotective effects of estrogens following ischemic stroke. *Frontiers in Neuroendocrinology, 30,* 201–211.

Svenningsson, P., Chergui, K., Rachleff, I., Flajolet, M., et al. (2006). Alterations in 5-HT$_{1B}$ receptor function by p11 in depression-like states. *Science, 311,* 77–80.

Sweet, W. H. (1973). Treatment of medically intractable mental disease by limited frontal leucotomy—Justifiable? *New England Journal of Medicine, 289,* 1117–1125.

Szalavitz, M. (2004, March 25). The accidental addict: Clearing away the myths surrounding the OxyContin "epidemic." *Slate* (http://slate.msn.com/id/2097786).

Szarfman, A., Doraiswamy, P. M., Tonning, J. M., and Levine, J. G. (2006). Association between pathologic gambling and parkinsonian therapy as detected in the Food and Drug Administration Adverse Event database. *Archives Neurology, 62,* 299–300.

Székely, T., Catchpole, C. K., DeVoogd, A., Marchl, Z., et al. (1996). Evolutionary changes in a song control area of the brain (HVC) are associated with evolutionary changes in song repertoire among European warblers (Sylviidae). *Proceedings of the Royal Society of London. Series B: Biological Sciences, 263,* 607–610.

Szente, M., Gajda, Z., Said Ali, K., and Hermesz, E. (2002). Involvement of electrical coupling in the in vivo ictal epileptiform activity induced by 4-aminopyridine in the neocortex. *Neuroscience, 115,* 1067–1078.

T

Taglialatela, J. P., Cantalupo, C., and Hopkins, W. D. (2006). Gesture handedness predicts asymmetry in the chimpanzee inferior frontal gyrus. *Neuroreport, 17,* 923–927.

Taipale, M., Kaminen, N., Nopola-Hemmi, J., Haltia, T., et al. (2003). A candidate gene for developmental dyslexia encodes a nuclear tetratricopeptide repeat domain protein dynamically regulated in brain. *Proceedings of the National Academy of Sciences, USA, 100,* 11553–11558.

Takahashi, H., Kato, M., Matsuura, M., Mobbs, D., et al. (2009). When your gain is my pain and your pain is my gain: Neural correlates of envy and schadenfreude. *Science, 323,* 937–939.

Takahashi, J. S. (1995). Molecular neurobiology and genetics of circadian rhythms in mammals. *Annual Review of Neuroscience, 18,* 531–554.

Takahashi, T., Svoboda, K., and Malinow, R. (2003). Experience strengthening transmission by driving AMPA receptors into synapses. *Science, 299,* 1585–1588.

Tallal, P., and Schwartz, J. (1980). Temporal processing, speech perception and hemispheric asymmetry. *Trends in Neurosciences, 3,* 309–311.

Tam, J., Duda, D. G., Perentes, J. Y., Quadri, R. S., et al. (2009). Blockade of VEGFR2 and not VEGFR1 can limit diet-induced fat tissue expansion: Role of local versus bone marrow-derived endothelial cells. *PLoS One, 4,* e4974.

Tamás, G., Lörincz, A., Simon, A., and Szabadics, J. (2003). Identified sources and targets of slow inhibition in the neocortex. *Science, 299,* 1902–1905.

Tamgüney, G., Miller, M. W., Wolfe, L. L., Sirochman, T. M., et al. (2009). Asymptomatic deer excrete infectious prions in faeces. *Nature, 461,* 529–532.

Tamminga, C. A., and Schulz, S. C. (1991). *Schizophrenia research.* New York: Raven.

Tanaka, K. (1993). Neuronal mechanisms of object recognition. *Science, 262,* 685–688.

Tanaka, Y., Kamo, T., Yoshida, M., and Yamadori, A. (1991). "So-called" cortical deafness. Clinical, neurophysiological and radiological observations. *Brain, 114,* 2385–2401.

Tanda, G., Munzar, P., and Goldberg, S. R. (2000). Self-administration behavior is maintained by the psychoactive ingredient of marijuana in squirrel monkeys. *Nature Neuroscience, 3,* 1073–1074.

Tang, N. M., Dong, H. W., Wang, X. M., Tsui, Z. C., et al. (1997). Cholecystokinin antisense RNA increases the analgesic effect induced by electroacupuncture or low dose morphine: Conversion of low responder rats into high responders. *Pain, 71,* 71–80.

Tang, Y. P., Shimizu, E., Dube, G. R., Rampon, C., et al. (1999). Genetic enhancement of learning and memory in mice. *Nature, 401,* 63–69.

Tang, Y. P., Wang, H., Feng, R., Kyin, M., et al. (2001). Differential effects of enrichment on learning and memory function in NR2B transgenic mice. *Neuropharmacology, 41,* 779–790.

Tanila, H., Shapiro, M., Gallagher, M., and Eichenbaum, H. (1997). Brain aging: Changes in the nature of information coding by the hippocampus. *Journal of Neuroscience, 17,* 5155–5166.

Tanji, J. (2001). Sequential organization of multiple movements: Involvement of cortical motor areas. *Annual Review of Neuroscience, 24,* 631–651.

Taub, E. (1976). Movement in nonhuman primates deprived of somatosensory feedback. *Exercise and Sport Sciences Reviews, 4,* 335–374.

Taub, E., Uswatte, G., and Elbert, T. (2002). New treatments in neurorehabilitation founded on basic research. *Nature Reviews. Neuroscience, 3,* 228–235.

Teasdale, J. D., Howard, R. J., Cox, S. G., Ha, Y., et al. (1999). Functional study of the cognitive generation of affect. *American Journal of Psychiatry, 156,* 209–215.

Temple, E., Deutsch, G. K., Poldrack, R. A., Miller, S. L., et al. (2003). Neural deficits in children with dyslexia ameliorated by behavioral remediation: Evidence from functional MRI. *Proceedings of the National Academy of Sciences, USA, 100,* 2860–2865.

Templeton, C. N., Greene, E., Davis, K. (2005). Allometry of alarm calls: Black-capped chickadees encode information about predator size. *Science, 308,* 1934–1937.

Tenn, W. (1968). *The seven sexes.* New York: Ballantine.

Terkel, J., and Rosenblatt, J. S. (1972). Humoral factors underlying maternal behavior at parturition: Cross transfusion between freely moving rats. *Journal of Comparative and Physiological Psychology, 80,* 365–371.

Terman, G. W., Shavit, Y., Lewis, J. W., Cannon, J. T., et al. (1984). Intrinsic mechanisms of pain inhibition: Activation by stress. *Science, 226,* 1270–1277.

Terpstra, N. J., Bolhuis, J. J., Riebel, K., van der Burg, J. M., et al. (2006). Localized brain activation specific to auditory memory in a female songbird. *Journal of Comparative Neurology, 494,* 784–791.

Terrace, H. S. (1979). *Nim.* New York: Knopf.

Terrazas, A., and McNaughton, B. L. (2000). Brain growth and the cognitive map. *Proceedings of the National Academy of Sciences, USA, 97,* 4414–4416.

Terzian, H. (1964). Behavioural and EEG effects of intracarotid sodium amytal injection. *Acta Neurochirurgica, 12,* 230–239.

Tessier-Lavigne, M., and Placzek, M. (1991). Target attraction: Are developing axons guided by chemotropism? *Trends in Neurosciences, 14,* 303–310.

Tessier-Lavigne, M., Placzek, M., Lumsden, A. G., Dodd, J., et al. (1988). Chemotropic guidance of developing axons in the mammalian central nervous system. *Nature, 336,* 775–778.

Tetel, M. J. (2000). Nuclear receptor coactivators in neuroendocrine function. *Journal of Neuroendocrinology, 12,* 927–932.

Teuber, H.-L., Milner, B., and Vaughan, H. G. (1968). Persistent anterograde amnesia after stab wound of the basal brain. *Neuropsychologia, 6,* 267–282.

Tewksbury, J. J., and Nabhan, G. P. (2001). Seed dispersal: Directed deterrence by capsaicin in chillies. *Nature, 412,* 403–404.

Thannickal, T. C., Moore, R. Y., Nienhuis, R., Ramanathan, L., et al. (2000). Reduced number of hypocretin neurons in human narcolepsy. *Neuron, 27,* 469–474.

Thaw, A. K., Frankmann, S., and Hill, D. L. (2000). Behavioral taste responses of developmentally NaCl-restricted rats to various concentrations of NaCl. *Behavioral Neuroscience, 114,* 437–441.

Thiruchelvam, M., Richfield, E. K., Baggs, R. B., Tank, A. W., et al. (2000). The nigrostriatal system as a preferential target of repeated exposures to combined parquat and maneb: Implications for Parkinson's disease. *Journal of Neuroscience, 20,* 9207–9214.

Thompson, P. M., Giedd, J. N., Woods, R. P., MacDonald, D., et al. (2000). Growth patterns in the developing brain detected by using continuum mechanical tensor maps. *Nature, 404,* 190–193.

Thompson, P. M., Vidal, C., Giedd, J. N., Gochman, P., et al. (2001). Mapping adolescent brain change reveals dynamic wave of accelerated gray matter loss in very early-onset schizophrenia. *Proceedings of the National Academy of Sciences, USA, 98,* 11650–11655.

Thompson, R. F. (1990). Neural mechanisms of classical conditioning in mammals. *Philosophical Transactions of the Royal Soci-*

ety of London. *Series B: Biological Sciences,* *329,* 161–170.

Thompson, R. F., and Krupa, D. J. (1994). Organization of memory traces in the mammalian brain. *Annual Review of Neuroscience, 17,* 519–549.

Thompson, R. F., and Steinmetz, J. E. (2009). The role of the cerebellum in classical conditioning of discrete behavioral responses. *Neuroscience, 162,* 732–755.

Thompson, T., and Schuster, C. R. (1964). Morphine self-administration, food reinforced and avoidance behaviour in rhesus monkeys. *Psychopharmacologia, 5,* 87–94.

Thorndike, E. L. (1898). *Animal intelligence, an experimental study of the associative processes in animals.* New York: Macmillan.

Thornton, A. E., Cox, D. N., Whitfield, K., and Fouladi, R. T. (2008). Cumulative concussion exposure in rugby players: Neurocognitive and symptomatic outcomes. *Journal of Clinical and Experimental Neuropsychology, 30,* 398–409.

Thornton, J. W., Need, E., and Crews, D. (2003). Resurrecting the ancestral steroid receptor: Ancient origin of estrogen signaling. *Science, 301,* 1714–1717.

Thornton-Jones, Z. D., Kennett, G. A., Benwell, K. R., Revell, D. F., et al. (2006). The cannabinoid CB1 receptor inverse agonist, rimonabant, modifies body weight and adiponectin function in diet-induced obese rats as a consequence of reduced food intake. *Pharmacology, Biochemistry, and Behavior, 84,* 353–359.

Thorpe, S. J., and Fabre-Thorpe, M. (2001). Seeking categories in the brain. *Science, 291,* 260–263.

Timmann, D., Drepper, J., Frings, M., Maschke, M., et al. (2009, July 3). The human cerebellum contributes to motor, emotional and cognitive associative learning. A review. *Cortex.* [Epub ahead of print]

Tissir, F., and Goffinet, A. M. (2003). Reelin and brain development. *Nature Reviews. Neuroscience, 4,* 496–505.

Tobias, P. V. (1980). L'evolution du cerveau humain. *La Recherche, 11,* 282–292.

Todorov, A., Said, C. P., Engell, A. D., and Oosterhof, N. N. (2008). Understanding evaluation of faces on social dimensions. *Trends in Cognitive Science, 12,* 455–460.

Tolman, E. C. (1949). There is more than one kind of learning. *Psychological Review, 56,* 144–155.

Tolman, E. C., and Honzik, C. H. (1930). Introduction and removal of reward, and maze performance in rats. *University of California Publications in Psychology, 4,* 257–275.

Tom, S. M., Fox, C. R., Trepel, C., and Poldrack, R. A. (2007). The neural basis of loss aversion in decision-making under risk. *Science, 315,* 515–518.

Tomizawa, K., Iga, N., Lu, Y. F., Moriwaki, A., et al. (2003). Oxytocin improves long-lasting spatial memory during motherhood through MAP kinase cascade. *Nature Neuroscience, 6,* 384–390.

Toni, N., Laplagne, D. A., Zhao, C., Lombardi, G., et al. (2008). Neurons born in the adult dentate gyrus form functional synapses with target cells. *Nature Neuroscience, 11,* 901–907.

Tootell, R. B. H., Hadjikhani, N. K., Vanduffel, W., Liu, A. K., et al. (1998). Functional analysis of primary visual cortex (V1) in humans. *Proceedings of the National Academy of Sciences, USA, 95,* 811–817.

Tootell, R. B., Silverman, M. S., Hamilton, S. L., De Valois, R. L., et al. (1988). Functional anatomy of macaque striate cortex. III. Color. *Journal of Neuroscience, 8,* 1569–1593.

Tootell, R. B., Silverman, M. S., Switkes, E., and De Valois, R. L. (1982). Deoxyglucose analysis of retinotopic organization in primate striate cortex. *Science, 218,* 902–904.

Tootell, R. B., Tsao, D., and Vanduffel, W. (2003). Neuroimaging weighs in: Humans meet macaques in "primate" visual cortex. *Journal of Neuroscience, 23,* 3981–3989.

Toran-Allerand, C. D. (2005). Estrogen and the brain: Beyond ER-alpha, ER-beta, and 17beta-estradiol. *Annals of the New York Academy of Sciences, 1052,* 136–144.

Tordoff, M., Rawson, N., and Friedman, M. (1991). 2,5-Anhydro-d-mannitol acts in liver to initiate feeding. *American Journal of Physiology, 261,* R283–R288.

Torrey, E. F. (2002). Severe psychiatric disorders may be increasing. *Psychiatric Times, 19,* 1–6.

Torrey, E. F., Bowler, A. E., Taylor, E. H., and Gottesman, I. I. (1994). *Schizophrenia and manic depressive disorder.* New York: Basic Books.

Trachtenberg, J. T., Chen, B. E., Knott, G. W., Feng, G., et al. (2002). Long-term in vivo imaging of experience-dependent synaptic plasticity in adult cortex. *Nature, 420,* 788–794.

Treesukosol, Y., Lyall, V., Heck, G. L., Desimone, J. A., et al. (2007). A psychophysical and electrophysiological analysis of salt taste in *Trpv1* null mice. *American Journal of Physiology, Regulatory, Integrative, and Comparative Physiology, 292,* R1799–R1809.

Treisman, A. [M]. (1996). The binding problem. *Current Opinion in Neurobiology, 6,* 171–178.

Treisman, A. M., and Gelade, G. (1980). A feature-integration theory of attention. *Cognitive Psychology, 12,* 97–136.

Treisman, M. (1977). Motion sickness—Evolutionary hypotheses. *Science, 197,* 493–495.

Trimble, M. R. (1991). Interictal psychoses of epilepsy. *Advances in Neurology, 55,* 143–152.

Tronick, R., and Reck, C. (2009). Infants of depressed mothers. *Harvard Review of Psychiatry, 17,* 147–156.

Truitt, W. A., and Coolen, L. M. (2002). Identification of a potential ejaculation generator in the spinal cord. *Science, 297,* 1566–1569.

Ts'o, D. Y., Frostig, R. D., Lieke, E. E., and Grinvald, A. (1990). Functional organization of primate visual cortex revealed by high resolution optical imaging. *Science, 249,* 417–420.

Tsuchiya, N., and Adolphs, R. (2007). Emotion and consciousness. *Trends in Cognitive Sciences, 11,* 158–167.

Tsutsui, K., Bentley, G. E., Ubuka, T., Saigoh, E., et al. (2006). The general and comparative biology of gonadotropin-inhibitory hormone (GnIH). *General and Comparative Endocrinology, 153,* 365–370.

Tuller, D. (2002, January 8). A quiet revolution for those prone to nodding off. *The New York Times* (http://query.nytimes.com/gst/fullpage.html?sec=health&res=980DE5DD1439F93BA35752C0A9649C8B63).

Tulving, E. (1972). Episodic and semantic memory. In E. Tulving and W. Donaldson (Eds.), *Organization of memory* (pp. 381–403). New York: Academic Press.

Tulving, E. (1989). Memory: Performance, knowledge, and experience. *European Journal of Cognitive Psychology, 1,* 3–26.

Tulving, E., Hayman, C. A., and Macdonald, C. A. (1991). Long-lasting perceptual priming and semantic learning in amnesia: A case experiment. *Journal of Experimental Psychology: Learning, Memory, and Cognition, 17,* 595–617.

Tulving, E., Markowitsch, H. J., Craik, F. E., Habib, R., et al. (1996). Novelty and familiarity activations in PET studies of memory encoding and retrieval. *Cerebral Cortex, 6,* 71–79.

Turgeon, J. L., McDonnell, D. P., Martin, K. A., and Wise, P. M. (2004). Hormone therapy: Physiological complexity belies therapeutic simplicity. *Science, 304,* 1269–1273.

Turner, E. H., Matthews, A. M., Linardatos, E., Tell, R. A., et al. (2008). Selective publication of antidepressant trials and its influence on apparent efficacy. *New England Journal of Medicine, 358,* 252–260.

Twain, M. (1897). *Following the Equator: A journey around the world.* Hartford, CT: American.

Tyack, P. L. (2003). Dolphins communicate about individual-specific social relationships. In F. de Waal and P. L. Tyack (Eds.), *Animal social complexity: Intelligence, culture, and individualized societies* (pp. 342–361). Cambridge, MA: Harvard University Press.

Tyzio, R., Cossart, R., Khalilov, I., Minlebaeve, M., et al. (2006). Maternal oxytocin triggers a transient inhibitory switch in GABA signaling in the fetal brain during delivery. *Science, 314,* 1788–1792.

U

Umilta, M. A., Kohler, E., Galiese, V., Fogassi, L., et al. (2001). I know what you are doing: A neurophysiological study. *Neuron, 31,* 155–165.

Ungerleider, L. G., Courtney, S. M., and Haxby, J. V. (1998). A neural system for human visual working memory. *Proceedings of the National Academy of Sciences, USA, 95,* 883–890.

Upile, T., Sipaul, F., Jerjes, W., Singh, S., et al. (2007). The acute effects of alcohol on auditory thresholds. *BMC Ear, Nose, and Throat Disorders, 7,* 4.

Ursin, H., Baade, E., and Levine, S. (1978). *Psychobiology of stress: A study of coping men.* New York: Academic Press.

V

Valenstein, E. S. (1986). *Great and desperate cures: The rise and decline of psychosurgery and other radical treatments for mental illness.* New York: Basic Books.

Vallortigara, G., Rogers, L. J., and Bisazza, A. (1999). Possible evolutionary origins of cognitive brain lateralization. *Brain Research. Brain Research Reviews, 30,* 164–175.

Vance, C., Rogelj, B., Hortobágyi, T., De Vos, K. J., et al. (2009). Mutations in FUS, an RNA processing protein, cause familial amyotrophic lateral sclerosis type 6. *Science, 323,* 1208–1211.

Van Dongen, H. P., Maislin, G., Mullington, J. M., and Dinges, D. F. (2003). The cumulative cost of additional wakefulness: Dose-response effects on neurobehavioral functions and sleep physiology from chronic sleep restriction and total sleep deprivation. *Sleep, 26,* 117–126.

VanDoren, M. J., Matthews, D. B., Janis, G. C., Grobin, A. C., et al. (2000). Neuroactive steroid 3 alpha-hydroxy-5alpha-pregnan-20-one modulates electrophysiological and behavioral actions of ethanol. *Journal of Neuroscience, 20,* 1982–1989.

Van Essen, D. C., and Drury, H. A. (1997). Structural and functional analyses of human cerebral cortex using a surface-based atlas. *Journal of Neuroscience, 17,* 7079–7102.

Van Gaal, L. F., Rissanen, A. M., Scheen, A. J., Ziegler, O., et al. (2005). Effects of the cannabinoid-1 receptor blocker rimonabant on weight reduction and cardiovascular risk factors in overweight patients: 1-year experience from the RIO-Europe study. *Lancet, 365,* 1389–1397.

Vann, S. D., and Aggleton, J. P. (2004). The mammillary bodies: Two memory systems in one? *Nature Reviews. Neuroscience, 5,* 35–44.

van Nas, A., Guhathakurta, D., Wang, S. S., Yehya, N., et al. (2009). Elucidating the role of gonadal hormones in sexually dimorphic gene coexpression networks. *Endocrinology, 150,* 1235–1249.

van Praag, H., Kempermann, G., and Gage, F. H. (2000). Neural consequences of environmental enrichment. *Nature Reviews. Neuroscience, 1,* 191–198.

Van Valen, L. (1974). Brain size and intelligence in man. *American Journal of Physical Anthropology, 40,* 417–423.

Van Zoeren, J. G., and Stricker, E. M. (1977). Effects of preoptic, lateral hypothalamic, or dopamine-depleting lesions on behavioral thermoregulation in rats exposed to the cold. *Journal of Comparative and Physiological Psychology, 91,* 989–999.

Vargas, C. D., Aballéa, A., Rodrigues, E. C., Reilly, K. T., et al. (2009). Re-emergence of hand-muscle representations in human motor cortex after hand allograft. *Proceedings of the National Academy of Sciences, USA, 106,* 7197–7202.

Vasey, P. L. (1995). Homosexual behaviour in primates: A review of evidence and theory. *International Journal of Primatology, 16,* 173–204.

Vassar, R., Ngai, J., and Axel, R. (1993). Spatial segregation of odorant receptor expression in the mammalian olfactory epithelium. *Cell, 74,* 309–318.

Vaughan, W., and Greene, S. L. (1984). Pigeon visual memory capacity. *Journal of Experimental Psychology: Animal Behavior Processes, 10,* 256–271.

Velliste, M., Perel, S., Spalding, M. C., Whitford, A. S., et al. (2008). Cortical control of a prosthetic arm for self-feeding. *Nature, 453,* 1098–1101.

Veraa, R. P., and Grafstein, B. (1981). Cellular mechanisms for recovery from nervous system injury: A conference report. *Experimental Neurology, 71,* 6–75.

Verhagen, A. M., Ekert, P. G., Pakusch, M., Silke, J., et al. (2000). Identification of DIABLO, a mammalian protein that promotes apoptosis by binding to and antagonizing IAP proteins. *Cell, 102,* 43–53.

Vertes, R. P., and Eastman, K. E. (2000). The case against memory consolidation in REM sleep. *Behavioral and Brain Sciences, 23,* 867–876.

Villalobos, M. E., Mizuno, A., Dahl, B. C., Kemmotsu, N., et al. (2005). Reduced functional connectivity between V1 and inferior frontal cortex associated with visuomotor performance in autism. *Neuroimage, 25,* 916–925.

Villringer, A., and Chance, B. (1997). Non-invasive optical spectroscopy and imaging of human brain function. *Trends in Neurosciences, 20,* 435–442.

Virkkunen, M., and Linnoila, M. (1993). Brain serotonin, type II alcoholism and impulsive violence. *Journal of Studies on Alcohol. Supplement, 11,* 163–169.

Vogt, B. A. (2005). Pain and emotion interactions in subregions of the cingulate gyrus. *Nature Reviews. Neuroscience, 6,* 533–544.

Volkow, N. D., Wang, G-J., Telang, F., Fowler, J. S., et al. (2006). Cocaine cues and dopamine in dorsal striatum: Mechanism of craving in cocaine addiction. *Journal of Neuroscience, 26,* 6583–6588.

Volkow, N. D., Wang, G. J., Kollins, S. H., Wigal, T. L., et al. (2009). Evaluating dopamine reward pathway in ADHD: Clinical implications. *JAMA, 302,* 1084–1091.

Volkow, N. D., and Wise, R.A. (2005). How can drug addiction help us understand obesity? *Nature Neuroscience, 8,* 555–560.

Voneida, T. J. (1990). The effect of rubrospinal tractotomy on a conditioned limb response in the cat. *Society for Neuroscience Abstracts, 16,* 279.

Vrontou, E., Nilsen, S. P., Demir, E., Kravitz, E. A., et al. (2006). *fruitless* regulates aggression and dominance in *Drosophila. Nature Neuroscience, 9,* 1469–1471.

Vythilingam, M., Anderson, E. R., Goddard, A., Woods, S. W., et al. (2000). Temporal lobe volume in panic disorder—A quantitative magnetic resonance imaging study. *Psychiatry Research, 99,* 75–82.

W

Wada, J. A., Clarke, R., and Hamm, A. (1975). Cerebral hemispheric asymmetry in humans. Cortical speech zones in 100 adults and 100 infant brains. *Archives of Neurology, 32,* 239–246.

Wada, J. A., and Rasmussen, T. (1960). Intracarotid injection of sodium amytal for the lateralization of cerebral speech dominance: Experimental and clinical observations. *Journal of Neurosurgery, 17,* 266–282.

Waddell, J., and Shors, T. J. (2008). Neurogenesis, learning and associative strength. *European Journal of Neuroscience, 27,* 3020–3028.

Wager, T. D., Rilling, J. K., Smith, E. E., Sokolik, A., et al. (2004). Placebo-induced changes in fMRI in the anticipation and experience of pain. *Science, 303,* 1162–1167.

Wager, T. D., Scott, D. J., and Zubieta, J. K. (2007). Placebo effects on human mu-opioid activity during pain. *Proceedings of the National Academy of Sciences, USA, 104,* 11056–11061.

Wagner, A. D., Desmond, J. E., Demb, J. B., Glover, G. H., et al. (1997). Semantic repetition priming for verbal and pictorial knowledge: A functional MRI study of left inferior prefrontal cortex. *Journal of Cognitive Neuroscience, 9,* 714–726.

Wagner, A. D., Schacter, D. L., Rotte, M., Koutstaal, W., et al. (1998). Building memories: Remembering and forgetting of verbal experiences as predicted by brain activity. *Science, 281,* 1188–1191.

Wagner, G. C., Beuving, L. J., and Hutchinson, R. R. (1980). The effects of gonadal hormone manipulations on aggressive target-biting in mice. *Aggressive Behavior, 6,* 1–7.

Wagner, U., Gais, S., Haider, H., Verleger, R., et al. (2004). Sleep inspires insight. *Nature, 427,* 352–355.

Wahl, O. F. (1976). Monozygotic twins discordant for schizophrenia: A review. *Psychological Bulletin, 83*, 91–106.

Wahlstrom, J. (2002). Changing times: Findings from the first longitudinal study of later high school start times. *National Association of Secondary School Principals Bulletin, 86*, 3–21.

Walker, E. F. (1991). *Schizophrenia: A life-course developmental perspective.* San Diego, CA: Academic Press.

Wallis, J. D. (2007). Orbitofrontal cortex and its contribution to decision-making. *Annual Review of Neuroscience, 30*, 31–56.

Walls, G. L. (1942). *The vertebrate eye: Vol. 1.* Bloomfield Hills, MI: Cranbrook Institute of Science.

Walsh, E. J., Wang, L. M., Armstrong, D. L., Curro, T., et al. (2003). Acoustic communication in *Panthera tigris*: A study of tiger vocalization and auditory receptivity. In Special Session on: Nature's orchestra: Acoustics of singing and calling animals—Production and reception of sound for communication by underwater and terrestrial animals. *Journal of the Acoustical Society of America, 113*, 2275.

Walters, R. J., Hadley, S. H., Morris, K. D. W., and Amin, J. (2000). Benzodiazepines act on GABA$_A$ receptors via two distinct and separable mechanisms. *Nature Neuroscience, 3*, 1273–1280.

Walther, S., Goya-Maldonado, R., Stippich, C., Weisbrod, M., et al. (2010). A supramodal network for response inhibition. *Neuroreport, 21*, 191–195.

Wang, F., Nemes, A., Mendelsohn, M., and Axel, R. (1998). Odorant receptors govern the formation of a precise topographic map. *Cell, 93*, 47–60.

Wang, H., Yu, M., Ochani, M., Amella, C. A., et al. (2003). Nicotinic acetylcholine receptor α7 subunit is an essential regulator of inflammation. *Nature, 421*, 384–388.

Wang, J. B., Imai, Y., Eppler, C. M., Gregor, P., et al. (1993). μ Opiate receptor: cDNA cloning and expression. *Proceedings of the National Academy of Sciences, USA, 90*, 10230–10234.

Wareing, M., Fisk, J. E., and Murphy, P. N. (2000). Working memory deficits in current and previous users of MDMA ("ecstasy"). *British Journal of Psychology, 91*, 181–188.

Waters, G. S., and Fouts, R. S. (2002). Sympathetic mouth movements accompanying fine motor movements in chimpanzees (*Pan troglodytes*) with implications toward the evolution of language. *Neurological Research, 24*, 174–180.

Watkin, P. M. (2001). Neonatal screening for hearing impairment. *Seminars in Neonatology, 6*, 501–509.

Watson, N. V. (2001). Sex differences in throwing: Monkeys having a fling. *Trends in Cognitive Sciences, 5*, 98–99.

Watson, N. V., Freeman, L. M., and Breedlove, S. M. (2001). Neuronal size in the spinal nucleus of the bulbocavernosus: Direct modulation by androgen in rats with mosaic androgen insensitivity. *Journal of Neuroscience, 21*, 1062–1066.

Webb, W. B. (1992). *Sleep, the gentle tyrant.* Bolton, MA: Anker.

Wedekind, C., Seebeck, T., Bettens, F., and Paepke, A. J. (1995). MHC-dependent mate preferences in humans. *Proceedings of the Royal Society of London. Series B: Biological Sciences, 260*, 245–249.

Wehr, T. A., Sack, D. A., Duncan, W. C., Mendelson, W. B., et al. (1985). Sleep and circadian rhythms in affective patients isolated from external time cues. *Psychiatry Research, 15*, 327–339.

Wei, F., Wang G. D., Kerchner, G. A., Kim, S. J., et al. (2001). Genetic enhancement of inflammatory pain by forebrain NR2B overexpression. *Nature Neuroscience, 4*, 164–169.

Weinberger, D. R., Aloia, M. S., Goldberg, T. E., and Berman, K. F. (1994). The frontal lobes and schizophrenia. *Journal of Neuropsychiatry and Clinical Neurosciences, 6*, 419–427.

Weinberger, D. R., Bigelow, L. B., Kleinman, J. E., Klein, S. T., et al. (1980). Cerebral ventricular enlargement in chronic schizophrenia. An association with poor response to treatment. *Archives of General Psychiatry, 37*, 11–13.

Weinberger, N. M. (1998). Physiological memory in primary auditory cortex: Characteristics and mechanisms. *Neurobiology of Learning and Memory, 70*, 226–251.

Weindruch, R., and Walford, R. L. (1988). *The retardation of aging and disease by dietary restriction.* Springfield, IL: Thomas.

Weiner, R. D. (1994). Treatment optimization with ECT. *Psychopharmacology Bulletin, 30*, 313–320.

Weiss, L. A., Arking, D. E., and The Gene Discovery Project of Johns Hopkins & the Autism Consortium. (2009). A genome-wide linkage and association scan reveals novel loci for autism. *Nature, 461*, 802–808.

Weitzman, E. D. (1981). Sleep and its disorders. *Annual Review of Neurosciences, 4*, 381–417.

Weitzman, E. D., Czeisler, C. A., Zimmerman, J. C., and Moore-Ede, M. C. (1981). Biological rhythms in man: Relationship of sleep-wake, cortisol, growth hormone, and temperature during temporal isolation. In J. B. Martin, S. Reichlin, and K. L. Bick (Eds.), *Neurosecretion and brain peptides* (pp. 475–499). New York: Raven.

Welch, D. M., and Meselson, M. (2000). Evidence for the evolution of bdelloid rotifers without sexual reproduction or genetic exchange. *Science, 288*, 1211–1215.

Weller, L., and Weller, A. (1993). Human menstrual synchrony: A critical assessment. *Neuroscience and Biobehavioral Reviews, 17*, 427–439.

Wesensten, N. J., Belenky, G., Kautz, M. A., Thorne, D. R., et al. (2002). Maintaining alertness and performance during sleep deprivation: Modafinil versus caffeine. *Psychopharmacology (Berlin), 159*, 238–247.

Wessberg, J., Stambaugh, C. R., Kralik, J. D., Beck, P. D., et al. (2000). Real-time predictions of hand trajectory by ensembles of cortical neurons in primates. *Nature, 408*, 361–365.

Westergaard, G. C., Kuhn, H. E., and Suomi, S. J. (1998). Bipedal posture and hand preference in humans and other primates. *Journal of Comparative Psychology, 112*, 55–64.

Wettschureck, N., and Offermanns, S. (2005). Mammalian G proteins and their cell type specific functions. *Physiological Reviews, 85*, 1159–1204.

Wever, E. G. (1974). The evolution of vertebrate hearing. In W. D. Keidel and W. D. Neff (Eds.), *Handbook of sensory physiology: Vol. 5. Auditory system* (pp. 423–454). New York: Springer.

Wever, R. A. (1979). Influence of physical workload on freerunning circadian rhythms of man. *Pflügers Archiv European Journal of Physiology, 381*, 119–126.

Wexler, N. S., Rose, E. A., and Housman, D. E. (1991). Molecular approaches to hereditary diseases of the nervous system: Huntington's disease as a paradigm. *Annual Review of Neuroscience, 14*, 503–529.

Whitaker, D., and McGraw, P. V. (2000). Long-term visual experience recalibrates human orientation perception. *Nature Neuroscience, 3*, 13.

White, N. M., and Milner, P. M. (1992). The psychobiology of reinforcers. *Annual Review of Psychology, 43*, 443–471.

White, P. M., Doetzlhofer, A., Lee, Y. S., Groves, A. K., et al. (2006). Mammalian cochlear supporting cells can divide and trans-differentiate into hair cells. *Nature, 441*, 984–987.

Whitlock, J. R., Heynen, A. J., Shuler, M. G., and Bear, M. F. (2006). Learning induces long-term potentiation in the hippocampus. *Science, 313*, 1093–1097.

Wible, C. G., Shenton, M. E., Hokama, H., Kikinis, R., et al. (1995). Prefrontal cortex and schizophrenia. A quantitative magnetic resonance imaging study. *Archives of General Psychiatry, 52*, 279–288.

Wiesel, T. N., and Hubel, D. H. (1963). Single-cell responses in striate cortex of kittens deprived of vision in one eye. *Journal of Neurophsyiology, 26*, 1002–1017.

Wiesel, T. N., and Hubel, D. H. (1965). Extent of recovery from the effects of visual deprivation in kittens. *Journal of Neurophysiology, 28*, 1060–1072.

Wiklund, C., and Sillén-Tullberg, B. (1985). Why distasteful butterflies have aposematic larvae and adults, but cryptic pupae: Evidence from predation experiments on the monarch and the European swallowtail. *Evolution, 39*, 1155–1158.

Wildman, D. E., Uddin, M., Liu, G., Grossman, L. I., et al. (2003). Implications of natural selection in shaping 99.4% non-synonymous DNA identity between humans and chimpanzees: Enlarging genus *Homo*. *Proceedings of the National Academy of Sciences, USA, 100,* 7181–7188.

Wilens, T. E., Prince, J. B., Spencer, T. J., and Biederman, J. (2006). Stimulants and sudden death: What is a physician to do? *Pediatrics, 118,* 1215–1219.

Will, B., Galani, R., Kelche, C., and Rosenzweig, M. R. (2004). Recovery from brain injury in animals: Relative efficacy of environmental enrichment, physical exercise or formal training (1990–2002). *Progress in Neurobiology, 72,* 167–182.

Williams, D. (1969). Neural factors related to habitual aggression. *Brain, 92,* 503–520.

Williams, J. H., Waiter, G. D., Gilchrist, A., Perrett, D. I., et al. (2006). Neural mechanisms of imitation and "mirror neuron" functioning in autistic spectrum disorder. *Neuropsychologia, 44,* 610–621.

Williams, S. R., and Stuart, G. J. (2003). Role of dendritic synapse location in the control of action potential output. *Trends in Neurosciences, 26,* 147–154.

Williams, T. J., Pepitone, M. E., Christensen, S. E., Cooke, B. M., et al. (2000). Finger-length ratios and sexual orientation. *Nature, 404,* 455–456.

Williams, Z. M., Bush, G., Rauch, S. I., Cosgrove, G. R., et al. (2004). Human anterior cingulate neurons and the integration of monetary reward with motor responses. *Nature Neuroscience, 7,* 1370–1374.

Willis, S. L., Tennstedt, S. L., Marsiske, M., Ball, K., et al. (2006). Long-term effects of cognitive training on everyday functional outcomes in older adults. *JAMA, 296,* 2805–2814.

Wingfield, J. C., Ball, G. F., Dufty, A. M., Hegner, R. E., et al. (1987). Testosterone and aggression in birds. *American Scientist, 75,* 602–608.

Winkowski, D. E., and Knudsen, E. I. (2006). Top-down gain control of the auditory space map by gaze control circuitry in the barn owl. *Nature, 439,* 336–339.

Winocur, G. (1990). Anterograde and retrograde amnesia in rats with dorsal hippocampal or dorsomedial thalamic lesions. *Behavioural Brain Research, 38,* 145–154.

Winocur, G., Wojtowicz, J. M., Sekeres, M., Snyder, J. S., et al. (2006). Inhibition of neurogenesis interferes with hippocampus-dependent memory function. *Hippocampus, 16,* 296–304.

Winslow, J. T., and Insel, T. R. (2002). The social deficits of the oxytocin knockout mouse. *Neuropeptides, 36,* 221–229.

Wise, R. A. (1996). Neurobiology of addiction. *Current Opinion in Neurobiology, 6,* 243–251.

Wise, R. A., Bauco, P., Carlezon, W. A., Jr., and Trojniar, W. (1992). Self-stimulation and drug reward mechanisms. *Annals of the New York Academy of Sciences, 654,* 192–198.

Woldorff, M. G., Gallen, C. C., Hampson, S. A., Hillyard, S. A., et al. (1993). Modulation of early sensory processing in human auditory cortex during auditory selective attention. *Proceedings of the National Academy of Sciences, USA, 90,* 8722–8726.

Woldorff, M. G., and Hillyard, S. A. (1991). Modulation of early auditory processing during selective listening to rapidly presented tones. *Electroencephalography and Clinical Neurophysiology, 79,* 170–191.

Wolf, S. S., Jones, D. W., Knable, M. B., Gorey, J. G., et al. (1996). Tourette syndrome: Prediction of phenotypic variation in monozygotic twins by caudate nucleus D2 receptor binding. *Science, 273,* 1225–1227.

Wolfe, J. M. (1994). Guided search 2.0: A revised model of visual search. *Psychonomic Bulletin & Review, 1,* 202–238.

Wolfe, J. M., Alvarez, G. A., and Horowitz, T. S. (2000). Attention is fast but volition is slow. *Nature, 406,* 691.

Wolinsky, E., and Way, J. (1990). The behavioral genetics of *Caenorhabditis elegans*. *Behavior Genetics, 20,* 169–189.

Wolk, D. A., Price, J. C., Saxton, J. A., Snitz, B. E., et al. (2009). Amyloid imaging in mild cognitive impairment subtypes. *Annals of Neurology, 65,* 557–568.

Wolkowitz, O. M., Lupien, S. J., Bigler, E., Levin, R. B., et al. (2004). The "steroid dementia syndrome": An unrecognized complication of glucocorticoid treatment. *Annals of the New York Academy of Sciences, 1032,* 191–194.

Womelsdorf, T., Anton-Erxleben, K., Pieper, F., and Treue, S. (2006). Dynamic shifts of visual receptive fields in cortical area MT by spatial attention. *Nature Neuroscience, 9,* 1156–1160.

Womelsdorf, T., Anton-Erxleben, K., and Treue, S. 2008. Receptive field shift and shrinkage in macaque middle temporal area through attentional gain modulation. *Journal of Neuroscience, 28,* 8934–8944.

Wood, J. M., Bootzin, R. R., Kihlstrom, J. F., and Schacter, D. L. (1992). Implicit and explicit memory for verbal information presented during sleep. *Psychological Science, 3,* 236–239.

Wood, N., and Cowan, N. (1995). The cocktail party phenomenon revisited: How frequent are attention shifts to one's name in an irrelevant auditory channel? *Journal of Experimental Psychology. Learning, Memory, and Cognition, 21,* 255–260.

Woodruff-Pak, D. S., and Jaeger, M. E. (1998). Predictors of eyeblink classical conditioning over the adult age span. *Psychology and Aging, 13,* 193–205.

Woolf, C. J., and Salter, M. W. (2000). Neuronal plasticity: Increasing the gain in pain. *Science, 288,* 1765–1769.

Woolsey, T. A., Durham, D., Harris, R. M., Simous, D. T., et al. (1981). Somatosensory development. In R. S. Aslin, J. R. Alberts, and M. R. Peterson (Eds.), *Sensory and perceptual development: Influence of genetic and experiential factors* (pp. 259–292). New York: Academic Press.

Woolsey, T. A., and Wann, J. R. (1976). Areal changes in mouse cortical barrels following vibrissal damage at different postnatal ages. *Journal of Comparative Neurology, 170,* 53–66.

World Health Organization. (2001). *The world health report.* Geneva, Switzerland: World Health Organization.

World Health Organization. (2004). *Burden of disease in DALYs by cause, sex, and mortality stratum in WHO regions, estimates for 2002.* Geneva, Switzerland: World Health Organization.

Wren, A. M., Seal, L. J., Cohen, M. A., Brynes, A. E., et al. (2001). Ghrelin enhances appetite and increases food intake in humans. *Journal of Clinical Endocrinology and Metabolism, 86,* 5992–5995.

Wren, A. M., Small, C. J., Ward, H. L., Murphy, K. G., et al. (2000). The novel hypothalamic peptide ghrelin stimulates food intake and growth hormone secretion. *Endocrinology, 141,* 4325–4328.

Wright, A. A., Santiago, H. C., Sands, S. F., Kendrick, D. F., et al. (1985). Memory processing of serial lists by pigeons, monkeys, and people. *Science, 229,* 287–289.

Wright, R. D., and Ward, L. M. (2008). *Orienting of attention.* New York: Oxford University Press.

Wuethrich, B. (2000). Learning the world's languages—before they vanish. *Science, 288,* 1156–1159.

Wurtz, R. H., and Goldberg, M. E. (1972). Activity of superior colliculus in behaving monkey. 3. Cells discharging before eye movements. *Journal of Neurophysiology, 35,* 575–586.

Wurtz, R. H., Goldberg, M. E., and Robinson, D. L. (1982). Brain mechanisms of visual attention. *Scientific American, 246*(6), 124–135.

X

Xerri, C., Coq, J., Merzenich, M., and Jenkins, W. (1996). Experience-induced plasticity of cutaneous maps in the primary somatosensory cortex of adult monkeys and rats. *Journal de Physiologie, 90,* 277–287.

Xerri, C., Stern J. M., and Merzenich, M. M. (1994). Alterations of the cortical representation of the rat ventrum induced by nursing behavior. *Journal of Neuroscience, 14,* 1710–1721.

Xu, H., Delling, M., Jun, J. C., and Clapham, D. E. (2006). Oregano, thyme and clove-derived flavors and skin sensitizers activate specific TRP channels. *Nature Neuroscience, 9,* 628–635.

Xu, L., Furukawa, S., and Middlebrooks, J. C. (1999). Auditory cortical responses in the cat to sounds that produce spatial illusions. *Nature, 399,* 688–691.

Y

Yaffe, K., Lui, L. Y., Zmuda, J., and Cauley, J. (2002). Sex hormones and cognitive function in older men. *Journal of the American Geriatrics Society, 50,* 707–712.

Yamazaki, S., Numano, R., Abe, M., Hida, A., et al. (2000). Resetting central and peripheral circadian oscillators in transgenic rats. *Science, 288,* 682–685.

Yanagisawa, K., Bartoshuk, L. M., Catalanotto, F. A., Karrer, T. A., et al. (1992). Anesthesia of the chorda tympani nerve: Insights into a source of dysgeusia. *Chemical Senses, 17,* 724.

Yang, S. H., Cheng, P. H., Banta, H., Piotrowska-Nitsche, K., et al. (2008). Towards a transgenic model of Huntington's disease in a non-human primate. *Nature, 453,* 921–924.

Yang, T. T., Gallen, C. C., Ramachandran, V. S., Cobb, S., et al. (1994). Noninvasive detection of cerebral plasticity in adult human somatosensory cortex. *Neuroreport, 5,* 701–704.

Yasuda, K., Raynor, K., Kong, H., Breder, C., et al. (1993). Cloning and functional comparison of kappa and delta opioid receptors from mouse brain. *Proceedings of the National Academy of Sciences, USA, 90,* 6736–6740.

Yehuda, R. (2002). Post-traumatic stress disorder. *New England Journal of Medicine, 346,* 108–114.

Yehuda, R., Kahana, B., Binder-Brynes, K., Southwick, S., et al. (1995). Low urinary cortisol excretion in Holocaust survivors with posttraumatic stress disorder. *American Journal of Psychiatry, 152,* 982–986.

Yin, J. C., Del Vecchio, M., Zhou, H., and Tully, T. (1995). CREB as a memory modulator: Induced expression of a dCREB2 activator isoform enhances long-term memory in *Drosophila. Cell, 81,* 107–115.

Yin, L., Wang, J., Klein, P. S., and Lazar, M. A. (2006). Nuclear receptor Rev-erbα is a critical lithium-sensitive component of the circadian clock. *Science, 311,* 1002–1004.

Yoon, H., Enquist, L. W., and Dulac, C. (2005). Olfactory inputs to hypothalamic neurons controlling reproduction and fertility. *Cell, 123,* 669–682.

Young, A. B. (1993). Role of excitotoxins in heredito-degenerative neurologic diseases. *Research Publications—Association for Research in Nervous and Mental Disease, 71,* 175–189.

Young, A. W., Hellawell, D. J., Van De Wal, C., and Johnson, M. (1996). Facial expression processing after amygdalotomy. *Neuropsychologia, 34,* 31–39.

Young, B., Coolen, L., and McKenna, K. (2009). Neural regulation of ejaculation. *Journal of Sexual Medicine, 6* (Suppl. 3), 229–233.

Young, L. J. (2009). Being human: love: Neuroscience reveals all. *Nature, 457,* 148.

Yu, S., Pritchard, M., Kremer, E., Lynch, M., et al. (1991). Fragile X genotype characterized by an unstable region of DNA. *Science, 252,* 1179–1181.

Z

Zadikoff, C., and Lang, A. E. (2005). Apraxia in movement disorders. *Brain, 128,* 1480–1497.

Zaidel, E. (1976). Auditory vocabulary of the right hemisphere following brain bisection or hemidecortication. *Cortex, 12,* 191–211.

Zarate, C. A., Jr., Singh, J. B., Carlson, P. J., Brutsche, N. E., et al. (2006). A randomized trial of an N-methyl-D-aspartate antagonist in treatment-resistant major depression. *Archives of General Psychiatry, 63,* 856–864.

Zatorre, R. J., Evans, A. C., and Meyer, E. (1994). Neural mechanisms underlying melodic perception and memory for pitch. *Journal of Neuroscience, 14,* 1908–1919.

Zeki, S. (1993). *A vision of the brain.* London: Blackwell.

Zeki, S., Watson, J. D., Lueck, C. J., Friston, K. J., et al. (1991). A direct demonstration of functional specialization in human visual cortex. *Journal of Neuroscience, 11,* 641–649.

Zeman, A. (2002). *Consciousness: A user's guide.* New Haven, CT: Yale University Press.

Zendel, B. R., and Alain, C. (2009). Concurrent sound segregation is enhanced in musicians. *Journal of Cognitive Neuroscience, 21,* 1488–1498.

Zhang, C. L., Zou, Y., He, W., Gage, F. H., et al. (2008). A role for adult TLX-positive neural stem cells in learning and behaviour. *Nature, 451,* 1004–1007.

Zhang, J. V., Ren, P.-G., Avsian-Kretchmer, O., Luo, C.-W., et al. (2005). Obestatin, a peptide encoded by the ghrelin gene, opposes ghrelin's effects on food intake. *Science, 310,* 996–999.

Zhang, S. D., and Odenwald, W. F. (1995). Misexpression of the white (w) gene triggers male-male courtship in *Drosophila. Proceedings of the National Academy of Sciences, USA, 92,* 5525–5529.

Zhang, T. Y., and Meaney, M. J. (2010). Epigenetics and the environmental regulation of the genome and its function. *Annual Review of Psychology, 61,* C1–C3.

Zhang, Y., Proenca, R., Maffei, M., Barone, M., et al. (1994). Positional cloning of the mouse obese gene and its human homologue. *Nature, 372,* 425–432.

Zhang, Z., and Bourque, C. W. (2003). Osmometry in osmosensory neurons. *Nature Neuroscience, 6,* 1021–1022.

Zhao, G. Q., Zhang, Y., Hoon, M. A., Chandrashekar, J., et al. (2003). The receptors for mammalian sweet and umami taste. *Cell, 115,* 255–266.

Zheng, J. L., and Gao, W. Q. (2000). Overexpression of Math1 induces robust production of extra hair cells in postnatal rat inner ears. *Nature Neuroscience, 3,* 580–586.

Zheng, J., Shen, W., He, D. Z., Long, K. B., et al. (2000). Prestin is the motor protein of cochlear outer hair cells. *Nature, 405,* 149–155.

Zhong, Z., Deane, R., Ali, Z., Parisi, M., et al. (2008). ALS-causing SOD1 mutants generate vascular changes prior to motor neuron degeneration. *Nature Neuroscience, 11,* 420–422.

Zhou, Y., Morais-Cabral, J. H., Kaufman, A., and MacKinnon, R. (2001). Chemistry of ion coordination and hydration revealed by a K⁺ channel-Fab complex at 2.0 A resolution. *Nature, 414,* 43–48.

Zihl, J., von Cramon, D., and Mai, N. (1983). Selective disturbance of movement vision after bilateral brain damage. *Brain, 106,* 313–340.

Zimmer, C. (2004). *The soul made flesh: The discovery of the brain—and how it changed the world.* New York: Basic Books.

Zola, S. M., Squire, L. R., Teng, E., Stefanacci, L., et al. (2000). Impaired recognition memory in monkeys after damage limited to the hippocampal region. *Journal of Neuroscience, 20,* 451–463.

Zola-Morgan, S., and Squire, L. R. (1986). Memory impairment in monkeys following lesions of the hippocampus. *Behavioral Neuroscience, 100,* 155–160.

Zola-Morgan, S. M., and Squire, L. R. (1990). The primate hippocampal formation: Evidence for a time-limited role in memory storage. *Science, 250,* 288–290.

Zola-Morgan, S., Squire, L. R., and Ramus, S. J. (1994). Severity of memory impairment in monkeys as a function of locus and extent of damage within the medial temporal lobe memory system. *Hippocampus, 4,* 483–495.

Zonta, M., Angulo, M. C., Gobbo, S., Rosengarten, B., et al. (2003). Neuron-to-astrocyte signalling is central to the dynamic control of brain microcirculation. *Nature Neuroscience, 6,* 43–49.

Zou, Z., and Buck, L. B. (2006). Combinatorial effects of odorant mixes in olfactory cortex. *Science, 311,* 1477–1481.

Zou, Z., Horowitz, L. F, Montmayeur, J. P., Snapper, S., et al. (2001). Genetic tracing reveals a stereotyped sensory map in the olfactory cortex. *Nature, 414,* 173–179.

Zou, Z., Li, F., and Buck, L. B. (2005). Odor maps in the olfactory cortex. *Proceedings of the National Academy of Sciences, USA, 102,* 7724–7729.

Zucker, I. (1976). Light, behavior, and biologic rhythms. *Hospital Practice, 11,* 83–91.

Zucker, I. (1988). Seasonal affective disorders: Animal models non fingo. *Journal of Biological Rhythms, 3,* 209–223.

Zucker, I., Boshes, M., and Dark, J. (1983). Suprachiasmatic nuclei influence circannual and circadian rhythms of ground squirrels. *American Journal of Physiology, 244,* R472–R480.

Zucker, L. M., and Zucker, T. F. (1961). "Fatty," a mutation in the rat. *Journal of Heredity, 52,* 275–278.

Zuo, Y., Yang, G., Kwon, E., and Wen-Biao, G. (2005). Long-term sensory deprivation prevents dendritic spine loss in primary somatosensory cortex. *Nature, 436,* 261–265.

Zurek, P. M. (1981). Spontaneous narrow-band acoustic signals emitted by human ears. *Journal of the Acoustical Society of America, 69,* 514–523.

Author Index

Subject Index

About the Book

Editor: Graig Donini

Project Editor: Kathaleen Emerson

Copy Editor: Stephanie Hiebert

Production Manager: Christopher Small

Book Production: Jefferson Johnson

Art: Dragonfly Media Group *and* Elizabeth Morales Scientific Illustration

Photo Researcher: David McIntyre

Book and Cover Design: Jefferson Johnson

Book and Cover Manufacturer: Courier Companies, Inc.